classrooms around the world!

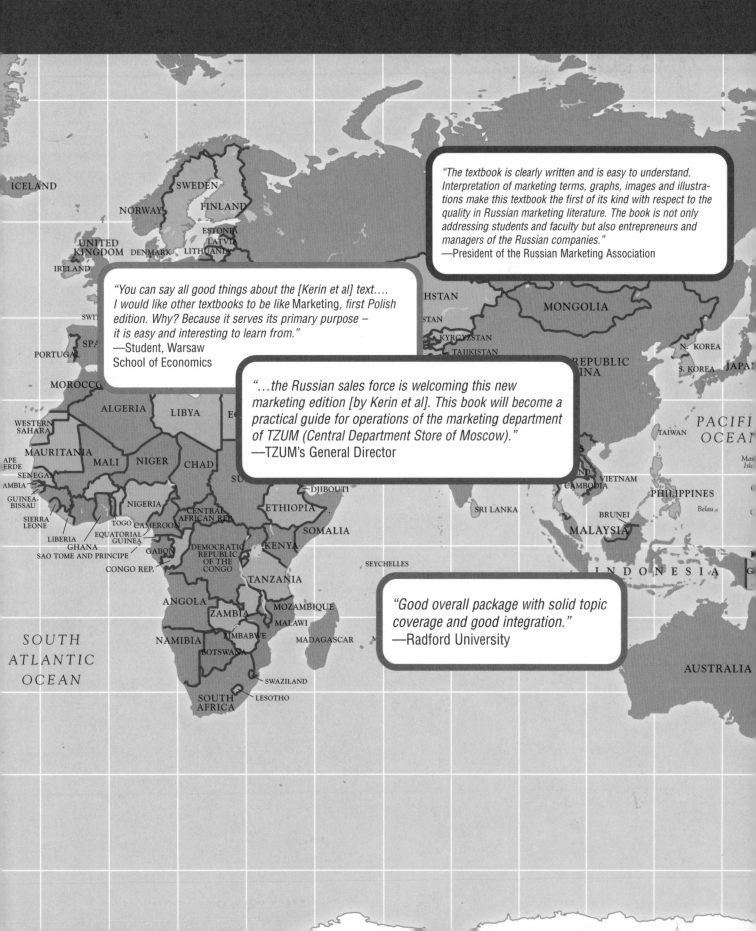

"The textbook is clearly written and is easy to understand. Interpretation of marketing terms, graphs, images and illustrations make this textbook the first of its kind with respect to the quality in Russian marketing literature. The book is not only addressing students and faculty but also entrepreneurs and managers of the Russian companies."
—President of the Russian Marketing Association

"You can say all good things about the [Kerin et al] text…. I would like other textbooks to be like Marketing, first Polish edition. Why? Because it serves its primary purpose – it is easy and interesting to learn from."
—Student, Warsaw School of Economics

"…the Russian sales force is welcoming this new marketing edition [by Kerin et al]. This book will become a practical guide for operations of the marketing department of TZUM (Central Department Store of Moscow)."
—TZUM's General Director

"Good overall package with solid topic coverage and good integration."
—Radford University

MARKETING

7th EDITION

Roger A. Kerin
Southern Methodist University

Eric N. Berkowitz
University of Massachusetts

Steven W. Hartley
University of Denver

William Rudelius
University of St. Thomas

McGraw-Hill
Irwin

Boston   Burr Ridge, IL   Dubuque, IA   Madison, WI   New York   San Francisco   St. Louis
Bangkok   Bogotá   Caracas   Kuala Lumpur   Lisbon   London   Madrid   Mexico City
Milan   Montreal   New Delhi   Santiago   Seoul   Singapore   Sydney   Taipei   Toronto

McGraw-Hill Higher Education

A Division of The McGraw-Hill Companies

MARKETING

Published by McGraw-Hill/Irwin, a business unit of The McGraw-Hill Companies, Inc., 1221 Avenue of the Americas, New York, NY, 10020. Copyright © 2003, 2000, 1997, 1994, 1992, 1989, 1986 by The McGraw-Hill Companies, Inc. All rights reserved. No part of this publication may be reproduced or distributed in any form or by any means, or stored in a database or retrieval system, without the prior written consent of The McGraw-Hill Companies, Inc., including, but not limited to, in any network or other electronic storage or transmission, or broadcast for distance learning.

Some ancillaries, including electronic and print components, may not be available to customers outside the United States.

This book is printed on acid-free paper.

domestic   3 4 5 6 7 8 9 0 QWV/QWV 0 9 8 7 6 5 4 3

international   1 2 3 4 5 6 7 8 9 0 QWV/QWV 0 9 8 7 6 5 4 3 2

ISBN 0-07-241075-2

Publisher: *John E. Biernat*
Executive editor: *Gary L. Bauer*
Developmental editors: *Gina M. Huck/Tracy L. Jensen*
Marketing manager: *Kim Kanakes Szum*
Senior project manager: *Kimberly D. Hooker*
Lead production supervisor: *Heather D. Burbridge*
Media producer: *Craig Atkins*
Supplement producer: *Susan Lombardi*
Photo research coordinator: *Ira C. Roberts*
Photo researcher: *Michael Hruby*
Cover design: *Laurie Entringer*
Interior design: *Laurie Entringer*
Cover illustration: *©tom white.Images*
Typeface: *10.5/12 Times Roman*
Compositor: *GTS Graphics, Inc.*
Printer: *Quebecor World Versailles Inc.*

Library of Congress Cataloging-in-Publication Data

Marketing / Roger A. Kerin . . . [et al.]. — 7th ed.
       p.   cm. — (the Irwin/McGraw-Hill series in marketing)
       Includes bibliographical references and index.
       ISBN 0-07-241075-2
       1. Marketing   I. Kerin, Roger A.   II. Series.
HF5415.M29474   2002
658.8—dc21   12595516

INTERNATIONAL EDITION ISBN 0-07-121725-8

Copyright © 2003. Exclusive rights by The McGraw-Hill Companies, Inc., for manufacture and export. This book cannot be re-exported from the country to which it is sold by McGraw-Hill.

The International Edition is not available in North America.

www.mhhe.com

PREFACE

Dynamic . . . Exciting . . . Challenging . . . and Surprising! The 21st century is an extraordinary time for instructors, students, and managers to be involved in the field of marketing. Virtual advertising, multichannel retailing, eCRM, cashless vending, everyday fair pricing, online coupons, data mining, and brand equity are just a few of the many indications that marketing is racing into a new era. At the same time, many traditional elements of the discipline such as segmentation, new product development, and pricing are growing in importance and use. The combination of the contemporary and the traditional elements of marketing create a truly exceptional topic to study and understand. We appreciate the opportunity to share our enthusiasm for the field with you and welcome you to your introduction to marketing!

The Seventh Edition of *Marketing* is the result of a detailed and rigorous development process designed to provide customer value in several ways. First, we continue to use the active-learning approach that has been the foundation of our previous editions. Second, we have incorporated many new examples, tools, and design elements that are consistent with the learning styles of today's students. Third, we have added, deleted, and modified topics and content based on our own expertise and the advice of many knowledgeable reviewers. Finally, we have invested in the most effective of the many evolving educational technologies. Overall, the Seventh Edition of *Marketing* represents our efforts to guarantee the high quality of previous editions and to continue our tradition of growth and improvement.

We are gratified by the growing interest in our approach to the study of marketing. Feedback from students and instructors from around the world continues to reinforce our pedagogical style. The text and its translations and adaptations are now used extensively throughout the United States, and in Canada, Poland, Russia, China, and many other countries. We hope that you will enjoy the text and your exploration of the knowledge, skills, and tools of the marketing discipline!

DISTINCTIVE FEATURES OF OUR APPROACH

The innovative pedagogical approach we developed through our own classroom experiences was introduced in the first edition in 1986. While each new edition has offered new content, cases, and examples to reflect changes in the marketing discipline and the marketplace, the distinctive features of our approach have remained as the foundation of the text and the supporting supplements. The features which you may recognize from previous editions and which are prominent in this edition include:

- An easy-to-read, high-involvement, interactive writing style that engages students through active learning techniques, timely and interesting examples, and challenging applications.
- A vivid and accurate description of businesses and marketing professionals—through cases, exercises, and testimonials—that allows students to "personalize" marketing and identify possible career interests and role models.
- The use of extended examples, involving people making marketing decisions, that students can easily relate to text concepts and that emphasize a decision-making orientation.
- Comprehensive and integrated coverage of traditional and contemporary scholarly concepts illustrated through relevant practitioner-related literature.
- A rigorous pedagogical framework based on the use of learning objectives, concept checks, key words, chapter summaries, and supportive student supplements such as the Student CD-ROM and Study Guide.

- A package of support materials to accommodate a wide variety of instructor teaching styles and student learning styles.

Feedback from many of the 2,500 instructors and 600,000 students who have used our text and package in the past has encouraged us to build on these strengths as we developed the Seventh Edition of *Marketing*.

NEW AND REVISED CONTENT

- **The Role of the Internet and Technology in Marketing Today:** *Marketing*, 7/e recognizes that the Internet and other digital technologies provide us with powerful new tools that can greatly enhance communication and commerce. From cover to cover, *Marketing, 7/e* integrates coverage of e-Commerce topics such as e-marketplaces, dynamic pricing, viral marketing, permission marketing, personalization, multichannel retailing, eCRM, collaborative commerce, file sharing and peer-to-peer communication, cyberservices, Internet appliances, interactive television, online secondary data sources, and virtual advertising.
- **New Chapter 21: "Implementing Interactive and Multichannel Marketing":** This new chapter provides a framework for how to think about and implement marketing strategy in an Internet/Web-enabled marketspace. Emphasis is placed on interactive marketing practice and the growing application of multichannel marketing. Students will also find this chapter of interest because they will see how important it is for companies to forge collaborative channel relationships to improve their global market competitiveness.
- **Consumer Behavior and Organizational Behavior Chapters Earlier in Text:** In response to reviewer feedback the global chapter has been moved to follow the behavior chapters allowing earlier coverage of these key chapters (now Chapters 5 and 6).
- **Increased Emphasis on Customer Value:** Chapter 1 presents an enhanced emphasis on customer value, the role of brands and how they make firms accountable to consumers, new products, the breadth of marketing and how it is used by many types of organizations, and a complete update of Rollerblade's marketing program.
- **Updated Overview of the Marketing Environment:** Chapter 3 now includes a discussion of Napster's dramatic impact on the music industry; an introduction to current electronic business technologies including the Internet, the World Wide Web, e-Commerce, and the growth of collaborative commerce; the shifting age distribution of the population; and the changing attitudes and roles of women.
- **Updated CB Coverage:** Chapter 5 includes new examples related to the stages of the consumer-decision process; new discussions of customer satisfaction and retention, and marketing strategies for high- and low-involvement products; and an updated discussion of VALS profiles.
- **New Organizational Buying Coverage:** Chapter 6 features new sections on online buying in organizational markets, e-marketplaces, and online auctions.
- **Updated Global Coverage:** Chapter 7 includes discussions of the emergence of a networked global marketspace, the influence of the World Trade Organization on the global rules of trade between nations, and important differences in the economic infrastructures of China, India, Eastern Europe, and the countries of the former Soviet Union. Discussions of global regulatory influences, such as the Economic Espionage Act and the Foreign Corrupt Practices Act, have been updated to reflect the latest regulatory changes.
- **Expanded Coverage of Marketing Research Technology:** Chapter 8 opens with an exciting example—the *Lord of the Rings* movie trilogy—and introduces

up-to-date and comprehensive coverage of online databases and Internet resources. The chapter also includes new discussions of creative research techniques such as hiring "cool hunters" to identify important cultural trends, and new coverage of Internet and fax survey techniques, data mining, and the impact of research on marketing actions.

- **Expanded Segmentation, Positioning, and Customization Material:** Chapter 9 includes coverage of the mass customization of shoes at Customatix.com, Apple's segmentation strategy, the chocolate milk positioning challenge, and updated coverage of product-market grids.

- **Updated Coverage of Brand Equity:** Chapter 11 now includes the Customer-based Brand Equity Pyramid, which helps explain the relationship between brand awareness and how consumers think and feel about a brand. This helps students understand how the added value of a brand name gives a product competitive and price advantage.

- **Updated Channels Coverage:** Chapter 15 includes new material and examples related to multiple channels of distribution, strategic alliances, vertical marketing, exclusive distribution, slotting allowances, and satisfying buyer requirements that show students how marketing channels are a necessity as a company builds sustainable market value.

- **Updated Supply Chain and Logistics Coverage:** Chapter 16 features current examples, such as "Dell Computer Corporation: A Responsive Supply Chain," and "Wal-Mart, Inc.: An Efficient Supply Chain," and current topics, such as "Information's Role in Supply Chain Responsiveness and Efficiency." Reverse logistics are used to explain the role of supply chains and logistics management in marketing and how a firm balances distribution costs against the need for effective customer service.

- **Updated Retailing Coverage:** Chapter 17 offers a new discussion of the repositioning of Target as an "upscale discount store," updated coverage of the global expansion of many retailers and e-tailers, and popular retail formats such as franchising. In addition, the chapter provides coverage of important new technologies, including cashless vending systems and interactive television shopping, as well as new concepts, such as everyday fair pricing and multi-channel retailing.

- **Updated Advertising Coverage:** Chapter 19 now includes virtual advertising, interactive television, satellite radio, as well as Internet advertising. Up-to-date examples of the latest forms of promotion, including sweepstakes, product placement, and online coupons are also provided.

ORGANIZATION

The Seventh Edition of *Marketing* is divided into five parts. Part 1, "Initiating the Marketing Process," looks first at what marketing is and how it creates customer value and customer relationships (Chapter 1). Then Chapter 2 provides an overview of the strategic marketing process that occurs in an organization—which provides a framework for the text. Appendix A provides a sample marketing plan as a reference for students. Chapter 3 analyzes the five major environmental factors in our changing marketing environment, while Chapter 4 provides a framework for including ethical and social responsibility considerations in marketing decisions.

Part 2, "Understanding Buyers and Markets," first describes, in Chapter 5, how individual consumers reach buying decisions. Next, Chapter 6 looks at organizational buyers and how they make purchase decisions. And finally, in Chapter 7, the nature and scope of world trade and the influence of cultural differences on global marketing practices are explored.

In Part 3, "Targeting Marketing Opportunities," the marketing research function and how information about prospective consumers is linked to marketing strategy and decisions is discussed in Chapter 8. The process of segmenting and targeting markets and positioning products appears in Chapter 9.

Part 4, "Satisfying Marketing Opportunities," covers the four Ps—the marketing mix elements. The product element is divided into the natural chronological sequence of first developing new products and services (Chapter 10) and then managing the existing products (Chapter 11) and services (Chapter 12). Pricing is covered in terms of underlying pricing analysis (Chapter 13), followed by actual price setting (Chapter 14), and Appendix B, Financial Aspects of Marketing. Three chapters address the place (distribution) aspects of marketing: Managing Marketing Channels and Wholesaling (Chapter 15), Integrating Supply Chain and Logistics Management (Chapter 16), and Retailing (Chapter 17). Retailing is a separate chapter because of its importance and interest as a career for many of today's students. Promotion is also covered in three chapters. Chapter 18 discusses integrated marketing communications and direct marketing, topics that have grown in importance in the marketing discipline recently. The primary forms of mass market communication—advertising, sales promotion, and public relations—are covered in Chapter 19. Personal selling and sales management is covered in Chapter 20.

Part 5, "Managing the Marketing Process," discusses issues and techniques related to interactive marketing technologies and the strategic marketing process. Chapter 21 describes how interactive technologies influence customer value and the customer experience through context, content, community, customization, connectivity, and commerce. Chapter 22 expands on Chapter 2 to describe specific techniques and issues related to blending the four marketing mix elements to plan, implement, and control marketing programs.

The book closes with several useful supplemental sections. Appendix C, "Planning a Career in Marketing," discusses marketing jobs and how to get them, and Appendix D provides 22 alternate cases. In addition, a detailed glossary and three indexes (name, company/product, and subject) complete the book.

ACKNOWLEDGMENTS

DEVELOPMENT OF THE TEXT AND PACKAGE

To ensure continuous improvement of our product we have utilized an extensive review and development process for each of our past editions. Building on that history, the Seventh Edition development process included several phases of evaluation and a variety of stakeholder audiences (e.g., students, instructors, etc.).

- The first phase of the review process asked adopters to suggest improvements to the text and supplements through a detailed review of each component while used in the classroom. We also surveyed students to find out what they liked about the book and what changes they would suggest.
- The second phase utilized user and non-user focus groups. These sessions focused specifically on the supplements package and its effectiveness for instructors and students.
- Finally, a group of experienced marketing instructors gave us feedback on selected chapters of the Sixth Edition and the supplements package.

Reviewers who were vital in the changes made to this edition include:

Christie Amato
University of North Carolina, Charlotte

Gerard Athaide
Loyola College

Andy Aylesworth
Bentley College

Karen Becker-Olsen
New York University

Joseph Belonax
Western Michigan University

Parimal Bhagat
William Paterson University

Jeff Blodgett
University of Mississippi

Charles Bodkin
University of North Carolina, Charlotte

Thomas Brashear
University of Massachusetts, Amherst

Martin Bressler
Thomas College

Bruce Brown
New River Community College

Alan Bush
University of Memphis

S. Choi Chan
Rutgers University

Clare Comm
University of Massachusetts, Lowell

Cristanna Cook
Husson College

John Coppett
University of Houston, Clear Lake Campus

John Cox
Campbellsville University

Scott Cragin
Missouri Southern College

Hugh Daubek
Purdue University, Calumet

Tino DeMarco
SUNY, Albany

Michael Drafke
College of DuPage

Eric Ecklund
Cambria Rowe Business College

Lori Feldman
Purdue University, Calumet

Kevin Feldt
University of Akron

Theresa Flaherty
Old Dominion University

Renee Foster
Delta State University

Stan Garfunkel
Queensborough Community College

James Ginther
Northern Virginia Community College

Susan Godar
William Paterson University

Dan Goebel
University of Southern Mississippi

Darrell Goudge
University of Central Oklahoma

Dotty Harpool
Wichita State University

Lynn Harris
Shippensburg University

Jonathan Hibbard
Boston University

Deb Jansky
Milwaukee Area Technical College

Sudhir Karunakaran
New York University

George Kelley
Erie Community College

Nanda Kumar
University of Texas, Dallas

Ann Kuzma
Minnesota State University, Mankato

John Kuzma
Minnesota State University, Mankato

Jay Lambe
Virginia Polytechnic Institute

Ron Larson
Western Michigan University

Robert Lawson
William Paterson University

Ann Little
High Point University

James Lollar
Radford University

Ann Lucht
Milwaukee Area Technical College

Richard Lutz
University of Florida

Rhonda Mack
College of Charleston

Phyllis McGinnis
Boston University

Jo Ann McManamy
Middlesex Community College

George Miaoulis
University of New Hampshire

Melissa Moore
Mississippi State University

Bill Murphy
Winona State University

Bob Newberry
Winona State University

Stephen Pirog
Seton Hall University

Cathie Rich-Duval
Merrimack College

William Rodgers
St. Cloud State University

Vicki Rostedt
University of Akron

Roberta Schultz
Western Michigan University

Jim Spiers
Arizona State University

Joe Stasio
Merrimack College

Tom Stevenson
University of North Carolina, Charlotte

Michael Swenson
Brigham Young University

Sue Umashankar
University of Arizona

Jeff von Freymann
Wingate College

Mark Weber
University of Minnesota

Don Weinrauch
Tennessee Tech

Sheila Wexler
University of Virginia

Janice Williams
University of Central Oklahoma

Wendy Wood
Bevill State Community College

Mark Young
Winona State University

Leon Zurawicki
University of Massachusetts, Boston

The preceding section demonstrates the amount of feedback and developmental input that went into this project, and we are deeply grateful to the numerous people who have shared their ideas with us. Reviewing a book or supplement takes an incredible amount of energy and attention. We are glad so many of our colleagues took the time to do it. Their comments have inspired us to do our best.

Reviewers who contributed to the first six editions of this book include:

Nadia J. Abgrab
Kerri Acheson
Roy Adler
Linda Anglin
William D. Ash
Patricia Baconride
Siva Balasubramanian
A. Diane Barlar
James H. Barnes
Frederick J. Beier
Thom J. Belich
Thomas M. Bertsch
Kevin W. Bittle
Nancy Bloom
William Brown
William G. Browne
Stephen Calcich
William J. Carner
Gerald O. Cavallo
S. Tamer Cavusgil
Sang Choe
Kay Chomic
Clare Comm
Clark Compton
Ken Crocker
Joe Cronin
James Cross
Lowell E. Crow
John H. Cunningham
Bill Curtis
Dan Darrow
Martin Decatur
Francis DeFea
Linda M. Delene
Paul Dion
William B. Dodds

James H. Donnelly
Eddie V. Easley
Roger W. Egerton
Steven Engel
Barbara Evans
Charles Ford
Donald Fuller
Marc Goldberg
Leslie A. Goldgehn
Kenneth Goodenday
James Gould
James L. Grimm
Pola B. Gupta
Richard Hansen
Donald V. Harper
Robert C. Harris
James A. Henley, Jr.
Richard M. Hill
Al Holden
Kristine Hovsepian
Jarrett Hudnal
Mike Hyman
Donald R. Jackson
Kenneth Jameson
James C. Johnson
Robert Jones
Mary Joyce
Jacqueline Karen
Herbert Katzenstein
Ram Kesaran
Roy Klages
Douglas Kornemann
Terry Kroeten
Priscilla LaBarbera
Duncan G. LaBay
Richard Lapidus

Irene Lange
Ed Laube
Debra Laverie
Gary Law
Wilton Lelund
Karen LeMasters
Richard C. Leventhal
Leonard Lindenmuth
Lynn Loudenback
Mike Luckett
Robert Luke
Michael R. Luthy
Richard J. Lutz
Barton L. Macchietta
Patricia Manninen
Kenneth Maricle
Elena Martinez
James McAlexander
Peter J. McClure
Jim McHugh
Gary F. McKinnon
Lee Meadow
James Meszaros
Ronald Michaels
Stephen W. Miller
William G. Mitchell
Linda Morable
Fred Morgan
William Motz
Donald F. Mulvihill
Janet Murray
Keith Murray
Joseph Myslivec
Donald G. Norris
Carl Obermiller
Dave Olson

James Olver
Philip Parron
Allan Palmer
Dennis Pappas
Richard Penn
June E. Parr
John Penrose
William Pertula
Michael Peters
William S. Piper
Gary Poorman
Vonda Powell
Joe Puzi
James P. Rakowski
Barbara Ribbens
Heikki Rinne
Jean Romeo
Larry Rottmeyer
Robert W. Ruekert

Maria Sanella
Eberhard Scheuing
Charles Schewe
Starr F. Schlobohm
Stan Scott
Harold S. Sekiguchi
Doris M. Shaw
Eric Shaw
Bob E. Smiley
Allen Smith
Ruth Ann Smith
James V. Spiers
Craig Stacey
Miriam B. Stamps
Scott Swan
Robert Swerdlow
Vincent P. Taiani
Clint Tankersley
Ruth Taylor

Andrew Thacker
Fred Trawick
Thomas L. Trittipo
Sue Umashankar
Ottilia Voegtli
Gerald Waddle
Randall E. Wade
Blaise Waguespack, Jr.
Harlan Wallingford
Robert S. Welsh
Ron Weston
Max White
James Wilkins
Kaylene Williams
Robert Williams
Jerry W. Wilson
Robert Witherspoon
Van R. Wood
William R. Wynd

Thanks are also due to many faculty members who contributed to the text chapters and cases. They include: Linda Rochford of the University of Minnesota, Duluth; David Gobeli of Oregon State University and Corrine Gobeli; Kenneth Goodpaster, Thomas Holloran, David Brennan, and Mark Spriggs of the University of St. Thomas; Thomas Belich of Bethel College; and Kathy Chadwick of St. Olaf College. Krzysztof Przybylowski of the Warsaw School of Economics and Olga Saguinova of the Plekhanov Academy of Economics provided a number of international materials. Michael Vessey provided cases, research assistance, many special images, and led our efforts on the In-Class Activities and Instructor's Survival Kit. Rick Armstrong produced the videos. William Carner of the University of Texas provided the study guide. Thomas K. Pritchett of Kennesaw College and Betty M. Pritchett were responsible for the revision of the test bank. Steve Engel of the University of Colorado and David Nowell of Sheridan College produced the interactive exercises. Milton Pressley and Steve Henson of the University of New Orleans produced the PowerPoint package. Steven White, University of Massachusetts, Dartmouth wrote the marketing plan guidelines and the sample marketing plan included on the Student CD. Our Russian edition coauthors provided the idea for the new descriptive case titles. Finally, Anne Harbour provided assistance with the glossary and was responsible for the revision of the Instructor's Manual.

Many businesspeople also provided substantial assistance by making available information that appears in the text and supplements—much of it for the first time in college materials. Thanks are due to Jimmy Jam, Terry Lewis, and Susan Owens of Flyte Tyme Productions; Carol Watzke of CNS; David Ford of Ford Consulting Group; Maureen Cahill of Mall of America; Jack McKeon and Frank Lynch of Golden Valley Microwave Foods; Wayne Johansen of HOM Furniture; Sarah Casanova of McDonald's in Russia; Donald Dunham of BP plc; Ken Hart of 3M; Debra Kennedy and Keith Nowak of Nokia; Monica Noordam, Umberto Milletti, and Shelly Berkowitz of DigitalThink; and Mark Rehborg of Tony's Pizza. We also acknowledge the special help of a team that worked with us on the Fallon Worldwide video case: Fred Senn, Bruce Bildsten, Kevin Flatt, Ginny Grossman, Kim Knutson, Julie Smith, Erin Tait, and Rob White.

Staff support from Southern Methodist University, the University of Denver, and the University of St. Thomas was essential. We gratefully acknowledge the help of Wanda Hanson, Louise Holt, Jeanne Milazzo, Gloria Valdez, and Karin Zeller for their many contributions.

Finally, we acknowledge the professional efforts of the McGraw-Hill/Irwin staff. Completion of our book and its many supplements required the attention and commitment of many editorial, production, marketing, and research personnel. Our Burr

Ridge–based team included John Biernat, Gary Bauer, Tracy Jensen, Scott Becker, Kimberly Kanakes, Mike Beamer, Erwin Llereza, Dave Kapoor, Kimberly Hooker, Laurie Entringer, Heather Burbridge, Melanie Becker, Sue Lombardi, Craig Atkins, Nick Barrett, Ira Roberts, and many others! In addition we relied on Claudia McCowan of GTS Graphics and Michael Hruby for constant attention regarding composition and photo elements of the text. Finally, our development editor, Gina Huck of Imaginative Solutions, provided outstanding assistance, advice, coordination, editing, and guidance with extraordinary professionalism and enthusiasm. Handling the countless details of our text, supplement, and support technologies has become an incredibly complex challenge. We thank all these people for their efforts and—in the end—their good work and good humor!

Roger A. Kerin
Eric N. Berkowitz
Steven W. Hartley
William Rudelius

A STUDENT'S GUIDE TO *MARKETING*, 7/e

Marketing, 7/e offers an array of pedagogical features to help you learn and apply the concepts at hand.

Chapter-Opening Vignettes—*Over 95% are new or revised!*

Chapter-opening vignettes introduce you to the chapter concepts ahead, using a recognizable and interesting company example. For instance in Chapter 9, the authors use Heelys (a shoe with built-in wheels targeted at skateboard and inline skate enthusiasts) and the segmentation strategies of Reebok, Nike, New Balance, Vans, and others to grab your interest.

The chapter-opening discussion is then woven throughout parts of the narrative, exhibits, and boxed features as well.

MARKETING NEWSNET

Communicating with Gen Y . . . 29.8 Hours per Day!

Recent research indicates that consumers have created 29.8-hour days by using more than one communication medium at the same time—a behavior often called "multitasking." Generation Y seems to be particularly adept at this new phenomenon. For example, it would not be unusual for a college freshman to log onto the Internet while listening to the radio and checking out Web addresses in a magazine! One reason is that media is pervasive—the average student may be exposed to 5000 messages each day—but another reason is the desire to be informed and to "keep in touch." As a result, this group of consumers probably doesn't give its full attention to any single message. Instead it uses continuous partial attention to scan the media.

Marketers can still communicate with Gen Y by utilizing a variety of promotional tools—from advertising to packaging to word-of-mouth communication—with an integrated message. Which media work particularly well with Gen Y? The most popular television channel is MTV. The most popular magazines are *Sports Illustrated* and *Seventeen*.

Favorite websites include anything with content related to their interests: celebrities, music, sports, and videogames. Another tactic growing in popularity is viral, or *"buzz" marketing*. Volkswagen of America, for example, holds contests on college campuses to see how many people can fit into a Volkswagen Beetle (the current record is 26). The participants and the observers end up experiencing and talking about the product for at least part of their 29.8-hour day!

Marketing NewsNet— *Nearly 75% new or updated!*

This boxed feature provides exciting, current examples of marketing applications in action, organized around the following themes: Technology & E-Commerce, Customer Value, Global, and Cross Functional.

Ethics and Social Responsibility Alert—*Over 50% new or updated!*

These boxes increase your awareness and assessment of current topics of ethical and social concern.

Web Link—*Over 70% new or updated!*

Integrated throughout the text, Web Links encourage you to explore digital strategies that innovative companies and organizations are employing online.

Concept Checks

Found at the end of each major chapter section, these checkpoints offer critical thinking and memory recall questions, helping you reflect on the text and test your comprehension of the material before reading on.

Concept Check

1. How does a product manager help manage a product's life cycle?

2. What does "creating new use situations" mean in managing a product's life cycle?

3. Explain the difference between trading up and trading down in repositioning.

Firms use actors or athletes as spokespersons to represent their products, such as Pierce Brosnan and Anna Kournikova for Omega watches, in the hope that they are opinion leaders.

Omega
www.omega.com

Pierce Brosnan's Choice

Anna Kournikova's Choice

Website Addresses

The URLs of companies and organizations discussed in the text are easily located in the text margin—facilitating further exploration of these real-world examples.

Internet Exercises—*Over 70% new or updated!*

These end-of chapter exercises ask you to go online and think critically about a specific company's use of the Internet—helping you apply your knowledge of key chapter concepts, terms, and topics, as well as evaluate the success or failure of the company's efforts.

INTERNET EXERCISE

Jalapeño soda? Aerosol mustard? Fingos? These are just three of the more than 65,000 products (both successes and failures) on the shelves of the NewProductWorks Showcase in Ann Arbor, Michigan. The Showcase includes food, beverages, health and beauty care, household, and pet products appearing from 1965 to the present. Although you probably can't personally visit the company, you can visit its new website (www.newproductworks.

ture is in doubt; "Failures," which are recent products that have failed miserably; and "Favorite Failures," which are those that cause people to ask *"What were they thinking?"* Study several of the failed products listed on the website and

VIDEO CASE 1–1 Rollerblade®: Rediscovering Growth

In the fiercely competitive in-line skate marketplace, what does the future hold for Rollerblade®?

As David Samuels, senior director for Sports Innovation at Rollerblade explains, innovative technology—in the form of new and better skates—will continue to be key for Rollerblade to stay ahead of the competition. Rollerblade must also find ways to expand the market for in-line skates. "Our challenge is to provide new venues, new reasons for people to skate. There's a lot of growth for us to catch up on in terms of household penetration," says Samuels.

THE SITUATION TODAY

When Rollerblade was founded, it was the only manufacturer of in-line skates in the world. Today the industry has more than 30 competitors, many that sell lower-priced skates than Rollerblade through mass-merchandising chains. Some of the large sporting goods manufacturers, like Nike, that have not traditionally sold in-line skates are now looking for ways to grow and are exploring the in-line skate market.

In addition, both Rollerblade and other in-line skate manufacturers are facing increased competition from

---

VIDEO CASE 3–1 Flyte Tyme Productions, Inc.: The Best Idea Wins!

"Terry was looking for a keyboard player to be in the band he was just starting," remembers Jimmy Jam of Flyte Tyme Productions, Inc. "I had sort of rebelled because I had first thought of myself as a drummer," says Jam. But after he listened and heard how good the drummer was, he told Terry, "I'll be the keyboard player."

The conversation took place a few weeks after Terry Lewis and Jimmy Jam met at a summer math program for gifted junior high school students, sponsored by a local university. The two came to prominence in the early 1980s as members of the funk band "The Time" that appeared as the opener on many of Prince's early tours. The pair still credit Prince for much of their tenacious work ethic and eclectic musical tastes. After leaving the band, Terry and Jimmy started a mu~~...~~
Flyte Tyme—creating the nev~~...~~
one. Now in their early 40s,~~...~~
gether for 20 years, most of it~~...~~
(www.flytetyme.com), where~~...~~
J. Blige, Boyz II Men, Mar~~...~~
Michael Jackson, Patti LaBel~~...~~
others!

THE MUSIC

Flyte Tyme's successes are impressive. Recently they produced Usher's No. 1 pop hit "U Remind Me," which held the top spot on the charts for four weeks. They also produced Sting's Oscar-nominated song "My Funny Friend and Me" for the film *The Emperor's New Clothes*. And their work on Hikaru Utada's album helped it climb to the top of Japan's pop charts, selling 4 million copies in two weeks!

These and other hits put Flyte Tyme in extraordinary company. Having produced 16 No. 1 singles on *Billboard*'s pop chart, they are second only to the producer for the Beatles (with 23) and tied with the producer for Elvis Presley. Flyte Tyme has managed to stay at the top throughout the 1980s, '90s, and '00s, thanks in large part

---

VIDEO CASE 9–1 Nokia: A Phone for Every Segment

"While practically everybody today is a potential mobile phone customer, everybody is simultaneously different in terms of usage, needs, lifestyles, and individual preferences," explains Nokia's Media Relations Manager, Keith Nowak. Understanding those differences requires that Nokia conduct ongoing research among different consumer groups throughout the world. The approach is reflected in the company's business strategy:

> We intend to exploit our leadership role by continuing to target and enter segments of the communications market that we believe will experience rapid growth or grow faster than the industry as a whole. . . .

In fact, Nowak believes that "to be successful in the mobile phone business of today and tomorrow, Nokia has to fully understand the fundamental nature and rationale of segmentation."

THE COMPANY

tures that were sold mainly in North America. In the 1990s, second generation (2G) devices consisted of voice/data digital cell phones with higher data transfer rates, expanded range, and more features. Sales of these devices expanded to Europe and Asia. In the twenty-first century, Nokia and other companies are combining several digital technologies into third generation (3G) communication devices that reach globally and feature the convergence of the cell phone, personal digital assistant (PDA), Internet services, and multimedia applications.

The global demand for cell phones has increased significantly over the years—from 284 million in 1999 to 410 million units in 2000 to 510 million units in 2001.

Producers of first and second generation cell phones used a geographic segmentation strategy as wireless communication networks were developed. Most started with the U.S. and then proceeded to Western Europe and Asia. However, each market grew ~~...~~ diff~~...~~

Alternate Cases (Appendix D)

Not only do you get 22 end-of-chapter video cases, but 22 alternate cases found in Appendix D—now that's a lot of learning opportunities!

Appendix A: Creating an Effective Marketing Plan

Following Chapter 2, this sample marketing plan of Howlin' Coyote Chili provides you with an effective reference early on in the text.

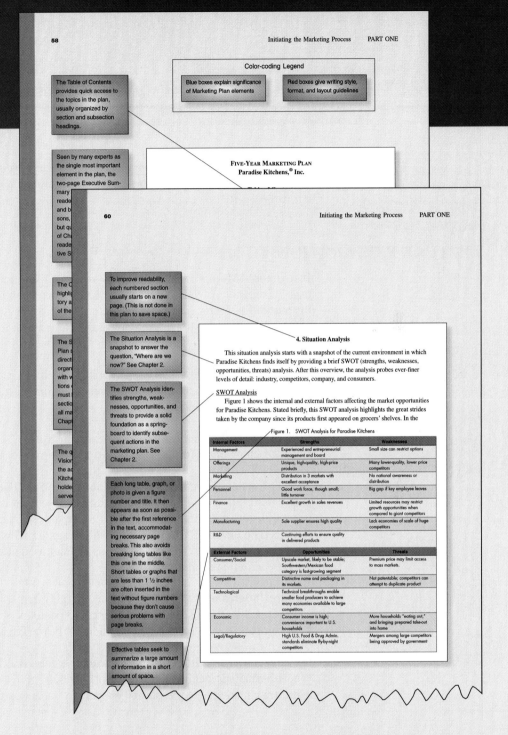

58   Initiating the Marketing Process   PART ONE

Color-coding Legend

| Blue boxes explain significance of Marketing Plan elements | Red boxes give writing style, format, and layout guidelines |

The Table of Contents provides quick access to the topics in the plan, usually organized by section and subsection headings.

Seen by many experts as the single most important element in the plan, the two-page Executive Summary...

FIVE-YEAR MARKETING PLAN
Paradise Kitchens,® Inc.

60   Initiating the Marketing Process   PART ONE

To improve readability, each numbered section usually starts on a new page. (This is not done in this plan to save space.)

The Situation Analysis is a snapshot to answer the question, "Where are we now?" See Chapter 2.

The SWOT Analysis identifies strengths, weaknesses, opportunities, and threats to provide a solid foundation as a springboard to identify subsequent actions in the marketing plan. See Chapter 2.

Each long table, graph, or photo is given a figure number and title. It then appears as soon as possible after the first reference in the text, accommodating necessary page breaks. This also avoids breaking long tables like this one in the middle. Short tables or graphs that are less than 1 ½ inches are often inserted in the text without figure numbers because they don't cause serious problems with page breaks.

Effective tables seek to summarize a large amount of information in a short amount of space.

4. Situation Analysis

This situation analysis starts with a snapshot of the current environment in which Paradise Kitchens finds itself by providing a brief SWOT (strengths, weaknesses, opportunities, threats) analysis. After this overview, the analysis probes ever-finer levels of detail: industry, competitors, company, and consumers.

SWOT Analysis

Figure 1 shows the internal and external factors affecting the market opportunities for Paradise Kitchens. Stated briefly, this SWOT analysis highlights the great strides taken by the company since its products first appeared on grocers' shelves. In the

Figure 1. SWOT Analysis for Paradise Kitchens

Internal Factors	Strengths	Weaknesses
Management	Experienced and entrepreneurial management and board	Small size can restrict options
Offerings	Unique, high-quality, high-price products	Many lower-quality, lower price competitors
Marketing	Distribution in 3 markets with excellent acceptance	No national awareness or distribution
Personnel	Good work force, though small; little turnover	Big gap if key employee leaves
Finance	Excellent growth in sales revenues	Limited resources may restrict growth opportunities when compared to giant competitors
Manufacturing	Sole supplier ensures high quality	Lack economies of scale of huge competitors
R&D	Continuing efforts to ensure quality in delivered products	

External Factors	Opportunities	Threats
Consumer/Social	Upscale market, likely to be stable; Southwestern/Mexican food category is fast-growing segment	Premium price may limit access to mass markets.
Competitive	Distinctive name and packaging in its markets.	Not patentable; competitors can attempt to duplicate product
Technological	Technical breakthroughs enable smaller food producers to achieve many economies available to large competitors	
Economic	Consumer income is high; convenience important to U.S. households	More households "eating out," and bringing prepared take-out into home
Legal/Regulatory	High U.S. Food & Drug Admin. standards eliminate fly-by-night competitors	Mergers among large competitors being approved by government

Plus, when combined with the Marketing Planning Software on the enclosed Student CD-ROM, you can't lose when it comes to learning!

AN INSTRUCTOR'S GUIDE TO SUPPLEMENTS

With the greatly enhanced Seventh Edition package, you and your students are covered from the basic supplements to the latest in educational technologies. Check it out for yourself!

LECTURE PREPARATION TOOLS

Instructor's Manual: The thoroughly revised Instructor's Manual includes: lecture notes; discussions of the Marketing NewsNet boxes, Web Link boxes, Ethics and Social Responsibility Alerts, Internet Exercises; answers to the Applying Marketing Concepts and Applications questions; supplemental lecture notes; teaching suggestions; and detailed information about integrating other supplements into the course and classroom.

Instructor's CD-ROM: The CD-ROM includes the print and electronic supplements, so you have access to all of the supplements on one disk. It also contains the seventh edition Computest package.

Video Case and Appendix D Case Teaching Notes: This media resource guide includes teaching notes for the video cases and alternate cases.

New PowerPoint Lecture Presentation Assembly Guide: This printed guide contains a description of all of the individual multimedia assets from which you can construct a custom presentation. The assets are organized by chapter and by topic, and are contained on the CD-ROM packaged with the guide. This guide also includes instructions on how to import the video, audio, art, photos, and other files into new or existing PowerPoint presentations.

Online Updates and Current Events: Adopters can sign up to be emailed updates on cases and material specific to the text, and postings of new *BusinessWeek* articles, all accompanied with teaching notes and new PowerPoint slides as appropriate.

In-Class Activities Guide in the Instructor's Survival Kit: This resource provides you with detailed teaching notes, relevant handouts, props, and products for use in-class to illustrate marketing concepts and encourage student participation and collaboration.

LECTURE PRESENTATION TOOLS

New and Revised **Video Case Studies:** A unique series of 22 contemporary marketing cases is available on cassette. Each video case corresponds with chapter-specific topics and an end-of-chapter case in the text. Selected new videos include Flyte Tyme, Nokia, Ford Consulting and substantially revised/updated videos, including Fallon Worldwide, Mall of America, and Golden Valley Microwave Foods.

New and Enhanced **PowerPoint Presentation:** Featuring a high-quality photo and art program including figure slides, commercials, product shots, advertisements, marketing-in-practice shots, and video segments from the video package. The presentation is contained on CD-ROMs packaged with the new **PowerPoint Lecture Presentation Assembly Guide**.

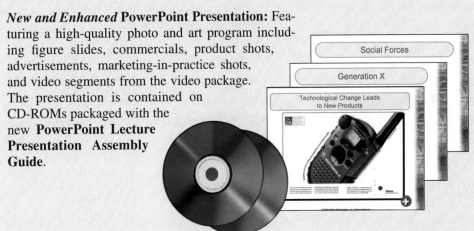

Instructor's Survival Kit (ISK): The kit offers new ways to spark classroom discussion and collaboration! Contents include:

- **In-Class Activities Guide** with learning objectives, transparency masters, appropriate handouts and templates, and detailed instructions for conducting the exercise.
- **In-Class Activities:** Popular activities from our past editions include brainstorming new advertising ideas for Breathe Right Strips, figuring out features of a better mousetrap, the Coke versus Pepsi taste test, and the "Ethics Quiz."
- **"Props":** To help implement the in-class activities and save instructor time, "props" such as labels for the Coke versus Pepsi taste test, the Breathe Right Strips for an in-class product test, and an example of the America Online direct mail software offer are included.
- **Sample Products:** A number of new products are included in the survival kit, such as 3M VHS pull apart strips and Breathe Right Strips. Also, when appropriate, related ads are included in transparencies and PowerPoint.

Instructor Survival Kit Updates: Twice each year two new In-Class Activities with related props or sample products and teaching notes will be made available to adopters of the text free of charge.

Color Acetates: 200 four-color overhead transparency acetates! 50% of these have been developed from information supplemental to the text and are accompanied by lecture notes to assist integration of this material into lectures.

ASSESSMENT TOOLS

Expanded 5,000+ Question Test Bank: Dramatically expanded and improved, the test bank now contains 5,000 questions categorized by topic and level of learning (definitional, conceptual, or application). The number of conceptual and application questions has been augmented with over 1,000 additional questions.

Expanded Computest Program: This Computest is revised to contain all of the multiple-choice questions from the Test Bank, Web and Student CD-ROM Quizzes, Study Guide, and PowerWeb readings so you can include questions from these supplements in tests and quizzes. This allows you to reward students who go the extra mile and utilize these study aids. The Computest program allows you to select any of the questions, make changes if desired, or add new questions—and quickly print out a finished set customized to your course.

PageOut Quizzes with Instructor Gradebook: Assign quizzes in PageOut to give students incentive to read the text and prepare for class. Grades for each student will automatically post to your class gradebook.

Online Learning Center and Student CD-ROM Quizzes: Helps to prepare students for taking tests: www.mhhe.com/kerin.

STUDENT LEARNING TOOLS

Print Study Guide: To go beyond mere memorization and actually apply marketing principles, the Study Guide provides students with chapter outlines for note-taking, sample tests, critical thinking questions, and flash cards.

Student CD-ROM: Packaged free-of-charge with every textbook, this CD-ROM contains a Narrated Concept Review for each chapter of the book. This study outline in PowerPoint features all key concepts from the text and narrated explanations of key figures. The CD-ROM also contains Self Assessment Quizzes with Feedback for each chapter, and Marketing Planning Software.

Student Online Learning Center: Students can visit this rich book-specific website to find current *BusinessWeek* articles, lots of self study and quizzing resources, and the Kerin et al., Seventh Edition PowerWeb resources, including Daily News Feed, Weekly Case Updates, *Readings in Marketing,* PowerSearch research engine, Career Resources, Web Research guidance, and Study Tips.

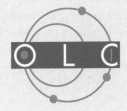

***BusinessWeek* Edition:** Students can subscribe to *BusinessWeek* at a special rate with purchase of the text. This real-world complement to the Seventh Edition is a great way to keep your course and classroom discussion current.

***The Wall Street Journal* Edition:** Students can obtain a 15-week subscription to the *WSJ* at a special rate with purchase of the text.

***Marketing, 7/e* PowerText:** Interactive Multimedia e-book . . . *Marketing,* 7/e online! PowerText offers an integrated learning experience that combines the traditional content of a textbook with the media-rich environment of the Internet. The content is designed to appeal to all learning styles, as material is presented through integrated components including text, animated illustrations, video resources, quizzes, interactive critical thinking exercises, and career resources. Students can purchase access to PowerText to complement their textbook or as an alternative to buying the printed textbook.

ONLINE TECHNOLOGY

Online Learning Center with PowerWeb

This robust book-specific website includes resources for both instructors and students. For the instructor, we offer downloadable supplement materials and continuous updates. Students have a 24-7 study center to keep them up-to-date, to provide examples for application, and to prepare for a test. The website also includes PowerWeb, featuring its online readings and daily newsfeed.

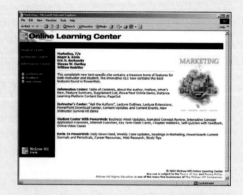

Instructor Center

- **"Ask the Authors"**
- **Instructor's Manual**
- **PowerPoint:** Includes concept screens and art from the text and notes on other digital assets available in the PowerPoint Presentation Assembly Guide.
- **Content Updates and Current Events:** You can sign up for e-mail updates on material specific to the text, postings of new *BusinessWeek* articles, and new case updates on PowerWeb—all accompanied with teaching notes and new PowerPoint slides as appropriate.
- **New Instructor's Survival Kit Items:** Twice during the school year, we will offer two new activities along with appropriate props and products for use in-class.

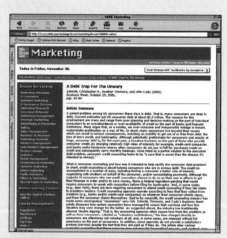

Student Center with PowerWeb

- *BusinessWeek* **Updates:** Important articles related to marketing will be posted.
- **Narrated Concept Review:** A study guide in PowerPoint covers major concepts in the text with narrated reviews of key figures.
- **Marketing Workshop, including:**
  - **Interactive Concept Application Exercises:** Engaging interactive exercises pose an issue or scenario and then require the student to make a choice. Feedback is provided for all student choices.
  - **Internet Exercises**
  - **Key Term Flash Cards**
  - **Chapter Web Links**
  - **Self Quizzes with Feedback**
  - **Online Video Cases:** Includes video case text and several video clips.

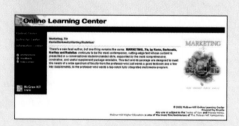

PowerWeb

- **Daily News Feed:** Headlines with annotations from the leading periodicals and news sources—searchable by topic.
- **Weekly Case Updates:** Each week a new short case dealing with a company in the headlines is presented.
- *Readings in Marketing:* A collection of important articles selected by a team of marketing professors provides deeper topical study.
- **PowerSearch Current Journals and Periodicals:** Search engine powered by Northern Lights.
- **Career Resources**
- **Web Research**
- **Study Tips**

PowerWeb elements have been integrated into the OLC to give students quicker access to additional online resources.

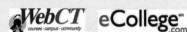

Fully compatible

You can use *Marketing,* 7/e online material with any online platform—including Blackboard, WebCT, and eCollege—to expand the reach of your course and open up distance learning options.

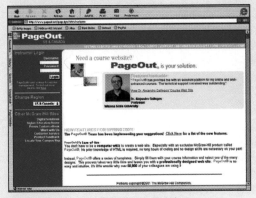

PageOut

This unique point-and-click course website tool enables you to create a high-quality course website without knowing HTML coding. With PageOut you can post your syllabus online, assign McGraw-Hill Online Learning Center or e-Book content, add links to important off-site resources, and maintain student results in the online gradebook.

Create a course website in no time!

BRIEF CONTENTS

DETAILED CONTENTS

Part 4
Satisfying Marketing Opportunities 264

10 DEVELOPING NEW PRODUCTS AND SERVICES 266

Part 5   Managing the Marketing Process   556

BOXED FEATURES

Stay up to date with these timely and interesting boxed features

MARKETING NEWSNET

WEB LINK

ETHICS AND SOCIAL RESPONSIBILITY ALERT

1

INITIATING THE MARKETING PROCESS

Developing customer relationships and value. This is the essence of the marketing process described in Part 1. Chapter 1 introduces the marketing process by describing the actions of Rollerblade as it faces the challenges of finding strategies to build on the phenomenal success of the product that created an entirely new industry. Chapter 2 describes how organizations such as Ben & Jerry's utilize the strategic marketing process to better serve its customers. Following Chapter 2 is a sample marketing plan (Appendix A) that illustrates the outcome of the strategic marketing process and provides a reference for students to study and use. Chapter 3 scans the business environment and identifies its important trends. The changes are described in terms of social, economic, technological, competitive, and regulatory forces. Finally, Chapter 4 provides a framework for including ethical and social responsibility considerations in marketing decisions.

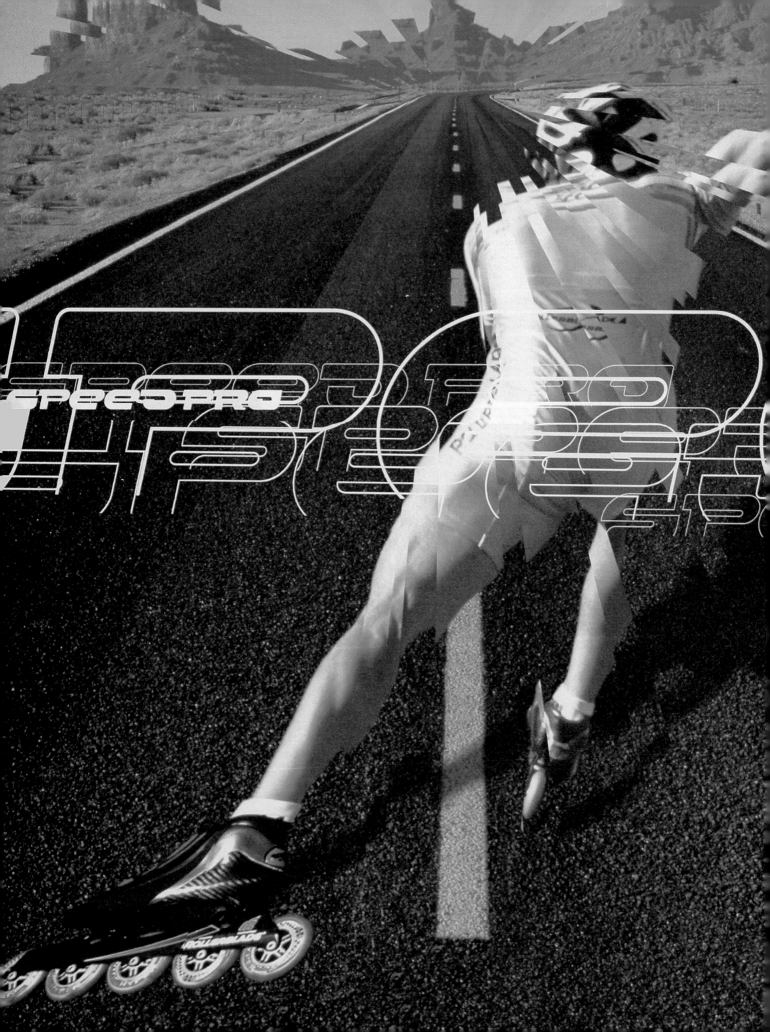

1

DEVELOPING CUSTOMER RELATIONSHIPS AND VALUE THROUGH MARKETING

AFTER READING THIS CHAPTER YOU SHOULD BE ABLE TO:

- Define marketing and explain the importance of (1) discovering and (2) satisfying consumer needs and wants.

- Distinguish between marketing mix elements and environmental factors.

- Understand how organizations build strong customer relationships using current thinking about customer value and relationship marketing.

- Describe how today's market orientation era differs from prior eras oriented to production and selling.

- Understand the meaning of ethics and social responsibility and how they relate to the individual, organizations, and society.

- Know what is required for marketing to occur and how it creates customer value and utilities for consumers.

FUSION, CORE, AND LIGHTNING! PHYSICS 101?

Well, . . . not quite!

This manufacturer has the classic marketing problem of any mind-bending company that has created an entire industry! What does it do for an encore? What does it do to innovate, to provide products that prospective buyers want . . . that build continuing, loyal customer relationships? A big part of the answer *is* fusion, core, and lightning or—more properly—Fusion™, Core™, and Lightning™. But that puts us ahead of the Rollerblade® story.

The Three-Century Old Innovation In the early 1700s a Dutch inventor trying to simulate ice skating in the summer created the first roller skates by attaching spools to his shoes. His in-line arrangement was the standard design until 1863 when the first skates with rollers set as two pairs appeared. This design became the standard, and in-line skates virtually disappeared from the market.

In 1980, two Minnesota hockey-playing brothers found an old pair of in-line skates while browsing through a sporting goods store. Working in their garage, they modified the design to add polyurethane wheels, a molded boot shell, and a toe brake. They sold their product, which they dubbed "Rollerblade skates," out of the back of their truck to hockey players and skiers as a means of staying in shape during the summer. In the mid-1980s an entrepreneur bought the company from the brothers and then hired marketing executive Mary Horwath to figure out how to market Rollerblade skates.

Understanding the Consumer   "When I came here," remembers Horwath, "I knew there had to be a change." By focusing only on serious athletes who used in-line skates to train for other sports, Rollerblade had developed an image as a training product. Conversations with in-line skaters, however, convinced Horwath that using Rollerblade skates:

• Was incredible fun.
• Was a great aerobic workout and made the skater stronger and healthier.
• Was quite different from traditional roller skating, which was practiced alone, mostly inside, and by young girls.
• Would have great appeal to people other than just off-season ice hockey skaters and skiers.

Horwath saw her task as changing the image in people's minds—or "repositioning"—Rollerblade skates to highlight the benefits people saw in in-line skating. Using what she called "guerilla marketing," Horwath used her tiny $200,000 annual marketing budget to gain national exposure for Rollerblade skates using inexpensive, nontraditional promotional methods such as "demo vans" loaded with skates that people could try for free.

What a Difference a Decade Makes   Fast-forward from the late 1980s to the early 21st century. The marketing problems of Rollerblade today are a far cry from those faced by Mary Horwath in the late 1980s. As shown in Figure 1–1[1], she and the company succeeded in popularizing in-line skating—and actually succeeded in launching an entirely new industry, as evidenced by the 27.8 million U.S. in-line skaters in 1997 (the peak year). One measure of the success of in-line skating is that it appeared in the first Extreme Games competition in 1995. However, the flattening of participation in in-line skating in the late 1990s is a source of concern to Rollerblade.

FIGURE 1–1
Number of in-line skaters in the United States. Where is the trend headed? For some answers, see the text.

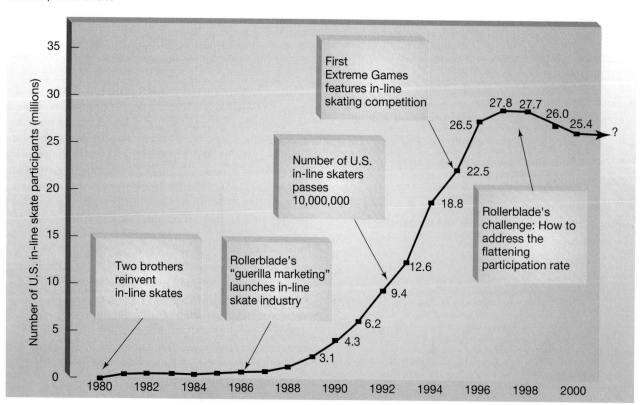

But Rollerblade's success in launching an industry carries its own dangers: competitors. There are more than 30 of them facing off with Rollerblade as the 21st century starts. Rollerblade has 35 percent of the annual industry sales, with no other competitor having more than 10 percent. Thus, Rollerblade's goal is to develop new skating products for current and new segments of buyers, forging strong, loyal customer relationships in the process. This is where breakthrough innovations on Rollerblade's in-line skates such as Fusion, Core, and Lightning come in. This situation presents a huge marketing lesson: Changing consumer tastes and changing competitive offerings require that organizations search continuously for ways to provide genuine value to customers, or the organizations will die. Thus, the future of organizations such as Rollerblade rely on the in-depth understanding of their customers' wants and needs and developing and marketing innovative products to satisfy them.

Rollerblade Skates, Marketing, and You   What marketing strategy is the Rollerblade marketing team using to try to rediscover the skyrocketing growth of in-line skating in the early 1990s shown in Figure 1–1? By the time you reach the end of this chapter, you will know some of the answers to this question.

One key to how well Rollerblade succeeds lies in the subject of this book: marketing. In this chapter and in the rest of the book we'll introduce you to many of the people, organizations, ideas, activities, and jobs in marketing that have spawned the products and services that have been towering successes, shattering failures, or something in between.

Marketing affects all individuals, all organizations, all industries, and all countries. This text seeks not only to teach you marketing concepts, but also to demonstrate its many applications and how it affects our lives. This knowledge should make you a better consumer, help you in your career, and enable you to be a more informed citizen.

In this chapter and those that follow, you will feel the excitement of marketing. You will be introduced to the dynamic changes that will affect all of us in the future. You will also meet many men and women whose marketing creativity sometimes achieved brilliant, extraordinary results. And who knows? Somewhere in these pages you may find a career.

WHAT IS MARKETING?

Being a Marketing Expert: Good News–Bad News

In many respects you are a marketing expert already. But just to test your expertise, try the "marketing expert" questions in Figure 1–2. These questions—some of them easy, others mind-boggling—show the diverse problems marketing executives grapple with every day. You'll find the answers in the next few pages.

The Good News: You Already Have Marketing Experience   You are somewhat of an expert because you do many marketing activities every day. You already know many marketing terms, concepts, and principles. For example, would you sell more 43-inch Hitachi Big Screen HDTV monitors for $1799 or $499 each? The answer is $499, of course, so your experience in shopping for products—and maybe even selling them—already gives you great insights into the world of marketing. As a consumer, you've already been involved in thousands of marketing decisions—but mainly on the buying, not the marketing, side.

The Bad News: Surprises about the Obvious   Unfortunately, common sense doesn't always explain some marketing decisions and actions. An actress's saying that she often "rollerbladed" (question 1, Figure 1–2) sounds like great publicity,

FIGURE 1–2
The see-if-you're-really-a-marketing-expert test

ANSWER THE QUESTIONS BELOW. THE CORRECT ANSWERS ARE GIVEN LATER IN THE CHAPTER.

1. In a magazine article, a well-known actress said she often "rollerbladed" for fun and exercise. What was Rollerblade's reaction? (*a*) delighted, (*b*) upset, or (*c*) somewhere in-between. Why?
2. The name is real so (*a*) what benefits might Kimberly Clark (maker of Kleenex) provide consumers in its *Avert Virucidal Tissues* and (*b*) what things might kill this new product?
3. At graduation the average U.S. college student has two credit cards and how much credit card debt? (*a*) $500; (*b*) $1,000; (*c*) $2,000; (*d*) $5,000; (*e*) $10,000
4. True or False: For the kids' segment, Rollerblade has a skate that expands as the kids' feet grow.
5. Besides wool, to be socially responsible 3M puts what recycled material into its very successful Scotchbrite™ Never Rust Wool Soap Pads? (*a*) aluminum cans, (*b*) steel-belted tires, (*c*) plastic bottles, (*d*) computer screens, (*e*) cardboard.

right? But Rollerblade was upset. Legally, Rollerblade® is a trademark registered at the U.S. Patent and Trademark Office (USPTO)—as shown by the ®—and, as a brand name, should be used only to identify that firm's products and services. With letters to offenders and advertisements like the one below, Rollerblade is trying to protect a precious asset: its brand identity. The ™ after the Fusion™ brand shows that Rollerblade claims trademark rights to the name at the USPTO but that it has not received official registration.[2] For simplicity, in books and reports these symbols only appear the first time the trademark or brand appears.

Under American trademark law, if consumers generally start using a brand name as the generic term to describe the product rather than the source of the product, then the company loses its exclusive rights to the name. "Rollerblade" skates would become "rollerblade"—just another English word to describe all kinds of in-line skating. That fate has already befallen some famous American products such as linoleum, aspirin, cellophane, escalator, yo-yo, corn flakes, and trampoline.[3]

American firms now spend billions of dollars annually in promotion and court cases to protect the integrity of their brand names. As described in the Marketing

Rollerblade ran this ad to communicate a specific message. It's also part of a "reminder" letter sent to people who *slip*. What is the message? For the answer and why it is important, see the text.

Everyday, irregardless of his homework, Jeffrey went "rollerblading" because it was to nice to lay around with his nose in a english book.

Of the seven errors in this headline, the use of "rollerblading" as a verb strikes us as the most extreme. Rollerblade® is a brand name. It is, also, technically incorrect to use "rollerblader" and "rollerblades" as nouns. Remember, the careful writer skates on in-line skates known as Rollerblade® skates.

© 1992 Rollerblade, Inc. Rollerblade and The Skate Logo are trademarks of Rollerblade, Inc.

MARKETING NEWSNET

The Challenge and Changing Role of Successful Brands

CUSTOMER VALUE

Brands are suddenly under major attack!

From the Critics

Criticism of Western—especially American—brands runs something like this: In today's global economy, brands are a huge portion of a company's value and profits. So rather than simply sell products, companies are in the business of marketing aspirations, images, and lifestyles. The sad part of this is that the companies shift production to third world countries where they pay poor wages and even exploit child labor. The "McDonaldsization of the globe" means that brands are so powerful that they make us all act alike and be alike—undermining our moral values.

From the Advocates

In contrast, *The Economist* magazine says "far from being instruments of oppression, [brands] make firms accountable to consumers." Brands started as a form of consumer protection, not consumer exploitation. Today brands not only simplify choices and guarantee a consistency of quality but, says *The Economist,* "they add fun and interest"—whether the example is Disney, Nokia, or Gap. As with Rollerblade's concern over "rollerblading," firms spend millions of dollars to protect their brand names to assure consumers get what they think they are buying.

Brands Today and Tomorrow

In today's competition carelessness or arrogance can devastate decades spent building a strong brand. Kellogg's, second among the world's top brands less than a decade earlier, in 2001 languished in thirty-ninth place according to Interbrand, a brand consultant. World Bank studies show that branded multinationals help developing economies by paying the best wages and offering the best working conditions. And for the future, firms may need to learn lessons from Nike, which revamped its supply chain after activists accused it of operating third world sweatshops. Brands of the future may need to go beyond sending signals to consumers about quality and consistency of the product to encompass a good feeling about the company itself.

The Result

All kinds of products, organizations, and causes—from Nike and Sony to the Red Cross and American Heart Association—are fighting to preserve the integrity of their brand names.

NewsNet, some critics see brands as simply selling images and undermining moral values.[4] But, as discussed there and in Chapter 11, brands save consumers time and simplify their choices by assuring a consistent quality. Further, the free market competition among high-quality brands ensures better product choices for consumers. Because legal and ethical issues such as the Rollerblade skates trademark problem are so central to many marketing decisions, they are addressed throughout the book.

Your common sense plus your in-depth study of the marketing concepts in the book will enable you to make better decisions and choices in the marketplace.

Marketing: Using Exchanges to Satisfy Needs

The American Marketing Association, representing marketing professionals, states that "**marketing** is the process of planning and executing the conception, pricing, promotion, and distribution of ideas, goods, and services to create exchanges that satisfy individual and organizational objectives."[5] Many people incorrectly believe that marketing is the same thing as advertising or personal selling; this definition shows marketing to be a far broader activity. Further, this definition stresses the importance of beneficial exchanges that satisfy the objectives of both those who buy and those who sell ideas, goods, and services—whether they be individuals or organizations.

To serve both buyers and sellers, marketing seeks (1) to discover the needs and wants of prospective customers and (2) to satisfy them. These prospective customers include both individuals buying for themselves and their households, and organizations that buy for their own use (such as manufacturers) or for resale (such as wholesalers and retailers). The key to achieving these two objectives is the idea of **exchange**, which is the trade of things of value between buyer and seller so that each is better off after the trade. This vital concept of exchange in marketing is covered below in more detail.

The Diverse Factors Influencing Marketing Activities

Although an organization's marketing activity focuses on assessing and satisfying consumer needs, countless other people, groups, and forces interact to shape the nature of its activities (Figure 1–3). Foremost is the organization itself, whose mission and objectives determine what business it is in and what goals it seeks. Within the organization, management is responsible for establishing these goals. The marketing department works closely with a network of other departments and employees to help provide the customer-satisfying products required for the organization to survive and prosper.

Figure 1–3 also shows the key people, groups, and forces outside the organization that influence marketing activities. The marketing department is responsible for facilitating relationships, partnerships, and alliances with the organization's customers, its shareholders (or often representatives of groups served by a nonprofit organization), its suppliers, and other organizations. Environmental forces such as social, technological, economic, competitive, and regulatory factors also shape an organization's marketing activities. Finally, an organization's marketing decisions are affected by and, in turn, often have an important impact on society as a whole.

The organization must strike a continual balance among the sometimes differing interests of these individuals and groups. For example, it is not possible to simultaneously provide the lowest-priced and highest-quality products to customers and pay the highest prices to suppliers, highest wages to employees, and maximum dividends to shareholders.

FIGURE 1–3
An organization's marketing department relates to many people, groups, and forces

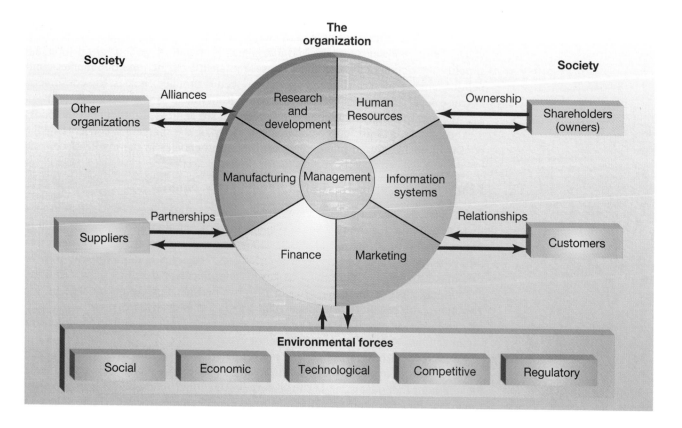

Requirements for Marketing to Occur

For marketing to occur, at least four factors are required: (1) two or more parties (individuals or organizations) with unsatisfied needs, (2) a desire and ability on their part to be satisfied, (3) a way for the parties to communicate, and (4) something to exchange.

Two or More Parties with Unsatisfied Needs   Suppose you've developed an unmet need—a desire for information about how computer and telecommunications are interacting to reshape the workplace—but you didn't yet know that *ComputerWorld* magazine existed. Also unknown to you was that several copies of *ComputerWorld* were sitting on the magazine rack at your nearest bookstore, waiting to be purchased. This is an example of two parties with unmet needs: you, with a need for technology-related information, and your bookstore owner, needing someone to buy a copy of *ComputerWorld.*

Desire and Ability to Satisfy These Needs   Both you and the bookstore owner want to satisfy these unmet needs. Furthermore, you have the money to buy the item and the time to get to the bookstore. The store's owner has not only the desire to sell *ComputerWorld* but also the ability to do so since it's stocked on the shelves.

A Way for the Parties to Communicate   The marketing transaction of buying a copy of *ComputerWorld* will never occur unless you know the product exists and its location. Similarly, the store owner won't stock the magazine unless there's a market of potential buyers nearby. When you receive a free sample in the mail or see the magazine on display in the bookstore, this communications barrier between you (the buyer) and your bookstore (the seller) is overcome.

Something to Exchange   Marketing occurs when the transaction takes place and both the buyer and seller exchange something of value. In this case, you exchange your money for the bookstore's magazine. Both you and the bookstore have gained something and also given up something, but you are both better off because you have each satisfied your unmet needs. You have the opportunity to read *ComputerWorld,* but you gave up some money; the store gave up the magazine but received money, which enables it to remain in business. This exchange process and, of course, the ethical and legal foundations of exchange are central to marketing.[6]

Concept Check

1. What is marketing?
2. Marketing focuses on _____ and _____ consumer needs.
3. What four factors are needed for marketing to occur?

HOW MARKETING DISCOVERS AND SATISFIES CONSUMER NEEDS

The importance of discovering and satisfying consumer needs is so critical to understanding marketing that we look at each of these two steps in detail next.

Discovering Consumer Needs

The first objective in marketing is discovering the needs of prospective consumers. Sound simple? Well, it's not. In the abstract, discovering needs looks easy, but when you get down to the specifics of marketing, problems crop up.

Yes, they're all for real! For these products, identify (1) what benefits the product provides buyers and (2) what "showstoppers" might kill the product in the marketplace. Answers are discussed in the text.

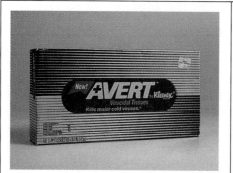

Kimberly Clark's Avert
Virucidal tissues

Pfizer's Body Smarts
crunch bars and fruit chews

Toro's iMow
lawn mower

Samsung's 17-inch SyncMaster
flat-panel PC screen

The Challenge of Launching Winning New Products   New-product experts generally estimate that 80 to 94 percent of the over 25,000 new consumable products (food, beverage, health, beauty, and other household and pet products) introduced in the United States annually "don't succeed in the long run." Robert M. Mc-Math, who has studied over 40,000 of these new-product launches, has two key suggestions: (1) focus on what the customer benefit is and (2) learn from the past.[7]

The solution to preventing such product failures seems embarrassingly obvious. First, find out what consumers need and want. Second, produce what they need and want and don't produce what they don't need and want. This is far more difficult than it sounds. The four products shown above illustrate just how hard it is with today's competition to achieve new-product success, a topic covered in more detail in Chapter 10.

In terms of potential benefits to customers and possible showstoppers, let's look first at the two consumable products:

- *Kimberly Clark's Avert Virucidal tissues.* Like the launch of Garlic Cake, the name confused consumers who couldn't quite understand what benefit a "virucidal" tissue provided. (It contained Vitamin C derivatives that were supposed to keep the germs from spreading when you blew into it.) Another problem: McMath observes that words that end in *cidal*—like homicidal or suicidal—don't put people in a buying mood. The clear showstoppers: Prospects were simply too confused and scared to risk their noses to Avert Virucidals (question 2, Figure 1–2).[8]
- *Pfizer's Body Smarts crunch bars and fruit chews.* Containing as much iron as a cup of spinach and as much fiber as a slice of bread, these chocolate and fruit-chew "nutraceuticals" let munchers indulge their sweet tooth believing they're getting solid nutrition, too. Launched in mid-2001 with a $70 million market-

ing campaign, the potential showstopper for Body Smarts is a carryover from bad past experiences: Good taste! If they're still on your candy counter when you read this, they probably taste good and are a winner.[9]

A bad buying decision with a consumable product may waste a dollar or two. But high-priced technical equipment involves a lot more thought during the buying process. So the revolutionary new lawn mower and computer monitor shown on page 12 still must demonstrate potential benefits to buyers:

- *Toro's iMow lawn mower.* Launched in 2001, this $900 robot mower lets lazy or gadget-happy homeowners lie in their hammocks and watch their iMow cut their grass. The first step is to lay down a low-voltage perimeter wire to limit the cutting area. The potential time-saving benefit will confront the iMow's final exam question: Will it work as planned?[10]
- *Samsung's 17-inch SyncMaster 760TFT flat-panel PC screen.* The benefits compared to a bulky, heavy cathode-ray tube (CRT) computer monitor are that flat-panel screens save space and are easier to move. Introduced in Fall 2001, the $790 SyncMaster faces both traditional CRTs and newly arriving flat-panel displays from competitors. Without quite the CRT's flexibility in pixel resolution, the flat-panel displays are leading-edge technology. But the potential showstoppers: Are the price, quality, and timing right? Watch your computer store or Internet seller for the answer.[11]

Firms spend billions of dollars annually on marketing and technical research that significantly reduces—but doesn't eliminate—new-product failure.

Consumer Needs and Consumer Wants   Should marketing try to satisfy consumer needs or consumer wants? The answer is both! Heated debates rage over this question, depending on the definitions of needs and wants and the amount of freedom given to prospective customers to make their own buying decisions.

A *need* occurs when a person feels physiologically deprived of basic necessities such as food, clothing, and shelter. A *want* is a felt need that is shaped by a person's knowledge, culture, and personality. So if you feel hungry, you have developed a basic need and desire to eat something. Let's say you then want to eat an apple or a candy bar because, based on your past experience and personality, you know these will satisfy your hunger need. Effective marketing, in the form of creating an awareness of good products at convenient locations, can clearly shape a person's wants.

At issue is whether marketing persuades prospective customers to buy the "wrong" things—say, a candy bar rather than an apple to satisfy hunger pangs. Of increasing concern, as described in the Ethics and Social Responsibility Alert, is student credit card debt. This debt is even forcing some students to drop out of college.[12]

Certainly, marketing tries to influence what we buy. A question then arises—at what point do we want government and society to step in to protect consumers? Most consumers would say they want government to protect us from harmful drugs and unsafe cars but not from candy bars and soft drinks. To protect students, should government limit the number of credit cards or amount of debt they can have? Such questions have no clear-cut answers, which is why legal and social issues are central to marketing. Because even psychologists and economists still debate the exact meanings of *need* and *want*, we shall avoid the semantic arguments and use the terms interchangeably throughout the rest of the book.

As shown in Figure 1–4, discovering needs involves looking carefully at prospective customers, whether they are children buying M&M's candy, college students buying Rollerblade in-line skates, or firms buying Xerox photocopying machines. A principal activity of a firm's marketing department is to scrutinize carefully its consumers to understand what they need, to study industry trends, to examine competitors' products, and even to analyze the needs of a customer's customer.

ETHICS AND SOCIAL RESPONSIBILITY ALERT

Student Credit Cards: Ultimate Benefit or the Disaster Waiting to Happen?

ETHICS

Tens of thousands of college students and other adults across the nation are drowning in credit card debt. In mid-2001 there were about 1.5 billion credit cards issued and $560 billion in outstanding credit card debt in the United States. This works out to about five credit cards and $2,000 in credit card debt for every man, woman, and child in the country.

College students are part of the under-25 age group that represents the fastest-growing bankruptcy filers in the country. In fact, in 1999, over 100,000 under-25 people filed for bankruptcy. The Consumer Federation of America reports that the average college graduate has two credit cards with a $5,000 balance between them (question 3, Figure 1–2). When adding in student loans—exempt from bankruptcy—rent, car payments, utilities, telephone, taxes, and interest, few starting salaries of college graduates will be high enough to cover much beyond minimum payments on the credit card debt.

What can students do who are over their heads in credit card debt? Some universities offer on-campus financial counseling. Or students can find savings in their utilities, wireless, long-distance and Internet services, insurance, and credit cards by logging onto www.lowermybills.com. Nellie Mae, the nation's lending education funder, provides students with debt-management tools and help at www.nelliemae.com. Financial counselors have two other bits of advice for students: (1) reduce the number of credit cards you have and (2) pay cash. Paying cash forces some hard thinking that is avoided by simply bringing out a plastic credit card.

What should be done to help students address their credit card debt problems? Require them to take personal finance training? Restrict the number of cards they own? Lower the maximum credit line? Have Congress pass laws to rein in credit card companies? What do you think?

What a Market Is   Potential consumers make up a **market**, which is (1) people (2) with the desire and (3) with the ability to buy a specific product. All markets ultimately are people. Even when we say a firm bought a Xerox copier, we mean one or several people in the firm decided to buy it. People who are aware of their unmet needs may have the desire to buy the product, but that alone isn't sufficient. People must also have the ability to buy, such as the authority, time, and money. People may even "buy" an idea that results in an action, such as having their blood pressure checked annually or turning down their thermostat to save energy.

Satisfying Consumer Needs

Marketing doesn't stop with the discovery of consumer needs. Because the organization obviously can't satisfy all consumer needs, it must concentrate its efforts on certain needs of a specific group of potential consumers. This is the **target market**—one or more specific groups of potential consumers toward which an organization directs its marketing program.

The Four Ps: Controllable Marketing Mix Factors   Having selected the target market consumers, the firm must take steps to satisfy their needs. Someone in the organization's marketing department, often the marketing manager, must take action and develop a complete marketing program to reach consumers by using a combination of four tools, often called the four Ps—a useful shorthand reference to them first published by Professor E. Jerome McCarthy:[13]

- *Product.* A good, service, or idea to satisfy the consumer's needs.
- *Price.* What is exchanged for the product.
- *Promotion.* A means of communication between the seller and buyer.
- *Place.* A means of getting the product into the consumer's hands.

We'll define each of the four Ps more carefully later in the book, but for now it's important to remember that they are the elements of the marketing mix, or simply the

FIGURE 1–4
Marketing's first task:
discovering consumer needs

marketing mix. These are the marketing manager's controllable factors, the marketing actions of product, price, promotion, and place that he or she can take to solve a marketing problem. The marketing mix elements are called controllable factors because they are under the control of the marketing department in an organization.

The Uncontrollable, Environmental Factors   There are a host of factors largely beyond the control of the marketing department and its organization. These factors can be placed into five groups (as shown in Figure 1–3): social, economic, technological, competitive, and regulatory forces. Examples are what consumers themselves want and need, changing technology, the state of the economy in terms of whether it is expanding or contracting, actions that competitors take, and government restrictions. These are the **environmental factors** in a marketing decision, the uncontrollable factors involving social, economic, technological, competitive, and regulatory forces. These five forces may serve as accelerators or brakes on marketing, sometimes expanding an organization's marketing opportunities and other times restricting them. These five environmental factors are covered in Chapter 3.

Wal-Mart and Lands' End provide customer value using two very different approaches. For their strategies, see the text.

Wal-Mart
www.wal-mart.com

Lands' End Direct Merchants
www.landsend.com

Traditionally, many marketing executives have treated these environmental factors as rigid, absolute constraints that are entirely outside their influence. However, recent studies and marketing successes have shown that a forward-looking, action-oriented firm can often affect some environmental factors, for example, by achieving technological or competitive breakthroughs.

THE MARKETING PROGRAM: HOW CUSTOMER RELATIONSHIPS ARE BUILT

A firm's marketing program connects the firm to its customers. To clarify this link, we shall first discuss the critically important concepts of customer value, customer relationships, and relationship marketing, and then illustrate these concepts with the marketing program at Rollerblade.

Global Competition, Customer Value, and Customer Relationships

Intense competition in today's fast-paced domestic and global markets has caused massive restructuring of many American industries and businesses. American managers are seeking ways to achieve success in this new, more intense level of global competition.[14]

This has prompted many successful U.S. firms to focus on "customer value." That firms gain loyal customers by providing unique value is the essence of successful marketing. What is new, however, is a more careful attempt at understanding how a firm's customers perceive value. For our purposes, **customer value** is the unique combination of benefits received by targeted buyers that includes quality, price, convenience, on-time delivery, and both before-sale and after-sale service. Firms now actually try to place a dollar value on a loyal, satisfied customer. As pointed out in Chapter 5, loyal Kleenex customers average 6.7 boxes a year, about $994 over 60 years in today's dollars.[15]

Research suggests that firms cannot succeed by being all things to all people.[16] Instead, firms must find ways to build long-term customer relationships to provide unique value that they alone can deliver to targeted markets. Many successful firms have chosen to deliver outstanding customer value with one of three value strategies— best price, best product, or best service.

Companies such as Wal-Mart, Southwest Airlines, Price/Costco, and Dell Computer have all been successful offering consumers the best price. Other companies such as Nike, Starbucks, Microsoft, and Johnson & Johnson claim to provide the best products on the market. Finally, companies such as Lands' End and Home Depot deliver value by providing exceptional service.

But changing tastes can devastate once-successful marketing strategies. Sears now must focus on strategies to defeat new groups of competitors: boutique specialty stores, catalog retailers, and Internet sellers (Chapter 2).

Relationship Marketing and the Marketing Program

Meaningful customer relationships are achieved by the firm's identifying creative ways to connect closely to its customers through specific marketing mix actions implemented in its marketing program.

Relationship Marketing: Easy to Understand   The hallmark of developing and maintaining effective customer relationships is today called **relationship marketing**, linking the organization to its individual customers, employees, suppli-

ers, and other partners for their mutual long-term benefits. Note that these mutual long-term benefits between the organization and its customers require links to other vital stakeholders—including suppliers, employees, and "partners" such as wholesalers or retailers in a manufacturer's channel of distribution. In an ideal setting, relationship marketing involves a personal, ongoing relationship between the organization and an individual customer.

Relationship Marketing: Difficult to Implement   Huge manufacturers find this rigorous standard of relationship marketing difficult to achieve. Today's information technology, along with cutting-edge manufacturing and marketing processes, have led to tailoring goods or services to the tastes of individual customers in high volumes at a relatively low cost. Thus, you can place an Internet order for all the components of a Dell or Apple computer and have it delivered in four or five days—in a configuration tailored to your unique wants.

But there are other forces working against these kinds of personal relationships between company and customer. Researchers Fournier, Dobscha, and Mick observe that "the number of one-on-one relationships that companies ask consumers to maintain is untenable,"[17] as evidenced by the dozens of credit card and financing offers a typical consumer gets in a year. A decade ago you might have gone to a small store to buy a book or music record, being helped in your buying decision by a sales-clerk or the store owner. With today's Internet purchases, you will probably have difficulty achieving the same personal, tender-loving-care connection that you once had with your own special book or music store.

The Marketing Program

Effective relationship marketing strategies help marketing managers discover what prospective customers need. They must translate this information into some concepts for products the firm might develop (Figure 1–5). These concepts must then be converted into a tangible **marketing program**—a plan that integrates the marketing mix to provide a good, service, or idea to prospective buyers. These prospects then react to the offering favorably (by buying) or unfavorably (by not buying), and the process is repeated. As shown in Figure 1–5, in an effective organization this process is continuous: Consumer needs trigger product concepts that are translated into actual products that stimulate further discovery of consumer needs.

FIGURE 1–5
Marketing's second task: satisfying consumer needs

A Marketing Program for Rollerblade

To see some specifics of an actual marketing program, let's return to the earlier example of Rollerblade and its in-line skates. Looking at the in-line skating horizon, Rollerblade's long-run strategy is to focus on three areas: (1) expand the market, (2) use the company's strengths in technology, and (3) "stay ahead of the trends." These three areas are covered below.

Expanding the Market for Rollerblade Skates

In terms of expanding the market, one Rollerblade marketing manager comments, "Our challenges are to find new venues, new reasons for people to skate." The foundation on which to build marketing programs reaching these new settings rests on two key elements:

- Finding the right benefits—or competitive points of difference (discussed in detail in Chapter 10)—to stress in reaching potential buyers. Three key benefits and points of difference for customers underlie all of Rollerblade's marketing efforts: (1) fun, (2) fitness and health, and (3) excitement.
- Targeting key segments of prospective customers and satisfying them with the specific kinds of Rollerblade brands of skates that they want.

Today, while the fundamental customer benefits remain the same, Rollerblade is now trying to reach narrower, more focused segments of customers than in the past. Let's look at several of these market segments and the products that Rollerblade has developed to provide key benefits to satisfy their needs:[18]

- *Children segment.* Most parents can't afford to buy a new set of in-line skates each season as their children's feet grow. No problem now! With the Junior™ line, the skate "grows" in four extensions to provide a skate for four sizes of a child's feet (question 4, Figure 1–2).
- *Fitness segment.* Want a skate to get you to exercise, whether you're a beginner or intermediate skater? Then try a Core or Fusion skate that utilizes Rollerblade's key technologies.
- *Speed segment.* You're a really serious in-line skater? How about a five-wheeled Lightning or Road Runner™ that retails for up to $649?
- *Terrain/"aggressive" segment.* Like to skate down snowless ski hills in the summer? The Coyote™ fills the bill. Its pneumatic tires provide a full inch of shock absorption plus good traction on slick surfaces—an in-line skate for aggressive, all-terrain skating.

Rollerblade's various product lines meet the needs of distinctly different segments of users.

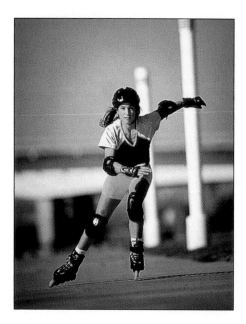

Rollerblade has more than 20 lines of skates targeted to different market segments. As illustrated in Figure 1–6 for the Junior and Core/Fusion brands, most Rollerblade brands require a slightly different marketing program to reach their targeted segments of potential customers.

Exploiting Strengths in Technology In 1995 Rollerblade was sold to Nordica, an Italian ski company owned by the Benetton organization. This provided huge technology synergies for the two firms. Examples of exploiting tomorrow's technology—some with Nordica, some on Rollerblade's own—include:

- *CoolMax*™. A performance fabric used to keep a skater's feet dry, even with intense skating.
- *ABT*®*Lite*. A light, integral braking system that allows skaters to brake by sliding their foot forward, without compromising balance or performance.
- *Shock Eraser*™. A cushioning support system that absorbs vibrations while skating and improves overall performance.
- *Progressive Fit System*™. A series of liners and footbeds that bring fit and comfort to skaters of all abilities.

Rollerblade's stress on the technology is reflected in the more than 200 patents it holds on key elements of its in-line skate line.

Staying Ahead of the Trends Consumer tastes change—and quickly! This is the reason for Rollerblade's concerns that it stay ahead of trends in the marketplace.[19] The recent downturn in consumer participation in in-line skating shown in Figure 1–1 has sent up a red flag for Rollerblade executives. Competition is coming from directions in wheeled vehicles never anticipated even two or three years earlier. Rollerblade has always had to compete with skateboards and also mountain bikes used in both on-road and off-road cycling. But few in the in-line skate industry foresaw sales of 8 million scooters in 2000, which cut heavily into skate sales, or foresaw a million pairs of

FIGURE 1–6
Marketing programs for two of Rollerblade's skates, targeted at two distinctly different customer segments: fast-growing kids and fitness skaters

MARKETING PROGRAM ACTIVITY TO REACH:

MARKETING MIX ELEMENT	FAST-GROWING KIDS SEGMENT	FITNESS SEGMENT	RATIONALE FOR MARKETING PROGRAM ACTIVITY
Product	Offer the Junior, a skate for children that "extends" so that it changes four shoe sizes as the children grow	Offer the Core and Fusion skates for beginning and intermediate skaters simply wanting fun and exercise	Use new-product research and the latest technology to offer high-quality skates to satisfy the needs of key customer segments
Price	Price up to $99 a pair	Price up to $199 a pair	Set prices that provide genuine value to the customer segment that is targeted
Promotion	Use demo vans to introduce children to in-line skating and place ads in local newspapers	Feature Rollerblade in sports competitions and magazines like *Shape, Mademoiselle,* and *Inline,* and local newspapers	Increase awareness of in-line skating to those new to the sport while offering specific skate designs for more advanced segments
Place	Distribute the Junior through sporting goods stores	Distribute the Core and Fusion lines through specialty and regular sporting goods stores	Make it easy for buyers in the segment to buy at an outlet that is convenient and where they feel comfortable

"Heelys"—a sneaker with an embedded, detachable wheel in the heel—flying off retail shelves in 2001 (see Chapter 9).

Appearing on the horizon in 2001: the Segway HT (human transporter)—initially known mysteriously as "It!" This may even impact a minor business segment of in-line skate sales, skates sold to those using them for delivery purposes, as mentioned in the Internet Exercise at the end of the chapter.

Having created a new sport and an entirely new industry, Rollerblade must address these new, competitive challenges. In a free market system, success encourages competition and imitations. The Rollerblade case at the end of the chapter lets us look at the marketing strategies that Rollerblade is developing for the 21st century.

Concept Check

1. An organization can't satisfy the needs of all consumers, so it must focus on one or more subgroups, which are its _____.

2. What are the four marketing mix elements that make up the organization's marketing program?

3. What are uncontrollable variables?

HOW MARKETING BECAME SO IMPORTANT

Marketing is a driving force in the modern global economy. To understand why this is so and some related ethical aspects, let us look at the (1) evolution of the market orientation, (2) ethics and social responsibility in marketing, and (3) breadth and depth of marketing activities.

Evolution of the Market Orientation

Many market-oriented manufacturing organizations have experienced four distinct stages in the life of their firms. We can use Pillsbury, now part of General Mills, and General Electric as examples.

Production Era   Goods were scarce in the early years of the United States, so buyers were willing to accept virtually any goods that were produced and make do with them as best they could. The central notion was that products would sell themselves, so the major concern of business firms was production, not marketing. Robert Keith, a Pillsbury president, described his company at this stage: "We are professional flour millers. . . . Our basic function is to mill quality flour."[20] As shown in Figure 1–7, this production era generally continued in America through the 1920s.

FIGURE 1–7
Four different orientations in the history of American business

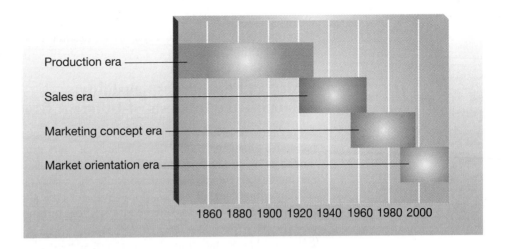

Sales Era   About that time, many firms discovered that they could produce more goods than their regular buyers could consume. Competition grew. The usual solution was to hire more salespeople to find new buyers. Pillsbury's philosophy at this stage was summed up simply by Keith: "We must hire salespersons to sell it [the flour] just as we hire accountants to keep our books." The role of the Pillsbury salesforce was simply to find consumers for the goods that the firm could produce best. This sales era continued into the 1950s for Pillsbury and into the 1960s for many other American firms (see Figure 1–7).

The Marketing Concept Era   In the 1960s, marketing became the motivating force among many American firms. Then the policy became: "we are in the business of satisfying needs and wants of consumers." This is really a brief statement of what has come to be known as the **marketing concept**; the idea is that an organization should (1) strive to satisfy the needs of consumers (2) while also trying to achieve the organization's goals.

The statement of a firm's commitment to satisfying consumer wants and needs that probably launched the marketing concept appeared in a 1952 annual report of General Electric:[21] "The concept introduces . . . marketing . . . at the beginning rather than the end of the production cycle and integrates marketing into each phase of the business." This statement emphasizes that marketing ideas are fed into the production cycle from *after* an item is produced to *before* it is designed. Clearly the marketing concept is a focus on the consumer. Unfortunately, many companies found that actually implementing the concept was very difficult.

The Market Orientation Era   Many of the implementation issues are now being addressed by the total quality management movement. Firms such as General Electric, Marriott, and Toyota have achieved great success by putting huge effort into implementing the marketing concept, giving their firms what has been called a *market orientation*. An organization that has a **market orientation** focuses its efforts on (1) continuously collecting information about customers' needs and competitors' capabilities, (2) sharing this information across departments, and (3) using the information to create customer value.[22]

An important outgrowth of this market orientation is the recent attention placed on **customer relationship management (CRM)**, the process of identifying prospective buyers, understanding them intimately, and developing favorable long-term perceptions of the organization and its offerings so that buyers will choose them in the marketplace.[23] This process requires the involvement and commitment of managers and employees throughout the organization and a growing application of information, communication, and Internet technology, as will be described throughout this book.

Ethics and Social Responsibility: Balancing the Interests of Different Groups

As organizations have changed their orientation, society's expectations of marketers have also changed. Today, the standards of marketing practice have shifted from an emphasis on producers' interests to consumers' interests. In addition, organizations are increasingly encouraged to consider the social and environmental consequences of their actions for all parties. Guidelines for ethical and socially responsible behavior can help managers balance consumer, organizational, and societal interests.

Ethics   Many marketing issues are not specifically addressed by existing laws and regulations. Should information about a firm's customers be sold to other organizations? Should advertising by professional service providers, such as accountants and attorneys, be restricted? Should consumers be on their own to assess the safety of a product? These questions raise difficult ethical issues. Many companies, industries, and professional associations have developed codes of ethics to assist managers.

Social Responsibility   While many ethical issues involve only the buyer and seller, others involve society as a whole. For example, suppose you change the oil in your old Chevy yourself and dump the used oil in a corner of your backyard. Is this just a transaction between you and the oil manufacturer? Not quite! The used oil may contaminate the soil, so society will bear a portion of the cost of your behavior. This example illustrates the issue of social responsibility, the idea that organizations are accountable to a larger society. The well-being of society at large should also be recognized in an organization's marketing decisions. In fact, some marketing experts stress the **societal marketing concept**, the view that an organization should discover and satisfy the needs of its consumers in a way that also provides for society's well-being.[24] For example, Scotchbrite™ Never Rust Wool Soap Pads from 3M—which are made from recycled plastic bottles—are more expensive than competitors (SOS and Brillo) but superior because they don't rust or scratch (question 5, Figure 1–2).

The societal marketing concept is directly related to **macromarketing**, which looks at the aggregate flow of a nation's goods and services to benefit society.[25] Macromarketing addresses broad issues such as whether marketing costs too much, whether advertising is wasteful, and what resource scarcities and pollution side effects result from the marketing system. While macromarketing issues are addressed briefly in this book, the book's main focus is on how an individual organization directs its marketing activities and allocates its resources to benefit its customers, or **micromarketing**. An overview of this approach appears in Chapter 2. Because of the importance of ethical and social responsibility issues in marketing today, Chapter 4 focuses on them but they are touched on throughout the book.

The Breadth and Depth of Marketing

Marketing today affects every person and organization. To understand this, let's analyze (1) who markets, (2) what they market, (3) who buys and uses what is marketed, (4) who benefits from these marketing activities, and (5) how they benefit.

Who Markets?   Every organization markets! It's obvious that business firms involved in manufacturing (Tommy Hilfiger, Heinz), retailing (Abercrombie & Fitch, Toys "Я" Us), and providing services (America Online, Chicago Cubs) market their offerings. Today many other types of marketing are also popular. Nonprofit organizations (San Francisco Opera, your local hospital) also engage in marketing.[26] Your col-

Marketing is used by nonprofit organizations, causes, and places, as well as businesses. Direct messages like those illustrated here can reach their target audiences very effectively.

lege or university, for example, probably has a marketing program to attract students, faculty members, and donations. Places (cities, states, countries) often use marketing efforts to attract tourists, conventions, or businesses. Special events or causes use marketing to inform and influence a target audience. These marketing activities range from government agencies discouraging smoking to private groups promoting a social cause such as literacy. Finally, individuals such as political candidates often use marketing to gain attention and preference.

What Is Marketed?   Goods, services, and ideas are marketed. Goods are physical objects, such as toothpaste, cameras, or computers, that satisfy consumer needs. Services are intangible items such as airline trips, financial advice, or telephone calls. Ideas are intangibles involving thoughts about actions or causes.

Financial pressures have caused art museums to embark on creative marketing activities to attract visitors and generate revenues. New York's Guggenheim Museum challenged the concept of what an art museum is when it organized an exhibition on "The Art of the Motorcycle."[27] As described in the Web Link, the Hermitage Museum has partnered with IBM to give you a computerized "virtual tour" of its exhibits in hopes that some day you may visit it personally.[28] The Guggenheim and Hermitage are themselves partnering to open a new "Jewel Box" museum . . . in Las Vegas! These museum marketing activities also show how goods and services in today's global marketplace are increasingly likely to cross national boundaries and involve multinational teams.

Who Buys and Uses What Is Marketed?   Both individuals and organizations buy and use goods and services that are marketed. **Ultimate consumers** are the people—whether 80 years or 8 months old—who use the goods and services purchased for a household. In contrast, **organizational buyers** are units such as manufacturers, retailers, or government agencies that buy goods and services for their own use or for resale. Although the terms *consumers, buyers,* and *customers* are sometimes used for both ultimate consumers and organizations, there is no consistency on this. In this book you will be able to tell from the example whether the buyers are ultimate consumers, organizations, or both.

Who Benefits?   In our free-enterprise society there are three specific groups that benefit from effective marketing: consumers who buy, organizations that sell, and society as a whole. True competition between products and services in the marketplace

WEB LINK

Marketing the Hermitage, a World-Class Russian Art Museum—with a Virtual Tour!

Founded in 1764 by Catherine the Great, the Hermitage is one of a handful of world-class museums—like the Louvre in Paris or the Metropolitan Museum in New York City—and is the main tourist attraction in St. Petersburg, Russia. Today, the Hermitage consists of five buildings of over 1,000 rooms that contain more than 3 million items, only 5 percent ever exhibited at one time!

But since the Berlin Wall fell in 1989, the Hermitage has struggled financially. Gone is most of its government funding. As a result, the number of visitors to the Hermitage has fallen from 3.5 million in 1989 to under 2 million in 2000, far less than the Louvre's 6.2 million.

Dr. Mikhail Piotrovsky, the Hermitage's director since 1992, decided to face this funding crisis head on. By using inno-

vative strategic alliances and marketing initiatives, Piotrovsky has begun to bring in the resources needed to improve and expand the museum.

To take a "virtual tour" of the Hermitage, go to its Internet address: www.hermitagemuseum.org/html_en/index.html and click on the "Virtual Visit" link.

This website allows people all over the world to view more Hermitage treasures and consider a personal visit. A $2 million IBM grant to the Hermitage made possible this state-of-the-art Internet website and a digital library of the Hermitage collection. The website allows users to "walk through" Hermitage rooms and see its artwork. Users can zoom in to examine the artwork more closely.

ГОСУДАРСТВЕННЫЙ ЭРМИТАЖ

THE STATE HERMITAGE MUSEUM

ensures that we consumers can find value from the best products, the lowest prices, or exceptional service. Providing choices leads to the consumer satisfaction and quality of life that we have come to expect from our economic system.

Organizations that provide need-satisfying products with effective marketing programs—for example, McDonald's, IBM, and Avon—have blossomed. But competition creates problems for ineffective competitors, such as eToys and hundreds of other dot-com businesses that failed in the last few years.[29] Effective marketing actions result in rewards for organizations that serve consumers and in millions of marketing jobs such as those described in Appendix C.

Finally, effective marketing benefits society. It enhances competition, which, in turn, improves both the quality of products and services and lowers their prices. This makes countries more competitive in world markets and provides jobs and a higher standard of living for their citizens.

How Do Consumers Benefit?   Marketing creates **utility**, the benefits or customer value received by users of the product. This utility is the result of the marketing exchange process. There are four different utilities: form, place, time, and possession. The production of the good or service constitutes *form utility. Place utility* means having the offering available where consumers need it, whereas *time utility* means having it available when needed. *Possession utility* is getting the product to consumers so they can use it.

Thus, marketing provides consumers with place, time, and possession utilities by making the good or service available at the right place and right time for the right consumer. Although form utility usually arises in manufacturing activity and could be seen as outside the scope of marketing, an organization's marketing activities influence the product features and packaging. Marketing creates its utilities by bridging space (place utility) and hours (time utility) to provide products (form utility) for consumers to own and use (possession utility).

Concept Check

1. Like Pillsbury and General Electric, many firms have gone through four distinct orientations for their business: starting with the _____ era and ending with today's _____ era.

2. What are the two key characteristics of the marketing concept?

3. In this book the term *product* refers to what three things?

SUMMARY

1 Combining personal experience with more formal marketing knowledge will enable us to identify and solve important marketing problems.

2 Marketing is the process of planning and executing the conception, pricing, promotion, and distribution of ideas, goods, and services to create exchanges that satisfy individual and organizational objectives. This definition relates to two primary goals of marketing: (*a*) assessing the needs of consumers and (*b*) satisfying them.

3 For marketing to occur, it is necessary to have (*a*) two or more parties with unmet needs, (*b*) a desire and ability to satisfy them, (*c*) communication between the parties, and (*d*) something to exchange.

4 Because an organization doesn't have the resources to satisfy the needs of all consumers, it selects a target market of potential customers—a subset of the entire market—on which to focus its marketing program.

5 Four elements in a marketing program designed to satisfy customer needs are product, price, promotion, and place. These elements are called the *marketing mix,* the *four Ps,* or the *controllable variables* because they are under the general control of the marketing department.

6 Environmental factors, also called *uncontrollable variables,* are largely beyond the organization's control. These include social, technological, economic, competitive, and regulatory forces.

7 Building on customer value and relationship marketing concepts, successful firms develop mutually beneficial long-term relationships with their customers.

8 In marketing terms, U.S. business history is divided into four periods: the production era, the sales era, the marketing concept era, and the current market orientation era.

9 Marketing managers must balance consumer, organizational, and societal interests. This involves issues of ethics and social responsibility.

10 Both profit-making and nonprofit organizations perform marketing activities. They market products, services, and ideas that benefit consumers, organizations, and countries. Marketing creates utilities that give benefits, or customer value, to users.

KEY TERMS AND CONCEPTS

customer relationship management (CRM) p. 21
customer value p. 16
environmental factors p. 15
exchange p. 10
macromarketing p. 22
market p. 14
market orientation p. 21
marketing p. 9
marketing concept p. 21

marketing mix p. 15
marketing program p. 17
micromarketing p. 22
organizational buyers p. 23
relationship marketing p. 16
societal marketing concept p. 22
target market p. 14
ultimate consumers p. 23
utility p. 24

APPLYING MARKETING CONCEPTS AND PERSPECTIVES

1 What consumer wants (or benefits) are met by the following products or services? (*a*) Carnation Instant Breakfast, (*b*) Adidas running shoes, (*c*) Hertz Rent-A-Car, and (*d*) television home shopping programs.

2 Each of the four products, services, or programs in question 1 has substitutes. Respective examples are (*a*) a ham and egg breakfast, (*b*) regular tennis shoes, (*c*) taking a bus, and (*d*) a department store. What consumer benefits might these substitutes have in each case that some consumers might value more highly than those mentioned in question 1?

3 What are the characteristics (e.g., age, income, education) of the target market customers for the following products or services? (*a*) *National Geographic* magazine, (*b*) *Wired* magazine, (*c*) New York Giants football team, and (*d*) the U.S. Open tennis tournament.

4 A college in a metropolitan area wishes to increase its evening-school offerings of business-related courses such as marketing, accounting, finance, and management. Who are the target market customers (students) for these courses?

5 What actions involving the four marketing mix elements might be used to reach the target market in question 4?

6 What environmental factors (uncontrollable variables) must the college in question 4 consider in designing its marketing program?

7 Polaroid introduced instant still photography, which proved to be a tremendous success. Yet Polavision, its instant movie system, was a total disaster. (*a*) What benefits does each provide to users? (*b*) What factors do you think contributed to Polavision's failure? (*c*) What research could have been undertaken that might have revealed Polavision's drawbacks?

8 Rollerblade is now trying to grow in-line skating globally. What are the advantages and disadvantages of trying to reach new global markets?

9 Does a firm have the right to "create" wants and try to persuade consumers to buy goods and services they didn't know about earlier? What are examples of "good" and "bad" want creation? Who should decide what is good and bad?

INTERNET EXERCISE

"It!" "Ginger!" "Jetson's scooter!" These were early names given the revolutionary Segway HT (human transporter), a technology shrouded in secrecy and mystery until it was launched with much fanfare in late 2001. Dean Kamen, the inventor of Segway HT, has also developed other high-tech innovations. The Segway HT relies on computers and gyroscopes to control its speed, balance, and direction. It weighs about 80 pounds and can travel up to 15 mph on a six-hour battery charge. A commercial version is expected to sell for $8,000 while the consumer version may sell for $3,000 when it becomes available.

Go to the Segway HT website (www.segway.com) and view both the consumer and business sections of the site.

1 What do you see as the advantages and disadvantages of the Segway HT?

2 For businesses, what applications could the Segway HT be used for?

3 Why would consumers want to purchase a Segway HT?

VIDEO CASE 1–1   Rollerblade®: Rediscovering Growth

In the fiercely competitive in-line skate marketplace, what does the future hold for Rollerblade®?

As David Samuels, senior director for Sports Innovation at Rollerblade explains, innovative technology—in the form of new and better skates—will continue to be key for Rollerblade to stay ahead of the competition. Rollerblade must also find ways to expand the market for in-line skates. "Our challenge is to provide new venues, new reasons for people to skate. There's a lot of growth for us to catch up on in terms of household penetration," says Samuels.

THE SITUATION TODAY

When Rollerblade was founded, it was the only manufacturer of in-line skates in the world. Today the industry has more than 30 competitors, many that sell lower-priced skates than Rollerblade through mass-merchandising chains. Some of the large sporting goods manufacturers, like Nike, that have not traditionally sold in-line skates are now looking for ways to grow and are exploring the in-line skate market.

In addition, both Rollerblade and other in-line skate manufacturers are facing increased competition from other wheeled sports. This includes everything from scooters and skateboards to on-road and off-road rides for mountain bikes. Even the Segway HT (see Internet Exercise) is a competitor in some situations. Further, as shown earlier in Figure 1–1, Samuels is concerned that the exploding growth of the in-line skate market seen in the early 1990s has turned to decline.

THE MARKETING PROGRAM

Expanding the market and continuing to be the leader in product innovation gives Rollerblade a strategic advantage in the marketplace. Yet it is a solid and creative marketing mix that will enable Rollerblade to pass these advantages along to the customer.

The product is the most important "P" in Rollerblade's marketing mix. This involves both innovative technologies and new skate designs. In terms of technologies, Rollerblade has pioneered the ABT and ABT Lite braking systems, more breathable fabrics, and vibration-absorbing cushioning systems. New skate designs include expandable skates for kids, the five-wheeled Lightning™ for speed skaters, the three-wheeled Coyote™ for off-road skaters, and specially-designed skates to fit women's feet.

Rollerblade's promotional strategy continues to set it apart from the competitors, too. Its catalogs feature both its new technologies and new skate designs. The Rollerblade website (www. rollerblade.com) is one of the most popular promotional tools with Rollerblade's loyal customers.

Since Rollerblade does not have the resources of an industry giant like Nike, it finds ways to communicate with customers that do not entail huge cash outlays. For example, Rollerblade provides information or product samples to media that, in turn, do in-line-skating features for articles or broadcast programs. It also develops promotional partnerships through sponsoring events and creating sweepstakes with other companies. Recently Rollerblade teamed up with Taco Bell, Curad, Wise Snacks, and Honeywell for joint advertising that benefits the partners but is less expensive for Rollerblade than purchasing nationwide television or radio ads by itself.

Finally, Rollerblade sponsors a competitive team of aggressive skaters and racers that competes around the world and regularly wins such events as ESPN's X-Games. It is creative and unorthodox approaches such as these that Samuels believes will keep Rollerblade ahead of the competition in the 21st century.

Rollerblade practices an across-the-board strategy when it comes to distribution and price. Samuels says, "Our distribution channels run the gamut. We are everywhere from the large mass market stores to specialty in-line dealers. Additionally, Rollerblade has chosen to hit every single price point possible. We have skates that are at the very high end, as well as skates as low as $79 under the Rollerblade brand. We also take a different brand name called Blade Runner and bring those products to the large mass markets of the world." Giving the lower-priced skates

an alternate brand name allows Rollerblade to uphold its high-quality image in the marketplace while still providing an opportunity for beginners to test out the sport.

ISSUES FOR THE FUTURE

Some of the pressing issues in the future are global expansion, creating new segments of skaters, and expanding the product line. As Samuels explains, "Currently, the U.S. makes up over 50 percent of the marketplace worldwide. But Europe has been significant also. Germany is definitely one of the strongest countries for in-line skating." Other areas of growth include Australia and New Zealand, Japan, Mexico, and Korea. Rollerblade hopes to widen its global reach as the company continues to grow.

The youth segment should prove to be one of the most important segments in the future. "One of the biggest changes that's happened to us, and to the world really, is the power of youth. Kids who are anywhere from 10 to 12 years old on up into their twenties have been able to make a significant impact with so little money," explains Samuels. Rollerblade expects young people to continue to shape the recreational sports markets well into the future. Finally, Rollerblade has begun to offer products that are not in-line skates, such as accessories like helmets; wrist, elbow, and knee pads; skate bags; and skate tools. Rollerblade will continue to introduce products that respond to consumer needs and desires—constantly working to improve skate comfort, durability, and technologies.

Questions

1 What trends in the environmental forces (social, economic, technological, competitive, and regulatory) identified in Figure 1–3 in the chapter (*a*) work for and (*b*) work against Rollerblade's potential growth in the 21st century?

2 What are the differences in marketing goals for Rollerblade (*a*) in 1986 when Rollerblade was launched and (*b*) today?

3 What are the (*a*) advantages and (*b*) disadvantages of having Rollerblade become part of the Benetton sport group? Refer to the text as well as the video case.

4 In searching for global markets to enter, (*a*) what are some criteria that Rollerblade should use to select countries to enter and (*b*) what three or four countries meet these criteria best and are the most likely candidates?

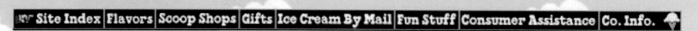

Site Index | Flavors | Scoop Shops | Gifts | Ice Cream By Mail | Fun Stuff | Consumer Assistance | Co. Info.

 # Statement Of Mission

BEN & JERRY'S IS DEDICATED TO the creation & demonstration of a new corporate concept of linked prosperity. Our mission consists of three interrelated parts.

UNDERLYING THE MISSION is the determination to seek new and creative ways of addressing all three parts, while holding a deep respect for individuals inside and outside the company, and for the communities of which they are a part.

PRODUCT

To make, distribute and sell the finest quality all natural ice cream and related products in a wide variety

[United States] [United Kingdom] [The Netherlands] [France] [Japan] [Page Blank?]

CHAPTER

2

LINKING MARKETING AND CORPORATE STRATEGIES

AFTER READING THIS CHAPTER YOU SHOULD BE ABLE TO:

- Describe the three organizational levels of strategy and how they relate to each other and the marketing function.

- Describe why business, mission, culture, and goals are important in organizations.

- Understand how organizations set strategic directions by assessing where they are now and seek to be in the future.

- Describe the strategic marketing process and its three key phases: planning, implementation, and control.

- Explain how the marketing mix elements are blended into a cohesive marketing program.

- Describe how marketing control compares actual results with planned objectives and acts on deviations from the plan.

WHERE DOES A CORRESPONDENCE SCHOOL "A" IN ICE CREAM MAKING LEAD? PLEASE STAY TUNED!

These two entrepreneurs aren't just your typical Tom, Dick, or Harry! Consider some facts about the company they founded:

- It recently launched a program letting customers send "Ice Cream by Mail" via its website.

- It contributes 7.5 percent of its pretax profits to philanthropic efforts.

- Its franchised PartnerShops are available to nonprofit organizations to provide training and job opportunities for people such as at-risk youth.

- It buys all of its milk and cream from one dairy cooperative whose members guarantee a bovine growth hormone-free supply.

- It just introduced KaBerry KaBoom! Flavor to help fund KaBoom!, a nonprofit organization that helps build playgrounds for kids.[1]

By now you know the company: Ben & Jerry's, or more formally, Ben & Jerry's Homemade, Inc.! Its website (opposite page) reflects its creative, funky approach to business—linked to a genuine concern for social causes.

Ben & Jerry's is proof that the American dream is still alive and well. Ben Cohen and Jerry Greenfield were grade school classmates on Long Island. In 1978 they headed north to Vermont and started an ice cream parlor in a renovated gas station.[2] Buoyed with enthusiasm, $12,000 they had borrowed and saved, and ideas from the $5 they spent on a Penn State correspondence course in ice cream making (with perfect scores on their open-book tests!) they were off and running.[3]

By 2000, Ben & Jerry's Homemade, Inc., had more than $200 million in sales— mainly from selling its incredibly rich ice cream. It had franchised more than 200 of its "Scoop Shop" retail outlets.

The company has international sales in Europe, the Mideast, and Asia. Not bad for two guys who started with a single ice cream parlor two decades ago.

In terms of its social mission, Ben & Jerry's in its own workplace has (1) committed to paying a "livable wage," (2) improved its employee benefits, and (3) sought to purchase its supplies from socially responsible suppliers. Outside its internal operations, Ben & Jerry's is a leader in protecting the environment, peaceful conflict resolution, and corporate philanthropy.

So where's the problem? In the late 1990s Ben and Jerry concluded the company's sales were flattening and it needed additional financial resources to grow. So in the spring of 2000 Ben & Jerry's agreed to be acquired by Unilever, a huge multinational firm. Key details: Ben & Jerry's would operate separately from Unilever's current U.S. ice cream business to preserve the company's legendary concern for the environment and social responsibility, and both cofounders would continue their involvement.[4]

Chapter 2 describes how organizations set their mission and overall direction and link these activities to marketing strategies. Because of today's intense competition, firms must continuously revisit these tasks—as Ben and Jerry have been forced to do. In essence, this chapter describes how organizations try to implement the marketing concept to provide genuine value to their customers.

LEVELS OF STRATEGY IN ORGANIZATIONS

This chapter first distinguishes among different kinds of organizations and the different levels within them. We then compare strategies at three different levels in an organization, emphasizing the importance of activities at the functional level.

Today's Organizations: Kinds, Levels, and Teams

Large organizations today are extremely complex. All of us deal in some way with huge organizations every day, so it is useful to understand (1) the two basic kinds of organizations, (2) the levels that exist in them and their link to marketing, and (3) the functional areas and cross-functional teams.

Kinds of Organizations   Today's organizations can be divided into business firms and nonprofit organizations. A *business firm* is a privately owned organization that serves its customers in order to earn a profit. Business firms must earn profits to survive. **Profit** is the reward to a business firm for the risk it undertakes in offering a product for sale; the money left over after a firm's total expenses are subtracted from its total revenues. In contrast to business firms, a *nonprofit organization* is a nongovernmental organization that serves its customers but does not have profit as an organizational goal. For simplicity in the rest of the book, however, the terms *firm, company, corporation,* and *organization* are used to cover both business and nonprofit operations.

Levels in Organizations and How Marketing Links to Them   Whether explicit or implicit, organizations such as Ben & Jerry's have a strategic direction. Marketing not only helps set this direction but must also help the organization move there. Figure 2–1 summarizes the focus of this direction at each of the three levels in an organization.

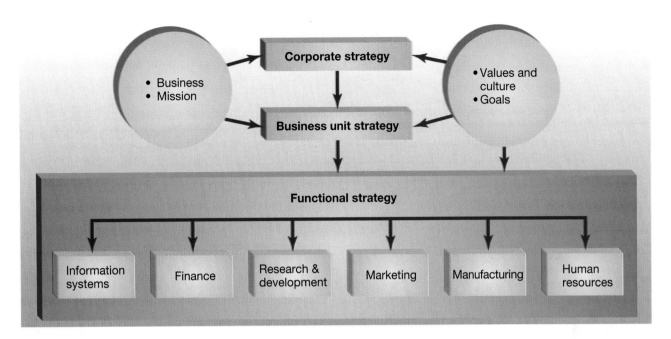

FIGURE 2-1
The three levels of strategy in organizations: corporate, business unit, and functional

The **corporate level** is where top management directs overall strategy for the entire organization. Multimarket, multiproduct firms such as General Electric or Johnson & Johnson really manage a portfolio of businesses, variously termed strategic business units (SBUs), strategic business segments, and product-market units (PMUs).[5] This level creates value for the shareholders of the firm, as measured by stock performance and profitability.

The term **business unit** refers to an organization that markets a set of related products to a clearly defined group of customers. The **business unit level** is the level at which business unit managers set the direction for their products and markets to exploit value-creating opportunities. The strategic direction is more specific at the business level of an organization. For less complex firms with a single business focus, such as Ben & Jerry's, the corporate and business unit levels may merge.

Each business unit has marketing and other specialized activities (e.g., finance, research and development, or human resource management) at the **functional level**, which is where groups of specialists *actually* create value for the organization. The term *department* generally refers to these specialized functions, such as the marketing department or information systems department. At the functional level, the strategic direction becomes more specific and focused. So, just as there is a hierarchy of levels within organizations, there is also a hierarchy of strategic directions set by management at that level.

Because marketing's major role is to look outward—to keep the organization focused on contributing to customer value—its activities tie to each of the three levels in Figure 2–1. In a large corporation with multiple business units, marketing may be called on to assess consumer trends as an aid to corporate planning. At the business unit level, marketing may be asked to provide leadership in developing a new, integrated customer service program across all business units.

Where Things Happen: Functional Areas and Cross-Functional Teams   At the lowest level in Figure 2–1, marketing serves as part of a team of functional specialists. This is the level at which most of the organization's work gets done—customers are listened to, products are designed and produced, customers' needs are satisfied. The marketing department does not work alone but works with *all* departments to deliver this customer value and satisfaction.

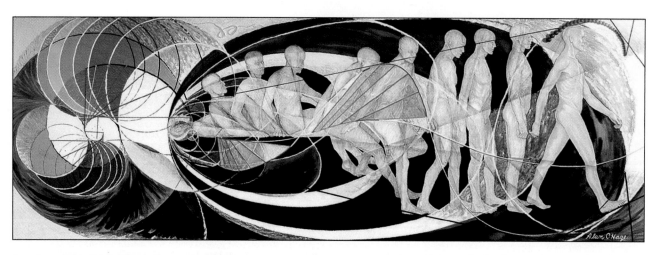

People see this "rising figure" mural in the headquarters of a world-class corporation. What does it signify? What does it say to employees? To others? For some insights and why it is important, see the text.

In practice, new-product development and other activities in many organizations involve **cross-functional teams**, a small number of people from different departments in an organization who are mutually accountable to a common set of performance goals. Boeing's cross-functional teams blend not only employees from different functional areas within the firm but also from its suppliers and customers as well. Listening to airline passengers like you, one Boeing cross-functional team helped develop the Boeing 777, with customer-value innovations like more aisle headroom, TV screens in seatbacks, and seats 1.5 inches wider than most economy jetliner seats.

Cross-functional conflict can arise because in marketing's drive to implement the marketing concept and increase customer value, other departments may see this as making their jobs more difficult. For example, widening the Boeing 777 seats adds design and space problems for the engineering department and causes the finance department concerns about cost overruns. It is marketing's job to make these departments understand that without happy, satisfied customers who buy the organization's product, there is no company and there are no jobs.

Strategy Issues in Organizations

Organizations need a *raison d'etre*—a reason for their existence—and a direction. This is where their business, mission, values and culture, and goals converge. As shown in Figure 2–1, business and mission apply to the corporate and business unit levels, while values and culture, and goals relate to all three levels.

The Business   Organizations like Ben & Jerry's, the Red Cross, and your college exist for a purpose—to accomplish something for someone. At birth, most organizations have clear ideas about what "something" and "someone" mean. But as the organization grows over time, often its purpose gets fuzzy, unclear.

This is where the organization repeatedly asks some of the most difficult questions it ever faces: What is our business? Who are our customers? What offerings should we provide to give these customers value? One guideline in defining the company's business: Try to understand the people served by the organization and the value they receive, which emphasizes the critical customer-driven focus that successful organizations have.

In a now-famous article, Harvard professor Theodore Levitt cited American railroads as organizations that had a narrow, production-oriented statement of their business: "We are in the railroad business!" This narrow definition of their business lost sight of who their customers were and how railroads served them. So a railroad saw only other railroads as competitors—failing to design strategies to compete with airlines, barges, pipelines, trucks, bus lines, and cars. Railroads would probably have fared better over the past century by recognizing they are in "the transportation business."[6]

With this focus on the customer, Disney *is not* in the movie and theme park business, but rather it *is* in the business of creating fun and fantasy for customers. Similarly, as we'll see shortly, Medtronic *is not* in the medical device business but *is* in the business of alleviating pain, restoring health, and extending life. In this respect Medtronic's business somewhat overlaps its mission, the next topic.

The Mission   By understanding its business, an organization can take steps to define its **mission**, a statement of the organization's scope, often identifying its customers, markets, products, technology, and values. Today often used interchangeably with "vision," the "mission" statement frequently has an inspirational theme—something that can ignite the loyalty of employees and others with whom the organization comes in contact. This is probably the best-known mission statement in America:

> To explore strange new worlds, to seek out new life and new civilizations, to boldly go where no one has gone before.

This continuing mission for the starship *Enterprise,* as Gene Rodenberry wrote it for the *Star Trek* adventure series, is inspirational and focuses the advanced technology, strong leadership, and skilled crew of the *Enterprise* on what is to be accomplished. This inspiration and focus appears in the mission of nonprofit organizations, like the American Red Cross:

> To improve the quality of human life; to enhance self-reliance and concern for others; and to help people avoid, prepare for, and cope with emergencies.

Today Medtronic is *the* world leader in developing, producing, and marketing heart pacemakers, but four decades ago it was struggling and near bankruptcy. Meeting monthly in the early 1960s in the garage where Medtronic started, the board of directors pressed Earl Bakken, the CEO and one of the founders, to describe "what the company was about."[7] So Bakken went to the blackboard and sketched out Medtronic's mission statement—one almost identical to its present-day mission shown in Figure 2–2. In an abbreviated form, this mission encompasses six ordered priorities: (1) contribution to human welfare; (2) focused growth, both what Medtronic *will* and *will not* do; (3) unsurpassed quality; (4) fair profit; (5) the personal worth of employees; and (6) good citizenship in its communities. This mission is inscribed in a stone wall at the entrance to corporate headquarters, a constant reminder to all.[8]

Values and Culture   Organizations must connect not just with their employees but with all their **stakeholders**, individuals or groups, either within or outside an organization, that relate to it in what it does and how well it performs. Internal stakeholders include employees, officers, and board members. External stakeholders typically include customers, suppliers, distributors, governments, unions, local communities, and the general public.[9] The "rising figure" wall painting at Medtronic's corporate headquarters (opposite page) clearly communicates to all these stakeholders what Earl Bakken wrote on the blackboard for his board of directors—that Medtronic "is about" making devices to help restore health and normal lives.

Whether at the corporate, business, or functional level, a **culture** exists in the unit, which is a system of shared values, attitudes, and behaviors that distinguish it

FIGURE 2–2
Medtronic's mission

- To contribute to human welfare by application of biomedical engineering in the research, design, manufacture, and sale of instruments or appliances that alleviate pain, restore health, and extend life.
- To direct our growth in the areas of biomedical engineering where we display maximum strength and ability; to gather people and facilities that tend to augment these areas; to continuously build on these areas through education and knowledge assimilation; to avoid participation in areas where we cannot make unique and worthy contributions.
- To strive without reserve for the greatest possible reliability and quality in our products; to be the unsurpassed standard of comparison and to be recognized as a company of dedication, honesty, integrity, and service.
- To make a fair profit on current operations to meet our obligations, sustain our growth, and reach our goals.
- To recognize the personal worth of employees by providing an employment framework that allows personal satisfaction in work accomplished, security, advancement opportunity, and means to share in the company's success.
- To maintain good citizenship as a company.

from others. At Medtronic, a corporate officer presents each new employee with a medallion with the "rising figure" on one side and the mission on the other. Each December five or six patients, accompanied by their physicians, describe to a large employee holiday celebration how Medtronic products have changed their lives. These activities send clear messages to employees and other stakeholders about Medtronic's cohesive corporate culture.[10]

When corporations merge or are acquired, corporate cultures can collide and conflict, often resulting from conflicts in missions and goals (discussed in the following section). Ben & Jerry's is an example. With $45 billion of annual sales and dozens of well-known brands (Wisk, Dove, Lipton), Unilever has 180 times the annual sales of Ben & Jerry's. This really makes Ben & Jerry's only a small business unit in the Unilever Corporation. The preacquisition press releases of April 2000 proclaimed Unilever's continuing commitment to the Ben & Jerry's social mission. However, after Unilever's acquisition was completed in August 2000, the honeymoon was apparently short-lived, at least partly based on conflict over social missions and cultures. Rumors surfaced that Ben and Jerry were threatening to leave Unilever.[11] The Internet Exercise at the end of the chapter asks you to compare missions and goals for both Ben & Jerry's and Unilever and get an update of where things stand today.

Goals   **Goals** or **objectives** (terms used interchangeably in this textbook) convert the mission into targeted levels of performance to be achieved, often by a specific time. So these goals measure how well a mission is being accomplished. As shown in Figure 2–1, goals exist at the corporate, business unit, and functional levels. All lower-level goals must contribute to achieving goals at the next, higher level. In fact, the pattern of goals provides strategic direction because organizations often get what they measure. Business firms can pursue several different types of goals:

- *Profit.* Classic economic theory assumes a firm seeks to maximize long-run profit, achieving as high a financial return on its investment as possible. In practice, many firms seek to maximize shareholder value and improve stock performance.
- *Sales revenue.* If profits are acceptable, a firm may elect to maintain or increase its sales level even though profitability may not be maximized. Increased sales revenue may gain promotions for key executives.
- *Market share.* A firm may choose to maintain or increase its market share, sometimes at the expense of greater profits if industry status or prestige is at

ETHICS AND SOCIAL RESPONSIBILITY ALERT

The Global Dilemma: How to Achieve Sustainable Development

ETHICS

Corporate executives and world leaders are increasingly asked to address the issue of "sustainable development," a term that involves having each country find an ideal balance between meeting the needs of the present generation at the expense of future ones. This often involves adding jobs today in highly polluting industries, thereby pushing cleanup actions into the future.

Eastern Europe and the nations of the former Soviet Union provide an example. Tragically, poisoned air and dead rivers are the legacies of seven decades of communist rule.

With more than half of the households of many of these nations below the poverty level, should the immediate goal be a cleaner environment or more food, clothing, housing, and consumer goods? What should the heads of these governments do? What should Western firms trying to enter these new, growing markets do? What will be the impact on future generations?

Should the environment or economic growth come first? What are the societal trade-offs?

stake. **Market share** is the ratio of sales revenue of the firm to the total sales revenue of all firms in the industry, including the firm itself.

- *Unit sales.* Sales revenue may be deceiving because of the effects of inflation, so a firm may choose to maintain or increase the number of units it sells, such as cars, cases of breakfast cereal, or TV sets.
- *Quality.* A firm may target the highest quality as Medtronic does with its medical devices and as 3M does with its Six Sigma program (Chapter 10).
- *Customer satisfaction.* Customers are the reasons the organization exists so their perceptions and actions are of vital importance. Their satisfaction can be measured directly with surveys or tracked with proxy measures like number of customer complaints or percent of orders shipped within 24 hours of receipt.
- *Employee welfare.* A firm may recognize the critical importance of its employees by having an explicit goal stating its commitment to good employment opportunities and working conditions for them.
- *Social responsibility.* A firm may seek to balance conflicting goals of consumers, employees, and stockholders to promote overall welfare of all these groups, even at the expense of profits. U.S. firms manufacturing products abroad increasingly seek to be "good global citizens" by paying reasonable wages and reducing pollution to facilitate sustainable development, the topic of the Ethics and Social Responsibility Alert.

Many private organizations that do not seek profits also exist. Examples are museums, symphony orchestras, private hospitals, and research institutes. These organizations strive to serve consumers with the greatest efficiency and the least cost. Although technically not falling under the definition of "nonprofit organization," government agencies also perform marketing activities in trying to achieve their goal of serving the public good.

Concept Check

1. What are the three levels in today's large organizations?

2. What is the difference between an organization's mission and its culture?

3. Give an example of a goal for a business and a goal for a nonprofit organization.

SETTING STRATEGIC DIRECTIONS

Setting strategic directions involves answering two other difficult questions: (1) Where are we now? and (2) Where do we want to go?

A Look Around: Where Are We Now?

Asking an organization where it is at the present time involves identifying its customers, competencies, competitors, and business sectors. More detailed approaches of assessing "where are we now?" include both SWOT analysis (Figure 2–9) and environmental scanning (Chapter 3), which may both be done at each of the three levels in the organization.

Customers   Ben & Jerry's customers are ice cream and frozen yogurt eaters. But they are not all the same, because they have different flavor preferences, fat preferences, convenience preferences, and so on. Medtronic's "customers" are cardiologists and heart surgeons that serve patients. But, as we'll see later in the chapter, practical considerations may require "customers" to be served differently in Asia than in the United States. The crucial point: Strategic directions must be customer-focused and provide genuine value and benefits to present and prospective customers.

Competencies   "What do we do best?" asks about our organization's capabilities or competencies. **Competencies** are an organization's special capabilities, including skills, technologies, and resources that distinguish it from other organizations. Exploiting these competencies can lead to success.[12] In Medtronic's case its competencies include world-class technology plus training, service, and marketing activities that respond to both standard and urgent, life-threatening medical needs and wants! Competencies should be distinctive enough to provide a **competitive advantage**, a unique strength relative to competitors, often based on quality, time, cost, or innovation.[13]

For example, if 3M has a goal of generating a specific portion of its sales from new products, it must have a supporting competency in research and development and new-product marketing. In the 1990s Hewlett-Packard had a truly competitive advantage with its fast cycle time, which allowed it to bring innovative products to markets in large volume rapidly.[14]

Another strategy is to develop a competency in total quality management (TQM). **Quality** here means those features and characteristics of a product that influence its ability to satisfy customer needs. The Marketing NewsNet box describes W. Edwards Deming's "quality chain" that has revolutionized global thinking about quality and is the foundation of many of today's quality initiatives.[15] Firms often try to improve quality or reduce new product cycles through **benchmarking**—discovering how

How well do you think these websites do? For the answers see Figure 2–4 and a description of Lands' End's strategy in the text.

L. L. Bean, Inc.
www.llbean.com

Lands' End, Inc.
landsend.com.

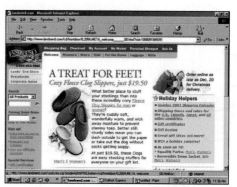

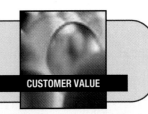

MARKETING NEWSNET

Adding Customer Value through the Quality Chain Reaction

CUSTOMER VALUE

When W. Edwards Deming went to Japan in 1950 to help rebuild postwar Japan, he shared a very profound model with Japanese industry. This model helped launch the quality revolution that has contributed to dramatic global change in countless industries.

The model is shown below. It has become a mantra for the quality movement. Assuming an organization has an otherwise effective strategy and management structure in place, the model shows the additional benefits from improving the quality of products, services, and processes. The first benefit is a decrease in costs as a direct result of less waste. A consequence of less waste is greater process productivity. This allows lower prices, which combines with the

improved products and services to allow the organization to compete more effectively. The ultimate payoff is that the firm stays in business and provides jobs because it provides greater value to the customers.

The amount of benefit can be quantified by looking at the cost of poor quality. Experts claim that 10 percent to 20 percent of sales revenues are needed to cover the cost of poor quality in the form of production waste and rework, complaints and warranty costs, and defective products. Through well-designed marketing programs, marketers can help reduce the cost of poor quality and contribute directly to a firm's performance.

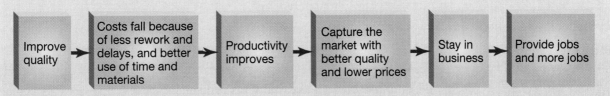

others do something better than your own firm so you can imitate or leapfrog competition. Benchmarking often involves studying operations in completely different businesses. When General Mills sought ideas on how to reduce the time to convert its production lines from one cereal to another, it sent a team to observe the pit crews at the Indianapolis 500 race. The result: General Mills cut its plant changeover time by more than half.

Competitors   In today's global competition the lines among competitive sectors are increasingly blurred. Lands' End started as a catalog retailer. But defining its competitors simply as other catalog retailers (Figure 2–3) is a huge oversimplification. In what is called "intertype competition" in Chapter 17, Lands' End now competes not only with other catalog retailers of clothing but with traditional department stores, mass merchandisers, specialty shops, and well-known brands of clothing sold in all these kinds of retailers. While only parts of the clothing lines sold by these competitors overlap those of Lands' End, all have websites for Internet sales.

To exploit its competencies Lands' End now operates both "inlet" and "outlet" stores, ones that complement both its catalog and Internet operations. Like all Internet retailers, it has a goal of increasing its "conversion rate," the percentage of browsers who actually buy something on visits to the website. Figure 2–4 shows that among big name e-tailers, Lands' End's conversion rate of 9.0 percent trails only L.L. Bean's 10.1 percent. Lands' End has invested heavily in technology to make its site more consumer friendly (easier to move from the home page to the sales-confirmation window) with a "virtual model" of a customer to let him or her "try things on" online (see Chapter 17) and "synchronized screens" to let Lands' End's service rep see exactly the same screen the customer is viewing at home.[16]

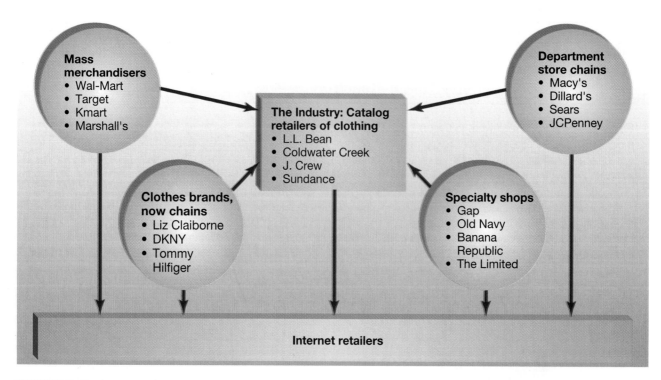

FIGURE 2–3

Who are Lands' End's competitors? They go far beyond traditional catalog retailers for clothes.

Lands' End's experience is typical of the complex array of competitors today's business firms face. So successful firms continuously assess both who the competitors are and how they are changing in order to respond with their own strategies.

Growth Strategies: Where Do We Want to Go?

Knowing where the organization is at the present time enables managers to set a direction for the firm and start to allocate resources to move toward that direction. Two techniques to aid in these decisions are (1) portfolio and (2) market-product analyses.

FIGURE 2–4

How some big-name Internet retailers (e-tailers) compare on "conversion rates," the percentage of browsers who actually buy something

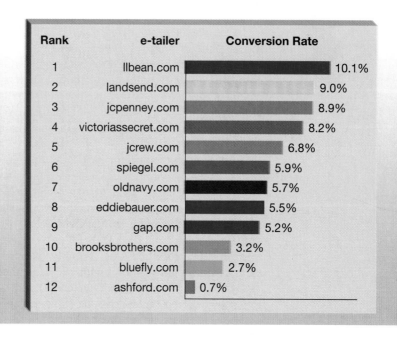

Rank	e-tailer	Conversion Rate
1	llbean.com	10.1%
2	landsend.com	9.0%
3	jcpenney.com	8.9%
4	victoriassecret.com	8.2%
5	jcrew.com	6.8%
6	spiegel.com	5.9%
7	oldnavy.com	5.7%
8	eddiebauer.com	5.5%
9	gap.com	5.2%
10	brooksbrothers.com	3.2%
11	bluefly.com	2.7%
12	ashford.com	0.7%

The Portfolio of Businesses: BCG Analysis   The Boston Consulting Group's (BCG) *business portfolio analysis* uses quantified performance measures and growth targets to analyze a firm's business units (called strategic business units, or SBUs, in the BCG analysis) as though they were a collection of separate investments.[17] While used at the business unit level here, this BCG analysis has also been applied at the product line or individual product or brand level. The popularity of this kind of portfolio analysis is shown by the fact that more than 75 percent of the largest U.S. firms have used it in some form. BCG, a nationally known management consulting firm, advises its clients to locate the position of each of its SBUs on a growth-share matrix (Figure 2–5). The vertical axis is the *market growth rate,* which is the annual rate of growth of the specific market or industry in which a given SBU is competing. This axis in the figure runs from 0 to 20 percent, although in practice it might run even higher. The axis has arbitrarily been divided at 10 percent into high-growth and low-growth areas.

The horizontal axis is the *relative market share,* defined as the sales of the SBU divided by the sales of the largest firm in the industry. A relative market share of 10× (at the left end of the scale) means that the SBU has 10 times the *share* of its largest competitor, whereas a share of 0.1× (at the right end of the scale) means it has only 10 percent of the *sales* of its largest competitor. The scale is logarithmic and is arbitrarily divided into high and low relative market shares at a value of 1×.

BCG has given specific names and descriptions to the four resulting quadrants in its growth-share matrix based on the amount of cash they generate for or require from the firm:

- Cash cows (lower-left quadrant) are SBUs that typically generate large amounts of cash, far more than they can invest profitably in their own product line. They have a dominant share of a slow-growth market and provide cash to pay large amounts of company overhead and to invest in other SBUs.
- Stars (upper-left quadrant) are SBUs with a high share of high-growth markets that may not generate enough cash to support their own demanding needs for future growth. When their growth slows, they are likely to become cash cows.

FIGURE 2–5
Boston Consulting Group growth-share matrix for a strong, diversified firm showing some strategic plans

Boston Consulting Group
www.bcg.com

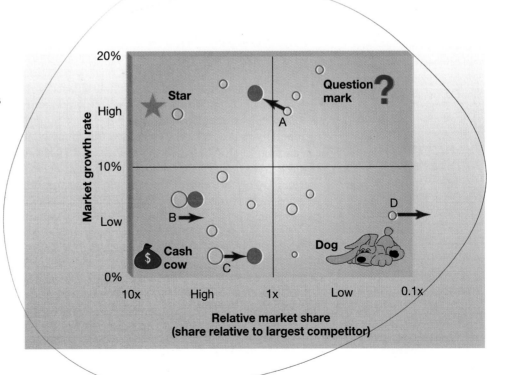

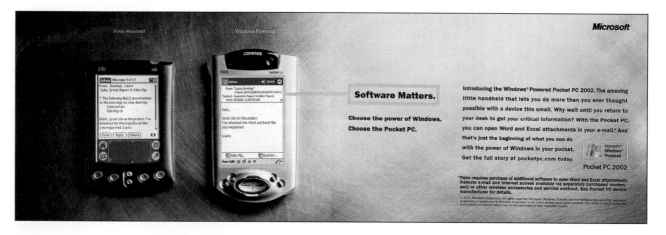

Strategies emerging from a business portfolio analysis: Microsoft "builds" its hand-held business while Procter & Gamble "divests" its Duncan Hines cake mix line to Aurora Foods.

- Question marks or problem children (upper-right quadrant) are SBUs with a low share of high-growth markets. They require large injections of cash just to maintain their market share, much less increase it. Their name implies management's dilemma for these SBUs: choosing the right ones to invest in and phasing out the rest.
- Dogs (lower-right quadrant) are SBUs with a low share of low-growth markets. Although they may generate enough cash to sustain themselves, they do not hold the promise of ever becoming real winners for the firm. Dropping SBUs in this quadrant from a business portfolio is generally advocated except when relationships with other SBUs, competitive considerations, or potential strategic alliances exist.[18]

The 14 circles in Figure 2–5 show the current SBUs in a strong, diversified firm. The area of each circle is proportional to the corresponding SBU's annual sales revenue.

The portfolio in Figure 2–5 is a mixed one. On the favorable side, one-half of its SBUs are large and have high market shares, but, unfortunately, the other half are small with low market shares. Because most firms have limited influence on the market growth rate (the factor shown on the vertical axis), their main alternative in a growth-share matrix framework is to try to change the relative market share (the factor on the horizontal axis).

To accomplish this, management makes conscious decisions on what role each SBU should have in the future and either injects or removes cash from it. Four alternative strategies are available for each SBU. The firm can invest more in the SBU to *build* its share (SBU A in Figure 2–5), as Microsoft has done with its handheld computer product lines. Or it can invest just enough to *hold* the SBU's share at about its current level (SBU B in the figure). Or it can *harvest* the SBU (SBU C in the figure), trying to milk its short-term cash flow even though it may lose share and become a dog in the longer run. Finally, the firm can *divest* the SBU (SBU D) by phasing it out or actually selling it to gain cash, as Procter & Gamble did by selling its Duncan Hines cake mix line to Aurora Foods.

The primary strengths of business portfolio analysis include (1) forcing a firm to assess each of its SBUs in terms of its relative market share and industry market growth rate, which, in turn, (2) requires the firm to forecast which SBUs will be cash producers and cash users in the future. Weaknesses are that (1) it is often difficult to get the information needed to locate each SBU on the growth-share matrix, (2) there are other important factors missing from the analysis such as possible synergies among the SBUs when they use the same salesforce or research and development facilities, and (3) there are problems in motivating people in an SBU that has been labeled a dog or even a cash cow and is unlikely to get new resources from the firm to grow and provide opportunities for promotion.[19] In addition, planners have had difficulty incorporating competitive information into portfolio analysis, and formal experiments show the technique may not provide as effective an allocation of resources as more traditional methods of financial analysis.[20]

Market-Product Analysis   Firms can also view growth opportunities in terms of four combinations of (1) current and new markets and (2) current and new products, as shown in Figure 2–6.

As Unilever attempts to increase sales revenues of its Ben & Jerry's business, it must consider all four of the alternative market-product strategies shown in Figure 2–6. For example, it can try to use a strategy of *market penetration*—increasing sales of present products in its existing markets, in this case by increasing sales of Ben & Jerry's present ice cream products to U.S. consumers. There is no change in either the basic product line or the market served, but increased sales are possible through finding innovative pricing, promotion, or distribution strategies to reach existing customer segments. For example, Ben & Jerry's might find efficiencies by hooking into Unilever's Breyers and Good Humor ice cream brands or through developing new flavors.

Market development, which here means selling existing Ben & Jerry's products to new markets, is a reasonable alternative. South American consumers are good candidates as possible new markets. There is good news and bad news for this strategy: increasing incomes of households in those markets present great opportunities, but the Ben & Jerry's brand is relatively unknown.

An expansion strategy using *product development* involves selling a new product to existing markets. Figure 2–6 shows that the firm could try leveraging the Ben & Jerry's brand, as mentioned earlier, by selling its own Ben & Jerry's brand of children's clothing in the United States. This, of course, has dangers because Americans may not be able to see a clear connection between the company's expertise in ice cream and, say, children's clothing.

Diversification involves developing new products and selling them in new markets. This is a potentially high-risk strategy for Ben & Jerry's—and for most firms—because the company has neither previous production experience nor marketing experience on which to draw. For example, in trying to sell a Ben & Jerry's brand of children's clothing in South America, the company has expertise neither in producing children's clothing nor in marketing to South American consumers.[21]

FIGURE 2–6
Four market-product strategies: alternative ways to expand sales revenues for Ben & Jerry's

Markets	PRODUCTS	
	Current	**New**
Current	**Market penetration** Selling more Ben & Jerry's super premium ice cream to Americans	**Product development** Selling a new product such as children's clothing under the Ben & Jerry's brand to Americans
New	**Market development** Selling more Ben & Jerry's super premium ice cream in South American markets for the first time	**Diversification** Selling a new product such as children's clothing in South American markets for the first time

Which strategies will Unilever (and Ben and Jerry?) follow for Ben & Jerry's? Keep your eyes, ears, and taste buds working to discover the marketing answers!

Building Blocks for an Organization's Success

Management theorists have attempted to identify key factors that are essential to a firm's success. One such structure appears in Figure 2–7, which identifies four critical factors: (1) customer relationships, to deliver genuine value for customers; (2) innovation, to create new and unique value; (3) quality, to ensure an excellence and consistency in what is sold; and (4) efficiency, to lower costs and, hence, the price paid by customers. Note that improving each of these factors at a particular time might cause other factors to decline. Thus, it is a continuing challenge for an organization to strike the right balance among these four "building blocks" that are the foundation of an organization's success.[22]

Lands' End provides an example of these building blocks. Its stores and website give a remarkable statement about its commitments to customer relationships and quality of its products with these unconditional words:

GUARANTEED. PERIOD.®

Its website points out the Lands' End guarantee has always been an unconditional one and it has read: "If you are not completely satisfied with any item you buy from us, at any time during your use of it, return it and we will refund your full purchase price." But to get the message across more clearly to its customers, it put it in the two-word guarantee above.

In terms of the innovation building block, Lands' End continuously improves its search engines to allow customers to use plain-language searches to find items more easily on its website. And what about the efficiency block in Lands' End's arsenal? In 2000 Lands' End launched a new service, "My Personal Shopper,"

FIGURE 2–7

A combination of customer relationships, innovation, quality, and efficiency are the building blocks of an organization's success.

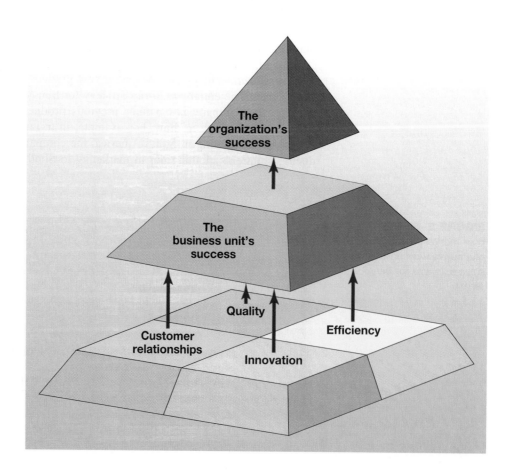

Lands' End's unconditional guarantee for its products is part of its "success" strategy. Others are described in the text.

that guides web shoppers and helps simplify their buying decisions. Its conversion rate with this? About 80 percent higher among those who used the Personal Shopper compared to those who used its nonpersonalized recommendations from its website.[23]

Concept Check

1. What are "competencies" and why are they important?

2. What is business portfolio analysis?

3. What are the four building blocks of an organization's success?

THE STRATEGIC MARKETING PROCESS

After the organization assesses where it's at and where it wants to go, other questions emerge:

1. How do we allocate our resources to get where we want to go?
2. How do we convert our plans to actions?
3. How do our results compare with our plans, and do deviations require new plans?

This same approach is used in the **strategic marketing process**, whereby an organization allocates its marketing mix resources to reach its target markets. This process is divided into three phases: planning, implementation, and control (Figure 2–8).

The strategic marketing process is so central to the activities of most organizations that they formalize it as a **marketing plan**, which is a road map for the marketing activities of an organization for a specified future period of time, such as one year or five years. Appendix A at the end of this chapter provides guidelines for writing a marketing plan and also presents a sample marketing plan for Paradise Kitchens,® Inc., a firm that produces and distributes a line of spicy chilies under the Howlin' Coyote® brand name. The sequence of activities that follow parallels the elements of the marketing plan that appear in Appendix A.

Ben & Jerry's develops and introduces its flavors of ice cream, yogurts, and sherbets in response to both consumer . . . ahem! . . . tastes and important social causes it supports. For more than a decade, the brownies for the Ben & Jerry's very popular Chocolate Fudge Brownie ice cream and low-fat frozen yogurt have been supplied by Greystone Bakery in Yonkers, New York—a nonprofit organization that trains and employs homeless and low-income people for self-sufficiency. As for Phish Food, the Vermont-based rock band Phish donates all the royalties it received from the sales of Phish Food ice cream to support efforts toward environmental preservation of Lake Champlain, on the border between New York and Vermont.

But not all flavors last. The ones that don't, wind up in Ben & Jerry's "Flavor Graveyard." To see Ben & Jerry's current flavors and those in the Flavor Graveyard, visit: www. benjerry.com/product/graveyard.tmpl.

The following section gives an overview of the strategic marketing process that places Chapters 3 through 21 in perspective. In Chapter 22 we examine the strategic marketing process again in more depth.

Strategic Marketing Process: The Planning Phase

As shown in Figure 2–8, the planning phase of the strategic marketing process consists of the three steps shown at the top of the figure: (1) situation analysis, (2) market-product focus and goal setting, and (3) the marketing program. Let's use the recent marketing planning experiences of several companies to look at each of these steps.

Step 1: Situation (SWOT) Analysis   The essence of **situation analysis** is taking stock of where the firm or product has been recently, where it is now, and where it is headed in light of the organization's plans and the external factors and trends affecting it. The situation analysis box in Figure 2–8 is the first of the three steps in the planning phase.

An effective short-hand summary of the situation analysis is a **SWOT analysis**, an acronym describing an organization's appraisal of its internal strengths and weaknesses and its external opportunities and threats. Both the situation and SWOT analyses can be done at the level of the entire organization, the business unit, the product line, or the specific product. As an analysis moves from the level of the

A SWOT analysis can suggest ways for Ben & Jerry's to leverage these well-known products and flavors.

Ben & Jerry's Homemade, Inc.
www.benjerry.com

Unilever N.V.
unilever.com

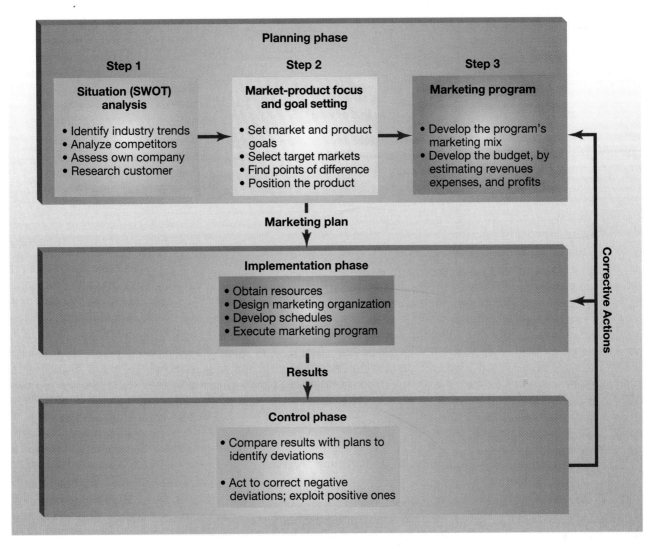

FIGURE 2–8
The strategic marketing process

entire organization to the specific product, it, of course, gets far more detailed. For small firms or those with basically a single product line, an analysis at the firm or product level is really the same thing.

Let's assume you are the Unilever vice president responsible for integrating Ben & Jerry's into Unilever's business. You might do the SWOT analysis shown in Figure 2–9. Note that your SWOT table has four cells formed by the combination of internal versus external factors (the rows) and favorable versus unfavorable factors (the columns) that summarize Ben & Jerry's strengths, weaknesses, opportunities, and threats. This SWOT analysis can identify Ben & Jerry's flavors that don't meet customer tastes and wind up in its "Flavor Graveyard," as described in the Web Link.

A SWOT analysis helps a firm identify the strategy-related factors in these four cells that can have a major effect on the firm. The ultimate goal is to identify the *critical* factors affecting the firm and then build on vital strengths, correct glaring weaknesses, exploit significant opportunities, and avoid disaster-laden threats. That is a big order. The ultimate goal is not simply to develop the SWOT analysis but to translate the results of the analysis into specific actions to help the firm grow and succeed.

Although the SWOT analysis is a shorthand look at the situation analysis, it is based on an exhaustive study of the four areas shown in step 1 of the planning phase

FIGURE 2–9
Ben & Jerry's: a "SWOT" to
get it growing again

Location of Factor	TYPE OF FACTOR	
	Favorable	**Unfavorable**
Internal	**Strengths** • Prestigious, well-known brand name among U.S. consumers • 40% share of the U.S. super premium ice cream market • Can complement Unilever's existing ice cream brands	**Weaknesses** • Danger that B&J's social responsibility actions may add costs, reduce focus on core business • Need for experienced managers to help growth • Flat sales and profits in recent years
External	**Opportunities** • Growing demand for quality ice cream in overseas markets • Increasing U.S. demand for frozen yogurt and other low-fat desserts • Success of many U.S. firms in extending successful brand in one product category to others	**Threats** • Consumer concern with fatty desserts; B&J customers are the type who read new government-ordered nutritional labels • Competes with giant Pillsbury and its Haagen-Dazs brand • International downturns increase the risks for B&J in European and Asian markets

of the strategic marketing process in Figure 2–8 that are the foundation on which the firm builds its marketing program:

- Identifying trends in the firm's industry.
- Analyzing the firm's competitors.
- Assessing the firm itself.
- Researching the firm's present and prospective customers.

Examples of more in-depth study in these four areas appear in the SWOT analysis in Figure 1 in the marketing plan in Appendix A and the chapters in this textbook cited in that plan.

Step 2: Market-Product Focus and Goal Setting   Finding a focus on what product offerings will be directed toward which customers (step 2 of the planning phase in Figure 2–8) is essential for developing an effective marketing program (step 3). This focus often comes from the firm's using **market segmentation**, which involves aggregating prospective buyers into groups, or segments, that (1) have common needs and (2) will respond similarly to a marketing action. Ideally a firm can use market segmentation to identify the segments on which it will focus its efforts—its target market segments—and develop one or more marketing programs to reach them.

Goal setting here involves setting measurable marketing objectives to be achieved—possibly for a specific market, a specific product or brand, or an entire marketing program. We can illustrate steps 2 and 3 in the planning phase of the strategic marketing process by using Medtronic's "Champion" brand heart pacemaker that it was developing for Asian patients needing them (Case D-10, Appendix D).[24] Stated simply, Medtronic's five-year marketing plan for its Champion pacemaker specifies these step 2 activities:

- *Set marketing and product goals.* As mentioned later in Chapter 10, the chances of new-product success are increased by specifying both market and product goals. Talks with cardiologists in India and China by Medtronic executives

IMPORTANT MESSAGE

FOR _____

DATE _____ TIME _____ A.M. / P.M.

M _____

OF _____

PHONE _____

☐ FAX   AREA CODE   NUMBER   EXTENSION

☐ MOBILE   AREA CODE   NUMBER   TIME TO CALL

TELEPHONED		PLEASE CALL	
CAME TO SEE YOU		WILL CALL AGAIN	
WANTS TO SEE YOU		RUSH	
RETURNED YOUR CALL		SPECIAL ATTENTION	

MESSAGE _____

_____

_____

_____

_____

SIGNED _____

Office DEPOT

Cop - A - Tan
310 . 392 . 8989

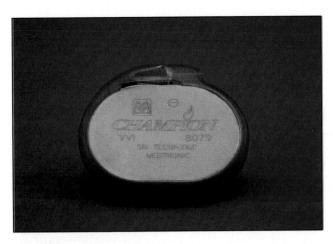

The "Champion": Medtronic's high-quality, long-life, low-cost heart pacemaker for Asian markets.

Medtronic, Inc.

medtronic.com

showed that these doctors saw some of the current state-of-the-art features as unnecessary. Instead, they preferred an affordable pacemaker that featured reliability and ease of use. Medtronic's goals: Design and market such a pacemaker in the next three years that could be manufactured in China for the Asian market.

- *Select target markets.* The Champion pacemaker will be targeted at cardiologists and medical clinics in India, China, and other Asian countries performing heart surgery.
- *Find points of difference.* **Points of difference** are those characteristics of a product that make it superior to competitive substitutes. (Chapter 10 points out that this is the single most important factor in the success or failure of a new product.) For the Champion pacemaker, the key points of difference are *not* the state-of-the-art features that drive up production costs and are important to only a minority of patients. Instead, they are high quality, long life, reliability, ease of use, and low cost.
- *Position the product.* The pacemaker will be "positioned" in cardiologists' and patients' minds as a medical device that is high quality and reliable with a long, nine-year life. The name "Champion" is selected after testing acceptable names among doctors in India, China, Pakistan, Singapore, and Malaysia.

Details in these four elements of step 2 provide a solid foundation to use in developing the marketing program—the next step in the planning phase of the strategic marketing process.

Step 3: Marketing Program   Activities in step 2 tell the marketing manager which customers to target and which customer needs the firm's product offerings can satisfy—the *who* and *what* aspects of the strategic marketing process. The *how* aspect—step 3 in the planning phase—involves developing the program's marketing mix and its budget.

Figure 2–10 shows components of each marketing mix element that are combined to provide a cohesive marketing program. For the five-year marketing plan of Medtronic, these marketing mix activities include the following:

- *Product strategy.* Offer a "Champion" brand heart pacemaker with features needed by Asian patients at an affordable price.
- *Price strategy.* Manufacture Champion to control costs so that it can be priced below $1,000 (in U.S. dollars)—a fraction of the price of the state-of-the-art pacemakers offered in Western markets.
- *Promotion strategy.* Feature demonstrations at cardiologist and medical conventions across Asia to introduce the Champion and highlight the device's features and application.
- *Place (distribution) strategy.* Search out, utilize, and train reputable medical distributors across Asia to call on cardiologists and medical clinics.

Putting this marketing program into effect requires that the firm commit time and money to it in the form of a budget. The budgeting process starts with a sales forecast based on estimates of units expected to be sold—probably by month, quarter, and year. Estimated expenses for the marketing mix activities comprising the marketing program are estimated and balanced against expected revenues to estimate the program's profitability. This budget is really the "sales" document presented to top management to gain approval for the budgeted resources to implement the marketing program.

FIGURE 2-10
Elements of the marketing mix
that comprise a cohesive
marketing program

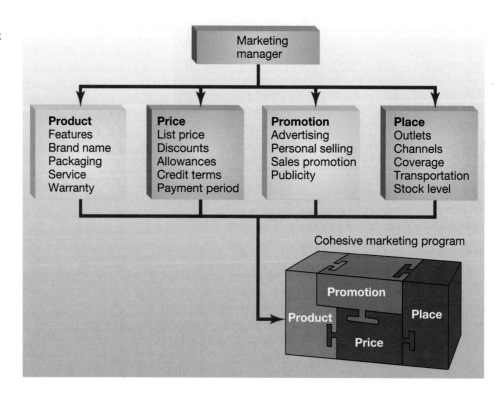

Concept Check	
	1. What is the difference between a strength and an opportunity in a SWOT analysis?
	2. What is market segmentation?
	3. What are "points of difference" and why are they important?

Strategic Marketing Process: The Implementation Phase

As shown in Figure 2–8, the result of the tens or hundreds of hours spent in the planning phase of the strategic marketing process is the firm's marketing plan. Implementation, the second phase of the strategic marketing process, involves carrying out the marketing plan that emerges from the planning phase. If the firm cannot put the marketing plan into effect—in the implementation phase—the planning phase was a waste of time. Figure 2–8 also shows the four components of the implementation phase: (1) obtaining resources, (2) designing the marketing organization, (3) developing schedules, and (4) actually executing the marketing program designed in the planning phase. Eastman Kodak provides a case example.

Fortune magazine has called Kodak "one of the most bureaucratic, wasteful, paternalistic, slow-moving, isolated, and beloved companies in America,"[25] and one that requires the kind of restructuring IBM has gone through to compete in today's global marketplace. The first agent of change for Kodak's restructuring was George Fisher, its chief executive officer (CEO) in the late 1990s. His early decisions are classic management and marketing lessons in implementing and controlling the activities of a corporate giant.

Obtaining Resources   When George Fisher arrived at Kodak in the mid-1990s, he observed, "There are textbook types of things that are wrong with this company. Decisions are too slow. People don't take risks."[26] So he pushed some revolutionary decisions that seemed obvious to him:

- Focus on Kodak's core business: imaging.
- Serve customer needs better, and stress quality.
- Shorten product-development cycles.
- Encourage a more dynamic, risk-taking, fast-decision culture.

Fisher needed money to implement these ideas, however, so he obtained $8 billion by selling off divisions not related to Kodak's core imaging business.

Designing the Marketing Organization

A marketing program needs a marketing organization to implement it. Figure 2–11 shows the organization chart of a typical manufacturing firm, giving some details of the marketing department's structure. Four managers of marketing activities are shown to report to the vice president of marketing. Several regional sales managers and an international sales manager may report to the manager of sales. This marketing organization is responsible for converting marketing plans to reality.

Developing Schedules

In early 2000 Daniel Karp became Kodak's CEO. Karp immediately launched a two-prong strategy: (1) move aggressively into digital camera and imaging technology while (2) improving Kodak's traditional cash cow film and film processing services. The focus—ugh!—on film comes about because 90 percent of Americans are still happy using film cameras and Kodak's paper, chemicals, and technical savvy are needed to complete the picture and make great prints.[27] Effective implementation requires deadlines. Karp set these deadlines for Kodak for 2001:

- Launch the mc3 digital camera line ($250–$350) targeted at 18- to 28-year-olds that combines still camera, video camera, and MP3 player.
- Introduce a family (DX 3500, DX 3600) of EasyShare digital cameras ($400–$600) and docking stations ($80) facilitating easy uploading of photo to a PC and the Internet.
- Emphasize its Kodak.com website (800,000 visits per month in 2001) that does everything from selling cameras to consumers to processing their film, arranging their photo albums, and letting them edit their images online.[28]

FIGURE 2–11
Organization of a typical manufacturing firm, showing a breakdown of the marketing department

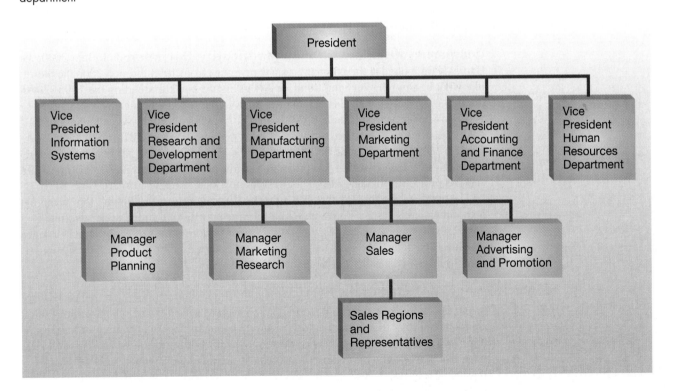

Executing the Marketing Program   Marketing plans are meaningless pieces of paper without effective execution of those plans. This effective execution requires attention to detail for both marketing strategies and marketing tactics. A **marketing strategy** is the means by which a marketing goal is to be achieved, usually characterized by a specified target market and a marketing program to reach it. Although the term *strategy* is often used loosely, it implies both the end sought (target market) and the means to achieve it (marketing program).

To implement a marketing program successfully, hundreds of detailed decisions are often required, such as writing ads or setting prices. These decisions, called **marketing tactics**, are detailed day-to-day operational decisions essential to the overall success of marketing strategies. Here are examples of both kinds of decisions at Kodak:

- *Marketing strategy decision:* Kodak looked at the surprising success cameras targeted at 18- to 28-year-olds (the "Generation Y" or "Gen Y" consumers discussed in Chapter 3) and teenagers: Nintendo's Game Boy digital camera that printed out tiny, grainy images on sticky paper and Polaroid's I-Zone Instant Pocket camera (Chapter 10). Kodak's strategy decision: Launch a new product targeted at Gen Y.
- *Marketing tactics decision:* Concurrently Kodak engineers were toying with the idea of hooking the computing power of digital cameras to digital MP3 music files. "We proposed the technology of the product," recalls engineer Clay Dunsmore, "but we didn't have a clear idea of who we would sell it to!" Kodak's tactics decision: Form a cross-functional team to work on the gadget—that became the mc3.[29]

Marketing strategies and marketing tactics shade into each other. Effective marketing program implementation requires excruciating concern for both.

Strategic Marketing Process: The Control Phase

The control phase of the strategic marketing process seeks to keep the marketing program moving in the direction set for it (see Figure 2–8). Accomplishing this requires the marketing manager (1) to compare the results of the marketing program with the goals in the written plans to identify deviations and (2) to act on these deviations—correcting negative deviations and exploiting positive ones.

Comparing Results with Plans to Identify Deviations   In late 2000, as Daniel Karp looked at the company's sales revenues from 1995 through 2000, he didn't like what he saw: the very flat trend, or AB in Figure 2–12. Extending the 1995–2000 trend to 2005 shows flat sales revenues, a totally unacceptable, no-growth strategy.

Kodak never achieved its late 1990s annual growth goal of 13 percent. Cutting this goal in half gives a more realistic target sales revenue line of BD from 2001 to 2005. This reveals a wedge-shaped shaded gap in the figure. Planners call this the *planning gap,* the difference between the projection of the path to reach a new goal (line BD) and the projection of the path of the results of a plan already in place (line BC).

The ultimate purpose of the firm's marketing program is to "fill in" this planning gap—in Kodak's case, to move its future sales revenue line from the no-growth line BC up to the challenging target of line BD. But poor performance can result in actual sales revenues being far less than the targeted levels. This is the essence of evaluation—comparing actual results with planned objectives.

Acting on Deviations   When evaluation shows that actual performance fails to meet expectations, managers need to take corrective actions. And when actual results are far better than the plan called for, creative managers find ways to exploit the situation. Two recent Kodak "midcourse corrections" for both positive and negative deviations from targets illustrate these management actions:

FIGURE 2-12
Evaluation and control of
Kodak's marketing program

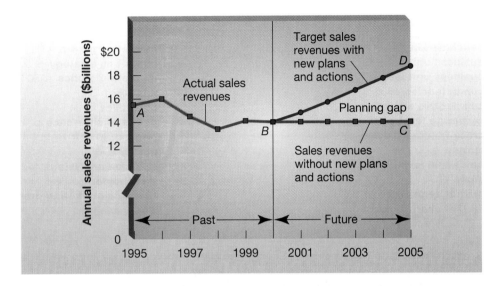

- *Exploiting a positive deviation.* Consumers like to take their film to Kodak mini-labs at retailers and get two sets of prints, but some also want to be able to edit their prints. So Kodak has strengthened its strategic partnerships with retailers like Wal-Mart, Kmart, and Kinko's/AOL to let the "second set of prints" be a CD-ROM that can be digitally edited.
- *Correcting a negative deviation.* Months of marketing research on digital camera users showed Kodak they wanted to get exact digital photos linked to PCs and the Internet with easy-to-use software, a problem with early designs. The fix: technical improvements leading to today's EasyShare camera-and-dock system.[30]

The strategic marketing process is discussed in greater detail again in Chapter 22.

Concept Check

1. What is the control phase of the strategic marketing process?

2. How do the objectives set for a marketing program in the planning phase relate to the control phase of the strategic marketing process?

SUMMARY

1 Today's large organizations, both business firms and nonprofit organizations, are often divided into three levels: the corporate, business unit, and functional levels.

2 Marketing has a role in all three levels by keeping a focus on customers and finding ways to add genuine customer value. At the lowest level, marketing serves as part of a team of functional specialists whose day-to-day actions actually involve customers and create customer value.

3 Organizations exist to accomplish something for someone. To give organizations focus, they continuously assess their business, mission, values and culture, and goals.

4 Setting strategic directions for an organization involves asking "Where are we now?" to assess the organization's customers, competencies, and competitors. It also involves asking "Where do we want to go?" that uses techniques like portfolio analysis and market-product analysis.

5 An organization's success rests on four building blocks: customer relationships, innovation, quality, and efficiency.

6 The strategic marketing process involves an organization allocating its marketing mix resources to reach its target markets using three phases: planning, implementation, and control.

7 The planning phase of the strategic marketing process has three steps, each with more specific elements: situation (SWOT) analysis, market-product focus and goal setting, and marketing program.

8 The implementation phase of the strategic marketing process has four key elements: obtaining resources, designing the marketing organization, developing schedules, and executing the marketing program.

9 The control phase of the strategic marketing process involves comparing results with the planned targets to identify deviations and taking actions to correct negative deviations and exploit positive ones.

KEY TERMS AND CONCEPTS

benchmarking p. 36
business unit p. 31
business unit level p. 31
competencies p. 36
competitive advantage p. 36
corporate level p. 31
cross-functional team p. 32
culture p. 33
functional level p. 31
goals p. 34
market segmentation p. 46
market share p. 35

marketing plan p. 43
marketing strategy p. 50
marketing tactics p. 50
mission p. 33
objectives p. 34
points of difference p. 47
profit p. 30
quality p. 36
situation analysis p. 44
stakeholders p. 33
strategic marketing process p. 43
SWOT analysis p. 44

APPLYING MARKETING CONCEPTS AND PERSPECTIVES

1 (*a*) Explain what a mission statement is. (*b*) Using Medtronic as an example from the chapter, explain how it gives a strategic direction to its organization. (*c*) Create a mission statement for your own career.

2 (*a*) How might top management try to change the "culture" of its organization? (*b*) What did George Fisher do at Kodak to try to change its culture?

3 What competencies best describe (*a*) your college or university, (*b*) your favorite restaurant, and (*c*) the company that manufactures the computer you own or use most often?

4 Look at Figure 2–3 that shows the four main groups of competitors Lands' End faces. For Wal-Mart, Sears, Old Navy, and Liz Claiborne, explain in which ways each is a competitor of Lands' End.

5 Why does a product often start as a question mark and then move counterclockwise around BCG's growth-share matrix shown in Figure 2–5?

6 Many American liberal arts colleges have traditionally offered an undergraduate degree in liberal arts (the product) to full-time 18- to 22-year-old students (the mar-

ket). How might such a college use the four market-product expansion strategies shown in Figure 2–6 to compete in the twenty-first century?

7 What is the main result of each of the three phases of the strategic marketing process? (*a*) planning, (*b*) implementation, and (*c*) control.

8 Select one strength, one weakness, one opportunity, and one threat from the SWOT analysis for Ben & Jerry's shown in Figure 2–9, and suggest a specific possible action that Unilever might take to exploit or address each one.

9 The goal-setting step in the planning phase of the strategic marketing process sets quantified objectives for use in the control phase. What actions are suggested for a marketing manager if measured results are below objectives? Above objectives?

10 Read Appendix A, "Creating an Effective Marketing Plan." Then write a 600-word executive summary for the marketing plan using the numbered headings shown in the plan.

INTERNET EXERCISE

In April 2000, Unilever N.V., a multinational consumer products firm bought Ben & Jerry's, adding to its portfolio of other famous North American ice cream brands, such as Breyers All Natural, Good-Humor, Klondike, and Popsicle. As a condition of the buyout, Unilever will continue to donate 7.5 percent of all pretax profits to the Ben & Jerry's Foundation and other organizations that engage in socially responsive activities. Go to Ben & Jerry's website (www.benjerry.com/mission.html) and

Unilever's website (www.unilever.com/co/op.html) to compare the mission statements of each firm. How are they similar? How are they different? Which mission statement do you believe will lead to "sustainable, profitable growth for the brand or businesses and the long-term creation of value for shareholders and employees" (from the "Introducing Unilever" promotional brochure)?

VIDEO CASE 2–1   Specialized Bicycle Components, Inc.: Ride the Red "S"

The speaker leans forward with both intensity and pride in his voice. "We're in the business of creating a bike that delivers the customer their best possible ride," he explains. "When the customer sees our red 'S,' they say this is the company that understands the cyclist. It's a company of riders. The products they make are the rider's products." The speaker is Chris Murphy, Director of Marketing for Specialized Bicycle Components, Inc.— or just "Specialized" to serious riders.

THE COMPANY

Specialized was founded in 1974 by Mike Sinyard, a cycling enthusiast who sold his VW van for the $1,500 start-up capital. Mike started out importing hard-to-find "specialized" bike components, but the company began to produce its own bike parts by 1976. Specialized introduced the first major production mountain bike in the world in 1980, revolutionizing the bike industry, and since then has maintained a reputation as the technological leader in the bike and bike accessory market. In fact, since the company's founding, its formal mission statement has remained unchanged: "To give everyone the best ride of their life!"

The company continues to innovate. It also sells road bikes and an extensive line of bike accessories, including helmets, water bottles, jerseys, and shoes. As Chris says, "The customer is buying the ride from us, not just the bike."

The first professional mountain bike racing team was created by Specialized in 1983. Team members often serve as design consultants. The company banks on the perception, and reality, that this race-proven technology trickles down to the entire line of Specialized bikes and products.

THE ENVIRONMENT

The bike market is driven by innovation and technology, and with the market becoming more crowded and competitive. Specialized divides the bike market into two categories: (1) the independent retailer, and (2) the end-user consumer. While its focus in designing the product is on the end-user consumer, it only sells directly to the retailer, and realizes a strong relationship with the dealers is a key factor for success. Steve Meineke, president of Specialized USA (the domestic unit of Specialized), refers to the on-floor salesperson as "our most important partner."

The end-user consumer is broken down into two target age groups: the 18- to 25-year-old college students and the 30- to 40-year-old professional "techies." To differentiate itself from the rest of the market, Specialized

positions itself as the innovator in mountain bikes—its models are what the rest of the industry imitates.

Mountain bikes account for approximately two-thirds of total industry bike sales, with road bikes accounting for the other third. The sport of mountain biking experienced a huge surge from 1989 to 1993, but in the mid-1990s sales began to flatten. Does Chris believe this trend will hurt Specialized? "We believe we will see growth in the next six or seven years as the entry level participants trade up-trade their lower end bikes for higher end bikes," he explains.

Specialized now has an extensive global distribution network with subsidiaries in 25 countries in Asia, North America, South America, Europe, and Australia.

THE ISSUES

How can Specialized stay at the forefront of an industry that now includes more than 20 manufacturers? Strategic placement in the marketplace is one way. Specialized recently designed its own server, the World Ride Web, on the Internet (www.specialized.com/bikes). The website offers international mountain bike trail and road bike trail directories, e-mail access to Specialized engineers, a trail preservation network, and a dealer directory that connects users directly to dealer home pages. Specialized believes guest appearances on TV talk shows and displays in retail shops help to keep the Specialized name in front of the end-user consumer.

Targeting its other market segment, the dealers, Specialized launched a "Best Ride Tour." It loaded up trailers full of the new models and visited 30 cities nationwide, enabling retailers and shop employees to test ride the bikes they will be ordering for the coming year— "Ride Before You Buy."

Specialized is also eager to become involved in joint ventures to keep its technological edge, including one with Du Pont that led to a more aerodynamic wheel. Specialized also entered into a distribution relationship with GripShift in 1994, allowing the high-end gear manufacturer access to its extensive dealer network.

Specialized sponsors races, provides racer support teams, initiates mountain biking safety programs, and is involved in trail-access advocacy groups all over the world. But, as it was in Specialized's early years, Mike sees a commitment to top quality and design as the most important factor for future success: "Even though we've been around for 20 years, this company still feels like it has something to prove. I expect it will always be that way."

Questions

1 Do a SWOT analysis for Specialized. Use Figure 2–9 in Chapter 2 and Figure 1 in Appendix A as guides. In assessing internal factors (strengths and weaknesses), use the material provided in the case. In assessing external factors (opportunities and threats) augment the case material with what you see happening in the bicycle industry.

2 As part of step 2 of the planning phase, and using your SWOT analysis, select target markets on which you might focus for present and potential bikers.

3 As part of step 3 of the planning phase and using your answers in questions 1 and 2 above, outline Specialized's marketing programs for the target market segments you chose.

CREATING AN EFFECTIVE MARKETING PLAN

"New ideas are a dime a dozen," observes Arthur R. Kydd, "and so are new products and new technologies." Kydd should know. As chief executive officer of St. Croix Venture Partners, he and his firm have provided the seed money and venture capital to launch more than 60 startup firms in the last 25 years. Today those firms have more than 5,000 employees. Kydd explains:

> I get 200 to 300 marketing and business plans a year to look at, and St. Croix provides startup financing for only two or three. What sets a potentially successful idea, product, or technology apart from all the rest is markets and marketing. If you have a real product with a distinctive point of difference that satisfies the needs of customers, you may have a winner. And you get a real feel for this in a well-written marketing or business plan.[1]

This appendix (1) describes what marketing and business plans are—including their purposes and guidelines in writing effective plans—and (2) provides a sample marketing plan.

MARKETING PLANS AND BUSINESS PLANS

After explaining the meanings, purposes, and audiences of marketing plans and business plans, this section describes some writing guidelines for them and what external funders often look for in successful plans.

Meanings, Purposes, and Audiences

A *marketing plan* is a road map for the marketing activities of an organization for a specified future period of time, such as one year or five years.[2] It is important to note that no single "generic" marketing plan applies to all organizations and all situations. Rather, the specific format for a marketing plan for an organization depends on the following:

- *The target audience and purpose.* Elements included in a particular marketing plan depend heavily on (1) who the audience is and (2) what its purpose is. A marketing plan for an internal audience seeks to point the direction for future marketing activities and is sent to all individuals in the organization who must implement the plan or who will be affected by it. If the plan is directed to an external audience, such as friends, banks, venture capitalists, or potential investors, for the purpose of raising capital, it has the additional function of being an important sales document. In this case it contains elements such as the strategic plan/focus, organization, structure, and biographies of key personnel that would rarely appear in an internal marketing plan. Also, the financial information is far more detailed when the plan is used to raise outside capital. The elements of a marketing plan for each of these two audiences are compared in Figure A–1.

- *The kind and complexity of the organization.* A small neighborhood restaurant has a somewhat different marketing plan than Nestlé, which serves international markets. The restaurant's plan would be relatively simple and directed at serving customers in a local market. In Nestlé's case, because there is a hierarchy of marketing plans, various levels of detail would be used—such as the entire organization, the business unit, or the product/product line.

- *The industry.* Both the restaurant serving a local market and Medtronic, selling heart pacemakers globally, analyze competition. Not only are their geographic thrusts far different, but the complexities of their offerings and, hence, the time periods likely to be covered by their plans also differ. A one-year marketing plan may be adequate for the restaurant, but Medtronic may need a five-year planning horizon because product-development cycles for complex, new medical devices may be three or four years.

In contrast to a marketing plan, a *business plan* is a road map for the entire organization for a specified future period of time, such as one year or five years.[3] A key difference between a marketing plan and a business plan is that the business plan contains details on the research and development (R&D)/operations/manufacturing activities of the organization. Even for a manufacturing business, the marketing plan is probably 60 or 70 percent of the entire business plan. For businesses like a small restaurant or auto repair shop, their marketing and business plans are virtually identical. The elements of a business plan typically targeted at internal and external audiences appear in the two right-hand columns in Figure A-1.

The Most-Asked Questions by Outside Audiences

Lenders and prospective investors reading a business or marketing plan that is used to seek new capital are probably the toughest audiences to satisfy. Their most-asked questions include the following:

1. Is the business or marketing idea valid?
2. Is there something unique or distinctive about the product or service that separates it from substitutes and competitors?
3. Is there a clear market for the product or service?
4. Are the financial projections realistic and healthy?
5. Are the key management and technical personnel capable, and do they have a track record in the industry in which they must compete?
6. Does the plan clearly describe how those providing capital will get their money back and make a profit?

Rhonda M. Abrahms, author of *The Successful Business Plan*, observes that "within the first five minutes of reading your . . . plan, readers must perceive that the answers to these questions are favorable."[4] While her comments apply to plans seeking to raise capital, the first five questions just listed apply equally well to plans for internal audiences.

Writing and Style Suggestions

There are no magic one-size-fits-all guidelines for writing successful marketing and business plans. Still, the following writing and style guidelines generally apply:[5]

- Use a direct, professional writing style. Use appropriate business terms without jargon. Present and future tenses with active voice are generally better than past tense and passive voice.
- Be positive and specific to convey potential success. At the same time, avoid superlatives ("terrific," "wonderful"). Specifics are better than glittering generalities. Use numbers for impact, justifying projections with reasonable quantitative assumptions, where possible.
- Use bullet points for succinctness and emphasis. As with the list you are reading, bullets enable key points to be highlighted effectively.
- Use "A-level" (the first level) and "B-level" (the second level) headings under the numbered section headings to help readers make easy transitions from one topic to another. This also forces the writer to organize the plan more carefully. Use these headings liberally, at least one every 200 to 300 words.
- Use visuals where appropriate. Photos, illustrations, graphs, and charts enable massive amounts of information to be presented succinctly.
- Shoot for a plan 15 to 35 pages in length, not including financial projections and appendixes. An uncomplicated small business may require only 15 pages, while a high-technology startup may require more than 35 pages.
- Use care in layout, design, and presentation. Laser or ink-jet printers give a more professional look than dot matrix printers do. Use 11 or 12 point type (you are now reading 10.5 point type) in the text. Use a serif type (with "feet," like that you are reading now) in the text because it is easier to read, and sans serif (without "feet") in graphs and charts like Figure A-1. A bound report with a nice cover and clear title page adds professionalism.

These guidelines are used, where possible, in the sample marketing plan that follows.

SAMPLE FIVE-YEAR MARKETING PLAN FOR PARADISE KITCHENS,® INC.

To help interpret the marketing plan for Paradise Kitchens,® Inc. that follows, we will describe the company and suggest some guidelines in interpreting the plan.

Background on Paradise Kitchens, Inc.

With a degree in chemical engineering, Randall F. Peters spent 15 years working for General Foods and Pillsbury with a number of diverse responsibilities: plant operations, R&D, restaurant operations, and new business development. His wife Leah, with degrees in both molecular cellular biology and food science, held various Pillsbury executive positions in new category development and packaged goods, and restaurant R&D. In the company's startup years, Paradise Kitchens survived on the savings of Randy and Leah—the cofounders. With their backgrounds, they decided Randy should serve as president and CEO of Paradise Kitchens, and Leah should focus on R&D and corporate strategy. The first products entered distribution in 1990.

Interpreting the Marketing Plan

The marketing plan that follows for Paradise Kitchens, Inc. is based on an actual plan developed by the company.[6] To protect proprietary information about the company, some details have been altered, but the basic logic of the plan has been kept.

Notes in the margins next to the Paradise Kitchens plan fall into two categories:

1. *Substantive notes* are in blue boxes. These notes elaborate on the significance of an element in the marketing plan and are keyed to chapter references in this textbook.
2. *Writing style, format, and layout notes* are in red boxes and explain the editorial or visual rationale for the element.

A closing word of encouragement! Writing an effective marketing plan is hard—but challenging and satisfying—work. Dozens of the authors' students have used effective marketing plans they wrote for class in their interviewing portfolio to show prospective employers what they could do and to help them get their first job.

FIGURE A–1
Elements in typical marketing and business plans targeted at different audiences

Element of the plan	Marketing plan		Business plan	
	For internal audience (to direct the firm)	For external audience (to raise capital)	For internal audience (to direct the firm)	For external audience (to raise capital)
1. Executive summary	✔	✔	✔	✔
2. Description of company		✔		✔
3. Strategic plan/focus		✔		✔
4. Situation analysis	✔	✔	✔	✔
5. Market-product focus	✔	✔	✔	✔
6. Marketing program strategy and tactics	✔	✔	✔	✔
7. R&D and operations program			✔	✔
8. Financial projections	✔	✔	✔	✔
9. Organization structure		✔		✔
10. Implementation plan	✔	✔	✔	✔
11. Evaluation and control	✔		✔	
Appendix A: Biographies of key personnel		✔		✔
Appendix B, etc.: Details on other topics	✔	✔	✔	✔

The Table of Contents
provides quick access to
the topics in the plan,
usually organized by
section and subsection
headings.

Seen by many experts as
the single most important
element in the plan, the
two-page Executive Sum-
mary "sells" the plan to
readers through its clarity
and brevity. For space reasons, it is not shown here,
but question 10 at the end
of Chapter 2 asks the
reader to write an Execu-
tive Summary for this plan.

The Company Description
highlights the recent history and recent successes
of the organization.

The Strategic Focus and
Plan sets the strategic
direction for the entire
organization, a direction
with which proposed ac-
tions of the marketing plan
must be consistent. This
section is not included in
all marketing plans. See
Chapter 2.

The qualitative Mission/
Vision statement focuses
the activities of Paradise
Kitchens for the stake-
holder groups to be
served. See Chapter 2.

FIVE-YEAR MARKETING PLAN
Paradise Kitchens,® Inc.

Table of Contents

1. Executive Summary

2. Company Description

Paradise Kitchens®, Inc. was started in 1989 by cofounders Randall F. Peters and
Leah E. Peters to develop and market Howlin' Coyote® Chili, a unique line of single
serve and microwaveable Southwestern/Mexican style frozen chili products. The
Howlin' Coyote line of chili was introduced into the Minneapolis–St. Paul market in
1990. The line was subsequently expanded to Denver in 1992 and Phoenix in 1994.

To the Company's knowledge, Howlin' Coyote is the only premium-quality, authentic Southwestern/Mexican style, frozen chili sold in U.S. grocery stores. Its high
quality has gained fast, widespread acceptance in these markets. In fact, same-store
sales doubled in the last year for which data are available. The Company believes
the Howlin' Coyote brand can be extended to other categories of Southwestern/
Mexican food products.

Paradise Kitchens believes its high-quality, high-price strategy has proven
successful. This marketing plan outlines how the Company will extend its
geographic coverage from 3 markets to 20 markets by the year 2003.

3. Strategic Focus and Plan

This section covers three aspects of corporate strategy that influence the marketing plan: (1) the mission/vision, (2) goals, and (3) core competence/sustainable
competitive advantage of Paradise Kitchens.

Mission/Vision

The mission and vision of Paradise Kitchens is to market lines of high-quality
Southwestern/Mexican food products at premium prices that satisfy consumers in
this fast-growing food segment while providing challenging career opportunities for
employees and above-average returns to stockholders.

The Goals section sets both the financial and non-financial targets—where possible in quantitative terms—against which the company's performance will be measured. See Chapter 2.

Lists use parallel construction to improve readability—in this case a series of infinitives starting with "To . . ."

Goals

For the coming five years Paradise Kitchens seeks to achieve the following goals:

• Nonfinancial goals

1. To retain its present image as the highest-quality line of Southwestern/Mexican products in the food categories in which it competes.
2. To enter 17 new metropolitan markets.
3. To achieve national distribution in two convenience store or supermarket chains by 2001 and five by 2003.
4. To add a new product line every third year.
5. To be among the top three chili lines—regardless of packaging (frozen, canned) in one-third of the metro markets in which it competes by 2001 and two-thirds by 2003.

• Financial goals

1. To obtain a real (inflation-adjusted) growth in earnings per share of 8 percent per year over time.
2. To obtain a return on equity of at least 20 percent.
3. To have a public stock offering by the year 2001.

In keeping with the goal of achieving national distribution through chains, Paradise Kitchens recently obtained distribution through a convenience store chain where it uses this point-of-purchase ad that adheres statically to the freezer case.

Core Competency and Sustainable Competitive Advantage

In terms of core competency, Paradise Kitchens seeks to achieve a unique ability (1) to provide distinctive, high-quality chilies and related products using Southwestern/Mexican recipes that appeal to and excite contemporary tastes for these products and (2) to deliver these products to the customer's table using effective manufacturing and distribution systems that maintain the Company's quality standards.

To translate these core competencies into a sustainable competitive advantage, the Company will work closely with key suppliers and distributors to build the relationships and alliances necessary to satisfy the high taste standards of our customers.

To improve readability, each numbered section usually starts on a new page. (This is not done in this plan to save space.)

The Situation Analysis is a snapshot to answer the question, "Where are we now?" See Chapter 2.

The SWOT Analysis identifies strengths, weaknesses, opportunities, and threats to provide a solid foundation as a springboard to identify subsequent actions in the marketing plan. See Chapter 2.

Each long table, graph, or photo is given a figure number and title. It then appears as soon as possible after the first reference in the text, accommodating necessary page breaks. This also avoids breaking long tables like this one in the middle. Short tables or graphs that are less than 1 ½ inches are often inserted in the text without figure numbers because they don't cause serious problems with page breaks.

Effective tables seek to summarize a large amount of information in a short amount of space.

4. Situation Analysis

This situation analysis starts with a snapshot of the current environment in which Paradise Kitchens finds itself by providing a brief SWOT (strengths, weaknesses, opportunities, threats) analysis. After this overview, the analysis probes ever-finer levels of detail: industry, competitors, company, and consumers.

SWOT Analysis

Figure 1 shows the internal and external factors affecting the market opportunities for Paradise Kitchens. Stated briefly, this SWOT analysis highlights the great strides taken by the company since its products first appeared on grocers' shelves. In the

Figure 1.   SWOT Analysis for Paradise Kitchens

Internal Factors	Strengths	Weaknesses
Management	Experienced and entrepreneurial management and board	Small size can restrict options
Offerings	Unique, high-quality, high-price products	Many lower-quality, lower price competitors
Marketing	Distribution in 3 markets with excellent acceptance	No national awareness or distribution
Personnel	Good work force, though small; little turnover	Big gap if key employee leaves
Finance	Excellent growth in sales revenues	Limited resources may restrict growth opportunities when compared to giant competitors
Manufacturing	Sole supplier ensures high quality	Lack economies of scale of huge competitors
R&D	Continuing efforts to ensure quality in delivered products	

External Factors	Opportunities	Threats
Consumer/Social	Upscale market, likely to be stable; Southwestern/Mexican food category is fast-growing segment	Premium price may limit access to mass markets.
Competitive	Distinctive name and packaging in its markets.	Not patentable; competitors can attempt to duplicate product
Technological	Technical breakthroughs enable smaller food producers to achieve many economies available to large competitors	
Economic	Consumer income is high; convenience important to U.S. households	More households "eating out," and bringing prepared take-out into home
Legal/Regulatory	High U.S. Food & Drug Admin. standards eliminate fly-by-night competitors	Mergers among large competitors being approved by government

The text discussion of Figure 1 (the SWOT Analysis table) elaborates on its more important elements. This "walks" the reader through the information from the vantage of the plan's writer. In terse plans this accompanying discussion is sometimes omitted, but is generally desirable to give the reader an understanding of what the company sees as the critical SWOT elements.

The Industry Analysis section provides the backdrop for the subsequent, more detailed analysis of competition, the company, and the company's customers. Without an in-depth understanding of the industry, the remaining analysis may be misdirected. See Chapter 2.

Even though relatively brief, this in-depth treatment of the Spicy Southwestern/Mexican food industry in the United States demonstrates to the plan's readers the company's understanding of the industry in which it competes. It gives both external and internal readers confidence that the company thoroughly understands its own industry.

Company's favor internally are its strengths of an experienced management team and board of directors, excellent acceptance of its lines in the three metropolitan markets in which it competes, and a strong manufacturing and distribution system to serve these limited markets. Favorable external factors (opportunities) include the increasing appeal of Southwestern/Mexican foods, the strength of the upscale market for the Company's products, and food-processing technological breakthroughs that make is easier for smaller food producers to compete.

Among unfavorable factors, the main weakness is the limited size of Paradise Kitchens relative to its competitors in terms of the depth of the management team, available financial resources, and national awareness and distribution of product lines. Threats include the danger that the Company's premium prices may limit access to mass markets and competition from the "eating-out" and "take-out" markets.

<u>Industry Analysis: Trends in Spicy and Mexican Foods</u>

Total spice consumption increased 50 percent from 1985 to 1995, and consumption of spices jumped from an annual average of 2 pounds per American in 1988 to 2.7 pounds in 1994. Currently, Mexican food and ingredients are used in 64 percent of American households. Burritos, enchiladas, and taco dinner kits, which had insignificant numbers in 1981, reached between 4 percent and 11 percent of American households in 1996. Age Wave, Inc.'s *1998 Boomer Report* also stated that Baby Boomers consumed 84 percent more Mexican food in 1995 than they did in 1986.

According to *Grocery Marketing,* as the general population becomes more accustomed to different ethnic cuisines and styles of eating, spicy foods and unusual flavors are turning up on the dinner tables of middle America and the aisles of supermarkets, as well. As Baby Boomers grow older, their taste buds will become less sensitive, and they will want stronger-tasting foods. In addition to age, growth in population, incomes, and tastes in the American diet should continue to fuel the trend for spicy foods in the United States. Retail sales of fiery food could top $1.8 billion in the year 2000, according to *Packaged Facts,* up from $1 billion in 1994.

These trends reflect a generally more favorable attitude toward spicy foods on the part of Americans. The Southwestern/Mexican market includes the foods shown in Figure 2.

This summary of sales in the Southwestern/Mexican product category shows it is significant and provides a variety of future opportunities for Paradise Kitchens.

As with the Industry Analysis, the Competitors Analysis demonstrates that the company has a realistic understanding of who its major competitors are and what their marketing strategies are. Again, a realistic assessment gives confidence to both internal and external readers that subsequent marketing actions in the plan rest on a solid foundation. See Chapters 2, 3, 8, 9, and 21.

This page uses a "block" style and does *not* indent each paragraph, although an extra space separates each paragraph. Compare this page with page 63, which has indented paragraphs. Most readers find indented paragraphs in marketing plans and long reports are easier to follow.

Figure 2. Some Foods Included in the Southwestern/Mexican Product Category, 1996

Item	Percent of Sales	Sales in Millions
Salsa	39%	$624
Cheese/bean dips	13	208
Refried beans	9	144
Seasoning mix	8	128
Chilies	7	112
Taco shells	7	112
Dinner kits	5	80
Taco sauce	3	48
Enchilada sauce	2	32
Other	7	112
Total	100%	$1,600

Competitors in Southwestern/Mexican Market

The chili market represents $495 million in annual sales. The products fall primarily into two groups: canned chili (62 percent of sales) and dry chili (16 percent of sales). The remaining 22 percent of sales go to frozen chili products. Besides Howlin' Coyote, Stouffers and Marie Callender's offer frozen chilies as part of their broad line of frozen dinners and entrees. Major canned chili brands include Hormel, Wolf, Dennison, Stagg, Chili Man, Chili Magic, and Castleberry's. Their retail prices range from $0.99 to $1.79.

Bluntly put, the major disadvantage of the segment's dominant product, canned chili, is that it does not taste very good. A taste test described in the October 1990 issue of *Consumer Reports* magazine ranked 26 canned chili products "poor" to "fair" in overall sensory quality. The study concluded, "Chili doesn't have to be hot to be good. But really good chili, hot or mild, doesn't come out of a can."

Dry mix brands include such familiar spice brands as Lawry's, McCormick, French's, and Durkee, along with smaller offerings such as Wick Fowler's and Carroll Shelby's. Their retail prices range from $0.99 to $1.99. The *Consumer Reports* study was more favorable about dry chili mixes, ranking them from "fair" to "very good." The magazine recommended, "If you want good chili, make it with fresh ingredients and one of the seasoning mixes we tested." A major drawback of dry mixes is that they require the preparers to add their own meat, beans, and tomatoes and take more preparation time than canned or frozen chilies.

The *Consumer Reports* study did not include the frozen chili entrees from Stouffer's or Marie Callender's (Howlin' Coyote was not yet on the market at the time of the test). However, it is fair to say that these products—consisting of ground beef, chili beans, and tomato sauce—are of average quality. Furthermore, they are not singled out for special marketing or promotional programs by their manufacturers. Marie Callender's (including cornbread) retails for $3.09, and Stouffer's retails for $2.99.

The Company Analysis provides details of the company's strengths and marketing strategies that will enable it to achieve the mission, vision, and goals identified earlier. See Chapters 2, 8, and 22.

The higher-level "A heading" of Customer Analysis has a more dominant typeface and position than the lower-level "B heading" of Customer Characteristics. These headings introduce the reader to the sequence and level of topics covered. The organization of this textbook uses this kind of structure and headings.

Satisfying customers and providing genuine value to them is why organizations exist in a market economy. This section addresses the question of "Who are the customers for Paradise Kitchens's products?" See Chapters 5, 6, 7, 8, and 9.

Company Analysis

The husband-and-wife team that cofounded Paradise Kitchens, Inc. in 1989 has 44 years of experience between them in the food-processing business. Both have played key roles in the management of the Pillsbury Company. They are being advised by a highly seasoned group of business professionals, who have extensive understanding of the requirements for new product development.

Currently, Howlin' Coyote products compete in the chili and Mexican frozen entree segments of the Southwestern/Mexican food market. While the chili obviously competes as a stand-alone product, its exceptional quality means it can complement such dishes as burritos, nachos, and enchiladas and can be readily used as a smothering sauce for pasta, rice, or potatoes. This flexibility of use is relatively rare in the prepared food marketplace. With Howlin' Coyote Paradise Kitchens is broadening the position of frozen chili in a way that can lead to impressive market share for the new product category.

The Company now uses a single outside producer with which it works closely to maintain the consistently high quality required in its products. The greater volume has increased production efficiencies, resulting in a steady decrease in the cost of goods sold.

Customer Analysis

In terms of customer analysis, this section describes (1) the characteristics of customers expected to buy Howlin' Coyote products and (2) health and nutrition concerns of Americans today.

Customer Characteristics. Demographically, chili products in general are purchased by consumers representing a broad range of socioeconomic backgrounds. Howlin' Coyote chili is purchased chiefly by consumers who have achieved higher levels of education and whose income is $30,000 and higher. These consumers represent 57 percent of canned and dry mix chili users.

The five Howlin' Coyote entrees offer a quick, tasty meal with high-quality ingredients.

The household buying Howlin' Coyote has one to three people in it. Among married couples, Howlin' Coyote is predominantly bought by households in which both spouses work. While women are a majority of the buyers, single men represent a significant segment. Anecdotally, Howlin' Coyote has heard from fathers of teenaged boys who say they keep a freezer stocked with the chili because the boys devour it.

Because the chili offers a quick way to make a tasty meal, the product's biggest users tend to be those most pressed for time. Howlin' Coyote's premium pricing also means that its purchasers are skewed toward the higher end of the income range. Buyers range in age from 25 to 55. Because consumers in the western United States have adopted spicy foods more readily than the rest of the country, Howlin' Coyote's initial marketing expansion efforts will be concentrated in that region.

Health and Nutrition Concerns. Coverage of food issues in the U.S. media is often erratic and occasionally alarmist. Because Americans are concerned about their diets, studies from organizations of widely varying credibility frequently receive significant attention from the major news organizations. For instance, a study of fat levels of movie popcorn was reported in all the major media. Similarly, studies on the healthfulness of Mexican food have received prominent "play" in print and broadcast reports. The high caloric levels of much Mexican and Southwestern-style food has been widely reported and often exaggerated.

Less certain is the link between these reports and consumer buying behavior. Most indications are that while Americans are well-versed in dietary matters, they are not significantly changing their eating patterns. The experience of other food manufacturers is that Americans expect certain foods to be high in calories and are not drawn to those that claim to be low-calorie versions. Low-fat frozen pizza was a flop. Therefore, while Howlin' Coyote is already lower in calories, fat, and sodium than its competitors, those qualities are not being stressed in its promotions. Instead, in the space and time available for promotions, Howlin' Coyote's taste, convenience, and flexibility are stressed.

5. Market-Product Focus

This section describes the five-year marketing and product objectives for Paradise Kitchens and the target markets, points of difference, and positioning of its lines of Howlin' Coyote chilies.

Marketing and Product Objectives

Howlin' Coyote's marketing intent is to take full advantage of its brand potential

---

This section demonstrates the company's insights into a major trend that has a potentially large impact.

Size of headings should give a professional look to the report and not overwhelm the reader. These two headings are too large.

As noted in Chapter 10, the chances of success for a new product are significantly increased if objectives are set for the product itself and if target market segments are identified for it. This section makes these explicit for Paradise Kitchens. The objectives also serve as the planned targets against which marketing activities are measured in program implementation and control.

A heading should be spaced closer to the text that follows (and that it describes) than the preceding section to avoid confusion for the reader. This rule is not followed for the Target Markets heading, which now unfortunately appears to "float" between the preceding and following paragraphs.

This section identifies the specific niches or target markets toward which the company's products are directed. When appropriate and when space permits, this section often includes a market-product grid. See Chapter 9.

---

while building a base from which other revenues sources can be mined—both in and out of the retail grocery business. These are detailed in four areas below:

- **Current markets.** Current markets will be grown by expanding brand and flavor distribution at the retail level. In addition, same-store sales will be grown by increasing consumer awareness and repeat purchases. With this increase in same-store sales, the more desirable broker/warehouse distribution channel will become available, increasing efficiency and saving costs.

- **New markets.** By the end of Year 5, the chili and salsa business will be expanded to a total of 20 metropolitan areas. This will represent 72 percent of U.S. food store sales.

- **Food service.** Food service sales will include chili products and smothering sauces. Sales are expected to reach $693,000 by the end of Year 3 and $1.5 million by the end of Year 5.

- **New products.** Howlin' Coyote's brand presence will be expanded at the retail level through the addition of new products in the frozen-foods section. This will be accomplished through new product concept screening in Year 1 to identify new potential products. These products will be brought to market in Years 2 and 3. Additionally, the brand may be licensed in select categories.

Target Markets

The primary target market for Howlin' Coyote products is households with one to three people, where often both adults work, with individual income typically above $30,000 per year. These households contain more experienced, adventurous consumers of Southwestern/Mexican food and want premium quality products.

To help buyers see the many different uses for Howlin' Coyote chili, recipes are even printed on the *inside* of the packages.

An organization cannot grow by offering only "me-too products." The greatest single factor in a new product's failure is the lack of significant "points of difference" that sets it apart from competitors' substitutes. This section makes these points of difference explicit. See Chapter 10.

A positioning strategy helps communicate the company's unique points of difference of its products to prospective customers in a simple, clear way. This section describes this positioning. See Chapters 9 and 10.

Everything that has gone before in the marketing plan sets the stage for the marketing mix actions— the 4 Ps—covered in the marketing program. See Chapters 10 through 20.

The section describes in detail three key elements of the company's product strategy: the product line, its quality and how this is achieved, and its "cutting edge" packaging. See Chapters 10, 11, and 12.

Points of Difference

The "points of difference"—characteristics that make Howlin' Coyote chilies unique relative to competitors—fall into three important areas:

- Unique taste and convenience. No known competitor offers a high-quality, "authentic" frozen chili in a range of flavors. And no existing chili has the same combination of quick preparation and home-style taste.

- Taste trends. The American palate is increasingly intrigued by hot spices, and Howlin' Coyote brands offer more "kick" than most other prepared chilies.

- Premium packaging. Howlin' Coyote's high-value packaging graphics convey the unique, high-quality product contained inside and the product's nontraditional positioning.

Positioning

In the past chili products have been either convenient or tasty, but not both. Howlin' Coyote pairs these two desirable characteristics to obtain a positioning in consumers' minds as very high-quality "authentic Southwestern/Mexican tasting" chilies that can be prepared easily and quickly.

6. Marketing Program

The four marketing mix elements of the Howlin' Coyote chili marketing program are detailed below. Note that "chile" is the vegetable and "chili" is the dish.

Product Strategy

After first summarizing the product line, the approach to product quality and packaging are covered.

Product Line. Howlin' Coyote chili, retailing for $2.99 for a 10- or 11.5-ounce serving, is available in five flavors. The five are:

- Green Chile Chili: braised extra-lean pork with fire-roasted green chilies, onions, tomato chunks, bold spices, and jalapeno peppers, based on a Southwestern favorite.

- Red Chile Chili: extra-lean cubed pork, deep-red chilies, and sweet onions; known as the "Texas Bowl of Red."

- Beef and Black Bean Chili: lean braised beef with black beans, tomato chunks, and Howlin' Coyote's own blend of red chilies and authentic spicing.

> Using parallel structure, this bulleted list presents the product line efficiently and crisply.

- Chicken Chunk Chili: hearty chunks of tender chicken, fire-roasted green chilies, black beans, pinto beans, diced onions, and zesty spices.

- Mean Bean Chili: vegetarian, with nine distinctive bean varieties and fire-roasted green chilies, tomato chunks, onion, and a robust blend of spices and rich red chilies.

Unique Product Quality. The flavoring systems of the Howlin' Coyote chilies are proprietary. The products' tastiness is due to extra care lavished upon the ingredients during production. The ingredients used are of unusually high quality. Meats are low-fat cuts and are fresh, not frozen, to preserve cell structure and moistness. Chilies are fire-roasted for fresher taste, not the canned variety used by more mainstream products. Tomatoes and vegetables are select quality. No preservatives or artificial flavors are used.

Packaging. Reflecting the "cutting edge" marketing strategy of its producers, Howlin' Coyote bucks conventional wisdom in packaging. It avoids placing predictable photographs of the product on its containers. (Head to any grocer's freezer and you will be hardpressed to find a product that does not feature a heavily stylized photograph of the contents.) Instead, Howlin' Coyote's package shows a Southwestern motif that communicates the product's out-of-the-ordinary positioning. This approach signals the product's nontraditional qualities: "adventurous" eating with minimal fuss—a frozen meal for people who do not normally enjoy frozen meals.

> A brief caption on photos and sample ads ties them to the text and highlights the reason for being included.

The Southwestern motif makes Howlin' Coyote's packages stand out in a supermarket's freezer case.

> This Price Strategy section makes the company's price point very clear, along with its price position relative to potential substitutes. When appropriate and when space permits, this section might contain a break-even analysis. See Chapters 13 and 14.

Price Strategy

Howlin' Coyote Chili is, at $2.99 for a 10- to 11.5-ounce package, priced comparably to the other frozen offerings and higher than the canned and dried chili varieties. However, the significant taste advantages it has over canned chilies and the convenience advantages over dried chilies justify this pricing strategy.

This "introductory overview" sentence tells the reader the topics covered in the section—in this case in-store demonstrations, recipes, and cents-off coupons. While this sentence may be omitted in short memos or plans, it helps readers see where the text is leading. These sentences are used throughout this plan. This textbook also generally utilizes these introductory overview sentences to aid your comprehension.

Elements of the Promotion Strategy are highlighted in terms of the three key promotional activities the company is emphasizing: in-store demonstrations, recipes, and cents-off coupons. For space reasons the company's on-line strategies are not shown in the plan. See Chapters 18, 19, 20 and 21.

Photos or sample ads can illustrate key points effectively, even if they are not in color as they appear here.

Promotion Strategy

Key promotion programs feature in-store demonstrations, recipes, and cents-off coupons.

In-Store Demonstrations. In-store demonstrations will be conducted to give consumers a chance to try Howlin' Coyote products and learn about their unique qualities. Demos will be conducted regularly in all markets to increase awareness and trial purchases.

Recipes. Because the products' flexibility of use is a key selling point, recipes will be offered to consumers to stimulate use. The recipes will be given at all in-store demonstrations, on the back of packages, and through a mail-in recipe book offer. In addition, recipes will be included in coupons sent by direct-mail or free-standing inserts. For new markets, recipes will be included on in-pack coupon inserts.

Cents-Off Coupons. To generate trial and repeat-purchase of Howlin' Coyote products, coupons will be distributed in four ways:

- In Sunday newspaper inserts. Inserts are highly read and will help generate awareness. Coupled with in-store demonstrations, this has been a very successful technique so far.

Sunday newspaper inserts encourage consumer trial and provide recipes to show how Howlin' Coyote chili can be used in summer meals.

Another bulleted list adds many details for the reader, including methods of gaining customer awareness, trial, and repeat purchases as Howlin' Coyote enters new metropolitan areas.

The Place Strategy is described here in terms of both (1) the present method and (2) the new one to be used when the increased sales volume makes it feasible. See Chapters 15, 16, and 17.

All the marketing mix decisions covered in the just-described marketing program have both revenue and expense effects. These are summarized in this section of the marketing plan. See Appendix B.

Note that this section contains no introductory overview sentence. While the sentence is not essential, many readers prefer to see it to avoid the abrupt start with Past Sales Revenues.

The graph shows more clearly the dramatic growth of sales revenue than data in a table would do.

- In-pack coupons. Inside each box of Howlin' Coyote chili will be coupons for $1 off two more packages of the chili. These coupons will be included for the first three months the product is shipped to a new market. Doing so encourages repeat purchases by new users.
- Direct-mail chili coupons. Those households that fit the Howlin' Coyote demographics described previously will be mailed coupons. This is likely to be an efficient promotion due to its greater audience selectivity.
- In-store demonstrations. Coupons will be passed out at in-store demonstrations to give an additional incentive to purchase.

Place (Distribution) Strategy

Howlin' Coyote is distributed in its present markets through a food distributor. The distributor buys the product, warehouses it, and then resells and delivers it to grocery retailers on a store-by-store basis. This is typical for products that have moderate sales—compared with, say, staples like milk or bread. As sales grow, we will shift to a more efficient system using a broker who sells the products to retail chains and grocery wholesalers.

7. Financial Data and Projections

Past Sales Revenues

Historically, Howlin' Coyote has had a steady increase in sales revenues since its introduction in 1990. In 1994, sales jumped spectacularly, due largely to new promotion strategies. Sales have continued to rise, but at a less dramatic rate. The trend in sales revenues appears in Figure 3.

Figure 3.   Sales Revenues for Paradise Kitchens, Inc.

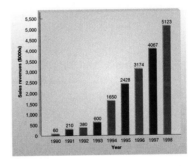

Because this table is very short, it is woven into the text, rather than given a figure number and title.

Because the plan proposes to enter 17 new metropolitan markets in the coming five years (for a total of 20), it is not possible to simply extrapolate the trend in Figure 3. Instead, management's judgment must be used. Methods of making sales forecasts—including the "lost horse technique used here—are discussed in Chapter 8.

The Five-Year Financial Projections section starts with the judgment forecast of cases sold and the resulting net sales. Gross profit and then operating profit—critical for the company's survival—are projected and show the company passes breakeven and becomes profitable in Year 2. An actual plan often contains many pages of computer-generated spreadsheet projections, usually shown in an appendix to the plan.

Five-Year Projections

Five-year financial projections for Paradise Kitchens appear below:

			Projections				
Financial Element	Units	Actual 1998	Year1 1999	Year 2 2000	Year 3 2001	Year 4 2002	Year 5 2003
Cases sold	1,000	353	684	889	1,249	1,499	1,799
Net sales	$1,000	5,123	9,913	12,884	18,111	21,733	26,080
Gross profit	$1,000	2,545	4,820	6,527	8,831	10,597	12,717
Operating profit (loss)	$1,000	339	985	2,906	2,805	3,366	4,039

These projections reflect the continuing growth in number of cases sold (with 8 packages of Howlin' Coyote chili per case) and increasing production and distribution economies of scale as sales volume increases.

8. Organization

Paradise Kitchens's present organization appears in Figure 4. It shows the four people reporting to the President. Below this level are both the full-time and part-time employees of the Company.

At present Paradise Kitchens operates with full-time employees in only essential positions. It now augments its full-time staff with key advisors, consultants, and subcontractors. As the firm grows, people with special expertise will be added to the staff.

Figure 4. The Paradise Kitchens Organization

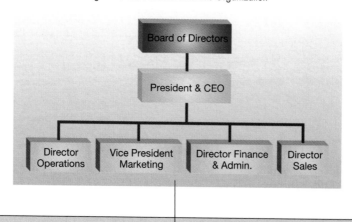

The Organization of Paradise Kitchens appears here. It reflects the bare-bones organizational structure of successful small businesses. Often a more elaborate marketing plan will show the new positions expected to be added as the firm grows. See Chapter 22.

The Implementation Plan shows how the company will turn plans into results. Gantt charts are often used to set deadlines and assign responsibilities for the many tactical marketing decisions needed to enter a new market. See Chapter 22.

The essence of Evaluation and Control is comparing actual sales with the targeted values set in the plan and taking appropriate actions. Note that the section briefly describes a contingency plan for alternative actions, depending on how successful the entry into a new market turns out to be. See Chapter 22.

Various appendixes may appear at the end of the plan, depending on the purpose and audience for them. For example, resumes of key personnel or detailed financial spreadsheets often appear in appendixes. For space reasons these are not shown here.

9. Implementation Plan

Introducing Howlin' Coyote chilies to new metropolitan areas is a complex task and requires that creative promotional activities gain consumer awareness and initial trial among the target market households identified earlier. The anticipated rollout schedule to enter these metropolitan markets appears in Figure 5.

Figure 5.   Rollout Schedule to Enter New U.S. Markets

Year	New Markets Added	Cumulative Markets	Cumulative Percentage of U.S. Market
Today (1998)	2	5	16
Year 1 (1999)	3	8	21
Year 2 (2000)	4	12	29
Year 3 (2001)	2	14	37
Year 4 (2002)	3	17	45
Year 5 (2003)	3	20	53

The diverse regional tastes in chili will be monitored carefully to assess whether minor modifications may be required in the chili recipes. For example, what is seen as "hot" in Boston may not be seen as "hot" in Dallas. As the rollout to new metropolitan areas continues, Paradise Kitchens will assess manufacturing and distribution trade-offs. This is important in determining whether to start new production with selected high-quality regional contract packers.

10. Evaluation and Control

Monthly sales targets in cases have been set for Howlin' Coyote chili for each metropolitan area. Actual case sales will be compared with these targets and tactical marketing programs modified to reflect the unique sets of factors in each metropolitan area. The speed of the roll-out program will increase or decrease, depending on the Paradise Kitchens's performance in the successive metropolitan markets it enters. Similarly, as described above in the section on the implementation plan, Paradise Kitchens may elect to respond to variations in regional tastes by using contract packers, which will reduce transportation and warehousing costs but will require special efforts to monitor production quality.

Appendix A. Biographical Sketches of Key Personnel

Appendix B. Detailed Financial Projections

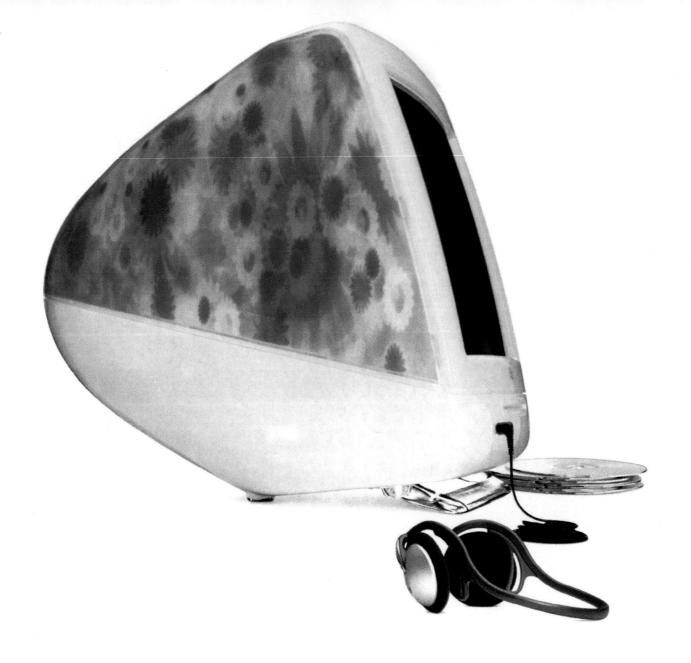

Rip. Mix. Burn.

The new iMac™ with iTunes + CD-RW. Take your favorite songs, put them in the order you want and burn a CD. After all, it's your music.

Think different.

CHAPTER 3

SCANNING THE MARKETING ENVIRONMENT

AFTER READING THIS CHAPTER YOU SHOULD ABLE TO:

- Understand how environmental scanning provides information about social, economic, technological, competitive, and regulatory forces.

- Explain how social forces such as demographics and culture and economic forces such as macroeconomic conditions and consumer income affect marketing.

- Describe how technological changes can affect marketing.

- Understand the forms of competition that exist in a market, key components of competition, and the impact of competition on corporate structures.

- Explain the major legislation that ensures competition and regulates the elements of the marketing mix.

HOW AN 18-YEAR-OLD CHANGED THE WORLD . . . WITH MUSIC!

Have you ever ripped a song from the Internet? Mixed a collection of music hits on your computer? Burned a CD of your favorites? If you have you may be one of 50 million users of Internet-based music file-sharing services like Shawn Fanning's Napster. Shawn was just 18 when he devised the software program that allowed computer users to share music files and, subsequently, changed almost everything about the music industry. Suddenly musicians, recording companies, computer companies like Apple, retail stores, and consumers like you are part of a completely different music marketplace. How did this happen? The marketing environment changed!

First, consumers changed. As one expert explains, the music industry "forces consumers to go to unpleasant stores to buy high-priced CDs, bundles bad songs along with good, encases its products in cheap plastic boxes that frequently break, then deliberately wraps the boxes in hard-to-open cellophane."[1] As a result music buyers started searching for a more customer-friendly distribution system.

Second, changes in technology facilitated the development of new products and services previously impossible to offer consumers. New computers with improved speed and storage capabilities were introduced. CD drives that could "burn" a customized CD became available. The Internet reached millions of computer users. And Shawn designed software that let almost anyone "share" a music file with anyone else on the Internet.

The creation of Napster, and other file-sharing services like it, has led to other changes in the marketing environment. Regulatory factors, for example, are influencing the activities of the services. The Recording Industry

Association of America sued Napster and several other music-swapping services for copyright violations. In response, U.S. courts have ruled that Napster must stop helping its users exchange copyrighted material, and Napster is trying to develop new technology that will operate as a pay subscription service.

Similarly, competitive factors have changed as music labels EMI, Bertelsmann, and Warner Music have created an online clearinghouse for their music called MusicNet, and Sony and Universal have created a joint venture called Pressplay. Consumers will also see a variety of new products designed to respond to file sharing. Intel's new Pentium processor campaign suggests that their product can "Give your whole music collection an upgrade," and Apple's new iMac is sold with iTunes software so users can "Rip. Mix. Burn"![2]

Changes such as these are clearly changing the marketing environment. Anticipating changes such as these and responding to them often means the difference between marketing success and failure. This chapter describes how the marketing environment has changed in the past and how it is likely to change in the future.

ENVIRONMENTAL SCANNING IN THE NEW MILLENNIUM

Changes in the marketing environment are a source of opportunities and threats to be managed. The process of continually acquiring information on events occurring outside the organization to identify and interpret potential trends is called **environmental scanning**.

Tracking Environmental Trends

Environmental trends typically arise from five sources: social, economic, technological, competitive, and regulatory forces. As shown in Figure 3–1 and described later in this chapter, these forces affect the marketing activities of a firm in numerous ways. To illustrate how environmental scanning is used, consider the following trend:[3]

> Coffee industry marketers have observed that the percentage of adults who drink coffee has declined from 75 percent in 1962 to 54 percent in 2000. Age-specific analysis, however, indicates that the percentage of 18- to 24-year-olds who drink coffee has risen from 19 percent in 1998 to 25 percent in 2000.

FIGURE 3–1

Environmental forces affecting the organization, as well as its suppliers and customers

What types of businesses are likely to be influenced by this trend? What future would you predict for coffee?

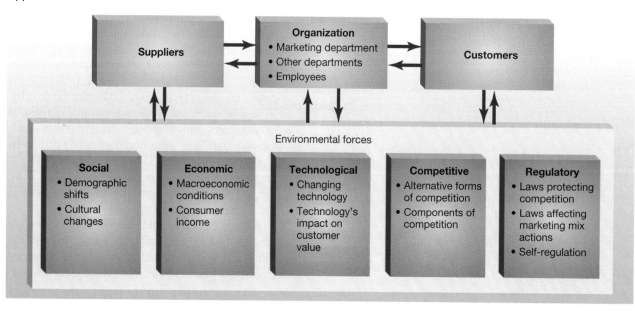

You may have concluded that this trend is likely to influence coffee manufacturers and supermarkets. If so, you are absolutely correct—manufacturers have responded by offering new flavors, and supermarkets have added coffee boutiques and gourmet brands to try to reverse the trend. Predicting the future of coffee requires assumptions about the number of years the trends will continue and the rate of increase or decline in various age groups. Did you consider these issues in your analysis? Because experts make different assumptions, their forecasts range from a 30 percent decline to a 7 percent increase by 2005—a range that probably includes your forecast!

Environmental scanning also involves explaining trends. Why has coffee consumption been declining? One explanation is that consumers are switching from coffee to other beverages such as soft drinks, juices, or water. This idea is supported by the fact that soft drink consumption has increased from 23 gallons per person in 1970 to 55 gallons in 2000. Another explanation is that preferences have shifted to more expensive types of coffee, and consumers have reduced their use to maintain the same level of expenditure. Identifying and interpreting trends, such as the decline in coffee consumption, and developing explanations, such as those offered in this paragraph, are essential to successful environmental scanning.

An Environmental Scan of the United States

What other trends might affect marketing in the future? A firm conducting an environmental scan of the United States might uncover key trends such as those listed in Figure 3–2 for each of the five environmental factors.[4] Although the list of trends is far from complete, it reveals the breadth of an environmental scan—from population shifts to remote suburbs and small towns, to the growth of wireless messaging, to the emergence of "network corporations." These trends affect consumers and the businesses and nonprofit organizations that serve them. Trends such as these are covered as the five environmental forces are described in the following pages.

FIGURE 3–2
An environmental scan of the
United States

ENVIRONMENTAL FORCE	TREND IDENTIFIED BY AN ENVIRONMENTAL SCAN
Social	• Movement toward healthful products and lifestyles. • Growing number and importance of Hispanic Americans. • Population shifts to remote suburbs and small towns.
Economic	• Increase in per capita income and standard of living. • Increase in savings as many workers approach retirement. • Slow economic growth and stock market adjustment, following 9-11-01 terrorism.
Technological	• Increased use of wireless messaging technology. • Declining cost of computer power and growth of "smart" products. • Advances in biotechnology and cancer drugs.
Competitive	• Increased focus on empowering workers to improve performance. • The emergence of fast, responsive "network corporations." • More international competition from emerging countries.
Regulatory	• New legislation related to digital copyright and intellectual property protection. • Greater concern for privacy and personal information collection. • New legislation on Internet taxation, e-mail spam, and domain names.

SOCIAL FORCES

The **social forces** of the environment include the demographic characteristics of the population and its values. Changes in these forces can have a dramatic impact on marketing strategy.

Demographics

Describing the population according to selected characteristics such as age, gender, ethnicity, income, and occupation is referred to as **demographics**. The 2000 Census indicates that the American population is growing older, becoming more ethnically diverse, and increasingly living in nontraditional families.[5]

The Population Trend
In 2001 the U.S. population was estimated to be 284 million people. In 1960 only 9 percent of the population was over age 65; by 2000 this percentage had increased to more than 12 percent.[6] This observation suggests a significant demographic trend—the graying of America. Figure 3–3 shows the age distributions of the population in 1960, 1990, and 2020.

In response to the changing age distribution of America's population, greater marketing attention has been focused on the **mature household**. Such households are headed by people over 50 years old, who represent the fastest-growing age segment in the population. In 2000 this group represented 28 percent of the population, but this percentage will climb to 32 percent by the year 2010 and to 36 percent by 2025.[7] People over 50 control 75 percent of the net worth of U.S. households, and the over-50 category includes the period (between 55 and 60) when a person's income peaks.

Environmental scanning of the trend has led some companies to begin to respond to this important market. AT&T, for example, has developed products aimed at seniors, such as emergency dialing mechanisms and amplifiers. Lennar Corporation in Miami is building retirement homes in "active adult communities" with clubhouses, concierge services, computer labs, and gyms. Kimberly Clark, maker of Huggies diapers for babies, has introduced Poise and Depend brands for adults. Finally, Bank of America introduced its "Private Bank" service to appeal to mature households.[8]

FIGURE 3–3
The changing age distribution of population in the United States
SOURCE: U.S. Bureau of the Census
Note: ■ Baby Boom

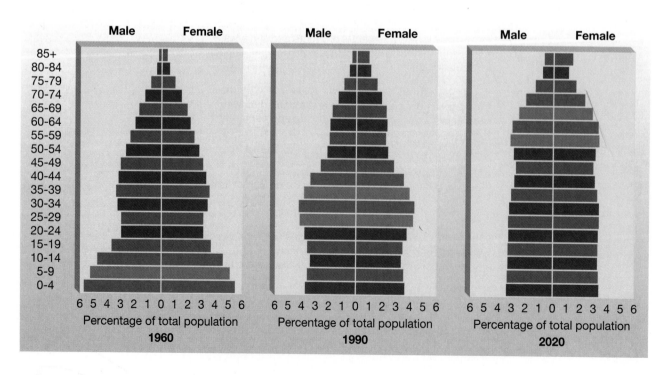

Which population groups are these advertisers trying to reach?

The Baby Boom, Generation X, and Generation Y

A major reason for the graying of America is that the **baby boomers**—the generation of children born between 1946 and 1964—are growing up. Figure 3–3 shows the baby boomers movement through the population distribution in red. As the 82 million boomers have aged, their participation in the work force and their earnings have increased, making them an important consumer market. It has been estimated that this group accounts for 56 to 58 percent of the purchases in most consumer product and service categories. In the future, boomers' interests will reflect concern for their children's future, their own health, and their own retirement, and companies will need to position products to respond to these interests. Generally, baby boomers are receptive to anything that makes them feel younger. L'Oreal, for example, introduced Absolue, a new skin-care line designed specifically for this age group.

Generation X includes the 15 percent of the U.S. population born between 1965 and 1976—a period known as the baby bust because the number of children born each year was declining. It is a generation of consumers who are self-reliant, entrepreneurial, supportive of racial and sexual diversity, and better educated than any previous generation. They are not prone to extravagance and are likely to pursue lifestyles and prefer products and services that are very different from baby boomers. For example, Generation X is planning for retirement and taking advantage of 401(k) plans and investment services much earlier than the boomer generation. Because they are likely to become a key influence on popular culture, marketers are now tracking this generation to identify the dominant consumption values of the twenty-first century.[9]

Generation Y refers to Americans born after 1976, the year that many baby boomers began having children. The increase in birthrate is also described as the echo-boom and the baby boomlet. Generation Y already exerts influence on music, sports, computers, and videogame purchases. Later in the twenty-first century, this group will influence markets, attitudes, and society much like the baby boomers do now and Generation X will soon.[10]

Because the members of each generation are distinctive in their attitudes and consumer behavior, marketers have been studying the many groups or cohorts that make up the marketplace and have developed *generational marketing* programs for them. The Marketing NewsNet box on the next page describes six generations that are often target markets in the United States.[11]

The American Family

As the population profile has changed, so has the structure of the American family. In 1960, 45 percent of all households consisted of married

MARKETING NEWSNET   Talking about Your Generation

Businesses have discovered that they can grow bigger by targeting smaller—smaller groups of consumers that is. These groups are increasingly defined as a generation or cohort related to important life experiences. The reason is that events occurring when people first become economic adults (usually between ages 17 and 21) affect their lifelong attitudes and values. These attitudes and values are unlikely to change as a person ages. So the kind of music that is popular during these formative years often remains the preferred type of music for life. Similarly, early lifetime experiences influence preferences in many other product and service categories.

Studies of the U.S. population have identified six distinct groups described in the table below. Which generation are you? Your parents?

COHORT	DEFINING EVENTS	BORN	FAVORITE MUSIC
The Depression cohort	The Great Depression	1912–1921	Big Band
The World War II cohort	World War II	1922–1927	Swing
The Postwar cohort	Korean War, Sputnik	1928–1945	Frank Sinatra
The Baby Boomers cohort	Woodstock, Kennedy assassination, Vietnam	1946–1964	Rock and roll
The Generation X cohort	Growth of divorce, AIDS	1965–1976	Grunge, rap, retro
The Generation Y cohort	The Internet	1977–	Hip hop

couples with children. Today, that type of household is just 23.5 percent of the population. More than one-fourth of all households now consist of people who live alone, and another 28 percent are married without children. The fastest-growing types of households are those with single parents (now 16 percent of the population), and those with unmarried partners (now 6 percent of the population). Advertisers are trying to develop campaigns that reflect the changing structure of U.S. households. Schwab financial services, for example, used Sarah Ferguson, a single mother, to reach single women with an interest in personal finance.[12]

The increase in cohabitation (households with unmarried partners) may be one reason that the divorce rate has declined slightly in recent years. Even so, the likelihood that a couple will divorce exceeds 40 percent and the total number of divorced people is 19.8 million. The majority of divorced people eventually remarry, which has given rise to the **blended family**, one formed by the merging into a single household of two previously separated units. Today, one of every three Americans is a stepparent, stepchild, stepsibling, or some other member of a blended family. Hallmark Cards, Inc. now has specially designed cards and verses for blended families.[13]

Population Shifts   A major regional shift in the U.S. population toward western and sunbelt states occurred in the 1990s. During the period of 1990 to 2000 the states of Nevada, Arizona, Colorado, Utah, and Idaho grew at the fastest rates, while North Dakota and West Virginia were the slowest-growing states. Three states—California, Texas, and Florida—accounted for 33 percent of the net population change in the United States, gaining more than 3 million persons each.[14]

Populations are also shifting within states. In the early 1900s the population shifted from rural areas to cities. From the 1930s through the 1980s the population shifted from the cities to suburbs. During the 1990s the population began to shift again, from suburbs to more remote suburbs called *exurbs* and to smaller towns called *penturbia*.[15] To assist marketers in gathering data on the population, the Census Bureau has developed a three-level classification system that reflects the varying locations of the population. From the largest to the smallest, these three areas are the consolidated metropolitan statistical area (CMSA), primary metropolitan statistical area (PMSA), and metropolitan statistical area (MSA), as shown in the margin and described here:

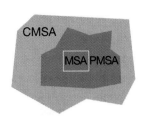

www.census.gov/
population/estimates/
about metro.html

- *Consolidated metropolitan statistical area (CMSA).* The largest designation in terms of geographical area and market size. It is made up of component PMSAs, defined next, that total at least 1 million people.
- *Primary metropolitan statistical area (PMSA).* An area that is part of a larger CMSA that has a total population of 1 million or more. It must also contain counties that conform to the following standards: (1) a total population of at least 100,000, (2) a population that is at least 60 percent urban, and (3) fewer than 50 percent of the resident workers commute to jobs outside the county.
- *Metropolitan statistical area (MSA).* (1) A city having a population of at least 50,000 or (2) an urbanized area with a population in excess of 50,000, with a total metropolitan population of at least 100,000. An MSA may include counties that have close economic and social ties to the central county.

There are currently 258 MSAs and 18 CMSAs comprised of 73 PMSAs in the United States.

Racial and Ethnic Diversity   A notable trend is the changing racial and ethnic composition of the U.S. population. Approximately one in four U.S. residents is African-American, American Indian, Asian, Pacific Islander, or a representative of another racial or ethnic group. Diversity is further evident in the variety of peoples that make up these groups. For example, Asians consist of Asian-Indians, Chinese, Filipinos, Japanese, Koreans, and Vietnamese. For the first time, the 2000 Census allowed respondents to choose more than one of the six race options, and more than 6 million reported more than one race. Hispanics, who may be from any race, currently make up 12 percent of the U.S. population and are represented by Mexicans, Puerto Ricans, Cubans, and others of Central and South American ancestry. While the United States is becoming more diverse, Figure 3–4 suggests that the racial and ethnic groups tend to be concentrated in geographic regions.[16]

FIGURE 3–4
Racial and ethnic concentrations in the United States

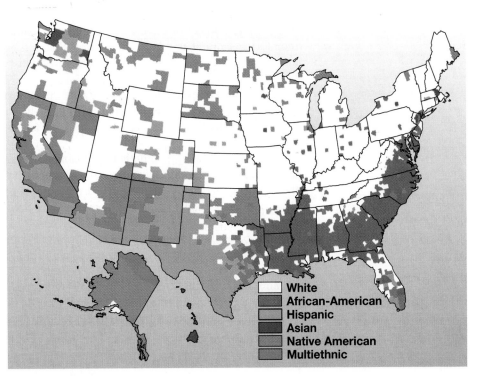

SOURCE: American Demographics, June 2001

The racial and ethnic composition of the U.S. population is expected to change even more by 2010. Since 1990 the Hispanic and Asian populations grew by more than 35 percent each, the African-American population by 11 percent, and the white population by only 3.6 percent.[17] When one considers that 38 percent of children in the United States will be African-American, Hispanic, or Asian by 2010, the long-term consequences of their buying patterns must be understood. Marketers who recognize and respond to diversity in the U.S. population will be rewarded for their efforts because consumer needs will be better satisfied. The unique purchasing patterns of different racial and ethnic groups are highlighted in Chapter 5.

Regional Marketing A new trend within marketing focuses not only on the shifting of consumers geographically but also on the differences in their product preferences based on where they live. This concept has been referred to as **regional marketing**, which is developing marketing plans to reflect specific area differences in taste preferences, perceived needs, or interests. For example, Procter & Gamble observed that vacuum brick-packs of coffee were relatively more popular than cans in the South. The company repackaged their Folgers brand coffee for those markets and developed a new advertising campaign. Sales of Folgers coffee increased 32 percent in the targeted markets.[18] In Chapter 9, you will learn more about this approach to the market referred to as *geographical segmentation*.

Because several ethnic groups are geographically concentrated, ethnic marketing is an increasingly important part of regional marketing. Consider, for example, that 48 percent of U.S. Asians live in Los Angeles, New York City, and San Francisco and that two-thirds of Hispanics live in Florida, Texas, and California. Saturn combined ethnic and regional marketing by running a Spanish-language advertising campaign, using a testimonial from San Antonio, Texas, firefighter Ernest Imperial, in Texas and California. The ads were not used in Florida, where more than 55 percent of the Hispanic population is Cuban—a group for which a different Hispanic dialect was needed.[19]

Culture

A second social force, **culture**, incorporates the set of values, ideas, and attitudes of a homogeneous group of people that are transmitted from one generation to the next. Because many of the elements of culture influence consumer buying patterns, monitoring cultural trends in the United States is important for marketing. Cross-cultural analysis needed for global marketing is discussed in Chapter 7.

The Changing Attitudes and Roles of Women One of the most notable changes in the United States in the past 30 years has been in the attitudes and roles of women in the marketplace. These changes have had a significant impact on marketing practices.

Your mothers and grandmothers probably remember advertising targeted at them that focused on the characteristics of household products—like laundry detergent that got clothes "whiter than white"! In the 1970s and 1980s ads began to create a bridge between genders with messages such as Secret's "strong enough for a man, but made for a woman." In the 1990s marketing to women focused on their challenge of balancing family and career interests. Women, and men, often struggled to encourage the slow movement toward equality in the marketplace. Today's Generation Y, however, represents the first generation of women who have no collective memory of the dramatic changes we have undergone. As one expert explains: "Feminism today is like fluoride, we scarcely notice that we have it."

Several factors have contributed to the shift in attitudes. First, many young women had career mothers who provided a reference point for lifestyle choices. Second, increased participation in organized sports eliminated one of the most visible inequal-

Saturn combined ethnic and regional marketing by using Spanish-language promotions in some states.

Saturn

www.saturnbp.com

ities in opportunities for women. And finally, the Internet has provided exposure to the marketplace through a mechanism that makes gender, race, and ethnicity invisible. Most of the 35 million Generation Y women view themselves as confident, strong, and feminine. They are not likely to respond to "we know you are busy" appeals; they know they are busy and thrive on it.

So how are companies changing to respond to this cultural transformation? The sporting goods industry started by simply placing a "for women" label on their men's products. Female consumers responded by saying the products didn't address their individual interests. Manufacturers then introduced lower-quality women's merchandise, and women simply bought the men's product. Now most manufacturers offer equal quality products designed specifically for each gender. Burton Snowboard Company also recognized the different needs. The company makes boards and clothing for women and redesigned its website to reflect feedback from female riders. The financial services, insurance, and health-care industries are also working on marketing programs that acknowledge women's individual interests and needs as consumers.[20]

Changing Values   Culture also includes values, which vary with age but tend to be very similar for men and women. All age groups, for example, rank "protecting the family" and "honesty" as the most important values. Consumers under 20 rank "friendship" third, while the 20 to 29, and 30 to 39 age groups rank "self-esteem" and "health and fitness" as their third most important values, respectively. These values are reflected in the growth of products and services that consumers believe are consistent with their values. Concern for health and fitness is one reason 51 million people in the United States report that they are trying to control their weight. But they are less likely to "diet" than they are to create a healthy and balanced lifestyle. Stouffer's Lean Cuisine is trying to respond to the trend by suggesting that health-conscious consumers don't have to sacrifice taste for nutrition with its "Do something good for yourself" campaign. Similarly, Jenny Craig's primary market is 35- to 55-year-old people who are interested in a healthier lifestyle. Other products related to this trend include vitamins, exercise equipment, fitness drinks, and magazines such as *Fitness, Runner's World,* and *Walking.*[21]

A change in consumption orientation is also apparent. Today, and for the foreseeable future, **value consciousness**—or the concern for obtaining the best quality, features, and performance of a product or service for a given price—will drive consumption behavior. Innovative marketers have responded to this new orientation in numerous ways. Holiday Inn Worldwide has opened Holiday Express hotels, designed to offer comfortable accommodations with room rates lower than Holiday Inns. Revlon's Charles of the Ritz, known for its upscale and expensive cosmetics, has introduced the Express Bar, a collection of modified, medium-priced cosmetics. Even American Express is adding low-fee credit cards to its line of well-known, high-priced, and exclusive green, gold, and platinum charge cards.[22]

Concept Check

1. Explain the term *regional marketing.*

2. What are the marketing implications of blended families?

3. How are important values such as "health and fitness" reflected in the marketplace today?

ECONOMIC FORCES

The third component of the environmental scan, the **economy**, pertains to the income, expenditures, and resources that affect the cost of running a business and household. We'll consider two aspects of these economic forces: a macroeconomic view of the marketplace and a microeconomic perspective of consumer income.

Macroeconomic Conditions

Of particular concern at the macroeconomic level is the inflationary or recessionary state of the economy, whether actual or perceived by consumers or businesses. In an inflationary economy, the cost to produce and buy products and services escalates as prices increase. From a marketing standpoint, if prices rise faster than consumer incomes, the number of items consumers can buy decreases. This relationship is evident in the cost of a college education. Today, average annual tuition is the equivalent of 250 hours of pay for an average worker, up from 110 hours of pay in 1960.[23]

Whereas inflation is a period of price increases, recession is a time of slow economic activity. Businesses decrease production, unemployment rises, and many consumers have less money to spend. The U.S. economy experienced recessions in the early 1970s, early 1980s, and early 1990s. From 1998 through early 2000 the U.S. economy grew rapidly as businesses invested in "new economy" technology and as consumers spent their stock market gains. Following this period of growth, however, the economy again entered a slow-growth recessionary period.[24]

Consumer expectations of an inflationary and recessionary U.S. economy is an important element of environmental scanning. Consumer spending, which accounts for two-thirds of U.S. economic activity, is affected by expectations of the future. Surveys of consumer expectations are tracked over time by research organizations, who ask questions such as "Do you expect to be better or worse off financially a year from now?" Surveyors record the share of positive and negative responses to these and related questions and construct an index. The higher the index, the more favorable are consumer expectations. Figure 3–5 shows the fluctuations in the Consumer Sentiment Index and annual vehicle sales. As can be seen, sales are closely related to expectations. This relationship has helped Chrysler plan its automobile production and avoid producing too many or too few cars. Levitz, the largest U.S.

FIGURE 3–5
University of Michigan
Consumer Sentiment Index
and automobile sales:
1970–2000

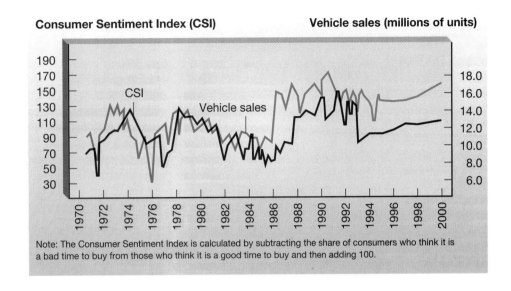

furniture retailer, also tracks consumer economic expectations since furniture sales reflect perceptions of the future economic environment.[25]

Consumer Income

The microeconomic trends in terms of consumer income are also important issues for marketers. Having a product that meets the needs of consumers may be of little value if they are unable to purchase it. A consumer's ability to buy is related to income, which consists of gross, disposable, and discretionary components.

Gross Income   The total amount of money made in one year by a person, household, or family unit is referred to as **gross income**. While the typical U.S. household earned only about $8,700 of income in 1970, it earned about $40,816 in 1999. When gross income is adjusted for inflation, however, income of that typical U.S. household was relatively stable from 1970 to 1999 (e.g., adjusted for inflation the 1970 salary was $35,200). Figure 3–6 shows the distribution of annual income among U.S. households.[26] Are you from a typical household? Read the accompanying Web Link to learn how you can determine the median household income in your home town.

FIGURE 3–6
Income distribution of U.S.
households

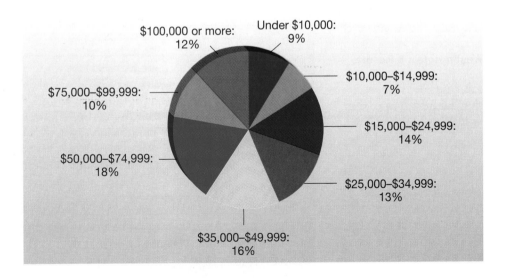

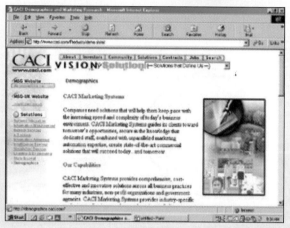
Disposable Income   The second income component, **disposable income**, is the money a consumer has left after paying taxes to use for food, shelter, and clothing. Thus, if taxes rise at a faster rate than does income, consumers must economize. In recent years consumers' allocation of income has shifted. As the marketplace has become more efficient, producing products that are more durable and use less energy, consumers have increased their disposable income. Car maintenance costs, for example, have declined 28 percent since 1985, because automobile quality has improved. Much of the money is being spent on new categories of "necessities" such as vitamins and supplements; antibacterial bodywashes, lotions, and deodorants; anti-wrinkle creams; and children's shampoos, toothpaste, and bath products.[27]

Discretionary Income   The third component of income is **discretionary income**, the money that remains after paying for taxes and necessities. Discretionary

As consumers' discretionary income increases, so does the enjoyment of pleasure travel.

Westin Hotels & Resorts
www.westin.com

income is used for luxury items such as vacations at a Westin resort. An obvious problem in defining discretionary versus disposable income is determining what is a luxury and what is a necessity.

The Department of Labor has calculated a budget for a household of four persons. Using these budget amounts, the Census Bureau defines a household as having discretionary income if its spendable income exceeds that of an average, similarly sized family by 30 percent or more. Recent studies suggest that two-thirds of all American households have some discretionary income. Two-person households have the highest average discretionary income at \$15,500, compared with an average of \$13,480 for all households with discretionary income.[28]

TECHNOLOGICAL FORCES

Our society is in a period of dramatic technological change. **Technology**, a major environmental force, refers to inventions or innovations from applied science or engineering research. Each new wave of technological innovation can replace existing products and companies. Do you recognize the items pictured below and what they may replace?

Technology of Tomorrow

Technological change is the result of research, so it is difficult to predict. Some of the most dramatic technological changes occurring now, however, include the following:

1. Advances in nanotechnology, the science of unimaginably small electronics, will lead to denser hard drives, smaller chips, and better medicine.
2. The convergence of personal computer and telephone technologies.
3. The Internet will become the communication backbone of information-intensive industries.
4. The emergence of biotechnology as a key component of the economy.

These trends in technology are already seen in today's marketplace. IBM has developed a 1-square-inch storage system that can record 400 gigabits of data. PDAs (personal digital assistants) such as Palm and Visor offer computing capabilities and wireless messaging. ImClone's new cancer drug, C225, will probably generate \$1 billion in annual sales. Other technologies such as satellite dishes, HDTV, and digital cameras are likely to replace or substitute for existing technologies such as cable, low-resolution TV, and film.[29]

Technological change leads to new products. What products might be replaced by these innovations?

Technology's Impact on Customer Value

Advances in technology are having important effects on marketing. First, the cost of technology is plummeting—causing the customer value assessment of technology-based products to focus on other dimensions such as quality, service, and relationships. When Computer Associates International introduced its software program Simply Money, it gave away the first million copies. Computer Associates reasoned that satisfied customers would later buy upgrades and related products. A similar approach is now used by many cellular telephone vendors, who charge little for the telephone if the purchase leads to a telephone service contract.[30]

Technology also provides value through the development of new products. Oldsmobile now offers customers an auto-navigation system that uses satellite signals to help the driver reach any destination. Under development are radarlike collision avoidance systems that disengage cruise control, reduce the engine speed, and even apply the brakes.[31] Other new products likely to be available soon include a "smart ski" with an embedded microprocessor that will adjust the flexibility of the ski to snow conditions; injectable health monitors that will send glucose, oxygen, and other clinical information to a wristwatch-like monitor; and electronic books that will allow you to download any volume and view it on pages coated with electronic "ink" and embedded electrodes.[32]

Technology can also change existing products and the ways they are produced. Many companies are using technological developments to allow *recycling* products through the manufacturing cycle several times. The National Association for Plastic Container Recovery, for example, estimates that 50 percent of all plastic bottles are now recycled—usually to make polyester fibers that are spun into everything from sweaters to upholstery. In Southern California, Tomra Systems has launched a chain of 200 rePlanet recycling kiosks that it hopes to spread across the United States. Consumers receive between 2.5 and 10 cents per recycled container. Another approach is *precycling*—efforts by manufacturers to reduce waste by decreasing the amount of packaging they use. The development of new packaging materials, for example, has allowed Du Pont to produce a collapsible pouch as an alternative to milk cartons in school lunch programs.[33]

Electronic Business Technologies

The transformative power of technology may be best illustrated by the rapid growth of the **marketspace**, an information- and communication-based electronic exchange environment mostly occupied by sophisticated computer and telecommunication technologies and digitized offerings. Any activity that uses some form of electronic communication in the inventory, exchange, advertisement, distribution, and payment of goods and services is often called **electronic commerce**. Although electronic commerce has existed through proprietary networks—such as those used to connect ATMs to your bank—for many years, in 1996 the World Wide Web burst onto the scene and started a new era of *electronic business*. Network technologies are now used for everything from filing expense reports, to monitoring daily sales, to sharing information with employees, to communicating instantly with suppliers.

The most widely visible application of electronic commerce exists in business-to-consumer interactive marketing, involving the Internet, the World Wide Web, and commercial online services. Many people view these three as being the same. They are not. The **Internet** is an integrated global network of computers that gives users access to information and documents. The **World Wide Web** is part of the Internet that supports a retrieval system that formats information and documents into Web pages. **Commercial online services** such as America Online offer electronic information and marketing services to subscribers who are charged a monthly fee.

Examples of recycling by rePlanet and precycling by Lever.

The combination of these technologies caused electronic commerce activity to sky-rocket to more than $30 billion last year![34]

Many companies have adapted Internet-based technology internally to support their electronic business strategies. An **Intranet**, for example, is an Internet/Web-based network used within the boundaries of an organization. It is a private Internet that may or may not be connected to the public Internet. **Extranets**, which use Internet-based technologies, permit communication between a company and its supplier, distributors, and other partners (such as advertising agencies). The accompanying Marketing NewsNet describes how these technologies have transformed some companies into e-businesses![35]

COMPETITIVE FORCES

The fourth component of the environmental scan, **competition**, refers to the alternative firms that could provide a product to satisfy a specific market's needs. There are various forms of competition, and each company must consider its present and potential competitors in designing its marketing strategy.

Alternative Forms of Competition

There are four basic forms of competition that form a continuum from pure competition to monopolistic competition to oligopoly to monopoly. Chapter 13 contains further discussions on pricing practices under these four forms of competition.

At one end of the continuum is *pure competition,* in which every company has a similar product. Companies that deal in commodities common to agribusiness (for example, wheat, rice, and grain) often are in a pure competition position in which distribution (in the sense of shipping products) is important but other elements of marketing have little impact.

In the second point on the continuum, *monopolistic competition,* the many sellers compete with their products on a substitutable basis. For example, if the price of coffee rises too much, consumers may switch to tea. Coupons or sales are frequently used marketing tactics.

Oligopoly, a common industry structure, occurs when a few companies control the majority of industry sales. For example, AT&T, WorldCom, and Sprint control approximately 80 percent of the $16 billion international long-distance telephone

MARKETING NEWSNET — The Net Worked!

TECHNOLOGY & E-COMMERCE

Despite the recent failures of many dot-com businesses it is clear that the Internet is changing many industries. Because the Internet can dramatically reduce the cost of communication, information-intensive businesses such as financial services, entertainment, health care, education, government, and many others are benefiting substantially from the Net. Success stories include E*Trade which offers online stock trading, Bank of America which has more than 3 million Internet customers, Monster.com which charges employers to post employment opportunities, Merck-Medco which offers prescription drugs through traditional and online channels, and Homestore.com which lists real estate offerings and sells ad space.

In addition, Net technologies are changing the way work is done within companies. For example, the Internet can increase the speed at which new product ideas spread among employees, between companies, within economies, and across countries. At Procter and Gamble, a Web-based information-sharing network facilitates the collection and evaluation of new product ideas from the company's 110,000 employees.

What's next? Some experts predict the World Wide Web will be bypassed by new Net technologies such as wireless services, peer-to-peer communication software, instant messaging, and machine-to-machine communication!

service market. Similarly, the entertainment industry in the United States is dominated by Viacom, Disney, and AOL Time Warner, and the U.S. defense contractor industry consists of Boeing, United Technologies, and Lockheed Martin. Critics of oligopolies suggest that because there are few sellers, price competition among firms is not desirable because it leads to reduced profits for all producers.[36]

The final point on the continuum, *monopoly,* occurs when only one firm sells the product. Monopolies are common for producers of goods considered essential to a community: water, electricity, and telephone service. Typically, marketing plays a small role in a monopolistic setting because it is regulated by the state or federal government. Government control usually seeks to ensure price protection for the buyer, although deregulation in recent years has encouraged price competition in the electricity market.[37] The U.S. Court of Appeals recently ruled that Microsoft is a monopoly, claiming that its 86 percent share of the PC operating system market has given the company excessive control of the computer and software industries.[38]

Components of Competition

In developing a marketing program, companies must consider the factors that drive competition: entry, bargaining power of buyers and suppliers, existing rivalries, and substitution possibilities.[39] Scanning the environment requires a look at all of them. These factors relate to a firm's marketing mix decisions and may be used to create a barrier to entry, increase brand awareness, or intensify a fight for market share.

Entry   In considering the competition, a firm must assess the likelihood of new entrants. Additional producers increase industry capacity and tend to lower prices. A company scanning its environment must consider the possible **barriers to entry** for other firms, which are business practices or conditions that make it difficult for new firms to enter the market. Barriers to entry can be in the form of capital requirements, advertising expenditures, product identity, distribution access, or switching costs. The higher the expense of the barrier, the more likely it will deter new entrants. For example, Lucent Technologies is the largest supplier of phone network equipment in the world, and its past customers find it less expensive to upgrade their equipment than switch to another supplier.[40]

Power of Buyers and Suppliers   A competitive analysis must consider the power of buyers and suppliers. Powerful buyers exist when they are few in number, there are low switching costs, or the product represents a significant share of the buyer's total costs. This last factor leads the buyer to exert significant pressure for price competition. A supplier gains power when the product is critical to the buyer and when it has built up the switching costs.

Existing Competitors and Substitutes   Competitive pressures among existing firms depend on the rate of industry growth. In slow-growth settings, competition is more heated for any possible gains in market share. High fixed costs also create competitive pressures for firms to fill production capacity. For example, airlines offer discounts for making early reservations and charge penalties for changes or cancellations in an effort to fill seats, which represent a high fixed cost.

Start-Ups, Entrepreneurs, and Small Businesses

The early 1980s saw employment peak in large corporations. A study appeared about this time asserting that small firms generated 66 percent of all new jobs created in the U.S.—middle-sized and large firms providing relatively few.[41] Some researchers have suggested that success for start-ups and small businesses lie more in effective execution than strategic planning, a lesson learned in the late 1990s by many failed dot-coms. While the recession of 2001 contributed to the downsizing of giant corporations and the failure of hundreds of start-ups, it also led to the formation of hundreds of new start-ups. For all the risks and uncertainties, the early 21st century continues as an era of start-ups, entrepreneurs, and small businesses.

The New Look in American Corporations

LOTUS FOR COLLABORATIVE COMMERCE

American corporations are rapidly changing the way they compete. For many managers the common practices that often ensured success in the past won't work any longer. The need to expand beyond the domestic markets, a general increase in the importance of intellectual capital, and the use of Internet technologies as competitive tools have all necessitated changes. Today's organization requires (1) constant change rather than stability, (2) networks rather than hierarchies, and (3) partnerships and alliances rather than self-sufficiency. United States corporations are adopting a new business model that consists of small business units, empowered workers with responsibility and accountability, and managers who "support" rather than control. Increases in productivity come by leveraging the creativity of individuals.

How will corporations facilitate these changes? One approach utilizes the Web as a management tool and leads to a model called the "network organization" or the "e-corporation." The Web gives everyone in the organization the ability to access and process information at any time and from any location. In addition, the Web allows employees to manage formal and informal networks of contractors, designers, manufacturers, and distributors. Software developer Ray Ozzie created Lotus Notes to help people quickly spread knowledge and information across organizations. It has been a huge success; more than 68 million users have purchased the product!

Concept Check

1. What is the difference between a consumer's disposable and discretionary income?

2. In pure competition there are a _____ number of sellers.

3. What is a network organization?

REGULATORY FORCES

For any organization, the marketing and broader business decisions are constrained, directed, and influenced by regulatory forces. **Regulation** consists of restrictions state and federal laws place on business with regard to the conduct of its activities. Regulation exists to protect companies as well as consumers. Much of the regulation from the federal and state levels has been passed to ensure competition and fair business practices. For consumers, the focus of legislation is to protect them from unfair trade practices and ensure their safety.

Protecting Competition

Major federal legislation has been passed to encourage competition, which is deemed desirable because it permits the consumer to determine which competitor will succeed and which will fail. The first such law was the *Sherman Antitrust Act* (1890). Lobbying by farmers in the Midwest against fixed railroad shipping prices led to the passage of this act, which forbids (1) contracts, combinations, or conspiracies in restraint of trade and (2) actual monopolies or attempts to monopolize any part of trade or commerce. Because of vague wording and government inactivity, however, there was only one successful case against a company in the nine years after the act became law, and the Sherman Act was supplemented with the *Clayton Act* (1914). This act forbids certain actions that are likely to lessen competition, although no actual harm has yet occurred.

In the 1930s the federal government had to act again to ensure fair competition. During that time, large chain stores appeared, such as the Great Atlantic & Pacific Tea Company (A&P). Small businesses were threatened, and they lobbied for the *Robinson-Patman Act* (1936). This act makes it unlawful to discriminate in prices charged to different purchasers of the same product, where the effect may substantially lessen competition or help to create a monopoly.

Product-Related Legislation

Various federal laws in existence specifically address the product component of the marketing mix. Some are aimed at protecting the company, some at protecting the consumer, and at least one at protecting both.

Company Protection
A company can protect its competitive position in new and novel products under the patent law, which gives inventors the right to exclude others from making, using, or selling products that infringe the patented invention. The federal copyright law is another way for a company to protect its competitive position in a product. The copyright law gives the author of a literary, dramatic, musical, or artistic work the exclusive right to print, perform, or otherwise copy that work. Copyright is secured automatically when the work is created. However, the published work should bear an appropriate copyright notice, including the copyright symbol, the first year of publication, and the name of the copyright owner, and it must be registered under the federal copyright law. Digital technology has necessitated new copyright legislation to improve protection of copyrighted digital products. Producers of DVD movies, music recordings, and software want protection from devices designed to circumvent antipiracy elements of their products.[42] Read the Ethics and Social Responsibility Alert and ask yourself: Should file-sharing be illegal?[43]

Consumer Protection
There are many consumer-oriented federal laws regarding products. One of the oldest is the *Meat Inspection Act* (1906), which provides for meat products to be wholesome, unadulterated, and properly labeled. The *Food, Drug and Cosmetics Act* (1938) is one of the most important of the federal regulatory laws. This act is aimed principally at preventing the adulteration or misbranding of the three

ETHICS AND SOCIAL RESPONSIBILITY ALERT   Should File-Sharing Be Illegal?

The answer to this question is difficult and complicated considering the simplicity of the idea that led to it. Shawn Fanning's Napster was a program that would allow computer users to swap music files with one another directly, without going through a centralized server. The success of the program shocked record companies and recording artists who claimed that Napster was guilty of contributing to and facilitating other people's infringement of copyright laws. One of the laws, the Digital Millennium Copyright Act, is designed to protect intellectual property owners but is controversial because it appears to infringe on the free speech provision of the U.S. Constitution. While the courts have ruled that Napster must prevent users from freely trading copyrighted songs, other software (e.g., Aimster, Gnutella, Bearshear) has become available. File-sharing advocates argue that it's perfectly legal for consumers to copy music for their own noncommercial use. Critics suggest that other software will soon allow sharing of movies, books, and photos—all of which are likely to be protected by copyrights. Finally, some observers worry that whatever U.S. courts decide won't in-

fluence file-swapping services in other countries, like Israel-based iMesh or Canada-based WinMX. What solution would you recommend? If file-sharing were illegal in the U.S. would you use a service based in another country?

categories of products. The various federal consumer protection laws include more than 30 amendments and separate laws relating to food, drugs, and cosmetics, such as the *Poison Prevention Packaging Act* (1970), the *Infant Formula Act* (1980) and the *Nutritional Labeling and Education Act* (1990). Various other consumer protection laws have a broader scope, such as the *Fair Packaging and Labeling Act* (1966), the *Child Protection Act* (1966), and the *Consumer Product Safety Act* (1972), which established the Consumer Product Safety Commission to monitor product safety and establish uniform product safety standards. Many of these recent laws came about because of **consumerism**, a grassroots movement started in the 1960s to increase the influence, power, and rights of consumers in dealing with institutions. The *Clean Air Act* (1990), designed to curb acid rain and air pollution, the *Telephone Consumer Protection Act* (1991), focusing on telemarketing abuses, and the *Children's Online Privacy Protection Act* (1998), requiring parental permission before collecting personal information from minors,[44] are recent responses to consumer interests. This movement continues and is reflected in growing consumer demands for ecologically safe products, and ethical and socially responsible business practices. One hotly debated issue concerns liability for environmental abuse.

Both Company and Consumer Protection   Trademarks are intended to protect both the firm selling a trademarked product and the consumer buying it. A Senate report states that:

> The purposes underlying any trademark statute [are] twofold. One is to protect the public so that it may be confident that, in purchasing a product bearing a particular trademark which it favorably knows, it will get the product which it asks for and wants to get. Secondly, where the owner of a trademark has spent energy, time, and money in presenting to the public the product, he is protected in this investment from misappropriation in pirates and cheats.

These products are identified by protected trademarks. Are any of these trademarks in danger of becoming generic?

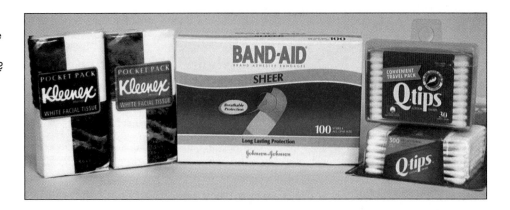

This statement was made in connection with another product-related law, the *Lanham Act* (1946), which provides for registration of a company's trademarks. Historically, the first user of a trademark in commerce had the exclusive right to use that particular word, name, or symbol in its business. Registration under the Lanham Act provides important advantages to a trademark owner that has used the trademark in interstate or foreign commerce, but it does not confer ownership. A company can lose its trademark if it becomes generic, which means that it has primarily come to be merely a common descriptive word for the product. Coca-Cola, Whopper, and Xerox are registered trademarks, and competitors cannot use these names. Aspirin and escalator are former trademarks that are now generic terms in the United States and can be used by anyone. In 1988, the *Trademark Law Revision Act* resulted in a major change to the Lanham Act—allowing a company to secure rights to a name before actual use by declaring an intent to use the name.[45]

One of the most recent changes in trademark law is the U.S. Supreme Court's ruling that companies may obtain trademarks for colors associated with their products. The reason is that, over time, consumers may begin to associate a particular color with a specific brand. Examples of products that may benefit from the new law include NutraSweet's sugar substitute in pastel blue packages and Owens-Corning Fiberglas Corporation's pink insulation.[46] Another area of growing interest is the registration of Internet addresses, or domain names, as trademarks.

Pricing-Related Legislation

The pricing component of the marketing mix is the focus of regulation from two perspectives: price fixing and price discounting. Although the Sherman Act did not outlaw price fixing, the courts view this behavior as *per se illegal* (*per se* means "through or of itself"), which means the courts see price fixing itself as illegal.

Certain forms of price discounting are allowed. Quantity discounts are acceptable; that is, buyers can be charged different prices for a product provided there are differences in manufacturing or delivery costs. Promotional allowances or services may be given to buyers on an equal basis proportionate to volume purchased. Also, a firm can meet a competitor's price "in good faith." Legal aspects of pricing are covered in more detail in Chapter 14.

Distribution-Related Legislation

The government has four concerns with regard to distribution—earlier referred to as "place" actions in the marketing mix—and the maintenance of competition. The first, *exclusive dealing*, is an arrangement with a buyer to handle only the products of one manufacturer and not those of competitors. This practice is only illegal under the Clayton Act when it substantially lessens competition.

Requirement contracts require a buyer to purchase all or part of its needs for a product from one seller for a period of time. These contracts are not always illegal but depend on the court's interpretation of their impact on distribution.

Exclusive territorial distributorships are a third distribution issue often under regulatory scrutiny. In this situation, a manufacturer grants a distributor the sole rights to sell a product in a specific geographical area. The courts have found few violations with these arrangements.

The fourth distribution strategy is a *tying arrangement,* whereby a seller requires the purchaser of one product to also buy another item in the line. These contracts may be illegal when the seller has such economic power in the tying product that the seller can restrain trade in the tied product. Legal aspects of distribution are reviewed in greater detail in Chapter 15.

Advertising- and Promotion-Related Legislation

Promotion and advertising are aspects of marketing closely monitored by the Federal Trade Commission (FTC), which was established by the *FTC Act of 1914.* The FTC has been concerned with deceptive or misleading advertising and unfair business practices and has the power to (1) issue cease and desist orders and (2) order corrective advertising. In issuing a *cease and desist order,* the FTC orders a company to stop practices it considers unfair. With *corrective advertising,* the FTC can require a company to spend money on advertising to correct previous misleading ads. The enforcement powers of the FTC are so significant that often just an indication of concern from the commission can cause companies to revise their promotion.

A landmark legal battle regarding deceptive advertising involved the Federal Trade Commission and Campbell Soup Co. It had been Campbell's practice to insert clear glass marbles into the bottom of soup containers used in print advertisements to bring the soup ingredients (for example, noodles or chicken) to the surface. The FTC ruled that the advertising was deceptive because it misrepresented the amount of solid ingredients in the soup, and it issued a cease and desist order. Campbell and its advertising agency agreed to discontinue the practice. Future ads used a ladle to show the ingredients.[47]

Other laws designed to regulate advertising practices include the *Federal Cigarette Labeling and Advertising Act* (1967), which requires health warnings on cigarette ads and packages, the *Public Health Cigarette Smoking Act* (1971), which prohibits advertising tobacco products on radio and television, and the *Children's Television Act* (1990), which limits the maximum amount of advertising during children's television programs to 10.5 minutes per hour on weekends and 12 minutes per hour on weekdays.

Control through Self-Regulation

The government has provided much legislation to create a competitive business climate and protect the consumer. An alternative to government control is **self-regulation**, where an industry attempts to police itself. The major television networks, for example, have used self-regulation to set their own guidelines for TV ads for children's toys. These guidelines have generally worked well. There are two problems with self-regulation, however: noncompliance by members and enforcement. In addition, if attempts at self-regulation are too strong, they may violate the Robinson-Patman Act. The best-known self-regulatory group is the Better Business Bureau (BBB). This agency is a voluntary alliance of companies whose goal is to help maintain fair practices. Although the BBB has no legal power, it does try to use "moral suasion" to get members to comply with its ruling. The BBB recently developed a reliability assurance program, called BBB Online, to provide objective consumer protection for Internet shoppers. Before they display the BBB Online logo on their

website, participating companies must be members of their local Better Business Bureau, have been in business for at least one year, have agreed to abide by BBB standards of truth in advertising, and have committed to work with the BBB to resolve consumer disputes that arise over goods or services promoted or advertised on their site.[48]

Concept Check

1. The _____ Act was punitive toward monopolies, whereas the _____ Act was preventive.

2. Describe some of the recent changes in trademark law.

3. How does the Better Business Bureau encourage companies to follow its standards for commerce?

SUMMARY

1 The population of the United States is aging as the over-65 population grows. Baby boomers, Generation X, and Generation Y are important target markets with very different interests as consumers. The structure of American families is changing as blended families become more common. The population is shifting to western and sunbelt states and to remote suburbs and small towns.

2 Recognition of racial, ethnic, and geographical differences in product preferences has given rise to companies developing tailored marketing plans.

3 Culture incorporates values, ideas, and attitudes. Womens' attitudes about their roles and products are changing. Common values include family, honesty, self-esteem, and health.

4 Disposable income is the number of dollars left after taxes. Discretionary income is the money consumers have after purchasing their necessities. The median gross income (dollars before taxes) of U.S. households has been stable since 1970 in real income terms.

5 Technology increases customer value by reducing the cost of products, providing new products, and improving existing products. The most important new development for marketers may be advances in electronic business technologies that allow improved communication with customers, employees, and suppliers.

6 Competition has caused corporations to utilize the Web as a management tool and become "network organizations."

7 The Sherman Antitrust Act of 1890 made monopolies illegal, whereas the Clayton Act tried to outlaw actions believed to lead to monopolies.

8 A company's brand name or symbol can be protected under the Lanham Act, but if the name becomes generic, the company no longer has sole right to the trademark.

9 Price fixing has been viewed as illegal by the courts. However, price discounting is allowed to meet competition or to account for differences in the cost of manufacture or distribution.

10 There are four aspects of distribution reviewed by courts: exclusive dealing arrangements, requirement contracts, exclusive territorial distributorships, and tying arrangements.

11 The Federal Trade Commission monitors unfair business practices and deceptive advertising. Two methods used in enforcement are (*a*) cease and desist orders and (*b*) corrective advertising.

12 Self-regulation attempts are common to some industries and are facilitated by organizations such as the Better Business Bureau. However, the effectiveness of self-regulation is coming under greater scrutiny by the courts.

KEY TERMS AND CONCEPTS

baby boomers p. 77
barriers to entry p. 88
blended family p. 78
commercial online services p. 86
competition p. 87
consumerism p. 91
culture p. 80
demographics p. 76
discretionary income p. 84
disposable income p. 84
economy p. 82
electronic commerce p. 86
environmental scanning p. 74
Extranets p. 87

Generation X p. 77
Generation Y p. 77
gross income p. 83
Internet p. 86
Intranet p. 87
marketspace p. 86
mature household p. 76
regional marketing p. 80
regulation p. 90
self-regulation p. 93
social forces p. 76
technology p. 85
value consciousness p. 82
World Wide Web p. 86

APPLYING MARKETING CONCEPTS AND PERSPECTIVES

1   For many years Gerber has manufactured baby food in small, single-sized containers. In conducting an environmental scan, identify three trends or factors that might significantly affect this company's future business, and then propose how Gerber might respond to these changes.

2   Describe the new features you would add to an automobile designed for the mature household. In what magazines would you advertise to appeal to this target market?

3   The population shift from suburbs to exurbs and penturbia was discussed in this chapter. What businesses and industries are likely to benefit from this trend? How will retailers need to change to accommodate these consumers?

4   New technologies are continuously improving and replacing existing products. Although technological change is often difficult to predict, suggest how the following companies and products might be affected by the Internet and digital technologies: (*a*) Kodak cameras and film, (*b*) American Airlines, and (*c*) the Metropolitan Museum of Art.

5   In recent years in the brewing industry, a couple of large firms that have historically had most of the beer sales (Anheuser-Busch and Miller) have faced competition from many small "micro" brands. In terms of the continuum of competition, how would you explain this change?

6   The Johnson Company manufactures buttons and pins with slogans and designs. These pins are inexpensive to produce and are sold in retail outlets such as discount stores, hobby shops, and bookstores. Little equipment is needed for a new competitor to enter the market. What strategies should Johnson consider to create effective barriers to entry?

7   Why would Xerox be concerned about its name becoming generic?

8   Develop a "Code of Business Practices" for a new online vitamin store. Does your code address advertising? Privacy? Use by children? Why is self-regulation important?

INTERNET EXERCISE

There are many sources of information that might be useful in an environmental scan. Two particularly useful websites include FEDSTATS (www.fedstats.gov) and *American Demographics* (www.demographics.com). The FEDSTATS page links 100 federal agencies including the U.S. Census Bureau, the Department of Commerce, and the Bureau of Labor Statistics. The *American Demographics* page provides text, tables, graphics, and a search tool for articles describing consumer trends. Use the sites to help answer the following questions:

1   What is the current (to the minute) population of the United States? The World? What is the projected population of the United States in 2050?

2   What social or consumer trends are described in a recent edition of *American Demographics*?

VIDEO CASE 3–1   Flyte Tyme Productions, Inc.: The Best Idea Wins!

"Terry was looking for a keyboard player to be in the band he was just starting," remembers Jimmy Jam of Flyte Tyme Productions, Inc. "I had sort of rebelled because I had first thought of myself as a drummer," says Jam. But after he listened and heard how good the drummer was, he told Terry, "I'll be the keyboard player."

The conversation took place a few weeks after Terry Lewis and Jimmy Jam met at a summer math program for gifted junior high school students, sponsored by a local university. The two came to prominence in the early 1980s as members of the funk band "The Time" that appeared as the opener on many of Prince's early tours. The pair still credit Prince for much of their tenacious work ethic and eclectic musical tastes. After leaving the band, Terry and Jimmy started a music production company—Flyte Tyme—creating the new name by adapting the old one. Now in their early 40s, the two have worked together for 20 years, most of it in Flyte Tyme Productions (www.flytetyme.com), where their clients include Mary J. Blige, Boyz II Men, Mariah Carey, Janet Jackson, Michael Jackson, Patti LaBelle, Usher, TLC, and many others!

THE MUSIC

Sunglasses, fedoras, and sharp suits are Jam and Lewis's signature image, but—curiously—they have no signature sound. Instead, their approach is to tailor tunes for each artist. Janet Jackson's steamy bedroom ballads don't sound anything like Patti LaBelle's big Diane Warren ballads. They also work in a wide variety of music genres—from gospel (Yolanda Adams) and reggae (Shaggy) to jazz (Herb Alpert) and pop (Mariah Carey).

Flyte Tyme's successes are impressive. Recently they produced Usher's No. 1 pop hit "U Remind Me," which held the top spot on the charts for four weeks. They also produced Sting's Oscar-nominated song "My Funny Friend and Me" for the film *The Emperor's New Groove*. And their work on Hikaru Utada's album helped it climb to the top of Japan's pop charts, selling 4 million copies in two weeks!

These and other hits put Flyte Tyme in extraordinary company. Having produced 16 No. 1 singles on *Billboard*'s pop chart, they are second only to the producer for the Beatles (with 23) and tied with the producer for Elvis Presley. Flyte Tyme has managed to stay at the top throughout the 1980s, '90s, and '00s, thanks in large part to Janet Jackson, who accounts for 10 of their 16 No. 1 songs. Recently, they wrote and produced their fifth successive album for Janet Jackson, which set an industry record when "All For You" became the first single to be played by 100 percent of the pop, R & B, and rhythm radio stations reporting to trade publication *Radio & Records*, in the first week after its release.

THE TEAM AND ITS FORMULA FOR SUCCESS

How have Jam and Lewis stayed at the top of the music game so long? Janet Jackson's answer: "There are no egos involved." Terry Lewis echoes this and says about his relationship with Jam: "He's the best partner a person could have. We've never had a contract—we've never had one argument in twenty-something years, not saying we don't disagree about things but our attitudes are the *best* idea wins. Not the right, not the wrong, but the *best*!"

"What we try to do is get everybody relaxed—check the egos at the door, that kind of thing. We find that we do it a lot more with new artists than with the older, more established artists," explains Jam. "Psychology is a big part of producing. Some artists like to work right away, others like to play pool, have lunch, talk on the phone, then they mosey in and record," he says. "If you think of Janet Jackson or Mariah Carey—the people who you would think of as superstars, you would think that they would bring a superstar ego with them. But it's almost the opposite," says Jam. "New artists often come to Flyte Tyme with a feeling they have to prove something. And what happens is, you don't really get a natural performance," says Jam.

Another of Flyte Tyme's special strengths: adapting the music and lyrics to an artist's unique talents, not the other way around. Their interest in many types of music and their experience with many artists allow them to add new ideas to the creative process. Still, Flyte Tyme may work on several different versions based on its perceptions of what radio stations or MTV will play.

Jam and Lewis work on both the music and lyrics for many of their songs, but Jam leans slightly more toward the melodies and Lewis toward the vocals and lyrics. In fact, Lewis keeps "The Book of Titles," and any time someone says something clever or in an interesting way it goes into the book. "Music is the soundtrack of life," says Lewis. "The inspiration for words I just take from watching people, and life has a lot of verses in it," he adds.

MARKETING, DISTRIBUTION, COMPETITION

Selecting the best music ideas requires an instinct to find the right blend of art and business. The elements of the art include a huge respect for and understanding of the artists, an interest in a broad palette of musical sounds, and a good ear for melodies and vocals. The business components of their formula include understanding many of the factors—such as marketing, distribution, and competition—that influence their business.

Music artists walking in the door of Flyte Tyme receive an array of services: A studio facility with Jam, Lewis, and an experienced staff providing ideas, direction, and focus—"trying to get things out of them they didn't know they had in them," says Lewis. Flyte Tyme

Records, the marketing arm, develops the artist's image, the marketing plan, advertising, and distribution—everything to get the record or CD on the rack to be sold. "If you have $100,000 to spend on promotion, you can do a nice music video and then you can spend a lot of time trying to get it played on MTV or BET or VH1 or any of the appropriate video channels," says Jam. Or sometimes the music calls for a different strategy, Flyte Tyme's "groundhog approach." For example, in the early 1990s with one of its bands, Flyte Tyme piled the band in a Winnebago and hit college campuses.

Today Flyte Tyme creates a lot of that same groundhog buzz with its website, where the music audience can learn about Flyte Tyme's artists and activities. Jam and Lewis note that Napster was a great tool in exposing music to the public. The delivery system—buying an album at a retail store, downloading music from the Internet, or burning a CD—doesn't affect the process of Flyte Tyme's making the music in its studio. But Lewis and Jam are concerned that the people who write the songs and the artists who deliver them get compensated fairly. "The record companies and everybody will eventually work it out," says Jam. "They have to because it's too valuable a commodity not to."

Questions

1 Based on the case information and what you know about today's music industry, conduct an environmental scan for Flyte Tyme to identify key trends. For each of the five environmental forces (social, economic, technological, competitive, and regulatory), identify trends likely to influence it in the near future.

2 Compared to many start-up businesses—80 percent of which fail within 5 years—what reasons explain Flyte Tyme's continuing success?

3 What marketing factors and actions must Jimmy Jam and Terry Lewis consider in developing music (*a*) for a new, unknown artist and (*b*) an established artist like Janet Jackson?

4 What promotional and distribution strategies should Flyte Tyme use to get its music in front of prospective buyers?

TEENAGE DRINKING IS DOWN BECAUSE PARENTS ARE DOING THEIR
HOMEWORK.

Susan knows if Emily has all the facts, she'll make a better decision about any subject. Even underage drinkir
So she took advantage of "Family Talk About Drinking," a free guide offered by Anheuser-Busch
to help parents talk to their kids. In the past decade alone, Anheuser-Busch and its distributors
have provided more than 5.2 million guides. It's people like Susan and programs like this
that have helped reduce teenage drinking by 47% since 1982.*

TEENAGE DRINKING DOWN 47%

For a free family guidebook, call 1-800-359-TALK, or download it at www.beeresponsible.com.

WE ALL MAKE A DIFFERENCE.®

CHAPTER

4 ETHICS AND SOCIAL RESPONSIBILITY IN MARKETING

AFTER READING THIS CHAPTER YOU SHOULD BE ABLE TO:

- Appreciate the nature and significance of ethics in marketing.

- Understand the differences between legal and ethical behavior in marketing.

- Identify factors that influence ethical and unethical marketing decisions.

- Distinguish among the different concepts of ethics and social responsibility.

- Recognize the importance of ethical and socially responsible consumer behavior.

THERE IS MORE TO ANHEUSER-BUSCH THAN MEETS THE PALATE

Why would a company spend more than $375 million since 1982 trying to convince people not to abuse its products and millions more to decrease litter and solid waste? Ask Anheuser-Busch, the world's largest brewer.

Anheuser-Busch has been an advocate for responsible drinking for two decades. The company began an aggressive campaign to fight alcohol abuse and underage drinking with its landmark "Know When to Say When" campaign in 1982. In 1989, a Consumer Awareness and Education Department was established within the company. This department was charged with developing and implementing programs, advertising and partnerships that promote responsible drinking, helping prevent alcohol abuse, and helping stop underage drinking before it starts. For example, more than 5.3 million copies of the company's *Family Talk About Drinking* guidebook have been distributed to parents and educators in the past decade. In 1999, the brewer began a new chapter in its awareness and education efforts with the launch of its "We All Make a Difference" advertising campaign. This effort reinforced the good practices of drinkers who exercise personal responsibility, designate a driver or call a cab, and salutes parents who talk to their children about illegal underage drinking. Anheuser-Busch believes these efforts have contributed to a sizable decline in drunk-driving accidents and a 64 percent drop in teenage drunk-driving deaths since 1982.

Responsibility at Anheuser-Busch is broader than its successful alcohol awareness and education initiatives. The company is an advocate and sponsor of numerous efforts to preserve the natural environment. A notable example is its massive recycling effort through Anheuser-

Busch Recycling Corporation (ABRC). ABRC is the world's largest recycler of aluminum cans. ABRC recycles over 700 million pounds of aluminum annually—the equivalent of about 120 percent of the beer cans Anheuser-Busch ships domestically. The rationale for founding ABRC was simple: voluntary recycling reduces litter and solid waste while conserving natural resources.

Anheuser-Busch acts on what it views as an ethical obligation to its customers and the general public with its alcohol awareness and education programs. At the same time, the company's efforts to protect the environment reflect its broader social responsibility.[1]

NATURE AND SIGNIFICANCE OF MARKETING ETHICS

Ethics are the moral principles and values that govern the actions and decisions of an individual or group.[2] They serve as guidelines on how to act rightly and justly when faced with moral dilemmas.

Ethical/Legal Framework in Marketing

A good starting point for understanding the nature and significance of ethics is the distinction between legality and ethicality of marketing decisions. Figure 4–1 helps visualize the relationship between laws and ethics.[3] Whereas ethics deal with personal moral principles and values, **laws** are society's values and standards that are enforceable in the courts. This distinction can sometimes lead to the rationalization that if a behavior is within reasonable ethical and legal limits, then it is not really illegal or unethical. When a recent survey asked the question, "Is it OK to get around the law if you don't actually break it?" 61 percent of businesspeople who took part responded "Yes."[4] How would you answer this question?

There are numerous situations in which judgment plays a large role in defining ethical and legal boundaries. Consider the following situations. After reading each, assign it to the cell in Figure 4–1 that you think best fits the situation along the ethical–legal continuum.[5]

1. More than 70 percent of the physicians in the Maricopa County (Arizona) Medical Society agreed to establish a maximum fee schedule for health services to curb rising medical costs. All physicians were required to adhere to this schedule as a condition for membership in the society. The U.S. Supreme Court ruled that this agreement to set prices violated the Sherman Act and represented price fixing, which is illegal.

2. A company in California sells a computer program to auto dealers showing that car buyers should finance their purchase rather than paying cash. The program omits the effect of income taxes and misstates the interest earned on savings over the loan period. The finance option always provides a net benefit over the cash option. Company employees agree that the program does mislead buyers, but say the company will "provide what [car dealers] want as long as it is not against the law."

3. China is the world's largest tobacco-producing country and has 300 million smokers. Approximately 700,000 Chinese die annually from smoking-related illnesses. This figure is expected to rise to more than 2 million by 2025. China restricts tobacco imports. U.S. trade negotiators advocate free trade, thus allowing U.S. tobacco companies to market their products in China. Critics say that the U.S. government should not assist in the promotion of smoking in China.

Did these situations fit neatly into Figure 4–1 as clearly ethical and legal or unethical and illegal? Probably not. As you read further in this chapter, you will be asked to consider other ethical dilemmas.

FIGURE 4–1

Classifying marketing decisions according to ethical and legal relationships

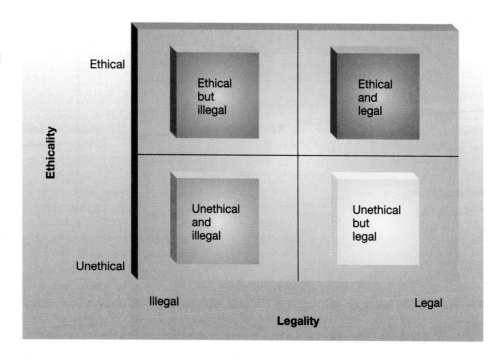

Current Perceptions of Ethical Behavior

There has been a public outcry about the ethical practices of businesspeople.[6] Public opinion surveys show that 58 percent of U.S. adults rate the ethical standards of business executives as only "fair" or "poor"; 90 percent think white-collar crime is "very common" or "somewhat common"; 76 percent say the lack of ethics in businesspeople contributes to tumbling societal moral standards; only the U.S. government is viewed as less trustworthy than corporations among institutions in the United States; and advertising practitioners, insurance agents, and car salespeople are thought to be among the least ethical occupations. A recent survey of 1,694 corporate employees generally confirms this public perception. When asked if they were aware of ethical problems in their companies, 41 percent answered yes.

There are at least four possible reasons the state of perceived ethical business conduct is at its present level. First, there is increased pressure on businesspeople to make decisions in a society characterized by diverse value systems. Second, there is a growing tendency for business decisions to be judged publicly by groups with different values and interests. Third, the public's expectations of ethical business behavior has increased. Finally, and most disturbing, ethical business conduct may have declined.

Concept Check

1. What are ethics?

2. What are four possible reasons for the present state of ethical conduct in the United States?

UNDERSTANDING ETHICAL MARKETING BEHAVIOR

Researchers have identified numerous factors that influence ethical marketing behavior.[7] Figure 4–2 presents a framework that shows these factors and their relationships.

FIGURE 4–2

A framework for
understanding ethical
behavior

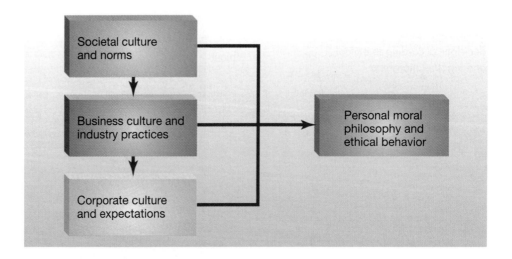

Societal Culture and Norms

As described in Chapter 3, *culture* refers to the set of values, ideas, and attitudes of
a homogeneous group of people that are transmitted from one generation to the next.
Culture also serves as a socializing force that dictates what is morally right and just.
This means that moral standards are relative to particular societies.[8] These standards
often reflect the laws and regulations that affect social and economic behavior, which
can create moral dilemmas. For example, Levi Strauss decided to end much of its
business dealings in China because of what the company called "pervasive human
rights abuses." According to its vice president for corporate marketing: "There are
wonderful commercial opportunities in China. But when ethical issues collide with
commercial appeal, we try to ensure ethics as the trump card. For us, ethical issues
precede all others."[9]

Societal values also affect ethical and legal relationships among individuals,
groups, and the institutions and organizations they create, including business practices. Consider the use of another's ideas, copyright, trademark, or patent. These are
viewed as intellectual property, and unauthorized use is deemed unethical and illegal in the United States. However, this is not the case elsewhere.[10] In Korea, for
instance, copying is partly rooted in its society's culture. According to a U.S. trade
official, many Koreans "have the idea that the thoughts of one man should benefit
all," and the Korean government rarely prosecutes infringements. United States companies estimate that the unauthorized use of their intellectual property in global markets costs them $250 billion annually in lost revenue.

Copyright infringement in the global business software industry is particularly
widespread with the explosive growth of the Internet. Copies of software can be distributed and downloaded quickly and globally, with the click of a mouse. Read the
accompanying Marketing NewsNet to find out where the unauthorized use of business software is most prevalent.[11]

Business Culture and Industry Practices

Societal culture provides a foundation for understanding moral behavior in business
activities. *Business cultures* "comprise the effective rules of the game, the boundaries between competitive and unethical behavior, [and] the codes of conduct in business dealings."[12] Consumers have witnessed numerous instances where business cultures in the brokerage (inside trading), insurance (deceptive sales practices), and
defense (bribery) industries went awry. Business culture affects ethical conduct both
in the exchange relationship between sellers and buyers and in the competitive
behavior among sellers.

MARKETING NEWSNET

Global Business Software Piracy

TECHNOLOGY & E-COMMERCE

By 2005, the Internet will link an estimated 1.17 billion Internet users worldwide. The many benefits of the Internet often overshadow its dark side: business software piracy. The explosive growth of the Internet is making piracy easy, because pirated copies of software can be distributed and downloaded quickly and globally, with the click of a mouse. The Software & Information Industry Association (SIIA) and the Business Software Alliance (BSA) estimate that one in every three business software applications in use in the world is pirated. Piracy means lost jobs, wages, tax revenues, and a potential barrier to success for software start-up companies around the globe.

It is estimated that the unauthorized copying of business software costs U.S. producers about $12 billion in worldwide sales annually. Software piracy has become pandemic in many countries. According to SIIA/BSA estimates, 70 percent of the software in eastern Europe is pirated followed by a piracy rate of 60 percent in the Middle East and 59 percent in Africa and Latin America. Countries with the highest piracy rates are Vietnam (98 percent), China

(91 percent), Russia (89 percent), and Lebanon and Oman (88 percent each). For comparison, the piracy rate in the United States is 25 percent and Canada, 41 percent.

Ethics of Exchange   The exchange process is central to the marketing concept. Ethical exchanges between sellers and buyers should result in both parties being better off after a transaction.

Prior to the 1960s, the legal concept of **caveat emptor**—let the buyer beware—was pervasive in the American business culture. In 1962 President John F. Kennedy outlined a **Consumer Bill of Rights** that codified the ethics of exchange between buyers and sellers. These were the right (1) to safety, (2) to be informed, (3) to choose, and (4) to be heard. Consumers expect and often demand that these rights be protected, as have American businesses.

The right to safety manifests itself in industry and federal safety standards for most products sold in the United States. In fact, the U.S. Consumer Product Safety Commission routinely monitors the safety of 15,000 consumer products. However, even the most vigilant efforts to ensure safe products cannot foresee every possibility. Mattel's experience with its Cabbage Patch Snacktime Kids doll is a case in point.[13] The doll was designed to "eat" plastic french fries, celery, and other tidbits by drawing them into its motorized mouth. Despite exhaustive laboratory and in-home testing, Mattel executives did not consider that a child's hair might get caught in the doll's mouth and cause harm. It did! Mattel immediately informed buyers of the safety issue, pulled the dolls from store shelves, refunded buyers, and discontinued the product.

The right to be informed means that marketers have an obligation to give consumers complete and accurate information about products and services, but this is not always the case. For example, three U.S. advertising agencies recently agreed to settle Federal Trade Commission (FTC) claims that they failed to disclose the actual costs of car leases and credit transactions in their advertising for three Japanese car

The Federal Trade Commission plays an active role in educating consumers and businesses about the importance of personal information privacy on the Internet. FTC initiatives are detailed on its website.

Federal Trade Commission
www.ftc.gov

makers.[14] This right also applies to the solicitation of personal information over the Internet and its subsequent use by marketers.[15] A FTC survey of websites indicated that 92 percent collect personal information such as consumer e-mail addresses, telephone numbers, shopping habits, and financial data. Yet, only two-thirds of websites inform consumers of what is done with this information once obtained. The FTC wants more than posted privacy notices that merely inform consumers of a company's data-use policy, which critics say are often vague, confusing, or too legalistic to be understood. This view is shared by two-thirds of consumers who worry about protecting their personal information online. The consumer right to be informed has spawned numerous federal legislation, such as the Children's Online Privacy Protection Act, and self-regulation initiatives restricting disclosure of personal information.

Relating to the third right, today many supermarket chains demand "slotting allowances" from manufacturers, in the form of cash or free goods, to stock new products.[16] This practice could limit the number of new products available to consumers and interfere with their right to choose. One critic of this practice remarked: "If we had had slotting allowances a few years ago, we might not have had granola, herbal tea, or yogurt."

Finally, the right to be heard means that consumers should have access to public-policy makers regarding complaints about products and services. This right is illustrated in limitations put on telemarketing practices. Consumer complaints about late-night and repeated calls resulted in the Telephone Consumer Protection Act of 1991. Additional curbs on misrepresentation have been enacted by the FTC as a result of continued consumer complaints.

Ethics of Competition   Business culture also affects ethical behavior in competition. Two kinds of unethical behavior are most common: (1) economic espionage and (2) bribery.

Economic espionage is the clandestine collection of trade secrets or proprietary information about a company's competitors. This practice is illegal and unethical and carries serious criminal penalties for the offending individual or business.[17] Espionage activities include illegal trespassing, theft, fraud, misrepresentation, wiretapping, the search of a competitor's trash, and violations of written and implicit employment agreements with non-compete clauses. About 50 percent of large U.S. and Canadian firms have uncovered espionage in some form, costing them more than $100 billion annually in lost sales.

Economic espionage is most prevalent in high-technology industries such as electronics, specialty chemicals, industrial equipment, aerospace, and pharmaceuticals, where technical know-how and trade secrets separate industry leaders from followers. But espionage can occur anywhere—even in the ready-to-eat cookie industry! Procter & Gamble charged that competitors photographed its plants and production lines, stole a sample of its cookie dough, and infiltrated a confidential sales presentation to learn about its technology, recipe, and marketing plan. The competitors paid Procter & Gamble $120 million in damages after a lengthy dispute.[18]

The second form of unethical competitive behavior is giving and receiving bribes and kickbacks. Bribes and kickbacks are often disguised as gifts, consultant fees, and favors. This practice is more common in business-to-business and government marketing than in consumer marketing. For example, two American Honda Motor

WEB LINK   The Corruption Perceptions Index

Bribery as a means to win and retain business varies widely by country. Transparency International, based in Germany, periodically polls employees of multinational firms and institutions, and political analysts and ranks countries on the basis of their perceived level of bribery to win or retain business. To obtain the most recent ranking, visit the Transparency International website at www.transparency.org and click Info Center.

Scroll the Corruption Perceptions Index to see where the United States stands in the worldwide rankings as well as its neighbors, Canada and Mexico. Any surprises? Which country listed in the most recent ranking has the highest ranking and which has the lowest ranking?

Company executives were recently fined and sentenced to prison for extracting $15 million in kickbacks from Honda dealers and advertising agencies, and a series of highly publicized trials uncovered widespread bribery in the U.S. Defense Department's awarding of $160 billion in military contracts.[19]

In general, bribery is most evident in industries experiencing intense competition and in countries in earlier stages of economic development. According to a recent United Nations' study, 15 percent of all companies in industrialized countries have to pay bribes to win or retain business. In Asia, this figure is 40 percent. In countries of the former Soviet Union, 60 percent of all companies must pay bribes to do business! A recent poll of senior executives engaged in global marketing revealed that Cameroon and Nigeria were the most likely countries to evidence bribery to win or retain business. Denmark and Finland were the least likely.[20] Bribery on a worldwide scale is monitored by Transparency International. Visit its website described in the accompanying Web Link box, and view the most recent country rankings on this practice.

The prevalence of economic espionage and bribery in international marketing has prompted laws to curb these practices. Two significant laws, the Economic Espionage Act and the Foreign Corrupt Practices Act, address these practices in the United States. Both are detailed in Chapter 7, Reaching Global Markets.

Corporate Culture and Expectations

A third influence on ethical practices is corporate culture. *Corporate culture* reflects the shared values, beliefs, and purpose of employees that affect individual and group behavior. The culture of a company demonstrates itself in the dress ("We don't wear ties"), sayings ("The IBM Way"), and manner of work (team efforts) of employees. Culture is also apparent in the expectations for ethical behavior present in formal codes of ethics and the ethical actions of top management and co-workers.

Codes of Ethics   A **code of ethics** is a formal statement of ethical principles and rules of conduct. It is estimated that 80 percent of U.S. companies have some sort of ethics code and one of every five large companies has corporate ethics officers. At United Technologies, for example, 160 corporate ethics officers distribute the

CODE OF ETHICS

Members of the American Marketing Association (AMA) are committed to ethical professional conduct. They have joined together in subscribing to this Code of Ethics embracing the following topics:

Responsibilities of the Marketer   Marketers must accept responsibility for the consequence of their activities and make every effort to ensure that their decisions, recommendations, and actions function to identify, serve, and satisfy all relevant publics: customers, organizations, and society.
Marketers' professional conduct must be guided by:

1. The basic rule of professional ethics: not knowingly to do harm.
2. The adherence to all applicable laws and regulations.
3. The accurate representation of their education, training, and experience.
4. The active support, practice, and promotion of this Code of Ethics.

Honesty and Fairness   Marketers shall uphold and advance the integrity, honor, and dignity of the marketing profession by:

1. Being honest in serving consumers, clients, employees, suppliers, distributors, and the public.

2. Not knowingly participating in conflict of interest without prior notice to all parties involved.
3. Establishing equitable fee schedules including the payment or receipt of usual, customary, and/or legal compensation or marketing exchanges.

Rights and Duties of Parties in the Marketing Exchange Process   Participants in the marketing exchange process should be able to expect that:

1. Products and services offered are safe and fit for their intended uses.
2. Communications about offered products and services are not deceptive.
3. All parties intend to discharge their obligations, financial and otherwise, in good faith.
4. Appropriate internal methods exist for equitable adjustment and/or redress of grievances concerning purchases.

It is understood that the above would include, *but is not limited to,* the following responsibilities of the marketer:

In the area of product development and management

- Disclosure of all substantial risks associated with product or service usage.
- Identification of any product component substitution that might materially change the product or impact on the buyer's purchase decision.
- Identification of extra-cost added features.

FIGURE 4–3
American Marketing
Association Code of Ethics

**American Marketing
Association**

www.marketingpower.com

company's ethics code, translated into 24 languages, to employees who work for this defense and engineering giant around the world.[21] Ethics codes and committees typically address contributions to government officials and political parties, relations with customers and suppliers, conflicts of interest, and accurate recordkeeping. For example, General Mills provides guidelines for dealing with suppliers, competitors, and customers, and recruits new employees who share these views. However, an ethics code is rarely enough to ensure ethical behavior. Johnson & Johnson has an ethics code and emphasizes that its employees be just and ethical in their behavior. But neither prohibited some of its employees from shredding papers to hinder a recent government probe into the firm's marketing of an acne cream, Retin-A.[22]

The lack of specificity is one of the major reasons for the violation of ethics codes.[23] Employees must often judge whether a specific behavior is really unethical. The American Marketing Association has addressed this issue by providing a detailed code of ethics, which all members agree to follow. This code is shown in Figure 4–3.

Ethical Behavior of Top Management and Co-Workers   A second reason for violating ethics codes rests in the perceived behavior of top management and co-workers.[24] Observing peers and top management and gauging responses to unethical behavior play an important role in individual actions. A recent study of business executives reported that 40 percent had been implicitly or explicitly rewarded for engaging in ethically troubling behavior. Moreover, 31 percent of those who refused to engage in unethical behavior were penalized, either through outright punishment or a diminished status in the company.[25] Clearly, ethical dilemmas often bring personal and

FIGURE 4–3
(Continued)

In the area of promotions

- Avoidance of false and misleading advertising.
- Rejection of high-pressure manipulation, or misleading sales tactics.
- Avoidance of sales promotions that use deception or manipulation.

In the area of distribution

- Not manipulating the availability of a product for purpose of exploitation.
- Not using coercion in the marketing channel.
- Not exerting undue influence over the reseller's choice to handle the product.

In the area of pricing

- Not engaging in price fixing.
- Not practicing predatory pricing.
- Disclosing the full price associated with any purchase.

In the area of marketing research

- Prohibiting selling or fund raising under the guise of conducting research.

- Maintaining research integrity by avoiding misrepresentation and omission of pertinent research data.
- Treating outside clients and suppliers fairly.

Organizational Relationships   Marketers should be aware of how their behavior may influence or impact on the behavior of others in organizational relationships. They should not demand, encourage, or apply coercion to obtain unethical behavior in their relationships with others, such as employees, suppliers, or customers.

1. Apply confidentiality and anonymity in professional relationships with regard to privileged information.
2. Meet their obligations and responsibilities in contracts and mutual agreements in a timely manner.
3. Avoid taking the work of others, in whole or in part, and represent this work as their own or directly benefit from it without compensation or consent of the originator or owner.
4. Avoid manipulation to take advantage of situations to maximize personal welfare in a way that unfairly deprives or damages the organization or others.

Any AMA members found to be in violation of any provision of this Code of Ethics may have his or her Association membership suspended or revoked.

professional conflict. For this reason, 35 states have laws protecting **whistle-blowers**, employees who report unethical or illegal actions of their employers. Some firms, such as General Dynamics and Dun & Bradstreet, have appointed ethics officers responsible for safeguarding these individuals from recrimination.

Personal Moral Philosophy and Ethical Behavior

Ultimately, ethical choices are based on the personal moral philosophy of the decision maker. Moral philosophy is learned through the process of socialization with friends and family and by formal education. It is also influenced by the societal, business, and corporate culture in which a person finds him- or herself.[26] Two prominent personal moral philosophies have direct bearing on marketing practice: (1) moral idealism and (2) utilitarianism.[27]

Moral Idealism   **Moral idealism** is a personal moral philosophy that considers certain individual rights or duties as universal, regardless of the outcome. This philosophy exists in the Consumer Bill of Rights and is favored by moral philosophers and consumer interest groups. For example, the right to know applies to probable defects in an automobile that relate to safety.

This philosophy also applies to ethical duties. A fundamental ethical duty is to do no harm. Adherence to this duty prompted the recent decision by 3M executives to phase out production of a chemical 3M had manufactured for nearly 40 years. The substance, used in far-ranging products from pet food bags, candy wrappers, carpeting, and 3M's popular Scotchguard fabric protector, had no known harmful health or environmental effect. However, the company discovered that the chemical appeared in miniscule amounts in humans and animals around the world and accumulated in tissue. Believing that the substance could be possibly harmful in large doses, 3M voluntarily stopped its production acknowledging that the outcome of this action was a potential loss of $500 million in annual sales.[28]

Utilitarianism   An alternative perspective on moral philosophy is **utilitarianism**, which is a personal moral philosophy that focuses on "the greatest good for the greatest number," by assessing the costs and benefits of the consequences of ethical behavior. If the benefits exceed the costs, then the behavior is ethical. If not, then the behavior is unethical. This philosophy underlies the economic tenets of capitalism and, not surprisingly, is embraced by many business executives and students.[29]

Utilitarian reasoning was apparent in Nestlé Food Corporation's marketing of Good Start infant formula, sold by Nestlé's Carnation Company. The formula, promoted as hypoallergenic, was designed to prevent or reduce colic caused by an infant's allergic reaction to cow's milk—a condition suffered by 2 percent of babies. However, some severely milk-allergic infants experienced serious side effects after using Good Start, including convulsive vomiting. Physicians and parents charged that the hypoallergenic claim was misleading, and the Food and Drug Administration investigated the matter. A Nestlé vice president defended the claim and product, saying, "I don't understand why our product should work in 100 percent of cases. If we wanted to say it was foolproof, we would have called it allergy-free. We call it hypo-, or less, allergenic."[30] Nestlé officials seemingly believed that most allergic infants would benefit from Good Start—"the greatest good for the greatest number." However, other views prevailed, and the claim was dropped from the product label.

An appreciation for the nature of ethics, coupled with a basic understanding of why unethical behavior arises, alerts a person to when and how ethical issues exist in marketing decisions. Ultimately, ethical behavior rests with the individual, but the consequences affect many.

Concept Check

1. What rights are included in the Consumer Bill of Rights?

2. Economic espionage includes what kinds of activities?

3. What is meant by moral idealism?

UNDERSTANDING SOCIAL RESPONSIBILITY IN MARKETING

As we saw in Chapter 1, the societal marketing concept stresses marketing's social responsibility by not only satisfying the needs of consumers but also providing for society's welfare. **Social responsibility** means that organizations are part of a larger society and are accountable to that society for their actions. Like ethics, agreement on the nature and scope of social responsibility is often difficult to come by, given the diversity of values present in different societal, business, and corporate cultures.[31]

Concepts of Social Responsibility

Figure 4–4 shows three concepts of social responsibility: (1) profit responsibility, (2) stakeholder responsibility, and (3) societal responsibility.

FIGURE 4–4
Three concepts of social
responsibility

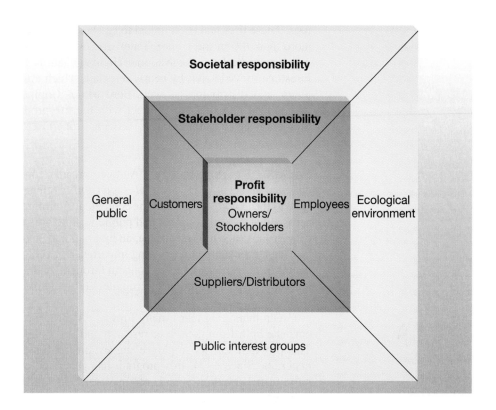

Profit Responsibility   *Profit responsibility* holds that companies have a simple duty—to maximize profits for their owners or stockholders. This view is expressed by Nobel Laureate Milton Friedman, who said, "There is one and only one social responsibility of business—to use its resources and engage in activities designed to increase its profits so long as it stays within the rules of the game, which is to say, engages in open and free competition without deception or fraud."[32] Genzyme, the maker of Ceredase, a drug that treats a genetic illness called Gaucher's disease that affects 20,000 people worldwide, has been criticized for apparently adopting this view in its pricing practices. Genzyme charges up to $200,000 for a year's worth of Ceredese. Critics claim this practice takes advantage of the federal "orphan drug" law, which grants companies a seven-year monopoly on drugs for rare diseases, and is engaged in profiteering. A Genzyme spokesperson responded by saying that Ceredase profits are below industry standards and that the company freely gives the drug to patients without insurance.[33]

Stakeholder Responsibility   Frequent criticism of the profit view has led to a broader concept of social responsibility. *Stakeholder responsibility* focuses on the obligations an organization has to those who can affect achievement of its objectives. These constituencies include customers, employees, suppliers, and distributors. Source Perrier S.A., the supplier of Perrier bottled water, exercised this responsibility when it recalled 160 million bottles of water in 120 countries after traces of a toxic chemical were found in 13 bottles. The recall cost the company $35 million, and $40 million more was lost in sales. Even though the chemical level was not harmful to humans, Source Perrier's president believed he acted in the best interests of the firm's consumers, distributors, and employees by removing "the least doubt, as minimal as it might be, to weigh on the image of the quality and purity of our product"—which it did.[34]

Failure to consider a company's broader constituencies can have negative consequences. For example, Bridgestone/Firestone, Inc., executives were widely criticized for how they responded to complaints about the safety of selected Firestone-brand tires. These tires had been linked to crashes that killed at least 174 people and injured more than 700 in the United States. In 2000, the company recalled 6.5 million tires under pressure from the National Highway Traffic Administration. After the recall, Firestone tire sales fell by nearly one-half, which affected Firestone employees, suppliers, and distributors as well. Ford Motor Company, a large buyer of Firestone tires, ended its exclusive contract with the tire producer and began using Michelin tires on selected 2002 vehicles.[35] Bridgestone/Firestone subsequently stopped selling its tires to Ford entirely.

Societal Responsibility   An even broader concept of social responsibility has emerged in recent years. *Societal responsibility* refers to obligations that organizations have to the (1) preservation of the ecological environment and (2) general public. Concerns about the environment and public welfare are represented by interest and advocacy groups such as Greenpeace, an international environmental organization.

Chapter 3 detailed the growing importance of ecological issues in marketing. Companies have responded to this concern through what is termed **green marketing**—marketing efforts to produce, promote, and reclaim environmentally sensitive products.

Green marketing takes many forms.[36] At 3M, product development opportunities emanate both from consumer research and its "Pollution Prevention Pays" program. This program solicits employee suggestions on how to reduce pollution and recycle materials. Since 1974, this program has generated over 4,000 ideas that eliminated more than 1.6 billion pounds of air, water, and solid waste pollutants from the environment. Xerox's "Design for the Environment" program focuses on ways to make its equipment recyclable and remanufacturable. Today, 90 percent of Xerox-designed products are remanufacturable. Home Depot, the home-and-garden center chain, discontinued the sale of wood products from endangered forests in 2002. The aluminum industry recycles two-thirds of aluminum cans for reuse and pays consumers more than $1 billion annually for used cans. These voluntary responses to environmental issues have been implemented with little or no additional cost to consumers.

A global undertaking to further green marketing efforts is the ISO 14000 initiative developed by the International Standards Organization (ISO) in Geneva, Switzerland. **ISO 14000** consists of worldwide standards for environmental quality and green marketing practices. These standards are embraced by 84 countries, including the United States, members of the European Union, and many Pacific Rim nations. Over 14,000 companies around the world have met ISO 14000 standards for environmental quality and green marketing. About 20 percent of all ISO 14000 certified companies are Japanese firms making Japan a world leader in environmental protection.[37]

Socially responsible efforts on behalf of the general public are becoming more common. A formal practice is **cause-related marketing**, which occurs when the charitable contributions of a firm are tied directly to the customer revenues produced through the promotion of one of its products.[38] This definition distinguishes cause-related marketing from a firm's standard charitable contributions, which are outright donations. For example, Procter & Gamble raises funds for the Special Olympics when consumers purchase selected company products, and MasterCard International links usage of its card with fund raising for institutions that combat cancer, heart disease, child abuse, drug abuse, and muscular dystrophy. Barnes & Noble promotes literacy, and Coca-Cola sponsors local Boys and Girls Clubs. Avon Products, Inc., focuses on different issues in different countries: breast cancer in the United States, Canada, Philippines, Mexico, Venezuela, Malaysia, and Spain; programs for women who care for senior citizens in Japan; emotional and financial support for mothers in Germany; and AIDS in Thailand. Cause-related marketing programs incorporate all three concepts of social responsibility by addressing public concerns and satisfying customer needs. They can also enhance corporate sales and profits as described in the accompanying Marketing NewsNet.[39]

MARKETING NEWSNET

Will Consumers Switch Brands for a Cause? Yes, If . . .

CUSTOMER VALUE

American Express Company pioneered cause-related marketing (CRM) when it sponsored the renovation of the Statue of Liberty. This effort raised $1.7 million for the renovation, increased card usage among cardholders, and attracted new cardholders. In 2001, U.S. companies raised more than $5 billion for causes they champion. It is estimated that CRM will raise over $8 billion in 2005.

Cause-related marketing benefits companies as well as causes. Research indicates that 82 percent of U.S. consumers say they have a more favorable opinion of companies that support causes. Also, 67 percent of consumers say they will switch to a brand or retailer that supports a good cause if the price and quality of brands or retailers are equal. In short, CRM may be a valued point of difference for brands and companies, all other things being equal.

For more information, including news, links, and case studies, visit the Cause Related Marketing Campaign website at www.crm.org.uk.

The Social Audit: Doing Well by Doing Good

Converting socially responsible ideas into actions involves careful planning and monitoring of programs. Many companies develop, implement, and evaluate their social responsibility efforts by means of a **social audit**, which is a systematic assessment of a firm's objectives, strategies, and performance in the domain of social responsibility. Frequently, marketing and social responsibility programs are integrated, as is the case with McDonald's. The company's concern for the needs of families with children who are chronically or terminally ill was converted into some 200 Ronald McDonald Houses around the world. These facilities, located near treatment centers, enable families to stay together during the child's care. In this case, McDonald's is contributing to the welfare of a portion of its target market.

A social audit consists of five steps:[40]

1. Recognition of a firm's social expectations and the rationale for engaging in social responsibility endeavors.
2. Identification of social responsibility causes or programs consistent with the company's mission.
3. Determination of organizational objectives and priorities for programs and activities it will undertake.
4. Specification of the type and amount of resources necessary to achieve social responsibility objectives.
5. Evaluation of social responsibility programs and activities undertaken and assessment of future involvement.

Corporate attention to social audits will increase as companies seek to achieve sustainable development and improve the quality of life in a global economy. **Sustainable development** involves conducting business in a way that protects the natural environment while making economic progress. Ecologically responsible

Marketing and social responsibility programs are often integrated, as is the case with McDonald's. Its concern for ill children is apparent in the opening of another Ronald McDonald House for children and their families.

McDonald's

www.mcdonalds.com

initiatives such as green marketing represent one such initiative. Recent initiatives related to working conditions at offshore manufacturing sites that produce goods for U.S. companies focus on quality-of-life issues. Public opinion surveys show that 90 percent of U.S. citizens are concerned about working conditions under which products are made in Asia and Latin America. Companies such as Reebok, Nike, Liz Claiborne, Levi Strauss, and Mattel have responded by imposing codes of conduct to reduce harsh or abusive working conditions at offshore manufacturing facilities.[41] Reebok, for example, now monitors production of its sporting apparel and equipment to ensure that no child labor is used in making its products.

Companies that evidence societal responsibility have been rewarded for their efforts. Research has shown that these companies (1) benefit from favorable word-of-mouth among consumers and (2) typically outperform less responsible companies on financial performance.[42]

Turning the Table: Consumer Ethics and Social Responsibility

Consumers also have an obligation to act ethically and responsibly in the exchange process and in the use and disposition of products. Unfortunately, consumer behavior is spotty on both counts.

Unethical practices of consumers are a serious concern to marketers. These practices include filing warranty claims after the claim period, misredeeming coupons, making fraudulent returns of merchandise, providing inaccurate information on credit applications, tampering with utility meters, tapping cable TV lines, recording copyrighted music and videocassettes, and submitting phony insurance claims. The cost to marketers in lost sales revenue and prevention expenses is huge.[43] For example, consumers who redeem coupons for unpurchased products or use coupons destined for other products cost manufacturers $1 billion each year. The record industry alone loses $1 billion annually as a result of illegal recording, and about 12 percent of VCR owners make illegal copies of videotapes, costing producers millions of dol-

Reebok has been a leader in improving workplace conditions in factories that produce its sporting apparel and equipment.

Reebok

www.reebok.com

lars in lost revenue. Electrical utilities lose between 1 percent and 3 percent of yearly revenues because of meter tampering.

Consumer purchase, use, and disposition of environmentally sensitive products relate to consumer social responsibility. Research indicates that consumers are sensitive to ecological issues.[44] However, research also shows that consumers (1) may be unwilling to sacrifice convenience and pay potentially higher prices to protect the environment and (2) lack the knowledge to make informed decisions dealing with the purchase, use, and disposition of products.[45]

Consumer confusion over which products are environmentally safe is also apparent, given marketers' rush to produce "green products." For example, few consumers realize that nonaerosol "pump" hairsprays are the second-largest cause of air pollution, after drying paint. In California alone, 27 tons of noxious hairspray fumes are expelled every day. And "biodegradable" claims on a variety of products, including trash bags, have not proven to be accurate, thus leading to buyer confusion. The FTC has drafted guidelines that describe the circumstances when environmental claims can be made and would not constitute misleading information. For example, an advertisement or product label touting a package as "50 percent more recycled content than before" could be misleading if the recycled content has increased from 2 percent to 3 percent.[46]

Ultimately, marketers and consumers are accountable for ethical and socially responsible behavior. The twenty-first century will prove to be a testing period for both.

Concept Check

1. What is meant by social responsibility?

2. Marketing efforts to produce, promote, and reclaim environmentally sensitive products are called _____.

3. What is a social audit?

SUMMARY

1   Ethics are the moral principles and values that govern the actions and decisions of an individual or group. Laws are society's values and standards that are enforceable in the courts. Operating according to the law does not necessarily mean that a practice is ethical.

2   Ethical behavior of businesspeople has come under severe criticism by the public. There are four possible reasons for this criticism: (*a*) increased pressure on businesspeople to make decisions in a society characterized by diverse value systems, (*b*) a growing tendency to have business decisions judged publicly by groups with different values and interests, (*c*) an increase in the public's expectations for ethical behavior, and (*d*) a possible decline in business ethics.

3   Numerous external factors influence ethical behavior of businesspeople. These include the following: (*a*) societal culture and norms, (*b*) business culture and industry practices, and (*c*) corporate culture and expectations. Each factor influences the opportunity to engage in ethical or unethical behavior.

4   Ultimately, ethical choices are based on the personal moral philosophy of the decision maker. Two moral philosophies are most prominent: (*a*) moral idealism and (*b*) utilitarianism.

5   Social responsibility means that organizations are part of a larger society and are accountable to that society for their actions.

6   There are three concepts of social responsibility: (*a*) profit responsibility, (*b*) stakeholder responsibility, and (*c*) societal responsibility.

7   Growing interest in societal responsibility has resulted in systematic efforts to assess a firm's objectives, strategies, and performance in the domain of social responsibility. This practice is called a social audit.

8   Consumer ethics and social responsibility are as important as business ethics and social responsibility.

KEY TERMS AND CONCEPTS

cause-related marketing p. 110
caveat emptor p. 103
code of ethics p. 105
Consumer Bill of Rights p. 103
economic espionage p. 104
ethics p. 100
green marketing p. 110
ISO 14000 p. 110

laws p. 100
moral idealism p. 107
social audit p. 111
social responsibility p. 108
sustainable development p. 111
utilitarianism p. 108
whistle-blowers p. 107

APPLYING MARKETING CONCEPTS AND PERSPECTIVES

1   What concepts of moral philosophy and social responsibility are applicable to the practices of Anheuser-Busch described in the introduction to this chapter? Why?

2   Five ethical situations were presented in this chapter: (*a*) a medical society's decision to set fee schedules, (*b*) the use of a computer program by auto dealers to arrange financing, (*c*) smoking in China, (*d*) the copying of trademarks and patents in Korea, and (*e*) the pricing of Ceredase for the treatment of a rare genetic illness. Where would each of these situations fit in Figure 4–1?

3   The American Marketing Association Code of Ethics shown in Figure 4–3 details the rights and duties of parties in the marketing exchange process. How do these rights and duties compare with the Consumer Bill of Rights?

4   Compare and contrast moral idealism and utilitarianism as alternative personal moral philosophies.

5   How would you evaluate Milton Friedman's view of the social responsibility of a firm?

6   The text lists several unethical practices of consumers. Can you name others? Why do you think consumers engage in unethical conduct?

7   Cause-related marketing programs have become popular. Describe two such programs that you are familiar with.

INTERNET EXERCISE

Business for Social Responsibility (BSR) is a membership organization for companies seeking to sustain their commercial success in ways that demonstrate respect for ethical values, people, communities, and the environment. As part of its mission, BSR scans more than 130 publications and news services each month to identify what is new in corporate social responsibility.

Choose a topic from Chapter 4 pertaining to ethics or social responsibility that interests you, such as economic espionage, current perceptions of ethical behavior, sustainable development or green marketing. Visit the BSR website at www.bsr.org and go to the Library. Can you update at least one example in the text related to your chosen topic?

VIDEO CASE 4-1   Energy Performance Systems, Inc.: Clean, Green Electricity

"Inexpensive, nonpolluting electricity is a global problem," says David Ostlie. "It's what is needed to provide people around the world with the standard of living they want."

In his next breath he suggests one answer to the problem: "What we need," says Ostlie matter of factly, "is just one electric utility to say 'yes'—to try our technology. Then the Whole-Tree Energy™ technology will speak for itself." David Ostlie is president of Energy Performance Systems, Inc. (EPS), a firm he founded in 1988 to produce environmentally clean, cheap electricity by growing, harvesting, transporting, drying, burning *whole* hardwood trees (trunks, branches, and all) in either (1) old retrofitted coal and oil (fossil fuel) power plants or (2) new power plants.

THE IDEA

Dave Ostlie points to three key features that make the EPS-owned and patented Whole-Tree Energy™ (WTE) technology unique:

1 Using *whole* hardwood trees. The use of whole trees saves a tremendous amount of time and energy over using wood chips—a common form for wood burned to produce electricity. "Hardwood trees" here means all broadleaf trees—mainly species such as cottonwood, aspen, birch, maple, and poplar (essentially all trees but conifers).

2 Drying the whole trees. Moisture is the culprit that leads to incomplete wood combustion and reduced energy output, resulting in emissions that lead to air pollution and acid rain. So the WTE process dries the trees to remove about 70 percent of the moisture prior to combustion, using waste heat from the combustion process itself.

3 Three-stage combustion. The whole trees burn at three levels in the furnace: (*a*) as trees in a 12-foot deep, mid-level pile, (*b*) as wood char that falls and is burned on a grate below the pile, and (*c*) as volatile gases (gasified wood) above the pile that burns cleanly like natural gas. The result is an incredibly *environmentally clean,* efficient combustion process.

The simplicity of the technology is a big plus compared to many of the current alternative energy technologies being studied around the world.

THE COMPANY

EPS is based on the Whole-Tree Energy™ technology and owns U.S., Canadian, European, and Japanese patents. The WTE™ technology has been scaled up in four successive tests that have demonstrated the feasibility of large-scale power production from sustained burning of whole trees. The mission of EPS: To commercialize the Whole-Tree Energy™ technology.

THE ISSUES

In assessing the Whole-Tree Energy™ technology, three critical issues soon emerge: (1) the environment and pollution, (2) jobs and economic development, and (3) buying interest of utilities.

The Environment and Pollution

Conventional coal-fired power plants, the staple for utilities, produce large volumes of SO_2, NO_x, ash, and extra CO_2 that contribute to air pollution, acid rain, and global warming. Based on test results, a WTE™ plant produces far less pollution than comparable fossil-fuel plants. Compared to a coal plant, the following levels of pollution have been demonstrated for a WTE™ plant:

- SO_2—less than $1/400$ of that for coal (on a fuel comparison basis) because wood contains virtually no sulfur.
- NO_x—approximately $1/10$ of that for coal due to the naturally low nitrogen content of wood fuel and the multistage WTE™ combustion process.
- Ash—less than $1/10$ of that for coal. The ash produced can be returned to the forest or sold as a fertilizer. Coal ash is considered a hazardous waste and must be stored indefinitely in specially designed storage ponds.
- Extra CO_2—Coal plants release enormous amounts of CO_2 to the atmosphere by burning the remnants of prehistoric plant life—coal—in large quantities. The rapidly increasing level of atmospheric CO_2 due to the burning of fossil fuels is a significant cause of global climate change. In contrast, using biomass—including trees—as a fuel results in no net addition of CO_2 to the atmosphere because the amount of CO_2 removed over the life of the tree is equal to that released by the tree, regardless of the tree's end use.

The net effect of burning a renewable biomass—trees—instead of fossil fuels will be a reduction in air pollution, acid rain, and global warming.

Jobs and Economic Development

WTE™ plants will burn (1) hardwoods that are unsalable (not wanted by other forest product firms), (2) fast-growing energy trees raised on plantations that can be harvested as often as every five to six years and add agricultural jobs, and (3) waste wood left over by other forest product firms. Harvesting overage hardwoods actually stimulates forest regeneration and often provides better habitat for wildlife. The U.S. Forest Service reports that much of the 20 billion tons of U.S. hardwoods are overage, not wanted by the logging, paper, and pulp industries and should be harvested.

A 100-megawatt WTE™ plant—providing enough electricity for a city of 100,000 people—will provide over 600 jobs in growing, harvesting, and transporting whole trees and in the plant producing electricity. In the search for local jobs, this is a huge benefit for economic development organizations trying to increase local employment.

Buying Interest of Utilities

To avoid more electrical blackouts, U.S. utilities must add new electrical generating capacity. For EPS, this provides an opportunity, either (1) by retrofitting to use in WTE™ some of the hundreds of coal and oil-fired plants throughout the United States that are operated infrequently because of their pollution problems or (2) by building new plants to use the WTE™ technology.

In an electric utility, capacity planners project the demand for electricity by industrial, commercial, and residential users and assess the utility's ability to supply the demand. The chief executive officer makes the recommendation to add new capacity, a decision reviewed by the board of directors. The vice president of power supply probably recommends the technology to be used and the site for the new power plant.

As Ostlie talks to prospective utility customers about the WTE™ technology, six concerns emerge that are covered below.

1   Can enough heat be generated by burning wood to produce electricity? "All the skeptics said we couldn't get a high enough temperature by burning wood," says Ostlie. "But in one recent heat-release test we produced values higher than those of state-of-the-art coal plants."

2   Can whole trees be loaded, transported, and dried? Forestry experts told Ostlie he couldn't load and transport whole trees on a truck because the branches wouldn't compress. So he hired a logger and did it. The WTE™ technology calls for large-scale drying of whole trees in an air-supported dome like those used in a sports stadium and stacked 35 meters high (see photo).

3 Are there enough trees available at reasonable cost to support commercial-size power plants? In about 75 percent of the United States enough biomass in the form of trees exists within a 50-mile radius to support a 100-megawatt power plant using the WTE™ technology. To support such a power plant, only about 0.1 percent of the land in a 50-mile radius of the plant would be harvested each year. Residential biomass and waste wood from pulp and timber mill operations are potential fuel sources, as are natural stands. Ultimately, much of the tree resource may come from short-rotation, hybrid tree plantations that provide farmers with an alternative cash crop.

4 What are the environmental benefits of WTE™ for utilities? Besides being increasingly sensitive to environmental concerns, a utility retrofitting a polluting electric power plant with Whole-Tree Energy™ can gain over a million dollars a year in SO_2 credits—an incentive for a utility to offset power produced by its high-pollution plants with electricity produced by nonpolluting plants.

5 What will it cost to build a retrofitted or new WTE™ power plant? A major appeal of the WTE™ process is its simplicity relative to say, coal-fired power plants. To retrofit an existing 100-megawatt coal plant, it will cost about $25 million—thereby putting back into production an existing plant that is of little value. To build a new 100-megawatt WTE™ plant would take about $100 million, about 25 to 30 percent less than a new fossil-fuel plant.

6 What will the cost be of electricity produced by a WTE™ plant? A recent feasibility study evaluating the WTE™ technology estimated that a WTE™ power plant could produce a kilowatt-hour of electricity for 20 to 40 percent less than today's fossil-fuel plants.

"It's not far away, but we've still got to make that first sale," adds Dave Ostlie.

Questions

1 Assume EPS builds a 100-megawatt Whole Tree Energy plant that proves successful and meets design objectives. What are the (*a*) benefits and (*b*) costs to these six groups: society as a whole, government agencies that helped with initial research and development funding, EPS, other utilities with competing technologies, energy users in the region of the plant, and households living near the plant?

2 (*a*) If the WTE plant is built and is a failure, how does this affect the benefits and cost in Question #1? (*b*) Should governments support new technologies like WTE? Explain your answer.

3 What are some of the key elements EPS should have in developing its strategy to market WTE™ to prospective utility buyers?

4 As a concerned citizen, (*a*) what do you see as the key benefits of the WTE™ technology and (*b*) what do you personally see as the potential "show stoppers" for WTE™—the critical things that can prevent it from being commercialized and becoming a reality?

5 A new product or technology like WTE™ requires educating a number of key groups, or "influencers," about the technology. Excluding the electric utilities themselves, (*a*) what groups, or market segments, should EPS try to reach, (*b*) what key benefits should be emphasized to each, and (*c*) what promotional methods or media should EPS use to reach each segment?

2

UNDERSTANDING BUYERS AND MARKETS

CHAPTER 5
Consumer Behavior

CHAPTER 6
Organizational Markets and Buyer Behavior

CHAPTER 7
Reaching Global Markets

Using local and global perspectives to understand people as individual consumers and as members of companies that become organizational buyers is the focus of Part 2. Chapter 5 examines the actions buyers take in purchasing and using products, and explains how and why one product or brand is chosen over another. In Chapter 6 John Baetz, the purchasing manager at JCPMedia, helps illustrate how he and a team of purchasing professionals buy over 260,000 tons of paper annually for JCPenney catalogs, newspaper inserts, and direct-mail pieces. Chapter 7 describes the nature and scope of world trade and examines the global marketing activities of companies such as Breathe Right Strips maker CNS, Inc., Coca-Cola, Ericsson, IBM, IKEA, and Nestlé. Together these chapters help marketing students understand individual, family, and organizational purchases in a variety of cultural environments.

CHAPTER 5

CONSUMER BEHAVIOR

AFTER READING THIS CHAPTER YOU SHOULD BE ABLE TO:

- Outline the stages in the consumer decision process.

- Distinguish among three variations of the consumer decision process: routine, limited, and extended problem solving.

- Explain how psychological influences affect consumer behavior, particularly purchase decision processes.

- Identify major sociocultural influences on consumer behavior and their effects on purchase decisions.

- Recognize how marketers can use knowledge of consumer behavior to better understand and influence individual and family purchases.

SAVVY AUTOMAKERS KNOW THY CUSTOM(H)ER

Who buys about 60 percent of new cars and light trucks? Who spends more than $85 billion on new and used cars and trucks and automotive accessories? Who influences 80 percent of all vehicle buying decisions? Women— yes, women.

Women are a driving force in the U.S. automotive industry. Enlightened automakers have hired women design engineers and marketing executives to help them understand this valuable custom(h)er. What have they learned? First, women prefer "sporty" vehicles that are relatively inexpensive and fun to drive rather than "sports" cars, luxury cars, and full-sized trucks with bigger engines and higher price tags. Second, a vehicle's "feel" is important to women. Sleek exteriors and interior designs that fit proportions of smaller drivers as well as opening ease for doors, trunks, and hoods are equally important. What is the number 1 women's fantasy car? It's Ford's Jaguar, according to womanmotorist.com.

Third, women approach car buying in a deliberate manner. They approach car buying, usage, and maintenance from a woman's point of view. They often visit auto-buying websites and scan car advertisements to gather information, but recommendations of friends and relatives matter most. Women shop an average of three dealerships before making a purchase decision—one more than men. Fourth, although men and women look for the same car features, their priorities differ. Both sexes value dependability most, but more women consider it a higher priority. Women also rank low price, ease of maintenance, and safety higher than men. Men view horsepower and acceleration as being more important than women. Finally, automakers have learned that 78 percent of women dislike the car-buying process.

Recognition of women as purchasers and influencers in car and truck buying has also altered the behavior of dealers. Many dealers now use a one-price policy and have stopped negotiating a vehicle's price. Industry research indicates that 68 percent of new-car buyers dread the price negotiation process involved in buying a car, and women often refuse to do it at all![1]

This chapter examines **consumer behavior**, the actions a person takes in purchasing and using products and services, including the mental and social processes that precede and follow these actions. This chapter shows how the behavioral sciences help answer questions such as why people choose one product or brand over another, how they make these choices, and how companies use this knowledge to provide value to consumers.

CONSUMER PURCHASE DECISION PROCESS

Behind the visible act of making a purchase lies an important decision process that must be investigated. The stages a buyer passes through in making choices about which products and services to buy is the **purchase decision process**. This process has the five stages shown in Figure 5–1: (1) problem recognition, (2) information search, (3) alternative evaluation, (4) purchase decision, and (5) postpurchase behavior.

Problem Recognition: Perceiving a Need

Problem recognition, the initial step in the purchase decision, is perceiving a difference between a person's ideal and actual situations big enough to trigger a decision.[2] This can be as simple as finding an empty milk carton in the refrigerator; noting, as a first-year college student, that your high school clothes are not in the style that other students are wearing; or realizing that your laptop computer may not be working properly.

In marketing, advertisements or salespeople can activate a consumer's decision process by showing the shortcomings of competing (or currently owned) products. For instance, an advertisement for a compact disc (CD) player could stimulate problem recognition because it emphasizes the sound quality of new CD players over the one you may now own.

Information Search: Seeking Value

After recognizing a problem, a consumer begins to search for information, the next stage in the purchase decision process. First, you may scan your memory for previous experiences with products or brands.[3] This action is called *internal search.* For frequently purchased products such as shampoo and conditioner, this may be enough. Or a consumer may undertake an *external search* for information.[4] This is especially needed when past experience or knowledge is insufficient, the risk of making a wrong purchase decision is high, and the cost of gathering information is low. The primary sources of external information are: (1) *personal sources,* such as relatives and friends whom the consumer trusts; (2) *public sources,* including various product-rating orga-

FIGURE 5–1
Purchase decision process

Brand	Model	Price	Headphones	Error correction	Bump immunity	Battery life (hours)	Controls
Sony	D-MJ95	$130	◓	◓	◉	26	◓
Sony	DSJ17CK	$160	○	◓	◉	29	◉
Sony	DSJ01	$200	○	◓	◉	33	◒
Sony	DEJ611	$ 80	○	○	◉	26	◒
Sony	DSJ15	$130	○	○	◉	25	◉
Panasonic	SL-SX280	$ 50	○	◒	◒	23	◒
Philips	AZ9213	$ 80	○	○	◒	17	○
Philips	EXP103/17	$180	○	○	◒	8	◒
GPX	C394881	$ 60	◒	○	◒	8	○
Lenoxx Sound	CD-91	$ 55	○	◒	◒	7	◒

Rating: ◉ Excellent   ◓ Very Good   ○ Good   ◒ Fair   ● Poor

FIGURE 5–2
Consumer Reports' evaluation of portable compact disc players (abridged)

Consumer Reports

www.consumerreports.org

nizations such as *Consumer Reports,* government agencies, and TV "consumer programs"; and (3) *marketer-dominated sources,* such as information from sellers that include advertising, company websites, salespeople, and point-of-purchase displays in stores.

Suppose you consider buying a portable CD player. You will probably tap several of these information sources: friends and relatives, portable CD-player advertisements, brand and company websites, and stores carrying CD players (for demonstrations). You might study the comparative evaluation of portable CD players that appeared in *Consumer Reports,* published by a product-testing organization, a portion of which appears in Figure 5–2.[5]

Alternative Evaluation: Assessing Value

The information search stage clarifies the problem for the consumer by (1) suggesting criteria to use for the purchase, (2) yielding brand names that might meet the criteria, and (3) developing consumer value perceptions. Based only on the information shown in Figure 5–2, what selection criteria would you use in buying a portable CD player? Would you use price, the quality of headphones, ease of using the controls, or some other combination of these and other criteria?

For some of you, the information provided may be inadequate because it does not contain all the factors you might consider when evaluating portable CD players. These factors are a consumer's **evaluative criteria**, which represent both the objective attributes of a brand (such as the locate speed) and the subjective ones (such as prestige) you use to compare different products and brands.[6] Firms try to identify and capitalize on both types of criteria to create the best value for the money sought by you and other consumers. These criteria are often displayed in advertisements.

Consumers often have several criteria for evaluating brands. (Didn't you in the preceding exercise?) Knowing this, companies seek to identify the most important evaluative criteria that consumers use when judging brands. For example, among the evaluative criteria shown in the columns of Figure 5–2, suppose that you use three in considering brands of portable CD players: (1) a list price under $150, (2) a battery life of more than 12 hours, and (3) ease of using the controls. These criteria establish the brands in your **evoked set**—the group of brands that a consumer would consider acceptable from among all the brands in the product class of which he or she is aware.[7] Your three evaluative criteria result in five models and three brands (Sony, Panasonic, and Philips) in your evoked set. If these alternatives don't satisfy you, you can change your evaluative criteria to create a different evoked set of models and brands.

Purchase Decision: Buying Value

Having examined the alternatives in the evoked set, you are almost ready to make a purchase decision. Two choices remain: (1) from whom to buy and (2) when to buy. For a product like a portable CD player, the information search process probably involved visiting retail stores, seeing different brands in catalogs, viewing portable CD-player promotions on a home shopping television channel, or visiting a seller's website. The choice of which seller to buy from will depend on such considerations as the terms of sale, your past experience buying from the seller, and the return policy. Often a purchase decision involves a simultaneous evaluation of both product attributes and seller characteristics. For example, you might choose the second-most preferred portable CD player brand at a store with a liberal refund and return policy versus the most preferred brand at a store with more conservative policies.

Deciding when to buy is frequently determined by a number of factors. For instance, you might buy sooner if one of your preferred brands is on sale or its manufacturer offers a rebate. Other factors such as the store atmosphere, pleasantness of the shopping experience, salesperson persuasiveness, time pressure, and financial circumstances could also affect whether a purchase decision is made or postponed.[8]

Use of the Internet to gather information, evaluate alternatives, and make buying decisions adds a technological dimension to the consumer purchase decision process. Consumer benefits and costs associated with this technology and its marketing implications are detailed in Chapter 21.

Postpurchase Behavior: Value in Consumption or Use

After buying a product, the consumer compares it with his or her expectations and is either satisfied or dissatisfied. If the consumer is dissatisfied, marketers must decide whether the product was deficient or consumer expectations too high. Product deficiency may require a design change; if expectations are too high, perhaps the company's advertising or the salesperson oversold the product's features.

Sensitivity to a customer's consumption or use experience is extremely important in a consumer's value perception. For example, research on long-distance telephone services provided by WorldCom, Sprint, and AT&T indicates that satisfaction or dissatisfaction affects consumer value perceptions.[9] Studies show that satisfaction or dissatisfaction affects consumer communications and repeat-purchase behavior. Satisfied buyers tell three other people about their experience. Dissatisfied buyers complain to nine people![10] Satisfied buyers also tend to buy from the same seller each time a purchase occasion arises. The financial impact of repeat-purchase behavior is significant, as described in the accompanying Marketing NewsNet.[11] Accordingly, firms such as General Electric (GE), Johnson & Johnson, Coca-Cola, and British Airways focus attention

A satisfactory or unsatisfactory consumption or use experience is an important factor in postpurchase behavior. Marketer attention to this stage can pay huge dividends as described in the text.

MARKETING
NEWSNET   The Value of a Satisfied Customer

CUSTOMER VALUE

Customer satisfaction is an important focus of the marketing concept. But how much is a satisfied customer worth? This question has prompted firms to calculate the financial value of a satisfied customer over time. Frito-Lay, for example, estimates that the average loyal consumer in the southwestern United States eats 21 pounds of salty snack chips a year. At a price of $2.50 a pound, this customer spends $52.50 annually on the company's salty snacks such as Lays and Ruffles potato chips and Doritos and Tostitos tortilla chips. Exxon estimates that a loyal customer will spend $500 annually for its branded gasoline, not including candy, snacks, oil, or repair services purchased at its gasoline stations. Kimberly-Clark reports that a loyal customer will buy 6.7 boxes of its Kleenex tissues each year and will spend $994 on facial tissues over 60 years, in today's dollars.

These calculations have focused marketer attention on customer satisfaction and retention. Ford Motor Company has set a target of increasing customer retention—the percentage of Ford owners whose next car is also a Ford—from 60 percent to 80 percent. Why? Ford executives say that each additional percentage point is worth a staggering $100 million in profits! This calculation is not unique to Ford. Research shows that a 5 percent improvement in customer retention can increase a company's profits by 70 to 80 percent.

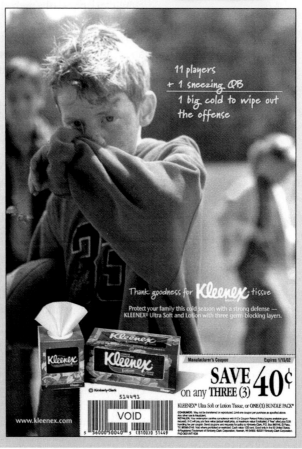

on postpurchase behavior to maximize customer satisfaction and retention.[12] These firms, among many others, now provide toll-free telephone numbers, offer liberalized return and refund policies, and engage in staff training to handle complaints, answer questions, and record suggestions. For example, GE operates a database that stores 750,000 answers about 8,500 of its models in 120 product lines to handle 3 million calls annually.[13] Such efforts produce positive postpurchase communications among consumers and contribute to relationship building between sellers and buyers.

Often a consumer is faced with two or more highly attractive alternatives, such as a Panasonic or Sony portable CD player. If you choose the Panasonic, you may think, "Should I have purchased the Sony?" This feeling of postpurchase psychological tension or anxiety is called **cognitive dissonance**. To alleviate it, consumers often attempt to applaud themselves for making the right choice. So after your purchase, you may seek information to confirm your choice by asking friends questions like, "Don't you like my portable CD player?" or by reading ads of the brand you chose. You might even look for negative features about the brand you didn't buy and decide that Sony's headphones, which were rated "good" in Figure 5–2, were actually a deficiency because they didn't feel right. Firms often use ads or follow-up calls from salespeople in this postpurchase stage to try to convince buyers that they made the right decision. For many years, Buick ran an advertising campaign with the message, "Aren't you really glad you bought a Buick?"

Involvement and Problem-Solving Variations

Sometimes consumers don't engage in the five-step purchase decision process. Instead, they skip or minimize one or more steps depending on the level of **involvement**, the personal, social, and economic significance of the purchase to the consumer.[14] High-involvement purchase occasions typically have at least one of three characteristics—the item to be purchased (1) is expensive, (2) can have serious personal consequences, or (3) could reflect on one's social image. For these occasions, consumers engage in extensive information search, consider many product attributes and brands, form attitudes, and participate in word-of-mouth communication. Low-involvement purchases, such as toothpaste and soap, barely involve most of us, whereas audio and video systems and automobiles are very involving. Researchers have identified three general variations in the consumer purchase process based on consumer involvement and product knowledge. Figure 5–3 summarizes some of the important differences between the three problem-solving variations.[15]

Routine Problem Solving   For products such as table salt and milk, consumers recognize a problem, make a decision, and spend little effort seeking external information and evaluating alternatives. The purchase process for such items is virtually a habit and typifies low-involvement decision making. Routine problem solving is typically the case for low-priced, frequently purchased products.

Limited Problem Solving   In limited problem solving, consumers typically seek some information or rely on a friend to help them evaluate alternatives. In general, several brands might be evaluated using a moderate number of different attributes. You might use limited problem solving in choosing a toaster, a restaurant for dinner, and other purchase situations in which you have little time or effort to spend.

Extended Problem Solving   In extended problem solving, each of the five stages of the consumer purchase decision process is used in the purchase, including considerable time and effort on external information search and in identifying and evaluating alternatives. Several brands are in the evoked set, and these are evaluated on many attributes. Extended problem solving exists in high-involvement purchase situations for items such as automobiles and financial investments.

FIGURE 5–3
Comparison of problem-solving variations

CHARACTERISTICS OF PURCHASE DECISION PROCESS	EXTENDED PROBLEM SOLVING	LIMITED PROBLEM SOLVING	ROUTINE PROBLEM SOLVING
Number of brands examined	Many	Several	One
Number of sellers considered	Many	Several	Few
Number of product attributes evaluated	Many	Moderate	One
Number of external information sources used	Many	Few	None
Time spent searching	Considerable	Little	Minimal

HIGH ◄ CONSUMER INVOLVEMENT ► LOW

Involvement and Marketing Strategy   Low and high consumer involvement has important implications for marketing strategy. If a company markets a low-involvement product and its brand is a market leader, attention is placed on (1) maintaining product quality, (2) avoiding stock-out situations so that buyers don't substitute a competing brand, and (3) advertising messages that reinforce a consumer's knowledge or assures buyers they made the right choice. Market challengers have a different task. They must break buying habits and use free samples, coupons, and rebates to encourage trial of their brand. Advertising messages will focus on getting their brand into a consumer's evoked set. For example, Campbell's V-8 vegetable juice advertising message—"I could have had a V-8!"—was targeted at consumers who routinely purchased fruit juices and soft drinks. Challengers can also link their brand attributes with high involvement issues. Tropicana does this by linking the natural attributes of orange juice with adult health concerns.

Marketers of high-involvement products recognize that their customers constantly seek and process information about objective and subjective brand attributes, form evaluative criteria, rate product attributes in various brands, and combine these ratings for an overall brand evaluation—like that described in the portable CD player purchase decision. Market leaders freely ply customers with product information through advertising and personal selling and create chat rooms on their company or brand websites. Market challengers capitalize on this behavior through comparative advertising that focuses on existing product attributes and often introduce novel evaluative criteria for judging competing brands. Increasingly, challengers benefit from Internet search engines such as MSN Search, Google, and Alta Vista that assist buyers of high-involvement products.

Situational Influences

Often the purchase situation will affect the purchase decision process. Five **situational influences** have an impact on your purchase decision process: (1) the purchase task, (2) social surroundings, (3) physical surroundings, (4) temporal effects, and (5) antecedent states.[16] The purchase task is the reason for engaging in the decision in the first place. Information searching and evaluating alternatives may differ depending on whether the purchase is a gift, which often involves social visibility, or for the buyer's own use. Social surroundings, including the other people present when a purchase decision is made, may also affect what is purchased. Physical surroundings such as decor, music, and crowding in retail stores may alter how purchase decisions are made. Temporal effects such as time of day or the amount of time available will influence where consumers have breakfast and lunch and what is ordered. Finally, antecedent states, which include the consumer's mood or the amount of cash on hand, can influence purchase behavior and choice.

Figure 5–4 on the next page shows the many influences that affect the consumer purchase decision process. The decision to buy a product also involves important psychological and sociocultural influences, the two important topics discussed during the remainder of this chapter. Marketing mix influences are described in Chapters 10 through 20.

Concept Check

1. What is the first step in the consumer purchase decision process?

2. The brands a consumer considers buying out of the set of brands in a product class of which the consumer is aware is called the _____.

3. What is the term for postpurchase anxiety?

FIGURE 5–4
Influences on the consumer
purchase decision process

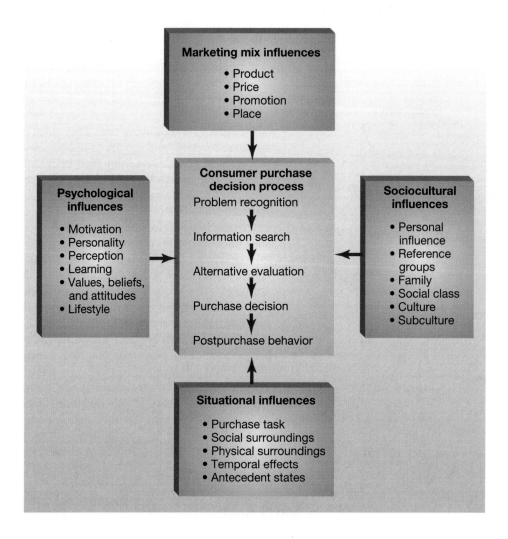

PSYCHOLOGICAL INFLUENCES ON CONSUMER BEHAVIOR

Psychology helps marketers understand why and how consumers behave as they do. In particular, concepts such as motivation and personality; perception; learning; values, beliefs, and attitudes; and lifestyle are useful for interpreting buying processes and directing marketing efforts.

Motivation and Personality

Motivation and personality are two familiar psychological concepts that have specific meanings and marketing implications. They are both used frequently to describe why people do some things and not others.

Motivation   **Motivation** is the energizing force that causes behavior that satisfies a need. Because consumer needs are the focus of the marketing concept, marketers try to arouse these needs.

An individual's needs are boundless. People possess physiological needs for basics such as water, sex, and food. They also have learned needs, including esteem, achievement, and affection. Psychologists point out that these needs are hierarchical; that is, once physiological needs are met, people seek to satisfy their learned needs. Figure 5–5 shows one need hierarchy and classification scheme that contains five need classes.[17] *Physiological needs* are basic to survival and must be satisfied first. A Burger King advertisement featuring a juicy hamburger attempts to activate

FIGURE 5–5
Hierarchy of needs

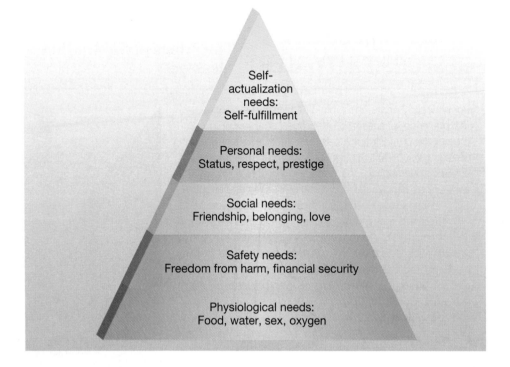

the need for food. *Safety needs* involve self-preservation and physical well-being. Smoke detector and burglar alarm manufacturers focus on these needs. *Social needs* are concerned with love and friendship. Dating services and fragrance companies try to arouse these needs. *Personal needs* are represented by the need for achievement, status, prestige, and self-respect. The American Express Gold Card and Brooks Brothers Clothiers appeal to these needs. Sometimes firms try to arouse multiple needs to stimulate problem recognition. Michelin combined security with parental love to promote tire replacement for automobiles. *Self-actualization needs* involve personal fulfillment. For example, a long-running U.S. Army recruiting program invited enlistees to "Be all you can be."

Personality   **Personality** refers to a person's consistent behaviors or responses to recurring situations. Although numerous personality theories exist, most identify key traits—enduring characteristics within a person or in his or her relationship with others. Such traits include assertiveness, extroversion, compliance, dominance, and aggression, among others. Research suggests that compliant people prefer known brand names and use more mouthwash and toilet soaps. In contrast, aggressive types use razors, not electric shavers, apply more cologne and after-shave lotions, and purchase signature goods such as Gucci, Yves St. Laurent, and Donna Karan as an indicator of status.[18] Cross-cultural analysis also suggests that residents of different countries have a **national character**, or a distinct set of personality characteristics common among people of a country or society.[19] For example, Americans and Germans are relatively more assertive than Russians and the English.

These personality characteristics are often revealed in a person's **self-concept**, which is the way people see themselves and the way they believe others see them.[20] Marketers recognize that people have an actual self-concept and an ideal self-concept. The actual self refers to how people actually see themselves. The ideal self describes how people would like to see themselves. These two self "images" are reflected in the products and brands a person buys including automobiles, home appliances and furnishings, magazines, clothing, grooming and leisure products, and frequently, the stores a person shops. The importance of self-concept is summed up

ETHICS AND SOCIAL RESPONSIBILITY ALERT

The Ethics of Subliminal Messages

ETHICS

For almost 50 years, the topic of subliminal perception and the presence of subliminal messages embedded in commercial communications has sparked debate. Although there is no substantive scientific support for the concept of subliminal perception, the Federal Communications Commission has denounced subliminal messages as deceptive. Still, consumers spend $50 million a year for audiotapes with subliminal messages designed to help them raise their self-esteem, quit smoking, or lose weight.

Subliminal messages are not illegal in the United States, however, and marketers occasionally pursue opportunities to create these messages. For example, Time Warner Interactive's Endorfun, a CD-ROM puzzle game, has a music soundtrack with more than 100 subliminal messages meant to make players feel good about themselves, even if they can't solve the puzzle. One message says, "I am a winner." Puzzle players are informed that subliminal messages exist and instructions on how to turn off the soundtrack are provided.

Do you believe that attempts to implant subliminal messages are a deceptive practice and unethical, regardless of their intent?

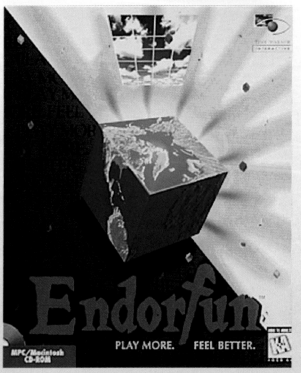

by a senior executive at Barnes & Noble: "People buy books for what the purchase says about them—their taste, their cultivation, their trendiness."[21]

Perception

One person sees a Cadillac as a mark of achievement; another sees it as ostentatious. This is the result of **perception**—the process by which an individual selects, organizes, and interprets information to create a meaningful picture of the world.

Selective Perception　　Because the average consumer operates in a complex environment, the human brain attempts to organize and interpret information with a process called *selective perception,* a filtering of exposure, comprehension, and retention. *Selective exposure* occurs when people pay attention to messages that are consistent with their attitudes and beliefs and ignore messages that are inconsistent. Selective exposure often occurs in the postpurchase stage of the consumer decision process, when consumers read advertisements for the brand they just bought. It also occurs when a need exists—you are more likely to "see" a McDonald's advertisement when you are hungry rather than after you have eaten a pizza.

Selective comprehension involves interpreting information so that it is consistent with your attitudes and beliefs. A marketer's failure to understand this can have disastrous results. For example, Toro introduced a small, lightweight snowblower called

Why does the Good Housekeeping seal for Clorox's new Fresh Step Crystals cat litter appear in the ad and why does Mary Kay, Inc. offer a free sample of its new Velocity brand fragrance through its mkvelocity.com website? The answer appears in the text.

The Clorox Company
www.freshstep.org

Mary Kay, Inc.
www.mkvelocity.com

the Snow Pup. Even though the product worked, sales failed to meet expectations. Why? Toro later found out that consumers perceived the name to mean that Snow Pup was a toy or too light to do any serious snow removal. When the product was renamed "Snow Master," sales increased sharply.[22]

Selective retention means that consumers do not remember all the information they see, read, or hear, even minutes after exposure to it. This affects the internal and external information search stage of the purchase decision process. This is why furniture and automobile retailers often give consumers product brochures to take home after they leave the showroom.

Because perception plays such an important role in consumer behavior, it is not surprising that the topic of subliminal perception is a popular item for discussion. **Subliminal perception** means that you see or hear messages without being aware of them. The presence and effect of subliminal perception on behavior is a hotly debated issue, with more popular appeal than scientific support. Indeed, evidence suggests that such messages have limited effects on behavior.[23] If these messages did influence behavior, would their use be an ethical practice? (See the accompanying Ethics and Social Responsibility Alert.[24])

Perceived Risk Perception plays a major role in the perceived risk in purchasing a product or service. **Perceived risk** represents the anxieties felt because the consumer cannot anticipate the outcomes of a purchase but believes that there may be negative consequences. Examples of possible negative consequences are the size of the financial outlay required to buy the product (Can I afford $300 for those skis?), the risk of physical harm (Is bungee jumping safe?), and the performance of the product (Will the hair coloring work?). A more abstract form is psychosocial (What will my friends say if I wear that sweater?). Perceived risk affects information search because the greater the perceived risk, the more extensive the external search phase is likely to be.

Recognizing the importance of perceived risk, companies develop strategies to reduce the consumer's risk and encourage purchases. These strategies and examples of firms using them include the following:

- Obtaining seals of approval: the Good Housekeeping seal for Fresh Step Crystals cat litter.
- Securing endorsements from influential people: The National Fluid Milk Processor Promotion Board "Got Milk" advertising campaign.
- Providing free trials of the product: samples of Mary Kay's Velocity fragrance.
- Giving extensive usage instructions: Clairol hair coloring.
- Providing warranties and guarantees: Cadillac's four-year, 50,000-mile, Gold Key Bumper-to-Bumper warranty.

Learning

Much consumer behavior is learned. Consumers learn which information sources to use for information about products and services, which evaluative criteria to use when assessing alternatives, and, more generally, how to make purchase decisions. **Learning** refers to those behaviors that result from (1) repeated experience and (2) thinking.

Behavioral Learning   *Behavioral learning* is the process of developing automatic responses to a situation built up through repeated exposure to it. Four variables are central to how consumers learn from repeated experience: drive, cue, response, and reinforcement. A *drive* is a need that moves an individual to action. Drives, such as hunger, might be represented by motives. A *cue* is a stimulus or symbol perceived by consumers. A *response* is the action taken by a consumer to satisfy the drive, and a *reinforcement* is the reward. Being hungry (drive), a consumer sees a cue (a billboard), takes action (buys a hamburger), and receives a reward (it tastes great!).

Marketers use two concepts from behavioral learning theory. *Stimulus generalization* occurs when a response elicited by one stimulus (cue) is generalized to another stimulus. Using the same brand name for different products is an application of this concept, such as Tylenol Cold & Flu and Tylenol P.M. *Stimulus discrimination* refers to a person's ability to perceive differences in stimuli. Consumers' tendency to perceive all light beers as being alike led to Budweiser Light commercials that distinguished between many types of "lights" and Bud Light.

Cognitive Learning   Consumers also learn through thinking, reasoning, and mental problem solving without direct experience. This type of learning, called *cognitive learning,* involves making connections between two or more ideas or simply observing the outcomes of others' behaviors and adjusting your own accordingly. Firms also influence this type of learning. Through repetition in advertising, messages such as "Advil is a headache remedy" attempt to link a brand (Advil) and an idea (headache remedy) by showing someone using the brand and finding relief.

Brand Loyalty   Learning is also important because it relates to habit formation—the basis of routine problem solving. Furthermore, there is a close link between habits and **brand loyalty**, which is a favorable attitude toward and consistent purchase of a single brand over time. Brand loyalty results from the positive reinforcement of previous actions. So a consumer reduces risk and saves time by consistently purchasing the same brand of shampoo and has favorable results—healthy, shining hair. There is evidence of brand loyalty in many commonly purchased products in the United States and the global marketplace. However, the incidence of brand loyalty appears to be declining in North America, Mexico, Western European nations, and Japan.[25]

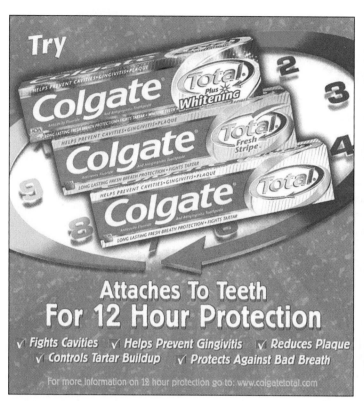

Attitudes toward Colgate toothpaste and Extra Strength Bayer aspirin were successfully changed by these ads. How? Read the text to find out how marketers can change consumer attitudes toward products and brands.

Colgate-Palmolive
www.colgate.com

Bayer Corporation
www.bayerus.com

Values, Beliefs, and Attitudes

Values, beliefs, and attitudes play a central role in consumer decision making and related marketing actions.

Attitude Formation   An **attitude** is a "learned predisposition to respond to an object or class of objects in a consistently favorable or unfavorable way."[26] Attitudes are shaped by our values and beliefs, which are learned. Values vary by level of specificity. We speak of American core values, including material well-being and humanitarianism. We also have personal values, such as thriftiness and ambition. Marketers are concerned with both, but focus mostly on personal values. Personal values affect attitudes by influencing the importance assigned to specific product attributes. Suppose thriftiness is one of your personal values. When you evaluate cars, fuel economy (a product attribute) becomes important. If you believe a specific car has this attribute, you are likely to have a favorable attitude toward it.

Beliefs also play a part in attitude formation. **Beliefs** are a consumer's subjective perception of *how well* a product or brand performs on different attributes. Beliefs are based on personal experience, advertising, and discussions with other people. Beliefs about product attributes are important because, along with personal values, they create the favorable or unfavorable attitude the consumer has toward certain products and services.

Attitude Change   Marketers use three approaches to try to change consumer attitudes toward products and brands, as shown in the following examples.[27]

1. *Changing beliefs about the extent to which a brand has certain attributes.* To allay consumer concern that aspirin use causes an upset stomach, Bayer Corporation successfully promoted the gentleness of its Extra Strength Bayer Plus aspirin.

2. *Changing the perceived importance of attributes.* Pepsi-Cola made freshness an important product attribute when it stamped freshness dates on its cans. Prior to doing so, few consumers considered cola freshness an issue. After Pepsi spent about $25 million on advertising and promotion, a consumer survey found that 61 percent of cola drinkers believed freshness dating was an important attribute![28]

3. *Adding new attributes to the product.* Colgate-Palmolive included a new antibacterial ingredient, tricloson, in its Colgate Total toothpaste and spent $100 million marketing the brand. The result? Colgate replaced Crest as the market leader for the first time in 25 years.[29]

Lifestyle

Lifestyle is a mode of living that is identified by how people spend their time and resources (activities), what they consider important in their environment (interests), and what they think of themselves and the world around them (opinions). The analysis of consumer lifestyles (also called *psychographics*) has produced many insights into consumers' behavior. For example, lifestyle analysis has proven useful in segmenting and targeting consumers for new and existing products (see Chapter 8).

Psychographics, the practice of combining psychology and demographics, is often used to study consumer behavior. The most prominent example of this type of analysis is the VALS™ Program developed by SRI International and currently run by SRI Consulting Business Intelligence.[30] The VALS Program has identified eight interconnected categories of adult lifestyles based on a person's self-orientation and resources. Self-orientation describes the patterns of attitudes and activities that help people reinforce their social self-image. Three patterns have been uncovered; they are oriented toward principles, status, and action. A person's resources encompass income, education, self-confidence, health, eagerness to buy, intelligence, and energy level. This dimension is a continuum ranging from minimal to abundant. Figure 5–6 shows the eight lifestyle types and their relationships, and highlights selected behavioral characteristics of each. Before reading further, visit the VALS Program website shown in the accompanying Web Link. Complete the short survey and find out your lifestyle category within seconds. Does it describe you?

The VALS Program seeks to explain why and how consumers make purchase decisions. For example, *principle-oriented consumers* try to match their behavior with their views of how the world is or should be. These older consumers divide into two categories. Fulfilleds are mature, satisfied, and reflective people who value

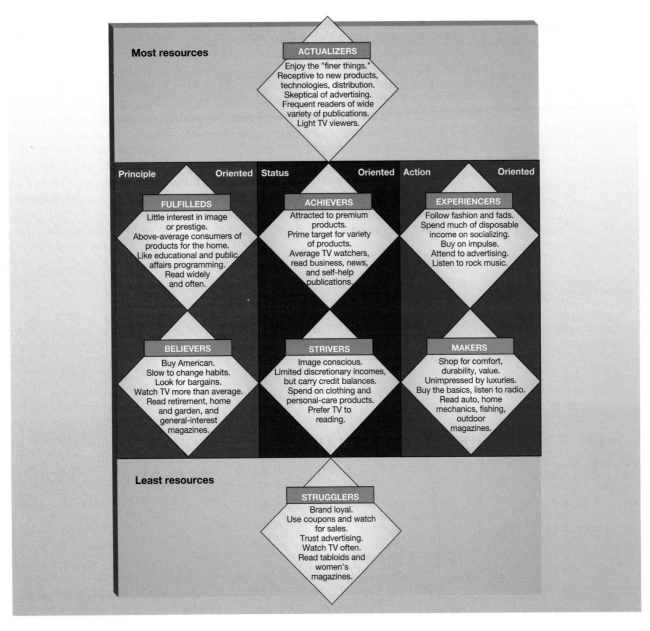

FIGURE 5–6
VALS™ psychographic
segments

order, knowledge, and responsibility. Most are well-educated and employed in a profession. Believers, with fewer resources to draw on, are conservative, conventional people with concrete beliefs and strong attachments to family, church, and community. *Status-oriented consumers* are motivated by the actions and opinions of others. These consumers include Achievers, who are successful and career-oriented; value duty, structure, prestige and material rewards; and have abundant resources at their disposal. Strivers, with fewer resources, seek motivation, self-definition, and social approval, and define success in purely financial terms. *Action-oriented consumers* are intensely involved in social and physical activity, enjoy variety, and are risk-takers. Experiencers are young, enthusiastic, impulsive, and rebellious consumers who are still formulating life values and behavior patterns. Makers too are energetic but focus their attention on practical matters related to family, work, and physical recreation. While Experiencers maintain a vicarious relationship with their surroundings, Makers experience life by working on it—building a house and raising children.

Two consumer types stand apart. Actualizers are successful, sophisticated, active, take-charge people with high self-esteem and abundant resources of all kinds. Image is important to them, not as evidence of power or status, but as an expression of taste, independence, and character. Strugglers are poor, often uneducated, and frequently concerned about their well-being. They have the oldest average age of the VALS consumer types.

Each of these categories exhibits different buying behavior and media preferences. For example, Believers and Makers typically own pickup trucks and fishing gear. Actualizers are likely to own a foreign car, a home computer, and have Internet access. Experiencers and Strivers are the most likely to visit Internet chat rooms. Actualizers, Fulfilleds, and Achievers tend to read business magazines such as *Fortune* and *Forbes*. Experiencers read sports magazines while Makers read automotive magazines. Believers are the heaviest readers of *Reader's Digest*. Along with Strugglers, they are the least likely to have a home computer and Internet access.

Concept Check

1. The problem with the Toro Snow Pup was an example of selective _____ .

2. What three attitude-change approaches are most common?

3. What does *lifestyle* mean?

SOCIOCULTURAL INFLUENCES ON CONSUMER BEHAVIOR

Sociocultural influences, which evolve from a consumer's formal and informal relationships with other people, also exert a significant impact on consumer behavior. These involve personal influence, reference groups, the family, social class, culture, and subculture.

Personal Influence

A consumer's purchases are often influenced by the views, opinions, or behaviors of others. Two aspects of personal influence are important to marketing: opinion leadership and word-of-mouth activity.

Opinion Leadership Individuals who exert direct or indirect social influence over others are called **opinion leaders**. Opinion leaders are more likely to be important for products that provide a form of self-expression. Automobiles, clothing, club membership, home audio and video equipment, and personal computers are products affected by opinion leaders, but appliances are not.[31] A study by *Popular Mechanics* magazine identified 18 million men who influence the purchases of some 85 million consumers for "do-it-yourself" products.[32]

About 10 percent of U.S. adults are opinion leaders.[33] Identifying, reaching, and influencing opinion leaders is a major challenge for companies. Some firms use sports figures or celebrities as spokespersons to represent their products, such as actor Pierce Brosnan and tennis player Anna Kournikova for Omega watches, in the hope that they are opinion leaders. Others promote their products in media believed to reach opinion leaders. Still others use more direct approaches. For example, Chrysler Corporation recently invited influential community leaders and business executives to test-drive its Dodge Intrepid, Chrysler Concorde, and Eagle Vision models. Some 6,000 accepted the offer, and 98 percent said they would recommend their tested car. Chrysler estimated that the number of favorable recommendations totaled 32,000.[34]

Firms use actors or athletes as spokespersons to represent their products, such as Pierce Brosnan and Anna Kournikova for Omega watches, in the hope that they are opinion leaders.

Omega

www.omega.com

Word of Mouth   People influencing each other during their face-to-face conversations is called **word of mouth**. Word of mouth is perhaps the most powerful information source for consumers because it typically involves friends viewed as trustworthy. When U.S. consumers were asked in a recent survey what most influences their buying decisions, 37 percent mentioned a friend's recommendation, and 20 percent said advertising. When a similar question was posed to Russian consumers, 72 percent said advice from friends, and 24 percent said advertising.[35]

The power of personal influence has prompted firms to promote positive and retard negative word of mouth.[36] For instance, "teaser" advertising campaigns are run in advance of new-product introductions to stimulate conversations. Other techniques such as advertising slogans, music, and humor also heighten positive word of mouth. On the other hand, rumors about Kmart (snake eggs in clothing), McDonald's (worms in hamburgers), and Corona Extra beer (contaminated beer) have resulted in negative word of mouth, none of which was based on fact. Overcoming or neutralizing negative word of mouth is difficult and costly. Firms have found that supplying factual information, providing toll-free numbers for consumers to call the company, and giving appropriate product demonstrations also have been helpful. Negative word of mouth is particularly challenging for global marketers as described in the Marketing NewsNet on the next page.[37]

The power of word of mouth has been magnified by the Internet and e-mail. Chapter 21 describes how marketers initiate and manage word of mouth in this setting.

Reference Groups

Reference groups are people to whom an individual looks as a basis for self-appraisal or as a source of personal standards. Reference groups affect consumer purchases because they influence the information, attitudes, and aspiration levels that help set a consumer's standards. For example, one of the first questions one asks others when planning to attend a social occasion is, "What are you going to wear?" Reference groups have an important influence on the purchase of luxury products but not of necessities—reference groups exert a strong influence on the brand chosen when its use or consumption is highly visible to others.[38]

MARKETING NEWSNET

Psst. Have You Heard . . . ? The Nemesis of Negative Word of Mouth in Global Marketing

GLOBAL

Global marketers have learned painfully that word of mouth is a powerful information source in developing countries. Rumors that result in negative word of mouth are particularly common. For example, several food products in Indonesia, including some sold by Nestlé, were rumored to contain pork, which is prohibited to the 160 million Muslim consumers in that country. Nestlé spent $250,000 in advertising to counteract the rumor. In Russia, Mars, Inc. had to confront the untrue claim that 200,000 Moscow children acquired diabetes from Snickers candy bars. Pabst Blue Ribbon beer was hit by a rumor in China that its beer was poisoned. Actually, a home-brewed beer had been poured into an empty Pabst bottle and resold.

Negative word of mouth has been shown to reduce the credibility of a company's advertising and consumers' intention to buy products. Its effect can be particularly damaging for companies that have recently entered a new country.

СУПЕРПИТАТЕЛЬНЫЙ БАТОНЧИК!

Consumers have many reference groups, but three groups have clear marketing implications. A *membership group* is one to which a person actually belongs, including fraternities and sororities, social clubs, and the family. Such groups are easily identifiable and are targeted by firms selling insurance, insignia products, and charter vacations. An *aspiration group* is one that a person wishes to be a member of or wishes to be identified with, such as a professional society. Firms frequently rely on spokespeople or settings associated with their target market's aspiration group in their advertising. A *dissociative group* is one that a person wishes to maintain a distance from because of differences in values or behaviors.

Family Influence

Family influences on consumer behavior result from three sources: consumer socialization, passage through the family life cycle, and decision making within the family or household.

Consumer Socialization   The process by which people acquire the skills, knowledge, and attitudes necessary to function as consumers is **consumer socialization**.[39] Children learn how to purchase (1) by interacting with adults in purchase situations and (2) through their own purchasing and product usage experiences. Research shows that children evidence brand preferences at age two, and these prefer-

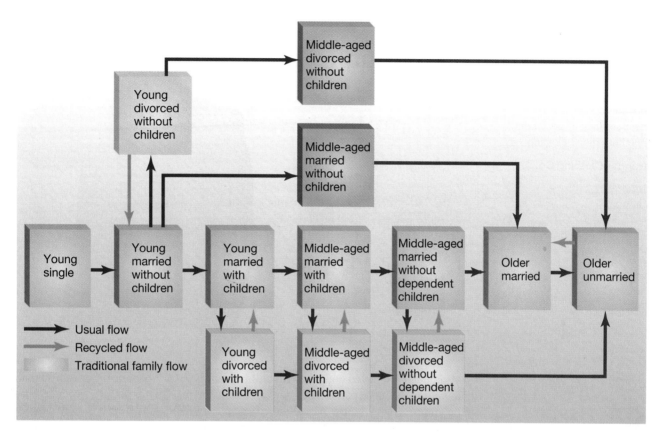

FIGURE 5–7
Modern family life cycle

ences often last a lifetime.[40] This knowledge has prompted Sony to introduce "My First Sony," a line of portable audio equipment for children; Time, Inc. to launch *Sports Illustrated for Kids;* Polaroid to develop the Cool Cam camcorder for children between ages 9 and 14; and Yahoo! and America Online to create special areas where young audiences can view their children's menu—Yahooligans! and Kids Only, respectively.

Family Life Cycle   Consumers act and purchase differently as they go through life. The **family life cycle** concept describes the distinct phases that a family progresses through from formation to retirement, each phase bringing with it identifiable purchasing behaviors.[41] Figure 5–7 illustrates the traditional progression as well as contemporary variations of the family life cycle. Today, the traditional family—married couples with children younger than 18 years—constitute just 23.5 percent of all U.S. households. The remaining 76.5 percent of U.S. households include single parents, unmarried couples, divorced, never-married, or widowed individuals, and older married couples whose children no longer live at home.

Young singles' buying preferences are for nondurable items, including prepared foods, clothing, personal care products, and entertainment. They represent a target market for recreational travel, automobile, and consumer electronics firms. Young married couples without children are typically more affluent than young singles because usually both spouses are employed. These couples exhibit preferences for furniture, housewares, and gift items for each other. Young marrieds with children are driven by the needs of their children. They make up a sizeable market for life insurance, various children's products, and home furnishings. Single parents with children are the least financially secure of households with children. Their buying preferences are affected by a limited economic status and tend toward convenience foods, child care services, and personal care items.

The Haggar Clothing Co. recognizes the important role women play in the choice of men's clothing. The company directs a large portion of its advertising toward women because they influence and purchase men's clothing.

Haggar Clothing Co.

www.haggar.com

Middle-aged married couples with children are typically better off financially than their younger counterparts. They are a significant market for leisure products and home improvement items. Middle-aged couples without children typically have a large amount of discretionary income. These couples buy better home furnishings, status automobiles, and financial services. Persons in the last two phases—older married and older unmarried—make up a sizeable market for prescription drugs, medical services, vacation trips, and gifts for younger relatives.

Family Decision Making   A third influence in the decision-making process occurs within the family. Two decision-making styles exist: spouse-dominant and joint decision making. With a joint decision-making style, most decisions are made by both husband and wife. Spouse-dominant decisions are those for which either the husband or the wife is responsible. Research indicates that wives tend to have the most say when purchasing groceries, children's toys, clothing, and medicines. Husbands tend to be more influential in home and car maintenance purchases. Joint decision making is common for cars, vacations, houses, home appliances and electronics, medical care, and long-distance telephone services. As a rule, joint decision making increases with the education of the spouses.[42]

Roles of individual family members in the purchase process are another element of family decision making. Five roles exist: (1) information gatherer, (2) influencer, (3) decision maker, (4) purchaser, and (5) user. Family members assume different roles for different products and services. This knowledge is important to firms.[43] For example, 89 percent of wives either influence or make outright purchases of men's clothing. Knowing this, Haggar Clothing, a menswear marketer, now advertises in women's magazines such as *Vanity Fair* and *Redbook*. Even though women are often the grocery decision maker, they are not necessarily the purchaser. More than 40 percent of all food-shopping dollars are spent by male customers. Increasingly, preteens and teenagers are the information gatherers, influencers, decision makers, and purchasers of products and services items for the family, given the prevalence of working parents and single-parent households.[44] Children under 12 directly influence about $300 billion in annual family purchases. Teenagers influence another $450 billion. These figures help explain why, for example, Nabisco, Johnson & Johnson, Apple Computer, Kellogg, P&G, Sony, and Oscar Mayer, among countless other companies, spend more than $32 billion annually in media that reach preteens and teens.

Social Class

A more subtle influence on consumer behavior than direct contact with others is the social class to which people belong. **Social class** may be defined as the relatively permanent, homogeneous divisions in a society into which people sharing similar values, interests, and behavior can be grouped. A person's occupation, source of income (not level of income), and education determine his or her social class. Generally speaking, three major social class categories exist—upper, middle, and lower—with subcategories within each. This structure has been observed in the United States, Great Britain, Western Europe, and Latin America.[45]

To some degree, persons within social classes exhibit common attitudes, lifestyles, and buying behaviors. Compared with the middle classes, people in the lower classes have a more short-term time orientation, are more emotional than rational in their reasoning, think in concrete rather than abstract terms, and see fewer personal opportunities. Members of the upper classes focus on achievements and the future and think in abstract or symbolic terms.

Companies use social class as a basis for identifying and reaching particularly good prospects for their products and services. For instance, AT&T has used social class for identifying preferences for different styles of telephones, JCPenney has historically appealed to the middle classes, and *New Yorker* magazine reaches the upper classes. In general, people in the upper classes are targeted by companies for items such as financial investments, expensive cars, and evening wear. The middle classes represent a target market for home improvement centers, automobile parts stores, and personal hygiene products. Firms also recognize differences in media preferences among classes: lower and working classes prefer sports and scandal magazines, middle classes read fashion, romance, and celebrity (*People*) magazines, and upper classes tend to read literary, travel, and news magazines.

Culture and Subculture

As described in Chapter 3, culture refers to the set of values, ideas, and attitudes that are accepted by a homogeneous group of people and transmitted to the next generation. Thus we often refer to the American culture, the Latin American culture, or the Japanese culture. Cultural underpinnings of American buying patterns were described in Chapter 3; Chapter 7 will explore the role of culture in global marketing.

Subgroups within the larger, or national, culture with unique values, ideas, and attitudes are referred to as **subcultures**. Various subcultures exist within the American culture. The three largest racial/ethnic subcultures in the United States are Hispanics, African-Americans, and Asians. Collectively, they annually spend about $1 trillion for goods and services.[46] Each of these groups exhibits sophisticated social and cultural behaviors that affect their buying patterns.

African-American Buying Patterns   African-Americans have the largest spending power of the three racial/ethnic subcultures in the United States. Consumer research on African-American buying patterns have focused on similarities and differences with whites. When socioeconomic status differences between African-Americans and whites are removed, there are more similarities than points of difference. Differences in buying patterns are greater within the African-American subculture, due to levels of socioeconomic status, than between African-Americans and whites of similar status.

Even though similarities outweigh differences, there are consumption patterns that do differ between African-Americans and whites.[47] For example, African-Americans spend far more than whites on boy's clothing, rental goods, and audio equipment. Adult African-Americans are twice as likely to own a pager and spend twice as much for online services, on a per capita basis, than whites. African-American women spend three times more on health and beauty products than white women. Furthermore, the typical African-American family is five years younger than the typical white family.

African-American women represent a large market for health and beauty products. Cosmetic companies such as Bonne Bell Cosmetics, Inc. actively seek to serve this market.

Bonne Bell Cosmetics, Inc.
www.bonnebell.com

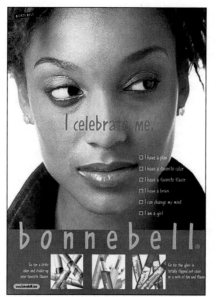

This factor alone accounts for some of the observed differences in preferences for clothing, music, shelter, cars, and many other products, services, and activities. Finally, it must be emphasized that, historically, African-Americans have been deprived of employment and educational opportunities in the United States. Both factors have resulted in income disparities between African-Americans and whites, which influence purchase behavior.

Recent research indicates that while African-Americans are price conscious, they are strongly motivated by quality and choice. They respond more to products such as apparel and cosmetics and advertising that appeal to their African-American pride and heritage as well as address their ethnic features and needs regardless of socioeconomic status.

Appreciation for the context in which African-Americans make purchase decisions is a necessary first step in understanding their buying patterns. Current research on African-American purchase behavior reveals that stereotypes are often misleading, as they also are for the Hispanic and Asian subcultures.

Hispanic Buying Patterns
Hispanics represent the largest racial/ethnic subculture in the United States in terms of population. About 50 percent of Hispanics in the United States are immigrants and the majority are under the age of 25.[48]

Research on Hispanic buying practices has uncovered several consistent patterns:[49]

1. Hispanics are quality and brand conscious. They are willing to pay a premium price for premium quality and are often brand loyal.
2. Hispanics prefer buying American-made products, especially those offered by firms that cater to Hispanic needs.
3. Hispanic buying preferences are strongly influenced by family and peers.
4. Hispanics consider advertising a credible product information source, and U.S. firms spend $2.5 billion annually on Spanish-language advertising.
5. Convenience is not an important product attribute to Hispanic homemakers with respect to food preparation or consumption, nor is low caffeine in coffee and soft drinks, low fat in dairy products, and low cholesterol in packaged foods.

Despite some consistent buying patterns, marketing to Hispanics has proven to be a challenge for two reasons. First, the Hispanic subculture is diverse and composed of Mexicans, Puerto Ricans, Cubans, and others of Central and South American ancestry. Cultural differences among these nationalities often affect product preferences. For example, Campbell Soup Company sells its Casera line of soups, beans, and sauces using different recipes to appeal to Puerto Ricans on the East Coast and Mexicans in the Southwest. Second, a language barrier exists, and commercial messages are frequently misinterpreted when translated into Spanish. A U.S. airline painfully learned this lesson when the Spanish translation of its "We Earn Our Wings Daily" message implied that passengers often ended up dead. Campbell Soup has overcome the language issue. It provides Spanish and English labels on its soups in parts of the western and southwestern United States.

Sensitivity to the unique needs of Hispanics by firms has paid huge dividends. For example, Metropolitan Life Insurance is the largest insurer of Hispanics. Goya Foods dominates the market for ethnic food products sold to Hispanics. Best Foods' Mazola Corn Oil captures two thirds of the Hispanic market for this product category. Time, Inc. has more than 200,000 subscribers to its *People en Espanol*.

PepsiCo often uses Spanish language advertising to promote its soft drinks to the Hispanic community in the United States.

PepsiCo, Inc.
www.pepsi.com

Asian Buying Patterns   About 70 percent of Asians in the United States are immigrants, and most are under the age of 30. Recent U.S. census figures indicate that Asian-Americans are the fastest-growing racial/ethnic subculture in the United States.

The Asian subculture is composed of Chinese, Japanese, Filipinos, Koreans, Asian-Indians, people from Southeast Asia, and Pacific Islanders. The diversity of the Asian subculture is so great that generalizations about buying patterns of this group are difficult to make.[50] Consumer research on Asian-Americans suggests that individuals and families divide into two groups. "Assimilated" Asian-Americans are conversant in English, highly educated, hold professional and managerial positions, and exhibit buying patterns very much like the typical American consumer. This group buys 15 percent of the 2,500 pianos Steinway makes every year in North America. "Nonassimilated" Asian-Americans are recent immigrants who still cling to their native languages and customs. The diversity of Asian-Americans evident in language, customs, and tastes requires marketers to be sensitive to different Asian nationalities. For example, Anheuser-Busch's agricultural products division sells eight different varieties of California-grown rice, each with a different Asian label to cover a range of nationalities and tastes. The company's advertising also addresses the preferences of Chinese, Japanese, and Koreans for different kinds of rice bowls.

Studies also show that the Asian-American subculture as a whole is characterized by hard work, strong family ties, appreciation for education, and median family incomes exceeding those of white families. Moreover, this subculture is the most entrepreneurial in the United States, as evidenced by the number of Asian-owned businesses. These qualities led Metropolitan Life Insurance to identify Asians as a target for insurance following the company's success in marketing to Hispanics.

Concept Check

1. What are the two primary forms of personal influence?

2. Marketers are concerned with which types of reference groups?

3. What two challenges must marketers overcome when marketing to Hispanics?

SUMMARY

1 When a consumer buys a product, it is not an act but a process. There are five steps in the purchase decision process: problem recognition, information search, alternative evaluation, purchase decision, and postpurchase behavior.

2 Consumers evaluate alternatives on the basis of attributes. Identifying which attributes are most important to consumers, along with understanding consumer beliefs about how a brand performs on those attributes, can make the difference between successful and unsuccessful products.

3 Consumer involvement with what is bought affects whether the purchase decision process involves routine, limited, or extended problem solving. Situational influences also affect the process.

4 Perception is important to marketers because of the selectivity of what a consumer sees or hears, comprehends, and retains.

5 Much of the behavior that consumers exhibit is learned. Consumers learn from repeated experience and reasoning. Brand loyalty is a result of learning.

6 Attitudes are learned predispositions to respond to an object or class of objects in a consistently favorable or unfavorable way. Attitudes are based on a person's values and beliefs concerning the attributes of objects.

7 Lifestyle is a mode of living reflected in a person's activities, interests, and opinions of himself or herself and the world.

8 Personal influence takes two forms: opinion leadership and word-of-mouth activity. A specific type of personal influence exists in the form of reference groups.

9 Family influences on consumer behavior result from three sources: consumer socialization, family life cycle, and decision making within the household.

10 Within the United States there are social classes and subcultures that affect a consumer's values and behavior. Marketers must be sensitive to these sociocultural influences when developing a marketing mix.

KEY TERMS AND CONCEPTS

attitude p. 133
beliefs p. 133
brand loyalty p. 132
cognitive dissonance p. 125
consumer behavior p. 122
consumer socialization p. 138
evaluative criteria p. 123
evoked set p. 124
family life cycle p. 139
involvement p. 126
learning p. 132
lifestyle p. 134
motivation p. 128

national character p. 129
opinion leaders p. 136
perceived risk p. 131
perception p. 130
personality p. 129
purchase decision process p. 122
reference groups p. 137
self-concept p. 129
situational influences p. 127
social class p. 141
subcultures p. 141
subliminal perception p. 131
word of mouth p. 137

APPLYING MARKETING CONCEPTS AND PERSPECTIVES

1 Review Figure 5–2 in the text, which shows the CD-player attributes identified by *Consumer Reports.* Which attributes are important to you? What other attributes might you consider? Which brand would you prefer?

2 Suppose research at Panasonic reveals that prospective buyers are anxious about buying high-definition television sets. What strategies might you recommend to the company to reduce consumer anxiety?

3 A Porsche salesperson was taking orders on new cars because he was unable to satisfy the demand with the limited number of cars in the showroom and lot. Several persons had backed out of the contract within two weeks of signing the order. What explanation can you give for this behavior, and what remedies would you recommend?

4 Which social class would you associate with each of the following items or actions: (*a*) tennis club membership, (*b*) an arrangement of plastic flowers in the kitchen, (*c*) *True Romance* magazine, (*d*) *Smithsonian* magazine, (*e*) formally dressing for dinner frequently, and (*f*) being a member of a bowling team.

5 Assign one or more levels of the hierarchy of needs and the motives described in Figure 5–5 to the following products: (*a*) life insurance, (*b*) cosmetics, (*c*) *The Wall Street Journal,* and (*d*) hamburgers.

6 With which stage in the family life cycle would the purchase of the following products and services be most closely identified: (*a*) bedroom furniture, (*b*) life insurance, (*c*) a Caribbean cruise, (*d*) a house mortgage, and (*e*) children's toys?

7 "The greater the perceived risk in a purchase situation, the more likely that cognitive dissonance will result." Does this statement have any basis given the discussion in the text? Why?

INTERNET EXERCISE

The size and economic significance of racial/ethnic sub-cultures in the United States has been documented by the 2000 Census. Population statistics supplied by the U.S. Census are readily accessible as www.census.gov. These statistics coupled with data useful for marketing purposes offer valuable insights into the growing diversity of the U.S. population.

The Selig Center for Economic Growth at the University of Georgia provides useful information on the buying power of African-Americans, Hispanics, and Asian-Americans—the three largest racial/ethnic sub-

cultures in the United States. Visit the Center's website at www.selig.uga.edu/ for answers to the following questions.

1   What is the most recent estimate of the buying power of African-Americans, Hispanics, and Asian-Americans in the United States.

2   In which states is African-American buying power the highest? Which states have the highest Hispanic and Asian-American buying power?

VIDEO CASE 5–1   Ken Davis Products, Inc: Barbecue Sauces for "Non-Improvisers"

"Cooking is a lot like music," explains Barbara Jo Davis. "There are musicians who are excellent musicians and they can play any of the classical music to perfection, but they don't know how to improvise. And then there are the jazz musicians who can do both of these things."

"The same thing is true of cooks," continues Barbara. "There are the cooks who can follow a recipe . . . and will be the best cooks in the world as long as they have a recipe. But if they have to improvise, then they're lost. So what we want to do is help those who aren't the improvisers."

THE COMPANY

Barbara Jo Davis is president of Ken Davis Products, Inc., a small regional business that develops and markets barbecue sauces. The company was founded by Barbara Davis's late spouse Ken Davis. Ken owned a restaurant where he served his grandmother's recipe for barbecue sauce, and he received such positive feedback from his customers he decided to write the recipe down to ensure it would taste the same every time he made it. He called in Barbara, then a home economist for a large consumer foods corporation, to help him do it. Shortly afterward Ken closed the restaurant, married Barbara, and began marketing his barbecue sauce full time. Barbara Davis stayed with the consumer foods corporation, becoming a manager for the test kitchens and for the cookbooks, until 1988 when she left to work for Ken Davis Products full time.

While Ken Davis Products is a market leader in its region, it has not expanded nationwide. Barbara Davis explains, "What I hear consumers say again and again is

the reason they buy Ken Davis barbecue sauces is because it's a local company. I think the reason we're the market leaders is because it's a personal product. People know who the person is. They can see me driving around in my car."

PRODUCTS, CUSTOMERS, AND ENVIRONMENT

In addition to the Original Ken Davis Barbecue Sauce, the company also sells Smooth and Spicy Barbecue Sauce, with jalapeno peppers added to it, and a line of marinade sauces called Jazz It Up. Through consumer testing and focus groups, Barbara Davis discovered the real problem consumers are facing when they cook is how to add flavor to the meats they are eating. Hence the Jazz It Up line of marinade sauces was born. Ken Davis Products now offers four varieties of cooking sauces—Orange Citrus, Lemon Lime, Southwestern, and Mesquite. "They're really a hybrid between marinades and cooking sauces because you can use them as an ingredient, a marinade, or even as a dipping sauce," explains Barbara Davis. This was a natural product line extension for Ken Davis Products based on its reputation in the barbecue sauce market.

The company does not target specific consumer segments because it seems the consumers are just about everybody. Barbara Davis has discovered through consumer focus groups that the barbecue sauce buying decision is still made by the female head of the household, but everybody in the family seems to participate in the decision. "Kids especially like our sauce a lot," explains Barbara Davis, "and elderly people like the Original Recipe because it's got a lot of flavor but it's not hot or spicy."

The Food and Drug Administration (FDA) recently passed legislation requiring all consumer food products to nutrition label their products in a standardized way. For small companies such as Ken Davis Products, this meant the added expense of finding an independent laboratory to analyze the products and redesigning the labels. Barbara Davis thinks this new legislation works to the advantage of Ken Davis Products, though. "New people can compare and see Ken Davis is indeed lower in sodium than most of the other barbecue sauces on the market."

THE ISSUES

Ken Davis Products prides itself on staying abreast of changing consumer tastes and trends. In addition to conducting focus groups, Barbara Davis solicits informal feedback from current and potential Ken Davis customers. She will talk to testers at an in-store sampling or even walk up to shoppers in the barbecue sauce aisle and ask them about their purchases. Barbara Davis believes, "You have to listen to your consumer because you're not in this business to please yourself. You're in business to please your consumer." In addition to discovering the latest tastes, she has learned from her customers that the primary promotional vehicle used to spread the word about Ken Davis Products is word of mouth.

To make the most of this strategy, Ken Davis Products participates in event marketing and in-store sampling. Ken Davis used to always say, "The best way to sell a food product is to get people to taste it, because it's ultimately the taste that will keep them as customers." Barbara Davis has found that another successful strategy to get people talking about Ken Davis Products is to become involved in the community. She regularly talks to groups of young entrepreneurs or invites school children to her test kitchen to learn how to cook. "You do all of these little things just to get people thinking Ken Davis. And they don't even know they're thinking Ken Davis half the time. But it's so ingrained that when they go to the grocery store, why would they look at those other brands?" Barbara Davis also sends out a newsletter twice a year to Ken Davis Products users with new recipe ideas and stories about the company. Today's busy family is always on the look out for quick and easy recipes.

Ken Davis Products also uses some more traditional promotional vehicles, such as Free Standing Inserts (FSIs) in the Sunday paper and radio advertising. The FSIs include a coupon to induce new customers to try the product. The radio ads reflect the local, homegrown differentiation strategy used by Ken Davis Products. Barbara Davis does the commercials herself, which are completely unrehearsed. "That way I don't have to pay talent," she chuckles.

THE MULTIPLE ROLES OF A SMALL BUSINESSPERSON

After working for a large corporation and then becoming a small business entrepreneur, Barbara Davis is in a unique position to comment on the satisfactions and hardships of owning your own business. She stresses that you have to know everything about your business—you can't specialize as in a large corporation. You also get to make all the decisions and have the satisfaction of being a part of the process every step of the way. "But," Barbara adds, "you have to work harder than you have ever worked in your life. You have to always be working. When I was working for a corporation, I resented working all those hours because it wasn't for me. But now when I'm working all these hours I love it because I am doing it for myself. That's the reward—it's all for you."

Questions

1 In what ways have American eating habits changed over the past decade that affect a barbecue sauce manufacturer?

2 What are the two or three main (*a*) objective evaluative criteria and (*b*) subjective evaluative criteria consumers of Ken Davis barbecue sauces might use?

3 How can Ken Davis Products do marketing research on consumers to find out what they eat, to learn how they use barbecue sauces, and to get ideas for new products?

4 (*a*) Do you think a small, local company such as Ken Davis Products should have entered the market as a premium-priced product or a low-priced product? (*b*) What should its pricing strategy be today?

5 What do you see are the (*a*) satisfactions and (*b*) concerns of being in business for yourself?

6

ORGANIZATIONAL MARKETS AND BUYER BEHAVIOR

AFTER READING THIS CHAPTER YOU SHOULD BE ABLE TO:

- Distinguish among industrial, reseller, and government markets.

- Recognize key characteristics of organizational buying that make it different from consumer buying.

- Understand how buying centers and buying situations influence organizational purchasing.

- Recognize the growing importance of online buying in industrial, reseller, and government markets.

BUYING PAPER IS SERIOUS BUSINESS AT JCPENNEY

John Baetz views paper very differently from most people. As the purchasing manager at JCPMedia, he and a team of purchasing professionals buy over 260,000 tons of paper annually at a cost exceeding hundreds of millions of dollars.

JCPMedia is the print and paper purchasing arm for JCPenney, the fifth-largest retailer in the United States and the largest catalog merchant of general merchandise in the Western Hemisphere. Paper is serious business at JCPMedia which buys paper for JCPenney catalogs (see opposite page), newspaper inserts, and direct-mail pieces. Some 20 companies from around the world, including International Paper in the United States, Stora Enso in Sweden, and UPM-Kymmene, Inc., a Finnish paper company, supply paper to JCPMedia.

JCPMedia paper buyers work closely with JCPenney marketing personnel to assure that the right quality and quantity of paper is purchased at the right price point for merchandise featured in the millions of catalogs, newspaper inserts, and direct-mail pieces distributed every year. In addition to paper quality and price, buyers also consider supplier capabilities. These include a supplier's capacity to deliver selected grades of paper from specialty items to magazine papers, the availability of specific types of paper to meet printing deadlines, and ongoing environmental programs. For example, a supplier's environment program, including forestry management and antipollution practices, are considered in the buying process at JCPMedia.[1]

The next time you thumb through a JCPenney catalog, newspaper insert, or direct-mail piece, take a moment to notice the paper. Considerable effort and attention was given to its selection and purchase.

Purchasing paper for JCPenney's catalogs, newspaper inserts, and direct-mail pieces is one example of organizational buying. This chapter examines the types of organizational buyers, key characteristics of organizational buying including online buying, and some typical buying decisions in organizational markets.

THE NATURE AND SIZE OF ORGANIZATIONAL MARKETS

Understanding organizational markets and buying behavior is a necessary prerequisite for effective business marketing. **Business marketing** is the marketing of goods and services to commercial enterprises, governments, and other profit and not-for-profit organizations for use in the creation of goods and services that they then produce and market to other business customers, as well as individuals and ultimate consumers.[2] Because over half of all U.S. business school graduates take jobs in firms that engage in business marketing, it is important to understand the characteristics of organizational buyers and their buying behavior.

Organizational buyers are those manufacturers, wholesalers and retailers, and government agencies that buy goods and services for their own use or for resale. For example, these organizations buy computers and telephone services for their own use. However, manufacturers buy raw materials and parts that they reprocess into the finished goods they sell, whereas wholesalers and retailers resell the goods they buy without reprocessing them. Organizational buyers include all buyers in a nation except ultimate consumers. These organizational buyers purchase and lease large volumes of capital equipment, raw materials, manufactured parts, supplies, and business services. In fact, because they often buy raw materials and parts, process them, and sell the upgraded product several times before it is purchased by the final organizational buyer or ultimate consumer, the aggregate purchases of organizational buyers in a year are far greater than those of ultimate consumers.

Organizational buyers are divided into three different markets: (1) industrial, (2) reseller, and (3) government markets (Figure 6-1).[3]

Industrial Markets

There are over 11.2 million firms in the industrial, or business, market. These **industrial firms** in some way reprocess a product or service they buy before selling it again to the next buyer. This is certainly true of Corning, Inc. which

FIGURE 6–1
Type and number of organizational customers

TYPE OF ORGANIZATION	NUMBER	KIND OF MARKET
Manufacturers	378,000	Industrial (business)
Mining	25,000	markets—11,221,000
Construction	639,000	
Farms, timber, and fisheries	1,912,000	
Service	7,290,000	
Finance, insurance, and real estate	661,000	
Transportation, communications, and public utilities	294,000	
Not-for-profit associations	22,000	
Wholesalers	521,000	Reseller markets—2,082,000
Retailers	1,561,000	
Government units	88,000	Government markets—88,000

SATISFYING THE DEMANDS OF METROPOLITAN NETWORKS HAS NEVER BEEN SO EASY. Everyone wants more bandwidth, and with Corning® MetroCor™ optical fiber everyone can have more – for less. MetroCor fiber, which enables transparent optical networking in metropolitan areas, is optimized for cost-effective DWDM transmission up to 10 Gbps. So not only is it ideal for today's networks, but also for tomorrow's. With its dispersion-optimized profile, MetroCor fiber lowers the cost of transmission equipment by making longer and less expensive ring architectures possible. MetroCor fiber also allows you to reduce your network's complexity while increasing its reliability. So in the city, less is clearly more.

Move it with MetroCor™ fiber.

CORNING
Discovering Beyond Imagination

www.corning.com/opticalfiber / 800.525.2524, ext. 5107 [us & canada] / 607.786.8125, ext. 5107 [international]

Corning, Inc. is a world leader in fiber-optic technology.

Corning, Inc.
www.corning.com

transforms an exotic blend of materials to create optical fiber capable of carrying much of the telephone traffic in the United States at once on a single strand. It is also true (if you stretch your imagination) of a firm selling services, such as a bank that takes money from its depositors, reprocesses it, and "sells" it as loans to borrowers.

The importance of services in the United States today is emphasized by the composition of the industrial markets shown in Figure 6–1. The first four types of industrial firms (manufacturers; mining; construction; and farms, timber, and fisheries) sell physical products and represent 26 percent of all the industrial firms, or about 1.9 million. The services market sells diverse services such as legal advice, auto repair, and dry cleaning. Along with finance, insurance, and real estate businesses, and transportation, communication, and public utility firms, these service firms represent about 73 percent of all industrial firms, or about 8.2 million. Because of the size and importance of service firms and some 22,000 not-for-profit organizations (such as the American Red Cross), service marketing is discussed in detail in Chapter 12.

Reseller Markets

Wholesalers and retailers who buy physical products and resell them again without any reprocessing are **resellers**. In the United States there are almost 1.6 million retailers and 521,000 wholesalers. In Chapters 15 through 17 we shall see how manufacturers use wholesalers and retailers in their distribution ("place") strategies as channels through which their products reach ultimate consumers. In this chapter we look at these resellers mainly as organizational buyers in terms of (1) how they make their own buying decisions and (2) which products they choose to carry.

Government Markets

Government units are the federal, state, and local agencies that buy goods and services for the constituents they serve. There are about 88,000 of these government units in the United States. Their annual purchases vary in size from the $898 million the Federal Aviation Administration intends to spend for 3,000 computerized workstations for 22 major air traffic control centers in the United States to lesser amounts spent by local school or sanitation districts.[4]

Global Organizational Markets

Industrial, reseller, and government markets also exist on a global scale. International trade statistics indicate that the largest exporting industries in the United States focus on organizational customers, not ultimate consumers.

The majority of world trade involves manufacturers, resellers, and government agencies buying goods and services for their own use or for resale to others. The exchange relationships often involve numerous transactions spanning the globe. For example, Volvo Aero of Sweden, Ishikawajima-Harima Heavy Industries of Japan, and Chemical Automatics Design Bureau of Russia provide key components used in the high-performance liquid hydrogen-fueled rocket engine made for space exploration by U.S.-based Pratt & Whitney. This engine is deployed in the Atlas, Titan, and Delta launch vehicles made by Lockheed-Martin and Boeing, which are sold to space agencies of many countries for use in deploying communication satellites. Even the familiar Yellow Pages, sold in Moscow, is the product of a global purchasing and marketing effort. The Moscow Yellow Pages lists more than 22,000 industrial, trade, joint venture, and government office telephone numbers and addresses. A New York City firm solicits advertising for and a German publisher prints the directory in English on behalf of the Moscow city government and telephone system for resale to businesses through stores, hotels, and international trade centers such as the Armand Hammer Center in Red Square.

MEASURING DOMESTIC AND GLOBAL INDUSTRIAL, RESELLER, AND GOVERNMENT MARKETS

The measurement of industrial, reseller, and government markets is an important first step for a firm interested in gauging the size of one, two, or all three of these markets in the United States and around the world. This task has been made easier with the **North American Industry Classification System (NAICS)**.[5] NAICS provides common industry definitions for Canada, Mexico, and the United States, which facilitate the measurement of economic activity in the three member countries of the North American Free Trade Agreement (NAFTA). NAICS replaced the Standard Industrial Classification (SIC) system, a version of which has been in place for more than 50 years in the three NAFTA member countries. The SIC neither permitted comparability across countries nor accurately measured new or emerging industries. Furthermore, NAICS is consistent with the International Standard Industrial Classification of All Economic Activities, published by the United Nations, to facilitate measurement of global economic activity.

The NAICS groups economic activity to permit studies of market share, demand for goods and services, import competition in domestic markets, and similar studies. NAICS designates industries with a numerical code in a defined structure. A six-digit coding system is used. The first two digits designate a sector of the economy, the third digit designates a subsector, and the fourth digit represents an industry group. The fifth digit designates a specific industry and is the most detailed level at which comparable data is available for Canada, Mexico, and the United States. The sixth digit designates individual country-level national industries. Figure 6–2 presents an abbreviated breakdown within the Information Industries Sector (code 51) to illustrate the classification scheme.

The NAICS permits a firm to find the NAICS codes of its present customers and then obtain NAICS-coded lists for similar firms. Also, it is possible to monitor NAICS categories to determine the growth in various sectors and industries to identify promising marketing opportunities. However, NAICS codes, like the earlier SIC codes, have important limitations. The NAICS assigns one code to each organization based on its major economic activity, so large firms that engage in many different activities are still given only one NAICS code. A second limitation is that five-digit national industry codes are not available for all three countries because the respective governments will not reveal data when too few organizations exist in a category. Despite these limitations, the NAICS represents yet another effort toward economic integration in North America and the world.

Concept Check

1. What are the three main types of organizational buyers?

2. What is the North American Industry Classification System (NAICS)?

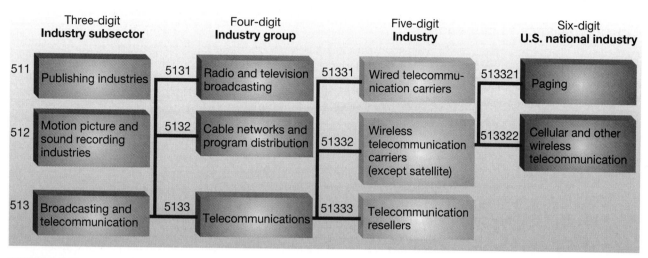

FIGURE 6–2
NAICS breakdown for
information industries sector:
NAICS code 51 (abbreviated)

CHARACTERISTICS OF ORGANIZATIONAL BUYING

Organizations are different from individuals, so buying for an organization is different from buying for yourself or your family.[6] True, in both cases the objective in making the purchase is to solve the buyer's problem—to satisfy a need or want. But unique objectives and policies of an organization put special constraints on how it makes buying decisions. Understanding the characteristics of organizational buying is essential in designing effective marketing programs to reach these buyers. Key characteristics of organizational buying are listed in Figure 6–3 on the next page and discussed next.[7]

Demand Characteristics

Consumer demand for products and services is affected by their price and availability and by consumers' personal tastes and discretionary income. By comparison, industrial demand is derived. **Derived demand** means that the demand for industrial products and services is driven by, or derived from, demand for consumer products and services. For example, the demand for Weyerhaeuser's pulp and paper products is based on consumer demand for newspapers, Domino's "keep warm" pizza-to-go boxes, Federal Express packages, and disposable diapers. Derived demand is often based on expectations of future consumer demand. For instance, Whirlpool purchases parts for its washers and dryers in anticipation of consumer demand, which is affected by the replacement cycle for these products and by consumer income.

Size of the Order or Purchase

The size of the purchase involved in organizational buying is typically much larger than that in consumer buying. The dollar value of a single purchase made by an organization often runs into the thousands or millions of dollars. For example, Motorola was recently awarded a $63 million contract to install a cellular phone system in Brazil.[8] With so much money at stake, most organizations place constraints on their buyers in the form of purchasing policies or procedures. Buyers must often get competitive bids from at least three prospective suppliers when the order is above a specific amount, such as $5,000. When the order is above an even higher amount, such as $50,000, it may require the review and approval of a vice president or even

CHARACTERISTICS   **DIMENSIONS**

Market characteristics

- Demand for industrial products and services is derived.
- Few customers typically exist, and their purchase orders are large.

Product or service characteristics

- Products or services are technical in nature and purchased on the basis of specifications.
- There is a predominance of raw and semifinished goods purchased.
- Heavy emphasis is placed on delivery time, technical assistance, postsale service, and financing assistance.

Buying process characteristics

- Technically qualified and professional buyers exist and follow established purchasing policies and procedures.
- Buying objectives and criteria are typically spelled out, as are procedures for evaluating sellers and products (services).
- Multiple buying influences exist, and multiple parties participate in purchase decisions.
- Reciprocal arrangements exist, and negotiation between buyers and sellers is commonplace.
- Online buying over the Internet is widespread.

Marketing mix characteristics

- Direct selling to organizational buyers is the rule, and physical distribution is very important.
- Advertising and other forms of promotion are technical in nature.
- Price is often negotiated, evaluated as part of broader seller and product (service) qualities, typically inelastic owing to derived demand, and frequently affected by trade and quantity discounts.

FIGURE 6–3
Key characteristics of organizational buying behavior

the president of the company. Knowing how the size of the order affects buying practices is important in determining who participates in the purchase decision and makes the final decision, and also the length of time required to arrive at a purchase agreement.

Number of Potential Buyers

Firms selling consumer products or services often try to reach thousands or millions of individuals or households. For example, your local supermarket or bank probably serves thousands of people, and Kellogg tries to reach 80 million American households with its breakfast cereals and probably succeeds in selling to a third or half of these in any given year. In contrast, firms selling to organizations are often restricted to far fewer buyers. Gulfstream Aerospace Corporation can sell its business jets to a few thousand organizations throughout the world, and B. F. Goodrich sells its original equipment tires to fewer than 10 car manufacturers.

Derived demand, the size of the purchase order, and the number of potential buyers will play a part in the commercial success of the new A380 superjumbo jet being developed by Europe's Airbus Industrie. Read the accompanying Market NewsNet to learn more about the largest airplane ever built.[9]

Organizational Buying Objectives

Organizations buy products and services for one main reason: to help them achieve their objectives. For business firms the buying objective is usually to increase profits through reducing costs or increasing revenues. 7-Eleven buys automated inven-

MARKETING NEWSNET

The Airbus A380 Superjumbo Jet Is About to Take Flight

GLOBAL

Rapidly expanding demand for intercontinental passenger air traffic and the growth of the global air freight industry bodes well for aircraft manufacturers. Europe's Airbus Industrie expects to transport future air travelers and cargo in the largest airplane ever built—its A380 superjumbo jet. Scheduled to begin service in 2006, the A380 features passenger models seating 555 to 800 people, spread over two full decks, and a freightliner model capable of delivering 331,000 pounds of cargo. The A380 has a list price of about $220 million.

The demand for the A380 will depend on prospective buyers' expectation of future air transport traffic. If initial orders are an indication, the future is bright for superjumbo jet aircraft. Airbus has already taken orders for the A380 from buyers on five continents, including Singapore Airlines, Qantas Airways, Virgin Atlantic Airways, Air France, Qatar

Airways, and FedEx, which has 10 freightliners on order with an option to buy even more.

tory systems to increase the number of products that can be sold through its convenience stores and to keep them fresh. Nissan Motor Company switched its advertising agency because it expects the new agency to devise a more effective ad campaign to help it sell more cars and increase revenues. To improve executive decision making, many firms buy advanced computer systems to process data. The objectives of nonprofit firms and government agencies are usually to meet the needs of the groups they serve. Thus, a hospital buys a high-technology diagnostic device to serve its patients better. Understanding buying objectives is a necessary first step in marketing to organizations. Recognizing the high costs of energy, Sylvania promotes to prospective buyers cost savings and increased profits made possible by its fluorescent and halogen lights.

Many companies today have broadened their buying objectives to include an emphasis on buying from minority- and women-owned suppliers and vendors. Companies such as Chrysler, Coca-Cola, Coors, and JCPenney report that sales, profits, and customer satisfaction have increased because of their minority- and women-owned supplier and vendor initiatives.[10] The successful efforts of Sears Roebuck are described in the accompanying Marketing NewsNet on the next page.[11]

Organizational Buying Criteria

In making a purchase the buying organization must weigh key buying criteria that apply to the potential supplier and what it wants to sell. **Organizational buying criteria** are the objective attributes of the supplier's products and services and the capabilities of the supplier itself. These criteria serve the same purpose as the evaluative criteria used by consumers and described in Chapter 5. Seven of the most commonly used criteria are (1) price, (2) ability to meet the quality specifications required for the item, (3) ability to meet required delivery schedules, (4) technical capability, (5) warranties and claim policies in the event of poor performance, (6) past performance on previous contracts, and (7) production facilities and capacity.[12] Suppliers that meet or exceed these criteria create customer value.

MARKETING NEWSNET

Minority- and Women-Owned Suppliers Create Customer Value at Sears, Roebuck and Co.

CUSTOMER VALUE

Sears is a leader in forging innovative links with minority- and women-owned suppliers and vendors. According to a Sears senior executive, "Minority- and women-owned suppliers have helped transform our apparel and merchandising strategies."

A visible and successful result of Sears's efforts is the Anthony Mark Hankins Signature line of clothing for women introduced into Sears in 1996. Anthony Mark Hankins is an award-winning African-American designer. Pictured here is one of his designs from his Fall 2001 Signature Collection for Sears.

The Sears commitment to furthering its involvement with minority- and women-owned suppliers and vendors is consistent with the diversity of customers that the retailer serves. "We want African-Americans, Hispanic-Americans, and Asian-Americans to know Sears is their store," says the company's director of ethnic marketing. He added: "Sears knows how important the ethnic customer is—and Sears is out front developing product lines and marketing approaches that tell these customers in no uncertain terms: You are welcome here."

Organizational buyers who purchase products and services in the global marketplace often supplement their buying criteria with supplier ISO 9000 standards certification. **ISO 9000** standards, developed by the International Standards Organization (ISO) in Geneva, Switzerland, refer to standards for registration and certification of a manufacturer's quality management and assurance system based on an on-site audit of practices and procedures. 3M, which buys and markets its products globally, has over 80 percent of its manufacturing and service facilities ISO 9000 certified. According to the company's director of quality control, certification also gives 3M confidence in the consistent quality of its suppliers' manufacturing systems and products.[13]

Many organizational buyers today are transforming their buying criteria into specific requirements that are communicated to prospective suppliers. This practice, called **reverse marketing**, involves the deliberate effort by organizational buyers to build relationships that shape suppliers' products, services, and capabilities to fit a buyer's needs and those of its customers.[14] For example, consider the case of Johnson Controls, Inc., the supplier of seats for the Plymouth Neon.[15] Johnson was able to meet Plymouth's cost target but not its safety, weight, and comfort requirements. After five 11-hour days, Johnson and Plymouth engineering and marketing staffs jointly worked out the technical details to satisfy Plymouth's performance requirements at a price acceptable to both parties. Ongoing reverse marketing efforts also exist. Harley-Davidson expects even its long-term suppliers to provide written plans of their efforts to improve quality, and it monitors the progress of these suppliers toward achieving these goals.

With many U.S. manufacturers using a "just-in-time" (JIT) inventory system that reduces the inventory of production parts to those to be used within hours or days, on-time delivery is becoming an even more important buying criterion and, in some instances, a requirement. Caterpillar trains its key suppliers at its Quality Institute in

Harley-Davidson works closely with its suppliers to assure quality parts and timeliness of delivery.

Harley-Davidson

www.harley-davidson.com

THE SONG ISN'T "BORN TO BE STATUS QUO."

JIT inventory systems and conducts supplier seminars on how to diagnose, correct, and implement continuous quality improvement programs. The just-in-time inventory system is discussed further in Chapter 16.

Buyer-Seller Relationships and Supply Partnerships

Another distinction between organizational and consumer buying behavior lies in the nature of the relationship between organizational buyers and suppliers. Specifically, organizational buying is more likely to involve complex and lengthy negotiations concerning delivery schedules, price, technical specifications, warranties, and claim policies. These negotiations can last for more than a year. This was the case when Los Alamos National Laboratory recently purchased a $35 million Cray Research T90 supercomputer that performs up to 60 million calculations per second.[16]

Reciprocal arrangements also exist in organizational buying. **Reciprocity** is an industrial buying practice in which two organizations agree to purchase each other's products and services. The U.S. Justice Department frowns on reciprocal buying because it restricts the normal operation of the free market. However, the practice exists and can limit the flexibility of organizational buyers in choosing alternative suppliers. Regardless of the legality of reciprocal buying, do you believe this practice is ethical? (See the Ethics and Social Responsibility Alert on page 158.)[17]

Long-term contracts are also prevalent.[18] As an example, the U.S. Department of Defense recently announced it intends to spend $6.9 billion over five years for computer and computer technology provided by Electronic Data Systems. Dana Corporation has engaged in a 10-year, $2 billion contract to supply Mack Trucks with axles, clutches, and frame assemblies.

In some cases, buyer-seller relationships develop into supply partnerships.[19] A **supply partnership** exists when a buyer and its supplier adopt mutually beneficial objectives, policies, and procedures for the purpose of lowering the cost and/or increasing the value of products and services delivered to the ultimate consumer. Intel, the world's largest manufacturer of microprocessors and the "computer inside" most personal computers, is a case in point. Intel supports its suppliers by offering them quality management programs and by investing in supplier equipment that produces fewer product defects and boosts supplier productivity. Suppliers, in turn,

ETHICS AND SOCIAL RESPONSIBILITY ALERT

Scratching Each Other's Back: The Ethics of Reciprocity in Organizational Buying

ETHICS

Reciprocity, the buying practice in which two organizations agree to purchase each other's products and services, is frowned upon by the U.S. Justice Department because it restricts the normal operation of the free market. Reciprocal buying practices do exist, however, in a variety of forms, including certain types of countertrade arrangements in international marketing. Furthermore, the extent to which reciprocity is viewed as an ethical issue varies across cultures. In many Asian countries, for instance, reciprocity is often a positive and widespread practice.

Reciprocity is occasionally addressed in the ethics codes of companies or their purchasing policies. For instance, IBM describes its reciprocity policy in the company's Global Procurement Principles and Practices Statement:

> IBM's goal is to buy goods and services which have the best prices, quality, delivery, and technology. IBM has a policy against reciprocal buying arrangements because those arrangements can interfere with this goal.

Do you think reciprocal buying is unethical?

provide Intel with consistent high-quality products at a lower cost for its customers, the makers of personal computers, and finally you, the ultimate customer. Retailers, too, are forging partnerships with their suppliers. Wal-Mart and Kmart have such a relationship with Procter & Gamble for ordering and replenishing P&G's products in their stores. By using computerized cash register scanning equipment and direct electronic linkages to P&G, these retailers can tell P&G what merchandise is needed, along with how much, when, and to which store to deliver it on a daily basis. Because supply partnerships also involve the physical distribution of goods, they are again discussed in Chapter 16 in the context of supply chains.

The Buying Center: A Cross-Functional Group

For routine purchases with a small dollar value, a single buyer or purchasing manager often makes the purchase decision alone. In many instances, however, several people in the organization participate in the buying process. The individuals in this group, called a **buying center**, share common goals, risks, and knowledge important to a purchase decision. For most large multistore chain resellers, such as Sears, 7-Eleven convenience stores, Kmart, or Safeway, the buying center is highly formalized and is called a *buying committee*. However, most industrial firms or government units use informal groups of people or call meetings to arrive at buying decisions.

The importance of the buying center requires that a firm marketing to many industrial firms and government units understand the structure, technical and business functions represented, and behavior of these groups. One researcher has suggested four questions to provide guidance in understanding the buying center in these organizations:[20] Which individuals are in the buying center for the product or service? What is the relative influence of each member of the group? What are the buying criteria of each member? How does each member of the group perceive our firm, our products and services, and our salespeople?

Answers to these questions are difficult to come by, particularly when dealing with industrial firms, resellers, and governments outside the United States.[21] For example, U.S. firms are often frustrated by the fact that Japanese buyers "ask a thousand questions" but give few answers, sometimes rely on third-party individuals to convey views on proposals, are prone to not "talk business," and often say yes to be courteous when they mean no. U.S. firms in the global chemical industry recognize that production engineering personnel have a great deal of influence in Hungarian buying groups, while purchasing agents in the Canadian chemical industry have relatively more influence in buying decisions.

People in the Buying Center

The composition of the buying center in a given organization depends on the specific item being bought. Although a buyer or purchasing manager is almost always a member of the buying center, individuals from other functional areas are included depending on what is to be purchased. In buying a million-dollar machine tool, the president (because of the size of the purchase) and the production vice president or manager would probably be members. For key components to be incorporated in a final manufactured product, a cross-functional group of individuals from research and development (R&D), engineering, and quality control are likely to be added. For new word-processing equipment, experienced secretaries who will use the equipment would be members. Still, a major question in penetrating the buying center is finding and reaching the people who will initiate, influence, and actually make the buying decision.

Roles in the Buying Center

Researchers have identified five specific roles that an individual in a buying center can play.[22] In some purchases the same person may perform two or more of these roles.

- *Users* are the people in the organization who actually use the product or service, such as a secretary who will use a new word processor.
- *Influencers* affect the buying decision, usually by helping define the specifications for what is bought. The information systems manager would be a key influencer in the purchase of a new mainframe computer.
- *Buyers* have formal authority and responsibility to select the supplier and negotiate the terms of the contract. The purchasing manager probably would perform this role in the purchase of a mainframe computer.
- *Deciders* have the formal or informal power to select or approve the supplier that receives the contract. Whereas in routine orders the decider is usually the buyer or purchasing manager, in important technical purchases it is more likely to be someone from R&D, engineering, or quality control. The decider for a key component being incorporated in a final manufactured product might be any of these three people.
- *Gatekeepers* control the flow of information in the buying center. Purchasing personnel, technical experts, and secretaries can all keep salespeople or information from reaching people performing the other four roles.

Buying Situations and the Buying Center

The number of people in the buying center largely depends on the specific buying situation. Researchers who have studied organizational buying identify three types of buying situations, called **buy classes**. These buy classes vary from the routine reorder, or *straight rebuy,* to the completely new purchase, termed *new buy.* In between these extremes is the *modified rebuy.* Some examples will clarify the differences.[23]

- *Straight rebuy.* Here the buyer or purchasing manager reorders an existing product or service from the list of acceptable suppliers, probably without even checking with users or influencers from the engineering, production, or quality control departments. Office supplies and maintenance services are usually obtained as straight rebuys.
- *Modified rebuy.* In this buying situation the users, influencers, or deciders in the buying center want to change the product specifications, price, delivery schedule, or supplier. Although the item purchased is largely the same as with the straight rebuy, the changes usually necessitate enlarging the buying center to include people outside the purchasing department.

BUYING CENTER DIMENSION	BUY-CLASS SITUATION	
	NEW BUY	STRAIGHT/MODIFIED REBUY
People involved	Many	Few
Decision time	Long	Short
Problem definition	Uncertain	Well-defined
Buying objective	Good solution	Low-price supplier
Suppliers considered	New/present	Present
Buying influence	Technical/operating personnel	Purchasing agent

FIGURE 6–4
How the buying situation
affects buying center behavior

- *New buy.* Here the organization is a first-time buyer of the product or service. This involves greater potential risks in the purchase, so the buying center is enlarged to include all those who have a stake in the new buy. Procter & Gamble's recent purchase of a multimillion-dollar fiber-optic network from Corning, Inc., linking its corporate offices in Cincinnati, represented a new buy.[24]

Figure 6–4 summarizes how buy classes affect buying center tendencies in different ways.[25]

The marketing strategies of sellers facing each of these three buying situations can vary greatly because the importance of personnel from functional areas such as purchasing, engineering, production, and R&D often varies with (1) the type of buying situation and (2) the stage of the purchasing process.[26] If it is a new buy for the manufacturer, you should be prepared to act as a consultant to the buyer, work with technical personnel, and expect a long time for a buying decision to be reached. However, if the manufacturer has bought the component part from you before (a straight or modified rebuy), you might emphasize a competitive price and a reliable supply in meetings with the purchasing agent.

Concept Check

1. What one department is almost always represented by a person in the buying center?

2. What are the three types of buying situations or buy classes?

CHARTING THE ORGANIZATIONAL BUYING PROCESS

Organizational buyers, like consumers, engage in a decision process when selecting products and services. **Organizational buying behavior** is the decision-making process that organizations use to establish the need for products and services and identify, evaluate, and choose among alternative brands and suppliers. There are important similarities and differences between the two decision-making processes. To better understand the nature of organizational buying behavior, we first compare it with consumer buying behavior and then describe an actual organizational purchase in detail.

Stages in the Organizational Buying Process

As shown in Figure 6–5 (and covered in Chapter 5), the five stages a student might use in buying a portable CD player also apply to organizational purchases. However, comparing the two right-hand columns in Figure 6–5 reveals some key differences. For example, when a portable CD player manufacturer buys earphones for its units

STAGE IN THE BUYING DECISION PROCESS	CONSUMER PURCHASE: PORTABLE CD PLAYER FOR A STUDENT	ORGANIZATIONAL PURCHASE: EARPHONES FOR A PORTABLE CD PLAYER
Problem recognition	Student doesn't like the features of the portable CD player now owned and desires a new portable CD player.	Marketing research and sales departments observe that competitors are improving the earphones on their portable CD models. The firm decides to improve the earphones on their own new models, which will be purchased from an outside supplier.
Information search	Student uses past experience, that of friends, ads, the Internet, and *Consumer Reports* to collect information and uncover alternatives.	Design and production engineers draft specifications for earphones. The purchasing department identifies suppliers of portable CD player earphones.
Alternative evaluation	Alternative portable CD players are evaluated on the basis of important attributes desired in a portable CD player, and several stores are visited.	Purchasing and engineering personnel visit with suppliers and assess (1) facilities, (2) capacity, (3) quality control, and (4) financial status. They drop any suppliers not satisfactory on these factors.
Purchase decision	A specific brand of portable CD player is selected, the price is paid, and the student leaves the store.	They use (1) quality, (2) price, (3) delivery, and (4) technical capability as key buying criteria to select a supplier. Then they negotiate terms and award a contract.
Postpurchase behavior	Student reevaluates the purchase decision, may return the portable CD player to the store if it is unsatisfactory, and looks for supportive information to justify the purchase.	They evaluate suppliers using a formal vendor rating system and notify a supplier if earphones do not meet their quality standard. If the problem is not corrected, they drop the firm as a future supplier.

FIGURE 6–5
Comparing the stages in consumer and organizational purchases

from a supplier, more individuals are involved, supplier capability becomes more important, and the postpurchase evaluation behavior is more formalized.

The earphone-buying decision process is typical of the steps made by organizational buyers. Let's now examine in detail the decision-making process for a more complex product—machine vision systems.

Buying a Machine Vision System

Machine vision is widely regarded as one of the keys to the factory of the future. The chief elements of a machine vision system are its optics, light source, camera, video processor, and computer software. Vision systems are mainly used for product inspection. They are also becoming important as one of the chief elements in the information feedback loop of systems that control manufacturing processes. Vision systems, selling in the price range of $5,000, are mostly sold to original equipment manufacturers (OEMs) who incorporate them in still larger industrial automation systems, which sell for $50,000 to $100,000.

Finding productive applications for machine vision involves the constant search for technology and designs that satisfy user needs. The buying process for machine vision components and assemblies is frequently a new buy because many machine vision systems contain elements that require some custom design. Let's track five purchasing stages that a company such as the Industrial Automation

Division of Siemens, a large German industrial firm, would follow when purchasing components and assemblies for the machine vision systems it produces and installs.

Problem Recognition

Sales engineers constantly canvass industrial automation equipment users such as American National Can, Ford Motor Company, Grumman Aircraft, and many Asian and European firms for leads on upcoming industrial automation projects. They also keep these firms current on Siemens' technology, products, and services. When a firm needing a machine vision capability identifies a project that would benefit from Siemens' expertise, company engineers typically work with the firm to determine the kind of system required to meet the customer's need.

After a contract is won, project personnel must often make a **make-buy decision**—an evaluation of whether components and assemblies will be purchased from outside suppliers or built by the company itself. (Siemens produces many components and assemblies.) When these items are to be purchased from outside suppliers, the company engages in a thorough supplier search and evaluation process.

Information Search

Companies such as Siemens employ a sophisticated process for identifying outside suppliers of components and assemblies. For standard items such as connectors, printed circuit boards, and components such as resistors and capacitors, the purchasing agent consults the company's purchasing databank, which contains information on hundreds of suppliers and thousands of products. All products in the databank have been prenegotiated as to price, quality, and delivery time, and many have been assessed using **value analysis**—a systematic appraisal of the design, quality, and performance of a product to reduce purchasing costs.

For one-of-a-kind components or assemblies such as new optics, cameras, and light sources, the company relies on its engineers to keep current on new developments in product technology. This information is often found in technical journals and industry magazines or at international trade shows where suppliers display their most recent innovations. In some instances, supplier representatives might be asked to make presentations to the buying center at Siemens. Such a group often consists of a project engineer; several design, system, and manufacturing engineers; and a purchasing agent.

The purchase of machine vision systems involves a lengthy organizational buying process.

Alternative Evaluation   Three main buying criteria are used to select suppliers: price, performance, and delivery. Other important criteria include assurance that a supplier will not go out of business during the contractual period, assurance that the supplier will meet product quality and performance specifications, and service during the contractual period. Typically, two or three suppliers for each standard component and assembly are identified from a **bidder's list**—a list of firms believed to be qualified to supply a given item. This list is generated from the company's purchasing databank as well as from engineering inputs. Specific items that are unique or one-of-a-kind may be obtained from a single supplier after careful evaluation by the buying center.

Firms selected from the bidder's list are sent a quotation request from the purchasing agent, describing the desired quantity, delivery date(s), and specifications of the components or assemblies. Suppliers are expected to respond within 30 days.

Purchase Decision   Unlike the short purchase stage in a consumer purchase, the period from supplier selection to order placement to product delivery can take several weeks or even months. Even after bids for components and assemblies are submitted, further negotiation concerning price, performance, and delivery terms is likely. Sometimes conditions related to warranties, indemnities, and payment schedules have to be agreed on. The purchase decision is further complicated by the fact that two or more suppliers of the same item might be awarded contracts. This practice can occur when large orders are requested. Furthermore, suppliers who are not chosen are informed why their bids were not selected.

Postpurchase Behavior   As in the consumer purchase decision process, postpurchase evaluation occurs in the industrial purchase decision process, but it is formalized and often more sophisticated. All items purchased are examined in a formal product acceptance process. The performance of the supplier is also monitored and recorded. Performance on past contracts determines a supplier's chances of being asked to bid on future purchases, and poor performance may result in a supplier's name being dropped from the bidder's list.

This example of an organizational purchase suggests four lessons for marketers to increase their chances of selling products and services to organizations. Firms selling to organizations must (1) understand the organization's needs, (2) get on the right bidder's list, (3) find the right people in the buying center, and (4) provide value to organizational buyers.

| Concept Check | **1.** What is a make-buy decision? |
| | **2.** What is a bidder's list? |

ONLINE BUYING IN ORGANIZATIONAL MARKETS

Organizational buying behavior and business marketing continues to evolve with the application of Internet/Web technology. Organizations dwarf consumers both in terms of online transactions made and purchase volume.[27] In fact, organizational buyers account for about 80 percent of the total worldwide dollar value of all online transactions. It is projected that online organizational buyers around the world will purchase between $6 and $7.5 trillion worth of products and services by 2005. Organizational buyers in the United States will account for about 60 percent of these purchases.

Prominence of Online Buying in Organizational Markets

Online buying in organizational markets is prominent for three major reasons.[28] First, organizational buyers depend heavily on timely supplier information that describes product availability, technical specifications, application uses, price, and delivery schedules. This information can be conveyed quickly via Internet/Web technology. Second, this technology has been shown to substantially reduce buyer order processing costs. At General Electric, online buying has cut the cost of a transaction from $50 to $100 per purchase to about $5. Third, business marketers have found that Internet/Web technology can reduce marketing costs, particularly sales and advertising expense, and broaden their potential customer base for many types of products and services. For these reasons, online buying is popular in all three kinds of organizational markets. For example, airlines order over $400 million in spare parts from the Boeing Company website each year. Customers of W. W. Grainger, a large U.S. wholesaler of maintenance, repair and operating supplies, buy about $425 million worth of these products annually online. Supply and service purchases totaling $650 million each year are made online by the Los Angeles County government.

Online buying can assume many forms. Organizational buyers can purchase directly from suppliers. For instance, a buyer might acquire a dozen desktop photocopiers from Xerox.com. This same buyer might purchase office furniture and supplies through a reseller such as Office Depot at officedepot.com. Increasingly, organizational buyers and business marketers are using e-marketplaces and online auctions to purchase and sell products and services.

E-Marketplaces: Virtual Organizational Markets

A significant development in organizational buying has been the creation and growth of online trading communities, called **e-marketplaces**, that bring together buyers and supplier organizations.[29] These online communities go by a variety of names, including B2B exchanges and e-hubs, and make possible the real-time exchange of information, money, products and services. E-marketplaces will account for almost one-half of all online organizational purchases in 2005.

E-marketplaces can be independent trading communities or private exchanges.[30] Independent e-marketplaces typically focus on a specific product or service, or serve a particular industry. They act as a neutral third-party and provide an Internet/Web technology trading platform and a centralized market that enable exchanges between buyers and sellers. Independent e-marketplaces charge a fee for their service and exist in settings that have one or more of the following features: (1) thousands of geographically dispersed buyers and sellers, (2) volatile prices caused by demand and supply fluctuations, (3) time sensitivity due to perishable offerings and changing technologies, and (4) easily comparable offerings between a variety of suppliers. Well-known independent e-marketplaces include e-Steel (steel products), PaperExchange (paper products), PlasticNet (plastics), Altra Energy (electricity, natural gas, and crude oil), and MRO.com (maintenance, repair, and operating supplies). Small business buyers and sellers, in particular, benefit from independent e-marketplaces. These e-marketplaces offer them an economical way to expand their customer base and reduce the cost of purchased products and services.

Large companies tend to favor private exchanges that link them with their network of qualified suppliers and customers.[31] Private exchanges focus on streamlining a company's purchase transactions with its suppliers and customers. Like independent e-marketplaces, they provide a technology trading platform and central market for buyer-seller interactions. They are not a neutral third party, however, but represent the interests of their owners. For example, Worldwide Retail Exchange performs the buying function for its 11 members, including Kmart, Target, Safeway, and Tesco, a large British supermarket chain. Rooster.com, formed by Du Pont, Cargill, Inc., and Cenex Harvest States Cooperatives, sells pesticides and herbicides to farmers.[32] The

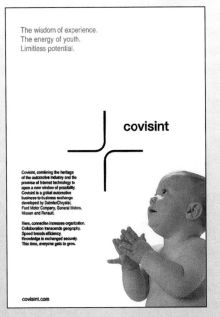
most ambitious e-marketplace yet devised is Covisint, which is expected to revolutionize the worldwide automotive industry. Owned principally by General Motors, Ford, and Daimler Chrysler, Covisint will be the world's largest B2B exchange when it is fully operational and will process $750 billion in transactions annually. Learn about Covisint in the accompanying Web Link.[33]

Online Auctions in Organizational Markets

Online auctions have grown in popularity among organizational buyers and business marketers. Many e-marketplaces offer this service. Two general types of auctions are common: (1) a traditional auction, and (2) a reverse auction.[34] Figure 6–6 shows how buyer and seller participants and price behavior differ by type of auction. Let's look at each auction type more closely to understand the implications of each for buyers and sellers.

In a **traditional auction** a seller puts an item up for sale and would-be buyers are invited to bid in competition with each other. As more would-be buyers become involved, there is an upward pressure on bid prices. Why? Bidding is sequential. Prospective buyers observe the bids of others and decide whether or not to increase the bid price. The auction ends when a single bidder remains and "wins" the item with its highest price. Traditional auctions are frequently used to dispose of excess merchandise. For example, Dell Computer sells surplus, refurbished, or closeout computer merchandise at its dellauction.com website.

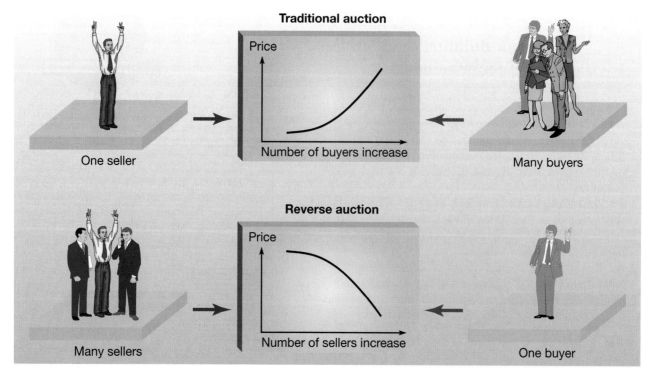

Traditional auction

Price

Number of buyers increase

One seller

Many buyers

Reverse auction

Price

Number of sellers increase

Many sellers

One buyer

FIGURE 6–6
How buyer and seller participants and price behavior differ by type of online auction

A reverse auction works in the opposite direction from a traditional auction. In a **reverse auction**, a buyer communicates a need for a product or service and would-be suppliers are invited to bid in competition with each other. As more would-be suppliers become involved, there is a downward pressure on bid prices for the buyer's business. Why? Like traditional auctions, bidding is sequential and prospective suppliers observe the bids of others and decide whether or not to decrease the bid price. The auction ends when a single bidder remains and "wins" the business with its lowest price. Reverse auctions benefit organizational buyers by reducing the cost of their purchases. As an example, General Electric's Global eXchange Services unit, which runs online reverse auctions for the company, claims it recently saved $780 million on the purchase of $6 billion worth of products and services.[35]

Clearly, buyers welcome the lower prices generated by reverse auctions. Some suppliers also favor reverse auctions because they give them a chance to capture business that they might not have otherwise had because of a long-standing purchase relationship between the buyer and another supplier. On the other hand, suppliers argue that reverse auctions put too much emphasis on prices, discourage consideration of other important buying criteria, and threaten supply partnership opportunities.[36]

Concept Check

1. What are e-marketplaces?

2. In general, which type of online auction creates upward pressure on bid prices and which type creates downward pressure on bid prices?

SUMMARY

1 Organizational buyers are divided into three different markets: industrial, reseller, and government. There are about 11.2 million industrial firms, 2 million resellers, and 88,000 government units.

2 Measuring industrial, reseller, and government markets is an important first step for firms interested in gauging the size of one, two, or all three markets. The North American Industry Classification System (NAICS) is a convenient starting point to begin this process.

3 Many aspects of organizational buying behavior are different from consumer buying behavior. Some key differences between the two include demand characteristics, number of potential buyers, buying objectives, buying criteria, size of the order or purchase, buyer-seller relationships and partnerships, and multiple buying influences within companies.

4 The buying center concept is central to understanding organizational buying behavior. Knowing who composes the buying center and the roles they play in making purchase decisions is important in marketing to organizations. The buying center usually includes a person from the purchasing department and possibly representatives from R&D, engineering, and production, depending on what is being purchased. These people can play one or more of five roles in a purchase decision: user, influencer, buyer, decider, or gatekeeper.

5 The three types of buying situations, or buy classes, are the straight rebuy, the modified rebuy, and the new buy. These form a scale ranging from a routine reorder to a totally new purchase.

6 The stages in an organizational buying decision are the same as those for consumer buying decisions: problem recognition, information search, alternative evaluation, purchase decision, and postpurchase behavior. Examples of organizational purchases described are the purchase of earphones by a portable CD player manufacturer and machine vision technology components by an electronics manufacturer.

7 Online buying is prevalent in industrial, reseller, and government markets. E-marketplaces will account for almost one-half of all online organizational purchases in 2005. Online auctions are commonly used by organizational buyers and business marketers.

KEY TERMS AND CONCEPTS

bidder's list p. 163
business marketing p. 150
buy classes p. 159
buying center p. 158
derived demand p. 153
e-marketplaces p. 164
government units p. 151
industrial firms p. 150
ISO 9000 p. 156
make-buy decision p. 162
North American Industry Classification System (NAICS) p. 152

organizational buyers p. 150
organizational buying behavior p. 160
organizational buying criteria p. 155
reciprocity p. 157
resellers p. 151
reverse auction p. 166
reverse marketing p. 156
supply partnership p. 157
traditional auction p. 165
value analysis p. 162

APPLYING MARKETING CONCEPTS AND PERSPECTIVES

1 Describe the major differences among industrial firms, resellers, and government units in the United States.

2 Explain how the North American Industry Classification System (NAICS) might be helpful in understanding industrial, reseller, and government markets, and discuss the limitations inherent in this system.

3 List and discuss the key characteristics of organizational buying that make it different from consumer buying.

4 What is a buying center? Describe the roles assumed by people in a buying center and what useful questions should be raised to guide any analysis of the structure and behavior of a buying center.

5 Effective marketing is of increasing importance in today's competitive environment. How can firms more effectively market to organizations?

6 A firm that is marketing multimillion-dollar wastewater treatment systems to cities has been unable to sell a new type of system. This setback has occurred even though the firm's systems are cheaper than competitive systems and meet U.S. Environmental Protection Agency (EPA) specifications. To date, the firm's marketing efforts have been directed to city purchasing departments and the various state EPAs to get on approved bidder's lists. Talks with city-employed personnel have indicated that the new system is very different from current systems and therefore city sanitary and sewer department engineers, directors of these two departments, and city council members are unfamiliar with the workings of the system. Consulting engineers, hired by cities to work on the engineering and design features of these systems and paid on a percentage of system cost, are also reluctant to favor the new system. (*a*) What roles do the various individuals play in the purchase process for a wastewater treatment system? (*b*) How could the firm improve the marketing effort behind the new system?

INTERNET EXERCISE

The North American Industrial Classification System (NAICS) structures industrial sectors into their component industries. The NAICS can be accessed at www.census.gov by first clicking NAICS followed by NAICS to SIC. Industry information can be obtained by navigating through the codes.

You have been hired as a market analyst by a textile company that is looking for opportunities outside its normal business. The vice president of marketing has asked you to look into the upholstered wood furniture manufacturing industry to determine its size. She suggests that

a good place to start is the NAICS, beginning with the two-digit manufacturing sectors (codes 31–33).

1 What is the three-digit industry subsector code for Furniture and Related Products Manufacturing?

2 What is the six-digit U.S. code for Upholstered Household Furniture Manufacturing?

3 How many establishments and what is the value of shipments sold by the U.S. upholstered household furniture industry based on the latest government statistics? (Hint: You will need to click Economic Census to get this information.)

VIDEO CASE 6-1   Lands' End: Where Buyers Rule

Organizational buying is a part of the marketing effort that influences every aspect of business at Lands' End. As Senior Vice President of Operations Phil Schaecher explains, "When we talk about purchasing at Lands' End, most people think of the purchase of merchandise for resale, but we buy many other things aside from merchandise, everything from the simplest office supply to the most sophisticated piece of material-handling equipment." As a result, Lands' End has developed a sophisticated approach to organizational buying, which is one of the keys to its incredible success!

THE COMPANY

The company started by selling sailboat equipment, duffle bags, rainsuits, and sweaters from a basement location in Chicago's old tannery district. In its first catalog, the company name was printed with a typing error—the apostrophe in the wrong place—but the fledgling company couldn't afford to correct and reprint it. So, ever since the company name has been Lands' End—with the misplaced apostrophe!

When the company outgrew its Chicago location, founder Gary Comer relocated it to Dodgeville, Wisconsin, where he had fallen in love with the rolling hills and changing seasons. The original business ideas were simple: "Sell only things we believe in, ship every order the day it arrives, and unconditionally guarantee everything." Over time the company developed eight principles of doing business:

1. Never reduce the quality of a product to make it cheaper.
2. Price products fairly and honestly.
3. Accept any return for any reason.
4. Ship items in stock the day after the order is received.

5. What is best for the customer is best for Lands' End.
6. Place contracts with manufacturers who are cost-conscious and efficient.
7. Operate efficiently.
8. Keep overhead low.

These principles became the guidelines for the company's dedicated local employees and helped create extraordinary expectations from Lands' End customers.

Today, Lands' End is one of the world's largest direct merchants, with annual sales of traditionally styled clothing, luggage, and home products exceeding $1.4 billion. The products are offered through catalogs, the Internet, and retail stores. Last year, Lands' End distributed more than 260 million catalogs designed for specific segments, including *The Lands' End Catalog, Lands' End Men, Lands' End Women, Lands' End Kids, Lands' End for School, Lands' End Home,* and *Lands' End Corporate*. In a typical day, catalog shoppers place more than 40,000 telephone calls to the company. The Lands' End website (www.landsend.com) also offers every Lands' End product and a wide variety of internet shopping innovations such as a 3-D model customized to each customer (called My Virtual Model™); a "personal shopper," to suggest products that match the consumer's preferences; and a feature that allows customers to "chat" online directly with a customer service representative. Lands' End also operates 19 stores in the United States, the United Kingdom, and Japan.

The company's goal is to please customers with the highest levels of quality and service in the industry. Lands' End maintains the high quality of its products through several important activities. For example, the company works directly with mills and manufacturers to retain control of quality and design. "The biggest difference between Lands' End and some other retailers or catalog businesses is that we actually design all the product here and we do all the specifications. Therefore, the manufacturer is building that product directly to our specs, we are not buying off of somebody else's line," explains Joan Mudget, Vice President of Quality Assurance. In addition, Lands' End tests its products for comfort and fit by paying real people (local residents and children) to "wear-test" and "fit-test" all types of garments!

Service has also become an important part of the Lands' End reputation. Customers expect prompt, professional service at every step—initiating the order, making selections, shipping, and follow-up (if necessary). Some of the ways Lands' End meets these expectations include offering the simplest guarantee in the industry—"Guaranteed. Period."—toll-free telephone lines open 24 hours-a-day, 364 days a year, continuous product training for telephone representatives, and 2-day shipping. Lands' End operators even send personal responses to all e-mail messages—approximately 230,000 per year!

ORGANIZATIONAL BUYING AT LANDS' END

The sixth Lands' End business principle (described above) is accomplished through the company's organizational buying process. First, its buyers specify fabric quality, construction, and sizing standards, which typically exceed industry standards, for current and potential Lands' End products. Then the buyers literally search around the world for the best possible source of fabrics and products. Once a potential supplier is identified, one of the company's 150 quality assurance personnel makes an information-gathering visit. The purpose of the visit is to understand the supplier's values, to assess four criteria (economic, quality, service, and vendor), and to determine if the Lands' End standards can be achieved.

Lands' End evaluations of potential suppliers lead to the selection of what the company hopes will become long-term partners. As Mudget explains, "When we're looking for new manufacturers we are looking for the long term. I think one of the most interesting things is we're not out there looking for new vendors every year to fill the same products." In fact, Lands' End believes that the term "supplier" does not adequately describe the importance the company places on the relationships. Lands' End suppliers are viewed as allies, supporters, associates, colleagues, and stakeholders in the future of the company. Once an alliance is formed the product specifications and the performance on those specifications are regularly evaluated.

Lands' End buyers face a variety of buying situations. Straight rebuys involve reordering an existing product—such as shipping boxes—without evaluating or changing specifications. Modified rebuys involve changing some aspect of a previously ordered product—such as the collar of a knit shirt—based on input from consumers, retailers, or other people involved in the purchase decision.

Finally, new buys involve first-time purchases—such as Lands' End addition of men's suits to its product line. The complexity of the process can vary with the type of purchase. Schaecher explains, "As you get more complicated in the purchase there are more things you look at to decide on a vendor."

FUTURE CHALLENGES FOR LANDS' END

Lands' End faces several challenges as it pursues improvements in its organizational buying process. First, new technologies offer opportunities for fast, efficient, and accurate communication with suppliers. Ed Smidebush, General Inventory Manager, describes a new system at Lands' End: "Our quick response system is a computerized system where we transmit electronically to our vendors each Sunday night, forecast information as well as stock positions and purchase order information so that on Monday morning this information will be incorporated directly into their manufacturing reports so that they can prioritize their production." Occasionally Lands' End must work with its suppliers to improve their technology and information system capabilities.

Another challenge for Lands' End is to anticipate changes in consumer interests. While it has many years of experience with retail consumers, preferences for colors, fabrics, and styles change frequently, requiring buyers to constantly monitor the marketplace. In addition, Lands' End's more recent offerings to corporate customers require constant attention "because business customers' wants and incentives, and the environment in which they're shopping, are very different from consumers at home," explains marketing manager Hilary Kleese.

Finally, Lands' End must anticipate the quantities of each of its products consumers are likely to order. To do this, historical information is used to develop forecasts. One of the best tests of their forecast accuracy is the holiday season, when Lands' End receives more than 100,000 calls each day. Having the right products available is important because, as every employee knows from Principle 4, every order must be shipped the day after it is received!

Questions

1 Who is likely to comprise the buying center in the decision to select a new supplier for Lands' End? Which of the buying center members are likely to play the roles of users, influencers, buyers, deciders, and gatekeepers?

2 Which stages of the organizational buying decision process does Lands' End follow when it selects a new supplier? What selection criteria does the company utilize in the process?

3 Describe purchases Lands' End buyers typically face in each of the three buying situations: straight rebuy, modified rebuy, new buy.

gros rhume, nez bouché...
Besoin d'air ?

BREATHE RIGHT
tellement efficace pour soulager les congestions nasales dues aux rhumes ou aux allergies !

Découvrez immédiatement l'effet *Breathe Right*.

En étirant les parois de la cloison nasale, *Breathe Right* permet de soulager aussitôt les nez bouchés par une congestion.

Maintenant, imaginez quel soulagement cela peut procurer si, vous ou l'un de vos proches, a un rhume ou une sinusite...

EN VENTE EN PHARMACIE

NE PAS UTILISER CHEZ L'ENFANT DE MOINS DE 5 ANS.

L'essayer, c'est déjà mieux respirer !

CHAPTER

7

REACHING GLOBAL MARKETS

AFTER READING THIS CHAPTER YOU SHOULD BE ABLE TO:

- Describe the nature and scope of world trade from a global perspective and its implications for the United States.

- Explain the effects of economic protectionism and the implications of economic integration for global marketing practices.

- Understand the importance of environmental factors (cultural, economic, and political) in shaping global marketing efforts.

- Describe alternative approaches firms use to enter and compete in global markets.

- Identify specific challenges marketers face when crafting worldwide marketing programs.

NOW THE WORLD CAN BREATHE EASIER . . . ONE NOSE AT A TIME

"I knew instantly *it* would be huge when I talked to *him,*" says Dr. Dan Cohen, chief executive officer of CNS, Inc. The "it" was a rudimentary spring-loaded adhesive device to stick to your nose to open up the nasal passages and improve breathing. The "him" was Bruce Johnson, the device's inventor, whose breathing and snoring problems had even driven him to put straws or paper clips up his nose at night to breathe better.

After millions of dollars of additional research and development, the meeting resulted in the spectacularly successful Breathe Right® nasal strips targeted at athletes, those with allergies, those who snore, . . . and those who *sleep* with those who snore.

Breathe Right® strips were an immediate marketing success in the United States, so Dr. Cohen counted the world's noses and sought to enter the global marketplace. But could this success story be repeated in other countries and cultures? In a word—yes! Today, CNS, Inc. distributes its Breathe Right® nasal strips on four continents due in large measure to the universal need satisfied by this innovative product supported by an effective marketing program described in this chapter.[1]

American marketers cannot ignore the vast potential of global markets. About 95 percent of the world's population having two-thirds of the world's purchasing power live outside the United States. In fact, many global markets are growing faster than comparable markets in the United States.

Pursuit of global markets by American and foreign marketers ultimately results in world trade. This chapter describes the nature and scope of world trade and highlights challenges firms such as CNS face when they undertake global marketing.

DYNAMICS OF WORLD TRADE

The dollar value of world trade has more than doubled in the past decade and will exceed $11.5 trillion in 2005. Manufactured goods and commodities account for 75 percent of world trade. Service industries, including telecommunications, transportation, insurance, education, banking, and tourism, represent the other 25 percent of world trade.

World Trade Flows

All nations and regions of the world do not participate equally in world trade. World trade flows reflect interdependencies among industries, countries, and regions and manifest themselves in country, company, industry, and regional exports and imports.

Global Perspective

Figure 7–1 shows the estimated dollar value of exports and imports among North American countries, Western Europe, Asian/Pacific Rim countries, and the rest of the world, including intraregional trade flows.[2] The United States, Western Europe, Canada, and Japan together account for two-thirds of world trade.

Not all trade involves the exchange of money for goods or services. In a world where 70 percent of all countries do not have convertible currencies or where government-owned enterprises lack sufficient cash or credit for imports, other means of payment are used. An estimated 15 to 20 percent of world trade involves **countertrade**, the practice of using barter rather than money for making global sales.[3]

FIGURE 7–1

Illustrative world trade flows for manufactured goods and commodities (billions of dollars)

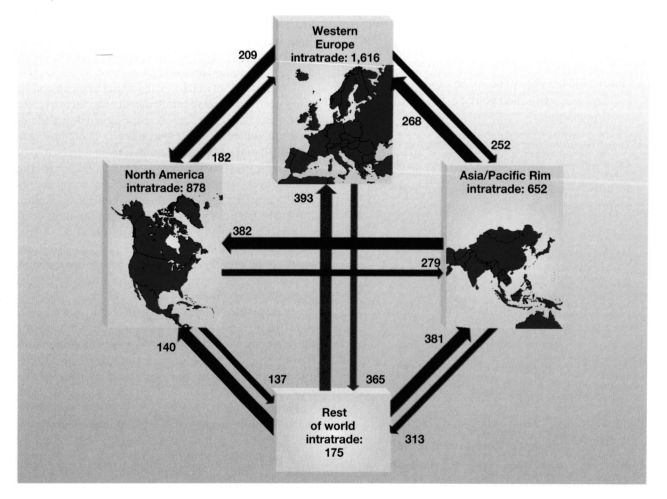

Countertrade is popular with many Eastern European nations, Russia, and Asian countries. For example, the Malaysian government recently exchanged 20,000 tons of rice for an equivalent amount of Philippine corn. Volvo of North America delivered automobiles to the Siberian police force when Siberia had no cash to pay for them. It accepted payment in oil, which it then sold for cash to pay for media advertising in the United States.[4]

A global perspective on world trade views exports and imports as complementary economic flows: A country's imports affect its exports and exports affect its imports. Every nation's imports arise from the exports of other nations. As the exports of one country increase, its national output and income rise, which, in turn, leads to an increase in the demand for imports. This nation's greater demand for imports stimulates the exports of other countries. Increased demand for exports of other nations energizes their economic activity, resulting in higher national income, which stimulates their demand for imports. In short, imports affect exports and vice versa. This phenomenon is called the **trade feedback effect** and is one argument for free trade among nations.

United States Perspective   The United States is the world's perennial leader in terms of **gross domestic product** (GDP), which is the monetary value of all goods and services produced in a country during one year. The United States is also among the world's leaders in exports due in large part to its global prominence in the aircraft, chemical, office equipment, information technology, pharmaceutical, telecommunications, and professional service industries. However, the U.S. percentage share of world exports has shifted downward over the past 30 years, whereas its percentage share of world imports has increased. Therefore, the relative position of the United States as a supplier to the world has diminished despite an absolute growth in exports. At the same time, its relative role as a marketplace for the world has increased, particularly for automobile, oil, textile, apparel, and consumer electronics products.

The difference between the monetary value of a nation's exports and imports is called the **balance of trade**. When a country's exports exceed its imports, it incurs a surplus in its balance of trade. When imports exceed exports, a deficit results. World trade trends in U.S. exports and imports are reflected in the U.S. balance of trade. Since 1975 two important things have happened in U.S. exports and imports. First, imports have significantly exceeded exports each year, indicating that the United States has a continuing balance of trade deficit. Second, the volume of both exports and imports is about 10 to 15 times what it was in the mid-1970s—showing why almost every American is significantly affected. The effect varies from the products they buy (Samsung VCRs from South Korea, Waterford crystal from Ireland, Louis Vuitton luggage from France) to those they sell (Cisco Systems' Internet technology to Europe, Du Pont's chemicals to the Far East) and the additional jobs and improved standard of living that result.

World trade flows to and from the United States reflect demand and supply interdependencies for goods and services among nations and industries. The three largest importers of U.S. goods and services are Canada, Mexico, and Japan. These countries purchase approximately 44 percent of U.S. exports. The four largest exporters to the United States are China, Japan, Canada, and Mexico.

The United States is Asia's largest export market, buying about one-third of the exports of Japan, Taiwan, South Korea, and China, a quarter of Hong Kong's exports, and 40 percent of the Philippines's exports. The trade imbalance between the United States and Asia is illustrated by the fact that Japan, South Korea, and China combine for about half of the total U.S. balance of trade deficit.

Competitive Advantage of Nations

As companies in many industries find themselves competing against foreign competitors at home and abroad, government policy makers around the world are increasingly asking why some companies and industries in a country succeed globally

FIGURE 7–2
Porter's "diamond" of national
competitive advantage

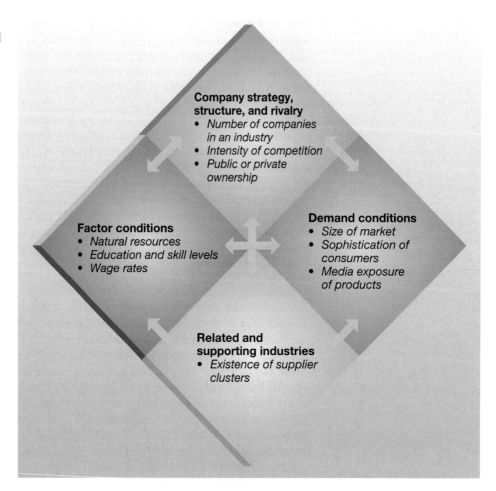

while others lose ground or fail. Harvard Business School Professor Michael Porter suggests a "diamond" to explain a nation's competitive advantage and why some industries and firms become world leaders.[5] He identified four key elements, which appear in Figure 7–2:

1. *Factor conditions.* These reflect a nation's ability to turn its natural resources, education, and infrastructure into a competitive advantage. Consider Holland, which exports 59 percent of the world's cut flowers. The Dutch lead the world in the cut-flower industry because of their research in flower cultivation, packaging, and shipping—not because of their weather.

2. *Demand conditions.* These include both the number and sophistication of domestic customers for an industry's product. Japan's sophisticated consumers demand quality in their TVs and radios, thereby making Japan's producers such as Sony, Sanyo, Matsushita, and Hitachi among the world leaders in the electronics industry.

3. *Related and supporting industries.* Firms and industries seeking leadership in global markets need clusters of world-class suppliers that accelerate innovation. The German leadership in scientific and industrial instrumentation relates directly to the cluster of supporting German precision engineering suppliers.

4. *Company strategy, structure, and rivalry.* These factors include the conditions governing the way a nation's businesses are organized and managed, along with the intensity of domestic competition. The Italian shoe industry has become a world leader because of intense domestic competition among firms such as MAB, Bruno Magli, and Rossimoda, which has made shoes for Christian Dior and Anne Klein Couture.

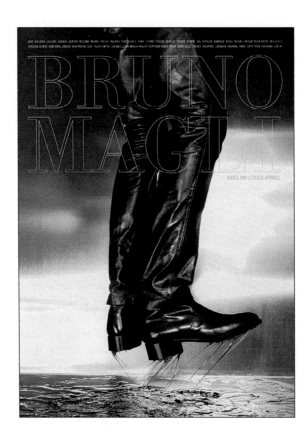

Sony and Bruno Magli have succeeded in the global marketplace as well as in their domestic markets.

Sony

www.sony.com

Bruno Magli

www.brunomagli.it

In Porter's study, case histories of firms in more than 100 industries were analyzed. While the strategies employed by the most successful global competitors were different in many respects, a common theme emerged—a firm that succeeds in global markets has first succeeded in intense domestic competition. Hence competitive advantage for global firms grows out of relentless, continuing improvement, innovation, and change.

However, pursuit of a country's competitive advantage in global markets has a dark side—economic espionage.[6] Economic espionage is the clandestine collection of trade secrets or proprietary information about competitors. This practice is common in high-technology industries such as electronics, specialty chemicals, industrial equipment, aerospace, and pharmaceuticals, where technical know-how and trade secrets separate global industry leaders from followers. It has been estimated that the intelligence services of some 23 nations routinely target U.S. firms for information about research and development strategies, manufacturing and marketing plans, and customer lists. To counteract this threat, the **Economic Espionage Act** makes the theft of trade secrets by foreign entities a federal crime in the United States. This act prescribes prison sentences of up to 15 years and fines up to $500,000 for individuals. Agents of foreign governments found guilty of economic espionage face a 25-year prison sentence and a $10 million fine.

Concept Check

1. What is the trade feedback effect?

2. What variables influence why some companies and industries in a country succeed globally while others lose ground or fail?

EMERGENCE OF A BORDERLESS ECONOMIC WORLD

Four trends in the past decade have significantly affected world trade. One trend is the gradual decline of economic protectionism exercised by individual countries. A second trend is apparent in the formal economic integration and free trade among nations. A third trend is evident in global competition among global companies for global consumers. The fourth trend is the emergence of a networked global market-space.

Decline of Economic Protectionism

Protectionism is the practice of shielding one or more sectors of a country's economy from foreign competition through the use of tariffs or quotas. The economic argument for protectionism is that it preserves jobs, protects a nation's political security, discourages economic dependency on other countries, and encourages the development of domestic industries. Read the accompanying Ethics and Social Responsibility Alert and ask yourself if protectionism has an ethical and social responsibility dimension.[7]

Tariffs and quotas discourage world trade as depicted in Figure 7–3. **Tariffs**, which are a government tax on goods or services entering a country, primarily serve to raise prices on imports. For example, the average tariff on manufactured goods in industrialized countries is 4 percent.

The effect of tariffs on world trade and consumer prices is substantial.[8] Consider U.S. rice exports to Japan. The U.S. Rice Millers' Association claims that if the Japanese rice market were opened to imports by lowering tariffs, lower prices would save Japanese consumers $6 billion annually, and the United States would gain a large share of the Japanese rice market. Similarly, tariffs imposed on bananas by Western European countries cost consumers $2 billion a year. Ecuador (the world's largest banana exporter), Mexico, Guatemala, and Honduras have negotiated a reduction in this levy by 2006.

A **quota** is a restriction placed on the amount of a product allowed to enter or leave a country. Quotas can be mandated or voluntary and may be legislated or negotiated by governments. Import quotas seek to guarantee domestic industries access to a certain percentage of their domestic market. The best-known quota concerns the

FIGURE 7–3
How protectionism affects world trade

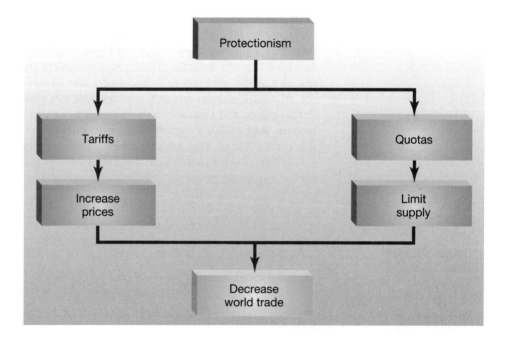

ETHICS AND SOCIAL RESPONSIBILITY ALERT

Global Ethics and Global Economics: The Case of Protectionism

ETHICS

World trade benefits from free and fair trade among nations. Nevertheless, governments of many countries continue to use tariffs and quotas to protect their various domestic industries. Why? Protectionism earns profits for domestic producers and tariff revenue for the government. There is a cost, however. Protectionist policies cost Japanese consumers between $75 billion and $110 billion annually. U.S. consumers pay about $70 billion each year in higher prices because of tariffs and other protective restrictions.

Sugar import quotas in the United States, automobile import quotas and banana import tariffs in many European countries, beer import tariffs in Canada, and rice import tariffs in Japan protect domestic industries but also interfere with world trade for these products. Regional trade agreements, such as those found in the provisions of the European Union and the North American Free Trade Agreement, may also pose a situation whereby member nations can obtain preferential treatment in quotas and tariffs whereas nonmember nations cannot.

Protectionism, in its many forms, raises an interesting global ethical question. Is protectionism, no matter how applied, an ethical practice?

mandatory or voluntary limits of foreign automobile sales in many countries. Quotas imposed by European countries make European cars 25 percent more expensive than similar models in the United States or Japan, costing European customers $40 billion per year. Less visible quotas apply to the importation of mushrooms, heavy motorcycles, color TVs, and sugar. For example, U.S. sugar import quotas have existed for over 50 years and preserve about half of the U.S. sugar market for domestic producers. American consumers pay almost $2 billion annually in extra food costs because of this quota.[9]

Every country engages in some form of protectionism. However, protectionism has declined over the past 50 years due in large part to the *General Agreement on Tariffs and Trade (GATT)*. This international treaty was intended to limit trade barriers and promote world trade through the reduction of tariffs, which it did. However, GATT did not explicitly address nontariff trade barriers, such as quotas and world trade in services, which often sparked heated trade disputes between nations.

World Trade Organization
www.wto.org

As a consequence, the major industrialized nations of the world formed the **World Trade Organization** (WTO) in 1995 to address a broad array of world trade issues.[10] There are 143 WTO member countries, including the United States, which account for more than 90 percent of world trade. The WTO is a permanent institution that sets rules governing trade between its members through panels of trade experts who (1) decide on trade disputes between members and (2) issue binding decisions. The WTO reviews more than 200 disputes annually. For instance, the WTO denied Eastman Kodak's multimillion-dollar damage claim that the Japanese government protected Fuji Photo from import competition. In another decision, the WTO allowed Britain, Ireland, and the European Union to reclassify U.S.-produced local area network (LAN) computer equipment as telecommunications gear. The new classification effectively doubled the import tariff on these U.S. goods.

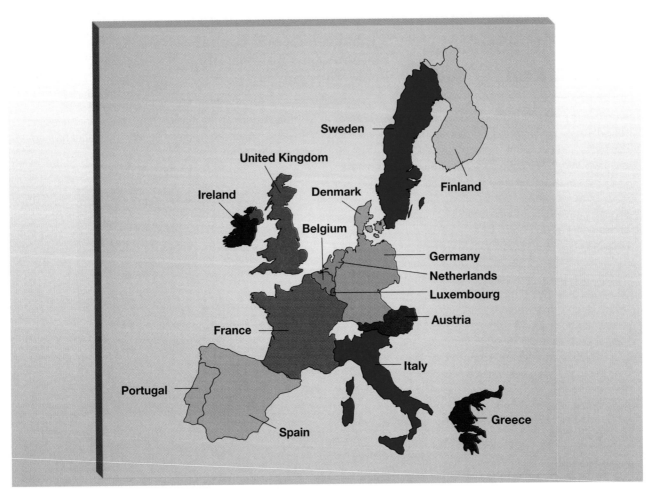

FIGURE 7–4
The countries of the European
Union in 2002

European Union

www.europa.eu.int

Rise of Economic Integration

In recent years a number of countries with similar economic goals have formed
transnational trade groups or signed trade agreements for the purpose of promoting
free trade among member nations and enhancing their individual economies. Three
of the best-known examples are the European Union (or simply EU), the North
American Free Trade Agreement (NAFTA), and Asian Free Trade Areas.

European Union   In 1993, 12 European countries effectively eliminated most of
the barriers to the free flow of goods, services, capital, and labor across their borders.
This event, after decades of negotiation, formed a single market composed of more
than 375 million consumers with a combined gross domestic product larger than that
of the United States. Original members of the European Union were Great Britain, Ireland, Denmark, Belgium, the Netherlands, Luxembourg, Germany, France, Italy,
Greece, Portugal, and Spain. Austria, Finland, and Sweden joined the European Union
in 1995, bringing its membership to 15 countries (see Figure 7–4). The Swiss have
elected not to join the European Union.

    The European Union creates abundant marketing opportunities because firms no
longer find it necessary to market their products and services on a nation-by-nation
basis. Rather, Pan-European marketing strategies are possible due to greater unifor-
mity in product and packaging standards; fewer regulatory restriction on transportation, advertising, and promotion imposed by countries; and removal of most tariffs
that affect pricing practices.[11] For example, Colgate-Palmolive Company now markets its Colgate toothpaste with one formula and package across EU countries at one

price. This practice was previously impossible because of different government regulations and tariffs. Europeanwide distribution from fewer locations is also feasible given open borders. French tire maker Michelin recently closed 180 of its European distribution centers and now uses just 20 to serve all EU countries. Pan-European marketing opportunities will benefit further from the issuance of a common currency called the "euro," which replaced national currencies in 2002 in 12 EU countries. Great Britain, Denmark, and Sweden have retained their own currencies.

NAFTA

www.mac.doc.gov/
nafta/nafta2

North American Free Trade Agreement The North American Free Trade Agreement (NAFTA) became effective in 1994 and lifted many trade barriers between the United States and Mexico. This agreement, when coupled with the 1988 U.S.–Canada Fair Trade Agreement, established a North American trade arrangement similar to that of the European Union. The reduction of tariffs and other provisions of NAFTA promoted relatively free trade among the United States, Canada, and Mexico and created a marketplace with over 400 million consumers. Negotiations are under way to expand NAFTA to create a 34-country Free Trade Area of the Americas by 2005. This agreement would include the United States, Canada, Mexico, and Latin American and Caribbean countries.[12]

NAFTA has stimulated trade flows among member nations as well as cross-border manufacturing and investment. For example, Whirlpool Corporation's Canadian subsidiary stopped making washing machines in Canada and moved that operation to Ohio. Whirlpool then shifted the production of household trash compactors, kitchen ranges, and compact dryers to Canada. Ford invested $60 million in its Mexico City manufacturing plant to produce smaller cars and light trucks for global sales.

Asian Free Trade Agreements Efforts to liberalize trade in East Asia—from Japan and the four "Little Dragons" (Hong Kong, Singapore, South Korea, and Taiwan) through Thailand, Malaysia, and Indonesia—are also growing. Although the trade agreements are less formal than those underlying the European Union and NAFTA, they have reduced tariffs among countries and promoted trade.

A New Reality: Global Competition among Global Companies for Global Consumers

The emergence of a largely borderless economic world has created a new reality for marketers of all shapes and sizes. Today, world trade is driven by global competition among global companies for global consumers.

Global Competition **Global competition** exists when firms originate, produce, and market their products and services worldwide. The automobile, pharmaceutical, apparel, electronics, aerospace, and telecommunication fields represent well-known industries with sellers and buyers on every continent. Other industries that are increasingly global in scope include soft drinks, cosmetics, ready-to-eat cereals, snack chips, and retailing.

Global competition broadens the competitive landscape for marketers. The familiar "cola war" waged by Pepsi-Cola and Coca-Cola in the United States has been repeated around the world, including India, China, and Argentina. Procter & Gamble's Pampers and Kimberly-Clark's Huggies have taken their disposable diaper rivalry from the United States to Western Europe. Boeing and Europe's Airbus Industrie vie for lucrative commercial aircraft contracts on virtually every continent.

Collaborative relationships also are becoming a common way to meet the demands of global competition. Global **strategic alliances** are agreements among two or more independent firms to cooperate for the purpose of achieving common goals such as a competitive advantage or customer value creation. For instance, several of the world's largest telecommunication equipment makers, including Ericsson (Sweden), Northern Telecom (Canada), Siemens (Germany), and 3Com and Worldcom (two U.S. firms), have formed Juniper Networks, Inc., an alliance created to build

Pepsi-Cola is available in more than 190 countries and territories and accounts for a quarter of all soft drinks sold internationally. This Brazilian ad—"How to make jeans last 10 years"—features the popular Diet Pepsi brand targeted at weight-conscious consumers.

PepsiCo, Inc.

www.pepsico.com

devices to speed global Internet communications. General Mills and Nestlé of Switzerland created Cereal Partners Worldwide for the purpose of fine-tuning Nestlé's European cereal marketing and distributing of General Mills cereals worldwide. This global alliance is expected to produce more than $1 billion in worldwide sales by 2005.[13]

Global Companies   Three types of companies populate and compete in the global marketplace: (1) international firms, (2) multinational firms, and (3) transnational firms.[14] All three employ people in different countries, and many have administrative, marketing, and manufacturing operations (often called divisions or subsidiaries) around the world. However, a firm's orientation toward and strategy for global markets and marketing defines the type of company it is or attempts to be.

An *international firm* engages in trade and marketing in different countries as an extension of the marketing strategy in its home country. Generally speaking, these firms market their existing products and services in other countries the same way they do in their home country. Avon, for example, successfully distributes its product line through direct selling in Asia, Europe, and South America, employing virtually the same marketing strategy used in the United States.

A *multinational firm* views the world as consisting of unique parts and markets to each part differently. Multinationals use a **multidomestic marketing strategy**, which means that they have as many different product variations, brand names, and advertising programs as countries in which they do business. For example, Lever Europe—a division of Unilever—markets its fabric softener known as Snuggle in the United States in 10 different European countries under seven brand names, including Kuschelweich in Germany, Coccolino in Italy, and Mimosin in France. These products have different packages, different advertising programs, and occasionally different formulas.[15]

A *transnational firm* views the world as one market and emphasizes cultural similarities across countries or universal consumer needs and wants more than differences. Transnational marketers employ a **global marketing strategy**—the practice of standardizing marketing activities when there are cultural similarities and adapting them when cultures differ. This approach benefits marketers by allowing them to realize economies of scale from their production and marketing activities.

MARKETING NEWSNET

The Global Teenager: A Market of 500 Million Consumers with $100 Billion to Spend

GLOBAL

The "global teenager" market consists of 500 million 13- to 19-year-olds in Europe, North and South America, and industrialized nations of Asia and the Pacific Rim who have experienced intense exposure to television (MTV broadcasts in some 139 countries), movies, travel, the Internet, and global advertising by companies such as Bennetton, Sony, Nike, and Coca-Cola. The similarities among teens across these countries are greater than their differences. For example, a global study of middle-class teenagers' rooms in 25 industrialized countries indicated it was difficult, if not impossible, to tell whether the rooms were in Los Angeles, Mexico City, Tokyo, Rio de Janeiro, Sidney, or Paris. Why? Teens spend $100 billion annually for a common gallery of products: Sony video games, Tommy Hilfiger

apparel, Levi's blue jeans, Nike athletic shoes, Procter & Gamble Cover Girl makeup, and Clearasil facial medicine.

Teenagers around the world appreciate fashion and music, and desire novelty and trendier designs and images. They also acknowledge an "Americanization" of fashion and culture based on another study of 6,500 teens in 26 countries. When asked what country had the most influence on their attitudes and purchase behavior, the United States was named by 54 percent of teens from the United States, 87 percent of those from Latin America, 80 percent of the Europeans, and 80 percent of those from the Far East. This phenomenon has not gone unnoticed by parents. As one parent in India said, "Now the youngsters dress, talk, and eat like Americans."

Global marketing strategies are popular among many business-to-business marketers such as Caterpillar and Komatsu (heavy construction equipment), and Texas Instruments, Intel, Hitachi, and Motorola (semiconductors). Consumer goods marketers such as Timex, Seiko, and Citizen (watches), Coca-Cola and Pepsi-Cola (cola soft drinks), Gillette (personal care products), L'Oréal and Shiseido (cosmetics), and McDonald's (fast foods) successfully execute this strategy.

Global Consumers Global competition among global companies often focuses on the identification and pursuit of global consumers as described in the accompanying Marketing NewsNet.[16] **Global consumers** consist of customer groups living in many countries or regions of the world who have similar needs or seek similar features and benefits from products or services.[17] Evidence suggests the emergence of a global middle-income class, a youth market, and an elite segment, each consuming or using a common assortment of products and services regardless of geographic location. A variety of companies have capitalized on the global consumer. Whirlpool, Sony, and IKEA have benefited from the growing global middle-income class desire for kitchen appliances, consumer electronics, and home furnishings, respectively. Levi's, Nike, Coca-Cola, and Bennetton have tapped the global youth market. DeBeers, Chanel, Gucci, Rolls Royce, and Sotheby's and Christie's, the world's largest fine art and antique auction houses, cater to the elite segment for luxury goods worldwide.

Emergence of a Networked Global Marketspace

The use of Internet/Web-based technology as a tool for exchanging goods, services, and information on a global scale is the fourth trend affecting world trade.[18] Some 785 million businesses, educational institutions, government agencies, and households worldwide are expected to have Internet access by 2005. The broad reach of this technology suggests that its potential for promoting world trade is huge. In fact, sales arising from electronic commerce are projected to represent 9 percent of world trade in 2005, up from about 1 percent in 2001.

The promise of a networked global marketspace is that it enables the exchange of goods, services, and information from companies *anywhere* to customers *anywhere* at *any time* and at a lower cost. This promise has become a reality for buyers and sellers in industrialized countries that possess the telecommunications infrastructure necessary to support Internet/Web-based technology. In particular, companies engaged in business-to-business marketing have spurred the growth of global electronic commerce. Ninety percent of global electronic commerce revenue arises from business-to-business transactions among a dozen countries in North America, Western Europe, and the Asia/Pacific Rim region. Industries that have benefited from this technology include industrial chemicals and controls, maintenance, repair, and operating supplies, computer and electronic equipment and components, aerospace parts, and agricultural and energy products. The United States, Canada, United Kingdom, Germany, Sweden, Japan, and Taiwan are among the most active participants in worldwide business-to-business electronic commerce.

Nestlé features multiple country and language websites that customize content and communicate with consumers in their native tongue. The website for Colombia shown here is an example. Read the text to learn how many websites and languages Nestlé uses.

Nestlé S. A.

www.nestle.com

Marketers recognize that the networked global marketspace offers unprecedented access to prospective buyers on every continent. Companies that have successfully capitalized on this access manage multiple country and language websites that customize content and communicate with consumers in their native tongue. Nestlé, the world's largest packaged food manufacturer, coffee roaster, and chocolate maker is a case in point. The company operates 31 individual country websites in 16 languages that span 5 continents. Amazon.com has Spanish, Japanese, French, and German language websites.

Concept Check

1. What is protectionism?

2. The North American Free Trade Agreement was designed to promote free trade among which countries?

3. What is the difference between a multidomestic marketing strategy and a global marketing strategy?

A GLOBAL ENVIRONMENTAL SCAN

Global companies conduct continuing environmental scans of the five sets of environmental factors described earlier in Figure 3–1 (social, economic, technological, competitive, and regulatory forces). This section focuses on three kinds of uncontrollable environmental variables—cultural, economic, and political-regulatory variables—that affect global marketing practices in strikingly different ways than those in domestic markets.

Cultural Diversity

Marketers must be sensitive to the cultural underpinnings of different societies if they are to initiate and consummate mutually beneficial exchange relationships with global consumers. A necessary step in this process is **cross-cultural analysis**, which involves the study of similarities and differences among consumers in two or more nations or societies.[19] A thorough cross-cultural analysis involves an understanding of and an appreciation for the values, customs, symbols, and language of other societies.

Values   A society's **values** represent personally or socially preferable modes of conduct or states of existence that are enduring. Understanding and working with these aspects of a society are important factors in global marketing. For example,[20]

- McDonald's does not sell hamburgers in its restaurants in India because the cow is considered sacred by almost 85 percent of the population. Instead, McDonald's sells the McMaharajah: two all-mutton patties, special sauce, lettuce, cheese, pickles, onions on a sesame-seed bun.
- Germans have not been overly receptive to the use of credit cards such as Visa or MasterCard and installment debt to purchase goods and services. Indeed, the German word for debt, *Schuld,* is the same as the German word for guilt.

These examples illustrate how cultural values can influence behavior in different societies. Cultural values become apparent in the personal values of individuals that affect their attitudes and beliefs and the importance assigned to specific behaviors

What cultural lesson did Coca-Cola executives learn when they used the Eiffel Tower and the Parthenon in a recent global advertising campaign?

and attributes of goods and services. These personal values affect consumption-specific values, such as the use of installment debt by Germans, and product-specific values, such as the importance assigned to credit card interest rates.

Customs   **Customs** are the norms and expectation about the way people do things in a specific country. Clearly customs can vary significantly from country to country. For example, 3M Company executives were perplexed when the company's Scotch-Brite floor-cleaning product initially produced lukewarm sales in the Philippines. When a Filipino employee explained that consumers there customarily clean floors by pushing coconut shells around with their feet, 3M changed the shape of the pad to a foot and sales soared! Some other customs may seem unusual to Americans. Consider, for example, that in France, men wear more than twice the number of cosmetics than women do and that Japanese women give Japanese men chocolates on Valentine's Day.

The custom of giving token business gifts is popular in many countries where they are expected and accepted.[21] However, bribes, kickbacks, and payoffs offered to entice someone to commit an illegal or improper act on behalf of the giver for economic gain is considered corrupt in any culture. The prevalence of bribery in global marketing has led to an agreement among the world's major exporting nations to make bribery of foreign government officials a criminal offense. This agreement is patterned after the **Foreign Corrupt Practices Act**, which makes it a crime for U.S. corporations to bribe an official of a foreign government or political party to obtain or retain business in a foreign country. Bribery paid to foreign companies is another matter. In France and Greece, bribes paid to foreign companies are a tax-deductible expense!

Customs also relate to nonverbal behavior of individuals in different cultural settings. The story is told of U.S. executives negotiating a purchase agreement with their Japanese counterparts. The chief American negotiator made a proposal that was met with silence by the Japanese head negotiator. The American assumed the offer was not acceptable and raised the offer, which again was met with silence. A third offer was made, and an agreement was struck. Unknown to the American, the silence of the Japanese head negotiator meant that the offer was being considered, not rejected. The Japanese negotiator obtained several concessions from the American because of a misreading of silence! Unlike U.S. businesspeople, who tend to express opinions early in meetings and negotiations, Japanese executives prefer to wait and listen. The higher their position, such as chief negotiator, the more they listen.[22]

Cultural Symbols   **Cultural symbols** are things that represent ideas and concepts. Symbols or symbolism play an important role in cross-cultural analysis because different cultures ascribe different meanings to things. So important is the role of symbols that a field of study, called **semiotics**, has emerged that examines the correspondence between symbols and their role in the assignment of meaning for people. By adroitly using cultural symbols, global marketers can tie positive symbolism to their products and services to enhance their attractiveness to consumers. However, improper use of symbols can spell disaster. A culturally sensitive global marketer will know that[23]

- North Americans are superstitious about the number 13, and Japanese feel the same way about the number 4. *Shi,* the Japanese word for four, is also the word for death. Knowing this, Tiffany & Company sells its fine glassware and china in sets of five, not four, in Japan.
- "Thumbs-up" is a positive sign in the United States. However, in Russia and Poland, this gesture has an offensive meaning when the palm of the hand is shown, as AT&T learned. The company reversed the gesture depicted in ads, showing the back of the hand, not the palm.

Cultural symbols evoke deep feelings. Consider how executives at Coca-Cola Company's Italian office learned this lesson. In a series of advertisements directed at Italian vacationers, the Eiffel Tower, Empire State Building, and the Tower of Pisa were turned into the familiar Coca-Cola bottle. However, when the white marble columns in the Parthenon that crowns Athens's Acropolis were turned into Coca-Cola bottles, the Greeks were outraged. Greeks refer to the Acropolis as the "holy rock," and a government official said the Parthenon is an "international symbol of excellence" and that "whoever insults the Parthenon insults international culture." Coca-Cola apologized for the ad.[24]

Global markets are also sensitive to the fact that the "country of origin or manufacture" of products and services can symbolize superior or poor quality in some countries. For example, Russian consumers believe products made in Japan and Germany are superior in quality to products from the United States and the United Kingdom. Japanese consumers believe Japanese products are superior to those made in Europe and the United States. About 48 percent of Americans say the quality of products from Asia is not as good as products made in the United States.[25]

Language   Global marketers should not only know the native tongues of countries in which they market their products and services but also the nuances and idioms of a language. Even though about 100 official languages exist in the world, anthropologists estimate that at least 3,000 different languages are spoken. There are 11 official languages spoken in the European Union, and Canada has two official languages (English and French). Seventeen major languages are spoken in India alone.

English, French, and Spanish are the principal languages used in global diplomacy and commerce. However, the best language to communicate with consumers is their own, as any seasoned global marketer will attest to. Unintended meanings of brand names and messages have ranged from the absurd to the obscene:[26]

- When the advertising agency responsible for launching Procter & Gamble's successful Pert shampoo in Canada realized that the name means "lost" in French, it substituted the brand name Pret, which means "ready."
- In Italy, Cadbury Schweppes, the world's third-largest soft drink manufacturer, realized that its Schweppes Tonic Water brand had to be renamed Schweppes Tonica because "il water" turned out to be the idiom for a bathroom.
- The Vicks brand name common in the United States is German slang for sexual intimacy; therefore, Vicks is called Wicks in Germany.

Do you see anything offensive in the logo design for a line of Nike athletic shoes? Read the text to understand the importance of language in global marketing.

Experienced global marketers use **back translation**, where a translated word or phrase is retranslated into the original language by a different interpreter to catch errors.[27] For example, IBM's first Japanese translation of its "Solution for a small planet" advertising message yielded "Answers that make people smaller." The error was caught and corrected. Nevertheless, unintended meanings still occur in the most unlikely situations. Just ask the logo designers for a line of Nike athletic shoes. The designers intended to portray "air" with stylized flames on the shoe heel. Unfortunately, the logo inadvertently resembled the Arabic script for the word "Allah," the Arabic word for God. After receiving complaints from Muslim leaders, Nike apologized and withdrew the offending shoes from the market.[28]

The importance of language in global marketing is assuming greater importance in an increasingly networked and borderless economic world. For example, Oracle Corporation, a leading worldwide supplier of software, now markets its products by language groups instead of through 145 country-specific efforts. The French group markets to France, Belgium, Switzerland, and Canada. A Spanish-language group oversees Spain and Latin America. Eight other language groups—English, Japanese, Korean, Chinese, Portuguese, Italian, Dutch, and German—cover Oracle's top revenue-producing countries.[29]

Cultural Ethnocentricity   The tendency for people to view their own values, customs, symbols, and language favorably is well-known. However, the belief that aspects of one's culture are superior to another's is called *cultural ethnocentricity* and is a sure impediment to successful global marketing.

An outgrowth of cultural ethnocentricity exists in the purchase and use of goods and services produced outside of a country. Global marketers are acutely aware that certain groups within countries disfavor imported products, not on the basis of price, features, or performance, but purely because of their foreign origin. **Consumer ethnocentrism** is the tendency to believe that it is inappropriate, indeed immoral, to purchase foreign-made products.[30] Ethnocentric consumers believe that buying imported products is wrong because such purchases are unpatriotic, harm domestic industries, and cause domestic unemployment. Consumer ethnocentrism has been observed among a segment of the population in the United States, France, Japan, Korea, and Germany as well as other parts of Europe and Asia. The prevalence of consumer ethnocentrism makes the task of global marketers more difficult.[31]

Economic Considerations

Global marketing is also affected by economic considerations. Therefore, a scan of the global marketplace should include (1) a comparative analysis of the economic development in different countries, (2) an assessment of the economic infrastructure in these countries, (3) measurement of consumer income in different countries, and (4) recognition of a country's currency exchange rates.

Stage of Economic Development   There are about 200 countries in the world today, each of which is at a slightly different point in terms of its stage of economic development. However, they can be classified into two major groupings that will help the global marketer better understand their needs:

- *Developed* countries have somewhat mixed economies. Private enterprise dominates, although they have substantial public sectors as well. The United States, Canada, Japan, and most of Western Europe can be considered developed.
- *Developing* countries are in the process of moving from an agricultural to an industrial economy. There are two subgroups within the developing category: (1) those that have already made the move and (2) those that remain locked in a preindustrial economy. Countries such as Poland, Hungary, Slovenia, Australia, Israel, Venezuela, and South Africa fall into the first group. In the second group are Pakistan, Sri Lanka, Tanzania, and Chad, where living standards are low and improvement will be slow.

A country's stage of economic development affects and is affected by other economic factors, as described next.

Economic Infrastructure   The *economic infrastructure*—a country's communications, transportation, financial, and distribution systems—is a critical consideration in determining whether to try to market to a country's consumers and organizations. Parts of the infrastructure that North Americans or Western Europeans take for granted can be huge problems elsewhere—not only in developing nations but even in countries of the former Soviet Union, Eastern Europe, the Indian subcontinent, and China where such an infrastructure is assumed to be in place.[32] Two-lane roads outside major urban centers that limit average speeds to 35 to 40 miles per hour are commonplace, and a nightmare for firms requiring prompt truck delivery in these countries. In China, the bicycle is the preferred mode of transportation. This is understandable because China has few navigable roads outside its major cities where 80 percent of the population lives. In India, Coca-Cola uses large tricycles to distribute cases of Coke along narrow streets in many cities. Wholesale and retail institutions tend to be small, and a majority are operated by new owner–managers in many of these countries who are still learning the ways of a free market system. These conditions have prompted firms such as Danone, a French food company, to establish its own wholesale, retail,

Procter & Gamble has successfully adapted to the economic infrastructure in China since beginning operations in that country in 1988.

The Coca-Cola Company has made a huge financial investment in bottling and distribution facilities in Russia.

The Coca-Cola Company
www.thecoca-colacompany.com

and delivery systems. Danone delivers its products to 700 shops in Russia and has set up 60 shops-in-shops, where it has its own retail sales associates and cash registers.[33]

The communication infrastructure in these countries also differ. This infrastructure includes telecommunication systems and networks in use, such as telephones, cable television, broadcast radio and television, computer, satellite, and wireless telephone. In general, the communication infrastructure in many developing countries is limited or antiquated compared with that of developed countries.

Even the financial and legal system can cause problems. Formal operating procedures among financial institutions and private properties did not exist under communism and are still limited. As a consequence, it is estimated that two-thirds of the commercial transactions in Russia involve nonmonetary forms of payment.[34] The legal red tape involved in obtaining titles to buildings and land for manufacturing, wholesaling, and retailing operations also has been a huge problem. Nevertheless, the Coca-Cola Company has invested $750 million from 1991 through 1998 to build bottling and distribution facilities in Russia, Allied Lyons has spent $30 million to build a plant to make Baskin-Robbins ice cream, and Mars recently opened a $200 million candy factory outside Moscow.[35]

Consumer Income and Purchasing Power   A global marketer selling consumer goods must also consider what the average per capita or household income is among a country's consumers and how the income is distributed to determine a nation's purchasing power. Per capita income varies greatly between nations. Average yearly per capita income in EU countries is $20,000 and is less than $200 in some developing countries such as Vietnam. A country's income distribution is important because it gives a more reliable picture of a country's purchasing power. Generally speaking, as the proportion of middle-income households in a country increases, the greater a nation's purchasing power tends to be. Figure 7–5 shows the worldwide disparity in the percentage distribution of households by level of purchasing power. In established market economies such as those in North America and Western Europe, 65 percent of households have an annual purchasing capability of $20,000 or more. In comparison, 75 percent of households in the developing countries of South Asia have an annual purchasing power of less than $5,000.[36]

Seasoned global marketers recognize that people in developing countries often have government subsidies for food, housing, and health care that supplement their income. Accordingly, people with seemingly low incomes are actually promising

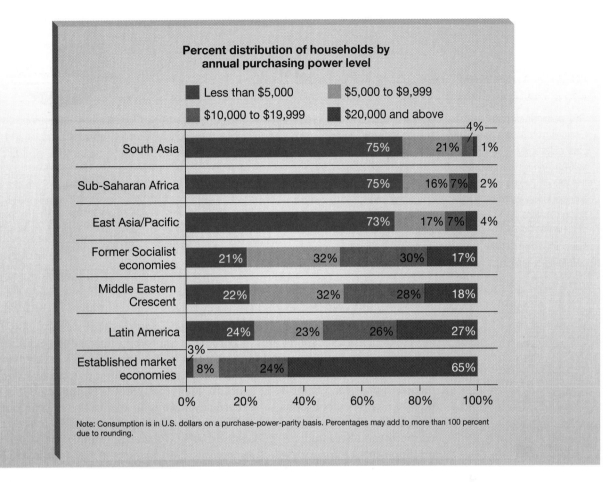

Percent distribution of households by annual purchasing power level

■ Less than $5,000   ■ $5,000 to $9,999
■ $10,000 to $19,999   ■ $20,000 and above

South Asia: 75% | 21% | 4% | 1%

Sub-Saharan Africa: 75% | 16% | 7% | 2%

East Asia/Pacific: 73% | 17% | 7% | 4%

Former Socialist economies: 21% | 32% | 30% | 17%

Middle Eastern Crescent: 22% | 32% | 28% | 18%

Latin America: 24% | 23% | 26% | 27%

Established market economies: 3% | 8% | 24% | 65%

0%   20%   40%   60%   80%   100%

Note: Consumption is in U.S. dollars on a purchase-power-parity basis. Percentages may add to more than 100 percent due to rounding.

FIGURE 7–5
How purchasing power differs around the world

customers for a variety of products. For example, a consumer in South Asia earning the equivalent of $250 per year can afford Gillette razors. When that consumer's income rises to $1,000, a Sony television becomes affordable, and a new Volkswagen or Nissan can be bought with an annual income of $10,000. In developing countries of Eastern Europe, a $1,000 annual income makes a refrigerator affordable, and $2,000 brings an automatic washer within reach.

Income growth in developing countries of Asia, Latin America, and Central and Eastern Europe is expected to stimulate world trade well into the twenty-first century. The number of consumers in these countries earning the equivalent of $10,000 per year is expected to surpass the number of consumers in the United States, Japan, and Western Europe combined by 2005.[37]

Currency Exchange Rates   Fluctuations in exchange rates among the world's currencies are of critical importance in global marketing. Such fluctuations affect everyone—from international tourists to global companies.

A **currency exchange rate** is the price of one country's currency expressed in terms of another country's currency, such as the U.S. dollar expressed in Brazilian reals, Japanese yen, or Swiss francs. Failure to consider exchange rates when pricing products for global markets can have dire consequences. Mattel learned this lesson the hard way. The company was recently unable to sell its popular Holiday Barbie doll and accessories in many international markets because they were too expensive. Why? Barbie prices, expressed in U.S. dollars, were set without regard for how they would translate into foreign currencies and were too high for many buyers.[38]

Exchange rate fluctuations have a direct impact on the sales and profits made by global companies. When foreign currencies can buy more U.S. dollars, for example,

WEB LINK   Checking a Country's Political Risk

The political climate in every country is regularly changing. Governments can make new laws or enforce existing policies differently. Numerous consulting firms prepare political risk analyses that incorporate a variety of variables such as the risk of internal turmoil, external conflict, government restrictions on company operations, and tariff and nontariff trade barriers.

The PRS Group maintains multiple databases of country-specific information and projections, including country political risk ratings. These ratings can be accessed at

www.prsgroup.com. Click "Top Ranked Countries." What country has the most favorable business climate and the least favorable business climate?

U.S. products are less expensive for the foreign customer. This was the case during the 1990s, and U.S. exports grew accordingly. Short-term fluctuations, however, can have a significant effect on the profits of global companies. Hewlett-Packard recently gained nearly a half million dollars of additional profit through exchange rate fluctuation in one year. On the other hand, Honda recently lost $408 million on its European operations alone because of currency swings in the Japanese yen compared with the euro and British pound.[39] Severe and protracted fluctuations in a country's currency can affect trade as well. For example, Procter & Gamble suspended product shipments to Turkey, one of its largest export markets, because of instability of the Turkish currency in 2001.[40]

Political-Regulatory Climate

The political and regulatory climate for marketing in a country or region of the world lies not only in identifying the current climate but in determining how long a favorable or unfavorable climate will last. An assessment of a country or regional political-regulatory climate includes an analysis of its political stability and trade regulations.

Political Stability   Trade among nations or regions depends on political stability. Billions of dollars have been lost in the Middle East, the former Federal Republic of Yugoslavia, and Africa as a result of internal political strife, terrorism, and war. Losses such as these encourage careful selection of politically stable countries and regions of the world for trade.

Political stability in a country is affected by numerous factors, including a government's orientation toward foreign companies and trade with other countries. These factors combine to create a political climate that is favorable or unfavorable for marketing and financial investment in a country or region of the world. Marketing managers monitor political stability using a variety of measures and often track country risk ratings supplied by agencies such as the PRS Group. Visit the PRS Group website shown in the accompanying Web Link and see the most recent political risk ratings for countries.

Trade Regulations   Countries have a variety of rules that govern business practices within their borders. These rules often serve as trade barriers.[41] For example, Japan has some 11,000 trade regulations. Japanese car safety rules effectively require all automobile replacement parts to be Japanese and not American or European; public health rules make it illegal to sell aspirin or cold medicine without a pharmacist present. The Malaysian government has advertising regulations stating that "advertisements must not project or promote an excessively aspirational lifestyle," Greece bans toy advertising, and Sweden outlaws all advertisements to children.

Trade regulations also appear in free trade agreements among countries. European Union nations abide by some 10,000 rules that specify how goods are to be made and marketed. For instance, the rules for a washing machine's electrical system are detailed on more than 100 typed pages. Regulations related to contacting consumers via telephone, fax, and e-mail without their prior consent also exist. The European Union's ISO 9000 quality standards, though not a trade regulation, have the same effect on business practice. These standards, described in Chapter 6, involve registration and certification of a manufacturer's quality management and quality assurance system. Many European companies require suppliers to be ISO 9000 certified as a condition of doing business with them. Certified companies have undergone an on-site audit that includes an inspection of its facilities to ensure that documented quality control procedures are in place and that all employees understand and follow them. More than 150 countries have adopted ISO 9000 standards, and 340,000 certificates have been issued worldwide with about 30,000 going to U.S. firms.[42]

Concept Check

1. Semiotics involves the study of _____.

2. When foreign currencies can buy more U.S. dollars, are U.S. products more or less expensive for a foreign consumer?

GLOBAL MARKET-ENTRY STRATEGIES

Once a company has decided to enter the global marketplace, it must select a means of market entry. Four general options exist: (1) exporting, (2) licensing, (3) joint venture, and (4) direct investment.[43] As Figure 7–6 demonstrates, the amount of financial commitment, risk, marketing control, and profit potential increases as the firm moves from exporting to direct investment.

FIGURE 7–6
Alternative global market-entry strategies

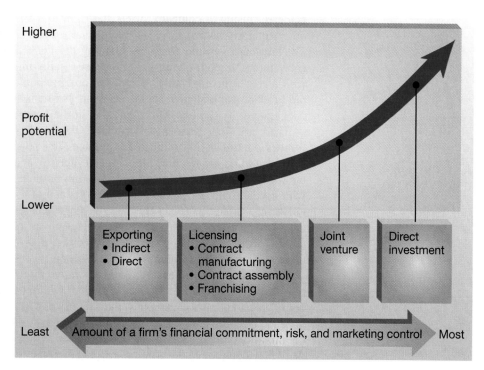

Exporting

Exporting is producing goods in one country and selling them in another country. This entry option allows a company to make the least number of changes in terms of its product, its organization, and even its corporate goals. Host countries usually do not like this practice because it provides less local employment than under alternative means of entry.

Indirect exporting is when a firm sells its domestically produced goods in a foreign country through an intermediary. It involves the least amount of commitment and risk but will probably return the least profit. This kind of exporting is ideal for the company that has no overseas contacts but wants to market abroad. The intermediary is often a distributer that has the marketing know-how and the resources necessary for the effort to succeed. Fran Wilson Creative Cosmetics of New York uses an indirect exporting approach to sell its products in Japan. Read the accompanying Marketing NewsNet to find out how this innovative marketer and its Japanese distributors sell 20 percent of the lipsticks exported to Japan by U.S. companies.[44]

Direct exporting is when a firm sells its domestically produced goods in a foreign country without intermediaries. Most companies become involved in direct exporting when they believe their volume of sales will be sufficiently large and easy to obtain so that they do not require intermediaries. For example, the exporter may be approached by foreign buyers that are willing to contract for a large volume of purchases. Direct exporting involves more risk than indirect exporting for the company but also opens the door to increased profits. The Boeing Company applies a direct exporting approach. Boeing is not only the world's largest aerospace company, but also the largest U.S. exporter, generating almost one-half of its total revenue from export sales.[45]

Even though exporting is commonly employed by large firms, it is the prominent global market-entry strategy among small- and medium-sized companies. For example, 60 percent of U.S. firms exporting products have fewer than 100 employees. These firms account for about 30 percent of total U.S. merchandise exports.[46]

Licensing

Under licensing, a company offers the right to a trademark, patent, trade secret, or other similarly valued items of intellectual property in return for a royalty or a fee. The advantages to the company granting the license are low risk and a capital-free entry into a foreign country. The licensee gains information that allows it to start with a competitive advantage, and the foreign country gains employment by having the product manufactured locally. Yoplait yogurt is licensed from Sodima, a French cooperative, by General Mills for sales in the United States.

There are some serious drawbacks to this mode of entry, however. The licensor forgoes control of its product and reduces the potential profits gained from it. In addition, while the relationship lasts, the licensor may be creating its own competition. Some licensees are able to modify the product somehow and enter the market with product and marketing knowledge gained at the expense of the company that got them started. To offset this disadvantage, many companies strive to stay innovative so that the licensee remains dependent on them for improvements and successful operation. Finally, should the licensee prove to be a poor choice, the name or reputation of the company may be harmed.

Two variations of licensing, *contract manufacturing* and *contract assembly,* represent alternative ways to produce a product within the foreign country. With contract manufacturing, a U.S. company may contract with a foreign firm to manufacture products according to stated specifications. The product is then sold in the foreign country or exported back to the United States. With contract assembly, the U.S. company may contract with a foreign firm to assemble (not manufacture) parts and com-

MARKETING NEWSNET

Creative Cosmetics and Creative Export Marketing in Japan

How does a medium-sized U.S. cosmetics firm sell 1.5 million tubes of lipstick in Japan annually? Fran Wilson Creative Cosmetics can attribute its success to a top-quality product, effective advertising, and a novel export marketing program. The firm's Moodmatcher lip coloring comes in green, orange, silver, black, and six other hues that change to a shade of pink, coral, or red, depending on a woman's chemistry when it's applied.

The company does not sell to department stores. According to a company spokesperson, "Shiseido and Kanebo (two large Japanese cosmetics firms) keep all the other Japanese or import brands out of the major department stores." Rather, the company sells its Moodmatcher lipstick through Japanese distributors that reach Japan's 40,000 beauty salons. The result? The company, with its savvy Japanese distributors, accounts for 20 percent of the $4.3 million of lipsticks exported annually to Japan by U.S. companies.

ponents that have been shipped to that country. In both cases, the advantage to the foreign country is the employment of its people, and the U.S. firm benefits from the lower wage rates in the foreign country. Contract manufacturing and assembly in developing countries has sparked controversy in the toy, textile, and apparel industries where poor working conditions, low pay, and child labor practices have been documented. However, this practice has been an economic boon to Taiwan where 55 percent of the world's notebook computers are made. In a typical year, U.S. companies such as Compaq Computer, Dell Computer, and IBM will have Taiwanese firms supply at least 65 percent of their notebook computer needs.[47]

A third variation of licensing is *franchising*. Franchising is one of the fastest-growing market-entry strategies. More than 35,000 franchises of U.S. firms are located in countries throughout the world. Franchises include soft-drink, motel, retailing, fast-food, and car rental operation and a variety of business services. McDonald's is a premier global franchiser: more than 70 percent of the company's stores are franchised, and over 60 percent of the company's sales come from non-U.S. operations.[48]

Joint Venture

When a foreign company and a local firm invest together to create a local business, it is called a **joint venture**. These two companies share ownership, control, and profits of the new company. Investment may be made by having either of the companies buy shares in the other or by creating a third and separate entity. This was done by Caterpillar, Inc., the world's largest manufacturer of earth-moving and construction equipment. It created NEVAMASH with its joint venture partner, Kirovsky Zvod, a large Russian manufacturer of heavy equipment.[49]

The advantages of this option are twofold. First, one company may not have the necessary financial, physical, or managerial resources to enter a foreign market alone. The joint venture between Ericsson, a Swedish telecommunications firm, and CGCT,

McDonald's uses franchising as a market-entry strategy and over 60 percent of the company's sales come from non-U.S. operations.

McDonald's

www.mcdonalds.com

a French switch maker, enabled them together to beat out AT&T for a $100 million French contract. Ericsson's money and technology combined with CGCT's knowledge of the French market helped them to win the contract that neither of them could have won alone. Similarly, Ford and Volkswagen formed a joint venture to make four-wheel-drive vehicles in Portugal. Second, a government may require or strongly encourage a joint venture before it allows a foreign company to enter its market. This is the case in China. Today, more than 75,000 Chinese-foreign joint ventures operate in China.[50]

The disadvantages arise when the two companies disagree about policies or courses of action for their joint venture or when governmental bureaucracy bogs down the effort. For example, U.S. firms often prefer to reinvest earnings gained, whereas some foreign companies may want to spend those earnings. Or a U.S. firm may want to return profits earned to the United States, while the local firm or its government may oppose this—the problem now faced by many potential joint ventures in Eastern Europe, Russia, Latin America, and South Asia.

Direct Investment

The biggest commitment a company can make when entering the global market is **direct investment**, which entails a domestic firm actually investing in and owning a foreign subsidiary or division.[51] Examples of direct investment are Nissan's Smyrna, Tennessee, plant that produces pickup trucks and the Mercedes-Benz factory in Vance, Alabama, that makes the Daimler Chrysler M-class sports utility vehicle. Many U.S.-based global companies also use this mode of entry. Reebok entered Russia by creating a subsidiary known as Reebok Russia, Motorola established a wholly owned Chinese subsidiary that manufactures mobile phones and other telecommunication equipment, and Ford built a $1.9 billion automobile plant in Brazil.

For many firms, direct investment often follows one of the other three market-entry strategies.[52] For example, Ernst & Young, an international accounting and management consulting firm, entered Hungary first by establishing a joint venture with a local company. Ernst & Young later acquired the company, making it a subsidiary with headquarters in Budapest. Following on the success of its European and Asian exporting strategy, Harley-Davidson now operates wholly owned marketing and sales subsidiaries in Germany, Italy, the United Kingdom, and Japan, among other countries.

The advantages to direct investment include cost savings, better understanding of local market conditions, and fewer local restrictions. Firms entering foreign markets using direct investment believe that these advantages outweigh the financial commitments and risks involved.

1. What mode of entry could a company follow if it has no previous experience in global marketing?

2. How does licensing differ from a joint venture?

CRAFTING A WORLDWIDE MARKETING EFFORT

The choice of a market-entry strategy is a necessary first step for a marketer when joining the community of global companies. The next step involves the challenging task of designing, implementing, and controlling marketing programs worldwide.

Product and Promotion Strategies

Global companies have five strategies for matching products and their promotion efforts to global markets. As Figure 7–7 shows, the strategies focus on whether a company extends or adapts its product and promotion message for consumers in different countries.

A product may be sold globally in one of three ways: (1) in the same form as in its home market, (2) with some adaptations, or (3) as a totally new product:[53]

1. *Product extension.* Selling virtually the same product in other countries is a product extension strategy. It works well for products such as Coca-Cola, Gillette razors, Breathe Right nasal strips, Wrigley's gum, and Levi's jeans. However, it didn't work for Jell-O (a more solid gelatin was preferred to the powder in England) or Duncan Hines cakes (which were seen as too moist and crumbly to eat with tea in England).

2. *Product adaptation.* Changing a product in some way to make it more appropriate for a country's climate or consumer preferences is a product adaptation strategy. Exxon sells different gasoline blends based on each country's climate. Gerber baby food comes in different varieties in different countries. Vegetable and Rabbit Meat is a favorite food in Poland. Freeze-Dried Sardines and Rice is popular in Japan. Maybelline's makeup is formulaically adapted in labs to local skin types and weather across the globe, including an Asia-specific mascara that doesn't run during the rainy season.

FIGURE 7–7

Five product and promotion strategies for global marketing

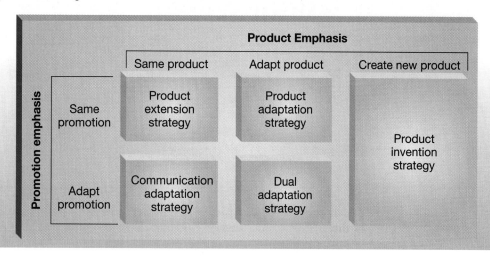

3. *Product invention.* Alternatively, companies can invent totally new products designed to satisfy common needs across countries. Black & Decker did this with its Snake Light Flexible Flashlight. Created to address a global need for portable lighting, the product became a best seller in North America, Europe, Latin America, and Australia, and is the most successful new product developed by Black & Decker.

An identical promotion message is used for the product extension and product adaptation strategies around the world. Gillette uses the same global message for its men's toiletries: "Gillette, the Best a Man Can Get." Even though Exxon adapts its gasoline for different countries, the promotion message is unchanged: "Put a Tiger in Your Tank."

Global companies may also adapt their promotion message. For instance, the same product may be sold in many countries but advertised differently. As an example, L'Oreal, a French health and beauty products marketer, introduced its Golden Beauty brand of sun care products through its Helena Rubenstein subsidiary in Western Europe with a communication adaptation strategy. Recognizing that cultural and buying motive differences related to skin care and tanning exist, Golden Beauty advertising features dark tanning for Northern Europeans, skin protection to avoid wrinkles among Latin Europeans, and beautiful skin for Europeans living along the Mediterranean Sea, even though the products are the same. Other companies use a dual adaptation strategy by modifying both their products and promotion messages. Nestlé does this with Nescafé coffee. Nescafé is marketed using different coffee blends and promotional campaigns to match consumer preferences in different countries. These examples illustrate a simple rule applied by global companies today: standardize product and promotion strategies whenever possible and adapt them wherever necessary. This is the art of global marketing.[54]

Distribution Strategy

Distribution is of critical importance in global marketing. The availability and quality of retailers and wholesalers as well as transportation, communication, and warehousing facilities are often determined by a country's stage of economic development. Figure 7–8 outlines the channel through which a product manufactured in one country must travel to reach its destination in another country. The first step involves the seller; its headquarters is the starting point and is responsible for the successful distribution to the ultimate consumer.

Gillette delivers the same global message whenever possible, as shown in the Gillette for Women Venus ads from Greece, Germany, and the United States.

The Gillette Company
www.gillette.com

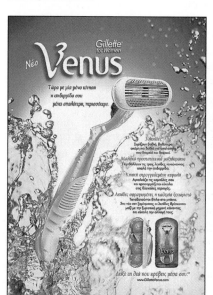
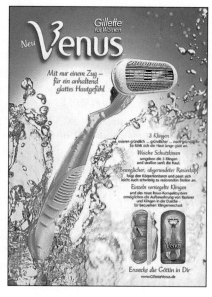
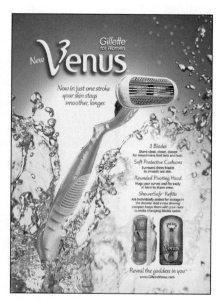

FIGURE 7–8
Channels of distribution in
global marketing

The next step is the channel between two nations, moving the product from one country to another. Intermediaries that can handle this responsibility include resident buyers in a foreign country, independent merchant wholesalers who buy and sell the product, or agents who bring buyers and sellers together.

Once the product is in the foreign nation, that country's distribution channels take over.[55] These channels can be very long or surprisingly short, depending on the product line. In Japan fresh fish go through three intermediaries before getting to a retail outlet. Conversely, shoes only go through one intermediary. In other cases, the channel does not even involve the host country. Procter & Gamble sells its soap door to door in the Philippines because there are no other alternatives in many parts of that country. The sophistication of a country's distribution channels increase as its economic infrastructure develops. Supermarkets facilitate selling products in many nations, but they are not popular or available in many others where culture and lack of refrigeration dictate shopping on a daily rather than a weekly basis. For example, when Coke and Pepsi entered China, both had to create direct-distribution channels, investing in refrigerator units for small retailers.

Pricing Strategy

Global companies also face many challenges in determining a pricing strategy as part of their worldwide marketing effort. Individual countries, even those with free trade agreements, may impose considerable competitive, political, and legal constraints on the pricing latitude of global companies. For example, Wal-Mart Stores were told by German antitrust authorities that their prices were too low, relative to competitors, and faced a fine for violating the country's trade if the prices weren't raised![56] Of course, economic factors such as the costs of production, selling, and tariffs, plus transportation and storage costs, also affect global pricing decisions.

Pricing too low or too high can have dire consequences. When prices appear too low in one country, companies can be charged with dumping, a practice subject to severe penalties and fines. **Dumping** is when a firm sells a product in a foreign country below its domestic price or below its actual cost. This is often done to build a company's share of the market by pricing at a competitive level. Another reason is that the products being sold may be surplus or cannot be sold domestically and, therefore, are already a burden to the company. The firm may be glad to sell them at almost any price. A recent trade dispute involving U.S. apple growers and Mexico is a case in point. Mexican trade officials claimed that U.S. growers were selling their red and golden delicious apples in Mexico below the actual cost of production. They imposed a 101 percent tariff on U.S. apples, and a severe drop in U.S. apple exports to Mexico resulted. Subsequent negotiations set a price floor on the price of U.S. apples sold to Mexico.[57]

When companies price their products very high in some countries but competitively in others, they face a gray market problem. A **gray market**, also called parallel importing, is a situation where products are sold through unauthorized channels of distribution. A gray market comes about when individuals buy products in a lower-priced country from a manufacturer's authorized retailer, ship them to higher-priced countries, and then sell them below the manufacturer's suggested retail price through unauthorized retailers. Many well-known products have been sold through gray markets, including Olympus cameras, Seiko watches, IBM personal computers, and Mercedes-Benz cars. Parallel importing is legal in the United States. It is illegal in the European Union.[58]

Concept Check

1. Products may be sold globally in three ways. What are they?

2. What is dumping?

SUMMARY

1 The dollar value of world trade has more than doubled in the past decade and will exceed $11.5 trillion in 2005. Manufactured goods and commodities account for 75 percent of world trade, while services account for 25 percent.

2 A global perspective on world trade views exports and imports as complementary economic flows. A country's exports affect its imports and vice versa. This phenomenon is called the *trade feedback effect*.

3 The United States is the world's perennial leader in terms of gross domestic product and among the world's leaders in exports. Nevertheless, the United States has incurred a continuing balance of trade deficit since 1975.

4 The reason some companies and some industries in a country succeed globally while others do not lies in their nation's competitive advantage. A nation's competitive advantage arises from specific conditions in a nation that foster success.

5 Four recent trends have significantly affected world trade: (*a*) a gradual decline of economic protectionism, (*b*) an increase in formal economic integration and free trade among

nations, (*c*) global competition among global companies for global consumers, and (*d*) the emergence of a networked global marketspace.

6 Although global and domestic marketing are based on the same marketing principles, many underlying assumptions must be reevaluated when a firm pursues global opportunities. A global environmental scan typically considers three kinds of uncontrollable environmental variables. These include cultural diversity, economic conditions, and political-regulatory climate.

7 Four global market-entry strategies are exporting, licensing, joint venture, and direct investment. The relative difficulty of global marketing, as well as the amount of financial commitment, risk, marketing control, and profit potential, increase in moving from exporting to direct investment.

8 Crafting a worldwide marketing effort involves designing, implementing, and controlling a marketing program that standardizes marketing mix elements when there are cultural similarities and adapting them when cultures differ.

KEY TERMS AND CONCEPTS

back translation p. 186
balance of trade p. 173
consumer ethnocentrism p. 186
countertrade p. 172
cross-cultural analysis p. 183
cultural symbols p. 185
currency exchange rate p. 189
customs p. 184
direct investment p. 194
dumping p. 197
Economic Espionage Act p. 175
exporting p. 192
Foreign Corrupt Practices Act p. 184
global competition p. 179

global consumers p. 181
global marketing strategy p. 180
gray market p. 197
gross domestic product p. 173
joint venture p. 193
multidomestic marketing strategy p. 180
protectionism p. 176
quota p. 176
semiotics p. 185
strategic alliances p. 179
tariffs p. 176
trade feedback effect p. 173
values p. 183
World Trade Organization p. 177

APPLYING MARKETING CONCEPTS AND PERSPECTIVES

1 What is meant by this statement: "Quotas are a hidden tax on consumers, whereas tariffs are a more obvious one"?

2 Is the trade feedback effect described in the text a long-run or short-run view on world trade flows? Explain your answer.

3 The United States is considered to be a global leader in the development and marketing of pharmaceutical products, and Merck & Co. of New Jersey is a world

leader in prescription drug sales. What explanation can you give for this situation based on the text discussion concerning the competitive advantage of nations?

4 How successful would a television commercial in Japan be if it featured a husband surprising his wife in her dressing area on Valentine's Day with a small box of chocolates containing four candies? Why?

5 As a novice in global marketing, which alternative for global market-entry strategy would you be likely to start with? Why? What other alternatives do you have for a global market entry?

6   Coca-Cola is sold worldwide. In some countries, Coca-Cola owns the bottling facilities; in others, it has signed contracts with licensees or relies on joint ventures. When selecting a licensee in each country, what factors should Coca-Cola consider?

INTERNET EXERCISE

The World Trade Organization (WTO) is the only international organization dealing with the global rules of trade between nations. Its intended function is to ensure that trade flows as smoothly, predictably, and freely as possible. Understanding how the WTO operates is a necessary prerequisite for global marketing.

Visit the WTO website at www.wto.org to learn more about how this organization functions and the issues it faces. A useful starting point for familiarizing yourself with the WTO is to find answers to the following questions:

1   Countries are constantly seeking WTO membership. How many countries are now members of this organization? Which country is the newest member?

2   What are the 10 most common misunderstandings about the WTO identified by this organization?

VIDEO CASE 7–1   CNS Breathe Right® Strips: Reaching the World's Noses

"When we first began marketing this product, what was so gratifying, particularly as a physician, were the literally thousands of letters and phone calls we would receive talking about how much better people slept at night. Almost all the letters began with 'thank you, thank you, thank you!' Just three thank you's. It was, 'I haven't gotten a good night's sleep like this in 10 years.'"

What is Dr. Dan Cohen, CEO of CNS, Inc., talking about? It's Breathe Right® nasal strips, the innovative adhesive pad with a small spring inside that, when attached to the nose, pulls the nasal passages open and makes it easier to breathe. Since its introduction in the United States, Breathe Right® strips have been coveted by athletes hoping to improve their performance through increased oxygen flow, snorers (and, more often, snorers' spouses) hoping for a sound night's sleep, and allergy and cold sufferers looking for relief for their stuffed noses.

HOW THIS WEIRD-LOOKING STRIP CAME ABOUT

The Breathe Right® strip was invented by Bruce Johnson, who suffered from chronic nasal congestion. At times he would put straws or paper clips up his nose at night to keep his nasal passages open. After tinkering in his workshop for years, he came up with a prototype design for the Breathe Right® strip. He brought the prototype to CNS, which was in the sleep disorders diagnostic equipment business at the time. Dr. Cohen knew instantly the market for the strips would be huge. After the products received Food and Drug Administration (FDA) approval and became successful in the market, CNS divested its other interests and went to work marketing the strips full time.

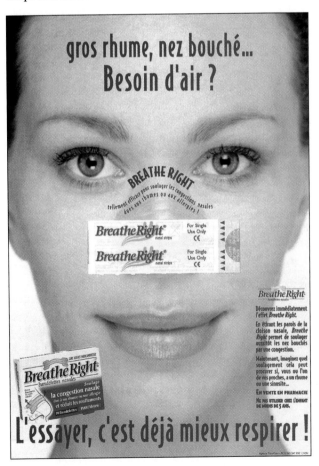

Being a small company, CNS did not have the budget to launch a large-scale marketing campaign. But it got the break it needed when Jerry Rice, the wide receiver for the San Francisco 49ers, wore one of the strips on national TV when the 49ers won the 1995 Super Bowl. The entire nation became aware of the product overnight, and demand for the strips increased dramatically. An indication of this national awareness was discussion on TV talk shows and even appearances of the strip in cartoons.

EVERYBODY HAS A NOSE: THE DECISION TO GO INTERNATIONAL

The problems that the Breathe Right® strips solve—snoring, congestion—are not unique to the U.S. population. Also, with the media being so global today, people around the world were seeing U.S. athletes wearing the strip and wondering how they could get their noses on some. CNS decided to take Breathe Right® international. But because it was still a relatively small company and had no experience in the global marketplace, it opted to take on a distribution partner that had extensive global outlets already in place as well as the ability to market the product abroad. 3M, makers of such products as Post-It™ notes and the leader in stick-to-skin products around the world, became the international distributor for Breathe Right® strips.

David Reynolds-Gooch, International Business Manager at 3M, explains that the strips fit in well with 3M's existing adhesive line of first-aid products and are sold in channels with which 3M has extensive leverage: pharmacies, hypermarkets, and food markets. 3M agreed to take control of all the marketing and communication responsibilities in addition to the distribution in return for a percentage of the sales revenue of the strips. The strips are "co-branded" in the international markets: The packages say both Breathe Right® and 3M.

BREATHING RIGHT AROUND THE WORLD

3M introduced the Breathe Right® strip in Japan, then it was rolled out in Europe, and now can be found in more than 40 countries from Australia to South America. 3M used a similar approach to that used by CNS in the United States: Create awareness during the introduction phase through public relations—sports related and otherwise. "The first year we had incredible PR success," remembers Reynolds-Gooch. "We believe we got about $14 million worth of free TV, radio, and print time around the world." This was done through such tactics as having the South African rugby team wear the strips while it won the World Cup of rugby and having pulmonologists and breathing experts describe the benefits of the product on talk shows in Japan, Australia, Europe, and Latin America.

CNS quickly discovered some major differences in marketing the product here and abroad. For instance, as Gary Tschautscher, Vice President of International Marketing at CNS explains, "In the United States, we positioned and distributed the strips as part of the cough/cold category of products. As we rolled it out internationally, suddenly we realized in some countries that section in the store doesn't even exist. So where do you position your product?" Additionally, says Reynolds-Gooch, "There really aren't many large drug chains or pharmacy chains. The stores are independent in most countries by law. So what that means is you have to go through multiple layers of distribution, and ultimately we were able to influence the pharmacists because of the other products 3M distributes in the stores." Finally, there is no couponing in most countries in the world. That vehicle for inducing trial of a new product is not available, and hence a lot more in-store sampling is needed.

BREATHE RIGHT® IN THE TWENTY-FIRST CENTURY

Both CNS and 3M face some issues for the future as Breathe Right strips gain in popularity around the globe. While the athletic segment of the market gets most of the publicity, the snorers are the bulk of the market for the strips internationally. Reynolds-Gooch has identified creating heavy users—those who use the strip every night—as the most important marketing point for the future, ahead of people with seasonal colds or allergies.

Also, many of the markets that have been identified as "hot" new markets throughout the business community may not be appropriate for the Breathe Right strips. For example, Latin America and Asia (especially China) are emerging markets with steadily increasing income levels and large populations, but the average age in these countries is under 30, and people under 30 typically do not have snoring problems with the frequency that older people do.

Questions

1 What are the advantages and disadvantages of CNS taking its Breathe Right® strip into international markets?

2 What advantages does CNS gain by having 3M as its international licensing partner? What are the advantages for 3M?

3 What criteria might CNS and 3M use in selecting countries to enter? Using these criteria, which five or six countries would you enter?

4 Which market segment would you target in entering the international markets—snorers, athletes, people with chronic congestion and allergies, or a new segment?

5 Which marketing mix variables do you think CNS should concentrate on the most to succeed in a global arena? Why?

3

TARGETING MARKETING OPPORTUNITIES

CHAPTER 8
Turning Marketing Information into Action

CHAPTER 9
Identifying Market Segments and Targets

Part 3 focuses on targeting marketing opportunities. Chapter 8 describes how people with similar wants and needs become the target of marketing opportunities. This chapter details how information about prospective consumers is linked to marketing strategy and decisive actions, and how information technology improves the process. Chapter 9 describes how shoe manufacturing giants like Reebok and Nike, and upstarts like Heelys and Customatix, design shoes to satisfy different customers. In addition, this chapter covers the steps a firm uses in segmenting and targeting a market and then positioning its offering in the marketplace. The application of segmentation, targeting, and positioning are illustrated with Apple Computer's strategy for its hardware and software.

THE
LORD OF THE RINGS
THE FELLOWSHIP OF THE RING

8

TURNING MARKETING INFORMATION INTO ACTION

AFTER READING THIS CHAPTER YOU SHOULD BE ABLE TO:

- Identify a five-step marketing research approach leading to marketing actions.

- Describe how secondary and primary data are used in marketing, including the uses of questionnaires, observations, experiments, and panels.

- Understand how information technology enables information systems to be used to link massive amounts of marketing information to meaningful marketing actions.

- Recognize alternative methods to forecast sales and use the lost-horse and linear trend extrapolation methods to make a simple forecast.

TEST SCREENINGS: LISTENING TO CONSUMERS TO REDUCE MOVIE RISKS!

"Blockbuster" movies are essential for today's fiercely competitive world of filmmaking—examples being *The Lord of the Rings* trilogy (opposite page), *Shoeless Joe, Teenie Weenies,* and *3000!*

What's in a Movie Name? Can't remember those last three movies—even after scratching your head? Well, test screenings by the studios—a form of marketing research—found that moviegoers had problems with those titles, too. Here's the title these three movies started with, where they wound up, and the reason:

- *Shoeless Joe* became *Field of Dreams* because audiences thought Kevin Costner might be playing a homeless person.
- *Teenie Weenies* became *Honey, I Shrunk the Kids* when moviegoers couldn't relate the original title to what they saw in the movie.
- *3000* became *Pretty Woman* when audiences didn't have a clue what the number meant. Hint: It was the number of dollars to spend an evening with Julia Roberts.[1]

Filmmakers want movie titles that are concise, attention-getting, capture the essence of the film, and have no legal restrictions—basically the same factors that make a good brand name.

How Filmmakers Try to Reduce Risk Is research on movie titles expensive? Very! But the greater expense is selecting a bad title that can kill a movie and cost the studio millions of dollars, not to mention the careers of producers and directors! So with

205

today's films averaging over $54 million to produce and $27 million to market,[2] movie studios use market research to reduce their risk of losses by hiring firms like the National Research Group to conduct test screenings and tracking studies.

For test screenings, 300 to 400 prospective moviegoers are recruited to attend a "sneak preview" of a film before its release. After viewing the movie, the audience fills out an exhaustive survey to critique the title, plot, characters, music, and ending as well as the marketing program (posters, trailers, etc.) to identify improvements to make in the final edit of the movie. Director Ron Howard *(How the Grinch Stole Christmas, Apollo 13, Cocoon)* says, "[While] the whole preview experience is not fun . . . you never want to be proven to be mistaken about anything."[3]

Without reading ahead, think about the answers to these questions:

- Whom would you recruit for movie test screenings?
- What questions would you ask to help you edit or modify the title or other aspects of a film?

Virtually every major U.S. movie produced today uses test screenings to obtain the key reactions of consumers likely to be in the target audience. Figure 8–1 summarizes some of the key questions that are used in these test screenings, both to select the people for the screenings and to obtain key reactions of those sitting in the screenings.

Here are some examples of changes to movies that have resulted from this kind of marketing research:

- *Making the plot move faster.* Disney cut a duet by Pocahontas and John Smith in *Pocahontas* because it got in the way of the action and confused test audiences.[4]
- *Reaching a market segment more effectively.* More action footage was added for Kevin Costner when preview screening showed young males were less enthusiastic about *The Bodyguard* than young females.[5]
- *Changing an ending.* *Fatal Attraction* had probably the most commercially successful "ending-switch" of all time. In its sneak previews, audiences liked everything but the ending, which had Alex (Glenn Close) committing suicide and managing to frame Dan (Michael Douglas) as her murderer by leaving his fingerprints on the knife she used. The studio shot $1.3 million of new scenes for the ending that audiences eventually saw.[6]

Sometimes studios get the pleasant news in its test screenings that a movie or plot "works" with an audience. This was the case when James Cameron, writer-director-producer of *Titanic,* sat in on a test screening of his $200 million epic and watched the audience go wild, a huge relief after months of cost overruns and delayed premieres.[7] *Titanic* went on to become the biggest "blockbuster" ever, grossing over $1.8 billion in worldwide box office sales.[8]

www.lordoftherings.net

New Line Cinema hopes to replicate *Titanic's* success with its *Lord of the Rings* trilogy, which will cost the studio $270 million to produce and an additional $50 million to market! Its first test screening at the Cannes Film Festival in May 2001 was a huge success. However, because each episode of the trilogy is being released during the Christmas season over the next three years (*The Fellowship of the Ring* in 2001, *The Two Towers* in 2002, and *The Return of the King* in 2003), New Line faces perhaps even more titanic risks: managing audience expectations in re-creating J. R. R. Tolkien's classic epic fantasy. Success involves maintaining audience interest over the three-year release period—a major challenge if moviegoers are disappointed with the first episode—and recouping the staggering $320 million (or more?) the studio will invest in the project!

Movie studios also use tracking studies, in which prospective moviegoers in the target audience are asked three key questions about an upcoming film release:[9]

- Are you aware of a particular film?
- Are you interested in seeing it?
- Would it be your first choice on a certain weekend?

FIGURE 8–1

Marketing research questions asked in test screenings of movies, and how they are used

POINT WHEN ASKED	KEY QUESTIONS	USE OF QUESTION(S)
Before the test screening	• How old are you? • How frequently do you pay to see movies? • What movies have you seen in the last three months?	Decide if person fits profile of target audience for movie. If yes, invite to test screening. If not, don't invite.
After the test screening	• What do you think of the title? What title would you suggest? • Were there any characters too distasteful? Who? How? • Did any scenes offend you? Which ones? How? • How did you like the ending? If you don't like it, how would you change it? • Would you recommend the movie to a friend?	Change movie title Change aspects of some characters Change scenes Change or clarify ending Overall indicator of liking and/or satisfaction with movie

Studios then use the data collected to forecast the movie's opening weekend box office sales, run last minute ads to increase its awareness and interest—the "buzz" or word of mouth for the film. In some cases, a studio may postpone or advance a movie's release date depending on the results for other movies scheduled for release at that time.

These examples show how marketing research is the link between marketing strategy and decisive actions, the main topic of this chapter. Also, marketing research is often used to help a firm develop sales forecasts, the final topic in the chapter.

THE ROLE OF MARKETING RESEARCH

To place marketing research in perspective, we can describe (1) what it is, (2) some of the difficulties in conducting it, and (3) the process marketing executives can use to make effective decisions.

What Marketing Research Is and Does

Marketing research is the process of defining a marketing problem and opportunity, systematically collecting and analyzing information, and recommending actions to improve an organization's marketing activities.[10]

A Means of Reducing Risk and Uncertainty Marketing research attempts to identify and define both marketing problems and opportunities and to generate and evaluate marketing actions. Although marketing research isn't perfect, it can reduce risk and uncertainty to improve decisions made by marketing managers.

Why Good Marketing Research Is Difficult

Marketing researchers face difficulties in asking consumers questions about new, unknown products. For example,

- Do consumers really know whether they are likely to buy a particular product that they probably have never thought about before?

- Even if they know the answer, will they reveal it? When personal or status questions are involved, will people give honest answers?
- Will their actual purchase behavior be the same as their stated interest or intentions? Will they buy the same brand they say they will?

A task of marketing research is to overcome these difficulties.

Steps in Making Effective Decisions

A **decision** is a conscious choice from among two or more alternatives. All of us make many such decisions daily. At work we choose from alternative ways to accomplish an assigned task. At college we choose from alternative courses. As consumers we choose from alternative brands. No magic formula guarantees correct decisions.

Managers and researchers have tried to improve the outcomes of decisions by using more formal, systematic approaches to *decision making,* the act of consciously choosing from alternatives. People who do not use some kind of system—and many do not—may make poor decisions. The systematic approach to making marketing decisions described in this chapter uses five steps and is shown in Figure 8–2. Although the five-step approach described next is used here to focus on marketing decisions, it provides a mental checklist for making both business and personal decisions.

Concept Check

1. What is marketing research?

2. What are the five steps marketing research uses to help lead to marketing actions?

STEP 1: DEFINE THE PROBLEM

Designers at Fisher-Price, the nation's top marketer of infant and preschool toys, seek to develop toys they think kids will like, but how can they be certain? To research the problem, Fisher-Price gets children to play at its state-licensed nursery

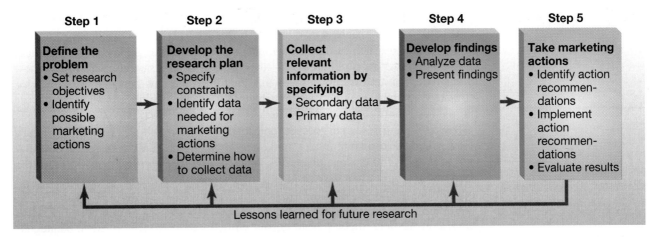

FIGURE 8-2

Five-step marketing research approach leading to marketing actions

school in East Aurora, New York. Behind one-way mirrors Fisher-Price designers and marketing researchers watch the children use—and abuse—the toys to develop better products.

Fisher-Price's toy testing shows how to define the problem and its two key elements: setting the research objectives and identifying resulting marketing actions suggested by the research. For example, the original model of a classic Fisher-Price toy, the Chatter Telephone™, was simply a wooden phone with a dial that rang a bell. Observers noted, however, that the children kept grabbing the receiver like a handle to pull the phone along behind them, so a designer added wheels, a noisemaker, and eyes that bobbed up and down on an experimental version of the toy.

Set the Research Objectives

Objectives are specific, measurable goals the decision maker seeks to achieve in solving a problem. Typical marketing objectives are increasing revenues and profits, discovering what consumers are aware of and want, and finding out why a product isn't selling well. For Fisher-Price, the immediate research objective was to decide whether to market the old or new telephone design.

Identify Possible Marketing Actions

Effective decision makers specify **measures of success**, which are criteria or standards used in evaluating proposed solutions to the problem. Different research outcomes—based on the measure of success—lead to different marketing actions. For the Fisher-Price problem, if a measure of success were the total time children spent playing with each of the two telephone designs, the results of observing them would lead to clear-cut actions as follows:

MEASURE OF SUCCESS: PLAYTIME	POSSIBLE MARKETING ACTION
• Children spent more time playing with old design.	Continue with old design; don't introduce new design.
• Children spent more time playing with new design.	Introduce new design; drop old design.

One test of whether marketing research should be undertaken is if different outcomes will lead to different marketing actions. If all the research outcomes lead to the same action—such as top management sticking with the older design regardless of what the observed children liked—the research is useless and a waste of money. In this case, research results showed that kids liked the new design, so Fisher-Price introduced its noise-making pull-toy Chatter Telephone, which became a toy classic and sold millions.

Toy marketing research goes beyond manufacturers such as Fisher-Price. Every summer Digital Research, Inc., a marketing research firm, evaluates almost 500 new toys from over 160 toy manufacturers to select *Family Fun* magazine's "Toy of the Year" award. More than 700 children "toy testers" are involved. And they've been right on the money in selecting Barney the TV dinosaur, Tickle Me Elmo, Sing & Snore Ernie, and Fisher-Price's Love to Dance Bear™ as hot toys—ones that jumped off retailers' shelves—but missed Furby (which arrived too late to be judged) and Tiger Electronic's robotic puppy, Poo-Chi.[11]

Most marketing researchers would agree with philosopher John Dewey's observations that "a problem well-defined is half-solved," but they know that defining a problem is an incredibly difficult, although essential, task. For example, if the objectives are too broad, the problem may not be researchable. If they are too narrow, the value of the research results may be seriously lessened. This is why marketing researchers spend so much time in defining a marketing problem precisely and writing a formal proposal that describes the research to be done.[12]

STEP 2: DEVELOP THE RESEARCH PLAN

The second step in the marketing research process involves (1) specifying the constraints on the research activity, (2) identifying the data needed for marketing actions, and (3) determining how to collect the data.

Marketing research turned up Fisher-Price's Love to Dance Bear "toy of the year" but missed Tiger Electronic's Poo-Chi, the robotic puppy.

Specify Constraints

The **constraints** in a decision are the restrictions placed on potential solutions by the nature and importance of the problem. Common constraints in marketing problems are limitations on the time and money available to solve the problem. Thus, Fisher-Price might set two constraints on its decision to select either the old or new version of the Chatter Telephone: the decision must be made in 10 weeks and no research budget is available beyond that needed for collecting data in its nursery school.

Identify Data Needed for Marketing Actions

Often marketing research studies wind up collecting a lot of data that are interesting but are irrelevant for the marketing decisions that result in marketing actions. In the Fisher-Price Chatter Telephone case, it might be nice to know the children's favorite colors, whether they like wood or plastic toys better, and so on. In fact, knowing answers to these questions might result in later modifications of the toy, but right now the problem is to select one of two toy designs. So this study must focus on collecting data that help managers make a clear choice between the two telephone designs.

Determine How to Collect Data

Determining how to collect useful marketing research data is often as important as actually collecting the data—Step 3 in the process, which is discussed later. Two key elements in deciding how to collect the data are (1) concepts and (2) methods.

Concepts   One valuable type of concept, a *hypothesis,* is a conjecture or idea about the relationship of two or more factors or what might happen in the future. Hypotheses that lead to marketing actions can come from many sources: from technical breakthroughs to marketing studies and customer suggestions.

For example, with the Chatter Telephone, Fisher-Price managers had the hypothesis that adding a noisemaker, wheels, and eyes to the basic design would make the toy more fun for children and increase sales. The proposed design is really a *new-product concept,* a tentative description of a product or service the firm might offer for sale.

Methods   *Methods* are the approaches that can be used to collect data to solve all or part of a problem. For example, if you are the marketing researcher at Fisher-Price responsible for the Chatter Telephone, you face a number of methods issues in developing your research plan, including the following:

- Can we actually ask three- or four-year-olds meaningful questions they can answer about their liking or disliking of the two designs?
- Are we better off not asking them questions but simply observing their behavior?
- If we simply observe the children's behavior, how can we do this in a way to get the best information without biasing the results?

Millions of other people have asked similar questions about millions of other products and services. How can you find and use the methodologies that other marketing researchers have found successful? Information on useful methods is available in tradebooks, textbooks, and handbooks that relate to marketing and marketing research. Some periodicals and technical journals, such as the *Journal of Marketing* and the *Journal of Marketing Research* published by the American Marketing Association, summarize methods and techniques valuable in addressing marketing problems. Special methods vital to marketing are (1) sampling and (2) statistical inference.

Marketing researchers often select a group of distributors, customers, or prospects, ask them questions, and treat their answers as typical of all those in whom they are interested. There are two ways of sampling, or selecting representative elements from a population: probability and nonprobability sampling. **Probability sampling** involves using precise rules to select the sample such that each element of the population has a specific known chance of being selected. For example, if a college wants to know how last year's 1,000 graduates are doing, it can put their names in a bowl and randomly select 50 names to contact. The chance of being selected— 50/1,000 or 0.05—is known in advance, and all graduates have an equal chance of being contacted. This procedure helps select a sample (the 50 graduates) that is representative of the entire population (the 1,000 graduates) and allows conclusions to be drawn about the entire population.

When time and budget are limited, researchers may opt for **nonprobability sampling** and use arbitrary judgments to select the sample so that the chance of selecting a particular element may be unknown or 0. If the college decides to select the 50 graduates from last year's class who live closest to the college, many members of the class have been arbitrarily excluded. This has introduced a bias that makes it dangerous to draw conclusions about the population from this geographically restricted sample.

The method of **statistical inference** involves drawing conclusions about a *population* (the "universe" of all people, stores, or salespeople about which researchers wish to generalize) from a *sample* (some elements of the universe) taken from that population. To draw accurate inferences about the population, the sample elements should be representative of that universe. If the sample is not typical, bias can be introduced, resulting in bad marketing decisions.

Concept Check

1. How do research objectives relate to marketing actions?

2. What does *constraints* mean?

3. What is the difference between concepts and methods?

STEP 3: COLLECT RELEVANT INFORMATION

Collecting enough relevant information to make a rational, informed marketing decision sometimes simply means using your knowledge to decide immediately. At other times it entails collecting an enormous amount of information at great expense.

Figure 8–3 shows how the different kinds of marketing information fit together. **Data**, the facts and figures pertinent to the problem, are divided into two main parts: secondary data and primary data. **Secondary data** are facts and figures that have already been recorded before the project at hand, whereas **primary data** are facts and figures that are newly collected for the project.

Secondary Data

Secondary data divide into two parts—internal and external secondary data— depending on whether the data come from inside or outside the organization needing the research.

Internal Secondary Data
Data that have already been collected and exist inside the business firm or other organization are internal secondary data. These include product sales data, and sales reports on customer calls.

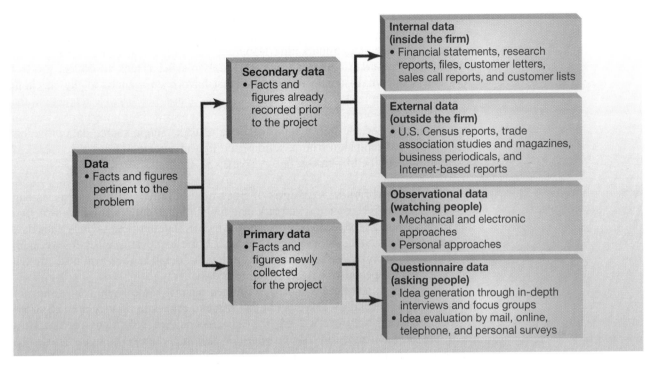

FIGURE 8–3
Types of marketing information

External Secondary Data Published data from outside the organization are external secondary data. The U.S. Census Bureau publishes a variety of useful reports. Best known is the Census 2000, which is a decennial count of the U.S. population containing detailed information on American households, such as the number of people per household and their age, sex, race/ethnic background, income, occupation, and education. Marketers use these data to identify characteristics and trends of ultimate consumers.

The Census Bureau also publishes other reports that are vital to business firms selling products and services to organizations. The Economic Census, which now encompasses the former U.S. Census of Manufacturers, U.S. Census of Retail Trade, and others, is conducted every five years. The 2002 Economic Census will contain data on the number and size of establishments in the United States that produce a good or service on the basis of its North American Industry Classification (NAICS) and the new North American Product Classification System (NAPCS). Special emphasis will be placed on the collection of information from women- and minority-owned businesses. The Current Industrial Reports are periodic studies that provide data on the production quantity and shipment value of selected products. Marketers use all these data to estimate market size, calculate market share, assess new market-product opportunities, and take marketing actions (see Chapter 9). Finally, trade associations, universities, and business periodicals provide detailed data of value to market researchers and planners. These data are now available online via the Internet, which can be identified and located using a search engine like Yahoo! The Web Link box provides examples.

A variety of marketing research organizations serves the needs of marketers. Specialized syndicated services provide a standard set of data on a regular basis, such as the Nielsen Media Research's TV ratings or J. D. Powers with its automotive quality and customer satisfaction research. Other market research suppliers contract with clients to conduct complete marketing research projects.

New marketing data services have recently emerged that offer *single-source data,* which is information provided by a single firm on household demographics and lifestyle, product purchases, TV viewing behavior, and responses to coupon and free-sample promotions. The principal advantage of single-source data is the ability of one service to collect, analyze, interrelate, and present all this information. For consumer product firms like Procter & Gamble, sales data from various channels are critical to allocate scarce marketing resources. As a result, they use firms such as Information Resources' InfoScan and AC Nielsen's ScanTrack to collect product sales and coupon/free-sample redemptions that have been scanned at the checkout counter from supermarket, drug, convenience, and mass merchandise retailers in the United States and other international markets.[13] Campbell Soup, maker of Swanson frozen dinners, used the information from one of these single-source data providers to shift a TV ad campaign from a serious to a light theme, which increased sales of Swanson dinners by 14 percent.[14]

Advantage and Disadvantages of Secondary Data   A general rule among marketing people is to obtain secondary data first and then collect primary data. Two important advantages of secondary data are (1) the tremendous time savings if the data have already been collected and published and (2) the low cost, such as free or inexpensive census reports. Furthermore, a greater level of detail is often available through secondary data, especially U.S. Census Bureau data.

However, these advantages must be weighed against some significant disadvantages. First, the secondary data may be out of date, especially if they are U.S. Census data collected only every 5 or 10 years. Second, the definitions or categories might not be quite right for your project. For example, the age groupings might be wrong for your project. Finally, because the data are collected for another purpose, they may not be specific enough for your project. In such cases it may be necessary to collect primary data.

Concept Check

1. What are methods?

2. What is the difference between secondary and primary data?

3. What are some advantages and disadvantages of secondary data?

Primary Data

The two principal ways to collect new or primary data for a marketing study are by: (1) observing people and (2) asking them questions.

Observational Data   Facts and figures obtained by watching, either mechanically or in person, how people actually behave is the way marketing researchers collect **observational data**. National TV ratings, such as those of Nielsen Media Research shown in Figure 8–4, are an example of mechanical observational data collected by a "people meter." The people meter is a box that (1) is attached to TV sets, VCRs, cable boxes, and satellite dishes in 5,000 homes across the country; (2) has a remote that operates the meter when a viewer begins and finishes watching a TV program; and (3) stores and then transmits the viewing information each night to Nielsen Media Research. Also, Nielsen Media Research employs a much larger sample of households in 210 TV markets in the United States to record their viewing behavior in TV diaries or booklets (not a mechanical but a manual measurement system) during the months of February, May, July, and November, which are known as "the sweeps."[15]

On the basis of all this observational data, Nielsen Media Research then calculates the "rating" and "share" of each TV program. With 105.5 million TV households in the United States based on the 2000 U.S. Census, a single ratings point equals 1 percent or 1,055,000 TV households.[16] A share point is the percentage of

WEB LINK

Online Databases and Internet Resources Useful for Marketers

Information contained in online databases available via the Internet consists of indexes to articles in periodicals and statistical or financial data on markets, products, and organizations that are accessed either directly or via Internet search engines or portals through key word searches.

Online databases of indexes, abstracts, and full-text information from periodicals include:

- LexisNexis™ Academic Universe (www.lexisnexis.com), which provides full-text documents from over 5,600 news, business, legal, medical, and reference publications.
- ProQuest databases (www.proquest.com), which provide summaries of management, marketing, and other business articles from over 8,000 publications.

Statistical and financial data on markets, products, and organizations include:

- Bloomberg (www.bloomberg.com), *Investor's Business Daily* (www.investors.com), and *The Wall Street Journal* (www.dowjones.com) all providing up-to-the-minute business news and security prices plus research reports on companies, industries, and countries.

- FISonline (www.fisonline.com) has created a database that contains information on over 28,000 companies worldwide (11,000 U.S. public companies and 17,000 non-U.S. public companies).
- STAT-USA (www.stat-usa.gov) from the Department of Commerce provides information on U.S. business, economic, and trade activity collected by the federal government.

Portals and search engines include:

- Firstgov.gov (www.firstgov.gov) is a portal to all U.S. government websites. Users click on links to browse by topic or enter keywords for specific searches.
- Yahoo! (www.yahoo.com) is a portal to the entire Internet. Users click on links to browse by topic or enter key words for specific searches.

Some of these websites are accessible only if your educational institution has paid a subscription fee. To see if you can access these sites for free, log on to your institution's website, click on the "library" icon, and then click on these or other useful databases to which your institution subscribes.

TV sets in use tuned to a particular program. Because network and local broadcast stations, cable systems, and other TV programmers use this information to set advertising rates and make programming decisions, precision in the Nielsen data is critical. Thus, a change of 1 percentage point in a rating can mean gaining or losing up to $50 million in advertising revenue because advertisers pay rates on the basis of the size of the audience for a TV program. As a result, broadcast and cable networks may change the time slot or even cancel a TV program if its ratings are consistently poor and advertisers are unwilling to pay a rate based on a higher guaranteed rating.

The people meter's limitations—as with all observational data collected mechanically (or manually)—relate to how the measurements are taken. Critics don't believe the devices accurately measure who is watching a given TV program or what is being watched. Moreover, people meters can't measure large segments of the population that watch TV programs at parties or sports bars. Recently, Nielsen Media Research and Arbitron, a service that also measures TV, cable, and radio listening behavior, have tested a "passive, portable people meter" that transmits the data directly to Nielsen/Arbitron for analysis.[17]

Nielsen//NetRatings also uses an electronic meter to record Internet user behavior. These data are collected by tracking the actual "mouse clicks" made by users from over 225,000 individuals in 26 countries as they surf the Internet via a meter installed on their home or work computers. Nielsen//NetRatings identifies the top

FIGURE 8–4
Nielsen ratings of the top 10 national television programs from January 28, 2002 through February 3, 2002

RANK	PROGRAM	NETWORK	RATING	SHARE
1	Super Bowl XXXVI	Fox	40.4	61.0
2	Fox Super Bowl Post Game	Fox	24.7	39.0
3	Friends	NBC	17.8	28.0
4	Friends—SP.	NBC	16.6	25.0
5	ER	NBC	16.0	25.0
6	CSI: Crime Scene	CBS	14.8	22.0
7	Law and Order	NBC	13.7	23.0
8	Everybody Loves Raymond	CBS	13.1	19.0
9	Will & Grace	NBC	13.0	19.0
10	West Wing	NBC	12.3	19.0

websites that have the largest unique audiences, the top advertising banners viewed, the top Internet advertisers, and global Internet usage for selected European and Asian countries. Figure 8–5 shows the top 10 Internet websites.

Watching consumers in person or by videotaping them are other observational approaches. For example, Aurora Foods observes how consumers bake cakes in its test kitchens to see if baking instructions on the cake box are understood and followed correctly. Gillette marketing researchers actually videotaped consumers brushing their teeth in their own bathrooms to see how they really brush—not just how they *say* they brush. The new-product result: Gillette's new Oral-B CrossAction toothbrush that's supposed to do a better job—at $4.99 each![18]

A specialized observational approach is *ethnographic research* in which anthropologists and other trained observers seek to discover subtle emotional reactions as consumers encounter products in their "natural use environment," such as in their home, car, or hotel. For example, Best Western International, Inc., a national hotel chain, paid couples to videotape themselves as they spent 3 to 7 days on a cross-country car trip. From this Best Western found that women usually decide when to pull off the road and where to stay—the reverse of focus group research. The result: Target more promotional messages to women.[19]

How do you do marketing research on things as diverse as toothbrushes, soap pads, and fashion products for teenagers? For some creative answers, see the text.

Oral-B Laboratories
www.oralb.com

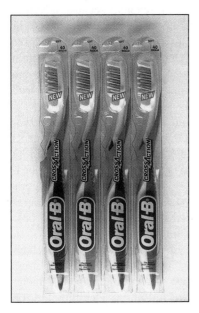

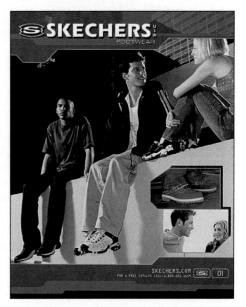

RANK	PROPERTY	UNIQUE AUDIENCE (MILLIONS)	REACH %	MINUTES PER PERSON
1	AOL Time Warner	39.7	50.8	15: 40
2	Yahoo!	33.5	42.8	32: 16
3	MSN	30.1	38.4	27: 40
4	Microsoft	13.0	16.6	07: 24
5	Google	8.8	11.2	07: 30
6	eBay	8.5	10.8	55: 26
7	About-Primedia	8.4	10.8	08: 42
8	Lycos Network	8.3	10.6	07: 40
9	Amazon	8.1	10.3	08: 23
10	Walt Disney Internet Group	6.6	8.5	14: 26

Personal observation is both useful and flexible, but it can be costly and unreliable when different observers report different conclusions in watching the same event. Also, although observation can reveal what people do, it cannot easily determine why they do it, such as why they are buying or not buying a product. This is the principal reason for using questionnaires.

Questionnaire Data   **Questionnaire data** are facts and figures obtained by asking people about their attitudes, awareness, intentions, and behaviors. Because so many questions might be asked in questionnaires, it is essential that the researcher concentrate on those directly related to the marketing problem at hand. Many marketing researchers divide questionnaire data used for hypothesis generation from those used for hypothesis evaluation.

Marketing studies for *hypothesis generation* involve a search for ideas that can be evaluated in later research. Hamburger Helper didn't fare too well with consumers when General Mills introduced it. Initial instructions called for cooking a half pound of hamburger separately from the noodles or potatoes, which were later mixed with the hamburger. *Individual interviews* (a single researcher asking questions of one respondent) showed that consumers (1) didn't think it contained enough meat and (2) didn't want the hassle of cooking in two different pots. So the Hamburger Helper product manager changed the recipe to call for a full pound of meat and to allow users to prepare it in one dish; this converted a potential failure into a success.[20]

Focus groups are informal sessions of 6 to 10 past, present, or prospective customers in which a discussion leader, or moderator, asks their opinions about the firm's and its competitors' products, how they use these products, and special needs they have that these products don't address. Often tape recorded and conducted in special interviewing rooms with a one-way mirror, these groups enable marketing researchers and managers to hear and watch consumer reactions. The informality and peer support in an effective focus group uncover ideas that are often difficult to obtain with individual interviews.

In the mid-1990s 3M sought ways to push further into the home-care business and decided to target the wool soap pads niche, which was dominated by giants SOS and Brillo. 3M ran eight focus groups around the United States and heard consumers complain that standard wool pads scratched their expensive cookware. These interviews led to 3M's internationally successful Scotch-Brite® Never Scratch wool soap pad.[21]

Finding "the next big thing" for consumers has become the obsession not only for consumer product firms but also for firms in many other industries.[22] The result is that marketing researchers have come to rely on techniques that are far more basic—many would say bizarre—than more traditional individual or focus group interviews. These "fuzzy front end" methods attempt to identify elusive consumer tastes or trends far before typical consumers have recognized them themselves. Two examples of unusual ways to collect consumer data and their results include the following:

- Having consumers take a photo of themselves every time they snack. This resulted in General Mills' "Homestyle" Pop Secret popcorn, which delivers the real butter and bursts of salt in microwave popcorn that consumers thought they could only get from the stovetop variety.[23]
- Having children and teenagers compete in a contest to submit designs for a new ketchup label. This resulted in 60,000 designs from which Heinz picked three to test on 10 million bottles of ketchup.[24]

Unusual techniques are also being used to try to spot consumer trends early. Two examples include:

- Having teenagers complete a drawing. This is used by researchers at Teenage Research Unlimited (TRU) to help discover what teenagers like, wear, listen to, read, and watch. TRU surveys 2,000 teens twice a year to identify their lifestyles, attitudes, trends, and behaviors. With its "Coolest Brand Meter™," TRU asks teens to specify the coolest brands within specific product categories, such as sneakers (Nike) and clothing (Abercrombie & Fitch).[25]

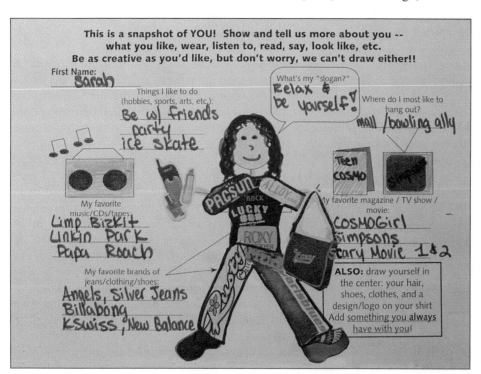

- Hiring "cool hunters," people with tastes far ahead of the curve. This is used to identify the "next big things" likely to sweep popular teen culture. Many marketers consult Look-Look, a marketing research firm that uses 500 "correspondents" who specialize in hunting for "trendsetters" for ideas, products, and fashions that are deemed to be "cool" in large cities around the world.[26] For example, Wet Seal uses this method to anticipate teenage girls' fashions while Skechers uses it to spot footwear trends.

In *hypothesis evaluation* the marketing researcher tests ideas discovered in the hypothesis generation stage to help the marketing manager recommend marketing actions. This test usually is a mail, telephone, personal, e-mail, fax, or Internet survey of a large sample of past, present, or prospective consumers.

In choosing between these alternatives, the marketing researcher has to make important trade-offs to balance cost against the expected quality of information obtained. Personal interview surveys have a major advantage of enabling the interviewer to be flexible in asking probing questions or getting reactions to visual materials, but are very costly to conduct. Mail surveys are usually biased because those most likely to respond have had especially positive or negative experiences with the product or brand. While telephone interviews allow flexibility, they are increasingly difficult to complete because respondents may hang up on the interviewer. Fax and Internet surveys are restricted to respondents having the technologies but are expanding rapidly.[27]

The high cost of reaching respondents in their homes using personal interviews has led to a dramatic increase in the use of *mall intercept interviews,* which are personal interviews of consumers while on visits to shopping centers. These face-to-face interviews reduce the cost of personal visits to consumers in their homes while providing the flexibility to show respondents visual cues such as ads or actual product samples. However, a critical disadvantage of mall intercept interviews is that the people selected for the interviews may not be representative of the consumers targeted for the interviews, giving a biased result.

Figure 8–6 shows typical problems to guard against in wording questions to obtain meaningful answers from respondents. For example, in a question of whether you eat at fast-food restaurants regularly, the word *regularly* is ambiguous. Two people might answer "yes" to the question, but one might mean "once a day" while the other means "once or twice a month." Both answers appear as "yes" to the researcher who tabulates them, but they suggest that dramatically different marketing actions be directed to each of these two prospective consumers. Therefore, it is essential that marketing research questions be worded precisely so that all respondents interpret the same question similarly.

Figure 8–7 shows a number of different formats for questions taken from a Wendy's survey that assessed fast-food restaurant preferences among present and prospective consumers. Question 1 is an example of an *open-ended question,* which allows respondents to express opinions, ideas, or behaviors in their own words without being forced to choose among alternatives that have been predetermined by a marketing researcher. This information is invaluable to marketers because it captures the "voice" of respondents, which is useful in understanding consumer behavior, identifying product benefits, or developing advertising messages. In

FIGURE 8–6
Typical problems in wording questions

PROBLEM	SAMPLE QUESTION	EXPLANATION OF PROBLEM
Leading question	Why do you like Wendy's fresh meat hamburgers better than those of competitors?	Consumer is led to make statement favoring Wendy's hamburgers.
Ambiguous question	Do you eat at fast-food restaurants regularly? ☐ Yes ☐ No	What is meant by word *regularly*—once a day, once a month, or what?
Unanswerable question	What was the occasion for eating your first hamburger?	Who can remember the answer? Does it matter?
Two questions in one	Do you eat Wendy's hamburgers and chili? ☐ Yes ☐ No	How do you answer if you eat Wendy's hamburgers but not chili?
Nonexhaustive question	Where do you live? ☐ At home ☐ In dormitory	What do you check if you live in an apartment?
Nonmutually exclusive answers	What is your age? ☐ Under 20 ☐ 20–40 ☐ 40 and over	What answer does a 40-year-old check?

1. What things are most important to you when you decide to eat out and go to a fast-food restaurant?

_____

_____

_____

2. Have you eaten at a fast-food restaurant in the past month?

☐ Yes   ☐ No

3. If you answered "yes" to question 2, how often do you eat fast food?

☐ Once a week   ☐ 2 to 3 times a month   ☐ Once a month or less

4. How important is it to you that a fast-food restaurant satisfies you on the following characteristics? [Check the box that describes your feelings for each item listed]

CHARACTERISTIC	VERY IMPORTANT	SOMEWHAT IMPORTANT	IMPORTANT	UNIMPORTANT	SOMEWHAT UNIMPORTANT	VERY UNIMPORTANT
• Taste of food	☐	☐	☐	☐	☐	☐
• Cleanliness	☐	☐	☐	☐	☐	☐
• Price	☐	☐	☐	☐	☐	☐
• Variety of menu	☐	☐	☐	☐	☐	☐

5. For each of the characteristics listed below, check the space on the scale that describes how you feel about Wendy's. Mark an "X" on only **one** of the five spaces listed for each item listed.

CHARACTERISTIC		CHECK THE SPACE THAT DESCRIBES THE DEGREE TO WHICH WENDY'S IS . . .	
• Taste of food	Tasty	_____ _____ _____ _____ _____	Not tasty
• Cleanliness	Clean	_____ _____ _____ _____ _____	Dirty
• Price	Inexpensive	_____ _____ _____ _____ _____	Expensive
• Variety of menu	Broad	_____ _____ _____ _____ _____	Narrow

FIGURE 8–7
Sample questions from
Wendy's survey

contrast, *closed-end* or *fixed alternative questions* require respondents to select one or more response options from a set of predetermined choices. Question 2 is an example of a *dichotomous question,* the simplest form of a fixed alternative question that allows only a "yes" or "no" response.

A fixed alternative question with three or more choices uses a *scale.* Question 5 is an example of a question that uses a *semantic differential scale,* a five-point scale in which the opposite ends have one-or two-word adjectives that have opposite meanings. For example, depending on how clean the respondent feels that Wendy's is, he or she would check the left-hand space on the scale, the right-hand space, or one of the five intervening points. Question 6 uses a *Likert scale,* in which the respondent indicates the extent to which he or she agrees or disagrees with a statement.

6. Check one box that describes your agreement or disagreement with each statement listed below:

STATEMENT	STRONGLY AGREE	AGREE	DON'T KNOW	DISAGREE	STRONGLY DISAGREE
• Adults like to take their families to fast-food restaurants	☐	☐	☐	☐	☐
• Our children have a say in where the family chooses to eat	☐	☐	☐	☐	☐

7. How important are each of the following sources of information to you when selecting a fast-food restaurant to eat at? [Check one box for each source listed]

SOURCE OF INFORMATION	VERY IMPORTANT	SOMEWHAT IMPORTANT	NOT AT ALL IMPORTANT
• Television	☐	☐	☐
• Newspapers	☐	☐	☐
• Radio	☐	☐	☐
• Billboards	☐	☐	☐
• Flyers	☐	☐	☐

8. How important are each of the following sources of information to you when selecting a fast-food restaurant to eat at? [Check one box for each source listed]

RESTAURANT	ONCE A WEEK OR MORE	2 TO 3 TIMES A MONTH	ONCE A MONTH OR LESS
• Burger King	☐	☐	☐
• McDonald's	☐	☐	☐
• Wendy's	☐	☐	☐

9. Please answer the following questions about you and your household. [Check only one for each item]

a. What is your gender? ☐ Male ☐ Female

b. What is your marital status? ☐ Single ☐ Married ☐ Other (widowed, divorced, etc.)

c. How many children under age 18 live in your home? ☐ 0 ☐ 1 ☐ 2 ☐ 3 or more

d. What is your age? ☐ Under 25 ☐ 25–44 ☐ 45 or older

e. What is your total annual individual or household income?
☐ <$15,000 ☐ $15,000–$49,000 ☐ $50,000 or more

FIGURE 8–7
(Continued)

The questionnaire in Figure 8–7 is an excerpt of a precisely worded survey that provides valuable information to the marketing researcher at Wendy's.[28] Questions 1 to 8 inform him or her about the likes and dislikes in eating out, frequency of eating out at fast-food restaurants generally and at Wendy's specifically, and sources of information used in making decisions about fast-food restaurants. Question 9 gives details about the personal or household characteristics, which can be used in trying to segment the fast-food market, a topic discussed in Chapter 9.

Electronic technology has revolutionized traditional concepts of "interviews" or "surveys." Today, respondents can walk up to a kiosk in a shopping center, read questions off a screen, and key their answers into a computer on a touch screen. Even fully automated telephone interviews exist: an automated voice questions respondents over the telephone, who then key their replies on a touch-tone telephone.

Wendy's changes continuously in response to changing customer wants, while keeping its "Fresh, hot'n juicy®" image.

Wendy's Restaurant

www.wendys.com

Panels and Experiments   Two special ways that observations and questionnaires are sometimes used are panels and experiments.

Marketing researchers often want to know if consumers change their behavior over time, and so they take successive measurements of the same people. A *panel* is a sample of consumers or stores from which researchers take a series of measurements. For example, The NPD Group collects data about consumer purchases such as apparel, food, and electronics from its Online Panel, which consists of over 2.7 million individuals worldwide. So a firm like General Mills can measure a consumer's switching behavior from one brand of its breakfast cereal (Wheaties) to another (Cheerios) or to a competitor's (Kellogg's Special K). A disadvantage of panels is that the marketing research firm needs to recruit new members continually to replace those who drop out. These new recruits must match the characteristics of those they replace to keep the panel representative of the marketplace.

An *experiment* involves obtaining data by manipulating factors under tightly controlled conditions to test cause and effect. The interest is in whether changing one of the independent variables (a cause) will change the behavior of the dependent variable that is studied (the result). In marketing experiments, the independent variables of interest—sometimes called the marketing "drivers"—are often one or more of the marketing mix elements, such as a product's features, price, or promotion (like advertising messages or coupons). The ideal dependent variable usually is a change in purchases (incremental unit or dollar sales) of individuals, households, or organizations. For example, food companies often use "test markets," a kind of marketing experiment discussed in Chapter 10, to determine if consumers will buy a new product or brand. In 1988, Wal-Mart opened three "experimental" stand-alone supercenters to gauge consumer acceptance before deciding to open others. Today, Wal-Mart operates over 1,000 supercenters nationwide.[29]

A potential difficulty with experiments is that outside factors (such as actions of competitors) can distort the results of an experiment and affect the dependent variable (such as sales). A researcher's task is to identify the effect of the marketing variable of interest on the dependent variable when the effects of outside factors in an experiment might hide it.

Advantages and Disadvantages of Primary Data   Compared with secondary data, primary data have the advantage of being more specific to the problem being studied. The main disadvantages are that primary data are usually far more costly and time consuming to collect than secondary data.

Concept Check

1. A mail questionnaire asks: "Do you eat pizza?" What kind of question is this?

2. Which survey provides the greatest flexibility for asking probing questions: mail, telephone, or personal interview?

3. What is the difference between a panel and an experiment?

Using Information Technology to Trigger Marketing Actions

Today's marketing managers can be drowned in such an ocean of data that they need to adopt strategies for dealing with complex, changing views of the competition, the market, and the consumer. The Internet and the desktop PC power of today provide a gateway to exhaustive data sources that vary from well organized and correct to disorganized and incorrect.

The Marketing Manager's View of Sales "Drivers"   Figure 8–8 shows a marketing manager's view of the product or brand "drivers," the factors that influence buying decisions of a household or organization and, hence, sales. These drivers include both the controllable marketing mix factors like product and distribution as well as uncontrollable factors like competition and the changing tastes of households or organizational buyers.

FIGURE 8–8
Product and brand drivers: factors that influence sales

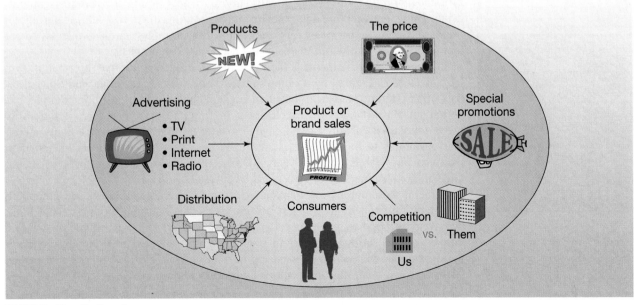

SOURCE: Ford Consulting Group, Inc.

Understanding these drivers involves managing this ocean of data. Sometimes hundreds of thousands of bits of data are created each week. Sources feeding this database ocean range from internal data about sales and customers to external data from syndication services and TV ratings. The marketer's task is to convert this data ocean into useful information on which to base informed decisions. In practice, some market researchers distinguish "data"—the facts and figures—from "information"— the distilled facts and figures whose interpretation leads to actions.

Current information about products, competitors, and customers is almost always accessed and analyzed by computer. So today, these activities fall under the broader term of **information technology**, which involves designing and managing computer and communication networks to provide a system to satisfy an organization's needs for data storage, processing, and access leading to effective marketing actions.

Key Elements of an Information System

Figure 8–9 shows how marketing researchers and managers use information technology to frame questions that provide answers leading to marketing actions. At the bottom of Figure 8–9 the marketer queries the databases in the information system with marketing questions needing answers. These questions go through statistical models that analyze the relationships that exist among the data. The databases form the core or "data warehouse" where the ocean of data is collected and stored. After the search of this data warehouse, the models select and link the pertinent data—often presenting them in tables and graphics for easy interpretation. Marketers can also use *sensitivity analysis* to query the database with "what if . . . ?" questions to determine how a hypothetical change in a driver like advertising can affect sales.

The Challenge in Mining Marketing Data

Making decisions from marketing information has many frustrations. Yet, timely, useful facts and insights about the market and competition play a key role in shaping the marketing manager's spending to drive sales. Many of these databases and models are very powerful, but major hurdles stand in the way of marketers getting to both the answers they need and the resulting actions: Time is scarce and the information is incredibly complex. Seasoned professionals must organize and interpret information clearly, quickly, and simply to initiate timely marketing actions.

Data Mining: A New Approach to Searching the Data Ocean

Traditional marketing research typically involves developing a hypothesis about a driver and then collecting data: Increasing couponing (the driver) during spring will increase trial by first-time buyers (the result). Marketing researchers then try to collect information to attempt to verify the truth of the hypothesis.

In contrast, **data mining** is the extraction of hidden predictive information from large databases. Catalog companies such as Lands' End, Fingerhut, and Spiegel use data mining to find statistical links that suggest marketing actions. For example, Fingerhut studies about 3,500 variables over the lifetime of a consumer's relationship. It has found that customers who change residences are three times as likely as regular customers to buy tables, fax machines, and decorative products but no more likely to buy jewelry or footwear. So Fingerhut has created a catalog especially targeted at consumers who have recently moved.[30]

Some of these purchase patterns are common sense: Peanut butter and grape jelly purchases link and might suggest a joint promotion between Skippy peanut butter and Welch's grape jelly. Other patterns link seemingly unrelated purchases: Supermarkets mined checkout data from scanners and discovered men buying diapers in the evening sometimes buy a six-pack of beer as well. So they placed diapers and beer near each other. Placing potato chips between them increased sales on all three.

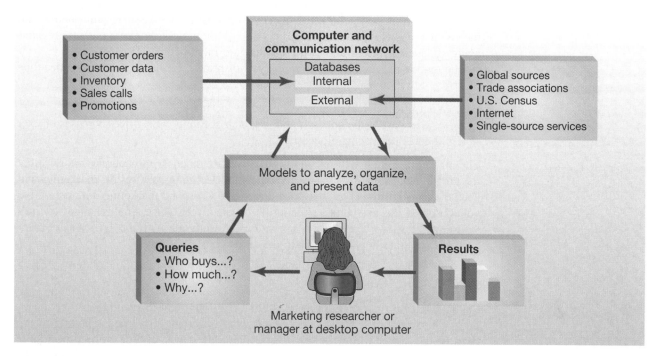

FIGURE 8–9
How marketing researchers
and managers use information
technology to turn information
into action

Still the success in data mining ultimately depends on humans—the judgments of the marketing managers and researchers in how to select, analyze, and interpret the information.

STEP 4: DEVELOP FINDINGS

Are retailers increasing shelf price unreasonably? To see how marketing and sales managers at Tony's Pizza might assess this question, read the text.

Mark Twain once observed, "Collecting data is like collecting garbage. You've got to know what you're going to do with the stuff before you collect it." Thus, marketing data and information have little more value than garbage unless they are analyzed carefully and translated into findings and recommendations for the marketing managers responsible for the action. How do we ensure that an analysis is carefully done? How do we prepare the work so that managers can use it to support actions?

Analyze the Data

Data are available, and it is possible to answer many questions. In today's fast-paced business world, answers that are clear, visual, and concise are a competitive advantage to decision makers. However, it takes time, expertise, and creativity to deliver clear analysis.

Assume Tony's® Pizza, which recently took a small price increase to cover a significant increase in the cost of ingredients and packaging materials, is facing an information challenge. Marketing does not anticipate any decline in sales from the 5-cent-at-the-shelf increase. After the increase, word filters back to headquarters that prices are increasing "too much." (To protect the proprietary information in this example, the data have been simplified and modified. The Ford Consulting Group case at the end of the chapter extends this discussion.)[31]

Tony's East Coast sales manager sends an e-mail to marketing at headquarters saying that three of the grocery chains in his region have moved the price on Tony's

Pizza up 25 cents! This is well above the target increase of 5 cents. With such a steep increase in price, the sales manager is concerned that sales will decline and the volume targets will be missed. He is also alerting marketing to a potentially damaging situation if prices across the country are increased by 25 cents.

The marketing team initiates an analysis of price information, and sets a deadline of Friday to report on:

1. What price increases have occurred in the market?
2. In what part of the country, and in which accounts have price increases of over 20 cents per package occurred?

The marketing action will depend on the facts. If much of the country has overshot the target for the price increase, and sales are declining as a result, marketing will need to take steps to (1) get the price down, and (2) spend marketing dollars to drive volume up. If the East Coast situation is isolated, then some small changes to sales volume targets may be necessary, as well as a discussion with the Tony's sales manager to determine how to deal with the situation.

Present the Findings

Findings must be clear. Those responsible for actions want to spend their time deciding what to do, not trying to understand what is shown. This means getting to the heart of the matter while avoiding distracting side issues, and delivering the results in "pictures" and in a single page if possible. The quadrant format in Figure 8–10 shows a creative way to prepare results to answer the questions asked by the marketing team about the price increase.

The lower left quadrant in Figure 8–10 summarizes the total U.S. performance. The bars answer the question, what percent of the stores (weighted for their size)

FIGURE 8–10
Converting data into marketing actions: What to do about supermarket chains that have increased retail prices by more than 20 cents per package?

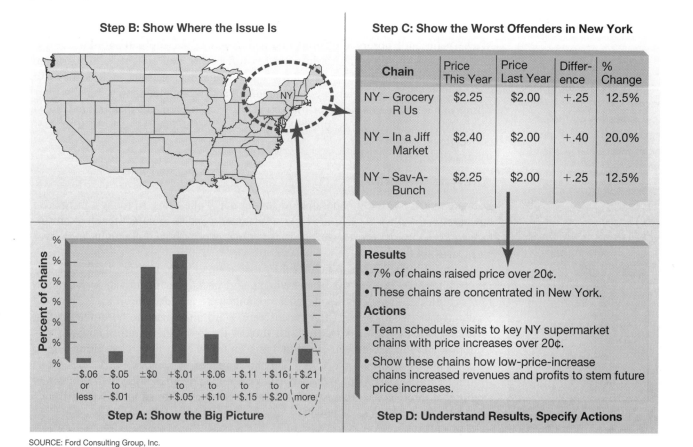

have taken various price changes? Thus, this chart provides information that answers the questions above and shows the percentage of chains raising prices by over 20 cents per package.

Where these price increases have occurred requires two views. The first is a map in the upper left quadrant, showing the states (in beige) where price increases exceed expectations. Green states are within the target price increase range. The other way to answer this question is with a list of grocery retailers who are most out of line with expectations, shown in the upper right quadrant.

The conclusions are that a very small percentage of stores have taken a significant price increase. In addition, these accounts are isolated in the state of New York at this time.

STEP 5: TAKE MARKETING ACTIONS

Effective marketing research doesn't stop with findings and recommendations—someone has to identify the actions, put them into effect, and monitor how the decisions turn out, which is the essence of Step 5.

Identify the Action Recommendations

The marketing team met to resolve the next steps from the price information provided. After a brief discussion the following action steps were noted:

- Look into steps with a New York sales team to address issues and to determine impact of large price increases on sales.
- Alert whole salesforce that price increases are a very isolated problem being dealt with.

The assistant marketing manager was assigned the duty of completing these action steps.

Implement the Action Recommendations

The assistant marketing manager took the following implementation steps:

- Forward the price analysis to the New York sales team and schedule a meeting for next week.
- Have the team visit NY accounts with large price increases to show them how chains with small price increases have achieved better revenues and profits.
- Deliver another price analysis in 90 days to the market research manager.

In the end, is the price increase a problem? No. This is just one of dozens of activities that involve research and marketing action that the marketing team handles every day.

These actions are the whole point of the research: You have to know what's going on in the market, and if you find that there is a problem, you have to take steps to fix it.

Evaluate the Results

Evaluating results is a continuing way of life for effective marketing managers. There are really two aspects of this evaluation process:

- Evaluating the decision itself: This involves monitoring the marketplace and setting up proactive systems to determine if action is necessary in the future. Are sales on Tony's Pizza still hitting targets? Is the price of Tony's Pizza creeping upward? Yes, but it is a slow, steady increase in the average prices around the country that isn't as dramatic as the 25 cent increase that sounds alarm bells.
- Evaluating the decision process used: Was the price evaluation and summary flawed? It is possible that the analyst erroneously used an inappropriate price

fact, or too large a time period that inaccurately reflects current prices. This sort of mistake is not uncommon, and the marketing team must be vigilant for other news from the marketplace that corroborates or refutes the price analysis.

Again, systematic analysis does not guarantee success. But it can improve a firm's success rate for its marketing decisions.

Concept Check

1. What does a marketing manager mean when she talks about a sales "driver"?

2. How does data mining differ from traditional marketing research?

3. In the marketing research for Tony's Pizza, what is an example of (a) a finding and (b) an action?

MARKET AND SALES FORECASTING

Forecasting or estimating the actual size of a market is often a key goal in a marketing research study. Good sales forecasts are important for a firm as it schedules production.[32] We will discuss (1) some basic forecasting terms, (2) two major approaches to forecasting, and (3) specific forecasting techniques.

Basic Forecasting Terms

Unfortunately, there are no standard definitions for some forecasting concepts, so it's necessary to take care in defining the terms used.

Market or Industry Potential

The term **market potential**, or **industry potential**, refers to the maximum total sales of a product by all firms to a segment during a specified time period under specified environmental conditions and marketing efforts of the firms. For example, the market potential for cake mix sales to U.S. consumers in 2005 might be 12 million cases—what Pillsbury, Betty Crocker, Aurora Foods, and other cake mix producers would sell to American consumers under the assumptions that (1) past patterns of dessert consumption continue and (2) the same level of promotional effort continues relative to other desserts. If one of these assumptions proves false, the estimate of market potential will be wrong. For example, if American consumers suddenly become more concerned about eating refined sugar and shift their dessert preferences from cakes to fresh fruits, the estimate of market potential will be too high.

Sales or Company Forecast

The term **sales forecast**, or **company forecast**, refers to the maximum total sales of a product that a firm expects to sell during a specified time period under specified environmental conditions and its own marketing efforts. For example, Betty Crocker might develop its sales forecast of 4 million cases of cake mix for U.S. consumers in 2005, assuming past dessert preferences continue with the same relative level of advertising expenditures among it, Pillsbury, and Aurora Foods. If Aurora Foods suddenly cuts its advertising in half, Betty Crocker's old sales forecast will probably be too low.

With both market potential estimates and sales forecasts, it is necessary to specify some significant details: the product involved (all cake mixes, only white cake mixes, or only Bundt cake mixes); the time period involved (month, quarter, or year); the segment involved (United States, Southwest region, upper-income buyer, or single-person households); controllable marketing mix factors (price and level of advertising support); uncontrollable factors (consumer tastes and actions of competitors); and the units of measurement (number of cases sold or total sales revenues).

Two Basic Approaches to Forecasting

A marketing manager rarely wants a single number for an annual forecast, such as 5,000 units sold or $75 million in sales revenue. Rather, the manager wants this total subdivided into elements the manager works with, such as sales by product line or sales by market segment. The two basic approaches to sales forecasting are (1) subdividing the total sales forecast (top-down forecast) or (2) building the total sales forecast by summing up the components (buildup forecast).

Top-Down Forecast

A **top-down forecast** involves subdividing an aggregate forecast into its principal components. A shoe manufacturer can use a top-down forecast to estimate the percentage of its total shoe sales in a state and develop state-by-state forecasts for shoe sales for the coming year. The "Survey of Buying Power," published annually by *Sales and Marketing Management* magazine, is a widely used source of such top-down forecasting information.[33]

For example, the state of New York has 5.72 percent of the U.S. retail sales. If the shoe manufacturer wanted to use a single factor related to expected shoe sales, it would choose the factor that has been most closely related to shoe sales historically, in this case the percentage of U.S. retail sales. The top-down forecast would then be that 5.72 percent of the firm's sales would be made in the state of New York. Sometimes multiple factors are considered so that the forecast might use an index that includes the population and consumer income in New York, as well as retail sales.

Buildup Forecast

A **buildup forecast** involves summing the sales forecasts of each of the components to arrive at the total forecast. It is a widely used method when there are identifiable components such as products, product lines, or market segments in the forecasting problem.

Figure 8–11 shows how Apple Computer uses the buildup approach to develop an aggregate two-quarter sales forecast involving its four principal product lines (iMac, iBook, PowerMac, and PowerBook). The total quarterly sales revenue for

FIGURE 8–11
Buildup approach to a two-quarter sales forecast for Apple Computer products

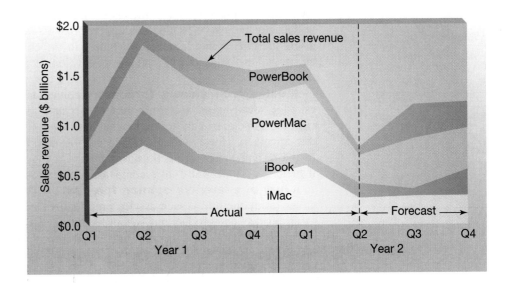

Apple is the sum of the individual forecasts for each product line. These are based on the forecasts for each model in that line, which for simplicity are not shown, and relates to Apple's segmentation strategy, discussed in Chapter 9.

Specific Sales Forecasting Techniques

Three main sales forecasting techniques can be used in the top-down or buildup approaches. Ordered from least to most costly, these are (1) judgments of the decision maker, (2) surveys of knowledgeable groups, and (3) statistical methods.

Judgments of the Decision Maker

Probably 99.9 percent of all sales forecasts are judgments of the person who must act on the results of the forecast—the individual decision maker. An example is the forecasts of likely sales, and hence the quantity to order, for the thousands of items stocked in a typical supermarket that must be forecast by the stock clerk or manager. A **direct forecast** involves estimating the value to be forecast without any intervening steps. Examples appear daily: How many quarts of milk should I buy? How much money should I get out of the ATM? Your mind may go through some intervening steps but so quickly you're unaware of it.

Thus, in estimating the amount of money to get from the ATM, you probably made some intervening estimates (such as counting the cash in your pocket or the special events you need cash for) to obtain your direct estimate. Lost-horse forecasting does this in a more structured way. A **lost-horse forecast** involves starting with the last known value of the item being forecast, listing the factors that could affect the forecast, assessing whether they have a positive or negative impact, and making the final forecast. The technique gets its name from how you'd find a lost horse: go to where it was last seen, put yourself in its shoes, consider those factors that could affect where you might go (to the pond if you're thirsty, the hayfield if you're hungry, and so on), and go there. For example, a product manager for Wilson's tennis rackets in 2002 who needed to make a sales forecast through 2006 would start with the known value of 2002 sales and list the positive factors (more tennis courts, more TV publicity) and the negative ones (competition from other sports, high prices of graphite and ceramic rackets) to arrive at the final series of annual sales forecasts.

Surveys of Knowledgeable Groups

If you wonder what your firm's sales will be next year, ask people who are likely to know something about future sales. Four common groups that are surveyed to develop sales forecasts are prospective buyers, the firm's salesforce, its executives, and experts.

A **survey of buyers' intentions forecast** involves asking prospective customers whether they are likely to buy the product during some future time period. For industrial products with few prospective buyers, this can be effective. There are only a few hundred customers in the entire world for Boeing's largest airplanes, so Boeing surveys them to develop its sales forecasts and production schedules.

A **salesforce survey forecast** involves asking the firm's salespeople to estimate sales during a coming period. Because these people are in contact with customers and are likely to know what customers like and dislike, there is logic to this approach. However, salespeople can be unreliable forecasters—painting too rosy a picture if they are enthusiastic about a new product and too grim a forecast if their sales quota and future compensation are based on it.

A **jury of executive opinion forecast** involves asking knowledgeable executives inside the firm—such as vice presidents of marketing, research and development, finance, and production—about likely sales during a coming period. Although this approach is fast and includes judgments from diverse functional areas, it can be biased by a dominant executive whose judgments are deferred to by the others. Also, how valuable are judgments from executives who rarely come in contact with customers—such as vice presidents of finance and production.

FIGURE 8–12

Linear trend extrapolation of sales revenues of Xerox, made at the start of 1999

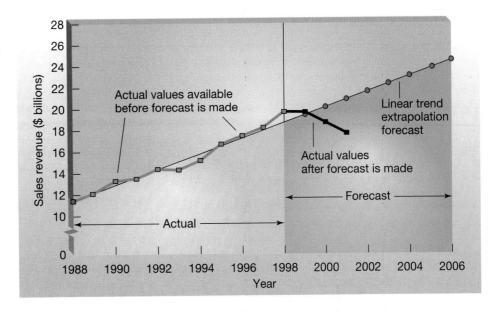

A **survey of experts forecast** involves asking experts on a topic to make a judgment about some future event. For example, 20 electronics and TV experts might be asked when a 25-inch high-definition television (HDTV) set might sell to consumers for less than $500. One form of a survey of experts forecast is a *technological forecast,* which involves estimating when breakthroughs in basic science will occur. Such a technological forecast might help HDTV executives estimate when major cost reductions in key HDTV components might occur.

Statistical Methods   The best-known statistical method of forecasting is **trend extrapolation**, which involves extending a pattern observed in past data into the future. When the pattern is described with a straight line, it is *linear trend extrapolation.* Suppose that in early 1999 you were a sales forecaster for the Xerox Corporation and had actual sales revenues running from 1988 to 1998 (Figure 8–12). Using linear trend extrapolation, you draw a line to fit the past data and project it into the future to give the forecast values shown for 1999 to 2006.[34]

If in 2002 you want to compare your forecasts with actual results, you are in for a surprise—illustrating the strength and weakness of trend extrapolation. Trend extrapolation assumes that the underlying relationships in the past will continue into the future, which is the basis of the method's key strength: simplicity. If this assumption proves correct, you have an accurate forecast. However, if this proves wrong, the forecast is likely to be wrong. In this case your forecasts from 1999 through 2001 were too high, as shown in Figure 8–12, largely because of fierce competition in the photocopying industry.

In practice, marketing managers often use several of the forecasting techniques to estimate the size of markets important to them. Also, they often do three separate forecasts based on different sets of assumptions: (1) "best case" with optimistic assumptions, (2) "worst case" with pessimistic ones, and (3) "most likely case" with most reasonable assumptions.

Concept Check

1. What is the difference between the top-down and buildup approaches to forecasting sales?

2. How do you make a lost-horse forecast?

3. What is linear trend extrapolation?

SUMMARY

1 Marketing research is the process of defining a marketing problem and opportunity, systematically collecting and analyzing information, and recommending actions to improve an organization's marketing activities. The chapter uses a five-step marketing research sequence that can lead to better decisions.

2 Defining the problem, step 1 in the sequence, involves setting the research objectives and identifying possible marketing actions.

3 Developing the research plan, step 2, requires specifying constraints on the problem, identifying data needed, and determining how to collect it.

4 Collecting relevant information, step 3, includes considering pertinent secondary and primary data. Secondary data have been recorded prior to the project and include those pieces of information internal and external to the organization. Primary data are collected specifically for the project and are obtained by either observing or questioning people.

5 Information technology enables massive amounts of marketing data to be stored, processed, and accessed. Databases can be queried using data mining to find statistical relationships useful in marketing.

6 Developing findings is step 4. It involves analyzing data and presenting findings to decision makers.

7 Step 5 in the sequence involves identifying and implementing marketing action recommendations and evaluating results.

8 Two basic approaches to forecasting sales are the top-down and buildup methods. Three forecasting techniques are judgments of individuals, surveys of groups, and statistical methods.

9 Individual judgments are the most widely used forecasting methods. Two common examples are direct and lost-horse forecasts.

10 Asking questions of groups of people who are knowledgeable about likely future sales is another frequently used method of forecasting. Four such groups are prospective buyers, the salesforce, executives, and experts.

11 Statistical forecasting methods, such as linear trend extrapolation, extend a pattern in past data into the future.

KEY TERMS AND CONCEPTS

buildup forecast p. 229
constraints p. 211
data p. 212
data mining p. 224
decision p. 208
direct forecast p. 230
information technology p. 223
jury of executive opinion forecast p. 230
lost-horse forecast p. 230
market or industry potential p. 228
marketing research p. 207
measures of success p. 209
nonprobability sampling p. 212

objectives p. 209
observational data p. 214
primary data p. 212
probability sampling p. 212
questionnaire data p. 217
sales or company forecast p. 228
salesforce survey forecast p. 230
secondary data p. 212
statistical inference p. 212
survey of buyers' intentions forecast p. 230
survey of experts forecast p. 231
top-down forecast p. 229
trend extrapolation p. 231

APPLYING MARKETING CONCEPTS AND PERSPECTIVES

1 Nielsen Media Research obtains ratings of local TV stations by having households fill out diary questionnaires. These give information on (*a*) who is watching TV and (*b*) what program. What are the limitations of this questionnaire method?

2 A rich aunt has decided to set you up in a business of your own choosing. To her delight, you decide on a service business—giving flying lessons in ultralight planes to your fellow college students. Some questions from the first draft of a mail questionnaire you plan to use are shown below. In terms of Figure 8–6, (*a*) identify the problem with each question and (*b*) correct it. NOTE: Some questions may have more than one problem.

a. Have you ever flown in commercial airliners and in ultralight planes?   ☐Yes   ☐No

b. Why do you think ultralights are so much safer than hang gliders? _____

c. At what age did you first know you like to fly?
   ☐Under 10   ☐10 to 20   ☐21 to 30   ☐Over 30

d. How much did you spend on recreational activities last year?
   ☐ $100 or less   ☐ $801 to $1,201
   ☐ $101 to $400   ☐ $1,201 to $1,600
   ☐ $401 to $800   ☐ $1,600 or more

e. How much would you pay for ultralight flying lessons? _____

f. Would you sign up for a class that met regularly?
   ☐ Yes   ☐No

3 The format in which information is presented to a harried marketing manager is often vital. (*a*) If you were a marketing manager and queried your information system, would you rather see the results in tables or charts and graphs? (*b*) What are one or two strengths and weaknesses of each format?

4   Aim Toothpaste puts a cents-off coupon in the Sunday paper across the entire country (free-standing insert, or FSI). In addition, Aim provides retailers with incentives to set up an in-store display and advertise the toothpaste in their local market newspapers. Using retail sales data for Aim, an analysis of sales performance is made contrasting the retailers without displays and local ads, to the retailers with these added promotions. Assume that the retailers who promoted Aim with displays and ads received a special payment in the form of product discounts of 25 percent. (*a*) What measures of success are appropriate? (*b*) Depending on the answer to "*a*," what recommendations might be made?

5   Another field experiment with coupons and in-store advertising for Wisk detergent is run. The index of sales is as follows:

	WEEKS BEFORE COUPON	WEEK OF COUPON	WEEK AFTER COUPON
Without in-store ads	100	144	108
With in-store ads	100	268	203

What are your conclusions and recommendations?

6   Suppose Fisher-Price wants to run an experimental and control group experiment to evaluate a proposed Chatter Telephone design. It has two different groups of children on which to run an experiment for one week each. The control group has the old toy telephone, whereas the experimental group is exposed to the newly designed pull toy with wheels, a noisemaker, and bobbing eyes. The dependent variable is the average number of minutes during the two-hour play period that one of the children is playing with the toy, and the results are as follows:

ELEMENT IN EXPERIMENT	EXPERIMENTAL GROUP	CONTROL GROUP
Experimental variable	New design	Old design
After measurement	62 minutes	13 minutes

Should Fisher-Price introduce the new design? Why?

7   Which of the following variables would linear trend extrapolation be more accurate for? (*a*) Annual population of the United States or (*b*) annual sales of cars produced in the United States by General Motors. Why?

INTERNET EXERCISE

WorldOpinion calls its website "The World's Market Research Web Site." To check out the latest marketing research news, job opportunites, and details of more than 8,500 research locations in 99 countries, go to www.world opinion.com and do the following:

1   Click on the "News" banner on WorldOpinion's home page to read about the current news and issues facing the market research industry.

2   Click on "Periodicals" for *The Frame,* a set of online articles published by Survey Sampling, Inc.

VIDEO CASE 8–1   Ford Consulting Group, Inc.: From Data to Actions

"The fast pace of working as a marketing professional isn't getting any easier," agrees David Ford, as he talks with Mark Rehborg—Tony's® Pizza brand manager. "The speed of communication, the availability of real-time market information, and the responsibility for a brand's profit make marketing one of the most challenging professional jobs today."

Mark responds, "Ten years ago, we could reach 80 percent of our target market with 3 television spots—but today, to reach the same 80 percent, we would have to buy 97 spots. We haven't the luxury to be complacent—our core consumer, the 6- to 14-year-old 'big kid,' is part of a savvy, wired culture that is changing rapidly."

THE COMPANY AND ITS CLIENTS

David Ford, president of Ford Consulting Group (FCG) assists clients such as Tony's in translating the market and sales information into insights and marketing activities. While Mark focuses part of his time on the execution of ideas that will draw consumers to Tony's, part of his time is managing sales and profit performance. He allocates budgeted funds to promote the product. Feedback from the salesforce requesting promotion funds is a common occurrence. Mark must balance the competing requests and make judgments about where to allocate the budget.

The information that FCG consultants and Tony's use most often for this analysis are single source data like AC Nielsen's ScanTrack and Information Resources' InfoScan (IRI) that summarize sales data from grocery stores and other outlets that scan at the checkout. Additionally, AC Nielsen and IRI provide insights into household shopping habits through their home-panel based services.

FCG's typical consulting project involves helping clients make sense of their existing information, *not* in helping clients collect more information. Most often the client has a critical time deadline for FCG's data analysis and action recommendations: The client "wants" the answer a week ago, about four days *before* it hires FCG for the project. The project that follows is typical of the work Ford Consulting Group (www.fordconsultinggroup.com) undertakes for a client. However, the data are hypothetical, but the situation is a very typical one in the grocery products industry. Here's a snapshot of some of the terms in the case:

- "You" have just come on the job, as "the new marketing person"
- "NE" is the Northeastern sales region of Tony's
- "SE, NW, SW" are the other sales regions

PART 1: A TYPICAL QUESTION, ON A TYPICAL DAY

Let's dive into the background of a typical question, on a typical day! Here are some memos that appear.

TO: Mark Rehborg, Tony's Brand Manager
FROM: Steve Quam, Tony's Field Sales
CC: Margaret Loiaza, NE Sales Region Manager

RE: Feedback on Sales Call at Food-Fast

Hi Mark—

Our sales call at Food-Fast wasn't so great. They don't see how our Tony's is going to sell well enough to justify the additional shelf-space. I also talked to Margaret and she said that second quarter may be weaker than planned across all the NE, and I should give you a heads-up. (She's on vacation this week, Aruba!) She's planning to schedule some time with you to talk about additional promotion money to do catch-up in the third quarter. She'll be there next week.

Steve

TO: You, the New Marketing Person
FROM: Mark Rehborg, Tony's Brand Manager (Your Boss)

RE: Small Project due Friday

Hi You,

Can you help out here?

I've got a meeting with Margaret on Friday afternoon, and she's concerned that Food-Fast and the whole NE is going to need some additional promotion dollars to fix some volume shortfalls.

Lauretta started the analysis and was hurt in a kick-boxing accident yesterday and won't be back to work until next week. Her files are attached. Can you look through these and prepare a summary of what's going on in the NE and the rest of the U.S.? Do you think we need more promotion money for Margaret?

Put some time on my calendar for Friday AM so we can go over this.

Mark

TABLE 1. COMPARISON OF TONY'S PERFORMANCE, BY REGION

REGION	QUARTERLY CHANGE IN VOLUME (%)	DISTRIBUTION (a) (%)	PRICE ($)	PRICE GAP (b) ($)	PROMOTION	
					SUPPORT (c) (%)	VOLUME (d) (%)
NE	3%	93%	$1.29	+8	7%	14%
SE	5%	95%	$1.11	-1	9%	16%
NW	8%	98%	$1.19	+1	8%	15%
SW	6%	96%	$1.25	0	8%	15%
U.S.	6%	97%	$1.19	0	8%	15%

a % of outlets carrying Tony's
b "Price gap" = (Our price) − (Competitor's price)
c Promotion support = % of the time brand was promoted
d Promotion volume = % of the volume sold on promotion

TABLE 2. COMPARISON OF MAJOR SUPERMARKET CHAINS IN THE NORTHEAST

SUPER-MARKET CHAIN	QUARTERLY CHANGE IN VOLUME (%)	DISTRIBUTION (a) (%)	PRICE ($)	PRICE GAP (b) ($)	PROMOTION	
					SUPPORT (c) (%)	VOLUME (d) (%)
Save-a-lot	5%	95%	$1.39	+10	10%	19%
Food-Fast	0%	90%	$1.28	-1	3%	4%
Get-Fresh	0%	90%	$1.30	+1	3%	4%
Dollars-Off	7%	97%	$1.34	+5	7%	14%

You dig into Lauretta's data files and develop Table 1 that shows how Tony's is doing in the company's four sales regions and the entire U.S. on key marketing dimensions. Without reading further, take a deep breath and try to answer Question #1.

PART 2: UNCOVERING THE TRUTH

Let's assume your analysis (Question #1) shows NE is a problem, so we need to understand what's going on in the NE. You dig into the data and develop Table 2. It shows the situation for the four largest supermarket chains in the Northeast sales region that carry Tony's. Now answer Question #2.

Questions

1 Study Table 1. (*a*) How does the situation in the Northeast compare to the other regions in the U.S.? (*b*) What appears to be the reason(s) that sales are soft? (*c*) Write a 150-word e-mail with attachments to Mark Rehborg, your boss, giving your answers to "b."

2 Study Table 2. (*a*) What do you conclude from this information? (*b*) Summarize your conclusions in a 150-word e-mail with attachments to Mark, who needs them for a meeting tomorrow with Margaret, the Northeast sales region manager. (*c*) What actions might your memo suggest?

3 Compare the strengths and weaknesses of using (*a*) the kind of syndicated transaction data present in this case (*b*) primary data collection like questionnaires in addressing marketing problems at Tony's.

9 IDENTIFYING MARKET SEGMENTS AND TARGETS

AFTER READING THIS CHAPTER YOU SHOULD BE ABLE TO:

- Explain what market segmentation is, when to use it, and the five steps involved in segmentation.

- Recognize the different factors used to segment consumer and organizational markets.

- Understand the significance of heavy, medium, and light users and nonusers in targeting markets.

- Develop a market-product grid to use in segmenting and targeting a market.

- Interpret a cross-tabulation to analyze market segments.

- Understand how marketing managers position products in the marketplace.

SNEAKERS MARKETING WARS: HEELYS, AIR PUMPS, AND 3 BILLION TRILLION CHOICES

Late for a flight out of the Dallas/Ft. Worth airport, Roger Adams rushed to the gate . . . by "heeling"! Adams, a former psychologist and skateboarder, had just invented Heelys, the latest craze (or fad) in sneakers.

Heelys combine the thrill of in-line skating, skateboarding, and scooting—along with running and walking—in one set of shoes! The sneakers come with an imbedded, detachable wheel located in the heel of each shoe. To "heel," you lift up the foot at the heel on one shoe, push off on the other foot, and glide (carefully). In 2001, Heelys (www.heelys.com), which average $90 to $100 per pair, were so hot that retailers couldn't keep them on their shelves. Heelying Sports LTD sold 1 million pairs of Heelys sneakers in 2001, its first full year of operations.[1]

Finding the Segments   What do you need in the sneaker business to stand out from the pack when consumers are faced with hundreds of athletic shoe choices, often on sneaker "walls" like that shown in the chapter opener? This is the multibillion-dollar question for manufacturers around the world: Today the global market athletic footwear or "sneakers" exceeds $25 billion. Adams and Heelying Sports believe they've found a unique "niche," or market segment of buyers.

But all sneaker manufacturers continue to search for new market segments of consumers and ways to differentiate their products from the competition. This challenge applies to the giants like Reebok and Nike, to upstarts like Heelys and Customatix (www.customatix.com) which markets an Internet design-your-own-shoe that it says offers more than 3 billion trillion design combinations.

Competitive Trends   Changing consumer tastes and global competition have forced sneaker manufacturers to come up with new product technologies, advertising campaigns, and endorsements to develop and position their new and existing products for their target market segments. Recently, Reebok gave a $40 million endorsement contract to Venus Williams for a signature line of tennis footwear and apparel and millions more to Alan Iverson for a line of basketball shoes. Reebok also signed 10-year mega deals with both the NBA (about $175 million) and NFL (about $250 million) to be their exclusive team uniform providers and also offer branded apparel to consumers. The Sporting Goods Manufacturers Association (SGMA) and the NPD Group identify the following U.S. trends to consider in planning for the sneaker wars for 2002 and beyond:

- *Age segments.* Teenagers are 23 percent of total sales, are the largest segment, and are willing to spend more for sneakers than older consumers.
- *Gender segments.* Both women and men are important segments—women because their sales growth is higher than men and men because they still buy more in total at higher average prices.
- *Price.* Almost 60 percent of sneakers purchased in 2000 cost less than $50 per pair.
- *Kinds of sports.* In the United States running shoes are number 1 ($4.4 billion in 2000); basketball shoes, number 2 ($2.5 billion); and cross-training, number 3 ($2.2 billion). Running and cross-training sales are up and basketball is down slightly.
- *Styles and use.* Most of the sales growth in sneakers is due to casual styles that have a strong fashion component, where colors or the "retro" look are prominent. Almost three-fourths of all sneakers are purchased for casual rather than for sports or fitness purposes.
- *Sweatshop and child labor.* Pressed by public outcry, firms such as Reebok and Nike joined together to approve a monitoring system and code of conduct to curtail use of sweatshop and child labor abroad.

The strategies sneaker manufacturers use to satisfy needs of different customers illustrate successful market segmentation, the main topic of this chapter. After discussing why markets need to be segmented, this chapter covers the steps a firm uses in segmenting and targeting a market and then positioning its offering to the marketplace.

WHY SEGMENT MARKETS?

A business firm segments its markets so it can respond more effectively to the wants of groups of prospective buyers and thus increase its sales and profits. Nonprofit organizations also segment the clients they serve to satisfy client needs more effectively while achieving the organization's goals. Let's use the dilemma of sneaker buyers finding their ideal Reebok shoes to describe (1) what market segmentation is and (2) when it is necessary to segment markets.

What Market Segmentation Means

People have different needs and wants, even though it would be easier for marketers if they didn't. **Market segmentation** involves aggregating prospective buyers into groups that (1) have common needs and (2) will respond similarly to a marketing action. The groups that result from this process are **market segments**, a relatively homogeneous collection of prospective buyers.

The existence of different market segments has caused firms to use a marketing strategy of **product differentiation**, a strategy that has come to have two different but related meanings. In its broadest sense, product differentiation involves a firm's using different marketing mix activities, such as product features and advertising, to help consumers perceive the product as being different and better than competing products. The perceived differences may involve physical features or nonphysical ones, such as image or price.

In a narrower sense, product differentiation involves a firm's selling two or more products with different features targeted to different market segments. A firm can get into trouble when its different products blend together in consumers' minds and don't reach distinct market segments successfully. The Reebok example discussed below shows how the company is using both market segmentation and product differentiation strategies.

Segmentation: Linking Needs to Actions
The definition of market segmentation first stresses the importance of aggregating—or grouping—people or organizations in a market according to the similarity of their needs and the benefits they are looking for in making a purchase. Second, such needs and benefits must be related to specific, tangible marketing actions the firm can take. These actions may involve separate products or other aspects of the marketing mix such as price, advertising or personal selling activities, or distribution strategies—the four Ps (product, price, promotion, place).

The process of segmenting a market and selecting specific segments as targets is the link between the various buyers' needs and the organization's marketing program (Figure 9–1). Market segmentation is only a means to an end: In an economist's terms, it relates supply (the organization's actions) to demand (customer needs). A basic test of the usefulness of the segmentation process is whether it leads to tangible marketing actions to increase sales and profitability. The Marketing NewsNet box[2] describes how firms from Reebok and Nike to Customatix have succeeded in using market segmentation and product differentiation strategies to reach special groups of customers.

FIGURE 9–1
Market segmentation links market needs to an organization's marketing program

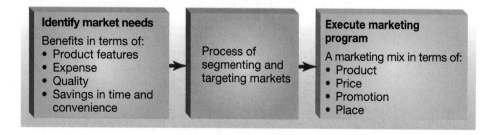

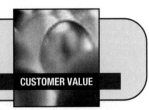

MARKETING NEWSNET   Sneaker Strategies: Who's Doing What   CUSTOMER VALUE

Microchips, air pumps and cushions, and wheels. Off-the-shelf versus design-your-own-shoe with trillions of design combinations. As outlined below, these are just a few of the innovative technologies and strategies used by sneaker manufacturers to attract new consumers and differentiate their products from those offered by competitors.

Reebok

The 2001 Traxtar™ 2.0 line ($65) of kids' shoes not only features a computer chip and motion sensor to measure their running and jumping ability but also plays games and songs to motivate children. The adult version, called the Smart Train DMX ($110–$250) also appeared in 2001 and has a microprocessor with a programmable speedometer, odometer, and calorie counter.

Nike

Originally launched in 1985, the 2002 "Michael-inspired" Air Jordan XVII ($200) basketball shoe incorporates the latest technologies for providing air cushioning in the heel and forefoot and for reducing painful turf toe. And it's packed in a metallic silver briefcase instead of a shoebox.

New Balance

Talk about boring: How about a marketing strategy that includes moderate prices, extra-wide shoe widths, more sizes, and links to podiatrists—all actions that target "baby boomers" like Steve Jobs and Dustin Hoffman who are most concerned with fit and comfort? To meet their needs, New Balance shoes incorporate shock absorbing (ABSORB®), foot rotation control (Rollbar® Stability System), and air cushioning (N-ergy S.C. System™) technologies.

Vans

Vans has targeted the rising wave of skateboard, snowboard, biking, and outdoor enthusiasts. To reach its targeted skateboard shoe market, Vans relies heavily on its endorsing athletes to design and market its signature lines and promote its skateboard events. Vans had a breakthrough when Foot Locker started selling its shoes in more than 1,000 retail outlets.

Customatix

Customatix has a website where you can completely design your own running or skateboarding shoes using up to three billion trillion combinations of colors, graphics, logos, and materials per shoe! Shoe prices range from $65 to $100 per pair and are delivered within two weeks. Using the Shoe Designer™, you start by selecting either a blank shoe model or one of many predesigned versions. See the Web Link box later in the chapter to design your own shoe.

Whether you want off-the-shelf or personally designed sneakers, they're available.

How Reebok's Segmentation Strategy Developed   In 1979, Paul Fireman, who had dropped out of college to run his family's business, wandered through an international trade fair and saw Reebok's custom track shoes. He bought the U.S. license from the British manufacturer and started producing top-of-the-line running shoes at about the time the running boom had peaked.

In a brilliant marketing decision, Fireman introduced the first soft-leather aerobic dance shoe—the Reebok "Freestyle"—in 1982. The flamboyant colors of these Reebok designer sneakers captured the attention of aerobic dance instructors and students alike. Figure 9–2 shows that Reebok has introduced a variety of shoes since 1982—from tennis and basketball shoes in 1984 to high-technology kids and adult shoes in 2001. For simplicity, Figure 9–2 covers only shoes and does not show nonshoe lines—like Greg Norman apparel (1993), "fitness water" (2001), and a line of NFL/NBA/Olympics apparel (2001). These nonshoe lines have the advantage for Reebok of cutting across many of the segments shown in the rows.

A $3 billion-a-year sneaker business has a huge need to generate revenues from new opportunities. As a result, Reebok has expanded both the markets it targets and the products it develops to satisfy this need. For example, Reebok:[3]

- Developed a line of "DMX-enhanced" running shoes that its ads said were "the best running shoe in the history of the world" and which gave its users extra

MARKET SEGMENT		PRODUCT									
GENERAL	GROUP WITH NEED	RUNNING SHOES	AEROBIC SHOES	TENNIS SHOES	BASKETBALL SHOES	KIDS SHOES	WALKING SHOES	CROSS-TRAINING SHOES	GOLF SHOES	KIDS TRAXTAR SHOES	ADULT SMART TRAIN DMX SHOES
		(1981)	(1982)	(1984)	(1984)	(1984)	(1986)	(1988)	(1997)	(2001)	(2001)
Performance-oriented 27%	Runners	P						P			P
	Aerobic/fitness exercisers		P					P			P
	Tennis players			P				P			
	Basketball players				P			P			
	Golfers								P		
	Adventure seekers							P			P
Nonathletic-oriented 73%	Walkers	S	S	S	S		P	P			S
	Children					P				P	
	Comfort/Style-conscious	S	S	S	S		S	S			S

Key: P = Primary market   S = Secondary market

FIGURE 9–2
Market-product grid showing how different Reebok shoes reach segments of customers with different needs

cushioning by distributing air through chambers in the shoe. Reebok plans to extend this technology to other shoe lines in 2001 and beyond.

- Launched its Traxtar™ line of children's shoes in 1999. In 2001, the Traxtar 2.0 line was launched. In late 2001, Reebok introduced the Smart Train DMX line of adult shoes, which incorporates the Traxtar microprocessor and DMX technologies.
- Relaunched its "The Pump" line of running and basketball shoes that allows users to manually inflate air sacs surrounding the foot to obtain a better fit by squeezing "the pump" located in the shoe's tongue.
- Launched notable marketing activities in 2000–2001, such as sponsoring several teams and athletes in the 2000 Summer Olympics and the CBS TV show *Survivor* (both Island and Outback series) and offering Reebok-branded merchandise.
- Operates over 200 Reebok, Rockport, Ralph Lauren, and Greg Norman stores in the United States that sell its respective branded footware, apparel, and accessories. It also sells its Reebok, Rockport, and Greg Norman products directly to consumers via the Internet.

What segmentation strategy will Reebok use to take it further into the twenty-first century? Only Reebok knows, but it will certainly involve trying to differentiate its products more clearly from its global competitors and perhaps target new or retarget existing global consumers.

Using Market-Product Grids   A **market-product grid** is a framework to relate the segments of a market to products offered or potential marketing actions by the firm. The grid in Figure 9–2 shows different market segments of sneaker users as rows in the grid, whereas the columns show the different shoe product lines (or marketing actions) chosen by Reebok. Thus, each cell in a market-product grid can depict the estimated market size of a given product sold to a specific market segment.

The red cells in Figure 9–2, labeled "P," represent Reebok's primary target market segment when it introduced each type of shoe. The blue cells, labeled "S," represent the secondary target market segments that also bought these products. In some cases, Reebok discovered that large numbers of people in a segment not originally targeted for a particular shoe style bought it anyway. Thus, Reebok products are purchased by two types of segments: "performance-oriented" consumers (27 percent), who buy sneakers and apparel for athletic purposes; and "nonathletic-oriented" consumers (73 percent), who buy sneakers and apparel for comfort, style, price, or other nonathletic reasons. But as Figure 9–2 depicts, two segments of consumers in the "nonathletic-oriented" category, "comfort/style conscious" and "walker" (who may object to be referred to as "nonathletes"), bought running, aerobic, and cross-trainer shoes not initially targeted at their respective segments. When this trend became apparent to Reebok in 1986, it introduced its walking shoe line directly at the walker segment.

Figure 9–2 also suggests one of the potential dangers faced by a firm that uses market segmentation: By subdividing an entire market into two or more segments, the firm runs the risk of diffusing its marketing efforts, thereby enabling competitors to attack these segments. To reach specific segments more effectively, Reebok uses "strategic business units," as discussed in Chapter 2, to focus its marketing efforts.[4]

When to Segment Markets

A business firm goes to the trouble and expense of segmenting its markets when this increases its sales revenue, profit, and return on investment. When its expenses more than offset the potentially increased revenues from segmentation, it should not attempt to segment its market. The specific situations that illustrate this point are the cases of (1) one product and multiple market segments, (2) multiple products and multiple market segments, and (3) "segments of one," or mass customization.

One Product and Multiple Market Segments

When a firm produces only a single product or service and attempts to sell it to two or more market segments, it avoids the extra costs of developing and producing additional versions of the product, which often entail extremely high research, engineering, and manufacturing expenses. In this case, the incremental costs of taking the product into new product segments are typically those of a separate promotional campaign or a new channel of distribution. Although these expenses can be high, they are rarely as large as those for developing an entirely new product.

Movies, magazines, and books are single products frequently directed to two or more distinct market segments. Movie companies often run different TV commercials or magazine ads featuring different aspects of a newly released film (love, or drama, or spectacular scenery) that are targeted to different market segments. *Time* magazine now publishes more than 200 different U.S. editions and more than 100 international editions, each targeted at unique geographic and demographic segments using a special mix of advertisements. As shown on the opposite page, Street & Smith's spring *Baseball* issue uses different covers in different regions of the United States, featuring a baseball star from that region.

Does Harry Potter appeal only to the kids' segment? See the text for the answer to this amazing publishing success.

Harry Potter's phenomenal four-book success is based both on author J. K. Rowling's fiction-writing wizardry and her publisher's creativity in marketing to preteen, teen, and adult segments of readers. By 2001 more than 40 million Harry Potter books had been sold in the United States, and the books were often at the top of *The New York Times* fiction best-seller list—for *adults*.[5] Although multiple TV commercials for movies and separate covers or advertisements for magazines or books are expensive, they are minor compared with the costs of producing an entirely new movie, magazine, or book for another market segment.

Multiple Products and Multiple Market Segments

Reebok's different styles of shoes, each targeted at a different type of user, are an example of multiple products aimed at multiple markets. Manufacturing these different styles of shoes is clearly more expensive than producing only a single style but seems worthwhile if it

serves customers' needs better, doesn't reduce quality or increase price, and adds to the sales revenues and profits.

Marketing experts increasingly stress the two-tier marketing strategies—what some call "Tiffany/Wal-Mart strategies"—that will be necessary for the United States in the twenty-first century.[6] Since 1980 the U.S. middle class has declined in size; the wealthiest fifth has seen its income grow, and the bottom three-fifths have seen their incomes stagnate or even decline. The result is that many firms are now offering different variations of the same basic product or service to high-end and low-end segments:

- Gap's Banana Republic chain sells blue jeans for $58, whereas its Old Navy stores sell a slightly different version for $22.
- General Motors' Saturn unit not only sells its no-haggling-on-price new cars but is aggressively marketing its "preowned" cars to reduce customer fears about buying a used car.
- The Walt Disney Company carefully markets two distinct Winnie-the-Poohs— such as the original line-drawn figures on fine china sold at Nordstroms and a cartoonlike Pooh on polyester bedsheets sold at Wal-Mart—and these Poohs don't play together on the shelves of the same retailer.

The lines between customer segments often blur, however, as shown by the Cadillacs and Mercedes in Wal-Mart parking lots.

Segments of One: Mass Customization   American marketers are rediscovering today what their ancestors running the corner general store knew a century ago: Every customer is unique, has unique wants and needs, and desires special tender loving care from the seller—the essence of customer relationship marketing (CRM). Economies of scale in manufacturing and marketing during the past century made mass-produced goods so affordable that most customers were willing to compromise their individual tastes and settle for standardized products. Today's Internet ordering and flexible manufacturing and marketing processes have made *mass customization* possible, tailoring goods or services to the tastes of individual customers on a high-volume scale. The Web Link shows how mass customization lets you design your own personalized running shoe or hiking boot.

Mass customization is the next step beyond *build-to-order* (BTO), manufacturing a product only when there is an order from a customer. Dell Computer uses BTO systems that trim work-in-progress inventories and shorten delivery times to customers. Dell's three-day deliveries (see Chapter 16) are made possible by restricting its computer line to only a few basic modules and stocking a variety of each. This gives customers a good choice with quick delivery—Dell PCs being assembled in four minutes. Most Dell customization comes from spending 90 minutes loading the unique software each customers selects. But even this system falls a bit short of total mass customization with virtually unlimited specification of features by customers.[7]

WEB LINK   Mass Customizing Your Own "Designer" Sneakers

Don't like the looks of those things on your feet right now? If you think your style instincts could design you a better running shoe or hiking boot, go to www.customatix.com! There you can design your own shoe—customizing 15 elements of your shoe. All possible combinations of these 15 design elements are the basis for Customatix's claim of offering more than 3 billion trillion design variations.

A bit too complex? Design a simpler sneaker on Nike's website: www.nike.com/nike_id.

The Segmentation Trade-Off: CRM versus Synergies   The key to successful product differentiation and market segmentation strategies is finding the ideal balance between satisfying a customer's individual wants and achieving organizational **synergy**, the increased customer value achieved through performing organizational functions more efficiently. The "increased customer value" can take many forms: more products, improved quality on existing products, lower prices, easier access to product through improved distribution, and so on. So the ultimate criterion for an organization's marketing success is that customers should be better off as a result of the increased synergies.

Customized perfumes from Procter & Gamble, customized jeans from Levi's, and customized employee uniforms from Lands' End are common today.[8] But are their customers really happy, given all the special technology? In spite of the critical importance of customer relationship management discussed in Chapter 1, a recent study found that two-thirds of such CRM projects fail. The essence of good customer relations is not the elegance of the latest technology but relentless attention to detail: good products, prompt service, a dedicated staff willing to take an extra step to handle those special customer needs.[9]

Concept Check

1. Market segmentation involves aggregating prospective buyers into groups that have two key characteristics. What are they?

2. What is product differentiation?

3. The process of segmenting and targeting markets is a bridge between what two marketing activities?

STEPS IN SEGMENTING AND TARGETING MARKETS

The process of segmenting a market and then selecting and reaching the target segments is divided into the five steps discussed in this section, as shown in Figure 9–3. Segmenting a market is not a science—it requires large doses of common sense and managerial judgment.

Market segmentation and target markets can be abstract topics, so put on your entrepreneur's hat to experience the process. Suppose you own a Wendy's fast-food restaurant next to a large urban university that offers both day and evening classes. Your restaurant specializes in the Wendy's basics: hamburgers, french fries, Frosty milkshakes, and chili. Even though you are part of a chain and have some restrictions on menu and decor, you are free to set your hours of business and to undertake local advertising. How can market segmentation help?

Form Prospective Buyers into Segments

Grouping prospective buyers into meaningful segments involves meeting some specific criteria for segmentation and finding specific variables to segment the consumer or organizational market being analyzed.

Criteria to Use in Forming the Segments
A marketing manager should develop segments for a market that meet five principal criteria:

- *Potential for increased profit and ROI.* The best segmentation approach is the one that maximizes the opportunity for future profit and ROI. If this potential is maximized through no segmentation, don't segment. For nonprofit organizations, the analogous criterion is the potential for serving client users more effectively.
- *Similarity of needs of potential buyers within a segment.* Potential buyers within a segment should be similar in terms of a marketing activity, such as product features sought or advertising media used.
- *Difference of needs of buyers among segments.* If the needs of the various segments aren't appreciably different, combine them into fewer segments. A different segment usually requires a different marketing action that, in turn, means greater costs. If increased revenues don't offset extra costs, combine segments and reduce the number of marketing actions.
- *Feasibility of a marketing action to reach a segment.* Reaching a segment requires a simple but effective marketing action. If no such action exists, don't segment.
- *Simplicity and cost of assigning potential buyers to segments.* A marketing manager must be able to put a market segmentation plan into effect. This means being able to recognize the characteristics of potential buyers and then assigning them to a segment without encountering excessive costs.

FIGURE 9–3
The process of segmenting and targeting markets involves five key steps

DILBERT   by Scott Adams

The Russians' love of the dark meat on a chicken—like legs and thighs—is an example of using these five criteria in global market segmentation. Americans prefer the white chicken meat. The result is that in the late 1990s about one in every four legs of U.S. chickens were eaten by Russians.[10]

Ways to Segment Consumer Markets   Figure 9–4 shows a number of variables that can be used to segment U.S. consumer markets, many based on those from the 2000 U.S. Census. They are divided into two general categories: customer characteristics and buying situations. Some examples of how certain characteristics can be used to segment specific markets:

- *Region* (a geographical customer characteristic). Campbell's found that its canned nacho cheese sauce, which could be heated and poured directly onto nacho chips, was too hot for Americans in the East and not hot enough for those in the West and Southwest. The result: Today Campbell's plants in Texas and California produce a hotter nacho cheese sauce than that produced in the other plants to serve their regions better.

- *Age and household size* (demographic customer characteristics). In 2005 the United States will have 29 million teenagers and 86 million people 50 and over—the size of these age segments warranting much marketing effort. More than half of all U.S. households are made up of only one or two persons, so Campbell's packages meals with only one or two servings—from Great Starts breakfasts to L'Orient dinners.

- *Lifestyle* (a psychographic customer characteristic). Psychographic variables are consumer activities, interests, and opinions. As shown in Figure 9–4, firms such as SRI (VALS) and Claritas provide lifestyle segmentation services to marketers. Claritas's lifestyle segmentation is based on the old adage "Birds of a feather flock together" or in its case, "You are Where You Live." Thus, Claritas believes that people of similar lifestyle characteristics tend to live near one another, have similar interests, and buy similar products and services. Claritas offers services such as MicroVision that classifies every *household* in the United States into one of 48 unique market segments.[11]

What special benefit does a MicroFridge offer, and to which market segment might this appeal? The answer appears in the text.

MAIN DIMENSION	SEGMENTATION VARIABLES	TYPICAL BREAKDOWNS
CUSTOMER CHARACTERISTICS		
Geographic	Region	Northeast; Midwest; South; West; etc.
	City size	Under 10,000; 10,000–24,999; 25,000–49,999; 50,000–99,999; 100,000–249,999; 250,000–499,999; 500,000–999,999; 1,000,000 or more
	Metropolitan area	Metropolitan statistical areas (MSAs); etc.
	Density	Urban; suburban; small town; rural
Demographic	Gender	Male; female
	Age	Under 6 yrs; 6–11 yrs; 12–17 yrs; 18–24 yrs; 25–34 yrs; 35–44 yrs; 45–54 yrs; 55–64 yrs; 65–74 yrs; 75 yrs plus
	Race	African-American; Asian; Hispanic; White/Caucasian; etc.
	Life stage	Infant; preschool; child; youth; collegiate; adult; senior
	Birth era	Baby boomer (1949–1964); Generation X (1965–1976); baby boomlet/Generation Y (1977–present)
	Household size	1; 2; 3–4; 5 or more
	Residence tenure	Own home; rent home
	Marital status	Never married; married; separated; divorced; widowed
Socioeconomic	Income	< $15,000; $15,000–$24,999; $25,000–34,999; $35,000–$49,999; $50,000–$74,999; $75,000 +
	Education	Some high school or less; high school graduate (or GED); etc.
	Occupation	Managerial and professional specialty; technical, sales, and administrative support; service; farming, forestry, and fishing; etc.
Psychographic	Personality	Gregarious; compulsive; introverted; aggressive; ambitious; etc.
	Values (VALS)	Actualizers; fulfilleds; achievers; experiencers; believers; strivers; makers; strugglers
	Lifestyle (Claritas)	Settled in; white picket fence; and 46 other household segments
BUYING SITUATIONS		
Outlet type	In-store	Department; specialty; outlet; convenience; supermarket; superstore/mass merchandiser; catalog
	Direct	Mail order/catalog; door-to-door; direct response; Internet
Benefits sought	Product features	Situation specific; general
	Needs	Quality; service; price/value; financing; warranty; etc.
Usage	Usage rate	Light user; medium user; heavy user
	User status	Nonuser; ex-user; prospect; first-time user; regular user
Awareness and intentions	Product knowledge	Unaware; aware; informed; interested; intending to buy; purchaser; rejection
Behavior	Involvement	Minimum effort; comparison; special effort

FIGURE 9–4

Segmentation variables and breakdowns for U.S. consumer markets

- *Benefits sought* (a buying situations characteristic). Important benefits offered to different customers are often a useful way to segment markets because they can lead directly to specific marketing actions, such as a new product, ad campaign, or distribution system. For example, MicroFridge targets its combination microwave/refrigerator/freezer at college dorm residents, who are often woefully short of space. Busy, convenience-oriented consumers are beginning to use online grocery shopping and delivery from services like Peapod, which is currently located in Chicago, Boston, Washington, D.C., among other markets.[12]

- **Usage rate** (quantity consumed or patronage—store visits—during a specific period; varies significantly among different customer groups). Airlines have developed frequent-flyer programs to encourage passengers to use the same airline repeatedly—a technique sometimes called "frequency marketing," which focuses on usage rate.

To obtain usage rate data, the Simmons Market Research Bureau semi-annually surveys about 33,000 adults 18 years of age and older to discover how the products and services they buy and the media they watch relate to their lifestyle and demographic characteristics. Figure 9–5 shows the results of a question Simmons asks about the respondent's frequency of use (or patronage) of "fast-food restaurants."[13]

As shown in the right column of Figure 9–5, the importance of the segment increases as we move up the table. Among nonusers of these restaurants, prospects (who *might become* users) are more important than nonprospects (who are *never likely* to become users). Moving up the rows to the users, it seems logical that light users of these restaurants (1 to 5 times per month) are important but less so than medium users (6 to 13 times per month), who, in turn, are a less important segment than the critical group—the heavy users (14 or more times per month). The "Actual Consumption" column in Figure 9–5 shows how much of the total monthly usage of these restaurants are accounted for by the heavy, medium, and light users.

Usage rate is sometimes referred to in terms of the **80/20 rule**, a concept that suggests 80 percent of a firm's sales are obtained from 20 percent of its customers. The percentages in the 80/20 rule are not really fixed at exactly 80 percent and 20 percent, but suggest that a small fraction of customers provide a large fraction of a firm's sales. For example, Figure 9–5 shows that the 17.1 percent of the U.S. population who are heavy users of fast-food restaurants provide 38.4 percent of the consumption volume.

The "Usage Index per Person" column in Figure 9–5 emphasizes the importance of the heavy-user group even more. Giving the light users (1 to 5 restaurant visits per month) an index of 100, the heavy users have an index of 467. In other words, for every $1.00 spent by a light user in one of these restaurants in a month, each heavy user spends $4.67. This is the reason for the emphasis in almost all marketing strategies on effective ways to reach these heavy users. Thus, as a Wendy's restaurant owner you want to keep the heavy-user segment constantly in mind.

As part of the Simmons fast-food survey, restaurant patrons were asked if each restaurant was (1) the sole restaurant they went to, (2) the primary one, or (3) one of several secondary ones. This national information, shown in Figure 9–6, might

FIGURE 9–5
Patronage of fast-food restaurants by adults 18 years and older: Simmons Market Research Bureau Spring 2001 Choices System National Consumer Survey

USER OR NONUSER	SPECIFIC SEGMENT	NUMBER (1,000S)	PERCENTAGE	ACTUAL CONSUMPTION (%)	USAGE INDEX PER PERSON	IMPORTANCE OF SEGMENT
Users	Heavy users (14+ per month)	34,111	17.1%	38.4	467	High
	Medium users (6–13 per month)	52,951	26.6%	40.5	317	
	Light users (1–5 per month)	87,380	43.8%	21.1	100	
Total users		174,442	87.5%	100.0	237	
Nonusers	Prospects	3,032	1.5%	0	0	
	Nonprospects	21,827	11.0%	0	0	
Total nonusers		24,859	12.5%	0	0	Low
Total	Users and nonusers	199,301	100.0%	100.0	—	

Welcome to online grocery shopping! With her son looking on, Patti Landry picks out what she wants at a nearby Jewel store.

Peapod

www.peapod.com

give you, as a Wendy's owner, some ideas in developing your local strategy. The Wendy's bar in Figure 9–6 shows that your sole (0.8 percent), primary (19.6 percent), and secondary (12.2 percent) user segments are somewhat behind Burger King and far behind McDonald's, so a natural strategy is to look at these two competitors and devise a marketing program to win customers from them.[14]

The "nonusers" part of your own bar in Figure 9–6 also provides ideas. It shows that 11.0 percent of adult Americans don't go to fast-food restaurants in a typical month (also shown in Figure 9–5) and are really nonprospects—unlikely to ever patronize your restaurant. But the 56.4 percent of the Wendy's bar shown as prospects may be worth detailed thought. These adults use the product category (fast-food restaurants) but *do not* go to Wendy's. New menu items or new promotional strategies might succeed in converting these "prospects" to "users." One key conclusion emerges about usage: in market segmentation studies, some measure of usage or revenues derived from various segments is central to the analysis.

In determining one or two variables to segment the market for your Wendy's restaurant, very broadly we find two main markets: students and nonstudents. To segment the students, we could try a variety of demographic variables, such as age, sex, year in school, or college major, or psychographic variables, such as personality characteristics, attitudes, or interests. But none of these variables really meets the five criteria listed previously—particularly the fourth criterion about leading to a feasible marketing action to reach the various segments. Four student segments that *do* meet these criteria include the following:

- Students living in dormitories (college residence halls, sororities, fraternities).
- Students living near the college in apartments.
- Day commuter students living outside the area.
- Night commuter students living outside the area.

These segmentation variables are really a combination of where the student lives and the time he or she is on campus (and near your restaurant). For nonstudents who might be customers, similar variables might be used:

- Faculty and staff members at the university.
- People who live in the area but aren't connected with the university.
- People who work in the area but aren't connected with the university.

FIGURE 9–6

Comparison of various kinds of users and nonusers for Wendy's, Burger King, and McDonald's restaurants

Simmons Market Research Bureau

www.smrb.com

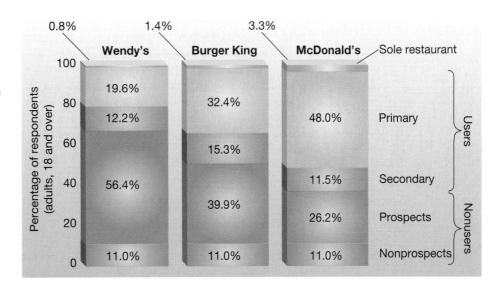

What variables might Xerox use to segment the organizational markets for its answer to color copying problems? For the possible answer and related marketing actions, see the text.

People in each of these segments aren't quite as similar as those in the student segments, which makes them harder to reach with a marketing program or action. Think about (1) whether the needs of all these segments are different and (2) how various advertising media can be used to reach these groups effectively.

Ways to Segment Organizational Markets

Variables for segmenting organizational markets are shown in Figure 9–7. A product manager at Xerox responsible for its new network color printer might use a number of these segmentation variables, as follows:

- *Location.* Firms located in a metropolitan statistical area (MSA) might receive a personal sales call, whereas those outside the MSA might be contacted by telephone.
- *NAICS code.* Firms categorized by the North American Industry Classification System (NAICS) code as manufacturers that deal with customers throughout the world might have different fax and document handling needs than do retailers or lawyers serving local customers.
- *Number of employees.* The size of the firm is related to the volume of digital documents produced for a given industry or NAICS, so firms with varying numbers of employees might be a specific target market for different Xerox systems.
- *Benefits sought.* Xerox can target organizations needing the high copying speed available with its new network color printer.

Form Products to Be Sold into Groups

As important as grouping customers into segments is finding a means of grouping the products you're selling into meaningful categories. If the firm has only one product or service, this isn't a problem, but when it has dozens or hundreds, these must be grouped in some way so buyers can relate to them. This is why department stores and supermarkets are organized into product groups, with the departments or aisles containing related merchandise. Likewise, manufacturers have product lines that are the groupings they use in the catalogs sent to customers.

What are the groupings for your restaurant? It could be the item purchased, such as a Frosty, chili, hamburgers, and french fries, but this is where judgment—the qualitative aspect of marketing—comes in. Students really buy an eating experience, or a meal that satisfies a need at a particular time of day, so the product grouping can be defined by meal or time of day as breakfast, lunch, between-meal snack, dinner, and after-dinner snack. These groupings are more closely related to the way purchases are actually made and permit you to market the entire meal, not just your french fries or Frosties.

Develop a Market-Product Grid and Estimate Size of Markets

Developing a market-product grid means labeling the markets (or horizontal rows) and products (or vertical columns), as shown in Figure 9–8. In addition, the size of the market in each cell, or the market-product combination, must be estimated. For your restaurant this involves estimating the number of, or sales revenue obtained from, each kind of meal that can reasonably be expected to be sold to

MAIN DIMENSION	SEGMENTATION VARIABLES	TYPICAL BREAKDOWNS
CUSTOMER CHARACTERISTICS		
Geographic	U.S. region	Northeast; Midwest; South; West; etc.
	Metropolitan area	Metropolitan statistical areas (MSAs); etc.
	Density	Urban; suburban; small town; rural
Demographic	NAICS code	2-digit: Sector (Information—51); 3-digit: Subsector (Broadcasting & Telecommunications—513); 4-digit: Industry Group (Telecommunications—5133); etc.
	NAICS sector	Agriculture, Forestry, Fishing, and Hunting (11); Mining (21); Utilities (22); Construction (23); Manufacturing (31–33); etc.
	Number of employees	1–99; 100–499; 500–999; 1,000–4,999; 5,000 +
	Annual sales	< $1 million; $1 million–$9.9 million; $10 million–$49.9 million; $50 million–$99.9 million; $100 million–$499.9 million; $500 million–$999.9 million; $1 billion–$4.9 billion; $5 billion +
	Number of locations	1–9; 10–49; 50–99; 100–499; 500–999; 1,000 and over
BUYING SITUATIONS*		
Nature of good	Kind	Product; service
	Where used	Installation; component; supplies
	Application	Office use; limited production use; heavy production use
Buying condition	Purchase location	Centralized; decentralized
	Who buys	Individual buyer; groups of buyers
	Type of buy	New buy; modified rebuy; straight rebuy

*Benefits sought, usage rate, and awareness and intentions are similar to consumer market variables in Figure 9–4.

FIGURE 9–7
Segmentation variables and
breakdowns for U.S.
organizational markets

each market segment. This is a form of the usage rate analysis discussed earlier in the chapter.

The market sizes in Figure 9–8 may be simple "guesstimates" if you don't have time for formal marketing research (as discussed in Chapter 8). But even such crude estimates of the size of specific markets using a market-product grid are far better than the usual estimates of the entire market.

Select Target Markets

A firm must take care to choose its target market segments carefully. If it picks too narrow a group of segments, it may fail to reach the volume of sales and profits it needs. If it selects too broad a group of segments, it may spread its marketing efforts so thin that the extra expenses more than offset the increased sales and profits.

Criteria to Use in Picking the Target Segments   There are two different kinds of criteria present in the market segmentation process: (1) those to use in dividing the market into segments (discussed earlier) and (2) those to use in actually picking the target segments. Even experienced marketing executives often confuse these two different sets of criteria. The five criteria to use in actually selecting the target segments apply to your Wendy's restaurant this way:

* *Market size.* The estimated size of the market in the segment is an important factor in deciding whether it's worth going after. There is really no market for

FIGURE 9–8
Selecting a target market for
your fast-food restaurant next
to an urban university (target
market is shaded)

| | **PRODUCTS: MEALS** | | | | |
MARKETS	**BREAK-FAST**	**LUNCH**	**BETWEEN-MEAL SNACK**	**DINNER**	**AFTER-DINNER SNACK**
STUDENT					
Dormitory	0	1	3	0	3
Apartment	1	3	3	1	1
Day commuter	0	3	2	1	0
Night commuter	0	0	1	3	2
NONSTUDENT					
Faculty or staff	0	3	1	1	0
Live in area	0	1	2	2	1
Work in area	1	3	0	1	0

Key: 3 = Large market; 2 = Medium market; 1 = Small market; 0 = No market.

breakfasts among dormitory students (Figure 9–8), so why devote any marketing effort toward reaching a small or nonexistent market?

• *Expected growth.* Although the size of the market in the segment may be small now, perhaps it is growing significantly or is expected to grow in the future. Between now and 2007 sales of fast-food meals eaten outside the restaurants are projected to grow three times as fast as those eaten inside. And Wendy's is the fast-food leader in average time to serve a drive-thru order—for example, 150.3 seconds per order, 16.7 seconds faster than McDonald's. This speed and convenience is potentially very important to night commuters in adult education programs.[15]

• *Competitive position.* Is there a lot of competition in the segment now or is there likely to be in the future? The less the competition, the more attractive the segment is. For example, if the college dormitories announce a new policy of "no meals on weekends," this segment is suddenly more promising for your restaurant.

• *Cost of reaching the segment.* A segment that is inaccessible to a firm's marketing actions should not be pursued. For example, the few nonstudents who live in the area may not be economically reachable with ads in newspapers or other media. As a result, do not waste money trying to advertise to them.

• *Compatibility with the organization's objectives and resources.* If your restaurant doesn't have the cooking equipment to make breakfasts and has a policy against spending more money on restaurant equipment, then don't try to reach the breakfast segment.

As is often the case in marketing decisions, a particular segment may appear attractive according to some criteria and very unattractive according to others.

Choose the Segments   Ultimately, a marketing executive has to use these criteria to choose the segments for special marketing efforts. As shown in Figure 9–8, let's assume you've written off the breakfast market for two reasons: too small of a market size and incompatibility with your objectives and resources. In terms of competitive position and cost of reaching the segment, you choose to focus on the four student segments and not the three nonstudent segments (although you're certainly not going to turn away business from the nonstudent segments). This combination of market-product segments—your target market—is shaded in Figure 9–8.

Take Marketing Actions to Reach Target Markets

The purpose of developing a market-product grid is to trigger marketing actions to increase revenues and profits. This means that someone must develop and execute an action plan.

How can Wendy's target different market segments like drive-thru customers with different advertising programs? For the answer, see the text and Figure 9–9.

Your Wendy's Segmentation Strategy With your Wendy's restaurant you've already reached one significant decision: There is a limited market for breakfast, so you won't open for business until 10:30 A.M. In fact, Wendy's first attempt at a breakfast menu was a disaster and was discontinued in 1986. Wendy's evaluates possible new menu items continuously, not only to compete with McDonald's and Burger King but with a complex array of supermarkets, convenience stores, and gas stations that sell reheatable packaged foods as well as new "easy-lunch" products.

Another essential decision is where and what meals to advertise to reach specific market segments. An ad in the student newspaper could reach all the student segments, but you might consider this "shotgun approach" too expensive and want a more focused "rifle approach" to reach smaller segments. If you choose three segments for special actions (Figure 9–9), advertising actions to reach them might include:

- *Day commuters* (an entire market segment). Run ads inside commuter buses and put flyers under the windshield wipers of cars in parking lots used by day commuters. These ads and flyers promote all the meals at your restaurant to a single segment of students—a horizontal cut through the market-product grid.
- *Between-meals snacks* (directed to all four student markets). To promote eating during this downtime for your restaurant, offer "Ten percent off all purchases between 2:00 and 4:30 P.M. during winter quarter." This ad promotes a single meal to all four student segments—a vertical cut through the market-product grid.

FIGURE 9–9
Advertising actions to reach specific student segments

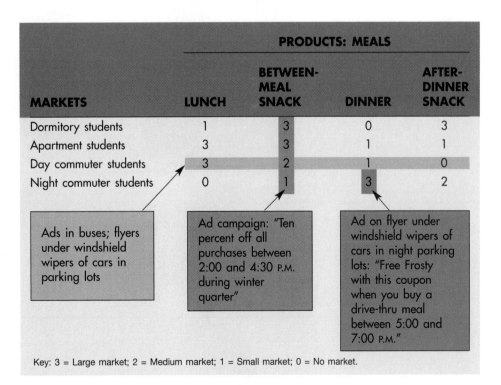

MARKETS	LUNCH	BETWEEN-MEAL SNACK	DINNER	AFTER-DINNER SNACK
Dormitory students	1	3	0	3
Apartment students	3	3	1	1
Day commuter students	3	2	1	0
Night commuter students	0	1	3	2

Ads in buses; flyers under windshield wipers of cars in parking lots

Ad campaign: "Ten percent off all purchases between 2:00 and 4:30 P.M. during winter quarter"

Ad on flyer under windshield wipers of cars in night parking lots: "Free Frosty with this coupon when you buy a drive-thru meal between 5:00 and 7:00 P.M."

Key: 3 = Large market; 2 = Medium market; 1 = Small market; 0 = No market.

- *Dinners to night commuters.* The most focused of all three campaigns, this ad promotes a single meal to a single student segment. The campaign might consist of a windshield flyer offering a free Frosty with the coupon when the person buys a drive-thru meal between 5:00 and 7:00 P.M.—which exploits the efficiency of Wendy's in its drive-thru business.

Depending on how your advertising actions work, you can repeat, modify, or drop them and design new campaigns for other segments you feel warrant the effort. This example of advertising your Wendy's restaurant is just a small piece of a complete marketing program using all the elements of the marketing mix.

Apple's Ever-Changing Segmentation Strategy   Steve Jobs and Steve Wozniak didn't realize they were developing today's multibillion-dollar PC industry when they invented the Apple I in a garage on April Fool's Day, 1976. Hobbyists, the initial target market, were not interested in the product. However, when the Apple II was displayed at a computer trade show in 1977, consumers loved it and Apple Computer was born. Typical of young companies, Apple focused on its products and had little concern for its markets. When IBM—"Big Blue"—entered the PC market in 1981, Apple was forced to become a "real company," much to the chagrin of its creative young engineers who were likened to "Boy Scouts without adult supervision."

With the introduction of the IBM PC, Big Blue quickly dominated the fledgling market, having licensed the DOS operating system from Bill Gates of Microsoft. By 1983, Apple had lost significant market share. During the Super Bowl in 1984, Apple launched the Macintosh with an Orwellian TV ad that has been described as the best commercial ever. And while the new Macintosh initially sold well, sales fell off dra-

What market segments for Apple's computers are represented by these products? The Marketing NewsNet and text discussion provide insights into Apple's market segmentation strategy.

Apple Computer

www.apple.com

matically, eventually leading to the departure of Steve Jobs from Apple in 1985. Unfortunately, Apple continued to languish under new, changing leadership as it constantly altered its market-product strategies. By the end of 1996, Apple's losses mounted and it was time for a bold move: Bring back Steve Jobs.[16]

When Steve Jobs returned in 1997, he detailed his vision for a reincarnated Apple by describing a new market segmentation strategy that he called the "Apple Product Matrix." This strategy consisted of developing two general types of computers (desktops and portables) targeted at two general kinds of market segments (consumer and professional). He also announced the controversial "Think Different" advertising campaign, deleted several models from Apple's existing PC line, launched The Apple Store in which Apple would sell its computers direct via the Internet or by telephone. In 1998, Apple retargeted the consumer and educational markets by introducing the revolutionary new iMac, the greatest PC product launch in history.[17]

In 1999, Apple introduced the clamshell-looking iBook portable computer, based on the same innovative design principles as the iMac. In January 2001, Steve Jobs again changed the strategic direction of Apple. According to Jobs, the PC industry has now entered into the third golden age of personal computing. The first era, which occurred from 1980 to 1994, featured the PC as an office productivity tool. Users bought PCs for their word processing, spreadsheet analysis, desktop publishing, and so forth capabilities. The second era occurred from 1995 to 2000 when the PC became the primary access tool for the Internet. As PC sales slowed in 2000, experts began to ask, "What's next?" They believed that a variety of small digital devices would replace personal computers. Steve Jobs says they're wrong and is betting the company on his conviction.

Jobs believes that the personal computer entered the Age of the Digital Lifestyle in 2001. In a keynote address, Jobs said that "the proliferation of digital devices— CD players, MP3 players, cell phones, handheld organizers (PDAs), digital cameras, digital camcorders, and more—will never have enough processing power and memory to stand alone." Jobs enthusiastically proclaimed "the Mac can become the digital hub of this new digital lifestyle by adding tremendous value to these devices." By repositioning Apple as the "digital hub" with "killer apps," such as iTunes, iMovie, iDVD, iPhoto, and so on, Jobs believes consumers can take full advantage of the new digital lifestyle era.

As in most segmentation situations, a single product does not fit into an exclusive market niche. Rather, there is overlap among products in the product line and also among the markets to which they are directed. But a market segmentation strategy enables Apple to offer different products to meet the needs of different market segments, as shown in the accompanying Marketing NewsNet.[18]

What does Steve Jobs have in store for Apple in the near future? Here are some plans and successes to build on for 2002 and beyond:[19]

- Redesigning the iMac (which sold over 6 million units by early 2002) and Power Mac G4 lines, which were both introduced in 1998.
- Adding more Apple Retail Stores, which were launched in May 2001, in the hopes of expanding its market share to 10 percent.
- Strengthening its relationship with the education market, which is Apple's largest target market segment, accounting for about 40 percent of its total sales.
- Developing new "killer apps," which include: Mac OS X, a completely rewritten operating system that significantly reduces "crashes"; iTunes, that allows users to record CDs and play MP3 music; iMovie, that enables users to create and edit home movies recorded on digital media; iDVD, that allows users to create DVDs that can be played on their Mac or DVD player at home; and iPhoto, which enables Mac users to import, edit, and print images from digital cameras.

Stay tuned to see if Steve Jobs and these market-product strategies for his vision of the digital lifestyle era are on target. He's betting the company on it!

MARKETING NEWSNET

Apple's Segmentation Strategy: Camp Runamok No Longer

CUSTOMER VALUE

"Camp Runamok" was the nickname given to Apple Computer in the early 1980s because the innovative company had no coherent series of product lines directed at identifiable market segments.

Today, Apple has targeted its various lines of Macintosh computers and software at specific market segments. Because the market-product grid shifts as a firm's strategy changes, the one shown below is based on Apple's market-product grid as of early 2002. This market-product grid is a simplification because each "product grouping" consists of a line of Macintosh computers or software. Nevertheless, the grid suggests the following market segmentation strategy used by Apple, based on the Apple Product Matrix and digital lifestyle described in the text.

MARKETS		PRODUCTS							
		HARDWARE				SOFTWARE			
SECTOR	SEGMENT	Power Macintosh G4	PowerBook G4	iMac	iBook	iTunes	iMovies	iDVD	iPhoto
CONSUMER	Individuals			✓	✓	✓	✓	✓	✓
	Small/home office	✓	✓	✓	✓	✓	✓	✓	✓
	Students			✓	✓	✓	✓		✓
	Teachers	✓	✓	✓	✓				✓
PROFESSIONAL	Medium/large business	✓	✓	✓				✓	✓
	Creative	✓	✓			✓	✓	✓	✓
	College faculty	✓	✓	✓	✓			✓	✓
	College staff	✓	✓						✓

Concept Check

1. What are some of the variables used to segment consumer markets?

2. What are some criteria used to decide which segments to choose for targets?

3. Why is usage rate important in segmentation studies?

ANALYZING MARKET SEGMENTS USING CROSS-TABULATIONS

To do a more precise market segmentation analysis of your Wendy's restaurant, suppose you survey fast-food patrons throughout the metropolitan area where your restaurant is located, using the questionnaire shown in Figure 8–6. You want to use this information as best you can to study the market's segments and develop your strategy. Probably the most widely used approach today in marketing is to develop and interpret cross-tabulations of data obtained by questionnaires.

Developing Cross-Tabulations

A **cross-tabulation**, or "cross-tab," is a method of presenting and relating data having two or more variables. It is used to analyze and discover relationships in the data. Two important aspects of cross-tabulations are deciding which of two variables to pair together to help understand the situation and forming the resulting cross-tabulations.

Pairing the Questions   Marketers pair two questions to understand marketing relationships and to find effective marketing actions. The Wendy's questionnaire in Figure 8–6 gives many questions that might be paired to understand the fast-food business better and help reach a decision about marketing actions to increase revenues. For example, if you want to study your hypothesis that as the age of the head of household increases, patronage of fast-food restaurants declines, you can cross tabulate questions 9*d* and 3.

Forming Cross-Tabulations   Using the answers to question 3 as the column headings and the answers to question 9*d* as the row headings gives a cross-tabulation, as shown in Figure 9–10, using the answers 586 respondents gave to both questions. The figure shows two forms of the cross-tabulation:

- The raw data or answers to the specific questions are shown in Figure 9–10A. For example, this cross-tab shows that 144 households whose head was 24 years or younger ate at fast-food restaurants once a week or more.
- Answers on a percentage basis, with the percentages running horizontally, are shown in Figure 9–10B. Of the 215 households headed by someone 24 years or younger, 67.0 percent ate at a fast-food restaurant at least once a week and only 8.8 percent ate there once a month or less.

Two other forms of cross-tabulation using the raw data shown in Figure 9–10A are described in problem 7 at the end of the chapter.

Interpreting Cross-Tabulations

A careful analysis of Figure 9–10 shows that patronage of fast-food restaurants is related to the age of the head of the household. Note that as the age of the head of

FIGURE 9–10
Two forms of a cross-tabulation relating age of head of household to fast-food restaurant patronage

A. ABSOLUTE FREQUENCIES

AGE OF HEAD OF HOUSEHOLD (YEARS)	FREQUENCY			
	ONCE A WEEK OR MORE	2 OR 3 TIMES A MONTH	ONCE A MONTH OR LESS	TOTAL
24 or less	144	52	19	215
25 to 39	46	58	29	133
40 or over	82	69	87	238
Total	272	179	135	586

B. ROW PERCENTAGES: RUNNING PERCENTAGES HORIZONTALLY

AGE OF HEAD OF HOUSEHOLD (YEARS)	FREQUENCY			
	ONCE A WEEK OR MORE	2 OR 3 TIMES A MONTH	ONCE A MONTH OR LESS	TOTAL
24 or less	67.0%	24.2%	8.8%	100.0%
25 to 39	34.6	43.6	21.8	100.0
40 or over	34.4	29.0	36.6	100.0
Total	46.4%	30.6%	23.0%	100.0%

the household increases, fast-food restaurant patronage declines, as shown by the boxed percentages on the diagonal in Figure 9–10B. This means that if you want to reach the heavy-user segment, you should direct your marketing efforts to the segment that is 24 years old or younger.

As discussed earlier in the chapter, there are various ways to segment a consumer market besides according to age. For example, you could make subsequent cross-tabulations to analyze patronage related to where students live and the meals they eat to obtain more precise information for the market-product grid in Figure 9–8.

Value of Cross-Tabulations

Probably the most widely used technique for organizing and presenting marketing data, cross-tabulations have some important advantages. The simple format permits direct interpretation and an easy means of communicating data to management. They have great flexibility and can be used to summarize experimental, observational, and questionnaire data. Also, cross-tabulations may be easily generated by today's personal computers.

Cross-tabulations also have some disadvantages. For example, they can be misleading if the percentages are based on too small a number of observations. Also, cross-tabulations can hide some relations because each typically only shows two or three variables. Balancing both advantages and disadvantages, more marketing decisions are probably made using cross-tabulations than any other method of analyzing data.

The ultimate value of cross-tabulations to a marketing manager lies in obtaining a better understanding of the wants and needs of buyers and targeting key segments. This enables a marketing manager to "position" the offering in the minds of buyers, the topic discussed next.

POSITIONING THE PRODUCT

When a company offers a product commercially, a decision critical to its long-term success is how to position it in the market upon introduction. **Product positioning** refers to the place an offering occupies in consumers' minds on important attributes relative to competitive offerings.

Two Approaches to Product Positioning

There are several approaches to positioning a new product in the market. Head-to-head positioning involves competing directly with competitors on similar product attributes in the same target market. Using this strategy, Dollar competes directly with Avis and Hertz.

Differentiation positioning involves seeking a less competitive, smaller market niche in which to locate a brand. McDonald's, trying to appeal to the health-conscious segment, introduced its low-fat McLean Deluxe hamburger to avoid direct competition with Wendy's and Burger King. Companies also follow a differentiation positioning strategy among brands within their own product line to try to minimize cannibalization of a brand's sales or shares.

Product Positioning Using Perceptual Maps

A key to positioning a product effectively is the perceptions of consumers. In determining a brand's position and the preferences of consumers, companies obtain three types of data from consumers:

1. Evaluations of the important attributes for a product class.
2. Judgments of existing brands with the important attributes.
3. Ratings of an "ideal" brand's attributes.

Finding the "right" positioning for a product or service is hard work for a marketing manager. To try your positioning skills:

- Study the two late-1990s General Motors car ads below and identify what its "positioning challenge" is. (A hint: What brands are advertised and what features are stressed?)
- Suggest a (1) positioning and (2) target market for chocolate milk.

Compare your ideas with the discussion in the text.

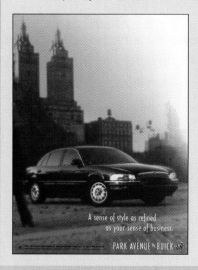

FIGURE 9–11
The challenge: Try to position General Motors and chocolate milk

From these data, it is possible to develop a **perceptual map**, a means of displaying or graphing in two dimensions the location of products or brands in the minds of consumers to enable a manager to see how consumers perceive competing products or brands and then take marketing actions. Look at Figure 9–11 and develop positioning ideas for General Motors and chocolate milk.

GM's Positioning Nightmare   Over the past three decades General Motors has had what is probably the most costly positioning challenge of any American company. Consumers simply couldn't keep its brands straight in their own minds—they couldn't tell a Chevrolet from a Pontiac or Oldsmobile from Buick and Cadillac. In the 1990s GM spent tens of millions of dollars trying to reposition its brands, for example to try to make Oldsmobile "the larger medium-priced brand" and Buick the "premium, near-luxury brand."[20]

How has it turned out? Judge for yourself by looking at the Oldsmobile and Buick ads in Figure 9–11. Can you see an important difference? Strikingly unique car features? No? Apparently most Americans have the same trouble, and in 2001 GM quietly announced the death of Oldsmobile—an American brand for eight decades!

Repositioning Chocolate Milk for Adults   **Repositioning** involves changing the place an offering occupies in a consumer's mind relative to competitive offerings. Figure 9–12 shows the positions that consumer beverages might occupy in the minds of American adults. Note that even these positions vary from one consumer to another. But for simplicity, let's assume these are the typical positions on the beverage perceptual map of adult Americans.

United States dairies, struggling to increase milk sales, hit on a wild idea: Try to target adults by repositioning chocolate milk to the location of the star shown in the

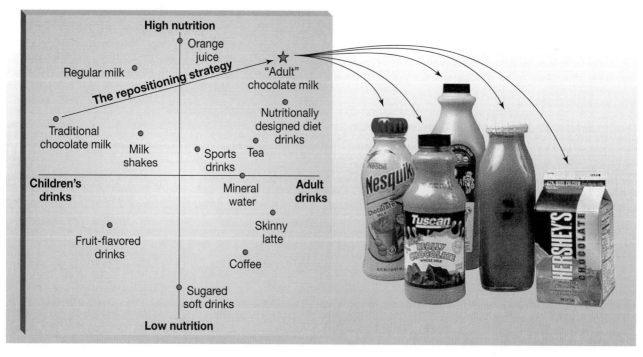

FIGURE 9–12
The strategy for repositioning
chocolate milk to reach adults

perceptual map in Figure 9–12. Their arguments are nutritionally powerful. For women chocolate milk provides calcium, critically important in female diets. And dieters can get a more filling, nutritious beverage than with a soft drink for about the same calories. The result: Chocolate milk sales increased dramatically in 2000, much of it because of adult consumption.[21]

Concept Check

1. What is cross-tabulation?

2. What are some advantages of cross-tabulations?

3. Why do marketers use perceptual maps in product positioning decisions?

SUMMARY

1 Market segmentation is aggregating prospective buyers into groups that have common needs and will respond similarly to a marketing action.

2 A straightforward approach to segmenting, targeting, and reaching a market involves five steps: (*a*) form prospective buyers into segments by characteristics such as their needs, (*b*) form products to be sold into groups, (*c*) develop a market-product grid and estimate size of markets, (*d*) select target markets, and (*e*) take marketing actions to reach the target markets.

3 Marketing variables are often used to represent customer needs in the market segmentation process. For consumer markets, typical customer variables are region, metropolitan statistical area, age, income, benefits sought, and usage rate. For industrial markets, comparable variables are geographical location, size of firm, and North American Industry Classification (NAICS) code.

4 Usage rate is an important factor in a market segmentation study. Users are often divided into heavy, medium, and light users.

5 Nonusers are often divided into prospects and non-prospects. Nonusers of a firm's brand may be important because they are prospects—users of some other brand in the product class that may be convinced to change brands.

6 Criteria used (*a*) to segment markets and (*b*) to choose target segments are related but different. The former includes potential to increase profits, similarity of needs of buyers within a segment, difference of needs among segments, and feasibility of a resulting marketing action. The latter includes market size, expected growth, the competitive position of the firm's offering in the segment, and the cost of reaching the segment.

7 A market-product grid is a useful way to display what products can be directed at which market segments, but the grid must lead to marketing actions for the segmentation process to be worthwhile.

8 Cross-tabulations are widely used today in market segmentation studies to identify needs of various customer segments and the actions to reach them.

9 A company can position a product head-to-head against the competition or seek a differentiated position. A concern with positioning is often to avoid cannibalization of the existing product line. In positioning, a firm often uses consumer judgments in the form of perceptual maps to locate its product relative to competing ones.

KEY TERMS AND CONCEPTS

cross-tabulation p. 256
80/20 rule p. 248
market-product grid p. 241
market segmentation p. 239
market segments p. 239
perceptual map p. 259

product differentiation p. 239
product positioning p. 258
repositioning p. 259
synergy p. 244
usage rate p. 248

APPLYING MARKETING CONCEPTS AND PERSPECTIVES

1 What variables might be used to segment these consumer markets? *(a)* lawnmowers, *(b)* frozen dinners, *(c)* dry breakfast cereals, and *(d)* soft drinks.

2 What variables might be used to segment these industrial markets? *(a)* industrial sweepers, *(b)* photocopiers, *(c)* computerized production control systems, and *(d)* car rental agencies.

3 In Figure 9–8 the dormitory market segment includes students living in college-owned residence halls, sororities, and fraternities. What market needs are common to these students that justify combining them into a single segment in studying the market for your Wendy's restaurant?

4 You may disagree with the estimates of market size given for the rows in the market-product grid in Figure 9–8. Estimate the market size, and give a brief justification for these market segments: *(a)* dormitory students, *(b)* day commuters, and *(c)* people who work in the area.

5 Suppose you want to increase revenues for your fast-food restaurant shown in Figure 9–9 even further. What advertising actions might you take to increase revenues from *(a)* dormitory students, *(b)* dinners, and *(c)* after-dinner snacks from night commuters?

6 Look back at Figure 8–6. Which questions would you pair to form a cross-tabulation to uncover the following relationships? *(a)* frequency of fast-food restaurant patronage and restaurant characteristics important to the customer, *(b)* age of the head of household and source of information used about fast-food restaurants, *(c)* frequency of patronage of Wendy's and source of information used about fast-food restaurants, or *(d)* how much children have to say about where the family eats and number of children in the household.

7 Look back at Figure 9–10A. *(a)* Run the percentages vertically and tell what they mean. *(b)* Express all numbers in the table as a percentage of the total number of people sampled (586) and tell what the percentages mean.

8 In Figure 9–10, *(a)* what might be other names for the three patronage levels shown in the columns? *(b)* Which is likely to be of special interest to Wendy's and why?

INTERNET EXERCISE

In its 25-year history, Apple Computer has initiated a series of creative market segmentation strategies, with new product lines targeted at specific market segments. For the latest updates of Apple's market-product strategies, go to www.apple-history.com and click on the "Intro" and "History" menu options. As you read the narrative, identify the new and remaining markets Apple has targeted with new and existing products compared to those described in the text and the Marketing NewsNet. Do you think Apple will succeed in its quest to lead us into the digital lifestyle age of personal computing? Can Apple survive as a niche PC marketer like BMW has with autos? Why or why not?

VIDEO CASE 9-1   Nokia: A Phone for Every Segment

"While practically everybody today is a potential mobile phone customer, everybody is simultaneously different in terms of usage, needs, lifestyles, and individual preferences," explains Nokia's Media Relations Manager, Keith Nowak. Understanding those differences requires that Nokia conduct ongoing research among different consumer groups throughout the world. The approach is reflected in the company's business strategy:

> We intend to exploit our leadership role by continuing to target and enter segments of the communications market that we believe will experience rapid growth or grow faster than the industry as a whole. . . .

In fact, Nowak believes that "to be successful in the mobile phone business of today and tomorrow, Nokia has to fully understand the fundamental nature and rationale of segmentation."

THE COMPANY

Nokia started in 1865, when a mining engineer built a wood-pulp mill in southern Finland to manufacture paper. Over the next century, the company diversified into industries ranging from paper to chemicals and rubber. In the 1960s, Nokia ventured into telecommunications by developing a digital telephone exchange switch. In the 1980s, Nokia developed the first "transportable" car mobile phone and the first "handportable" one. During the early 1990s, Nokia divested all of its non-telecommunications operations to focus on its telecommunications and mobile handset businesses.

Today, Nokia is the world leader in mobile communications. The company generates sales of more than $27 billion in a total of 130 countries and employs more than 60,000 people. Its simple mission: to "connect people."

The mission is accomplished by understanding consumer needs and providing offerings that meet or exceed those needs. Nokia believes that excellence in three areas—product design; services such as mobile Internet, messaging, and network security; and state-of-the-art technology—is the most important aspect of its offerings.

THE CELLULAR PHONE MARKET

In the 1980s, first generation (1G) cell phones consisted of voice-only analog devices with limited range and fea-

tures that were sold mainly in North America. In the 1990s, second generation (2G) devices consisted of voice/data digital cell phones with higher data transfer rates, expanded range, and more features. Sales of these devices expanded to Europe and Asia. In the twenty-first century, Nokia and other companies are combining several digital technologies into third generation (3G) communication devices that reach globally and feature the convergence of the cell phone, personal digital assistant (PDA), Internet services, and multimedia applications.

The global demand for cell phones has increased significantly over the years—from 284 million in 1999 to 410 million units in 2000 to 510 million units in 2001.

Producers of first and second generation cell phones used a geographic segmentation strategy as wireless communication networks were developed. Most started with the U.S. and then proceeded to Western Europe and Asia. However, each market grew at different rates. By 2001, Asia had the largest number of handsets—170 million units. Western Europe was a close second at 167 million units, followed by North America at 90 million units. Latin America had sales of 42 million units while the rest of the world had sales of 38 million units. In terms of market share, Nokia led all producers with 32 percent in 2000 and 35 percent in 2001. Motorola and Ericsson, the second and third share leaders respectively, each had less than 20 percent of the market in 2001.

The total number of worldwide wireless subscribers reached 1 billion in 2001 and is expected to increase to 2.3 billion by 2005. Demand should increase due to the growing demand by teens for high-speed handsets that will provide Internet and multimedia applications. According to the Cellular Telecommunications & Internet Association (CTIA), U.S. wireless subscribers spend an average of $45 per month on calls.

HOW NOKIA SEGMENTS ITS MARKETS

According to Debra Kennedy, Director of America's Brand Marketing at Nokia, "Different people have different usage needs. Some people want and need all of the latest and most advanced data-related features and functions, while others are happy with basic voice connectivity. Even people with similar usage needs often have differing lifestyles representing various value sets. For example, some people have an active lifestyle in which sports and fitness play an important role, while for others arts, fashion and trends may be very important."

Based on its information about consumer usage, lifestyles, and individual preferences, Nokia currently defines six segments: "Basic" consumers who need voice connectivity and a durable style; "Expression" consumers who want to customize and personalize features; "Classic" consumers who prefer a traditional appearance and web browser function; "Fashion" consumers who want a very small phone as a fashion item; "Premium" consumers who are interested in all technological and service features; and "Communicator" consumers who want to combine all of their communication devices (e.g., telephone, pager, PDA).

NOKIA'S PRODUCT LINE

To meet the needs of these segments, Nokia has recently introduced several innovative products. For example, for the Communicator segment, Nokia's 7650 features a built-in digital camera, an enhanced user interface, large color display, and multimedia messaging (MMS) functionality that allows users to combine audio, graphic, text, and imaging content in one message. Once the user has selected a picture, written text, and included an audio clip, a multimedia message can be sent directly to another multimedia messaging-capable terminal as well as to the recipient's email address.

Nokia's 6340 phone allows Classic consumers to roam between various global networks; has a new wallet feature that stores the user's credit and debit card information for quick wireless Internet e-commerce transactions; supports voice-activated dialing, control of the user interface, and three minutes of voice memo recording; and includes a personal information manager (phone book and calendar).

To target the Basic segment, Nokia provides very easy-to-use, low-priced phones that are likely to be used primarily for voice communication. They are designed for consumers who are buying their first cell phone. "We want it to be a very easy choice for the consumer," explains Kennedy. Products designed for the Expression segment are still in the low price range but allow young adults to have fun while communicating with friends. Nokia recently introduced the 5210, a cell phone that offers a youthful and vibrant style with improved durability, for this group. Features include a removable shell, a built-in stopwatch, a thermometer, downloadable game packs, a personalized logo, and a personal information manager.

Nokia also designs phones for the Fashion segment—people who want a phone to "show off." The Nokia 8260 and 8390 products are in this category. They provide basic communication and other features but are not designed for heavy use. One of Nokia's television commercials for fashion phones showed two people sitting on a couch trying to talk to each other at a loud party—so they call each other on their phones! In addition, Nokia offers phones for the Premium segment—people who also want a distinctive and elegant design, but as a fine item to appreciate rather than to show off. The Nokia 8890, a phone with a chrome case and blue back light, was designed for this group. In addition, Nokia recently introduced the all-in-one 5510, which features an MP3 player that can store up to 2 hours of music, an FM radio, a messaging machine with full keyboard, a game platform with game controls for two hands and keys located on either side of the screen, and of course, the cell phone.

THE FUTURE FOR NOKIA

A fast-growing segment for wireless mobile cell phones is the automobile. According to the ARC Group, the number of cars with "telematic" systems will increase from 1 million units to 56 million units by 2005. Ford, Nissan, and other automobile manufacturers have recently introduced systems in selected models. One reason for the expected popularity of these devices is their "hands-free, voice-activated" operation, which is designed to reduce cell phone-related automobile accidents. The CTIA has recently developed a public service announcement (PSA) to curb this dangerous behavior and forestall legislation designed to eliminate cell phone use in the car entirely.

Nokia Executive Vice President Olli-Pekka Kallasvuo is so optimistic he recently commented that "our ambition should be extremely high," as the company has set its sights on capturing 50 percent of the worldwide mobile-phone market.

Questions

1 Why has segmentation been a successful marketing strategy for Nokia?

2 What customer characteristics were used by cellular phone manufacturers during the industry's early stages of growth? Which customer characteristics and segmentation variables are used by Nokia today?

3 Create a market-product grid for Nokia today. What potential new markets could you add to the grid?

4

SATISFYING MARKETING OPPORTUNITIES

Part 4 covers the unique combination of products, price, place, and promotion that results in an offering for potential customers. How products and services are developed and managed is the focus of Chapters 10, 11, and 12. Pricing is covered in Chapters 13, 14, and Appendix B. Three chapters address the place (distribution) element with examples such as Avon's use of multiple marketing channels, Dell's responsive supply chain, and Target's investment in "smart cards" and other retailing innovations. Finally, three promotion chapters cover topics ranging from Disney's integrated marketing communications program, to "virtual advertisements" that don't really exist, to Xerox CEO Anne Mulcahy's efforts to increase market share by "selling the way customers want to buy."

"I see. And how long have you had these feelings of inferiority to tape?"

10

DEVELOPING NEW PRODUCTS AND SERVICES

AFTER READING THIS CHAPTER YOU SHOULD BE ABLE TO:

- Understand the ways in which consumer and business goods and services can be classified and marketed.

- Explain the implications of alternative ways of viewing "newness" in new products.

- Analyze the factors contributing to a product's success or failure.

- Recognize and understand the purposes of each step of the new-product process.

3M: CONTINUOUS INNOVATION
+ GENUINE BENEFITS
= SATISFIED CUSTOMERS

Ken Hart, Ph.D., 3M™ Business Development Manager for its VHB™ tape, knows that "having a better mousetrap"—or in his case an innovative 3M industrial adhesive—isn't enough!

He knows that before potential customers will buy and use it, he must help them learn about the adhesive, understand its benefits, and think about ways to actually use it in their designs.[1] And every customer application differs a little bit from the last. Here's a quick take on the marketing issues he faced recently.

- *The product?* A revolutionary 3M VHB (for "very high bond") tape made with high-strength acrylic, pressure-sensitive adhesives that can make a continuous metal bond stronger than spot welds or rivets for applications such as on cargo trailers and highway signs.
- *The target market?* Mechanical engineers responsible for the designs of everything from trucks, airplanes, and cars to ceilings in buildings.
- *The special marketing task?* To get the target mechanical engineers to seriously consider the 3M VHB tape adhesive and actually use it in applications where decades of tradition make them normally specify welds, screws, or rivets in their designs.

Ken Hart and his marketing staff developed the tongue-in-cheek ad shown on the opposite page that runs in design engineering magazines and confronts an engineer's inertia in breaking free from traditional design solutions. The team's continuing challenge is to do marketing research on customer needs to develop an integrated marketing communications strategy (Chapter 18) with advertising, public relations, and direct marketing to explain VHB's benefits to the design engineers. Although 3M received the original adhesive patent two decades ago, continuous innovation requires upgrading the formula and mechanical delivery system with new applications.[2]

A brief look at some 3M products provides us with insights into how its new-product research has enabled 3M to become a global leader in adhesive technology, leading to dozens of revolutionary 3M adhesive products, including:

- Post-it® Notes. The adhesive enables you to stick and unstick that note to your friend over and over again.
- Nexcare™ Tattoo™ Waterproof™ Bandages for kids. The bandage combines superior, waterproof wound protection with fun designs.
- Scotch™ Pop-up Tape. This is the latest version of the tape everyone uses to wrap gifts and mend well-worn pages in textbooks.
- Latitude™ Transdermal Drug Delivery System. This uses drug-in-adhesive technology contained in a skin patch to deliver sustained doses of medications.

The essence of marketing is in developing products such as a new, technologically advanced adhesive to meet buyer needs. A **product** is a good, service, or idea consisting of a bundle of tangible and intangible attributes that satisfies consumers and is received in exchange for money or some other unit of value. Tangible attributes include physical characteristics such as color or sweetness, and intangible attributes include becoming healthier or wealthier. Hence, a product includes the breakfast cereal you eat, the accountant who fills out your tax return, or your local art museum.

The life of a company often depends on how it conceives, produces, and markets new products. This is the exact reason that 3M encourages its researchers to spend up to 15 percent of their time on new technologies and innovative product ideas of their own choosing—"scouting time" they call it. This strategy contributes to more than 500 3M patents a year, routinely placing 3M among the top 10 U.S. corporations each year in patents received.[3] Later we describe how 3M strives to "delight its customers" using cross-functional teams, "Six Sigma," and "lead user" initiatives.

This chapter covers decisions involved in developing and marketing new products and services. Chapters 11 and 12 discuss the process of managing existing products and services, respectively.

THE VARIATIONS OF PRODUCTS

A product varies in terms of whether it is a consumer or business good. For most organizations the product decision is not made in isolation because companies often offer a range of products. To better appreciate the product decision, let's first define some terms pertaining to products.

Product Line and Product Mix

A **product line** is a group of products that are closely related because they satisfy a class of needs, are used together, are sold to the same customer group, are distributed through the same type of outlets, or fall within a given price range.[4] Polaroid has two major product lines consisting of cameras and film; Nike's product lines are shoes and clothing; the Mayo Clinic's product lines consist of inpatient hospital care, outpatient physician services, and medical research. Each product line has its own marketing strategy.

Within each product line is the *product item,* a specific product as noted by a unique brand, size, or price. For example, Downy softener for clothes comes in 20-ounce and 40-ounce sizes; each size is considered a separate item or *stock keeping unit* (SKU), which is a unique identification number that defines an item for ordering or inventory purposes.

Out here you're nobody. Perfect.

Sometimes you find yourself in the middle of nowhere. And sometimes in the middle of nowhere you find yourself. The legendary H1.

HUMMER like nothing else.

Hummer's striking ads gain attention for its product line of unique, upscale vehicles.

The third way to look at products is by the **product mix**, or the number of product lines offered by a company. The Cray, Inc. division of Tera Computer Company has a single product line consisting of supercomputers, which are sold mostly to governments and large businesses. Fortune Brands, however, has many product lines that include sporting equipment (Titleist golf balls), distilled beverages (Jim Beam liquors), and office products (Swingline staplers).

Classifying Products

Both the federal government and companies classify products, but for different purposes. The government's classification method helps it collect information on industrial activity. Companies classify products to help develop similar marketing strategies for the wide range of products offered. Two major ways to classify products are by type of user and degree of product tangibility.

Type of User   The first major type of product classification is according to the user. **Consumer goods** are products purchased by the ultimate consumer, whereas **business goods** (also called *B2B goods, industrial goods, or organizational goods*) are products that assist directly or indirectly in providing products for resale. In many instances the differences are distinct: Oil of Olay face moisturizer and Bass shoes are clearly consumer products, whereas Cray computers and high-tension steel springs are industrial goods used in producing other products or services.

There are difficulties, however, with this classification because some products can be considered both consumer and business items. A Compaq computer can be sold to consumers as a final product or to business firms for office use. Each classification results in different marketing actions. Viewed as a consumer product, the Compaq computer would be sold through computer stores or directly from the

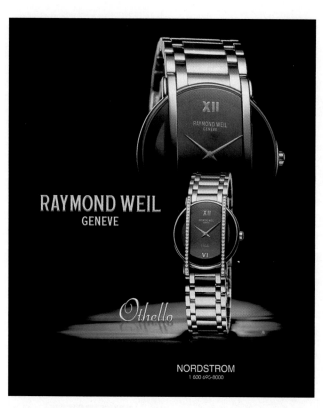

Specialty goods like Raymond Weil watches require distinct marketing programs to reach narrow target markets.

Raymond Weil

company website. As a business product, the Compaq computer might be sold by a salesperson offering discounts for multiple purchases.

Degree of Tangibility   Classification by degree of tangibility divides products into one of three categories. First is a *nondurable* good, an item consumed in one or a few uses, such as food products and fuel. A *durable* good is one that usually lasts over an extended number of uses, such as appliances, automobiles, and stereo equipment. *Services* are defined as activities, benefits, or satisfactions offered for sale, such as marketing research, health care, and education. According to this classification government data indicate that the United States is becoming a service economy, which is the reason for a separate chapter (Chapter 12) on the topic.

This classification method also provides direction for marketing actions. For nondurable products like Wrigley's gum, inexpensive and purchased frequently, consumer advertising and wide distribution in retail outlets is essential. Durable products like cars, however, generally cost more than nondurable goods and last longer, so personal selling is an important marketing activity in answering consumer questions and concerns.

Services and New-Product Development   "New-product" development in services like buying a stock or airline ticket or watching TV occurs but, being intangible, is often difficult to observe step by step. Nevertheless, service innovations can have a huge impact on our lives. For example, online brokerage firms have revolutionized the financial services industry. And in mid-2001, Priceline.com Inc.—the name-your-own-price travel retailer—announced its first-ever profitable quarter, a stark contrast to the hundreds of failed dot-coms.[5] Impacting us even more will be Gemstar-TV Guide's interactive TV that by 2005 will enable you to use your TV to see the 500-channel listing, click on the Internet, buy products, or download the latest movie.[6]

CLASSIFYING CONSUMER AND BUSINESS GOODS

Because the buyer is the key to marketing, consumer and business product classifications are discussed in greater detail.

Classification of Consumer Goods

Convenience, shopping, specialty, and unsought products are the four types of consumer goods. They differ in terms of (1) effort the consumer spends on the decision, (2) attributes used in purchase, and (3) frequency of purchase. **Convenience goods** are items that the consumer purchases frequently, conveniently, and with a minimum of shopping effort. **Shopping goods** are items for which the consumer compares several alternatives on criteria, such as price, quality, or style. **Specialty goods** are items, such as Tiffany sterling silver, that a consumer makes a special effort to search out and buy. **Unsought goods** are items that the consumer either does not know about or knows about but does not initially want. Figure 10–1 shows how the classification of a consumer product into one of these four types results in different aspects of the marketing mix being stressed. Different degrees of brand loyalty and amounts of shopping effort are displayed by the consumer for a product in each of the four classes.

TYPE OF CONSUMER GOOD

BASIS OF COMPARISON	CONVENIENCE	SHOPPING	SPECIALTY	UNSOUGHT
Product	Toothpaste, cake mix, handsoap, laundry detergent	Cameras, TVs, briefcases, clothing	Rolls Royce cars, Rolex watches	Burial insurance, thesaurus
Price	Relatively inexpensive	Fairly expensive	Usually very expensive	Varies
Place (distribution)	Widespread; many outlets	Large number of selective outlets	Very limited	Often limited
Promotion	Price, availability, and awareness stressed	Differentiation from competitors stressed	Uniqueness of brand and status stressed	Awareness is essential
Brand loyalty of consumers	Aware of brand, but will accept substitutes	Prefer specific brands, but will accept substitutes	Very brand loyal; will not accept substitutes	Will accept substitutes
Purchase behavior of consumers	Frequent purchases; little time and effort spent shopping	Infrequent purchases; needs much comparison shopping time	Infrequent purchases; needs extensive search and decision time	Very infrequent purchases; some comparison shopping

FIGURE 10–1
Classification of consumer goods

The manner in which a consumer good is classified depends on the individual. One person may view a camera as a shopping good and visit several stores before deciding on a brand, whereas a friend may view cameras as a specialty good and will only buy a Nikon.

Classification of Business Goods

A major characteristic of business goods is that their sales are often the result of *derived demand;* that is, sales of industrial products frequently result (or are derived) from the sale of consumer goods. For example, if consumer demand for Ford cars (a consumer product) increases, the company may increase its demand for paint spraying equipment (a business product). Business goods may be classified as production or support goods.

Production Goods
Items used in the manufacturing process that become part of the final product are **production goods**. These include raw materials such as grain or lumber, as well as component parts. For example, a company that manufactures door hinges used by GM in its car doors is producing a component part. As noted in Chapter 6, the marketing of production goods is based on factors such as price, quality, delivery, and service. Marketers of these products tend to sell directly to industrial users.

Support Goods
The second class of business goods is **support goods**, which are items used to assist in producing other goods and services. Support goods include installations, accessory equipment, supplies, and services.

- *Installations* consist of buildings and fixed equipment. Because a significant amount of capital is required to purchase installations, the industrial buyer deals directly with construction companies and manufacturers through sales representatives. The pricing of installations is often by competitive bidding.
- *Accessory equipment* includes tools and office equipment and is usually purchased in small-order sizes by buyers. As a result, instead of dealing directly with buyers, sellers of industrial accessories use distributors to contact a large number of buyers.
- *Supplies* are similar to consumer convenience goods and consist of products such as stationery, paper clips, and brooms. These are purchased with little effort, using the straight rebuy decision sequence discussed in Chapter 6. Price and delivery are key factors considered by the buyers of supplies.
- *Services* are intangible activities to assist the industrial buyer. This category can include maintenance and repair services and advisory services such as tax or legal counsel, where the seller's reputation is critical.

Concept Check

1. Explain the difference between product mix and product line.
2. What are the four main types of consumer goods?
3. To which type of good (business or consumer) does the term *derived demand* generally apply?

NEW PRODUCTS AND WHY THEY SUCCEED AND FAIL

New products are the lifeblood of a company and keep it growing, but the financial risks are large. Before discussing how new products reach the stage of commercialization when they are in the market, we'll begin by looking at *what* a new product is.

What Is a New Product?

The term *new* is difficult to define. Is Sony's PlayStation 2 *new* when there was a PlayStation 1? Is Microsoft's Xbox *new* when Microsoft hasn't been a big player in video games before? What does *new* mean for new-product marketing? Newness from several points of view and some marketing implications of this newness are discussed below.

Newness Compared with Existing Products   If a product is functionally different from existing products, it can be defined as new. Sometimes this newness is revolutionary and creates a whole new industry, as in the case of the Apple II computer. We often think that newness in terms of more features or advanced technology is automatically better for everyone in the market. But simpler can be better for many potential customers, as described later in the chapter. One surprise: Innovation research shows that firms using "disruptive innovation" and creating newness by simplifying the product are often *not* the industry leaders selling the more sophisticated high-end products with more features.[7]

Newness in Legal Terms   The U.S. Federal Trade Commission (FTC) advises that the term *new* be limited to use with a product up to six months after it enters regular distribution. The difficulty with this suggestion is in the interpretation of the term *regular distribution.*

As you read the discussion about what "new" means in new-product development, think about how it affects the marketing strategies of Sony and Microsoft in their *new* video-game launches.

Sony Corporation

www.sony.com

Microsoft Corporation

www.microsoft.com

Newness from the Company's Perspective   Successful companies are starting to view newness and innovation in their products at three levels. At the lowest level, which usually involves the least risk, is a product line extension. This is an incremental improvement of an existing product for the company, such as Frosted Cheerios or Diet Cherry Coke or Gillette Venus for Women—extensions of the basic Cheerios or Diet Coke or men's Gillette Mach 3 product lines, respectively. At the next level is a significant jump in the innovation or technology, such as Sony's leap from the micro tape recorder to the Walkman. The third level is true innovation, a truly revolutionary new product, like the first Apple computer in 1976. Effective new product programs in large firms deal at all three levels.

Newness from the Consumer's Perspective   A fourth way to define new products is in terms of their effects on consumption. This approach classifies new products according to the degree of learning required by the consumer, as shown in Figure 10–2.

With *continuous innovation,* no new behaviors must be learned. Samsung's ad on the next page communicates the message that its stylish cell phone with several functions is easy to use. Clearly, Samsung is marketing a user-friendly cell phone, but a continuous innovation *not* requiring new learned behaviors. Under these conditions, the beauty of this innovation is that effective marketing simply depends on generating awareness and having strong distribution in appropriate outlets, not completely reeducating customers.

With *dynamically continuous innovation,* only minor changes in behavior are required for use. An example is built-in, fold-down child seats such as those available in Chrysler minivans. Built-in car seats for children require only minor bits of education and changes in behavior, so the marketing strategy is to educate prospective buyers on their benefits, advantages, and proper use.

A *discontinuous innovation* involves making the consumer learn entirely new consumption patterns in order to use the product. After decades of research, IBM

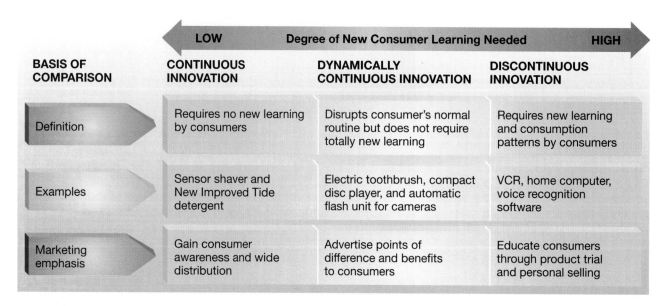

	LOW ← Degree of New Consumer Learning Needed → HIGH		
BASIS OF COMPARISON	**CONTINUOUS INNOVATION**	**DYNAMICALLY CONTINUOUS INNOVATION**	**DISCONTINUOUS INNOVATION**
Definition	Requires no new learning by consumers	Disrupts consumer's normal routine but does not require totally new learning	Requires new learning and consumption patterns by consumers
Examples	Sensor shaver and New Improved Tide detergent	Electric toothbrush, compact disc player, and automatic flash unit for cameras	VCR, home computer, voice recognition software
Marketing emphasis	Gain consumer awareness and wide distribution	Advertise points of difference and benefits to consumers	Educate consumers through product trial and personal selling

FIGURE 10–2
Consumption effects define newness

With Samsung's continuous-innovation cell phone, no new behaviors need to be learned.

introduced its ViaVoice speech recognition software. If you are using ViaVoice early in the twenty-first century, you are to speak to your computer and watch your own words appear on your computer screen, and you also can open Windows programs with your voice. The risk that IBM faced in introducing this discontinuous innovation was that you had to learn new behaviors in producing your word-processed memos and reports. Hence, marketing efforts for discontinuous innovations involve not only gaining initial consumer awareness but also educating consumers on both the benefits and proper use of the innovative product, activities that can cost millions of dollars.

Why Products Succeed and Fail

We all know the giant product successes—such as Microsoft Windows, Swatch watches, CNN. Yet the thousands of failures every year that slide quietly into oblivion cost American businesses billions of dollars. Recent research suggests that it takes about 3,000 raw unwritten ideas to produce a single commercially successful new product.[8] To learn marketing lessons and convert potential failures to successes, we can analyze why new products fail and then study several failures in detail. As we go through the new-product process later in the chapter, we can identify ways such failures might have been avoided—admitting that hindsight is clearer than foresight.

Marketing Reasons for New-Product Failures   Both marketing and nonmarketing factors contribute to new-product failures, as shown in the accompanying Marketing NewsNet. Using the research results from several studies[9] on new-product success and failure and also those described in the Marketing NewsNet, we can identify critical marketing factors—sometimes overlapping—that often separate new-product winners and losers:

MARKETING NEWSNET

What Separates New-Product Winners and Losers

CUSTOMER VALUE

What makes some products winners and others losers? Knowing this answer is a key to a new-product strategy. R. G. Cooper and E. J. Kleinschmidt studied 203 new industrial products to find the answers shown below.

The researchers defined the "product success rate" of new products as the percentage of products that reached the company's own profitability criteria. Product "winners" are the best 20 percent of performers and "losers" are the worst 20 percent. For example, for the first factor in the table below, 98 percent of the winners had a major point of difference compared with only 18 percent of the losers.

Note that the table below includes both marketing and nonmarketing factors. Most of the marketing factors tie directly to the reasons cited in the text for new-product failures that are taken from a number of research studies.

FACTOR AFFECTING PRODUCT SUCCESS RATE	PRODUCT "WINNERS" (BEST 20%)	PRODUCT "LOSERS" (WORST 20%)	% DIFFERENCE (WINNERS–LOSERS)
• Point of difference, or uniquely superior product	98%	18%	80%
• Well-defined product before actual development starts	85	26	59
• Synergy, or fit, with firm's R&D and manufacturing capabilities	80	29	51
• Quality of execution of technological activities	76	30	46
• Quality of execution of activities before actual development starts	75	31	44
• Synergy, or fit, with marketing mix activities	71	31	40
• Quality of execution of marketing mix activities	71	32	39
• Market attractiveness, ones with large markets, high growth	74	43	31

1. *Insignificant "point of difference."* Shown as the most important factor in the Marketing NewsNet, a distinctive "point of difference" is essential for a new product to defeat competitive ones—through having superior characteristics that deliver unique benefits to the user. In the mid-1990s General Mills introduced "Fingos," a sweetened cereal flake about the size of a corn chip. Consumers were supposed to snack on them dry, but they didn't.[10] The point of difference was not important enough to get consumers to give up eating competing snacks such as popcorn, potato chips, or Cheerios from the box late at night.

2. *Incomplete market and product definition before product development starts.* Ideally, a new product needs a precise **protocol**, a statement that, before product development begins, identifies (1) a well-defined target market; (2) specific customers' needs, wants, and preferences; and (3) what the product will be and do. Without this precision, loads of money disappear as research and development (R&D) tries to design a vague product for a phantom market. Apple

New product success or
failure? For the special
problems these products
face, see the text.

Computer's hand-sized Newton computer that intended to help keep the user organized fizzled badly because no clear protocol existed.

3. *Too little market attractiveness.* Market attractiveness refers to the ideal situation every new-product manager looks for: a large target market with high growth and real buyer need. But often, when looking for ideal market niches, the target market is too small and competitive to warrant the R&D, production, and marketing expenses necessary to reach it. In the early 1990s Kodak discontinued its Ultralife lithium battery with its 10-year shelf life, although the battery was touted as lasting twice as long as an alkaline battery. Yet the product was only available in the 9-volt size, which accounted for less than 10 percent of the U.S. battery market.

4. *Poor execution of the marketing mix: name, package, price, promotion, distribution.* Coca-Cola thought its Minute Maid Squeeze-Fresh frozen orange juice concentrate in a squeeze bottle was a hit. The idea was that consumers could make one glass of juice at a time, and the concentrate stayed fresh in the refrigerator for over a month. After two test markets, the product was finished. Consumers loved the idea, but the product was messy to use, and the advertising and packaging didn't educate them effectively on how much concentrate to mix.

5. *Poor product quality or sensitivity to customer needs on critical factors.* Overlapping somewhat with point 1, this factor stresses that problems on one or two critical factors can kill the product, even though the general quality is high. For example, the Japanese, like the British, drive on the left side of the road. Until 1996 U.S. carmakers sent Japan few right-drive cars—unlike German carmakers who exported right-drive models in a number of their brands.[11] As described in the Marketing NewsNet "When Less Is More," sometimes large markets can be served by taking features out of a product and actually making it simpler.

6. *Bad timing.* The product is introduced too soon, too late, or at a time when consumer tastes are shifting dramatically. Bad timing gives new-product managers nightmares. IBM, for example, killed several laptop computer prototypes because competitors introduced better, more advanced machines to the marketplace before IBM could get there.

7. *No economical access to buyers.* Grocery products provide an example. Today's mega-supermarkets carry 30,000 different SKUs. With about 34 new food products introduced each day, the fight for exposure is tremendous in terms of

MARKETING NEWSNET

When Less Is More: How Reducing the Number of Features Can Open Up Huge Markets

TECHNOLOGY & E-COMMERCE

New products! To invent them the natural thing is to add more features, new technologies, more glitz. Many new product successes in the chapter do just that.

But huge new markets can open up in moving to the opposite direction by taking features away and simplifying the product. "Less-is-more" building design introduced in the United States by Mies van der Rohe in the 1930s revolutionized American architecture. Here are some "less-is-more" new product breakthroughs that revolutionized national or global markets:

1. Canon's tabletop copiers. Canon found it couldn't sell its little copiers to big companies, which were happy with their large Xerox machines. So Canon sold its little machines to little companies with limited copying needs by the zillions.

2. Palm Computing's PalmPilot PDA. Apple Computer's Newton personal digital assistant (PDA) seemed like a great idea but users found it too complicated. Enter: PalmPilot inventors Donna Dubinsky and Jeff Hawkins who deleted features to achieve the market breakthrough.

3. Intuit's QuickBooks accounting software. Competitors offered complex accounting software containing every feature professional accountants might possibly want. Intuit then introduced QuickBooks, a smaller, cheaper program with less functionality that won 70 percent of the huge market for small-business accounting software within two years.

4. Swatch watches. In 1983 a slim plastic watch with only 51 components appeared on the global market. That simplicity—plus top quality, affordable price, and creative designs—is the reason that by 2001 more than 250 million Swatch watches had been sold.

Sometimes much less is much, much more!

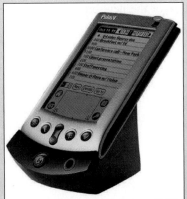

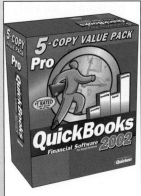

costs for advertising, distribution, and shelf space.[12] Because shelf space is judged in terms of sales per square foot, Thirsty Dog! (a zesty beef-flavored, vitamin-enriched, mineral-loaded, lightly carbonated bottled water for your dog) must displace an existing product on the supermarket shelves, a difficult task with the precise measures of revenues per square foot these stores use.

A Look at Some Failures   Before reading further and trying to remember a lesson from Chapter 1, study the product failures described in Figure 10–3. Then try to identify which of the seven reasons listed in the text is the most likely explanation for their failure. The two examples are discussed in greater detail below.

Kimberly Clark's Avert Virucidal tissues lasted 10 months in test market in upstate New York before being pulled from the shelves. People didn't believe the claims and were frightened by the "-cidal" in the name—that they connected to events like "suicidal." So the tissue probably failed because of not having a clear point of difference and a bad name, and, hence, bad marketing mix execution—probably reasons 1 and 4 in the list in the text.

FIGURE 10-3
Why did these new products
fail?

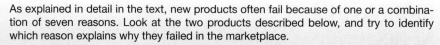

As explained in detail in the text, new products often fail because of one or a combination of seven reasons. Look at the two products described below, and try to identify which reason explains why they failed in the marketplace.

- Kimberly Clark's "Avert Virucidal" tissues that contained vitamin C derivatives scientifically designed to kill cold and flu germs when users sneezed, coughed, or blew their nose into them.

- OUT! International's Hey! There's A Monster In My Room spray that was designed to rid scary creatures from kids' rooms and had a bubble-gum fragrance.

Compare your insights with those in the text.

OUT! International's Hey! There's A Monster In My Room spray was creative and cute when introduced in 1993. But the name probably kept the kids awake at night more than their fear of the monsters because it suggested the monster was still hiding in the room. Question: Wouldn't calling it the "Monster-Buster Spray"—the secondary name shown at the bottom of the package—have licked the name problem? It looks like the spray was never really defined well in a protocol (reason 2) and definitely had poor name execution (reason 4).

Simple marketing research on consumers should have revealed the problems. Developing successful new products may sometimes involve luck, but more often it involves having a product that really meets a need and has significant points of difference over competitive products. The likelihood of success is improved by paying attention to the early steps of the new-product process described in the next section of the text.

Concept Check

1. From a consumer's viewpoint, what kind of innovation would an improved electric toothbrush be?

2. What does "insignificant point of difference" mean as a reason for new-product failure?

THE NEW-PRODUCT PROCESS

Companies such as General Electric, Sony, and Procter & Gamble take a sequence of steps before their products are ready for market. Figure 10–4 shows the seven stages of the **new-product process**, the sequence of activities a firm uses to identify business opportunities and convert them to a salable good or service. This sequence begins with new-product strategy development and ends with commercialization.

New-Product Strategy Development

For companies, **new-product strategy development** involves defining the role for a new product in terms of the firm's overall corporate objectives. This step in the new-product process has been added by many companies recently to provide a needed focus for ideas and concepts developed in later stages.

Objectives of the Stage: Identify Markets and Strategic Roles   During this new-product strategy development stage the company uses the environmental scanning process described in Chapter 3 to identify trends that pose either opportunities or threats. Relevant company strengths and weaknesses are also identified. The outcome of new-product strategy development is not only new-product ideas but identifying markets for which new products will be developed and strategic roles new products might serve—the vital protocol activity explained earlier in the discussion of the Marketing NewsNet on new-product winners and losers.

3M: Cross-Functional Teams, Six Sigma, and Lead Users

Key to 3M's success in new-product development is its use of *cross-functional teams,* a small number of people from different departments in an organization who are mutually accountable to a common set of performance goals. Today in 3M, teams are especially important in new-product development so that individuals from R&D, marketing, sales, manufacturing, and finance can simultaneously search in a constructive environment for new-product and market opportunities. In the past 3M and other firms often utilized these department people in sequence—possibly resulting in R&D designing new products that the manufacturing department couldn't produce economically and that the marketing department couldn't sell.

Important today in 3M's cross-functional teams is **Six Sigma**, a means to "delight the customer" by achieving quality through a highly disciplined process to focus on developing and delivering near-perfect products and services. "Near perfect" here means being 99.9997 percent perfect or allowing 3.4 defects per million products produced or transactions processed—getting as close as possible to "zero defects." Six Sigma's success lies in determining what variables impact the results, measuring them, and making decisions based on data, not gut feelings.[13]

In the late-1990s 3M became concerned that its new-product development too often involved making incremental improvements to existing lines. Innovation research shows that many revolutionary product breakthroughs are prototyped by "lead users"—*not* the manufacturers actually providing and selling the product. Lead users are companies, organizations, or individuals that have needs going far beyond normal user needs, so that they may have come up with innovations on their own. By putting cross-functional teams into contact with these lead users, the approach has resulted in several dozen new-product concepts for 3M.[14]

Idea Generation

Developing a pool of concepts as candidates for new products, or **idea generation**, must build on the previous stage's results. New-product ideas are generated by consumers, employees, basic R&D, and competitors.

Customer and Supplier Suggestions

Companies often analyze consumer complaints or supplier ideas to discover new-product opportunities. Listening to growing concerns about cholesterol and fat in its food, McDonald's reformulated its shakes

FIGURE 10–4
Stages in the new-product process

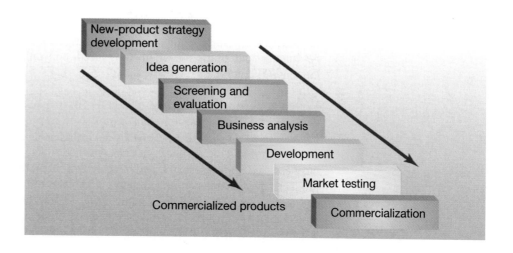

See the text for the unusual source of the new-product idea for Polaroid's very successful I-Zone Instant Pocket camera.

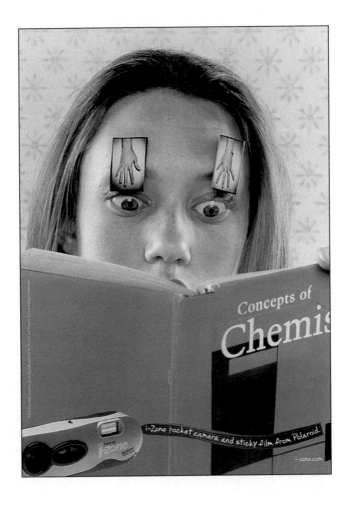

with a low-fat mixture and introduced a low-fat hamburger. Whirlpool, trying to reduce costs by cutting the number of different product platforms in half, got ideas on ways to standardize components.[15]

Employee and Co-Worker Suggestions   Employees may be encouraged to suggest new-product ideas through suggestion boxes or contests. The idea for Nature Valley Granola Bars from General Mills came when one of its marketing managers observed co-workers bringing granola to work in plastic bags.

In 1997 a Polaroid employee in Tokyo saw a group of teenage girls crammed into a photo booth that took instant minipictures. Over objections from many company scientists, this idea became the $25 Polaroid I-Zone Instant Pocket camera, the number 1 selling camera in the United States in early 2000, only four months after introduction. Its small photos are good enough for high schoolers, the original target market, and adults for whom fun, speed, convenience, and reasonable price are key buying criteria.[16]

Research and Development Breakthroughs   Another source of new products is a firm's basic research, but the costs can be huge. As described in the Marketing NewsNet, Sony is the acknowledged world leader in new-product development in electronics. Its scientists and engineers produce an average of four new products each business day. Sony's research and development breakthroughs have led to innovative products, and its ability to manufacture and market those products has made it a legend in the electronics industry, popularizing VCRs, the Walkman, and—coming into your future?—flat-panel Organic Electroluminescence (OEL) monitors about the thickness of a credit card providing brighter images on large, 30-inch screens.

MARKETING NEWSNET

The World's Consumer Electronics Champ: and Its Name Is . . . ?

TECHNOLOGY & E-COMMERCE

The "battle for the living room" begins this company's twenty-first century. To win, it will have to keep linking its cool digital hardware technology, design, and entertainment content. With over $63 billion in global sales for 2000, it was voted one of America's "most respected brands" and known—along with Coke, Nike, and MTV—as one of the four most creative companies in the world. What is this firm, whose first product was a rice cooker launched shortly after its founding in 1946? Yes, it's Sony!

This Japan-based company with operations around the globe made the first transistor radio (1955) and television (1960), Walkman (1979), CD player (1982), and PlayStation video console (1995). And Sony innovation continues, from its DVD video player (1998), Clié hand-held PDA (2000), and flat-panel Organic Electroluminescence (OEL) monitors and TVs that are a little thicker than a credit card but have brighter images on the screen (2003).

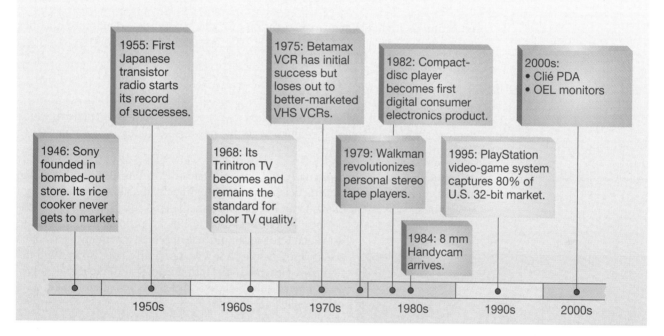

Not all R&D labs have Sony's genius for moving electronic breakthroughs into the marketplace. Take Xerox Corporation's Palo Alto Research Center (PARC). In maybe the greatest electronic fumble of all time, by 1979 PARC had what's in your computer system now—graphical user interfaces, mice, windows and pull-down menus, laser printers, and distributed computing. Concerned with aggressive competition from Japan in its core photocopier business, Xerox didn't even bother to patent these breakthroughs. Apple Computer's Steven Jobs visited PARC in 1979, adapted many of the ideas for the Macintosh, and the rest is history.[17]

Professional R&D laboratories also provide new-product ideas. Labs at Arthur D. Little helped put the crunch in Cap'n Crunch cereal and the flavor in Carnation Instant Breakfast. As described in the Web Link, IDEO is a world-class new-product development firm, having designed more than 4,000 of them. These range from the Apple mouse and Heartstream portable defibrillator to Crest's neat squeeze toothpaste dispenser and Nike's all-terrain sunglasses.

Competitive Products   New-product ideas can also be found by analyzing the competition. A six-person intelligence team from the Marriott Corporation spent six months traveling around the country staying at economy hotels. The team assessed the

WEB LINK

IDEO—"Where Design Is Not a Noun–It's a Verb"

The Apple mouse. The Handspring Visor Edge PDA. The Crest Neat Squeeze toothpaste dispenser. The Specialized Wedlock bike lock. These are just some of the over 4,000 new products designed by a firm you've probably never heard of but benefit from everyday. For David Kelley, co-founder of IDEO, product design includes both artistic and functional design elements. And to foster this creativity, IDEO allows its designers and engineers much freedom— its offices look like schoolrooms, employees can hang their bicycles from the ceiling, there are rubber band fights, and on Monday mornings, there are "show-and-tell" sessions.

Visit IDEO's website (www.ideo.com/client.htm) to view its recent inventions and innovations for clients such as Pepsi's Twist 'n Go 32-ounce cup, SoftBook's electronic book reader, and Nike's all-terrain sunglasses.

competition's strengths and weaknesses on everything from the soundproof qualities of the rooms to the softness of the towels. Marriott then budgeted $500 million for a new economy hotel chain, Fairfield Inns.

Screening and Evaluation

The third stage of the new product process is **screening and evaluation**, which involves internal and external evaluations of the new-product ideas to eliminate those that warrant no further effort.

Internal Approach   Internally, the firm evaluates the technical feasibility of the proposal and whether the idea meets the objectives defined in the new-product strategy development step. In the 1990s Penn Racquet Sports, the largest U.S. producer of tennis balls, faced flat sales because of a decade-long lull in recreational tennis. What to do? Penn Racquet employees observed that many used tennis balls were given as a toy to the family dog. So in 1998 the company designed and introduced R. P. Fetchem—a dye-free "natural felt fetch toy" that looks remarkably like . . . a tennis ball![18]

A year's worth of consumer interviews went into the development of Sun Chips.

External Approach Concept tests are external evaluations that consist of preliminary testing of the new-product idea (rather than the actual product) with consumers. Concept tests usually rely on written descriptions of the product but may be augmented with sketches, mockups, or promotional literature. Several key questions are asked during concept testing: How does the customer perceive the product? Who would use it? How would it be used?

Frito-Lay spent a year interviewing 10,000 consumers about the concept of a multigrain snack chip. The company experimented with 50 different shapes before settling on a thin, rectangular chip with ridges and a slightly salty, nutty flavor. The product, Sun Chips, is highly successful.

Concept Check

1. What step in the new-product process has been added in recent years?

2. What are four sources of new-product ideas?

3. What is the difference between internal and external screening and evaluation approaches used by a firm in the new-product process?

To learn how University of Texas students contributed their wisdom (teeth) to Merck's very successful Vioxx arthritis and pain drug, see the text.

Business Analysis

Business analysis involves specifying the features of the product and the marketing strategy needed to commercialize it and making necessary financial projections. This is the last checkpoint before significant capital is invested in creating a prototype of the product. Economic analysis, marketing strategy review, and legal examination of the proposed product are conducted at this stage. It is at this point that the product is analyzed relative to the firm's marketing and technological synergies, two criteria noted in the Marketing NewsNet shown earlier in the chapter.

The marketing strategy review studies the new-product idea in relation to the marketing program to support it. The proposed product is assessed to determine whether it will help or hurt sales of existing products. Likewise, the product is examined to assess whether it can be sold through existing channels or if new outlets will be needed. Profit projections involve estimating the number of units expected to be sold but also the costs of R&D, production, and marketing.

As an important aspect of the business analysis, the proposed new product is studied to determine whether it can be protected with a patent or copyright. An attractive new-product proposal is one in which the technology, product, or brand cannot easily be copied. All of these critical business issues emerged in Merck's huge research and development gamble on its Vioxx drug for arthritis sufferers, discussed in the next section.

Development

Product ideas that survive the business analysis proceed to actual **development**, turning the idea on paper into a prototype. This results in a demonstrable, producible product in hand. Outsiders seldom understand the technical complexities of the development stage, which involves not only manufacturing the product but also performing laboratory and consumer tests to ensure that it meets the standards set. Design of the product becomes an important element.

Some new products can be so important and costly that the company is literally betting its very existence on success. And creative, out-of-the-box thinking can be critical. In the pharmaceutical industry no more than one out of every 5,000 to 10,000 new compounds developed in the labs emerges as an approved drug.[19]

Talking to a Merck colleague at a medical convention, Dr. Peppi Prosit discovered that the colleague's lab had made a breakthrough and developed a test to determine if a painkiller drug was less likely to cause the upset stomach that is a bad side effect of most pain and arthritis medicines. Moments later he saw a poster display from a Japanese researcher claiming to have developed just such a painkiller, but one not yet fit for humans. His challenge: Build a similar pain and arthritis drug for people that could pass Merck's new lab test.

Dr. Prosit's team cooked up hundreds of compounds costing tens of millions of dollars. The two best were sent to an Austin, Texas, oral surgeon who yanks the wisdom teeth of University of Texas students, hands them a pain pill, and puts them into a dorm attached to his clinic to measure their suffering. One of the two Merck compounds had outstanding "minimum-suffering results" among the students.

Merck's cross-functional team of marketing, manufacturing, and research people cut five weeks off the normal market-launch cycle for the drug—now branded "Vioxx." In a remarkable feat, Vioxx was stocked in 40,000 pharmacies within 11 days of receiving U.S. Food and Drug Administration approval. The result: A spectacular success and continuing research to develop a better, second-generation Vioxx. Top management at Merck has said that if Vioxx had failed, Merck might have been forced to merge with another pharmaceutical firm.[20]

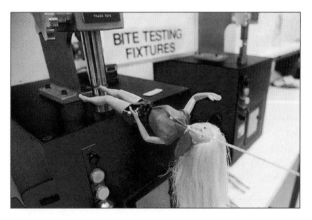

Merck's Vioxx drug prototype went through exhaustive lab and clinical tests to see if it met design criteria set for it if used the way it is intended. But safety tests are also critical for when the product isn't used as planned. To make sure seven-year-olds can't bite Barbie's head off and choke, Mattel clamps her foot in steel jaws in a test stand and then pulls on her head with a wire. Similarly, car manufacturers have done extensive safety tests by crashing their cars into concrete walls. As mentioned in the Ethics and Social Responsibility Alert box, consumer groups are increasingly concerned about what happens when a pickup truck or sport utility vehicle hits a small car when their bumpers don't line up.[21] Auto industry tests are identifying some feasible, but costly, solutions.

Market Testing

The **market testing** stage of the new-product process involves exposing actual products to prospective consumers under realistic purchase conditions to see if they will buy. Often a product is developed, tested, refined, and then tested again to get consumer reactions through either test marketing or simulated test markets.

Test Marketing   Test marketing involves offering a product for sale on a limited basis in a defined area. This test is done to determine whether consumers will actually buy the product and to try different ways of marketing it. Only about a third of the products test marketed do well enough to go on to the next phase. These market tests are usually conducted in cities that are viewed as being representative of U.S. consumers like the six shown in Figure 10–5. Of these cities, Wichita Falls,

ETHICS AND SOCIAL RESPONSIBILITY ALERT

SUVs versus Cars: Godzilla Meets a Chimp?

ETHICS

Make car wrecks safe. Sound silly? But . . . the problem is death! The high and heavy pickups, vans, and sport utility vehicles (SUVs) are now involved in nearly 20 percent of all U.S. highway deaths. When one huge vehicle meets a compact car, the larger, higher one, which weighs in about a ton more than a compact car, smashes the smaller one's passenger compartment, instead of going head-to-head at bumper level. The people in the car become 81 percent of the deaths in these accidents.

The problem is also money. These mega-vehicles now account for nearly 50 percent of Detroit's sales and most of its profits. Improving the cars—with side air bags and steel supports—is cheaper than lowering the frame or adding a crumple zone for the frame of the bigger vehicle. Nothing is easy.

Change may have to come from National Highway & Transportation Safety Administration mandates, which point to the complete redesign of Mercedes Benz's M-class SUV as the model for what should be done by having its SUV frame and bumper as much as 9 inches lower than Detroit's SUVs. This makes the bumpers of Mercedes SUVs and those of small cars more likely to meet in a crash, dramatically increasing the safety for small-car passengers.

Who should address the problem here? The National Highway & Transportation Safety Administration? The insurance companies? The vehicle manufacturers? Consumers?

To see how your vehicle measures up on various crash tests, go to the website of the Insurance Institute of Highway Safety (www.hwysafety.org) and click on "Vehicle Ratings."

Texas, most closely matches the U.S. average found in the 2000 Census. Other criteria used in selecting test market cities are brand purchase patterns resembling the U.S. average, small towns far enough from big markets to allow low-cost advertising purchases, cable systems to deliver different ads to different homes, and tracking systems like those of AC Nielsen to measure sales resulting from different advertising campaigns.[22]

This gives the company an indication of potential sales volume and market share in the test area. Market tests are also used to check other elements of the marketing mix besides the product itself such as price, level of advertising support, and distribution. These market tests also are time consuming and expensive because production lines as well as promotion and sales programs must be set up. Costs can run several million dollars. Market tests also reveal plans to competitors, sometimes enabling them to get a product into national distribution first. Competitors can also

FIGURE 10–5

Six important U.S. test markets and the "demographics winner"—Wichita Falls, Texas, Metropolitan Statistical Area (MSA)

Grand Junction, CO
Cedar Rapids, IA   Eau Claire, WI
Pittsfield, MA
Odessa-Midland, TX
Wichita Falls, TX

Demographic Characteristic	USA	Wichita Falls, TX
2000 population	281.4 mil.	140,518
Median age (years)	35.3	33.6
% of family households with children under 18	32.8%	33.8%
% Hispanic or Latino of any race	12.5%	11.8%
% African-American	12.3%	9.6%
% Asian-American	3.6%	1.7%
% Native-American	1.5%	1.7%

try to sabotage test markets. With such problems, some firms skip test markets completely or use simulated test markets.

Simulated Test Markets   Because of the time, cost, and confidentiality problems of test markets, consumer packaged goods companies often turn to *simulated* (or *laboratory*) *test markets* (*STM*), a technique that simulates a full-scale test market but in a limited fashion. STMs are often run in shopping malls, where consumers are questioned to identify who uses the product class being tested. Willing participants are questioned on usage, reasons for purchase, and important product attributes. Qualified persons are then shown TV commercials or print ads for the test product along with competitors' advertising and are given money to make a decision to buy or not buy a package of the product (or the competitors') from a real or simulated store environment. STMs are used early in the development process to screen new-product ideas and later in the process to make sales projections.

When Test Markets Don't Work   Test marketing is a valuable step in the new-product process, but not all products can use it. Testing a service beyond the concept level is very difficult because the service is intangible and consumers can't see what they are buying. Similarly, test markets for expensive consumer products such as cars or VCRs or costly industrial products such as jet engines or computers are impractical. For these products consumer reactions to mockup designs or one-of-a-kind prototypes are all that is feasible. Carmakers test new style designs on "early adopters" (discussed in Chapter 11) who are more willing than the average customer to buy new designs or products.[23]

Commercialization

Finally, the product is brought to the point of **commercialization**—positioning and launching it in full-scale production and sales. Companies proceed very carefully at the commercialization stage because this is the most expensive stage for most new products, especially consumer products.

Figure 10–6 identifies the purpose of each stage of the new-product process and the kinds of marketing information and methods used. The figure also suggests information that might help avoid some new-product failures. Although using the new-product process does not guarantee successful products, it does increase a firm's success rate.

Burger King's French Fries: The Complexities of Commercialization   Burger King's "improved french fries" are an example of what can go wrong at the commercialization stage. In the fast-food industry, McDonald's french fries are the "gold standard" against which all other fries are measured. In 1996 Burger King decided to take on McDonald's fries and spent millions of R&D dollars developing a starch-coated fry designed to retain heat longer and "add crunch."

In Burger King's 19-page french fry specifications, one requirement astounded even veteran food scientists: Crispiness was to be determined "by an audible crunch that should be present for seven or more chews . . . loud enough to be apparent to the evaluator." A 100-person team set to work and developed the starch-coated fry that beat McDonald's fries in taste tests, 57 percent to 35 percent, with 8 percent no opinion. After "certifrying" 300,000 managers and employees on the new frying procedures, the fries were launched in early 1998 with a $70 million marketing budget. The launch turned to disaster. The reason: The new fry proved too complicated to get right day after day in Burger King restaurants, except under ideal conditions.[24]

Commercializing a new french fry: To learn how Burger King's "audible crunches" confronted McDonald's fries, see the text.

STAGE OF PROCESS	PURPOSE OF STAGE	MARKETING INFORMATION AND METHODS USED
New-product strategy development	Identify new-product niches to reach in light of company objectives	Company objectives; assessment of firm's current strengths and weaknesses in terms of market and product
Idea generation	Develop concepts for possible products	Ideas from employees and co-workers, consumers, R&D, and competitors; methods of brainstorming and focus groups
Screening and evaluation	Separate good product ideas from bad ones inexpensively	Screening criteria, concept tests, and weighted point systems
Business analysis	Identify the product's features and its marketing strategy, and make financial projections	Product's key features, anticipated marketing mix strategy; economic, marketing, production, legal, and profitability analyses
Development	Create the prototype product, and test it in the laboratory and on consumers	Laboratory and consumer tests on product prototypes
Market testing	Test product and marketing strategy in the marketplace on a limited scale	Test markets, simulated test markets (STMs)
Commercialization	Position and offer product in the marketplace	Perceptual maps, product positioning, regional rollouts

FIGURE 10–6
Marketing information and methods used in the new-product process

By summer 2000 Burger King realized something had to be done. Solution: Launch a "new," coated fry in early 2001—not requiring "seven audible crunches." A commercialization stage success? You be the judge.

The Risks and Uncertainties of the Commercialization Stage

As the Burger King french fries show, the job is far from over when the new product gets to the commercialization stage. If the firm moves quickly, sometimes a potential commercialization stage disaster can be averted, as with Coca-Cola's decision to reintroduce old Coke three months after New Coke was launched in 1985. In spite of brilliant technologies, the hundreds of dot-com failures in 2000 and 2001 show the difficulty of launching successful new products.

Grocery products pose special commercialization problems. Because shelf space is so limited, many supermarkets require a **slotting fee** for new products, a payment a manufacturer makes to place a new item on a retailer's shelf. This can run to several million dollars for a single product. But there's even another potential expense. If a new grocery product does not achieve a predetermined sales target, some retailers require a **failure fee**, a penalty payment by a manufacturer to compensate the retailer for sales its valuable shelf space never made. To minimize the financial risk of a new-product failure, many grocery product manufacturers use *regional rollouts,* introducing the product sequentially into geographical areas of

the United States to allow production levels and marketing activities to build up gradually.

Speed as a Factor in New-Product Success   In recent years, companies have discovered that speed or "time to market" (TtM) is often vital in introducing a new product. Recent studies have shown that high-tech products coming to market on time are far more profitable than those arriving late. So some companies—such as Sony, Honda, AT&T, and Hewlett-Packard—have overlapped the sequence of stages described in this chapter. With this approach, termed *parallel development,* cross-functional team members who conduct the simultaneous development of both the product and the production process stay with the product from conception to production. This has enabled Hewlett-Packard to reduce the development time for computer printers from 54 months to 22. In software development, *fast prototyping* uses a "do it, try it, fix it" approach—encouraging continuing improvements even after the initial design.

Effective cross-functional teams at Hewlett-Packard have reduced new-product development times significantly.

Concept Check

1. How does the development stage of the new-product process involve testing the product inside and outside the firm?

2. What is a test market?

3. What is commercialization of a new product?

SUMMARY

1   A product is a good, service, or idea consisting of a bundle of tangible and intangible attributes that satisfies consumers and is received in exchange for money or some other unit of value. A company's product decisions involve the product item, product line, and range of its product mix.

2   Products can be classified by user and tangibility. By user, the major distinctions are consumer or business goods. Consumer goods consist of convenience, shopping, and specialty products. Business goods are for either production or support. By degree of tangibility, products divide into nondurable goods, durable goods, and services.

3   There are several ways to define a new product, such as the degree of distinction from existing products, a time base specified by the FTC, a company perspective, or effect on a consumer's usage pattern.

4   In terms of its effect on a consumer's use of a product, a discontinuous innovation represents the greatest change and a continuous innovation the least. A dynamically continuous innovation is disruptive but not totally new.

5   The failure of a new product is usually attributable to one of seven marketing reasons: insignificant point of difference, incomplete market and product definition before product development begins, too little market attractiveness, poor execution of the marketing mix, poor product quality on critical factors, bad timing, and no economical access to buyers.

6   The new-product process consists of seven stages. Objectives for new products are determined in the first stage, new-product strategy development; this is followed by idea generation, screening and evaluation, business analysis, development, market testing, and commercialization.

7   Ideas for new products come from several sources, including consumers, employees, R&D laboratories, and competitors.

8   Screening and evaluation can be done internally or externally.

9   Business analysis involves defining the features of the new product, a marketing strategy to introduce it, and a financial forecast.

10   Development involves not only producing a prototype product but also testing it in the lab and on consumers to see that it meets the standards set for it.

11   In market testing new products, companies often rely on market tests to see that consumers will actually buy the product when it's offered for sale and that other marketing mix factors are working. Products surviving this stage are commercialized—taken to market.

KEY TERMS AND CONCEPTS

APPLYING MARKETING CONCEPTS AND PERSPECTIVES

1 Products can be classified as either consumer or business goods. How would you classify the following products: (*a*) Johnson's baby shampoo, (*b*) a Black & Decker two-speed drill, and (*c*) an arc welder?

2 Are products such as Nature Valley Granola bars and Eddie Bauer hiking boots convenience, shopping, specialty, or unsought goods?

3 Based on your answer to problem 2, how would the marketing actions differ for each product and the classification to which you assigned it?

4 In terms of the behavioral effect on consumers, how would a PC, such as a Macintosh PowerBook or an IBM ThinkPad, be classified? In light of this classification, what actions would you suggest to the manufacturers of these products to increase their sales in the market?

5 Several alternative definitions were presented for a new product. How would a company's marketing strategy be affected if it used (*a*) the legal definition or (*b*) a behavioral definition?

6 What methods would you suggest to assess the potential commercial success for the following new products: (*a*) a new, improved ketchup, (*b*) a three-dimensional television system that took the company 10 years to develop, and (*c*) a new children's toy on which the company holds a patent?

7 Concept testing is an important step in the new-product process. Outline the concept tests for (*a*) an electrically powered car and (*b*) a new loan payment system for automobiles that is based on a variable interest rate. What are the differences in developing concept tests for products as opposed to services?

INTERNET EXERCISE

Jalapeño soda? Aerosol mustard? Fingos? These are just three of the more than 65,000 products (both successes and failures) on the shelves of the NewProductWorks Showcase in Ann Arbor, Michigan. The Showcase includes food, beverages, health and beauty care, household, and pet products appearing from 1965 to the present. Although you probably can't personally visit the company, you can visit its new website (www.newproductworks. com). Study the "Hits and Misses" categories (www. newproductworks.com/resources/resources_hm_index. html), such as "This Month's Picks," which are new products that have the potential for success; "We Expect Them to Be Successes," which are those that probably will be commercial successes; "Jury Is Out," products whose future is in doubt; "Failures," which are recent

products that have failed miserably; and "Favorite Failures," which are those that cause people to ask *"What were they thinking?"* Study several of the failed products listed on the website and try to identify the reasons discussed earlier in the chapter that may have led to their failure. Contrast these failed products with those that are deemed successes to learn why they became "sure-fire winners!"

VIDEO CASE 10–1   Palm Inc.: Developing Competitive New Products

Developing new products often requires a complicated and challenging sequence of activities. "It's not as simple as taking what the customer wants and creating a product," says Joe Sipher, director—Wireless Products at Palm Inc. "If we did that, we would have ended up with something like Apple Computer's Newton, which was a failure because it incorporated too many features into the product." While this perspective seems counterintuitive, it has proven highly successful for Palm Inc. as a pioneer in the development of the handheld computers often called personal digital assistants (PDAs).

THE COMPANY

The inventors of the first Palm products, Jeff Hawkins and Donna Dubinsky, started out developing personal computing connectivity and shorthand software for other PDA manufacturers in the spring of 1994. According to Dubinsky, "We started out as an applications software company. We worked with Casio, Sharp, Hewlett-Packard, Apple, and others—everybody who was working in the field at that time. But none of the platforms were compelling. Most people thought a PDA should be a smaller version of a laptop computer." Although Palm Inc. was the leading software developer for these PDA entrants, sales were too low to keep the company running. "The reasons why early hand-held computers failed were because they had too many features, making them too big, too slow, too heavy, and too expensive," explains Andrea Butter, vice president of marketing.

Palm managers saw a dismal future in being the leading applications provider for a nonexistent market. However, as Butter states, "We felt we knew what customers wanted to do in handheld computing and one day an investor challenged us and said, 'If you know how to do it, why don't you do it?'" They accepted the challenge and today Palm Inc. is the leading provider of handheld computers with 55 percent of the worldwide market. In addition, Palm's operating system software is used by licensees and strategic partners such as Acer, Franklin Covey, HandEra, Handspring, IBM, and Sony in 71 percent of all PDAs.

THE POSITIONING DILEMMA

Defining this type of product has been a challenge. These products have been referred to as information appliances, handheld computers, personal information managers, and personal digital assistants (PDA). Physically, these products have a thin, panel-like body measuring about 5″ × 3″ × 0.5″. They typically use a pen or stylus and handwriting recognition software to allow users to

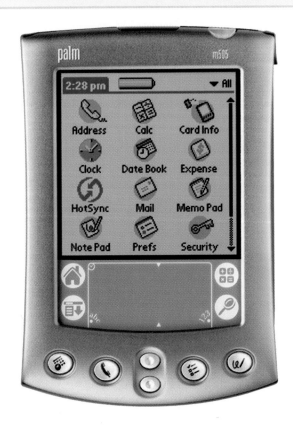

store addresses and telephone numbers, enter appointments on a calendar, make notes and to-do lists, and interface with personal computers to transfer e-mail and other data. Some versions also have tiny keyboards. Hawkins and Dubinsky viewed PDAs as digital replacements for paper-based systems, such as DayTimers, Rolodexes, and Post-it® Notes.

PALM INC.'S NEW PRODUCT PROCESS

Hawkins used his own experience with the "GRiDPad," the first handheld computer developed in the mid-1980s, and "Graffiti," a shorthand-type of handwriting recognition software developed for other entrants in the PDA market, to design the first Palm product—the PalmPilot. Hawkins's R&D consisted of carrying a rectangular block of wood in his shirt pocket with "function buttons" glued to it. When people asked him if he was free for lunch, he would take out his "connected organizer," tap on a "button," and observe their reactions. Hawkins tried several variations before settling on a final design: the PalmPilot had only four function buttons (calendar, addresses and phone numbers, to-do lists, and memos) because those were the most frequently used applications. In addition, Palm Computing conducted a survey among customers of Casio's "Zoomer" PDA. The most important finding was that 90 percent used a personal computer. As a result, the PalmPilot also included PC connectivity. Finally, the PalmPilot was sold only in computer and office supply stores because their salespersons were perceived to have greater skills in selling technology-based products.

The original PalmPilot was launched in 1996 at Demo'96, a trade show whose attendees were technology opinion leaders. The PalmPilot was the "media darling of the show" and sales skyrocketed. The original PalmPilot has since been retired. The Palm product line, however, has evolved to include a variety of new models. Each model has maintained the same commitment to the design philosophy of the original PalmPilot: they must be simple, small, and connected.

COMPETITION AND THE PDA MARKET

When Windows CE, an alternative to the Palm operating system, came out in 1997, Dubinsky recalls, "We said 'Oh-oh, it's all over for us now.'" Hardware manufacturers such as Hewlett-Packard, Casio, and Philips partnered with Microsoft to create products that had functions similar to Palm and offered simplified versions of Microsoft's popular Word and Excel programs, the familiar Windows-like interface, and Internet searching and paging via a PC card interface. However, these products were pricey, sluggish, and consumed more power than the Palm products. In addition, consumers weren't interested in devices that were positioned between PDAs and personal computers.

Palm also faced competition from Web-based personal information managers (PIM), which performed identical functions as the PalmPilot. These organizers were stored at the user's Internet service provider and accessed via browsers such as Netscape or Internet Explorer, or portals such as Yahoo! or America Online (AOL).

Finally, the PDA market is facing pressure from consumers to converge with other digital technologies and provide expansion capabilities such as a wireless modem, a digital camera, and a mobile telephone. This trend has created new competitors such as mobile telephone manufacturer Nokia.

THE FUTURE OF PALM COMPUTING

Palm has responded by developing new products to meet consumers' needs. For example, the Palm m100 handheld series is the lowest-priced Palm and offers users who are new to PDAs easy personalization through changeable faceplates. The Palm III offers better screen contrast, a faster processor, expanded memory, color display, and longer battery life. The best-selling product, the Palm V, offers a sleek, ultra slim industrial design, re-

cessed buttons, and a rechargeable battery for continuous operation.

The Palm VII revolutionized the PDA marketplace by targeting the rapidly growing wireless and mobile market which has an estimated potential of 20 million subscribers in 2002. The Palm VII offers wireless Internet access through the proprietary Palm.Net "web clipping" technology. E-trade, Ticketmaster, *The Wall Street Journal* Interactive Edition, the Weather Channel, *USA Today*, Yahoo!, and other content partners provide information optimized for the small screen of a PDA. In addition, users can send and receive e-mail messages and conduct e-commerce transactions.

Similar in design to the Palm V series, the Palm m500 series brings two sleek, expandable additions to the Palm product line: the Palm m500 monochrome handheld and the Palm m505 color handheld. Along with the traditional functions and features of other Palm products, both models feature Palm's new SD Card and Multi-MediaCard expansion slot and the Palm Universal Connector, which provides either serial or USB connectivity. The expansion slot offers an easy way for users to add storage; applications; content; and add-ons, such as a portable keyboard, wireless modem and camera. Both products contain software such as Palm's Mobil Connectivity, Palm Reader, DataViz Documents To Go, MGI PhotoSuite Mobil Edition, Infinity Softworks power-One Personal calculator, AvantGo, and Chapura Pocket Mirror.

Finally, Palm has encouraged third-party software developers to extend the Palm operating system functionality by developing applications such as contact and schedule management, sales force and field automation, personal productivity, groupware, and financial management. There are currently more than 175,000 developers registered to provide Palm platform solutions. In the future, Palm products will create "Personal Area Networks" that will allow Palm users to interact with other PDAs, printers, and corporate networks!

Questions

1   Which of the steps in the new product process discussed in Chapter 10 did Palm Computing use to develop the PalmPilot? What activities did Palm Computing use in each step?

2   What are the characteristics of the PalmPilot target market?

3   What kinds of learning or behavioral changes were required by consumers who purchased the PalmPilot?

4   What are the key "points of difference" of the PalmPilot when compared to substitute products?

5   How would you rate the PalmPilot on the following reasons for success or failure: significant points of difference; size of market; product quality; market timing; and access to consumers?

SOME RELIGIONS ARE PRACTICED SEVEN DAYS A WEEK.

CHAPTER 11

MANAGING PRODUCTS AND BRANDS

AFTER READING THIS CHAPTER YOU SHOULD BE ABLE TO:

- Explain the product life-cycle concept and relate a marketing strategy to each stage.

- Recognize the differences in product life cycles for various products and their implications for marketing decisions.

- Understand alternative approaches to managing a product's life cycle.

- Describe elements of brand personality and brand equity and the criteria for the good brand name.

- Explain the rationale for alternative branding strategies employed by companies.

- Understand the role of packaging, labeling, and warranties in the marketing of a product.

GATORADE: A THIRST FOR COMPETITION

The thirst for Gatorade is unquenchable as far as Sue Wellington is concerned. She should know. Wellington has forged a brilliant marketing career nurturing the Gatorade brand for 13 years. Today, Gatorade is a brand powerhouse that commands 85 percent of the U.S. sports beverage market.

Like Kleenex in the tissue market and Jello among gelatin desserts, Gatorade has become synonymous with sports beverages. Concocted in 1965 at the University of Florida as a rehydration beverage for the school's football team, the drink was coined "Gatorade" by an opposing team's coach after watching his team lose to the Florida Gators in the Orange Bowl. The name stuck, and a new beverage product class was born.

Stokely–Van Camp Co. bought the Gatorade formula in 1967 and commercialized the product. The original Gatorade was a liquid with a lemon-lime flavor. An orange flavor was introduced in 1971 and a fruit punch flavor in 1983. Instant Gatorade was launched in 1979. Quaker Oats purchased Stokely–Van Camp in 1983, at which time Gatorade sales were $85 million. Quaker Oats executives quickly grew sales through a variety of means. More flavors were added and multiple package sizes were offered using different containers—glass and plastic bottles and aluminum cans. Distribution expanded first to include convenience stores and supermarkets followed by vending machines and fountain service. Consistent advertising and promotion effectively conveyed the product's unique benefits and links to athletic competition using popular athletes such as Michael Jordan and Mia Hamm as spokespersons. International opportunities were vigorously pursued. Gatorade is sold in 47 countries in North America, Europe, Latin America, Africa, and Asia and has become a global brand.

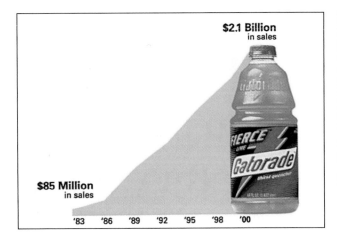

Gatorade's uninterrupted sales growth is a direct result of masterful product and brand management.

Gatorade

Brand development has been a key factor in Gatorade's success. Under Wellington's direction, Quaker Oats introduced Gatorade Frost in 1997, with a "lighter, crisper" taste aimed at expanding the brand's reach beyond participants in organized sports to other usage occasions that she terms "intense sweaty situations." "We're a brand for the active thirst market, anytime anybody is hot and parched." Gatorade Frost proved to be a welcome relief for parched palates, racking up annual sales of $200 million. Gatorade Fierce, with a "bolder" taste, was launched in 1999 and posts annual sales of $250 million. But Wellington notes, "Remember, our main competitor is tap water." Not surprisingly, Gatorade recently entered the bottled water category with Propel Fitness Water, a lightly flavored and sweetened water fortified with B-vitamins and antioxidants. Gatorade sales exceeded $2 billion in 2001 when PepsiCo, Inc., acquired Quaker Oats. As for Sue Wellington, she was named senior vice president and president—U.S. beverages.[1]

The marketing of Gatorade illustrates effective product and brand management in a dynamic marketplace. This chapter shows how the actions taken by Gatorade executives are typical of those made by successful marketers.

THE PRODUCT LIFE CYCLE

Products, like people, have been viewed as having a life cycle. The concept of the **product life cycle** describes the stages a new product goes through in the marketplace: introduction, growth, maturity, and decline (Figure 11–1).[2] There are two curves shown in this figure, total industry sales revenue and total industry profit, which represent the sum of sales revenue and profit of all firms producing the product. The reasons for the changes in each curve and the marketing decisions involved are discussed in the following pages.

Introduction Stage

The introduction stage of the product life cycle occurs when a product is first introduced to its intended target market. During this period, sales grow slowly, and profit is minimal. The lack of profit is often the result of large investment costs in product development, such as the $1 billion spent by Gillette to develop and launch the MACH 3 razor shaving system. The marketing objective for the company at this stage is to create consumer awareness and stimulate trial—the initial purchase of a product by a consumer.

Companies often spend heavily on advertising and other promotion tools to build awareness among consumers in the introduction stage. For example, Gillette budgeted $300 million in advertising alone to introduce the MACH 3 razor to consumers.[3] These expenditures are often made to stimulate *primary demand,* or desire

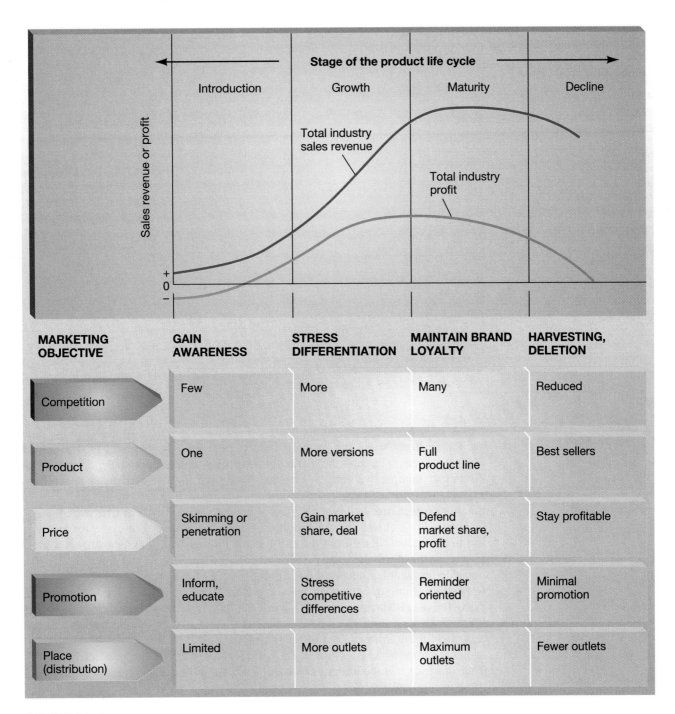

	Stage of the product life cycle			
	Introduction	Growth	Maturity	Decline
MARKETING OBJECTIVE	**GAIN AWARENESS**	**STRESS DIFFERENTIATION**	**MAINTAIN BRAND LOYALTY**	**HARVESTING, DELETION**
Competition	Few	More	Many	Reduced
Product	One	More versions	Full product line	Best sellers
Price	Skimming or penetration	Gain market share, deal	Defend market share, profit	Stay profitable
Promotion	Inform, educate	Stress competitive differences	Reminder oriented	Minimal promotion
Place (distribution)	Limited	More outlets	Maximum outlets	Fewer outlets

FIGURE 11–1

How stages of the product life cycle relate to a firm's marketing objectives and marketing mix actions

for the product class rather than for a specific brand since there are few competitors with the same product. As more competitors introduce their own products and the product progresses along its life cycle, company attention is focused on creating *selective demand,* or demand for a specific brand.

Other marketing mix variables also are important at this stage. Gaining distribution can be a challenge because channel intermediaries may be hesitant to carry a new product. Moreover, in this stage a company often restricts the number of variations of the product to ensure control of product quality. For example, Gatorade came in only one flavor. Gillette offered only a single version of the MACH 3 razor.

During introduction, pricing can be either high or low. A high initial price may be used as part of a *skimming* strategy to help the company recover the costs of development as well as capitalize on the price insensitivity of early buyers. 3M is a

FIGURE 11–2

Product life cycle for the stand-alone fax machine for business use: 1970–2001

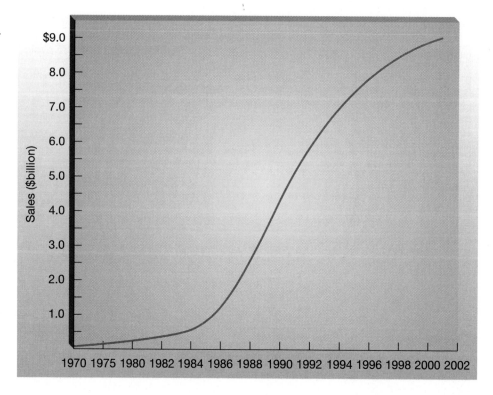

master of this strategy. According to a 3M manager, "We hit fast, price high, and get the heck out when the me-too products pour in."[4] High prices tend to attract competitors eager to enter the market because they see the opportunity for profit. To discourage competitive entry, a company can price low, referred to as *penetration pricing*. This pricing strategy helps build unit volume, but a company must closely monitor costs. These and other pricing techniques are covered in Chapter 14.

Figure 11–2 charts the stand-alone fax machine product life cycle for business use in the United States from the early 1970s through 2001.[5] As shown, sales grew slowly in the 1970s and early 1980s after Xerox pioneered the first portable fax machine that sent and received documents. Fax machines were originally sold direct to businesses through company salespeople and were premium priced. The average price for a fax machine in 1980 was $12,700. By today's standards, those fax machines were primitive. They contained mechanical parts, not electronic circuitry, and offered few features seen in today's models.

Several product classes are in the introductory stage of the product life cycle. These include high-definition television (HDTV) and "hybrid" (gasoline- and electric-powered) automobiles.

Growth Stage

The second stage of the product life cycle, growth, is characterized by rapid increases in sales. It is in this stage that competitors appear. For example, Figure 11–2 shows the dramatic increase in sales of fax machines from 1986 to 1992. The number of companies selling fax machines was also increasing, from one in the early 1970s to four in the late 1970s to seven manufacturers in 1983, which sold nine brands. By 1992 there were some 25 manufacturers and 60 brands from which to choose.

The result of more competitors and more aggressive pricing is that profit usually peaks during the growth stage. For instance, the average price for a fax machine declined from $3,300 in 1985 to $1,500 in 1992. At this point the emphasis of advertising shifts to stimulating selective demand, in which product benefits are compared with those of competitors' offerings.

Product sales in the growth stage grow at an increasing rate because of new people trying or using the product and a growing proportion of *repeat purchasers*—people who tried the product, were satisfied, and bought again. As a product moves through the life cycle, the ratio of repeat to trial purchasers grows. Failure to achieve substantial repeat purchasers usually means an early death for a product. Alberto-Culver introduced Mr. Culver's Sparklers, which were solid air fresheners that looked like stained glass. The product moved quickly from the introduction to the growth stage, but then sales plummeted. The problem was there were almost no repeat purchasers because buyers treated the product like cheap window decorations, left them there, and didn't buy new ones. Durable fax machines meant that replacement purchases were rare; however, it was common for more than one machine to populate a business as their use became more widespread. In 1995, there was one fax machine for every eight people in a business in the United States.

Changes start to appear in the product during the growth stage. To help differentiate a company's brand from its competitors, an improved version or new features are added to the original design, and product proliferation occurs. Changes in fax machines included (1) models with built-in telephones; (2) models that used plain, rather than thermal, paper for copies; (3) models that integrated telex for electronic mail purposes; and (4) models that allowed for secure (confidential) transmissions. For Gatorade, new flavors and package sizes were added during the growth stage.

In the growth stage it is important to gain as much distribution for the product as possible. In the retail store, for example, this often means that competing companies fight for display and shelf space. Expanded distribution in the fax industry is an example. In 1986, early in the growth stage, only 11 percent of office machine dealers carried this equipment. By the mid-1990s, more than 70 percent of these dealers carried fax equipment, distribution was expanded to other stores selling electronic equipment, and the fight continues for which brands will be displayed.

Hybrid automobiles made by Honda are in the introductory stage of the product life cycle. DVD players produced by Toshiba are in the growth stage. Each product and company faces unique challenges based on its product life cycle stage.

Honda
www.honda.com

Toshiba
www.toshiba.com

It's an environmental movement all by itself.

How many cars does it take to change the world? Just one, perhaps. Introducing the all-new Honda Insight. It's America's first gasoline-electric hybrid automobile.

Nothing short of an engineering breakthrough, the Insight achieves a terrific 68 miles per gallon on the highway, 61 miles per gallon in the city, and an astounding 700-mile range on one tank of fuel. How? By combining an efficient three-cylinder gasoline engine with an electric motor powered by nickel-metal hydride batteries that never need to be plugged in. Then add a world-class aerodynamic design, and an extremely lightweight body, and you have the ultra-low-emission† Insight.

It's the culmination of years of research and development into lighter, cleaner, more efficient automobiles. In other words, technology with a conscience. Then again, what else would you expect from a car powered by Honda?

HONDA
The power of dreams·

IT'S HARD TO IMAGINE YOU EVER LIVED

WITHOUT HER.

TOSHIBA
DIGITAL HOME MEDIA

It's that kind of love

Numerous product classes or industries are in the growth stage of the product life cycle. Examples include DVD players and personal digital assistants (PDAs).

Maturity Stage

The third stage, maturity, is characterized by a slowing of total industry sales or product class revenue. Also, marginal competitors begin to leave the market. Most consumers who would buy the product are either repeat purchasers of the item or have tried and abandoned it. Sales increase at a decreasing rate in the maturity stage as fewer new buyers enter the market. Profit declines because there is fierce price competition among many sellers and the cost of gaining new buyers at this stage increases.

Marketing attention in the maturity stage is often directed toward holding market share through further product differentiation and finding new buyers. Gillette, for example, differentiated its MACH 3 razor through new product features specifically designed for women and then launched the Gillette for Women Venus razor just as the MACH 3 razor entered its maturity stage. Fax machine manufacturers developed Internet-enabled models and introduced product features suitable for small and home businesses, which today represent a substantial portion of industry sales. Still, a major consideration in a company's strategy in this stage is to reduce overall marketing cost by improving promotional and distribution efficiency.

Stand-alone fax machines for business use approached the maturity stage in the late 1990s. By 2001, over 80 percent of industry sales were captured by four producers (Brother, Canon, Panasonic, and Sharp), reflecting the departure of marginal competitors. Industry sales slowed in the late 1990s compared with triple-digit average annual dollar sales increases in the late 1980s. By early 2002, 100 million stand-alone fax machines for business use were installed throughout the world.

Numerous product classes and industries are in the maturity stage of their product life cycle. These include carbonated soft drinks, automobiles, and TVs.

Decline Stage

The decline stage occurs when sales and profits begin to drop. Frequently, a product enters this stage not because of any wrong strategy on the part of the company but because of environmental changes. Technological innovation often precedes the decline stage as newer technologies replace older technologies. The word-processing capability of personal computers pushed typewriters into decline. Compact discs did the same to cassette tapes in the prerecorded music industry. Will Internet technology and e-mail spell doom for fax machines? The accompanying Marketing NewsNet offers one perspective on this question.[6]

Products in the decline stage tend to consume a disproportionate share of management time and financial resources relative to their potential future worth. A company will follow one of two strategies to handle a declining product: deletion or harvesting.

Deletion   Product *deletion,* or dropping the product from the company's product line, is the most drastic strategy. Because a residual core of consumers still consume or use a product even in the decline stage, product elimination decisions are not taken lightly. For example, Gillette continues to sell its Liquid Paper correction fluid for use with typewriters in the era of word-processing equipment.

Harvesting   A second strategy, *harvesting,* is when a company retains the product but reduces marketing costs. The product continues to be offered, but salespeople do not allocate time in selling nor are advertising dollars spent. The purpose of harvesting is to maintain the ability to meet customer requests. Coca-Cola, for instance, still sells Tab, its first diet cola to a small group of die-hard fans. According to Coke's CEO, "It shows you care. We want to make sure those who want Tab, get Tab."[7]

MARKETING NEWSNET

Will E-Mail Spell Doom for the Familiar Fax?

TECHNOLOGY & E-COMMERCE

Technological substitution often causes the decline stage in the product life cycle. Will the Internet and e-mail replace fax machines?

This question has caused heated debates. Even though sales of Internet host computers are in the growth stage of the product life cycle, fax machine sales continue to grow as well. Industry analysts estimate that there are 1 billion e-mail mailboxes worldwide. However, the growth of e-mail has not affected faxing because the two technologies do not directly compete for the same messaging applications.

E-mail is used for text messages and faxing is predominately used for communicating formatted documents by business users. Fax usage is expected to increase through 2005, and sales of stand-alone fax machines are expected to increase as well. Internet technology may eventually replace facsimile technology, but not in the immediate future.

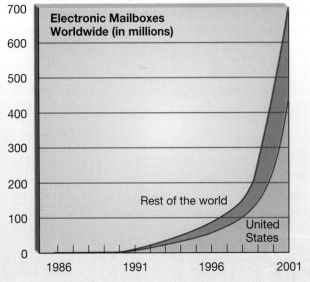

Some Dimensions of the Product Life Cycle

Some important aspects of product life cycles are (1) their length, (2) the shape of their curves, and (3) how they vary with different levels of products.

Length of the Product Life Cycle   There is no exact time that a product takes to move through its life cycle. As a rule, consumer products have shorter life cycles than business products. For example, many new consumer food products such as Frito-Lay's WOW brand potato chips move from the introduction stage to maturity in 18 months. The availability of mass communication vehicles informs consumers faster and shortens life cycles. Also, technological change tends to shorten product life cycles as new product innovation replaces existing products.

Shape of the Product Life Cycle   The product life-cycle curve shown in Figure 11–1 is the *generalized life cycle,* but not all products have the same shape to their curve. In fact, there are several different life-cycle curves, each type suggesting different marketing strategies. Figure 11–3 shows the shape of life-cycle curves for four different types of products: high learning, low learning, fashion, and fad products.

A *high learning product* is one for which significant education of the customer is required and there is an extended introductory period (Figure11–3A). Products such as personal computers had this type of life-cycle curve because consumers had to understand the benefits of purchasing the product or be educated in a new way of performing a familiar task. Convection ovens, for example, necessitate that the consumer learn a new way of cooking and alter familiar recipes.

In contrast, for a *low learning product* sales begin immediately because little learning is required by the consumer, and the benefits of purchase are readily understood (Figure 11–3B). This product often can be easily imitated by competitors, so the marketing strategy is to broaden distribution quickly. In this way, as competitors rapidly enter, most retail outlets already have the innovator's product. It is also important to have the manufacturing capacity to meet demand. An example of a

FIGURE 11–3
Alternative product life cycles

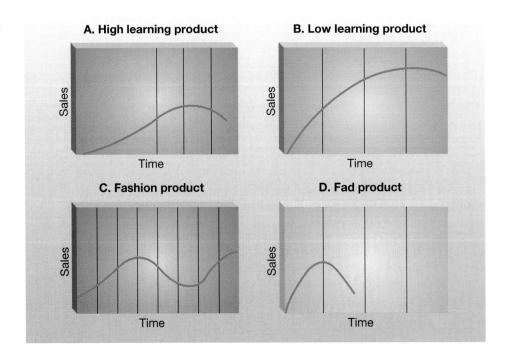

successful low learning product is Gillette's MACH 3 razor. Introduced in mid-1998, MACH 3 recorded $1 billion in sales in the brief span of three years.[8]

A *fashion product* (Figure 11–3C), such as hemline lengths on skirts or lapel widths on jackets, is introduced, declines, and then seems to return. Life cycles for fashion products most often appear in women's and men's clothing styles. The length of the cycles may be years or decades.

A *fad* experiences rapid sales on introduction and then an equally rapid decline (Figure 11–3D). These products are typically novelties and have a short life cycle. They include car tattoos sold in southern California and described as the first removable and reusable graphics for automobiles, and vinyl dresses, fleece bikinis, and an AstroTurf miniskirt made by Thump, Inc., a Minnesota clothing company.[9]

The Product Level: Class and Form   The product life cycle shown in Figure 11–1 is a total industry or product class curve. Yet, in managing a product it is important to often distinguish among the multiple life cycles (class and form) that may exist. **Product class** refers to the entire product category or industry, such as video game consoles and software shown in Figure 11–4.[10] **Product form** pertains to variations within the class. For video games, product form exists in the computing capability of game consoles such as 8-, 16-, 32/64-, and the new 128-bit machines such as Sony's PlayStation 2, Nintendo's Game cube, and Microsoft's Xbox. Game consoles and software have a life cycle of their own and typically move from the introduction stage to maturity in five years.

The Life Cycle and Consumers   The life cycle of a product depends on sales to consumers. Not all consumers rush to buy a product in the introductory stage, and the shapes of the life-cycle curves indicate that most sales occur after the product has been on the market for some time. In essence, a product diffuses, or spreads, through the population, a concept called the *diffusion of innovation*.[11]

Some people are attracted to a product early, while others buy it only after they see their friends with the item. Figure 11–5 shows the consumer population divided into five categories of product adopters based on when they adopt a new product. Brief profiles accompany each category. For any product to be successful, it must

FIGURE 11–4
Video game console and software life cycles by product class and product form

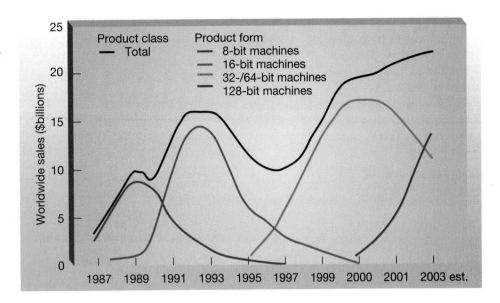

be purchased by innovators and early adopters. This is why manufacturers of new pharmaceuticals try to gain adoption by leading hospitals, clinics, and physicians that are widely respected in the medical field. Once accepted by innovators and early adopters, the adoption of new products moves on to the early majority, late majority, and laggard categories.

Several factors affect whether a consumer will adopt a new product or not. Common reasons for resisting a product in the introduction stage are usage barriers (the product is not compatible with existing habits), value barriers (the product provides no incentive to change), risk barriers (physical, economic, or social), and psychological barriers (cultural differences or image).[12]

Companies attempt to overcome these barriers in numerous ways. They provide warranties, money-back guarantees, extensive usage instructions, demonstrations, and free samples to stimulate initial trial of new products. For example, software

FIGURE 11–5
Five categories and profiles of product adopters

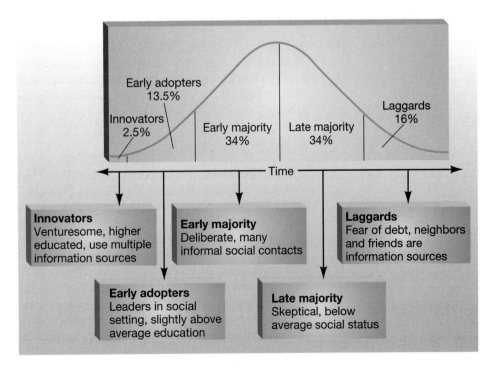

For the first time since the introduction of the Dyna Glide line in 1990, Harley-Davidson introduced a brand new family of motorcycles—starting with the VRSCA V-Rod™ motorcycle. Visit the company's website to experience the VRSCA V-Rod™.

Harley-Davidson, Inc.
www.harley-davidson.com

developers offer demonstrations downloaded from the Internet. Maybelline allows consumers to browse through the Cover Girl Color Match system on its website to find out how certain makeup products will look. Free samples are one of the most popular means to gain consumer trial. In fact, 71 percent of consumers consider a sample to be the best way to evaluate a new product.[13]

Concept Check

1. Advertising plays a major role in the _____ stage of the product life cycle, and _____ plays a major role in maturity.

2. How do high learning and low learning products differ?

3. What does the life cycle of a fashion product look like?

MANAGING THE PRODUCT LIFE CYCLE

An important task for a firm is to manage its products through the successive stages of their life cycles. This section discusses the role of the product manager who is usually responsible for this, and analyzes three ways to manage a product through its life cycle: modifying the product, modifying the market, and repositioning the product.

Role of a Product Manager

The product manager (sometimes called *brand manager*) manages the marketing efforts for a close-knit family of products or brands.[14] Introduced by Procter & Gamble in 1928, the product manager style of marketing organization is used by consumer goods firms such as General Mills and PepsiCo and by industrial firms such as Intel and Hewlett-Packard. The U.S. Postal Service recently began using product managers as well. All product managers are responsible for managing existing products through the stages of the life cycle. Some are also responsible for developing new products. Product managers' marketing responsibilities include developing and executing a marketing program for the product line described in an annual marketing plan and approving ad copy, media selection, and package design. The role of product managers in planning, implementing, and controlling marketing strategy is covered in Chapter 22.

Modifying the Product

Product modification involves altering a product's characteristic, such as its quality, performance, or appearance, to try to increase and extend the product's sales. Wrinkle-free cotton slacks sold by Levi Strauss, Haggar, and Farah revitalized sales of men's casual pants and now account for 60 percent of the men's cotton pants product class sales. Harley-Davidson recently introduced the V-Rod™ motorcycle— the company's first new model in over a decade—to appeal to a new generation of buyers. With its aerodynamic look, clamshell-style instrument panel and unpainted aluminum-and-steel frame, the V-Rod is billed as Harley's first "performance custom" motorcycle.[15]

New features, packages, or scents can be used to change a product's characteristics and give the sense of a revised product. Procter & Gamble revamped Pantene shampoo and conditioner with a new vitamin formula and relaunched the brand with a multimillion-dollar advertising and promotion campaign. The result? Pantene, a brand first introduced in the 1940s, became the top-selling shampoo and conditioner in the United States in an industry with more than 1,000 competitors.[16]

Modifying the Market

With **market modification** strategies, a company tries to find new customers, increase a product's use among existing customers, or create new use situations.

Finding New Users   Produce companies have begun marketing and packaging prunes as dried plums for the purpose of attracting younger buyers. Sony has expanded its user base by developing PlayStation 2 video games for children under 13 years old.[17]

Increasing Use   Promoting more frequent usage has been a strategy of Campbell Soup Company. Because soup consumption rises in the winter and declines during the summer, the company now advertises more heavily in warm months to encourage consumers to think of soup as more than a cold-weather food. Similarly, The Florida Orange Growers Association advocates drinking orange juice throughout the day rather than for breakfast only.

Creating New Use Situation   Finding new uses for an existing product has been the strategy behind Woolite, a laundry soap. Originally intended for the hand washing of woolen material, Woolite now promotes itself for use with all fine clothing items. The Milk Processor Education Program suggests a new use situation by substituting milk for water or other ingredients in preparing food.

The Milk Processor Education Program (MilkPEP) promotes the use of milk rather than water or other ingredients in preparing food. According to a MilkPEP executive, "If every household one day a week added milk rather than water to instant coffee and made a caffe latte, it would add [up to] $100 million to the bottom line of the milk industry."

The Milk Processor Education Program
www.whymilk.com

Repositioning the Product

Often a company decides to reposition its product or product line in an attempt to bolster sales. *Product repositioning* is changing the place a product occupies in a consumer's mind relative to competitive products. A firm can reposition a product by changing one or more of the four marketing mix elements. Four factors that trigger a repositioning action are discussed next.

Reacting to a Competitor's Position   One reason to reposition a product is because a competitor's entrenched position is adversely affecting sales and market share. Procter & Gamble repositioned its venerable Ivory soap bar in response to the success of Lever 2000, sold by Lever Brothers. Lever 2000, a bar soap that moisturizes, deodorizes, and kills bacteria, eroded P&G's dominance of the bar soap market. P&G responded with its own triple-threat soap called New Ivory Ultra Safe Skin Care Soap. The problem? The new Ivory doesn't float![18]

Reaching a New Market   When Unilever introduced iced tea in Britain in the mid-1990s, sales were disappointing. British consumers viewed it as leftover hot tea, not suitable for drinking. The company made its tea carbonated and repositioned it as a cold soft drink to compete as a carbonated beverage and sales improved. New Balance, Inc. has repositioned its athletic shoes for aging baby boomers. Instead of competing head-on against Nike, Reebok, and Fila, the company offers an expansive range of widths tailored for an older consumer's heavier weight and networks with podiatrists who use the wide models to insert foot-support devices.[19]

Catching a Rising Trend   Changing consumer trends can also lead to repositioning. Consumer interest in "functional foods" is an example.[20] These foods offer health and dietary benefits beyond nutrition. A number of products have capitalized on this trend. Quaker Oats now makes the FDA-approved claim that oatmeal, as part of a low saturated fat, low cholesterol diet, may reduce the risk of heart disease. Calcium-enriched products, such as Nutri-Grain bars and Uncle Ben's Calcium Plus rice, emphasize healthy bone structure for children and adults. Marketers of juices, such as V-8 and Tropicana, focus on the natural health benefits of their product.

Changing the Value Offered   In repositioning a product, a company can decide to change the value it offers buyers and trade up or down. **Trading up** involves adding value to the product (or line) through additional features or higher-quality materials. Michelin and Goodyear have done this with a "run-flat" tire that can travel up to 50 miles at 55 miles-per-hour after suffering total air loss. Dog food manufacturers, such as Ralston Purina, also have traded up by offering super premium foods based on "life-stage nutrition." Mass merchandisers, such as Sears and JCPenney, can trade up by adding a designer clothes section to their stores.

Trading down involves reducing the number of features, quality, or price. For example, airlines have added more seats, thus reducing leg room, and eliminated extras, such as snack service and food portions. Trading down often exists when companies engage in **downsizing**—reducing the content of packages without changing package size and maintaining or increasing the package price. Firms have been criticized for this practice, as described in the accompanying Ethics and Social Responsibility Alert.[21]

Concept Check	
	1. How does a product manager help manage a product's life cycle?
	2. What does "creating new use situations" mean in managing a product's life cycle?
	3. Explain the difference between trading up and trading down in repositioning.

BRANDING AND BRAND MANAGEMENT

A basic decision in marketing products is **branding**, in which an organization uses a name, phrase, design, symbols, or combination of these to identify its products and distinguish them from those of competitors. A **brand name** is any word, "device" (design, sound, shape, or color), or combination of these used to distinguish a seller's goods or services. Some brand names can be spoken, such as a Gatorade or Rollerblade. Other brand names cannot be spoken, such as the rainbow-colored apple (the *logotype* or *logo*) that Apple Computer originally put on its machines and in its ads. A **trade name** is a commercial, legal name under which a company does business. The Campbell Soup Company is the trade name of that firm.

A **trademark** identifies that a firm has legally registered its brand name or trade name so the firm has its exclusive use, thereby preventing others from using it. In the United States, more than a million trademarks are registered with the U.S. Patent and Trademark Office, and these trademarks are protected under the Lanham Act. A well-known trademark can help a company advertise its offerings to customers and develop their brand loyalty.

Because a good trademark can help sell a product, *product counterfeiting,* which involves low-cost copies of popular brands not manufactured by the original producer, has been a growing problem. Counterfeit products can steal sales from the original manufacturer or hurt the company's reputation. Counterfeiting losses to U.S. companies exceed $50 billion in every year. To protect against counterfeiting, the U.S. government passed the Trademark Counterfeiting Act, which makes counterfeiting a federal offense with offenders subject to prison sentences, damage payments, and seizure of counterfeit merchandise.

Trademark protection is a major issue in global marketing. For instance, the transformation of the Soviet Union into individual countries meant that U.S. firms, such as Xerox, had to reregister trademarks in each of the republics to prohibit misuse and generic use ("xeroxing") of their trademarks by competitors and consumers.

Consumers may benefit most from branding. Recognizing competing products by distinct trademarks allows them to be more efficient shoppers. Consumers can recognize and avoid products with which they are dissatisfied, while becoming loyal to other, more satisfying brands. As discussed in Chapter 5, brand loyalty often eases consumers' decision making by eliminating the need for an external search.

Can you describe the brand personality traits for these two brands? Not sure? Try visiting their websites for more information.

got2b
www.got2b.com

Mambo
www.lizclaiborne.com/mambo

Brand Personality and Brand Equity

Product managers recognize that brands offer more than product identification and a means to distinguish their products from competitors. Successful and established brands take on a **brand personality**, a set of human characteristics associated with a brand name.[22] Research shows that consumers often assign personality traits to products—traditional, romantic, rugged, sophisticated, rebellious—and choose brands that are consistent with their own or desired self-image. Marketers can and do imbue a brand with a personality through advertising that depicts a certain user or usage situation and conveys certain emotions or feelings to be associated with the brand. For example, the personality traits associated with Coca-Cola are all-American, real, and cool; with Pepsi, young, exciting, and hip; and with Dr Pepper, nonconforming, unique, and fun.

Brand name importance to a company has led to a concept called **brand equity**, the added value a given brand name gives to a product beyond the functional benefits provided.[23] This value has two distinct advantages. First, brand equity provides a competitive advantage, such as the Sunkist label that implies quality fruit and the Disney name that defines children's entertainment. A second advantage is that consumers are often willing to pay a higher price for a product with brand equity. Brand equity, in this instance, is represented by the premium a consumer will pay for one brand over another when the functional benefits provided are identical. Intel microchips, Bose audio systems, Duracell batteries, Microsoft computer software, and Louis Vuitton luggage all enjoy a price premium arising from brand equity.

Creating Brand Equity   Brand equity doesn't just happen. It is carefully crafted and nurtured by marketing programs that forge strong, favorable and unique consumer associations and experiences with a brand. Brand equity resides in the minds of consumers and results from what they have learned, felt, seen, and heard about a brand over time. Marketers recognize that brand equity is not easily or quickly achieved. Rather, it arises from a sequential building process consisting of four steps (Figure 11–6).[24] The first step is to develop positive brand awareness and an association of the brand in consumers' minds with a product class or need to give the brand an identity. Gatorade and Kleenex have done this in the sports drink and facial tissue product classes, respectively. Next, a marketer must establish a brand's meaning in the minds of consumers. Meaning arises from what a brand stands for and has two dimensions—a functional, performance-related dimension and an abstract, imagery-related dimension. Nike has done this through continuous product development and improvement and its links to peak athletic performance in its integrated marketing communications program. The third step is to elicit the proper consumer responses to a brand's identity and meaning. Here attention is placed on how consumers think and feel about a brand. Thinking focuses on a brand's perceived quality, credibility, and superiority relative to other brands. Feeling relates to the consumer's emotional reaction to a brand. Michelin elicits both responses for its tires. Not only is Michelin thought of as a credible and superior-quality brand, but consumers also acknowledge a warm and secure feeling of safety, comfort, and self-assurance without worry or concern about the brand. The final, and most difficult, step is to create a consumer-brand resonance evident in an intense, active loyalty relationship between consumers and the brand. A deep psychological bond characterizes consumer-brand resonance and the personal identification consumers have with the brand. Examples of brands that have achieved this status include Harley-Davidson, Apple, and eBay.

Valuing Brand Equity   Brand equity also provides a financial advantage for the brand owner.[25] Successful, established brand names, such as Gillette, Nike, Gatorade, and Nokia, have an economic value in the sense that they are intangible assets. The recognition that brands are assets is apparent in the decision to buy and sell brands. For example, Procter & Gamble bought the Hawaiian Punch brand from Del Monte in 1990 for $150 million and sold it to Cadbury Schweppes in 1999 for $203 million. This

FIGURE 11–6

Customer-based brand equity pyramid

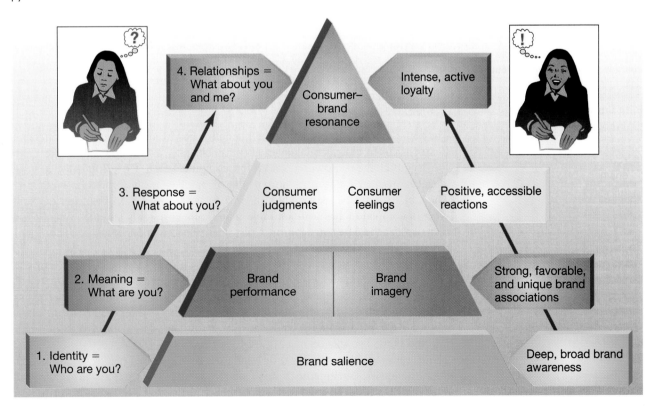

Ruffles and Chee-tos are in Israel now, and more Frito-Lay snack items may follow. Entry into Israel was made possible through a licensing agreement with Elite Foods in Israel.

Elite Company
www.elite.co.il

example illustrates that brands, unlike physical assets that depreciate with time and use, appreciate in value when effectively managed. However, brands can lose value when they are not managed properly. The purchase and sale of Snapple by Quaker Oats is a case in point. Quaker bought Snapple for $1.7 billion in 1994, only to sell it to Triarc Companies in 1997 for $300 million.

Licensing

The value of brand equity also is evident in the strategy of licensing. **Licensing** is a contractual agreement whereby a company allows another firm to use its brand name, patent, trade secret, or other property for a royalty or a fee. Licensing can be very profitable to a licensor and a licensee as annual worldwide retail sales of licensed products exceed $200 billion.[26] Playboy has earned more than $260 million licensing its name for merchandise ranging from shoes in the United States to wallpaper in Europe and cooking classes in Brazil. Murjani has sold more than $500 million of clothing worldwide bearing the Coca-Cola logo. Disney earns about $300 million annually licensing its classic Disney characters such as Mickey Mouse and Winnie the Pooh to Mattel.

Licensing also assists companies in entering global markets with minimal risk. Frito-Lay licensed Elite Foods in Israel to produce and market Frito-Lay's Ruffles potato chips and Chee-tos cheese-flavored corn puffs. These brands capture a significant percent of the salty snack market in Israel.

Picking a Good Brand Name

We take brand names such as Dial, Sanyo, Porsche, and Adidas for granted, but it is often a difficult and expensive process to pick a good name. Companies will spend between $25,000 and $100,000 to identify and test a new brand name.[27] For instance, Intel spent $45,000 for the Pentium name given its family of microchips.[28] There are five criteria mentioned most often when selecting a good brand name.[29]

- The name should suggest the product benefits. For example, Accutron (watches), Easy Off (oven cleaner), Glass Plus (glass cleaner), Cling-Free (antistatic cloth for drying clothes), Powerbook (laptop computer), and Tidy Bowl (toilet bowl cleaner) all clearly describe the benefits of purchasing the product.
- The name should be memorable, distinctive, and positive. In the auto industry, when a competitor has a memorable name, others quickly imitate. When Ford named a car the Mustang, Pintos, Colts, and Broncos soon followed. The Thunderbird name led to the Phoenix, Eagle, Sunbird, and Firebird.
- The name should fit the company or product image. Sharp is a name that can apply to audio and video equipment. Excedrin, Anacin, and Nuprin are scientific-sounding names, good for an analgesic. However, naming a personal computer PCjr, as IBM did with its first computer for home use, neither fit the company nor the product. PCjr, sounded like a toy and stalled IBM's initial entry into the home-use market.
- The name should have no legal or regulatory restrictions. Legal restrictions produce trademark infringement suits, and regulatory restrictions arise through improper use of words. For example, the U.S. Food and Drug Administration

discourages the use of the word *heart* in food brand names. This restriction led to changing the name of Kellogg's Heartwise cereal to Fiberwise, and Clorox's Hidden Valley Ranch Take Heart Salad Dressing had to be modified to Hidden Valley Ranch Low-Fat Salad Dressing.[30] Increasingly, brand names need a corresponding address on the Internet. This further complicates name selection because millions of domain names are already registered.

• Finally, the name should be simple (such as Bold laundry detergent, Sure deodorant, and Bic pens) and should be emotional (such as Joy and Obsession perfumes). In the development of names for international use, having a non-meaningful brand name has been considered a benefit. A name such as Exxon does not have any prior impressions or undesirable images among a diverse world population of different languages and cultures. The 7Up name is another matter. In Shanghai, China, the phrase means "death through drinking" in the local dialect, and sales have suffered as a result.[31]

Do you have an idea for a brand name? If you do, check to see if the name has been already registered with the U.S. Patent and Trademark Office by visiting its website described in the accompanying Web Link.

Branding Strategies

In deciding to brand a product, companies have several possible strategies, including manufacturer branding, reseller branding, or mixed branding approaches.

Manufacturer Branding   With **manufacturer branding**, the producer dictates the brand name using either a multiproduct or multibrand approach. **Multiproduct branding** is when a company uses one name for all its products. This approach is often referred to as a *blanket* or *family* branding strategy (Figure 11–7).

There are several advantages to multiproduct branding. Capitalizing again on brand equity, consumers who have a good experience with the product will transfer this favorable attitude to other items in the product class with the same name. Therefore, this brand strategy makes possible *line extensions,* the practice of using a current brand name to enter a new market segment in its product class. Campbell Soup Company effectively employs a multiproduct branding strategy with soup line extensions. It offers regular Campbell soup, home-cooking style, and chunky varieties and more than 100 soup flavors. This strategy can also result in lower advertising and promotion costs because the same name is used on all products, thus raising the level of brand awareness. A risk with line extension is that sales of an extension may come at the expense of other items in the company's product line. Therefore, line extensions work best when they provide incremental company revenue by taking sales away from competing brands or attracting new buyers.[32]

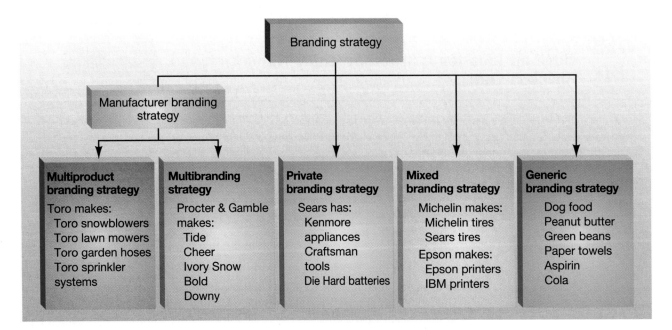

FIGURE 11–7
Alternative branding strategies

Some companies employ *subbranding,* which combines a family brand with a new brand. For example, ThinkPad is a subbrand to the IBM name. Quaker Oats has successfully used subbranding for Gatorade with the introduction of Gatorade Frost and Gatorade Fierce, with unique flavors developed for each.

A strong brand equity also allows for *brand extension,* the practice of using a current brand name to enter a completely different product class.[33] For instance, the equity in the Tylenol name as a trusted pain reliever allowed Johnson & Johnson to successfully extend this name to Tylenol Cold & Flu and Tylenol PM, a sleep aid. Fisher-Price, an established name in children's toys, was able to extend this name to children's shampoo and conditioners and baby bath and lotion products.

However, there is a risk with brand extensions. Too many uses for one brand name can dilute the meaning of a brand for consumers. Marketing experts claim this has happened to the Arm & Hammer brand given its use for toothpaste, laundry detergent, gum, cat litter, air freshener, carpet deodorizer, and antiperspirant.[34]

A recent variation on brand extensions is the practice of **co-branding**, the pairing of two brand names of two manufacturers on a single product.[35] For example, Hershey Foods has teamed with General Mills to offer a co-branded breakfast cereal called Reese's Peanut Butter Puffs and with Nabisco to provide Chips Ahoy cookies using Hershey's chocolate morsels. Citibank co-brands MasterCard and Visa with American Airlines and Ford. Co-branding benefits firms by allowing them to enter new product classes and capitalize on an already established brand name in that product class.

An alternative manufacturer's branding strategy, **multibranding**, involves giving each product a distinct name. Multibranding is a useful strategy when each brand is intended for a different market segment. P&G makes Camay soap for those concerned with soft skin and Safeguard for those who want deodorant protection. Black & Decker markets its line of tools for the household do-it-yourselfer segment with the Black & Decker name, but uses the DeWalt name for its professional tool line. Disney uses the Miramax and Touchstone Pictures names for films directed at adults and its Disney name for children's films.

Multibranding strategies become more complex in the global marketplace. As an example, P&G uses multiple brand names for the same product when competing internationally. For instance, PertPlus shampoo is sold as Rejoice in Hong Kong, Pert-

Black & Decker uses a multibranding strategy to reach different market segments. Black & Decker markets its line of tools for the do-it-yourselfer market with the Black & Decker name, but uses the DeWalt name for its professional tool line.

Black & Decker
www.blackanddecker.com

Plus in the Middle East, and Vidal Sassoon in the United Kingdom. However, international branding strategies do differ. In Japan, where corporate names are important, P&G markets the company's name prominently with the brand name of the product.

Compared with the multiproduct approach, promotional costs tend to be higher with multibranding. The company must generate awareness among consumers and retailers for each new brand name without the benefit of any previous impressions. The advantages of this approach are that each brand is unique to each market segment and there is no risk that a product failure will affect other products in the line. Nevertheless, some large multibrand firms have found that the complexity and expense of implementing this strategy can outweigh the benefits. For example, Unilever is presently pruning its brands from some 1,600 to 400 through product deletion and sales to other companies.[36]

The multibranding approach in Europe is slowly being replaced by **euro-branding**, the strategy of using the same brand name for the same product across all countries in the European Union. This strategy has many of the benefits linked with multiproduct branding in addition to making Pan-European advertising and promotion programs possible.

Private Branding   A company uses **private branding**, often called *private labeling* or *reseller branding,* when it manufactures products but sells them under the brand name of a wholesaler or retailer. Rayovac, Paragon Trade Brands, and Ralcorp Holding are major suppliers of private label alkaline batteries, diapers, and grocery products, respectively. Radio Shack, Sears, Kmart, and Kroger are large retailers that have their own brand names. Private branding is popular because it typically produces high profits for manufacturers and resellers. Consumers also buy them. It is estimated that one of every five items purchased at U.S. supermarkets, drugstores, and mass merchandisers such as Wal-Mart bears a private brand.[37]

MARKETING NEWSNET

Creating Customer Value through Packaging: Pez Heads Dispense More Than Candy

CUSTOMER VALUE

Customer value can assume numerous forms. For Pez Candy, Inc. (www.pez.com), customer value manifests itself in some 250 Pez character candy dispensers. Each 99 cent refillable dispenser ejects tasty candy tablets in a variety of flavors that delight preteen and teens alike.

Pez was formulated in 1927 by Austrian food mogul Edward Haas III and successfully sold in Europe as an adult breath mint. Pez, which comes from the German word for peppermint, *pfefferminz,* was originally packaged in a hygienic, headless plastic dispenser. Pez first appeared in the United States in 1953 with a headless dispenser, marketed to adults. After conducting extensive marketing research, Pez was repositioned with fruit flavors, repackaged with licensed character heads on top of the dispenser, and remarketed as a children's product in the mid-1950s. Since then, most top-level licensed characters and hundreds of other characters have become Pez heads. Consumers eat more than 3 billion Pez tablets annually, and company sales growth exceeds that of the candy industry as a whole.

The unique Pez package dispenses a "use experience"

for its customers beyond the candy itself, namely, fun. And fun translates into a 98 percent awareness level for Pez among teenagers and 89 percent among mothers with children. Pez has not advertised its product for years. With that kind of awareness, who needs advertising?

Mixed Branding   A compromise between manufacturer and private branding is **mixed branding**, where a firm markets products under its own name and that of a reseller because the segment attracted to the reseller is different from their own market. Sanyo and Toshiba manufacture television sets for Sears as well as for themselves. This process is similar to Michelin's, which manufactures tires for Sears as well as under its own name. Kodak uses a mixed branding approach in Japan to increase its sales of 35-mm film. In addition to selling its Kodak brand, the company now makes "COOP" private label film for the Japanese Consumer Cooperative Union, which is a group of 2,500 stores. Priced significantly below its Kodak brand, the private label seeks to attract the price-sensitive Japanese consumer.[38]

Generic Branding   An alternative branding approach is the **generic brand**, which is a no-brand product such as dog food, peanut butter, or green beans. There is no identification other than a description of the contents. The major appeal is that the price is up to one-third less than that of branded items. Generic brands account for less than 1 percent of total grocery sales. The limited appeal of generics has been attributed to the popularity of private brands and greater promotional efforts for manufacturer brand name items. Consumers who use generics see these products as being as good as brand name items, and in light of what they expect, users of these products are relatively pleased with their purchases.

PACKAGING AND LABELING

The **packaging** component of a product refers to any container in which it is offered for sale and on which label information is conveyed. A **label** is an integral part of the package and typically identifies the product or brand, who made it, where

Can you name this soft drink brand? If you can, then the package has fulfilled its purpose.

and when it was made, how it is to be used, and package contents and ingredients. To a great extent, the customer's first exposure to a product is the package and label and both are an expensive and important part of marketing strategy. For Pez Candy, Inc. the character head-on-a-stick plastic container that dispenses a miniature brick candy is the central element of its marketing strategy as described in the accompanying Marketing NewsNet.[39]

Creating Customer Value through Packaging and Labeling

Packaging and labeling costs companies about $100 billion annually and account for about 15 cents of every dollar spent by consumers for products.[40] Despite the cost, packaging and labeling are essential because both provide important benefits for the manufacturer, retailer, and ultimate consumer.

Communication Benefits
A major benefit of packaging is the label information on it conveyed to the consumer, such as directions on how to use the product and the composition of the product, which is needed to satisfy legal requirements of product disclosure. For example, the labeling system for packaged and processed foods, which created a uniform format for nutritional and dietary information, became effective in the mid-1990s at a cost of $2 billion to food companies. Other information consists of seals and symbols, either government required or commercial seals of approval (such as the Good Housekeeping seal).

Packaging also can have brand equity benefits for a company. According to the director of marketing for L'eggs hosiery, "Packaging is important to the equity of the L'eggs brand." Why? Packaging has been shown to enhance brand recognition and facilitate the formation of strong, favorable, and unique brand associations.[41]

Functional Benefits
Packaging often plays an important functional role, such as convenience, protection, or storage. Quaker State changed its oil containers to eliminate the need for a separate spout, and Borden changed the shape of its Elmer's Wonder Bond adhesive to prevent clogging of the spout.

The unique cylindrical packaging for Pringles provides both functional and perceptual benefits and serves as a major point of difference for the snack chip.

Pringles

www.pringles.com

The convenience dimension of packaging is becoming increasingly important. Kraft Miracle Whip salad dressing and Heinz ketchup are sold in squeeze bottles, microwave popcorn has been a major market success, and Chicken of the Sea tuna and Folgers coffee are packaged in single-serving portions.

Consumer protection has become an important function of packaging, including the development of tamper-resistant containers. Today, companies commonly use safety seals or pop-tops that reveal previous opening. Nevertheless, no package is truly tamper resistant. U.S. law now provides for maximum penalties of life imprisonment and $250,000 fines for package tampering. Consumer protection through labeling exists in "open dating," which states the expected shelf life of the product.

Perceptual Benefits   A third component of packaging and labeling is the perception created in the consumer's mind. Just Born Inc., a candy manufacturer of such brands as Jolly Joes and Mike and Ike Treats, discovered the importance of this component of packaging. For many years the brands were sold in old-fashioned black and white packages, but when the packaging was changed to four color, with animated grape and cherry characters, sales increased 25 percent. Coca-Cola brought back its famous pale-green, contoured 8-ounce bottle to attract consumers who remember drinking soft drinks from glass bottles, not from aluminum cans and large plastic bottles. A worldwide sales increase of 8 percent was linked to the new-old bottle.[42]

A package can connote status, economy, and product quality. Procter & Gamble's Original Pringles, with its unique cylindrical packaging, offers uniform chips, minimal breakage, freshness, and better value for the money than flex-bag packages for chips.

In the past, the color of packages was selected subjectively. For example, the famous Campbell's soup can was the inspiration of a company executive who liked Cornell

University's red and white football uniforms. Today, there is greater recognition that color affects consumers' perceptions.[43] When the color of the can of Barrelhead Sugar-Free Root Beer changed to beige from blue, consumers said it tasted more like old-fashioned root beer. And Owens-Corning judged the pink color of its fiber insulation to be so important that the color was given trademark status by the courts.

Because labels list a product's source, brands competing in the global marketplace can benefit from "country of origin or manufacture" perceptions as described in Chapter 7. Consumers tend to have stereotypes about country-product pairings that they judge "best"—English tea, French perfume, Italian leather, and Japanese electronics—which can affect a brand's image.[44] Increasingly today, Chinese firms are adopting the English language and Roman letters for their brand's labels. This is being done because of the perception in many Asian countries that "things Western are good," even if consumers cannot understand the meaning of the English words![45]

Global Trends in Packaging

Two global trends in packaging originating in the mid-1990s continue into the twenty-first century. One trend involves the environmental effects of packaging, the other focuses on packaging health and safety concerns.

Environmental Sensitivity

Environmental Sensitivity   Because of widespread worldwide concern about the growth of solid waste and the shortage of viable landfill sites, the amount, composition, and disposal of packaging material continues to receive much attention.[46] Recycling packaging material is a major thrust. Procter & Gamble now uses recycled cardboard in 70 percent of its paper packaging and is packaging Tide, Cheer, Era, and Dash detergents in jugs that contain 25 percent recycled plastic. Spic and Span liquid cleaner is packaged in 100 percent recycled material. Other firms, such as the large U.K. retailer Sainsbury, emphasize the use of less packaging material. Sainsbury examines every product it sells to ensure that each uses only the minimum material necessary for shipping and display.

European countries have been trendsetters concerning packaging guidelines and environmental sensitivity. Many of these guidelines now exist in provisions governing trade to and within the European Union. In Germany, 80 percent of packaging material must be collected, and 80 percent of this amount must be recycled or reused to reduce solid waste in landfills. U.S. firms marketing in Europe have responded to these guidelines, and ultimately benefited U.S. consumers.

Increasingly, firms are using life-cycle analysis (LCA) to examine the environmental effect of their packaging at every stage from raw material sources and production through distribution and disposal. A classic use of LCA was the decision by McDonald's to abandon the polystyrene clam shells it used to package its hamburger. LCA indicated that the environment would be better served if the amount of solid waste packaging was reduced than if the polystyrene shells were recycled. McDonald's elected to package its hamburgers in a light wrap made of paper and polyethylene and eliminate the polystyrene package altogether.

Health and Safety Concerns

Health and Safety Concerns   A second trend involves the growing health and safety concerns of packaging materials. Today, a majority of U.S. and European consumers believe companies should make sure products and their packages are safe, regardless of the cost, and companies are responding to this view in numerous ways.[47] Most butane lighters sold today, such as those made by BIC, contain a child-resistant safety latch to prevent misuse and accidental fire. Child-proof caps on pharmaceutical products and household cleaners and sealed lids on food packages are now common. New packaging technology and materials that extend a product's *shelf life* (the time a product can be stored) and prevent spoilage continue to be developed with special applications for less-developed countries.

PRODUCT WARRANTY

A final component for product consideration is the **warranty**, which is a statement indicating the liability of the manufacturer for product deficiencies. There are various types of product warranties with different implications for manufacturers and customers.[48]

Some companies offer *express warranties,* which are written statements of liabilities. In recent years the FTC has required greater disclosure on express warranties to indicate whether the warranty is a limited-coverage or full-coverage alternative. A *limited-coverage warranty* specifically states the bounds of coverage and, more important, areas of noncoverage. A *full warranty* has no limits of noncoverage. Cadillac is a company that boldly touts its warranty coverage. The Magnuson-Moss Warranty/FTC Improvement Act (1975) regulates the content of consumer warranties and so has strengthened consumer rights with regard to warranties.

With greater frequency, manufacturers are being held to *implied warranties,* which assign responsibility for product deficiencies to the manufacturer. Studies show that warranties are important and affect a consumer's product evaluation. Brands that have limited warranties tend to receive less positive evaluations compared with full-warranty items.

Warranties are also important in light of increasing product liability claims. In the early part of this century the courts protected companies, but the trend now is toward "strict liability" rulings, where a manufacturer is liable for any product defect, whether it followed reasonable research standards or not. This issue is hotly contested between companies and consumer advocates.

Warranties represent much more to the buyer than just protection from negative consequences—they can hold a significant marketing advantage for the producer. Sears has built a strong reputation for its Craftsman tool line with a simple warranty: if you break a tool, it's replaced with no questions asked. Zippo has an equally simple guarantee: "If it ever fails, we'll fix it free."

Concept Check

1. How does a generic brand differ from a private brand?

2. Explain the role of packaging in terms of perception.

3. What is the difference between an expressed and an implied warranty?

SUMMARY

1 Products have a finite life cycle consisting of four stages: introduction, growth, maturity, and decline. The marketing objectives for each stage differ.

2 In the introductory stage the need is to establish primary demand, whereas the growth stage requires selective demand strategies. In the maturity stage the need is to maintain market share; the decline stage necessitates a deletion or harvesting strategy.

3 There are various shapes to the product life cycle. High learning products have a long introductory period, and low learning products rapidly enter the growth stage. There are also different curves for fashions and fads. Different product life-cycle curves can exist for the product class and product form.

4 In managing a product's life cycle, changes can be made in the product itself or in the target market. Product modification approaches include changes in the quality, performance, or appearance. Market modification approaches entail increasing a product's use among existing customers, creating new use situations, or finding new users.

5 Product repositioning can come about by reacting to a competitor's position, reaching a new market, capitalizing on a rising trend, or changing the value offered in a product.

6 Branding enables a firm to distinguish its product in the marketplace from those of its competitors. Successful and established brands take on a brand personality, a set of human characteristics associated with a brand name. A good brand name should suggest the product benefits, be memorable, fit the company or product image, be free of legal restrictions, and be simple and emotional. A good brand name is of such importance that is has led to a concept of brand equity, the added value a given brand name gives to a product beyond the functional benefits provided.

7 Licensing of a brand name is being used by many companies. The company allows the name to be used without having to manufacture the product.

8 Manufacturers can follow one of three branding strategies: a manufacturer's brand, a reseller brand, or a mixed brand approach. With a manufacturer's branding approach, the company can use the same brand name for all products in the line (multiproduct, or family, branding) or can give products different brands (multibranding).

9 A reseller, or private, brand is used when a firm manufactures a product but sells it under the brand name of a wholesaler or retailer. A generic brand is a product with no identification of manufacturer or reseller that is offered on the basis of price appeal.

10 Packaging and labeling provide communication, functional, and perceptual benefits. The two global emerging trends in packaging are greater concerns regarding the environmental impact and the health and safety of packaging materials.

11 The warranty, a statement of a manufacturer's liability for product deficiencies, is an important aspect of a manufacturer's product strategy.

KEY TERMS AND CONCEPTS

brand equity p. 306
brand name p. 305
brand personality p. 306
branding p. 305
co-branding p. 310
downsizing p. 305
euro-branding p. 311
generic brand p. 312
label p. 312
licensing p. 308
manufacturer branding p. 309
market modification p. 303
mixed branding p. 312

multibranding p. 310
multiproduct branding p. 309
packaging p. 312
private branding p. 311
product class p. 300
product form p. 300
product life cycle p. 294
product modification p. 302
trade name p. 305
trademark p. 305
trading down p. 305
trading up p. 304
warranty p. 316

APPLYING MARKETING CONCEPTS AND PERSPECTIVES

1 Listed here are three different products in various stages of the product life cycle. What marketing strategies would you suggest to these companies? (*a*) GTE cellular telephone company—growth stage, (*b*) Mountain Stream tap-water purifying systems—introductory stage, and (*c*) hand-held manual can openers—decline stage.

2 It has often been suggested that products are intentionally made to break down or wear out. Is this strategy a planned product modification approach?

3 The product manager of GE is reviewing the penetration of trash compactors in American homes. After more than two decades in existence, this product is in relatively few homes. What problems can account for this poor acceptance? What is the shape of the trash compactor life cycle?

4 For several years Ferrari has been known as the manufacturer of expensive luxury automobiles. The company plans to attract the major segment of the car-buying market who purchase medium-priced automobiles. As Ferrari considers this trading-down strategy, what branding strategy would you recommend? What are the trade-offs to consider with your strategy?

5 The nature of product warranties has changed as the federal court system reassesses the meaning of warranties. How does the regulatory trend toward warranties affect product development?

INTERNET EXERCISE

New Product News provides a central Internet location on the latest new products. It provides a forum for companies to present their most recent new products. New Product News is updated daily with company press releases from the entire world. Some 30 product categories with one or more new products are typically listed by New Product News each day. A unique feature of New Product News is that a company website address that can be accessed immediately follows each new product description.

Visit the New Product News website at <u>www.newproductnews.com</u> and go to "new items this week." Your assignment is outlined below:

1 Identify and describe how a new product listed promotes more frequent usage, creates a new use situation, reaches a new market or new users, or changes the value offered to consumers.

2 Identify and describe a new product that is branded using a family branding strategy, a subbranding strategy, or a brand extension strategy.

VIDEO CASE 11–1   BMW: "Newness" and the Product Life Cycle

"We're fortunate right now at BMW in that all of our products are new and competitive," says Jim McDowell, vice president of marketing at BMW, as he explains BMW's product life cycle. "Now, how do you do that? You have to introduce new models over time. You have to logically plan out the introductions over time, so you're not changing a whole model range at the same time you're changing another model range."

BMW's strategy is to keep its products in the introduction and growth stages by periodically introducing new models in each of its product lines. In fact, BMW does not like to have any products in the maturity or decline stage of the product life cycle. Explains McDowell, "If a product is declining, we would prefer to withdraw it from the market, as opposed to having a strategy for dealing with the declining product. We're kind of a progressive, go get 'em company, and we don't think it does our brand image any good to have any declining products out there. So that's why we work so hard at managing the growth aspect."

BMW—THE COMPANY AND ITS PRODUCTS

BMW is one of the preeminent luxury car manufacturers in Europe, North America, and the world today. BMW produces several lines of cars, including the 3 series, the 5 series, the 7 series, the Z line (driven by Pierce Brosnan as James Bond in *Goldeneye*), and the new X line, BMW's "sport activity" vehicle line. In addition, BMW is now selling Rovers, a British car line anchored by the internationally popular Land Rover sport utility vehicle, and will begin selling Rolls Royce vehicles in 2003. Sales of all the BMW, Rover, and Land Rover vehicles have been on the rise globally. High-profile image campaigns (such as the James Bond promotion) and the award-winning BMW website (where users can design their own car) continue to increase the popularity of BMW's products.

PRODUCT LIFE CYCLE

BMW cars typically have a product life cycle of seven years. To keep products in the introductory and growth stages, BMW regularly introduces new models for each of its series to keep the entire series "new." For instance, with the 3 series, it will introduce the new sedan model one year, the new coupe the next year, then the convertible, then the station wagon, and then the sport hatchback. That's a new product introduction for five of the seven years of the product life cycle. McDowell explains, "So, even though we have seven-year life cy-

cles, we constantly try and make the cars meaningfully different and new about every three years. And that involves adding features and other capabilities to the cars as well." How well does this strategy work? BMW often sees its best sales numbers in either the sixth or seventh year after the product introduction.

As global sales have increased, BMW has become aware of some international product life-cycle differences. For example, it has discovered that some competitive products have life cycles that are shorter or longer than seven years. In Sweden and Britain automotive product life cycles are eight years, while in Japan they are typically only four years long.

BRANDING

"BMW is fortunate—we don't have too much of a dilemma as to what we're going to call our cars." McDowell is referring to BMW's trademark naming system that consists of the product line number and the motor type. For example, the designation "328" tells you the car is in the 3 series and the engine is 2.8 liters in size. BMW has found this naming system to be clear and logical and can be easily understood around the world. The Z and X series don't quite fit in with this system. BMW had a tradition of building experimental, open-air cars and calling them Z's, and hence when the prototype for the Z3 was built, BMW decided to continue with the Z name. For the sport activity vehicle, BMW also used a letter name—the X series—since the four-wheel drive vehicle didn't fit with the sedan-oriented 3, 5, and 7 series. Other than the Z3 (the third in the Z series) and the X5 (named 5 to symbolize its mid-sized status within that series), the BMW branding strategy is quite simple, unlike the evocative names many car manufacturers choose to garner excitement for their new models.

MANAGING THE PRODUCT THROUGH THE WEB—THE WAVE OF THE FUTURE

One of the ways BMW is improving its product offerings even further is through its innovative website (www.bmwusa.com). At the site, customers can learn about the particular models, e-mail questions, and request literature or test-drives from their local BMW dealership. What really sets BMW's website apart from other car manufacturers, though, is the ability for customers to configure a car to their own specifications (interior choices, exterior choices, engine, packages, and options) and then transfer that information to their local

dealer. As Carol Burrows, product communications manager for BMW, explains, "The BMW website is an integrated part of the overall marketing strategy for BMW. The full range of products can be seen and interacted with online. We offer pricing options online. Customers can go to their local dealership via the website to further discuss costs for purchase of a car. And it is a distribution channel for information that allows people access to the information 24 hours a day at their convenience."

Questions

1 Compare the product life cycle described by BMW for its cars to the product life cycle shown in Figure 11–1. How are they (*a*) similar and (*b*) dissimilar?

2 Based on BMW's typical product life cycle, what marketing strategies are appropriate for the 3 series? The X5?

3 Which of the three ways to manage the product life cycle does BMW utilize with its products—modifying the product, modifying the market, or repositioning the product?

4 How would you describe BMW's branding strategy (manufacturer branding, private branding, or mixed branding)? Why?

5 Go to the BMW website (www.bmwusa.com) and design a car to your own specifications. How does this enable you as a customer to evaluate the product differently than would be otherwise possible?

CHAPTER

12

MANAGING SERVICES

AFTER READING THIS CHAPTER YOU SHOULD BE ABLE TO:

- Describe four unique elements of services.

- Recognize how services differ and how they can be classified.

- Understand the way in which consumers purchase and evaluate services.

- Develop a customer contact audit to identify service advantages.

- Understand the important role of internal marketing in service organizations.

- Explain the role of the four Ps in the services marketing mix.

THE HARD ROCK CAFÉ KNOWS WHAT YOU WANT: AN EXCEPTIONAL EXPERIENCE!

Hard Rock Cafés "offer exciting nightlife, great food, and live entertainment" explains CEO and president Pete Beaudrault. In fact, the mission of Hard Rock Café International is "to spread the spirit of rock 'n' roll by delivering an exceptional entertainment and dining experience." If you've ever been to one of the cafés you'll probably agree—they are designed to emphasize the rock 'n' roll theme and provide a unique and distinctive experience for customers!

It all started more than 30 years ago when Eric Clapton gave the original Hard Rock Café in London his guitar to be displayed at his favorite table. Soon another guitar arrived from The Who's Pete Townshend, and ever since the restaurants have displayed memorabilia from rock's favorite musicians and bands including Elvis Presley, Jimi Hendrix, Aerosmith, The Red Hot Chili Peppers, Madonna, U2, Creed, and Matchbox Twenty. Today, there are more than 100 Hard Rock Cafés in 40 countries and the music memorabilia collection is worth $32 million.

To add to the experience the company is using streaming video to bring local musical performances to all of its locations. According to Scott Little, Hard Rock's strategic planner, "we'll use the Web to create a forum for up-and-coming artists and to bring national bands that play our large concert venues into the smaller locations." In Chicago the live video is shown on 64 huge flat-screen monitors! There is also an e-commerce aspect to the experience now because Hard Rock fans can use the Hard Rock Web page as an entertainment portal to listen to and purchase music, buy memorabilia through a special eBay auction service, and subscribe to digital-music programming.[1]

The Hard Rock Café is one of many service organizations today competing for customers by offering enjoyable, memorable experiences rather than traditional service transactions. Walt Disney was one of the first to recognize the importance of sights, sounds, tastes, aromas, and textures to provide a unique experience when he created Disneyland. Chuck E. Cheese's uses a similar approach to sell birthday party experiences that include entertainment, food, music, and a fun environment. Companies that sell goods with a service element are also offering experiences. Nike, for example, offers fun activities and promotional events in its own store, Niketown, and Steinway provides a free concert including a pianist, invitations, and hors d'oeuvres in its customers' homes. These businesses are increasing the value of their offering to customers by engaging them in experiential elements of their service.

Some experts believe we are on the verge of a new economic era driven by an *experience economy.*[2] Coffee can be purchased as a commodity in a grocery store and brewed at home at a cost of about 10 cents per cup. Coffee can also be purchased from 7-11, where consumers pay for the convenience of the service, for a cost of about 75 cents per cup. But most of us have often paid about $3 per cup at a Starbucks where the look of the shop, the jazz music, and the barrista's knowledge of the beans creates a "coffee experience" that is still a good value. ESPN Zone, Home Depot, Planet Hollywood, and many other companies are responding to consumers' preferences for compelling experiences.

As the actions of the Hard Rock Café and the other examples above illustrate, the marketing of services is dynamic and challenging. In this chapter we discuss how services differ from traditional products (goods), how consumers make purchase decisions, and the ways in which the marketing mix is used.

THE UNIQUENESS OF SERVICES

As noted in Chapter 1, **services** are intangible items such as airline trips, financial advice, or automobile repair that an organization provides to consumers. To obtain these services, consumers exchange money or something else of value, such as their own time.

Services have become one of the most important components of the U.S. economy. While goods-producing firms employ approximately 25 million people, services employ more than 100 million, and they have continued to grow despite the recent economic downturn. In addition, approximately 40 percent of the gross domestic product (GDP) now comes from services. As shown in Figure 12–1, services accounted for $3.9 trillion in 2000, which was an increase of more than 350 percent since 1980. Services also represent a large export business—the $317 billion of services exports in 2000 is one of the few areas in which the United States has a trade surplus.[3]

The growth in this sector is the result of increased demand for services that have been available in the past and the increasing interest in new services. Concierge services, for example, have expanded beyond hotels and are now popular in department stores such as Nordstrom, real estate firms such as Century 21, and large office buildings. Families can call services such as Concierge Atelier, where owner Jeanne Clarey and her staff help with parenting questions, event planning, travel arrangements, shopping, and even taking pets to the veterinarian! New services include: Yahoo!Broadcast which offers a wide variety of audio and video content including radio stations, classic TV programs, full-length movies and live concerts; "Care Alert," a free service offered by the U.S. airline consortium and travel agency Orbitz, notifies customers by e-mail, pager, or telephone of flight status changes because of weather or mechanical problems; and the DNA Copyright Institute now offers a service to copyright the unique DNA contained in your genes! These firms and many others like them are examples of the imaginative services that will play a role in our economy in the future.[4]

FIGURE 12–1
Importance of services in the
U.S. gross domestic product
(GDP)

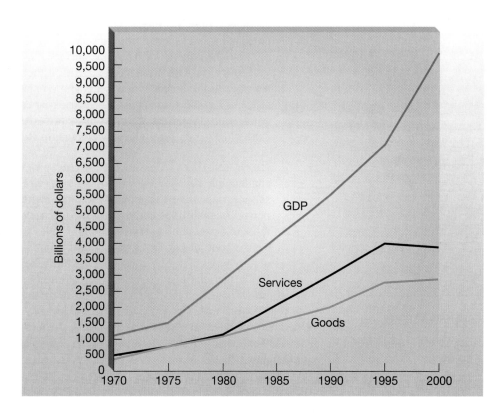

The Four I's of Services

There are four unique elements to services: intangibility, inconsistency, inseparability, and inventory. These four elements are referred to as the **four I's of services**.

Intangibility   Services are intangible; that is, they can't be held, touched, or seen before the purchase decision. In contrast, before purchasing a traditional product, a consumer can touch a box of laundry detergent, kick the tire of an automobile, or sample a new breakfast cereal. Because services tend to be a performance rather than

Why do many services
emphasize their tangible
benefits? The answer appears
in the text.

Virgin Atlantic
www.virgin.com

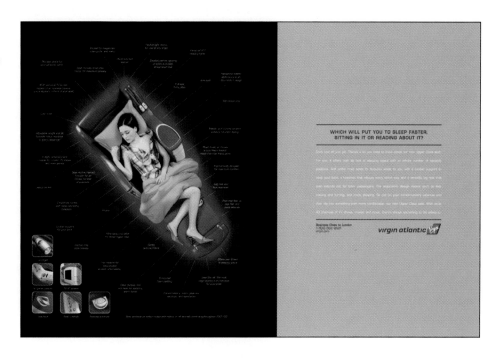

American Express Co.

an object, they are much more difficult for consumers to evaluate. To help consumers assess and compare services marketers try to make them tangible or show the benefits of using the service.

The Virgin Atlantic advertisement on the previous page shows a traveler sleeping in the airline's new seats and emphasizes features such as 6 feet of space, a TV and game console, electric seat controls, lights, and laptop power connection. American Express also provides tangible benefits by offering cardholders gifts through its Membership Rewards program.

Inconsistency   Developing, pricing, promoting, and delivering services is challenging because the quality of a service is often inconsistent. Because services depend on the people who provide them, their quality varies with each person's capabilities and day-to-day job performance. Inconsistency is much more of a problem in services than it is with tangible goods. Tangible products can be good or bad in terms of quality, but with modern production lines the quality will at least be consistent. On the other hand, one day the Philadelphia Phillies baseball team may have great hitting and pitching and look like a pennant winner and the next day lose by 10 runs. Or a soprano at New York's Metropolitan Opera may have a bad cold and give a less-than-perfect performance. Whether the service involves tax assistance at Arthur Andersen or guest relations at the Ritz-Carlton, organizations attempt to reduce inconsistency through standardization and training.[5]

Inseparability   A third difference between services and goods, and related to problems of consistency, is inseparability. In most cases, the consumer cannot (and does not) separate the deliverer of the service from the service itself. For example, to receive an education, a person may attend a university. The quality of the education may be high, but if the student has difficulty interacting with instructors, finds counseling services poor, or does not receive adequate library or computer assistance, he or she may not be satisfied with the educational experience. Students' evaluations of their education will be influenced primarily by their perceptions of instructors, counselors, librarians, and other people at the university.

The amount of interaction between the consumer and the service provider depends on the extent to which the consumer must be physically present to receive

People play an important role in the delivery of many services.

IBM Business Consultants

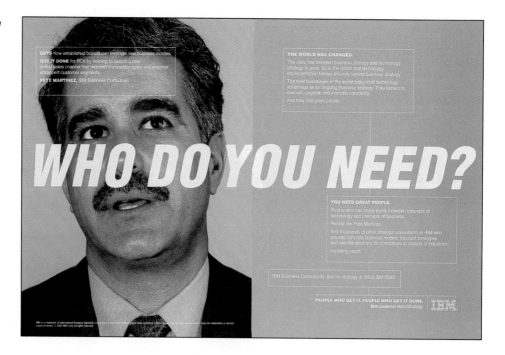

the service. Some services such as haircuts, golf lessons, medical diagnoses, and food service require the customer to participate in the delivery of the services. Other services such as car repair, dry cleaning, and waste disposal process tangible objects with less involvement from the customer. Finally, services such as banking, consulting, education, and insurance can now be delivered electronically, often requiring no face-to-face customer interaction.[6]

Inventory   Inventory of services is different from that of goods. Inventory problems exist with goods because many items are perishable and because there are costs associated with handling inventory. With services, inventory carrying costs are more subjective and are related to **idle production capacity**, which is when the service provider is available but there is no demand. The inventory cost of a service is the cost of paying the person used to provide the service along with any needed equipment. If a physician is paid to see patients but no one schedules an appointment, the fixed cost of the idle physician's salary is a high inventory carrying cost. In some service businesses, however, the provider of the service is on commission (the Merrill Lynch stockbroker) or is a part-time employee (a clerk at Sears). In these businesses, inventory carrying costs can be significantly lower or nonexistent because the idle production capacity can be cut back by reducing hours or having no salary to pay because of the commission compensation system. Figure 12–2 shows a scale of inventory carrying costs represented on the high end by airlines and hospitals and on the low end by real estate agencies and hair salons. The inventory carrying costs of airlines is high because of high-salaried pilots and very expensive equipment. In contrast, real estate agencies and hair salons have employees who work on commission and need little expensive equipment to conduct business. One reason service providers must maintain production capacity is because of the importance of time to today's customers. People don't want to wait long at the emergency room!

The Service Continuum

The four Is differentiate services from goods in most cases, but many companies are not clearly service-based or good-based organizations. Is IBM a computer company or service business? Although IBM manufactures computers and other goods, more than half the company's employees work in its services division providing systems integration, networking, consulting, education, and product support.[7] As companies look at what they bring to the market, there is a range from the tangible to the intangible or good-dominant to service-dominant offerings referred to as the **service continuum** (Figure 12–3).

Teaching, nursing, and the theater are intangible, service-dominant activities, and intangibility, inconsistency, inseparability, and inventory are major concerns in their marketing. Salt, neckties, and dog food are tangible goods, and the problems represented by the four Is are not relevant in their marketing. However, some

FIGURE 12–2
Inventory carrying costs of services

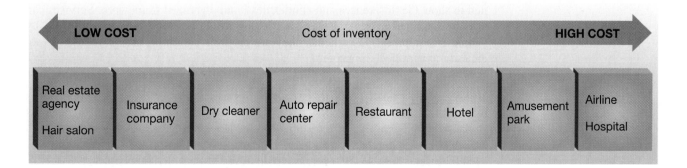

FIGURE 12-3
Service continuum

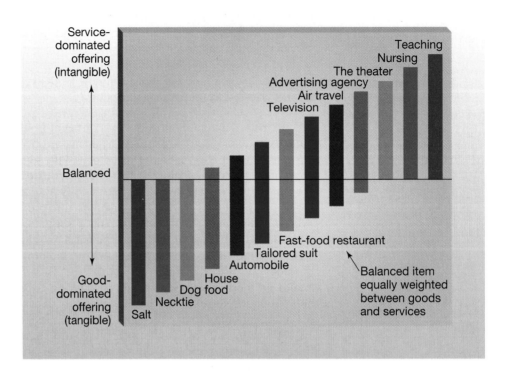

businesses are a mix of intangible service and tangible good factors. A clothing tailor provides a service but also a good, the finished suit. How pleasant, courteous, and attentive the tailor is to the customer is an important component of the service, and how well the clothes fit is an important part of the product. As shown in Figure 12–3, a fast-food restaurant is about half tangible goods (the food) and half intangible services (courtesy, cleanliness, speed, convenience).

For many businesses today it is useful to distinguish between their core product—either a good or a service—and supplementary services. A core service offering such as a bank account, for example, also has supplementary services such as deposit assistance, parking or drive-through availability, ATMs, and monthly statements. Supplementary services often allow service providers to differentiate their offering from competitors, and they may add value for consumers. While there are many potential supplementary services, key categories of supplementary services include information delivery, consultation, order taking, billing procedures, and payment options.[8] See the accompanying Marketing NewsNet to learn why sports teams try to augment their core offering.[9]

Classifying Services

Throughout this book, marketing organizations, techniques, and concepts are classified to show the differences and similarities in an organized framework. Services can also be classified in several ways, according to (1) whether they are delivered by people or equipment, (2) whether they are profit or nonprofit, or (3) whether or not they are government sponsored.

Delivery by People or Equipment As seen in Figure 12–4, many companies offer services. Professional services include management consulting firms such as Booz, Allen & Hamilton or Accenture. Skilled labor is required to offer services such as Sears appliance repair or Sheraton catering service. Unskilled labor such as that used by Brinks store-security forces is also a service provided by people.

MARKETING NEWSNET

Sports Get a Gold Medal. In Marketing!

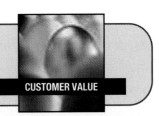

CUSTOMER VALUE

Like most services, sports teams know that inconsistency can reduce consumer interest. How well a team will play from game to game or year to year is difficult to control and predict. So in addition to providing a core service such as football or baseball games, many teams have invested in marketing programs that build an image and increase the entertainment value for fans. Promotional events, merchandise licensing, and new facilities with luxury seats have all become important marketing activities for sports teams. Some baseball stadiums have even added "beaming stations" to send statistics to fans' personal digital assistants.

While individual teams compete with each other, they also compete with other sports. The big four—baseball, football, basketball, and hockey—have seen significant shifts in popularity in recent years. Baseball, for example, has seen attendance and TV ratings steadily decline. Football has become the most popular sport in the United States through strong promotion of Monday Night Football, Sunday afternoon programs, and preseason training camp. Hockey has improved through expansion into southern states. Finally, basketball has been the fastest-growing sport in the world (after soccer).

The competition isn't limited to major sports though. Marketing efforts by many other familiar sports such as golf, tennis, gymnastics, soccer, and figure skating have been increasing. In addition, women's leagues are vying for fans' attention. And finally, many new and unfamiliar sports such as skysurfing, kite boarding, ice climbing, bull riding, bass fishing, and bicycle riding are developing growing fan interest.

Which sports marketing program is the most sophisticated? Probably the Olympics. Companies now pay $55 million for the privilege of being official Olympic sponsors, and TV rights are $1.3 billion. The $600 million marketing program includes public relations and advertising programs that have made the five rings the most recognizable sports logo on earth!

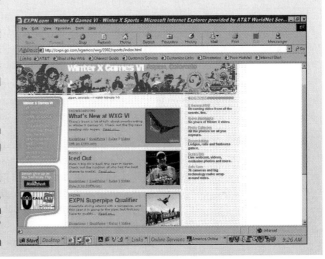

FIGURE 12–4
Service classifications

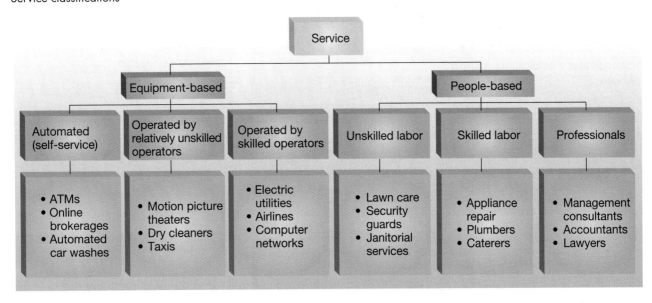

Equipment-based services do not have the marketing concerns of inconsistency because people are removed from the provision of the service. Electric utilities, for example can provide service without frequent personal contact with customers. Motion picture theaters have projector operators that consumers never see. And a growing number of customers use self-service technologies such as Schwab's online stock trading service without interacting with any service employees.[10]

Profit or Nonprofit Organizations   Many organizations involved in services also distinguish themselves by their tax status as profit or nonprofit organizations. In contrast to *profit organizations, nonprofit organizations'* excesses in revenue over expenses are not taxed or distributed to shareholders. When excess revenue exists, the money goes back into the organization's treasury to allow continuation of the service. Based on the corporate structure of the nonprofit organization, it may pay tax on revenue-generating holdings not directly related to its core mission. The 1.1 million nonprofit organizations in the United States now generate 7 percent of the gross domestic product.[11]

The American Red Cross, United Way, Greenpeace, Outward Bound, the Salvation Army, and the University of Florida are nonprofit organizations. Historically, misconceptions have limited the use of marketing practices by such organizations.[12] In recent years, however, nonprofit organizations such as hospitals, universities, and museums have turned to marketing to increase their revenues. The Girl Scouts of America is a good example. Faced with eight years of falling membership, they adopted a marketing orientation that reversed its membership trend and attracted more than 2.7 million young girls to become Girl Scouts.[13] Where can you get ideas for nonprofit marketing programs? See the Web Link to learn about several excellent resources!

Government Sponsored or Not   A third way to classify services is based on whether they are government sponsored. Although there is no direct ownership and they are nonprofit organizations, governments at the federal, state, and local levels provide a broad range of services. The United States Postal Service, for example, has adopted many marketing activities. Its "The U.S. Postal Service Is Everywhere So You Can Be Anywhere" campaign is designed to change its image of a huge bureaucracy, to focus its efforts on customer satisfaction, and to allow it to compete with UPS, FedEx, foreign postal services, and electronic communication technologies. Because faxes and e-mail

Nonprofit and government-sponsored services often advertise.

Outward Bound
www.outwardbound.com

United States Postal Service
www.usps.com

WEB LINK   Nonprofit Organizations Are Becoming Marketing Experts

Although nonprofit organizations may be relatively inexperienced with marketing practices, several websites are helping the industry catch up quickly. The Internet Nonprofit Center (www.nonprofit-info.org) offers answers to hundreds of questions including many on marketing. The GB3 Group's

site "Nonprofit Marketing Solutions," (www.gb3group.com) offers an answer center, book reviews, and a free marketing newsletter. Use the sites to collect ideas about marketing at nonprofit organizations.

have reduced first-class postage revenue, the Postal Service now tries to attract customers to its global package delivery service. Another marketing program has converted 700 postal offices to retail outlets that sell collector stamps, Pony Express sweatshirts, and even neckties! Government sponsorship does not limit competition, however. Britain's Royal Mail recently opened an office in Manhattan to compete for international direct-mail business.[14]

Concept Check	1. What are the four I's of services?
	2. Would inventory carrying costs for an accounting firm with certified public accountants be (a) high, (b) low, or (c) nonexistent?
	3. To eliminate service inconsistencies, companies rely on _____ and _____.

HOW CONSUMERS PURCHASE SERVICES

Colleges, hospitals, hotels, and even charities are facing an increasingly competitive environment. Successful service organizations, like successful product-oriented firms, must understand how the consumer makes a service purchase decision and quality evaluation and in what ways a company can present a differential advantage relative to competing offerings.

The Purchase Process

Many aspects of services affect the consumer's evaluation of the purchase. Because services cannot be displayed, demonstrated, or illustrated, consumers cannot make a prepurchase evaluation of all the characteristics of services.[15] Similarly, because service providers may vary in their delivery of a service, an evaluation of a service may change with each purchase. Figure 12–5 on the next page portrays how different types of goods and services are evaluated by consumers. Tangible goods such as clothing, jewelry, and furniture have *search* properties, such as color, size, and style, which can be determined before purchase. Services such as restaurants and child care have *experience* properties, which can only be discerned after purchase or during consumption. Finally, services provided by specialized professionals such as medical diagnoses and legal services have *credence* properties, or characteristics that the consumer may find impossible to evaluate even after purchase and consumption.[16] To reduce the uncertainty created by these properties, service consumers turn to personal sources of information such as early adopters, opinion leaders, and reference group members during the purchase decision process.[17]

FIGURE 12–5
How consumers evaluate
goods and services

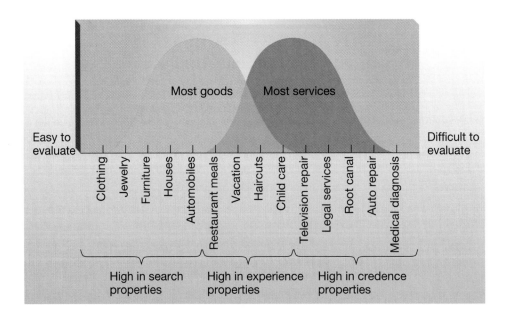

Assessing Service Quality

Once a consumer tries a service, how is it evaluated? Primarily by comparing expectations about a service offering to the actual experience a consumer has with the service.[18] Differences between the consumer's expectations and experience are identified through **gap analysis**. This type of analysis asks consumers to assess their expectations and experiences on dimensions of service quality such as those described in Figure 12–6.[19] Expectations are influenced by word-of-mouth communications, personal needs, past experiences, and promotional activities, while actual experiences are determined by the way an organization delivers its service.[20] The relative importance of the various dimensions of service quality varies by the type

FIGURE 12–6
Dimensions of service quality

DIMENSION	DEFINITION	EXAMPLES OF QUESTIONS AIRLINE CUSTOMERS MIGHT ASK
Reliability	Ability to perform the promised service dependably and accurately	Is my flight on time?
Tangibles	Appearance of physical facilities, equipment, personnel, and communication materials	Is the plane, the gate, the baggage area clean?
Responsiveness	Willingness to help customers and provide prompt service	Are the flight attendants willing to answer my questions?
Assurance	Knowledge and courtesy of employees and their ability to convey trust and confidence	Are the ticket counter attendants, flight attendants, and pilots knowledgeable about their jobs?
Empathy	Caring, individualized attention provided to customers	Do the employees determine if I have special seating, meal, baggage, transfer or rebooking needs?

of service.[21] What if someone is dissatisfied and complains? See the Marketing NewsNet on the next page for four steps that can help.[22]

Customer Contact and Relationship Marketing

Consumers judge services on the entire sequence of steps that make up the service process. To focus on these steps or "service encounters," a firm can develop a **customer contact audit**—a flowchart of the points of interaction between consumer and service provider.[23] This is particularly important in high-contact services such as hotels, educational institutions, and automobile rental agencies. Figure 12–7 is a consumer contact audit for renting a car from Hertz. The interactions identified in a customer contact audit often serve as the basis for developing relationships with customers.

A Customer's Car Rental Activities   A customer decides to rent a car and (1) contacts the rental company (see Figure 12–7). A customer service representative receives the information (2) and checks the availability of the car at the desired location. When the customer arrives at the rental site (3), the reservation system is again accessed, and the customer provides information regarding payment, address, and driver's license (4). A car is assigned to the customer (5), who proceeds by bus to the car pickup (6). On return to the rental location (7), the car is parked and the customer checks in (8), providing information on mileage, gas consumption, and damages (9). A bill is subsequently prepared (10).

Each of the steps numbered 1 to 10 is a customer contact point where the tangible aspects of Hertz service are seen by the customer. Figure 12–7, however, also shows a series of steps lettered A to E that involve two levels of inspections on the automobile. These steps are essential in providing a car that runs, but they are not points of customer interaction. To create a service advantage, Hertz must create a

FIGURE 12–7

Customer contact in car rental (green shaded boxes indicate customer activity)

The Hertz Corporation

www.hertz.com

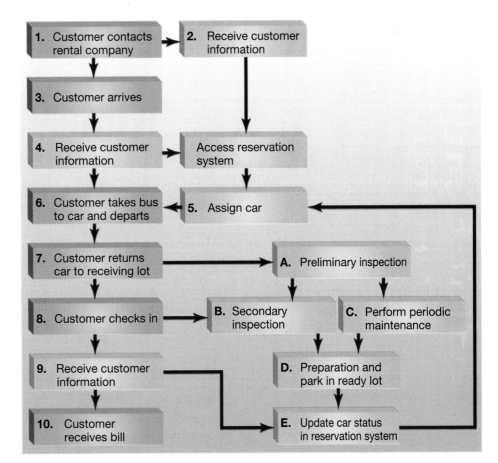

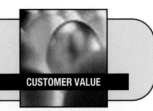

MARKETING NEWSNET

What if Someone Complains? How Services Can Recover from Failure to Satisfy a Customer!

CUSTOMER VALUE

Many service companies have developed strategies to encourage customer satisfaction and loyalty. Despite these efforts, however, every company has some service failures that lead to customer complaints. How can services recover from these situations? Professors Stephen Tax and Stephen Brown suggest four steps:

Step 1: Identify service failures. Only 5 to 10 percent of dissatisfied customers choose to complain—the rest simply switch companies or make negative comments to other people. One way companies encourage customers to express concerns is through 800 numbers.

Step 2: Resolve customer problems. Once customers complain, they want fair procedures, interactions, and outcomes. Because most complaints are first expressed to "front-line" employees, a key to resolving complaints is training employees to handle likely situations and giving them the authority to resolve problems. Federal Express, for example, gives new customer service representatives five weeks of training before assigning them to a location.

Step 3: Communicate and classify service failures. This step reflects the concept of organizational learning, or the capacity to improve performance based on experience. AT&T, for example, adds all complaints to its database in real time.

Step 4: Integrate data and improve overall service. Because only a small percentage of customers complain, other sources of relevant, timely information are needed. Information from surveys, focus groups, advisory panels, and other sources must be integrated with the complaint information to identify areas for service quality improvement.

Many firms are improving their methods of dealing with complaints. Scandanavian Airlines set up kiosks outside arrival gates to collect feedback from passengers. Xerox uses a Customer Action Request Form to facilitate its response to complaints. And at the Ritz-Carlton Hotels all 19,000 employees carry a plastic laminated card with the company's "Gold Standards." Number 13 of 20 guidelines: "Never lose a guest. Instant guest pacification is the responsibility of each employee. Whoever receives a complaint will own it, resolve it to the guest's satisfaction and record it."

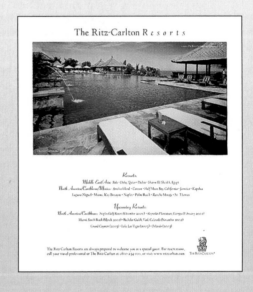

competitive advantage in the sequence of interactions with the customer. For example, Hertz has attempted to eliminate step 4 for some customers.

Relationship Marketing   The contact between a service provider and a customer represents a service encounter that is likely to influence the customer's assessment of the purchase. The number of encounters in a service experience may vary. Disney, for example, estimates that a park visitor will have 74 encounters with Disney employees in a single visit. These encounters represent opportunities to develop social bonds, or relationships, with customers. The relationship may also be developed through loyalty incentives such as airline frequent flyer programs and through service delivery systems such as the label-printing and package-tracking software given to high-volume customers by Federal Express. These elements are the basis for relationship marketing, which provides several benefits for service customers including the continuity of a single provider, customized service delivery, reduced stress due to a repetitive purchase process, and an absence of switching costs. Recent surveys of consumers have indicated that while customers of many services are interested in being "relationship customers," they also require that the relationship be balanced in terms of loyalty, benefits, and respect for privacy.[24]

Concept Check	1. What are the differences between search, experience, and credence properties?
	2. Hertz created its differential advantage at the points of _____ in their customer contact audit?

MANAGING THE MARKETING OF SERVICES

Just as the unique aspects of services necessitate changes in the consumer's purchase process, the marketing management process requires special adaptation.[25] As emphasized earlier in the chapter, in services marketing the employee plays a central role in attracting, building, and maintaining relationships with customers.[26] This aspect of services marketing has led to a concept called internal marketing.[27]

Internal marketing is based on the notion that a service organization must focus on its employees, or internal market, before successful programs can be directed at customers.[28] The internal marketing concept holds that an organization's employees (its "internal market") will be influenced to develop a market orientation if marketing-like activities are directed at them. This idea suggests that employees and employee development through recruitment, training, communication, and administration are critical to the success of service organizations.[29]

Let's use the four Ps framework of the text for discussing the marketing mix for services.

Product (Service)

To a large extent, the concepts of the product component of the marketing mix discussed in Chapters 10 and 11 apply equally well to Cheerios (a good) and to American Express (a service). Yet there are three aspects of the product/service element of the mix that warrant special attention: exclusivity, brand name, and capacity management.

Exclusivity   Chapter 10 pointed out that one favorable dimension in a new product is its ability to be patented. Remember that a patent gives the manufacturer of a product exclusive rights to its production for 17 years. A major difference between products and services is that services cannot be patented. Hence the creator of a successful fast-food hamburger chain could quickly discover the concept being copied by others. Domino's Pizza, for example, has seen competitors copy the quick delivery advantage that propelled the company to success. Many businesses today try to distinguish their core product with new or improved supplementary services through outsourcing: hotels outsource concierge services, airlines outsource maintenance, and banks outsource the mailing of monthly statements.[30]

Branding   An important aspect in marketing goods is the branding strategy used. However, because services are intangible and, therefore, more difficult to describe, the brand name or identifying logo of the service organization is particularly important in consumer decisions.[31] The financial services industry, for example, has failed to use branding to distinguish what consumers perceive to be similar offerings by banks, mutual fund companies, brokerage firms, and insurance companies. Federal Express, however, is a strong service brand name because it suggests the possibility that it is government sanctioned, and it describes the nature and benefit (speed) of the service.[32] Take a look at the figures on the next page to determine how successful some companies have been in branding their service by name, logo, or symbol.

Logos create service identities.

Capacity Management   Most services have a limited capacity due to the inseparability of the service from the service provider and the perishable nature of the service. For example, a patient must be in the hospital at the same time as the surgeon to "buy" an appendectomy, and only one patient can be helped at that time. Similarly, no additional surgery can be conducted tomorrow because of an unused operating room or an available surgeon today—the service capacity is lost if it is not used. So the service component of the mix must be integrated with efforts to influence consumer demand.[33] This is referred to as **capacity management**.

Service organizations must manage the availability of the offering so that (1) demand matches capacity over the duration of the demand cycle (for example, one day, week, month, year), and (2) the organization's assets are used in ways that will maximize the return on investment (ROI).[34] Figure 12–8 shows how a hotel tries to manage its capacity during the high and low seasons. Differing price structures are assigned to each segment of consumers to help moderate or adjust demand for the service. Airline contracts fill a fixed number of rooms throughout the year. In the slow season, when more rooms are available, tour packages at appealing prices are used to attract groups or conventions, such as an offer for seven nights in Orlando at a reduced price. Weekend packages are also offered to buyers. In the high-demand season, groups are less desirable because guests who will pay high prices travel to Florida on their own.

FIGURE 12–8
Managing capacity in a hotel

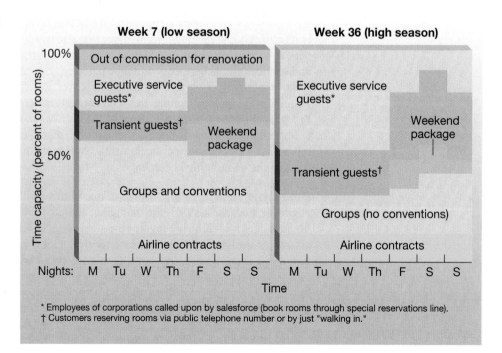

* Employees of corporations called upon by salesforce (book rooms through special reservations line).
† Customers reserving rooms via public telephone number or by just "walking in."

Pricing

In the service industries, *price* is referred to in various ways. Hospitals refer to charges; consultants, lawyers, physicians, and accountants to fees; airlines to fares; and hotels to rates. Regardless of the term used, price plays two essential roles: (1) to affect consumer perceptions and (2) to be used in capacity management. Because of the intangible nature of services, price can indicate the quality of the service. Would you wonder about the quality of a $100 surgery? Studies have shown that when there are few well-known cues by which to judge a product, consumers use price.[35] Look at the accompanying ad for eye surgery. Would you have concerns about the offer or think it's a good value for the money?

The capacity management role of price is also important to movie theaters, airlines, restaurants, and hotels. Many service businesses use **off-peak pricing**, which consists of charging different prices during different times of the day or days of the week to reflect variations in demand for the service. Airlines offer discounts for weekend travel, and movie theaters offer matinee prices. The New York State Thruway Authority has been testing different toll amounts for different times of the day to try to reduce traffic during rush hour.[36]

Place (Distribution)

Place or distribution is a major factor in developing a service marketing strategy because of the inseparability of services from the producer. Historically in services marketing, little attention has been paid to distribution. But as competition grows, the value of convenient distribution is being recognized. Hairstyling chains such as Cost Cutters Family Hair Care, tax preparation offices such as H & R Block, and accounting firms such as Deloitte and Touche all use multiple locations for the distribution of services. In the banking industry, customers of participating banks using the Cirrus system can access any one of thousands of automatic teller systems throughout the United States. The availability of electronic distribution through the World Wide Web now provides global coverage for travel services, banking, entertainment, and many other information-based services.

Promotion

The value of promotion, specifically advertising, for many services is to show the benefits of purchasing the service. It is valuable to stress availability, location, consistent quality, and efficient, courteous service.[37] The Princeton Review ad on the next page, for example, describes the benefits available to its customers—higher test scores. In addition, services must be concerned with their image. Promotional efforts,

Price influences perceptions of services.

Services need promotional programs.

The Princeton Review

www.princetonreview.com

Accenture

www.accenture.com

such as Accenture's "Now it gets interesting" campaign or Merrill Lynch's use of the bull in its ads, contribute to image and positioning strategies.[38] In most cases promotional concerns of services are similar to those of products.

In the past, advertising has been viewed negatively by many nonprofit and professional service organizations. In fact, professional groups such as law, dentistry, and medicine had previously used their respective professional codes of conduct to prevent their members from advertising. A Supreme Court case in 1976, however, struck down this constraint on professional services advertising.[39] Although opposition to advertising remains strong in some professional groups, the barriers to promotion are gradually disappearing. In recent years, advertising has been used by religious groups; legal, medical, and dental services; educational institutions; and many other service organizations. Attorney Rosalie Osias of Long Island, New York, more than doubled the number of cases at her real estate and banking law practice by running ads in two trade newspapers covering the mortgage banking industry in New York.[40]

Another form of promotion, publicity, has played a major role in the promotional strategy of nonprofit services and some professional organizations. Nonprofit organizations such as public school districts, the Chicago Symphony Orchestra, religious organizations, and hospitals have used publicity to disseminate their messages. Because of the heavy reliance on publicity, many services use public service announcements (PSAs), and because PSAs are free, nonprofit groups have tended to rely on them as the foundation of their media plan.[41] However, as discussed in Chapter 19, the timing and location of a PSA are under the control of the medium, not the organization. So the nonprofit service group cannot control who sees the message or when the message is given.

SERVICES IN THE FUTURE

What can we expect from the services industry in the future? New and better services, of course, and an unprecedented variety of choices. Many of the changes will be the result of two factors—deregulation and technological development.

One by one, transportation, telecommunications, financial services, professional services, and others have gone through some kind of regulatory changes. The

Telecommunications Act of 1996, for example, was designed to open the telecommunications markets to competition and provide better local phone services, more innovative wireless services, and easier access to broadband Internet connections. In the banking industry, deregulation in 2000 has led to car companies, retailers, and universities opening their own banks. Nordstrom Federal Savings Bank already has 5 million customers! Even more recently 24 states have instituted electricity utility deregulation to encourage competition. Although the new approach has led to difficulties in some states such as California, in other states it has encouraged investment in new power plants and kept power rates low.[42]

Technological advances are also changing the service industry. New "cyberservices" will include online photography websites such as AOL's You've Got Pictures which develop film, post the photos online, provide editing software to crop or touch up the images, and allow you to custom order prints. New Internet-based services will also make it possible to obtain videos, movies, and even textbooks like this one electronically. What is the hottest trend in new services? Matchmaking—some experts claim that there may soon be as many as 10,000 dating services available! Match.com, for example, boasts 5 million members and more than 1,000 marriages. In Japan, the services are so popular they are offered in I-mode, the technology that allows Web access from cell phones.[43]

Concept Check

1. Matching demand with capacity is the focus of _____ management.

2. How does a movie theater use off-peak pricing?

3. What factors will influence future changes in services?

SUMMARY

1 Services have four unique elements: intangibility, inconsistency, inseparability, and inventory.

2 Intangibility refers to the difficulty of communicating the service benefits. Inconsistency refers to the difficulty of providing the same level of quality each time a service is purchased. Inseparability means that consumers cannot separate the deliverer of the service from the service itself. Inventory costs for services are related to the cost of maintaining production capacity.

3 Services can be classified in several ways. The primary distinction is whether they are provided by people or equipment. Other distinctions of services are in terms of tax status (profit versus nonprofit) or whether the service is provided by a government agency.

4 Consumers can evaluate three aspects of goods or services: search properties, experience properties, and credence properties.

5 A gap analysis determines if consumers' expectations are different from their actual experiences.

6 A customer contact audit is a flowchart of the points of interaction between a service provider and its customers. Interactions are opportunities for relationship marketing.

7 Internal marketing, which focuses on an organization's employees, is critical to the success of a service organization.

8 Because services cannot be patented, unique offerings are difficult to protect. In addition, because services are intangible, brands and logos (which can be protected) are particularly important to help distinguish among competing service providers.

9 The inseparability of production and consumption of services means that capacity management is important in the service element of the mix. This process involves matching demand to meet capacity.

10 The intangible nature of services makes price an important cue to indicate service quality to the consumer.

11 Distribution has become an important marketing tool for services, and electronic distribution allows some services to provide global coverage.

12 Historically, promotion has not been viewed favorably by many nonprofit and professional service organizations. In recent years this attitude has changed, and service organizations have increased their promotional activities.

KEY TERMS AND CONCEPTS

capacity management p. 334
customer contact audit p. 331
four I's of services p. 323
gap analysis p. 330
idle production capacity p. 325

internal marketing p. 333
off-peak pricing p. 335
service continuum p. 325
services p. 322

APPLYING MARKETING CONCEPTS AND PERSPECTIVES

1 Explain how the four I's of services would apply to a Marriott Hotel.

2 Idle production capacity may be related to inventory or capacity management. How would the pricing component of the marketing mix reduce idle production capacity for (*a*) a car wash, (*b*) a stage theater group, and (*c*) a university?

3 What are the search, experience, and credence properties of an airline for the business traveler and pleasure traveler? What properties are most important to each group?

4 Outline the customer contact audit for the typical deposit you make at your neighborhood bank.

5 The text suggests that internal marketing is necessary before a successful marketing program can be directed at consumers. Why is this particularly true for service organizations?

6 Outline the capacity management strategies that an airline must consider.

7 Draw the channel of distribution for the following services: (*a*) a restaurant, (*b*) a hospital, and (*c*) a hotel.

8 How does off-peak pricing influence demand for services?

9 In recent years, many service businesses have begun to provide their employees with uniforms. Explain the rationale behind this strategy in terms of the concepts discussed in this chapter.

10 Look back at the service continuum in Figure 12–3. Explain how the following points in the continuum differ in terms of consistency: (*a*) salt, (*b*) automobile, (*c*) advertising agency, and (*d*) teaching.

INTERNET EXERCISE

The American Marketing Association provides a variety of useful services for anyone interested in the latest services marketing concepts and strategies. Go to AMA's home page (www.marketingpower.com), type "services marketing" in the search engine to review the information and services available. If you click on "AMA" and "publications," articles from a variety of publications, including *Marketing Health Services*, can be reviewed. Investigate a services marketing topic of interest to you.

1 What publications are available regarding the topic you selected?

2 Describe two insights you obtained from the summaries of the publications.

VIDEO CASE 12–1   DigitalThink: Marketing E-Learning Services

"In 1996, two colleagues and I started discussing the possibilities that the Internet was opening up for corporate training," said Umberto Milletti, vice president of marketing and solutions management at DigitalThink. "We realized that we could harness the power of the same technologies that had revolutionized other parts of the business world to help organizations better disseminate skills and knowledge to their people."

Milletti's observation was very insightful. Over the last several decades, computer technology and—more recently—the Internet have changed the way that companies around the world do business. Desktop computers help employees work more productively; processes that once were laborious and manual are lightning fast; and geographically dispersed people can communicate and collaborate in cyberspace faster than ever before.

DigitalThink, a company that has grown from three employees to more than 500 in a few years, is at the forefront of a revolution in corporate training and education

services. DigitalThink and other e-learning companies are supplementing—and occasionally replacing—traditional classroom-based training in much of the business world. The effectiveness of e-learning is causing many firms to reconsider their methods of providing training and education to employees, partners, and customers.

MARKET OPPORTUNITIES

Large companies with many locations and dispersed workforces, such as car rental agencies, hotels, airlines, retail stores, banks, and consulting firms, need to train thousands of employees frequently throughout the year. In the past, employees would gather in central locations for training courses that could last anywhere from a few days to one month. This approach to training and education was very costly and time consuming, and its effectiveness was influenced by inconsistencies in the capabilities of the trainers and the difficulty of requiring the trainers and the students to be in the same location. Using personalized, technology-based instruction saves the company time and money by increasing the reliability and effectiveness of the service and by putting the learner in control of the location and the pace of the learning experience. DigitalThink is leading the e-learning movement. Its methods have been shown to compress training time by as much as 50 percent and reduce the cost of development, maintenance, and delivery by 64 percent. A recent study estimates that the global market for e-learning will grow at a 100 percent annual growth rate to $33.6 billion in 2005!

HOW DOES DIGITALTHINK ACHIEVE THESE MIRACULOUS RESULTS?

DigitalThink e-learning is very results-focused. Courses are designed to develop the specific knowledge and skills that employees or salespeople need to do their jobs and to give them the opportunity to test their knowledge and apply what they've learned with a real-world situation or problem that they might encounter on the job. "Learning is most effective when students practice and demonstrate performance in a way that closely matches the performance expected of them," explains Shelly Berkowitz, manager of instructional design at DigitalThink. "We design relevant, realistic practice and assessment activities that require students to solve problems that are as complex as those they encounter in actual work situations."

Trainees can go through the courses at their own pace, allowing people to take as much or as little time as they need. Advanced students can skip over material that they already know and go directly to the exercise or assessment section to test their mastery of the material. DigitalThink e-learning can also be delivered to the learner through different media: on a CD, via a company intranet, or through a browser on the Internet. The Web-based versions of DigitalThink's training courses are the most popular—these allow companies to update and maintain the training program very easily and cost-effectively, as well as to reach all their employees smoothly and quickly.

THE MARKET

DigitalThink sees its target market as the Global 2000 companies, the largest corporations in the United States and around the world. These companies have the critical mass needed to justify large training programs, as well as continued need for training and re-training. Within these companies, key decision makers with large staffs might include the director of a call center, the vice president of sales, or the chief information officer. Hardware and software manufacturers, travel and leisure companies, major retailers, and other organizations that have been tradi-

tionally dependent on massive instructor-led training efforts are key markets where DigitalThink has had success selling its e-learning products and services. Specific customer needs vary from ready-made courseware, to custom course development, to comprehensive learning management systems which include virtual classrooms, content management systems, and consulting services.

CUSTOMER EXAMPLES

DigitalThink developed a customized training program for an international airline's baggage and reservations departments. This airline is very geographically dispersed, so it did not make sense for it to constantly transport new employees to a central location for training. Also, with the large number of people performing these jobs, the training needs are almost constant. The content of the training is very process-oriented, which is one of the best applications for e-learning. The airline and its employees have been pleased with its decision to transition its training program to a technology-based system.

Circuit City is another of DigitalThink's prominent customers. "The e-learning program that we provide to Circuit City is centered around customer service, products that the sales counselors sell, general sales skills, and managerial skills," explains Milletti. DigitalThink has helped Circuit City create more effective, interactive training that takes half as long as classroom based–learning and costs half as much. And the retailer expects to see continued improvement in customer satisfaction and sales.

Check out DigitalThink's website (www.digitalthink. com/catalog/demos.html) to see a demo that includes some of the custom courses that DigitalThink has created for its customers.

Questions

1 What are (*a*) the advantages and (*b*) the disadvantages of DigitalThink's technology-based instruction over conventional classroom-based educational services?

2 Given your answer to question 1 above, (*a*) what are the key criteria DigitalThink should use in identifying prospective customers for its service, (*b*) what market segments meet your criteria, and (*c*) what are possible sales objections these segments might have that you have to address?

3 Suppose a large international hotel chain asks DigitalThink to make a proposal to train its thousands of front-desk clerks and receptionists. (*a*) How would you design an e-learning program to train them how to check-in a customer? (*b*) How can DigitalThink demonstrate the points of difference or benefits to the hotel chain of its technology-based instruction to obtain a contract to design an e-learning program?

Edit   Window   Sign Off   Help

Write   Mail Center   Print   My Files   My AOL   Favorites   Internet   Char

http://leisure.travelocity.com/Vacations/Tours/Location/0,2607,TRAV

Travelocity.com
A Sabre Company

Home   Dream, Plan, Go   Flights   Lodging   Cars/Rail   Vaca

cations Home | Vacation Finder | Shop By Destination | Shop By Inte

Vacations > Asia > China > **Tours**

TOUR TYPES
Escorted Tours

MORE ASIA TOUR DESTINATIONS

Select from list ▼   Go!

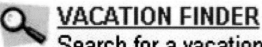 **VACATION FINDER**
Search for a vacation package or
cruise that meets all your needs.

TOUR OPERATORS
Read more about vendors offering
Tours.

The Great Wall of China i
can be seen from space. (

CHINA TOUR HIGHLI
Ancient history and the
a fascinating array of c

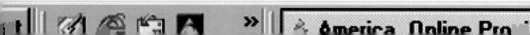

13

BUILDING THE PRICE FOUNDATION

AFTER READING THIS CHAPTER YOU SHOULD BE ABLE TO:

- Identify the elements that make up a price.

- Recognize the constraints on a firm's pricing latitude and the objectives a firm has in setting prices.

- Explain what a demand curve is and how it affects a firm's total and marginal revenue.

- Recognize what price elasticity of demand means to a manager facing a pricing decision.

- Explain the role of costs in pricing decisions.

- Calculate a break-even point for various combinations of price, fixed cost, and unit variable cost.

WHERE DOT-COMS STILL THRIVE: HELPING YOU GET A $100 A NIGHT HOTEL ROOM OVERLOOKING NEW YORK'S CENTRAL PARK!

"When I travel, I always go through Internet sites," Utah State student Catherine C. Woolley tells *Business Week* magazine.[1] She used this strategy recently with Priceline.com Inc. to reserve a $100 a night hotel room overlooking Central Park, a glitzy area in New York City.

Even with a sluggish economy, Internet startups specializing in online travel bookings hit $23 billion in sales in 2001, up 59 percent over 2000. These online websites—such as that for Travelocity on the opposite page—book airline tickets, hotel rooms, and special travel and cruise packages for travelers. In terms of market share of U.S. online travel websites, the three leaders are Travelocity (35 percent), Expedia (25 percent), and Priceline (17 percent)—Catherine Woolley's hotel reservation supplier. By 2001 all were profitable, a rarity for dot-coms, although the September 11, 2001 attacks have made their lives more difficult.

Why Travel Dot-Coms Haven't Tanked

"There are a bunch of businesses that don't make sense at all on the Internet, says Mitchell J. Rubin, a money manager who has a lot of his fund invested in Internet travel companies. "Travel is the quintessential one that does," he continues.[2] Travel companies have beaten the dot-com odds by providing two key benefits to customers:

1. *Saving time.* User friendliness makes getting Internet travel and hotel reservations easy, often saving much time and misunderstanding.
2. *Saving money.* Customers can achieve substantial price savings using the travel dot-coms over using many of the competing conventional booking services.

ANSWER THE QUESTIONS BELOW. THE CORRECT ANSWERS ARE GIVEN LATER IN THE CHAPTER.

1. If you are marketing vice president of Airbus Industries planning to introduce your 555-seat Airbus A380 Super Jumbo passenger jet in 2006, which price would you set? (a) $120 million, (b) $220 million, (c) $320 million, (d) $420 million.
2. In terms of long-run sensitivity to price, rank these commodities from the most sensitive to least sensitive: jewelry and watches, gasoline, wine, clothing.
3. As an airline, what are the circumstances under which you'd be happy to have Travelocity sell a ticket at half the "regular full-fare price"?
4. In automating a manufacturing plant, which of these would definitely increase in the short run? (a) price, (b) fixed cost, (c) total revenue, (d) variable cost.

FIGURE 13–1
Quick-take quiz on price:
Answers that are part
numbers, part good judgment

Although time and money savings for customers are a big part in the success of travel dot-coms, they also have huge advantages over those dot-coms selling physical products such as food and books.

Travel Dot-Com Prices: A Win-Win for Both Buyers and Sellers!

The benefits to customers buying airline tickets and hotel reservations from dot-com travel companies are clear. But what are the benefits for airlines and hotels? The easy answer: The extra revenue, say, of Travelocity selling an airline ticket on United Airlines more than offsets the expenses United incurs in providing the airline trip to the customer. But it's a bit more complex than that and involves carefully assessing prices, revenues, fixed costs, and variable costs. And if the answers were that easy, hundreds of failed dot-com firms with brilliant ideas, technologies, and marketing plans would still be going strong today. So question 3 in Figure 13–1 asks you when an airline would be happy to have, say, Travelocity sell low-priced tickets. Spend a couple of minutes on the "quiz" and then compare your answers to those given throughout the chapter.

Among all marketing and operations factors in a business firm, price is unique! It is the common denominator where all other business decisions come together. The price must be "right"—in the sense that customers must be willing to pay it to generate revenues, which in turn validates the thousands of decisions on topics like product features, manufacturing trade-offs, and promotional activities. In fact, among 1,000 large U.S. companies, research shows that a 1 percent price increase translates to a 12 percent increase in profitability, other factors remaining the same.[3]

Welcome to the fascinating—and intense—world of pricing, where myriad forces come together in the price prospective buyers are asked to pay. This chapter and Chapter 14 cover important factors used in setting prices.

NATURE AND IMPORTANCE OF PRICE

The price paid for goods and services goes by many names. You pay *tuition* for your education, *rent* for an apartment, *interest* on a bank credit card, and a *premium* for car insurance. Your dentist or physician charges you a *fee,* a professional or social organization charges *dues,* and airlines charge a *fare.* In business, an executive is given a *salary,* a salesperson receives a *commission,* and a worker is paid a *wage.* Of course, what you pay for clothes or a haircut is termed a *price.*

PRICE EQUATION

ITEM PURCHASED	PRICE	= LIST PRICE	INCENTIVES AND – ALLOWANCES	+ EXTRA FEES
New car bought by an individual	Final price	= List price	– Rebate Cash discount Old car trade-in	+ Financing charges Special accessories Destination charges
Term in college bought by a student	Tuition	= Published tuition	– Scholarship Other financial aid Discounts for number of credits taken	+ Special activity fees
Bank loan obtained by a small business	Principal and interest	= Amount of loan sought	– Allowance for collateral	+ Premium for uncertain creditworthiness
Merchandise bought from a wholesaler by a retailer	Invoice price	= List price	– Quantity discount Cash discount Seasonal discount Functional or trade discount	+ Penalty for late payment

FIGURE 13–2
The price of four different purchases

What Is a Price?

These examples highlight the many varied ways that price plays a part in our daily lives. From a marketing viewpoint, **price** is the money or other considerations (including other goods and services) exchanged for the ownership or use of a good or service. Recently Wilkinson Sword exchanged some of its knives for advertising used to promote its razor blades. This practice of exchanging goods and services for other goods and services rather than for money is called **barter**. These transactions account for billions of dollars annually in domestic and international trade. For example, Internet exchanges such as FastParts, Inc., and FairMarket Inc. help barter $18 billion annually of excess inventory generated by U.S. firms that otherwise would have been sold at low prices.[4]

Figure 13–2 illustrates how the price equation applies to a variety of different products and services. One new twenty-first century variable: strange "special fees" and "surcharges." These are driven by the ease of making price comparisons on the Internet and consumers' zeal for low prices. Examples of these special fees are a Green Bay Packer "user fee" that can add $1,400 to the price of a season ticket or a 5 percent "environmental surcharge" by dry cleaners around the country. The reason: Sellers see this as a way of showing a lower list price, and buyers are more willing to pay for the extra fees than a higher list price.[5]

For most products, money is exchanged, although the amount is not always the same as the list or quoted price, because of the discounts, allowances, and extra fees shown in Figure 13–2. Suppose you decide to buy a 2002 Lamborghini Murciélago ("bat" in Spanish) because its 6.2 liter, 571-horsepower V-12 engine moves you from 0 to 62 mph in 3.8 seconds at a top speed of 205 mph. The list price is $300,000. As a rebate for buying

Lamborghini Murciélago

How do consumers relate value to price, as in the new Kohler walk-in bathtub that is safe for children and elderly alike? For a discussion of this important issue, see the text.

Kohler Company

www.kohler.com

within the year, you receive $20,000 off the list price. You agree to pay half down ($140,000) and the other half when the car is delivered in six months, which results in a financing fee of $3,285. To ship the car from Italy, you will pay a $5,000 destination charge. For your 1996 Honda Civic DX 4-door sedan that has 60,000 miles and is in fair condition, you are given a trade-in allowance of $5,000, which is the *Kelley Blue Book* (www.kbb.com) trade-in value of your car.[6]

Applying the "price equation" (as shown in Figure 13–2) to your purchase, your final price is:

$$\text{Final Price} = \text{List price} - (\text{Incentives} + \text{Allowances}) + \text{Extra fees}$$

$$= \$300,000 - (\$20,000 + \$5,000) + (\$3,285 + \$5,000)$$

$$= \$283,285$$

Your monthly payment for the six-month loan of $140,000 is $23,880.79. Are you still interested?

Price as an Indicator of Value

From a consumer's standpoint, price is often used to indicate value when it is paired with the perceived benefits of a product or service. Specifically, **value** can be defined as the ratio of perceived benefits to price, or:[7]

$$\text{Value} = \frac{\text{Perceived benefits}}{\text{Price}}$$

This relationship shows that for a given price, as perceived benefits increase, value increases. Also, for a given price, value decreases when perceived benefits decrease. Creative marketers engage in **value-pricing**, the practice of simultaneously increasing product and service benefits and maintaining or decreasing price.

For some products, price influences the perception of overall quality, and ultimately value, to consumers.[8] For example, in a survey of home furnishing buyers, 84 percent agreed with the following statement: "The higher the price, the higher the quality."[9]

Consumer value assessments are often comparative. Here value involves the judgment by a consumer of the worth and desirability of a product or service relative to substitutes that satisfy the same need. In this instance a "reference value" emerges, which involves comparing the costs and benefits of substitute items. For example, Kohler recently introduced a walk-in bathtub that is safe for children and the elderly.

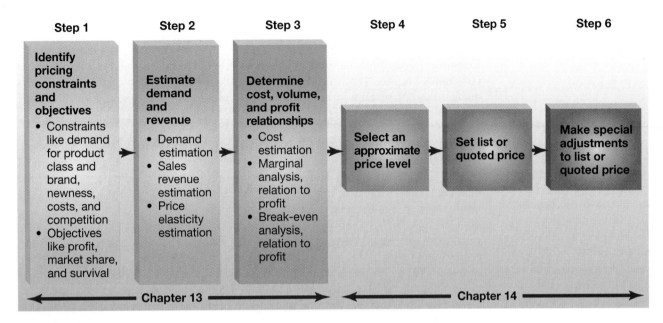

Step 1	Step 2	Step 3	Step 4	Step 5	Step 6

Identify pricing constraints and objectives
- Constraints like demand for product class and brand, newness, costs, and competition
- Objectives like profit, market share, and survival

Estimate demand and revenue
- Demand estimation
- Sales revenue estimation
- Price elasticity estimation

Determine cost, volume, and profit relationships
- Cost estimation
- Marginal analysis, relation to profit
- Break-even analysis, relation to profit

Select an approximate price level

Set list or quoted price

Make special adjustments to list or quoted price

◄——————— Chapter 13 ———————►   ◄——————— Chapter 14 ———————►

FIGURE 13–3
Steps in setting price

Although priced higher than conventional step-in bathtubs, it has proven very successful because buyers place great "value" on the extra safety.

Price in the Marketing Mix

Pricing is also a critical decision made by a marketing executive because price has a direct effect on a firm's profits. This is apparent from a firm's **profit equation**:

Profit = Total revenue − Total cost

or

Profit = (Unit price × Quantity sold) − Total cost

What makes this relationship even more important is that price affects the quantity sold, as illustrated with demand curves later in this chapter. Furthermore, since the quantity sold sometimes affects a firm's costs because of efficiency of production, price also indirectly affects costs. Thus, pricing decisions influence both total revenue and total cost, which makes pricing one of the most important decisions marketing executives face.

The importance of price in the marketing mix necessitates an understanding of six major steps involved in the process organizations go through in setting prices (Figure 13–3):

- Identify pricing constraints and objectives.
- Estimate demand and revenue.
- Determine cost, volume, and profit relationships.
- Select an approximate price level.
- Set list or quoted price.
- Make special adjustments to list or quoted price.

The first three steps are covered in this chapter and the last three in Chapter 14.

STEP 1: IDENTIFY PRICING CONSTRAINTS AND OBJECTIVES

To define a problem, it is important to consider both the objectives and constraints that narrow the range of alternatives available to solve it. These same principles apply in solving a pricing problem. Let's first review the pricing constraints so that we can better understand the nature of pricing alternatives.

Identifying Pricing Constraints

Factors that limit the latitude of prices a firm may set are **pricing constraints**. Consumer demand for the product clearly affects the price that can be charged. Other constraints on price vary from factors within the organization to competitive factors outside the organization. Legal and regulatory constraints on pricing are discussed in Chapter 14.

Are these real "collectibles" or "trashables"? The text describes factors that affect a product's price. And you can check the Web Link box to see if those old Beanie Babies or Nikes in your attic or a new Ichiro Suzuki bobble head doll have value.

Demand for the Product Class, Product, and Brand   The number of potential buyers for the product class (such as cars), product (sports cars), and brand (Ford Thunderbird) clearly affects the price a seller can charge. So does whether the item is a luxury—like a Thunderbird—or a necessity—like bread and a roof over your head. The nature of demand is discussed later in the chapter.

Newness of the Product: Stage in the Product Life Cycle   The newer a product and the earlier it is in its life cycle, the higher is the price that can usually be charged. Willing to spend up to $1,600 for a new electronic book? The high initial price is possible because of patents and limited competition early in its product life cycle. By the time you read this, the price will probably be much lower.

Sometimes—when nostalgia or fad factors come into play—prices may rise later in the product life cycle. As described in the Web Link box, collectibles such as a 1952 Mickey Mantle baseball card or old sneakers can experience skyrocketing prices.[10] But they can take a nosedive, too. Publishing competitive prices on the Internet for the same or similar brands of products has revolutionized access to price comparisons for both "collectors" and buyers of more traditional products.

Single Product versus a Product Line   When Sony introduced its CD player, not only was it unique and in the introductory stage of its product life cycle but also it was the *only* CD player Sony sold, so the firm had great latitude in setting a price. Now, with a wide range of Sony CD products and technologies, the price of individual models has to be consistent with the others based on features provided and meaningful price differentials that communicate value to consumers.

Cost of Producing and Marketing the Product   In the long run, a firm's price must cover all the costs of producing and marketing a product. If the price doesn't cover the cost, the firm will fail, so in the long run a firm's costs set a floor under its price. Regent Air and McClain Airlines painfully learned this lesson. Both airlines provided luxury transcontinental air service for one-way airfares as high as $1,000. Unfortunately, the total cost of providing this red-carpet service exceeded the total revenue and both companies failed.

Prices of "collectibles"—such as toys or old sneakers—are set by demand and supply forces discussed in this chapter. And for fads, the prices can fluctuate wildly. Some other recent collectibles prices, besides those mentioned above:

- Zip, a cat, Beanie Baby: $177 (if it has black paws).
- 1985 Nike Dunks, high-top, blue-and-black basketball shoes: $2,300.
- 2001 Ichiro Suzuki bobble head doll: $305

To get a feel for prices of some of these collectibles, visit: www.ebay.com.

Marathon runner Malcolm East now wishes he had done a little more research on sneaker prices. At his wife's insistence he threw out six pairs of old shoes—that he now thinks would have fetched $15,000!

Want in on the collectibles business? Think twice. Zip the Cat Beanie Baby sold for $2,250 in 1998, over $2,000 more than in 2001.

Setting hundreds of prices that will be valid for the life of a catalog involves many risky decisions.

Cost of Changing Prices and Time Period They Apply   If Scandinavian Airlines asks General Electric (GE) to provide spare jet engines to power the new Boeing 737 it just bought, GE can easily set a new price for the engines to reflect its latest information since only one buyer has to be informed. But if The Territory Ahead decides that sweater prices are too low in its catalogs after thousands of catalogs have been mailed to customers, it has a big problem, so it must consider the cost of changing prices and the time period for which they apply in developing the price list for its catalog items. A recent study of four supermarket chains found the average annual cost of these price changes was $105,887, which represents 0.70 percent of revenues and an astounding 35.2 percent of net margins.[11] In actual practice, research indicates that most firms change the prices of their major products once a year.[12] But on a website, prices can change from minute to minute.[13]

Type of Competitive Markets   The seller's price is constrained by the type of market in which it competes. Economists generally delineate four types of competitive markets: pure monopoly, oligopoly, monopolistic competition, and pure competition. Figure 13–4 shows that the type of competition dramatically influences the latitude of price competition and, in turn, the nature of product differentiation and extent of advertising. A firm must recognize the general type of competitive market it is in to understand the latitude of both its price and nonprice strategies. For example, prices can be significantly affected by four competitive situations:

- *Pure monopoly.* In 1994 Johnson & Johnson (J&J) revolutionized the treatment of coronary heart diseases by introducing the "stent"—a tiny mesh tube "spring" that props open clogged arteries. Initially a monopolist, J&J stuck with its early $1,595 price and achieved $1 billion in sales and 91 percent market share by the end of 1996. But its reluctance to give price reductions for large-volume purchases to hospitals antagonized them. When competitors introduced an improved stent at lower prices, J&J's market share plummeted to 8 percent two years later.[14] Microsoft is another example. Its competitors and customers have argued in court that it engaged in illegal acts that reduced competition and increased prices.[15]

- *Oligopoly.* The few sellers of aluminum (Reynolds, Alcoa) or large jetliners try to avoid price competition because it can lead to disastrous price wars in which all lose money. Yet firms in such industries stay aware of a competitor's price cuts or increases and may follow suit. The products can be undifferentiated

TYPE OF COMPETITIVE MARKET

STRATEGIES AVAILABLE	PURE MONOPOLY (One seller who sets the price for a unique product)	OLIGOPOLY (Few sellers who are sensitive to each other's prices)	MONOPOLISTIC COMPETITION (Many sellers who compete on nonprice factors)	PURE COMPETITION (Many sellers who follow the market price for identical, commodity products)
Extent of price competition	None: sole seller sets price	Some: price leader or follower of competitors	Some: compete over range of prices	Almost none: market sets price
Extent of product differentiation	None: no other producers	Various: depends on industry	Some: differentiate products from competitors	None: products are identical
Extent of advertising	Little: purpose is to increase demand for product class	Some: purpose is to inform but avoid price competition	Much: purpose is to differentiate firm's products from competitors	Little: purpose is to inform prospects that seller's products are available

FIGURE 13–4

Pricing, product, and advertising strategies available to firms in four types of competitive markets

(aluminum) or differentiated (large jetliners), and informative advertising that avoids head-to-head price competition is used.[16]

- *Monopolistic competition.* Dozens of regional, private brands of peanut butter compete with national brands like Skippy and Jif. Both price competition (regional, private brands being lower than national brands) and nonprice competition (product features and advertising) exist.
- *Pure competition.* Hundreds of local grain elevators sell corn whose price per bushel is set by the marketplace. Within strains, the corn is identical, so advertising only informs buyers that the seller's corn is available.

Competitors' Prices   A firm must know or anticipate what specific price its present and potential competitors are charging now or will charge. When the NutraSweet Company planned the market introduction of Simplesse® all natural fat substitute, it had to consider the price of fat replacements already available as well as potential competitors, including Procter & Gamble's Olestra, Pfizer Inc.'s VeriLo, and the Stellar brand made by A. E. Staley Company.

Identifying Pricing Objectives

Expectations that specify the role of price in an organization's marketing and strategic plans are **pricing objectives**. To the extent possible, these organizational pricing objectives are also carried to lower levels in the organization, such as in setting objectives for marketing managers responsible for an individual brand. H. J. Heinz, for example, has specific pricing objectives for its Heinz ketchup brand that vary by country. Chapter 2 discussed six broad objectives that an organization may pursue, which tie in directly to the organization's pricing policies.

Profit   Three different objectives relate to a firm's profit, usually measured in terms of return on investment (ROI) or return on assets. One objective is *managing for long-run profits,* which is followed by many Japanese firms that are willing to forgo immediate profit in cars, TV sets, or computers to develop quality products that can

FIGURE 13–5
Where each dollar of your movie ticket goes

penetrate competitive markets in the future. A *maximizing current profit* objective, such as during this quarter or year, is common in many firms because the targets can be set and performance measured quickly. American firms are sometimes criticized for this short-run orientation. A *target return* objective involves a firm such as Du Pont or Exxon setting a goal (such as 20 percent) for pretax ROI. These three profit objectives have different implications for a firm's pricing objectives.

Another profit consideration for firms such as movie studios and manufacturers, discussed in more depth in Chapter 14, is to ensure that those firms in their channels of distribution make adequate profits. Without profits for these channel members, the movie studio or manufacturer is cut off from its customers. For example, Figure 13–5 shows where each dollar of your movie ticket goes. The 51 cents the movie studio gets must cover its profit plus the cost of making and marketing the movie, which averaged an all-time high of $81 million in 2000.[17] Although the studio would like more than 51 cents of your dollar, it settles for this amount to make sure theaters and distributors are satisfied and willing to handle its movies.

Sales   Given that a firm's profit is high enough for it to remain in business, its objectives may be to increase sales revenue. The hope is that the increase in sales revenue will in turn lead to increases in market share and profit. Cutting price on one product in a firm's line may increase its sales revenue but reduce those of related products. Objectives related to sales revenue or unit sales have the advantage of being translated easily into meaningful targets for marketing managers responsible for a product line or brand—far more easily than with an ROI target, for example.

Market Share   Market share is the ratio of the firm's sales revenues or unit sales to those of the industry (competitors plus the firm itself). Companies often pursue a market share objective when industry sales are relatively flat or declining. In the late 1990s, Boeing cut prices drastically to try to maintain its 60 percent market share and encountered huge losses. Although increased market share is a primary goal of some firms, others see it as a means to other ends: increasing sales and profits.

Unit Volume   Many firms use unit volume, the quantity produced or sold, as a pricing objective. These firms often sell multiple products at very different prices and need to match the unit volume demanded by customers with price and production capacity. Using unit volume as an objective can be counterproductive if a volume objective is achieved, say, by drastic price cutting that drives down profit.

Survival   In some instances, profits, sales, and market share are less important objectives of the firm than mere survival. Continental Airlines has struggled to attract passengers with low fares, no-penalty advance-booking policies, and aggressive promotions to improve the firm's cash flow. This pricing objective has helped Continental to stay alive in the competitive airline industry.

Social Responsibility   A firm may forgo higher profit on sales and follow a pricing objective that recognizes its obligations to customers and society in general. Medtronics followed this pricing policy when it introduced the world's first heart pacemaker. Gerber supplies a specially formulated product free of charge to children who cannot tolerate foods based on cow's milk. Government agencies, which set many prices for services they offer, use social responsibility as a primary pricing objective.

Concept Check

1. What factors impact the list price to determine the final price?

2. How does the type of competitive market a firm is in affect its latitude in setting price?

STEP 2: ESTIMATE DEMAND AND REVENUE

Basic to setting a product's price is the extent of customer demand for it. Marketing executives must also translate this estimate of customer demand into estimates of revenues the firm expects to receive.

Fundamentals of Estimating Demand

Newsweek decided to conduct a pricing experiment at newsstands in 11 cities throughout the United States.[18] At that time, Houston newsstand buyers paid $2.25. In Fort Worth, New York, Los Angeles, San Francisco, and Atlanta, newsstand buyers paid the regular $2.00 price. In San Diego, the price was $1.50. The price in Minneapolis–St. Paul, New Orleans, and Detroit was only $1.00. By comparison, the regular newsstand price for *Time* and *U.S. News & World Report*, *Newsweek*'s competitors, was $1.95. Why did *Newsweek* conduct the experiment? According to a *Newsweek* executive, at that time, "We want to figure out what the demand curve for our magazine at the newsstand is."

The Demand Curve   A **demand curve** shows a maximum number of products consumers will buy at a given price. Demand curve D_1 in Figure 13–6 shows the newsstand demand for *Newsweek* under conditions existing. Note that as price falls, people buy more. But price is not the complete story in estimating demand. Economists stress three other key factors:

1. *Consumer tastes.* As we saw in Chapter 3, these depend on many factors such as demographics, culture, and technology. Because consumer tastes can change quickly, up-to-date marketing research is essential.

2. *Price and availability of other products.* As the price of close substitute products falls (the price of *Time*) and their availability increases, the demand for a product declines (the demand for *Newsweek*).

3. *Consumer income.* In general, as real consumer income (allowing for inflation) increases, demand for a product also increases.

The first of these two factors influences what consumers *want* to buy, and the third affects what they *can* buy. Along with price, these are often called **demand factors**, or factors that determine consumers' willingness and ability to pay for goods and services. As discussed earlier in Chapters 8 and 10, it is often very difficult to estimate demand for new products, especially because consumer likes and dislikes are often so difficult to read clearly. For example, Campbell Soup spent seven years and $55 million on a supersecret project to produce a line of Intelligent Quisine (IQ) food products. The company expected that its line of 41 breakfasts, lunches, dinners, and snacks would be the first foods "scientifically proven to lower high levels of cholesterol, blood sugar, and blood pressure."[19] After 15 months in an Ohio test market, Campbell Soup yanked the entire IQ line when it fell far short of expectations because customers found the line too pricey and lacking in variety.

Newsweek
www.newsweek.com

Movement Along versus Shift of a Demand Curve   Demand curve D_1 in Figure 13–6 shows that as the price is lowered from $2.00 to $1.50, the quantity demanded increases from 3 million (Q_1) to 4.5 million (Q_2) units per year. This is an example of a movement along a demand curve and assumes that other factors (consumer tastes, price and availability of substitutes, and consumer income) remain unchanged.

What if some of these factors change? For example, if advertising causes more people to want *Newsweek,* newsstand distribution is increased, and consumer incomes double, then the demand increases. This is shown in Figure 13–6 as a shift of the demand curve to the right, from D_1 to D_2. This increased demand means that more *Newsweek* magazines are wanted for a given price: At a price of $2, the demand is 6 million units per year (Q_3) on D_2 rather than 3 million units per year (Q_1) on D_1.

Fundamentals of Estimating Revenue

While economists may talk about "demand curves," marketing executives are more likely to speak in terms of "revenues generated." Demand curves lead directly to three related revenue concepts critical to pricing decisions: **total revenue**, **average revenue**, and **marginal revenue** (Figure 13–7).

Demand Curves and Revenue   Figure 13–8A again shows the demand curve for *Newsweek,* but it is now extended to intersect both the price and quantity axes. The demand curve shows that as price is changed, the quantity of *Newsweek* magazines sold throughout the United States changes. This relationship holds whether the price is increased from $2.50 to $3.00 on the demand curve or is reduced from $1 to $0 on the curve. In the former case the market demands no *Newsweek* magazines, whereas in the latter case 9 million could be given away at $0 per unit.

It is likely that if *Newsweek* was given away, more than 9 million would be demanded. This fact illustrates two important points. First, it can be dangerous to extend a demand curve beyond the range of prices for which it really applies. Second, most demand curves are rounded (or convex) to the origin, thereby avoiding an unrealistic picture of what demand looks like when a straight-line curve intersects either the price axis or the quantity axis.

Figure 13–8B shows the total revenue curve for *Newsweek* calculated from the demand curve shown in Figure 13–8A. The total revenue curve is developed by

FIGURE 13–6
Illustrative demand curves for *Newsweek* magazine

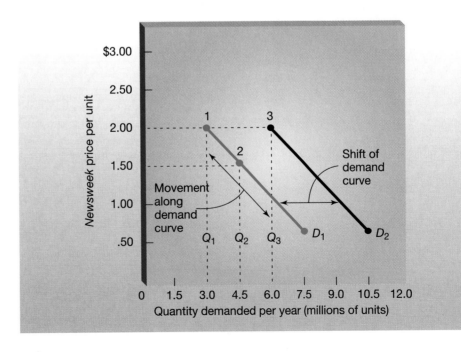

FIGURE 13–7
Fundamental revenue concepts

Total revenue (TR) is the total money received from the sale of a product. If:

    TR = Total revenue
     P = Unit price of the product
    Q = Quantity of the product sold

then:

$$TR = P \times Q$$

Average revenue (AR) is the average amount of money received for selling one unit of the product, or simply the price of that unit. Average revenue is the total revenue divided by the quantity sold:

$$AR = \frac{TR}{Q} = P$$

Marginal revenue (MR) is the change in total revenue obtained by selling one additional unit:

$$MR = \frac{\text{Change in TR}}{\text{1 unit increase in Q}} = \frac{\Delta TR}{\Delta Q} = \text{slope of TR curve}$$

FIGURE 13–8
How a downward-sloping demand curve affects total, average, and marginal revenue

simply multiplying the unit price times the quantity for each of the points on the demand curve. Total revenue starts at $0 (point *A*), reaches a maximum of $6,750,000 at point *D*, and returns to $0 at point *G*. This shows that as price is reduced in the *A*-to-*D* segment of the curve, total revenue is increased. However, cutting price in the *D*-to-*G* segment results in a decline in total revenue.

Marginal revenue, which is the slope of the total revenue curve, is positive but decreasing when the price lies in the range from $3 to above $1.50 per unit. Below

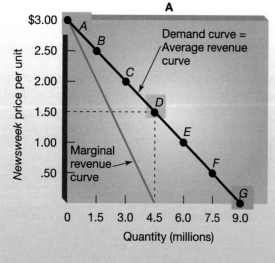
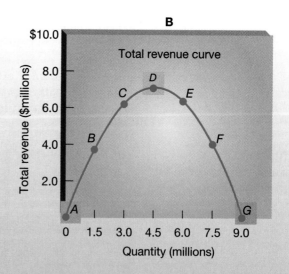

POINT ON DEMAND CURVE	PRICE (P)	QUANTITY SOLD (Q)	TOTAL REVENUE (P x Q)	AVERAGE REVENUE (TR/Q = P)	MARGINAL REVENUE (ΔTR/ΔQ)
A	$3.00	0	$ 0	$3.00	$3.00
B	2.50	1,500,000	3,750,000	2.50	2.00
C	2.00	3,000,000	6,000,000	2.00	1.00
D	1.50	4,500,000	6,750,000	1.50	0
E	1.00	6,000,000	6,000,000	1.00	−1.00*
F	.50	7,500,000	3,750,000	.50	−2.00*
G	0	9,000,000	0	0	−3.00*

*Not shown in Figure 13–8A. [Note that the marginal revenue (MR) curve in Figure 13–8A is the slope of the total revenue curve in Figure 13–8B.]

MARKETING NEWSNET

The Airbus versus Boeing Face-Off: How Many Can We Sell and at What Price . . . in 2006?

GLOBAL

Are you interested in flying the eighth wonder of the world? Airbus Industries is counting on it, when it introduces the new $220 million A380 super jumbo jet in 2006 (question 1, Figure 13–1). The A380 (below left) will carry 555 to 800 passengers in a double-decker bus design that may include sleeping berths, restaurants, and a casino. Airbus must sell 250 A380s to break even because development costs can reach $12 billion!

The A380 is targeted at the growing market for passenger jets that seat 400+ and large cargo jets, which Airbus forecasts will total 1,741 planes by 2019. Airbus gave early customers of the A380 deep discounts of up to 40 percent off the list price (or $140 million per plane). It had 67 firm orders for the A380 by mid-July 2001.

Boeing, too, took a careful look at the market for a large, over-the-ocean jet aircraft. Its in-depth marketing research on the priorities of its airline customers and their passengers for the 2006–2008 time frame showed that reducing travel time was their most critical need—far more important than features like sleeping berths or restaurants. So, in March 2001, Boeing announced that it would defer work on the 747X—a "stretch" version of its 747, the best-selling large passenger jet on the globe. Instead, Boeing started development of the $10 billion Sonic Cruiser (below right), which can cross oceans traveling at near the speed of sound.

Time—and the events of September 11, 2001—will tell what customers want.

$1.50 per unit, though, marginal revenue is actually negative, so the extra quantity of magazines sold is more than offset by the decrease in the price per unit.

For any downward-sloping, straight-line demand curve, the marginal revenue curve always falls at a rate twice as fast as the demand curve. As shown in Figure 13–8A, the marginal revenue becomes $0 per unit at a quantity sold of 4.5 million units—the very point at which total revenue is maximum (see Figure 13–8B). A rational marketing manager would never operate in the region of the demand curve in which marginal revenue is negative. This means that in Figure 13–8A this manager would set prices only in the *A*-to-*D* segment of the demand curve. Also, when market share falls, the easy answer is to cut price—often with devastating results: a 1 percent price cut in the food and drug industry results in a 24 percent decline in profits, other factors being equal.[20]

What price did *Newsweek* select after conducting its experiment? It kept the price at $2.00. However, through expanded newsstand distribution and more aggressive advertising, *Newsweek* was later able to shift its demand curve to the right and charge a price of $2.50 without affecting its newsstand volume.

Does forecasting future demand and revenue sound easy? Study the Marketing NewsNet above to understand the special difficulties that Airbus and Boeing face trying to forecast the demand and revenue for their revolutionary airliners five or six years before they roll off the production line.[21]

Is clothing or gasoline more sensitive to price changes? For the answer see the text and its discussion of price elasticity of demand.

Price Elasticity of Demand   With a downward-sloping demand curve, we have been concerned with the responsiveness of demand to price changes. This can be conveniently measured by **price elasticity of demand**, or the percentage change in quantity demanded relative to a percentage change in price. Price elasticity of demand (E) is expressed as follows:

$$E = \frac{\text{Percentage change in quantity demanded}}{\text{Percentage change in price}}$$

Because quantity demanded usually decreases as price increases, price elasticity of demand is usually a negative number. However, for the sake of simplicity and by convention, elasticity figures are shown as positive numbers.

Price elasticity of demand assumes three forms: elastic demand, inelastic demand, and unitary demand elasticity. *Elastic demand* exists when a 1 percent decrease in price produces more than a 1 percent increase in quantity demanded. Price elasticity is greater than 1 with elastic demand. *Inelastic demand* exists when a 1 percent decrease in price produces less than a 1 percent increase in quantity demanded. With inelastic demand, price elasticity is less than 1. *Unitary demand* exists when the percentage change in price is identical to the percentage change in quantity demanded. In this instance, price elasticity is equal to 1.

Price elasticity of demand is determined by a number of factors. First, the more substitutes a product or service has, the more likely it is to be price elastic. For example, butter has many possible substitutes in a meal and is price elastic, but gasoline has almost no substitutes and is price inelastic. Second, products and services considered to be necessities are price inelastic, so, open-heart surgery is price inelastic, whereas airline tickets for a vacation are price elastic. Third, items that require a large cash outlay compared with a person's disposable income are price elastic. Accordingly, cars and yachts are price elastic; books and movie tickets tend to be price inelastic.

Price elasticity is important to marketing managers because of its relationship to total revenue, so it is important that marketing managers recognize that price elasticity of demand is not the same over all possible prices of a product. Figure 13–8B illustrates this point using the *Newsweek* demand curve shown in Figure 13–8A. As the price decreases from $2.50 to $2.00, total revenue increases, indicating an elastic demand. However, when the price decreases from $1.00 to 50 cents, total revenue declines, indicating an inelastic demand. Unitary demand elasticity exists at a price of $1.50.

Price Elasticities for Brands and Product Classes   Marketing executives also recognize that the price elasticity of demand is not always the same for product classes (such as stereo receivers) and brands within a product class (such as Sony and Marantz). For example, marketing experiments on brands of cola, coffee, and snack and specialty foods generally show elasticities of 1.5 to 2.5, indicating they are price elastic.[22]

By comparison, here are the short-run and long-run price elasticities of demand for four product classes, running most to least price elastic (most to least price sensitive in question 2, Figure 13–1):

| | PRICE ELASTICITY | |
PRODUCT CLASS	SHORT RUN	LONG RUN
Clothing	0.90	2.90
Wine	0.88	1.17
Jewelry and watches	0.41	0.67
Gasoline	0.20	0.60

This shows that a 1 percent decrease in the price of clothing would result in only a 0.90 percent increase in the quantity sold in the short run but 2.90 percent increase in the long run. So, if you must have that new sweater today, you are much less responsive to a low price than if you can look for a sale price over the coming two or three months. But gasoline for your car or SUV is entirely different! The table shows that Americans aren't going to change their gasoline purchases much in the short or long run, regardless of slight price decreases or increases![23]

Because 12- to 17-year-olds often have limited "spending money," this group is very price elastic in its demand for cigarettes. As a result, many legislators recommend far higher excise taxes on cigarettes to increase their prices significantly with the goal of reducing teen-age smoking. Thus, price elasticity is not only a relevant concept for marketing managers, but also important for public policy affecting pricing practices.[24]

Concept Check

1. What is the difference between a movement along and a shift of a demand curve?

2. What does it mean if a product has a price elasticity of demand that is greater than 1?

STEP 3: DETERMINE COST, VOLUME, AND PROFIT RELATIONSHIPS

While revenues are the moneys received by the firm from selling its products or services to customers, costs or expenses are the moneys the firm pays out to its employees and suppliers. Marketing managers often use marginal analysis and break-even analysis to relate revenues and costs, topics covered in this section.

The Importance of Controlling Costs

Understanding the role and behavior of costs is critical for all marketing decisions, particularly pricing decisions. Four cost concepts are important in pricing decisions: **total cost**, **fixed cost**, **variable cost**, and **marginal cost** (Figure 13–9).

Many firms go bankrupt because their costs get out of control, causing their total costs to exceed their total revenues over an extended period of time. This is why sophisticated marketing managers make pricing decisions that balance both their revenues and costs. An example, described in the Marketing NewsNet, shows why travel dot-com firms have been more successful than their brick-and-mortar counterparts.[25] Besides the reasons in the box, an airline is delighted to sell last-day tickets for half of the full fare because the revenue obtained by filling the seat far exceeds the low unit variable cost of the passenger's meal and baggage handling (question 3, Figure 13–1).

Marginal Analysis and Profit Maximization

A basic idea in business, economics, and indeed everyday life is marginal analysis. In personal terms, marginal analysis means that people will continue to do something as long as the incremental return exceeds the incremental cost. This same idea holds true in marketing and pricing decisions. In this setting, **marginal analysis** means that as long as revenue received from the sale of an additional product (marginal revenue) is greater than the additional cost of producing and selling it (marginal cost), a firm will expand its output of that product.

FIGURE 13–9
Fundamental cost concepts

Total cost (TC) is the total expense incurred by a firm in producing and marketing the product. Total cost is the sum of fixed cost and variable cost.

Fixed cost (FC) is the sum of the expenses of the firm that are stable and do not change with the quantity of product that is produced and sold. Examples of fixed costs are rent on the building, executive salaries, and insurance.

Variable cost (VC) is the sum of the expenses of the firm that vary directly with the quantity of product that is produced and sold. For example, as the quantity sold doubles, the variable cost doubles. Examples are the direct labor and direct materials used in producing the product and the sales commissions that are tied directly to the quantity sold. As mentioned above:

$$TC = FC + VC$$

Variable cost expressed on a per unit basis is called *unit variable cost (UVC)*.

Marginal cost (MC) is the change in total cost that results from producing and marketing one additional unit:

$$MC = \frac{\text{Change in TC}}{\text{1 unit increase in Q}} = \frac{\Delta TC}{\Delta Q} = \text{slope of TC curve}$$

Why is Pets.com and its sock puppet only a memory? For the answers, see the text and the Marketing NewsNet box.

Marginal analysis is central to the concept of maximizing profits. In Figure 13–10A, marginal revenue and marginal cost are graphed. Marginal cost starts out high at lower quantity levels, decreases to a minimum through production and marketing efficiencies, and then rises again due to the inefficiencies of overworked labor and equipment. Marginal revenue follows a downward slope. In Figure 13–10B, total cost and total revenue curves corresponding to the marginal cost and marginal revenue curves are graphed. Total cost initially rises as quantity increases but increases at the slowest rate at the quantity where marginal cost is lowest. The total revenue curve increases to a maximum and then starts to decline, as shown in Figure 13–8B.

The message of marginal analysis, then, is to operate up to the quantity and price level where marginal revenue equals marginal cost (MR = MC). Up to the output quantity at which MR = MC, each increase in total revenue resulting from selling one additional unit exceeds the increase in the total cost of producing and marketing that unit. Beyond the point at which MR = MC, however, the increase in total revenue from selling one more unit is less than the cost of producing and marketing that unit. At the quantity at which MR = MC, the total revenue curve lies farthest above the total cost curve, they are parallel, and profit is a maximum.

Break-Even Analysis

Marketing managers often employ a simpler approach for looking at cost, volume, and profit relationships, which is also based on the profit equation. **Break-even analysis** is a technique that analyzes the relationship between total revenue and total cost to determine profitability at various levels of output. The **break-even point** (BEP) is the quantity at which total revenue and total cost are equal and beyond which profit occurs. In terms of the definitions in Figure 13–9:

$$BEP_{Quantity} = \frac{\text{Fixed cost}}{\text{Unit price} - \text{Unit variable cost}}$$

Calculating a Break-Even Point   Consider, for example, a corn farmer who wishes to identify how many bushels of corn he must sell to cover his fixed cost at a given price. Suppose the farmer had a fixed cost (FC) of $2,000 (for real estate taxes, interest on a bank loan, and other fixed expenses) and a unit variable cost (UVC) of $1

MARKETING NEWSNET

Pricing Lessons from the Dot-Coms: Understand Revenues and Expenses!

TECHNOLOGY & E-COMMERCE

Price, revenue, fixed cost, variable cost. Boring topics from finance or economics? But they are also critical to marketing success, as shown by lessons learned by the successful travel dot-coms so far.

Brick-and-Mortar Dot-Com Failures

In the 18 months ending mid-2001, 555 dot-coms failed, many of them brick-and-mortar businesses like Pets.com (pet products) and Webvan (online groceries). Some reasons for these failures:

- Setting prices too low to cover the huge brick-and-mortar fixed costs of inventory, warehouses, and order fulfillment—especially on low-margin goods like groceries (Webvan).
- Spending too much on promotion, such as Pets.com's $2.2 million on Super Bowl XXXV ads.
- Believing people would forgo shopping at traditional stores, a problem, for example, with Pets.com competing with Petsmart.

Travel Dot-Com Successes (So Far)

Besides time and money savings for customers, the travel dot-coms have special strategies for success:

- Reaching key customer segments that will actually pay *higher* prices for hotel rooms or airline tickets.
- Reaching customer segments (students, senior citizens) whose last-minute or last-week flexibility enables them to reserve hotel rooms or airline seats that would otherwise go unsold.
- Being able to conduct almost all operations electronically, without the warehousing and order fulfillment problems of their brick-and-mortar dot-com cousins.

Still, travel dot-coms face major uncertainties. One is the appearance of Orbitz.com in mid-2001—an online travel agency owned by five major U.S. airlines. Also very significant is the dramatic decrease in demand for airline tickets following the attacks of September 11, 2001.

per bushel (for labor, corn seed, herbicides, and pesticides). If the price (P) is $2 per bushel, his break-even quantity is 2,000 bushels:

$$BEP_{Quantity} = \frac{FC}{P - UVC} = \frac{\$2,000}{\$2 - \$1} = 2,000 \text{ bushels}$$

The shaded row in Figure 13–11 shows that the break-even quantity at a price of $2 per bushel is 2,000 bushels since, at this quantity, total revenue equals total cost.

FIGURE 13–10
Profit maximization pricing

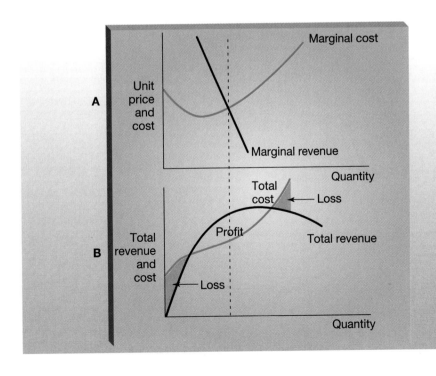

QUANTITY SOLD (Q)	PRICE PER BUSHEL (P)	TOTAL REVENUE (TR) (P × Q)	UNIT VARIABLE COST (UVC)	TOTAL VARIABLE COSTS (TVC) (UVC × Q)	FIXED COST (FC)	TOTAL COST (TC) (FC + VC)	PROFIT (TR – TC)
0	$2	$ 0	$1	$ 0	$2,000	$2,000	–$2,000
1,000	2	2,000	1	1,000	2,000	3,000	–1,000
2,000	2	4,000	1	2,000	2,000	4,000	0
3,000	2	6,000	1	3,000	2,000	5,000	1,000
4,000	2	8,000	1	4,000	2,000	6,000	2,000
5,000	2	10,000	1	5,000	2,000	7,000	3,000
6,000	2	12,000	1	6,000	2,000	8,000	4,000

FIGURE 13–11
Calculating a break-even point

At less than 2,000 bushels the farmer incurs a loss, and at more than 2,000 bushels makes a profit. Figure 13–12 shows a graphic presentation of the break-even analysis, called a **break-even chart**.

Applications of Break-Even Analysis   Because of its simplicity, break-even analysis is used extensively in marketing, most frequently to study the impact on profit of changes in price, fixed cost, and variable cost. The mechanics of break-even analysis are the basis of the widely used electronic spreadsheets offered by computer programs such as Microsoft *Excel* that permit managers to answer hypothetical "what if . . ." questions about the effect of changes in price and cost on their profit.

An example will show the power of break-even analysis. As described in Figure 13–13, if an electronic calculator manufacturer automates its production, thereby increasing fixed cost and reducing variable cost by substituting machines for workers, this increases the break-even point from 333,333 to 500,000 units per year. Note in this example that in the short run only the fixed costs definitely increase

FIGURE 13–12
Break-even analysis chart

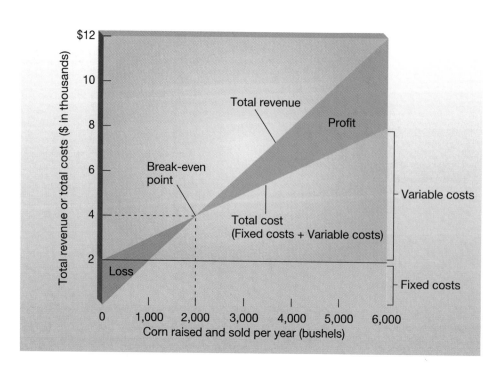

FIGURE 13–13
The cost trade-off: fixed versus variable costs

Executives in virtually every mass-production industry—from locomotives and cars to electronic calculators and breakfast cereals—are searching for ways to increase quality and reduce production costs to remain competitive in world markets. Increasingly they are substituting robots, automation, and computer-controlled manufacturing systems for blue- and white-collar workers.

To understand the implications of this on the break-even point and profit, consider this example of an electronic calculator manufacturer:

BEFORE AUTOMATION			**AFTER AUTOMATION**		
P	=	$10 per unit	P	=	$10 per unit
FC	=	$1,000,000	FC	=	$4,000,000
UVC	=	$7 per unit	UVC	=	$2 per unit

$$\text{BEP}_{Quantity} = \frac{FC}{P-UVC}$$

$$= \frac{\$1,000,000}{\$10-\$7}$$

$$= 333,333 \text{ units}$$

$$\text{BEP}_{Quantity} = \frac{FC}{P-UVC}$$

$$= \frac{\$4,000,000}{\$10-\$2}$$

$$= 500,000 \text{ units}$$

The automation increases the fixed cost and increases the break-even quantity from 333,333 to 500,000 units per year. So if annual sales fall within this range, the calculator manufacturer will incur a loss with the automated plant, whereas it would have made a profit if it had not automated.

But what about its potential profit if it sells 1 million units a year? Look carefully at the two break-even charts below, and see the text to check your conclusions:

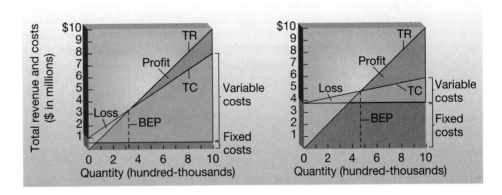

(question 4, Figure 13–1), hopefully offset in the longer run by reduced unit variable cost.

But what about the impact of the higher level of fixed costs on profit? Remember, profit at any output quantity is given by:

Profit = Total revenue − Total cost

$$= (P \times Q) - [FC + (UVC \times Q)]$$

So profit at 1 million units of sales before automation is:

Profit = $(P \times Q) - [FC + (UVC \times Q)]$

$$= (\$10 \times 1,000,000) - [\$1,000,000 + (\$7 \times 1,000,000)]$$

$$= \$10,000,000 - \$8,000,000$$

$$= \$2,000,000$$

After automation, profit is:

$$\text{Profit} = (P \times Q) - [FC + (UVC \times Q)]$$
$$= (\$10 \times 1,000,000) - [\$4,000,000 + (\$2 \times 1,000,000)]$$
$$= \$10,000,000 - \$6,000,000$$
$$= \$4,000,000$$

Automation, by adding to fixed costs, increases profit by $2 million at 1 million units of sales. Thus, as the quantity sold increases for the automated plant, the potential increase or leverage on profit is tremendous. This is why with large production and sales volumes, automated plants for Ford cars or Texas Instruments calculators produce large profits. Also, firms in other industries, such as airline, railroad, and hotel and motel industries, that require high fixed costs can reap large profits when they go even slightly beyond the break-even point.

Concept Check

1. What is the difference between fixed costs and variable costs?

2. What is a break-even point?

SUMMARY

1 Price is the money or other considerations exchanged for the ownership or use of a product or service. Although price typically involves money, the amount exchanged is often different from the list or quoted price because of allowances and extra fees.

2 Consumers use price as an indicator of value when it is paired with the perceived benefits of a good or service. Sometimes price influences consumer perceptions of quality itself and at other times consumers make value assessments by comparing the costs and benefits of substitute items.

3 Pricing constraints such as demand, product newness, costs, competitors, other products sold by the firm, and the type of competitive market restrict a firm's pricing latitude.

4 Pricing objectives, which specify the role of price in a firm's marketing strategy, may include pricing for profit, sales revenue, market share, unit sales, survival, or some socially responsible price level.

5 A demand curve shows the maximum number of products consumers will buy at a given price and for a given set of (*a*)

consumer tastes, (*b*) price and availability of other products, and (*c*) consumer income. When any of these change, there is a shift of the demand curve.

6 Important revenue concepts include total revenue, average revenue, and marginal revenue.

7 Price elasticity of demand measures the sensitivity of units sold to a change in price. When demand is elastic, a reduction in price is more than offset by an increase in units sold, so that total revenue increases.

8 It is necessary to consider cost behavior when making pricing decisions. Important cost concepts include total cost, variable cost, fixed cost, and marginal cost.

9 Break-even analysis shows the relationship between total revenue and total cost at various quantities of output for given conditions of price, fixed cost, and variable cost. The break-even point is where total revenue and total cost are equal.

KEY TERMS AND CONCEPTS

average revenue p. 351
barter p. 343
break-even analysis p. 356
break-even chart p. 356
break-even point p. 357
demand curve p. 350
demand factors p. 350
fixed cost p. 355
marginal analysis p. 355
marginal cost p. 355
marginal revenue p. 351

price p. 343
price elasticity of demand p. 354
pricing constraints p. 346
pricing objectives p. 348
profit equation p. 345
total cost p. 355
total revenue p. 351
variable cost p. 355
value p. 344
value-pricing p. 344

APPLYING MARKETING CONCEPTS AND PERSPECTIVES

1 How would the price equation apply to the purchase price of (*a*) gasoline, (*b*) an airline ticket, and (*c*) a checking account?

2 What would be your response to the statement, "Profit maximization is the only legitimate pricing objective for the firm"?

3 How is a downward-sloping demand curve related to total revenue and marginal revenue?

4 A marketing executive once said, "If the price elasticity of demand for your product is inelastic, then your price is probably too low." What is this executive saying in terms of the economic principles discussed in this chapter?

5 A marketing manager reduced the price on a brand of cereal by 10 percent and observed a 25 percent increase in quantity sold. The manager then thought that if the price were reduced by another 20 percent, a 50 percent increase in quantity sold would occur. What would be your response to the marketing manager's reasoning?

6 A student theater group at a university has developed a demand schedule that shows the relationship between ticket prices and demand based on a student survey, as follows:

TICKET PRICE	NUMBER OF STUDENTS WHO WOULD BUY
$1	300
2	250
3	200
4	150
5	100

(*a*) Graph the demand curve and the total revenue curve based on these data. What ticket price might be set based on this analysis? (*b*) What other factors should be considered before the final price is set?

7 Touché Toiletries, Inc. has developed an addition to its Lizardman Cologne line tentatively branded Ode d'Toade Cologne. Unit variable costs are 45 cents for a 3-ounce bottle, and heavy advertising expenditures in the first year would result in total fixed costs of $900,000. Ode d'Toade Cologne is priced at $7.50 for a 3-ounce bottle. How many bottles of Ode d'Toade must be sold to break even?

8 Suppose that marketing executives for Touché Toiletries reduced the price to $6.50 for a 3-ounce bottle of Ode d'Toade and the fixed costs were $1,100,000. Suppose further that the unit variable cost remained at 45 cents for a 3-ounce bottle. (*a*) How many bottles must be sold to break even? (*b*) What dollar profit level would Ode d'Toade achieve if 200,000 bottles were sold?

9 Executives of Random Recordings, Inc. produced an album entitled *Sunshine/Moonshine* by the Starshine Sisters Band. The cost and price information was as follows:

Album cover	$ 1.00 per album
Songwriter's royalties	0.30 per album
Recording artists' royalties	0.70 per album
Direct material and labor costs to produce the album	1.00 per album
Fixed cost of producing an album (advertising, studio fee, etc.)	100,000.00
Selling price	7.00 per album

(*a*) Prepare a chart like that in Figure 13–11 showing total cost, fixed cost, and total revenue for album quantity sold levels starting at 10,000 albums through 100,000 albums at 10,000 album intervals, that is, 10,000; 20,000; 30,000; and so on.

(*b*) What is the break-even point for the album?

INTERNET EXERCISE

It's Wednesday and you just completed your midterm exams. As a reward for your hard work, a friend sent you a pair of free tickets to a popular Broadway show in New York City for 7:00 P.M. Saturday night. Check out the following online travel services to book a round-trip ticket, leaving from Chicago's O'Hare (ORD) airport around 5:00 P.M. on Friday to New York City's La Guardia (LGA) airport. On Sunday, you'll leave La Guardia around 5:00 P.M. and return to O'Hare. Which of the following online travel services provides the cheapest fare and fewest restrictions? Check out our search and see if you can beat the prices we obtained in late 2001. And don't forget to eat at the Carnegie Deli while you're in New York!

- Cheap Tickets (www.cheaptickets.com). Lowest price: $210.00 from American Trans Air.
- Orbitz, the new online travel service owned by the major airlines (www.orbitz.com). Lowest price: $335.00 from Continental Airlines.
- Travelocity, the leading online travel service (www. travelocity.com). Lowest price: $317.50 from American Trans Air.

[NOTE: You were not asked to search Expedia.com or Priceline.com because you may accidentally order a ticket without meaning to do so.]

VIDEO CASE 13–1   Washburn International: Guitars and Break-Even Points

"The relationship between musicians and their guitars is something really extraordinary—and is a fairly strange one," says Brady Breen in a carefully understated tone of voice. Breen has the experience to know. He's production manager of Washburn International, one of the most prestigious guitar manufacturers in the world. Washburn's instruments range from one-of-a-kind, custom-made acoustic and electric guitars and basses to less-expensive, mass-produced ones.

THE COMPANY

The modern Washburn International started in 1977 when a small Chicago firm bought the century-old Washburn brand name and a small inventory of guitars, parts, and promotional supplies. At that time annual revenues of the company were $300,000 for the sale of about 2,500 guitars. Washburn's first catalog, appearing in 1978, told a frightening truth:

> Our designs are translated by Japan's most experienced craftsmen, assuring the consistent quality and craftmanship for which they are known.

At that time the American guitar-making craft was at an all-time low. Guitars made by Japanese firms such as Ibane and Yamaha were in use by an increasing number of professionals.

Times have changed for Washburn. Today the company sells about 250,000 guitars a year. Annual sales exceed $50 million. All this resulted from Washburn's aggressive marketing strategies to develop product lines with different price points targeted at musicians in distinctly different market segments.

THE PRODUCTS AND MARKET SEGMENTS

Arguably the most trendsetting guitar developed by the modern Washburn company appeared in 1980. This was the Festival Series of cutaway, thin-bodied flattops, with built-in bridge pickups and controls, which went on to become the virtual standard for live performances. John Lodge of the Moody Blues endorsed the 12-string version—his gleaming white guitar appearing in both concerts and ads for years. In the time since the Festival Series appeared, countless rock and country stars have used these instruments including Bob Dylan, Dolly Parton, Greg Allman, John Jorgenson, and George Harrison.

Until 1991 all Washburn guitars were manufactured in Asia. That year Washburn started building its high-end guitars in the United States. Today Washburn marketing executives divide its product line into four levels. From high end to low end these are:

- One-of-a-kind, custom units.
- Batch-custom units.
- Mass-customized units.
- Mass-produced units.

The one-of-a-kind custom units are for the many stars that use Washburn instruments. The mass-produced units targeted at first-time buyers are still manufactured in Asian factories.

PRICING ISSUES

Setting prices for its various lines presents a continuing challenge for Washburn. Not only do the prices have to reflect the changing tastes of its various segments of musicians, but the prices must also be competitive with the prices set for guitars manufactured and marketed globally. In fact, Washburn and other well-known guitar manufacturers have a prestige-niche strategy. For Washburn this involves endorsements by internationally known musicians who play its instruments and lend their names to lines of Washburn signature guitars. This has the effect of reducing the price elasticity or price sensitivity for these guitars. Stars playing Washburn guitars like Nuno Bettencourt, David Gilmour of Pink Floyd, Joe Perry of Aerosmith, and Darryl Jones of the Rolling Stones have their own lines of signature guitars—the "batch-custom" units mentioned earlier.

Joe Baksha, Washburn's executive vice president, is responsible for reviewing and approving prices for the company's lines of guitars. Setting a sales target of 2,000 units for a new line of guitars, he is considering a suggested retail price of $329 per unit for customers at one of the hundreds of retail outlets carrying the Washburn line. For planning purposes, Baksha estimates half of the final retail price will be the price Washburn nets when it sells its guitar to the wholesalers and dealers in its channel of distribution.

Looking at Washburn's financial data for its present Chicago plant, Baksha estimates that this line of guitars must bear these fixed costs:

Rent and taxes	= $12,000
Depreciation of equipment	= $ 4,000
Management and quality control program	= $20,000

In addition, he estimates the variable costs for each unit to be:

Direct materials	= $25/unit
Direct labor	= 8 hours/unit @ $14/hour

Carefully kept production records at Washburn's Chicago plant make Baksha believe that these are reasonable estimates. He explains, "Before we begin a production run, we have a good feel for what our costs will be. The U.S.-built N-4, for example, simply costs more than one of our foreign-produced Mercury or Wing series electrics."

Caught in the global competition for guitar sales, Washburn searches for ways to reduce and control costs. After much agonizing, the company decided to move to Nashville, Tennessee. In this home of country music, Washburn expects to lower its manufacturing costs because there are many skilled workers in the region, and its fixed costs will be reduced by avoiding some of the expenses of having a big city location. Specifically, Washburn projects that it will reduce its rent and taxes expense by 40 percent and the wage rate it pays by 15 percent in relocating from Chicago to Nashville.

Questions

1 What factors are most likely to affect the demand for the lines of Washburn guitars (*a*) bought by a first-time guitar buyer and (*b*) bought by a sophisticated musician who wants a signature model signed by David Gilmour or Joe Perry?

2 For Washburn what are examples of (*a*) shifting the demand curve to the right to get a higher price for a guitar line (movement *of* the demand curve) and (*b*) pricing decisions involving moving *along* a demand curve?

3 In Washburn's Chicago plant what is the break-even point for the new line of guitars if the retail price is (*a*) $329, (*b*) $359, and (*c*) $299? Also, (*d*) if Washburn achieves the sales target of 2,000 units at the $329 retail price, what will its profit be?

4 Assume that Washburn moves its production to Nashville and that the costs are reduced as projected in the case. Then, what will be the (*a*) new break-even point at a $329 retail price for this line of guitars and (*b*) the new profit if it sells 2,000 units?

5 If for competitive reasons, Washburn eventually has to move all its production back to Asia, (*a*) which specific costs might be lowered and (*b*) what additional costs might it expect to incur?

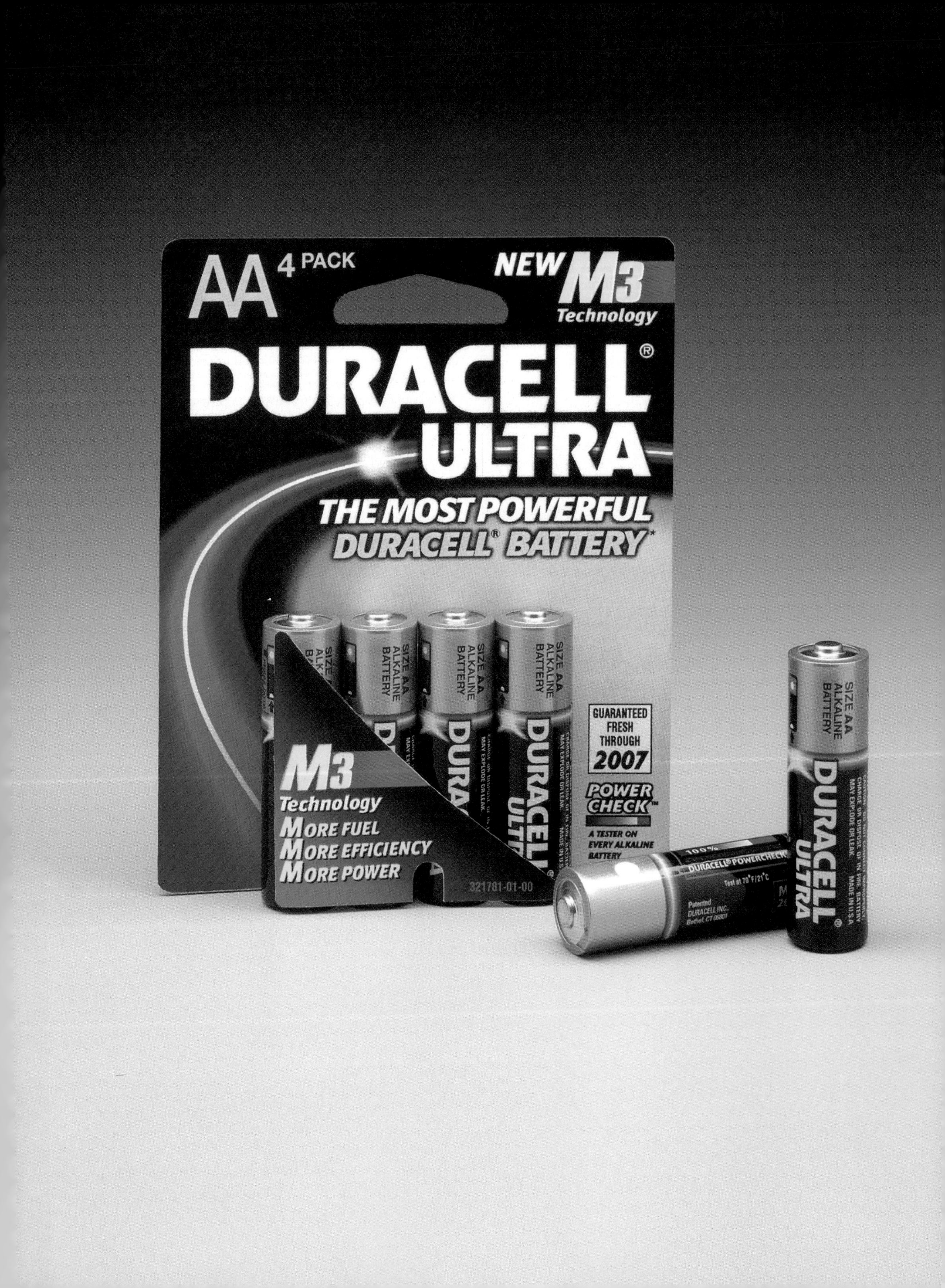
AA 4 PACK
NEW M3 Technology
DURACELL®
ULTRA
THE MOST POWERFUL DURACELL® BATTERY*
SIZE AA ALKALINE BATTERY
DURACELL
GUARANTEED FRESH THROUGH 2007
POWER CHECK™
A TESTER ON EVERY ALKALINE BATTERY
M3 Technology
MORE FUEL
MORE EFFICIENCY
MORE POWER
321781-01-00
DURACELL® POWERCHECK
DURACELL ULTRA

14

ARRIVING AT THE FINAL PRICE

AFTER READING THIS CHAPTER YOU SHOULD BE ABLE TO:

- Understand how to establish the initial "approximate price level" using demand-oriented, cost-oriented, profit-oriented, and competition-oriented approaches.

- Identify the major factors considered in deriving a final list or quoted price from the approximate price level.

- Describe adjustments made to the approximate price level on the basis of geography, discounts, and allowances.

- Prepare basic financial analyses useful in evaluating alternative prices and arriving at the final sales price.

- Describe the principal laws and regulations affecting pricing practices.

DURACELL KNOWS THE VALUE OF PORTABLE POWER

How is value defined for an alkaline battery? Ask Duracell, the world's leading manufacturer and marketer of high-performance alkaline batteries.

As the global leader of the $8 billion alkaline battery category, Duracell pioneered the high-performance segment of alkaline batteries with the launch of Duracell Ultra, the most successful new battery ever introduced. Duracell Ultra was designed to meet the extraordinary power requirements of today's portable electronic devices. Duracell Ultra with M3 Technology AA alkaline batteries last up to 180 percent longer than ordinary alkaline batteries in digital cell phones; up to 140 percent longer in hand-held personal computers; and up to 100 percent longer in camcorders. M3 Technology's patented and patent-pending advancements and design enhancements not only provide longer battery life, but also improve the performance of devices. For example, halogen flashlights shine brighter and camera flashes recycle faster with M3 Technology.

Product innovation that benefits the consumer is a critical ingredient in Duracell Ultra's marketing success. "M3 Technology is readily understood and appreciated by consumers because it answers their fundamental needs for portable power," says Duracell's senior vice president for business management and business development. "Moreover, consumers expect this type of advance from the leader in the category." Such innovation naturally translates into the price consumers are willing to pay. Duracell Ultra with M3 Technology is priced about 25 percent higher than Duracell alkaline batteries.[1]

The marketing success of Duracell Ultra illustrates the imaginative commercialization of new alkaline battery

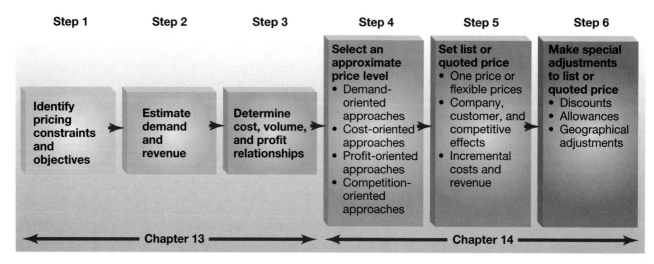

FIGURE 14–1
Steps in setting price

technology at a price point that creates value for the consumer. In addition to understanding consumer demand, cost, competition, and profit considerations played a role in Duracell's pricing decision which will be discussed later in the chapter.

This chapter describes how companies select an approximate price level, highlights important considerations in setting a list or quoted price, and identifies various price adjustments that can be made to prices set by the firm—the last three steps an organization uses in setting price (Figure 14–1). In addition, an overview of important legal and regulatory aspects of pricing is provided.

STEP 4: SELECT AN APPROXIMATE PRICE LEVEL

A key to a marketing manager's setting a final price for a product is to find an "approximate price level" to use as a reasonable starting point. Four common approaches to helping find this approximate price level are (1) demand-oriented, (2) cost-oriented, (3) profit-oriented, and (4) competition-oriented approaches (Figure 14–2). Although these approaches are discussed separately below, some of them overlap, and an effective marketing manager will consider several in searching for an approximate price level.

Demand-Oriented Approaches

Demand-oriented approaches weigh factors underlying expected customer tastes and preferences more heavily than such factors as cost, profit, and competition when selecting a price level.

Skimming Pricing   A firm introducing a new or innovative product can use **skimming pricing**, setting the highest initial price that customers really desiring the product are willing to pay. These customers are not very price sensitive because they weigh the new product's price, quality, and ability to satisfy their needs against the same characteristics of substitutes. As the demand of these customers is satisfied, the firm lowers the price to attract another, more price-sensitive segment. Thus, skimming pricing gets its name from skimming successive layers of "cream," or customer segments, as prices are lowered in a series of steps.

Skimming pricing is an effective strategy when (1) enough prospective customers are willing to buy the product immediately at the high initial price to make these sales profitable, (2) the high initial price will not attract competitors, (3) lowering price has only a minor effect on increasing the sales volume and reducing the unit costs, and (4) customers interpret the high price as signifying high quality. These

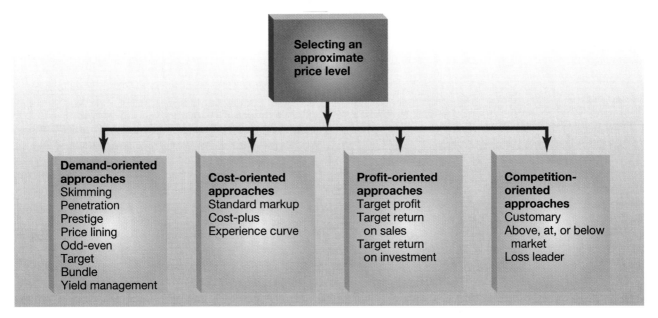

FIGURE 14–2
Four approaches for selecting an approximate price level

four conditions are most likely to exist when the new product is protected by patents or copyrights or its uniqueness is understood and valued by consumers. Duracell adopted a skimming strategy for the Duracell Ultra alkaline battery because many of these conditions applied.

Penetration Pricing   Setting a low initial price on a new product to appeal immediately to the mass market is **penetration pricing**, the exact opposite of skimming pricing. Nintendo consciously chose a penetration strategy when it introduced its Gamecube video game console first in Japan and later in the United States in 2001. Gamecube was launched with an introductory price of $199.95—$100.00 less than the list price for Microsoft's Xbox and Sony's Playstation 2 consoles.[2]

The conditions favoring penetration pricing are the reverse of those supporting skimming pricing: (1) many segments of the market are price sensitive, (2) a low initial price discourages competitors from entering the market, and (3) unit production and marketing costs fall dramatically as production volumes increase. A firm using penetration pricing may (1) maintain the initial price for a time to gain profit lost from its low introductory level or (2) lower the price further, counting on the new volume to generate the necessary profit.

In some situations penetration pricing may follow skimming pricing. A company might initially price a product high to attract price-insensitive consumers and recoup initial research and development costs and introductory promotional expenditures. Once this is done, penetration pricing is used to appeal to a broader segment of the population and increase market share.[3]

Prestige Pricing   As noted in Chapter 13, consumers may use price as a measure of the quality or prestige of an item so that as price is lowered beyond some point, demand for the item actually falls. **Prestige pricing** involves setting a high price so that quality- or status-conscious consumers will be attracted to the product and buy it (Figure 14–3A). The demand curve slopes downward and to the right between points A and B but turns back to the left between points B and C because demand is actually reduced between points B and C. From A to B buyers see the lowering of price as a bargain and buy more; from B to C they become dubious about the quality and prestige and buy less. A marketing manager's pricing strategy here is to stay above price P_0 (the initial price).

FIGURE 14–3
Demand curves for two types of demand-oriented approaches

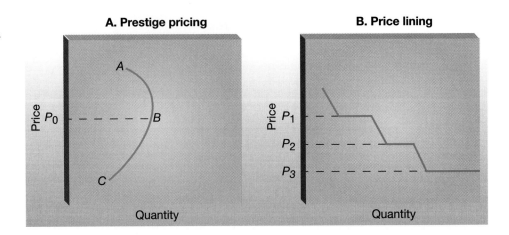

Rolls-Royce cars, Chanel perfume, Cartier jewelry, Lalique crystal, and Swiss watches have an element of prestige pricing in them and may sell worse at lower prices than at higher ones.[4] The recent success of Swiss watchmaker TAG Heuer is an example. The company raised the average price of its watches from $250 to $1,000, and its sales volume increased sevenfold![5] Recently, Energizer learned that buyers of high-performance alkaline batteries tend to associate a lower price with lower quality. The accompanying Marketing NewsNet describes the pricing lesson learned by Energizer.[6]

Price Lining   Often a firm that is selling not just a single product but a line of products may price them at a number of different specific pricing points, which is called **price lining**. For example, a discount department store manager may price a line of women's dresses at $59, $79, and $99. As shown in Figure 14–3B, this assumes that demand is elastic at each of these price points but inelastic between these price points. In some instances all the items might be purchased for the same cost and then marked up at different percentages to achieve these price points based on color, style, and expected demand. In other instances manufacturers design products for different price points, and retailers apply approximately the same markup percentages to achieve the three or four different price points offered to consumers. Sellers often feel that a limited number (such as three or four) of price points is preferable to 8 or 10 different ones, which may only confuse prospective buyers.[7]

Odd-Even Pricing   Sears offers a Craftsman radial saw for $499.99, the suggested retail price for a MACH 3 razor set (razor and two blades) is $6.99, and Kmart sells Windex glass cleaner on sale for 99 cents. Why not simply price these items at $500, $7, and $1, respectively? These firms are using **odd-even pricing**, which involves setting prices a few dollars or cents under an even number. The presumption is that consumers see the Sears radial saw as priced at "something over $400" rather than "about $500." In theory, demand increases if the price drops from $500 to $499.99. There is some evidence to suggest this does happen. However, research suggests that overuse of odd-ending prices tends to mute its effect on demand.[8]

Target Pricing   Manufacturers will sometimes estimate the price that the ultimate consumer would be willing to pay for a product. They then work backward through markups taken by retailers and wholesalers to determine what price they can charge wholesalers for the product. This practice, called **target pricing**, results in the manufacturer deliberately adjusting the composition and features of a product to achieve the target price to consumers. Canon uses this practice for pricing its cameras as does Heinz for its complete line of pet foods.[9]

Battery manufacturers are as tireless as a certain drum-thumping bunny in their efforts to create products that perform better, last longer, and not incidentally, outsell the competition. The commercialization of new alkaline battery technology at a price that creates value for consumers is not always obvious or easy. Just ask the marketing executives at Energizer about their experience with pricing Energizer Advanced Formula and Energizer e^2 AA alkaline batteries.

When Duracell launched its high-performance Ultra brand AA alkaline battery with a 25 percent price premium over standard Duracell batteries, Energizer quickly countered with its own high-performance battery—Energizer Advanced Formula. Believing that consumers would not pay the premium price, Energizer priced its Advanced Formula brand at the same price as its standard AA alkaline battery, expecting to gain market share from Duracell. It did not happen. Why? According to industry analysts, consumers associated Energizer's low price with inferior quality in the high-performance segment. Instead of gaining market share, Energizer lost market share to Duracell and Rayovac, the number three battery manufacturer.

Having learned its lesson, Energizer subsequently released its e^2 high-performance battery, this time priced 4 percent higher than Duracell Ultra and about 50 percent higher than Advanced Formula. The result? Energizer recovered lost sales and market share. The lesson learned? Value lies in the eye of the beholder.

Bundle Pricing   A frequently used demand-oriented pricing practice is **bundle pricing**—the marketing of two or more products in a single "package" price. For example, Delta Air Lines offers vacation packages that include airfare, car rental, and lodging. Bundle pricing is based on the idea that consumers value the package more than the individual items. This is due to benefits received from not having to make separate purchases and enhanced satisfaction from one item given the presence of another. Moreover, bundle pricing often provides a lower total cost to buyers and lower marketing costs to sellers.[10]

Yield Management Pricing   Have you noticed seats on airline flights are priced differently within coach class? What you observed is **yield management pricing**—the charging of different prices to maximize revenue for a set amount of capacity at any given time.[11] As described in Chapter 12, service businesses engage in capacity management, and an effective way to do this is by varying prices by time, day, week, or season. Yield management pricing is a complex approach that continually matches demand and supply to customize the price for a service. Airlines, hotels, cruise ships, and car rental companies frequently use it. American Airlines estimates that yield management pricing produces an annual revenue that exceeds $500 million.[12]

Concept Check

1. What are the circumstances in pricing a new product that might support skimming or penetration pricing?

2. What is odd-even pricing?

Cost-Oriented Approaches

With cost-oriented approaches a price setter stresses the cost side of the pricing problem, not the demand side. Price is set by looking at the production and marketing costs and then adding enough to cover direct expenses, overhead, and profit.

Standard Markup Pricing

Standard Markup Pricing   Managers of supermarkets and other retail stores have such a large number of products that estimating the demand for each product as a means of setting price is impossible. Therefore, they use **standard markup pricing**, which entails adding a fixed percentage to the cost of all items in a specific product class. This percentage markup varies depending on the type of retail store (such as furniture, clothing, or grocery) and on the product involved. High-volume products usually have smaller markups than do low-volume products. Supermarkets such as Kroger, Safeway, and Jewel have different markups for staple items and discretionary items. The markup on staple items like sugar, flour, and dairy products varies from 10 percent to 23 percent, whereas markups on discretionary items like snack foods and candy ranges from 27 percent to 47 percent. These markups must cover all expenses of the store, pay for overhead costs, and contribute something to profits. For supermarkets these markups, which may appear very large, result in only a 1 percent profit on sales revenue if the store is operating efficiently. By comparison, consider the markups on snacks and beverages purchased at your local movie theater. The markup on soft drinks is 87 percent, 65 percent on candy bars, and a whopping 90 percent on popcorn! An explanation of how to compute a markup, along with operating statement data and other ratios, is given in Appendix B to this chapter.

Cost-Plus Pricing

Cost-Plus Pricing   Many manufacturing, professional services, and construction firms use a variation of standard markup pricing. **Cost-plus pricing** involves summing

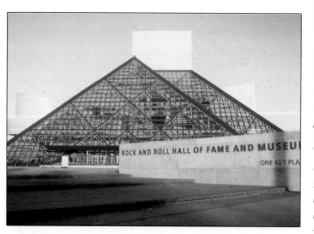

the total unit cost of providing a product or service and adding a specific amount to the cost to arrive at a price. Cost-plus pricing generally assumes two forms. With *cost-plus percentage-of-cost pricing,* a fixed percentage is added to the total unit cost. This is often used to price one- or few-of-a-kind items, as when an architectural firm charges a percentage of the construction costs of, say, the $92 million Rock and

Roll Hall of Fame and Museum in Cleveland, Ohio. In buying highly technical, few-of-a-kind products such as hydro-electric power plants or space satellites, country governments have found that general contractors are reluctant to specify a formal, fixed price for the procurement. Therefore, they use *cost-plus fixed-fee pricing,* which means that a supplier is reimbursed for all costs, regardless of what they turn out to be, but is allowed only a fixed fee as profit that is independent of the final cost of the project. For example, suppose that the National Aeronautics and Space Administration agreed to pay Boeing $1.2 billion as the cost of a space shuttle and agreed to a $100 million fee for providing that space shuttle. Even if Boeing's cost increased to $2 billion for the space shuttle, its fee would remain $100 million.

Cost-plus pricing is the most commonly used method to set prices for business products.[13] Increasingly, however, this method is finding favor among business-to-business marketers in the service sector. For example, the rising cost of legal fees has prompted some law firms to adopt a cost-plus pricing approach. Rather than billing business clients on an hourly basis, lawyers and their clients agree on a fixed fee based on expected costs plus a profit for the law firm. Many advertising agencies now use this approach. Here, the client agrees to pay the agency a fee based on the cost of its work plus some agreed-on profit, which is often a percentage of total cost.[14]

Experience Curve Pricing   The method of **experience curve pricing** is based on the learning effect, which holds that the unit cost of many products and services declines by 10 percent to 30 percent each time a firm's experience at producing and selling them doubles.[15] This reduction is regular or predictable enough that the average cost per unit can be mathematically estimated. For example, if the firm estimates that costs will fall by 15 percent each time volume doubles, then the cost of the 100th unit produced and sold will be about 85 percent of the cost of the 50th unit, and the 200th unit will be 85 percent of the 100th unit. Therefore, if the cost of the 50th unit is $100, the 100th unit would cost $85, the 200th unit would be $72.25, and so on. Because prices often follow costs with experience curve pricing, a rapid decline in price is possible. Japanese and U.S firms in the electronics industry often adopt this pricing approach. This cost-based pricing approach complements the demand-based pricing strategy of skimming followed by penetration pricing. For example, CD player prices have decreased from $900 to less than $200, fax machine prices have declined from $1,000 to under $300, and cellular telephones that once sold for $4,000 are now priced below $99. Panasonic, Sony, Samsung, Zenith, and other television manufacturers will use experience curve pricing for HDTV sets. Consumers will benefit because prices will decline as cumulative sales volume grows.

Profit-Oriented Approaches

A price setter may choose to balance both revenues and costs to set price using profit-oriented approaches. These might either involve a target of a specific dollar volume of profit or express this target profit as a percentage of sales or investment.

Panasonic expects to be a leader in the successful commercialization of HDTV.

Panasonic

www.panasonic.com

Target Profit Pricing   A firm may set an annual target of a specific dollar volume of profit, which is called **target profit pricing**. Suppose a picture framing store

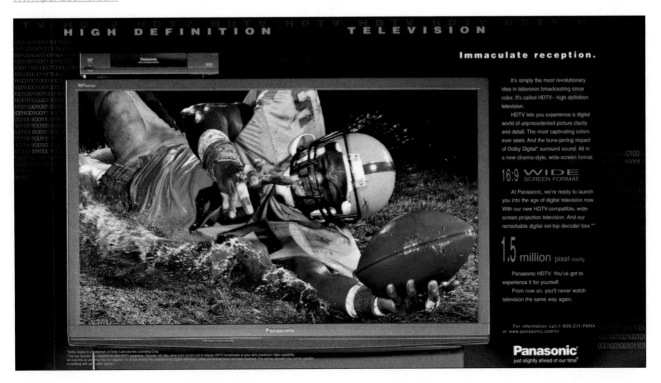

owner wishes to use target profit pricing to establish a price for a typical framed picture and assumes the following:

- Variable cost is a constant $22 per unit.
- Fixed cost is a constant $26,000.
- Demand is insensitive to price up to $60 per unit.
- A target profit of $7,000 is sought at an annual volume of 1,000 units (framed pictures).

The price can be calculated as follows:

$$\text{Profit} = \text{Total revenue} - \text{Total cost}$$

$$\text{Profit} = (P \times Q) - [FC + (UVC \times Q)]$$

$$\$7,000 = (P \times 1,000) - [\$26,000 + (\$22 \times 1,000)]$$

$$\$7,000 = 1,000P - (\$26,000 + \$22,000)$$

$$1,000P = \$7,000 + \$48,000$$

$$P = \$55$$

Note that a critical assumption is that this higher average price of a framed picture will not cause the demand to fall.

Target Return-on-Sales Pricing

A difficulty with target profit pricing is that although it is simple and the target involves only a specific dollar volume, there is no benchmark of sales or investment used to show how much of the firm's effort is needed to achieve the target. Firms such as supermarket chains often use **target return-on-sales pricing** to set typical prices that will give them a profit that is a specified percentage, say, 1 percent, of the sales volume. Suppose the owner decides to use target return-on-sales pricing for the frame shop and makes the same first three assumptions shown previously. The owner now sets a target of 20 percent return on sales at an annual volume of 1,250 units. This gives

$$\text{Target return on sales} = \frac{\text{Target profit}}{\text{Total revenue}}$$

$$20\% = \frac{TR - TC}{TR}$$

$$0.20 = \frac{P \times Q - [FC + (UVC \times Q)]}{TR}$$

$$0.20 = \frac{P \times 1,250 - [\$26,000 + (\$22 \times 1,250)]}{P \times + 1,250}$$

$$P = \$53.50$$

So at a price of $53.50 per unit and an annual quantity of 1,250 frames,

$$TR = P \times Q = \$53.50 \times 1,250 = \$66,875$$

$$TC = FC + (UVC \times Q) = \$26,000 + (\$22 \times 1,250) = \$53,500$$

$$\text{Profit} = TR - TC = \$66,875 - \$53,500 = \$13,375$$

As a check,

$$\text{Target return on sales} = \frac{\text{Target profit}}{\text{Total revenue}} = \frac{\$13,375}{\$66,875} = 20\%$$

Target Return-on-Investment Pricing

Firms such as General Motors and many public utilities set annual return-on-investment (ROI) targets such as ROI of 20 percent. **Target return-on-investment pricing** is a method of setting prices to achieve this target.

ASSUMPTIONS OR RESULTS	FINANCIAL ELEMENT	SIMULATION				
		LAST YEAR	A	B	C	D
ASSUMPTIONS	Price per unit (P)	$50	$54	$54	$58	$58
	Units sold (Q)	1,000	1,200	1,100	1,100	1,000
	Change in unit variable cost (UVC)	0%	+10%	+10%	+20%	+20%
	Unit variable cost	$22.00	$24.20	$24.20	$26.20	$26.40
	Total expenses	$8,000	Same	Same	Same	Same
	Owner's salary	$18,000	Same	Same	Same	Same
	Investment	$20,000	Same	Same	Same	Same
	State and federal taxes	50%	Same	Same	Same	Same
SPREADSHEET SIMULATION	Net sales (P x Q)	$50,000	$64,800	$59,400	$63,800	$58,000
	Less: COGS (Q x UVC)	22,000	29,040	26,620	29,040	26,400
	Gross margin	$28,000	$35,760	$32,780	$34,760	$31,600
	Less: total expenses	8,000	8,000	8,000	8,000	8,000
	Less: owner's salary	18,000	18,000	18,000	18,000	18,000
	Net profit before taxes	$2,000	$9,760	$6,780	$8,760	$5,600
	Less: taxes	1,000	4,880	3,390	4,380	2,800
	Net profit after taxes	$1,000	$4,880	$3,390	$4,380	$2,800
	Investment	$20,000	$20,000	$20,000	$20,000	$20,000
	Return on investment	5.0%	24.4%	17.0%	21.9%	14.0%

FIGURE 14–4

Results of computer spreadsheet simulation to select price to achieve a target return on investment

Suppose the store owner sets a target ROI of 10 percent, which is twice that achieved the previous year. She considers raising the average price of a framed picture to $54 or $58—up from last year's average of $50. To do this, she might improve product quality by offering better frames and higher-quality matting, which will increase the cost but will probably offset the decreased revenue from the lower number of units that can be sold next year.

To handle this wide variety of assumptions, today's managers use computerized spreadsheets to project operating statements based on a diverse set of assumptions. Figure 14–4 shows the results of computerized spreadsheet simulation, with assumptions shown at the top and the projected results at the bottom. A previous year's operating statement results are shown in the column headed "Last Year," and the assumptions and spreadsheet results for four different sets of assumptions are shown in columns A, B, C, and D.

In choosing a price or another action using spreadsheet results, the decision maker must (1) study the results of the computer simulation projections and (2) assess the realism of the assumptions underlying each set of projections. For example, the store owner sees from the bottom row of Figure 14–4 that all four spreadsheet simulations exceed the after-tax target ROI of 10 percent. But, after more thought, she judges it to be more realistic to set an average price of $58 per unit, allow the unit variable cost to increase by 20 percent to account for more expensive framing and matting, and settle for the same unit sales as the 1,000 units sold last year. She selects simulation D in this computerized spreadsheet approach to target ROI pricing and has a goal of 14 percent after-tax ROI. Of course, these same calculations can be done by hand, but this is far more time consuming.

Competition-Oriented Approaches

Rather than emphasize demand, cost, or profit factors, a price setter can stress what competitors or "the market" is doing.

Customary Pricing For some products where tradition, a standardized channel of distribution, or other competitive factors dictate the price, **customary pricing** is used. Tradition prevails in the pricing of Swatch watches. The $40 customary price for the basic model changed little in 10 years. Candy bars offered through standard vending machines have a customary price of 60 cents, and a significant departure from this price may result in a loss of sales for the manufacturer. Hershey typically has changed the amount of chocolate in its candy bars depending on the price of raw chocolate rather than vary its customary retail price so that it can continue selling through vending machines.

Above-, At-, or Below-Market Pricing For most products it is difficult to identify a specific market price for a product or product class. Still, marketing managers often have a subjective feel for the competitors' price or market price. Using this benchmark, they then may deliberately choose a strategy of **above-, at-, or below-market pricing**.

Among watch manufacturers, Rolex takes pride in emphasizing that it makes one of the most expensive watches you can buy—a clear example of above-market pricing. Manufacturers of national brands of clothing such as Hart Schaffner & Marx and Christian Dior and retailers such as Neiman-Marcus deliberately set premium prices for their products.

Large mass-merchandise chains such as Sears and JCPenney generally use at-market pricing. These chains often establish the going market price in the minds of their competitors. Similarly, Revlon and Cluett Peabody & Company (the maker of Arrow shirts) generally price their products "at market." They also provide a reference price for competitors that use above- and below-market pricing.

In contrast, a number of firms use below-market pricing. Manufacturers of generic products and retailers who offer their own private brands of products ranging from peanut butter to shampoo deliberately set prices for these products about 8 percent to 10 percent below the prices of nationally branded competitive products such as Skippy peanut butter, Vidal Sassoon shampoo, or Crest toothpaste. Below-market pricing also exists in business-to-business marketing. Hewlett-Packard, for instance, initially priced its line of office personal computers below Compaq and IBM to promote a value image among corporate buyers.[16]

Loss-Leader Pricing For a special promotion retail stores deliberately sell a product below its customary price to attract attention to it. The purpose of this **loss-leader pricing** is not to increase sales but to attract customers in hopes they will buy other products as well, particularly the discretionary items with large markups. Mass merchandisers such as Target have sold home videos at half their customary price to attract customers to their stores. According to an industry observer, "Video is one of the mass merchandisers' favorite traffic-building devices."[17]

Concept Check

1. What is standard markup pricing?

2. What profit-based pricing approach should a manager use if he or she wants to reflect the percentage of the firm's resources used in obtaining the profit?

3. What is the purpose of loss-leader pricing when used by a retail firm?

STEP 5: SET THE LIST OR QUOTED PRICE

The first four steps in setting price covered in Chapter 13 and this chapter result in an approximate price level for the product that appears reasonable. But it still remains for the manager to set a specific list or quoted price in light of all relevant factors.

One-Price versus Flexible-Price Policy

A seller must decide whether to follow a one-price or flexible-price policy. A **one-**

price policy, also called *fixed pricing,* is setting one price for all buyers of a product or service. For example, when you buy a Wilson Sting tennis racket from a discount store, you are offered the product at a single price. You can buy it or not, but there is no variation in the price under the seller's one-price policy. Saturn Corporation uses this approach in its stores and features a "no haggle, one price" price for its cars. Some retailers such as Dollar Tree Stores and 99¢ Only Stores have married this policy with a below-market approach and sell everything in their stores for $1 or less![18]

In contrast, a **flexible-price policy**, also called *dynamic pricing,* involves setting different prices for products and services depending on individual buyers and purchase situations. A flexible-price policy gives sellers considerable discretion in setting the final price in light of demand, cost, and competitive factors. Yield management pricing is a form of flexible pricing because prices vary by an individual buyer's purchase situation, company cost considerations, and competitive conditions.[19] Dell Computer Corporation recently adopted flexible pricing. It continually adjusts prices in response to changes in its own costs, competitive pressures, and demand from customers, from one segment of the personal computer market to another. "Our flexibility allows us to be [priced] different even within a day," says a Dell spokesperson.[20]

Most companies use a one-price policy. However, flexible pricing has grown in popularity because of increasingly sophisticated information technology. Today, many marketers have the ability to customize a price for an individual on the basis of his or her purchasing patterns, product preferences, and price-sensitivity, all of which are stored in company data warehouses. Price customization is particularly prevalent for products and services bought online. Online marketers routinely adjust prices in response to purchase situations and past purchase behaviors of online buyers. Some online marketers monitor an online shopper's "clickstream"—the way that person navigates through the website. If the visitor behaves like a price-sensitive shopper— perhaps by comparing many different products and prices—that person may be offered a lower price.

Flexible pricing means that some customers pay more and others less for the same product or service. And, flexible pricing is not without its critics because of this discriminatory potential. For example, car dealers have traditionally used flexible pricing on the basis of buyer-seller negotiations to agree on a final sales price. However,

ETHICS AND SOCIAL RESPONSIBILITY ALERT

Flexible Pricing: Is There Race and Gender Discrimination in Bargaining for a New Car?

ETHICS

What do 60 percent of prospective buyers dread when looking for a new car? That's right! They dread negotiating the price. Price bargaining, however, has a more serious side and demonstrates shortcomings of flexible pricing when purchasing a new car: the potential for price discrimination by race and gender. Recent research among 153 car dealers in a large midwestern city suggests that car dealers offer male and female African-Americans and white females higher prices than white males even though all buyers used identical bargaining strategies when negotiating the price of a new car. African-American males were typically offered

the highest price, followed by African-American females, white females, and white males.

New car price bargaining has been eliminated by an increasing number of car dealers, most notably Saturn dealers. Saturn's no haggle, one-price policy for new cars has been recently expanded to preowned or used Saturns. According to a Saturn executive, "People don't want to dicker on price, period, whether it's a house, suit of clothes, or a car. When you have to dicker, you feel uncomfortable because you always feel you paid too much." In certain instances, some consumers do.

flexible pricing may result in race and gender discrimination in car buying as detailed in the Ethics and Social Responsibility Alert box.[21] There are also legal issues associated with flexible pricing. As noted at the end of this chapter, there are constraints under the Robinson-Patman Act to prevent carrying a flexible-price policy to the extreme of price discrimination.

Company, Customer, and Competitive Effects

As the final list or quoted price is set, the effects on the company, customers, and competitors must be assessed.

Company Effects   For a firm with more than one product, a decision on the price of a single product must consider the price of other items in its product line or related product lines in its product mix. Within a product line or mix there are usually some products that are substitutes for one another and some that complement each other. Frito-Lay recognizes that its tortilla chip product line consisting of Baked Tostitos, Tostitos, and Doritos brands are partial substitutes for one another and its bean and cheese chip dip line and salsa sauces complement the tortilla chip line.

A manager's challenge when marketing multiple products is **product-line pricing**, the setting of prices for all items in a product line. When setting prices, the manager seeks to cover the total cost and produce a profit for the complete line, not necessarily for each item. For example, the penetration price for Nintendo's Gamecube video game console was likely below its cost, but the price of its video games (complementary products) was set high enough to cover the loss and deliver a profit for the Nintendo product line.

Product-line pricing involves determining (1) the lowest priced product and price, (2) the highest priced product and price, and (3) price differentials for all other products in the line.[22] The lowest and highest priced items in the product line play important roles. The highest priced item is typically positioned as the premium item in quality and features. The lowest priced item is the traffic builder designed to capture the attention of the hesitant or first-time buyer. Price differentials between items in the line should make sense to customers and reflect differences in their perceived value of the products offered. Behavioral research also suggests that the price differentials should get larger as one moves up the product line.

Frito-Lay recognizes that its tortilla chip products are partial substitutes for one another and its bean and cheese dips and salsa sauces complement tortilla chips. This knowledge is used for Frito-Lay product-line pricing.

Frito-Lay, Inc.

www.frito-lay.com

Customer Effects   In setting price, retailers weigh factors heavily that satisfy the perceptions or expectations of ultimate consumers, such as the customary prices for a variety of consumer products. Retailers have found that they should not price their store brands 20 to 25 percent below manufacturers' brands.[23] When they do, consumers often view the lower price as signaling lower quality and don't buy. Manufacturers and wholesalers must choose prices that result in profit for resellers in the channel to gain their cooperation and support. Toro failed to do this on its lines of lawn mowers and snow throwers. It decided to augment its traditional hardware outlet distribution by also selling through mass merchandisers such as Kmart and Target. To do so, it set prices for the mass merchandisers substantially below those for its traditional hardware outlets. Many unhappy hardware stores abandoned Toro products in favor of mowers and snow throwers from other manufacturers.

Competitive Effects   A manager's pricing decision is immediately apparent to most competitors, who may retaliate with price changes of their own. Therefore, a manager who sets a final list or quoted price must anticipate potential price responses from competitors. Regardless of whether a firm is a price leader or follower, it wants to avoid cutthroat price wars in which no firm in the industry makes a satisfactory profit. A **price war** involves successive price cutting by competitors to increase or maintain their unit sales or market share. Price wars erupt in a variety of industries, from consumer electronics to disposable diapers, from soft drinks to airlines, and from grocery retailing to telephone services. Managers expecting that a lower price will result in a larger market share, higher unit sales, and greater profit for their company often initiate them. This may occur. However, if competitors match the lower price, other things being equal, the expected market share, sales, and intended profit gain are lost. According to a recent analysis of large U.S. companies, a 1 percent price cut—assuming no change in unit volume or costs—lowers a company's net profit by an average of 8 percent![24] Marketers are advised to consider price cutting only when one or more conditions exist: (1) the company has a cost or technological advantage over its competitors, (2) primary demand for a product class will grow if prices are lowered, and (3) the price cut is confined to specific products or customers (as with airline tickets), and not across-the-board.[25]

FIGURE 14–5
The power of marginal analysis in real-world decisions

Suppose the owner of a picture framing store is considering buying a series of magazine ads to reach her up-scale target market. The cost of the ads is $1,000, the average price of a framed picture is $50, and the unit variable cost (materials plus labor) is $30.

This is a direct application of marginal analysis that an astute manager uses to estimate the incremental revenue or incremental number of units that must be obtained to at least cover the incremental cost. In this example, the number of extra picture frames that must be sold is obtained as follows:

$$\text{Incremental number of frames} = \frac{\text{Extra fixed cost}}{\text{Price} - \text{Unit variable cost}}$$

$$= \frac{\$1,000 \text{ of advertising}}{\$50 - \$30}$$

$$= 50 \text{ frames}$$

So unless there are other benefits of the ads, such as long-term goodwill, she should only buy the ads if she expects they will increase frame sales by at least 50 units.

Balancing Incremental Costs and Revenues

When a price is changed or new advertising or selling programs are planned, their effect on the quantity sold must be considered. This assessment, called *marginal analysis* (Chapter 13), involves a continuing, concise trade-off of incremental costs against incremental revenues.

Do marketing and business managers really use marginal analysis? Yes, they do, but they often don't use phrases such as *marginal revenue, marginal cost,* and *elasticity of demand.*

Think about these managerial questions:

- How many extra units do we have to sell to pay for that $1,000 advertisement?
- How much savings on unit variable cost do we have to get to keep the break-even point the same if we invest in a $10,000 labor-saving machine?
- Should we hire three more salespeople or not?

All these questions are a form of marginal or incremental analysis, even though these exact words are not used.

Figure 14–5 shows the power—and some limitations—of marginal analysis applied to a marketing decision. Note that the frame store owner must either conclude that a simple advertising campaign will more than pay for itself in additional sales or not undertake the campaign. The decision could also have been made to increase the average price of a framed picture to cover the cost of the campaign, but the principle still applies: Expected incremental revenues from pricing and other marketing actions must more than offset incremental costs.

The example in Figure 14–5 shows both the main advantage and difficulty of marginal analysis. The advantage is its commonsense usefulness, and the difficulty is obtaining the necessary data to make decisions. The owner can measure the cost quite easily, but the incremental revenue generated by the ads is difficult to measure. She could partly solve this problem by offering $2 off the purchase price with use of a coupon printed in the ad to see which sales resulted from the ad.

STEP 6: MAKE SPECIAL ADJUSTMENTS TO THE LIST OR QUOTED PRICE

When you pay 60 cents for a bag of M&Ms in a vending machine or receive a quoted price of $10,000 from a contractor to renovate a kitchen, the pricing sequence ends with the last step just described: setting the list or quoted price. But when you

FIGURE 14-6
Three special adjustments to list or quoted price

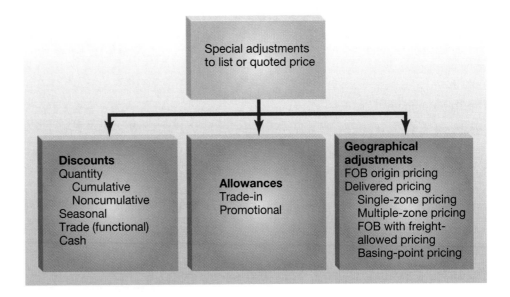

are a manufacturer of M&M candies or gas grills and sell your product to dozens or hundreds of wholesalers and retailers in your channel of distribution, you may need to make a variety of special adjustments to the list or quoted price. Wholesalers also must adjust list or quoted prices they set for retailers. Three special adjustments to the list or quoted price are (1) discounts, (2) allowances, and (3) geographical adjustments (Figure 14–6).

Discounts

Discounts are reductions from list price that a seller gives a buyer as a reward for some activity of the buyer that is favorable to the seller. Four kinds of discounts are especially important in marketing strategy: (1) quantity, (2) seasonal, (3) trade (functional), and (4) cash discounts.[26]

Quantity Discounts   To encourage customers to buy larger quantities of a product, firms at all levels in the channel of distribution offer **quantity discounts**, which are reductions in unit costs for a larger order. For example, an instant photocopying service might set a price of 10 cents a copy for 1 to 25 copies, 9 cents a copy for 26 to 100, and 8 cents a copy for 101 or more. Because the photocopying service gets more of the buyer's business and has longer production runs that reduce its order-handling costs, it is willing to pass on some of the cost savings in the form of quantity discounts to the buyer.

Quantity discounts are of two general kinds: noncumulative and cumulative. *Noncumulative quantity discounts* are based on the size of an individual purchase order. They encourage large individual purchase orders, not a series of orders. This discount is used by Federal Express to encourage companies to ship a large number of packages at one time. *Cumulative quantity discounts* apply to the accumulation of purchases of a product over a given time period, typically a year. Cumulative quantity discounts encourage repeat buying by a single customer to a far greater degree than do noncumulative quantity discounts.

Seasonal Discounts   To encourage buyers to stock inventory earlier than their normal demand would require, manufacturers often use seasonal discounts. A firm such as Toro that manufactures lawn mowers and snow throwers offers seasonal discounts to encourage wholesalers and retailers to stock up on lawn mowers in January

Toro uses seasonal discounts to stimulate consumer demand and smooth out seasonal manufacturing peaks and troughs.

The Toro Company
www.toro.com

and February and on snow throwers in July and August—five or six months before the seasonal demand by ultimate consumers. This enables Toro to smooth out seasonal manufacturing peaks and troughs, thereby contributing to more efficient production. It also rewards wholesalers and retailers for the risk they accept in assuming increased inventory carrying costs and having supplies in stock at the time they are wanted by customers.

Trade (Functional) Discounts   To reward wholesalers and retailers for marketing functions they will perform in the future, a manufacturer often gives trade, or functional, discounts. These reductions off the list or base price are offered to resellers in the channel of distribution on the basis of (1) where they are in the channel and (2) the marketing activities they are expected to perform in the future.

Suppose a manufacturer quotes price in the following form: list price—$100 less 30/10/5. The first number in the percentage sequence always refers to the retail end of the channel, and the last number always refers to the wholesaler or jobber closest to the manufacturer in the channel. The trade discounts are simply subtracted one at a time. This price quote shows $100 is the manufacturer's suggested retail price; 30 percent of the suggested retail price is available to the retailer to cover costs and provide a profit of $30 ($100 × 0.3 = $30); wholesalers closest to the retailer in the channel get 10 percent of their selling price ($70 × 0.1 = $7); and the final group of wholesalers in the channel (probably jobbers) that are closest to the manufacturer get 5 percent of their selling price ($63 × 0.05 = $3.15). Thus, starting with the manufacturer's retail price and subtracting the three trade discounts shows that the manufacturer's selling price to the wholesaler or jobber closest to it is $59.85 (Figure 14–7).

Traditional trade discounts have been established in various product lines such as hardware, food, and pharmaceutical items. Although the manufacturer may suggest the trade discounts shown in the example just cited, the sellers are free to alter the discount schedule depending on their competitive situation.

Cash Discounts   To encourage retailers to pay their bills quickly, manufacturers offer them cash discounts. Suppose a retailer receives a bill quoted at $1,000, 2/10 net 30. This means that the bill for the product is $1,000, but the retailer can take a 2 percent

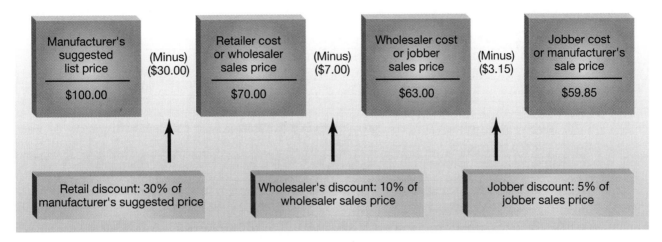

FIGURE 14–7
The structure of trade discounts

discount ($1,000 × 0.02 = $20) if payment is made within 10 days and send a check for $980. If the payment cannot be made within 10 days, the total amount of $1,000 is due within 30 days. It is usually understood by the buyer that an interest charge will be added after the first 30 days of free credit.

Naive buyers may think that the 2 percent discount offered is not substantial. What this means is that the buyer pays 2 percent on the total amount to be able to use that amount an extra 20 days—from day 11 to day 30. In a 360-day business year, this is an effective annual interest rate of 36 percent (2% × 360/20 = 36%). Because the effective interest rate is so high, firms that cannot take advantage of a 2/10 net 30 cash discount often try to borrow money from their local banks at rates far lower than the 36 percent they must pay by not taking advantage of the cash discount.

Retailers provide cash discounts to consumers as well to eliminate the cost of credit granted to consumers. These discounts take the form of discount-for-cash policies.

Allowances

Allowances—like discounts—are reductions from list or quoted prices to buyers for performing some activity.

Trade-in Allowances   A new car dealer can offer a substantial reduction in the list price of that new Toyota Camry by offering you a trade-in allowance of $500 for your Chevrolet. A trade-in allowance is a price reduction given when a used product is part of the payment on a new product. Trade-ins are an effective way to lower the price a buyer has to pay without formally reducing the list price.

Promotional Allowances   Sellers in the channel of distribution can qualify for **promotional allowances** for undertaking certain advertising or selling activities to promote a product. Various types of allowances include an actual cash payment or an extra amount of "free goods" (as with a free case of pizzas to a retailer for every dozen cases purchased). Frequently, a portion of these savings is passed on to the consumer by retailers.

Some companies, such as Procter & Gamble, have chosen to reduce promotional allowances for retailers by using everyday low pricing. **Everyday low pricing** (EDLP) is the practice of replacing promotional allowances with lower manufacturer list prices. EDLP promises to reduce the average price to consumers while minimizing promotional allowances that cost manufacturers billions of dollars every year. However, EDLP does not necessarily benefit supermarkets as described in the Marketing NewsNet on the next page.[27]

MARKETING NEWSNET

Everyday Low Prices at the Supermarket = Everyday Low Profits: Creating Customer Value at a Cost

CUSTOMER VALUE

Who wouldn't welcome low retail prices every day? The answer is supermarket chains—76 percent of U.S. grocery stores have not adopted this practice. Supermarkets prefer Hi-Lo pricing based on frequent specials where prices are temporarily lowered then raised again. Hi-Lo pricing reflects allowances that manufacturers give supermarkets to push their product. Consider a New York City supermarket whose advertisement is shown here. It regularly pays $1.15 for a can of Bumble Bee white tuna ($55.43 ÷ 48 = $1.15), but the allowances reduce the cost to 96 cents. A price special of 99 cents still provides a 3 cent retail markup ($0.99 retail price in ad—$0.96 cost). When the price on tuna returns to its regular level, the store's gross margin on tuna increases substantially on those cans that were bought with the allowance but not sold during the price special promotion.

Everyday low pricing (EDLP) eliminates manufacturer allowances and can reduce average retail prices by up to 10 percent. While EDLP provides lower average prices than Hi-Lo pricing, EDLP does not allow for deeply discounted price specials. EDLP can create everyday customer value and modestly increase supermarket sales—but at a cost. Already slim supermarket chain profits can slip by 18 percent

BUMBLE BEE white tuna	
List price per 48-can case:	$55.43
Allowance:	$9.50
Net cost per can:	96 cents

RAGÚ spaghetti sauce	
List price per 12-jar case:	$9.50
Allowance:	96 cents
Net cost per jar:	71 cents

MAXWELL HOUSE instant coffee	
List price per 18-jar case:	$83.72
Allowance:	$13.50
Net cost per jar:	$3.90

with EDLP without the benefit of allowances as described earlier. Also, some argue that EDLP without price specials is boring for many grocery shoppers who welcome price specials. EDLP has been hailed as "value pricing" by manufacturers, but supermarkets view it differently. For them, EDLP means "Everyday Low Profits!"

Geographical Adjustments

Geographical adjustments are made by manufacturers or even wholesalers to list or quoted prices to reflect the cost of transportation of the products from seller to buyer. The two general methods for quoting prices related to transportation costs are (1) FOB origin pricing and (2) uniform delivered pricing.

FOB Origin Pricing   FOB means "free on board" some vehicle at some location, which means the seller pays the cost of loading the product onto the vehicle that is used (such as a barge, railroad car, or truck). **FOB origin pricing** usually involves the seller's naming the location of this loading as the seller's factory or warehouse (such as "FOB Detroit" or "FOB factory"). The title to the goods passes to the buyer at the point of loading, so the buyer becomes responsible for picking the specific mode of transportation, for all the transportation costs, and for subsequent handling of the product. Buyers farthest from the seller face the big disadvantage of paying the higher transportation costs.

Uniform Delivered Pricing   When a **uniform delivered pricing** method is used, the price the seller quotes includes all transportation costs. It is quoted in a contract as "FOB buyer's location," and the seller selects the mode of transportation, pays the freight charges, and is responsible for any damage that may occur because the seller retains title to the goods until delivered to the buyer. Although they go by various names, four kinds of delivered pricing methods are (1) single-zone pricing, (2) multiple-zone pricing, (3) FOB with freight-allowed pricing, and (4) basing-point pricing.

In *single-zone pricing* all buyers pay the same delivered price for the products, regardless of their distance from the seller. This method is also called *postage stamp pricing* because it is the way that U.S. postal rates are set for first-class mail. So although a store offering free delivery in a metropolitan area has lower transportation costs for goods shipped to customers nearer the store than for those shipped to distant ones, customers pay the same delivered price.

In *multiple-zone pricing* a firm divides its selling territory into geographic areas or zones. The delivered price to all buyers within any one zone is the same, but prices across zones vary depending on the transportation cost to the zone and the level of competition and demand within the zone. The U.S. Postal Service uses multiple-zone pricing for mailing certain packages. This system is also used in setting prices on long-distance phone calls.

With *FOB with freight-allowed pricing*, also called *freight absorption pricing*, the price is quoted by the seller as "FOB plant—freight allowed." The buyer is allowed to deduct freight expenses from the list price of the goods, so the seller agrees to pay, or "absorb," the transportation costs.

Basing-point pricing involves selecting one or more geographical locations (basing point) from which the list price for products plus freight expenses are charged to the buyer. For example, a company might designate St. Louis as the basing point and charge all buyers a list price of $100 plus freight from St. Louis to their location. Basing-point pricing methods have been used in the steel, cement, and lumber industries where freight expenses are a significant part of the total cost to the buyer and products are largely undifferentiated.

Legal and Regulatory Aspects of Pricing

Arriving at a final price is clearly a complex process. The task is further complicated by legal and regulatory restrictions. Five pricing practices have received the most scrutiny: (1) price fixing, (2) price discrimination, (3) deceptive pricing, (4) geographical pricing, and (5) predatory pricing[28] (Figure 14–8).

Price Fixing   A conspiracy among firms to set prices for a product is termed **price fixing**. Price fixing is illegal per se under the Sherman Act (*per se* means in and of itself). When two or more competitors explicitly or implicitly set prices, this practice is called *horizontal price fixing*. For example, six foreign vitamin companies recently

FIGURE 14–8
Pricing practices affected by legal restrictions

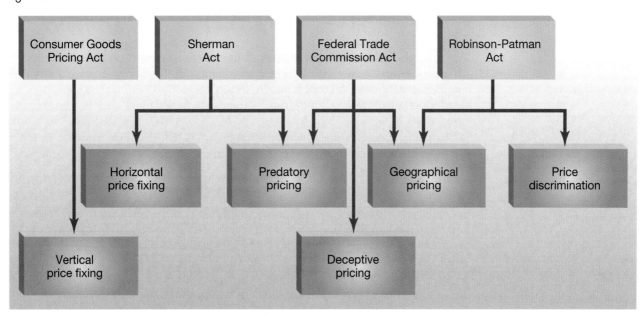

WEB LINK And You Thought That "Free" Is Simply Defined!

The offer of "free" merchandise or service is a promotional device often used to attract customers. The FTC acknowledges that such offers are a useful and valuable marketing practice. However, the FTC also recognizes that such offers must be made with extreme care so as to avoid any possibility that consumers will be misled or deceived.

The FTC has issued its "Guide Concerning Use of the Word 'Free' and Similar Representations" at www.ftc.gov/ bcp/guides/free.htm. This guide illustrates that the term "free" has multiple dimensions. Suppose a marketer substitutes similar words for "free," such as "gift," "given without charge," or "bonus." What is the FTC's position on this practice?

BUY ONE, GET ONE FREE

pled guilty to price fixing in the human and animal vitamin industry and paid the largest fine in U.S. history, $335 million.[29]

Vertical price fixing involves controlling agreements between independent buyers and sellers (a manufacturer and a retailer) whereby sellers are required to not sell products below a minimum retail price. This practice, called *resale price maintenance,* was declared illegal per se in 1975 under provisions of the Consumer Goods Pricing Act. Nevertheless, shoe supplier Nine West recently agreed to settle government charges that the company restricted competition by coercing retailers to adhere to its resale prices. Nine West agreed to pay $34 million in the settlement.[30] However, manufacturers and wholesalers can fix the maximum retail price for their products provided the price agreement does not create an "unreasonable restraint of trade" or is anticompetitive.

It is important to recognize that a manufacturer's "suggested retail price" is not illegal per se. The issue of legality only arises when manufacturers enforce such a practice by coercion. Furthermore, there appears to be a movement toward a "rule of reason" in pricing cases. This rule holds that circumstances surrounding a practice must be considered before making a judgment about its legality. The rule of reason perspective is the direct opposite of the per se rule, which holds that a practice is illegal in and of itself.

Price Discrimination   The Clayton Act as amended by the Robinson-Patman Act prohibits **price discrimination**—the practice of charging different prices to different buyers for goods of like grade and quality. However, not all price differences are illegal; only those that substantially lessen competition or create a monopoly are deemed unlawful. Moreover, "goods" is narrowly defined and does not include discrimination in services.

A unique feature of the Robinson-Patman Act is that it allows for price differentials to different customers under the following conditions:

1. When price differences charged to different customers do not exceed the differences in the cost of manufacture, sale, or delivery resulting from differing methods or quantities in which such goods are sold or delivered to buyers. This condition is called the *cost justification defense.*
2. Price differences resulting from meeting changing market conditions, avoiding obsolescence of seasonal merchandise including perishables or closing out sales.
3. When price differences are quoted to selected buyers in good faith to meet competitors' prices and are not intended to injure competition. This condition is called the *meet the competition defense.*

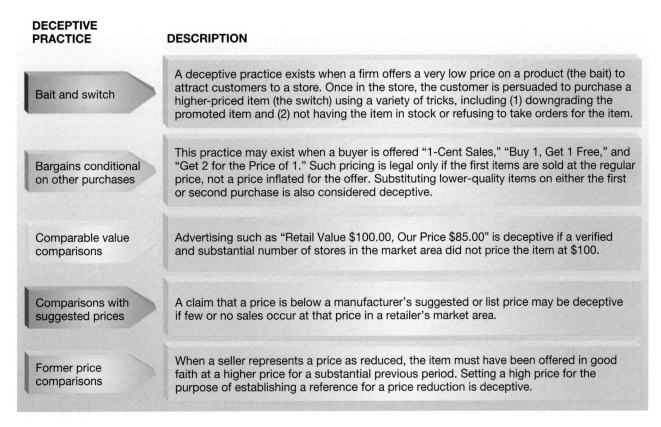

DECEPTIVE PRACTICE	DESCRIPTION
Bait and switch	A deceptive practice exists when a firm offers a very low price on a product (the bait) to attract customers to a store. Once in the store, the customer is persuaded to purchase a higher-priced item (the switch) using a variety of tricks, including (1) downgrading the promoted item and (2) not having the item in stock or refusing to take orders for the item.
Bargains conditional on other purchases	This practice may exist when a buyer is offered "1-Cent Sales," "Buy 1, Get 1 Free," and "Get 2 for the Price of 1." Such pricing is legal only if the first items are sold at the regular price, not a price inflated for the offer. Substituting lower-quality items on either the first or second purchase is also considered deceptive.
Comparable value comparisons	Advertising such as "Retail Value $100.00, Our Price $85.00" is deceptive if a verified and substantial number of stores in the market area did not price the item at $100.
Comparisons with suggested prices	A claim that a price is below a manufacturer's suggested or list price may be deceptive if few or no sales occur at that price in a retailer's market area.
Former price comparisons	When a seller represents a price as reduced, the item must have been offered in good faith at a higher price for a substantial previous period. Setting a high price for the purpose of establishing a reference for a price reduction is deceptive.

FIGURE 14–9
Five most common deceptive pricing practices

The Robinson-Patman Act also covers promotional allowances. To legally offer promotional allowances to buyers, the seller must do so on a proportionally equal basis to all buyers distributing the seller's products. In general, the rule of reason applies frequently in price discrimination cases and is often applied to cases involving flexible pricing practices of firms.

Deceptive Pricing   Price deals that mislead consumers fall into the category of deceptive pricing. Deceptive pricing is outlawed by the Federal Trade Commission Act. The FTC monitors such practices and has published a regulation titled "Guides against Deceptive Pricing" designed to help businesspeople avoid a charge of deception. The five most common deceptive pricing practices are described in Figure 14–9. As you read about these practices it should be clear that laws cannot be passed and enforced to protect consumers and competitors against all of these practices, so it is essential to rely on the ethical standards of those making and publicizing pricing decisions. A frequently used pricing practice is to offer products and services for free—a great price! It would seem that the meaning of "free" is obvious. Think again. Visit the FTC website described in the accompanying Web Link to learn what free means.

Geographical Pricing   FOB origin pricing is legal, as are FOB freight-allowed pricing practices, providing no conspiracy to set prices exists. Basing-point pricing can be viewed as illegal under the Robinson-Patman Act and the Federal Trade Commission Act if there is clear-cut evidence of a conspiracy to set prices. In general, geographical pricing practices have been immune from legal and regulatory restrictions, except in those instances in which a conspiracy to lessen competition exists under the Sherman Act or price discrimination exists under the Robinson-Patman Act.

Predatory Pricing   **Predatory pricing** is the practice of charging a very low price for a product with the intent of driving competitors out of business. Once competitors have been driven out, the firm raises its prices. This practice is illegal under the Sherman Act and the Federal Trade Commission Act. Proving the presence of this practice has been difficult and expensive because it must be shown that the predator explicitly attempted to destroy a competitor and the predatory price was below the defendant's average cost.[31]

Concept Check

1. Why would a seller choose a flexible-price policy over a one-price policy?

2. If a firm wished to encourage repeat purchases by a buyer throughout a year, would a cumulative or noncumulative quantity discount be a better strategy?

3. Which pricing practices are covered by the Sherman Act?

SUMMARY

1   Four general approaches for finding an approximate price level for a product or service are demand-oriented, cost-oriented, profit-oriented, and competition-oriented pricing.

2   Demand-oriented pricing approaches stress consumer demand and revenue implications of pricing and include eight types: skimming, penetration, prestige, price lining, odd-even, target, bundle, and yield management.

3   Cost-oriented pricing approaches emphasize the cost aspects of pricing and include three types: standard markup, cost-plus, and experience curve pricing.

4   Profit-oriented pricing approaches focus on a balance between revenues and costs to set a price and include three types: target profit, target return-on-sales, and target return-on-investment pricing.

5   Competition-oriented pricing approaches stress what competitors or the marketplace are doing and include three types: customary; above-, at-, or below-market; and loss-leader pricing.

6   Given an approximate price level for a product, a manager must set a list or quoted price by considering factors such as one-price versus a flexible-price policy; the effects of the proposed price on the company, customer, and competitors; and balancing incremental costs and revenues.

7   List or quoted price is often modified through discounts, allowances, and geographical adjustments.

8   Legal and regulatory issues in pricing focus on price fixing, price discrimination, deceptive pricing, geographical pricing, and predatory pricing.

KEY TERMS AND CONCEPTS

above-, at-, or below-market pricing p. 374
basing-point pricing p. 383
bundle pricing p. 369
cost-plus pricing p. 370
customary pricing p. 374
everyday low pricing p. 381
experience curve pricing p. 371
flexible-price policy p. 375
FOB origin pricing p. 382
loss-leader pricing p. 374
odd-even pricing p. 368
one-price policy p. 375
penetration pricing p. 367
predatory pricing p. 386
prestige pricing p. 367

price discrimination p. 384
price fixing p. 383
price lining p. 368
price war p. 377
product-line pricing p. 376
promotional allowances p. 381
quantity discounts p. 379
skimming pricing p. 366
standard markup pricing p. 370
target pricing p. 368
target profit pricing p. 371
target return-on-investment pricing p. 372
target return-on-sales pricing p. 372
uniform delivered pricing p. 382
yield management pricing p. 369

APPLYING MARKETING CONCEPTS AND PERSPECTIVES

1 Under what conditions would a camera manufacturer adopt a skimming price approach for a new product? A penetration approach?

2 What are some similarities and differences between skimming pricing, prestige pricing, and above-market pricing?

3 A producer of microwave ovens has adopted an experience curve pricing approach for its new model. The firm believes it can reduce the cost of producing the model by 20 percent each time volume doubles. The cost to produce the first unit was $1,000. What would be the approximate cost of the 4,096th unit?

4 The Hesper Corporation is a leading manufacturer of high-quality upholstered sofas. Current plans call for an increase of $600,000 in the advertising budget. If the firm sells its sofas for an average price of $850 and the unit variable costs are $550, then what dollar sales increase will be necessary to cover the additional advertising?

5 Suppose executives estimate that the unit variable cost for their VCR is $100, the fixed cost related to the product is $10 million annually, and the target volume for next year is 100,000 recorders. What sales price will be necessary to achieve a target profit of $1 million?

6 A manufacturer of motor oil has a trade discount policy whereby the manufacturer's suggested retail price is $30 per case with the terms of 40/20/10. The manufacturer sells its products through jobbers, who sell to wholesalers, who sell to gasoline stations. What will the manufacturer's sale price be?

7 What are the effective annual interest rates for the following cash discount terms? (*a*) 1/10 net 30, (*b*) 2/10 net 30, and (*c*) 2/10 net 60.

8 Suppose a manufacturer of exercise equipment sets a suggested price to the consumer of $395 for a particular piece of equipment to be competitive with similar equipment. The manufacturer sells its equipment to a sporting goods wholesaler who receives 25 percent of the selling price and a retailer who receives 50 percent of the selling price. What demand-oriented pricing approach is being used, and at what price will the manufacturer sell the equipment to the wholesaler?

9 Is there any truth in the statement, "Geographical pricing schemes will always be unfair to some buyers?" Why or why not?

INTERNET EXERCISE

Price discrimination, as defined by the Robinson-Patman Act, has been the subject of an enormous amount of litigation between buyers and sellers since its enactment in 1936. A unique website (www.lawmall.com/rpa) provides an up-to-date summary of price discrimination issues that is targeted toward businesspeople.

Visit the LawMall website to find answers to three frequently asked questions concerning Robinson-Patman Act lawsuits:

1 What are the litigation stages and estimated length of a Robinson-Patman Act lawsuit?

2 What are the estimated expenses of a Robinson-Patman Act price discrimination lawsuit?

3 What remedies are afforded plaintiffs in a Robinson-Patman Act price discrimination lawsuit?

VIDEO CASE 14-1   My Own Meals: Setting Retail Prices

"The kids generally like the fast-food meals. I tend to not like them because I try to stay away from the high fat," says Angela Harmon, mother of three young girls. "I have to have something that is nutritious and fast," remarks Mary Champlain, mother of two. Comments like these and her own experiences led Mary Anne Jackson to conclude that there was an opportunity to provide parents with better children's food options. As Mary explains, "Being a busy working mother, I knew that there was a need for this type of product in the marketplace."

THE IDEA

Mary's insight about the marketplace was supported by several socioeconomic trends. For example:

- More than 65 percent of working mothers now have school-age children, the highest percentage ever.
- About 90 percent of children under the age of 7 eat at McDonald's at least four times per month.
- More than 90 percent of homes in the United States now have microwave ovens.
- Women already represent almost half of the total workforce.

In addition, research has shown that children have a big influence on their parents' food and meal choices. Children aren't biased toward cooking a dinner from scratch; in fact, children love using microwave ovens. Children also respond to consumer advertising and packaging. Typical favorites for children include hot dogs, macaroni and cheese, pizza, chicken nuggets, and spaghetti. Most importantly, though, children like having their own meals.

With this evidence, some food industry experience and business education, and a lot of entrepreneurial spirit, Mary Anne Jackson set out to satisfy the need for nutritious, convenient children's meals. Her idea: develop a line of healthy, microwaveable meals for the 30 million children 2 to 10 years old.

THE COMPANY

Ms. Jackson started by founding a company, My Own Meals, Inc. (www.myownmeals.com), with a line of five healthy microwaveable meals. The meals were offered in shelf-stable "retort" packages, which are like flexible cans. This created a whole new category of prepared foods and raised more than a few eyebrows among the major food companies. Mary observed that "the need for children's meals was not being addressed in the past, and

I think this was because most major food companies are run by men." Eventually, however, the big companies challenged My Own Meals with their own entries into the new category. Tyson, Banquet (Con Agra), and Hormel each introduced new children's meals, although Tyson and Banquet launched frozen meals. The competition reinforced Mary's efforts, "Having competitors come into the marketplace justified the existence of the category," she explains.

The product line was developed using a lot of marketing research—hundreds of busy mothers provided input about product quality, usage rates, and price. The results indicated that customers would serve their children high-quality meals between three and four times each month and that they would be willing to pay approximately $2.30 for each meal. Based on this information Mary estimated that the potential retail market was $500 million!

My Own Meals, Inc. became the market leader of children's meals with its line of natural, refrigeration-free, long-life meals specifically developed for the taste and nutritional needs of children. The five-product line included "My Turkey Meatballs," "My Kind of Chicken," "My Meatballs and Shells," "Chicken, Please," and "My Favorite Pasta." My Own Meals, Inc. products were sold through grocery stores and by mail order throughout the United States. Organizations such as the Feingold Association which recommends products to parents of allergy-prone children, the American Dietetics Association, the Public Voice, and others became supporters of the new emphasis on nutrition and taste for children.

THE ISSUE: SETTING RETAIL PRICES

"We were trying to decide if we were priced appropriately and competitively for the marketplace, and we decided that we would look at the price elasticity for our product line," observes Mary Anne Jackson. "We found that the closer we came to $3.00 a unit, the lower the volume was, and overall we were losing revenues and profits," said Jackson.

To arrive at final retail prices for her company's products Mary Anne Jackson considered factors related to demand, cost, profit, and competition. For example, because lower-quality brands had entered the market, My Own Meals needed a retail price that reflected the superior quality of its products. "We're premium priced because we're a higher quality product than any of our competitors. If we weren't, our quality image would be lowered to the image that they have," explains Jackson.

At some stores, however, prices approached $3.00 and consumer demand decreased.

To estimate the prices consumers would see on their shelves, Jackson needed to estimate the cost of producing the meals and add My Own Meal's markup. Then she determined the markup each of the distribution channels—retail grocery stores, mass merchants, day care centers, and military commissaries—would add to reach the retail price. The grocery stores were very concerned about profitability and used a concept called direct product profitability (DPP) to determine prices and shelf space. "They want to know how much money they make on each square foot of the shelf dedicated to each product line. I had to do a DPP analysis to show them why they were making more on our products for our space than the competition," remarks Mary Anne Jackson. Finally, Mary considered competitors' prices, which were:

- Looney Toons (Tyson) $2.49
- Kid Cuisine (Banquet) $1.89
- Kid's Kitchen (Hormel) $1.19

Mary knew that it was important to consider all of these factors in her pricing decisions. The price would influence the interest of consumers and retailers, the reactions of competitors, and ultimately the success of My Own Meals!

Questions

1 In what ways are the demand factors of (*a*) consumer tastes, (*b*) price and availability of substitute products, and (*c*) consumer income important in influencing consumer demand for My Own Meals products?

2 How can (*a*) demand-based, (*b*) cost-based, (*c*) profit-based, and (*d*) competition-based approaches be used to help My Own Meals arrive at an approximate price level?

3 Why might the retail price of My Own Meal's products be different in grocery stores, mass merchants, day care centers, and military commissaries?

FINANCIAL ASPECTS OF MARKETING

Basic concepts from accounting and finance provide valuable tools for marketing executives. This appendix describes an actual company's use of accounting and financial concepts and illustrates how they assist the owner in making marketing decisions.

THE CAPLOW COMPANY

An accomplished artist and calligrapher, Jane Westerlund, decided to apply some of her experience to the picture framing business in Minneapolis. She bought an existing retail frame store, The Caplow Company, from a friend who owned the business and wanted to retire. She avoided the do-it-yourself end of the framing business and chose three kinds of business activities: (1) cutting the frame, mats, and glass for customers who brought in their own pictures or prints to be framed; (2) selling prints and posters that she had purchased from wholesalers; and (3) restoring high-quality frames and paintings.

To understand how accounting, finance, and marketing relate to each other, let's analyze (1) the operating statement for her frame shop, (2) some general ratios of interest that are derived from the operating statement, and (3) some ratios that pertain specifically to her pricing decisions.

The Operating Statement

The operating statement (also called an *income statement* or *profit-and-loss statement*) summarizes the profitability of a business firm for a specific time period, usually a month, quarter, or year. The title of the operating statement for The Caplow Company shows it is for a one-year period (Figure B–1). The purpose of an operating statement is to show the profit of the firm and the revenues and expenses that led to that profit. This information tells the owner or manager what has happened in the past and suggests actions to improve future profitability.

The left side of Figure B–1 shows that there are three key elements to all operating statements: (1) sales of the firm's goods and services, (2) costs incurred in making

and selling the goods and services, and (3) profit or loss, which is the difference between sales and costs.

Sales Elements The sales element of Figure B–1 has four terms that need explanation:

- *Gross sales* are the total amount billed to customers. Dissatisfied customers or errors may reduce the gross sales through returns or allowances.
- *Returns* occur when a customer gives the item purchased back to the seller, who either refunds the purchase price or allows the customer a credit on subsequent purchases. In any event, the seller now owns the item again.
- *Allowances* are given when a customer is dissatisfied with the item purchased and the seller reduces the original purchase price. Unlike returns, in the case of allowances the buyer owns the item.
- *Net sales* are simply gross sales minus returns and allowances.

The operating statement for The Caplow Company shows that

Gross sales	$80,500
Less: Returns and allowances	500
Net sales	$80,000

The low level of returns and allowances shows the shop generally has done a good job in satisfying customers, which is essential in building the repeat business necessary for success.

Cost Elements The *cost of goods sold* (COGS) is the total cost of the products sold during the period. This item varies according to the kind of business. A retail store purchases finished goods and resells them to customers without reworking them in any way. In contrast, a manufacturing firm combines raw and semifinished materials and parts, uses labor and overhead to rework these into finished goods, and then sells them to customers. All these activities are reflected in the cost of goods sold item on a manufacturer's operating

FIGURE B–1

Examples of an operating statement

THE CAPLOW COMPANY
Operating Statement
For the Year Ending December 31, 2001

Sales	Gross sales			$80,500
	Less: Returns and allowances			500
	Net sales			$80,000
Costs	Cost of goods sold:			
	Beginning inventory at cost		$ 6,000	
	Purchases at billed cost	$21,000		
	Less: Purchase discounts	300		
	Purchases at net cost	20,700		
	Plus freight-in	100		
	Net cost of delivered purchases		20,800	
	Direct labor (framing)		14,200	
	Cost of goods available for sale		41,000	
	Less: Ending inventory at cost		5,000	
	Cost of goods sold			36,000
	Gross margin (gross profit)			$44,000
	Expenses:			
	Selling expenses:			
	Sales salaries	2,000		
	Advertising expense	3,000		
	Total selling expense		5,000	
	Administrative expenses:			
	Owner's salary	18,000		
	Bookkeeper's salary	1,200		
	Office supplies	300		
	Total administrative expense		19,500	
	General expenses:			
	Depreciation expense	1,000		
	Interest expense	500		
	Rent expense	2,100		
	Utility expenses (heat, electricity)	3,000		
	Repairs and maintenance	2,300		
	Insurance	2,000		
	Social security taxes	2,200		
	Total general expense		13,100	
	Total expenses			37,600
Profit or loss	Profit before taxes			$ 6,400

statement. Note that the frame shop has some features of a pure retailer (prints and posters it buys that are resold without alteration) and a pure manufacturer (assembling the raw materials of molding, matting, and glass to form a completed frame).

Some terms that relate to cost of goods sold need clarification:

- *Inventory* is the physical material that is purchased from suppliers, may or may not be reworked, and is available for sale to customers. In the frame shop inventory includes molding, matting, glass, prints, and posters.
- *Purchase discounts* are reductions in the original billed price for reasons such as prompt payment of the bill or the quantity bought.
- *Direct labor* is the cost of the labor used in producing the finished product. For the frame shop this is the cost of producing the completed frames from the molding, matting, and glass.
- *Gross margin (gross profit)* is the money remaining to manage the business, sell the products or services, and give some profit. Gross margin is net sales minus cost of goods sold.

The two right-hand columns in Figure B–1 between "Net sales" and "Gross margin" calculate the cost of goods sold:

Net sales		$80,000
Cost of goods sold		
Beginning inventory at cost	$ 6,000	
Net cost of delivered purchases	20,800	
Direct labor (framing)	14,200	
Cost of goods available for sale	41,000	
Less: ending inventory at cost	5,000	
Cost of goods sold		36,000
Gross margin (gross profit)		$44,000

This section considers the beginning and ending inventories, the net cost of purchases delivered during the year, and the cost of the direct labor going into making the frames. Subtracting the $36,000 cost of goods sold from the $80,000 net sales gives the $44,000 gross margin.

Three major categories of expenses are shown in Figure B–1 below the gross margin:

- *Selling expenses* are the costs of selling the product or service produced by the firm. For The Caplow Company there are two such selling expenses: sales salaries of part-time employees waiting on customers and the advertising expense of simple newspaper ads and direct-mail ads sent to customers.
- *Administrative expenses* are the costs of managing the business, and for The Caplow Company include three expenses: the owner's salary, a part-time bookkeeper's salary, and office supplies expense.
- *General expenses* are miscellaneous costs not covered elsewhere; for the frame shop these include seven items: depreciation expense (on her equipment), inter-

Jane Westerlund (left) and an assistant assess the restoration of a gold frame for regilding.

est expense, rent expense, utility expenses, repairs and maintenance expense, insurance expense, and social security taxes.

As shown in Figure B–1, selling, administrative, and general expenses total $37,600 for The Caplow Company.

Profit Element   What the company has earned, the *profit before taxes,* is found by subtracting cost of goods sold and expenses from net sales. For The Caplow Company, Figure B–1 shows that profit before taxes is $6,400.

General Operating Ratios to Analyze Operations

Looking only at the elements of Caplow's operating statement that extend to the right-hand column highlights the firm's performance on some important dimensions. Using operating ratios such as *expense-to-sales ratios* for expressing basic expense or profit elements as a percentage of net sales gives further insights:

ELEMENT IN OPERATING STATEMENT	DOLLAR VALUE	PERCENTAGE OF NET SALES
Gross sales	$80,500	
Less: Returns and allowances	500	
Net sales	80,000	100%
Less: Cost of goods sold	36,000	45
Gross margin	44,000	55
Less: Total expenses	37,600	47
Profit (or loss) before taxes	$ 6,400	8%

Westerlund can use this information to compare her firm's performance from one time period to the next. To do so, it is especially important that she keep the same definitions for each element of her operating statement, also a significant factor in using the electronic spreadsheets discussed in Chapter 14. Performance comparisons between periods are more difficult if she changes definitions for the accounting elements in the operating statement.

She can use either the dollar values or the operating ratios (the value of the element of the operating statement divided by net sales) to analyze the firm's performance. However, the operating ratios are more valuable than the dollar values for two reasons: (1) the simplicity of working with percentages rather than dollars and (2) the availability of operating ratios of typical firms in the same industry, which are published by Dun & Bradstreet and trade associations. Thus, Westerlund can compare her firm's performance not only with that of *other* frame shops but also with that of *small* frame shops that have annual net sales, for example, under $100,000. In this way she can identify where her operations are better or worse than other similar firms. For example, if trade association data showed a typical frame shop of her size had a ratio of cost of goods sold to net sales of 37 percent, compared with her 45 percent, she might consider steps to reduce this cost through purchase discounts, reducing inbound freight charges, finding lower-cost suppliers, and so on.

Ratios to Use in Setting and Evaluating Price

Using The Caplow Company as an example, we can study four ratios that relate closely to setting a price: (1) markup, (2) markdown, (3) stockturns, and (4) return on investment. These terms are defined in Figure B–2 and explained below.

Markup   Both markup and gross margin refer to the amount added to the cost of goods sold to arrive at the selling price, and they may be expressed either in dollar or percentage terms. However, the term *markup* is more commonly used in setting retail prices. Suppose the average price Westerlund charges for a framed picture is $80. Then in terms of the first two definitions in Figure B–2 and the earlier information from the operating statement,

ELEMENT OF PRICE	DOLLAR VALUE
Cost of goods sold	$36
Markup (or gross margin)	44
Selling price	$80

The third definition in Figure B–2 gives the percentage markup on selling price:

$$\text{Markup on selling price (\%)} = \frac{\text{Markup}}{\text{Selling Price}} \times 100$$

$$= \frac{44}{80} \times 100 = 55\%$$

And the percentage markup on cost is obtained as follows:

$$\text{Markup on cost (\%)} = \frac{\text{Markup}}{\text{Cost of goods sold}} \times 100$$

$$= \frac{44}{36} \times 100 = 122.2\%$$

Inexperienced retail clerks sometimes fail to distinguish between the two definitions of markup, which (as the preceding calculations show) can represent a tremendous difference, so it is essential to know whether the base is cost or selling price. Marketers generally use selling price as the base for talking about "markups" unless they specifically state that they are using cost as a base.

Retailers and wholesalers that rely heavily on markup pricing (discussed in Chapter 14) often use standardized tables that convert markup on selling price to markup on cost, and vice versa. The two equations below show how to convert one to the other:

$$\text{Markup on selling price (\%)} = \frac{\text{Markup on cost (\%)}}{100\% + \text{Markup on cost (\%)}} \times 100$$

$$\text{Markup on cost (\%)} \quad = \frac{\text{Markup on selling price (\%)}}{100\% - \text{Markup on selling price (\%)}}$$

Using the data from The Caplow Company gives

$$\text{Markup on selling price (\%)} = \frac{\text{Markup on cost (\%)}}{100\% + \text{Markup on cost (\%)}} \times 100$$

$$= \frac{122.2}{100 + 122.2} \times 100 = 55\%$$

$$\text{Markup on cost (\%)} = \frac{\text{Markup on selling price (\%)}}{100\% - \text{Markup on selling price (\%)}} \times 100$$

$$= \frac{55}{100 + 55} \times 100 = 122.2\%$$

The use of an incorrect markup base is shown in Westerlund's business. A markup of 122.2 percent on her cost of goods sold for a typical frame she sells gives 122.2% × $36 = $44 of markup. Added to the $36 cost of goods sold, this gives her selling price of $80 for the framed picture. However, a new clerk working for her who

NAME OF FINANCIAL ELEMENT OR RATIO	WHAT IT MEASURES	EQUATION
Selling price ($)	Price customer sees	Cost of goods sold (COGS) + Markup
Markup ($)	Dollars added to COGS to arrive at selling price	Selling price − COGS
Markup on selling price (%)	Relates markup to selling price	$\dfrac{\text{Markup}}{\text{Selling price}} \times 100 = \dfrac{\text{Selling price} - \text{COGS}}{\text{Selling price}} \times 100$
Markup on cost (%)	Relates markup to cost	$\dfrac{\text{Markup}}{\text{COGS}} \times 100 = \dfrac{\text{Selling price} - \text{COGS}}{\text{COGS}} \times 100$
Markdown (%)	Ability of firm to sell its products at initial selling price	$\dfrac{\text{Markdowns}}{\text{Net sales}} \times 100$
Stockturn rate	Ability of firm to move its inventory quickly	$\dfrac{\text{COGS}}{\text{Average inventory at cost}}$ or $\dfrac{\text{Net sales}}{\text{Average inventory at selling price}}$
Return on investment (%)	Profit performance of firm compared with money invested in it	$\dfrac{\text{Net profit after taxes}}{\text{Investment}} \times 100$

FIGURE B–2

How to calculate selling price, markup, markdown, stockturn, and return on investment

erroneously priced the framed picture at 55 percent of cost of goods sold set the final price at $55.80 ($36 of cost of goods sold plus 55% × $36 = $19.80). The error, if repeated, can be disastrous: frames would be accidentally sold at $55.80, or $24.20 below the intended selling price of $80.

Markdown   A markdown is a reduction in a retail price that is necessary if the item will not sell at the full selling price to which it has been marked up. The item might not sell for a variety of reasons: the selling price was set too high or the item is out of style or has become soiled or damaged. The seller "takes a markdown" by lowering the price to sell it, thereby converting it to cash to buy future inventory that will sell faster.

The markdown percentage cannot be calculated directly from the operating statement. As shown in the fifth item of Figure B–2, the numerator of the markdown percentage is the total dollar markdowns. Markdowns are reductions in the prices of goods that are purchased by customers. The denominator is net sales.

Suppose The Caplow Company had a total of $700 in markdowns on the prints and posters that are stocked and available for sale. Since the frames are custom made for individual customers, there is little reason for a markdown there. Caplow's markdown percent is then

$$
\begin{aligned}
\text{Markdown (\%)} &= \frac{\text{Markdowns}}{\text{Net sales}} \times 100 \\
&= \frac{\$700}{\$80,000} \times 100 \\
&= 0.875\%
\end{aligned}
$$

Other kinds of retailers often have markdown ratios several times this amount. For example, women's dress stores have markdowns of about 25 percent, and menswear stores have markdowns of about 2 percent.

A customer discusses choices of framing and matting for her print with Jane Westerlund.

Stockturn Rate   A business firm is anxious to have its inventory move quickly, or "turn over." Stockturn rate, or simply stockturns, measures this inventory movement. For a retailer a slow stockturn rate may show it is buying merchandise customers don't want, so this is a critical measure of performance. When a firm sells only a single product, one convenient way to measure stockturn rate is simply to divide its cost of goods sold by average inventory at cost. The sixth item in Figure B–2 shows how to calculate stockturn rate using information in the operating statement:

$$\text{Stockturn rate} = \frac{\text{Cost of goods sold}}{\text{Average inventory at cost}}$$

The dollar amount of average inventory at cost is calculated by adding the beginning and ending inventories for the year and dividing by 2 to get the average. From Caplow's operating statement, we have

$$\text{Stockturn rate} = \frac{\text{Cost of goods sold}}{\text{Average inventory at cost}}$$

$$= \frac{\text{Cost of goods sold}}{\dfrac{\text{Beginning inventory} + \text{Ending inventory}}{2}}$$

$$= \frac{\$36,000}{\dfrac{\$6,000 + \$5,000}{2}}$$

$$= \frac{\$36,000}{\$5,500}$$

$$= 6.5 \text{ stockturns per year}$$

What is considered a "good stockturn" varies by the kind of industry. For example, supermarkets have limited shelf space for thousands of new products from manufacturers each year, so they watch stockturn carefully by product line. The stockturn rate in supermarkets for breakfast foods is about 17 times per year, for pet food about 22 times, and for paper products about 25 times per year.

Return on Investment   A better measure of the performance of a firm than the amount of profit it makes in a year is its ROI, which is the ratio of net income to the investment used to earn that net income. To calculate ROI, it is necessary to subtract income taxes from profit before taxes to obtain net income, then divide this figure by the investment that can be found on a firm's balance sheet (another accounting statement that shows the firm's assets, liabilities, and net worth). While financial and accounting experts have many definitions for "investment," an often-used definition is "total assets."

For our purposes, let's assume that Westerlund has total assets (investment) of $20,000 in The Caplow Company, which covers inventory, store fixtures, and framing equipment. If she pays $1,000 in income taxes, her store's net income is $5,400, so her ROI is given by the seventh item in Figure B–2:

$$\text{Return on investment} = \text{Net income/Investment} \times 100$$

$$= \$5,400/\$20,000 \times 100$$

$$= 27\%$$

If Westerlund wants to improve her ROI next year, the strategies she might take are found in this alternative equation for ROI:

$$\text{ROI} = \text{Net sales/Investment} \times \text{Net income/Net sales}$$

$$= \text{Investment turnover} \times \text{Profit margin}$$

This equation suggests that The Caplow Company's ROI can be improved by raising turnover or increasing profit margin. Increasing stockturns will accomplish the former, whereas lowering cost of goods sold to net sales will cause the latter.

15

MANAGING MARKETING CHANNELS AND WHOLESALING

AFTER READING THIS CHAPTER YOU SHOULD BE ABLE TO:

- Explain what is meant by a marketing channel of distribution and why intermediaries are needed.

- Recognize differences between marketing channels for consumer and business products and services in domestic and global markets.

- Describe the types and functions of firms that perform wholesaling activities.

- Distinguish among traditional marketing channels, electronic marketing channels, and different types of vertical marketing systems.

- Describe factors considered by marketing executives when selecting and managing a marketing channel, including channel conflict and legal restrictions.

AVON'S MAKEOVER IS MORE THAN COSMETIC

Avon Products, Inc. is in the midst of its own makeover. As the world's leading direct seller of beauty and related items to women in 139 countries, Avon has begun calling on new customers, in new ways, with new products.

Avon's makeover represents a noticeable expansion beyond its traditional manner of doing business. For more than 115 years, the company successfully marketed its products through an extensive network of independent representatives, which today number 3.4 million worldwide. However, Avon's marketing research indicated that 59 percent of women who don't buy Avon products would if they were more accessible. The message to Avon's senior management was clear: Give busy women a choice in how they do their buying—through an Avon representative, in a store, or online. According to Andrea Jung, Avon's chief executive officer, "While direct selling will always be our principal sales channel, expanding access to new customers will help accelerate top-line [sales] growth."

The goal of expanded access to new customers has materialized in novel ways. Avon earmarked $60 million to build a website (avon.com) focused around the company's representatives and brochures. In late 2001, Avon introduced a shop-within-a-store format in selected JCPenney stores. These shops feature Avon's new brand of makeup, skin care, fragrance and other personal care items called beComing that are not sold by Avon representatives. The stores are "not without risk, but with great opportunity," Ms. Jung says. "It's a giant step."

Is Avon's makeover achieving its goal? Yes. "We've learned that at retail, we attract new customers, not the same people that our representatives are serving directly," said Debora Coffey, an Avon spokeswoman.[1]

This chapter focuses on marketing channels of distribution and why they are an important component in the marketing mix. It then shows how such channels benefit consumers and the sequence of firms that make up a marketing channel. Finally, it describes factors that influence the choice and management of marketing channels, including channel conflict and legal restrictions.

NATURE AND IMPORTANCE OF MARKETING CHANNELS

Reaching prospective buyers, either directly or indirectly, is a prerequisite for successful marketing. At the same time, buyers benefit from distribution systems used by firms.

Defining Marketing Channels of Distribution

You see the results of distribution every day. You may have purchased Lay's Potato Chips at the 7-Eleven store, a book through Amazon.com, and Levi's jeans at Sears. Each of these items was brought to you by a marketing channel of distribution, or simply a **marketing channel**, which consists of individuals and firms involved in the process of making a product or service available for use or consumption by consumers or industrial users.

Marketing channels can be compared with a pipeline through which water flows from a source to terminus. Marketing channels make possible the flow of goods from a producer, through intermediaries, to a buyer. Intermediaries go by various names (Figure 15–1) and perform various functions.[2] Some intermediaries actually purchase items from the seller, store them, and resell them to buyers. For example, Sunshine Biscuits produces cookies and sells them to food wholesalers. The wholesalers then sell the cookies to supermarkets and grocery stores, which, in turn, sell them

FIGURE 15–1
Terms used for marketing intermediaries

TERM	DESCRIPTION
Middleman	Any intermediary between manufacturer and end-user markets
Agent or broker	Any intermediary with legal authority to act on behalf of the manufacturer
Wholesaler	An intermediary who sells to other intermediaries, usually to retailers; usually applies to consumer markets
Retailer	An intermediary who sells to consumers
Distributor	An imprecise term, usually used to describe intermediaries who perform a variety of distribution functions, including selling, maintaining inventories, extending credit, and so on; a more common term in business markets but may also be used to refer to wholesalers
Dealer	An even more imprecise term that can mean the same as distributor, retailer, wholesaler, and so forth

to consumers. Other intermediaries such as brokers and agents represent sellers but do not actually take title to products—their role is to bring a seller and buyer together. Century 21 real estate agents are examples of this type of intermediary. The importance of intermediaries is made even clearer when we consider the functions they perform and the value they create for buyers.

Value Created by Intermediaries

Few consumers appreciate the value created by intermediaries; however, producers recognize that intermediaries make selling goods and services more efficient because they minimize the number of sales contacts necessary to reach a target market. Figure 15–2 shows a simple example of how this comes about in the digital camera industry. Without a retail intermediary (such as Sears), Kodak, Sony, Panasonic, and Hewlett-Packard would each have to make four contacts to reach the four buyers shown who are in the target market. However, each producer has to make only one contact when Sears acts as an intermediary. Equally important from a macro marketing perspective, the total number of industry transactions is reduced from 16 to 8, which reduces producer cost and hence benefits the customer.

Functions Performed by Intermediaries
Intermediaries make possible the flow of products from producers to buyers by performing three basic functions (Figure 15–3). Most prominently, intermediaries perform a transactional function that involves buying, selling, and risk taking because they stock merchandise in anticipation of sales. Intermediaries perform a logistical function evident in the gathering, storing, and dispersing of products (see Chapter 16 on supply chain and logistics management). Finally, intermediaries perform facilitating functions, which assist producers in making goods and services more attractive to buyers.

All three groups of functions must be performed in a marketing channel, even though each channel member may not participate in all three. Channel members often negotiate about which specific functions they will perform. Sometimes disagreements result, and a breakdown in relationships among channel members occurs. This happened recently when PepsiCo's bottler in Venezuela switched to Coca-Cola. Because all marketing channel functions had to be performed, PepsiCo either had to set up its own bottling operation to perform the marketing channel functions, or find another bottler, which it did.[3]

FIGURE 15–2
How intermediaries minimize transactions

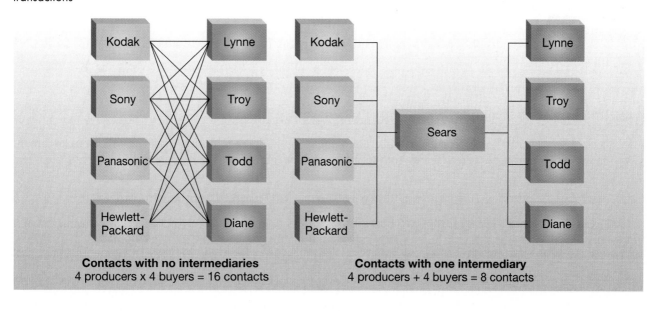

Contacts with no intermediaries
4 producers x 4 buyers = 16 contacts

Contacts with one intermediary
4 producers + 4 buyers = 8 contacts

TYPE OF FUNCTION   ACTIVITIES RELATED TO FUNCTION

Transactional function

- *Buying*: Purchasing products for resale or as an agent for supply of a product
- *Selling*: Contacting potential customers, promoting products, and soliciting orders
- *Risk taking*: Assuming business risks in the ownership of inventory that can become obsolete or deteriorate

Logistical function

- *Assorting*: Creating product assortments from several sources to serve customers
- *Storing*: Assembling and protecting products at a convenient location to offer better customer service
- *Sorting*: Purchasing in large quantities and breaking into smaller amounts desired by customers
- *Transporting*: Physically moving a product to customers

Facilitating function

- *Financing*: Extending credit to customers
- *Grading*: Inspecting, testing, or judging products, and assigning them quality grades
- *Marketing information and research*: Providing information to customers and suppliers, including competitive conditions and trends

FIGURE 15–3
Marketing channel functions
performed by intermediaries

Consumer Benefits from Intermediaries   Consumers also benefit from intermediaries. Having the goods and services you want, when you want them, where you want them, and in the form you want them is the ideal result of marketing channels. In more specific terms, marketing channels help create value for consumers through the four utilities described in Chapter 1: time, place, form, and possession. Time utility refers to having a product or service when you want it. For example, FedEx provides next-morning delivery. Place utility means having a product or service available where consumers want it, such as having a Texaco gas station located on a long stretch of lonely highway. Form utility involves enhancing a product or service to make it more appealing to buyers. For example, Compaq Computer delivers unfinished PCs to dealers, which then add memory, chips, modems, and other parts, based on consumer specifications. Possession utility entails efforts by intermediaries to help buyers take possession of a product or service, such as having airline tickets delivered by a travel agency.

Concept Check

1. What is meant by a marketing channel?
2. What are the three basic functions performed by intermediaries?

CHANNEL STRUCTURE AND ORGANIZATION

A product can take many routes on its journey from a producer to buyers, and marketers search for the most efficient route from the many alternatives available.

Marketing Channels for Consumer Goods and Services

Figure 15–4 shows the four most common marketing channels for consumer goods and services. It also shows the number of levels in each marketing channel, as evidenced by the number of intermediaries between a producer and ultimate buyers. As

FIGURE 15–4

Common marketing channels for consumer goods and services

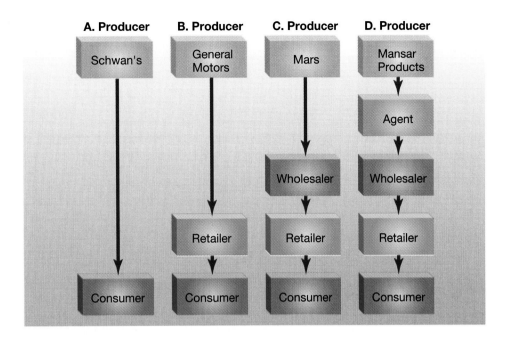

the number of intermediaries between a producer and buyer increases, the channel is viewed as increasing in length. Thus the producer → wholesaler → retailer → consumer channel is longer than the producer → consumer channel.

Channel A represents a **direct channel** because a producer and ultimate consumers deal directly with each other. Many products and services are distributed this way. A number of insurance companies sell their financial services using a direct channel and branch sales offices. Schwan's Sales Enterprises of Marshall, Minnesota, markets a full line of frozen foods in 48 states and parts of Canada using door-to-door salespeople who sell from refrigerated trucks. Because there are no intermediaries with a direct channel, the producer must perform all channel functions.

The remaining three channel forms are **indirect channels** because intermediaries are inserted between the producer and consumers and perform numerous channel functions. Channel B, with a retailer added, is most common when a retailer is large and can buy in large quantities from a producer or when the cost of inventory makes it too expensive to use a wholesaler. Manufacturers such as General Motors, Ford, and Daimler Chrysler use this channel, and a local car dealer acts as a retailer. Why is there no wholesaler? So many variations exist in the product that it would be impossible for a wholesaler to stock all the models required to satisfy buyers; in addition, the cost of maintaining an inventory would be too high. However, large retailers such as Sears, 7-Eleven, Safeway, and JCPenney buy in sufficient quantities to make it cost effective for a producer to deal with only a retail intermediary.

Adding a wholesaler in Channel C is most common for low-cost, low-unit value items that are frequently purchased by consumers, such as candy, confectionary items, and magazines. For example, Mars sells its line of candies to wholesalers in case quantities; then they can break down (sort) the cases so that individual retailers can order in boxes or much smaller quantities.

Channel D, the most indirect channel, is employed when there are many small manufacturers and many small retailers and an agent is used to help coordinate a large supply of the product. Mansar Products, Ltd. is a Belgian producer of specialty jewelry that uses agents to sell to wholesalers in the United States, which then sell to many small retailers.

FIGURE 15–5

Common marketing channels for business goods and services

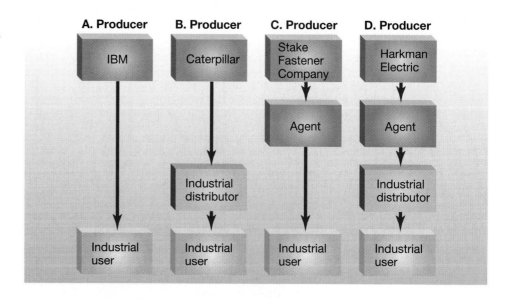

Marketing Channels for Business Goods and Services

The four most common channels for business goods and services are shown in Figure 15–5. In contrast with channels for consumer products, business channels typically are shorter and rely on one intermediary or none at all because business users are fewer in number, tend to be more concentrated geographically, and buy in larger quantities (see Chapter 6).

Channel A, represented by IBM's large, mainframe computer business, is a direct channel. Firms using this channel maintain their own salesforce and perform all channel functions. This channel is employed when buyers are large and well defined, the sales effort requires extensive negotiations, and the products are of high unit value and require hands-on expertise in terms of installation or use.

Channels B, C, and D are indirect channels with one or more intermediaries to reach industrial users. In Channel B an **industrial distributor** performs a variety of marketing channel functions, including selling, stocking, and delivering a full product assortment and financing. In many ways, industrial distributors are like wholesalers in consumer channels. Caterpillar relies on industrial distributors to sell its construction and mining equipment in almost 200 countries. In addition to selling, Caterpillar distributors stock 40,000 to 50,000 parts and service equipment using highly trained technicians.[4]

Channel C introduces a second intermediary, an *agent,* who serves primarily as the independent selling arm of producers and represents a producer to industrial users. For example, Stake Fastener Company, a California-based producer of industrial fasteners, has an agent call on industrial users rather than employing its own salesforce.

Channel D is the longest channel and includes both agents and distributors. For instance, Harkman Electric, a small Texas-based producer of electric products, uses agents to call on distributors who sell to industrial users.

Electronic Marketing Channels

These common marketing channels for consumer and business goods and services are not the only routes to the marketplace. Advances in electronic commerce have opened new avenues for reaching buyers and creating customer value.

Interactive electronic technology has made possible **electronic marketing channels** which employ the Internet to make goods and services available for consumption or use by consumers or business buyers. A unique feature of these chan-

FIGURE 15–6

Representative electronic
marketing channels

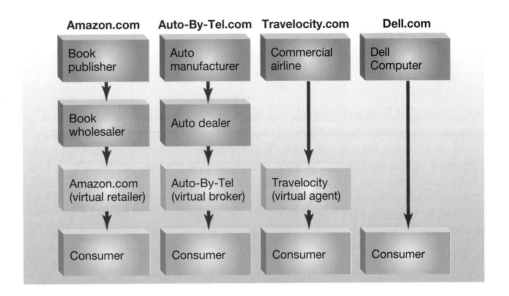

nels is that they combine electronic and traditional intermediaries to create time, place, form, and possession utility for buyers.[5]

Figure 15–6 shows the electronic marketing channels for books (Amazon.com), automobiles (Auto-By-Tel.com), reservation services (Travelocity.com), and personal computers (Dell.com). Are you surprised that they look a lot like common marketing channels? An important reason for the similarity resides in channel functions detailed in Figure 15–3. Electronic intermediaries can and do perform transactional and facilitating functions effectively and at a relatively lower cost than traditional intermediaries because of efficiencies made possible by information technology. However, electronic intermediaries are incapable of performing elements of the logistical function, particularly for products such as books and automobiles. This function remains with traditional intermediaries or with the producer, as evident with Dell Computer Corporation with its direct channel. In fact, the inability of many electronic intermediaries to master the logistical function in a cost-effective manner contributed to their demise in the "dot-com crash" of 2001.

Many services can be distributed through electronic marketing channels, such as travel reservation marketed by Travelocity.com, financial securities by Schwab.com, and insurance by MetLife.com. Software too can be marketed this way. However, many other services such as health care and auto repair still involve traditional intermediaries.

Direct Marketing Channels

Many firms also use direct marketing channels to reach buyers. **Direct marketing channels** allow consumers to buy products by interacting with various advertising media without a face-to-face meeting with a salesperson. Direct marketing channels includes mail-order selling, direct-mail sales, catalog sales, telemarketing, interactive media, and televised home shopping (for example, the Home Shopping Network). U.S. sales revenue attributed to direct marketing channels exceeds $1.7 trillion.[6]

Some firms sell products almost entirely through direct marketing channels. These firms include L.L. Bean (apparel), Sharper Image (expensive gifts and novelties), and Egghead.com (personal computers). Manufacturers such as Nestlé and Sunkist, in addition to using traditional channels composed of wholesalers and retailers, employ direct marketing through catalogs and telemarketing to reach more buyers.

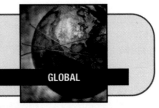

MARKETING NEWSNET
Nestlé and General Mills: Cereal Partners Worldwide

GLOBAL

Can you say Nestlé Cheerios *miel amandes*? Millions of French start their day with this European equivalent of General Mills' Honey Nut Cheerios, made possible by Cereal Partners Worldwide (CPW). CPW is the food industry's first strategic alliance designed to be a global business; it joined the cereal manufacturing and marketing capability of U.S.-based General Mills with the worldwide distribution clout of Swiss-based Nestlé.

From its headquarters near Lake Geneva, Switzerland, CPW first launched General Mills cereals under the Nestlé label in France, the United Kingdom, Spain, and Portugal in 1991. Today, CPW competes in 70 markets worldwide and soon expects to achieve its goal of $1 billion in profitable sales.

The General Mills–Nestlé strategic alliance is also likely to increase the ready-to-eat worldwide market share of these companies, which are already rated as the two best-managed firms in the world. CPW is on track to reach its goal of a 20 percent worldwide share.

At the same time, retailers such as JCPenney use direct marketing techniques to augment conventional store merchandising activities. Some experts believe that direct marketing accounts for 20 percent of all retail transactions in the United States and 10 percent of retail transactions in Europe. Direct marketing is covered in greater depth in Chapter 18.

Multiple Channels and Strategic Alliances

In some situations producers use **dual distribution**, an arrangement whereby a firm reaches different buyers by employing two or more different types of channels for the same basic product. For example, GE sells its large appliances directly to home and apartment builders but uses retail stores, including Wal-Mart, to sell to consumers. In some instances, firms pair multiple channels with a multibrand strategy (see Chapter 11). This is done to minimize cannibalization of the firm's family brand and differentiate the channels. For example, Hallmark sells its Hallmark greeting cards through Hallmark stores and select department stores, and its Ambassador brand of cards through discount and drugstore chains. Avon Products sells the Avon brand through its independent representatives and website, but markets the beComing brand through its JCPenney shop-within-a-store, as described in the chapter-opening example. In other instances a firm will distribute modified products through different channels. Zoecon Corporation sells its insect control chemicals to professional pest-control operators such as Orkin and Terminex. A modified compound is sold to Boyle-Midway for use in its Black-Flag Roach Ender brand.

A recent innovation in marketing channels is the use of **strategic channel alliances**, whereby one firm's marketing channel is used to sell another firm's products.[7] An alliance between Kraft Foods and Starbucks is a case in point. Kraft distributes Starbucks coffee in U.S. supermarkets and internationally. Strategic alliances are popular in global marketing, where the creation of marketing channel relationships is expensive and time consuming. For example, General Motors distributes the Swedish Saab through its Saturn dealers in Canada. General Mills and Nestlé have an extensive alliance that spans 70 international markets from Brazil to Poland to Thailand. Read the accompanying Marketing NewsNet so you won't be surprised when you are served Nestlé (not General Mills) Cheerios in Europe, South America, and parts of Asia.[8]

A Closer Look at Channel Intermediaries

Channel structures for consumer and business products assume various forms based on the number and type of intermediaries. Knowledge of the roles played by these intermediaries is important for understanding how channels operate in practice.

The terms *wholesaler, agent,* and *retailer* have been used in a general fashion consistent with the meanings given in Figure 15–1. However, on closer inspection, a variety of specific types of intermediaries emerges. These intermediaries engage in wholesaling activities—those activities involved in selling products and services to those who are buying for the purposes of resale or business use. Intermediaries engaged in retailing activities are discussed in detail in Chapter 17. Figure 15–7 describes the functions performed by major types of independent wholesalers.[9]

FIGURE 15–7
Functions performed by independent wholesaler types

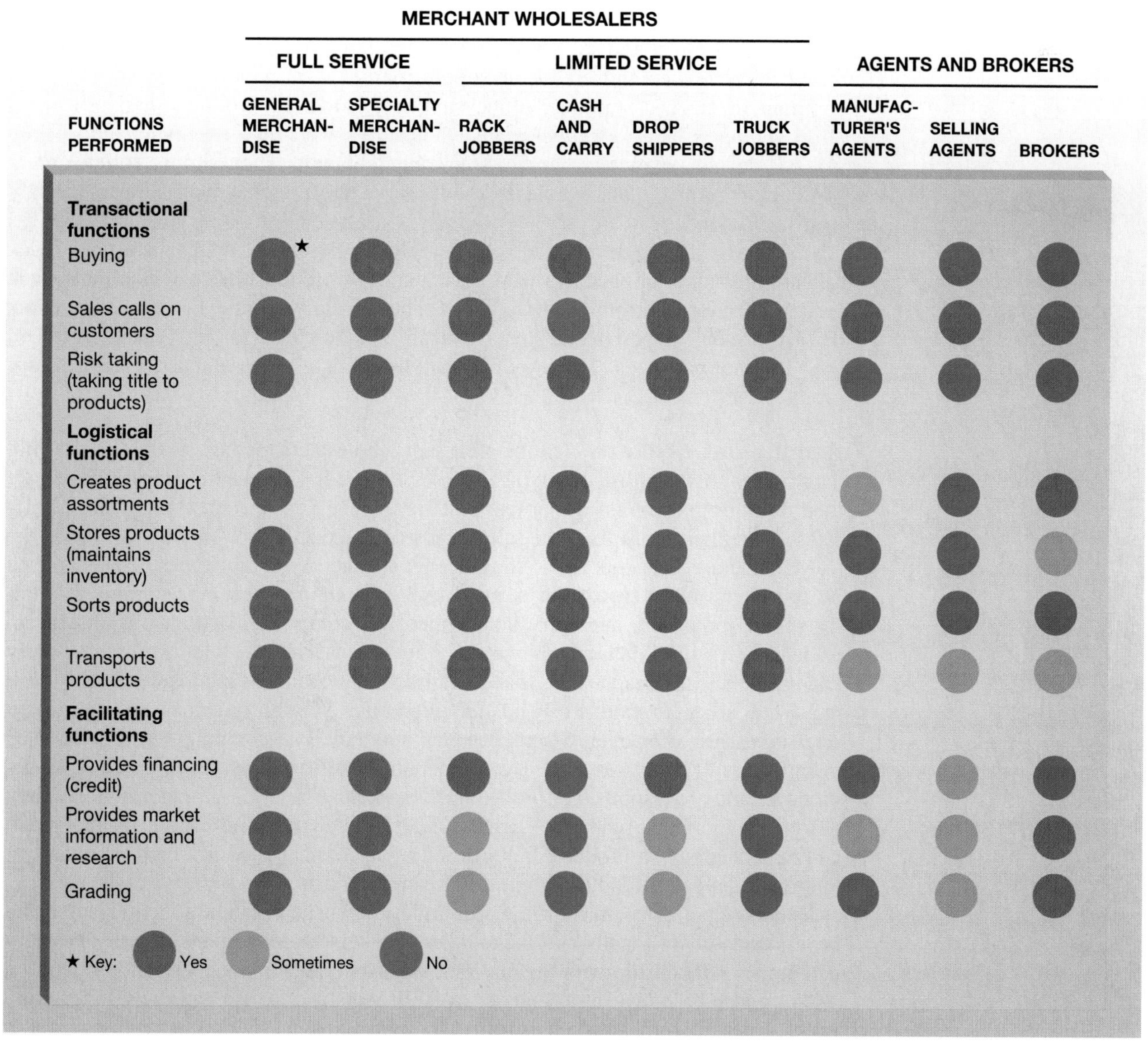

MERCHANT WHOLESALERS

FUNCTIONS PERFORMED	FULL SERVICE		LIMITED SERVICE				AGENTS AND BROKERS		
	GENERAL MERCHANDISE	SPECIALTY MERCHANDISE	RACK JOBBERS	CASH AND CARRY	DROP SHIPPERS	TRUCK JOBBERS	MANUFACTURER'S AGENTS	SELLING AGENTS	BROKERS
Transactional functions									
Buying									
Sales calls on customers									
Risk taking (taking title to products)									
Logistical functions									
Creates product assortments									
Stores products (maintains inventory)									
Sorts products									
Transports products									
Facilitating functions									
Provides financing (credit)									
Provides market information and research									
Grading									

★ Key: ● Yes   ● Sometimes   ● No

Merchant Wholesalers   **Merchant wholesalers** are independently owned firms that take title to the merchandise they handle. They go by various names, including industrial distributor (described earlier). About 83 percent of the firms engaged in wholesaling activities are merchant wholesalers.

Merchant wholesalers are classified as either full-service or limited-service wholesalers, depending on the number of functions performed. Two major types of full-service wholesalers exist. *General merchandise* (or *full-line*) *wholesalers* carry a broad assortment of merchandise and perform all channel functions. This type of wholesaler is most prevalent in the hardware, drug, and clothing industries. However, these wholesalers do not maintain much depth of assortment within specific product lines. *Specialty merchandise* (or *limited-line*) *wholesalers* offer a relatively narrow range of products but have an extensive assortment within the product lines carried. They perform all channel functions and are found in the health foods, automotive parts, and seafood industries.

Four major types of limited-service wholesalers exist. *Rack jobbers* furnish the racks or shelves that display merchandise in retail stores, perform all channel functions, and sell on consignment to retailers, which means they retain the title to the products displayed and bill retailers only for the merchandise sold. Familiar products such as hosiery, toys, housewares, and health and beauty aids are sold by rack jobbers. *Cash and carry wholesalers* take title to merchandise but sell only to buyers who call on them, pay cash for merchandise, and furnish their own transportation for merchandise. They carry a limited product assortment and do not make deliveries, extend credit, or supply market information. This wholesaler is common in electric supplies, office supplies, hardware products, and groceries. *Drop shippers,* or *desk jobbers,* are wholesalers who own the merchandise they sell but do not physically handle, stock, or deliver it. They simply solicit orders from retailers and other wholesalers and have the merchandise shipped directly from a producer to a buyer. Drop shippers are used for bulky products such as coal, lumber, and chemicals, which are sold in extremely large quantities. *Truck jobbers* are small wholesalers who have a small warehouse from which they stock their trucks for distribution to retailers. They usually handle limited assortments of fast-moving or perishable items that are sold for cash directly from trucks in their original packages. Truck jobbers handle products such as bakery items, dairy products, and meat.

Agents and Brokers   Unlike merchant wholesalers, agents and brokers do not take title to merchandise and typically provide fewer channel functions. They make their profit from commissions or fees paid for their services, whereas merchant wholesalers make their profit from the sale of the merchandise they own.

Manufacturer's agents and selling agents are the two major types of agents used by producers. **Manufacturer's agents**, or *manufacturer's representatives,* work for several producers and carry noncompetitive, complementary merchandise in an exclusive territory. Manufacturer's agents act as a producer's sales arm in a territory and are principally responsible for the transactional channel functions, primarily selling. They are used extensively in the automotive supply, footwear, and fabricated steel industries. However, Swank Jewelry and Japanese computer firms have used manufacturer's agents as well. By comparison, **selling agents** represent a single producer and are responsible for the entire marketing function of that producer. They design promotional plans, set prices, determine distribution policies, and make recommendations on product strategy. Selling agents are used by small producers in the textile, apparel, food, and home furnishing industries.

Brokers are independent firms or individuals whose principal function is to bring buyers and sellers together to make sales. Brokers, unlike agents, usually have no continuous relationship with the buyer or seller but negotiate a contract between two parties and then move on to another task. Brokers are used extensively by producers of seasonal products (such as fruits and vegetables) and in the real estate industry.

A unique broker that acts in many ways like a manufacturer's agent is a food broker, representing buyers and sellers in the grocery industry. Food brokers differ from conventional brokers because they act on behalf of producers on a permanent basis and receive a commission for their services. For example, Nabisco uses food brokers to sell its candies, margarine, and Planters peanuts, but it sells its line of cookies and crackers directly to retail stores.

Manufacturer's Branches and Offices

Unlike merchant wholesalers, agents, and brokers, manufacturer's branches and sales offices are wholly owned extensions of the producer that perform wholesaling activities. Producers assume wholesaling functions when there are no intermediaries to perform these activities, customers are few in number and geographically concentrated, or orders are large or require significant attention. A *manufacturer's branch office* carries a producer's inventory and performs the functions of a full-service wholesaler. A *manufacturer's sales office* does not carry inventory, typically performs only a sales function, and serves as an alternative to agents and brokers.

Vertical Marketing Systems and Channel Partnerships

The traditional marketing channels described so far represent a loosely knit network of independent producers and intermediaries brought together to distribute goods and services. However, new channel arrangements have emerged for the purpose of improving efficiency in performing channel functions and achieving greater marketing effectiveness. These new arrangements are called vertical marketing systems and channel partnerships. **Vertical marketing systems** are professionally managed and centrally coordinated marketing channels designed to achieve channel economies and maximum marketing impact.[10] Figure 15–8 depicts the major types of vertical marketing systems: corporate, contractual, and administered.

FIGURE 15–8
Types of vertical marketing systems

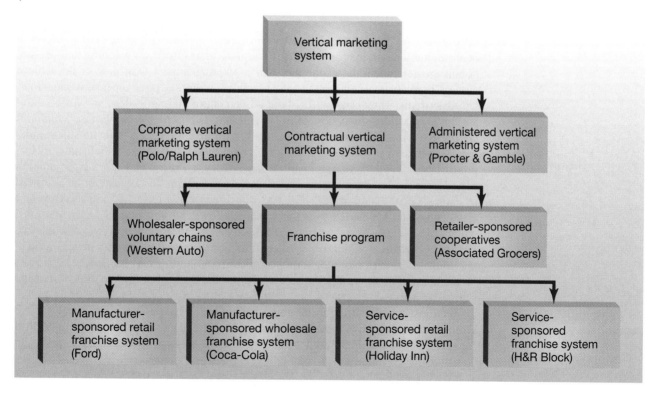

Sherwin Williams and Ace Hardware represent two different types of vertical marketing systems. Read the text to find out how they differ.

Sherwin Williams

www.sherwin-williams.com

Ace Hardware

www.acehardware.com

Corporate Systems   The combination of successive stages of production and distribution under a single ownership is a *corporate vertical marketing system.* For example, a producer might own the intermediary at the next level down in the channel. This practice, called *forward integration,* is exemplified by Polo/Ralph Lauren, which manufactures clothing and also owns apparel shops. Other examples of forward integration include Goodyear, Singer, Sherwin Williams, and the building materials division of Boise Cascade. Alternatively, a retailer might own a manufacturing operation, a practice called *backward integration.* For example, Kroger supermarkets operate manufacturing facilities that produce everything from aspirin to cottage cheese, for sale under the Kroger label. Companies seeking to reduce distribution costs and gain greater control over supply sources or resale of their products pursue forward and backward integration. However, both types of integration increase a company's capital investment and fixed costs. For this reason, many companies favor contractual vertical marketing systems to achieve channel efficiencies and marketing effectiveness.

Contractual Systems   Under a *contractual vertical marketing system,* independent production and distribution firms integrate their efforts on a contractual basis to obtain greater functional economies and marketing impact than they could achieve alone. Contractual systems are the most popular among the three types of vertical marketing systems. They account for about 40 percent of all retail sales.

Three variations of contractual systems exist. *Wholesaler-sponsored voluntary chains* involve a wholesaler that develops a contractual relationship with small, independent retailers to standardize and coordinate buying practices, merchandising programs, and inventory management efforts. With the organization of a large number of independent retailers, economies of scale and volume discounts can be achieved to compete with chain stores. IGA and Ben Franklin variety and craft stores represent wholesaler-sponsored voluntary chains. *Retailer-sponsored cooperatives* exist when small, independent retailers form an organization that operates a wholesale facility cooperatively. Member retailers then concentrate their buying power through the wholesaler and plan collaborative promotional and pricing activities. Examples of retailer-sponsored cooperatives include Associated Grocers, Ace Hardware, and Certified Grocers.

The most visible variation of contractual systems is **franchising**, a contractual arrangement between a parent company (a franchisor) and an individual or firm (a franchisee) that allows the franchisee to operate a certain type of business under an established name and according to specific rules. Franchises generate about $1 trillion in sales through about 700,000 outlets annually in the United States.[11] Four types of franchise arrangements are most popular. Manufacturer-sponsored retail franchise systems are prominent in the automobile industry, where a manufacturer such as Ford licenses dealers to sell its cars subject to various sales and service conditions. Manufacturer-sponsored wholesale systems are evident in the soft-drink industry, where Pepsi-Cola licenses wholesalers (bottlers) who purchase concentrate from Pepsi-Cola and then carbonate, bottle, promote, and distribute its products to supermarkets and restaurants. Service-sponsored retail franchise systems are provided by firms that have designed a unique approach for performing a service and wish to profit by selling the franchise to others. Holiday Inn, Avis, and McDonald's represent this franchising approach. Service-sponsored franchise systems exist when franchisors license individuals or firms to dispense a service under a trade name and specific guidelines. Examples include Snelling and Snelling, Inc. employment services, and H&R Block tax services. Service-sponsored franchise arrangements are the fastest-growing type of franchise. Franchising is discussed further in Chapter 17.

Administered Systems   In comparison, *administered vertical marketing systems* achieve coordination at successive stages of production and distribution by the size and influence of one channel member rather than through ownership. Procter & Gamble, given its broad product assortment ranging from disposable diapers to detergents, is able to obtain cooperation from supermarkets in displaying, promoting, and pricing its products. Wal-Mart can obtain cooperation from manufacturers in terms of product specifications, price levels, and promotional support, given its position as the world's largest retailer.

Channel Partnerships   Increasingly, channel members are forging channel partnerships akin to supply partnerships described in Chapter 6. A **channel partnership** consists of agreements and procedures among channel members for ordering and physically distributing a producer's products through the channel to the ultimate consumer.[12] A central feature of channel partnerships is the collaborative use of information and communication technology to better serve customers and reduce the time and cost of performing channel functions.

The partnership Levi Strauss & Company has with Modell's Sporting Goods in New York is a case in point.[13] By using point-of-sale scanning equipment and direct electronic linkage to Levi Strauss in San Francisco, Modell's can instantaneously inform Levi Strauss what styles and sizes of jeans are needed, create purchase orders, and convey shipping instructions without any human involvement. The result? The costs of performing transaction, logistic, and facilitating functions are substantially reduced, and the customer is virtually assured of having his or her preferred 501 Levi jeans in stock. The role of information and communication technology in supply chain and logistics management is discussed further in Chapter 16.

Concept Check

1. What is the difference between a direct and an indirect channel?

2. Why are channels for business products typically shorter than channels for consumer products?

3. What is the principal distinction between a corporate vertical marketing system and an administered vertical marketing system?

CHANNEL CHOICE AND MANAGEMENT

Marketing channels not only link a producer to its buyers but also provide the means through which a firm implements various elements of its marketing strategy. Therefore, choosing a marketing channel is a critical decision.

Factors Affecting Channel Choice and Management

The final choice of a marketing channel by a producer depends on a number of factors that often interact with each other.

Environmental Factors   The changing environment described in Chapter 3 has an important effect on the choice and management of a marketing channel. For example, Tupperware Corporation, a name synonymous with kitchen utensils and plastic storage containers sold in the home at Tupperware "parties," now uses shopping mall kiosks and recently began selling its products in Super Target stores. Changing family lifestyles with high employment among women prompted this action.[14] Advances in the technology of growing, transporting, and storing perishable cut flowers has allowed Kroger to eliminate flower wholesalers and buy direct from flower growers around the world. Kroger's annual cut flower sales exceed $100 million, making it the largest flower retailer in the world.[15] The Internet has created new marketing channel opportunities for a variety of products, including consumer electronics, books, music, video, and clothing and accessory items.

Consumer Factors   Consumer characteristics have a direct bearing on the choice and management of a marketing channel. Determining which channel is most appropriate is based on answers to fundamental questions such as: Who are potential customers? Where do they buy? When do they buy? How do they buy? What do they buy? These answers also indicate the type of intermediary best suited to reaching target buyers. For example, Ricoh Company, Ltd. studied the serious (as opposed to recreational) camera user and concluded that a change in marketing channels was

The Internet has created new marketing channel opportunities for the distribution of children's toys.

FAO Schwarz
www.faoschwarz.com

WEB LINK   Check the VISA ATM Locator

VISA offers a valuable Web resource in its ATM Locator that can be accessed at www.visa.com. VISA has some 460,000 automatic teller machines in 120 countries. One is probably in your neighborhood, wherever that is in the world! To find the nearest VISA ATM, follow the easy ATM Locator directions and request a site map. You'll be in the money in no time. Here's the map for McGraw-Hill Higher Education's neighborhood.

necessary. The company terminated its contract with a wholesaler who sold to mass merchandise stores and began using manufacturer's agents who sold to photo specialty stores. These stores agreed to stock and display Ricoh's full line and promote it prominently. Sales volume tripled within 18 months. Recognizing that car buyers now comparison shop on the Internet, automakers now have their own websites to provide price and model information.

Product Factors   In general, highly sophisticated products such as large, scientific computers, unstandardized products such as custom-built machinery, and products of high unit value are distributed directly to buyers. Unsophisticated, standardized products with low unit value, such as table salt, are typically distributed through indirect channels. A product's stage in the life cycle also affects marketing channels. This was shown in the description of the fax machine product life cycle in Chapter 11.

Company Factors   A firm's financial, human, or technological capabilities affect channel choice. For example, firms that are unable to employ a salesforce might use manufacturer's agents or selling agents to reach wholesalers or buyers. If a firm has multiple products for a particular target market, it might use a direct channel, whereas firms with a limited product line might use intermediaries of various types to reach buyers.

Company factors also apply to intermediaries. For example, personal computer hardware and software producers wishing to reach business users might look to value-added resellers such as Micro Age, which has its own salesforce and service staff that calls on businesses.

Channel Design Considerations

Recognizing that numerous routes to buyers exist and also recognizing the factors just described, marketing executives typically consider three questions when choosing a marketing channel and intermediaries:

1. Which channel and intermediaries will provide the best coverage of the target market?
2. Which channel and intermediaries will best satisfy the buying requirements of the target market?
3. Which channel and intermediaries will be the most profitable?

Target Market Coverage   Achieving the best coverage of the target market requires attention to the density and type of intermediaries to be used at the retail level of distribution.[16] Three degrees of distribution density exist: intensive, exclusive, and selective.

Intensive distribution means that a firm tries to place its products and services in as many outlets as possible. Intensive distribution is usually chosen for convenience products or services; for instance, candy, fast food, newspapers, and soft drinks. For example, Coca-Cola's retail distribution objective is to place its products "within an arm's reach of desire." Cash, yes cash, is also distributed intensively by VISA. Visit VISA's website described in the Web Link, to locate the nearest VISA automatic teller machine.

Exclusive distribution is the extreme opposite of intensive distribution because only one retail outlet in a specified geographical area carries the firm's product. Exclusive distribution is typically chosen for specialty products or services; for example, automobiles, some women's fragrances, men's and women's apparel and accessories, and yachts. Gucci, one of the world's leading luxury goods companies, uses exclusive distribution in the marketing of its Yves Saint Laurent, Sergio Rossi, Boucheron, Opium, and Gucci brands.[17] Sometimes retailers sign exclusive distribution agreements with manufacturers and suppliers.[18] For instance, Radio Shack sells only Compaq Personal computers and Thomson SA's RCA brand of audio and video products in its 7,000 stores.

Selective distribution lies between these two extremes and means that a firm selects a few retail outlets in a specific geographical area to carry its products. Selective distribution weds some of the market coverage benefits of intensive distribution to the control over resale evident with exclusive distribution. For this reason, selective distribution is the most common form of distribution intensity. It is usually associated with shopping goods or services such as Rolex watches, Ben Hogan golf clubs, and Hendredon furniture.

Satisfying Buyer Requirements   A second consideration in channel design is gaining access to channels and intermediaries that satisfy at least some of the interests buyers might want fulfilled when they purchase a firm's products or services. These interests fall into four categories: (1) information, (2) convenience, (3) variety, and (4) attendant services.

Information is an important requirement when buyers have limited knowledge or desire specific data about a product or service. Properly chosen intermediaries communicate with buyers through in-store displays, demonstrations, and personal selling. Personal computer manufacturers such as Gateway and Apple Computer have opened their own retail outlets staffed with highly trained personnel, to inform buyers how their products can better meet each customer's needs.[19]

Convenience has multiple meanings for buyers, such as proximity or driving time to a retail outlet. For example, 7-Eleven stores with more than 5,300 outlets nationwide satisfy this interest for buyers, and candy and snack food firms benefit by gaining display space in these stores. For other consumers, convenience means a minimum of time and hassle. Jiffy Lube and Q-Lube, which promise to change engine oil and filters quickly, appeal to this aspect of convenience. For those who shop on the Internet, convenience means that websites must be easy to locate and navigate, and image downloads must be fast. A commonly held view among website developers is the "eight second rule": Consumers will abandon their efforts to enter or navigate a website if download time exceeds eight seconds.[20]

Variety reflects buyers' interest in having numerous competing and complementary items from which to choose. Variety is evident in both the breadth and depth of products and brands carried by intermediaries, which enhances their attraction to buyers. Thus, manufacturers of pet food and supplies seek distribution through pet superstores such as Petco and PetsMart, which offer a wide array of pet products.

MARKETING NEWSNET

Apple Computer, Inc.: Think Different, Shop Different

CUSTOMER VALUE

Think Different

Apple Computer's catchy advertising conveys the company's spirit. Apple ignited the personal computer revolution in the 1970s with the Apple II, reinvented the personal computer in the 1980s with the Macin-tosh, and captured the imagination of personal computer buyers world-wide with the introduction of the Apple iMac—a de-sign and technological breakthrough.

Now Apple invites buyers to *shop different* at its new Apple stores that seek to satisfy the buying requirements of today's PC purchaser. At each Apple store, knowl-edgeable salespeople demonstrate Macs® running innovative applications like iTunes for burning custom CDs and iMovie™ for making home videos, as well as Mac® OS x, Apple's new operating

system. All of the Macs are connected to the Internet. Sev-eral Macs are connected to digital lifestyle products that compliment the Mac experience, such as digital cameras, digital camcorders, MP3 players, and handheld organizers.

The stores carry over 300 third-party software titles for creative profession-als, students, educators, and consumers, and maintain inventory for every Apple and third-party product to ensure immediate fulfillment of buyer requests. If a buyer has a question about specific applications, he or she can visit the "Ge-nius Bar," staffed by Apple-trained personnel, for the answer.

Interested in visiting an Apple store? Log on to the com-pany's website at www.apple.com to find a location near you or take a virtual tour.

Attendant services provided by intermediaries are an important buying require-ment for products such as large household appliances that require delivery, installa-tion, and credit. Therefore, Whirlpool seeks dealers that provide such services.

Steven P. Jobs, Apple Computer's CEO, is one person who believes that computer retailers have failed to satisfy the buying requirements of today's consumer. Believ-ing that "Buying a car is no longer the worst purchasing experience. Buying a computer is no. 1," he launched Apple stores in 2001 with the intent of operating as many as 110 nationwide. Read the accompanying Marketing NewsNet to see how Apple stores intend to satisfy the information, convenience, variety, and service inter-ests of consumers.[21]

Profitability   The third consideration in designing a channel is profitability, which is determined by the margins earned (revenues minus cost) for each channel member and for the channel as a whole. Channel cost is the critical dimension of profitability. These costs include distribution, advertising, and selling expenses associated with different types of marketing channels. The extent to which channel members share these costs de-termines the margins received by each member and by the channel as a whole.

Global Dimensions of Marketing Channels

Marketing channels around the world reflect traditions, customs, geography, and the economic history of individual countries and societies. Even so, the basic marketing channel functions must be performed. But differences do exist and are illustrated by

For the answer to how Schick became a razor and blade market share leader in Japan read the text.

Schick

www.schick.com

highlighting marketing channels in Japan—the world's second-largest economy and the second-largest U.S.–world trade partner.

Intermediaries outside Western Europe and North America tend to be small, numerous, and often owner operated as described in Chapter 7. Japan, for example, has less than one-half of the population and a land mass less than 5 percent of the United States. However, Japan and the United States have about the same number of wholesalers and retailers. Why? Japanese marketing channels tend to include many intermediaries based on tradition and lack of storage space. As many as five intermediaries are involved in the distribution of soap in Japan compared with one or two in the United States.

Understanding marketing channels in global markets is often a prerequisite to successful marketing. For example, Gillette attempted to sell its razors and blades through company salespeople in Japan as it does in the United States, thus eliminating wholesalers traditionally involved in marketing toiletries. However, Schick sold its razors and blades through the traditional Japanese channel involving wholesalers. The result? Schick achieved a commanding lead over Gillette in the Japanese razor and blade market.[22]

Channel relationships also must be considered. In Japan, the distribution *keiretsu* (translated as "alignments") bonds producers and intermediaries together.[23] The bond, through vertical integration and social and economic ties, ensures that each channel member benefits from the distribution alignment. The dominant member of the distribution *keiretsu,* which is typically a producer, has considerable influence over channel member behavior, including which competing products are sold by other channel members. Well-known Japanese companies such as Matsushita (electronics), Nissan and Toyota (automotive products), Nippon Gakki (musical instruments), and Kirin (and other brewers and distillers) employ the distribution *keiretsu* extensively. Shiseido and Kanebo, for instance, influence the distribution of cosmetics through Japanese department stores.

Channel Relationships: Conflict, Cooperation, and Law

Unfortunately, because channels consist of independent individuals and firms, there is always potential for disagreements concerning who performs which channel functions, how profits are allocated, which products and services will be provided by whom, and who makes critical channel-related decisions. These channel conflicts necessitate measures for dealing with them. Sometimes they result in legal action.

Conflict in Marketing Channels   **Channel conflict** arises when one channel member believes another channel member is engaged in behavior that prevents it from achieving its goals. Two types of conflict occur in marketing channels: vertical conflict and horizontal conflict.[24]

Vertical conflict occurs between different levels in a marketing channel; for example, between a manufacturer and a wholesaler or retailer or between a wholesaler and a retailer. Three sources of vertical conflict are most common. First, conflict arises when a channel member bypasses another member and sells or buys products direct, a practice called **disintermediation**. This conflict emerged when Jenn-Air, a producer of kitchen appliances, decided to terminate its distributors and sell direct to retailers. Second, disagreements over how profit margins are distributed among channel members produce conflict. This happened when Compaq Computer Corporation and one of its dealers disagreed over how price discounts were applied in the sale of Compaq's products. Compaq Computer stopped selling to the dealer for 13 months until the issue was resolved. A third conflict situation arises when manufacturers believe wholesalers or retailers are not giving their products adequate attention. For example, H. J. Heinz Company found itself in a conflict situation with its supermarkets in Great Britain when the supermarkets promoted and displayed private brands at the expense of Heinz brands.

ETHICS AND SOCIAL RESPONSIBILITY ALERT

The Ethics of Slotting Allowances

ETHICS

Have you ever wondered why your favorite cookies are no longer to be found at your local supermarket? Or that delicious tortilla chip you like to serve at parties is missing from the shelf and replaced by another brand?

Blame it on slotting allowances. Some large supermarket chains demand slotting allowances from food manufacturers, paid in the form of money or free goods to stock and display products. These allowances, which can run up to $25,000 per item for a supermarket chain, cost U.S. food makers about $1 billion annually. Not surprisingly, slotting

allowances have been labeled "ransom," "extortional allowances," and "commercial bribery" by manufacturers because they already pay supermarkets $25 billion a year in "trade dollars" to promote and discount their products. Small food manufacturers, in particular, view slotting allowances as an economic barrier to distribution for their products. Supermarket operators see these allowances as a reasonable cost of handling business for manufacturers.

Is the practice of charging slotting allowances unethical behavior?

Horizontal conflict occurs between intermediaries at the same level in a marketing channel, such as between two or more retailers (Target and Kmart) or two or more wholesalers that handle the same manufacturer's brands. Two sources of horizontal conflict are common. First, horizontal conflict arises when a manufacturer increases its distribution coverage in a geographical area. For example, a franchised Cadillac dealer in Chicago might complain to General Motors that another franchised Cadillac dealer has located too close to its dealership. Second, dual distribution causes conflict when different types of retailers carry the same brands. For instance, the launch of Elizabeth Taylor's Black Pearls fragrance by Elizabeth Arden was put on hold when department store chains such as May and Dillard refused to stock the item once they learned that mass merchants Sears and JCPenney would also carry the brand. Elizabeth Arden subsequently introduced the brand only through department stores.[25]

Cooperation in Marketing Channels   Conflict can have destructive effects on the workings of a marketing channel, so it is necessary to secure cooperation among channel members. One means is through a **channel captain**, a channel member that coordinates, directs, and supports other channel members. Channel captains can be producers, wholesalers, or retailers. P&G assumes this role because it has a strong consumer following in brands such as Crest, Tide, and Pampers. Therefore, it can set policies or terms that supermarkets will follow. McKesson, a pharmaceutical drug wholesaler, is a channel captain because it coordinates and supports the product flow from numerous small drug manufacturers to more than 20,000 drugstores and some 6,000 hospitals nationwide. Wal-Mart and Home Depot are retail channel captains because of their strong consumer image, number of outlets, and purchasing volume.

A firm becomes a channel captain because it is typically the channel member with the ability to influence the behavior of other members.[26] Influence can take four forms. First, economic influence arises from the ability of a firm to reward other members given its strong financial position or customer franchise. Microsoft Corporation and Toys "Я" Us have such influence. Expertise is a second source of influence over other channel members. For example, American Hospital Supply helps its customers (hospitals) manage inventory and streamline order processing for hundreds of medical supplies. Third, identification with a particular channel member may also create influence for that channel member. For instance, retailers may compete to carry the Ralph Lauren line, or clothing manufacturers may compete to be carried by Neiman-Marcus, Nordstrom's, or Bloomingdale's. In both instances the desire to be associated with a channel member gives that firm influence over others. Finally, influence can arise from the legitimate right of one channel member to direct

FIGURE 15–9
Channel strategies and
practices affected by legal
restrictions

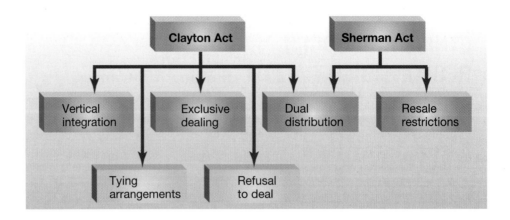

the behavior of other members. This situation would occur under contractual vertical marketing systems where a franchisor could legitimately direct how a franchisee behaves. Other means for securing cooperation in marketing channels rest in the different variations of vertical marketing systems.

Channel influence can be used to gain concessions from other channel members. For instance, some large supermarket chains expect manufacturers to pay allowances, in the form of cash or free goods, to stock and display their products. Some manufacturers call these allowances "extortion" as described in the Ethics and Social Responsibility Alert.[27]

Legal Considerations   Conflict in marketing channels is typically resolved through negotiation or the exercise of influence by channel members. Sometimes conflict produces legal action. Therefore, knowledge of legal restrictions affecting channel strategies and practices is important. Some restrictions were described in Chapter 14, namely vertical price-fixing and price discrimination. However, other legal considerations unique to marketing channels warrant attention.[28]

In general, suppliers can select whomever they want as channel intermediaries and may refuse to deal with whomever they choose. However, the Federal Trade Commission and the Justice Department monitor channel practices that restrain competition, create monopolies, or otherwise represent unfair methods of competition under the Sherman Act (1890) and the Clayton Act (1914). Six practices have received the most attention (Figure 15–9).

Dual distribution, although not illegal, can be viewed as anticompetitive in some situations. The most common situation arises when a manufacturer distributes through its own vertically integrated channel in competition with independent wholesalers and retailers that also sell its products. If the manufacturer's behavior is viewed as an attempt to lessen competition by eliminating wholesalers or retailers, then such action would violate both the Sherman and Clayton Acts.

Vertical integration is viewed in a similar light. Although not illegal, this practice is sometimes subject to legal action under the Clayton Act if it has the potential to lessen competition or foster monopoly.

The Clayton Act specifically prohibits exclusive dealing and tying arrangements when they lessen competition or create monopolies. *Exclusive dealing* exists when a supplier requires channel members to sell only its products or restricts distributors from selling directly competitive products. *Tying arrangements* occur when a supplier requires a distributor purchasing some products to buy others from the supplier. These arrangements often arise in franchising. They are illegal if the tied products could be purchased at fair market values from other suppliers at desired quality standards of the franchiser. Full-line forcing is a special kind of tying arrangement. This practice involves a supplier requiring that a channel member carry its full line of products in order to sell a specific item in the supplier's line.

Even though a supplier has a legal right to choose intermediaries to carry and represent its products, a *refusal to deal* with existing channel members may be illegal under the Clayton Act. *Resale restrictions* refer to a supplier's attempt to stipulate to whom distributors may resell the supplier's products and in what specific geographical areas or territories they may be sold. These practices have been prosecuted under the Sherman Act. Today, however, the courts apply the "rule of reason" in such cases and consider whether such restrictions have a "demonstrable economic effect."

Concept Check

1. What are the three degrees of distribution density?
2. What are the three questions marketing executives consider when choosing a marketing channel and intermediaries?
3. What is meant by "exclusive dealing"?

SUMMARY

1 A marketing channel consists of individuals and firms involved in the process of making a product or service available for use by consumers or business users.

2 Intermediaries make possible the flow of products and services from producers to buyers by performing transactional, logistical, and facilitating functions. At the same time, intermediaries create time, place, form, and possession utility.

3 Channel structure describes the route taken by products and services from producers to buyers. Direct channels represent the shortest route because producers interact directly with buyers. Indirect channels include intermediaries between producers and buyers.

4 In general, marketing channels for consumer products and services contain more intermediaries than do channels for business products and services. In some situations, producers use Internet, direct marketing, multiple channels and strategic channel alliances to reach buyers.

5 Numerous types of wholesalers can exist within a marketing channel. The principal distinction between the various types of wholesalers lies in whether they take title to the items they sell and the channel functions they perform.

6 Vertical marketing systems are channels designed to achieve channel function economies and marketing impact. A vertical marketing system may be one of three types: corporate, administered, or contractual.

7 Marketing managers consider environmental, consumer, product, and company factors when choosing and managing marketing channels.

8 Channel design considerations are based on the target market coverage sought by producers, the buyer requirements to be satisfied, and the profitability of the channel. Target market coverage comes about through one of three levels of distribution density: intensive, exclusive, and selective distribution. Buyer requirements are evident in the amount of information, convenience, variety, and service sought by consumers. Profitability relates to the margins obtained by each channel member and the channel as a whole.

9 Marketing channels in the global marketplace reflect traditions, customs, geography, and the economic history of individual countries and societies. These factors influence channel structure and relationships among channel members.

10 Conflicts in marketing channels are inevitable. Vertical conflict occurs between different levels in a channel. Horizontal conflict occurs between intermediaries at the same level in the channel.

11 Legal issues in the management of marketing channels typically arise from six practices: dual distribution, vertical integration, exclusive dealing, tying arrangements, refusal to deal, and resale restrictions.

KEY TERMS AND CONCEPTS

brokers p. 408
channel captain p. 417
channel conflict p. 416
channel partnership p. 411
direct channel p. 403
direct marketing channels p. 405
disintermediation p. 416
dual distribution p. 406
electronic marketing channels p. 404
exclusive distribution p. 414
franchising p. 410

indirect channels p. 403
industrial distributor p. 404
intensive distribution p. 414
manufacturer's agents p. 408
marketing channel p. 400
merchant wholesalers p. 408
selective distribution p. 414
selling agents p. 408
strategic channel alliances p. 406
vertical marketing systems p. 409

APPLYING MARKETING CONCEPTS AND PERSPECTIVES

1 A distributor for Celanese Chemical Company stores large quantities of chemicals, blends these chemicals to satisfy requests of customers, and delivers the blends to a customer's warehouse within 24 hours of receiving an order. What utilities does this distributor provide?

2 Suppose the president of a carpet manufacturing firm has asked you to look into the possibility of bypassing the firm's wholesalers (who sell to carpet, department, and furniture stores) and selling direct to these stores. What caution would you voice on this matter, and what type of information would you gather before making this decision?

3 What type of channel conflict is likely to be caused by dual distribution, and what type of conflict can be reduced by direct distribution? Why?

4 How does the channel captain idea differ among corporate, administered, and contractual vertical marketing systems with particular reference to the use of the different forms of influence available to firms?

5 Comment on this statement: "The only distinction among merchant wholesalers and agents and brokers is that merchant wholesalers take title to the products they sell."

6 How do specialty, shopping, and convenience goods generally relate to intensive, selective, and exclusive distribution? Give a brand name that is an example of each goods-distribution matchup.

INTERNET EXERCISE

Franchising is a large and growing industry both inside and outside the United States. For many individuals, franchising offers an opportunity to operate one's own business.

The Internet provides a number of websites that feature franchising opportunities. The International Franchise Association (www.franchise.org) features an extensive array of information, including answers to questions about franchising. Franchise.com (www.franchise.com)

shows franchise opportunities for the aspiring franchisee.

1 Visit the Franchise.com website, and go to Franchise Matchmaker. Which franchise opportunities fit you?

2 Visit the International Franchise Association website, and go to Frequently Asked Questions about Franchising. What are the current trends in franchising?

VIDEO CASE 15–1   Creston Vineyards: Facing Channel Challenges

Larry Rosenbloom's customers include individuals, retail stores, restaurants, hotels, and even the White House! Because of the many types and large numbers of customers, distribution is as important as production at Creston Vineyards. As Larry explains, "We need distributors in our business . . . as most other [businesses] do, to get the product to the end user, to the consumer."

THE COMPANY

In 1772 Franciscan Padres introduced wine to the La Panza Mountains of California when they founded Mission San Luis Obispo south of what is now San Francisco. The potential of the region for growing grapes remained a secret, however, until 1980 when Stephanie and Larry Rosenbloom purchased an abandoned ranch and started Creston Vineyards. Because it

takes several years for vines to grow and produce grapes, Creston did not sell its first wine until 1982. Today, the 569-acre ranch has 155 acres of planted vineyards and produces more than 55,000 cases of eight varieties of wines. The production facilities include a 15,000-square-foot winery and 2,000 square feet of laboratory and office space.

Since 1982 Creston wines have won more than 500 awards in wine tasting events and competitions. In addition, the Rosenblooms are particularly proud of the fact that their wine was served at the inaugurations of Presidents Reagan, Bush, and Clinton. It was at the inaugurations that Creston conceived the concept of an "Artist Collection" of labels—painted by James Paul Brown, who also painted the presidents' portraits. The artistic labels added another dimension of distinctiveness to the Creston products. In fact, Creston's success has attracted the attention of Mondavi, Beringer, Kendall-Jackson, J. Lohr, and several other large Northern California wineries, which have purchased land and started vineyards near the Creston location.

THE INDUSTRY AND DISTRIBUTION CHANNELS

The wine industry is undergoing several very interesting changes. First, sales have increased in recent years after a general decline since 1984. The decline was attributed to changing consumer demographics, shifting buying habits, and concerns about the economy. At least some of the recent interest in wine is related to the press reports suggesting the possible health benefits of red wine. A second change is the significant increase in the price of wine due to a low supply of good international wines and changing exchange rates, and an infestation of vine-eating insects (phylloxera) on over 20 percent of California's vineyards. Finally, many wine producers are trying to change the image of wine from a beverage only for special occasions and gourmet foods to a beverage for any occasion.

The industry also faces several distribution challenges. The large number of wine producers and the variety of consumers requires a sophisticated system of distribution channels. By combining different types of intermediaries, the industry is able to meet the requirements of many customers. In addition, because the sale of wine is regulated, the use of multiple distribution channels facilitates the sale of wine in many locations.

One of the most common channels of distribution involves a distributor buying wine directly from the vineyard and reselling it to retail stores and restaurants within a geographic area. Some distributors, however, may not need quantities large enough to warrant purchasing directly from the vineyard. They usually purchase several brands at the same time from a warehouse. A broker may facilitate sales by providing information to distributors, training the distributor's salesforce, and even assisting in sales calls to retailers. John Drady, 1 of 12 brokers for Creston Vineyards, explains: "It's very important that we translate our knowledge and our selling skills to the distributor's salespeople so they can, in turn, go out and [sell] more readily on their own."

Other channels are also used by Creston. In California, for example, Creston can sell directly to any customer. The vineyard also sells directly to some large retailers, such as Trader Joe's. Another channel of distribution is through wine clubs, which provide club members with information about wines and an average of six wines per year. The popularity of wine clubs has been increasing and they now account for 15 percent of Creston's sales.

THE ISSUES

In an industry with thousands of products and hundreds of producers, Creston is relatively new and small. Selecting and managing its distribution channels to best meet the needs of many constituents is a key task. Providing marketing assistance, product information, and appropriate assortment, transportation, storage, and credit are just a few of the functions the warehouse, brokers, distributors, and retailers may provide as the product moves from the vineyard to the end-user.

Creston also faces a situation where new, and possibly more efficient, channels are becoming available. Direct sales, wine clubs, and online services have generated substantial sales for Creston. Other channels, or new variations of existing channels, may also be available in the future. Overall, Creston must continue to utilize distribution channels to provide value to customers ranging from large retailers, to hotels and restaurants, to individuals, to the White House!

Questions

1   What functions must be performed by intermediaries in the wine industry?

2   What intermediaries and distribution channels are currently used by Creston Vineyards?

Supply Chain:
Managing Logistics For the 21st Century

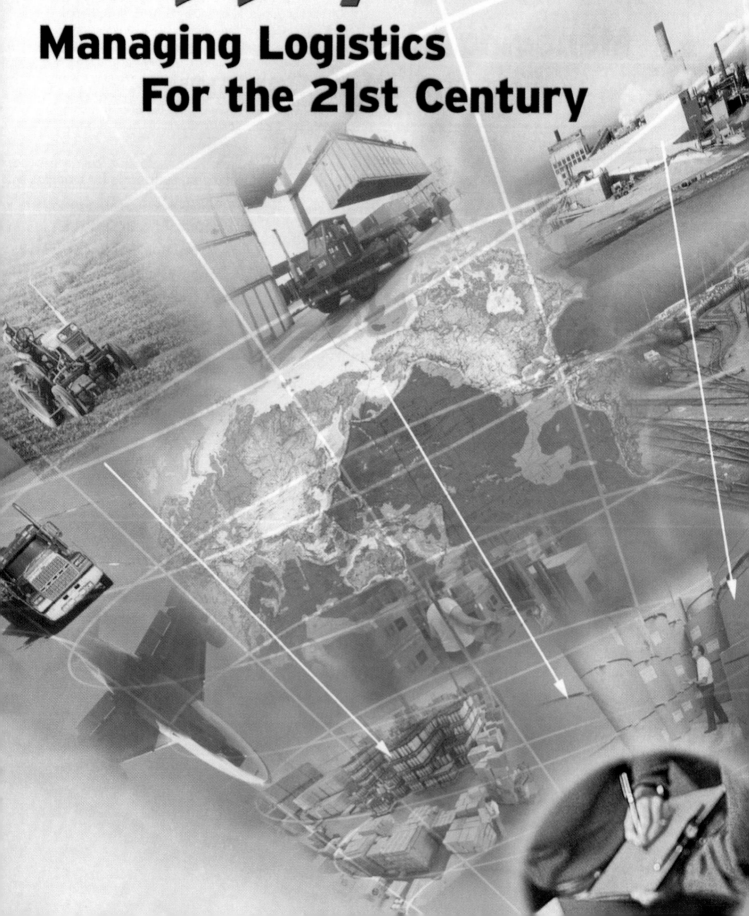

CHAPTER
16

INTEGRATING SUPPLY CHAIN AND LOGISTICS MANAGEMENT

AFTER READING THIS CHAPTER YOU SHOULD BE ABLE TO:

- Explain what supply chain and logistics management are and how they relate to marketing strategy.

- Understand the distinction between supply chain responsiveness and efficiency.

- Explain how managers trade off different "logistics costs" relative to customer service in order to make a supply chain decision.

- Recognize how customer service in logistics decisions contributes to customer value and successful marketing programs.

- Describe the key logistics functions of transportation, warehousing and materials handling, order processing, and inventory management and the role of third-party logistics providers.

SNAP! CRACK! POP! EVEN WORLD-CLASS COMPANIES CAN FEEL THE BULLWHIP'S STING

Bad things can happen to great companies. Just ask Boeing, Hewlett-Packard, Bristol-Myers Squibb, Nike, and Procter & Gamble. Each of these industry leaders have experienced the bullwhip's sting at one time or another for one or more of their products.

What is the bullwhip, and why does its sting hurt so bad? Companies define the bullwhip as too much or too little inventory to satisfy customer needs, missed production schedules, and ineffective transportation or delivery caused by miscommunication among material suppliers, manufacturers, and resellers of consumer and industrial goods. Its sting is poor customer service and lost revenue and profit opportunities.

Suppliers, manufacturers, and resellers know that to get a handle on the bullwhip, attention needs to focus on the technology and coordinated activities that make possible the physical flow and transformation of goods from the raw materials stage to the final consumer or industrial user. They also recognize that accurate, timely, and shared information can soften the bullwhip's sting, thereby benefiting customers and companies alike.[1]

Welcome to the critical world of supply chain and logistics management. The essence of the problem is simple: It makes no sense to have brilliant marketing programs to sell world-class products if the products aren't available at the right time, at the right place, and in the right form and condition that customers want them. It's finding the continuing solutions through time that's always the problem. This chapter describes the role of supply chains and logistics management in marketing and how a firm balances distribution costs against the need for effective customer service.

SIGNIFICANCE OF SUPPLY CHAIN AND LOGISTICS MANAGEMENT

We often hear or use the term physical distribution, but seldom appreciate its significance in marketing. U.S. companies spend almost $560 billion transporting raw materials and finished goods each year, another $332 billion on material handling, warehousing, storage, and holding inventory, and over $40 billion on managing the distribution process, including the cost of information technology. Worldwide, these activities and investments cost companies about $2 trillion each year.[2] In this section, we highlight contemporary perspectives on physical distribution, including supply chains and logistics, and describe the linkage between supply chain management and marketing strategy.

Relating Marketing Channels, Logistics, and Supply Chain Management

A marketing channel relies on logistics to actually make products available to consumers and industrial users—a point emphasized in the previous chapter. **Logistics** involves those activities that focus on getting the right amount of the right products to the right place at the right time at the lowest possible cost. The performance of these activities is **logistics management**, the practice of organizing the *cost-effective flow* of raw materials, in-process inventory, finished goods, and related information from point of origin to point of consumption to satisfy *customer requirements.*[3]

Three elements of this definition deserve emphasis. First, logistics deals with decisions needed to move a product from the source of raw materials to consumption, or the *flow* of the product. Second, those decisions have to be made in a *cost-effective* manner. While it is important to drive down logistics costs, there is a limit—the third point of emphasis. A firm needs to drive down logistics costs as long as it can deliver expected *customer service,* which means satisfying customer requirements. The role of management is to see that customer needs are satisfied in the most cost-effective manner. When properly done, the results can be spectacular. Procter & Gamble is a case in point. Beginning in the early 1990s, the company set out to meet the needs of consumers more effectively by collaborating and partnering with its suppliers and retailers to ensure that the right products reached store shelves at the right time and at a lower cost. The effort was judged a success when, during an 18-month period in the late 1990s, P&G's retail customers recorded a $65 million savings in logistics costs while customer service increased.[4]

The Procter & Gamble experience is not an isolated incident. Today, logistics management is embedded in a broader view of physical distribution, consistent with the emphasis on supply and channel partnering described in Chapters 6 and 15. Companies now recognize that getting the right items needed for consumption or production to the right place at the right time in the right condition at the right cost is often beyond their individual capabilities and control. Instead, collaboration, coordination, and information sharing among manufacturers, suppliers, and distributors are necessary to create a seamless flow of goods and services to customers. This perspective is represented in the concept of a supply chain and the practice of supply chain management.

A **supply chain** is a sequence of firms that perform activities required to create and deliver a good or service to consumers or industrial users.[5] It differs from a marketing channel in terms of membership. A supply chain includes suppliers who provide raw material inputs to a manufacturer as well as the wholesalers and retailers who deliver finished goods to you. The management process is also different. **Supply chain management** is the integration and organization of information and logistics activities *across firms* in a supply chain for the purpose of creating and delivering goods and services that provide value to consumers. The relation among marketing channels, logistics management, and supply chain management is shown in Figure 16–1. An important feature of supply chain management is its application

FIGURE 16-1
Relating marketing channels,
logistics management, and
supply chain management

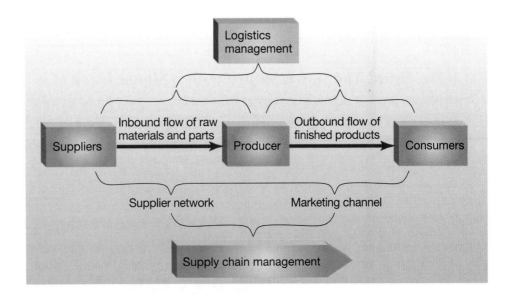

of sophisticated information technology that allow companies to share and operate systems for order processing, transportation scheduling, and inventory and facility management.

Sourcing, Assembling, and Delivering a New Car: The Automotive Supply Chain

All companies are members of one or more supply chains. A supply chain is essentially a sequence of linked suppliers and customers in which every customer is, in turn, a supplier to another customer until a finished product reaches the final consumer. Even a simplified supply chain diagram for car makers shown in Figure 16–2 illustrates how complex a supply chain can be.[6] A car maker's supplier network includes thousands of firms that provide the 5,000 or so parts in a typical automobile. They provide items ranging from raw materials such as steel and rubber to components, including transmissions, tires, brakes, and seats, to complex subassemblies and assemblies evident in chassis and suspension systems that make for a smooth, stable ride. Coordinating and scheduling material and component flows for their assembly into actual automobiles by car makers is heavily dependent on logistical activities, including transportation, order processing, inventory control, materials handling, and information technology. A central link is the car maker supply chain manager, who is responsible for translating customer requirements into actual orders and arranging for delivery dates and financial arrangements for automobile dealers. This is not an easy task given different consumer

FIGURE 16-2
The automotive supply chain

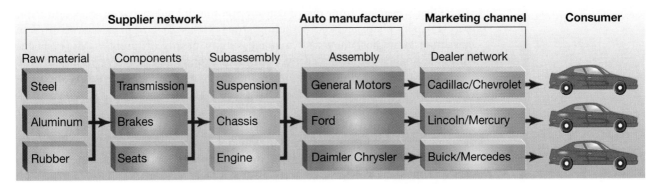

Supply chain managers are responsible for having the right products at the right place at the right time at the right price for customers. In the automotive industry, this task is complex given the variety of car options available. To appreciate the challenge, visit the Saturn website at www.saturnbp.com. Click Shop & Buy followed by Build Your Saturn. Assemble your own Saturn by choosing the features desired, immediately obtain the manufacturer's

suggested retail price (MSRP), and compare *your* assembled Saturn with a friend's Saturn.

This easy task for you represents a sizeable undertaking for a Saturn supply manager. You may not have realized it, but a Saturn comes in thousands of versions, including retailer-installed options you might want. A supply of these accessories has to be at the Saturn retailer for installation when you want to pick up your new car.

preferences and the amount consumers are willing to pay. To appreciate the challenge facing supply chain managers, visit the Saturn website described in the accompanying Web Link, and assemble your own car based on your preferences and price point.

Logistical aspects of the automobile marketing channel are also an integral part of the supply chain. Major responsibilities include transportation [which involves the selection and oversight of external carriers (trucking, airline, railroad, and shipping companies) for cars and parts to dealers], the operation of distribution centers, the management of finished goods inventories, and order processing for sales. Supply chain managers also play an important role in the marketing channel. They work with extensive car dealer networks to ensure that the right mix of automobiles are delivered to different locations. In addition, they make sure that spare and service parts are available so that dealers can meet the car maintenance and repair needs of consumers. All of this is done with the help of information technology that links the entire automotive supply chain. What does all of this cost? It is estimated that logistics costs represent 25 percent to 30 percent of the retail price of a typical new car.

Supply Chain Management and Marketing Strategy

The automotive supply chain illustration shows how information and logistics activities are integrated and organized across firms to create and deliver a car for you. What's missing from this illustration is the linkage between a specific company's supply chain and its marketing strategy. Just as companies have different marketing strategies, they also manage supply chains differently. More specifically, the goals to be achieved by a firm's marketing strategy determines whether its supply chain needs to be more responsive or efficient in meeting customer requirements.

Aligning a Supply Chain with Marketing Strategy   There are a variety of supply chain configurations, each of which is designated to perform different tasks well. Marketers today recognize that the choice of a supply chain follows from a clearly defined marketing strategy and involves three steps:[7]

MARKETING NEWSNET

Nike: The Swoosh Supply Chain Stumbles

TECHNOLOGY & E-COMMERCE

Ever innovative, Nike, the world's leading athletic shoe-maker, recently invested $400 million to streamline the way it produces, ships, and delivers shoes to retailers. The investment was intended to help Nike better match store supply with consumer demand, and avoid having warehouses full of shoes that had gone out of style, while boosting sales of trendier models. The multimillion-dollar investment, principally in supply chain management information technology, was intended to build more responsiveness into Nike's supply chain. The goal was to advance the company's well-earned reputation for delivering the right athletic shoes, at the right time, price, and quantity to satisfy the fashion and functional needs of its customers.

The result? It didn't happen. So what went wrong? Using the new information technology, Nike mistakenly sent double orders to its factories, resulting in an over-supply of many slow-selling shoes, a Nike spokeswoman said. Meanwhile, production of its hot-selling items, like the Air Force Ones basketball shoe, did not keep pace with demand. To offset shipping delays for its popular shoes, Nike had to transport them by plane at $4 to $8 a pair, compared with about 75 cents a pair by boat, according to an industry analyst. Company profitability suffered because of this supply chain stumble and Nike's stock price dropped.

1. *Understand the customer.* To understand the customer, a company must identify the needs of the customer segment being served. These needs, such as a desire for a low price or convenience of purchase, help a company define the relative importance of efficiency and responsiveness in meeting customer requirements.
2. *Understand the supply chain.* Second, a company must understand what a supply chain is designed to do well. Supply chains range from those that emphasize being responsive to customer requirements and demand to those that emphasize efficiency with a goal of supplying products at the lowest possible delivered cost.
3. *Harmonize the supply chain with the marketing strategy.* Finally, a company needs to ensure that what the supply chain is capable of doing well is consistent with the targeted customer's needs and its marketing strategy. If a mismatch exists between what the supply chain does particularly well and a company's marketing strategy, the company will either need to redesign the supply chain to support the marketing strategy or change the marketing strategy. The bottom line is that a poorly designed supply chain can do serious damage to an otherwise brilliant marketing strategy. Read the accompanying Marketing NewsNet box to learn how Nike's supply chain hampered the marketing of its popular Air Force Ones basketball shoe.[8]

How are these steps applied and how are efficiency and responsive considerations built into a supply chain? Let's briefly look at how two market leaders—Dell Computer Corporation and Wal-Mart, Inc.—have harmonized their supply chain and marketing strategy.

Dell Computer Corporation: A Responsive Supply Chain   The Dell marketing strategy targets customers who desire having the most up-to-date personal computer equipment customized to their needs. These customers are also willing to (1) wait to have their customized personal computer delivered in a few days, rather than picking out a model at a retail store; and (2) pay a reasonable, though not the lowest price in the marketplace. Given Dell's customer segment, the company has the option of adopting an efficient or responsive supply chain. An efficient supply chain may use inexpensive, but slower modes of transportation, emphasize economies of scale in its production process by reducing the variety of PC configurations offered, and limit its assembly and inventory storage facilities to a single location, say Austin, Texas, where the company is headquartered. If Dell

World-class marketers Dell Computer and Wal-Mart emphasize responsiveness and efficiency in their supply chains, respectively.

Dell Computer Corporation
www.dell.com

Wal-Mart, Inc.
www.wal-martstores.com

opted only for efficiency in its supply chain, it would be difficult if not impossible to satisfy its target customer's desire for rapid delivery and a wide variety of customizable products. Dell instead has opted for a responsive supply chain. It relies on more expensive express transportation for receipt of components from suppliers and delivery of finished products to customers. The company achieves product variety and manufacturing efficiency by designing common platforms across several products and using common components. Dell operates manufacturing facilities in Texas, Tennessee, Brazil, Ireland, Malaysia, and China to assure rapid delivery. Moreover, Dell has invested heavily in information technology to link itself with suppliers and customers.

Wal-Mart, Inc.: An Efficient Supply Chain   Now let's consider Wal-Mart. Wal-Mart's marketing strategy is to be a reliable, lower-price retailer for a wide variety of mass consumption consumer goods. This strategy favors an efficient supply chain designed to deliver products to consumers at the lowest possible cost. Efficiency is achieved in a variety of ways. For instance, Wal-Mart keeps relatively low inventory levels, and most is stocked in stores available for sale, not in warehouses gathering dust. The low inventory arises from Wal-Mart's innovative use of **cross-docking**—a practice that involves unloading products from suppliers, sorting products for individual stores, and quickly reloading products onto its trucks for a particular store. No warehousing or storing of products occurs, except for a few hours or, at most, a day. Cross-docking allows Wal-Mart to operate only a small number of distribution centers to service its vast network of Wal-Mart Stores, Supercenters, and SAM's Clubs which contributes to efficiency. On the other hand, the company runs its own fleet of trucks to service its stores. This does increase cost and investment, but the benefits in terms of responsiveness justify the cost in Wal-Mart's case. Wal-Mart has invested significantly more than its competitors in information technology to operate its supply chain. The company feeds information about customer requirements and demand from its stores back to its suppliers, which manufacture only what is being demanded. This large investment has improved the efficiency of Wal-Mart's supply chain and made it responsive to customer needs.

Three lessons can be learned from these two examples. First, there is no one best supply chain for every company. Second, the best supply chain is the one that is consistent with the needs of the customer segment being served and complements a company's marketing strategy. And finally, supply chain managers are often called upon to make trade-offs between efficiency and responsiveness on various elements of a company's supply chain.

Concept Check

1. What is the principal difference between a marketing channel and a supply chain?

2. The choice of a supply chain involves what three steps?

INFORMATION AND LOGISTICS MANAGEMENT OBJECTIVE IN A SUPPLY CHAIN

The objective of information and logistics management in a supply chain is to minimize logistics costs while delivering maximum customer service. The Dell Computer and Wal-Mart examples highlighted how two market leaders have realized this objective by different means. An important similarity between these two companies is that both use information to leverage logistics activities, reduce logistics costs, and improve customer service.

Information's Role in Supply Chain Responsiveness and Efficiency

Information consists of data and analysis regarding inventory, transportation, distribution facilities, and customers throughout the supply chain.[9] Continuing advances in information technology make it possible to track logistics activities and customer service variables and manage them for efficiency and responsiveness. For example, information on customer demand patterns allows pharmaceutical companies such as Eli Lilly and GlaxoSmithKline to produce and stock drugs in anticipation of customer needs. This improves supply chain responsiveness because customers will find the drugs when and where they want them. Demand information improves supply chain efficiency because pharmaceutical firms are better able to forecast customer needs and produce, transport, and store the required amount of inventory.

A variety of technologies are used to transmit and manage information in a supply chain. **Electronic data interchanges** (EDIs) combine proprietary computer and telecommunication technologies to exchange electronic invoices, payments, and

J.D. Edwards & Company is an internationally recognized supply chain management consulting firm.

J.D. Edwards & Company
www.jdedwards.com

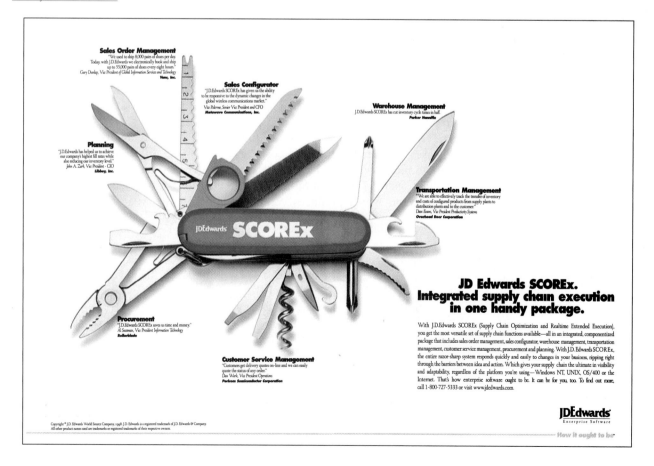

information among suppliers, manufacturers, and retailers. When linked with store scanning equipment and systems, EDI provides a seamless electronic link from a retail checkout counter to suppliers and manufacturers. Wal-Mart and Procter & Gamble actually pioneered the use of EDI. EDI is commonly used in retail, apparel, transportation, pharmaceutical, grocery, health-care, and insurance industries, as well as by local, state, and federal government agencies. About 95 percent of the companies listed in the Fortune 1000 use EDI. At Hewlett-Packard, for example, 1 million EDI transactions are made every month.

Another technology is the Extranet which is an Internet/Web-based network that permits secure business-to-business communication between a manufacturer and its suppliers, distributors, and sometimes other partners (such as advertising agencies). Extranets are less expensive and more flexible to operate than EDI because of their connection to the public Internet. This technology is prominent in private electronic exchanges described in Chapter 6. For example, WhirlpoolWebWorld.com allows Whirlpool to fulfill retailer orders quickly and inexpensively and better match appliance demand and supply.

Whereas EDI and Extranets transmit information, other technologies help manage information in a supply chain. Enterprise resource planning (ERP) technology and supply chain management software track logistics cost and customer service variables, both of which are described next.

Total Logistics Cost Concept

For our purposes **total logistics cost** includes expenses associated with transportation, materials handling and warehousing, inventory, stockouts (being out of inventory), order processing, and return goods handling.[10] Note that many of these costs are interrelated so that changes in one will impact the others. For example, as the firm attempts to minimize its transportation costs by shipping in larger quantities, it will also experience an increase in inventory levels. Larger inventory levels will not only increase inventory costs but should also reduce stockouts. It is important, therefore, to study the impact on all of the logistics decision areas when considering a change.

Figure 16–3 provides a graphic example. An oft-used supply chain strategy is for a firm to have a number of warehouses, which receive shipments in large quantities and then redistribute smaller shipments to local customers. As the number of warehouses increases, inventory costs rise and transportation costs fall. That is, more inventory is warehoused, but it is transported in volume closer to customers. The net effect is to minimize the total costs of logistics shown in Figure 16–3 by having 10 warehouses. This means the total cost curve is minimized at a point where neither of the two individual cost elements is at a minimum but the overall system is.

Studying its total logistics cost has had revolutionary consequences for National Semiconductor, which produces computer chips. In two years it cut its standard

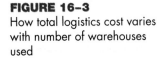

FIGURE 16–3

How total logistics cost varies with number of warehouses used

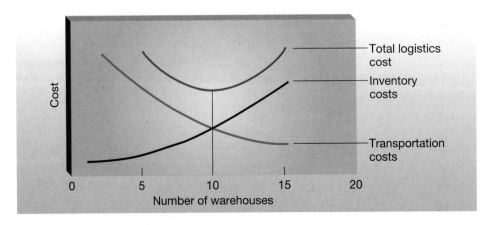

delivery time 47 percent, reduced distribution costs 2.5 percent, and increased sales 34 percent by shutting down six warehouses around the world and air-freighting its microchips from its huge distribution center in Singapore. It does this even though it has six factories in Israel, Britain, and the United States. National also discovered that a lot of its chips were actually profit-losers, and it cut the number of products it sells by 45 percent, thereby simplifying logistics and increasing profits.[11]

Customer Service Concept

If a supply chain is a *flow,* the end of it—or *output*—is the service delivered to customers. However, service can be expensive. One firm found that to increase on-time delivery from a 95 percent rate to a 100 percent rate tripled total logistics costs. Higher levels of service require tactics such as more inventory to reduce stockouts, more expensive transportation to improve speed and lessen damage, and double or triple checking of orders to ensure correctness. A firm's goal should be to provide adequate customer service while controlling logistics costs. Customer service is now seen not merely as an expense but as a means to increase customer satisfaction and sales. For example, a 3M survey about customer service among 18,000 European customers in 16 countries revealed surprising agreement in all countries about the importance of customer service. Respondents stressed factors such as condition of product delivered, on-time delivery, quick delivery after order placement, and effective handling of problems.[12]

Within the context of a supply chain, **customer service** is the ability of logistics management to satisfy users in terms of time, dependability, communication, and convenience. As suggested by Figure 16–4, a supply chain manager's key task is to balance these four customer service factors against total logistics cost factors.

Time   In a supply chain setting, time refers to **lead time** for an item, which means the lag from ordering an item until it is received and ready for use or sale. This is also referred to as *order cycle time* or *replenishment time* and may be more important to retailers or wholesalers than consumers. The various elements that make up the typical order cycle include recognition of the need to order, order transmittal, order processing, documentation, and transportation. A current emphasis in supply chain management is to reduce lead time so that the inventory levels of customers may be minimized. Another emphasis is to make the process of reordering and receiving products as simple as possible, often through electronic data and inventory systems called

FIGURE 16–4

Supply chain managers balance total logistics cost factors against customer service factors

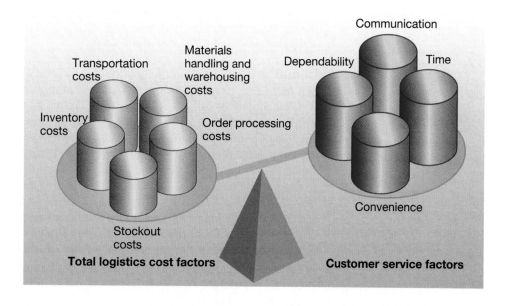

MARKETING NEWSNET

For Fashion and Food Merchandising, Haste Is as Important as Taste

CUSTOMER VALUE

Fashion and food have a lot in common. Both depend a lot on taste and both require timely merchandising. By its nature, fashion dictates that suppliers and retailers be able to adjust to new styles, colors, and different seasons. Fashion retailers need to identify what's hot so it can be ordered quickly and what's not to avoid markdowns. Saks Fifth Avenue has employed a *quick response* delivery system for fashion merchandise since the mid 1990s. Saks' point-of-sale scanner system records each day's sales. When stock falls below a minimum level, the system automatically generates a replenishment order. Vendors of fashion merchandise, such as Donna Karan (DKNY), receive an electronic order, which is processed within 48 hours.

Food marketers and retailers use the term *efficient consumer response* to describe their replenishment systems. All major food companies, including General Mills, Del Monte,

Heinz, Nestlé, and Beatrice Foods, and many supermarket chains such as Kroger, Safeway, and A&P rely on electronic replenishment systems to minimize stockouts of popular items and overstocks of slow-moving items. Lowered retailer inventories and efficient logistics practices have been projected to save U.S. grocery shoppers $30 billion a year.

quick response and **efficient consumer response** delivery systems.[13] These inventory management systems are designed to reduce the retailer's lead time for receiving merchandise, thereby lowering a retailer's inventory investment, improving customer service levels, and reducing logistics expense (see the accompanying Marketing NewsNet box).[14] The order processing portion of lead time will be discussed later in this chapter.

Dependability   Dependability is the consistency of replenishment. This is important to all firms in a supply chain and to consumers. It can be broken into three elements: consistent lead time, safe delivery, and complete delivery. Consistent service allows planning (such as appropriate inventory levels), whereas inconsistencies create surprises. Intermediaries may be willing to accept longer lead times if they know about them in advance and can thus make plans. While surprise delays may shut down a production line, early deliveries will be almost as troublesome because of the problems of storing the extra inventory. Dependability is essential for the just-in-time inventory strategies discussed at the end of the chapter.

Communication   Communication is a two-way link between buyer and seller that helps in monitoring service and anticipating future needs. Status reports on orders are a typical example of improved communication between buyer and seller. The increased communication capability of transportation carriers has enhanced the accuracy of such tracing information and improved the ability of buyers to schedule shipments. Note, however, that such information is still reactive and is not a substitute for consistent on-time deliveries. Therefore, some firms have partnered with firms specializing in logistics in an effort to institutionalize a more proactive flow of useful information that, in turn, improves on-time deliveries. Hewlett-Packard (HP), a high-tech computer printer manufacturer, recently turned its inbound raw materials over to a logistics firm, Roadway Logistics. HP lets Roadway manage the warehousing and coordinate parts delivery so that HP can focus on its printer business. In the process, HP estimates it has cut its warehouse operating costs by about 10 percent.[15]

Convenience   The concept of convenience for a supply chain manager means that there should be a minimum of effort on the part of the buyer in doing business with the seller. Is it easy for the customer to order? Are the products available from many outlets? Does the buyer have to buy huge quantities of the product? Will the seller arrange all necessary details, such as transportation? The seller must concentrate on removing unnecessary barriers to customer convenience. This customer service factor has promoted the use of vendor-managed inventory practices discussed later in the chapter.

Customer Service Standards

Firms that operate effective supply chains usually develop a set of written customer service standards. These serve as objectives and provide a benchmark against which results can be measured for control purposes. In developing these standards, information is collected on customers' needs. It is also necessary to know what competitors offer as well as the willingness of customers to pay a bit more for better service. After these and similar questions are answered, realistic standards are set and an ongoing monitoring program is established. The examples below suggest that customer service standards will differ by type of firm.

TYPE OF FIRM	CUSTOMER SERVICE STANDARD
Wholesaler	At least 98% of orders filled accurately
Manufacturer	Order cycle time of no more than 5 days
Retailer	Returns accepted within 30 days
Airline	At least 90% of arrivals on time
Trucker	A maximum of 5% loss and damage per year
Restaurant	Lunch served within 5 minutes of order

Concept Check

1. The objective of information and logistics management in a supply chain is to _____.

2. How does consumer demand information increase supply chain responsiveness and efficiency?

3. What is the relationship between the number of warehouses a company operates, its inventory costs, and its transportation costs?

KEY LOGISTICS FUNCTIONS IN A SUPPLY CHAIN

The four key logistic functions in a supply chain include (1) transportation, (2) warehousing and materials handling, (3) order processing, and (4) inventory management. These functions have become so complex and interrelated that many companies have outsourced them to third-party logistics providers. **Third-party logistics providers** are firms that perform most or all of the logistics functions that manufacturers, suppliers, and distributors would normally perform themselves.[16] Today, nearly 70 percent of manufacturers listed in the Fortune 500 outsource one or more logistics functions, at least on a limited basis. Ryder, UPS Logistics, FedEx, Roadway Logistics, Emery Worldwide, Global Logistics, and Penske are just a few of the companies that specialize in handling logistics functions for their clients. For example, UPS Logistics manages Compaq Computer Corporation's transportation carriers, service parts inventory, field stocking, central warehousing and distribution, returned goods

FedEx and Emery Worldwide
are two third-party logistics
providers that perform most or
all of the logistics functions
that manufacturers, suppliers,
and distributors would
normally perform.

FedEx

www.fedex.com

Emery Worldwide

www.emeryworld.com

handling, and order fulfillment. UPS Logistics also provides similar services for other computer manufacturers, including Dell Computer Corporation.[17] The four major logistics functions and the involvement of third-party logistics providers are described in detail next.

Transportation

Transportation provides the movement of goods necessary in a supply chain. There are five basic modes of transportation: railroads, motor carriers, air carriers, pipelines, and water carriers, and modal combinations involving two or more modes, such as highway trailers on a rail flatcar.

All transportation modes can be evaluated on six basic service criteria:

- *Cost.* Charges for transportation.
- *Time.* Speed of transit.
- *Capability.* What can be realistically carried with this mode.
- *Dependability.* Reliability of service regarding time, loss, and damage.
- *Accessibility.* Convenience of the mode's routes (such as pipeline availability).
- *Frequency.* Scheduling.

Figure 16–5 summarizes service advantages and disadvantages of five of the modes of transportation available.[18]

Railroads   Railroads carry heavy, bulky items over long distances. Of the commodities tracked by the rail industry, coal, farm products, chemicals, and nonmetallic minerals represent about 70 percent of the total tonnage. Railroads can carry larger shipments than trucks (in terms of total weight per vehicle), but their routes are less extensive. Service innovations include unit trains and intermodal service. A *unit train* is

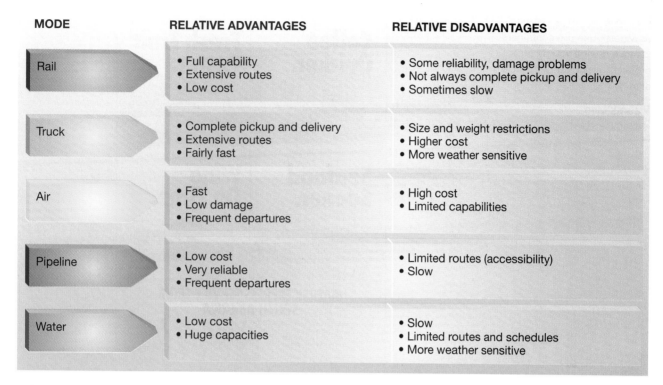

MODE	RELATIVE ADVANTAGES	RELATIVE DISADVANTAGES
Rail	• Full capability • Extensive routes • Low cost	• Some reliability, damage problems • Not always complete pickup and delivery • Sometimes slow
Truck	• Complete pickup and delivery • Extensive routes • Fairly fast	• Size and weight restrictions • Higher cost • More weather sensitive
Air	• Fast • Low damage • Frequent departures	• High cost • Limited capabilities
Pipeline	• Low cost • Very reliable • Frequent departures	• Limited routes (accessibility) • Slow
Water	• Low cost • Huge capacities	• Slow • Limited routes and schedules • More weather sensitive

FIGURE 16–5

Advantages and disadvantages of five modes of transportation

dedicated to one commodity (often coal), using permanently coupled cars that run a continuous loop from a single origin to a single destination and back. Even though the train returns empty, the process captures enough operating efficiencies to make it one of the lowest-cost transportation alternatives available. Unit trains keep to a specific schedule so that the customers can plan on reliable delivery and usually carry products that can be loaded and unloaded quickly and automatically.

Railroads also apply the unit train concept to **intermodal transportation**, which involves combining different transportation modes to get the best features of each. The result is a service that attracts high-valued freight, which would normally go by truck. The most popular combination is truck-rail, called *piggyback* or *trailer on flatcar (TOFC)*. The other popular use of an intermodal combination is associated with export/import traffic and uses containers in place of trailers. These containers can be loaded on ships, trains, and truck trailers, so in terms of the on-land segment of international shipments, a container is handled the same way as a trailer. Containers are used in international trade because they use less space on ocean-going vessels.

Motor Carriers   In contrast to the railroad industry, the for-hire motor carrier industry is composed of many small firms, including as many as 500,000 independent truckers and firms that own their own trucks for transporting their own products.

The greatest advantage of motor carriers is the complete door-to-door service. Trucks can go almost anywhere there is a road, and with the design of specialized equipment they can carry most commodities. Their physical limitations are size and weight restrictions enforced by the states. Trucks have the reputation for maintaining a better record than rail for loss and damage and providing faster, more reliable service, especially for shorter distances. As a result, trucks carry higher-valued goods that are time-sensitive and expensive to carry in inventory. The trade-off is that truck rates are substantially higher than rail rates.

Export/import shippers such as Maersk Line use containers to move a wide variety of products, including perishable ones.

Maersk Line

www.maerskline.com

Air Carriers and Express Companies   Air freight is costly, but its speed may create savings in lower inventory. The items that can be carried are limited by space constraints and are usually valuable, time-sensitive, and lightweight, such as perishable flowers, clothing, and electronic parts. Specialized firms provide ground support in terms of collecting shipments and delivering them to the air terminal. When air freight is handled by major airlines—such as American, United, Delta, or Northwest—it is often carried as cargo using the excess luggage space of scheduled passenger flights.

Freight Forwarders   **Freight forwarders**, already mentioned a number of times, are firms that accumulate small shipments into larger lots and then hire a carrier to move them, usually at reduced rates. Recall that transportation companies provide rate incentives for larger quantities. Forwarders collect many small shipments consigned to a common destination and pay the carrier the lower rate based on larger volume, so they often convert shipments that are less-than-truckload (LTL) into full truckloads, thereby receiving better shipping rates. The rates charged by the forwarder to the individual shippers, in turn, are somewhat less than the small quantity rate, and the difference is the forwarder's margin. In general, the shipment receives improved service at lower cost.

  Air freight forwarders are an example of specialization in one transportation mode. In some cases, airlines will subcontract excess space to *air freight forwarders* or *express companies,* which are firms that market air express services to the general public. Where markets are large enough, major airlines have responded with pure air freight service between specific airports—often involving international destinations.

Warehousing and Materials Handling

Warehouses may be classified in one of two ways: (1) storage warehouses and (2) distribution centers. In *storage warehouses* the goods are intended to come to rest for some period of time, as in the aging of products or in storing household goods. *Distribution*

United Airlines Cargo provides fast, global delivery—often utilizing containers.

United Airlines

www.ual.com

centers, on the other hand, are designed to facilitate the timely movement of goods and represent a very important part of a supply chain. They represent the second most significant cost in a supply chain after transportation.

Distribution centers not only allow firms to hold their stock in decentralized locations but are also used to facilitate sorting and consolidating products from different plants or different suppliers. Some physical transformation can also take place in distribution centers such as mixing or blending different ingredients, labeling, and repackaging. Paint companies such as Sherwin-Williams and Benjamin Moore use distribution centers for this purpose. In addition, distribution centers may serve as manufacture sales offices, described in Chapter 15, and order processing centers.

Materials handling, which involves moving goods over short distances into, within, and out of warehouses and manufacturing plants, is a key part of warehouse operations. The two major problems with this activity are high labor costs and high rates of loss and damage. Every time an item is handled, there is a chance for loss or damage. Common materials handling equipment includes forklifts, cranes, and conveyors. Today, materials handling in warehouses is automated by using computers and robots to reduce the cost of holding, moving, and recording inventories.

Order Processing

There are several stages in the processing of an order, and a failure at any one of them can cause a problem with the customer. The process starts with transmitting the order by a variety of means such as the Internet, an Extranet, or electronic data interchange (EDI). This is followed by entering the order in the appropriate databases and sending the information to those needing it. For example, a regional warehouse is notified to prepare an order. After checking inventory, a new quantity may need to be reordered from the production line, or purchasing may be requested to reorder from a vendor. If the item is currently out of stock, a "backorder" is created, and the whole process of

Materials handling through
automation is now common in
distribution centers.

keeping track of a small part of the original order must be managed. In addition, credit may have to be checked for some customers, all documentation for the order must be prepared, transportation must be arranged, and an order confirmation must be sent. Order processing systems are evaluated in terms of speed and accuracy.

Electronic order processing has replaced manual processing for most large companies.[19] For example, IBM soon expects to be doing business electronically with all of its suppliers, either on the Internet or through EDI. Kiwi Brands, the Douglassville, Pennsylvania, marketer of Kiwi shoe polish, Endust, Behold, and Ty-D-Bol, receives 75 percent of its retailers' purchase orders via EDI. The company has also implemented financial EDI, sending invoices to retailers and receiving payment order/remittance advice documents and electronic funds transfer (EFT) payments. Shippers as well are linked to the system, allowing Kiwi to receive shipment status messages electronically.

Inventory Management

Inventory management is one of the primary responsibilities of the supply chain manager. The major problem is maintaining the delicate balance between too little and too much. Too little inventory may result in poor service, stockouts, brand switching, and loss of market share; too much leads to higher costs because of the money tied up in inventory and the chance that it may become obsolete. Remember the sting of the bullwhip described at the beginning of the chapter?

Reasons for Inventory   Traditionally, carrying inventory has been justified on several grounds: (1) to offer a buffer against variations in supply and demand, often caused by uncertainty in forecasting demand; (2) to provide better service for those customers who wish to be served on demand; (3) to promote production efficiencies; (4) to provide a hedge against price increases by suppliers; (5) to promote purchasing and transportation discounts; and (6) to protect the firm from contingencies such as strikes and shortages. However, companies today view inventory as something to be moved, not stored, and more of a liability than an asset. The traditional justification for inventory has resulted in excessive inventories that have proven costly to maintain.

The key to Saturn's JIT system: a Ryder truck driver downloads a key-shaped floppy disk from an onboard computer to get delivery instructions.

Ryder System, Inc.

www.ryder.com

Consider the U.S. automobile industry. Despite efforts to streamline its supply chain, industry analysts estimate that $230 billion worth of excess inventory piles up annually in the form of unused raw materials, parts waiting to be delivered, and vehicles sitting on dealers' lots.[20]

Inventory Costs   Specific inventory costs are often hard to detect because they are difficult to measure and occur in many different parts of the firm. A classification of inventory costs includes the following:

- *Capital costs.* The opportunity costs resulting from tying up funds in inventory instead of using them in other, more profitable investments; these are related to interest rates.
- *Inventory service costs.* Items such as insurance and taxes that are present in many states.
- *Storage costs.* Warehousing space and materials handling.
- *Risk costs.* Possible loss, damage, pilferage, perishability, and obsolescence.

Storage costs, risk costs, and some service costs vary according to the characteristics of the item inventoried. For example, perishable products or highly seasonal items have higher risk costs than a commodity type product such as lumber. Capital costs are always present and are proportional to the *values* of the item and prevailing interest rates. The costs of carrying inventory vary with the particular circumstances but quite easily could range from 10 to 35 percent for different firms.

Supply Chain Inventory Strategies   Conventional wisdom a decade ago was that a firm should protect itself against uncertainty by maintaining a reserve inventory at each of its production and stocking points. This has been described as a "just-in-case" philosophy of inventory management and led to unnecessary high levels of inventory. In contrast is the **just-in-time (JIT) concept**, which is an inventory supply system that operates with very low inventories and requires fast, on-time delivery. When parts are needed for production, they arrive from suppliers "just in time," which means neither before nor after they are needed. Note that JIT is used in situations where demand forecasting is reliable, such as when supplying an automobile production line, and is not suitable for inventories that are to be stored over significant periods of time.

Saturn's manufacturing operation in Spring Hill, Tennessee, uses a sophisticated JIT system. A central computerized system directs trucks to deliver preinspected parts at specific times 21 hours a day, six days a week to one of the plant's 56 receiving docks. Incredibly, the JIT system must coordinate Saturn's 339 suppliers located in 39 states, each supplier being an average of 550 miles away from the Spring Hill facility. Does the JIT system work for Saturn? The answer is a resounding yes. The Saturn production line has been shut down only once—for 18 minutes!—because the right part was not delivered at the right place and time.

ETHICS AND SOCIAL RESPONSIBILITY ALERT

Reverse Logistics and Green Marketing Go Together at Estée Lauder Companies

ETHICS

Retailing industry research firms and trade groups report that U.S. consumers return an estimated $62 billion in merchandise to retailers each year. Until recently, returned merchandise was often disposed of in solid-waste landfills.

Estée Lauder Companies, Inc. used to dump about $60 million worth of its products into landfills each year, destroying more than one-third of its name-brand cosmetics returned by retailers. That changed recently when Estée Lauder developed a sophisticated reverse logistics system that cut the volume of destroyed products in half. During the system's first year of operation, the company was able to evaluate 24 percent more returned products, redistribute 150 percent more of its returns, and save $475,000 in labor costs. Estée Lauder still destroyed 27 percent of returned products because their shelf life had expired, but that was down from 37 percent the

previous year. The company expects to reduce its disposal rate to 15 percent as the reverse logistics system becomes even more efficient. The net effect of Estée Lauder's initiative has been a reduction in costs and a cleaner environment.

Ryder Integrated Logistics is charged with making Saturn's JIT system work smoothly. Ryder long-haul trucks and their drivers are the most expensive part of the system. The key—very literally—to this JIT system is a computer disk in the form of a plastic key that drivers plug into an on-truck computer. The computer screen then tells the driver where to go, the route to use, and how much time to spend getting there.[21]

Electronic data interchange and electronic messaging technology coupled with the constant pressure for faster response time in replenishing inventory have also changed the way suppliers and customers do business in a supply chain. The approach, called **vendor-managed inventory** (VMI), is an inventory-management system whereby the *supplier* determines the product amount and assortment a customer (such as a retailer) needs and automatically delivers the appropriate items.[22]

Campbell Soup's system illustrates how VMI works.[23] Campbell first establishes EDI links with retailers. Every morning, retailers electronically inform the company of their demand for all Campbell products and the inventory levels in their distribution centers. Campbell uses that information to forecast future demand and determine which products need replenishment based on upper and lower inventory limits established with each retailer. Trucks leave the Campbell shipping plant that afternoon and arrive at the retailer's distribution centers with the required replenishments the same day.

CLOSING THE LOOP: REVERSE LOGISTICS

The flow of goods in a supply chain does not end with the consumer or industrial user. Companies today recognize that a supply chain can work in reverse.[24] **Reverse logistics** is a process of reclaiming recyclable and reusable materials, returns, and reworks from the point of consumption or use for repair, remanufacturing, redistribution, or disposal. The effect of reverse logistics can be seen in the reduced waste in landfills and lowered operating costs for companies. The accompanying Ethics and Social Responsibility Alert describes the successful reverse logistics initiative at Estée Lauder Companies, Inc.[25]

Companies such as Eastman Kodak (reusable cameras), Hewlett-Packard (printer toner cartridges returned for filling), and Xerox and IBM (remanufacing and recycling equipment parts) have implemented acclaimed reverse logistics programs.[26] Other firms have enlisted third-party logistics providers to handle this process along with other supply chain functions. GNB Technologies, Inc., a manufacturer of lead-acid batteries for automobiles and boats, has outsourced much of its supply chain activity to UPS Logistics.[27] The company contracts with UPS to manage its shipments between plants, distribution centers, recycling centers, and retailers. This includes movement of both new batteries and used products destined for recycling and covers both truck and railroad shipments. This partnership along with the initiatives of other battery makers has paid economic and ecological dividends. By recycling 90 percent of the lead from used batteries, manufacturers have kept the demand for new lead in check, thereby holding down costs to consumers. Also, solid waste management costs and the environmental impact of lead in landfills is reduced.

Concept Check

1. What are the basic trade-offs between the modes of transportation?
2. What types of inventory should use storage warehouses and which type should use distribution centers?
3. What are the strengths and weaknesses of a just-in-time system?

SUMMARY

1 Logistics involves those activities that focus on getting the right amount of the right products to the right place at the right time at the lowest possible cost. Logistics management includes the coordination of the flows of both inbound and outbound goods, an emphasis on making these flows cost-effective, and customer service.

2 A supply chain is a sequence of firms that perform activities required to create and deliver a good or service to consumers or industrial users. Supply chain management is the integration and organization of information and logistics across firms for the purpose of creating value for consumers.

3 The goals to be achieved by a firm's marketing strategy determines whether its supply chain needs to be more responsive or efficient in meeting customer requirements. Marketers today recognize that the choice of a supply chain involves three steps: (*a*) understand the customer, (*b*) understand the supply chain, and (*c*) harmonize the supply chain with the marketing strategy.

4 The objective of information and logistics management in a supply chain is to minimize logistics costs while delivering maximum customer service. Information can leverage logistics activities, reduce total logistics costs, and improve customer service.

5 Minimizing total logistics cost is irrelevant without specifying an acceptable customer service level that must be maintained. Although key customer service factors depend on the situation, important elements of the customer service program

are likely to be time-related dependability, communications, and convenience.

6 Four key logistics functions in a supply chain include (*a*) transportation, (*b*) warehousing and material handling, (*c*) order processing, and (*d*) inventory management. Third-party logistics perform most or all of the logistics functions that manufacturers, suppliers, and distributors would normally perform themselves.

7 The modes of transportation (e.g., railroads, motor carriers, air carriers, and trucks) offer shippers different service benefits. Better service often costs more, although it should result in savings in other areas of the logistics system.

8 The function of warehousing and material handling in a supply chain is to facilitate storage and movement of goods. Distribution centers provide flexibility and facilitate sorting and consolidating products from different plants or different suppliers.

9 Inventory management and order processing go hand in hand in a supply chain. Both functions have benefited from information technology. Two popular supply chain inventory management practices are just-in-time and vendor-managed inventory management systems.

10 Reverse logistics closes the loop in a supply chain. Reverse logistics is the process of reclaiming recyclable and reusable materials, returns, and reworks from the point of consumption or use for repair, remanufacturing, redistribution, or disposal.

KEY TERMS AND CONCEPTS

cross-docking p. 428
customer service p. 431
efficient consumer response p. 432

electronic data interchange (EDI) p. 429
freight forwarders p. 436
intermodal transportation p. 435

APPLYING MARKETING CONCEPTS AND PERSPECTIVES

1 List several companies to which logistical activities might be unimportant. Also list several whose focus is only on the inbound or outbound side.

2 What are some types of businesses in which order processing may be among the paramount success factors?

3 What behavioral problems might arise to negate the logistics concept within the firm?

4 List the customer service factors that would be vital to buyers in the following types of companies: (*a*) manufacturing, (*b*) retailing, (*c*) hospitals, and (*d*) construction.

5 Name some cases when extremely high service levels (e.g., 99 percent) would be warranted.

6 Name the mode of transportation that would be the best for the following products: (*a*) farm machinery, (*b*) cut flowers, (*c*) frozen meat, and (*d*) coal.

7 The auto industry is a heavy user of the just-in-time concept. Why? What other industries would be good candidates for its application? What do they have in common?

8 Look again at Figure 16–3. Explain why as the number of warehouses increases, (*a*) inventory costs rise and (*b*) transportation costs fall.

INTERNET EXERCISE

The bullwhip effect is a common problem in supply chains. The bullwhip's significance is evident in the attention afforded it in the QuickMBA. QuickMBA's purpose is to offer a concise discussion on important issues facing today's manager.

The QuickMBA at www.quickmba.com/ops/scm, which also gives an overview of supply chain management, provides insights into the bullwhip effect. Visit

QuickMBA at the address given to learn more about the bullwhip effect and answer the following questions:

1 What are the principal contributors to the bullwhip effect?

2 How have companies reduced the sting of the bullwhip?

VIDEO CASE 16–1   Amazon: Delivering the Goods . . . Millions of Times Each Day!

"The new economy means that the balance of power has shifted toward the consumer," explains Jeff Bezos, CEO of Amazon.com, Inc. The global online retailer is a pioneer of fast, convenient, low-cost virtual shopping that has attracted millions of consumers. Of course, while Amazon has changed the way many people shop, the company still faces the traditional and daunting task of creating a seamless flow of deliveries to its customers—often millions of times each day!

THE COMPANY

Bezos started Amazon.com with a simple idea: to use the Internet to transform book buying into the fastest, easiest, and most enjoyable shopping experience possible.

The company was incorporated in 1994 and opened its virtual doors in July 1995. At the forefront of a huge growth of dot-com businesses, Amazon pursued a get-big-fast business strategy. Sales grew rapidly and Amazon began adding products and services other than books. In fact, Amazon soon set its goal on being the world's most customer-centric company, where customers can find and discover anything they might want to buy online!

Today Amazon claims to have the "Earth's Biggest Selection™" of products and services, including books, CDs, videos, toys and games, electronics, kitchenware, computers, free electronic greeting cards, and auctions. Other services allow customers to:

- search for books, music and videos with any word from the title or any part of the artist's name,

- browse hundreds of product categories, and
- receive personalized recommendations, based on past purchases, through e-mail or when they log on.

These products and services have attracted millions of people in more than 220 countries and made Amazon.com, along with its international sites in the United Kingdom, Germany, Japan, and France, the leading online retailer.

Despite its incredible success with consumers and continuing growth in sales to more than $3 billion annually, Amazon.com found it difficult to be profitable. Many industry observers questioned the viability of online retailing and Amazon's business model. Then, Amazon shocked many people by announcing its first profit in the fourth quarter of 2001. There are a variety of explanations for the turnaround. Generally, Bezos suggests that "efficiencies allow for lower prices, spurring sales growth across the board, which can be handled by existing facilities without much additional cost." More specifically, the facilities Bezos is referring to are the elements of its supply chain—which are one of the most complex and expensive aspects of the company's business.

SUPPLY CHAIN AND LOGISTICS MANAGEMENT AT AMAZON.COM

What happens after an order is submitted on Amazon's website but before it arrives at the customer's door? A lot! Amazon.com maintains seven huge distribution, or "fulfillment," centers where it keeps inventory of more than 2.7 million products. This is one of the key differences between Amazon.com and some of its competitors—it actually stocks products. So Amazon must manage the flow of products from its suppliers to its distribution centers and the flow of customer orders from the distribution centers to individuals' homes or offices.

The process begins with the suppliers. "Amazon's goal is to collaborate with our suppliers to increase efficiencies and improve inventory turnover," explains Jim Miller, vice president of supply chain at Amazon.com. "We want to bring to suppliers the kind of interactive relationship that has inspired customers to shop with us," he adds. For example, Amazon is using software to more accurately forecast purchasing patterns by region, which allows it to give its suppliers better information about delivery dates and volumes. Prior to the development of this software, 12 percent of incoming inventory was sent to the wrong location, leading to lost time and delayed orders. Now only 4 percent of the incoming inventory is mishandled.

At the same time, Amazon has been improving the part of the process that sorts the products into the individual orders. Jeffrey Wilke, Amazon's senior vice president of operations, says, "We spent the whole year really focused on increasing productivity." Again, technology has been essential. "The speed at which telecommunications networks allow us to pass information back and forth has enabled us to do the real-time work that we keep talking about. In the past it would have taken too long to get this many items through a system," explains Wilke. Once the order is in the system, computers ensure that all items are included in the box before it is taped and labeled. A network of trucks and regional postal hubs then conclude the process with delivery of the order.

The success of Amazon's logistics and supply chain management activities may be most evident during the year-end holiday shopping season. Amazon received orders for 37.9 million items between November 9 and December 21, including orders for 450,000 Harry Potter books and products, and orders for 36,000 items placed just before the holiday delivery deadline. Well over 99 percent of the orders were shipped and delivered on time!

AMAZON'S CHALLENGES

Despite all of Amazon's recent improvements, logistics experts estimate that the company's distribution centers are operating at approximately 40 percent of their capacity. This situation suggests that Amazon must reduce its capacity or increase its sales.

Several sales growth options are possible. First, Amazon can continue to pursue growth through sales of books, CDs, and videos. Expanded lists of books, music, and movies from throughout the world and convenient selection services may appeal to current and potential customers. Second, Amazon can continue its expansion into new product and service categories. This approach would prevent Amazon from becoming a niche merchant of books, music, and movies, and position it as an online department store. Finally, Amazon can pursue a strategy of providing access to its existing operations to other retailers. For example, Amazon took over the Toys "Я" Us website, adding it as a store on Amazon's site. Borders, Expedia, and Circuit City have begun similar partnerships.

Amazon.com has come a long way toward proving that online retailing can work. As the company strives to maintain profitability and continue its growth, its future success is likely to depend on the success of its logistics and supply chain management activities!

Questions

1 How do Amazon.com's logistics and supply chain management activities help the company create value for its customers?

2 What systems did Amazon develop to improve the flow of products from suppliers to Amazon distribution centers? What systems improved the flow of orders from the distribution centers to customers?

3 Why will logistics and supply chain management play an important role in the future success of Amazon.com?

17

RETAILING

AFTER READING THIS CHAPTER YOU SHOULD BE ABLE TO:

- Identify retailers in terms of the utilities they provide.

- Explain the alternative ways to classify retail outlets.

- Understand the many methods of nonstore retailing.

- Classify retailers in terms of the retail positioning matrix.

- Develop retailing mix strategies over the life cycle of a retail store.

SMART, CHIC, AND CHEAP: TARGET HITS THE BULL'S-EYE!

Since 1962 Target has been a discount store competing with rivals Kmart and Wal-Mart. Then it asked Dave Peterson, creative director of advertising agency Peterson Milla Hooks to suggest a campaign that would help the store implement its strategy to reposition Target as an up-scale discounter. Dave thought the simple red Target logo was "fun, designery and fashioney" and similar to an early Gucci or Chanel logo. The result was a funky retro pop campaign called "Bull's-Eye World" featuring the Target logo on everything in the ads—clothing, wallpaper, even dogs! The campaign was a huge success with consumers and established Target's logo in a class with those of McDonald's arches and Nike's swoosh. The repositioning of Target was acknowledged by its designation as Marketer of the Year, and led one industry expert to remark that Target has "been able to carve out the ultimate retail positioning with both a perception of having the highest quality products and at the same time, a perception of being a low price leader."

Target has continued its repositioning by adding a line of clothes and products designed by Italian Mossimo Giannulli, a line of makeup by professional makeup artist Sonia Kashuk, and line of high-fashion private label products designed by architect Michael Graves. To emphasize its high-quality brands Target is also using licensing agreements to offer lines of clothing designed with Twinkies, Mr. Clean, Sugar Daddy, and Mr. Potato Head brand names on them. For Valentine's Day the promotions emphasize Hershey's Kisses, Nestlé's SweetTarts, and Hot Tamales! New advertising campaigns—which include "Spotted at Target" and "Color My World" ads emphasizing the brands—are being used, and new advertising locations—such as on popcorn bags in movie theaters and in magazines such as Vogue and Glamour—have also been added.

Other marketing activities are taking advantage of the many new ways retailers can reach customers. Target's bridal registry, Club Wedd, is now the largest in the world. An extension of the bridal registry for new parents, called the Lullaby Club, is also growing in popularity. Its website, Target.com, provides an extension of its brand to locales where no stores exist. To encourage website traffic the retailer recently opened a four-story building in Manhattan called Target House to showcase Target's merchandise. In addition, during the next 10 years Target plans to open 200 Super Target stores, which include grocery stores.

Finally, Target's most exciting marketing activity may be its decision to be the first major U.S. retailer to issue "smart cards" to its shoppers. Smart cards hold much more information than traditional cards because they use an embedded computer chip rather than a magnetic strip. Consumers will be able to use the card to keep track of purchases, qualify for frequent purchase rewards, and even download electronic coupons. Target plans to install chip readers in all of its 1,000 stores during the next year, and begin issuing the new cards to its 36 million current card holders during the same period![1]

Target is just one example of many dynamic and exciting retailers you may encounter today. This chapter examines the critical role of retailing in the marketplace and the challenging decisions retailers face as they strive to create value for their customers.

What types of products will consumers buy directly through catalogs, television, the Web, or by telephone? In what type of store will consumers look for products they don't buy directly? How important is the location of the store? Will customers expect services such as alterations, delivery, installation, or repair? What price should be charged for each product? These are difficult and important questions that are an integral part of retailing. In the channel of distribution, retailing is where the customer meets the product. It is through retailing that exchange (a central aspect of marketing) occurs. **Retailing** includes all activities involved in selling, renting, and providing goods and services to ultimate customers for personal, family, or household use.

FIGURE 17–1
Which company best represents which utilities?

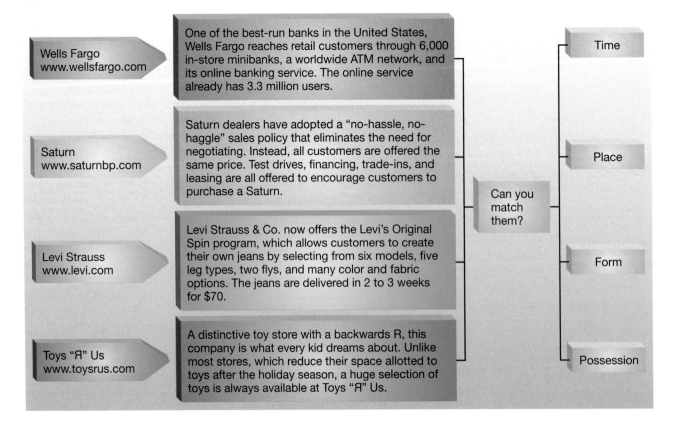

THE VALUE OF RETAILING

Retailing is an important marketing activity. Not only do producers and consumers meet through retailing actions, but retailing also creates customer value and has a significant impact on the economy. To consumers, the value of retailing is in the form of utilities provided (Figure 17–1). Retailing's economic value is represented by the people employed in retailing as well as by the total amount of money exchanged in retail sales (Figure 17–2).

Consumer Utilities Offered by Retailing

The utilities provided by retailers create value for consumers. Time, place, possession, and form utilities are offered by most retailers in varying degrees, but one utility is often emphasized more than others. Look at Figure 17–1 to see how well you can match the retailer with the utility being emphasized in the description.

Providing minibanks in supermarkets, as Wells Fargo does, puts the bank's products and services close to the consumer, providing place utility. By providing financing or leasing and taking used cars as trade-ins, Saturn makes the purchase easier and provides possession utility. Form utility—production or alteration of a product—is offered by Levi Strauss & Co. as it creates "Original Spin" jeans to meet each customer's specifications. Finding toy shelves stocked in May is the time utility dreamed about by every child (and many parents) who enters Toys "Я" Us. Many retailers offer a combination of the four basic utilities. Some supermarkets, for example, offer convenient locations (place utility) and are open 24 hours (time

FIGURE 17–2
Retail sales ($ billions), by type of business

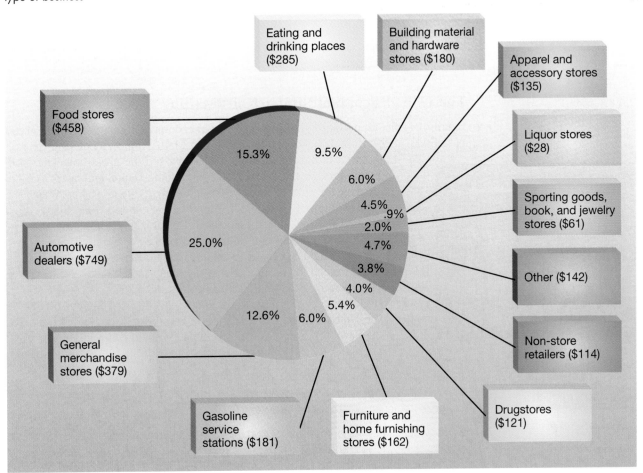

MARKETING NEWSNET

Bricks *and* Clicks Are Going Global

GLOBAL

Around the world, customer tastes are converging, trade restrictions are disappearing, and retailers are responding with global expansion. U.S.–based convenience store 7-Eleven, for example, plans to open one new store each month over the next five years, in Denmark alone! Swedish furniture manufacturer IKEA plans to open five new stores in the United States each year for the next 10 years. Office product retailer Staples opened 189 new stores outside the United States in 2000 and 160 new stores in 2001. And Italy's Benetton already has stores in 120 countries!

The biggest global expansion, however, may be in e-tailer growth. Companies such as Amazon.com, Yahoo!, and eBay are rapidly expanding into other countries. Amazon.com, for example, has opened a site and distribution center in Britain and has a French headquarters in development. Yahoo! is Europe's largest portal with twice as many visitors as Germany's T-Online, and online broker E*Trade has opened an office in Stockholm.

Why are retailers and e-tailers expanding? One reason is that local market growth rates are slowing so merchants are looking for new places to invest. As Wal-Mart's CFO John B. Menzer explains "someday the U.S. will slow down, and international will be the growth vehicle for the company." A second reason is that these companies want to benefit from strong brand names and create global brands!

utility). In addition, consumers may seek additional utilities such as entertainment, recreation, or information.[2]

The Global Economic Impact of Retailing

Retailing is also important to the U.S. and global economies. Three of the 30 largest businesses in the United States are retailers (Wal-Mart, Home Depot, and Sears).[3]

Wal-Mart's 193 billion of sales in 2000 surpassed the gross domestic product of Finland for that same year. Wal-Mart, Home Depot, and Sears together have more than 1.8 million employees—more than live in Austin, Texas, and Spokane, Washington, combined! Figure 17–2 shows that many other retailers, including food stores, automobile dealers, and general merchandise outlets, are also significant contributors to the U.S. economy.[4]

Outside the United States, large retailers include Daiei in Japan, Pinault-Printemps in France, Karstadtguelle in Germany, and Marks & Spencer in Britain.[5] In emerging economies such as China and Mexico, a combination of local and global retailers is evolving. Wal-Mart, for example, has 603 stores outside the United States, including joint ventures in China and Korea. The Marketing NewsNet describes the incredible expansion currently under way.[6]

Concept Check

1. When Levi Strauss makes jeans cut to a customer's exact preferences and measurements, what utility is provided?

2. Two measures of the importance of retailing in the global economy are _____ and _____.

CLASSIFYING RETAIL OUTLETS

For manufacturers, consumers, and the economy, retailing is an important component of marketing that has several variations. Because of the large number of alternative forms of retailing, it is easier to understand the differences among retail institutions by recognizing that outlets can be classified in several ways. First, **form of ownership** distinguishes retail outlets based on whether individuals, corporate chains, or contractual systems own the outlet. Second, **level of service** is used to describe the degree of service provided to the customer. Three levels of service include self-, limited-, and full-service retailers. Finally, the type of **merchandise line** describes how many different types of products a store carries and in what assortment. The alternative types of outlets are discussed in greater detail in the following pages.

Form of Ownership

Independent Retailer

One of the most common forms of retail ownership is the independent business, owned by an individual. Small retailers account for most of the 1.5 million retail establishments in the United States and include hardware stores, bakeries, clothing stores, and restaurants. In addition, there are 29,000 jewelry stores, 26,000 florists, and 24,000 sporting good and bicycle stores. The advantage of this form of ownership for the owner is that he or she can be his or her own boss. For customers, the independent store can offer convenience, quality personal service, and lifestyle compatibility.[7]

Corporate Chain

A second form of ownership, the corporate chain, involves multiple outlets under common ownership. If you've ever shopped at Marshall Field's, Mervyn's California, or Target, you've shopped at a chain outlet owned by the Target Corporation.

In a chain operation, centralization in decision making and purchasing is common. Chain stores have advantages in dealing with manufacturers, particularly as the size of the chain grows. A large chain can bargain with a manufacturer to obtain good service or volume discounts on orders. Target's large volume makes it a strong negotiator with manufacturers of most products. The buying power of chains is seen when consumers compare chain store prices with other types of stores. Consumers also benefit in dealing with chains because there are multiple outlets with similar merchandise and consistent management policies.

Retailing has become a high-tech business for many large chains. Wal-Mart, for example, has developed a sophisticated inventory management and cost control system that allows rapid price changes for each product in every store. Although the technology requires a substantial investment, it is a necessary competitive tool today—a lesson illustrated by Mexico's largest drugstore chain. When Wal-Mart and other discounters opened stores in Mexico, Formacias Benavides used its state-of-the-art computer system to match prices on popular pharmaceutical products that were also available in the new competitors' stores.[8]

Contractual System

Contractual systems involve independently owned stores that band together to act like a chain. The three kinds described in Chapter 15 are retailer-sponsored cooperatives, wholesaler-sponsored voluntary chains, and franchises. One retailer-sponsored cooperative is the Associated Grocers, which consists of neighborhood grocers that all agree with several other independent grocers to buy their meat from the same wholesaler. In this way, members can take advantage of volume discounts commonly available to chains and also give the impression of being a large chain, which may be viewed more favorably by some consumers. Wholesaler-sponsored voluntary chains such as Ace Hardware and Independent Grocers' Alliance (IGA) try to achieve similar benefits.

As noted in Chapter 15, in a franchise system an individual or firm (the franchisee) contracts with a parent company (the franchisor) to set up a business or retail outlet. McDonald's, Holiday Inn, Radio Shack, and Blockbuster Video all offer franchising opportunities. The franchisor usually assists in selecting the store location, setting up the store, advertising, and training personnel. In addition, in "business format" franchising the franchisor provides step-by-step procedures for the major aspects of the business, and guidelines for the most likely decisions a franchisee will confront. The franchisee pays a one-time franchise fee and an annual royalty, usually tied to the store's sales.

Although franchises might be seen as a relatively new phenomenon, this ownership approach has been used with gas stations since the early 1900s.[9] Franchising is attractive because it provides an opportunity for people to enter a well-known, established business where managerial advice is provided. Also, the franchise fee may be less than the cost of setting up an independent business. The International Franchise Association recently reported that there are 320,000 franchised businesses in the United States which generate $1 trillion in annual sales and employ more than 8 million people. Franchising is popular in international markets also—more than half of all U.S. franchisors have operations in other countries. What is the fastest-growing franchise? For the past year it has been 7-Eleven, which now has 21,000 locations, including 15,000 stores outside of the U.S.![10]

Franchise fees paid to the franchisor can range from $10,000 for a Subway franchise to $45,000 for a McDonald's restaurant franchise. When the fees are combined with other costs such as real estate and equipment, however, the total investment can be much higher. Figure 17–3 shows the top five franchises, as rated by *Entrepreneur* magazine, based on factors such as size, financial strength, stability, years in business, and costs. By selling franchises, an organization reduces the cost of expansion but loses some control. A good franchisor, however, will maintain strong control of the outlets in terms of delivery and presentation of merchandise and try to enhance recognition of the franchise name.[11]

Level of Service

Even though most customers perceive little variation in retail outlets by form of ownership, differences among retailers are more obvious in terms of level of service. In some department stores, such as Loehman's, very few services are provided. Some grocery stores, such as the Cub chain, have customers bag the food themselves. Other outlets, such as Neiman Marcus, provide a wide range of customer services from gift wrapping to wardrobe consultation.

FIGURE 17–3
The top five franchises

FRANCHISE	TYPE OF BUSINESS	TOTAL STARTUP COST	NUMBER OF FRANCHISES
Subway	Sandwich restaurant	$63,000 –175,000	15,200
Mail Boxes Etc.	Postal services	$126,000–196,000	4,400
McDonald's	Fast-food restaurant	$478,000–1,400,000	21,000
Jiffy Lube	Automobile fluid service	$174,000–194,000	1,700
Taco Bell	Fast-food restaurant	$236,000–515,000	4,500

Self-Service   Self-service is at the extreme end of the level of service continuum because the customer performs many functions and little is provided by the outlet. Home building supply outlets and gas stations are often self-service. Warehouse stores, usually in buildings several times larger than a conventional store, are self-service with all nonessential customer services eliminated. Several new forms of self-service include Federal Express's placement of hundreds of self-service package shipping stations in retail stores such as Sam's Club and a self-service scanning system called the Self-Checkout currently being installed by Kmart in 1,300 of its U.S. stores.[12]

Limited Service   Limited-service outlets provide some services, such as credit, and merchandise return, but not others, such as custom-made clothes. General merchandise stores such as Wal-Mart, Kmart, and Target are usually considered limited service outlets. Customers are responsible for most shopping activities, although salespeople are available in departments such as consumer electronics, jewelry, and lawn and garden.

Full-Service   Full-service retailers, which include most specialty stores and department stores, provide many services to their customers. Nordstrom, a Seattle-based retail chain, for example, is legendary for its customer service. The store typically has 50 percent more salespeople on the floor than similar-sized stores. Salespeople often write customers thank-you notes or deliver purchases to customers' homes. In most stores, customers are serenaded by the sounds of a grand piano. These activities are reflected in a biannual industry customer satisfaction survey—the Retail Satisfaction Index—which often ranks Nordstrom highest in terms of personalized attention and professional salespeople.[13]

Merchandise Line

Retail outlets also vary by their merchandise lines, the key distinction being the breadth and depth of the items offered to customers (Figure 17–4). **Depth of product line** means that the store carries a large assortment of each item, such as a shoe store that offers running shoes, dress shoes, and children's shoes. **Breadth of product line** refers to the variety of different items a store carries.

Depth of Line   Stores that carry a considerable assortment (depth) of a related line of items are limited-line stores. Oshman's sporting goods stores carry considerable depth in sports equipment ranging from weight-lifting accessories to running shoes. Stores that carry tremendous depth in one primary line of merchandise are single-line stores. Victoria's Secret, a nationwide chain, carries great depth in women's lingerie. Both limited- and single-line stores are often referred to as *specialty outlets.*

Specialty discount outlets focus on one type of product, such as electronics (Circuit City), office supplies (Staples), or books (Barnes and Noble) at very competitive

FIGURE 17–4
Breadth versus depth of merchandise lines

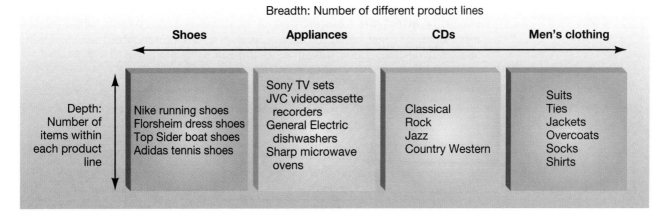

Breadth: Number of different product lines

FIGURE 17–5
Supercenters are a popular store format.

	WAL-MART SUPERCENTER	SUPER KMART	SUPER TARGET
Number of supercenters	977	106	37
Future plans	1,100	up to 1,000	200
Size (sq. feet)	110–230,000	140–180,000	175,000

prices. These outlets are referred to in the trade as *category killers* because they often dominate the market. Staples, for example, controls 37 percent of the office supply market.[14]

Breadth of Line　Stores that carry a broad product line, with limited depth, are referred to as *general merchandise stores*. For example, large department stores such as Dillard's, Macy's, Marshall Field's, and Neiman Marcus carry a wide range of different types of products but not unusual sizes. The breadth and depth of merchandise lines are important decisions for a retailer. Traditionally, outlets carried related lines of goods. Today, however, **scrambled merchandising**, offering several unrelated product lines in a single store, is common. The modern drugstore carries food, camera equipment, magazines, paper products, toys, small hardware items, and pharmaceuticals. Supermarkets rent video tapes, develop film, and sell flowers.

A form of scrambled merchandising, the **hypermarket**, has been successful in Europe since the late 1960s. These hypermarkets are large stores (more than 200,000 square feet) offering a mix of 40 percent food products and 60 percent general merchandise. Prices are typically 5 to 20 percent below discount stores. The general concept behind the stores is simple: offer consumers everything in a single outlet, eliminating the need to stop at more than one location.

Despite their success in Europe, hypermarkets have not been popular in the United States. When Wal-Mart opened four Hypermart USA stores and Kmart opened three American Fare stores, they discovered that U.S. shoppers were uncomfortable with the huge size of the stores. In addition, the competitive environment was tough: warehouse stores beat hypermarkets on price, category killers beat them on selection, and discounters beat them on location.[15]

Searching for a better concept, some retailers are trying new stores, called *supercenters,* which combine a typical merchandise store (typically 70,000 square feet) with a full-size grocery. Wal-Mart already operates more than 900 supercenters, whereas rival Kmart has close to 100 Super Kmart Centers, and Target has recently started building SuperTargets. Figure 17–5 shows the differences among the three major stores using the supercenter format in the United States.[16]

Scrambled merchandising is convenient for consumers because it eliminates the number of stops required in a shopping trip. However, for the retailer this merchandising policy means there is competition between very dissimilar types of retail outlets, or **intertype competition**. A local bakery may compete with a department store, discount outlet, or even a local gas station. Scrambled merchandising and intertype competition make it more difficult to be a retailer.

Concept Check

1. Centralized decision making and purchasing are an advantage of _____ ownership.

2. What are some examples of new forms of self-service retailers?

3. Would a shop for big men's clothes carrying pants in sizes 40 to 60 have a broad or deep product line?

NONSTORE RETAILING

Most of the retailing examples discussed earlier in the chapter, such as corporate chains, department stores, and limited- and single-line specialty stores, involve store retailing. Many retailing activities today, however, are not limited to sales in a store. Nonstore retailing occurs outside a retail outlet through activities that involve varying levels of customer and retailer involvement. Figure 17–6 shows six forms of nonstore retailing: automatic vending, direct mail and catalogs, television home shopping, online retailing, telemarketing, and direct selling.

Automatic Vending

Nonstore retailing includes vending machines, which make it possible to serve customers when and where stores cannot. Maintenance and operating costs are high, so product prices in vending machines tend to be higher than those in stores. Typically, small convenience products are available in vending machines. Of the 3 million vending machines currently in use in the United States, more than 1.8 million are soft-drink machines. In Japan, however, products available in vending machines include dried squid, hair tonic, boxers, green tea, beer, CDs, books, clothing, and even music downloaded from a satellite transmission system. Sanyo Electric recently introduced a fully automated convenience store![17]

Improved technology will soon make vending machines easier to use by reducing the need for cash. In Europe, for example, Marconi Online Systems has installed 6,000 vending machines which allow consumers to pay for products using a cell phone. Similarly, the world's largest vending machine company, Canteen Vending Services, is testing a cashless system called FreedomPay, which allows consumers to wave a small wand in front of a sensor to make a purchase. Another improvement in vending machines—the use of wireless technology to notify retailers when their machines are empty—is one reason automatic merchandising sales are expected to increase in the future.[18]

FIGURE 17–6
Forms of nonstore retailing

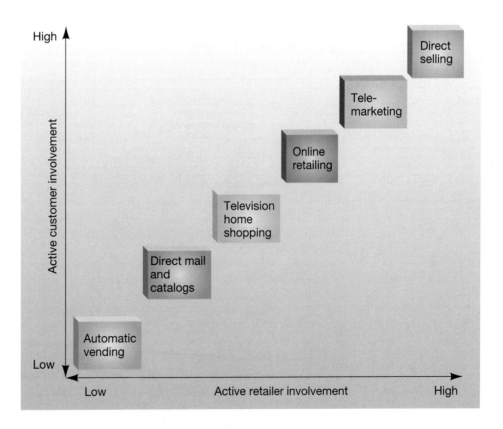

Direct Mail and Catalogs

Direct-mail and catalog retailing is attractive because it eliminates the cost of a store and clerks. For example, it costs a traditional retail store $34 to acquire a new customer whereas catalog customers are acquired for approximately $14. In addition, catalogs improve marketing efficiency through segmentation and targeting, and they create customer value by providing a fast and convenient means of making a purchase. In 2001 Americans increased their catalog spending to $121 billion.[19] International sales grew also. Direct marketers offer rural Japanese farmers outdoor gear at discount prices through direct-mail campaigns—and deliver within 72 hours![20]

One reason for the growth in catalog sales is that traditional retailers such as Office Depot are adding catalog operations. Another reason is that many Internet retailers such as Amazon.com have also added catalogs. As consumers' direct mail purchases have increased, the number of catalogs, and the number of products sold through catalogs has increased. A typical household now receives more than 50 of the 16 billion catalogs mailed each year. The competition combined with recent increases in postal rates, however, have caused catalog retailers to focus on proven customers rather than "prospects." Another successful new approach used by many catalog retailers is to send specialty catalogs to market niches identified in their databases. L. L. Bean, a longstanding catalog retailer, has developed an individual catalog for fly-fishing enthusiasts. Similarly, Lillian Vernon Corporation sends a specialty catalog called "Lilly's Kids" to customers with children or grandchildren and a "Welcome" catalog of household items to customers who change their address.[21]

Creative forms of catalog retailing are also being developed. Hallmark, for example, offers cards for businesses in their colorful 32-page "Business Expressions" catalog. Victoria's Secret mails as many as 45 catalogs a year to its customers to generate mail-order and 800-number business and to increase traffic in its 897 stores. Many catalog retailers such as the Sharper Image now allow telephone orders, mail orders, and e-mail orders![22]

Specialty catalogs appeal to market niches.

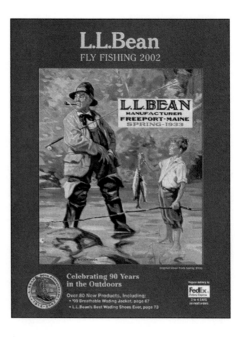

Television Home Shopping

Television home shopping is possible when consumers watch a shopping channel on which products are displayed; orders are then placed over the telephone or the Internet.

One popular program, Home Shopping Network (HSN), uses its 24-hour programming to reach more than 143 million households worldwide. The company generates sales of $1.8 billion by offering approximately 21,000 products and shipping 41 million packages each year! Because television home shopping programs typically attract women over age 35, other programs such as MTV's "House of Style" with host Molly Sims are designed to attract a younger audience. Another leading program, QVC, recently opened a store called QVC @ the Mall in the Mall of America to introduce people to the QVC concept and attract new customers. A limitation of TV shopping has been the lack of buyer-seller interaction. New Internet technologies, however, now allow consumers to simultaneously shop, chat, and interact with their favorite show host while watching TV.[23]

Online Retailing

Online retailing allows consumers to search for, evaluate, and order products through the Internet. For many consumers the advantages of this form of retailing are the 24-hour access, the ability to comparison shop, in-home privacy, and variety. Studies of online shoppers indicated that men were initially more likely than women to buy something online. As the number of online households increased to more than 50 percent, however, the profile of online shoppers changed to include all shoppers. In addition, the number of online retailers grew rapidly for several years and then declined as many stand-alone, Internet-only businesses failed or consolidated. Today, there has been a melding of traditional and online retailers—"bricks and clicks"—who are using experiences from both approaches to create better value and experiences for customers. At Walmart.com, for example, CEO Jeanne Jackson has advocated a streamlined and intuitive Web page layout and new services such as real-time inventories in individual stores that allow customers to decide whether to go to the store or to buy online. Experts predict that online sales will reach $107 billion by 2003.[24]

Online retail purchases can be the result of several very different approaches. First, consumers can pay dues to become a member of an online discount service such as www.netMarket.com. The service offers more than 800,000 items at very low prices to its 25 million subscribers. Another approach to online retailing is to use a shopping "bot" such as www.mysimon.com. This site searches the Web for a product specified by the consumer, and provides a report on the locations of the best prices available. Consumers can also use the Internet to go directly to online malls (www.fashionmall.com), apparel retailers (www.gap.com), book stores (www.amazon.com), computer manufacturers (www.dell.com), grocery stores (www.peapod.com), music and video stores (www.cdnow.com), and travel agencies (www.travelocity.com). A final, and quickly growing approach, to online retailing is the online auction, such as www.ebay.com, where consumers bid on more than 1,000 categories of products.[25]

One of the biggest problems online retailers face is that nearly two-thirds of online shoppers make it to "checkout" and then leave the website to compare shipping costs and prices on other sites. Of the shoppers who leave, 70 percent do not return. One way online retailers are addressing this issue is to offer consumers a comparison of competitors' offerings. At booksamillion.com, for example, consumers can use a "comparison engine" to compare prices with Amazon.com and Barnesandnoble.com.[26]

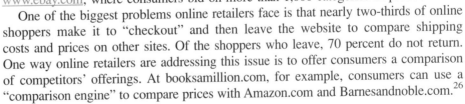

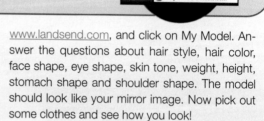

Online retailers are also trying to improve the online retailing experience by adding "experiential" or interactive activities to their websites. The Web Link describes how apparel stores use "virtual models" to involve consumers in the purchase process and help with product selection.[27] Other changes on the horizon include the growing availability of high-speed Internet connections through satellite services, high-speed digital telephone lines, and cable connections that run 50 to 100 times faster than typical telephone lines. In addition, the merger of television home shopping and online retailing will be possible through TV-based Web platforms such as WebTV, AOLTV, and UltimateTV, which use an "Internet appliance" attached to a television to connect to the Internet.[28] Owning a television or a computer isn't a necessity for online retailing, however, as 4,100 "Internet cafes" in 148 countries now provide guests with access to computer stations linked to the Internet.[29]

Telemarketing

Another form of nonstore retailing, called **telemarketing**, involves using the telephone to interact with and sell directly to consumers. Compared with direct mail, telemarketing is often viewed as a more efficient means of targeting consumers, although the two techniques are often used together. Information Management Network, a Dallas-based company, for example, sends direct mail to 30 million names each year to generate 650,000 responses from people who are then contacted by telemarketers. At Ryder Consumer Truck Rental, well-trained agents talk to 15 prospective customers each hour, while the staff of 24 at Lens Express makes 100,000 calls each month. Telemarketing has grown in popularity as companies search for ways to cut costs but still provide convenient access to their customers.

Internet cafes provide access to the Web.

According to the American Teleservices Association, telemarketing sales exceed $500 billion.[30]

As the use of telemarketing grows, consumer privacy has become a topic of discussion among consumers, Congress, the Federal Trade Commission, and businesses. Issues such as industry standards, ethical guidelines, and new privacy laws are evolving to provide a balance between the varying perspectives. An example is the industry self-regulation program, called Telewatch, which encourages legal, ethical, and professional business conduct among telemarketers. In addition, the Direct Marketing Association maintains a nationwide "Do Not Call" list with more than 3.5 million names, and several states have enacted "Do Not Call" laws.[31]

Direct Selling

Direct selling, sometimes called door-to-door retailing, involves direct sales of goods and services to consumers through personal interactions and demonstrations in their home or office. A variety of companies, including familiar names such as Fuller Brush, Avon, World Book, and Mary Kay Cosmetics, have created an industry with more than $16 billion in sales by providing consumers with personalized service and convenience. In the United States, however, sales have been declining as retail chains such as Wal-Mart begin to carry similar products at discount prices and as the increasing number of dual-career households reduces the number of potential buyers at home.

In response to the changes in the United States, many direct selling retailers are expanding into other markets. Avon, for example, already has 3 million sales representatives in 137 countries including Mexico, Poland, Argentina, and China.[32] Similarly, other retailers such as Amway, Herbalife, and Electrolux are rapidly expanding. More than 70 percent of Amway's $7 billion in sales now comes from outside the United States, and sales in Japan alone exceed sales in North America.[33] Direct selling is likely to continue to grow in markets where the lack of effective distribution channels increases the importance of door-to-door convenience and where the lack of consumer knowledge about products and brands will increase the need for a person-to-person approach.[34]

Concept Check

1. Successful catalog retailers often send _____ catalogs to _____ markets identified in their databases.

2. How are retailers increasing consumer interest and involvement in online retailing?

3. Where are direct selling retail sales growing? Why?

RETAILING STRATEGY

This section identifies how a retail store positions itself and describes specific actions it can take to develop a retailing strategy.

Positioning a Retail Store

The classification alternatives presented in the previous sections help determine one store's position relative to its competitors.

Retail Positioning Matrix   The **retail positioning matrix** is a matrix developed by the MAC Group, Inc., a management consulting firm.[35] This matrix positions retail outlets on two dimensions: breadth of product line and value added. As defined previously, breadth of product line is the range of products sold through each outlet. The second dimension, *value added,* includes elements such as location (as with 7-Eleven stores), product reliability (as with Holiday Inn or McDonald's), or prestige (as with Saks Fifth Avenue or Brooks Brothers).

The retail positioning matrix in Figure 17–7 shows four possible positions. An organization can be successful in any position, but unique strategies are required within each quadrant. Consider the four stores shown in the matrix:

1. Bloomingdale's has high value added and a broad product line. Retailers in this quadrant pay great attention to store design and product lines. Merchandise often has a high margin of profit and is of high quality. The stores in this position typically provide high levels of service.
2. Wal-Mart has low value added and a broad line. Wal-Mart and similar firms typically trade a lower price for increased volume in sales. Retailers in this position focus on price with low service levels and an image of being a place for good buys.
3. Tiffany's has high value added and a narrow line. Retailers of this type typically sell a very restricted range of products that are of high status quality. Customers are also provided with high levels of service.
4. Just for Feet has low value added and a narrow line. Such retailers are specialty mass merchandisers. Just for Feet, for example, carries athletic shoes at a discount.[36] These outlets appeal to value-conscious consumers. Economies of scale are achieved through centralized advertising, merchandising, buying, and distribution. Stores are usually the same in design, layout, and merchandise; hence they are often referred to as "cookie-cutter" stores.

FIGURE 17–7
Retail positioning matrix

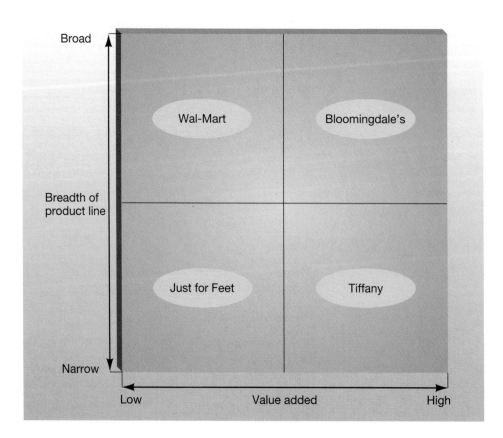

Keys to Positioning   To successfully position a store, it must have an identity that has some advantages over the competitors yet is recognized by consumers. A company can have outlets in several positions on the matrix, but this approach is usually done with different store names. Target Co., for example, owns Marshall Fields department stores (with high value added and a broad line) and Target discount stores (low value added and a broad line). Shifting from one box in the retail positioning matrix to another is also possible, but all elements of retailing strategy must be reexamined. For example, JCPenney has modified the visual presentation of its stores and changed the assortment of its merchandise to reposition itself from a mass merchandiser competing with Sears to a contemporary department store competing with stores such as Macy's.[37]

Retailing Mix

In developing retailing strategy, managers work with the **retailing mix**, which includes the (1) goods and services, (2) physical distribution, and (3) communications tactics chosen by a store (Figure 17–8).[38] Decisions relating to the mix focus on the consumer. Each of the areas shown is important, but we will cover only three basic areas: (1) pricing, (2) store location, and (3) image and atmosphere. The communications and promotion components are discussed in Chapter 19 on advertising and Chapter 20 on personal selling.

FIGURE 17–8
The retailing mix

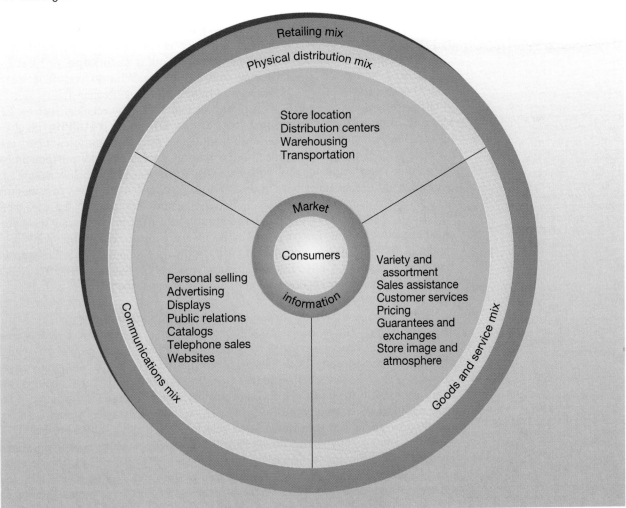

Retail Pricing In setting prices for merchandise, retailers must decide on the markup, markdown, and timing for markdowns. As mentioned in the appendix to Chapter 14 (Appendix B), the *markup* refers to how much should be added to the cost the retailer paid for a product to reach the final selling price. Retailers decide on the *original markup,* but by the time the product is sold, they end up with a *maintained markup.* The original markup is the difference between retailer cost and initial selling price. When products do not sell as quickly as anticipated, their price is reduced. The difference between the final selling price and retailer cost is the maintained markup, which is also called the *gross margin.*

Discounting a product, or taking a *markdown,* occurs when the product does not sell at the original price and an adjustment is necessary. Often new models or styles force the price of existing models to be marked down. Discounts may also be used to increase demand for complementary products.[39] For example, retailers might take a markdown on stereos to increase sales of CDs or reduce the price of cake mix to generate frosting purchases. The *timing* of a markdown can be important. Many retailers take a markdown as soon as sales fall off to free up valuable selling space and cash. However, other stores delay markdowns to discourage bargain hunters and maintain an image of quality. There is no clear answer, but retailers must consider how the timing might affect future sales.

Although most retailers plan markdowns, many retailers use price discounts a part of their regular merchandising policy. Wal-Mart and Home Depot, for example, emphasize consistently low prices and eliminate most markdowns with a strategy often called *everyday low pricing.*[40] Because consumers often use price as an indicator of product quality, however, the brand name of the product and the image of the store become important decision factors in these situations.[41] Another strategy, *everyday fair pricing,* is advocated by retailers which may not offer the lowest price but try to create value for customers through its service and the total buying experience.[42]

A special issue for retailers trying to keep prices low is **shrinkage**, or breakage and theft of merchandise by customers and employees. Who do you think steals more? For the answer see the accompanying Ethics and Social Responsibility Alert.[43]

Off-price retailing is a retail pricing practice that is used by retailers such as T.J. Maxx, Burlington Coat Factory, and Ross Stores. **Off-price retailing** involves selling brand-name merchandise at lower than regular prices. The difference between the off-price retailer and a discount store is that off-price merchandise is bought by the retailer from manufacturers with excess inventory at prices below wholesale prices, while the discounter buys at full wholesale price (but takes less of a markup than do traditional department stores). Because of this difference in the way merchandise is purchased by the retailer, selection at an off-price retailer is unpredictable, and searching for bargains has become a popular activity for many consumers. "It's more like a sport than it is like ordinary shopping," says Christopher Boring of Columbus, Ohio's Retail Planning Associates.[44] Savings to the consumer at off-price retailers are reported as high as 70 percent off the prices of a traditional department store.

There are several variations of off-price retailing. One is the warehouse club. These large stores (more than 100,000 square feet) began as rather stark outlets with no elaborate displays, customer service, or home delivery. They require an annual membership fee (ranging from $30 to $100) for the privilege of shopping there. While a typical Kmart stocks 100,000 items, warehouse clubs carry about 3,500 items and usually stock just one brand of appliance or food product. Service is minimal, and customers usually must pay by cash or check. Customers are attracted by the ultralow prices and surprise deals on selected merchandise, although several of the clubs have recently started to add "ancillary" services such as optical shops and pharmacies to differentiate themselves from competitors. The major warehouse clubs in the United States include Wal-Mart's Sam's Club, BJ's Wholesale Club, and Costco's Warehouse Club. Sales of these off-price retailers have grown faster than the rest of the retail industry and exceeded $62 billion in 2001.[45]

ETHICS AND SOCIAL RESPONSIBILITY ALERT

Who Takes the Five-Finger Discount? You'll Be Surprised

ETHICS

Retailers lose almost 2 percent of their sales to theft each year. To combat the problem many stores attempt to discourage consumers from shoplifting with magnetic detectors, locked cases, and other deterrents. What you may find surprising, though, is that more than 50 percent of the thefts are not made by consumers but by employees! The most popular items to steal are candy from convenience stores, shirts from department stores, batteries from discount stores, and cigarettes from drugstores. When does this happen? The most popular time is between 3 and 6 P.M. Why do you think shoplifting is such a large problem? What recommendations would you make to retailers?

A second variation is the outlet store. Factory outlets, such as Van Heusen Factory Store, Bass Shoe Outlet, and Oneida Factory Store, offer products for 25 to 30 percent off the suggested retail price. Manufacturers use the stores to clear excess merchandise and to reach consumers who focus on value shopping. Retail outlets such as Nordstrom's Rack and Brooks Brothers Outlet Store allow retailers to sell excess merchandise and still maintain an image of offering merchandise at full price in their primary store. The number of factory outlet centers has increased from 183 in 1990 to 312, with sales of $11.2 billion. Some experts expect the next trend to combine the various types of off-price retailers in "value-retail centers."[46]

A third variation of off-price retailing is offered by single-price, or extreme value, retailers such as Family Dollar, Dollar General, and Dollar Tree. These stores average about 6,000 square feet in size and attract customers who want value and a "corner store" environment rather than a large supercenter experience. Some experts predict extraordinary growth of these types of retailers. Dollar General, for example, already has 3,360 stores and plans for 500 new stores in the next year.[47]

Store Location   A second aspect of the retailing mix involves deciding where to locate the store and how many stores to have. Department stores, which started downtown in most cities, have followed customers to the suburbs, and in recent years more stores have been opened in large regional malls. Most stores today are near several others in one of five settings: the central business district, the regional center, the community shopping center, the strip, or the power center.

The **central business district** is the oldest retail setting, the community's downtown area. Until the regional outflow to suburbs, it was the major shopping area, but the suburban population has grown at the expense of the downtown shopping area. Detroit, experiencing a decade of population decline, lost its last major department store in 1982 when Hudson's left the central city.

Regional shopping centers consist of 50 to 150 stores which typically attract customers who live or work within a 5- to 10-mile range. These large shopping areas often contain two or three *anchor stores,* which are well-known national or regional stores such as Sears, Saks Fifth Avenue, and Bloomingdale's. The largest variation of a regional center is the West Edmonton Mall in Alberta, Canada. The shopping center is a conglomerate of 600 stores, six amusement centers, 110 restaurants, and a 355-room Fantasyland hotel.[48]

A more limited approach to retail location is the **community shopping center**, which typically has one primary store (usually a department store branch) and often about 20 to 40 smaller outlets. Generally, these centers serve a population of consumers who are within a 10- to 20-minute drive.

Not every suburban store is located in a shopping mall. Many neighborhoods have clusters of stores, referred to as a **strip location**, to serve people who are within a 5- to 10-minute drive. Gas station, hardware, laundry, grocery, and pharmacy outlets are commonly found in a strip location. Unlike the larger shopping centers, the composition of these stores is usually unplanned. A variation of the strip shopping location is called the **power center**, which is a huge shopping strip with multiple anchor (or national) stores. Power centers are seen as having the convenient location found in many strip centers and the additional power of national stores. These large strips often have two to five anchor stores and often contain a supermarket, which brings the shopper to the power center on a weekly basis.[49]

Several new types of retail locations include carts, kiosks, and wall units. These forms of retailing have been popular in airports and mall common areas because they provide consumers with easy access and rental income for the property owner. Retailers benefit from the relatively low cost compared with a regular store.

Retail Image and Atmosphere   Deciding on the image of a retail outlet is an important retailing mix factor that has been widely recognized and studied since the late 1950s. Pierre Martineau described image as "the way in which the store is defined in the shopper's mind," partly by its functional qualities and partly by an aura of psychological attributes.[50] In this definition, *functional* refers to mix elements such as price ranges, store layouts, and breadth and depth of merchandise lines. The psychological attributes are the intangibles such as a sense of belonging, excitement, style, or warmth. Image has been found to include impressions of the corporation that operates the store, the category or type of store, the product categories in the store, the brands in each category, merchandise and service quality, and the marketing activities of the store.[51]

Closely related to the concept of image is the store's atmosphere or ambiance. Many retailers believe that sales are affected by layout, color, lighting, and music in the store as well as by how crowded it is. In addition, the physical surroundings that influence customers may affect the store's employees.[52] In creating the right image and atmosphere, a retail store tries to identify its target audience and what the target audience seeks from the buying experience so the store will fortify the beliefs and the emotional reactions buyers are seeking.[53] Sears, for example, is attempting to shift from its appliance and tool image with advertising that speaks to all members of a family. The new "Sears. Where else?" campaign emphasizes a broad range of brand-name merchandise and one-stop shopping.[54]

Concept Check

1. What are the two dimensions of the retail positioning matrix?

2. How does original markup differ from maintained markup?

3. A huge shopping strip with multiple anchor stores is a _____ center.

THE CHANGING NATURE OF RETAILING

Retailing is the most dynamic aspect of a channel of distribution. Stores such as factory outlets show that new retailers are always entering the market, searching for a new position that will attract customers. The reason for this continual change is explained by two concepts: the wheel of retailing and the retail life cycle.

The Wheel of Retailing

The **wheel of retailing** describes how new forms of retail outlets enter the market.[55] Usually they enter as low-status, low-margin stores such as a drive-in

FIGURE 17–9
The wheel of retailing

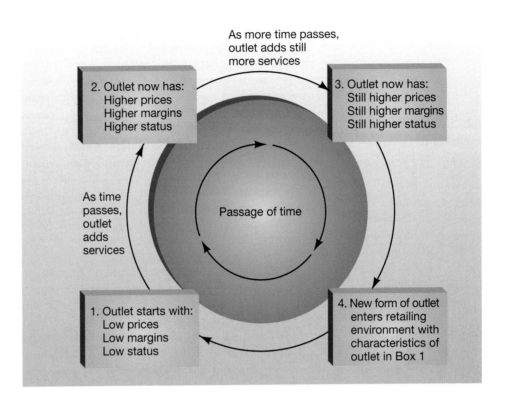

hamburger stand with no indoor seating and a limited menu (Figure 17–9, box 1). Gradually these outlets add fixtures and more embellishments to their stores (in-store seating, plants, and chicken sandwiches as well as hamburgers) to increase the attractiveness for customers. With these additions, prices and status rise (box 2). As time passes, these outlets add still more services and their prices and status increase even further (box 3). These retail outlets now face some new form of retail outlet that again appears as a low-status, low-margin operator (box 4), and the wheel of retailing turns as the cycle starts to repeat itself.

In the 1950s, McDonald's and Burger King had very limited menus of hamburgers and french fries. Most stores had no inside seating for customers. Over time, the wheel of retailing for fast-food restaurants has turned. These chains have changed by altering their stores and expanding their menus. Today, McDonald's is testing new products such as its Sourdough Supreme Burgers and Strawberry Cheesecake in Los Angeles, new formats such as its new gourmet coffee-and-dessert outlet called McCafe in Montreal, and new decor options such as the 50s-style store opened in Chicago. The changes are leaving room for new forms of outlets such as Checkers Drive-In Restaurants. The chain opened fast-food stores that offered only the basics—burgers, fries, and cola, a drive-through window, and no inside seating—and now has more than 845 stores.[56] The wheel is turning for other outlets too—Boston Market has added turkey, meat loaf, and ham to its original menu of chicken. For still others, the wheel has come full circle. Taco Bell is now opening small, limited-offering outlets in gas stations, discount stores, or "wherever a burrito and a mouth might possibly intersect."[57]

Discount stores were a major new retailing form in the 1960s and priced their products below those of department stores. As prices in discount stores rose, in the 1980s they found themselves overpriced compared with a new form of retail outlet—the warehouse retailer. Today, off-price retailers and factory outlets are offering prices even lower than warehouses!

The Retail Life Cycle

The process of growth and decline that retail outlets, like products, experience is described by the **retail life cycle**.[58] Figure 17–10 shows the retail life cycle and the position of various current forms of retail outlets on it. Early growth is the stage of emergence of a retail outlet, with a sharp departure from existing competition. Market share rises gradually, although profits may be low because of startup costs. In the next stage, accelerated development, both market share and profit achieve their greatest growth rates. Usually multiple outlets are established as companies focus on the distribution element of the retailing mix. In this stage some later competitors may enter. Wendy's, for example, appeared on the hamburger chain scene almost 20 years after McDonald's had begun operation. The key goal for the retailer in this stage is to establish a dominant position in the fight for market share.

The battle for market share is usually fought before the maturity phase, and some competitors drop out of the market. In the wars among hamburger chains, Jack In The Box, Gino Marchetti's, and Burger Chef used to be more dominant outlets. New retail forms enter in the maturity phase, stores try to maintain their market share, and price discounting occurs. For example, when McDonald's introduced its Extra Value Meal, a discounted package of burger, fries, and drink, Wendy's followed with a kid's Value Menu.

The challenge facing retailers is to delay entering the decline stage in which market share and profit fall rapidly. Specialty apparel retailers, such as the Gap, Limited, Benetton, and Ann Taylor, have noticed a decline in market share after a decade of growth. To prevent further decline, these retailers will need to find ways of discouraging their customers from moving to low-margin, mass-volume outlets or high-price, high-service boutiques.[59]

FIGURE 17–10
The retail life cycle

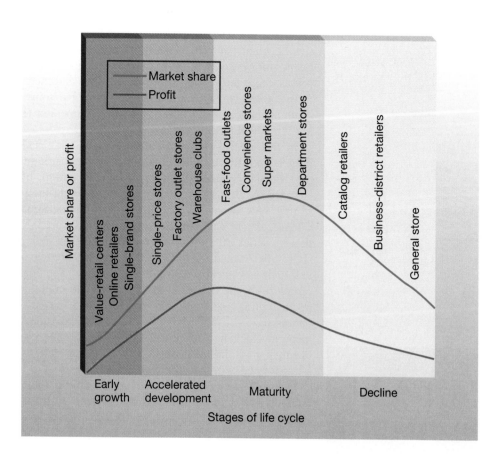

FUTURE CHANGES IN RETAILING

Three exciting trends in retailing—the growth of multi-channel retailing, the increasing impact of technology, the dramatic changes in the way we shop—are likely to lead to many changes for retailers and consumers in the future.

Multichannel Retailing

The retailing formats described previously in this chapter represent an exciting menu of choices for creating customer value in the marketplace. Each format allows retailers to offer unique benefits and meet particular needs of various customer groups. While each format has many successful applications, retailers in the future are likely to combine many of the formats to offer a broader spectrum of benefits and experiences. These **multichannel retailers** will utilize and integrate a combination of traditional store formats and nonstore formats such as catalogs, television, and online retailing. Barnes and Noble, for example, created Barnesandnoble.com to compete with Amazon.com. Similarly, Office Depot has integrated its store, catalog, and Internet operations.

Integrated channels can make shopping simpler and more convenient. A consumer can research choices online or in a catalog and then make a purchase online, over the telephone, or at the closest store. In addition, the use of multiple channels allows retailers to reach a broader profile of customers. While online retailing may cannibalize catalog business to some degree, a Web transaction costs about half as much to process as a catalog order. Multichannel retailers also benefit from the synergy of sharing information among the different channel operations. Online retailers, for example, have recognized that the Internet is more of a transactional medium than a relationship-building medium and are working to find ways to complement traditional customer interactions.[60]

The Impact of Technology

One of the most significant changes retailers may face in the future is the way consumers pay for purchases. Today, one of the most convenient and popular methods of payment is a credit card. Credit cards, however, are likely to be replaced by smart cards, which look the same as credit cards but store information on computer chips instead of magnetic strips. They will hold information about bank accounts and amounts of available funds, and they will contain customer purchase information such as airline seat preferences and clothing sizes. The idea is already popular in Europe and Asia where more than 33 million smart cards are in use. Benefits for consumers include faster service—a smart card transaction is much faster than having a check or credit card approved—and they are a convenient method of paying for small-dollar-amount transactions. Merchants will also benefit because they will save the 5 to 7 percent usually paid to credit card companies or lost in handling. Currently the absence of processing equipment is slowing the use of smart cards in the United States. Investments such as Target's move to smart cards, described earlier in the chapter, are likely to help, however.

Changing Shopping Behavior

In recent years consumers have become precision shoppers. The number of stores consumers visit and the number of times they visit those stores each month is declining. Shoppers are demanding convenient hours and locations, outstanding service, and reasonable prices from retailers. As a result, familiar forms of retailers such as supermarkets, travel agencies, and car dealerships are likely to change or be replaced by new types of retailers. Byerly's, a supermarket chain expanding from Minneapolis to Chicago, offers rushed shoppers a wide variety of premium ready-to-eat entrees, in a carpeted store. TravelFest Superstores in Austin, Texas, offer one-stop shopping for travelers. Visa applications, traveler's checks, luggage, newspapers from around the world, and traditional tickets and reservations are available in the stores from 9 A.M. to 11 P.M. Even car dealers are changing. CarMax offers no-haggle pricing, an inventory of 500 to 1,000 cars, written offers on trade-in vehicles, guarantees and extended warranties, financing, and one-hour transactions if a car is purchased.

Another response to the changes in consumers' preferences is a form of co-branding in which two retailers share a location. For example, McDonald's has developed partnerships with Wal-Mart, Home Depot, Amoco, and Chevron that will lead to thousands of satellite outlets in retail stores and gas stations. Starbucks Coffee Co. has opened cafes in more than 100 Barnes and Noble bookstores. And KFC, which attracts a strong dinner crowd, now also includes Taco Bell, which is stronger in the lunch market, at 800 of its stores. Retailers hope that consumers will appreciate the convenience of the new locations.[61]

Concept Check

1. According to the wheel of retailing, when a new retail form appears, how would you characterize its image?

2. Market share is usually fought out before the _____ stage of the retail life cycle.

3. What is a smart card?

SUMMARY

1 Retailing provides customer value in the form of various utilities: time, place, possession, and form. Economically, retailing is important in terms of the people employed and money exchanged in retail sales.

2 Retailing outlets can be classified along several dimensions: the form of ownership, level of service, or merchandise line.

3 There are several forms of ownership: independent, chain, retailer-sponsored cooperative, wholesaler-sponsored chain or franchise.

4 Stores vary in the level of service they provide. Three levels are self-service, limited service, or full service.

5 Retail outlets vary in terms of the breadth and depth of their merchandise lines. Breadth refers to the number of different items carried, and depth refers to the assortment of each item offered.

6 Nonstore retailing includes automatic vending, direct mail and catalogs, television home shopping, online retailing, telemarketing, and direct selling.

7 A retail store positions itself on two dimensions: breadth of product line and value added, which includes elements such as location, product reliability, and prestige.

8 Retailing strategy is based on the retailing mix, consisting of goods and services, physical distribution, and communication tactics.

9 In retail pricing, retailers must decide on the markup, markdown, and timing for the markdown. Off-price retailers offer brand-name merchandise at lower than regular prices. This retailing form includes warehouse clubs, outlet stores, and single-price retailers.

10 Retail store location is an important retail mix decision. The common alternatives are the central business district, a regional shopping center, a community shopping center, or a strip location. A variation of the strip location is the power center, which is a strip location with multiple national anchor stores and a supermarket.

11 Retail image and atmosphere help retailers create the appropriate buying experience for their target market.

12 New retailing forms are explained by the wheel of retailing. Stores enter as low-status, low-margin outlets. Over time, they add services and raise margins, which allows a new form of low-status, low-margin retailing outlet to enter.

13 Like products, retail outlets have a life cycle consisting of four stages: early growth, accelerated development, maturity, and decline.

14 Multichannel retailers utilize and integrate a combination of store and nonstore formats. Technology will change the way consumers pay for purchases in the future. Smart cards may lead to a cashless society.

KEY TERMS AND CONCEPTS

breadth of product line p. 451
central business district p. 461
community shopping center p. 461
depth of product line p. 451
form of ownership p. 449
hypermarket p. 452
intertype competition p. 452
level of service p. 449
merchandise line p. 449
multichannel retailers p. 465
off-price retailing p. 460

power center p. 462
regional shopping centers p. 461
retail life cycle p. 464
retail positioning matrix p. 458
retailing p. 446
retailing mix p. 459
scrambled merchandising p. 452
shrinkage p. 460
strip location p. 461
telemarketing p. 456
wheel of retailing p. 462

APPLYING MARKETING CONCEPTS AND PERSPECTIVES

1   Discuss the impact of the growing number of dual-income households on (*a*) nonstore retailing and (*b*) the retail mix.

2   How does value added affect a store's competitive position?

3   In retail pricing, retailers often have a maintained markup. Explain how this maintained markup differs from original markup and why it is so important.

4   What are the similarities and differences between the product and retail life cycles?

5   How would you classify Wal-Mart in terms of its position on the wheel of retailing versus that of an off-price retailer?

6   Develop a chart to highlight the role of each of the three main elements of the retailing mix across the four stages of the retail life cycle.

7   In Figure 17–7 Just for Feet was placed on the retail positioning matrix. What strategies should Just for Feet follow to move itself into the same position as Tiffany?

8   Breadth and depth are two important components in distinguishing among types of retailers. Discuss the breadth and depth implications of the following retailers discussed in this chapter: (*a*) Levi Strauss, (*b*) Wal-Mart, (*c*) L. L. Bean, and (*d*) Circuit City.

9   According to the wheel of retailing and the retail life cycle, what will happen to factory outlet stores?

10   The text discusses the development of online retailing in the United States. How does the development of this retailing form agree with the implications of the retail life cycle?

INTERNET EXERCISE

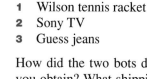

For many consumers comparison shopping is not appealing because of the inconvenience of traveling to multiple locations. Even on the Internet, finding and searching multiple websites can be tedious. One solution is a form of software called an "intelligent agent" or "bot" (derived from robot) which automatically searches for the best price. Try each of the following shopping bots—www.mysimon.com and www.dealtime.com—to find the best price for one of the following products:

1   Wilson tennis racket
2   Sony TV
3   Guess jeans

How did the two bots differ? What range of prices did you obtain? What shipping and handling charges would apply to each purchase? Why are different recommendation made by the agents?

VIDEO CASE 17–1   Mall of America: Shopping . . . and a Whole Lot More!

"Build it and they will come" not only worked in the movie *Field of Dreams* but applies—big time—to Mall of America!

Located in a suburb of Minneapolis, Mall of America (www.mallofamerica.com) is the largest completely enclosed retail and family-entertainment complex in the United States. "We're more than a mall, we're a destination," explains Maureen Cahill, an executive at Mall of America. More than 100,000 people each day—40 million visitors each year—visit the one-stop complex offering retail shopping, guest services, convenience, a huge variety of entertainment, and fun for all! "Guest services" include everything from high school and college classrooms to a doctor's office and wedding chapel.

THE CONCEPT AND CHALLENGE

The idea for Mall of America came from the West Edmonton Mall in Alberta, Canada. The Ghermezian Brothers, who developed that mall, sought to create a unique mall that would not only attract local families, but tourists from the Upper Midwest, the rest of the nation, and even abroad.

The two challenges for Mall of America: How can it (1) attract and keep the large number of retail establishments needed to (2) continue to attract even more millions of visitors than today? A big part of the answer is in Mall of America's positioning—"There is a place for fun in your life!"

THE STAGGERING SIZE AND OFFERINGS

Opened August 1992 amid tremendous worldwide publicity, Mall of America faced skeptics, who had their doubts because of its size, its unique retail-entertainment mix, and the nationwide recession. Despite these concerns, it opened with over 80 percent of its space leased and attracted more than one million visitors its first week.

Mall of America is 4.2 million square feet, the equivalent of 88 football fields. This makes it three to four times the size of most other regional malls. It includes four anchor-department stores—Nordstrom's, Macy's, Bloomingdale's, and Sears. It also includes over 520 specialty stores from Brooks Brothers and Sharper Image to Marshall's and DSW Shoe Warehouse. Approximately 36 percent of Mall of America's space is devoted to anchors with approximately 64 percent in specialty stores. This makes the space allocation the reverse of most regional malls.

The retail-entertainment mix of Mall of America is incredibly diverse. For example, there are over 100 apparel and accessory stores, 17 jewelry stores, and 24 shoe stores. Some retailers have more than one store. Two food courts with 27 restaurants plus over 30 other restaurants scattered throughout the building meet most food preferences of visitors. Another surprise: Mall of America is home to many "concept stores," where retailers introduce a new type of store or design. In addition, it has

an entrepreneurial program for people with an innovative retail idea and limited resources. They can open up a kiosk, wall unit, or small store for a specified time period or as a temporary seasonal tenant.

Unique features of Mall of America include:

- Camp Snoopy, a 7-acre theme park with over 50 attractions and rides that include a roller coaster, Ferris wheel, and games in a glass-enclosed, sky-lighted area with over 400 trees.
- Underwater World, where visitors are surrounded by tropical sharks, stingrays, and sea turtles; can adventure among fish native to the north woods; and can discover what lurks at the bottom of the Mississippi River.
- The Upper East Side, on the fourth floor with its bars, nightclubs, game rooms, 14-screen theater, comedy club, and state-of-the-art bowling alley.
- The LEGO Land Imagination Center, a 6,000 square-foot showplace with over 30 full-sized models that include dinosaurs and astronauts.
- Cereal World, a new theme park created by General Mills to let children actually see cereal "come to life" and enable them as well as adults to learn more about cereal grains, products, and health.

As a host to corporate events and private parties, Mall of America has a rotunda that opens to all four floors that facilitates presentations, demonstrations, and exhibits. Organizations like Pepsi, Visa-USA, and the U.S. Postal Service have used the facilities to gain shopper awareness. Mall of America is a rectangle with the anchor department stores at the corners and Camp Snoopy in the sky-lighted central area, making it easy for shoppers to understand and navigate. It has 12,750 free parking ramp spaces on-site with another 7,000 spaces nearby during peak times.

THE MARKETS

The Minneapolis-St. Paul metropolitan area is a market with 3 million people. A total of 28 million people live within 400 miles or a day's drive of Mall of America. A survey of its shoppers showed that 43 percent of the shoppers come from outside Minnesota and account for 56 percent of the sales revenues. Located three miles from the 13th-busiest international airport in the world, Mall of America provides a shuttle bus from the airport every half hour. It will also have light rail service from the airport and downtown Minneapolis in a few years.

About 6 percent of visitors come from outside the United States. Some come just to see and experience Mall of America while others take advantage of the savings available on goods (Japan) or taxes (Canada and states with sales taxes on clothing). Both situations have changed with the recession and arrival of discounters in Japan and the decline of the Canadian dollar.

THE FUTURE: FACING THE CHALLENGES

Where does Mall of America head in the future?

"We just did a brand study and found that Mall of America is one of the most recognized brands in the world," says Maureen Cahill. "They might not know where we are sometimes, but they've heard of Mall of America and they know they want to come."

"What we've learned since 1992 is to keep the Mall of America fresh and exciting," she explains. "We're constantly looking at what attracts people and adding to that. We're adding new stores, new attractions, and new events. We hold over 350 events a year and with everyone from Garth Brooks to Sarah Ferguson to *NSYNC."

Mall of America recently announced a plan for a 5.7 million square foot expansion, the area of another 117 football fields, connected by a pedestrian skyway to the present building. "The second phase will not be a duplicate of what we have," says Cahill. "We have plans for at least three hotels, a performing arts center, a business office complex, an art or history museum, and possibly even a television broadcast facility."

Questions

1 Why has Mall of America been such a marketing success so far?

2 What (*a*) retail and (*b*) consumer trends have occurred since Mall of America was opened in 1992 that it should consider when making future plans?

3 (*a*) What criteria should Mall of America use in adding new facilities to its complex? (*b*) Evaluate (1) retail stores, (2) entertainment offerings and (3) hotels on these criteria.

4 What specific marketing actions would you propose that Mall of America managers take to ensure its continuing success in attracting visitors (*a*) from the local metropolitan area and (*b*) from outside of it?

CHAPTER 18

INTEGRATED MARKETING COMMUNICATIONS AND DIRECT MARKETING

AFTER READING THIS CHAPTER YOU SHOULD BE ABLE TO:

- Explain the communication process and its elements.

- Understand the promotional mix and the uniqueness of each component.

- Select the promotional approach appropriate to a product's life-cycle stage and characteristics.

- Differentiate between the advantages of push and pull strategies.

- Appreciate the value of an integrated marketing communications approach.

- Understand the value of direct marketing for consumers and sellers.

INTEGRATED MARKETING COMMUNICATIONS MAKE MAGIC AT DISNEY!

How are you at remembering birthdays? Well even if you are usually forgetful, Disney is using its expertise at integrating many forms of communication to help you remember—and celebrate—the 100th anniversary of the company's founder, Walt Disney. The plan calls for a $250 million budget during a 15-month campaign, which includes advertising, partnerships with other companies, direct marketing, Internet promotions, and many other ways of getting its message to Disney fans.

The TV advertising includes four versions targeted at families, children, parents, and grandparents. The partnerships include agreements with McDonald's, Coca-Cola, American Express, Kellogg, and Hallmark Cards to run joint promotions. Direct marketing activities include special offers mailed to many of the 31 million households in Disney's database. The Web page, Disney-World.com, provides information about the events associated with the celebration, and allows consumers to make reservations and travel plans. The campaign also includes an anthem—"Then the dream began to grow and come alive . . . Touching every one of us, lighting up the skies"—and an in-park promotion called "100 Years of Magic!"

Disney applies a similar, integrated approach to the marketing of all its products, services, and events. Other promotional activities include advertising on Radio Disney, sponsorship of documentaries on the ABC Television network, Internet-linked kiosks to allow potential customers to check for location and availability of products at its stores, and contests and giveaways. Another component of Disney's promotion plan is a membership program called Disney Club which currently has 300,000 members who pay $39.95 annually to receive unique merchandise offers, VIP treatment at special events, and discounts. More than 4,000 members of the club, for example, were invited to preview the new California Adventure theme park at half-price before it opened to the public. To promote the release of its movie *Atlantis: The Lost Empire,* Disney gave away 13 million copies of a CD-based interactive game. Disney stores use in-store promotion which complements the online offering (at Disneystore.com) and the Disney catalogs.

Disney also uses "cross-media" deals, co-branding agreements, and joint ventures. A deal with Toys "Я" Us, for example, includes a $30 million multimedia promotion plan for magazine, newspaper, movie, radio, and television promotion. Ads will appear on Disney Kids Network and Toon Disney cable network and in a newspaper supplement reaching 50 million homes. The co-branding agreements include Minute Maid's 18-variety line of Disney Xtreme! Coolers and Kellogg's lines of Disney-based cereals, toaster pastries, and waffles. Cereals tied to the movie *Monsters, Inc.,* for example, screamed when opened! And Disney used a joint venture with Oriental Land to create and promote its newest theme park, the marine-themed DisneySea in Tokyo.[1]

All of the many types of promotion used by Disney are becoming an important part of marketing. Applications of the techniques demonstrate the importance of creativity in communicating with potential customers. In addition, to ensure that a consistent message is delivered through all promotional activities, a process that integrates marketing communications is a necessity.

Promotion represents the fourth element in the marketing mix. The promotional element comprises a mix of tools available for the marketer called the *promotional mix,* which consists of advertising, personal selling, sales promotion, public relations, and direct marketing. All of these elements can be used to (1) inform prospective buyers about the benefits of the product, (2) persuade them to try it, and (3) remind them later about the benefits they enjoyed by using the product. This chapter first gives an overview of the communication process and the promotional elements used in marketing and then discusses direct marketing. Chapter 19 covers advertising, sales promotion, and public relations, and Chapter 20 discusses personal selling.

THE COMMUNICATION PROCESS

Communication is the process of conveying a message to others and requires six elements: a source, a message, a channel of communication, a receiver, and the processes of encoding and decoding[2] (Figure 18–1). The **source** may be a company or person who has information to convey. The information sent by a source, such as a description of a new cellular telephone, forms the **message**. The message is conveyed by means of a **channel of communication** such as a salesperson, advertising media, or public relations tools. Consumers who read, hear, or see the message are the **receivers**.

Encoding and Decoding

Encoding and decoding are essential to communication. **Encoding** is the process of having the sender transform an abstract idea into a set of symbols. **Decoding** is the reverse, or the process of having the receiver take a set of symbols, the message, and transform them back to an abstract idea. Look at the accompanying automobile advertisement: Who is the source, and what is the message?

Decoding is performed by the receivers according to their own frame of reference: their attitudes, values, and beliefs.[3] In the ad on the next page, Mercedes-Benz is the source and the message is this advertisement, which appeared in *Wired* magazine (the channel). How would you interpret (decode) this advertisement? The

FIGURE 18–1
The communication process

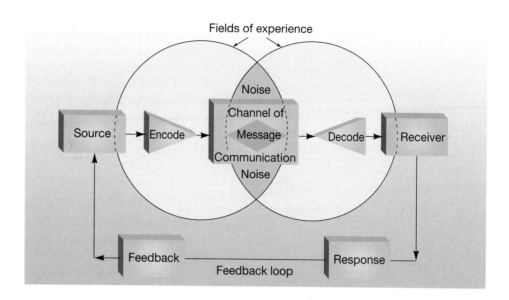

picture and text in the advertisement show that the source's intention is to generate interest in a vehicle with "the big engine that could"—a statement the source believes will appeal to the readers of the magazine.

The process of communication is not always a successful one. Errors in communication can happen in several ways. The source may not adequately transform the abstract idea into an effective set of symbols, a properly encoded message may be sent through the wrong channel and never make it to the receiver, the receiver may not properly transform the set of symbols into the correct abstract idea, or finally, feedback may be so delayed or distorted that it is of no use to the sender. Although communication appears easy to perform, truly effective communication can be very difficult.

A source and a message.

Mercedes-Benz
www.mbusa.com

For the message to be communicated effectively, the sender and receiver must have a mutually shared **field of experience**—similar understanding and knowledge. Figure 18–1 shows two circles representing the fields of experience of the sender and receiver, which overlap in the message. Some of the better-known communication problems have occurred when U.S. companies have taken their messages to cultures with different fields of experience. Many misinterpretations are merely the result of bad translations. For example, KFC made a mistake when its "finger-lickin' good" slogan was translated into Mandarin Chinese as "eat your fingers off!"[4]

Feedback

Figure 18–1 shows a line labeled *feedback loop,* which consists of a response and feedback. A **response** is the impact the message had on the receiver's knowledge, attitudes, or behaviors. **Feedback** is the sender's interpretation of the response and indicates whether the message was decoded and understood as intended. Chapter 19 reviews approaches called *pretesting* that ensure that messages are decoded properly.

Noise

Noise includes extraneous factors that can work against effective communication by distorting a message or the feedback received (Figure 18–1). Noise can be a simple error, such as a printing mistake that affects the meaning of a newspaper advertisement, or using words or pictures that fail to communicate the message clearly. Noise can also occur when a salesperson's message is misunderstood by a prospective buyer, such as when a salesperson's accent, use of slang terms, or communication style make hearing and understanding the message difficult.

Concept Check

1. What are the six elements required for communication to occur?

2. A difficulty for U.S. companies advertising in international markets is that the audience does not share the same _____.

3. A misprint in a newspaper ad is an example of _____.

THE PROMOTIONAL ELEMENTS

To communicate with consumers, a company can use one or more of five promotional alternatives: advertising, personal selling, sales promotion, public relations, and direct marketing. Figure 18–2 summarizes the distinctions among these five elements. Three of these elements—advertising, sales promotion, and public relations—are often said to use *mass selling* because they are used with groups of prospective buyers. In contrast, personal selling uses *customized interaction* between a seller and a prospective buyer. Personal selling activities include face-to-face, telephone, and interactive electronic communication. Direct marketing also uses messages customized for specific customers.

Advertising

Advertising is any paid form of nonpersonal communication about an organization, good, service, or idea by an identified sponsor. The *paid* aspect of this definition is important because the space for the advertising message normally must be bought. An occasional exception is the public service announcement, where the

PROMOTIONAL ELEMENT	MASS VERSUS CUSTOMIZED	PAYMENT	STRENGTHS	WEAKNESSES
Advertising	Mass	Fees paid for space or time	• Efficient means for reaching large numbers of people	• High absolute costs • Difficult to receive good feedback
Personal selling	Customized	Fees paid to salespeople as either salaries or commissions	• Immediate feedback • Very persuasive • Can select audience • Can give complex information	• Extremely expensive per exposure • Messages may differ between salespeople
Public relations	Mass	No direct payment to media	• Often most credible source in the consumer's mind	• Difficult to get media cooperation
Sales promotion	Mass	Wide range of fees paid, depending on promotion selected	• Effective at changing behavior in short run • Very flexible	• Easily abused • Can lead to promotion wars • Easily duplicated
Direct marketing	Customized	Cost of communication through mail, telephone, or computer	• Messages can be prepared quickly • Facilitates relationship with customer	• Declining customer response • Database management is expensive

FIGURE 18–2
The promotional mix

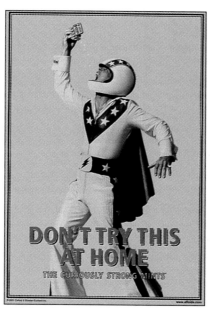

advertising time or space is donated. A full-page, four-color ad in *Time* magazine, for example, costs $192,000. The *nonpersonal* component of advertising is also important. Advertising involves mass media (such as TV, radio, and magazines), which are nonpersonal and do not have an immediate feedback loop as does personal selling. So before the message is sent, marketing research plays a valuable role; for example, it determines that the target market will actually see the medium chosen, and that the message will be understood.

There are several advantages to a firm using advertising in its promotional mix. It can be attention-getting—as with this Altoids ad—and also can communicate specific product benefits to prospective buyers. By paying for the advertising space, a company can control *what* it wants to say and, to some extent, to *whom* the message is sent. If an electronics company wants college students to receive its message about CD players, advertising space is purchased in a college campus newspaper. Advertising also allows the company to decide *when* to send its message (which includes how often). The nonpersonal aspect of advertising also has its advantages. Once the message is created, the same message is sent to all receivers in a market segment. If the message is properly pretested, the company can trust that the same message will be decoded by all receivers in the market segment.

Advertising has some disadvantages. As shown in Figure 18–2 and discussed in depth in Chapter 19, the costs to produce and place a message are significant, and the lack of direct feedback makes it difficult to know how well the message was received.

Personal Selling

The second major promotional alternative is **personal selling**, defined as the two-way flow of communication between a buyer and seller, designed to influence a person's or group's purchase decision. Unlike advertising, personal selling is usually face-to-face communication between the sender and receiver (although telephone and electronic sales are growing). Why do companies use personal selling?

There are important advantages to personal selling, as summarized in Figure 18–2. A salesperson can control to *whom* the presentation is made. Although some control is available in advertising by choosing the medium, some people may read the college newspaper, for example, who are not in the target audience for CD players. For the CD-player manufacturer, those readers outside the target audience are *wasted coverage*. Wasted coverage can be reduced with personal selling. The personal component of selling has another advantage over advertising in that the seller can see or hear the potential buyer's reaction to the message. If the feedback is unfavorable, the salesperson can modify the message.

The flexibility of personal selling can also be a disadvantage. Different salespeople can change the message so that no consistent communication is given to all customers. The high cost of personal selling is probably its major disadvantage. On a cost-per-contact basis, it is generally the most expensive of the five promotional elements.

Public Relations

Public relations is a form of communication management that seeks to influence the feelings, opinions, or beliefs held by customers, prospective customers, stockholders, suppliers, employees, and other publics about a company and its products or services.[5] Many tools such as special events, lobbying efforts, annual reports, and image management may be used by a public relations department, although publicity often plays the most important role. **Publicity** is a nonpersonal, indirectly paid presentation of an organization, good, or service. It can take the form of a news story, editorial, or product announcement. A difference between publicity and both advertising and personal selling is the "indirectly paid" dimension. With publicity a company does not pay for space in a mass medium (such as television or radio) but attempts to get the medium to run a favorable story on the company. In this sense there is an indirect payment for publicity in that a company must support a public relations staff.

An advantage of publicity is credibility. When you read a favorable story about a company's product (such as a glowing restaurant review), there is a tendency to believe it. Travelers throughout the world have relied on Arthur Frommer's guides such as *Ireland from $60 a Day*. These books outline out-of-the-way, inexpensive restaurants, hotels, inns, and bed-and-breakfast rooms, giving invaluable publicity to these establishments. Such businesses do not (nor can they) buy a mention in the guide, which in recent years has sold millions of copies.

The disadvantages of publicity relate to the lack of the user's control over it. A company can invite a news team to preview its innovative exercise equipment and hope for a favorable mention on the 6 P.M. newscasts. But without buying advertising time, there is no guarantee of any mention of the new equipment or that it will

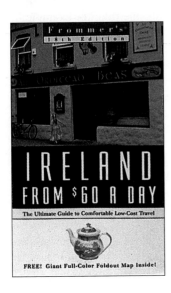

be aired when the target audience is watching. The company representative who calls the station and asks for a replay of the story may be told, "Sorry, it's only news once." With publicity there is little control over what is said, to whom, or when. As a result, publicity is rarely the main component of a promotional campaign.

Sales Promotion

A fourth promotional element is **sales promotion**, a short-term inducement of value offered to arouse interest in buying a good or service. Used in conjunction with advertising or personal selling, sales promotions are offered to intermediaries as well as to ultimate consumers. Coupons, rebates, samples, and sweepstakes are just a few examples of sales promotions discussed later in this chapter.

The advantage of sales promotion is that the short-term nature of these programs (such as a coupon or sweepstakes with an expiration date) often stimulates sales for their duration. Offering value to the consumer in terms of a cents-off coupon or rebate may increase store traffic from consumers who are not store-loyal.[6]

Sales promotions cannot be the sole basis for a campaign because gains are often temporary and sales drop off when the deal ends.[7] Advertising support is needed to convert the customer who tried the product because of a sales promotion into a long-term buyer.[8] If sales promotions are conducted continuously, they lose their effectiveness. Customers begin to delay purchase until a coupon is offered, or they question the product's value. Some aspects of sales promotions also are regulated by the federal government. These issues are reviewed in detail later in Chapter 19.

Direct Marketing

Another promotional alternative, **direct marketing**, uses direct communication with consumers to generate a response in the form of an order, a request for further information, or a visit to a retail outlet.[9] The communication can take many forms including face-to-face selling, direct mail, catalogs, telephone solicitations, direct response advertising (on television and radio and in print), and online marketing. Like personal selling, direct marketing often consists of interactive communication. It also has the advantage of being customized to match the needs of specific target markets. Messages can be developed and adapted quickly to facilitate one-to-one relationships with customers.

While direct marketing has been one of the fastest growing forms of promotion, it has several disadvantages. First, most forms of direct marketing require a comprehensive and up-to-date database with information about the target market. Developing and maintaining the database can be expensive and time-consuming. In addition, growing concern about privacy has led to a decline in response rates among some customer groups. Companies with successful direct marketing programs are sensitive to these issues and often use a combination of direct marketing alternatives together, or direct marketing combined with other promotional tools, to increase value for customers.

Concept Check

1. Explain the difference between advertising and publicity when both appear on television.

2. Which promotional element should be offered only on a short-term basis?

3. Cost per contact is high with the _____ element of the promotional mix.

INTEGRATED MARKETING COMMUNICATIONS—
DEVELOPING THE PROMOTIONAL MIX

A firm's **promotional mix** is the combination of one or more of the promotional elements it chooses to use. In putting together the promotional mix, a marketer must consider several issues. First, the balance of the elements must be determined. Should advertising be emphasized more than personal selling? Should a promotional rebate be offered? Would public relations activities be effective? Several factors affect such decisions: the target audience for the promotion,[10] the stage of the product's life cycle, characteristics of the product, decision stage of the buyer, and even the channel of distribution. Second, because the various promotional elements are often the responsibility of different departments, coordinating a consistent promotional effort is necessary. A promotional planning process designed to ensure integrated marketing communications can facilitate this goal.

The Target Audience

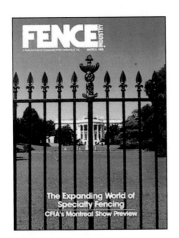

Promotional programs are directed to the ultimate consumer, to an intermediary (retailer, wholesaler, or industrial distributor), or to both. Promotional programs directed to buyers of consumer products often use mass media because the number of potential buyers is large. Personal selling is used at the place of purchase, generally the retail store. Direct marketing may be used to encourage first-time or repeat purchases. Combinations of many media alternatives are a necessity for some target audiences today. The Marketing NewsNet describes how Generation Y consumers give media only partial attention but can be reached through integrated programs.[11]

Advertising directed to business buyers is used selectively in trade publications, such as *Fence* magazine for buyers of fencing material. Because business buyers often have specialized needs or technical questions, personal selling is particularly important. The salesperson can provide information and the necessary support after sales.

Intermediaries are often the focus of promotional efforts. As with business buyers, personal selling is the major promotional ingredient. The salespeople assist intermediaries in making a profit by coordinating promotional campaigns sponsored by the manufacturer and by providing marketing advice and expertise. Intermediaries' questions often pertain to the allowed markup, merchandising support, and return policies.

The Product Life Cycle

All products have a product life cycle (see Chapter 11), and the composition of the promotional mix changes over the four life-cycle stages, as shown for Purina Dog Chow in Figure 18–3.

Introduction Stage Informing consumers in an effort to increase their level of awareness is the primary promotional objective in the introduction stage of the product life cycle. In general, all the promotional mix elements are used at this time, although the use of specific mix elements during any stage depends on the product and situation. News releases about Purina's new nutritional product are sent to veterinary magazines, trial samples are sent to registered dog owners, advertisements are placed in *Dog World* magazine, and the salesforce begins to approach supermarkets to get orders. Advertising is particularly important as a means of reaching as many people as possible to build up awareness and interest. Publicity may even begin slightly before the product is commercially available.

MARKETING NEWSNET

Communicating with Gen Y . . . 29.8 Hours per Day!

CROSS FUNCTIONAL

Recent research indicates that consumers have created 29.8-hour days by using more than one communication medium at the same time—a behavior often called "multi-tasking." Generation Y seems to be particularly adept at this new phenomenon. For example, it would not be unusual for a college freshman to log onto the Internet while listening to the radio and checking out Web addresses in a magazine! One reason is that media is pervasive—the average student may be exposed to 5,000 messages each day—but another reason is the desire to be informed and to "keep in touch." As a result, this group of consumers probably doesn't give its full attention to any single message. Instead it uses continuous partial attention to scan the media.

Marketers can still communicate with Gen Y by utilizing a variety of promotional tools—from advertising to packaging to word-of-mouth communication—with an integrated message. Which media work particularly well with Gen Y? The most popular television channel is MTV. The most popular magazines are *Sports Illustrated* and *Seventeen*.

Favorite websites include anything with content related to their interests: celebrities, music, sports, and videogames. Another tactic growing in popularity is viral, or *"buzz" marketing.* Volkswagen of America, for example, holds contests on college campuses to see how many people can fit into a Volkswagen Beetle (the current record is 26). The participants and the observers end up experiencing and talking about the product for at least part of their 29.8-hour day!

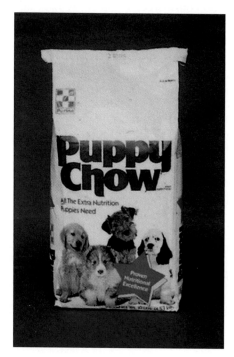

Purina Dog Chow: a product in the maturity stage of its life cycle.

Growth Stage   The primary promotional objective of the growth stage is to persuade the consumer to buy the product—Purina Dog Chow—rather than substitutes, so the marketing manager seeks to gain brand preference and solidify distribution. Sales promotion assumes less importance in this stage, and publicity is not a factor because it depends on novelty of the product. The primary promotional element is advertising, which stresses brand differences. Personal selling is used to solidify the channel of distribution. For consumer products such as dog food, the salesforce calls on the wholesalers and retailers in hopes of increasing inventory levels and gaining shelf space. For business products, the salesforce often tries to get contractual arrangements to be the sole source of supply for the buyer.

Maturity Stage   In the maturity stage the need is to maintain existing buyers, and advertising's role is to remind buyers of the product's existence. Sales promotion, in the form of discounts and coupons offered to both ultimate consumers and intermediaries, is important in maintaining loyal buyers. In a test of one mature consumer product, it was found that 80 percent of the product's sales at this stage resulted from sales promotions.[12] For the past four years Purina has sponsored the Incredible Dog Challenge, which is now covered by ESPN and USA Network![13] Direct marketing actions such as direct mail are used to maintain involvement with existing customers and to encourage repeat purchases. Price cuts and discounts can also significantly increase a mature brand's sales. The salesforce at this stage seeks to satisfy intermediaries. An unsatisfied customer who switches brands is hard to replace.

FIGURE 18-3
Promotional tools used over the product life cycle of Purina Dog Chow

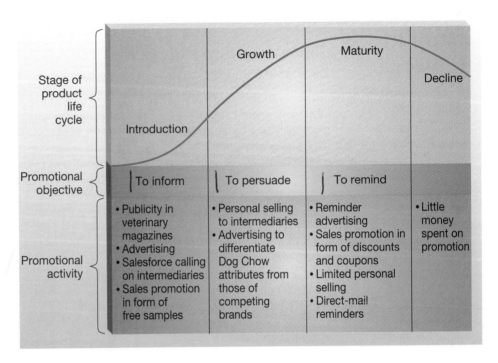

Decline Stage

Decline Stage   The decline stage of the product life cycle is usually a period of phaseout for the product, and little money is spent in the promotional mix.

Product Characteristics

The proper blend of elements in the promotional mix also depends on the type of product. Three specific characteristics should be considered: complexity, risk, and ancillary services. *Complexity* refers to the technical sophistication of the product and hence the amount of understanding required to use it. It's hard to provide much information in a one-page magazine ad or 30-second television ad, so the more complex the product, the greater the emphasis on personal selling. Gulfstream asks potential customers to call their senior vice president in its ads. No information is provided for simple products such as Heinz ketchup.

A second element is the degree of risk represented by the product's purchase. Risk for the buyer can be assessed in terms of financial risk, social risk, and physical risk. A private jet, for example, might represent all three risks—it is expensive, employees and customers may see and evaluate the purchase, and safety and reliability are important. Although advertising helps, the greater the risk, the greater the need for personal selling. Consumers are unlikely to associate any of these risks with cereal.

The level of *ancillary services* required by a product also affects the promotional strategy. Ancillary services pertain to the degree of service or support required after the sale. This characteristic is common to many industrial products and consumer purchases. Who will provide maintenance for the plane? Advertising's role is to establish the seller's reputation. Direct marketing can be used to describe how a product or service can be customized to individual needs. However, personal selling is essential to build buyer confidence and provide evidence of customer service.

Stages of the Buying Decision

Knowing the customer's stage of decision making can also affect the promotional mix. Figure 18–4 shows how the importance of the promotional elements varies with the three stages in a consumer's purchase decision.

How do Gulfstream aircraft and Heinz ketchup differ on complexity, risk, and ancillary services?

Gulfstream

www.gulfstreamvsp.com

Heinz

www.heinz.com

Prepurchase Stage   In the prepurchase stage advertising is more helpful than personal selling because advertising informs the potential customer of the existence of the product and the seller. Sales promotion in the form of free samples also can play an important role to gain low-risk trial. When the salesperson calls on the customer after heavy advertising, there is some recognition of what the salesperson represents. This is particularly important in industrial settings in which sampling of the product is usually not possible.

Purchase Stage   At the purchase stage the importance of personal selling is highest, whereas the impact of advertising is lowest. Sales promotion in the form of coupons, deals, point-of-purchase displays, and rebates can be very helpful in encouraging demand. In this stage, although advertising is not an active influence on the purchase, it is the means of delivering the coupons, deals, and rebates that are often important.

FIGURE 18–4
How the importance of promotional elements varies during the consumer's purchase decision

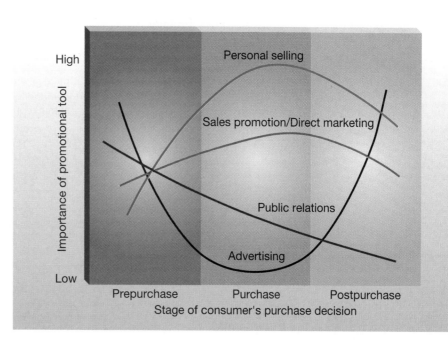

Postpurchase Stage   In the postpurchase stage the salesperson is still important. In fact, the more personal contact after the sale, the more the buyer is satisfied. Advertising is also important to assure the buyer that the right purchase was made. Advertising and personal selling help reduce the buyer's postpurchase anxiety.[14] Sales promotion in the form of coupons and direct marketing reminders can help encourage repeat purchases from satisfied first-time triers. Public relations plays a small role in the postpurchase stage.

Channel Strategies

Chapter 15 discussed the channel flow from producer to intermediaries to consumer. Achieving control of the channel is often difficult for the manufacturer, and promotional strategies can assist in moving a product through the channel of distribution. This is where a manufacturer has to make an important decision about whether to use a push strategy, pull strategy, or both in its channel of distribution.[15]

Push Strategy   Figure 18–5A shows how a manufacturer uses a **push strategy**, directing the promotional mix to channel members to gain their cooperation in ordering and stocking the product. In this approach, personal selling and sales promotions play major roles. Salespeople call on wholesalers to encourage orders and provide sales assistance. Sales promotions, such as case discount allowances (20 percent off the regular case price), are offered to stimulate demand. By pushing the product through the channel, the goal is to get channel members to push it to their customers.

Anheuser-Busch, for example, spends a significant amount of its marketing resources on maintaining its relationship with its distributors, and through them, with retailers. At a meeting of its wholesalers and salespeople, Anheuser-Busch announced that it would provide $250 million of marketing support for its Budweiser brand—an action designed to maintain channel dominance. The company also arranges group discounts on purchase of trucks, insurance, and the computers that wholesalers use to order beer. Even specialized computer software is provided to help retailers maximize the shelf space of Anheuser-Busch products.[16]

FIGURE 18–5

A comparison of push and pull promotional strategies

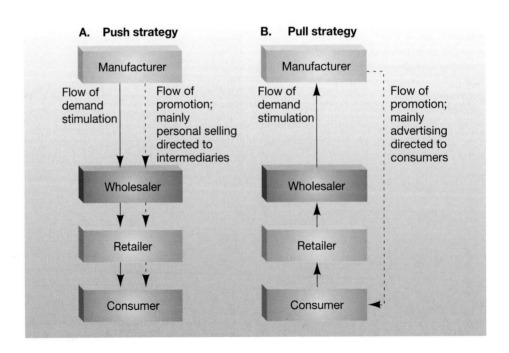

WEB LINK

Disney Takes IMC to China and the Rest of the World!

Integrated marketing communications within the United States is a difficult and challenging task for most organizations. At Disney, managers have added another level of complexity by trying to integrate their promotional activities around the world. Disney is currently planning for the opening of Hong Kong Disneyland in 2006. In addition, the 1.3 billion people in China are an attractive market for Disney, particularly because the 2008 Olympics are scheduled for China. Visit Disney's international portal, disneyinternational. com for access to Disney websites for Brazil, Australia,

China, Japan, France, Italy, Switzerland, the United Kingdom, and many others. The Australian site, for example, helps visitors find the location of the nearest Disney store in Australia, while the French site helps visitors make reservations for Disneyland Resort–Paris! Choose 5 of the 20 countries to compare. What similarities in Disney's approach to each country can you observe? What about differences? How does each country promote Disney's 100th birthday party?

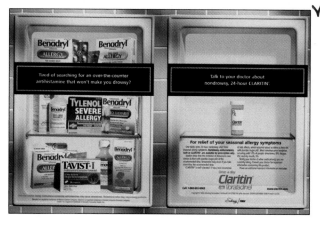

Claritin
www.claritin.com

Pull Strategy   In some instances manufacturers face resistance from channel members who do not want to order a new product or increase inventory levels of an existing brand. As shown in Figure 18–5B, a manufacturer may then elect to implement a **pull strategy** by directing its promotional mix at ultimate consumers to encourage them to ask the retailer for the product. Seeing demand from ultimate consumers, retailers order the product from wholesalers and thus the item is pulled through the intermediaries. Pharmaceutical companies, for example, have typically used marketing programs consisting of personal selling and free samples directed only to doctors.[17] They now also spend more than $1.2 billion annually to advertise prescription drugs directly to consumers. The strategy is designed to encourage consumers to ask their physicians for a specific drug by name—pulling it through the channel. Successful advertising strategies, such as Claritin's "Talk to your doctor . . ." campaign, can have dramatic effects on the sales of a product.[18]

Integrated Marketing Communications

In the past the promotional elements were regarded as separate functions handled by experts in separate departments. The salesforce designed and managed its activities independently of the advertising department, and sales promotion and public relations were often the responsibility of outside agencies or specialists. The result was often an overall communication effort that was uncoordinated and, in some cases, inconsistent. Today the concept of designing marketing communications programs that coordinate all promotional activities—advertising, personal selling, sales promotion, public relations, and direct marketing—to provide a consistent message across all audiences is referred to as **integrated marketing communications** (IMC).

The key to developing successful IMC programs is to create a process that facilitates their design and use. A tool used to evaluate a company's current process is the IMC audit. The audit analyzes the internal communication network of the company, identifies key audiences, evaluates customer databases, assesses messages in recent ads, public relations releases, packaging, video news releases, signage, sales promotion pieces, and direct mail, and determines managers' knowledge of IMC.[19] While many organizations are interested in improving their IMC process, a recent survey suggests that fewer than one-third have been successful at implementing IMC. The reasons include lack of expertise, lack of budget, and lack of management approval.[20]

Once the IMC process is implemented, most organizations want to assess its benefits. The tendency is to try to determine which element of promotion "works" better. In an integrated program, however, media advertising might be used to build awareness, sales promotion to generate an inquiry, direct mail to provide additional information to individual prospects, and a personal sales call to complete the transaction. The tools are used for different reasons, and their combined use creates a synergy that should be the focus of the assessment.[21] Another level of integration is necessary when firms have international promotion programs. The accompanying Web Link box describes Disney's effort to integrate its programs in 20 countries![22]

Concept Check

1. For consumer products, why is advertising emphasized more than personal selling?

2. Explain the differences between a push strategy and a pull strategy.

3. Integrated marketing communications programs provide a _____ message across all audiences.

DEVELOPING THE PROMOTION PROGRAM

Because media costs are high, promotion decisions must be made carefully, using a systematic approach. Paralleling the planning, implementation, and control steps described in the strategic marketing process (Chapter 2), the promotion decision process is divided into (1) developing, (2) executing, and (3) evaluating the promotion program (Figure 18–6). Development of the promotion program focuses on the four *W*s:

- *Who* is the target audience?
- *What* are (1) the promotion objectives, (2) the amounts of money that can be budgeted for the promotion program, and (3) the kinds of promotion to use?
- *Where* should the promotion be run?
- *When* should the promotion be run?

Identifying the Target Audience

The first decision in developing the promotion program is identifying the *target audience*, the group of prospective buyers toward which a promotion program is

FIGURE 18–6
The promotion decision process

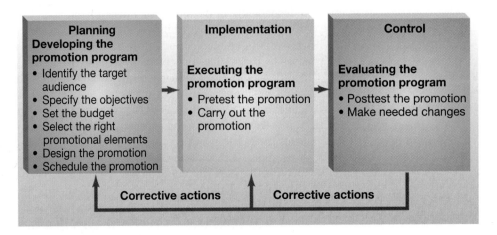

directed. To the extent that time and money permit, the target audience for the promotion program is the target market for the firm's product, which is identified from marketing research and market segmentation studies. The more a firm knows about its target audience's profile—including their lifestyle, attitudes, and values—the easier it is to develop a promotion program. If a firm wanted to reach you with television and magazine ads, for example, it would need to know what TV shows you watch and what magazines you read.

Specifying Promotion Objectives

After the target audience is identified, a decision must be reached on what the promotion should accomplish. Consumers can be said to respond in terms of a **hierarchy of effects**, which is the sequence of stages a prospective buyer goes through from initial awareness of a product to eventual action (either trial or adoption of the product).[23]

- *Awareness.* The consumer's ability to recognize and remember the product or brand name.
- *Interest.* An increase in the consumer's desire to learn about some of the features of the product or brand.
- *Evaluation.* The consumer's appraisal of the product or brand on important attributes.
- *Trial.* The consumer's actual first purchase and use of the product or brand.
- *Adoption.* Through a favorable experience on the first trial, the consumer's repeated purchase and use of the product or brand.

For a totally new product the sequence applies to the entire product category, but for a new brand competing in an established product category it applies to the brand itself. These steps can serve as guidelines for developing promotion objectives.

Although sometimes an objective for a promotion program involves several steps in the hierarchy of effects, it often focuses on a single stage. Regardless of what the specific objective might be, from building awareness to increasing repeat purchases,[24] promotion objectives should possess three important qualities. They should (1) be designed for a well-defined target audience, (2) be measurable, and (3) cover a specified time period.

Setting the Promotion Budget

From Figure 18–7 (on the next page) it is clear that the promotion expenditures needed to reach U.S. households are enormous. Note that six companies—General Motors, Philip Morris, Procter & Gamble, Ford, Pfizer, and Pepsi—each spend a total of more than $2 billion dollars annually on promotion.[25]

After setting the promotion objectives, a company must decide on how much to spend. Determining the ideal amount for the budget is difficult because there is no precise way to measure the exact results of spending promotion dollars. However, there are several methods used to set the promotion budget.[26]

Percentage of Sales   In the **percentage of sales budgeting** approach, funds are allocated to promotion as a percentage of past or anticipated sales, in terms of either dollars or units sold. A common budgeting method,[27] this approach is often stated in terms such as, "Our promotion budget for this year is 3 percent of last year's gross sales." The advantage of this approach is obvious: it's simple and provides a financial safeguard by tying the promotion budget to sales. However, there is a major fallacy in this approach, which implies that sales cause promotion. Using this method, a company may reduce its promotion budget because of a downturn in past sales or an

RANK	COMPANY	TOTAL (MILLIONS)	ADVERTISING (MILLIONS)	DIRECT MAIL, SALES PROMOTION, COUPONS, AND OTHER PROMOTIONS (MILLIONS)
1	General Motors	$3,935	$2,951	$ 984
2	Philip Morris	2,603	1,770	833
3	Procter & Gamble	2,363	1,542	821
4	Ford	2,345	1,196	1,149
5	Pfizer	2,265	803	1,462
6	PepsiCo	2,100	672	1,428
7	DaimlerChrysler	1,984	1,686	298
8	AOL Time Warner	1,770	1,469	301
9	Disney	1,757	1,054	703
10	Verizon	1,613	742	871
11	Johnson & Johnson	1,601	873	728
12	Sears	1,455	655	800
13	Unilever	1,454	698	756
14	AT&T	1,416	524	892
15	General Electric	1,310	458	852

FIGURE 18–7
U.S. promotion expenditures
by companies in 2000

anticipated downturn in future sales—situations where it may need promotion the most.

Competitive Parity A second common approach, **competitive parity budgeting**, is matching the competitor's absolute level of spending or the proportion per point of market share. This approach has also been referred to as *matching competitors* or *share of market*. It is important to consider the competition in budgeting.[28] Consumer responses to promotion are affected by competing promotional activities, so if a competitor runs 30 radio ads each week, it may be difficult for a firm to get its message across with only five messages.[29] The competitor's budget level, however, should not be the only determinant in setting a company's budget. The competition might have very different promotional objectives, which require a different level of promotion expenditures.

All You Can Afford Common to many small businesses is **all-you-can-afford budgeting**, in which money is allocated to promotion only after all other budget items are covered. As one company executive said in reference to this budgeting process, "Why, it's simple. First, I go upstairs to the controller and ask how much they can afford to give us this year. She says a million and a half. Later, the boss comes to me and asks how much we should spend, and I say 'Oh, about a million and a half.' Then we have our promotion appropriation."[30]

Fiscally conservative, this approach has little else to offer. Using this budgeting philosophy, a company acts as though it doesn't know anything about a promotion-sales relationship or what its promotion objectives are.

Objective and Task The best approach to budgeting is **objective and task budgeting**, whereby the company (1) determines its promotion objectives, (2) outlines the tasks to accomplish these objectives, and (3) determines the promotion cost of performing these tasks.[31]

This method takes into account what the company wants to accomplish and requires that the objectives be specified.[32] Strengths of the other budgeting methods are integrated into this approach because each previous method's strength is tied to the objectives. For example, if the costs are beyond what the company can afford, objectives are reworked and the tasks revised. The difficulty with this method is the judgment required to determine the tasks needed to accomplish objectives. Would two or four insertions in *Time* magazine be needed to achieve a specific awareness level? Figure 18–8 shows a sample media plan with objectives, tasks, and budget outlined. The total amount to be budgeted is $430,000. If the company can only afford $300,000, the objectives must be reworked, tasks redefined, and the total budget recalculated.

Selecting the Right Promotional Tools

Once a budget has been determined, the combination of the five basic IMC tools—advertising, personal selling, sales promotion, public relations, and direct marketing—can be specified. While many factors provide direction for selection of the appropriate mix, the large number of possible combinations of the promotional tools means that many combinations can achieve the same objective. Therefore, an analytical approach and experience are particularly important in this step of the promotion decision process. The specific mix can vary from a simple program using a single tool to a comprehensive program using all forms of promotion. The Olympics have become a very visible example of a comprehensive integrated communication program. Because the Games are repeated every two years, the promotion is almost continuous. Included in the program are advertising campaigns, personal selling efforts by the Olympic committee and organizers, sales promotion activities such as product tie-ins and sponsorships, public relations programs managed by the host cities, and direct marketing efforts targeted at a variety of audiences including governments, organizations, firms, athletes, and individuals.[33] At this stage, it is also important to assess the relative importance of the various tools. While it may be desirable to utilize and integrate several forms of promotion, one may deserve emphasis. The Olympics, for example, place exceptional importance on public relations and publicity.

Designing the Promotion

The central element of a promotion program is the promotion itself. Advertising consists of advertising copy and the artwork that the target audience is intended to see or hear. Personal selling efforts depend on the characteristics and skills of the salesperson. Sales promotion activities consist of the specific details of inducements such as coupons, samples, and sweepstakes. Public relations efforts are readily seen in tangible elements such as news releases, and direct marketing actions depend on written, verbal, and electronic forms of delivery. The design of the promotion will

FIGURE 18–8
The objective and task approach

OBJECTIVE

To increase awareness among college students for a new video game. Awareness at the end of one semester should be 20 percent of all students from the existing 0 percent today.

TASKS	COSTS
Advertisements once a week for a semester in 500 college papers	$280,000
Direct-mail samples to student leaders on 500 college campuses	50,000
Sponsor a national contest for video-game players	100,000
Total budget	$430,000

play a primary role in determining the message that is communicated to the audience. This design activity is frequently viewed as the step requiring the most creativity. In addition, successful designs are often the result of insight regarding consumer's interests and purchasing behavior. All of the promotion tools have many design alternatives. Advertising, for example, can utilize fear, humor, or other emotions in its appeal. Similarly, direct marketing can be designed for varying levels of personal or customized appeals. One of the challenges of IMC is to design each promotional activity to communicate the same message.

Scheduling the Promotion

Once the design of each of the promotional program elements is complete, it is important to determine the most effective timing of their use. The promotion schedule describes the order in which each promotional tool is introduced and the frequency of its use during the campaign. New Line Cinema, for example, developed one of the longest promotion schedules on record for its *Lord of the Rings* movie trilogy, planned for release in 2001, 2002, and 2003. To generate interest in the first movie months before its release, a movie "trailer" was shown on the television season premiere of *Angel*. Stickers and other products were then released to stores, followed by a global marketing program at Burger King's 10,000 restaurants.[34] Overall, the scheduling of the various promotions was designed to generate interest, bring consumers into theaters, and then encourage additional purchases after seeing the movie. Several factors such as seasonality and competitive promotion activity can also influence the promotion schedule. Businesses such as ski resorts, airlines, and professional sports teams are likely to reduce their promotional activity during the "off" season. Similarly, restaurants, retail stores, and health clubs are likely to increase their promotional activity when new competitors enter the market.

EXECUTING AND EVALUATING THE PROMOTION PROGRAM

As shown earlier in Figure 18–6, the ideal execution of a promotion program involves pretesting each design before it is actually used to allow for changes and modifications which improve its effectiveness. Similarly, posttests are recommended to evaluate the impact of each promotion and the contribution of the promotion toward achieving the program objectives. The most sophisticated pretest and posttest procedures have been developed for advertising and are discussed in Chapter 19. Testing procedures for sales promotion and direct marketing efforts currently focus on comparisons of different designs or responses of different segments. To fully benefit from IMC programs, companies must create and maintain a test-result database that allows comparisons of the relative impact of the promotional tools, and their execution options, in varying situations. Information from the database will allow informed design and execution decisions and provide support for IMC activities during internal reviews by financial or administrative personnel. The San Diego Padres baseball team, for example, developed a database of information relating attendance to its integrated campaign using a new logo, special events, merchandise sales, and a loyalty program.

Carrying out the promotion program can be expensive and time-consuming. One researcher estimates that "an organization with sales less than $10 million can successfully implement an IMC program in one year, one with sales between $200 million and $500 million will need about three years, and one with sales between $2 billion and $5 billion will need five years." To facilitate the transition there are approximately 200 integrated marketing communications agencies in operation. In addition, some of the largest advertising agencies are adopting approaches that embrace "total communications solutions." J. Walter Thompson, for example, now has a Total Solutions Group that is responsible for designing integrated programs such as the

"Shadows" diamond campaign for De Beers. The campaign has appeared in 23 countries on television, in print, and in other media and is supported by an extensive range of public relations, point-of-sale, and educational materials. While most agencies still have departments dedicated to promotion, direct marketing, and other specialties, the trend today is clearly toward a long-term perspective in which all forms of promotion are integrated.[35]

Concept Check

1. What are the characteristics of good promotion objectives?

2. What are the weaknesses of the percentage of sales budgeting approach?

3. How have advertising agencies changed to facilitate the use of IMC programs?

DIRECT MARKETING

Direct marketing has many forms and utilizes a variety of media. Several forms of direct marketing—direct mail and catalogs, television, telemarketing, and direct selling—were discussed as methods of nonstore retailing in Chapter 17. In addition, although advertising is discussed in Chapter 19, a form of advertising—direct response advertising—is an important form of direct marketing. Finally, interactive or online marketing is discussed in detail in Chapter 21. In this section the growth of direct marketing, its benefits, and key global, technological, and ethical issues are discussed.

The Growth of Direct Marketing

The increasing interest in customer relationship management is reflected in the dramatic growth of direct marketing. The ability to customize communication efforts and create one-to-one interactions is appealing to most marketers, particularly those with IMC programs. While direct marketing methods are not new, the ability to design and use them has increased with the availability of databases. In recent years direct marketing growth—in terms of spending, revenue generated, and employment—has outpaced total economic growth. Direct marketing expenditures of $205 billion in 2001 are expected to grow 31 percent by 2005. Similarly, 2001 revenues of $1.9 trillion are expected to grow to $2.7 trillion by 2005. Employment has also grown and now numbers more than 14 million employees. Figure 18–9 shows how the various forms of direct marketing contribute to the overall industry.[36]

FIGURE 18–9
Direct marketing expenditures, sales and employment by medium

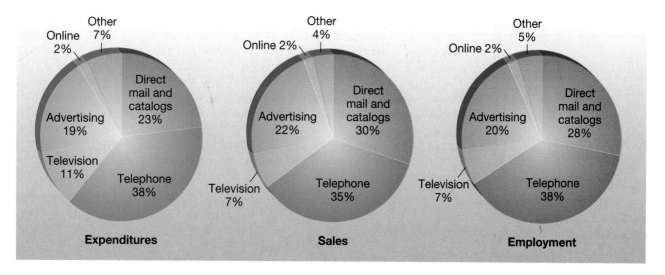

Columbia House is one example of the kinds of companies fueling the growth in direct marketing. You may have received the company's letters in the mail offering 12 free music CDs if you agree to buy 5 additional CDs over the next two years. In the past, the CDs were automatically delivered unless the customer told the company not to send them. Today, customers decide when to order. Columbia House also has similar offers for DVDs, videos, and television shows. With more than 16 million club members, Columbia House is the largest direct marketer of entertainment products. Because one of its largest customer bases is the college student, its business typically surges about 30 percent in August when students return to college![37]

Another component of the growth in direct marketing is the increasing popularity of the newest direct marketing channel—the Internet. As discussed in Chapter 21, total online sales have risen from close to nothing in 1996 to projections approaching 34 billion today. Continued growth in the number of consumers with Internet access and the number of businesses with websites and electronic commerce offerings is likely to contribute to the future growth of direct marketing.

The Value of Direct Marketing

One of the most visible indicators of the value of direct marketing for consumers is the level of use of various forms of direct marketing. For example, 68 percent of the U.S. population has ordered merchandise or services by phone or mail; more than 12 million adults have purchased items from a television offer; the average adult spends more than 30 hours per year accessing online services; and more than 21 percent of all adults make three to five purchases from a catalog each year. Consumers report many benefits, including the following: they don't have to go to a store, they can usually shop 24 hours a day, buying direct saves time, they avoid hassles with salespeople, they can save money, it's fun and entertaining, and direct marketing offers more privacy than in-store shopping. Many consumers also believe that direct marketing provides excellent customer service.[38] Toll-free telephone numbers, customer service representatives with access to information regarding purchasing preferences, overnight delivery services, and unconditional guarantees all help create value for direct marketing customers. At Landsend.com, when customers need assistance they can click a "help" icon and a sales rep will take control of their browser until the correct product is found. "It's like we were walking down the aisle in a store," says one Lands' End customer![39]

The value of direct marketing for sellers can be described in terms of the responses it generates.[40] **Direct orders** are the result of offers that contain all the information necessary for a prospective buyer to make a decision to purchase and complete the transaction. Club Med, for example, uses direct e-mail offers to sell "last-minute specials" to people in its database. The messages, which are sent midweek, describe rooms and air transportation available at a 30 to 40 percent discount if the customer can make the decision to travel on such short notice.[41] **Lead generation** is the result of an offer designed to generate interest in a product or service and a request for additional information. America Online announced a contest with direct advertising and used a direct-mail trial offer to generate interest in its latest release.[42] Finally, **traffic generation** is the outcome of an offer designed to motivate people to visit a business. Mitsubishi recently mailed a sweepstakes offer to 1 million prospective buyers to encourage them to visit a Mitsubishi dealer and test drive the new Galant. The names of prospects who took test drives were entered in the sweepstakes, which included a Galant, a trip to Hawaii, and large-screen TVs as prizes.[43]

Technological, Global, and Ethical Issues in Direct Marketing

The information technology and databases described in Chapter 8 are key elements in any direct marketing program. Databases are the result of organizations' efforts to collect demographic, media, and consumption profiles of customers so that direct marketing tools—such as catalogs—can be directed at specific customers. For example, Lillian Vernon started her very successful mail-order company four decades ago at her kitchen table by putting all her merchandise in a single catalog: laundry baskets and men's slippers on one page might be followed by toys on the next. But in the last few years Lillian Vernon has shifted to a database approach with the 150 million catalogs she mails annually. There are now home-oriented, children's, and Christmas-ornament catalogs targeted at customers who have purchased these kinds of merchandise from her main catalog in the past.[44]

While most companies try to keep records of their customers' past purchases, many other types of data are needed to use direct marketing to develop one-to-one relationships with customers. Data, however, have little value by themselves. To translate data into information the data must be unbiased, timely, pertinent, accessible, and organized in a way that helps the marketing manager make decisions that lead to direct marketing actions. Some data, such as lifestyles, media use, and consumption behavior, must be collected in consumers' homes. Other types of data can be collected from the businesses where purchases are made. Today, technology such as optical scanners helps collect data with as little intrusion on the customer as possible. Safeway supermarkets, for eample, use scanners to read bar codes and track customers' purchases in its database.

Technology may also prove to be important in the global growth of direct marketing. Compared with the United States, other countries' direct marketing systems are undeveloped. The mail and telephone systems in many countries are likely to improve, however, creating many new direct marketing opportunities. Developments in international marketing research and database management will also facilitate global growth. In Argentina, for example, mail service is very slow, telephone service is poor, and response to some forms of direct marketing such as coupons is negligible. The country is the first, however, to fully deregulate its postal service and expects rapid improvement from the private company, Correo Argentino. In Mexico direct marketing activities are more advanced. Pond's recently mailed 20,000 direct-mail offers within Mexico and was surprised by a 33 percent response.[45] Another issue for global direct marketers is payment. Because fewer consumers have credit cards, alternatives such as C.O.D. and bank deposits are needed.

Global and domestic direct marketers both face challenging ethical issues today. Of course there has been considerable attention given to some annoying direct marketing activities such as telephone solicitations during dinner and evening hours. Concerns about privacy, however, have led to various attempts to provide guidelines that balance consumer and business interests. The European Union recently passed a consumer privacy law, called the Data Protection Directive, after several years of discussion with the Federation of European Direct Marketing and the U.K.'s Direct Marketing Association. In the United States, the Federal Trade Commission and many state legislatures have also been concerned about privacy.[46] Another issue, the proliferation of e-mail advertising has received increasing attention from consumers and marketers recently. The accompanying Ethics and Social Responsibility Alert offers some of the details of the debate.[47]

Concept Check

1. The ability to design and use direct marketing programs has increased with the availability of _____ and _____.

2. What are the three types of responses generated by direct marketing activities?

ETHICS AND SOCIAL RESPONSIBILITY ALERT

How Do You Like Your E-Mail? "Opt-out" or "Opt-in" Are Your Choices

ETHICS

More than 1 billion e-mail messages are sent each day in the United States. You've probably noticed that many of them are direct-marketing messages—personalized offers from companies such as Pepsi, Victoria's Secret, Toyota, and the Phoenix Suns! In fact, e-mail advertisers spent more than $2 billion in 2001 on their campaigns. One reason is that e-mail offers one-to-one conversations with each prospective consumer. Another reason is that the average cost per e-mail message is less than $.01 compared to $0.75 to $2.00 for direct mail and $1 to $3 for telemarketing.

Some consumers have complained that they are inundated with unsolicited messages, sometimes called "spam," and ignore them, while marketers believe that better management of e-mail campaigns will improve the value of e-mail advertising for customers. Two general approaches to managing e-mail are being discussed. The "opt-out" system allows recipients to decline future messages after the first contact. The "opt-in" system requires advertisers to obtain e-mail addresses from registration questions on websites, business-reply cards, and even entry forms for contests or sweepstakes. Surveys indicate that about 77 percent of the unsolicited e-mails are deleted without being read, while only 2 percent of the e-mails received with the consumer's permission are deleted.

The European Union's Committee for Citizen's Freedoms and Rights recently debated the issue and gave a preliminary ruling in favor of an opt-out policy. Some companies, however, have adopted opt-in policies. What is your opinion? Why?

SUMMARY

1 Communication is the process of conveying a message to others and requires a source, a message, a channel of communication, a receiver, and the processes of encoding and decoding.

2 For effective communication to occur, the sender and receiver must have a shared field of experience. The receiver's response provides feedback to the sender and helps determine whether decoding has occurred or noise has distorted the message.

3 The promotional elements consist of advertising, personal selling, sales promotion, public relations, and direct marketing. These tools vary according to whether they are personal; can be identified with a sponsor; and can be controlled with regard to whom, when, where, and how often the message is sent.

4 In selecting the appropriate promotional mix, marketers must consider the target audience, the stage of the product's life cycle, characteristics of the product, decision stage of the buyer, and the channel of distribution.

5 The target for promotional programs can be the ultimate consumer, an intermediary, or both. Ultimate consumer programs rely more on advertising, whereas personal selling is more important in reaching business buyers and intermediaries.

6 The emphasis on the promotional tools varies with a product's life cycle. In introduction, awareness is important. During growth, creating brand preference is essential. Advertising is more important in the former stage and personal selling in the latter. Sales promotion helps maintain buyers in the maturity stage.

7 The appropriate promotional mix depends on the complexity of the product, the degree of risk associated with its purchase, and the need for ancillary services.

8 In the prepurchase stage of a customer's purchase decision, advertising and public relations are emphasized; at the purchase stage personal selling, sales promotion, and direct marketing are most important; and during the postpurchase stage advertising, personal selling, and sales promotion are used to reduce postpurchase anxiety.

9 When a push strategy is used, personal selling and sales promotions directed to intermediaries play major roles. In a pull strategy, advertising and sales promotions directed to ultimate consumers are important.

10 Integrated marketing communications programs coordinate all promotional activities to provide a consistent message across all audiences.

11 The promotion decision process involves developing, executing, and evaluating the promotion program. Developing the promotion program focuses on determining who is the target audience, what to say, where the message should be said, and when to say it.

12 Setting promotion objectives is based on the hierarchy of effects. Objectives should be measurable, have a specified time period, and state the target audience.

13 Budgeting methods often used are percentage of sales, competitive parity, and the all-you-can-afford approaches. The best budgeting approach is based on the objectives set and tasks required.

14 Selecting, designing, and scheduling promotional elements requires experience and creativity because of the large number of possible combinations of the promotion mix.

15 Direct marketing offers consumers convenience, entertainment, privacy, time savings, low prices, and customer service. Sellers benefit from direct orders, lead generation, and traffic generation.

16 Global opportunities for direct marketing will increase as mail and telephone systems improve worldwide. Consumer's concerns about privacy will be a key issue for direct marketers in the future.

KEY TERMS AND CONCEPTS

advertising p. 474
all-you-can-afford budgeting p. 486
channel of communication p. 472
communication p. 472
competitive parity budgeting p. 486
decoding p. 472
direct marketing p. 477
direct orders p. 490
encoding p. 472
feedback p. 474
field of experience p. 474
hierarchy of effects p. 485
integrated marketing communications p. 483
lead generation p. 490
message p. 472

noise p. 474
objective and task budgeting p. 486
percentage of sales budgeting p. 485
personal selling p. 476
promotional mix p. 478
public relations p. 476
publicity p. 476
pull strategy p. 483
push strategy p. 482
receivers p. 472
response p. 474
sales promotion p. 477
source p. 472
traffic generation p. 490

APPLYING MARKETING CONCEPTS AND PERSPECTIVES

1 After listening to a recent sales presentation, Mary Smith signed up for membership at the local health club. On arriving at the facility, she learned there was an additional fee for racquetball court rentals. "I don't remember that in the sales talk; I thought they said all facilities were included with the membership fee," complained Mary. Describe the problem in terms of the communication process.

2 Develop a matrix to compare the five elements of the promotional mix on three criteria—to *whom* you deliver the message, *what* you say, and *when* you say it.

3 Explain how the promotional tools used by an airline would differ if the target audience were (*a*) consumers who travel for pleasure and (*b*) corporate travel departments that select the airlines to be used by company employees.

4 Suppose you introduced a new consumer food product and invested heavily both in national advertising (pull strategy) and in training and motivating your field salesforce to sell the product to food stores (push strategy). What kinds of feedback would you receive from both the advertising and your salesforce? How could you increase both the quality and quantity of each?

5 Fisher-Price Company, long known as a manufacturer of children's toys, has introduced a line of clothing for children. Outline a promotional plan to get this product introduced in the marketplace.

6 Many insurance companies sell health insurance plans to companies. In these companies the employees pick the plan, but the set of offered plans is determined by the company. Recently Blue Cross–Blue Shield, a health insurance company, ran a television ad stating, "If your employer doesn't offer you Blue Cross–Blue Shield coverage, ask why." Explain the promotional strategy behind the advertisement.

7 Identify the sales promotion tools that might be useful for (*a*) Tastee Yogurt—a new brand introduction, (*b*) 3M self-sticking Post-it notes, and (*c*) Wrigley's Spearmint Gum.

8 Design an integrated marketing communications program—using each of the five promotional elements—for Music Boulevard, the online music store.

9 BMW recently introduced its first sport-utility vehicle, the X5, to compete with other popular 4X4 vehicles such as the Mercedes-Benz M-class and Jeep Grand Cherokee. Design a direct marketing program to generate (*a*) leads, (*b*) traffic in dealerships, and (*c*) direct orders.

10 Develop a privacy policy for database managers that provides a balance of consumer and seller perspectives. How would you encourage voluntary compliance with your policy? What methods of enforcement would you recommend?

INTERNET EXERCISE

Several large advertising agencies have described shifts in their philosophies to include IMC approaches to communication. In many cases the outcome has been campaigns that utilize a combination of the five promotional elements. Go to J. Walter Thompson's website at www.jwt.com, and review its integrated campaigns.

1 Describe the promotional elements of one of the campaigns. Why were these elements selected? How are they integrated?

2 How would you evaluate the effectiveness of each of the promotional elements used? How would you evaluate the effectiveness of the entire campaign?

VIDEO CASE 18–1 Airwalk, Inc.: Reaching the Youth Market with IMC

"To effectively communicate with the youth audience," observes Sharon Lee, "it is important to earn their respect by knowing what they think and how they think. You must stay one step ahead of them by constantly studying what they are reading, doing, listening to, playing, and watching."

Sharon Lee speaks from experience. She is an account director at Lambesis, the California advertising agency whose integrated marketing communications (IMC) program launched Airwalk shoes into the stratosphere. Lee's job is to be the key link between Airwalk and Lambesis. Her special insights into the youth market have helped make Airwalk's recent success possible. But it wasn't always so easy.

EARLY DAYS: THE STRUGGLE

George Yohn founded the company in 1986—searching for a piece of the fast-growing athletic shoe craze headed by Nike and Reebok. His first efforts marketing an aerobic shoe hit the wall, so he had to find a new product and marketing strategy. Then one of his designers found a sport that other sneaker manufacturers hadn't yet discovered: skateboarding. Yohn watched skateboarders drag their feet to turn and brake, so he developed a special athletic shoe that had extra layers of leather, more rubber in the sole, and double stitching to add longer life. Watching skateboarders do a popular trick of popping the board into the air, he named his new company "Airwalk."

The colorful skateboard shoes almost jumped off the shelves in the surf and skate shops stocking them, so Airwalk moved into other freestyle segments like snowboarding and BMX bike riding. Industry sources estimated that there were 10 million skateboarders, 3.5 to 5 million snowboarders, and 3.7 million BMX participants in the United States alone. Airwalk sales quickly hit $20 million!

REPOSITIONING AIRWALK: TARGETING MAINSTREAM YOUTHS

At this point Yohn got his great insight: if basketball shoes aren't just worn by basketball players, why should skateboarding shoes just be worn by skateboarders? This gave Yohn his new challenge: reposition Airwalk to bring its hotdogger image to mainstream youths who were looking for stylish shoes but weren't into skateboarding.

While this repositioning looked great on paper, making it actually happen was a big, big order! Although Airwalk was well-known among action-sport enthusiasts, the brand name was almost unknown among mainstream youths. It was at this point that Airwalk introduced its active/casual line of sneakers targeted at these youths, mainly teens.

RESEARCH: FINDING WHAT'S COOL!

Looking back, it's now possible to find some key elements that have led to Airwalk's success today. One example is the huge effort it puts into "trend spotting" research, discussed earlier in Chapter 8. Dee Gordon, a nationally known expert in trend spotting is on the staff of Lambesis. She authors the *L Report,* published quarterly by Lambesis, that surveys 18,000 trendsetter and mainstream respondents from ages 14 to 30 across the United States and touches on every aspect of their lives. Gordon's research gives other Lambesis employees like Sharon Lee and its clients in-depth insights into what the trendsetters and cool kids are thinking, doing, and buying. Dee Gordon also studies trends around the world as a foundation for global marketing strategies developed by Lambesis clients.

MAKING IT HAPPEN: THE IMC STRATEGY

Airwalk and Lambesis recognized that much of Nike's and Reebok's success is that they recognize their business is no longer simply about selling shoes—it's about creating a cool image for their shoes. Mastering the marketing of the hard-to-define concept known as "cool" was the task that Airwalk dropped in the lap of Lambesis when Airwalk launched its first active/casual footwear line, targeted at the youth market.

The special challenge for Lambesis was to expand the market for Airwalk shoes by reaching the new, broader cool segments for its shoes without diluting their image among the existing core segments. Chad Farmer, the creative director at Lambesis who is charged with coming up with ideas for Airwalk ads, saw an opportunity to position Airwalk to the youth market as the harbinger of style in casual footwear. At the same time, Airwalk's integrated marketing communications program must retain its shoes' reputation for quality and durability while featuring their original designs and colors.

Chad Farmer's IMC program illustrates the diversity of media and strategies available to creative agencies and clients trying to break through the media clutter. This clutter is reflected in today's youths often seeing about 3,000 advertising messages in a typical day. Airwalk's TV commercials and print ads are alive with humor, irreverence, and unrestrained attitude. In many of the 14 countries where Airwalks are sold, youths steal its outdoor posters to hang in their rooms. Airwalk's website (www.airwalk.com) not only displays its latest line of shoes, but also provides graphics, animation, and recent TV commercials that can be downloaded.

Airwalk's IMC strategy doesn't stop with conventional media. Airwalk team "riders" include the best competitive skateboarders, snowboarders, mountain bike riders, and surfers who represent the company in major competitions globally. Bands and musicians such as the Beastie Boys, Green Day, Pearl Jam, and R.E.M. wear Airwalks—gaining great visibility for the brand. Lambesis gets product placement everywhere from movies and music videos to skateboard/BMX camps and fashion magazine photos.

What has resulted from all of this? Sales increased 400 percent in a single year. Today's sales are more than $300 million. And Teen Research Unlimited, a marketing research group, reports that Airwalk is among the top 20 percent of "coolest" brands and still climbing.

Questions

1   What were Airwalk's promotional objectives when it decided to target mainstream youths with its line of shoes in its IMC program?

2   Airwalk has developed what it calls a "tripod" strategy to stress three simple one-word concepts to communicate to the youth it targets and to stress in its IMC program. From reading the case and from what you know about the youth market, what might these be?

3   Describe how Airwalk and Lambesis might use the following media or promotional elements in their IMC strategy to target the notoriously difficult-to-reach target market of youths: (*a*) TV, (*b*) billboards, (*c*) product placements in movies, (*d*) special events, and (*e*) website. Explain your answers.

4   As Airwalk sells its shoes around the world, it has chosen to use a *global* marketing strategy, as defined in Chapter 7. (*a*) What are the advantages and disadvantages for Airwalk of this strategy? (*b*) For example, in print ads how might Airwalk take advantage of this strategy?

ADVERTISING, SALES PROMOTION, AND PUBLIC RELATIONS

AFTER READING THIS CHAPTER YOU SHOULD BE ABLE TO:

- Explain the differences between product advertising and institutional advertising and the variations within each type.

- Understand the steps used to develop, execute, and evaluate an advertising program.

- Explain the advantages and disadvantages of alternative advertising media.

- Understand the strengths and weaknesses of consumer-oriented and trade-oriented sales promotions.

- Recognize public relations as an important form of communication.

WHAT'S THE FUTURE OF ADVERTISING? THE ANSWER IS PERSONAL!

Have you ever seen an advertisement for a product you probably would never buy? Maybe you saw a cat food ad, but you own three dogs! Or the program you like keeps running milk ads, but you are allergic to dairy products. Well, several new technologies hope to change the world of advertising so that what you see will better match your personal interests! Virtual advertising, personal video recorders, and interactive television are all contributing to the change, and some experts predict that in the future your TV will select commercials targeted specifically for you!

Virtual advertising, for example, uses a patented computer system that digitally inserts ads into sporting events and other broadcasts—not as a traditional 15-, 30-, or 60-second advertising message, but as a visual part of the program. On ESPN's coverage of baseball games, for example, television viewers see ads that appear to be on the backstop behind home plate that are invisible to fans at the game. Television broadcasts of soccer games show a Coca-Cola logo on the field, even though the players see only green grass!

Personal video recorders (PVRs), such as the units offered by Ultimate TV and TiVo, enable viewers to basically program their own personal network. Just specify the programs you want, and by updating its programming guide through a telephone connection the PVR records all the shows from any channel at any time for the entire season. In addition, by monitoring your recording preferences and using your answers to PVR set-up questions, the technology will also record programs that it "thinks" you will like. New versions of the personalization software will soon allow advertisers to insert ads that are specific to the viewer of that television. So if parents typically watch a different television than their children, the ads on the two TVs are likely to be different even if the same program is tuned in!

Finally, interactive television will bring consumers interactive advertising. Eventually, viewers will be able to access information on any product or service seen during a program—a piece of art on Frasier's wall, clothing worn by any of the Friends, or a vehicle driven by someone on the set of *The X-Files*. Using their remotes, interested viewers could click on a jacket worn by Chandler or Rachel to reach a menu of additional personalized information—photos of the jacket in the viewer's color preferences and sizes, reminders of how the jacket would fit with other wardrobe items purchased recently, a list of nearby stores currently carrying the jacket, or online order and payment options. This approach provides instant information requested by the consumer—perhaps the ultimate in personalized advertising![1]

Virtual advertising, personal video recorders, and interactive advertising are just a few of the many exciting changes taking place in the field of advertising today. Chapter 18 described **advertising** as any *paid* form of *nonpersonal* communication about an organization, good, service, or idea by an identified sponsor. This chapter describes alternative types of advertisements, the advertising decision process, sales promotion, and public relations.

TYPES OF ADVERTISEMENTS

As you look through any magazine, watch television, listen to the radio, or browse on the Web, the variety of advertisements you see or hear may give you the impression that they have few similarities. Advertisements are prepared for different purposes, but they basically consist of two types: product and institutional.

Product Advertisements

Focused on selling a good or service, **product advertisements** take three forms: (1) pioneering (or informational), (2) competitive (or persuasive), and (3) reminder. Look at the ads by Jeep, Xerox, and FTD, and determine the type and objective of each ad.

Used in the introductory stage of the life cycle, *pioneering* advertisements tell people what a product is, what it can do, and where it can be found. The key objective

Advertisements serve varying purposes. Which ad would be considered (1) pioneering, (2) competitive, and (3) a reminder?

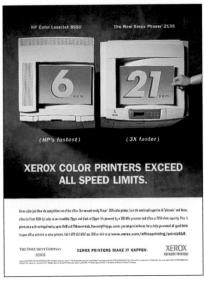

Dial soap uses reinforcement ads to encourage consumers to keep using the product.

of a pioneering advertisement (such as the ad for Jeep's new Liberty) is to inform the target market. Informative ads have been found to be interesting, convincing, and effective.[2]

Advertising that promotes a specific brand's features and benefits is *competitive*. The objective of these messages is to persuade the target market to select the firm's brand rather than that of a competitor. An increasingly common form of competitive advertising is comparative advertising, which shows one brand's strengths relative to those of competitors.[3] The Xerox ad, for example, highlights the competitive advantage of Xerox over its primary competitor Hewlett-Packard. Studies indicate that comparative ads attract more attention and increase the perceived quality of the advertiser's brand.[4] Firms that use comparative advertising need market research to provide legal support for their claims.[5]

Reminder advertising is used to reinforce previous knowledge of a product. The FTD ad shown reminds consumers about the association between its product and a special event—in this case, Valentine's Day. Reminder advertising is good for products that have achieved a well-recognized position and are in the mature phase of their product life cycle. Another type of reminder ad, *reinforcement,* is used to assure current users they made the right choice. One example: "Aren't you glad you use Dial? Don't you wish everybody did?"

Institutional Advertisements

The objective of **institutional advertisements** is to build goodwill or an image for an organization, rather than promote a specific good or service. Institutional advertising has been used by companies such as Texaco, Pfizer, and IBM to build confidence in the company name.[6] Often this form of advertising is used to support the public relations plan or counter adverse publicity. Four alternative forms of institutional advertisements are often used:

1. *Advocacy* advertisements state the position of a company on an issue. Lorillard Tobacco Company places ads discouraging teenagers from smoking, as shown on the next page. A unique form of advocacy advertisement is used when organizations make a statement or a request related to a particular event, such as the request by American Red Cross for blood donations to help terrorism victims.
2. *Pioneering institutional* advertisements, like the pioneering ads for products discussed earlier, are used for announcements about what a company is, what it can do, or where it is located. Recent Bayer ads stating "We cure more headaches than you think" are intended to inform consumers that the company produces many products in addition to aspirin.

An advocacy advertisement by Lorillard Tobacco Company discouraging teen smoking and a competitive institutional advertisement by dairy farmers trying to increase demand for milk

3. *Competitive institutional* advertisements promote the advantages of one product class over another and are used in markets where different product classes compete for the same buyers. The American Dairy Farmers and Milk Producers use their "Got Milk?" campaign to increase demand for milk as it competes against other beverages.

4. *Reminder institutional* advertisements, like the product form, simply bring the company's name to the attention of the target market again. The four branches of the U.S. military sponsor the "Today's Military" campaign to remind potential recruits of the opportunities in the active military, the National Guard, and the reserves.

Concept Check

1. What is the difference between pioneering and competitive ads?

2. What is the purpose of an institutional advertisement?

DEVELOPING THE ADVERTISING PROGRAM

The promotion decision process described in Chapter 18 can be applied to each of the promotional elements. Advertising, for example, can be managed by following the three steps (developing, executing, and evaluating) of the process.

Identifying the Target Audience

To develop an effective advertising program advertisers must identify the target audience. All aspects of an advertising program are likely to be influenced by the characteristics of the prospective consumer. Understanding the lifestyles, attitudes, and demographics of the target market is essential. Mary Quinlan, vice chair of the MacManus Group advertising agency, suggests that when women are the target it is important that the ad content reflects that women "like to see other women who are diverse, confident, and naturally beautiful," and that "women respond to emotional truth and real-life experience."[7] Similarly, the placement of ads depends on the audience. When Hummer, the biggest and most expensive sport utility vehicle in the market, began its $3 million campaign targeted at "rugged individualists" with incomes above $200,000, it selected *Wired, Spin, Red Herring, Business Week, Skiing,* and *Cigar Aficionado* to carry the ads.[8] Even scheduling can depend on the audience. Claritin, the nation's most prescribed allergy medication, schedules its use of brochures, in-store displays, coupons, and advertising to correspond to the allergy season, which varies by geographic region.[9] To eliminate possible bias that might result from subjective judgments about some population segments, the Federal Communications Commission suggests that advertising program decisions be based on market research about the target audience.[10]

√ Specifying Advertising Objectives

The guidelines for setting promotion objectives described in Chapter 18 also apply to setting advertising objectives. This step helps advertisers with other choices in the promotion decision process such as selecting media and evaluating a campaign. Advertising with an objective of creating awareness, for example, would be better matched with a magazine than a directory such as the Yellow Pages.[11] The Magazine Publishers of America believe objectives are so important that they offer a $100,000 prize each year to the campaign that best meets its objectives. The last winner, Volkswagen, won with its "Hey, There's a . . ." campaign, which helped achieve the objective of launching the new Beetle in the United States.[12] Similarly, the Advertising Research Foundation is collecting information about the effectiveness of advertising, particularly new forms such as online advertising.[13] Experts believe that factors such as product category, brand, and consumer involvement in the purchase decision may change the importance—and, possibly, the sequence—of the stages of the hierarchy of effects. Snickers, for example, knew that its consumers were unlikely to engage in elaborate information processing when it designed a recent campaign. The result was ads with simple humorous messages rather than extensive factual information.[14]

Setting the Advertising Budget

You might not remember who advertised during the 1990 Super Bowl, but it cost the companies $700,000 to place a 30-second ad. By 2002 the cost of placing a 30-second ad during Super Bowl XXXVI was $2.0 million (Figure 19–1). The reason for the escalating cost is the growing number of viewers: 41.3 million homes and 84.3 million people tune in. In addition, the audience is attractive to advertisers because research indicates that it is equally split between men and women and that prior to the game 54 percent of survey respondents were "looking forward" to watching the 59 "spots." As a result the Super Bowl attracts relatively new advertisers such as Monster.com and regular advertisers such as Anheuser-Busch.[15] Which ads were rated highest? Pepsi, AT&T Wireless, Charles Schwab, and M&M's. To see your favorite Super Bowl ads again, read the accompanying Web Link.

While not all advertising options are as expensive as the Super Bowl, most alternatives still represent substantial financial commitments and require a formal budgeting process. Pepsi and Coca-Cola, for example, have market shares of 13.8 and 20.3 percent and advertising budgets of $112 and $141 million, respectively. Using a competitive parity budgeting approach, each company spends between $7 and $8 million for each percent of market share. Using an objective and task approach, Sepracor allocated $100 million to introduce a new fast-acting allergy medication called Soltara.[16]

WEB LINK   See Your Favorite Super Bowl Ad Again!

If you missed some of the ads during the last Super Bowl, or if you liked some of them so much you want to see them again, you can review the ads at www.adforum.com. Just click on the Super Bowl icon. All ads for the past three Super Bowls, and classics like the "1984" Apple Computer ad are available to view. Which ads are your favorites? Compare their ratings!

Designing the Advertisement

An advertising message usually focuses on the key benefits of the product that are important to a prospective buyer in making trial and adoption decisions. The message depends on the general form or appeal used in the ad and the actual words included in the ad.

Message Content   Most advertising messages are made up of both informational and persuasional elements. These two elements, in fact, are so intertwined that it is sometimes difficult to tell them apart. For example, basic information contained in many ads such as the product name, benefits, features, and price are presented in a way that tries

FIGURE 19–1
Super Bowl, super dollars. Pepsi and Monster.com place ads on the Super Bowl.

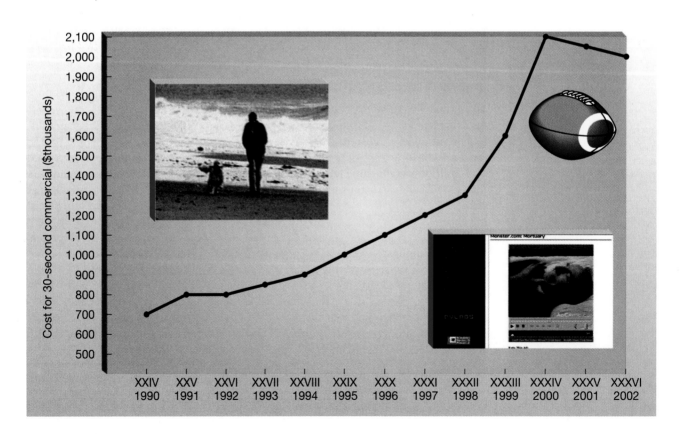

to attract attention and encourage purchase. On the other hand, even the most persuasive advertisements have to contain at least some basic information to be successful.

Information and persuasive content can be combined in the form of an appeal to provide a basic reason for the consumer to act. Although the marketer can use many different types of appeals, common advertising appeals include fear appeals,[17] sex appeals, and humorous appeals.

Fear appeals suggest to the consumer that he or she can avoid some negative experience through the purchase and use of a product or through a change in behavior. Insurance companies often try to show the negative effects of premature death on the relatives of those who don't carry enough life or mortgage insurance. Food producers encourage the purchase of low-fat, high-fiber products as a means of reducing cholesterol levels and the possibility of a heart attack.[18] When using fear appeals, the advertiser must be sure that the appeal is strong enough to get the audience's attention and concern, but not so strong that it will lead them to "tune out" the message. The Marketing NewsNet on the next page suggests some guidelines for developing an ad with a fear appeal.[19]

In contrast, *sex appeals* suggest to the audience that the product will increase the attractiveness of the user. Sex appeals can be found in almost any product category, from automobiles to toothpaste. The contemporary women's clothing store Bebe, for example, designs its advertising to "attract customers who are intrigued by the playfully sensual and evocative imagery of the Bebe lifestyle." Similarly, Diet Coke used this form of advertising when its advertising agency designed a campaign "to capture the sexual energy between men and women, and explore the traits that make them attractive to one another." Unfortunately, many commercials that use sex appeals are only successful at gaining the attention of the audience; they have little impact on how consumers think, feel, or act. Some advertising experts even argue that such appeals get in the way of successful communication by distracting the audience from the purpose of the ad. While Maybelline uses Sarah Michelle Gellar and Cover Girl uses Faith Hill as celebrity spokespersons, Revlon recently dropped its supermodel spokesperson, Cindy Crawford, because it is concerned that women remember the celebrity but not the brand they promote.[20]

Humorous appeals imply either directly or more subtly that the product is more fun or exciting than competitors' offerings. As with fear and sex appeals, the use of humor is widespread in advertising and can be found in many product categories. Of 32 awards recently given in *Advertising Age*'s Best Awards advertising competition, 23 were to ads using humor appeals. You may have a favorite humorous ad character such as the Energizer battery bunny, the Taco Bell talking dog, or the E-Trade monkey. Unfortunately for the advertiser, humor tends to wear out quickly, eventually boring the consumer. Another problem with humorous appeals is that their effectiveness may vary across cultures if used in a global campaign.[21]

Examples of a fear appeal
and a humor appeal

MARKETING NEWSNET

Designing Ads that Deal with Negative Issues

CUSTOMER VALUE

Have you ever developed anxiety over a message you've received from an advertisement? If your answer is yes, chances are that your reaction was the result of what advertisers call a *fear appeal*. Examples you may be familiar with include fire or smoke detector ads that depict a family home burning, political candidate endorsements that warn against the rise of other unpopular ideologies, or social cause ads warning of the serious consequences of drug use, alcoholism, or AIDS. This approach is based on three steps—the creation of a fearful situation by giving the audience information about the severity of the threat and the probability of its occurrence, describing the effectiveness of a solution or coping response, and suggesting how the solution can be implemented.

How individuals react to fear appeals, though, varies significantly with their prior knowledge and experience. Indeed, the varying levels of anxiety that result from the ads suggest several ethical concerns for the psychological well-being of consumers. Therefore, advertisers need to consider four guidelines when developing their ads:

1. Whenever possible, use low or moderate (rather than high) levels of fear.
2. Offer more than one alternative as a solution.
3. Avoid deceptive implications (e.g., that a product will completely eliminate a fearful condition).
4. Pretest each ad to ensure a balance between the message and the level of anxiety.

Some examples of fear appeals include the following:

SPONSOR	MEDIUM	THEME
American Express Travelers Checks	Television	A couple on a vacation was shown victimized by a robbery and left in a state of shock and desperation.
American Red Cross (CPR training)	Print	A photo shows a man with a baby. The copy reads: "What if the unthinkable happened? Would you know how to respond?"
Cease Fire	Print	The ads show a gun with a tag describing an accidental shooting of a child. The copy reads: "A gun in the home is much more likely to kill a family member than to kill an intruder."
Prudential Insurance	Television	A man was shown dying on an operating table. The message focused on who will take care of his children.
Partnership for a Drug-Free America	Print	An abstract illustration of a person's body includes copy claiming "sniffing can harm your nervous system."

∫ **Creating the Actual Message**   Advertising agency Goodby, Silverstein & Partners was recently designated as *Advertising Age* magazine's advertising Agency of the Year for "advertising that displays a classic narrative, providing 'a breathtaking combination of humanity and humility.'" One example of the agency's approach is the Discover Card ad showing a man going into the emergency room using his card, and enjoying the fact he will get money back after he is revived from a heart attack. Other successful campaigns include the E-Trade "What are you doing with your money?," *The Wall Street Journal* "Adventures in Capitalism," and the "Got Milk?" ads.[22]

Goodby, Silverstein & Partners' use of well-known personalities in the "Got Milk?" campaign is an example of a very popular form of advertising today—the use of a celebrity spokesperson. In homes across the United States, sports heroes, rock stars, movie stars, and many other celebrities are talking directly to consumers through ads in all of today's many media options. Advertisers who use a celebrity spokesperson believe that the ads are more likely to influence sales. The "Got Milk?" campaign features MTV star Carson Daly, supermodel Gisele Bundchen, legendary boxer Muhammad Ali and his daughter Laila Ali, Ronald McDonald, and many other celebrities, in an attempt to reverse the decline in per capita milk consumption. The two top celebrity spokespersons were Tiger Woods, who appears in American Express, Nike, Titleist, and Buick ads, and Michael Jordan, who appears in Nike, Hanes, Rayovac,

A creative advertisement by agency Goodby, Silverstein & Partners for Discover Card.

www.discovercard.com

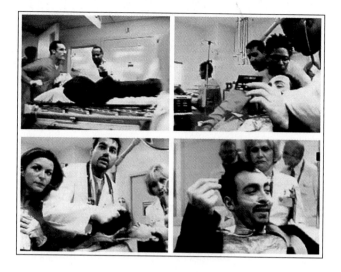

Gatorade, and Ballpark ads. Avon recently signed Venus and Serena Williams to endorse its line of cosmetics and its line of vitamins and nutritional supplements (Avon Wellness). Janice Spector, Avon's director of global advertising, says that the sisters were selected because they were "two very young women who were all about empowerment, and caring and sharing" and because "their appeal goes very far and wide." One potential shortcoming of this form of advertising is that the spokesperson's image may change to be inconsistent with the image of the company or brand. NFL football player Terrell Davis lost a contract with Campbell's Soup after being associated with a federal racketeering case, and tennis player Steffi Graf lost a contract with Opel after she was linked to a German tax-evasion case against her father.[23]

Print ads help attract readers to *The Wall Street Journal.*

www.wsj.com

THE WALL very few articles on dilly dallying or lollygagging STREET JOURNAL.

Adventures in Capitalism.

Translating the copywriter's ideas into an actual advertisement is a complex process. Designing quality artwork, layout, and production for the advertisements is costly and time-consuming. High-quality TV commercials typically cost about $268,000 to produce a 30-second ad, a task done by about 2,000 small commercial production companies across the United States. One reason for the high costs is that as companies have developed global campaigns, the need to shoot commercials in "exotic" locations has increased. Audi recently filmed commercials in Germany, Australia, and Morocco. Actors are expensive also. The Screen Actors Guild reports that an actor in a typical network TV car ad would earn between $12,000 and 15,000.[24]

Concept Check

1. What are characteristics of good advertising objectives?

2. What is a potential shortcoming of using a celebrity spokesperson?

✓ Selecting the Right Media

Every advertiser must decide where to place its advertisements. The alternatives are the *advertising media,* the means by which the message is communicated to the target audience. Newspapers, magazines, radio, and TV are examples of advertising media. This "media selection" decision is related to the target audience, type of product, nature of the message, campaign objectives, available budget, and the costs of the alternative media. Figure 19–2 shows the distribution of the $243 billion spent on advertising among the many media alternatives.[25]

Choosing a Medium and a Vehicle within That Medium   In deciding where to place advertisements, a company has several media to choose from and a number of alternatives, or vehicles, within each medium. Often advertisers use a mix of media forms and vehicles to maximize the exposure of the message to the target audience while at the same time minimizing costs. These two conflicting goals of (1) maximizing exposure and (2) minimizing costs are of central importance to media planning.

Basic Terms   Media buyers speak a language of their own, so every advertiser involved in selecting the right media for their campaigns must be familiar with some common terms used in the advertising industry. Figure 19–3 shows the most common terms used in media decisions.

Because advertisers try to maximize the number of individuals in the target market exposed to the message, they must be concerned with reach. ✓**Reach** is the number of different people or households exposed to an advertisement. The exact definition of reach sometimes varies among alternative media. Newspapers often use reach to describe their total circulation or the number of different households that buy the paper. Television and radio stations, in contrast, describe their reach using the term **rating**—the percentage of households in a market that are tuned to a particular TV show or radio station. In general, advertisers try to maximize reach in their target market at the lowest cost.

FIGURE 19–2
U.S. advertising expenditures, by category (data in millions of dollars)

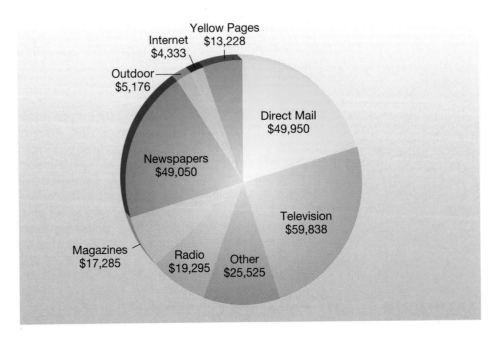

FIGURE 19–3
The language of the media
buyer

TERM	WHAT IT MEANS
Reach	The number of different people or households exposed to an advertisement.
Rating	The percentage of households in a market that are tuned to a particular TV show or radio station.
Frequency	The average number of times an individual is exposed to an advertisement.
Gross rating points (GRPs)	Reach (expressed as a percentage of the total market) multiplied by frequency.
Cost per thousand (CPM)	The cost of advertising divided by the number of thousands of individuals or households that are exposed.

Although reach is important, advertisers are also interested in exposing their target audience to a message more than once. This is because consumers often do not pay close attention to advertising messages, some of which contain large amounts of relatively complex information. When advertisers want to reach the same audience more than once, they are concerned with **frequency**, the average number of times a person in the target audience is exposed to a message or advertisement. Like reach, greater frequency is generally viewed as desirable.[26] Studies indicate that with repeated exposure to advertisements consumers respond more favorably to brand extensions.[27]

When reach (expressed as a percentage of the total market) is multiplied by frequency, an advertiser will obtain a commonly used reference number called **gross rating points** (GRPs). To obtain the appropriate number of GRPs to achieve an advertising campaign's objectives, the media planner must balance reach and frequency. The balance will also be influenced by cost. **Cost per thousand** (CPM) refers to the cost of reaching 1,000 individuals or households with the advertising message in a given medium (*M* is the Roman numeral for 1,000).

Different Media Alternatives

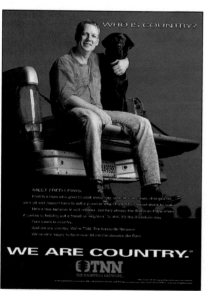

Figure 19–4 (on the next page) summarizes the advantages and disadvantages of the major advertising media, which are described in more detail below. Direct mail was discussed in Chapter 18.

Television   Television is a valuable medium because it communicates with sight, sound, and motion. Print advertisements alone could never give you the sense of a sports car cornering at high speed or communicate Ford's excitement about its new Mustang. In addition, network television is the only medium that can reach 95 percent of the homes in the United States.[28] Recent studies have shown that *out-of-home TV* reaches another 20 million viewers in bars, hotels, offices, and college campuses each week.[29]

Television's major disadvantage is cost: the price of a prime-time, 30-second ad run on *ER* is $620,000 and the average price for all prime-time programs is $194,000.[30] Because of these high charges, many advertisers choose less expensive "spot" ads, which run between programs in 10-, 15-, 30-, or 60-second lengths. Shorter ads reduce costs but severely restrict the amount of information and emotion that can be conveyed. Research indicates, however, that two different versions of a 15-second commercial, run back-to-back, will increase recall over long intervals.[31]

MEDIUM	ADVANTAGES	DISADVANTAGES
Television	Reaches extremely large audience; uses picture, print, sound, and motion for effect; can target specific audiences.	High cost to prepare and run ads; short exposure time and perishable message; difficult to convey complex information.
Radio	Low cost; can target specific local audiences; ads can be placed quickly; can use sound, humor, and intimacy effectively.	No visual element; short exposure time and perishable message; difficult to convey complex information.
Magazines	Can target specific audiences; high-quality color; long life of ad; ads can be clipped and saved; can convey complex information.	Long time needed to place ad; relatively high cost; competes for attention with other magazine features.
Newspapers	Excellent coverage of local markets; ads can be placed and changed quickly; ads can be saved; quick consumer response; low cost.	Ads compete for attention with other newspaper features; short life span; poor color.
Internet	Video and audio capabilities; animation can capture attention; ads can be interactive and link to advertiser.	Animation and interactivity require large files and more time to "load." Effectiveness is still uncertain.
Outdoor	Low cost; local market focus; high visibility; opportunity for repeat exposures.	Message must be short and simple; low selectivity of audience; criticized as a traffic hazard.
Direct mail	High selectivity of audience; can contain complex information and personalized messages; high-quality graphics.	High cost per contact; poor image (junk mail).

SOURCES: William F. Arens, *Contemporary Advertising*, 7th ed. (New York: McGraw-Hill/Irwin, 1999), pp. 268. R20: and William G. Nickels, James M. McHugh, and Susan M. McHugh, *Understanding Business*, 5th ed. (Burr Ridge, IL: McGraw-Hill/Irwin, 1999), p. 483.

FIGURE 19–4
Advantages and disadvantages of major advertising media

Another problem with television advertising is the likelihood of *wasted coverage*—having people outside the market for the product see the advertisement. The cost and wasted coverage problems of TV advertising can be reduced through the specialized cable and direct broadcast (satellite) channels. Advertising time is often less expensive on cable and direct broadcast channels than on the major networks. There are currently about 150 options—such as ESPN, MTV, Lifetime, The Nashville Network, the History Channel, Home and Garden Television, and the Outdoor Life Network—that reach very narrowly defined audiences. Other forms of television are changing television advertising also. Pay-per-view movie services and PVRs, for example, offer the potential of commercial-free viewing.

Another popular form of television advertising is the infomercial. **Infomercials** are program-length (30-minute) advertisements that take an educational approach to communication with potential customers. Today more than 90 percent of all TV stations air infomercials, and more than 25 percent of all consumers have purchased a product as a result of seeing an infomercial. Volvo, Club Med, General Motors, Bank of America, Mattel, Revlon, Texaco, and many other companies have used infomercials as a means of providing information that is relevant, useful, and entertaining to prospective customers. TiVo, the personal video recorder manufacturer, for example,

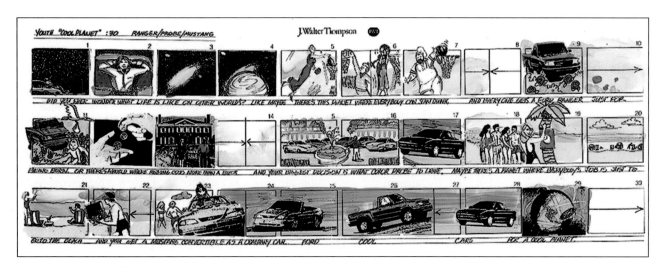

TV storyboards lead to commercials, which communicate with sight, sound, and motion.

is using infomercials to show "how the PVR works, with vignettes on how it adds value to the TV-viewing experience."[32]

Radio   There are seven times as many radio stations as television stations in the United States. The major advantage of radio is that it is a segmented medium. There are the Farm Radio Network, the Physicians' Network, all-talk shows, and hard rock stations, all listened to by different market segments. The average college student is a surprisingly heavy radio listener and spends more time during the day listening to radio than watching network television—2.2 hours versus 1.6 hours. Thus, advertisers with college students as their target market must consider radio.

The disadvantage of radio is that it has limited use for products that must be seen. Another problem is the ease with which consumers can tune out a commercial by switching stations. A new form of radio available through satellite services will offer up to 100 digital-quality coast-to-coast radio channels to consumers for a monthly subscription fee. Sirius Satellite Radio and XM Satellite Radio will offer commercial-free channels, and channels with only about 6 minutes of advertising per hour compared with 15 to 20 minutes heard on "free" channels.[33] Radio is also a medium that competes for people's attention as they do other activities such as driving, working, or relaxing. Peak radio listening time is during the drive times (6 to 10 A.M. and 4 to 7 P.M.).

Magazines   Magazines have become a very specialized medium, primarily because there are currently more than 5,000 magazines, and new magazines such as *O, The Oprah Magazine, CosmoGirl, eCompany Now, Revolution,* and *Elle Girl* are introduced each year. The marketing advantage of this medium is the great number of special-interest publications that appeal to narrowly defined segments. Runners read *Runner's World,* sailors buy *Yachting,* gardeners subscribe to *Garden Design,* and teenagers peruse *Teen People.* More than 675 publications focus on computers and technology, 669 are dedicated to travel, and 500 magazine titles are related to music.[34] Each magazine's readers often represent a unique profile. Take the *Rolling Stone* reader, who tends to listen to music more than most people—so Sony knows an ad for its new CLIE Handheld (which includes an MP3 audio player) in *Rolling Stone* is reaching the desired target audience. In addition to the distinct audience profiles of magazines, good color production is an advantage that allows magazines to create strong images.[35]

The cost of advertising in national magazines is a disadvantage, but many national publications publish regional and even metro editions, which reduce the absolute cost and wasted coverage. *Time* publishes well over 400 different editions, including Latin American, Canadian, Asian, South Pacific, European, and U.S. editions. The U.S.

editions include national, demographic, regional, state, and city options. In addition to cost, another limitation to magazines is their infrequency. At best, magazines are printed on a weekly basis, with many specialized publications appearing only monthly or less often. Although specialization can be an advantage of this medium, consumer interests can be difficult to translate into a magazine theme—a fact made clear by the hundreds of magazine failures during the past decade. *Virtual City, Mouth 2 Mouth, Top Model,* and *Esquire Sportsman,* for example, all failed to attract and keep a substantial number of readers or advertisers.[36]

Newspapers   Newspapers are an important local medium with excellent reach potential. Because of the daily publication of most papers, they allow advertisements to focus on specific current events, such as a "24-hour sale." Local retailers often use newspapers as their sole advertising medium. Newspapers are rarely saved by the purchaser, however, so companies are generally limited to ads that call for an immediate customer response (although customers can clip and save ads they select). Companies also cannot depend on newspapers for color reproduction as good as that in most magazines.

National advertising campaigns rarely include this medium except in conjunction with local distributors of their products. In these instances both parties often share the advertising costs using a cooperative advertising program, which is described later in this chapter. Another exception is the use of newspapers such as *The Wall Street Journal* and *USA Today,* which have national distribution.

Three trends are influencing newspapers today. The first is the dramatic increase in their cost of production and distribution. As printing and paper cost have increased, newspapers in cities such as Seattle and Denver have attempted to cut costs by merging their printing operations with another newspaper under a legal arrangement called a joint operating agreement (JOA). In cities such as Phoenix and Houston, population growth and suburban sprawl have increased the cost of distribution, requiring the newspapers to print outlying editions earlier, run multiple printing facilities, and use digital displays on the delivery vehicles to help control costs. The second trend is the growth in online newspapers. More than 60 newspapers, including *The Chicago Tribune, The New York Times,* the *Dallas Morning News,* the *San Jose Mercury News,* and the *Washington Post,* are already online and many others are expected soon. Finally, in many large cities free tabloid newspapers such as Boston's *Metro* and New York's *Daily News Express* are targeting commuters and creating new competition for traditional "paid-for" newspapers.[37]

Internet   The Internet represents a relatively new medium for advertisers although it has already attracted a wide variety of industries. Online advertising is similar to print advertising in that it offers a visual message. It has additional advantages, however, because it can also use the audio and video capabilities of the Internet. Sound and movement may simply attract more attention from viewers, or they may provide an element of entertainment to the message. Online advertising also has the unique feature of being interactive. Called *rich media,* these interactive ads have drop-down menus, built-in games, or search engines to engage viewers. Although online advertising is relatively small compared to other traditional media, it offers an opportunity to reach younger consumers who have developed a preference for online communication.[38]

There are a variety of online advertising options. The most common—banner ads—represent approximately 50 percent of online ad expenditures, although their effectiveness has declined to a current "click-through" rate of 0.3 percent. IBM used a banner ad with the question "What's on your mind?" to engage viewers by encouraging them to view a larger ad, and then click through to IBM's website. Other forms of online advertising include skyscrapers, pop-ups, interstitials, and minisites which use streaming video and audio, and are becoming similar to television advertising. Many advertisers are also adding entertainment elements. The online advertising

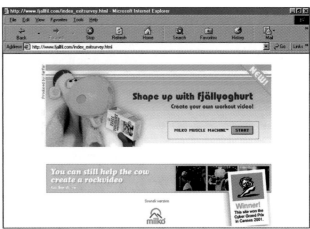

Internet advertising must
engage and entertain viewers.

grand prize winner of the Cannes International Advertising Festival, for example, was a website for Milko milk where visitors create their own workout video! Online advertising also includes e-mail marketing (discussed in Chapter 18). Lee Jeans sent 200,000 e-mail messages to young men who forwarded the message to an average of six friends each. The messages directed consumers to an online game, and ultimately to stores where secret codes for prizes were printed on price tags![39]

One disadvantage of online advertising is that because the medium is new, technical and administrative standards for the various formats are still evolving. This situation makes it difficult for advertisers to run national online campaigns across multiple sites. The Internet Advertising Bureau provides some guidance for online advertising standards and makes recommendations for new formats. Another disadvantage to online advertising is the difficulty of measuring impact. Online advertising lags behind radio, TV, and print in offering advertisers proof of effectiveness. To address this issue several companies are testing methods of tracking where viewers go on their computer in the days and weeks after seeing an ad. Nielsen's rating service, for example, measures actual click-by-click behavior through meters installed on the computers of 225,000 individuals in 26 countries both at home and at work (see www.nielsen-netratings.com for recent ratings). Another suggestion being tested by Volvo and Unilever is "permission-based" advertising where viewers agree to watch a commercial online in exchange for points, samples, or access to premium content and advertisers only pay for completed views! Internet advertising is discussed further in Chapter 21 in the context of interactive marketing.[40]

Outdoor   A very effective medium for reminding consumers about your product is outdoor advertising, such as the scoreboard at San Francisco's 3Com Park. The most common form of outdoor advertising, called *billboards,* often results in good reach and frequency and has been shown to increase purchase rates.[41] The visibility of this medium is good supplemental reinforcement for well-known products, and it is a relatively low-cost, flexible alternative. A company can buy space just in the desired geographical market. A disadvantage to billboards, however, is that no opportunity exists for lengthy advertising copy. Also, a good billboard site depends on traffic patterns and sight lines. In many areas environmental laws have limited the use of this medium.

If you have ever lived in a metropolitan area, chances are you might have seen another form of outdoor advertising, transit advertising. This medium includes messages on the interior and exterior of buses, subway cars, and taxis. As use of mass transit grows, transit advertising may become increasingly important. Selectivity is available to advertisers, who can buy space by neighborhood or bus route. One disadvantage to this medium is that the heavy travel times, when the audiences are the largest, are not conducive to reading advertising copy. People are standing shoulder to shoulder on the subway, hoping not to miss their stop, and little attention is paid to the advertising.

The outdoor advertising industry has experienced a surge of growth recently. Lower costs, faster technology, and a lot of creativity have attracted large, national advertisers such as Sony, Microsoft, and America Online.[42] Orlando's Transportation Authority utilizes a wireless system to receive advertising for flat screen monitors mounted in its 240 buses. Streetbeam is developing a service that will allow commuters with personal digital assistants (e.g., a Palm handheld) to receive enhanced messages from the displays![43] Although outdoor advertising expenditures grew to more than $5 billion in 2001, the industry must address environmental concerns through self-regulation or be restricted by legislation. For example, four states have banned billboards, and New York City's Metropolitan Transportation Authority has banned tobacco advertising on buses and subways.[44]

Captivate TV Network offers "TV in Elevators."

Other Media   As traditional media have become more expensive and cluttered, advertisers have been attracted to a variety of nontraditional advertising options, called *place-based media.* Messages are placed in locations that attract a specific target audience such as airports, doctors' offices, health clubs, theaters (where ads are played on the screen before the movies are shown), even bathrooms of bars, restaurants, and nightclubs![45] Soon there will be advertising on video screens on gas pumps, ATMs, and in elevators. New York's La Guardia airport has started putting ads on baggage conveyors, and Beach n Billboard will even imprint ads in the sand on a beach![46]

Selection Criteria   Choosing between these alternative media is difficult and depends on several factors. First, knowing the media habits of the target audience is essential to deciding among the alternatives. Second, occasionally product attributes necessitate that certain media be used. For example, if color is a major aspect of product appeal, radio is excluded. Newspapers allow advertising for quick actions to confront competitors, and magazines are more appropriate for complicated messages because the reader can spend more time reading the message. The final factor in selecting a medium is cost. When possible, alternative media are compared using a common denominator that reflects both reach and cost—a measure such as CPM.

Scheduling the Advertising

There is no correct schedule to advertise a product, but three factors must be considered. First is the issue of *buyer turnover,* which is how often new buyers enter the market to buy the product. The higher the buyer turnover, the greater is the amount of advertising required. A second issue in scheduling is the *purchase frequency;* the more frequently the product is purchased, the less repetition is required. Finally, companies must consider the *forgetting rate,* the speed with which buyers forget the brand if advertising is not seen.

Setting schedules requires an understanding of how the market behaves. Most companies tend to follow one of three basic approaches:

1. *Continuous (steady) schedule.* When seasonal factors are unimportant, advertising is run at a continuous or steady schedule throughout the year.
2. *Flighting (intermittent) schedule.* Periods of advertising are scheduled between periods of no advertising to reflect seasonal demand.

3. *Pulse (burst) schedule.* A flighting schedule is combined with a continuous schedule because of increases in demand, heavy periods of promotion, or introduction of a new product.

For example, products such as dry breakfast cereals have a stable demand throughout the year and would typically use a continuous schedule of advertising. In contrast, products such as snow skis and suntan lotions have seasonal demands and receive flighting-schedule advertising during the seasonal demand period. Some products such as toys or automobiles require pulse-schedule advertising to facilitate sales throughout the year and during special periods of increased demand (such as holidays or new car introductions). Some evidence suggests that pulsing schedules are superior to other advertising strategies.[47] In addition, recent research findings indicate that the effectiveness of a particular ad "wears out" quickly and, therefore, many alternative forms of a commercial may be more effective.[48]

Concept Check

1. You see the same ad in *Time* and *Fortune* magazines and on billboards and TV. Is this an example of reach or frequency?

2. Why has the Internet become a popular advertising medium?

3. What factors must be considered when choosing among alternative media?

EXECUTING THE ADVERTISING PROGRAM

Executing the advertising program involves pretesting the advertising copy and actually carrying out the advertising program. John Wanamaker, the founder of Wanamaker's Department Store in Philadelphia, remarked, "I know half my advertising is wasted, but I don't know what half." By evaluating advertising efforts marketers can try to ensure that their advertising expenditures are not wasted.[49] Evaluation is done usually at two separate times: before and after the advertisements are run in the actual campaign. Several methods used in the evaluation process at the stages of idea formulation and copy development are discussed below. Posttesting methods are reviewed in the section on evaluation.

Pretesting the Advertising

To determine whether the advertisement communicates the intended message or to select among alternative versions of the advertisement, **pretests** are conducted before the advertisements are placed in any medium.

Portfolio Tests   Portfolio tests are used to test copy alternatives. The test ad is placed in a portfolio with several other ads and stories, and consumers are asked to read through the portfolio. Afterward subjects are asked for their impressions of the ads on several evaluative scales, such as from "very informative" to "not very informative."

Jury Tests   Jury tests involve showing the ad copy to a panel of consumers and having them rate how they liked it, how much it drew their attention, and how attractive they thought it was. This approach is similar to the portfolio test in that consumer reactions are obtained. However, unlike the portfolio test, a test advertisement is not hidden within other ads.

FIGURE 19–5
Alternative structures of
advertising agencies used to
carry out the advertising
program

TYPE OF AGENCY	SERVICES PROVIDED
Full-service agency	Does research, selects media, develops copy, and produces artwork; also coordinates integrated campaigns with all marketing efforts
Limited-service (specialty) agency	Specializes in one aspect of creative process; usually provides creative production work; buys previously unpurchased media space
In-house agency	Provides range of services, depending on company needs

Theater Tests   Theater testing is the most sophisticated form of pretesting. Consumers are invited to view new television shows or movies in which test commercials are also shown. Viewers register their feelings about the advertisements either on hand-held electronic recording devices used during the viewing or on questionnaires afterward.

Carrying Out the Advertising Program

The responsibility for actually carrying out the advertising program can be handled in one of three ways, as shown in Figure 19–5. The **full-service agency** provides the most complete range of services, including market research, media selection, copy development, artwork, and production. Agencies that assist a client by both developing and placing advertisements have traditionally charged a commission of 15 percent of media costs. As corporations have introduced integrated marketing approaches, however, most (70 percent) advertisers have switched from paying commissions to incentives or fees based on performance. Brad Brinegar, CEO of advertising agency Leo Burnett USA, suggests that "a lot of value we offer is in strategic thinking, and how to pay for that is very different from traditional media spending." The most common performance criteria used are sales, brand and ad awareness, market share, and copy test results. Procter and Gamble's switch to sales-based incentives actually turned out better for its agency than media commissions would have. Global marketing director Bob Wehling explains: "P&G's goal in changing compensation wasn't to cut costs, the goal was to increase sales and support agencies in developing more comprehensive marketing plans that focus less exclusively on TV advertising and more on a broad array of reaching consumers."[50] **Limited-service agencies** specialize in one aspect of the advertising process such as providing creative services to develop the advertising copy or buying previously unpurchased media space. Limited-service agencies that deal in creative work are compensated by a contractual agreement for the services performed. Finally, **in-house agencies** made up of the company's own advertising staff may provide full services or a limited range of services.

EVALUATING THE ADVERTISING PROGRAM

The advertising decision process does not stop with executing the advertising program. The advertisements must be posttested to determine whether they are achieving their intended objectives, and results may indicate that changes must be made in the advertising program.

Posttesting the Advertising

An advertisement may go through **posttests** after it has been shown to the target audience to determine whether it accomplished its intended purpose. Five approaches common in posttesting are discussed here.[51]

Starch scores an advertisement.

Aided Recall (Recognition-Readership)   After being shown an ad, respondents are asked whether their previous exposure to it was through reading, viewing, or listening. The Starch test shown in the accompanying photo uses aided recall to determine the percentage of those (1) who remember seeing a specific magazine ad (*noted*), (2) who saw or read any part of the ad identifying the product or brand (*seen-associated*), and (3) who read at least half of the ad (*read most*). Elements of the ad are then tagged with the results, as shown in the picture.

Unaided Recall   A question such as, "What ads do you remember seeing yesterday?" is asked of respondents without any prompting to determine whether they saw or heard advertising messages.

Attitude Tests   Respondents are asked questions to measure changes in their attitudes after an advertising campaign, such as whether they have a more favorable attitude toward the product advertised.[52]

Inquiry Tests   Additional product information, product samples, or premiums are offered to an ad's readers or viewers. Ads generating the most inquiries are presumed to be the most effective.

Sales Tests   Sales tests involve studies such as controlled experiments (e.g., using radio ads in one market and newspaper ads in another and comparing the results) and consumer purchase tests (measuring retail sales that result from a given advertising campaign). The most sophisticated experimental methods today allow a manufacturer, a distributor, or an advertising agency to manipulate an advertising variable (such as schedule or copy) through cable systems and observe subsequent sales effects by monitoring data collected from checkout scanners in supermarkets.[53]

Making Needed Changes

Results of posttesting the advertising copy are used to reach decisions about changes in the advertising program. If the posttest results show that an advertisement is doing poorly in terms of awareness or cost efficiency, it may be dropped and other ads run in its place in the future. On the other hand, sometimes an advertisement may be so successful it is run repeatedly or used as the basis of a larger advertising program.

Concept Check

1. Explain the difference between pretesting and posttesting advertising copy.

2. What is the difference between aided and unaided recall posttests?

SALES PROMOTION

The Importance of Sales Promotion

Sales promotion has become a key element of the promotional mix, which now accounts for more than $100 billion in annual expenditures. In a recent survey by the Promotion Marketing Association, marketing professionals reported that approximately 53 percent of their budgets were allocated to advertising, 23 percent to consumer promotion, 18 percent to trade promotion, and 6 percent to public relations and customer service.[54] The allocation of marketing expenditures reflects the trend toward integrated promotion programs which include a variety of promotion elements. Selection and integration of the many promotion techniques require a good understanding of the advantages and disadvantages of each kind of promotion.[55]

Consumer-Oriented Sales Promotions

Directed to ultimate consumers, **consumer-oriented sales promotions**, or simply consumer promotions, are sales tools used to support a company's advertising and personal selling. The alternative consumer-oriented sales promotion tools include coupons, deals, premiums, contests, sweepstakes, samples, continuity programs, point-of-purchase displays, rebates, and product placement (see Figure 19–6).

Coupons   Coupons are sales promotions that usually offer a discounted price to the consumer, which encourages trial. Approximately 250 billion coupons are distributed in the United States each year. The redemption rate is typically about 2 percent, although it increases during recessionary cycles of the economy. In 2000, 4.5 billion coupons were redeemed for a value of $3.6 billion or an average of 77 cents per coupon. In recent years the average face value of coupons, the number of coupons with multiple-purchase requirements, and the time until expiration have all been increasing.

FIGURE 19–6
Sales promotion alternatives

KIND OF SALES PROMOTION	OBJECTIVES	ADVANTAGES	DISADVANTAGES
Coupons	Stimulate demand	Encourage retailer support	Consumers delay purchases
Deals	Increase trial; retaliate against competitor's actions	Reduce consumer risk	Consumers delay purchases; reduce perceived product value
Premiums	Build goodwill	Consumers like free or reduced-price merchandise	Consumers buy for premium, not product
Contests	Increase consumer purchases; build business inventory	Encourage consumer involvement with product	Require creative or analytical thinking
Sweepstakes	Encourage present customers to buy more; minimize brand switching	Get customer to use product and store more often	Sales drop after sweepstakes
Samples	Encourage new product trial	Low risk for consumer	High cost for company
Continuity programs	Encourage repeat purchases	Help create loyalty	High cost for company
Point-of-purchase displays	Increase product trial; provide in-store support for other promotions	Provide good product visibility	Hard to get retailer to allocate high-traffic space
Rebates	Encourage customers to purchase; stop sales decline	Effective at stimulating demand	Easily copied; steal sales from future; reduce perceived product value
Product placement	Introduce new products; demonstrate product use	Positive message in a noncommercial setting	Little control over presentation of product

ETHICS AND SOCIAL RESPONSIBILITY ALERT

Coupon Scams Cost Manufacturers $500 Million Each Year

ETHICS

Coupon fraud has become a serious concern for consumer goods manufacturers. How serious? The Coupon Information Center estimates that companies pay out coupon refunds of more than $500 million a year to retailers and individuals who don't deserve them. That adds a huge cost to promotions designed to help consumers.

The methods used by the cheaters are becoming very sophisticated. For example:

- Some scam artists set up a fake store and send coupons to manufacturers for payment.
- Coupon collectors often sell coupons to retailers who are paid full face value by manufacturers, even though the products were not sold.
- Retailers increase their refunds by adding extra coupons to those handed in by shoppers.

- Counterfeiters print rebate forms and proofs of purchase to collect big cash rebates without buying the products.

One of the newest forms of coupon fraud is the result of Internet coupon sites which allow coupons to be printed at home. The coupon bar code, value, or even the offer can be manipulated and copied with now-common computer equipment and skills.

Some of the steps being taken to reduce coupon and rebate fraud include requiring handwritten redemption requests and requesting a proof of purchase. In addition, to reduce online abuses, several stores are trying in-store kiosks to print the coupons and vendors are trying systems that send an electronic coupon credit directly to the retailer.

What are your reactions to misredemption? Should action be taken against coupon fraud?

In addition the number of coupons generated at Internet sites (e.g., www.valpak.com and www.couponsonline.com) has been increasing. Coupons are often viewed as a key element of an integrated marketing program. Sears, for example, offered coupons for $5 off purchases of $25 or more in kids' apparel and footwear for consumers who donated books to the Million Book March, a national cause-related campaign.[56]

Do coupons help increase sales? Studies suggest that market share does increase during the period immediately after coupons are distributed.[57] There are also indications, however, that couponing can reduce gross revenues by lowering the price paid by already-loyal consumers.[58] Therefore, the 9,000 manufacturers who currently use coupons are particularly interested in coupon programs directed at potential first-time buyers. One means of focusing on these potential buyers is through electronic in-store coupon machines that match coupons to your most recent purchases. A recent survey suggests that 81 percent of Americans use coupons when grocery shopping.[59]

Coupons are often far more expensive than the face value of the coupon; a 25 cent coupon can cost three times that after paying for the advertisement to deliver it, dealer handling, clearinghouse costs, and redemption. In addition, misredemption, or paying the face value of the coupon even though the product was not purchased, should be added to the cost of the coupon. See the accompanying Ethics and Social Responsibility Alert for additional information about misredemption.[60]

Deals   Deals are short-term price reductions, commonly used to increase trial among potential customers or to retaliate against a competitor's actions. For example, if a rival manufacturer introduces a new cake mix, the company responds with a "two packages for the price of one" deal. This short-term price reduction builds up the stock on the kitchen shelves of cake mix buyers and makes the competitor's introduction more difficult.

Premiums   A promotional tool often used with consumers is the premium, which consists of merchandise offered free or at a significant savings over its retail price. This latter type of premium is called *self-liquidating* because the cost charged to the consumer covers the cost of the item. McDonald's, for example, used a free premium in a promotional partnership with Disney/Pixar during the release of the movie *Monsters, Inc.* Collectable toys that portrayed movie characters were given away free with the purchase of a Happy Meal. Milk-Bone dog biscuits used a self-liquidating premium when it offered a ball toy for $8.99 and two proofs of purchase.[61] By offering a premium, companies encourage customers to return frequently or to use more of the product.

Contests   A fourth sales promotion in Figure 19–6, the contest, is where consumers apply their skill or analytical or creative thinking to try to win a prize. For example, the History Channel used a contest to generate viewership for its Founding Fathers miniseries. Five million pamphlets were distributed through 3,000 libraries to announce an essay contest with college scholarships as awards. More than 5,000 essays were submitted and the ratings for the four-day miniseries were double network averages.[62] If you like contests, you can even enter online now at websites such as www.playhere.com!

Sweepstakes   *Reader's Digest* and Publisher's Clearing House are two of the better-promoted sweepstakes. These sales promotions require participants to submit some kind of entry form but are purely games of chance requiring no analytical or creative effort by the consumer. The approach is very effective—*Time* magazine obtained 1.4 million new subscribers in one year through sweepstakes promotions.[63] A variation of a sweepstakes is the instant-win game such as Coca-Cola's "Pop the Top" promotion. The game offers the latest trend in contest prizes—an "experience," which in this game was going to a Christina Aguilera video shoot. According to Michael La Kier, Coca-Cola's manager of consumer promotions, "Consumers overwhelmingly have told us that experiences are more meaningful."[64] Federal laws, the Federal Trade Commission, and state legislatures have issued rules covering sweepstakes, contests, and games to regulate their fairness, ensure that the chance for winning is represented honestly, and guarantee that the prizes are actually awarded.[65]

Samples   Another common consumer sales promotion is sampling, which is offering the product free or at a greatly reduced price. Often used for new products, sampling puts the product in the consumer's hands. A trial size is generally offered that is smaller than the regular package size. If consumers like the sample, it is hoped they will remember and buy the product. When Mars changed its Milky Way Dark to Milky

Consumer-oriented promotions use games to attract prospective customers and continuity programs to reward loyal customers.

Way Midnight it gave away more than 1 million samples to college students at night clubs, several hundred campuses, and popular spring break locations. Awareness of the candy bar rose to 60 percent, trial rose 166 percent, and sales rose 25 percent! Overall, companies invest more than $1.2 billion in sampling programs each year.[66]

Continuity Programs   Continuity programs are a sales promotion tool used to encourage and reward repeat purchases by acknowledging each purchase made by a consumer and offering a premium as purchases accumulate. The most popular continuity programs today are the frequent flyer and frequent traveler programs used by airlines, hotels, and car rental services to reward loyal customers. American Airlines customers, for example, earn "points" for each mile they fly, and can then redeem the accumulated points for free tickets on the airline. American Airlines also offers a credit card which provides points for all charges made on the card. Some continuity programs, such as the American Express Membership Rewards program, require participants to pay a membership fee. For $40 per year, in addition to their annual card fees, 8 million people in 30 countries receive special offers and can redeem points for just about anything from airline miles to hotel stays to merchandise. What is the most outrageous award? One million points qualifies a member for a lease on a Mustang convertible![67]

Point-of-Purchase Displays   In a store aisle, you often encounter a sales promotion called a *point-of-purchase display.* These product displays take the form of advertising signs, which sometimes actually hold or display the product, and are often located in high-traffic areas near the cash register or the end of an aisle. The accompanying

picture shows a point-of-purchase display for Nabisco's annual back-to-school program. The display is designed to maximize the consumer's attention to lunch box and after-school snacks, and to provide storage for the products. A recent survey of retailers found that 87 percent plan to use more point-of-purchase materials in the future, particularly for products that can be purchased on impulse.[68]

Some studies estimate that two-thirds of a consumer's buying decisions are made in the store. This means that grocery product manufacturers want to get their message to you at the instant you are next to their brand in your supermarket aisle—perhaps through a point-of-purchase display. At a growing number of supermarkets this may be done with Floorgraphics—floor displays with animation and sound, and Shelfscents—displays that release a product's scent to potential consumers.[69] The advantage of these methods of promotion is that they do not rely on the consumers' ability to remember the message for long periods of time. Other in-store promotions such as interactive kiosks are also becoming popular.

Rebates   Another consumer sales promotion in Figure 19–6, the cash rebate, offers the return of money based on proof of purchase. This tool has been used heavily by car manufacturers facing increased competition. For example, to increase sales, General Motors offered recent college graduates an extra $400 rebate on the Chevrolet Cavalier, in addition to the $2,500 rebate already offered.[70] When the rebate is offered on lower-priced items, the time and trouble of mailing in a proof of purchase to get the rebate check often means that many buyers never take advantage of it. However, this "slippage" is less likely to occur with frequent users of rebate promotions.[71] In addition, online consumers are more likely to take advantage of rebates.

Can you identify these product placements?

Product Placement   A final consumer promotion, **product placement**, involves the use of a brand-name product in a movie, television show, video, or a commercial for another product. It was Steven Spielberg's placement of Hershey's Reese's Pieces in *E.T.* that first brought a lot of interest to the candy. Similarly, when Tom Cruise wore Bausch and Lomb's Ray-Ban sunglasses in *Risky Business* and its Aviator sunglasses in *Top Gun,* sales skyrocketed from 100,000 pairs to 7,000,000 pairs in five years. More recently you might remember seeing participants in the television show *Survivor* eating Doritos and drinking Mountain Dew, actors in the movie *Bandits* driving a Chrysler PT Cruiser, or women in the cast of *Ally McBeal* wearing BeBe clothing. And after driving a BMW in his last three movies, James Bond is driving Aston Martin's new V12 Vanquish once again (the only car he drove in the first 16 Bond movies). Another form of product placement uses new digital technology which can make "virtual" placements in any existing program. Reruns of *Seinfeld,* for example, could insert a Pepsi on a desktop, a Lexus parked on the street, or a box of Tide on the countertop![72] The photo above shows Beaver's father with a cell phone in his pocket!

Companies are usually eager to gain exposure for their products, and the studios believe that product placements add authenticity to the film or program. The studios receive fees—Warner Bros. reportedly charged America Online between $3 and $6 million for using its e-mail service in the movie *You've Got Mail*—in exchange for the on-screen exposure. How are product placements arranged? Many companies simply send brochures and catalogs to the studio resource departments; others are approached by agents who review scripts to find promising scenes where a product might be used.[73]

Trade-Oriented Sales Promotions

Trade-oriented sales promotions, or simply trade promotions, are sales tools used to support a company's advertising and personal selling directed to wholesalers, retailers, or distributors. Some of the sales promotions just reviewed are used for this purpose, but there are three other common approaches targeted uniquely to these intermediaries: (1) allowances and discounts, (2) cooperative advertising, and (3) training of distributors' salesforces.

Allowances and Discounts   Trade promotions often focus on maintaining or increasing inventory levels in the channel of distribution. An effective method for encouraging such increased purchases by intermediaries is the use of allowances and discounts. However, overuse of these "price reductions" can lead to retailers changing their ordering patterns in the expectation of such offerings. Although there are many variations that manufacturers can use with discounts and allowances, three common approaches include the merchandise allowance, the case allowance, and the finance allowance.[74]

Reimbursing a retailer for extra in-store support or special featuring of the brand is a *merchandise allowance.* Performance contracts between the manufacturer and trade member usually specify the activity to be performed, such as a picture of the product in a newspaper with a coupon good at only one store. The merchandise allowance then consists of a percentage deduction from the list case price ordered during the promotional period. Allowances are not paid by the manufacturer until it sees proof of performance (such as a copy of the ad placed by the retailer in the local newspaper).

A second common trade promotion, a *case allowance,* is a discount on each case ordered during a specific time period. These allowances are usually deducted from the invoice. A variation of the case allowance is the "free goods" approach, whereby retailers receive some amount of the product free based on the amount ordered, such as 1 case free for every 10 cases ordered.[75]

A final trade promotion, the *finance allowance,* involves paying retailers for financing costs or financial losses associated with consumer sales promotions. This trade promotion is regularly used and has several variations. One type is the floor stock protection program—manufacturers give retailers a case allowance price for products in their warehouse, which prevents shelf stock from running down during the promotional period. Also common are freight allowances, which compensate retailers that transport orders from the manufacturer's warehouse.

Cooperative Advertising
Resellers often perform the important function of promoting the manufacturer's products at the local level. One common sales promotional activity is to encourage both better quality and greater quantity in the local advertising efforts of resellers through **cooperative advertising**. These are programs by which a manufacturer pays a percentage of the retailer's local advertising expense for advertising the manufacturer's products.

Usually the manufacturer pays a percentage, often 50 percent, of the cost of advertising up to a certain dollar limit, which is based on the amount of the purchases the retailer makes of the manufacturer's products. In addition to paying for the advertising, the manufacturer often furnishes the retailer with a selection of different ad executions, sometimes suited for several different media. A manufacturer may provide, for example, several different print layouts as well as a few broadcast ads for the retailer to adapt and use.[76]

Training of Distributors' Salesforces
One of the many functions the intermediaries perform is customer contact and selling for the producers they represent. Both retailers and wholesalers employ and manage their own sales personnel. A manufacturer's success often rests on the ability of the reseller's salesforce to represent its products.

Thus, it is in the best interest of the manufacturer to help train the reseller's salesforce. Because the reseller's salesforce is often less sophisticated and knowledgeable about the products than the manufacturer might like, training can increase their sales performance. Training activities include producing manuals and brochures to educate the reseller's salesforce. The salesforce then uses these aids in selling situations. Other activities include national sales meetings sponsored by the manufacturer and field visits to the reseller's location to inform and motivate the salesperson to sell the products. Manufacturers also develop incentive and recognition programs to motivate reseller's salespeople to sell their products.

Concept Check

1. Which sales promotional tool is most common for new products?

2. What's the difference between a coupon and a deal?

3. Which trade promotion is used on an ongoing basis?

PUBLIC RELATIONS

As noted in Chapter 18, public relations is a form of communication management that seeks to influence the image of an organization and its products and services. Public relations efforts may utilize a variety of tools and may be directed at many distinct audiences. While public relations personnel usually focus on communicating positive aspects of the business, they may also be called on to minimize the negative impact of a problem or crisis. Firestone, for example, recalled 6.5 million tires when National Highway Traffic Safety Administration officials launched an investigation into consumer complaints about the tires. Debates with Ford Motor Company about the tire failures being due to overloading or underinflation, created a difficult situation for the public relations department.[77] The most frequently used public relations tool is publicity.

Publicity Tools

In developing a public relations campaign, several methods of obtaining nonpersonal presentation of an organization, good, or service without direct cost—**publicity tools**—are available to the public relations director. Many companies frequently use the *news release,* consisting of an announcement regarding changes in the company or the product line. The objective of a news release is to inform a newspaper, radio station, or other medium of an idea for a story. A recent study found that more than 40 percent of all free mentions of a brand name occur during news programs.[78]

A second common publicity tool is the *news conference.* Representatives of the media are all invited to an informational meeting, and advance materials regarding the content are sent. This tool is often used when negative publicity—as in the cases of the Ford Explorer rollover problem, the NASCAR Daytona 500 accident that killed Dale Earnhardt, and the *Exxon Valdez* oil spill—requires a company response.[79]

Nonprofit organizations rely heavily on *PSAs* (*public service announcements*), which are free space or time donated by the media. For example, the charter of the American Red Cross prohibits any local chapter from advertising, so to solicit blood donations local chapters often depend on PSAs on radio or television to announce their needs.

Cameron Diaz uses publicity to promote her movies.

Finally, today many high-visibility individuals are used as publicity tools to create visibility for their companies, their products, and themselves. Michael Eisner uses visibility to promote Disney, Cameron Diaz uses it to promote her movies, and U.S. senators use it to promote themselves as political candidates. These publicity efforts are coordinated with news releases, conferences, advertising, donations to charities, volunteer activities, endorsements, and any other activities that may have an impact on public perceptions.[80]

INCREASING THE VALUE OF PROMOTION

Today's customers seek value from companies that provide leading-edge products, hassle-free transactions at competitive prices, and customer intimacy.[81] Promotion practices have changed dramatically to improve transactions and increase customer intimacy by (1) emphasizing long-term relationships, and (2) increasing self-regulation.

Building Long-Term Relationships with Promotion

Many changes in promotional techniques have been driven by marketers' interest in developing long-term relationships with their customers. Promotion can contribute to brand and store loyalty by improving its ability to target individual preferences and by engaging customers in valuable and entertaining communication. New media such as the Internet have provided immediate opportunities for personalized promotion activities such as e-mail advertising. In addition, technological developments have helped traditional media such as TV and radio focus on individual preferences through services such as TiVo and XM Radio. Although the future holds extraordinary promise for the personalization of promotion, the industry will need to manage and balance consumers' concerns about privacy as it proceeds.

Changes that help engage consumers have also been numerous. Marketers have attempted to utilize interactive technologies and to integrate new media and technologies into the overall creative process. Ad agencies are increasingly integrating public relations, direct marketing, advertising, and promotion into comprehensive campaigns. In fact, some experts predict that advertising agencies will soon become "communications consulting firms." Further, increasingly diverse and global audiences necessitate multimedia approaches and sensitivity communication techniques that engage the varied groups.[82] Overall, companies hope that these changes will build customer relationships for the long term—emphasizing a lifetime of purchases rather than a single transaction.

Self-Regulation

Unfortunately, over the years many consumers have been misled—or even deceived—by some promotions. Examples include sweepstakes in which the gifts were not awarded, rebate offers that were a terrible hassle, and advertisements whose promises were great, until the buyer read the small print. In one of the worst scandals in promotion history, McDonald's assisted an FBI investigation of the firm responsible for its sweepstakes—because the promotion agency security director was suspected of stealing winning gamepieces.[83]

Promotions targeted at special groups such as children and the elderly also raise ethical concerns. For example, providing free samples to children in elementary schools or linking product lines to TV programs and movies have led to questions about the need for restrictions on promotions.[84] Although the Federal Trade Commission does provide some guidelines to protect consumers and special groups from misleading promotions, some observers believe more government regulation is needed.

To rely on formal regulation by federal, state, and local governments of all promotional activities would be very expensive. As a result, there are increasing efforts by advertising agencies, trade associations, and marketing organizations at *self-regulation.*[85] By imposing standards that reflect the values of society on their promotional activities, marketers can (1) facilitate the development of new promotional methods, (2) minimize regulatory constraints and restrictions, and (3) help consumers gain confidence in the communication efforts used to influence their purchases. As organizations strive for effective self-regulation, marketing executives will need to make sound ethical judgments about the use of existing and new promotional practices.

Concept Check

1. What is a news release?

2. What is the difference between government regulation and self-regulation?

SUMMARY

1 Advertising may be classified as either product or institutional. Product advertising can take three forms: pioneering, competitive, or reminder. Institutional ads are one of these three or advocacy.

2 The promotion decision process described in Chapter 18 can be applied to each of the promotional elements such as advertising.

3 Copywriters and art directors have the responsibility of identifying the key benefits of a product and communicating them to the target audience with attention-getting advertising. Common appeals include fear, sex, and humor.

4 In selecting the right medium, there are distinct trade-offs among television, radio, magazines, newspapers, direct mail, outdoor, and other media. The decision is based on media habits of the target audience, product characteristics, message requirements, and media costs.

5 In determining advertising schedules, a balance must be made between reach and frequency. Scheduling must take into account buyer turnover, purchase frequency, and the rate at which consumers forget.

6 Advertising is evaluated before and after the ad is run. Pretesting can be done with portfolio, jury, or theater tests. Posttesting is done on the basis of aided recall, unaided recall, attitude tests, inquiry tests, and sales tests.

7 To execute an advertising program, companies can use several types of advertising agencies. These firms can provide a full range of services or specialize in creative or placement activities. Some firms use their own in-house agency.

8 Almost equal amounts of money are spent on sales promotion and advertising. Selecting sales promotions requires a good understanding of the advantages and disadvantages of each option.

9 There is a wide range of consumer-oriented sales promotions: coupons, deals, premiums, contests, sweepstakes, samples, continuity programs, point-of-purchase displays, rebates, and product placements.

10 Trade-oriented promotions consist of allowances and discounts, cooperative advertising, and training of distributors' salesforces. These are used at all levels of the channel.

11 The most frequently used public relations tool is publicity—a nonpersonal, indirectly paid presentation of an organization, good, or service conducted through new releases, news conferences, or public service announcements.

12 Efforts to improve the value of promotion include emphasizing long-term relationships and increasing self-regulation.

KEY TERMS AND CONCEPTS

advertising p. 498
consumer-oriented sales promotions p. 516
cooperative advertising p. 521
cost per thousand p. 507
frequency p. 507
full-service agency p. 514
gross rating points p. 507
infomercials p. 508
in-house agencies p. 514
institutional advertisements p. 499

limited-service agencies p. 514
posttests p. 514
pretests p. 513
product advertisements p. 498
product placement p. 520
publicity tools p. 522
rating p. 506
reach p. 506
trade-oriented sales promotions p. 520

APPLYING MARKETING CONCEPTS AND PERSPECTIVES

1 How does competitive product advertising differ from competitive institutional advertising?

2 Suppose you are the advertising manager for a new line of children's fragrances. Which form of media would you use for this new product?

3 You have recently been promoted to be director of advertising for the Timkin Tool Company. In your first meeting with Mr. Timkin, he says, "Advertising is a waste! We've been advertising for six months now and sales haven't increased. Tell me why we should continue." Give your answer to Mr. Timkin.

4 A large life insurance company has decided to switch from using a strong fear appeal to a humorous approach. What are the strengths and weaknesses of such a change in message strategy?

5 Which medium has the lowest cost per thousand?

MEDIUM	COST	AUDIENCE
TV show	$5,000	25,000
Magazine	2,200	6,000
Newspaper	4,800	7,200
FM radio	420	1,600

6 Some national advertisers have found that they can have more impact with their advertising by running a large number of ads for a period and then running no ads at all for a period. Why might such a flighting schedule be more effective than a steady schedule?

7 Each year managers at Bausch and Lomb evaluate the many advertising media alternatives available to them as they develop their advertising program for contact lenses. What advantages and disadvantages of each alternative should they consider? Which media would you recommend to them?

8 What are two advantages and two disadvantages of the advertising posttests described in the chapter?

9 Federated Banks is interested in consumer-oriented sales promotions that would encourage senior citizens to direct deposit their Social Security checks with the bank. Evaluate the sales promotion options, and recommend two of them to the bank.

10 How can public relations be used by Firestone and Ford following investigations into complaints about tire failures?

11 Describe a self-regulation guideline you believe would improve the value of (*a*) an existing form of promotion and (*b*) a new promotional practice.

INTERNET EXERCISE

Most Web pages accept some form of advertising. If you were to advise your college or university to advertise on the Web, what three Web pages would you recommend? You can use the information at www.adhome.com to help make your recommendation.

1 What is the monthly rate for a full banner ad at each of the websites?

2 Describe the profile of the audience for each of the websites.

3 Calculate the CPM for each website.

WEBSITE	MONTHLY RATE	AUDIENCE PROFILE	CPM
1.			
2.			
3.			

VIDEO CASE 19–1   Fallon Worldwide: In the *Creativity* Business

"Most people think of Fallon as being in the advertising business, but we don't really think of ourselves that way," says Rob White, president of Fallon Worldwide. "We believe that we are a creativity company that happens to do some advertising," he continues.

As an example, he points out that Fallon starts upstream of a firm's communication issues to identify the key business problem and uses creativity to help solve it. Sometimes this involves a heavy dose of advertising and other times almost none. But it always takes a very creative flair.

Founded in 1981, Fallon Worldwide—or simply "Fallon"—has won dozens of advertising awards. This includes two "Agency of the Year" awards given by *Advertising Age* magazine. "I think Fallon's success is due to two important things," says White. "One is the people and the other one is the culture that bonds the people together. When you create a special kind of culture with collaboration and teamwork from a very high level and people with different backgrounds, amazing things can happen," he explains.

Bruce Bildsten, Fallon Creative Group Director, echoes this focus on creativity: "It's always a challenge as creative director to try to stay at the forefront and come up with something that people haven't seen. I desperately try not to look at other advertising for ideas. I always challenge our people to look at work from other parts of the world—film, novels, music—for inspiration."

A look at two promotional campaigns developed at Fallon show how creativity, teamwork, and not looking at traditional ads from other agencies come together to build award-winning campaigns. Both campaigns discussed below end before the actual media execution and ask for your ideas in the questions at the end of the case. Fallon people tell much of the story in their own words.

LEE DUNGAREES: OVERCOMING UNCOOL WITH BUDDY LEE

The marketing challenge for Lee and its jeans was clear. "Lee was uncool," explains Julie Smith, Fallon Senior Account Planner, "and it wasn't even on the radar screen for young people," Smith continues. So while Lee was doing well among women over 35, younger people had negative associations with the Lee brand.

This gave the promotional objectives a clear focus: Gain favorable perceptions of Lee among young people and make it acceptable for them to buy Lee jeans. The target market, too, became very specific: 17- to 22-year-old men and women. "Because the Lee brand had so much female imagery associated with it, we had to over-

compensate, so we leaned toward males as the epicenter of our target," says Smith. Lee and Fallon chose the 17- to 22-year-old age target because "before that people are brand promiscuous, they are trying out a lot of different brands," says Smith. After that they settle on one or two brands, so getting 17- to 22-year-olds to seriously consider Lee jeans is critical.

Many Lee ads in the past were seen as "cool" by younger people. The problem was that marketing research tracking studies showed that younger people attributed these ads twice as often to Levis as to Lee. In trying to find a creative idea that would always link Lee and its promotions, the Fallon team went to Lee's headquarters in Kansas City, dug through a century of archives, and looked for something that was very positive and closely associated with the Lee brand.

Enter Buddy Lee. When young consumers were asked what they wanted when they were wearing their ideal set of jeans it "was to feel like they could do anything." This resulted in the positioning for Lee's brand and the springboard for its communications: the indestructible spirit. Making this indestructible spirit strongly associated with the Lee brand is where Buddy Lee comes in. Although Buddy Lee is seen as interesting, intriguing, curious, and even a little spooky to young people, he has grabbed their attention.

Research also showed that the Lee brand was so strongly associated with older women, it probably could not be redirected to target young men and women. So Lee and Fallon created a "sub-brand," Lee Dungarees (www.leedungarees.com). This is the brand Buddy Lee is associated with and champions with his indomitable, indestructible spirit!

Then the new challenge emerged: How to connect Buddy Lee and his spirit to the 17- to 22-year-olds in the target market?

BMW: GRABBING ATTENTION WITH "THE HIRE"

Working closely together in the late 1990s, BMW and Fallon brainstormed, talked to consumers, and agonized over what the positioning of BMW should be. Their answer: "Responsiveness"—which means a performance vehicle that includes not only acceleration and braking but also its cornering, its safety.

The only problem with this was that soon major competitors like Mitsubishi and Ford were trying to adopt this "responsiveness" positioning for themselves. "So our first promotional objective was to separate BMW from its competitors as the only true, cool, legitimate, ultimate driving machine," says Ginny Grossman, Fallon Group Director. "We wanted the ownership of the 'responsiveness' position. We wanted people to associate that with BMW and only BMW."

"The target audience for 'The Hire' was BMW's future customer," says Erin Tait, Fallon Senior Account Planner. "Today the average age of a BMW driver is 42. So what we wanted to do was make sure that the future audience, the 20- and 30-year-olds felt as good about the BMW brand as the 40- and 50-year-olds did. So, this campaign 'The Hire' was about making sure that the BMW brand was relevant and attractive to that younger audience."

Overseen by Hollywood directors like Ang Lee and John Frankenheimer, "The Hire" is the title given to a series of five short films launched on the Internet that can be downloaded (www.bmwfilms.com). They feature Clive Owen as the driver and carry provocative titles: "Ambush," "Chosen," "The Follow," "Star," and "Powder Keg."

In trying to reach this younger market, a special problem emerged. "When we spoke to 20- and 30-year-olds about the BMW brand and what they thought it meant to them, they talked about things like being really into aggressive driving and risk-taking. That's the kind of person that would choose a BMW. But unfortunately, a lot of those attributes got taken in kind of a negative way," explains Tait.

"So our challenge was to take the positive value of the BMW brand. That's what Clive Owen in 'The Hire' really helped to do because the decisions he makes and the risks he takes are all for the good and for helping the person he's been hired to drive," says Tait. "You learn about this character through these movies which helps shape your perception of the kind of person that would choose

a BMW. Plus it gives you a great sense for how the car performs in treacherous, difficult driving situations."

BMW and Fallon's next challenge was how to use these creative films to attract the attention of 20- and 30-year-olds and achieve "water cooler talk" the next day after they saw them on the Internet.

PUSHING THE CREATIVE BARRIERS

How does Fallon keep the creative juices flowing—from developing new promotional campaigns to using new media like the Internet? This involves continuing to develop award-winning commercials like "cat herders" for EDS and "Mark," the 42-year-old in the Holiday Inn commercials who lives at home and sponges off his family, as well as the Lee Dungarees and BMW campaigns.

Concerning new media, Kevin Flatt, Fallon Creative-Interactive, talks about the increasing importance of the Internet: "A number of our clients are recognizing now that they can get more focused connections to meaningful consumers with the Internet and be able to measure whether it's working or not." For people thinking about going into advertising, he tells what his job means to him: "If you love it, it is the most rewarding job because of how wonderful it is to be able to go and tell somebody 'I love what I do!'"

Questions

1 Fallon Worldwide stresses its creativity, as shown by comments from the Fallon people in the case. (*a*) In what ways do the Lee Dungarees and BMW campaigns reflect their creativity? (*b*) Compare the sources of the ideas in the two campaigns.
2 In the Lee Dungarees and BMW campaigns how were (*a*) the target markets and (*b*) each brand's positioning changed from the situation prior to the campaign?
3 The case does not discuss the media used in the Buddy Lee campaign. What media and communication vehicles should it use initially (*a*) to reach the target market of 17- to 22-year-olds? (*b*) to continue to reach them after the first couple of years of the campaign?
4 The case also does not discuss the development of media in BMW's "The Hire" campaign. (*a*) How could BMW and Fallon launch the films most successfully on the Internet? (*b*) What other media might they use after that launch?
5 How might Fallon and its clients measure the success of (*a*) the Lee Dungarees and (*b*) the BMW campaigns?

CHAPTER

20

PERSONAL SELLING AND SALES MANAGEMENT

AFTER READING THIS CHAPTER YOU SHOULD BE ABLE TO:

- Recognize different types of personal selling.

- Describe the stages in the personal selling process.

- Specify the functions and tasks in the sales management process.

- Determine whether a firm should use manufacturer's representatives or a company salesforce and the number of people needed in a company's salesforce.

- Understand how firms recruit, select, train, motivate, compensate, and evaluate salespeople.

- Describe recent applications of salesforce automation and customer relationship management.

SELLING THE WAY CUSTOMERS WANT TO BUY

Anne Mulcahy has a tough assignment. As the newly named president and chief executive officer at Xerox Corporation, she is in the midst of successfully implementing one of the greatest feats in the annals of business history—restoring Xerox's legendary marketing and financial vitality. "As CEO of Xerox, I am ready and privileged to lead a team of dedicated employees who are as sharply focused and committed as I am in the successful turnaround of our company, transforming it to the realities of the digital age and putting Xerox back on a growth trajectory," said Mulcahy (shown on the opposite page).

Mulcahy is ideally suited to the task. She began her 25-year Xerox career as a field sales representative and assumed increasingly responsible management and executive positions. These included chief staff officer, president of Xerox's General Markets Operations, and, most recently, president and chief operating officer of Xerox. As CEO, Mulcahy has to muster the knowledge and experience gained from this varied background. Not surprisingly, her sales background has played a pivotal role.

"We will win back market share one customer at a time, one sale at a time," Mulcahy says. "We'll do that by providing greater value than our competitors—and that means selling the way customers want to buy." She adds that Xerox must offer a broad range of products and services at competitive prices through direct, indirect, Web, and telephone sales, and customer support. Her approach to sales, coupled with her considerable management experience, has already borne fruit as Xerox positions itself for the twenty-first century.[1]

This chapter examines the scope and significance of personal selling and sales management in marketing. It first highlights the many forms of personal selling and outlines the selling process. Sales management functions are then described, including recent advances in salesforce automation and customer relationship management.

SCOPE AND SIGNIFICANCE OF PERSONAL SELLING AND SALES MANAGEMENT

Chapter 18 described personal selling and management of the sales effort as being part of the firm's promotional mix. Although it is important to recognize that personal selling is a useful vehicle for communicating with present and potential buyers, it is much more. Take a moment to answer the questions in the personal selling and sales management quiz in Figure 20–1. As you read on, compare your answers with those in the text.

Nature of Personal Selling and Sales Management

Personal selling involves the two-way flow of communication between a buyer and seller, often in a face-to-face encounter, designed to influence a person's or group's purchase decision. However, with advances in telecommunications, personal selling also takes place over the telephone, through video teleconferencing and Internet/Web-enabled links between buyers and sellers.

Personal selling remains a highly human-intensive activity despite the use of technology. Accordingly, the people involved must be managed. **Sales management** involves planning the selling program and implementing and controlling the personal selling effort of the firm. The tasks involved in managing personal selling include setting objectives; organizing the salesforce; recruiting, selecting, training, and compensating salespeople; and evaluating the performance of individual salespeople.

Pervasiveness of Selling

"Everyone lives by selling something," wrote author Robert Louis Stevenson a century ago. His observation still holds true today. The Bureau of Labor Statistics reports that almost 16 million people are employed in sales positions in the United States. Included in this number are manufacturing sales personnel, real estate brokers,

FIGURE 20–1
Personal selling and sales management quiz

1. What percentage of chief executive officers in the 1,000 largest U.S. corporations have significant sales and marketing experience in their work history? (check one)

   10% _____   30% _____   50% _____
   20% _____   40% _____   60% _____

2. About how much does it cost for a field sales representative to make a single personal sales call? (check one)

   $100 _____ $200 _____ $300 _____
   $150 _____ $250 _____ $350 _____

3. "A salesperson's job is finished when a sale is made." True or false? (circle one)

                    True   False

4. About what percentage of U.S. companies includes customer satisfaction as a measure of salesperson performance? (check one)

   10% _____   30% _____   50% _____
   20% _____   40% _____   60% _____

Could this be a salesperson in the operating room? Read the text to find why Medtronic salespeople visit hospital operating rooms.

Medtronic

www.medtronic.com

stockbrokers, and salesclerks who work in retail stores. In reality, however, virtually every occupation that involves customer contact has an element of personal selling. For example, attorneys, accountants, bankers, and company personnel recruiters perform sales-related activities, whether or not they acknowledge it. About 20 percent of the chief executive officers in the 1,000 largest U.S. corporations have significant sales and marketing experience in their work history like Anne Mulcahy at Xerox.[2] (What percentage did you check for question 1 in Figure 20–1?) Thus, selling often serves as a stepping-stone to top management, as well as being a career path in itself.

Personal Selling in Marketing

Personal selling serves three major roles in a firm's overall marketing effort. First, salespeople are the critical link between the firm and its customers. This role requires that salespeople match company interests with customer needs to satisfy both parties in the exchange process. Second, salespeople *are* the company in a consumer's eyes. They represent what a company is or attempts to be and are often the only personal contact a customer has with the company. For example, the "look" projected by Gucci salespeople is an important factor in communicating the style of the company's apparel line. Third, personal selling may play a dominant role in a firm's marketing program. This situation typically arises when a firm uses a push marketing strategy, described in Chapter 18. Avon, for example, pays almost 40 percent of its total sales dollars for selling expenses. Pharmaceutical firms and office and educational equipment manufacturers also rely heavily on personal selling in the marketing of their products.

Creating Customer Value through Salespeople: Relationship and Partnership Selling

As the critical link between the firm and its customers, salespeople can create customer value in many ways. For instance, by being close to the customer, salespeople can identify creative solutions to customer problems. Salespeople at Medtronic, Inc., the world leader in the heart pacemaker market, are in the operating room for more than 90 percent of the procedures performed with their product, and are on call, wearing pagers, 24 hours a day. "It reflects the willingness to be there in every situation, just in case a problem arises—even though nine times out of ten the procedure goes just fine," notes a satisfied customer.[3] Salespeople can create value by easing the customer buying process. This happened at AMP, Inc., a producer of electrical products. Salespeople and customers had a difficult time getting product specifications and performance data on AMP's 70,000 products quickly and accurately. The company now records all information on CD-ROM disks that can be scanned instantly by salespeople and customers. Customer value is also created by salespeople who follow through after the sale. At Jefferson Smurfit Corporation, a multibillion-dollar supplier of packaging products, one of its salespeople juggled production from three of the company's plants to satisfy an unexpected demand for boxes from General Electric. This person's action led to the company being given GE's "Distinguished Supplier Award."

Customer value creation is made possible by **relationship selling**, the practice of building ties to customers based on a salesperson's attention and commitment to customer needs over time. Relationship selling involves mutual respect and trust among buyers and sellers. It focuses on creating long-term customers, not a one-time sale.[4] A recent survey of 300 senior sales executives revealed that 96 percent consider "building long-term relationships with customers" to be the most important activity affecting sales performance. Companies such as American Express, Electronic Data Systems, Motorola, and Owens-Corning have made relationship building a core focus of their sales effort.[5]

Some companies have taken relationship selling a step further and forged partnerships between buyer and seller organizations. With **partnership selling**, sometimes called *enterprise selling,* buyers and sellers combine their expertise and resources to create customized solutions; commit to joint planning; and share customer, competitive, and company information for their mutual benefit, and ultimately the customer.[6] As an approach to sales, partnership selling relies on cross-functional business specialists who apply their knowledge and expertise to achieve higher productivity, lower cost, and greater customer value. Partnership selling complements supplier and channel partnering described in Chapters 6, 15, and 16. This practice is embraced by companies such as IBM, Du Pont, and Honeywell, which have established partnerships with customers such as American Airlines, Ford, Milliken, and the U.S. government.[7]

Relationship and partnership selling represent another dimension of customer relationship management. Both emphasize the importance of learning about customer needs and wants tailoring solutions to customer problems as a means to customer value creation.

Concept Check

1. What is personal selling?

2. What is involved in sales management?

THE MANY FORMS OF PERSONAL SELLING

Personal selling assumes many forms based on the amount of selling done and the amount of creativity required to perform the sales task. Broadly speaking, three types of personal selling exist: order taking, order getting, and sales support activities. While some firms use only one of these types of personal selling, others use a combination of all three.

A Frito-Lay salesperson takes inventory of snacks for the store manager to sign. In this situation, the manager will make a straight rebuy decision.

Frito-Lay, Inc.

www.fritolay.com

Order Taking

Typically, an **order taker** processes routine orders or reorders for products that were already sold by the company. The primary responsibility of order takers is to preserve an ongoing relationship with existing customers and maintain sales. Two types of order takers exist. *Outside order takers* visit customers and replenish inventory stocks of resellers, such as retailers or wholesalers. For example, Frito-Lay salespeople call on supermarkets, neighborhood grocery stores, and other establishments to ensure that the company's line of snack products (such as Doritos and Tostitos tortilla chips) is in adequate supply. In addition, outside order takers often provide assistance in arranging displays. *Inside order takers,* also called *order clerks* or *salesclerks,* typically answer simple questions, take orders, and complete transactions with customers. Many retail clerks are inside order takers. Inside order takers are often employed by companies that use *inbound telemarketing,* the use of toll-free telephone numbers that customers can call to obtain information about products or services and make purchases. In business-to-business settings, order taking arises in straight rebuy situations. Order takers generally do little selling in a conventional sense and engage in only modest problem solving with customers. They often represent products that have few options, such as confectionary items, magazine subscriptions, and highly standardized industrial products. Inbound telemarketing is also an essential selling activity for more "customer service" driven firms, such as Dell Computer. At these companies, order takers undergo extensive training so that they can better assist callers with their purchase decisions.

Order Getting

An **order getter** sells in a conventional sense and identifies prospective customers, provides customers with information, persuades customers to buy, closes sales, and follows up on customers' use of a product or service. Like order takers, order getters can be inside (an automobile salesperson) or outside (a Xerox salesperson). Order getting involves a high degree of creativity and customer empathy and is typically required for selling complex or technical products with many options, so

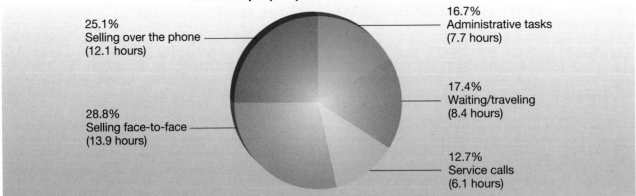

How salespeople spend their time each week

25.1%
Selling over the phone
(12.1 hours)

28.8%
Selling face-to-face
(13.9 hours)

16.7%
Administrative tasks
(7.7 hours)

17.4%
Waiting/traveling
(8.4 hours)

12.7%
Service calls
(6.1 hours)

FIGURE 20–2

How outside order-getting salespeople spend their time each week

considerable product knowledge and sales training are necessary. In modified rebuy or new buy purchase situations in business-to-business selling, an order getter acts as a problem solver who identifies how a particular product may satisfy a customer's need. Similarly, in the purchase of a service, such as insurance, a Metropolitan Life insurance agent can provide a mix of plans to satisfy a buyer's needs depending on income, stage of the family's life cycle, and investment objectives.

Order getting is not a 40-hour-per-week job. Industry research indicates that outside order getters, or field service representatives, work about 48 hours per week. As shown in Figure 20–2, 54 percent of their time is spent selling and another 13 percent is devoted to customer service calls. The remainder of their work is occupied by getting to customers and performing numerous administrative tasks.[8]

Order getting by outside salespeople is also expensive. It is estimated that the average cost of a single field sales call is almost $170.00, factoring in salespeople compensation, benefits, and travel-and-entertainment expenses.[9] (What amount did you check for question 2 in Figure 20–1?) This cost illustrates why outbound telemarketing is so popular today. *Outbound telemarketing* is the practice of using the telephone rather than personal visits to contact customers. A significantly lower cost per sales call (in the range of $20 to $25) and little or no field expense accounts for its widespread appeal. Some 40 million outbound telemarketing calls are made each year in the United States![10]

Customer Sales Support Personnel

Customer sales support personnel augment the selling effort of order getters by performing a variety of services. For example, **missionary salespeople** do not directly solicit orders but rather concentrate on performing promotional activities and introducing new products. They are used extensively in the pharmaceutical industry, where they persuade physicians to prescribe a firm's product. Actual sales are made through wholesalers or directly to pharmacists who fill prescriptions. A **sales engineer** is a salesperson who specializes in identifying, analyzing, and solving customer problems and brings know-how and technical expertise to the selling situation but often does not actually sell products and services. Sales engineers are popular in selling business products such as chemicals and heavy equipment.

In many situations firms engage in cross-functional **team selling**, the practice of using an entire team of professionals in selling to and servicing major customers.[11] Team selling is used when specialized knowledge is needed to satisfy the different interests of individuals in a customer's buying center. For example, a selling team might consist of a salesperson, a sales engineer, a service representative, and a financial executive, each of whom would deal with a counterpart in the customer's firm. Selling teams have grown in popularity due to partnering and take different forms.

MARKETING NEWSNET

Creating and Sustaining Customer Value through Cross-Functional Team Selling

CROSS FUNCTIONAL

The day of the lone salesperson calling on a customer is rapidly becoming history. Many companies today are using cross-functional teams of professionals to work with customers to improve relationships, find better ways of doing things, and, of course, create and sustain value for their customers.

Xerox and IBM pioneered cross-functional team selling, but other firms were quick to follow as they spotted the potential to create and sustain value for their customers. Recognizing that corn growers needed a herbicide they could apply less often, a Du Pont team of chemists, sales and marketing executives, and regulatory specialists created just the right product that recorded sales of $57 million in its first year. Procter & Gamble uses teams of marketing, sales, advertising, computer systems, and distribution personnel to work with its major retailers, such as Wal-Mart, to identify ways to develop, promote, and deliver products. Pitney Bowes, Inc., which produces sophisticated computer systems that weigh, rate, and track packages for firms such as UPS and Federal Express, also uses sales teams to meet customer needs. These teams consist of sales personnel, "carrier management specialists," and engineering and administrative executives who continually find ways to improve

the technology of shipping goods across town and around the world.

Efforts to create and sustain customer value through cross-functional team selling have become a necessity as customers seek greater value for their money. According to the vice president for procurement of a Fortune 500 company, "Today, it's not just getting the best price but getting the best value—and there are a lot of pieces to value."

In *conference selling,* a salesperson and other company resource people meet with buyers to discuss problems and opportunities. In *seminar selling,* a company team conducts an educational program for a customer's technical staff, describing state-of-the-art developments. IBM and Xerox pioneered cross-functional team selling in working with prospective buyers. Other firms have embraced this practice and created and sustained value for their customers, as described in the accompanying Marketing NewsNet.[12]

Concept Check

1. What is the principal difference between an order taker and an order getter?

2. What is team selling?

THE PERSONAL SELLING PROCESS: BUILDING RELATIONSHIPS

Selling, and particularly order getting, is a complicated activity that involves building buyer–seller relationships. Although the salesperson–customer interaction is essential to personal selling, much of a salesperson's work occurs before this meeting and continues after the sale itself. The **personal selling process** consists of six stages: (1) prospecting, (2) preapproach, (3) approach, (4) presentation, (5) close, and (6) follow-up (Figure 20–3).

FIGURE 20–3
Stages and objectives of the
personal selling process

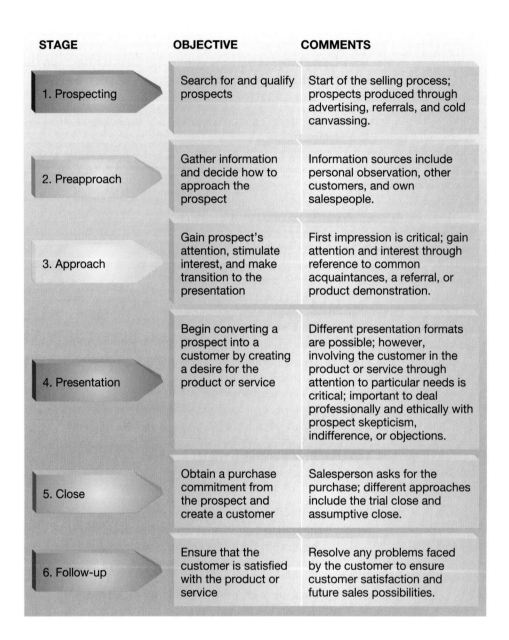

STAGE	OBJECTIVE	COMMENTS
1. Prospecting	Search for and qualify prospects	Start of the selling process; prospects produced through advertising, referrals, and cold canvassing.
2. Preapproach	Gather information and decide how to approach the prospect	Information sources include personal observation, other customers, and own salespeople.
3. Approach	Gain prospect's attention, stimulate interest, and make transition to the presentation	First impression is critical; gain attention and interest through reference to common acquaintances, a referral, or product demonstration.
4. Presentation	Begin converting a prospect into a customer by creating a desire for the product or service	Different presentation formats are possible; however, involving the customer in the product or service through attention to particular needs is critical; important to deal professionally and ethically with prospect skepticism, indifference, or objections.
5. Close	Obtain a purchase commitment from the prospect and create a customer	Salesperson asks for the purchase; different approaches include the trial close and assumptive close.
6. Follow-up	Ensure that the customer is satisfied with the product or service	Resolve any problems faced by the customer to ensure customer satisfaction and future sales possibilities.

Prospecting

Personal selling begins with *prospecting*—the search for and qualification of potential customers.[13] For some products that are one-time purchases such as encyclopedias, continual prospecting is necessary to maintain sales. There are three types of prospects. A *lead* is the name of a person who may be a possible customer. A *prospect* is a customer who wants or needs the product. If an individual wants the product, can afford to buy it, and is the decision maker, this individual is a *qualified prospect*.

Leads and prospects are generated using several sources. For example, advertising may contain a coupon or a toll-free number to generate leads. Some companies use exhibits at trade shows, professional meetings, and conferences to generate leads or prospects. Staffed by salespeople, these exhibits are used to attract the attention of prospective buyers and disseminate information. Others use lists and directories. Another approach for generating leads is through *cold canvassing* in person or by telephone. This approach simply means that a salesperson may open a directory, pick a name, and visit or call that individual or business. Although the refusal rate is high

Trade shows are a popular source for leads and prospects. Companies like TSCentral provide comprehensive trade show information.

TSCentral

www.tscentral.com

with cold canvassing, this approach can be successful. For example, 41 brokers at Lehman Brothers recently identified 18,004 prospects, qualified 1,208 of them, made 659 sales presentations, and opened 40 new accounts in four working days.[14] However, cold canvassing is frowned upon in most Asian and Latin American societies. Personal visits, based on referrals, are expected.[15]

Cold canvassing is often criticized by U.S. consumers and is now regulated. A recent survey reported that 75 percent of U.S. consumers consider this practice an intrusion on their privacy, and 72 percent find it distasteful.[16] The Telephone Consumer Protection Act contains provisions to curb abuses such as early morning or late night calling. Additional federal regulations require more complete disclosure regarding solicitations, include provisions that allow consumers to avoid being called at any time, and impose fines up to $10,000 for violations. Some companies, such as American Express Financial Advisors (AMEX), have banned cold canvassing altogether.[17]

Preapproach

Once a salesperson has identified a qualified prospect, preparation for the sale begins with the preapproach. The *preapproach* stage involves obtaining further information on the prospect and deciding on the best method of approach. Knowing how the prospect prefers to be approached, and what the prospect is looking for in a product or service, is essential regardless of cultural setting. For example, a Merrill Lynch stockbroker will need information on a prospect's discretionary income, investment objectives, and preference for discussing brokerage services over the telephone or in person. For business product companies such as Texas Instruments, the preapproach involves identifying the buying role of a prospect (for example, influencer or decision maker), important buying criteria, and the prospect's receptivity to a formal or informal presentation. Identifying the best time to contact a prospect is also important. For example, Northwestern Mutual Life Insurance Company suggests the best times to call on people in different occupations: dentists before 9:30 A.M., lawyers between 11:00 A.M. and 2:00 P.M., and college professors between 7:00 and 8:00 P.M.

This stage is very important in international selling where customs dictate appropriate protocol. In many South American countries, for example, buyers expect salespeople to be punctual for appointments. However, prospective buyers are routinely 30 minutes late. South Americans take negotiating seriously and prefer straightforward presentations, but a hard-sell approach will not work.[18]

Successful salespeople recognize that the preapproach stage should never be shortchanged. Their experience coupled with research on customer complaints indicate that failure to learn as much as possible about the prospect is unprofessional and the ruin of a sales call.[19]

Approach

The *approach* stage involves the initial meeting between the salesperson and prospect, where the objectives are to gain the prospect's attention, stimulate interest, and build the foundation for the sales presentation itself and the basis for a working relationship. The first impression is critical at this stage, and it is common for

salespeople to begin the conversation with a reference to common acquaintances, a referral, or even the product or service itself. Which tactic is taken will depend on the information obtained in the prospecting and preapproach stages.

The approach stage is very important in international settings. In many societies outside the United States, considerable time is devoted to nonbusiness talk designed to establish a rapport between buyers and sellers. For instance, it is common for two or three meetings to occur before business matters are discussed in the Middle East and Asia. Gestures are also very important. The initial meeting between a salesperson and a prospect in the United States customarily begins with a firm handshake. Handshakes also apply in France, but they are gentle, not firm. Forget the handshake in Japan. A bow is appropriate. What about business cards? Business cards should be printed in English on one side and the language of the prospective customer on the other. Knowledgeable U.S. salespeople know that their business cards should be handed to Asian customers using both hands, with the name facing the receiver. In Asia, anything involving names demands respect.[20]

Presentation

The *presentation* is at the core of the order-getting selling process, and its objective is to convert a prospect into a customer by creating a desire for the product or service. Three major presentation formats exist: (1) stimulus-response format, (2) formula selling format, and (3) need-satisfaction format.

Stimulus-Response Format   The **stimulus-response presentation** format assumes that given the appropriate stimulus by a salesperson, the prospect will buy. With this format the salesperson tries one appeal after another, hoping to "hit the right button." A counter clerk at McDonald's is using this approach when he or she asks whether you'd like an order of french fries or a dessert with your meal. The counter clerk is engaging in what is called *suggestive selling.* Although useful in this setting, the stimulus-response format is not always appropriate, and for many products a more formalized format is necessary.

Formula Selling Format   A more formalized presentation, the **formula selling presentation** format, is based on the view that a presentation consists of information that must be provided in an accurate, thorough, and step-by-step manner to inform the prospect. A popular version of this format is the *canned sales presentation,* which is a memorized, standardized message conveyed to every prospect. Used frequently by firms in telephone and door-to-door selling of consumer products (for example, Kirby vacuum cleaners), this approach treats every prospect the same, regardless of differences in needs or preference for certain kinds of information. Canned sales presentations can be advantageous when the differences between prospects are unknown or with novice salespeople who are less knowledgeable about the product and selling process than experienced salespeople. Although it guarantees a thorough presentation, it often lacks flexibility and spontaneity and, more important, does not provide for feedback from the prospective buyer—a critical component in the communication process and the start of a relationship.

Need-Satisfaction Format

The stimulus-response and formula selling formats share a common characteristic: The salesperson dominates the conversation. By comparison, the **need-satisfaction presentation** format emphasizes probing and listening by the salesperson to identify needs and interests of prospective buyers. Once these are identified, the salesperson tailors the presentation to the prospect and highlights product benefits that may be valued by the prospect. The need-satisfaction format, which emphasizes problem solving, is the most consistent with the marketing concept and relationship building. Two selling styles are associated with this format. **Adaptive selling** involves adjusting the presentation to fit the selling situation, such as knowing when to offer solutions and when to ask for more information.[21] Sales research and practice show that knowledge of the customer and sales situation are key ingredients for adaptive selling. Many consumer service firms such as brokerage and insurance firms and consumer product firms like AT&T and Gillette effectively apply this selling style. **Consultative selling** focuses on problem identification, where the salesperson serves as an expert on problem recognition and resolution.[22] With consultative selling, problem solution options are not simply a matter of choosing from an array of existing products or services. Rather, novel solutions often arise, thereby creating unique value for the customer. Consultative selling is prominent in business-to-business marketing. Johnson Controls' Automotive Systems Group, IBM's Global Services, and DHL Worldwide Express are often cited for their consultative selling style.[23]

Handling Objections

A critical concern in the presentation stage is handling objections. *Objections* are excuses for not making a purchase commitment or decision. Some objections are valid and are based on the characteristics of the product or service or price. However, many objections reflect prospect skepticism or indifference. Whether valid or not, experienced salespeople know that objections do not put an end to the presentation. Rather, techniques can be used to deal with objections in a courteous, ethical, and professional manner. The following six techniques are the most common:[24]

1. *Acknowledge and convert the objection.* This technique involves using the objection as a reason for buying. For example, a prospect might say, "The price is too high." The reply: "Yes, the price is high because we use the finest materials. Let me show you. . . ."
2. *Postpone.* The postpone technique is used when the objection will be dealt with later in the presentation: "I'm going to address that point shortly. I think my answer would make better sense then."
3. *Agree and neutralize.* Here a salesperson agrees with the objection, then shows that it is unimportant. A salesperson would say, "That's true and others have said the same. However, they concluded that issue was outweighed by the other benefits."
4. *Accept the objection.* Sometimes the objection is valid. Let the prospect express such views, probe for the reason behind it, and attempt to stimulate further discussion on the objection.
5. *Denial.* When a prospect's objection is based on misinformation and clearly untrue, it is wise to meet the objection head on with a firm denial.
6. *Ignore the objection.* This technique is used when it appears that the objection is a stalling mechanism or is clearly not important to the prospect.

MARKETING NEWSNET The Subtlety of Saying Yes in East Asia

GLOBAL

The economies of East Asia—spanning from Japan to Indonesia—almost equal that of the United States and total about four-fifths of the European Union. The marketing opportunities in East Asia are great, but effective selling in these countries requires a keen cultural ear. Seasoned global marketers know that in many Asian societies it is impolite to say *no*, and *yes* has multiple meanings.

Yes in Asian societies can have at least four meanings. It can mean that listeners are simply acknowledging that a speaker is talking to them even though they don't understand what is being said, or it can mean that a speaker's words are understood, but not that they are agreed with. A third meaning of *yes* conveys that a presentation is understood, but other people must be consulted before any com-

mitment is possible. Finally, *yes* can also mean that a proposal is understood and accepted. However, experienced negotiators also note that this *yes* is subject to change if the situation is changed.

This one example illustrates why savvy salespeople are sensitive to cultural underpinnings when engaged in cross-cultural sales negotiations.

Each of these techniques requires a calm, professional interaction with the prospect and is most effective when objections are anticipated in the preapproach stage. Handling objections is a skill requiring a sense of timing, appreciation for the prospect's state of mind, and adeptness in communication. Objections also should be handled ethically. Lying or misrepresenting product or service features are grossly unethical practices.

Close

The *closing* stage in the selling process involves obtaining a purchase commitment from the prospect. This stage is the most important and the most difficult because the salesperson must determine when the prospect is ready to buy. Telltale signals indicating a readiness to buy include body language (prospect reexamines the product or contract closely), statements ("This equipment should reduce our maintenance costs"), and questions ("When could we expect delivery?"). The close itself can take several forms. Three closing techniques are used when a salesperson believes a buyer is about ready to make a purchase: (1) trial close, (2) assumptive close, and (3) urgency close. A *trial close* involves asking the prospect to make a decision on some aspect of the purchase: "Would you prefer the blue or gray model?" An *assumptive close* entails asking the prospect to consider choices concerning delivery, warranty, or financing terms under the assumption that a sale has been finalized. An *urgency close* is used to commit the prospect quickly by making reference to the timeliness of the purchase: "The low interest financing ends next week," or, "That is the last model we have in stock." Of course, these statements should be used only if they accurately reflect the situation; otherwise, such claims would be unethical. When a prospect is clearly ready to buy, the final close is used, and a salesperson asks for the order.

Knowing when the prospect is ready to buy becomes even more difficult in cross-cultural buyer–seller negotiations where societal customs and language play a large role. Read the accompanying Marketing NewsNet to understand the multiple meanings of *yes* in Japan and other societies in East Asia.[25]

Follow-Up

The selling process does not end with the closing of a sale; rather, professional selling requires customer follow-up. One marketing authority equated the follow-up with courtship and marriage,[26] by observing, ". . . the sale merely consummates the courtship. Then the marriage begins. How good the marriage is depends on how well the relationship is managed." The *follow-up stage* includes making certain the customer's purchase has been properly delivered and installed and difficulties experienced with the use of the item are addressed. Attention to this stage of the selling process solidifies the buyer–seller relationship. Moreover, research shows that the cost and effort to obtain repeat sales from a satisfied customer is roughly half of that necessary to gain a sale from a new customer.[27] In short, today's satisfied customers become tomorrow's qualified prospects or referrals. (What was your answer to question 3 in the quiz?)

Concept Check

1. What are the six stages in the personal selling process?

2. What is the distinction between a lead and a qualified prospect?

3. Which presentation format is most consistent with the marketing concept? Why?

THE SALES MANAGEMENT PROCESS

Selling must be managed if it is going to contribute to a firm's overall objectives. Although firms differ in the specifics of how salespeople and the selling effort are managed, the sales management process is similar across firms. Sales management consists of three interrelated functions: (1) sales plan formulation, (2) sales plan implementation, and (3) evaluation and control of the salesforce (Figure 20–4).

Sales Plan Formulation

Formulating the sales plan is the most basic of the three sales management functions. According to the vice president of the Harris Corporation, a global communications company, "If a company hopes to implement its marketing strategy, it really needs a detailed sales planning process."[28] The **sales plan** is a statement describing what is to be achieved and where and how the selling effort of salespeople is to be deployed. Formulating the sales plan involves three tasks: (1) setting objectives, (2) organizing the salesforce, and (3) developing account management policies.

Setting Objectives   Setting objectives is central to sales management because this task specifies what is to be achieved. In practice, objectives are set for the total salesforce and for each salesperson. Selling objectives can be output related and focus

FIGURE 20–4
The sales management process

ETHICS AND SOCIAL RESPONSIBILITY ALERT

The Ethics of Asking Customers about Competitors

ETHICS

Salespeople are a valuable source of information about what is happening in the marketplace. By working closely with customers and asking good questions, salespeople often have first-hand knowledge of customer problems and wants. They also are able to spot the activities of competitors. However, should salespeople explicitly ask customers about competitor strategies such as pricing practices, product development efforts, and trade and promotion programs?

Gaining knowledge about competitors by asking customers for information is a ticklish ethical issue. Research indicates that 25 percent of U.S. salespeople engaged in business-to-business selling consider this practice unethical, and their companies have explicit guidelines for this practice. It is also noteworthy that Japanese salespeople

consider this practice to be more unethical than do U.S. salespeople.

Do you believe that asking customers about competitor practices is unethical? Why or why not?

on dollar or unit sales volume, number of new customers added, and profit. Alternatively, they can be input related and emphasize the number of sales calls and selling expenses. Output- and input-related objectives are used for the salesforce as a whole and for each salesperson. A third type of objective that is behaviorally related is typically specific for each salesperson and includes his or her product knowledge, customer service, and selling and communication skills. Increasingly, firms are also emphasizing knowledge of competition as an objective since salespeople are calling on customers and should see what competitors are doing.[29] But should salespeople explicitly ask their customers for information about competitors? Read the accompanying Ethics and Social Responsibility Alert to see how salespeople view this practice.[30]

Whatever objectives are set, they should be precise and measurable and specify the time period over which they are to be achieved. Once established, these objectives serve as performance standards for the evaluation of the salesforce—the third function of sales management.

Organizing the Salesforce   Establishing a selling organization is the second task in formulating the sales plan. Three questions are related to organization. First, should the company use its own salesforce, or should it use independent agents such as manufacturer's representatives? Second, if the decision is made to employ company salespeople, then should they be organized according to geography, customer type, or product or service? Third, how many company salespeople should be employed?

The decision to use company salespeople or independent agents is made infrequently. However, Coca-Cola's Food Division recently replaced its salesforce with independent agents (food brokers). The Optoelectronics Division of Honeywell, Inc., has switched back and forth between agents and its own salesforce over the last 25 years and now uses both. The decision is based on an analysis of economic and behavioral factors. An economic analysis examines the costs of using both types of salespeople and is a form of break-even analysis.

Consider a situation in which independent agents would receive a 5 percent commission on sales, and company salespeople would receive a 3 percent commission, salaries, and benefits. In addition, with company salespeople, sales administration costs would be incurred for a total fixed cost of $500,000 per year. At what sales

FIGURE 20–5

Break-even chart for comparing independent agents and a company salesforce

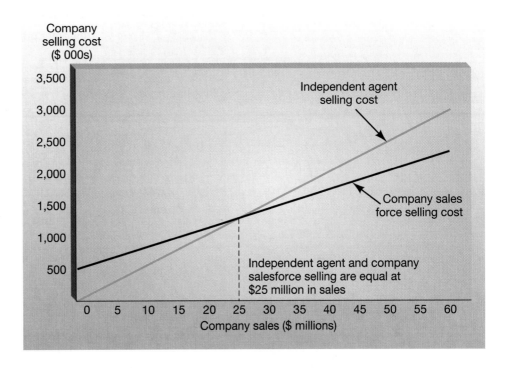

level would independent or company salespeople be less costly? This question can be answered by setting the costs of the two options equal to each other and solving for the sales level amount, as shown in the following equation:

Total cost of company salespeople = Total cost of independent agents

$$[0.03(X) + \$500,000] = 0.05(X)$$

where X = sales volume. Solving for X, sales volume equals $25 million, indicating that below $25 million in sales independent agents would be cheaper, but above $25 million a company salesforce would be cheaper. This relationship is shown in Figure 20–5.

Economics alone does not answer this question, however. A behavioral analysis is also necessary and should focus on issues related to the control, flexibility, effort, and availability of independent and company salespeople.[31] An individual firm must weigh the pros and cons of the economic and behavioral considerations before making this decision.

If a company elects to employ its own salespeople, then it must choose an organizational structure based on (1) geography, (2) customer, or (3) product (Figure 20–6). A geographical structure is the simplest organization, where the United States, or indeed the globe, is first divided into regions and each region is divided into districts or territories. Salespeople are assigned to each district with defined geographical boundaries and call on all customers and represent all products sold by the company. The principal advantage of this structure is that it can minimize travel time, expenses, and duplication of selling effort. However, if a firm's products or customers require specialized knowledge, then a geographical structure is not suitable.

When different types of buyers have different needs, a customer sales organizational structure is used. In practice this means that a different salesforce calls on each separate type of buyer or marketing channel. For example, Kodak recently switched from a geographical to a marketing channel structure with different sales teams serving specific retail channels: mass merchandisers, photo specialty outlets, and food and drug stores. The rationale for this approach is that more effective, specialized customer support and knowledge are provided to buyers. However, this structure often leads to higher administrative costs and some duplication of selling effort, because two separate salesforces are used to represent the same products.

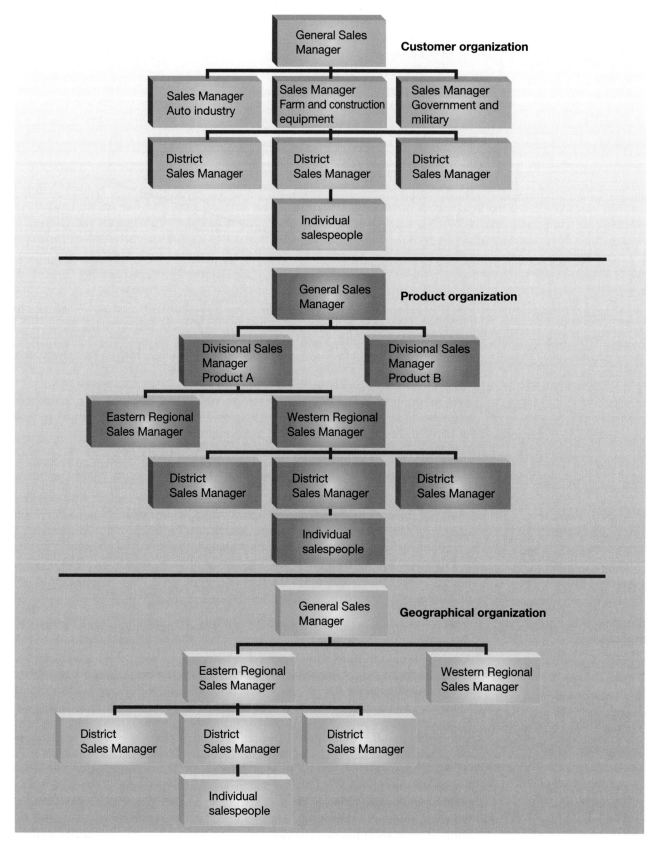

FIGURE 20–6
Organizing the salesforce by customer, product, and geography

A variation of the customer organizational structure is **major account management**, or *key account management,* the practice of using team selling to focus on important customers so as to build mutually beneficial, long-term, cooperative relationships.[32] Major account management involves teams of sales, service, and often technical personnel who work with purchasing, manufacturing, engineering, logistics, and financial executives in customer organizations. This approach, which often assigns company personnel to a customer account, results in "customer specialists" who can provide exceptional service. Procter & Gamble uses this approach with Wal-Mart as does Black & Decker with Home Depot.

When specific knowledge is required to sell certain types of products, then a product sales organization is used. For example, Lone Star Steel has a salesforce that sells drilling pipe to oil companies and another that sells specialty steel products to manufacturers. The primary advantage of this structure is that salespeople can develop expertise with technical characteristics, applications, and selling methods associated with a particular product or family of products. However, this structure also produces high administrative costs and duplication of selling effort because two company salespeople may call on the same customer.

In short, there is no one best sales organization for all companies in all situations. Rather, the organization of the salesforce should reflect the marketing strategy of the firm. Each year about 10 percent of U.S. firms change their sales organizations to implement new marketing strategies.

The third question related to salesforce organization involves determining the size of the salesforce. For example, why does Frito-Lay have about 17,500 salespeople who call on supermarkets, grocery stores, and other establishments to sell snack foods? The answer lies in the number of accounts (customers) served, the frequency of calls on accounts, the length of an average call, and the amount of time a salesperson can devote to selling.

A common approach for determining the size of a salesforce is the **workload method**. This formula-based method integrates the number of customers served, call frequency, call length, and available selling time to arrive at a figure for the salesforce size. For example, Frito-Lay needs about 17,500 salespeople according to the following workload method formula:

$$NS = \frac{NC \times CF \times CL}{AST}$$

where:

NS = Number of salespeople
NC = Number of customers
CF = Call frequency necessary to service a customer each year
CL = Length of an average call
AST = Average amount of selling time available per year

Frito-Lay sells its products to 350,000 supermarkets, grocery stores, and other establishments. Salespeople should call on these accounts at least once a week, or 52 times a year. The average sales call lasts an average of 81 minutes (1.35 hour). An average salesperson works 2,000 hours a year (50 weeks $\times$ 40 hours a week), but 12 hours a week are devoted to nonselling activities such as travel and administration, leaving 1,400 hours a year. Using these guidelines, Frito-Lay would need

$$NS = \frac{350,000 \times 52 \times 1.35}{1,400} = 17,550 \text{ salespeople}$$

The value of this formula is apparent in its flexibility; a change in any one of the variables will affect the number of salespeople needed. Changes are determined, in part, by the firm's account management policies.

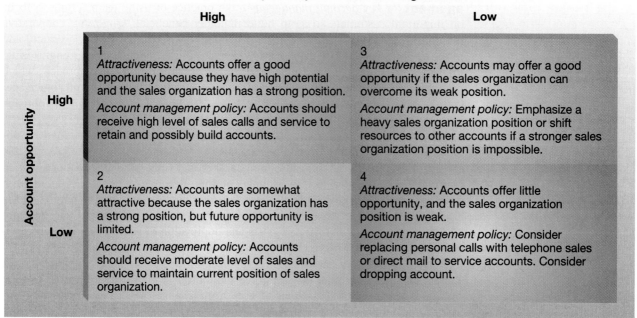

FIGURE 20–7
Account management
policy grid

Developing Account Management Policies   The third task in formulating a sales plan involves developing **account management policies** specifying whom salespeople should contact, what kinds of selling and customer service activities should be engaged in, and how these activities should be carried out. These policies might state which individuals in a buying organization should be contacted, the amount of sales and service effort that different customers should receive, and the kinds of information salespeople should collect before or during a sales call.

An example of an account management policy in Figure 20–7 shows how different accounts or customers can be grouped according to level of opportunity and the firm's competitive sales position.[33] When specific account names are placed in each cell, salespeople clearly see which accounts should be contacted, with what level of selling and service activity, and how to deal with them. Accounts in cells 1 and 2 might have high frequencies of personal sales calls and increased time spent on a call. Cell 3 accounts will have lower call frequencies, and cell 4 accounts might be contacted through telemarketing or direct mail rather than in person. For example, Union Pacific Railroad recently put its 20,000 smallest accounts on a telemarketing program. A subsequent survey of these accounts indicated that 84 percent rated Union Pacific's sales effort "very effective" compared with 67 percent before the switch.[34]

Sales Plan Implementation

The sales plan is put into practice through the tasks associated with sales plan implementation. Whereas sales plan formulation focuses on "doing the right things," implementation emphasizes "doing things right." The three major tasks involved in implementing a sales plan are (1) salesforce recruitment and selection, (2) salesforce training, and (3) salesforce motivation and compensation.

Salesforce Recruitment and Selection   Effective recruitment and selection of salespeople is one of the most crucial tasks of sales management. It entails finding people who match the type of sales position required by a firm. Recruitment and selection practices would differ greatly between order-taking and order-getting sales positions, given the differences in the demands of these two jobs. Therefore, recruitment

WEB LINK   What Is Your Emotional Intelligence?

A person's success at work depends on many talents, including intelligence and technical skills. Recent research indicates that an individual's emotional intelligence is also important, if not more important! Emotional intelligence (E-IQ) has five dimensions: (1) self-motivation skills; (2) self-awareness, or knowing one's own emotions; (3) the ability to manage one's emotions and impulses; (4) empathy, or the ability to sense how others are feeling;

and (5) social skills, or the ability to handle the emotions of other people.

What is your E-IQ? Visit the website at www.utne. com and click "What's Your E-IQ?" Answer the questions to learn what your E-IQ is and obtain additional insights.

and selection begin with a carefully crafted job analysis and job description followed by a statement of job qualifications.[35]

A *job analysis* is a study of a particular sales position, including how the job is to be performed and the tasks that make up the job. Information from a job analysis is used to write a *job description,* a written document that describes job relationships and requirements that characterize each sales position. It explains (1) to whom a salesperson reports, (2) how a salesperson interacts with other company personnel, (3) the customers to be called on, (4) the specific activities to be carried out, (5) the physical and mental demands of the job, and (6) the types of products and services to be sold. The job description is then translated into a statement of job qualifications, including the aptitudes, knowledge, skills, and a variety of behavioral characteristics considered necessary to perform the job successfully. Qualifications for order-getting sales positions often mirror the expectations of buyers: (1) imagination and problem-solving ability, (2) honesty, (3) intimate product knowledge, and (4) attentiveness reflected in responsiveness to buyer needs and customer loyalty and follow-up.[36] Firms use a variety of methods for evaluating prospective salespeople. Personal interviews, reference checks, and background information provided on application forms are the most frequently used methods.

Successful selling also requires a high degree of emotional intelligence. **Emotional intelligence** is the ability to understand one's own emotions and the emotions of people with whom one interacts on a daily basis. These qualities are important for adaptive selling and may spell the difference between effective and ineffective order-getting salespeople.[37] Are you interested in what your emotional intelligence might be? Read the accompanying Web Link and test yourself.

The search for qualified salespeople has produced an increasingly diverse salesforce in the United States. Women now represent half of all professional salespeople, and minority representation is growing. The fastest growth rate is among salespeople of Asian and Hispanic descent (see Figure 20–8).[38]

Salesforce Training   Whereas recruitment and selection of salespeople is a one-time event, salesforce training is an ongoing process that affects both new and seasoned salespeople. Sales training covers much more than selling practices. For example, IBM Global Services salespeople, who sell consulting and various information technology services, take at least two weeks of in-class and Web-based training on both consultative selling and the technical aspects of business.[39]

Training new salespeople is an expensive process. Almost 5 million U.S. salespeople receive employer-sponsored training annually at a cost of almost $10 billion per year.[40] On-the-job training is the most popular type of training, followed by individual instruction taught by experienced salespeople. Formal classes and seminars taught by sales trainers are also popular.

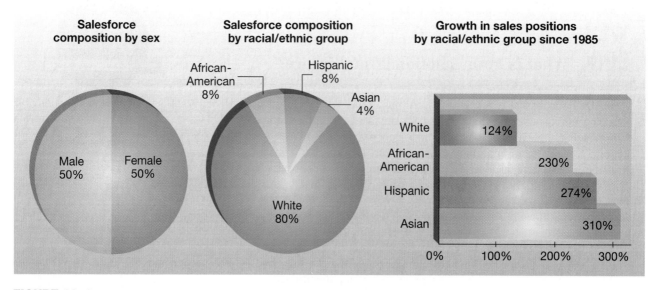

FIGURE 20–8
U.S. salesforce composition and change

Salesforce Motivation and Compensation   A sales plan cannot be successfully implemented without motivated salespeople. Research on salesperson motivation suggests that (1) a clear job description, (2) effective sales management practices, (3) a personal need for achievement, and (4) proper compensation, incentives, or rewards will produce a motivated salesperson.[41]

The importance of compensation as a motivating factor means that close attention must be given to how salespeople are financially rewarded for their efforts. Salespeople are paid using one of three plans: (1) straight salary, (2) straight commission, or (3) a combination of salary and commission. Under a *straight salary compensation plan* a salesperson is paid a fixed fee per week, month, or year. With a *straight commission compensation plan* a salesperson's earnings are directly tied to the sales or profit generated. For example, an insurance agent might receive a 2 percent commission of $2,000 for selling a $100,000 life insurance policy. A *combination compensation plan* contains a specified salary plus a commission on sales or profit generated.

Each compensation plan has its advantages and disadvantages. A straight salary plan is easy to administer and gives management a large measure of control over how salespeople allocate their efforts. However, it provides little incentive to expand sales volume. This plan is used when salespeople engage in many nonselling activities, such as account servicing. A straight commission plan provides the maximum amount of selling incentive but can detract salespeople from providing customer service. This plan is common when nonselling activities are minimal. Combination plans are most preferred by salespeople and attempt to build on the advantages of salary and commission plans while reducing potential shortcomings of each.[42] Today, 63 percent of companies use combination plans, 17 percent use straight salary, and 20 percent rely solely on commissions.

Mary Kay Cosmetics recognizes a top salesperson at its annual sales meeting.

Mary Kay Cosmetics, Inc.
www.marykay.com

Nonmonetary rewards are also given to salespeople for meeting or exceeding objectives. These rewards include trips, honor societies, distinguished salesperson awards, and letters of commendation. Some unconventional rewards include the new pink Cadillacs and Pontiacs, fur coats, and jewelry given by Mary Kay Cosmetics to outstanding salespeople. Mary Kay, with 10,000 cars, has the largest fleet of General Motors cars in the world![43]

Effective recruitment, selection, training, motivation, and compensation programs combine to create a productive salesforce. Ineffective practices often lead to costly salesforce turnover. U.S. firms experience an annual 11.6 percent turnover rate, which means that almost one of every nine salespeople are replaced each year.[44] The expense of replacing and training a new salesperson, including the cost of lost sales, can be high. Moreover, new recruits are often less productive than established salespeople.

Salesforce Evaluation and Control

The final function in the sales management process involves evaluating and controlling the salesforce. It is at this point that salespeople are assessed as to whether sales objectives were met and account management policies were followed. Both quantitative and behavioral measures are used to tap different selling dimensions.[45]

Quantitative Assessments   Quantitative assessments, called quotas, are based on input- and output-related objectives set forth in the sales plan. Input-related measures focus on the actual activities performed by salespeople such as those involving sales calls, selling expenses, and account management policies. The number of sales calls made, selling expense related to sales made, and the number of reports submitted to superiors are frequently used input measures.

Output measures focus on the results obtained and include sales produced, accounts generated, profit achieved, and orders produced compared with calls made. Dollar sales volume, last year/current year sales ratio, the number of new accounts, and sales of specific products are frequently used measures when evaluating salesperson output.

Behavioral Evaluation   Behavioral measures are also used to evaluate salespeople. These include assessments of a salesperson's attitude, attention to customers, product knowledge, selling and communication skills, appearance, and professional demeanor. Even though these assessments are sometimes subjective, they are frequently considered, and, in fact, inevitable, in salesperson evaluation. Moreover, these factors are often important determinants of quantitative outcomes.

About 60 percent of U.S. companies now include customer satisfaction as a behavioral measure of salesperson performance.[46] (What percentage did you check for question 4 in Figure 20–1?) Indianapolis Power & Light, for example, asks major customers to grade its salespeople from A to F. IBM Siebel Systems has been the most aggressive in using this behavioral measure. Forty percent of an IBM Siebel salesperson's evaluation is linked to customer satisfaction; the remaining 60 percent is linked to profits achieved. The relentless focus on customer satisfaction by Eastman Chemical Company salespeople contributed to the company being named a recipient of the prestigious Malcolm Baldrige National Quality Award.[47] Eastman surveys its customers with eight versions of its customer satisfaction questionnaire printed in nine languages. Some 25 performance items are studied, including on-time and correct delivery, product quality, pricing practice, and sharing of market information. The survey is managed by the salesforce, and salespeople review the results with customers. Eastman salespeople know that "the second most important thing they have to do is get their customer satisfaction surveys out to and back from customers," says Eastman's sales training director. "Number one, of course, is getting orders."

Salesforce Automation and Customer Relationship Management

Personal selling and sales management are undergoing a technological revolution with the integration of salesforce automation into customer relationship management

Computer and communication technologies have made it possible for Compaq Computer salespeople to work out of their homes.

Compaq Computer Corporation

www.compaq.com

processes. In fact, the convergence of computer, information, communication, and Internet/Web technologies has transformed the sales function in many companies and made the promise of customer relationship management a reality. **Salesforce automation** (SFA) is the use of these technologies to make the sales function more effective and efficient. SFA applies to a wide range of activities, including each stage in the personal selling process and management of the salesforce itself.

Salesforce automation represents both an opportunity and a challenge for companies. Examples of SFA applications include computer hardware and software for account analysis, time management, order processing and follow-up, sales presentations, proposal generation, and product and sales training. But applications are not free. It is estimated that companies worldwide spent $2.6 billion for SFA software alone in 2001 and will spend over $4 billion in 2004. In addition, companies are investing two to three times these amounts for SFA salesforce training and technology integration services.[48]

Salesforce Computerization Computer technology has become an integral part of field selling through innovations such as laptop, notebook, palmtop, pad, and tablet computers. For example, salespeople for Godiva Chocolates use their laptop computers to process orders, plan time allocations, forecast sales, and communicate with Godiva personnel and customers. While in a department store candy buyer's office, such as Neiman Marcus, a salesperson can calculate the order cost (and discount), transmit the order, and obtain a delivery date within minutes from Godiva's order processing department.[49]

Toshiba America Medical System salespeople now use laptop computers with built-in CD-ROM capabilities to provide interactive presentations for their computerized tomography (CT) and magnetic resonance imaging (MRI) scanners. In it the customer sees elaborate three-dimensional animations, high-resolution scans, and video clips of the company's products in operation as well as narrated testimonials from satisfied customers. Toshiba has found this application to be effective both for sales presentations and for training its salespeople.[50]

Toshiba America Medical System salespeople have found computer technology to be an effective sales tool and training device.

Toshiba America Medical Systems

www.toshiba.com

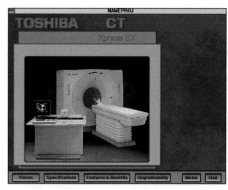

Salesforce Communication   Technology also has changed the way salespeople communicate with customers, other salespeople and sales support personnel, and management. Facsimile, electronic mail, and voice mail are three common communication technologies used by salespeople today. Cellular (phone) technology, which now allows salespeople to exchange data as well as voice transmissions, is equally popular. Whether traveling or in a customer's office, these technologies provide information at the salesperson's fingertips to answer customer questions and solve problems.

Advances in communication and computer technologies have made possible the mobile and home sales office. Some salespeople now equip minivans with a fully functional desk, swivel chair, light, computer, printer, fax machine, cellular phone, and a satellite dish. Jeff Brown, an agent manager with U.S. Cellular, uses such a mobile office. He says, "If I arrive at a prospect's office and they can't see me right away, then I can go outside to work in my office until they're ready to see me."[51] Home offices are now common. Compaq Computer Corporation is a case in point. The company recently shifted its entire 224-person U.S. salesforce into home offices, closed three regional sales offices, and saved $10 million in staff salaries and office rent. A fully equipped home office for each salesperson costs the company about $8,000 and includes a notebook computer, fax/copier, cellular phone, two phone lines, and office furniture.[52]

Perhaps the greatest impact on salesforce communication is the application of Internet/Web-based technology. Today, salespeople are using their company's Intranet for a variety of purposes. At EDS, a professional services firm, salespeople access its Intranet to download client material, marketing content, account information, technical papers, and competitive profiles. In addition, EDS offers 7,000 training classes that salespeople can take anytime, anywhere.[53]

Salesforce automation is clearly changing how selling is done and how salespeople are managed. Its numerous applications promise to boost selling productivity, improve customer relationships, and decrease selling cost. As applications increase, SFA has the potential to transform selling and sales management in the twenty-first century.

Concept Check

1. What are the three types of selling objectives?

2. What three factors are used to structure sales organizations?

3. How does emotional intelligence tie to adaptive selling?

SUMMARY

1 Personal selling involves the two-way flow of communication between a buyer and a seller, often in a face-to-face encounter, designed to influence a person's or group's purchase decision. Sales management involves planning the sales program and implementing and controlling the personal selling effort of the firm.

2 Personal selling is pervasive since virtually every occupation that involves customer contact has an element of selling attached to it.

3 Personal selling plays a major role in a firm's marketing effort. Salespeople occupy a boundary position between buyers and sellers; they *are* the company to many buyers and account for a major cost of marketing in a variety of industries; and they can create value for customers.

4 Three types of personal selling exist: order-taking, order-getting, and sales support activities. Each type differs from the others in terms of actual selling done and the amount of creativity required to perform the job.

5 The personal selling process, particularly for order getters, is a complex activity involving six stages: (1) prospecting, (2) preapproach, (3) approach, (4) presentation, (5) close, and (6) follow-up.

6 The sales management process consists of three interrelated functions: (1) sales plan formulation, (2) sales plan implementation, and (3) evaluation of the salesforce.

7 A sales plan is a statement describing what is to be achieved and where and how the selling effort of salespeople is to be deployed. Sales planning involves setting objectives, organizing the salesforce, and developing account management policies.

8 Effective salesforce recruitment and selection efforts, sales training that emphasizes selling skills and product knowledge, and motivation and compensation practices are necessary to successfully implement a sales plan.

9 Salespeople are evaluated using quantitative and behavioral measures that are linked to selling objectives and account management policies.

10 Salesforce automation involves the use of technology designed to make the sales function more effective and efficient. It applies to a wide range of activities, including each stage in the personal selling process and management of the salesforce itself.

KEY TERMS AND CONCEPTS

account management policies p. 546
adaptive selling p. 539
consultative selling p. 539
emotional intelligence p. 547
formula selling presentation p. 538
major account management p. 545
missionary salespeople p. 534
need-satisfaction presentation p. 539
order getter p. 533
order taker p. 533
partnership selling p. 532

personal selling p. 530
personal selling process p. 535
relationship selling p. 532
sales engineer p. 534
sales management p. 530
sales plan p. 541
salesforce automation p. 550
stimulus-response presentation p. 538
team selling p. 534
workload method p. 545

APPLYING MARKETING CONCEPTS AND PERSPECTIVES

1 Jane Dawson is a new sales representative for the Charles Schwab brokerage firm. In searching for clients, Jane purchased a mailing list of subscribers to *The Wall Street Journal* and called them all regarding their interest in discount brokerage services. She asked if they have any stocks and if they have a regular broker. Those people without a regular broker were asked their investment needs. Two days later Jane called back with investment advice and asked if they would like to open an account. Identify each of Jane Dawson's actions in terms of the steps of selling.

2 For the first 50 years of business the Johnson Carpet Company produced carpets for residential use. The salesforce was structured geographically. In the past five years a large percentage of carpet sales has been to industrial users, hospitals, schools, and architects.

The company also has broadened its product line to include area rugs, Oriental carpets, and wall-to-wall carpeting. Is the present salesforce structure appropriate, or would you recommend an alternative?

3 Where would you place each of the following sales jobs on the order-taker/order-getter continuum shown below? (*a*) Burger King counter clerk, (*b*) automobile insurance salesperson, (*c*) IBM computer salesperson, (*d*) life insurance salesperson, and (*e*) shoe salesperson.

Order taker	**Order getter**

4 Listed here are two different firms. Which compensation plan would you recommend for each firm, and what reasons would you give for your recommendations? *(a)* A newly formed company that sells lawn care equipment on a door-to-door basis directly to consumers; and *(b)* the Nabisco Company, which sells heavily advertised products in supermarkets by having the salesforce call on these stores and arrange shelves, set up displays, and make presentations to store buying committees.

5 The TDK tape company services 1,000 audio stores throughout the United States. Each store is called on 12 times a year, and the average sales call lasts 30 minutes. Assuming a salesperson works 40 hours a week, 50 weeks a year, and devotes 75 percent of the time to actual selling, how many salespeople does TDK need?

6 A furniture manufacturer is currently using manu-

facturer's representatives to sell its line of living room furniture. These representatives receive an 8 percent commission. The company is considering hiring its own salespeople and has estimated that the fixed cost of managing and paying their salaries would be $1 million annually. The salespeople would also receive a 4 percent commission on sales. The company has sales of $25 million dollars, and sales are expected to grow by 15 percent next year. Would you recommend that the company switch to its own salesforce? Why or why not?

7 Suppose someone said to you, "The only real measure of a salesperson is the amount of sales produced." How might you respond?

INTERNET EXERCISE

A unique resource for the latest developments in personal selling and sales management is the Sales Marketing Network (SMN) at www.info-now.com. SMN provides highly readable reports on a variety of topics including many discussed in this chapter, such as telemarketing, motivation, sales training, and sales management. These reports contain concise overviews, definitions, statistics, and reviews of critical issues. They also include references to additional information and links to related material elsewhere on the SMN

site. Registration (at no cost) is required to view some of the reports.

Visit the SMN site and do the following:

1 Select a chapter topic, and update the statistics for, say, sales training costs or the popularity of different salesforce incentives.

2 Select a topic covered in the chapter such as telemarketing, and summarize the critical issues identified for this practice.

VIDEO CASE 20–1   Reebok: Relationship Selling and Customer Value

"I think face-to-face selling is the most important and exciting part of this whole job. It's not writing the sales reports. It's not analyzing trends and forecasting. It's the two hours that you have to try to sell the buyer your products in a way that's profitable for both you and the retailer," relates Robert McMahon, key account sales representative for Reebok Northeast. As the person in charge of Reebok's largest accounts in New England—including MVP Sports, Modell's, and City Sports in Boston—McMahon's job encompasses a myriad of activities, from supervising other sales representatives to attending companywide computer training sessions to monitoring competitors' activities. But it's the actual selling that is most appealing to McMahon. "That's the challenging, stimulating part of the job. Selling to the buyer is a different challenge every day. Every sales call, as well as you may have preplanned it, can change based on shifts and trends in the market. So you need to be able to react to those changes and really think on your feet in front of the buyer."

REEBOK—HOT ON NIKE'S HEELS IN THE ATHLETIC SHOE AND APPAREL MARKET

Reebok is the second largest athletic shoe manufacturer behind the market leader, Nike. In addition to its athletic shoes, Reebok also sells Rockport, Greg Norman Collection, and Ralph Lauren Footwear shoes. The Reebok sporting goods line remains the flagship brand, though, and distinguishes itself on the market through the DMX cushioning technology in its footwear. Reebok concentrates its resources on getting its footwear and sporting goods gear into a diversified mix of distribution channels such as athletic footwear specialty stores, department stores, and large sporting goods stores. Reebok is unique in that it emphasizes relationships with the retailers as an integral part of its marketing strategy. As an employee at MVP Sports, one of Reebok's major retailers, puts it, "Reebok is the only company that comes in on a regular basis and gives us information. Nike

comes in once in a great while. New Balance comes in every six months. Saucony has come in twice. That's been it. Reebok comes in every month to update us on new information and new products. They tell us about the technology so we can tell the customers." Says Laurie Sipples, "vector" representative for Reebok, "There's a partnership that exists between Reebok and an account like MVP Sports that sets us apart. That relationship is a great asset that Reebok has because the retailer feels more in touch with us than other brands."

THE SELLING PROCESS AT REEBOK

Selling at Reebok includes three elements—building trust between the salesperson and the retailer, providing enough information to the retailer for them to be successful selling Reebok products, and finally supporting the retailer after the sale. Sean Neville, senior vice president and general manager of Reebok North America, explains, "Our goal is not to sell to the retailer; our goal is ultimately to sell to the consumer, and so we use the retailer as a partner. The salespeople are always keeping their eyes open and thinking like the retailer and selling to the consumer."

Reebok sells in teams that consist of the account representatives, who do the actual selling to the retailer, and the "vector" representatives, who spend their time in the stores training the store salespeople and reporting trends back to the account manager. The selling teams are organized geographically so that the salespeople live and work in the area they are selling in. This allows the sales team to understand the consumer intuitively. Neville explains, "If you have someone from New York City fly to L.A. and try to tell someone on the streets of Los Angeles what's happening from a trends standpoint and what products to purchase, it's very difficult."

On average, Reebok salespeople spend 70 percent of their time preparing for a sale and 30 percent of their time actually selling. The sales process at Reebok typically follows the six steps of the personal selling process identified in Figure 20–3: (1) Reebok identifies the outlets it would like to carry its athletic gear; (2) the salesforce prepares for the a presentation by familiarizing themselves with the store and its customers; (3) a Reebok representative approaches the prospect and suggests a meeting and presentation; (4) as the presentation begins, the salesperson summarizes relevant market conditions and consumer trends to demonstrate Reebok's commitment to a partnership with the retailer, states what s/he hopes to get out of the sales meeting, explains how the products work, and reinforces the benefits of Reebok products; (5) the salesperson engages in an action close (gets a signed document or a firm confirmation of the sale); and (6) later, various members of the salesforce frequently visit the retailer to provide assistance and monitor consumer preferences.

THE SALES MANAGEMENT PROCESS AT REEBOK

The sales teams at Reebok are organized based on Reebok's three major distribution channels: athletic specialty stores, sporting goods stores, and department stores. The smaller stores have sales teams assigned to them based on geographical location within the United States (west coast, central, southeast, and northeast). The salesforce is then further broken down into footwear and apparel teams. The salesforce is primarily organized by distribution channel because this is most responsive to customer needs and wants. The salesforce is compensated on both a short-term and long-term basis. In the short term, salespeople are paid based on sales results and profits for the current quarter as well as forecasting. In the long term, salespeople are compensated based on their teamwork and teambuilding efforts. As Neville explains, "Money is typically fourth or fifth on the list of pure motivation. Number one is recognition for a job well done. And that drives people to succeed." Management at Reebok is constantly providing feedback to the salesforce acknowledging their success, not just during annual reviews, and Neville feels this is the key to the high level of motivation, energy, and excitement that exists in the salesforce at Reebok.

WHAT'S NEW ON THE HORIZON FOR THE SALESFORCE AT REEBOK?

Reebok has recently issued laptop computers to its entire salesforce that enable the salespeople to check inventories in the warehouses, make sure orders are being shipped on time, and even enter orders while they're out in the field. Reebok is also focusing more on relationship selling. McMahon describes his relationship with a major buyer as "one of trust and respect. It's gotten to the point now where we're good friends. We go to a lot of sporting events together, which I think really helps." Another recent innovation is for the salesforce to incentivize the stores' sales clerks. For instance, whoever sells the most pairs of Reebok shoes in a month will get tickets to a concert or a football game.

Questions

1   How does Reebok create customer value for its major accounts through relationship selling?

2   How does Reebok utilize team selling to provide the highest level of customer value possible to its major accounts?

3   Is Reebok's salesforce organized based on geography, customer, or product?

4   What are some ways Reebok's selling processes are changing due to technical advancements?

PART

5

MANAGING THE MARKETING PROCESS

CHAPTER 21
Implementing Interactive and Multichannel Marketing

CHAPTER 22
Pulling It All Together: The Strategic Marketing Process

Part 5 discusses issues and techniques related to interactive marketing technologies and the planning, implementation, and control phases of the strategic marketing process. Chapter 21 describes how the evolution of a new exchange environment has led to a new marketing mantra: "Anytime, Anywhere, Anyway!" The chapter also illustrates how interactive technologies influence customer value and the customer experience through context, content, community, customization, communication, connectivity, and commerce. Chapter 22 explains how marketing executives search for a competitive advantage and allocate the firm's resources to maximize the effects of marketing efforts. Frameworks for improving marketing planning, guidelines for creating an effective marketing plan, and alternatives for organizing a marketing department are also discussed.

CHAPTER 21

IMPLEMENTING INTERACTIVE AND MULTICHANNEL MARKETING

AFTER READING THIS CHAPTER YOU SHOULD BE ABLE TO:

● Understand what interactive marketing is and how it creates customer value, customer relationships, and customer experiences in the new marketspace.

● Identify the demographic and lifestyle profile of online consumers.

● Explain why certain types of products and services are particularly suited for interactive marketing.

● Describe why consumers shop and buy online and how marketers influence online purchasing behavior.

● Distinguish between the use of multiple channels and multichannel marketing in reaching online consumers.

● Recognize the different roles played by transactional websites and promotional websites in multichannel marketing.

ANYTIME, ANYWHERE, ANYWAY: THE NEW MARKETING MANTRA

What a difference a year (or three) makes. Just yesterday it seems, the Internet and the World Wide Web's promise of immediacy and interactivity was hailed as a compelling new technology that would revolutionize marketing and forever change how consumers shop and purchase products and services. It's clear that Internet/Web technology has altered consumer behavior and marketing practice, but not in quite the manner pundits prognosticated.

Internet/Web technology has empowered consumers to seek information, evaluate alternatives, and make purchase decisions on their own terms and conditions. At the same time, this technology has challenged marketers to deliver to consumers *more* (selection, service, quality, enjoyment, convenience, and information) *for less* (money, time, effort). In short, the initial promise of immediacy and interactivity quickly transformed itself into a "straight A" customer value standard and marketing mantra: *Anytime, Anywhere, Anyway!*

Today, consumers expect to shop and buy their favorite products and services anytime, anywhere, and anyway without constraints. Marketers have responded by engaging in interactive and multichannel marketing. This chapter describes how companies design and implement marketing programs that capitalize on the unique value-creation capabilities of Internet/Web technology. We begin by explaining how this technology can create customer value, build customer relationships, and produce customer experiences in novel ways. Next, we describe how consumer behavior and marketing practice are affected by Internet/Web technology. Finally, we show how marketers integrate and leverage their communication and delivery channels using Internet/Web technology.[1]

CREATING CUSTOMER VALUE, RELATIONSHIPS, AND EXPERIENCES IN THE NEW MARKETSPACE

Consumers and companies populate two market environments today. One is the traditional marketplace. Here buyers and sellers engage in face-to-face exchange relationships in a material environment characterized by physical facilities (stores and offices) and mostly tangible objects. The other is the marketspace, an Internet/Web-enabled digital environment characterized by "face-to-screen" exchange relationships and electronic images and offerings.

The existence of two market environments has been a boon for consumers. Today, consumers can shop for and purchase a wide variety of products and services in either market environment. Actually, many consumers now browse and buy in both market environments and more are expected to do so in the future as access to and familiarity with Internet/Web technology grows.[2] As an illustration, Figure 21–1 shows the 10-year growth trend in Internet/Web users and estimated online retail sales in the United States.[3]

Marketing in two market environments also poses significant challenges for companies. Companies with origins in the traditional marketplace, such as Procter & Gamble, Wal-Mart, and General Motors, are challenged to define the nature and scope of their marketspace presence. These companies need to determine the role of Internet/Web technology in attracting, retaining, and building consumer relationships to improve their competitive positions in the traditional marketplace while achieving a marketspace presence. Consider Toys "Я" Us, a leading toy retailer in the traditional marketplace. It has formed an alliance with Amazon.com to create a marketspace presence—Toysrus.com. Toys "Я" Us leverages its toy merchandising know-how and immense store network with Amazon's knowledge and experience with Internet/Web technology. The result? Toys "Я" Us now has a presence in two market environments. On the other hand, companies with marketspace origins, including Amazon.com, eBay, E-Trade, and others, are challenged to continually refine, broaden, and deepen their marketspace presence, and consider what role, if any, the traditional marketplace will play in their future. Gateway Computer is a case in point.[4] This direct marketer and a marketspace pioneer has elected to operate a network of Gateway Country showrooms for personal computer buyers who prefer browsing in a store, physically handling the merchandise, and talking face-to-face with a salesperson. Regardless of origin, a company's success in achieving a meaningful marketspace presence hinges largely on designing and executing a marketing program that capitalizes on the unique customer value-creation capabilities of Internet/Web technology.

FIGURE 21–1
The 10-year trend in Internet/Web users and online retail sales revenue in the United States

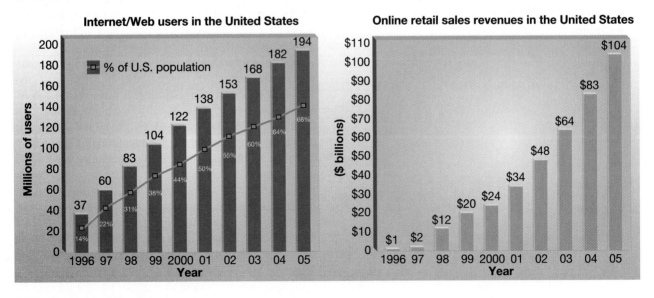

Customer Value Creation in Marketspace

Despite the widespread interest in marketspace, its economic significance remains small compared with the traditional marketplace. Electronic commerce is expected to represent less than 20 percent of total U.S. consumer and business goods and services expenditures in 2005, and less than 9 percent of global expenditures.[5] Why then has the new marketspace captured the eye and imagination of marketers?

Marketers believe that the possibilities for customer value creation are greater in marketspace than in the traditional marketplace. Recall from Chapter 1 that marketing creates time, place, form, and possession utilities for customers, thereby providing value. In marketspace, the provision of direct, on-demand information is possible from marketers *anywhere* to customers *anywhere at any time*. Why? Operating hours and geographical constraints do not exist in marketspace. For example, Recreational Equipment (www.rei.com), an outdoor gear marketer, reports that 35 percent of its orders are placed between 10:00 P.M. and 7:00 A.M., long after and before retail stores are open for business. This isn't surprising. About 58 percent of Internet/Web users prefer to shop and buy in their night clothes or pajamas![6] Similarly, a U.S. consumer from Chicago can access Marks & Spencer (www.marks-and-spencer. co.uk), the well-known British department store, to shop for clothing as easily as a person living near London's Piccadilly Square. Possession utility—getting a product or service to consumers so they can own or use it—is accelerated. Airline, car rental, and lodging electronic reservation systems such as Orbitz (www.orbitz.com) allow comparison shopping for the lowest fares, rents, and rates and almost immediate access to and confirmation of travel arrangements and accommodations.

The greatest marketspace opportunity for marketers, however, lies in its potential for creating form utility. Interactive two-way Internet/Web-enabled communication capabilities in marketspace invite consumers to tell marketers exactly what their requirements are, making customization of a product or service to fit the buyer's exact needs possible. For instance, Bluefly.com, an apparel company, encourages customers to develop their own catalog free of unwanted items. Consumers can specify the brands, clothing category, and sizes right for their needs. Bluefly.com will instantaneously create a personalized catalog just for them called MyCatalog.

Orbitz offers consumers the most low-cost airfares and flight options on the Web as well as rental cars, lodging, cruises, vacation packages, and other travel deals.

Orbitz

www.orbitz.com

Interactivity, Individuality, and Customer Relationships in Marketspace

Marketers also benefit from two unique capabilities of Internet/Web technology that promote and sustain customer relationships. One is *interactivity;* the other is *individuality.*[7] Both capabilities are important building blocks for buyer-seller relationships. For these relationships to occur, companies need to interact with their customers by listening and responding to their needs. Marketers must also treat customers as individuals and empower them to (1) influence the timing and extent of the buyer-seller interaction and (2) have a say in the kind of products and services they buy, the information they receive, and in some cases, the prices they pay.

Internet/Web technology allows for interaction, individualization, and customer relationship building to be carried out on a scale never before available and makes interactive marketing possible. **Interactive marketing** involves two-way buyer-seller electronic communication in a computer-mediated environment in which the buyer controls the kind and amount of information received from the seller. Interactive marketing today is characterized by sophisticated choiceboard and personalization systems that transform information supplied by customers into customized responses to their individual needs.

Choiceboards
A **choiceboard** is an interactive, Internet/Web-enabled system that allows individual customers to design their own products and services by answering a few questions and choosing from a menu of product or service attributes (or components), prices, and delivery options.[8] Customers today can design their own computers with Dell Computer's online configurator, create their own athletic shoe at Niketown.com, assemble their own investment portfolios with Schwab's mutual fund evaluator, and even mix their own cereal ingredients at General Mills's experimental MyCereal.com website. Because choiceboards collect precise information about the preferences and behavior of individual buyers, a company becomes more knowledgeable about the customer and better able to anticipate and fulfill that customer's needs. Read the accompanying Marketing NewsNet to learn how Reflect.com uses choiceboard technology to create made-to-order cosmetics and other personal care items for women.[9]

Most choiceboards are essentially transaction devices. However, companies such as Dell Computer have expanded the functionality of choiceboards using collaborative filtering technology. **Collaborative filtering** is a process that automatically groups people with similar buying intentions, preferences, and behaviors and predicts future purchases.[10] For example, say two people who have never met buy a few of the same CDs over time. Collaborative filtering software is programmed to reason that these two buyers might have similar musical tastes: If one buyer likes a particular CD, then the other will like it as well. The outcome? Collaborative filtering gives marketers the ability to make a dead-on sales recommendation to a buyer in *real time*!

Choiceboards and collaborative filtering represent two important capabilities of Internet/Web technology and have changed the way companies operate today. According to an electronic commerce manager at IBM, "The business model of the past was make and sell. Now instead of make and sell, it's sense and respond."[11]

Personalization
Choiceboards and collaborative filtering are marketer-initiated efforts to provide customized responses to the needs of individual buyers. Personalization systems are typically buyer-initiated efforts. **Personalization** is the consumer-initiated practice of generating content on a marketer's website that is custom tailored to an individual's specific needs and preferences. For example, Yahoo! (www.yahoo.com) allows users to create personalized MyYahoo pages. Users can add or delete a variety of types of information from their personal pages, including specific stock

MARKETING NEWSNET

Reflect.com: Creating Customized Cosmetics

TECHNOLOGY & E-COMMERCE

"We're learning that customization is powerful," says Ginger Kent, CEO of Reflect.com (www.reflect.com), based in San Francisco. Reflect.com is the first online marketer that allows users to create their own cosmetics—everything from skin and body care items to hair care, color cosmetics, fragrances, and accessories. The company lets customers tailor their own products by suggesting beauty ingredients they like most. "It's an incredibly powerful idea—like a throwback to the 1800s and how apothecaries mixed formulas for people," notes Kent.

Reflect.com is targeted to women who crave individualized products. In fact, no Reflect product exists before it is created by the consumer. Over a million "customizations" have been done for online shoppers and the incidence of new users continues to grow. Today, Reflect.com is considered the second most visited beauty website. Contrary to other beauty websites that have failed, Kent says confidently: "Our business model has a high profit margin, and also includes repeat customers." What's more, almost 90 percent of customers recommend the site to others.

quotes, weather conditions in any city in the world, and local television schedules. In turn, Yahoo! can use the buyer profile data entered when users register at the site to tailor e-mail messages, advertising, and content to the individual—and even post a happy birthday greeting on the user's special day!

An aspect of personalization is a buyer's willingness to have tailored communications brought to his or her attention. Obtaining this approval is called **permission marketing**—the solicitation of a consumer's consent (called "opt-in") to receive e-mail and advertising based on personal data supplied by the consumer. Permission marketing is a proven vehicle for building and maintaining customer relationships, provided it is properly used. Companies that successfully employ permission marketing adhere to three rules.[12] First, they make sure "opt-in" customers only receive information that is relevant and meaningful to them. Second, their customers are given the option of "opting out" or changing the kind, amount, or timing of information sent to them. Finally, their customers are assured that their name or buyer profile data will not be sold or shared with others. This assurance is important because 86 percent of Internet/Web users have expressed concern about the privacy of their personal information.[13]

Creating an Online Customer Experience

A continuing challenge for companies is the design and execution of marketing programs that capitalize on the unique and evolving customer value-creation capabilities of Internet/Web technology. Companies now realize that simply applying Internet/Web technology to create time, place, form, and possession utility is not enough to claim a meaningful marketspace presence. Today, the quality of the customer experience produced by a company is the standard by which a meaningful marketspace presence is measured.

From an interactive marketing perspective, **customer experience** is defined as the sum total of the interactions that a customer has with a company's website, from the initial look at a home page through the entire purchase decision process.[14] Companies produce a customer experience through seven website design elements. These elements are context, content, community, customization, communication, connection, and commerce, each of which is summarized in Figure 21–2. A closer look at these elements illustrates how each contributes to customer experience.

Context refers to a website's aesthetic appeal and functional look and feel reflected in site layout and design. A functionally oriented website focuses largely on the company's offering, be it products, services, or information. For instance, travel websites tend to be functionally oriented with an emphasis on destinations, scheduling, and prices. In contrast, the Reflect.com website, shown earlier, is a more aesthetically oriented site with its focus on beauty products. As these examples suggest, context attempts to convey the core consumer benefit provided by the company's offering(s). *Content* applies to all digital information on a website, including the presentation form—text, video, audio, and graphics. Content quality and presentation

FIGURE 21–2

Website design elements that drive customer experience

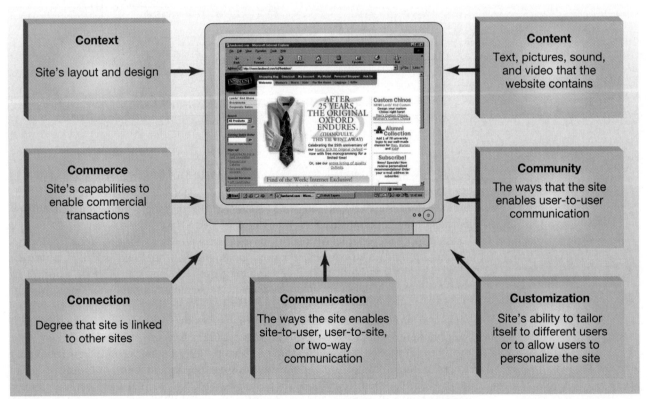

SOURCE: Rafi A. Mohammed, Robert J. Fisher, Bernard J. Jaworski, and Aileen M. Cahill, *Internet Marketing: Building Advantage in a Networked Economy,* (Burr Ridge, IL: McGraw-Hill/Irwin © 2002), p. 623.

along with context dimensions combine to engage a website visitor and provide a platform for the five remaining design elements.

Website *customization* is the ability of a site to modify itself to—or be modified by—each individual user. This design element is prominent in websites that offer personalized content, such as My eBay and MyYahoo. The *connection* element in website design is the network of formal linkages between a company's site and other sites. These links are embedded in the website; appear as highlighted words, a picture, or graphic; and allow a user to effortlessly visit other sites with a mouse click. Connection is a major design element for informational websites such as *The New York Times*. For example, users of NYTimes.com can access the book review section and link to Barnes & Noble to order a book or browse related titles without ever visiting a store.

Communication refers to the dialogue that unfolds between the website and its users. Consumers—particularly those who have registered at a site—now expect that communication be interactive and individualized in real time much like a personal conversation. In fact, some websites now enable a user to talk directly with a customer representative while shopping the site. For example, two-thirds of the sales through Dell Computer's website involve human sales representatives. In addition, an increasing number of company websites encourage user-to-user communications hosted by the company to create virtual communities, or simply, *community*. This design element is growing in popularity because it has been shown to enhance customer experience and build favorable buyer-seller relationships. Examples of communities range from the Parenting Community hosted by Kimberly-Clark (www.huggies.com) to the Harley Owners Group (H.O.G) sponsored by Harley-Davidson (www.harley-davidson.com).

The seventh design element is *commerce*—the website's ability to conduct sales transactions for products and services. Online transactions are quick and simple in

Harley-Davidson pays close attention to creating a favorable customer experience at its website.

Harley-Davidson
www.harley-davidson.com

well-designed websites. Amazon.com has mastered this design element with "one-click shopping," a patented feature that allows users to place and order products with a single mouse click.

All websites do not include all design elements. Although every website has context and content, they differ in the use of the remaining five elements. Why? Websites have different purposes. For example, only websites that emphasize the actual sale of products and services include the commerce element. Websites that are used primarily for advertising and promotion purposes emphasize the communication element. The difference between these two types of websites is discussed later in the chapter.

Concept Check

1. The greatest marketspace opportunity for marketers lies in the creation of what kind of utility?

2. The consumer-initiated practice of generating content on a marketer's website that is custom tailored to an individual's specific needs and preferences is called _____ .

3. Companies produce a customer experience through what seven website design elements?

ONLINE CONSUMER BEHAVIOR AND MARKETING PRACTICE IN MARKETSPACE

Who are online consumers, and what do they buy? Why do they choose to shop and purchase products and services in the new marketspace rather than or in addition to the traditional marketplace? Answers to these questions have a direct bearing on marketspace marketing practices.

The Online Consumer

Many labels are given online consumers—cybershoppers, Netizens, and e-shoppers—suggesting they are a homogeneous segment of the population. They are not, but as a group, they do differ demographically from the general population.

Profiling the Online Consumer
Online consumers differ from the general population in one important respect. They own or have access to a computer or an Internet/Web-enabled device, such as a wireless cellular telephone. Over 50 percent of U.S. households have a computer in their home with Internet/Web access, although access is often possible at work or school. Figure 21–3 profiles households with Internet/Web access at home.[15]

Online consumers are the subsegment of all Internet/Web users who employ this technology to research products and services and make purchases. Research indicates that about 80 percent of all adult Internet/Web users have sought online product or service information at one time or another.[16] For example, some 70 percent of prospective travelers have researched travel information online, even though fewer than 25 percent have actually made online travel reservations. Over 40 percent have researched automobiles before making a purchase, but only 8 percent of users actually bought a vehicle online.[17] About two-thirds of adult Internet/Web users have actually purchased a product or service online at one time or another.[18]

As a group, online consumers, like Internet/Web users, are evenly split between men and women, and tend to be better educated, younger, and more affluent than the general U.S. population, which makes them an attractive market. Even though

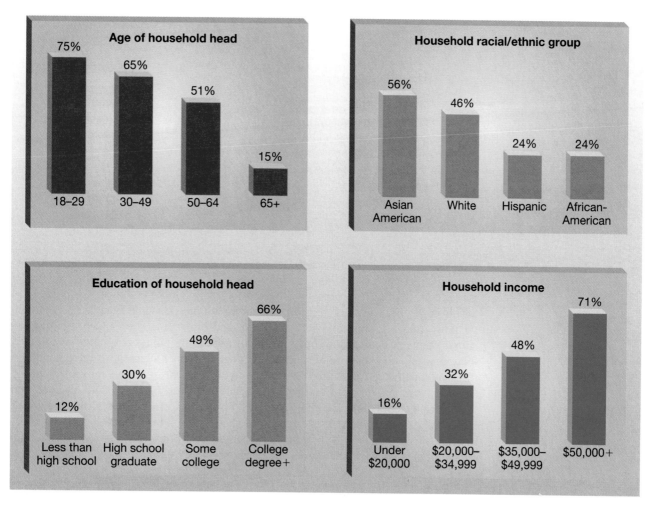

FIGURE 21–3
Internet/Web access at home among U.S. households

online shopping and buying is growing in popularity, a small percentage of online consumers still account for a disproportionate share of online retail sales in the United States. It is estimated that 20 percent of online consumers who spend $1,000-plus per year online account for 87 percent of total consumer online sales.[19]

Online Consumer Lifestyle Segmentation   Not all Internet/Web users use the technology the same way, nor are they likely to be exclusive online consumers. Numerous marketing research firms have studied the lifestyles and shopping and spending habits of online consumers. A recurrent insight is that online consumers are diverse and represent different kinds of people seeking different kinds of online experiences. As an illustration, Harris Interactive, a large U.S. research firm, has identified six distinct online consumer lifestyle segments.[20]

The largest online consumer lifestyle segment, called *click-and-mortar,* consists of female homemakers who tend to browse retailer websites, but actually buy products in traditional retail outlets. They make up 23 percent of online consumers and represent an important segment for multichannel retailers that also feature catalog and store operations, such as J. Crew and JCPenney. Twenty percent of online consumers are *hunter-gatherers*—married baby boomers with children at home who use the Internet like a consumer magazine to compare products and prices. They can be found visiting comparison shopping websites such as dealcatcher.com and mysimon.com on a regular basis. Nineteen percent of online consumers are *brand loyalists* who regularly visit their favorite bookmarked websites and spend the most money online. They are better-educated and more-affluent Internet/Web users who

effortlessly navigate familiar and trusted websites and enjoy the online browsing and buying experience. Next there are *time-sensitive materialists* who regard the Internet as a convenience tool for buying music, books, and computer software and electronics. They account for 17 percent of online consumers and can be found visiting Amazon.com, dell.com, sony.com, and bmg.com. The *hooked, online, and single* segment consists of young, affluent, and single online consumers who bank, play games, and spend more time online than any other segment as documented in the accompanying Web Link. They make up 16 percent of online consumers, enjoy auction websites such as eBay, and visit game websites like iWon.com, ea.com, and games.yahoo.com. Five percent of online consumers are the *ebivalent newbies*—newcomers to the Internet who rarely spend money online, but seek product information. This segment is populated by senior citizens, African-Americans, and Hispanics. Do any of these segments describe your online lifestyle and spending habits?

What Online Consumers Buy

Much still needs to be learned about online consumer purchase behavior. Although research has documented the most frequently purchased products and services bought online, marketers also need to know why these items are popular in the new marketspace.

There are six general product and service categories that dominate online consumer buying today and for the foreseeable future, as shown in Figure 21–4.[21] One category consists of items for which product information is an important part of the purchase decision, but prepurchase trial is not necessarily critical. Items such as computers, computer accessories, and consumer electronics sold by dell.com fall into this category. So do books, which accounts for the sales growth of Amazon.com and Barnes & Noble (www.barnesandnoble.com). Both booksellers publish short reviews of new books that visitors to their websites can read before making a purchase decision. According to an authority on electronic commerce, "You've read the reviews, you want it, you don't need to try it on."[22] A second category includes items for which audio or video demonstration is important. This category consists of CDs and videos sold by columbiahouse.com and cdnow.com. The third category contains items that can be delivered digitally, including computer software, travel and lodging reservations and confirmations, financial brokerage services, and electronic ticketing. Popular websites for these items include travelocity.com, ticketmaster.com, and schwab.com.

Unique items, such as collectibles, specialty goods, and foods and gifts, represent a fourth category. Collectible auction houses (www.sothebys.com and www.butterfields.com), wine merchant eVineyard (www.wine.com), and flower and gift marketer 1-800-Flowers (www.1800flowers.com) sell these products. A fifth category

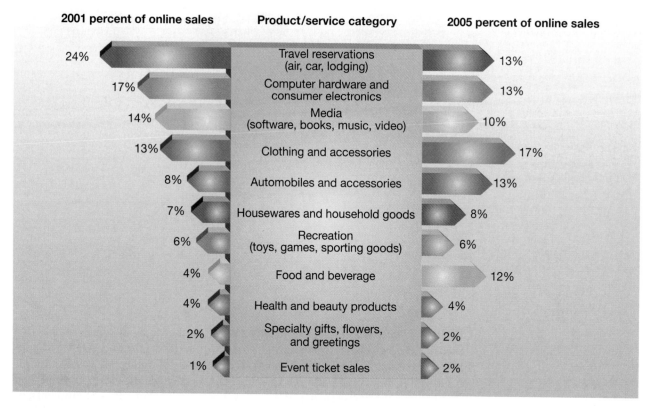

2001 percent of online sales	Product/service category	2005 percent of online sales
24%	Travel reservations (air, car, lodging)	13%
17%	Computer hardware and consumer electronics	13%
14%	Media (software, books, music, video)	10%
13%	Clothing and accessories	17%
8%	Automobiles and accessories	13%
7%	Housewares and household goods	8%
6%	Recreation (toys, games, sporting goods)	6%
4%	Food and beverage	12%
4%	Health and beauty products	4%
2%	Specialty gifts, flowers, and greetings	2%
1%	Event ticket sales	2%

FIGURE 21–4
Online consumer sales by product/service category: 2001 and 2005

includes items that are regularly purchased and where convenience is very important. Many consumer-packaged goods, such as grocery products, fall into this category. A final category of items consists of highly standardized products and services for which information about price is important. Certain kinds of insurance (auto and homeowners), home improvement products, casual apparel, and toys make up this category.

Why Consumers Shop and Buy Online

Marketers emphasize the customer value-creation possibilities, the importance of interactivity, individuality and relationship building, and producing customer experience in the new marketspace. However, consumers typically refer to six reasons why they shop and buy online: convenience, cost, choice, customization, communication, and control (Figure 21–5).

Convenience   Online shopping and buying is *convenient*. Consumers can visit Wal-Mart at www.wal-mart.com to scan and order from among thousands of displayed products without fighting traffic, finding a parking space, walking through long aisles, and standing in store checkout lines. Alternatively, online consumers can use **bots**, electronic shopping agents or robots that comb websites, to compare prices and product or service features. In either instance an online consumer has never ventured from his or her computer monitor. However, for convenience to remain a source of customer value creation, websites must be easy to locate and navigate, and image downloads must be fast. A commonly held view among online marketers is the **eight-second rule**: Customers will abandon their efforts to enter and navigate a website if download time exceeds eight seconds.[23] Furthermore, the more clicks and pauses between clicks required to access information or make a purchase, the more likely it is a customer will exit a website.

FIGURE 21–5
Why consumers shop and buy
online

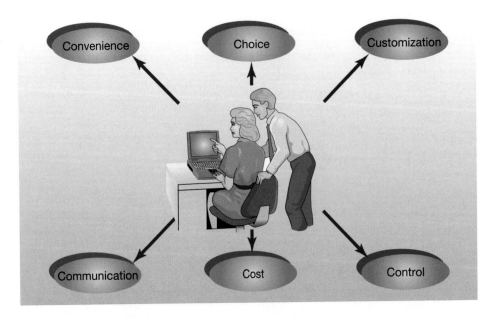

Choice   *Choice* is a second reason why consumers shop and buy online and has two
dimensions. First, choice exists in the product or service selection offered to consumers. Buyers desiring selection can avail themselves of numerous websites for almost anything they want. For instance, online buyers of consumer electronics can shop
individual manufacturers such as Bose (www.bose.com) or Sony (www.sony.com), or
visit iqvc.com, a general merchant, that offers more than 100,000 products. Choice
assistance is the second dimension. Here, the interactive capabilities of Internet/Web-
enabled technologies invite customers to engage in an electronic dialogue with marketers for the purpose of making informed choices. Lands' End (www.landsend.com)
provides choice assistance with its "My Virtual Model" apparel service. Men and
women submit their body shape, skin color, hair style, height, weight, and other attributes. The model then "tries on" outfits identified by the customer. Like any good salesperson, the service recommends flattering outfits for purchase.

Customization   Even with a broad selection and choice assistance, some customers prefer one-of-a-kind items that fit their specific needs. *Customization* arises
from Internet/Web-enabled capabilities that make possible a highly interactive and individualized information and exchange environment for shoppers and buyers.
Remember the earlier Reflect.com, Nike, Schwab, Dell Computer, and General Mills
examples? To varying degrees, online consumers also benefit from **customerization**—the growing practice of customizing not only a product or service, but also
personalizing the marketing and overall shopping and buying interaction for each
customer.[24] Customerization seeks to do more than offer consumers the right product,
at the right time, at the right price. It combines choiceboard and personalization systems to expand the exchange environment beyond a transaction and makes shopping
and buying an enjoyable, personal experience.

Communication   Online consumers particularly welcome the *communication* capabilities of Internet/Web-enabled technologies. This communication can take three
forms: (1) marketer-to-consumer e-mail notification, (2) consumer-to-marketer buying
and service requests, and (3) consumer-to-consumer chat rooms and instant messaging.[25] This communication capability is evidenced in the fact that over 4 trillion e-mail
messages are sent annually worldwide and some 656 million instant messages are sent
daily on America Online.[26]

Communication has proven to be a double-edged sword for online consumers. On the one hand, the interactive communication capabilities of Internet/Web-enabled technologies increase consumer convenience, reduce information search costs, and make choice assistance and customization possible. Communication also promotes the development of company-hosted and independent **web communities**—websites that allow people to congregate online and exchange views on topics of common interest. For instance, iVillage.com, the Women's Network, is a web community for women and includes topics such as career management, personal finances, parenting, relationships, beauty, and health. On the other hand, communication can take the form of electronic junk mail or unsolicited e-mail, called **spam**. The prevalence of spam has prompted some online services such as Hotmail to institute policies and procedures to prevent spammers from spamming their subscribers and 17 states have antispamming laws. In addition, pending Federal legislation will impose a fine of $500,000 and a jail sentence of one year on professional spammers.

Internet/Web-enabled communication capabilities also make possible *buzz,* a popular term for word-of-mouth behavior in marketspace. Chapter 5 described the importance of word of mouth in consumer behavior. Internet/Web technology has magnified its significance. In marketspace, the scope and speed of word of mouth has increased fourfold on average because of consumer chat rooms, instant messaging, and product and service review websites such as epinions.com and consumer-review.com.[27] Buzz is particularly influential for toys, cars, sporting goods, motion pictures, apparel, consumer electronics, pharmaceuticals, health and beauty products, and health care services. Some marketers have capitalized on this phenomenon by creating buzz through viral marketing.

Viral marketing is an Internet/Web-enabled promotional strategy that encourages individuals to forward marketer-initiated messages to others via e-mail.[28] There are three approaches to viral marketing. Marketers can embed a message in the product or service so that customers hardly realize they are passing it along. The classic example is Hotmail, which was one of the first companies to provide free, Web-based e-mail. Each outgoing e-mail message has the tagline: Get Your Private, Free Email from MSN Hotmail at http://www.hotmail.com. Today, Hotmail has some 80 million users! Marketers can also make the website content so compelling that viewers want to share it with others. De Beers has done this at www.adiamondisforever.com, where users can design their own rings and show them to others. One out of five website visitors e-mail their ring design to friends and relatives

De Beers effectively applied viral marketing in the launch of its custom ring website.

De Beers

www.adiamondisforever.com

who visit the site. Similarly, eBay reports that more than half its visitors were referred by other visitors. Finally, marketers can offer incentives (discounts, sweepstakes, or free merchandise) for referrals. Procter & Gamble did this for its Physique shampoo. People who referred 10 friends to the shampoo's website (www.physique.com) received a free, travel-sized styling spray and were entered in a sweepstakes to win a year's supply of the shampoo. The response? The promotion generated 2 million referrals and made Physique the most successful new shampoo ever launched in the United States.

Cost   Consumer *cost* is a fifth reason for online shopping and buying. Research indicates that many popular items bought online can be purchased at the same price or cheaper than in retail stores.[29] Lower prices also result from Internet/Web-enabled software that permits **dynamic pricing**, the practice of changing prices for products and services in real time in response to supply and demand conditions. As described in Chapter 14, dynamic pricing is a form of flexible pricing and can often result in lower prices. It is typically used for pricing time-sensitive items like airline seats, scarce items found at art or collectible auctions, and out-of-date items such as last year's models of computer equipment and accessories. A consumer's cost of external information search, including time spent and often the hassle of shopping, is also reduced. Greater shopping convenience and lower external search costs are two major reasons for the popularity of online shopping and buying among women, and particularly for those who work outside the home.

Control   The sixth reason consumers prefer to buy online is the *control* it gives them over their shopping and purchase decision process. Online shoppers and buyers are empowered consumers. They deftly use Internet/Web technology to seek information, evaluate alternatives, and make purchase decisions on their own time, terms, and conditions. Nearly 80 percent of online consumers regularly engage **portals** and "search engines," which are electronic gateways to the World Wide Web that supply a broad array of news and entertainment, information resources, and shopping services.[30] Well-known portals include Yahoo!, America Online, and MSN.com. To evaluate alternatives, consumers visit comparison shopping websites such as comparenet.com and price.com or employ bots such as Yahoo! Shopping and Excite's Product Finder, which provide product descriptions and prices for a wide variety of brands and models. The result of these activities is a more informed consumer and discerning shopper. In the words of one marketing consultant, "In the marketspace, the customer is in charge."[31]

Even though consumers have many reasons for shopping and buying online, a segment of Internet/Web users refrain from making purchases for privacy and security reasons as described in the accompanying Ethics and Social Responsibility Alert.[32] These consumers are concerned about a rarely mentioned seventh "C"— cookies. **Cookies** are computer files that a marketer can download onto the computer of an online shopper who visits the marketer's website. Cookies allow the marketer's website to record a user's visit, track visits to other websites, and store and retrieve this information in the future. Cookies also contain information provided by visitors, such as expressed product preferences, personal data, and financial information, including credit card numbers. Clearly, cookies make possible customized and personalized content for online shoppers. The controversy surrounding cookies is summed up by an authority on the technology: "At best a cookie makes for a user-friendly Web world: like a doorman or salesclerk who knows who you are. At worst, cookies represent a potential loss of privacy."[33]

When and Where Online Consumers Shop and Buy

Shopping and buying also happen at different times in marketspace than in the traditional marketplace.[34] About 80 percent of online retail sales occur Monday

ETHICS AND SOCIAL RESPONSIBILITY ALERT

Sweet and Sour Cookies in the New Marketspace

ETHICS

Privacy and security are two key reasons consumers are leery of online shopping and buying. A recent *Wall Street Journal/Harris Interactive* poll reported that 73 percent of online consumers are concerned about threats to their personal privacy on the Internet. Even more telling, 53 percent have stopped shopping a website or forgone an online purchase because of privacy concerns. Industry analysts estimate that poor consumer confidence in privacy and security has resulted in lost sales that exceed $2.8 billion annually.

The privacy and security concerns of online consumers are related to the "cookies" described in the text and how those cookies can be used or misused. A percolating issue is whether the U.S. government should pass Internet/Web privacy laws. About 70 percent of online consumers favor such action. Companies have adopted initiatives to develop their own privacy standards without government action. The Online Privacy Alliance (www.privacyalliance.org) is a consortium of businesses and associations that aims to promote electronic commerce through online privacy policies and self-regulation. TRUSTe (www.etrust.org) awards its trademark to websites that comply with standards of privacy protection and disclosure.

Do you think that governmental or self-regulation is the best way to deal with issues of privacy and security in the new marketspace?

through Friday. The busiest shopping day is Wednesday. By comparison, 35 percent of retail store sales are registered on the weekend. Saturday is the most popular shopping day. Monday through Friday online shopping and buying often occurs during normal work hours—some 40 percent of online consumers say they visit websites from their place of work, which partially accounts for the sales level during the workweek.[35] Favorite websites for workday shopping and buying include those featuring event tickets, online periodical subscriptions, flowers and gifts, consumer electronics, and travel. Websites offering health and beauty items, apparel and accessories, and music and video tend to be browsed and bought from a consumer's home.

Consumers are more likely to browse than buy online. Although 9 in 10 online consumers regularly shop in the marketspace of websites, over half (51 percent) confine their purchases to the traditional retail store marketplace.[36] Consumer marketspace browsing and buying in the traditional marketplace has popularized multichannel marketing, which is described next.

Concept Check

1. What is the eight-second rule?

2. Which online consumer lifestyle segment spends the most money online and which spends the most time online?

3. What are the six reasons consumers prefer to shop and buy online?

MULTICHANNEL MARKETING TO THE ONLINE CONSUMER

The fact that a large number of consumers browse and buy in two market environments means that few companies limit their marketing programs exclusively to the traditional marketplace or marketspace. Today, it is commonplace for companies to maintain a presence in both market environments of some kind and measure. This dual presence is called multichannel marketing.

Integrating and Leveraging Multiple Channels with Multichannel Marketing

Companies often employ multiple marketing channels for their products and services. *Dual distribution* is the term used to describe this practice, which focuses on reaching different consumers through different marketing channels. The Avon example that introduced Chapter 15 highlighted this practice. Avon markets its health and beauty products directly through Avon sales representatives, a brochure, shops in JCPenney stores, and an Avon website. The various communication (representatives and brochures) and delivery (shops) channels allow Avon to reach different consumers, feature different brands, and provide different shopping and buying experiences.

Multichannel marketing bears some resemblance to dual distribution. For example, different communication and delivery channels are used such as catalogs, kiosks, retail stores, and websites. In fact, retailers that employ two or more of these channels are labeled *multichannel retailers* as described in Chapter 17. However, the resemblance ends at this point. **Multichannel marketing** is the *blending* of different communication and delivery channels that are *mutually reinforcing* in attracting, retaining, and building relationships with consumers who shop and buy in the traditional marketplace and marketspace. Multichannel marketing seeks to integrate a firm's communication and delivery channels, not differentiate them. In doing so, consumers can browse and buy "anytime, anywhere, anyway" expecting that the experience will be similar regardless of channel. At Eddie Bauer, for example, every effort is made to make the apparel shopping and purchase process for its customers the same in its retail stores, with its catalog, and at its website. According to an Eddie Bauer marketing manager, "We don't distinguish between channels because it's all Eddie Bauer to our customers."[37]

Multichannel marketing also can leverage the value-adding capabilities of different channels.[38] For example, retail stores can leverage their physical presence by allowing customers to pick up their online orders at a nearby store or return or exchange nonstore purchases if they wish. Catalogs can serve as shopping tools for online purchasing, as they do for store purchasing. Websites can help consumers do their "homework" before visiting a store. Office Depot has leveraged its store, catalog, and website channels with impressive results. The company, which is the world's largest office supply retail chain, is the second largest Internet retailer in the world (behind Amazon.com), doing about $1 billion in online retail sales annually.[39] The benefits of multichannel marketing is also apparent in the spending behavior of consumers as described in the accompanying Marketing NewsNet.[40]

Implementing Multichannel Marketing

Not all companies employ websites for multichannel marketing the same way. This should not be surprising. Different companies apply the value-creation capabilities of Internet/Web technology differently depending on their overall marketing program.

Websites play a multifaceted role in multichannel marketing because they can serve as either a communication or delivery channel. Two general applications of websites exist based on their intended purpose: (1) transactional websites, and (2) promotional websites.

MARKETING NEWSNET   The Multichannel Marketing Multiplier

CUSTOMER VALUE

Multichannel marketing is the blending of different communication and delivery channels that are mutually reinforcing in attracting, retaining, and building relationships with consumers who shop and buy in the traditional marketplace and marketspace. Industry analysts refer to the complementary role of different communication and delivery channels as an "influence effect."

Retailers that integrate and leverage their stores, catalogs, and websites have seen a sizeable "lift" in yearly sales recorded from individual customers. Eddie Bauer is a case in point. Customers who shop only one of its channels spend $100 to $200 per year. Those who shop in two channels spend $300 to $500 annually. Customers who shop all these channels—store, catalog, and website—spend $800 to $1,000 per year. Moreover, multichannel customers have been found to be *three times* as profitable as single-channel customers!

JCPenney has seen similar results. The company is a leading multichannel retailer and reports that a JCPenney customer who shops in all three channels—store, catalog, and website—spends *four to eight times* as much as a customer who shops in only one channel, as shown in the chart below.

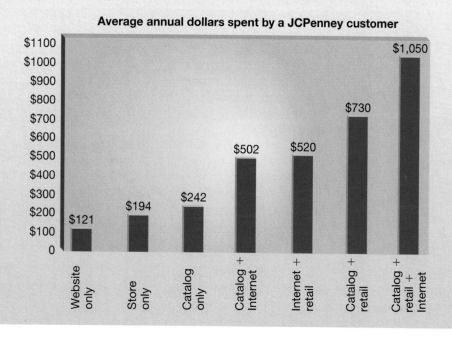

Average annual dollars spent by a JCPenney customer

Website only	$121
Store only	$194
Catalog only	$242
Catalog + Internet	$502
Internet + retail	$520
Catalog + retail	$730
Catalog + retail + Internet	$1,050

Multichannel Marketing with Transactional Websites   *Transactional websites* are essentially electronic storefronts. They focus principally on converting an online browser into an online, catalog, or in-store buyer using the website design elements described earlier. Transactional websites are most common among store and catalog retailers and direct selling companies, such as Tupperware. The Gap, for instance, generates more sales volume from its website (www.gap.com) than any one of its stores, save one.[41] Retailers and direct selling firms have found that their websites, while cannibalizing sales volume from stores, catalogs, and sales representatives, attract new customers and influence sales. Consider Victoria's Secret, the well-known specialty retailer of intimate apparel for women age 18 to 45. It reports that almost 60 percent of its website customers are men, most of whom generate new sales volume for the company.[42] Likewise, Sears.com is estimated to account for $500 million worth of Sears, Roebuck & Co. in-store appliance sales. Why? Sears customers first research appliances online before visiting a store.[43]

Transactional websites are used less frequently by manufacturers of consumer products. A recurring issue for manufacturers is the threat of *channel conflict,* described in Chapter 15, and the potential harm to trade relationships with their retailing intermediaries. Still, manufacturers do use transactional websites, often cooperating with retailers. For example, Ethan Allen, the furniture manufacturer, markets its product line at www.ethanallen.com. Whenever feasible, Ethan Allen retailers fill online orders, and receive 25 percent of the sales price. For items shipped directly from the Ethan Allen factory, the store nearest the customer receives 10 percent of the sales price.[44] In addition, Ethan Allen, like other manufacturers, typically lists stores on their website where their merchandise can be shopped and bought. More often than not, however, manufacturers engage multichannel channels, using websites as advertising and promotion vehicles.

Multichannel Marketing with Promotional Websites *Promotional websites* have a very different purpose than transactional sites. They advertise and promote a company's products and services and provide information on how items can be used and where they can be purchased. They often engage the visitor in an interactive experience involving games, contests, and quizzes with electronic coupons and other gifts as prizes. Procter & Gamble maintains separate websites for dozens of its leading brands, including Pringles potato chips (www.pringles.com), Vidal Sassoon hair products (www.vidalsassoon.com), Scope mouthwash (www.scope-mouthwash.com), and Pampers diapers (www.pampers.com).[45] Promotional sites can be effective in generating interest in and trial of a company's products and services (see Figure 21–6).[46] General Motors reports that 80 percent of the people visiting a Saturn store first visited the brand's website (www.saturn.com) and 70 percent of Saturn leads come from its website.

Promotional websites also can be used to support a company's traditional marketing channel and build customer relationships. This is the objective of the Clinique Division of Estee Lauder Companies, which markets cosmetics through department stores. Clinique reports that 80 percent of current customers who visit its website (www.clinique.com) later purchase a Clinique product at a department store; 37 percent of non-Clinique buyers make a Clinique purchase after visiting the company's website.

FIGURE 21–6

Implementing multichannel marketing with promotional websites

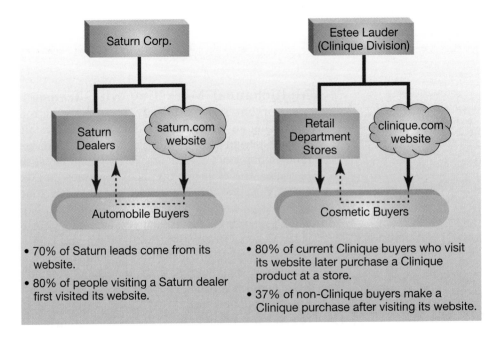

- 70% of Saturn leads come from its website.
- 80% of people visiting a Saturn dealer first visited its website.

- 80% of current Clinique buyers who visit its website later purchase a Clinique product at a store.
- 37% of non-Clinique buyers make a Clinique purchase after visiting its website.

The popularity of multichannel marketing is apparent in its growing impact on online retail sales. Fully 65 percent of U.S. online retail sales in 2001 were made by companies that practiced multichannel marketing. Multichannel marketers are expected to register about 85 percent of U.S. online retail sales in 2005.[47]

Concept Check

1. Multichannel marketing is _____ .

2. Channel conflict between manufacturers and retailers is likely to arise when manufacturers use _____ websites.

SUMMARY

1 Consumers and companies populate two market environments today—the traditional marketplace and the new marketspace. A company's marketspace success hinges largely on designing and executing a marketing program that capitalizes on the unique value-creation capabilities of Internet/Web technology.

2 Internet/Web technology creates time, place, form, and possession utility in novel ways, resulting in customer value.

3 Marketers benefit from two unique capabilities of Internet/Web-enabled technology that create customer relationships—interactivity and individuality—which make interactive marketing possible. Interactive marketing, in turn, is characterized by choiceboard and personalization systems that transform information supplied by customers into customized responses to their individual needs.

4 Customer experience is the standard by which a meaningful marketspace presence is measured and produced through seven website elements: context, content, community, customization, communication, connection, and commerce.

5 Online consumers represent a segment of all Internet/Web users, differ demographically from the general population, and exhibit distinct lifestyle and spending profiles. Six general product and service categories are bought by online consumers. However, travel reservations, computer hardware and consumer electronics, media, and clothing and accessories account for the majority of consumer purchases.

6 Consumers refer to six reasons they shop and buy online: convenience, cost, choice, customization, communication, and control. Marketers capitalize on these reasons using a variety of approaches including electronic shopping agents (bots), web communities, viral marketing, and dynamic pricing. However, consumers are concerned about electronic junk mail (spam) and online privacy and security.

7 The prevalence of consumer shopping online and buying in retail stores has made multichannel marketing popular. Multichannel marketing is the blending of different communication and delivery channels that are mutually reinforcing in attracting, retaining, and building relationships with consumers who shop and buy in the traditional marketplace and marketspace.

8 Not all companies approach multichannel marketing the same way. A major difference in approach is the use of transactional websites and promotional websites.

KEY TERMS AND CONCEPTS

bots p. 569
choiceboard p. 562
collaborative filtering p. 562
cookies p. 572
customer experience p. 564
customerization p. 570
dynamic pricing p. 572
eight-second rule p. 569
interactive marketing p. 562

multichannel marketing p. 574
online consumers p. 566
permission marketing p. 563
personalization p. 562
portals p. 572
spam p. 571
viral marketing p. 571
web communities p. 571

APPLYING MARKETING CONCEPTS AND PERSPECTIVES

1 By early 2002, about two-thirds of Internet/Web users had actually purchased something online. Have you made an online purchase? If so, why do you think so many people who have access to the Internet and the World Wide Web are not also online buyers? If not, why

are you reluctant to do so? Do you think that electronic commerce benefits consumers even if they don't make a purchase?

2 Like the traditional marketplace, marketspace offers marketers opportunities to create greater time, place, form, and possession utility. How do you think Internet/Web-enabled technology rates in terms of creating these values? Take a shopping trip at a virtual retailer of your choice (don't buy anything unless you really want to). Then compare the time, place, form, and possession utility provided by the virtual retailer with that you enjoyed during a nonelectronic experience shopping for the same product category.

3 Visit Amazon.com (www.amazon.com), or Barnes & Noble (barnesandnoble.com). As you tour the company's website, think about how shopping for books online compares with a trip to your university bookstore to buy books. Specifically, compare and contrast your shopping experiences with respect to convenience, choice, customization, communication, cost, and control.

4 Suppose you are planning to buy a new car so you decide to visit www.carpoint.com. Based on your experience visiting that site, do you think you would enjoy more or less control in negotiating with the dealer when you actually purchase your vehicle?

5 Visit the website for your university or college. Based on your visit, would you conclude that the site is a transactional site or a promotional site? Why? How would you rate the site in terms of the six website design elements that affect customer experience?

6 One of the benefits that interactive marketing provides for companies is the ability to obtain consumer information that can be used to more effectively manage the marketing mix. Catalina Marketing Corporation, for example, creates profiles of its online customers' product category and brand preferences and uses this information to generate personalized coupons. Some consumers, however, worry about their privacy as companies like Catalina create customer databases. Visit Catalina's website at www.valuepage.com to determine what information you must provide to obtain your own customized coupons. Is the added value of the coupons worth the price of the information you must reveal to get the coupons? Why or why not?

INTERNET EXERCISE

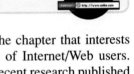

What are the most recent statistics and trends in interactive and multichannel marketing? Look no further than Nua Internet Surveys (Nua), an online service that abstracts up-to-date research on Internet/Web usage and applications from around the world. Nua conveniently organizes research by business, social, technical, demographic, and geographical categories for easy inspection.

Visit the Nua website at www.nua.ie/surveys. Your assignment is as follows:

1 Choose a topic covered in the chapter that interests you, such as the demographics of Internet/Web users. Compare and contrast the most recent research published in Nua with information contained in the chapter. Don't be surprised if you find differences!

2 Choose two regions of the world, such as North America and Europe. How do Internet/Web usage and interactive marketing differ between the two regions based on the most recent research?

VIDEO CASE 21–1 America Online, Inc.: Defining the Online Experience

"America Online started as a vision of Steve Case to provide basic e-mail and bulletin board communication services," says Wendy Brown, vice president of commerce strategy at America Online (AOL). This, of course, was several years before the commercialization of the World Wide Web (WWW) and the Internet. Over the years, AOL has added a variety of communication services, information "channels," shopping opportunities, and personalization features. Today, AOL has become the convenient tool that, according to Brown, "people use to be able to manage their lives, stay in touch with others, buy things, and learn." In fact, AOL's mission is to become the world's most respected and valued company by connecting, informing, and entertaining people everywhere in innovative ways that will enrich their lives.

THE COMPANY

Myer Berlow, senior vice president of interactive marketing, says, "the important thing to understand about our business model is that we have a dual income stream. We have subscriber revenues and we have other revenues, namely advertising and e-commerce." Currently, approximately 40 percent of revenues is generated from subscriptions, 25 percent from advertising, and 35 percent from e-commerce. To maintain its revenue growth, AOL has had to address several key challenges—including attracting new members and managing its network "access" capabilities.

The essence of AOL's growth strategy is to be the easiest and most convenient Internet online service. To increase the number of members, AOL has developed

several programs to get its software in the hands of potential customers. For example, AOL has mailed disks to computer users, shrinkwrapped copies with computer magazines, and placed freestanding displays in selected retailers. In addition, AOL has offered up to 1,000 free hours to potential customers to encourage them to explore the service during a 45-day trial period. To ensure that installation is easy, the software is designed so that trial users of AOL's service only need to "point and click" and the software installs itself. To make the access and navigation of its online service easy, AOL designed a well-organized, graphical user interface to allow users to quickly and easily navigate the service. These and other design features have been important elements in converting trial users to paying members.

AOL also negotiated an agreement to be included on the desktop of the new Windows XP operating system that ships with all Compaq brand computers. Managers at AOL had attempted to negotiate a deal directly with Microsoft. The pact would have added AOL to Windows XP shipped with any PC and added Microsoft's competitive web browser, MSN, as an option on AOL's online service. Microsoft also wanted AOL's messaging service to be compatible with MSN messenger as well as AOL to pledge not to file an antitrust suit against it. The two companies could not reach an agreement. So AOL is not currently included on Windows, and when PC makers add it to the desktop, Microsoft encourages the manufacturers to put MSN there too. Some industry sources suggest that a long-term solution to the conflict would be to require Microsoft to license Windows to all PC manufacturers—like Compaq—who could then configure it in their own way. "All we're trying to do is let consumers

find AOL instead of being stuck with Microsoft," explains AOL's Barry Shuler.

AOL has also grown through key acquisitions and alliances. In 1997, AOL purchased Internet pioneer CompuServe, which had approximately 2 million members worldwide. In 1998, AOL's acquisition of the leading Internet browser, Netscape, brought an additional 15 million members to the company. "Our merger with Netscape provided us with another world-class brand, a fast-growing portal, innovative talent, and cutting-edge technologies," said Steve Case. AOL also entered into strategic alliances with Sun Microsystems to provide software for e-commerce, Bell Atlantic to provide convenient and affordable high-speed online access to millions of AOL members across the United States, and DirectTV, Philips Electronics, and others to add interactivity to the television viewing experience.

In 2000 AOL added MapQuest, the leading service in mapping and navigation, to provide directions and real-time traffic information to consumers at any time. Then in early 2001, AOL and Time Warner combined in a $97 billion merger which was described as a one-of-a-kind union of new and old media that would usher in the "Internet Century." AOL provided a large and growing online customer base and Time Warner provided a vast resource for content in its media brands. Steven Case became chairman of the board of the new company, AOL Time Warner, Inc. Since the merger, AOL has continued to grow through strategic partnerships. For example, AOL has announced an alliance with Sony to develop a "gateway" device that will enable consumers to conveniently connect all their Web-linked devices—including PCs, stereos, TVs, and PDAs. AOL has also developed a partnership with Sprint to provide long-distance service on its website for as little as $5.95 a month.

AOL has now become the largest Internet service provider in the world with more than 33 million paid subscribers who connect to the service an average of over 60 minutes per day. Millions more access its website, www.aol.com. AOL also offers a variety of other services. In addition to its Netscape browser, Instant Messenger, and MapQuest, AOL offers Shop@AOL—a dynamic shopping experience offering millions of products from more than 300 merchants; Moviefone—a free directory of movies, showtimes, theater locations, and ticketing service; Digital City—an entertainment guide and visitors directory for more than 200 cities; AOL@School—a free online learning tool for K–12 classrooms; AOL Anywhere and AOLbyPhone—which provide access to its services from pagers, cell phones, and PDAs; You've Got Pictures—a tool for viewing and sharing photographs online; Radio@AOL—which provides access to more than 75 radio stations online; and Spinner.com and Winamp—media players for the Internet's audio and video content. For consumers who prefer an "always on" and faster connection to the Internet, the

company now also offers AOL High-Speed Broadband. The AOL International division, which is growing even faster than the U.S. division, operates localized online services in 17 countries in eight languages.

E-COMMERCE AT AOL

Nearly 153 million people in the United States were using the Internet in 2002, generating $48 billion in online retail sales. By 2005, more than 194 million people are likely to be online, producing $104 billion in revenues. "The Internet is the first medium that really solves the marketers' dilemma. It lets consumers seek information about a particular brand and enables them to buy it quickly, thereby simplifying the entire purchase process," says Berlow.

The potential of e-commerce became clear during the holiday season when AOL members spent $1.2 billion online. During this period, almost 1.25 million AOL members made their first purchase online. AOL estimates that 84 percent of its present members "window-shopped" and 44 percent bought merchandise through AOL or aol.com. Members who shopped online were very satisfied with the experience. They said they appreciated AOL's ease-of-use, convenience, and security of their online transactions, not to mention the great values offered by many of its retail partners. Moreover, research indicates that once members shop online, they develop an e-commerce habit, purchasing one to three items during the first three months alone.

This success was largely due to the merchants and "e-tailers" (such as Eddie Bauer, J. Crew, Toys "Я" Us, Macy's, Barnes & Noble, Digital Chef, etc.) AOL partnered with to enhance AOL's Shopping Channel. AOL's e-commerce goal is to offer consumers "one-stop shopping" convenience, branded products and services, and value. What are AOL shoppers buying? Based on traffic counts to AOL Shopping Channel departments, the Toys, Kids, and Babies category held the number-one spot, followed closely by apparel. The average AOL holiday shopper purchased two items online every week during the holiday shopping season and spent about $54. Since interactive marketing and e-commerce are growing rapidly, AOL continues to attract e-tailers, other mass merchandisers, and service providers to sell their wares through AOL. Agreements with Unilever, First USA (credit cards), Citibank, AmeriTrade and E-Trade (brokerage), eBay (online auctions), and *The Financial Times* (news) are among many companies partnering with AOL in long-term relationships.

ENSURING THE FUTURE OF E-COMMERCE

While the future of e-commerce looks bright, AOL faces several important issues. According to a Boston Consulting Group study, retailers must continue to offer consumers compelling reasons to shop online. Further advances in convenience, cost, choice, customization, communication, and control must be made for more consumers to change their shipping behavior. With respect to *convenience,* "portals" are expected to be the primary means consumers will use to access and browse the Internet. While AOL is the world's leading Internet online service, it will need to promote and defend its leadership position against the efforts made by Microsoft, Yahoo!, Disney, and other formidable competitors.

In terms of *cost,* consumers should benefit by reduced costs for products and services purchased online because they can order directly from the manufacturers, retailers, or service providers. Moreover, they can search the Internet for the best price for the products and services they desire. However, retailers often must resolve channel conflicts that arise as a result of selling online directly to consumers. Specifically, some potential online retailers may hesitate or choose not to sell online because it might cannibalize sales through existing channels, alienate existing distribution partners, and, more important, lower margins for all in the channel. Retailers who choose to sell online may be able to charge a premium if they provide superior service, enhanced features, and a strong brand presence not found on other online portals' or retailers' websites.

Giving consumers *choice* in their Internet experience will continue to be critical. AOL must continue to expand the choices available to its subscribers, both in terms of the types (shopping, e-mail, messaging, news, etc.) and depth (number of retail partners for each shopping category) of the services offered. These retail partners must provide AOL members with a broad array of goods and services available for browsing or purchasing online. To date, AOL has offered the most comprehensive array of top brand names and it must continue to do so.

As Dell Computer, Mattel, and other companies have demonstrated, "build-to-order" systems allow customers to *customize* their product and service purchases with the feature set they want and at a price they can afford. For AOL and its partners, the continued integration of manufacturing, database, customer service, and fulfillment or service delivery systems must provide consumers with the customization they desire. In addition, *communications* issues must be resolved. Cable modems, digital subscriber lines (DSL), fiber optics, and other technologies need to become more readily available to consumers.

Finally, online consumers want to *control* the personal and financial data that is gathered during an online visit or transaction. Specifically, they want to know whether their data is safeguarded, how it is used by e-tailers, and if it is disclosed to other organizations for marketing purposes. Consumers also want the ability to restrict access to morally objectionable websites and "chat rooms" and to protect their computers from "viruses." International Data Corporation estimates the market for Internet security software will reach $7.4 billion in 2002. While AOL has taken the lead in developing its "Parental Controls" as well as an extensive privacy policy, additional efforts may be required as international e-commerce grows and demands for a "safer" Internet increase.

Overall, AOL faces a challenging future. Consumers are becoming more and more comfortable with, and demanding of, online services. At the same time, competi-

tion from Microsoft, phone companies, and other Internet service providers is substantial and growing. Consumers are eager for more, though. One estimate suggests that subscribers would pay up to $159 per month for an online service that provided broadband access with telephone capabilities, online music, games, and films for multiple users!

Questions

1   How has the vision or mission of AOL changed from the early 1980s to the present?

2   How does AOL facilitate online shopping or e-commerce? What are the advantages and disadvantages of using AOL for online shopping versus the more traditional method you may use?

3   What challenges has AOL overcome to attract both consumers and retailer partners to engage in e-commerce? What challenges do they still need to overcome?

4   What are the six "C's" of e-commerce and what is AOL's marketing strategy in each of these areas?

CHAPTER

22

PULLING IT ALL TOGETHER: THE STRATEGIC MARKETING PROCESS

AFTER READING THIS CHAPTER YOU SHOULD BE ABLE TO:

- Explain how marketing managers allocate their limited resources, both in theory and in practice.

- Describe three marketing planning frameworks: Porter's generic strategies, profit enhancement options, and market-product synergies.

- Describe what makes an effective marketing plan and some problems that often exist with them.

- Describe the alternatives for organizing a marketing department and the role of a product manager.

- Schedule a series of tasks to meet a deadline using a Gantt chart.

- Understand how sales and profitability analyses and marketing audits are used to evaluate and control marketing programs.

MARKETING STRATEGY AT GENERAL MILLS: SHARES, SEGMENTS, AND SYNERGIES!

Assume you are a marketing manager at General Mills responsible for introducing successful new brands of cereal. Here are some facts to tell you how difficult your job is:

- Only one out of five new brands succeeds, which is defined as achieving 0.5 percent market share—or half of 1 percent—of the $7.5 billion-a-year U.S. ready-to-eat (RTE) cereal market.[1]
- A new-product launch typically costs up to $40 million.
- Busy Americans, who are on the run, are increasingly likely to eat a bagel, muffin, or yogurt for breakfast instead of cereal because of their convenience, causing cereal sales to plummet more than $1 billion from 1996 to 2000. So new cereal offerings must steal or "cannibalize" sales from existing brands for a successful launch.
- Consumers are concerned about the healthiness of RTE cereals. Some contain sugar and others contain genetically modified grains.
- Smaller competitors have entered the U.S. RTE cereal market by introducing "bagged" or generic, private label versions of well-known General Mills' and Kellogg's brands for about $1 less per bag than their branded counterparts.[2]

However, as a marketing manager at General Mills, you have some good news:

- Based on estimates for the period 1995 to 2010, the largest target markets for RTE cereal are consumers who are under 18, which will grow by 5 million, and 45 and older, which will grow by 34 million.[3]
- In 2000, General Mills became the RTE cereal market leader with a 32.2 percent share in terms of dollar value, surpassing Kellogg's, which garnered a 30.7 percent share. Other RTE cereal marketers had the following dollar market shares: Post (16 percent); Quaker Oats (9 percent); and private label and generic store brands (8 percent). Cheerios and Wheaties rank among the top five brands in terms of dollar and volume shares.[4]
- To capitalize on changing and fast-growing consumer trends, General Mills introduced several new products targeted at specific market segments:[5]

  - Wheaties Energy Crunch—"The Breakfast of Everyday Champions," which combines added protein, carbohydrates, and B vitamins for people who engage in active, healthy lifestyles and want "all-day energy."
  - Para Su Familia (For Your Family), a line of four cereals targeted at Hispanic consumers in the southwestern U.S. and Mexico. Hispanics spend over $720 million on RTE cereals annually.
  - Harmony, a "nutraceutical" cereal that is fortified with soy, antioxidants, folic acid, and calcium targeted at women who want a healthier breakfast.
  - Chex Morning Mix® in single-serve pouches to "grab the nutrition and skip the bowl!" Shades of Fingo's? See Chapter 10.[6]
  - Yoplait Exprèsse, the adult version of Yoplait's Go-Gurt yogurt in a plastic, squeezable tube, can be eaten chilled or frozen without a spoon.
  - Big G Milk 'n Cereal Bar, which combines cereal and a milk-based layer so that convenience-oriented consumers can "eat & go."

To make matters even a bit more complicated, General Mills acquired Pillsbury in October 2001, hoping to find important marketing, manufacturing, and supply-chain efficiencies and synergies. So in your marketing manager position at General Mills you'll face many tough challenges. But you can learn from both past successes and difficulties. Later in the chapter you can stretch your creative talents trying to find marketing synergies—and more "one-handedness"—in merging General Mills and Pillsbury product lines.[7]

This chapter discusses issues and techniques related to planning, implementation, and control phases of the strategic marketing process, the kind of topics marketing strategists at General Mills face in achieving growth. The individual elements of the strategic marketing process were introduced in Chapter 2.

STRATEGIC MARKETING'S GOAL: EFFECTIVE RESOURCE ALLOCATION

As noted in Chapter 2, corporate and marketing executives search continuously to find a competitive advantage—a unique strength relative to competitors, often based on quality, time, cost, or innovation. Having identified this competitive advantage, they must allocate their firm's resources to exploit it. The timing of product and market actions may also influence the magnitude and duration of a firm's competitive advantage.[8]

Allocating Marketing Resources Using Sales Response Functions

A **sales response function** relates the expense of marketing effort to the marketing results obtained.[9] For simplicity in the examples that follow, only the effects of annual marketing effort on annual sales revenue will be analyzed, but the concept applies to other measures of marketing success—such as profit, units sold, or level of awareness—as well.

Maximizing Incremental Revenue Minus Incremental Cost   Economists give managers a specific guideline for optimal resource allocation: allocate the firm's marketing, production, and financial resources to the markets and products where the excess of incremental revenues over incremental costs is greatest. This parallels the marginal revenue–marginal cost analysis of Chapter 13.

Figure 22–1 illustrates the resource allocation principle that is inherent in the sales response function. The firm's annual marketing effort, such as sales and advertising expenses, is plotted on the horizontal axis. As the annual marketing effort increases, so does the resulting annual sales revenue, which is plotted on the vertical axis. The relationship is assumed to be S-shaped, showing that an additional $1 million of marketing effort from $3 million to $4 million results in far greater increases of sales revenue in the midrange ($20 million) of the curve than at either end (an increase from $2 million to $3 million in spending yields an increase of $10 million in sales; an increase from $6 million to $7 million in spending leads to an increase of $5 million in sales).

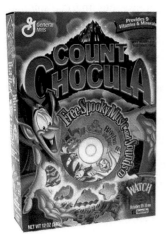

A Numerical Example of Resource Allocation   Suppose Figure 22–1 shows the situation for a General Mills product such as Count Chocula, a chocolate-flavored cereal with vitamins and minerals targeted at kids. Also assume that the sales response function doesn't change through time as a result of changing consumer tastes and incomes. Point A shows the position of the firm in year 1, whereas Point B shows it three years later in year 4. General Mills has decided to "recharacterize" Count Chocula with a series of playful new packages (shown at left) plus advertising and sales promotion that, let's say, increases its marketing effort on the brand from $3 million to $6 million a year. If the relationship in Figure 22–1 holds true and is a good picture of consumer purchasing behavior, the sales revenues of Count Chocula should increase from $30 million to $70 million a year.

Let's look at the major resource allocation question: What are the probable increases in sales revenue for Count Chocula in year 1 and year 4 if General Mills were to spend an additional $1 million in marketing effort? As Figure 22–1 reveals:

Year 1

Increase in marketing effort from $3 million to $4 million = $1 million
Increase in sales revenue from $30 million to $50 million = $20 million
Ratio of incremental sales revenue to effort = $20,000,000:$1,000,000 = 20:1

FIGURE 22–1
Sales response function showing the situation for two different years

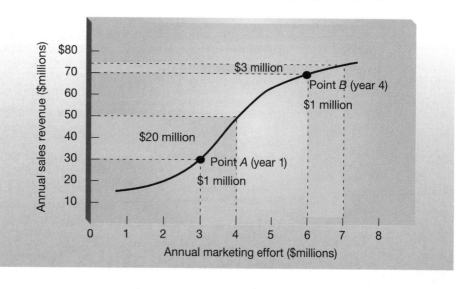

Year 4

Increase in marketing effort from \$6 million to \$7 million = \$1 million

Increase in sales revenue from \$70 million to \$73 million = \$3 million

Ratio of incremental sales revenue to effort = \$3,000,000:\$1,000,000 = 3:1

Thus, in year 1 a dollar of extra marketing effort returned \$20 in sales revenue, whereas in year 4 it returned only \$3. If no other expenses are incurred, it might make sense to spend \$1 million in year 4 to gain \$3 million in incremental sales revenue. However, it may be far wiser for General Mills to invest the money in products in one of its other business units, such as its new Wheaties Energy Crunch cereal or its new Yoplait Exprèsse. The essence of resource allocation is simple: put incremental resources where the incremental returns are greatest over the foreseeable future.

Allocating Marketing Resources in Practice

General Mills, like many firms in these businesses, does extensive analysis using **share points**, or percentage points of market share, as the common basis of comparison to allocate marketing resources effectively. This allows it to seek answers to the question "How much is it worth to us to try to increase our market share by another 1 (or 2, or 5, or 10) percentage point?"

This also enables higher-level managers to make resource allocation trade-offs among different kinds of business units owned by the company. To make these resource allocation decisions, marketing managers must estimate (1) the market share for the product, (2) the revenues associated with each point of market share (a share point in breakfast cereals may be five times what it is in cake mixes), (3) the contribution to overhead and profit (or gross margin) of each share point, and (4) possible cannibalization effects on other products in the line (for example new Wheaties Energy Crunch might reduce Wheaties sales).[10]

The resource allocation process helps General Mills choose wisely from among the many opportunities that exist in its various products and markets.

Resource Allocation and the Strategic Marketing Process

Company resources are allocated effectively in the strategic marketing process by converting marketing information into marketing actions. Figure 22–2 summarizes the strategic marketing process introduced in Chapter 2, along with some details of the marketing actions and information that compose it. Figure 22–2 is really a simplification of the actual strategic marketing process: while the three phases of the strategic marketing process have distinct separations in the figure and the marketing actions are separated from the marketing information, in practice these blend together and interact.

The upper half of each box in Figure 22–2 highlights the actions involved in that part of the strategic marketing process, and the lower half summarizes the information and reports used. Note that each phase has an output report:

PHASE	OUTPUT REPORT
Planning	Marketing plans (or programs) that define goals and the marketing mix strategies to achieve them
Implementation	Results (memos or computer outputs) that describe the outcomes of implementing the plans
Control	Corrective action memos, triggered by comparing results with plans, that (1) suggest solutions to problems and (2) take advantage of opportunities

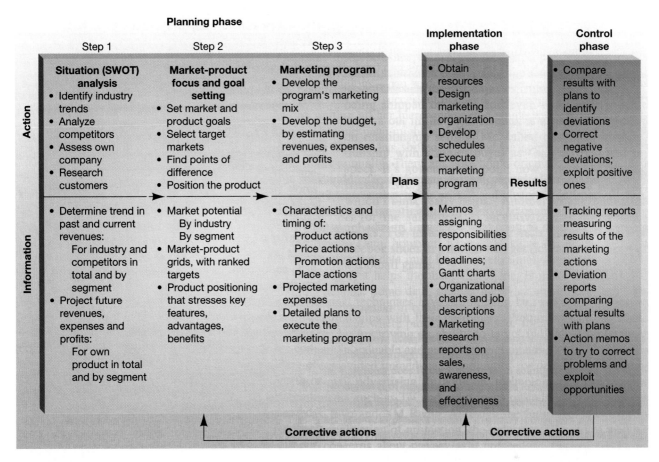

FIGURE 22-2
The strategic marketing process: actions and information

The corrective action memos become "feedback loops" in Figure 22–2 that help improve decisions and actions in earlier phases of the strategic marketing process.

THE PLANNING PHASE OF THE STRATEGIC MARKETING PROCESS

Three aspects of the strategic marketing process deserve special mention: (1) the varieties of marketing plans, (2) marketing planning frameworks that have proven useful, and (3) some marketing planning and strategy lessons.

The Variety of Marketing Plans

The planning phase of the strategic marketing process usually results in a marketing plan that sets the direction for the marketing activities of an organization. As noted earlier in Appendix A, a marketing plan is the heart of a business plan. Like business plans, marketing plans aren't all from the same mold; they vary with the length of the planning period, the purpose, and the audience. Let's look briefly at two kinds: long-range and annual marketing plans.

Long-Range Marketing Plans   Typically, long-range marketing plans cover marketing activities from two to five years into the future. Except for firms in industries such as autos, steel, or forest products, marketing plans rarely go beyond five years into the future because the tremendous number of uncertainties present make the benefits of planning less than the effort expended. Such plans are often directed at top-level executives and the board of directors.

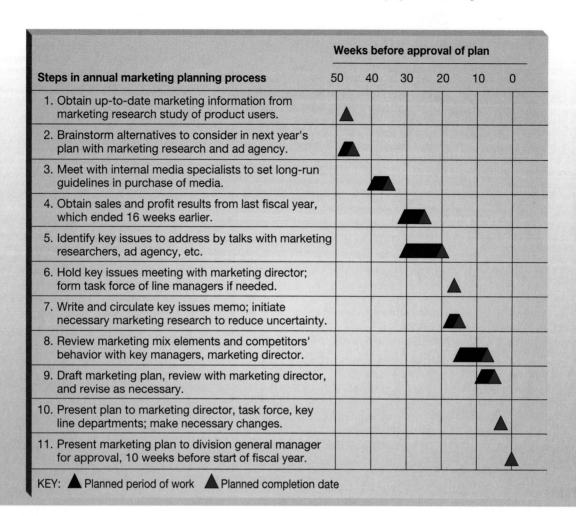

Steps in annual marketing planning process	Weeks before approval of plan					
	50	40	30	20	10	0
1. Obtain up-to-date marketing information from marketing research study of product users.	▲					
2. Brainstorm alternatives to consider in next year's plan with marketing research and ad agency.	▲					
3. Meet with internal media specialists to set long-run guidelines in purchase of media.		▲				
4. Obtain sales and profit results from last fiscal year, which ended 16 weeks earlier.			▲			
5. Identify key issues to address by talks with marketing researchers, ad agency, etc.			▲			
6. Hold key issues meeting with marketing director; form task force of line managers if needed.				▲		
7. Write and circulate key issues memo; initiate necessary marketing research to reduce uncertainty.				▲		
8. Review marketing mix elements and competitors' behavior with key managers, marketing director.					▲	
9. Draft marketing plan, review with marketing director, and revise as necessary.					▲	
10. Present plan to marketing director, task force, key line departments; make necessary changes.						▲
11. Present marketing plan to division general manager for approval, 10 weeks before start of fiscal year.						▲

KEY: ▲ Planned period of work   ▲ Planned completion date

FIGURE 22–3
Steps a large consumer package goods firm takes in developing its annual marketing plan

Annual Marketing Plans   Usually developed by a marketing or product manager (discussed later in the chapter) in a consumer products firm such as General Mills, annual marketing plans deal with marketing goals and strategies for a product, product line, or entire firm for a single year. Typical steps that firms such as 3M, Coca-Cola, and Johnson & Johnson take in developing their annual marketing plans for their existing products are shown in Figure 22–3.[11] This annual planning cycle typically starts with a detailed marketing research study of current users and ends after 48 weeks with the approval of the plan by the division general manager—10 weeks before the fiscal year starts. Between these points there are continuing efforts to uncover new ideas through brainstorming and key-issues sessions with specialists both inside and outside the firm. The plan is fine-tuned through a series of often excruciating reviews by several levels of management, which leaves few surprises and little to chance.[12]

Concept Check

1. What is the significance of the S-shape of the sales response function in Figure 22–1?

2. What are the main output reports from each phase of the strategic marketing process?

3. What are two kinds of marketing plans?

Marketing Planning Frameworks: The Search for Growth

Marketing planning for a firm with many products competing in many markets is a complex process. Yet in a business firm all these planning efforts are directed at finding the means for increased growth in sales and profits. Three techniques that are useful in helping corporate and marketing executives in such a firm make important resource allocation decisions are (1) Porter's generic business strategies, (2) profit enhancement options, and (3) market-product synergies. All three techniques relate to elements introduced in earlier chapters.

Porter's Generic Business Strategies

As shown in Figure 22–4, Michael E. Porter has developed a framework in which he identifies four basic, or "generic," strategies.[13] A **generic business strategy** is one that can be adopted by any firm, regardless of the product or industry involved, to achieve a competitive advantage. Some current research suggests that a firm needs several major competencies, not just one, to sustain its competitive advantage over longer periods;[14] other research suggests that the preferred strategy is to focus on a single discipline—such as operational excellence, product leadership, or customer intimacy.[15]

Although all of the techniques discussed here involve generic strategies, the phrase is most often associated with Porter's framework. In this framework the columns identify the two fundamental alternatives firms can use in seeking competitive advantage: (1) becoming the low-cost producer within the markets in which it competes or (2) differentiating itself from competitors by developing points of difference in its product offerings or marketing programs. In contrast, the rows identify the competitive scope: (1) a broad target by competing in many market segments or (2) a narrow target by competing in only a few segments or even a single segment. The columns and rows result in four generic business strategies, any one of which can provide a competitive advantage among similar business units in the same industry:

1. A **cost leadership strategy** (cell 1) requires a serious commitment to reducing expenses that, in turn, lowers the price of the items sold in a relatively broad array of market segments. One way is by securing raw materials from a lower-cost supplier. Also, significant investments in capital equipment may be necessary to improve the production or distribution process and achieve these lower unit costs. The cost leader still must have adequate quality levels. Wal-Mart's sophisticated systems of regional warehouses and electronic data interchange with its suppliers has led to huge cost savings and its cost leadership strategy.

2. A **differentiation strategy** (cell 2) requires innovation and significant points of difference in product offerings, brand image, higher quality, advanced technology, or superior service in a relatively broad array of market segments. This allows the firm to charge a price premium. Delphi Automobile Systems has used this strategy to use satellite communications to connect you and your

FIGURE 22–4
Porter's four generic business strategies

SOURCE OF COMPETITIVE ADVANTAGE

Competitive scope	Lower cost	Differentiation
Broad target	1. Cost leadership	2. Differentiation
Narrow target	3. Cost focus	4. Differentiation focus

Which of Porter's generic strategies are Wal-Mart and Volkswagen using? For the answer and a discussion of the strategies, see the text.

car to 24-hour-a-day emergency services, directions to a destination, and the opportunity to order a movie while on the road.

3. A **cost focus strategy** (cell 3) involves controlling expenses and, in turn, lowering prices, in a narrow range of market segments. Retail chains targeting only a few market segments in a restricted group of products—such as Office Max in office supplies—have used a cost focus strategy successfully. Southwest Airlines has been very successful in offering low fares between very restricted pairs of cities.

4. Finally, a **differentiation focus strategy** (cell 4) utilizes significant points of difference to reach one or only a few market segments. Volkswagen has achieved spectacular success by targeting the "nostalgia segment," 35- to 55-year-old baby boomers, with its technology-laden New Beetle.[16]

These strategies also form the foundation for Michael Porter's theory about what makes a nation's industries successful, as discussed in Chapter 7.

Profit Enhancement Options   If a business wants to increase, or "enhance," its profits, it can (1) increase revenues, (2) decrease expenses, or (3) do both. Among these "profit enhancement options," let's look first at the strategy options of increasing revenues and then at those for decreasing expenses.

The strategy option of increasing revenues can only be achieved by using one or a combination of four ways to address present or new markets and products (Figure 22–5): (1) market penetration, (2) product development, (3) market development, and (4) diversification (which are described in Chapter 2).

Procter & Gamble has followed a successful strategy of market penetration (present markets, present products) by concentrating its effort on becoming the market leader in each of its more than 30 product categories. It is currently first in market share in more than half these product categories. Recent research, however, suggests that while market share may be directly related to profitability in some industries, this is not true for all. Corporate goals such as increasing customer satisfaction may be more successful than simply maximizing market share.[17]

In contrast, Johnson & Johnson has succeeded with a product development strategy—finding new products for its present markets—to complement popular brands such as Tylenol pain reliever and Accuvue contact lenses. To compete with Bristol-

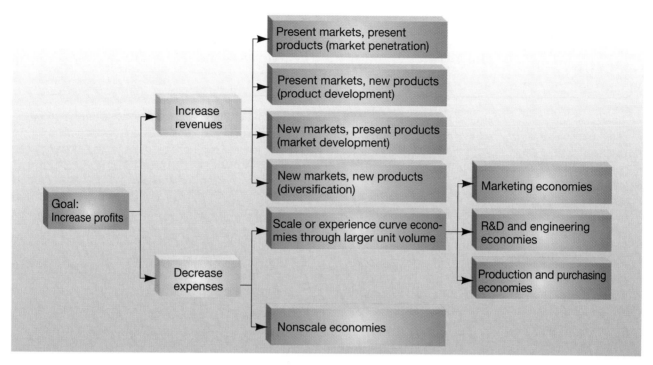

FIGURE 22–5
Profit enhancement options for increasing a firm's profits

Myers Squibb, American Home Products, and other companies, Johnson & Johnson developed Tylenol PM—a combination pain killer and sleeping pill—and Surevue—a long-lasting disposable contact lens.

Walt Disney Co. pursued a market development strategy (new market, present product) following the success of the original Disneyland in Anaheim, California. The first market expansion, of course, was to Orlando, Florida, and more recently Disney built theme parks in Tokyo and Paris.

Finally, Philip Morris, which depended on Marlboro cigarettes for 60 percent of its profits in the late 1980s, has used a diversification strategy (new market, new product) to reduce its dependence on a single brand. In recent years Philip Morris has purchased Seven-Up, Miller Brewing, General Foods, and Kraft to create a portfolio of consumer products.

Strategy options for decreasing expenses fall into two broad categories (Figure 22–5). One is relying on scale economies or experience curve benefits from an increased volume of production to drive unit costs down and gross margins up, the best-known examples being electronic devices such as fax or voice-mail machines whose prices fell by half in a few years. Scale economies may occur in marketing, as well as in R&D, engineering, production, and purchasing.

The other strategy option to decrease expenses is simply finding other ways to reduce costs, such as cutting the number of managers, increasing the effectiveness of the salesforce through more training, or reducing the product rejects by inspectors. Procter & Gamble concluded the world didn't really need 31 varieties of Head & Shoulders shampoo. Cutting the number of packages, sizes, and formulas in hair care alone, P&G has slashed the varieties almost in half—reducing expenses and increasing profits in the bargain.[18]

Market-Product Synergies   Using the market-product grid framework introduced in Chapter 9, we can see two kinds of synergy that are critical in developing corporate and marketing strategies: (1) marketing synergy and (2) R&D–manufacturing synergy. While the following example involves external synergies through mergers and acquisitions, the concepts apply equally well to internal synergies sought in adding new products or seeking new markets.

America Online (AOL) acquires Time Warner "to create entertainment synergies." General Mills (Big G) acquires Pillsbury "to get synergy." General Electric (GE) tries to acquire Honeywell (and fails because of antitrust concerns from the European Union) "to realize synergies." With the current emphasis of giant mergers and acquisitions, partners in these ventures look for synergies that for some are realized and for others have often proven elusive or impossible to achieve.

For example, AOL Time Warner believed that it could attain marketing synergies by cross-selling its AOL, Time Warner Cable, CNN, Time, Inc, services, such as promoting a Warner Bros. movie on CNN or placing an ad in *Time* magazine. Big G expects to generate distribution efficiencies by adding refrigerated and frozen products made by Pillsbury to its own lines of refrigerated products like Yoplait and Go-Gurt yogurts. GE sought to integrate Honeywell's avionics business with its jet engine business, creating the potential of offering airplane manufacturers like Boeing a "bundled" package at a lower price because of sales efficiencies.

To try your hand in this multibillion dollar synergy game, assume you are vice president of marketing for Great States Corp., which markets a line of nonpowered and powered walking and riding lawnmowers. A market-product grid for your business is shown in Figure 22–7. You distribute your nonpowered mowers in all three market segments shown and powered and walking mowers only in suburban markets. However, you don't offer powered riding mowers for any of the three markets.

Here are your strategy dilemmas:

1. Where are the marketing synergies (efficiencies)?
2. Where are the R&D and manufacturing synergies (efficiencies)?
3. What would a market-product grid look like for an ideal company that Great States could merge with in order to achieve both marketing and R&D-manufacturing synergies (efficiencies)?

For answers to these questions, read the text and study Figures 22–6 and 22–7.

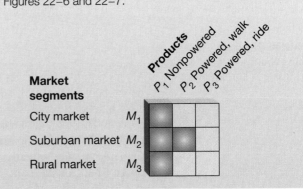

A critical step in the external analysis is to assess how these merger and acquisition strategies provide the organization with **synergy**, the increased customer value achieved through performing organizational functions more efficiently. The "increased customer value" can take many forms: more products, improved quality on existing products, lower prices, improved distribution, and so on. But the ultimate criterion is that customers should be better off as a result of the increased synergy. The firm, in turn, should be better off by gaining more satisfied customers.

A market-product grid helps identify important trade-offs in the strategic marketing process. As noted in the Marketing NewsNet,[19] assume you are vice president of marketing for Great States Corporation's line of nonpowered lawnmowers and powered walking mowers sold to the consumer market. You are looking for new product and new market opportunities to increase your revenues and profits.

You conduct a market segmentation study and develop a market-product grid to analyze future opportunities. You identify three major segments in the consumer market based on geography: (1) city, (2) suburban, and (3) rural households. These market segments relate to the size of lawn a consumer must mow. The product clusters are (1) nonpowered, (2) powered walking, and (3) powered riding mowers. Five alternative marketing strategies are shown in the market-product grids in Figure 22–6. As mentioned in Chapter 9, the important marketing efficiencies—or synergies—run horizontally across the rows in Figure 22–6. Conversely, the important R&D and production efficiencies—or synergies—run vertically down the columns. Let's look at the synergy effects for the five combinations in Figure 22–6.

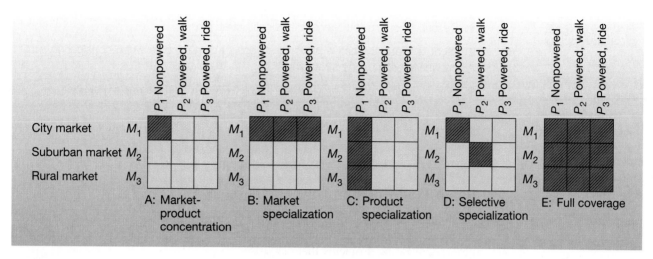

FIGURE 22–6
Market-product grid of alternative strategies for a lawnmower manufacturer

A. *Market-product concentration.* The firm benefits from "focus" on a single product line and market segment, but it loses opportunities for significant synergies in both marketing and R&D–manufacturing.

B. *Market specialization.* The firm gains marketing synergy through providing a complete product line, but R&D–manufacturing have the difficulty of developing and producing two new products.

C. *Product specialization.* The firm gains R&D–manufacturing synergy through production economies of scale, but gaining market distribution in the three different geographic areas will be costly.

D. *Selective specialization.* The firm doesn't get either marketing or R&D–manufacturing synergies because of the uniqueness of the market-product combinations.

E. *Full coverage.* The firm has the maximum potential synergies in both marketing and R&D–manufacturing. The question: Is it spread too thin because of the resource requirements needed to reach all market-product combinations?

The Marketing NewsNet posed the question of what the ideal partner for Great States would be if it merged with another firm, given the market-product combinations shown in the box. If, as vice president of marketing, you want to follow a full-coverage strategy, then the ideal merger partner is shown in Figure 22–7. This would give the maximum potential synergies—if you are not spreading your merged companies too thin. Marketing gains by having a complete product line in all regions, and R&D–manufacturing gains by having access to new markets that can provide production economies of scale through producing larger volumes of its existing products.

FIGURE 22–7
An ideal merger for Great States to obtain full market-product coverage

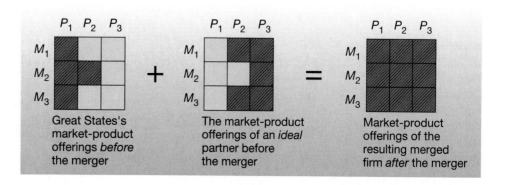

Concept Check

1. Describe Porter's four generic business strategies.

2. What are four alternative ways to increase a firm's profits when considering profit enhancement options strategies?

3. Where do (a) marketing synergies and (b) R&D–manufacturing synergies appear in a market-product grid framework?

Some Planning and Strategy Lessons

Applying these frameworks is not automatic but requires a great deal of managerial judgment. Commonsense requirements of an effective marketing plan are discussed next, followed by problems that can arise.

Guidelines for an Effective Marketing Plan   President Dwight D. Eisenhower, when he commanded Allied armies in World War II, made his classic observation, "Plans are nothing; planning is everything." It is the process of careful planning that focuses an organization's efforts and leads to success. The plans themselves, which change with events, are often secondary. Effective planning and plans are inevitably characterized by identifiable objectives, specific strategies or courses of action, and the means to execute them. Here are some guidelines in developing effective marketing plans:

- *Set measurable, achievable goals.* Ideally, goals should be quantified and measurable in terms of what is to be accomplished and by when. So, "Increase market share from 18 percent to 22 percent by December 31, 2005" is preferable to "Maximize market share given our available resources." Also, to motivate people the goals must be achievable.
- *Use a base of facts and valid assumptions.* The more a marketing plan is based on facts and valid assumptions, rather than guesses, the less uncertainty and risk are associated with executing it. Good marketing research helps.
- *Utilize simple, but clear and specific, plans.* Effective execution of plans requires that people at all levels in the firm understand what, when, and how they are to accomplish their tasks.
- *Have complete and feasible plans.* Marketing plans must incorporate all the key marketing mix factors and be supported by adequate resources.
- *Make plans controllable and flexible.* Marketing plans must enable results to be compared with planned targets, which allows replanning—the flexibility to update the original plans.

Problems in Marketing Planning and Strategy   From postmortems on company plans that did work and on those that did not work, a picture emerges of

Marketing 101 final exam: (1) What is the common feature among the Big G products? (2) How might that feature be woven into the Pillsbury products? Answers are provided in the text and Marketing NewsNet.

where problems occur in the planning phase of a firm's strategic marketing process. The following list explores these problems:

1. Plans may be based on very poor assumptions about environmental factors, especially changing economic conditions and competitors' actions. A Western Union plan failed because it didn't reflect the impact of deregulation and competitors' actions on business.

2. Planners and their plans may have lost sight of their customers' needs. The "better ingredients, better pizza" slogan makes the hair stand up on the back of the necks of Pizza Hut executives. The reason is that this slogan of Papa John's International pizza chain reflects the firm's obsessive attention to detail, which is stealing market share from five-times-bigger Pizza Hut! Sample detail: If the cheese on the pizza shows a single air bubble or the crust is not golden brown, the offending pizza is not served to the customer![20]

3. Too much time and effort may be spent on data collection and writing the plans. Westinghouse has cut its planning instructions for operating units "that looked like an auto repair manual" to five or six pages.

4. Line operating managers often feel no sense of ownership in implementing the plans. Andy Grove, when he was CEO of Intel, observed, "We had the very ridiculous system . . . of delegating strategic planning to strategic planners. The strategies these [planners] prepared had no bearing on anything we actually did."[21] The solution is to assign more planning activities to line operating managers—the people who actually carry them out.

Big G Plus Pillsbury: Increasing Emphasis on Synergies and Segments
Combining General Mills and Pillsbury operations gives a merged firm with $13 billion in annual sales. The merger is expected to generate major synergies in distribution and supply-chain operations by combining many administrative, purchasing, manufacturing, and shipping activities of the two firms.[22]

Steve Sanger, CEO of the merged firm, gets even more excited when he talks about carrying his consumer convenience and "one-handedness" synergies into the Pillsbury product line. He looks at what he calls "Pillsbury's marvelous dough technology" and points out that "if you think of hand-held foods, most of them are dough wrapped around something." So on the drawing boards may be a Pillsbury biscuit or the cookie dough "wrapped around something," a new product you might be able to buy soon. But the competition is tough: Kraft Foods' barbequed chicken on a stick covered in dough and 7-Eleven's macaroni and cheese on a push-up stick.[23]

As shown in the Marketing NewsNet box, General Mills has cereal brands targeted at many segments, some large and others only niche segments. With Big G's Milk 'n Cereal Bars, commuters on the way to work can try "dashboard dining"—eating a cereal breakfast without a bowl or spoon. The basic components: General Mills' traditional cereals bought in a box. General Mills is increasing its presence in global markets through joint ventures. Its Cereal Partners Worldwide (CPW), a joint venture with Nestlé, now holds 20 percent market share across 75 countries. This enables its traditional strengths in food product brands to reach new segments of international consumers.[24]

Balancing Value and Values in Strategic Marketing Plans
Two important trends are likely to influence the strategic marketing process in the future. The first, value-based planning, combines marketing planning ideas and financial planning techniques to assess how much a division or strategic business unit (SBU) contributes to the price of a company's stock (or shareholder wealth). Value is created when the financial return of a strategic activity exceeds the cost of the resources allocated to the activity.

MARKETING NEWSNET

Keeping Planning Simple at Big G: "One-Handed" Convenience plus Cover All the Bases

CUSTOMER VALUE

What do you do when you're chief executive officer of a firm in the low-growth food industry? This is the problem facing Steve Sanger, CEO of General Mills—or "Big G" from its cereal logo. His remarkable answers: one-handedness and covering all the bases, both built on a focus on today's consumers and keeping marketing planning simple and clear.

One-Handedness

When Steve Sanger gets proposals for a new food product or a way to reposition an old one, he asks one question, "Can we make it 'one handed'?" This doesn't mean *build* it one-handed but being able to *eat* it one-handed! With today's consumers, Sanger says, "You have to make every-thing more convenient"—like letting people have a free hand while eating and typing or driving. Go-Gurt (for kids) and Yoplait Exprèsse (for adults) yogurts, Chex Morning Mix, and Big G Milk 'n Cereal Bars are examples of Sanger's one-handed strategy.

Cover-All-the-Bases

Big G also faces the continuing challenge of finding growth in its cereal business with 60 percent of its profits coming from cereal sales in North America. To do this it monitors consumers' changing tastes and implements new-product and diversification strategies like those described earlier in Figure 2–6 and shown below:

PRODUCTS

Markets	Current	New
Current	**Market Penetration** Finding ways to make current products appeal to current customers: Cheerios, with games or CDs	**Product Development** Reaching current customers with a new product: Harmony, a nutritiously fortified cereal for women wanting a healthier breakfast
New	**Market Development** Reaching new customers with basically a current product: Wheaties Energy Crunch, for those needing "all-day energy"	**Diversification** Reaching new customers with a new product: Sunrise Organic, for those wanting a cereal grown without pesticides that receives formal organic certification

The second trend is the increasing interest in value-driven strategies, which incorporate concerns for ethics, integrity, employee health and safety, and environmental safeguards with more common corporate values such as growth, profitability, customer service, and quality. Some experts have observed that although many corporations cite broad corporate values in advertisements, press releases, and company newsletters, they have not yet changed their strategic plans to reflect the stated values.[25]

It is easier to talk about planning than to do it well. Try your hand as a consultant to help Trevor's Toys make some strategic marketing decisions, as described in the Web Link box.

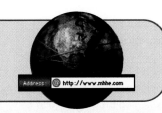

WEB LINK   **Want to Be a BCG Consultant? Solve the Trevor's Toys Online Case**

The Boston Consulting Group (BCG) is probably best known for its "growth-share" portfolio matrix discussed in Chapter 2.[26] As an active and respected management consulting firm, BCG maintains a website to describe its services. Included in the Careers section of the website is an interactive strategy case that asks potential employees to analyze the typical strategic challenges faced by BCG clients.

Go to the BCG website and assess the e-commerce strategy of Trevor's Toys. You can access the interactive case by going to www.bcg.com/careers/interview_prep/interactive_case/interactive_case.asp. After reading the welcome page, click on "Begin Interactive Case" to go to the Trevor's Toys online case. Read the case and directions carefully, solve it within the specified time limits, and consider becoming a BCG consultant after graduation!

THE IMPLEMENTATION PHASE OF THE STRATEGIC MARKETING PROCESS

The Monday morning diagnosis of a losing football coach often runs something like "We had an excellent game plan: we just didn't execute it."

Is Planning or Implementation the Problem?

The planning-versus-execution issue applies to the strategic marketing process as well: a difficulty when a marketing plan fails is determining whether the failure is due to a poor plan or poor implementation. Figure 22–8 shows the outcomes of (1) good and bad marketing planning and (2) good and bad marketing implementation.[27] Good planning and good implementation in cell 1 spell success, as with General Electric's continuing leadership in lighting that combines strong innovative products and the well-known GE brand with excellent advertising and distribution.

Most of the hundreds of failed dot-com firms fall into the "bad-bad" cell 4. The principal owner of the Expedia travel-booking website says, "You have to deliver a better product to your customer, not just offer an Internet retail option for the sake of dabbling in some new technology." What often happened with the dot-coms was bad planning focused mainly on getting start-up money from investors—not providing value to customers—and bad implementation with large expenditures on traditional ads to try to promote their failing websites. What is also clear is that while some Internet companies may have had good ideas for delivering

FIGURE 22–8
Results of good and bad marketing planning and implementation

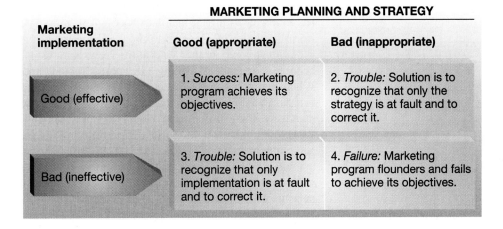

General Electric's army of innovative lights have benefited from having both good planning and implementation of their marketing programs—and by making it into one of Jack Welch's "three circles."

General Electric Company
www.ge.com

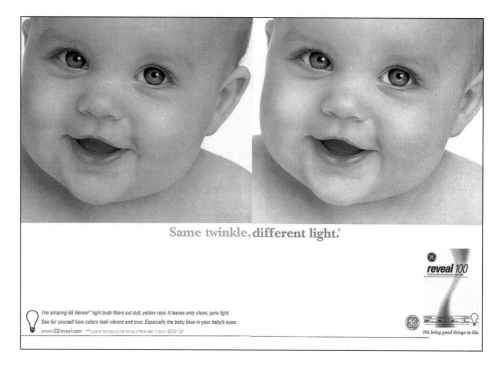

physical products—like toys books, and groceries—to their customer's door, they didn't understand inventories, warehouses, and physical distribution (cell 3 in Figure 22–8).[28]

Cells 2 and 3 indicate trouble because either the marketing planning *or* marketing implementation—not both—is bad. A firm or product does not stay permanently in cell 2 or 3. If the problem is solved, the result can be success (cell 1); if not, it is failure (cell 4).

Toyota used good implementation on a bad marketing strategy (cell 2) when it applied its superior automobile marketing skills to the introduction of its T100 pickup truck. Consumer response was well below forecasts because the truck was too big to compete with smaller "compact" pickups and too small and underpowered to compete with full-size options. Goodyear Tire and Rubber Co. found itself in cell 3 after it successfully developed all-season radial tires but created problems with the 640-dealer distribution network by raising wholesale prices. The poor implementation led to a two-point decline in market share—a drop of 3 million tires.

Increasing Emphasis on Marketing Implementation

In the new millennium, the implementation phase of the strategic marketing process has emerged as a key factor to success by moving many planning activities away from the duties of planners to those of line managers.

As described in the Marketing NewsNet, General Electric's Jack Welch has become a legend in making GE more efficient and far better at implementation. When Welch became CEO in 1981 he faced an organization mired in red tape, turf battles, and slow decision making. Further, Welch saw GE bogged down with 25,000 managers and close to a dozen layers between him and the factory floor. In his "delayering," he sought to cut GE's levels in half and to speed up decision making and implementation by building an atmosphere of trust and autonomy among his managers and employees. Although there are debates on some Welch strategies, businesses around the world are using his focus on implementation as a benchmark. One measure of GE's global impact: In 2000, *Fortune* magazine named General Electric "the world's most admired company."[29]

MARKETING NEWSNET

GE's Implementation Strategies: How Neutron Jack Became "One of the Most Acclaimed CEOs of the Twentieth Century"

CUSTOMER VALUE

Time magazine calls him "one of the most acclaimed CEOs (chief executive officers) of the 20th century." Yet employees at his company in the 1980s called him "Neutron Jack" because they said his corporate downsizings were alleged to leave the buildings standing with no people in them—like a neutron bomb would. However, his difficult strategy decisions and in-your-face leadership style probably assured the jobs of thousands of his firm's employees today.

He is Jack Welch, General Electric's CEO for two decades, up to mid-2001. Welch's implementation focus emerges in his five-box flowchart below:

- *Three Circle Strategy.* In the early 1980s Welch looked at the 350 businesses in 43 strategic business units he inherited. By focusing GE's businesses in three key areas as shown in the illustration, he set the strategic direction for GE's future.
- *#1, #2.* Welch concluded that GE "winners" would be either #1 or #2 in their industry.
- *Fix, close, or sell.* This became GE's mantra. Coupled with "#1, #2," more than 100 businesses were closed or sold. An example is GE's housewares (small appliance) division that was sold to Black & Decker. The rest were fixed.
- *Delayering.* Welch felt GE was drowning in layers, managers, and red tape. By eliminating a lot of these and "rituals, endless studies, and briefings," he gave employees more personal empowerment and accountability.
- *Downsizing.* Painful as it was to him, Welch thought the only way to create a competitive organization was ultimately to lay off one-third of GE's employees: 150,000 workers.

How important have Jack Welch's ideas become? Today they are studied—and often adapted—by hundreds of chief executive officers around the world!

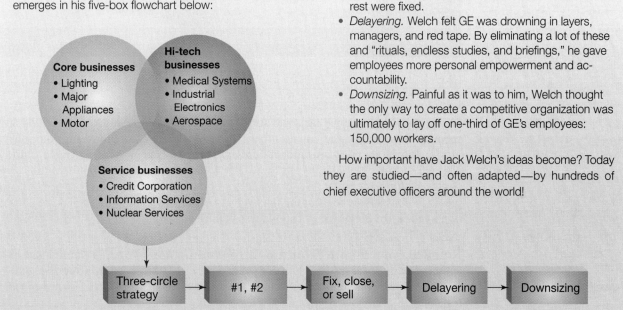

Improving Implementation of Marketing Programs

No magic formula exists to guarantee effective implementation of marketing plans. In fact, the answer seems to be equal parts of good management skills and practices, from which have come some guidelines for improving program implementation.

Communicate Goals and the Means of Achieving Them   Those called on to implement plans need to understand both the goals sought and how they are to be accomplished. Everyone in Papa John's—from founder John Schnatter to telephone order takers and make-line people—is clear on what the firm's goal is: to deliver better pizzas using better ingredients. The firm's orientation packet for employees lists its six "core values" that executives are expected to memorize. Sample: Core value no. 4 is "PAPA," or "People Are Priority No. 1, Always."[30]

Have a Responsible Program Champion Willing to Act   Successful programs almost always have a **product or program champion** who is able and willing to cut red tape and move the program forward. Such people often have the

For the unusual way General Motors avoided the "NIH syndrome" to help develop the Saturn, see the text.

uncanny ability to move back and forth between big-picture strategy questions and specific details when the situation calls for it. Program champions are notoriously brash in overcoming organizational hurdles. The U.S. Navy's Admiral Grace Murray Hopper not only gave the world the COBOL computer language but also the word *bug*—meaning any glitch in a computer or computer program. This program champion's famous advice for moving decisions to actions by cutting through an organization's red tape: "Better to ask forgiveness than permission."

Reward Successful Program Implementation   When an individual or a team is rewarded for achieving the organization's goal, they have maximum incentive to see a program implemented successfully because they have personal ownership and a stake in that success. At a General Electric surge protector plant, employees receive a bonus each quarter that the facility meets plantwide performance goals.

Take Action and Avoid "Paralysis by Analysis"   Management experts warn against paralysis by analysis, the tendency to excessively analyze a problem instead of taking action. To overcome this pitfall, they call for a "bias for action" and recommend a "do it, fix it, try it" approach.[31] Conclusion: Perfectionists finish last, so getting 90 percent perfection and letting the marketplace help in the fine tuning makes good sense in implementation.

Lockheed Martin's Skunk Works got its name from the comic strip *L'il Abner* and its legendary reputation from achieving superhuman technical feats with a low budget and ridiculously short deadlines by stressing teamwork. Under the leadership of Kelly Johnson, in 35 years the Skunk Works turned out a series of world-class aircraft from the world's fastest (the SR-71 Blackbird) to the nation's most untrackable aircraft (the F-117 Stealth fighter). Now on the drawing boards: The X-33 Venturestar, the planned replacement for the space shuttle. Two of Kelly Johnson's basic tenets: (1) make decisions promptly and (2) avoid paralysis by analysis. In fact, one U.S. Air Force audit showed that Johnson's Skunk Works could carry out a program on schedule with 126 people, whereas a competitor in a comparable program was behind schedule with 3,750 people.[32]

Foster Open Communication to Surface the Problems   Success often lies in fostering a work environment that is open enough so employees are willing to speak out when they see problems without fear of recrimination. The focus is placed on trying to solve the problem as a group rather than finding someone to blame. Solutions are solicited from anyone who has a creative idea to suggest—from the janitor to the president—without regard to status or rank in the organization.

Two more Kelly Johnson axioms from Lockheed Martin's Skunk Works apply here: (1) When trouble develops, surface the problem immediately, and (2) get help; don't keep the problem to yourself. This latter point is important even if it means getting ideas from competitors.

Saturn is General Motors' attempt to create a new company where participatory management and improved communications lead to a successful product. For example, to encourage discussion of possible cost reductions, each employee receives 100 to 750 hours of training, including balance sheet analysis. To avoid the "NIH syndrome"—the reluctance to accept ideas "not invented here" or not originated inside one's own firm—Saturn engineers bought 70 import cars to study for product design ideas and selected options that would most appeal to their target market.

Schedule Precise Tasks, Responsibilities, and Deadlines   Successful implementation requires that people know the tasks for which they are responsible and the deadline for completing them. To implement the thousands of tasks on a new aircraft design, Lockheed Martin typically holds weekly program meetings. The outcome of each of these meetings is an **action item list** that has three columns: (1) the task, (2) the name of the person responsible for accomplishing that task, and (3) the date by which the task is to be finished. Within hours of completing a program meeting, the action item list is circulated to those attending. This then serves as the starting agenda for the next meeting. Meeting minutes are viewed as secondary and backward looking. Action item lists are forward looking, clarify the targets, and put strong pressure on people to achieve their designated tasks by the deadline.

Related to the action item lists are formal *program schedules,* which show the relationships through time of the various program tasks. Scheduling an action program involves (1) identifying the main tasks, (2) determining the time required to complete each, (3) arranging the activities to meet the deadline, and (4) assigning responsibilities to complete each task.

Suppose, for example, that you and two friends are asked to do a term project on the problem, "How can the college increase attendance at its performing arts concerts?[33] And suppose further that the instructor limits the project in the following ways:

1. The project must involve a mail survey of the attitudes of a sample of students.
2. The term paper with the survey results must be submitted by the end of the 11-week quarter.

To begin the assignment, you need to identify all the project tasks and then estimate the time you can reasonably allocate to each one. As shown in Figure 22–9, it would take 15 weeks to complete the project if you did all the tasks sequentially; so to complete it in 11 weeks, your team must work on different parts at the same time, and some activities must be independent enough to overlap. This requires specialization and cooperation. Suppose that of the three of you (A, B, and C), only student C can type. Then you (student A) might assume the task of constructing the questionnaire and selecting samples, and student B might tabulate the data. This division of labor allows each student to concentrate on and become expert in one area, but you should also cooperate. Student C might help A and B in the beginning, and A and B might help C later on.

FIGURE 22–9
Tasks to complete a term project

Shown below are the tasks you might face as a member of a student team to complete a marketing research study using a mail questionnaire. Elapsed time to complete all the tasks is 15 weeks. How do you finish the project in an 11-week quarter? For an answer, see the text.

Task	Time (weeks)
1. Construct and test a rough-draft questionnaire for clarity (in person, not by mail) on friends.	2
2. Type and copy a final questionnaire.	2
3. Randomly select the names of 200 students from the school directory.	1
4. Address and stamp envelopes; mail questionnaires.	1
5. Collect returned questionnaires.	3
6. Tabulate and analyze data from returned questionnaires.	2
7. Write final report.	3
8. Type and submit final report.	1
Total time necessary to complete all activities	15

You must also figure out which activities can be done concurrently to save time. In Figure 22–9 you can see that task 2 must be completed before task 4. However, task 3 might easily be done before, at the same time as, or after task 2. Task 3 is independent of task 2.

Scheduling production and marketing activities—from a term project to a new product rollout to a space shuttle launch—can be done efficiently with Gantt charts. Figure 22–10 shows one variation of a Gantt chart used to schedule the class project, demonstrating how the concurrent work on several tasks enables the students to finish the project on time. Developed by Henry L. Gantt, this method is the basis for the scheduling techniques used today, including elaborate computerized methods. The key to all scheduling techniques is to distinguish tasks that *must* be done sequentially from those that *can* be done concurrently. As in the case of the term project, scheduling tasks concurrently often reduces the total time required for a project. Software programs, such as Microsoft Project, simplify the task of developing a schedule or Gantt chart.

FIGURE 22–10
Gantt chart for scheduling the term project

Task description	Students involved in task	Week of quarter 1 2 3 4 5 6 7 8 9 10 11
1. Construct and test a rough-draft questionnaire for clarity (in person, not by mail) on friends.	A	
2. Type and copy the final questionnaire.	C	
3. Randomly select the names of 200 students from the school directory.	A	
4. Address and stamp envelopes; mail questionnaires.	C	
5. Collect returned questionnaires.	B	
6. Tabulate and analyze data from returned questionnaires.	B	
7. Write final report.	A, B, C	
8. Type and submit final report.	C	

KEY: ▲ Planned completion date   ■ Planned period of work   Current date
△ Actual completion date   ▨ Actual period of work

Organizing for Marketing

A marketing organization is needed to implement the firm's marketing plans. Basic issues in today's marketing organizations include understanding (1) how line versus staff positions and divisional groupings interrelate to form a cohesive marketing organization and (2) the role of the marketing or product manager.

Line versus Staff and Divisional Groupings   Although simplified, Figure 22–11 shows the organization of a Pillsbury business unit that will be merged into General Mills. The similarity of marketing organizations in the two firms makes the merger process easier. This business unit consists of the Breakfast Products, Refrigerated Baked Goods, and Desserts & Baking Mixes groups. It highlights the distinction between line and staff positions in marketing. People in **line positions**, such as the senior marketing manager for Biscuits, have the authority and responsibility to issue orders to the people who report to them, such as the two product managers shown in Figure 22–11. In this organizational chart, line positions are connected with solid lines. Those in **staff positions** (shown by dotted lines) have the authority and responsibility to advise people in line positions but cannot issue direct orders to them.

Most marketing organizations use divisional groupings—such as product line, functional, geographical, and market-based—to implement plans and achieve their

FIGURE 22–11
Organization of a Pillsbury business unit, showing two product or brand groups

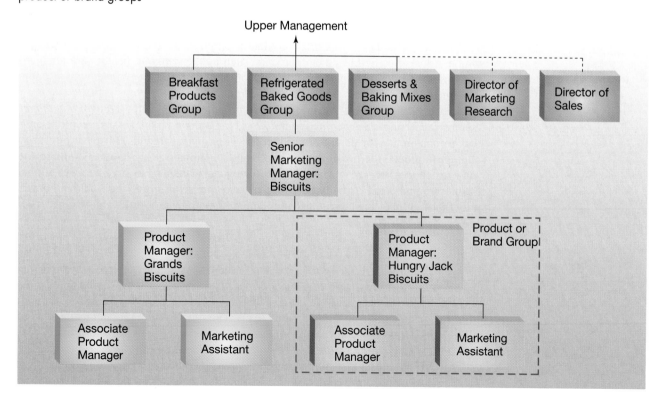

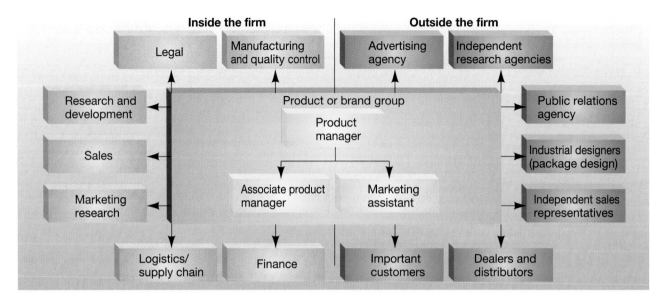

Inside the firm   **Outside the firm**

FIGURE 22–12
Units with which the product manager and product group work

organizational objectives. Three of these appear in some form in Pillsbury's organizational chart in Figure 22–11. At the top of the chart, Pillsbury organizes by **product line groupings** in which a unit is responsible for specific product offerings, such as Breakfast Products or Refrigerated Baked Goods.

At higher levels than shown in Figure 22–11, Pillsbury is organized by **functional groupings** such as manufacturing, marketing, and finance, which are the different business activities within a firm.

Pillsbury uses **geographical groupings** for its more than 500 field sales representatives throughout the United States. Each director of sales has several regional sales managers reporting to him or her, such as western, southern, and so on. These, in turn, have district managers reporting to them, with the field sales representatives at the lowest level.

A fourth method of organizing a company is to use **market-based groupings**, which utilize specific customer segments, such as the banking, health care, or manufacturing segments. When this method of organizing is combined with product groupings, the result is a *matrix organization.*

A relatively new position in consumer products firms is the *category manager* (senior marketing manager in Figure 22–11). Category managers have profit-and-loss responsibility for an entire product line—all biscuit brands, for example. They attempt to reduce the possibility of one brand's actions hurting another brand in the same category. Procter & Gamble uses category managers to organize by "global business units" such as baby care and beauty care. Cutting across country boundaries, these global business units implement standardized worldwide pricing, marketing, and distribution.[34]

Role of the Product Manager   The key person in the product or brand group shown in Figure 22–12 is the manager who heads it. As mentioned in Chapter 10, this person is often called the *product manager* or *brand manager.* This person and the assistants in the product group are the basic building blocks in the marketing department of most consumer and business product firms. The function of a product manager is to plan, implement, and control the annual and long-range plans for the products for which he or she is responsible.

There are both benefits and dangers to the product manager system. On the positive side, product managers become strong advocates for the assigned products, cut red tape to work with people in various functions both inside and outside the organization (Figure 22–12), and assume profit-and-loss responsibility for the performance of the product line. On the negative side, even though product managers have major responsibilities, they have relatively little direct authority, so most groups and functions shown in Figure 22–12 must be coordinated to meet the product's goals.[35] To coordinate the many units, product managers must use persuasion rather than orders.

THE CONTROL PHASE OF THE STRATEGIC MARKETING PROCESS

The essence of control, the final phase of the strategic marketing process, is to compare results with planned goals for the marketing program in order to take necessary corrective actions.

The Marketing Control Process

Ideally, quantified goals from the marketing plans developed in the planning phase have been accomplished by the marketing actions taken in the implementation phase (Figure 22–13) and measured as results in the control phase. A marketing manager then uses *management by exception,* which means identifying results that deviate from plans to diagnose their causes and take new actions. Often results fall short of plans, and a corrective action is needed. For example, after 50 years of profits Caterpillar accumulated losses of $1 billion. To correct the problem, Caterpillar focused its marketing efforts on core products and reduced its manufacturing costs. At other times the comparison shows that performance is far better than anticipated, in which case the marketing manager tries to identify the reason and move quickly to exploit the unexpected opportunity.

Measuring Results   Without some quantitative goal, no benchmark exists with which to compare actual results. Manufacturers of both consumer and business products are increasingly trying to develop marketing programs that have not only specific action programs but also specific procedures for monitoring key measures of performance. Today marketing executives measure not only financial targets such as sales revenues and profits but also marketing ones, such as customer satisfaction, time-to-market, and salesforce motivation.

Taking Marketing Actions   When results deviate significantly from plans, some kind of action is essential. Deviations can be the result of the process used to specify goals or can be due to changes in the marketplace. Beaten badly for years in

FIGURE 22–13
The control phase of the strategic marketing process

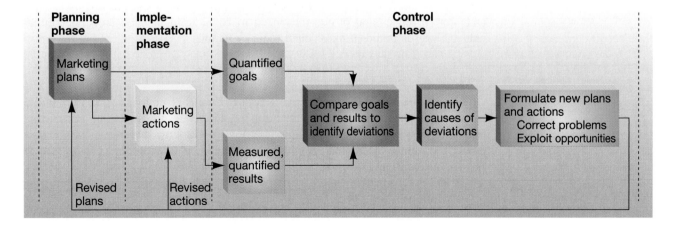

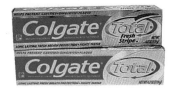

the U.S. toothpaste market by P&G's Crest, in the late 1990s Colgate went on the offensive. It took aggressive marketing action to introduce its Total toothpaste, the first "oral pharmaceutical" ever approved by the U.S. Food and Drug Administration. Not only does Total clean teeth, but its germ-fighting feature helps heal gingivitis, one of the bleeding-gum diseases of increasing concern to aging baby boomers. This has caused Colgate's share of the U.S. toothpaste market to rise from 25 percent in 1997 to 32 percent in 2000, an astonishing increase in a very stable product category.[36]

Sales Analysis

For controlling marketing programs, **sales analysis**—using the firm's sales records to compare actual results with sales goals and identify areas of strength and weakness—is critical. All the variables that might be used in market segmentation may be used in **sales component analysis** (also called *microsales analysis*), which traces sales revenues to their sources, such as specific products, sales territories, or customers. Common breakdowns include the following:

- Customer characteristics: demographics, NAICS, size, reason for purchase, and type of reseller (retailer or wholesaler).
- Product characteristics: model, package size, and color.
- Geographical region: sales territory, city, state, and region.
- Order size.
- Price or discount class.
- Commission to the sales representative.

Today's computers can easily produce these breakdowns, provided the input data contain these classifications. Therefore, it is critical that marketing managers specify the breakdowns they require from the accounting and information systems departments, so they get the needed information for decisions without information overload.

Profitability Analysis

To their surprise, marketing managers often discover the 80/20 principle the hard way—on the job. **Profitability analysis** enables the manager to measure the profitability of the firm's products, customer groups, sales territories, channels of distribution, and even order sizes. This leads to decisions to expand, maintain, reduce, or eliminate specific products, customer groups, or channels.

For example, following the 80/20 principle, a marketing manager will try to find the common characteristics among the 20 percent of the customers (or products, brands, sales districts, salespeople, or kinds of orders) that generate 80 percent (or the bulk) of revenues and profits to find more like them to exploit competitive advantages. Conversely, the 80 percent of customers, products, brands, and so on, that generate few revenues and profits may need to be reduced or even dropped entirely unless a way is found to make them more profitable.

The Marketing Audit

Often a broader marketing perspective is needed than is given by sales or profitability analyses, one that covers a longer time horizon and relates the marketing mix factors to environmental variables. This is the role of a **marketing audit**, which is a comprehensive, unbiased, periodic review of the strategic marketing process of a firm or

Products/services: The reason for existence

1. Is the product/service free from deadwood?
2. What is the life-cycle stage?
3. How will user demands or trends affect you?
4. Are you a leader in new-product innovation?
5. Are inexpensive methods used to estimate new-product potentials before consideration amounts are spent on R&D and market introduction?
6. Do you have different quality levels for different markets?
7. Are packages/brochures effective salespeople for the products/services they present?
8. Do you present products/services in the most appealing colors (formats) for markets being served?
9. Are there features or benefits to exploit?
10. Is the level of customer service adequate?
11. How are quality and reliability viewed by customers?

Customer: User profiles

1. Who are the current and potential customers?
2. Are there geographic aspects of use: regional, rural, urban?
3. Why do people buy the product/service; what motivates their preferences?
4. Who makes buying decisions; when; where?
5. What is the frequency and quantity of use?

Markets: Where products/services are sold

1. Have you identified and measured major segments?
2. Are small potential market segments overlooked in trying to satisfy the majority?
3. Are the markets for the products/services expanding or declining?
4. Should different segments be developed; are there gaps in penetration?

Competitors: Their influence

1. Who are the principal competitors, how are they positioned, and where are they headed?
2. What are their market shares?
3. What features of competitors' products/services stand out?
4. Is the market easily entered or dominated?

Pricing: Profitability planning

1. What are the objectives of current pricing policy: acquiring, defending, or expanding?
2. Are price policies set to produce volume or profit?
3. How does pricing compare with competition in similar levels of quality?
4. Does cost information show profitability of each item?
5. What is the history of price deals, discounts, and promotions?

FIGURE 22–14
Marketing audit questions

SBU. The purpose of the marketing audit, which serves as both a planning and control technique, is to identify new problems and opportunities that warrant an action plan to improve performance.

Many firms undertaking a marketing audit use a checklist such as that shown in Figure 22–14 as a part of their situation analysis in their strategic marketing process. The checklist used covers factors ranging from the marketing mix factors and customer profiles to markets and competitors.

For a meaningful, comprehensive marketing audit, the individual or team conducting the audit must have a free rein to talk to managers, employees, salespeople, distributors, and customers, as well as have access to all pertinent internal and external reports and memoranda. They need to involve all levels of the organization in the process to ensure that resulting action recommendations have widespread support.

Concept Check

1. What is the difference between a line and a staff position in a marketing organization?

2. What are four groupings used within a typical marketing organization?

3. What two components of the strategic marketing process are compared to control a marketing program?

SUMMARY

1 Marketing managers use the strategic marketing process to allocate their resources as effectively as possible. Sales response functions help them assess what the market's response to additional marketing effort will be.

2 The planning phase of the strategic marketing process usually results in a marketing plan that sets the direction for the marketing activities of an organization. There are two kinds of marketing plans: long-range and annual.

3 Three useful frameworks to improve marketing planning are (*a*) Porter's generic business strategies, (*b*) profit enhancement options, and (*c*) market-product synergies.

4 An effective marketing plan has measurable, achievable goals; uses facts and valid assumptions; is simple, clear, and specific; is complete and feasible; and is controllable and flexible.

5 The implementation phase of the strategic marketing process is concerned with executing the marketing program developed in the planning phase and has achieved increased attention the past decade.

6 Essential to good scheduling is separating tasks that can be done concurrently from those that must be done sequentially. Gantt charts are a simple, effective means of scheduling.

7 Organizing marketing activities necessitates recognition of two different aspects of an organization: (*a*) line and staff positions and (*b*) product line, functional, geographical, and market-based groupings.

8 The product manager performs a vital marketing role in both consumer and business product firms, interacting with numerous people and groups both inside and outside the firm.

9 The control phase of the strategic marketing process involves measuring the results of the actions from the implementation phase and comparing them with goals set in the planning phase. Sales analyses, profitability analyses, and marketing audits are used to control marketing programs.

KEY TERMS AND CONCEPTS

action item list p. 601
cost focus (generic) strategy p. 590
cost leadership (generic) strategy p. 589
differentiation focus (generic) strategy p. 590
differentiation (generic) strategy p. 589
functional groupings p. 604
generic business strategy p. 589
geographical groupings p. 604
line positions p. 603
market-based groupings p. 604

marketing audit p. 606
product line groupings p. 604
product or program champion p. 599
profitability analysis p. 606
sales analysis p. 606
sales component analysis p. 606
sales response function p. 584
share points p. 586
staff positions p. 603
synergy p. 592

APPLYING MARKETING CONCEPTS AND PERSPECTIVES

1 Assume a firm faces an S-shaped sales response function. What happens to the ratio of incremental sales revenue to incremental marketing effort at the (*a*) bottom, (*b*) middle, and (*c*) top of this curve?

2 What happens to the ratio of incremental sales revenue to incremental marketing effort when the sales response function is an upward-sloping straight line?

3 In 2001 General Mills invested millions of dollars in expanding its cereal and yogurt businesses. To allocate this money between these two businesses, what information would General Mills like to have?

4 Suppose your Great States lawnmower company has the market-product concentration situation shown in Figure 22–6A. What are both the synergies and potential pitfalls of following expansion strategies of (*a*) market specialization and (*b*) product specialization?

5 Are value-driven strategies inconsistent with value-based planning? Give an example that supports your position.

6 The first Domino's Pizza restaurant was near a college campus. What implementation problems are (*a*) similar and (*b*) different for restaurants near a college campus versus a military base?

7 A common theme among managers who succeed repeatedly in program implementation is fostering open communication. Why is this so important?

8 Parts of tasks 5 and 6 in Figure 22–10 are done both concurrently and sequentially. How can this be? How does it help the students meet the term paper deadline?

9 In Pillsbury's organizational chart in Figure 22–11, where do product line, functional, and geographical groupings occur?

10 Why are quantified goals in the planning phase of the strategic marketing process important for the control phase?

INTERNET EXERCISE

McKinsey & Company is a global management consulting firm with offices in over 40 countries. As a leading firm in this competitive industry, McKinsey conducts "engagements" (consulting projects) for clients in a variety of industry sectors. Its distinctive competence is its "integrative thinking," which combines the knowledge gained from other industries and then applies the lessons learned to the specific problems faced by its clients.

The McKinsey Quarterly summarizes the knowledge obtained from serving its clients. Articles are organized by functional area and industry sector. To browse these articles, go to www.mckinseyquarterly.com and click on their respective links.

1   Under the Functions heading, click on the "Marketing" link. Scroll down until you find the article "A New Way to Market." Then click on the "Read Full Text Link" to read the entire article. (Note: You will have to register with McKinsey to read or download the article for free.)

Why do the authors say that the traditional organizational structure based on product, channels, customer groups, and so forth, that focus on specific functional tasks, such as brand or segment management, hinders the strategic marketing process? What are the three principles that "new-style" marketing organizations must adhere to in order to seize market opportunities?

2   If you want to apply for a career at McKinsey, it, like the Boston Consulting Group, allows you to "try your hand" at solving a business problem. Go to www.mckinsey.com/careers/apply/solveacase/index.asp and select one of the case options. To frame the problem, you need to learn how to ask the right questions; in other words, like a physician, you need to diagnose the problem before you can offer your client a recommended solution. As McKinsey says, "Finding the solution is not as important as how you arrived at it. We hope you'll enjoy the challenge."

VIDEO CASE 22–1   Golden Valley Microwave Foods: The Surprising Channel

"We developed the technology that launched the microwave popcorn business and helped make ACT II the number one brand in the world," says Jack McKeon, president of Golden Valley Microwave Foods, a division of ConAgra Foods, Inc. "But we were also lucky along the way, as we backed into what has become one of the biggest distribution channels in the industry today, one that no one ever saw coming."

Founded in 1978, today Golden Valley is the global leader in producing and marketing microwave popcorn. Its ACT II brand is No. 1 in the industry. But it hasn't always been easy.

THE LAUNCH: THE IDEA AND THE TECHNOLOGY

In 1978 only about 15 percent of U.S. households had microwave ovens, so launching a microwave foods business was risky. Golden Valley's initial marketing research turned up two key points of difference or benefits that people wanted in their microwave popcorn: (1) fewer unpopped kernels and (2) good popping results in even low-powered ovens—the kind that half of U.S. households had at the time. Golden Valley's research and development (R&D) staff successfully addressed these

wants by developing a microwave popcorn bag utilizing a thin strip of material laminated between layers of paper, which focused the microwave energy to produce high-quality popped corn, regardless of an oven's power. This breakthrough significantly increased the size of the microwave popcorn market, and is still used in all microwave popcorn bags. Using its revolutionary package, Golden Valley introduced ACT II in 1984.

THE LUCKY DAY: BOTH CAPITAL AND MASS MERCHANDISERS

From its founding in 1978 until a public offering of its stock in September 1986, Golden Valley was privately owned and, like most startups, was severely undercapitalized. Due to the cost of developing and introducing ACT II, Golden Valley needed a partner to help develop the business. Its solution, in 1985, was to enter into a licensing agreement to share its technology for packaging microwave popcorn with one of the food giants under that firm's brand. In turn, Golden Valley agreed it would not distribute its ACT II brand in U.S. grocery stores for ten years. This meant that Golden Valley had to find channels outside the grocery and supermarket channel in which to sell its microwave popcorn so it could survive.

For the next ten years, the company sold ACT II through vending machines, video stores, institutions (movie theaters, colleges, military bases), drug stores, club stores, and convenience stores. "But the huge opportunity we discovered and developed was in the mass-merchandiser channel through chains like Wal-Mart and Target, which really got behind microwave popcorn in the late 80s," says McKeon. "ACT II microwave popcorn was the first item of any kind to sell a million units in a week for Target, and that happened in 1987. Wal-Mart, too, was on the front end of this market and today is the top seller of microwave popcorn in any channel, selling far more popcorn than the leading grocery chains. Mass merchandisers now account for over a third of all the microwave popcorn sold in the U.S. They created the ACT II business as we know it today, and it was accomplished without a dime of conventional consumer promotions. That's one of the really unique parts of the ACT II story."

THE SITUATION TODAY

In the U.S. today, over 90 percent of households own microwave ovens, and more than 60 percent of households are microwave popcorn consumers. "Our marketing research shows ACT II is especially strong in young families with kids," says Frank Lynch, vice president of Marketing at Golden Valley. This conjures up an image of mom and dad watching a movie on TV with the kids and eating ACT II popcorn, a picture close to reality. "ACT II has good market penetration in almost all age, income, urban versus rural, and ethnic segments," he continues.

"From the beginning, Golden Valley has been the leader in the microwave popcorn industry," says McKeon "and we plan to continue that record." As evidence, he cites a number of Golden Valley's "firsts":

- First mass-marketed microwave popcorn
- First flavored microwave popcorn
- First microwave popcorn tub
- First fat-free microwave popcorn
- First extra-butter microwave popcorn
- First one-step sweetened microwave popcorn

This list highlights a curious market segmentation phenomenon that has emerged in the last five years—the no-butter versus plenty-of-butter consumers. Originally popcorn was seen as junk food. Later studies by nutritionists pointed out its health benefits: low calories and high fiber. This caused Golden Valley to introduce its low-fat popcorn in the late-1990s to appeal to the health-conscious segment of consumers. But big surprise: popcorn eaters may be health-conscious in the rest of their daily lives, but when it comes to eating popcorn while watching a movie at home on TV, the more butter on their popcorn, the better. Early in the twenty-first century, much of the growth in popcorn sales is in the spoil-yourself-with-a-lot-of-butter-on-your-popcorn segment.

Because of these diverse consumer tastes in popcorn, Golden Valley has developed a variety of popcorn products around its ACT II brand. Besides the low-fat and extra butter versions, these include the original flavors (natural and butter), sweet glazed products, popcorn in tubs, and Kettle Corn. It also has a line of ACT II non-popcorn snacks such as soft pretzels and snack mixes.

Golden Valley positions ACT II as unpretentious, fun, and youthful—a great product at a reasonable price. By stressing the value aspect of ACT II, Golden Valley has positioned the brand to appeal to today's growing value consciousness of consumers seeking quality products at reasonable prices. In terms of market share, these strategies have enabled ACT II to become the leader in the microwave popcorn market.

OPPORTUNITIES FOR FUTURE GROWTH

During the 1980s and 1990s, the microwave popcorn industry could rely on sales growth that accompanied the growth of household ownership of microwave ovens from under 20 percent to over 90 percent. But now, with a microwave oven in virtually every U.S. home, Golden Valley is trying to identify new market segments, new products, and innovative ways to appeal to all the major marketing channels.

In the U.S., Golden Valley's strategy must include finding creative ways to continue to work with existing channels where it has special strength, such as the mass merchandiser channel. It also needs to further develop opportunities in the grocery store and supermarket channel, accessible to Golden Valley since 1995. Also important to Golden Valley are warehouse clubs, such as Sam's Club, Costco, and BJ's, which have become very significant outlets in the past decade.

Global markets, too, present opportunities. With sales in more than 30 countries, and the leading share in most of those markets, Golden Valley has followed the penetration of microwave ovens in countries around the world. However, foreign markets represent foreign tastes, something that does not always lend itself to standardized products. United Kingdom consumers, for example, think of popcorn as a candy or child's food rather than the salty snack it is in the United States. Even in the Disney Park in Paris, American-style popcorn is absent, as French consumers sprinkle sugar on their popcorn. Swedes like theirs very buttery while many Mexicans like jalapeno-flavored popcorn.

Questions

1 Visit ACT II's website at www.ACTII.com and examine the assortment of products. (*a*) In terms of the branding strategies discussed in Chapter 11, what kind of branding strategy is Golden Valley using today? (*b*) What are the benefits and dangers of this strategy?

2 Develop a SWOT analysis that addresses the business climate Golden Valley finds itself in today.

3 Compared to selling through the non-grocery channels, what kind of product, price, and promotion strategies might Golden Valley use to reach the grocery channel more effectively?

4 What special marketing issues does Golden Valley face as it pursues growth in global markets?

PLANNING A CAREER IN MARKETING

GETTING A JOB: THE PROCESS OF MARKETING YOURSELF

Getting a job is usually a lengthy process, and it is exactly that—a *process* that involves careful planning, implementation, and control. You may have everything going for you: a respectable grade point average (GPA), relevant work experience, several extracurricular activities, superior communication skills, and demonstrated leadership qualities. Despite these, you still need to market yourself systematically and aggressively; after all, even the best products lie dormant on the retailer's shelves unless marketed effectively.

The process of getting a job involves the same activities marketing managers use to develop and introduce products into the marketplace.[1] The only difference is that you are marketing yourself, not a product. You need to conduct marketing research by analyzing your personal qualities (performing a self-audit) and by identifying job opportunities. Based on your research results, select a target market—those job opportunities that are compatible with your interests, goals, skills, and abilities—and design a marketing mix around that target market. *You* are the "product";[2] you must decide how to "position" yourself in the job market. The price component of the marketing mix is the salary range and job benefits (such as health and life insurance, vacation time, and retirement benefits) that you hope to receive. Promotion involves communicating with prospective employers through written correspondence (advertising) and job interviews (personal selling). The place element focuses on how to reach prospective employers—at the career services office or job fairs, for example.

This appendix will assist you in career planning by (1) providing information about careers in marketing and (2) outlining a job search process.

CAREERS IN MARKETING

The diversity of marketing opportunities is reflected in the many types of marketing jobs, ranging from product management to marketing research to public relations.

The growing interest in marketing by service organizations such as athletic teams, law firms, and banks, and nonprofit organizations such as universities, the performing arts, and government agencies, has added to the numerous opportunities offered by traditional employers such as manufacturers, retailers, and advertising agencies. In addition, e-commerce has created a variety of new opportunities such as product development managers for application service providers, data miners, and permission marketing managers for graduates with marketing skills.[3] Examples of companies that have opportunities for graduates with degrees in marketing include Target, America Online, Genuity, Inc., Hallmark Cards, Xerox Corp., Wells Fargo, Pitney Bowes, General Motors, Sherwin Williams, Wal-Mart, and Office Depot.[4] Most of these career opportunities offer the chance to work with interesting people on stimulating and rewarding problems. Comments one product manager, "I love marketing as a career because there are different challenges every day."[5]

Recent studies of career paths and salaries suggest that marketing careers can also provide excellent opportunities for advancement and substantial pay. For example, about one of every five chief executive officers (CEOs) of the nation's 500 most valuable publicly held companies have a career history that is heaviest in marketing.[6] Similarly, reports of average starting salaries of college graduates indicate that salaries in marketing compare favorably with those in many other fields. The average starting salary of new marketing undergraduates in 2001 was $35,021, compared with $30,805 for journalism majors and $29,685 for advertising majors.[7] The future is likely to be even better. The U.S. Department of Labor reports that marketing and sales will be one of the five fastest-growing occupations through 2008. Employment is expected to grow by 15 percent or 2.3 million jobs![8]

Figure C–1 describes marketing occupations in six major categories: product management and physical distribution, advertising, retailing, sales, marketing research, and nonprofit marketing. One of these may be right for you! (Additional sources of marketing career information are provided at the end of this appendix.)

PRODUCT MANAGEMENT AND PHYSICAL DISTRIBUTION

Product development manager creates a "road map" for new products by working with customers to determine their needs and with designers to create the product.

Product manager is responsible for integrating all aspects of a product's marketing program including research, sales, sales promotion, advertising, and pricing.

Supply chain manager oversees the part of a company that transports products to consumers and handles customer service.

Operations manager supervises warehousing and other physical distribution functions and often is directly involved in moving goods on the warehouse floor.

Inventory control manager forecasts demand for stockpiled goods, coordinates production with plant managers, and tracks current levels of shipments to keep customers supplied.

Physical distribution specialist is an expert in the transportation and distribution of goods and also evaluates the costs and benefits of different types of transportation.

SALES

Direct or retail salesperson sells directly to consumers in the salesperson's office, the consumer's home, or a retailer's store.

Trade salesperson calls on retailers or wholesalers to sell products for manufacturers.

Industrial or semi-technical salesperson sells supplies and services to businesses.

Complex or professional salesperson sells complicated or custom-designed products to businesses. This requires understanding of the product technology.

Customer service manager maintains good relations with customers by coordinating the sales staff, marketing management, and physical distribution management.

NONPROFIT MARKETING

Marketing manager develops and directs marketing campaigns, fundraising, and public relations.

ADVERTISING

Account executive maintains contact with clients while coordinating the creative work among artists and copywriters. Account executives work as partners with the client to develop marketing strategy.

Media buyer deals with media sales representatives in selecting advertising media and analyzes the value of media being purchased.

Copywriter works with art director in conceptualizing advertisements and writes the text of print or radio ads or the storyboards of television ads.

Art director handles the visual component of advertisements.

Sales promotion manager designs promotions for consumer products and works at an ad agency or a sales promotion agency.

Public relations manager develops written or filmed messages for the public and handles contacts with the press.

RETAILING

Buyer selects products a store sells, surveys consumer trends, and evaluates the past performance of products and suppliers.

Store manager oversees the staff and services at a store.

MARKETING RESEARCH

Project manager for the supplier coordinates and oversees the market studies for a client.

Account executive for the supplier serves as a liaison between client and market research firm, like an advertising agency account executive.

In-house project director acts as project manager (see above) for the market studies conducted by the firm for which he or she works.

Competitive intelligence researcher uses new information technologies to monitor the competitive environment.

Data miner compiles and analyzes consumer data to identify behavior patterns, preferences, and "user profiles" for personalized marketing programs.

SOURCE: Adapted from David W. Rosenthal and Michael A. Powell, *Careers in Marketing*, ©1984, pp. 352–54.

FIGURE C–1
Marketing occupations

Product Management and Physical Distribution

Many organizations assign one manager the responsibility for a particular product. For example, Procter & Gamble (P&G) has separate managers for Tide, Cheer, Gain, and Bold. Product or brand managers are involved in all aspects of a product's marketing program, such as marketing research, sales, sales promotion, advertising, and pricing, as well as manufacturing. Managers of similar products typically report to a category manager and may be part of a *product management team.*[9]

College graduates with bachelor's and master's degrees—often in marketing and business—enter P&G as brand assistants, the only starting position in its product or brand group. Each year students from campuses throughout the United States accept positions with P&G.[10] As brand assistants, their responsibilities consist primarily of selling and sales training.

After one to two years of good performance, the brand assistant is promoted to assistant brand manager and after about the same period to brand (product) manager. These promotions often involve several brand groups. For example, a new employee might start as brand assistant for P&G's soap products, be promoted to assistant brand manager for Crest toothpaste, and subsequently become brand manager for

Folger's coffee, Charmin, or Pampers. The reason, as recruiter Henry de Montebello explains, is that "in the future everybody will have strategic alliances with everybody else, and the executives who thrive will be well-rounded."[11]

Several other jobs related to product management (Figure C–1) deal with physical distribution issues such as storing the manufactured product (inventory), moving the product from the firm to the customers (transportation), and engaging in many other aspects of the manufacture and sale of goods. Prospects for these jobs are likely to increase as wholesalers increase their involvement with selling and distribution activities and begin to take advantage of overseas opportunities.[12]

Advertising

Although we may see hundreds of advertisements in a day, what we can't see easily is the fascinating and complex advertising profession. The entry-level advertising positions filled every year include jobs with a variety of firms. Advertising professionals often remark that they find their jobs appealing because the days are not routine and they involve creative activities with many interesting people.

Advertising positions are available in three kinds of organizations: advertisers, media companies, and agencies. Advertisers include manufacturers, retail stores, service firms, and many other types of companies. Often they have an advertising department responsible for preparing and placing their own ads. Advertising careers are also possible with the media: television, radio stations, magazines, and newspapers. Finally, advertising agencies offer job opportunities through their use of account management, research, media, and creative services.

Starting positions with advertisers and advertising agencies are often as assistants to employees with several years of experience. An assistant copywriter facilitates the development of the message, or copy, in an advertisement. An assistant art director participates in the design of visual components of advertisements. Entry-level media positions involve buying the media that will carry the ad or selling air time on radio or television or page space in print media. Advancement to supervisory positions requires planning skills, a broad vision, and an affinity for spotting an effective advertising idea. Students interested in advertising should develop good communication skills and try to gain advertising experience through summer employment opportunities or internships.[13]

Retailing

There are two separate career paths in retailing: merchandise management and store management (Figure C–2). The key position in merchandising is that of a buyer, who is responsible for selecting merchandise, guiding the promotion of the merchandise, setting prices, bargaining with wholesalers, training the salesforce, and monitoring the competitive environment. The buyer must also be able to organize and coordinate many critical activities under severe time constraints. In contrast, store management involves the supervision of personnel in all departments and the

FIGURE C–2
Typical retailing career paths

general management of all facilities, equipment, and merchandise displays. In addition, store managers are responsible for the financial performance of each department and for the store as a whole. Typical positions beyond the store manager level include district manager, regional manager, and divisional vice president.[14]

Most starting jobs in retailing are trainee positions. A trainee is usually placed in a management training program and then given a position as an assistant buyer or assistant department manager. Advancement and responsibility can be achieved quickly because there is a shortage of qualified personnel in retailing and because superior performance of an individual is quickly reflected in sales and profits—two visible measures of success. In addition, the growth of multichannel retailing has created new opportunities such as website management and online merchandise procurement.[15]

Sales

College graduates from many disciplines are attracted to sales positions because of the increasingly professional nature of selling jobs and the many opportunities they can provide. A selling career offers benefits that are hard to match in any other field: (1) the opportunity for rapid advancement (into management or to new territories and accounts); (2) the potential for extremely attractive compensation (the average salary of regional sales managers is $114,200);[16] (3) the development of personal satisfaction, feelings of accomplishment, and increased self-confidence; and (4) independence—salespeople often have almost complete control over their time and activities. Many companies now offer two sales career paths—one for people who want to go into management, and another for those who want to remain in sales for their entire career.[17]

Employment opportunities in sales occupations are found in a wide variety of organizations, including insurance agencies, retailers, and financial service firms (Figure C–3). In addition, many salespeople work as manufacturer's representatives for organizations that have selling responsibilities for several manufacturers.[18] Activities in sales jobs include *selling duties,* such as prospecting for customers, demonstrating the product, or quoting prices; *sales-support duties,* such as handling complaints and helping solve technical problems; and *nonselling duties,* such as preparing reports, attending sales meetings, and monitoring competitive activities. Salespeople who can deal with these

FIGURE C–3

Employment opportunities in selected sales occupations (1998 to 2008)

OCCUPATION	1998 EMPLOYMENT	2008 EMPLOYMENT	PERCENTAGE CHANGE 1998–2008	AVERAGE ANNUAL GROWTH
Insurance agents and brokers	387,000	395,500	2%	850
Retail sales workers	4,582,000	5,147,000	12	56,500
Securities and financial services sales workers	303,000	427,000	41	12,400
Real estate agents and brokers	347,000	381,000	10	3,400
Travel agents	138,000	163,000	18	2,500
Service sales representatives	841,000	1,270,000	51	42,900

SOURCE: "The 1998–2008 Job Outlook in Brief," *Occupational Outlook Quarterly* (Washington, DC: U.S. Dept. of Labor, Bureau of Labor Statistics, Spring 2000), p. 22.

varying activities are critical to a company's success. According to RJR Nabisco, their recruiting priority is "finding quality people who can analyze data from customers, see things from the consumer's eyes, use available sales tools like laptops and syndicated data, and interface with the marketing people at headquarters."[19]

One of the fastest areas of growth in sales is in the direct marketing industry. Interest in information technology, relationship marketing, and integrated marketing has increased the demand for contact with customers. For many firms this means new or additional telemarketing efforts; for other firms it means increasing the amount of time salespeople spend with clients; for still others it means sophisticated e-mail marketing. "E-mail is the most valuable channel companies have to be interactive with their customers," says Gina Lambright, vice president for client services at marketing consulting firm Quris in San Francisco. At Dell Computer, the company recently selected by *Sales and Marketing Management* magazine for its Best E-Business Strategy award, online communication allows salespeople to concentrate on "value-added functions," and "the ultimate direct relationship with no intermediary."[20]

Marketing Research

Marketing researchers play important roles in many organizations today. They are responsible for obtaining, analyzing, and interpreting data to facilitate making marketing decisions. This means marketing researchers are basically problem solvers. Success in the area requires not only an understanding of statistics, computers, and the Internet, but also a broad base of marketing knowledge[21] and an ability to communicate with management. Individuals who are inquisitive, methodical, analytical, and solution oriented find the field particularly rewarding.

The responsibilities of the men and women currently working in the market research industry include defining the marketing problem, designing the questions, selecting the sample, collecting and analyzing the data, and, finally, reporting the results of the research. These jobs are available in three kinds of organizations. *Marketing research consulting firms* contract with large companies to provide research about their products or services.[22] *Advertising agencies* may provide research services to help clients with questions related to advertising and promotional problems. Finally, some companies have an *in-house research staff* to design and execute their research projects. Online marketing research is rapidly requiring understanding of new tools such as dynamic scripting, response validation, intercept sampling, and online consumer panels.[23]

Although marketing researchers may start as assistants performing routine tasks, they quickly advance to broader responsibilities. Survey design, interviewing, report writing, and all aspects of the research process create a challenging career. In addition, research projects typically deal with such diverse problems as consumer motivation, pricing, forecasting, and competition. The marketing research field has experienced a shortage of qualified candidates in recent years. Successful candidates, however, "like what they're doing and get excited over their work, whether it be listening to a focus group or running a complex datamining model," according to Carolyn Marconi, director of marketing research for the Vanguard Group, Inc.[24]

International Careers

Many of the careers just described can be found in international settings—in multinational U.S. corporations, small- to medium-size firms with export business, and franchises. The international public relations firm Burson-Marstellar, for example, has offices in New York, Sydney, Copenhagen, and Bangkok. Similarly, franchises such as Blockbuster Entertainment are expanding in many other markets outside of the United States. The changes in the European Union and among Asian countries may provide other opportunities. Variations of the permanent international career are also possible—for example, some companies may alternate periods of work at "headquarters" with "field" assignments in foreign countries.[25] Finally, a domestic international career—working for a foreign-owned company with an office in the United States—may be appealing.[26]

Applicants for international positions should first develop a skill that can be applied in an international setting. In addition, however, internationally competent employees will need language and cultural skills. A Conference Board description illustrates the point:

> The successful managers of the future will probably be those who speak both Japanese and English, who have a strong base in Brussels and contacts in the Pacific Rim, and who know the cafes and bars of Singapore.

Further, in many organizations, international experience has become a necessity for promotion and career advancement. "If you are going to succeed, an expatriate assignment is essential," says Eric Kraus of Gillette Co. in Boston. Of Gillette's top 20 executives, 19 have international experience.[27]

THE JOB SEARCH PROCESS

Activities you should consider during your job search process include assessing yourself, identifying job opportunities, preparing your résumé and related correspondence, and going on job interviews.

Assessing Yourself

You must know your product—you—so that you can market yourself effectively to prospective employers. Consequently, a critical first step in your job search is conducting a self-analysis, which involves critically examining yourself on the following dimensions: interests, abilities, education, experience, personality, desired job environment, and personal goals.[28] The importance of performing this assessment was stressed by a management consultant:[29]

> Many graduates enter the world of work without even understanding the fact that they are specific somebodies, much less knowing the kinds of competencies and motivations with which they have been endowed. . . . The tragedy of not knowing is awesome. Ignorant of who they are, most graduates are doomed to spend too much of their lives in work for which they are poorly suited. . . . Self-knowledge is critical to effectively managing your career.

Asking Key Questions   A self-analysis, in part, entails asking yourself some very important and difficult questions (Figure C–4). It is critical that you respond to the questions honestly, because your answers ultimately will be used as a guide in your job selection.[30] A less-than-candid appraisal of yourself might result in a job mismatch.

Identifying Strengths and Weaknesses   After you have addressed the questions posed in Figure C–4, you are ready to identify your strengths and weaknesses. To do so, draw a vertical line down the middle of a sheet of paper and label one side of the paper "strengths" and the other side "weaknesses." Based on your answers to the questions, record your strong and weak points in their respective column. Ideally this cataloging should be done over a few days to give you adequate time to reflect on your attributes. In addition, you might seek input from others who know you well (such as parents, close relatives, friends, professors, or employers) and can offer more objective views. They might even evaluate you on the questions in Figure C–4, and you can compare the results with your own evaluation. A hypothetical list of strengths and weaknesses is shown in Figure C–5.

What skills are most important? The answer, of course, varies by occupation and employer. Recent studies, however, suggest that problem-solving skills, communication skills, interpersonal skills, analytical and computer skills, and leadership skills

INTERESTS

How do I like to spend my time?
Do I enjoy working with people?
Do I like working with mechanical things?
Do I enjoy working with data?
Am I a member of many organizations?
Do I enjoy physical activities?
Do I like to read?

ABILITIES

Am I adept at analysis?
Am I adept at working with computers?
Do I have good verbal and written communication skills?
What special talents do I have?
At which abilities do I wish I were more adept?

EDUCATION

How have my courses and extracurricular activities
    prepared me for a specific job?
Which were my best subjects? My worst?
Is my GPA a good indication of my academic ability?
    Why?
Do I aspire to a graduate degree? Before beginning my
    job?
Why did I choose my major?

PERSONAL GOALS

What are my short-term and long-term goals? Why?
Am I career oriented, or do I have broader interests?
What are my career goals?
What jobs are likely to help me achieve my goals?
What do I hope to be doing in 5 years? In 10 years?
What do I want out of life?

PERSONALITY

What are my good and bad traits?
Am I competitive?
Do I work well with others?
Am I outspoken?
Am I a leader or a follower?
Do I work well under pressure?
Do I work quickly, or am I methodical?
Do I get along well with others?
Am I ambitious?
Do I work well independently of others?

DESIRED JOB ENVIRONMENT

Am I willing to relocate? Why?
Do I have a geographical preference? Why?
Would I mind traveling in my job?
Do I have to work for a large or nationally known firm to be
    satisfied?
Must my job offer rapid promotion opportunities?
If I could design my own job, what characteristics would it
    have?
How important is high initial salary to me?

EXPERIENCE

What previous jobs have I held? What were my responsi-
    bilities in each job?
What internships or co-op positions have I held? What
    were my responsibilities?
What volunteer positions have I held? What were my
    responsibilities?
Were any of my jobs or positions applicable to positions
    I may be seeking? How?
What did I like the most about my previous jobs? Like the
    least?
If I had it to do over again, would I work in these jobs?
    Why?

FIGURE C–4
Questions to ask in your self-analysis

are all valued by employers. Personal characteristics employers seek in a job candidate include honesty, integrity, motivation, initiative, self-confidence, flexibility, and enthusiasm. Finally, most employers also look for work experience, internship experience, or co-op experience.[31]

Taking Job-Related Tests   Personality and vocational interest tests, provided by many colleges and universities, can give you other ideas about yourself. After tests have been administered and scored, test takers meet with testing service counselors to discuss the results. Test results generally suggest jobs for which students have an inclination. The most common tests at the college level are the Strong Interest Inventory and the Campbell Interest and Skill Survey. Some counseling centers also administer the Myers-Briggs Type Indicator—a personality measure that helps identify professions you may enjoy.[32] If you have not already done so, you may wish to see whether your school offers such testing services.

Identifying Your Job Opportunities

To identify and analyze the job market, you must conduct some marketing research to determine what industries *and* companies offer promising job opportunities that relate to the results of your self-analysis. Several sources that can help in your search are discussed next.

FIGURE C-5
Hypothetical list of job candidate's strengths and weaknesses

STRENGTHS	WEAKNESSES
Enjoy being with people	Am not adept at working with computers
Am an avid reader	Have minimal work experience
Have good communication skills	Have a mediocre GPA
Am involved in many extracurricular activities	Am sometimes impatient
Work well with others	Resent close supervision
Work well independently	Work methodically (slowly)
Am honest and dependable	Will not relocate
Am willing to travel in the job	Anger easily sometimes
Am a good problem solver	Lack of customer orientation
Have a good sense of humor	Poor technical skills
Am a self-starter, have drive	

Career Services Office   Your career services office is an excellent source of job information. Personnel in that office can (1) inform you about which companies will be recruiting on campus, (2) alert you to unexpected job openings, (3) advise you about short-term and long-term career prospects, (4) offer advice on résumé construction, (5) assess your interviewing strengths and weaknesses, and (6) help you evaluate a job offer. In addition, the office usually contains a variety of written materials focusing on different industries and companies and tips on job hunting. One major publication available in most career services offices is the National Association of Colleges and Employers publication *Job Choices,* which contains a list of employers, kinds of job openings for college graduates, and whom to contact about jobs in those firms. Another publication for students is *jobpostings,* which is published seven times during the academic year.

Online Career and Employment Services   Many companies no longer make frequent on-campus visits. Instead, they may use the many online services available to advertise an employment opportunity or to search for candidate information. The National Association of Colleges and Employers, for example, maintains a site on the World Wide Web called JobWeb (www.jobweb.org). Similarly, monster.com and headhunter.net are online databases of employment ads, candidate resumes, and other career-related information. Some of the information resources include career guidance, a cover letter library, occupational profiles, and résumé templates.[33] Employers may contact students directly when the candidate's qualifications meet their specific job requirements. The advantage of this system for students is that regardless of the size or location of the campus they are attending, many companies have access to their résumé. Some job boards even allow applicants to post audio and video clips of themselves. One advantage for recruiters is that some of the job boards utilize software for performing background verification.[34] Your school's career center may also have a "home page" that offers online job search information and links to other World Wide Web sites.

Library   The public or college library can provide you with reference material that, among other things, describes successful firms and their operations, defines the content of various jobs, and forecasts job opportunities. For example, *Fortune* publishes a list of the 1,000 largest U.S. and global companies and their respective sales and profits; Dun & Bradstreet publishes directories of all companies in the United States with a net worth of at least $500,000. *Careers in Marketing,* a publication of the American Marketing Association, presents career opportunities in marketing. The *Occupational Outlook Handbook* is an annual publication of the U.S. Department of

Labor that provides projections for specific job prospects, as well as information pertaining to those jobs. A librarian can indicate reference materials that will be most pertinent to *your* job search.

Advertisements   Help-wanted advertisements provide an overview of what is happening in the job market. Local (particularly Sunday editions) and college newspapers, trade press (such as *Marketing News* or *Advertising Age*), and business magazines (such as *Sales and Marketing Management*) contain classified advertisement sections that generally have job opening announcements, often for entry-level positions. Reviewing the want ads can help you identify what kinds of positions are available and their requirements and job titles, which firms offer certain kinds of jobs, and levels of compensation.

Employment Agencies   An employment agency can make you aware of several job opportunities very quickly because of its large number of job listings available through computer databases. Many agencies specialize in a particular field (such as sales and marketing). The advantages of using an agency include that it (1) reduces the cost of a job search by bringing applicants and employers together, (2) often has exclusive job listings available only by working through the agency, (3) performs much of the job search for you, and (4) tries to find a job that is compatible with your qualifications and interests.[35] In the past some employment agencies have engaged in questionable business practices, so check with the Better Business Bureau or your business contacts to determine the quality of the various agencies.

Personal Contacts and Networking   An important source of job information that students often overlook is their personal contacts. People you know often may know of job opportunities, so you should advise them that you're looking for a job. Relatives and friends might aid your job search. Instructors you know well and business contacts can provide a wealth of information about potential jobs and even help arrange an interview with a prospective employer. They may also help arrange "informational interviews" with employers who do not have immediate openings. These interviews allow you to collect information about an industry or an employer and give you an advantage if a position does become available. It is a good idea to leave your résumé with all your personal contacts so they can pass it along to those who might be in need of your services. Student organizations (such as the student chapter of the American Marketing Association and Pi Sigma Epsilon, the professional sales fraternity) may be sources of job opportunities, particularly if they are involved with the business community. Local chapters of professional business organizations (such as the American Marketing Association and Sales and Marketing Executives International) also can provide job information; contacting their chapter president is a first step in seeking assistance from these organizations. In the past decade, small employers have provided the greatest growth in employment, and their most common source of new employees is through personal referrals.[36] Creating a network of professional contacts is one of the most important career planning activities you can undertake.[37]

State Employment Office   State employment offices have listings of job opportunities in their state and counselors to help arrange a job interview for you. Although state employment offices perform functions similar to employment agencies, they differ in listing only job opportunities in their state and providing their services free.

Direct Contact   Another means of obtaining job information is direct contact—personally communicating to prospective employers (either by mail, e-mail, or in person) that you would be interested in pursuing job opportunities with them. Often you may not even know whether jobs are available in these firms. If you correspond with the companies in writing, a letter of introduction and an attached résumé should serve as your initial form of communication. Your major goal in direct contact is ultimately to arrange a job interview.

Writing Your Résumé

A résumé is a document that communicates to prospective employers who you are. An employer reading a résumé focuses on two key questions: (1) What is the candidate like? and (2) What can the candidate do for me?[38] It is imperative that you design a résumé that addresses these two questions and presents you in a favorable light. Personnel in your career services office can provide assistance in designing résumés.

The Résumé Itself

A well-constructed résumé generally contains up to nine major sections: (1) identification (name, address, and telephone number), (2) job or career objective, (3) educational background, (4) extracurricular activities, (5) work experience or history, (6) skills or capabilities (that pertain to a particular kind of job for which you may be interviewing), (7) accomplishments or achievements, (8) personal interests, and (9) personal references.[39] There is no universally accepted format for a résumé, but three are more frequently used: chronological, functional, and targeted. A *chronological* format presents your work experience and education according to the time sequence in which they occurred (i.e., in chronological order). If you have had several jobs or attended several schools, this approach is useful to highlight what you have done. With a *functional* format, you group your experience into skill categories that emphasize your strengths. This option is particularly appropriate if you have no experience or only minimal experience related to your chosen field. A *targeted* format focuses on the capabilities you have for a specific job. This alternative is desirable if you know what job you want and are qualified for it.[40] In any of the formats, if possible, you should include quantitative information about your accomplishments and experience, such as "increased sales revenue by 20 percent" for the year you managed a retail clothing store. A résumé that illustrates the chronological format is shown in Figure C–6.[41]

Technology is creating a need for a new type of résumé—the electronic résumé. Although traditional versions of résumés may be visually appealing, today most career experts suggest that résumés accommodate delivery through mail, e-mail, and fax machines. In addition, résumés must accommodate employers who use scanning technology to enter résumés into their own databases or who search commercial online databases. To fully utilize online opportunities, an electronic résumé with a popular font (e.g., Times Roman), and relatively large font size (e.g., 10–14 pt.)—and without italic text, graphics, shading, underlining, or vertical lines—must be available. In addition, because online recruiting starts with a key word search, it is important to include key words, focus on nouns rather than verbs, and avoid abbreviations.[42]

Letter Accompanying a Résumé

The letter accompanying a résumé, or cover letter, serves as the job candidate's introduction. As a result, it must gain the attention and interest of the reader or it will fail to give the incentive to examine the résumé carefully. In designing a letter to accompany your résumé, address the following issues:[43]

- Address the letter to a specific person.
- Identify the position for which you are applying and how you heard of it.
- Indicate why you are applying for the position.
- Summarize your most significant credentials and qualifications.
- Refer the reader to the enclosed résumé.
- Request a personal interview, and advise the reader when and where you can be reached.

FIGURE C–6
Chronological résumé

SALLY WINTER

Campus address (until 6/1/2002):   Home address:
Elm Street Apartments #2B   123 Front Street
College Town, Ohio 44042   Teaneck, NJ 07666
Phone: (614) 424-1648   Phone: (201) 836-4995
swinter@osu.stu.edu

Education
B.S. in Business Administration, Ohio State University, 2002, cum laude—3.3 overall
GPA—3.6 GPA in major

Work Experience
Paid for 70 percent of my college expenses through the following part-time and summer
jobs:

Legal Secretary, Smith, Lee & Jones, Attorneys at Law, New York, NY—summer 2000
  • Took dictation and transcribed tapes of legal proceedings
  • Typed contracts and other legal documents
  • Reorganized client files for easier access
  • Answered the phone and screened calls for the partners

Salesclerk, College Varsity Shop, College Town, Ohio—1999–2001 academic years
  • Helped customers with buying decisions
  • Arranged stock and helped with window displays
  • Assisted in year-end inventories
  • Took over responsibilities of store manager when she was on vacation or ill

Assistant Manager, Treasure Place Gift Shop, Teaneck, NJ—summers and Christmas
vacations—1998–2001
  • Supervised two salesclerks
  • Helped select merchandise at trade shows
  • Handled daily accounting
  • Worked comfortably under pressure during busy seasons

Campus Activities
  • Elected captain of the women's varsity tennis team for two years
  • Worked as a reporter and night editor on campus newspaper for two years
  • Elected historian for Mortar Board chapter, a senior women's honorary society

Computer Skills
  • Word, Excel, Microsoft Publisher

Personal Interests
  • Collecting antique clocks, listening to jazz, swimming

References Available on Request

A sample letter comprising these six factors is presented in Figure C–7. Some students have tried creative approaches to making their letter stand out—sending a gift
with their letter or using creative packaging, for example. Although these tactics may
gain a recruiter's attention, most hiring managers say that a frivolous approach makes
for a frivolous employee. As a general rule, nothing works better than an impressive cover letter and good academic credentials.[44]

Interviewing for Your Job

The job interview is a conversation between a prospective employer and a job candidate that focuses on determining whether the employer's needs can be satisfied by
the candidate's qualifications. The interview is a "make or break" situation: If the

FIGURE C–7
Sample letter accompanying a résumé

Sally Winter
Elm Street Apartments, #2B
College Town, Ohio 44042
January 31, 2002

Mr. J. B. Jones
Sales Manager
Hilltop Manufacturing Company
Minneapolis, MN 55406

Dear Mr. Jones:

Dr. William Johnson, Professor of Business Administration at the Ohio State University, recently suggested that I write to you concerning your opening and my interest in a sales position. With a B.S. degree in business administration and courses in personal selling and sales management, I am confident that I could make a positive contribution to your firm.

During the past four years I have been a salesclerk in a clothing store and an assistant manager in a gift shop. These two positions required my performing a variety of duties including selling, purchasing, stocking, and supervising. As a result, I have developed an appreciation for the viewpoints of the customer, salesperson, and management. Given my background and high energy level, I feel that I am particularly well qualified to assume a sales position in your company.

My enclosed résumé better highlights my education and experience. My extracurricular activities should strengthen and support my abilities to serve as a sales representative.

I am eager to talk with you because I feel I can demonstrate to you why I am a strong candidate for the position. I have friends in Minneapolis with whom I could stay on weekends, so Fridays or Mondays would be ideal for an appointment. I will call you in a week to see if we can arrange a mutually convenient time for a meeting. I am hopeful that your schedule will allow this.

Thank you for your kind consideration. If you would like some additional information, please feel free to contact me at (614) 424-1648. I look forward to talking with you.

Sincerely,

Sally Winter

enclosure

interview goes well, you have increased your chances of receiving a job offer; if it goes poorly, you probably will be eliminated from further consideration.

Preparing for a Job Interview   To be successful in a job interview, you must prepare for it so you can exhibit professionalism and indicate to a prospective employer that you are serious about the job. When preparing for the interview, several critical activities need to be performed.

Before the interview, gather facts about the industry, the prospective employer, and the job. Relevant information might include the general description for the occupation; the firm's products or services; the firm's size, number of employees, and financial and competitive position; the requirements of the position; and the name and personality of the interviewer.[45] Obtaining this information will provide you with additional insight into the firm and help you formulate questions to ask the interviewer. This information might be gleaned, for example, from corporate annual reports, *The*

Wall Street Journal, Moody's manuals, Standard & Poor's *Register of Corporations, Directors, and Executives, The Directory of Corporate Affiliations,* selected issues of *Business Week,* or trade publications. If information is not readily available, you could call the company and indicate that you wish to obtain some information about the firm before your interview.

Preparation for the job interview should also involve role playing, or pretending that you are in the "hot seat" being interviewed. Before role playing, anticipate questions interviewers may pose and how you might address them (Figure C–8). Do not memorize your answers, though, because you want to appear spontaneous, yet logical and intelligent. Nonetheless, it is helpful to practice how you might respond to the questions. You should also anticipate a substance abuse screening process—now common among a wide variety of organizations.[46] In addition, develop questions you might ask the interviewer that are important and of concern to you (Figure C–9). "It's an opportunity to show the recruiter how smart you are," comments one recruiter.[47]

When role playing, you and someone with whom you feel comfortable should engage in a mock interview. Afterward, ask the stand-in interviewer to candidly appraise your interview content and style. You may wish to videotape the mock interview; ask the personnel in your career services office where videotaping equipment can be obtained for this purpose.

Before the job interview you should attend to several details. Know the exact time and place of the interview; write them down—do not rely on your memory. Get the full company name straight. Find out what the interviewer's name is and how to pronounce it. Bring a notepad and pen along on the interview, in case you need to record anything. Make certain that your appearance is clean, neat, professional, and conservative. And be punctual; arriving tardy to a job interview gives you an appearance of being unreliable.

Succeeding in Your Job Interview   You have done your homework, and at last the moment arrives and it is time for the interview. Although you may experience some apprehension, view the interview as a conversation between the prospective employer and you. Both of you are in the interview to look over the other party, to see whether there might be a good match. You know your subject matter (you); furthermore, because you did not have a job with the firm when you walked into the interview, you really have nothing to lose if you don't get it—so relax.[48]

When you meet the interviewer, greet him or her by name, be cheerful, smile, and maintain good eye contact. Take your lead from the interviewer at the outset. Sit down after the interviewer has offered you a seat. Sit up straight in your chair, and look alert and interested at all times. Appear relaxed, not tense. Be enthusiastic.

FIGURE C–8
Questions frequently asked by interviewers

FIGURE C–8
Questions frequently asked by interviewers

INTERVIEWER QUESTIONS

1. What are your long-range and short-range goals?
2. What do you consider to be your greatest strengths and weaknesses?
3. Describe your most rewarding college experiences.
4. What do you see yourself doing in 5 years? In 10 years?
5. Are you a leader? Explain.
6. What do you really want out of life?
7. How would you describe yourself?
8. Why did you choose your college major?
9. In which extracurricular activities did you participate? Why?
10. What jobs have you enjoyed the most? The least? Why?
11. How has your previous work experience prepared you for a marketing career?
12. Why do you want to work for our company?
13. What qualifications do you think a person needs to be successful in a company like ours?
14. What do you know about our company?
15. What criteria are you using to evaluate the company for which you hope to work?
16. In what kind of city would you prefer to live?
17. What can I tell you about our company?
18. Are you willing to relocate?
19. Are you willing to spend at least six months as a trainee?
20. Why should we hire you?

During the interview, be yourself. If you try to behave in a manner that is different from the "real" you, your attempt may be transparent to the interviewer or you may ultimately get the job but discover that you aren't suited for it. In addition to assessing how well your skills match those of the job, the interviewer will probably try to assess your long-term interest in the firm. William Kucker, a recruiter for General Electric, explains, "We're looking for people to make a commitment."[49]

FIGURE C–9
Questions frequently asked by interviewees

INTERVIEWEE QUESTIONS

1. Why would a job candidate want to work for your firm?
2. What makes your firm different from its competitors?
3. What is the company's promotion policy?
4. Describe the typical first-year assignment for this job.
5. How is an employee evaluated?
6. What are the opportunities for personal growth?
7. Do you have a training program?
8. What are the company's plans for future growth?
9. What is the retention rate of people in the position for which I am interviewing?
10. How can you use my skills?
11. Does the company have development programs?
12. What kind of image does the firm have in the community?
13. Why do you enjoy working for your firm?
14. How much responsibility would I have in this job?
15. What is the corporate culture in your firm?

As the interview comes to a close, leave it on a positive note. Thank the interviewer for his or her time and the opportunity to discuss employment opportunities. If you are still interested in the job, express this to the interviewer. The interviewer will normally tell you what the employer's next step is. Rarely will a job offer be made at the end of the initial interview. If it is and you want the job, accept the offer; if there is any doubt in your mind about the job, however, ask for time to consider the offer.

Following Up on Your Job Interview

After your interview, send a thank-you note to the interviewer and indicate whether you are still interested in the job. If you want to continue pursuing the job, "polite persistence" may help you get it. According to one expert, "Many job hunters make the mistake of thinking that their career fate is totally in the hands of the interviewer once the job interview is finished."[50] You *can* have an impact on the interviewer *after* the interview is over.

The thank-you note is a gesture of appreciation and a way of maintaining visibility with the interviewer. (Remember the adage, "Out of sight, out of mind.") Even if the interview did not go well, the thank-you note may impress the interviewer so much that his or her opinion of you changes. After you have sent your thank-you note, you may wish to call the prospective employer to determine the status of the hiring decision. If the interviewer told you when you would hear from the employer, make your telephone call *after* this date (assuming, of course, that you have not yet heard from the employer); if the interviewer did not tell you when you would be contacted, make your telephone call a week or so after you have sent your thank-you note.

As you conduct your follow-up, be persistent but polite. If you are too eager, one of two things could happen to prevent you from getting the job: the employer might feel that you are a nuisance and would exhibit such behavior on the job, or the employer may perceive that you are desperate for the job and thus are not a viable candidate.

Handling Rejection

You have put your best efforts into your job search. You developed a well-designed résumé and prepared carefully for the job interview. Even the interview appears to have gone well. Nevertheless, a prospective employer may send you a rejection letter. ("We are sorry that our needs and your superb qualification don't match.") Although you will probably be disappointed, not all interviews lead to a job offer because there normally are more candidates than there are positions available.

If you receive a rejection letter, you should think back through the interview. What appeared to go right? What went wrong? Perhaps personnel from your career services office can shed light on the problem, particularly if they are in the custom of having interviewers rate each interviewee. Try to learn lessons to apply in future interviews. Keep interviewing and gaining interview experience; your persistence will eventually pay off.

SELECTED SOURCES OF MARKETING CAREER INFORMATION

The following is a selected list of marketing information sources that you should find useful during your academic studies and professional career.

BUSINESS AND MARKETING PUBLICATIONS

Peter D. Bennett, ed., *Dictionary of Marketing Terms,* 3rd ed. (Lincolnwood, IL: NTC Publishing Group, 1998). This dictionary contains definitions of more than 3,000 marketing terms.

Patrick Butler, *Business Research Sources: A Reference Navigator* (New York: McGraw-Hill, 1999). This book is designed as a resource book to help students engage in business research. As a guidebook for students, the book answers three questions—what to look for, where to find the information, how to use the information.

Business Periodicals Index (BPI) (New York: H. W. Wilson Company). This is a monthly (except August) index of almost 400 periodicals from all fields of business and marketing.

Encyclopedia of Business Information Sources, 13th ed. (Detroit, MI: Gale Research, 1999). A bibliographic guide to over 21,000 citations covering more than 1,100 primary subjects of interest to business personnel.

Arlene Fink and Jacqueline B. Kosecoff, *How to Conduct Surveys: A Step-by-Step Guide,* 2nd ed. (Thousand Oaks, CA: Sage Publications, 1998). A simple guide to understand how to develop surveys, compare the uses and costs of different survey methods (paper, telephone, Internet, personal interview), analyze the data obtained from surveys, and present the survey results.

Joshua Grossnickle and Oliver Raskin, *Handbook of On-line Marketing Research* (New York: McGraw-Hill, 2001). This handbook describes techniques which take advantage of the Web's unique data-gathering characteristics, in a style that requires little prior knowledge on the part of the reader.

Jeffrey Heilbrunn, ed., *Marketing Encyclopedia* (Lincolnwood, IL: NTC Business Books, 1995). This book provides a collection of essays by professional and academic marketing experts on issues and trends shaping the future of marketing.

Larry Kahaner, *Competitive Intelligence: How to Gather, Analyze, and Use Information to Move Your Business to the Top* (New York: Simon & Schuster, 1998). This book takes readers beyond the information age and into the age of intelligence, explaining how to turn the raw facts, statistics, and numbers about competitors' activities and market trends into practical guidelines for making the right business decisions.

Barbara Lewis and Dale Littler, eds., *The Blackwell Encyclopedic Dictionary of Marketing* (Cambridge, MA: Blackwell Publishers, 1999). Part of the 10-volume *Blackwell Encyclopedia of Management,* this book provides clear, concise, up-to-the-minute, and highly informative definitions and explanations of the key concepts and terms in marketing management, consumer behavior, segmentation, organizational marketing, pricing, communications, retailing and distribution, product management, market research, and international marketing.

Jerry M. Rosenberg, *Dictionary of Marketing and Advertising* (New York: Wiley, 1995). This dictionary contains more than 5,500 concise definitions of marketing and advertising terms.

Jean L. Sears and Marilyn K. Moody, *Using Government Information Sources,* 3rd ed. (Phoenix, AZ: Oryx Press, 2001). An easy-to-use manual arranged by topics such as consumer expenditures, business and industry statistics, economic indicators, and projections. Each chapter contains a search strategy, a checklist of courses, and a narrative description of the sources.

Garrett Wasny, *World Business Resources.com* (New York: McGraw-Hill, 2000). A directory of over 8,000 international business, economic, and demographic resources online. Organized by topic and by region, this guide also offers more than 200 tips to speed up Internet searches.

CAREER PLANNING PUBLICATIONS

Richard N. Bolles, *The 2001 What Color Is Your Parachute? A Practical Manual for Job-Hunters and Career-Changers* (Berkeley, CA: Ten Speed Press, 2001). A companion workbook is also available. See www.jobhuntersbible.com.

Dennis V. Damp and Samuel Concialdi, *The Book of U.S. Government Jobs: Where They Are, What's Available, and How to Get One,* 7th ed. (Moon Township, PA: Bookhaven Press, 2000).

Jack Evans and Barry Berman, *Careers in Marketing,* 2nd ed. (Englewood Cliffs, NJ: Prentice Hall, 1995).

J. Michael Farr and LaVerne L. Ludden, *Best Jobs for the 21st Century for College Graduates* (Indianapolis: JIST Publishing, 2000). See www.jist.com.

Donna Fisher and Sandy Vilas, *Power Networking: 59 Secrets for Personal and Professional Success,* 2nd ed. (Austin, TX: Bard Press, 2000).

Katherine Hansen, *A Foot in the Door: Networking Your Way into the Hidden Job Market* (Berkeley, CA: Ten Speed Press, 2000).

Harvard Business School Career Guide for Marketing—2001 (Cambridge, MA: President and Fellows of Harvard College, 2001). See www.hbsp.harvard.edu/products/press/hbs_careerguides.html.

Fred E. Jardt and Mary B. Nemnich, *Cyberspace Resume Kit: How to Make and Launch a Snazzy Online Resume* (Indianapolis, IN: JIST Works, 2001). See www.jist.com.

Stephanie Lowell, *The Harvard Business School Guide to Careers in the Nonprofit Sector* (Cambridge, MA: President and Fellows of Harvard College, 2000). See www.hbsp.harvard.edu/products/press/hbs_careerguides.html.

Nancy Mueller, *Work Worldwide: International Career Strategies for the Adventurous Job Seeker* (Emeryville, CA: Avalon Travel Publishing, 2000).

The National Job Bank, 17th ed. (Avon, MA: Adams Media Corporation, 2001). See www.adamsmedia.com.

Anne Wolfinger, *The Quick Internet Guide to Career and Education Information* (Indianapolis, IN: JIST Works, 2000). See www.jist.com.

Martin Yate, *Knock 'Em Dead 2001 Edition; Cover Letters That Knock 'Em Dead; and Résumés That Knock 'Em Dead* (Holbrook, MA: Adams Media Corporation, 2001). See www.adamsmedia.com.

Websites: Resources on job searches, résumé writing, interviewing, U.S. and international job postings, etc.

www.accesssalesjobs.com	www.headhunter.net
www.ajb.dni.us	www.hotjobs.com
www.careercity.com	www.monster.com
www.careerXroads.com	www.jobbankusa.com
www.careers.org	www.studentcentral.com
www.careerbuilder.com	www.vault.com
www.careers-in-marketing.com	www.wetfeet.com

SELECTED PERIODICALS

Ad Week, BPI Communications, Inc. (47 issues). See www.adweek.com. (subscription rate: $140)

Advertising Age, Crain Communications, Inc. (weekly). See www.adage.com. (subscription rate: $119)

American Demographics, PRIMEDIA Intertec (monthly). See www.inside.com. (subscription rate $69)

Barron's, Dow Jones & Co., Inc. (weekly). See www.barrons.com or www.dowjones.work.com. (subscription rates: $145 print; $59 online; $29 online for current print subscribers)

Brand Week, BPI Communications, Inc. (47 issues). See www.adweek.com. (subscription rate: $140)

Business 2.0, Business 2.0 Inc. (monthly). See www.business2.com. (subscription rate: $9.99)

Business Horizons, Indiana University c/o JAI Press, Inc. (bimonthly). See www.jaipress.com. (subscription rate: $96)

Business Marketing (w/Net Marketing), Crain Communications, Inc. (weekly). See www.businessmarketing.com. (subscription rate: $59)

Business Week, McGraw-Hill Companies (weekly). See www.businessweek.com. (subscription rate: $39.95)

Chain Store Age, Lebhar-Friedman, Inc. (monthly). See www.chainstoreage.com. (subscription rate: $105)

Direct Marketing, Hoke Communications, Inc. (monthly). (subscription rate: $60)

eCommerce Times, eMarketer.com (daily). See www.emarketer.com.

Fortune, Time, Inc. (weekly). See www.fortune.com. (subscription rate: $119.92)

Forbes, Forbes Inc. (bimonthly). See www.forbes.com. (subscription rates: call 800-888-9896)

Harvard Business Review, Harvard University (bimonthly). See www.hbsp.harvard.edu. (subscription rate: $118)

Industrial Marketing Management, Elsevier Science Publishing (bimonthly). See www.elsevier.com.

International Journal of Electronic Commerce, M. E. Sharpe Publishing (quarterly). See www.mesharpe.com. (subscription rate: $69)

Internet Marketing & Technology Report, Internet Marketing Resources (monthly). See www.intermarketing.com. (subscription rate: $377)

Journal of the Academy of Marketing Science, Sage Publications, Inc. (quarterly). See www.sagepub.com. (subscription rate: $85)

Journal of Advertising Research, Advertising Research Foundation (bi-monthly). See www.amic.com or www.arfsite.org. (subscription rate: $110)

Journal of Business and Industrial Marketing, MCB University Press (bi-monthly). See www.mcb.co.uk. (subscription rate: $629)

Journal of Consumer Marketing, MCB University Press (bimonthly). See www.mcb.co.uk. (subscription rate: $629)

Journal of Consumer Research, University of Chicago Press (quarterly). See www.journals.uchicago.edu. (subscription rate: nonmembers: $90; members: $45; students: $25)

Journal of Interactive Marketing, Direct Marketing Educational Foundation (quarterly). See www.the-dma.com. (subscription rate: $199)

Journal of Marketing, American Marketing Association (quarterly). See www.marketingpower.com. (subscription rate: nonmembers: $80; members: $45).

Journal of Marketing Education, University of Colorado (three times per year). Write to: University of Colorado, Graduate School of Business Administration, Campus Box 420, Boulder, CO 80309. (subscription rate: $33)

Journal of Marketing Research, American Marketing Association (quarterly). See www.marketingpower.com. (subscription rate: nonmembers: $80; members: $45)

Journal of Personal Selling & Sales Management, CTC Press (quarterly). See www.mkt.cba.cmich.edu/jpssm. (subscription rate: $60)

Journal of Public Policy and Marketing, American Marketing Association (semiannually). See www.marketingpower.com. (subscription rate: nonmembers: $70; members: $45)

Journal of Retailing, Institute of Retailing Management, JAI Press (quarterly). See www.jaipress.com. (subscription rate: $112)

Marketing Education Review, CTC Press (three times per year). See www.ctcpress.com. (subscription rate: $32)

Marketing Health Services, American Marketing Association (quarterly). See www.marketingpower.com. (subscription rate: nonmembers: $70; members: $45)

Marketing Management, American Marketing Association (quarterly). See www.marketingpower.com. (subscription rate: nonmembers: $70; members: $45)

Marketing News, American Marketing Association (biweekly). See www.marketingpower.com. (subscription rate: nonmembers: $75; members: $30)

Marketing Research, American Marketing Association (quarterly). See www.marketingpower.com. (subscription rate: nonmembers: $70; members: $45)

Media Week, BPI Communications, Inc. (47 Issues). See www.adweek.com. (subscription rate: $149)

Sales and Marketing Management, BPI Communications, Inc. (weekly). See www.salesandmarketing.com. (subscription rate: $48)

Stores, National Retail Federation (weekly). See www.nrf.com or www.stores.org. (subscription rate: $49)

The Wall Street Journal Interactive, Dow Jones & Company, Inc. (daily). See www.wsj.com. (subscription rates: $175 print; $59 online; student: $98 for both print and online)

PROFESSIONAL AND TRADE ASSOCIATIONS

Alliance for Environmental Innovation
6 N. Market Bldg., Fanueil Hall Marketplace
Boston, MA 02109
(617) 723-2996
www.environmentaldefense.org/alliance

American Association of Advertising Agencies
405 Lexington Ave.
New York, NY 10174-1801
(212) 682-2500
www.aaaa.org

American Advertising Federation
1101 Vermont Ave. NW., Suite 500
Washington, DC 20005
(202) 898-0089
www.aaf.org

American e-Commerce Association
2346 Camp St.
New Orleans, LA 70130
(504) 495-1748
www.aeaus.com

American Marketing Association
311 S. Wacker Dr., Suite 5800
Chicago, IL 60606
(800) AMA-1150
www.marketingpower.com

American Society of Transportation and Logistics
5100 Poplar Ave., Suite 522
Memphis, TN 38137
(901) 415-6800
www.astl.org

Association for Interactive Media
1430 Broadway, 8th Floor
New York, NY 10018
(888) 337-0008
www.imarketing.org

Bank Marketing Association
1120 Connecticut Ave. NW
Washington, DC 20036
(800) 433-9013
www.bmanet.org

Business Marketing Association
400 N. Michigan Ave., 15th Floor
Chicago, IL 60611
(800) 664-4BMA (4262)
www.marketing.org

Direct Marketing Association
 1120 Avenue of the Americas
 New York, NY 10036
 (212) 768-7277
 www.the-dma.org

Direct Selling Association
 1275 Pennsylvania Ave. NE, Suite 800
 Washington, DC 20004
 (202) 347-8866
 www.dsa.org

International Advertising Association
 521 Fifth Ave., Suite 1807
 New York, NY 10175
 (212) 557-1133
 www.iaaglobal.org

International Franchise Association
 1350 New York Ave. NE, Suite 900
 Washington, DC 20005
 (202) 628-8000
 www.franchise.org

International Mass Retail Association
 1700 North Moore St., Suite 2250
 Arlington, VA 22209
 (703) 841-2300
 www.imra.org

Marketing Research Association
 1344 Silas Deane Hwy., Suite 306
 Rocky Hill, CT 06067
 (860) 257-4008
 www.mra-net.org

Marketing Science Institute
 1000 Massachusetts Ave.
 Cambridge, MA 02138
 (617) 491-2060
 www.msi.org

National Association of Purchasing Management
 P.O. Box 22160
 Tempe, AZ 85285-2160
 (602) 752-6276
 www.napm.org

National Association of Wholesale Distributors
 1725 K St. NW
 Washington, DC 20006
 (202) 872-0885
 www.naw.org

National Mail Order Association
 2807 Polk St. NE
 Minneapolis, MN 55418
 (612) 788-1673
 www.nmoa.org

National Retail Federation
 325 7th St. NW, Suite 1100
 Washington, DC 20004-2802
 (202) 783-7971
 www.nrf.com

Product Development and Management Association
 17000 Commerce Parkway, Suite C
 Mount Laurel, NJ 08054
 (800) 232-5241
 www.pdma.org

Public Relations Society of America
 33 Irving Place, 3rd Fl.
 New York, NY 10003
 (212) 995-2230
 www.prsa.org

Sales and Marketing Executives International
 P.O. Box 1390
 Sumas, WA 98295-1390
 (312) 893-0751
 www.smei.org

Society for Marketing Professional Services
 99 Canal Center Plaza, Suite 250
 Alexandria, VA 22314
 (800) 292-7677
 www.smps.org

U.S. Internet Industry Association (USIIA)
 Box 212
 5810 Kingstown Center Dr., Suite 120
 Alexandria, VA 22315
 (703) 924-0006
 www.usiia.org

Women in Advertising and Marketing of
 Metropolitan Washington
 4200 Wisconsin Ave. NW, Suite 106-238
 Washington DC 20016
 (301) 369-7400
 www.wamdc.org

D

ALTERNATE CASES

CASE D–1 Burton Snowboards: Building a Sport

At the age of 23, Jack Burton Carpenter quit a well-paid financial position to pursue his passion for snowboarding. He founded Burton Snowboards with a $20,000 inheritance in Manchester, Vermont, in 1977.

Carpenter first became interested in snowboarding when he received a Snurfer for Christmas in the late 1960s. The Snurfer was essentially two skis bound together with a rope for steering. Although the Snurfer was never a commercial success, Carpenter never forgot the product and it became the basis for the Burton snowboard. The early years were rough. He sold fewer than 1,500 boards in his first three years in business. The big break came in 1983 when Vermont's Stratton Mountain became the first ski resort to allow snowboarding. Burton (he dropped the Carpenter to avoid confusion) sent employees out to more than 300 ski resorts to lobby to allow boarders on the hills. Burton Snowboarding has grown to be the leading snowboard maker with offices in Japan, Austria, as well as Vermont. Estimated 2000 sales were $200 million.

held in Nagano, Japan. In spite of growing acceptance, snowboarding still maintains a slightly edgy, rebel image.

THE INDUSTRY

Snowboarding is a wintertime sport that resembles surfing on a ski hill. The modern snowboard industry began around 20 years ago. Currently snowboarding is considered one of the hottest sports around. With an annual growth rate of 31 percent, snowboarding was the fastest-growing sport of the 62 sports and recreation activities surveyed in 2000 by the National Sporting Goods Association. There were over 4.3 million snowboarders in the United States in 2000. Much of snowboarding's popularity has seemingly come at the expense of alpine skiing which has dropped more than 30 percent in the past 10 years.

Snowboarding is achieving worldwide attention and acceptance. The International Olympic Committee and the International Ski Federation first accepted snowboarding as a medal sport in the 1998 Winter Olympics,

THE PARTICIPANTS

Snowboarders are primarily male and young. More than 71 percent of skiers are men. The average age is 25, although over 60 percent of snowboarders are under age 25. Skiers, in contrast, are older—with an average age of 40—and more affluent. Snowboarders have an average household income of $53,800 compared to $92,600 for skiers.

There are about 3.7 million people in the United States that fit the description of "snowboarders only" in contrast to 10.5 million that consider themselves "skiers only." However, there are about 14.2 million that participate in both snowboarding and skiing and the profile for this group shows characteristics intermediate to those described above—63 percent male and with an average age of 31.

THE COMPETITION

Barriers to entry are relatively low so new entrants can be expected. Industry giants such as Burton, Sims, and Nitro account for the bulk of the market but companies such as Adidas-Salomon, K2, and others have made significant investments in the industry as well and there are a number of smaller companies.

Burton is not only the pioneer but has also been the trendsetter for snowboarding. Burton has the product line with the greatest depth and breadth with racing, free riding, park and pipe boards. Burton's line appeals to novice as well as professional boarders. Prices range from $250 to $800. In addition to boards, Burton offers helmets (through its wholly owned subsidiary, Red), bags, bindings, and boots. Burton offers more than 4,200 products under its name, more in the Red and Backhill programs. For information on Burton's product line, visit www.burton.com.

THE ISSUES

Burton uses print advertisements in such magazines as *Snowboarder* and *Transworld SNOWboarding*. The ads are often tied in with reader service cards at the back of the magazine so that additional information can be requested. Burton also sponsors riders—a very important promotional tool and vital to the sport's success. These team members are often role models for young boarders and even well-known celebrity boarders couldn't survive financially without such sponsorship. Burton also sponsors snowboarding events such as the U.S. Open. Other promotional items include posters and stickers.

Snowboard design is constantly changing. Currently boards are becoming longer (for better landings), are trending toward unidirectional styles (rather than the blunt-nosed boards that can ride in both directions), and now have more side cuts and narrower stances than in the past.

Burton has been very loyal to the distributors that have helped build the business. While Burton tends to be distributed primarily in specialty shops, there may be increasing pressure to offer the boards at national chains and competitors may start to offer products at lower-price point outlets.

An increasing concern in the industry is safety. Although the number of participants worldwide has increased from 1 million to an estimated 12 million, the number of injuries has skyrocketed. Whereas the actual injury rates of four to six injuries per 1,000 snowboarding visits is comparable to alpine skiing, a bigger percentage of the injured are beginners—49 to 60 percent of snowboard injuries are beginners compared with 34 percent of skiing injuries occurring among beginners.[1]

Questions

1 What are the environmental forces influencing the snowboarding industry?

2 What are the differences in marketing goals for Burton Snowboarding in (*a*) its early years while developing the industry and (*b*) today with growing competition?

3 Identify the elements of the marketing mix for Burton currently. What marketing mix would you recommend for Burton given the changes occurring in the snowboarding marketplace?

4 How will the image of snowboarding be affected if more skiers or older participants take up the sport?

CASE D–2   Clearly Canadian: How Marketing Strategies Lead to Growth

Clearly Canadian Beverage Corporation CEO Douglas L. Mason has a good understanding of the importance of linking marketing and corporate strategies. As he explains, the company's success requires that "our energy and resources must be concentrated in the areas where we can produce the greatest value." Mason describes the company's goal as "finding more ways to bring Clearly Canadian products to more people." To accomplish this goal, Clearly Canadian's marketing efforts have focused on expanding current products, developing new innovative products, and meeting the needs of existing and new market segments.

THE COMPANY

Clearly Canadian Beverage Corporation started as small entrepreneurial venture in Vancouver, British Columbia, in the late 1980s. Its first product, Clearly Canadian

Sparkling Flavored Water, was a huge success with consumers and led to extraordinary growth of the company. Today, Clearly Canadian is a leading producer of premium alternative beverages, the fastest-growing category in the $11.7 billion alternative beverage industry. The company markets and distributes its portfolio of beverages throughout Canada, the United States, and numerous countries around the world. Maintaining its position in the marketplace, however, has been a challenge!

When Clearly Canadian entered the beverage market it wanted to capitalize on the consumer trend toward innovative, good-tasting beverages. It carved out a niche using premium pricing and distinctive packaging to create a very sophisticated image. Premium pricing helped position Clearly Canadian as a high-quality product, and distinctive packaging allowed the product to stand out on crowded retail shelves. The company also achieved widespread distribution for its product in Canada and the

United States, which was key to its early success. By 1992, Clearly Canadian was selling about 22 million cases of its beverage annually.

The following year, though, sales of Clearly Canadian dropped to 7 million cases. Experts observed that the beverage market had attracted many competitors. Although many of the new brands were positioned to compete directly in the premium-priced niche with Clearly Canadian, others were using low-price strategies to attract customers. In addition, consumers' tastes were changing as new beverage types, such as ready-to-drink iced tea, became available. Clearly Canadian found itself losing market share in the market it had helped create!

THE STRATEGIC MARKETING PROCESS

Mason knew that if the company was to grow it needed a plan. A situation analysis revealed several strengths, weaknesses, opportunities, and threats. The company's strengths, for example, included a strong brand name that had pioneered the product category, distinct packaging, and a premium image. Its weaknesses were that it had been satisfied with its early success—reacting to market changes rather than being proactive, and it had limited resources compared to some of its competitors. Clearly Canadian's primary opportunity was that unlike the soft-drink market, which was mature and dominated by a few brands, the alternative beverage market was growing and dynamic. Threats included competition from other sparkling waters, iced tea, natural sodas, and "juice blends," and aggressive price discounting by many of its competitors.

The next step in Clearly Canadian's marketing plan was to consider growth opportunities in terms of its current products and markets, and possible new products and markets. Six months of research, for example, led to a new package design for its flagship brand. After the product's introduction in the United States and Canada, it was launched in international markets including the United Kingdom, Germany, the Netherlands, Denmark, and Kuwait. To better serve the variety of interests of its existing customers, Clearly Canadian introduced Tré Limone, a lemon-ginger drink inspired by European café sodas, and Cascade Clear, a noncarbonated pure drinking water. New products designed to attract new market segments were also introduced. Orbitz, a fruit-flavored beverage with gel spheres was targeted at teenagers, while Clearly Canadian O+2, an oxygen-enhanced water, and Reebok Fitness Water, a water beverage with vitamins, minerals, and electrolytes, were targeted at active, health-conscious consumers.

Clearly Canadian designed its marketing programs to increase "consumer awareness and brand imagery" in each of the product-market combinations. National promotions, including joint sampling programs with 20th Century Fox, Warner-Lambert Co. (Trident Gum), and Speedo, and regional TV and radio campaigns were used to introduce products and to encourage consumers to try them. The marketing program for Reebok Fitness Water, for example, included sampling teams that drove vans to major sporting events, key grocery and retail outlets, and Reebok-sponsored events in initial launch markets including New York, Boston, St. Louis, Phoenix, Portland, and Seattle. The company also provided additional training for its salesforce and created stronger strategic partnerships with its distributors throughout the world.

Although not all of the product and market initiatives were a success—Orbitz has been withdrawn from the market—the result of Clearly Canadian's overall plan was dramatic, reestablishing the company as a leading producer of premium alternative beverages. In fact, BevNet.com picked Clearly Canadian Sparkling Water as its number 1 choice in the summer's Top Ten Hottest Beverages! John Craven, president of BevNET.com observes, "with literally hundreds of new age products making their way to the shelves each year, it's difficult to pick a few." Today's consumers are looking for beverages that provide a unique thirst-quenching experience and an image of health and style. Clearly Canadian believes it has a competitive advantage in its ability to identify and implement quick and effective changes to meet the changing demands of consumers.

THE FUTURE

Clearly Canadian has sold more than 1.5 billion bottles of its products since it started business. Now its efforts are focused on selling the next billion bottles. To achieve this goal, the company must continue to utilize the strategic marketing process to maintain its position in the marketplace. New challenges include the expansion of the alternative beverage market to include sports beverages, ready-to-drink coffee, energy drinks, and vegetable/fruit blends. In addition, huge competitors such as Coke and Pepsi now offer water and sports drinks, and brands such as Snapple, AriZona, and SoBe have created new-product attributes for consumers to consider. Finally, new potential uses of the company's limited resources—such as new products for restaurants and offices (e.g., larger sizes), new beverage types (e.g., coffee), and national advertising campaigns—

continue to present themselves. So as long as the marketing environment continues to change, Doug Mason and Clearly Canadian will be asking "Where are we now? Where do we want to go? and How do we get there?"[2]

Questions

1 Which phases and steps of the strategic marketing process does Clearly Canadian utilize to develop a plan that will lead to growth of the company?

2 Discuss the product-market strategies utilized by Clearly Canadian. Which of its actions represents market penetration? Product development? Market development? Diversification?

3 What recent changes in the marketing environment are likely to have an impact on Clearly Canadian? What new strategies would you recommend?

CASE D–3   Jamba Juice: Scanning the Marketing Environment

What were you doing in 10th grade? Waiting to get your driver's license? Kirk Perron was thinking about his future and putting together a deal that would help launch the successful Jamba Juice chain. It sounds incredible but Kirk Perron bought the real estate for his first juice bar when he was in 10th grade. He borrowed money from a high school counselor, the librarian, and his school bus driver to put together the $12,000 down payment.

THE COMPANY

Kirk Perron opened up his first operation as The Juice Club in 1990 in San Luis Obispo, California. He hit on the idea for a convenient, delicious, healthful food store on a long weekend bike ride. An avid cyclist with a lifelong interest in health and nutrition, he wanted to offer an alternative to typical fast-food fare. The idea was a hit and quickly spread. In 1995, the company changed its name from The Juice Club to Jamba Juice. Today Jamba Juice has more than 325 stores nationwide offering a wide variety of healthy drinks and snacks. Jamba Juice is considered the industry leader in the smoothie market and Perron predicts that one day Jamba Juice will be as big a brand as Coca-Cola.

THE IDEA

Jamba Juice is all about healthy food and fun. Jamba is from an African word that means "to celebrate." Walk into a Jamba Juice store and customers can choose from a wide variety of Jamba Juice specialties including smoothies, fresh squeezed fruit and vegetable

juices, soups, breads, and pretzels. Jamba's offerings are healthy—for example its soups contain "5-a-day" servings of vegetables in each cup and are low in fat and calories.

Smoothies are the bulk of the Jamba Juice's business. They are made with juice and fruit and often yogurt, sherbet, or ice milk. A typical smoothie gets most of its calories from carbohydrates and protein providing a low or no-fat, nutritious meal. Jamba smoothies and soups are designed to meet "heart healthy" FDA requirements. Nutritional supplements called "boosts" such as "energy juice boost," containing ginseng and gingko biloba, and "immunity juice boost," with echinacea and antioxidants, are available and can be added to soups or smoothies. Learn more about Jamba at www.jambajuice.com.

As you sit at the counter in a Jamba Juice, you can watch friendly, well-schooled Jamba Juice employees whip, beat, and blend your smoothie right before your eyes. Stores also feature nutrition centers where customers can get a complete nutritional breakdown for each product. Outlets also feature a merchandising area which has Jamba Juice juicers, mugs, hats, and T-shirts.

THE COMPETITION

Juice bars have been part of a growing trend. Barriers to entry are fairly low. Single-store outlets or small chains within a city or region are common although there has been increased consolidation. For example, Jamba acquired its largest competitor, Utah-based Zuka juice, in 1999. New Orleans–based Smoothie King has 270 locations in 20 states and is planning to expand in the Midwest. Atlanta-based Planet Smoothie has 125 stores in 25 states and continues to expand. Jamba has positioned itself as a replacement for typical fast-food fare. This means it also considers fast-food restaurants indirect competitors.

Jamba has had to fight to maintain its trademark in a competitive market. Several years ago a San Francisco Juice bar called Jamm'n Juice was forced to change its name after Jamba complained that Jamm'n Juice and its animated fruit and vegetables were too close to the Jamba trademark and logo.

THE MARKET

Juice bars have existed for decades, often in health-food stores and gyms and were associated with what was a small group of intensely health-conscious customers. That small demographic group boomed in recent years fueling the market for fat-free foods, fitness equipment, and apparel. There has also been an increasing level of health consciousness among society generally. However, "the consumer always talks thin and eats fat" according to Allan Hickock, an industry analyst with U.S. Bancorp Piper Jaffray.

However, Jamba Juice is optimistic about the opportunities for expanding the market by replacing fast food with good-for-you food. Retail sales of juice and smoothies are expected to reach $663 million in 2001 compared with $552 million in 2000. About two-thirds of Jamba's customers are between the ages of 15 and 25—not exactly the same demographic group as the traditional health-conscious baby boomer. Age and education level are important selection criteria for opening new Jamba Juice outlets. Kirk Perron believes that the more highly educated potential customers are, the more likely they will be to stop in for a nutritious smoothie. In fact, many of current and planned Jamba outlets are in college towns and partnerships have been formed to open outlets in universities and airports. You can find Jamba in both the Los Angeles and San Francisco airports and on campus at the University of North Carolina, George Washington University, and the Univer-

sity of Nevada–Las Vegas, among others. Jamba also has agreements with Barnes & Noble and Whole Foods Markets, two partners that share Jamba's values and commitment to healthy living.

THE ISSUES

Purists insist that the best drinks come from completely fresh produce. Fresh produce can be hard to work with to provide consistent-tasting drinks. Also, the price of fresh produce can change drastically throughout the year.

With fairly limited menus, juice bars are considered great as an add-on rather than a stand-alone retail establishment because they are usually not strong enough to draw customer traffic on their own. Personnel are important to the success of a juice bar—described as "bartenders" they have to be able to put on a good show for the customer.

There is a seasonality effect for smoothie and juice operators. For example, in northern climates, operators in enclosed downtown skyways or mall locations often see their business fall off in the summer when people are outdoors walking around. Business surges in the winter. In order to offer a more winter-friendly fare, Jamba also offers a selection of soups and breads.[3]

Questions

1 Conduct an environmental scan for Jamba Juice as it considers a new juice bar to open near your university. Identify factors that you think have an impact on the juice bar market, and indicate whether these factors would tend to enhance opportunities or represent threats.

2 Given your environmental analysis, which environmental force do you believe is most critical for Jamba Juice and why?

3 Examine the competitive environment for juice bars. Consider the likelihood of new entrants, barriers to entry, existing competitors, and substitutes. How would you summarize the current competitive environment?

4 Do you think that the juice bar phenomenon is a fad or rooted in some fundamental environmental and market forces? Why?

CASE D–4   Ford and Firestone: Who's to Blame?

Ford Motor Company and Firestone Tire and Rubber enjoyed one of the longest running relationships in American business, built upon the friendship and business relationship among the founders, Harvey Firestone and Henry Ford. From 1908 when Firestone first outfitted the Model T Ford until 2000, Firestone was the primary tire supplier to Ford. A well-publicized

falling out over the "blame" for the deaths and accidents occurring in Ford Explorer vehicles equipped with Firestone tires buried the relationship. Firestone blamed Ford and consumers, whereas Ford blamed Firestone. Both companies have damaged their credibility and reputation among consumers. What went wrong?

THE FORD EXPLORER

To understand how the entire situation unfolded, it is useful to focus on the development and launch of earlier Ford automobiles. The Ford Pinto was designed in the early 1960s under the leadership of then Ford president Lee Iaccoca under the "limits of 2,000." To compete in the lower-priced auto segment, Ford's goal was to design a subcompact that weighed under 2,000 pounds with a price tag under $2,000 and that could be brought to market in under two years instead of the usual four to five years.

Ford engineers placed the Pinto's gas tank in a location vulnerable to rear-end collisions to cut costs. A Ford cost/benefit analysis estimated it would cost $11 per car to move the gas tank to a less vulnerable position. Given that Ford expected to produce 12.5 million Pintos over the life of the model, Ford decided not to redesign the car and spend $137 million to move the gas tank. Using insurance company claim values at the time, Ford estimated that they would "save" about $50 million in insurance claims by relocating the gas tank, netting an $87 million loss. Hence, it was cheaper to leave the gas tank in its rear-end position. The decision proved fatal. Ultimately, the recall of the Pinto and related expenses cost Ford at least $1.5 billion.

The history of the Explorer really begins with the Ford Bronco. The design of the Bronco was the basis for the Explorer. A line of light trucks using the "twin I-beam" suspension was developed to lift up the vehicle to travel over rough terrain. However, this meant that the center of gravity was higher and the vehicle became more prone to stability problems and rollovers. By the late 1980s, Ford faced more than 800 lawsuits from rollovers of the Bronco II and Ranger—forerunners of the Explorer.

The market was looking for a rugged vehicle that was primarily image and less performance in the mid-1980s. Ford delivered with the development of the Explorer. Because automobile manufacturing had a four- to five-year lead time for a new model, decisions were made about the Explorer before all the consequences of the earlier decisions on the Bronco and Ranger were in. Among the early decisions made—use of the same "twin I-beam" suspension of the Bronco II and manufacturing on the same assembly line used for the Ranger. Internal company documents of tests on the Explorer prototype showed a number of problems with rollovers and a tendency to lift its wheels and tip during turns made at speeds up to 55 mph—even worse performance than the Bronco II. As early as 1987, there were calls from designers to make changes in the design of the vehicle that would improve stability and that would maintain passenger safety.

Consumer Reports came out with a scathing review of the Bronco II in June 1989. *Consumer Reports* advised consumers to "steer clear" of the product. At this point, the Explorer's design, modeled on the Bronco II, was frozen, parts were ordered, and facilities were readied for production for 1990 delivery.

Another important design decision was that of the tires for the Explorer. Both Goodyear and Firestone tires were selected for the Explorer. Examining various Firestone models, a Ford engineer reported that there was a good probability of passing the Consumer's Union testing for the Explorer with Firestone P225 tires, less confidence with the Firestone P235. Ford chose the P235. Ford's engineer, Roger Stornant, claimed that "management is aware of the potential risk with the P235 tires and has accepted that risk. The Consumer's Union test is generally unrepresentative of the real world and I see no 'real' risk in failing except what may result in the way of spurious litigation."

Ford engineers suggested four ways to improve the stability of the Explorer: widening the chassis by 2 inches, lowering the engine, lowering the tire pressure, and stiffening the springs. Ford chose the latter two, reducing the recommended tire pressure from 30 to 35 psi to 26 psi. This produced more road gripping but also increased friction, increased the heat of the tires, and caused tread separations. The lower tire pressure also reduced fuel economy.

BRIDGESTONE/FIRESTONE

Firestone had its own history of recalls. In 1978, between 13 and 14 million Firestone "500" tires were recalled because of faulty manufacture costing the company more than $200 million. The National Highway Safety Administration (NHTSA) called for tougher new standards for tires and light trucks. If these standards had been in place in the late 1970s, the early and subsequent designs of SUVs would have been quite different—saving lives and money. However, the NHTSA was essentially dismantled by the Reagan administration that slashed the NHTSA's budget and revoked several new regulations—including a warning light for tire inflation problems.

In 1987, Firestone became a subsidiary of Bridgestone Tire Co. Ltd. Bridgestone, a Japanese company, was named for its founder Shojiro Ishibashi, whose name means "stone bridge." Bridgestone was proud of the its technological leadership—innovations in tire performance and design—as well as its dedication to quality—all of its plants were QS 9000 and ISO 9000 certified. The Firestone subsidiary was relabeled the Bridgestone/Firestone Company in 1990 with headquarters in Nashville, Tennessee. This division represented about half of Bridgestone's global profits in 1999.

The first tire separation lawsuits hit Firestone in 1992. This was followed by labor disputes and a strike at the Bridgestone/Firestone plant in Decatur, Illinois, following attempts to cut costs. Testing of both Goodyear and Firestone tire models used on the Explorer showed that the Goodyear tires significantly outperformed Firestone. In some instances, Firestone tires wore out twice as fast as Goodyear. The Firestone Wilderness tire earned the lowest acceptable NHTSA heat resistance rating—a "C." The comparable Goodyear tire received a "B."

Ford began to pressure Goodyear to lower tire prices in 1995. Goodyear decided it could not manufacture tires at a price that Ford was willing to pay and actually asked for a price increase because of higher material costs. At this point, Ford discontinued using Goodyear tires on its Explorer, relying entirely upon Firestone.

LAUNCH OF THE EXPLORER AND THE LAWSUITS

The Explorer was launched in 1990 and quickly became the best-selling SUV on the market. Granted, few consumers were using it for its off-road capabilities, but they looked adventuresome whizzing down the freeway to the mall. Ford engineers were well aware of the safety risk of the Explorer. Letters to dealerships warned of the dangers of failing to follow precautions on recommended tire usage stating that ignoring these precautions could lead to loss of control and vehicle rollover which could result in serious injury or death.

Ford also conducted a survey in 1993 of SUV drivers. They found that these drivers drove faster, were more likely to drive in bad weather, and followed other vehicles more closely—particularly troubling because the Explorer needed 20 to 30 feet more to stop when traveling at 60 mph than a typical family car.

By 1995, a Texas jury found Ford 100 percent at fault for the death of a 20-year-old college student driving a Bronco II that rolled over because of tire separation. The $25 million verdict was the largest SUV rollover verdict at the time. In 1996, a trainee test driver lost control of an Explorer during a lane change at 52.5 mph. The driver, overcorrecting, found the car in a four-wheel slide and then a 360-degree flip.

State Farm Insurance, the largest U.S. automobile insurer, notified Firestone and NHTSA in 1998 that they were experiencing an unusual number of claims on Firestone tires. Ford quietly began replacing Firestone tires on Explorers in Venezuela and Saudi Arabia because of rollover deaths in those countries.

POINTING FINGERS

An investigative report on a Houston television station started to blow the cover off the problems at Ford and Firestone in February 2000. The vice president of public affairs at Firestone accused the television station of unfairly characterizing Firestone radial ATX tires as dangerous. She stated that the television station would better serve viewers by telling them how to properly maintain their tires and suggested that many of the crashes were caused by external factors such as punctures.

By May 2000, NHTSA belatedly launched an investigation and sent a defect notice to Firestone. Ford accused Firestone of withholding data needed to determine which tires were defective. Ford accused NHTSA of sitting on Firestone data, and it was Ford that pinpointed where the bad tires were being produced and pressed for a recall. By late summer of 2000, the recall was announced.

Ford organized a "war room" of 500 people dedicated to the crisis—public affairs and media, engineering, legal, regulatory, purchasing, and finance people collecting and analyzing data, operating a 24-hour hot line for the public, and disseminating information with NHTSA and the public.

Meanwhile, Bridgestone executives in Japan had no real appreciation of what was happening with Firestone. There were few Explorers sold in Japan and very few tires subject to recall. The attitude was that the Japanese built better cars, therefore the problem must be Ford. The first public statement by Firestone's president, Masatoshi Ono, seemed to hold the Ford Explorer responsible and advised car owners to check tire pressure every month—even better, every two weeks.

Ford's CEO, Jacques Nasser, went on the offensive claiming that there were no problems with the design of the Explorer and that there was no data pointing to faults with the Explorer, insisting that this was a tire problem. Ford rolled out a $5 million advertising campaign to protect its reputation and brand.

In May 2001, a second recall of 13 million Firestone tires was announced by Ford in an attempt to clear the path for the 2002 Explorer. Ford claimed it did not have enough confidence in the Firestone tires, while Firestone countered that the real issue was the safety of the Explorer. Firestone-equipped Explorers accounted for most of the 174 deaths and 700 injuries sustained in accidents reported at that time. In addition, Ford faced lawsuits seeking more than $590 million in damages.

Congressional hearings were launched. Accusations and data flew back and forth. Bridgestone/Firestone announced its intention to close its Decatur, Illinois, plant in December 2001, laying off almost 1,400 people. The president of the local steelworkers union claimed that Ford blamed Firestone and then Firestone made a scapegoat of the Decatur plant.

Ford announced in July 2001 that it had taken an equity position in Top Driver, Inc., the largest chain of driving schools in the country, and would be developing a driver safety course for SUV owners. The implication was that accidents with Ford Explorers were due not only to defective Firestone tires but to driver error as well. Ford was criticized as hypocritical for presenting advertising images of invincible SUVs that can be driven with abandon, weaving in and out of traffic, giving drivers a false sense of security, while at the same time claiming that SUV drivers needed safety training.[4]

Questions

1 What moral philosophy appeared to guide the decision making at Ford? At Bridgestone/Firestone? Is there any evidence that either company changed its decision-making model as lawsuits mounted?

2 Do you see Ford's handling of the situation surrounding the development, marketing, and subsequent recall as ethical but illegal, ethical and legal, unethical but legal, or unethical and illegal? Why?

3 What actions would you recommend that Ford take to deal with the aftermath of this situation?

CASE D–5   The Johnsons Buy a Food Processor

At 4:52 P.M. on Friday, January 11, 2002, Brock and Alisha Johnson bought a food processor. There was no doubt about it. Any observer would agree that the purchase took place at precisely that time. Or did it?

When questioned after the transaction, neither Brock nor Alisha could remember which of them at first noticed or suggested the idea of getting a food processor. They do recall that in the summer of 2000 they attended a dinner party given by a friend who specialized in French and Chinese cooking. The meal was delicious, and their friend Brad was very proud of the Cuisinart food processor he had used to make many of the dishes. The item was expensive, however—over $300.

The following summer, Alisha noticed a comparison study of food processors in *Better Homes and Gardens*. The performance of four different brands was compared. At about the same time, Brock noticed that *Consumer Reports* also compared a number of brands of food processors. In both instances, the Cuisinart brand came out on top.

Later that fall, new models of the Cuisinart were introduced, and a model they liked was selling for $200 in department stores. The Johnsons searched occasionally for Cuisinarts in discount houses or in wholesale showroom catalogs, even searching the Internet, hoping to find a lower price for the product. They were simply not offered there.

For Christmas 2001, the Johnsons traveled from Atlanta to the family home in Michigan. While there, the Johnsons received a gift of a Sunbeam Mixmaster from a grandmother. While the mixer was beautiful, Alisha immediately thought how much more versatile a food processor would be. One private sentence to that effect brought immediate agreement from Brock. The box was (discreetly) not opened, although many thanks were expressed. The box remained unopened the entire time the Johnsons kept the item.

Back home in Atlanta in January, Alisha again saw the $200 Cuisinart advertised by Rich's, one of the major full-service department stores in Atlanta. Brock and Alisha visited a branch location on a Saturday afternoon and saw the item. The salesperson, however, was not knowledgeable about its features and not very helpful in explaining its attributes. The Johnsons left, disappointed.

Two days later, Alisha called the downtown location, where she talked to Ms. Evans, a seemingly knowledgeable salesperson who claimed to own and love exactly the model the Johnsons had in mind. Furthermore, Ms. Evans said that they did carry Sunbeam mixers and would make an exchange of the mixer, which had been received as a gift and for which no receipt was available.

On the following Friday morning, Brock put the mixer in his car trunk when he left for work downtown. That afternoon, Alisha and six-month-old Brock, Jr., rode downtown with a friend to meet Brock and make the transaction. After meeting downtown, they drove through heavy rainy-day traffic to Rich's to meet Ms. Evans, whom they liked as much in person as they did on the telephone. After a brief, dry-run demonstration of the use and operation of the attachments for all of the models, the Johnsons confirmed their initial decision to take the $200 Cuisinart model (DLC-85). They then asked about exchanging the Sunbeam mixer that they had brought with them. "No problem," said Ms. Evans.

After making a quick phone call, Ms. Evans returned with bad news. Rich's had not carried that particular model of mixer. This model mixer was a single-color model that is usually carried at discount houses, catalog sales houses, and jewelry stores. The one carried by the better department stores, such as Rich's, was a two-tone model. Ms. Evans was sorry she could not make the exchange, but suggested that other stores might carry the item. She even offered to allow the Johnsons to use her phone to verify the availability of the item. The Johnsons did exactly that.

Alisha dialed several of the suggested stores, looking for a retailer who carried both the Cuisinart and the Sunbeam model, but she quickly learned that they were distributed through different types of retail stores. A young man who answered the phone at one store, however, seemed friendly and helpful, and Alisha was able to obtain his agreement to take the item as a return if she could get there that afternoon.

The store was about 1/2 mile away. Brock volunteered to babysit for Brock, Jr., at Rich's while Alisha returned the mixer. She took the downtown shoppers' bus to the store with the still unopened mixer box under her arm.

About an hour later, Alisha returned, cold and wet, with a refund. Brock, having run out of ways to entertain a six-month-old, was very happy to see her. Together they bought the Cuisinart at 4:52 P.M. and proudly took it home.[5]

Questions

1   Which of the Johnsons decided to buy a food processor? The Cuisinart?

2   When was the decision to buy made?

3   What were the important attributes in the evaluation of the Cuisinart brand?

4   Would you characterize the Johnsons' purchase decision process as routine problem solving, limited problem solving, or extended problem solving? Why?

CASE D–6   Honeywell, Inc.: The Optoelectronics Division Studies Buying Behavior

After several years of developing fiber-optic technology for U.S. Department of Defense projects, executives in the Optoelectronics Division of Honeywell, Inc., decided to pursue commercial applications for their products and technology. The task would not be easy because fiber optics was a new technology that many firms would find unfamiliar. Fiber optics is the technology of transmitting light through long, thin, flexible fibers of glass, plastic, or other transparent materials. When it is used in a commercial application, a light source emits infrared light flashes corresponding to data. Millions of light flashes per second send streams through a transparent fiber. A light sensor at the other end of the fiber "reads" the data transmitted. It is estimated that sales of fiber-optic technology could exceed $3 billion in 1997. Almost half the dollar sales volume would come from telecommunications, about 25 percent from government or military purchases, and about 25 percent from commercial applications in computers, robotics, cable TV, and other products.

Interest in adapting fiber-optic technology and products for commercial applications had prompted Honeywell executives to carefully review buying behavior associated with the adoption of a new technology. The buying process appeared to contain at least six phases: (1) need recognition, (2) identification of available products, (3) comparison with existing technology, (4) vendor or seller evaluation, (5) the decision itself, and (6) follow-up on technology performance. Moreover, there appeared to be several people within the buying organization who would play a role in the adoption of a new technology. For example, top management (such as the president and executive vice presidents) would certainly be involved. Engineering and operations management (e.g., vice presidents of engineering and manufacturing) and design engineers (e.g., persons who develop specifications for new products) would also play a major role. Purchasing personnel would have a say in such a decision and particularly in the vendor-evaluation process. The role played by each person in the buying organization was still unclear to Honeywell. It seemed that engineering management personnel could slow the adoption of fiber optics if they did not feel it was appropriate for the products made by the company. Design engineers, who would actually apply fiber optics in product design, might be favorably or unfavorably disposed to the technology depending on whether they knew how to use it. Top management personnel would participate in any final decisions to use fiber optics and could generate interest in the technology if stimulated to do so.

This review of buying behavior led to questions about how to penetrate a company's buying organization and have fiber optics used in the company's products. Although Honeywell was a large, well-known company with annual sales exceeding $8 billion, its fiber-optic technology capability was much less familiar. Therefore the executives thought it was necessary to establish Honeywell's credibility in fiber optics. This was done, in part, through an advertising image campaign that featured Honeywell Optoelectronics as a leader in fiber optics. For more information about Honeywell and its fiber-optics products, visit the company website at www.honeywell.com.[6]

Questions

1   What type of buying situation is involved in the purchase of fiber optics, and what will be important buying criteria used by companies considering using fiber optics in their products?

2   Describe the purchase decision process for adopting fiber optics, and state how members in the buying center for this technology might play a part in this process.

3   What effect will perceived risk have on a company's decision of whether to use fiber optics in its products?

4   What role does the image advertising campaign play in Honeywell Optoelectronics' efforts to market fiber optics?

CASE D–7   Callaway Golf: The Global Challenge

Callaway Golf got its start when the late Ely R. Callaway purchased one-half of a hickory-shafted golf club company called Hickory Stick in 1982 for $400,000. Callaway–Hickory Stick, later renamed Callaway Golf, made golf history with the introduction of its stainless steel, oversized driver, the Big Bertha in 1991. The Big Bertha driver was followed by a Big Bertha line of irons and fairway woods, the Great Big Bertha oversized driver, and then in 1997, the Biggest Big Bertha. This club was so big, and for many golfers at that time, so cumbersome or awkward, that it did not catch on in popularity like the previous two Big Bertha driver products. Even so, Callaway sales were $800 million in 1998, compared with $22 million in 1990.

BUYER BEHAVIOR

Most golfers, pros and amateurs alike, probably experiment more with new drivers, fairway woods, and putters than other clubs. In fact, many top professionals and amateurs choose to play with their favorite irons for years and years before changing. Callaway Golf was extremely smart to enter the club market the way it did by introducing drivers and then following up with specialty clubs that golfers enjoy tinkering with more than irons.

THE GLOBAL GOLF MARKET

The golf industry has a strong worldwide appeal. The game is extremely popular in countries around the world including Scotland (golf's birthplace), England, Sweden, Spain, South Africa, South America, Australia, New Zealand, and Japan, where golf enthusiasm rises to unheard of levels. Many countries and continents from around the world are represented both professionally and at the amateur level in worldwide competitions. The golf tours around the world have done much to link golf as a global sport. The Ryder Cup and the Solheim Cup, for example, have matched the European and U.S. PGA and LPGA tour players in competition for many years. And the recently formed Presidents Cup matches the best of the PGA Tour against the best of the international players from outside of Europe. The newly formed World Golf Championships pits the best players from around the world in match play and stroke play competitions. The Five World Professional Golf Tours, the PGA, the European PGA, the Japan PGA, the Australasian PGA, and the South African PGA tour are all represented in these newly formed World Golf Championships.

Golf enthusiasts from around the world follow the sport through televised tournaments, daily newspaper coverage, golf magazines, weekly golf journals, sports reports, as well as Internet websites. Golf-related websites are among the largest categories of Internet sites.

Golf is truly a global sport. Courses and competitions are held in many countries and on almost every continent—except Antarctica. Professional and amateur players from around the world compete and interact with a high degree of etiquette and sportsmanship. Professional players represent equipment manufacturers from around the world. International players may use and represent American golf equipment manufacturers, whereas American players may choose to endorse and represent international equipment manufactures. Golfers, at both the professional and amateur levels, share ideas and experiences from the game they play.

The golf equipment market is a highly congested and very competitive marketplace. Many players exist and the field is constantly changing with new start-ups, mergers, and acquisitions. Major players today include Fortune Brands (Titleist), Karsten Manufacturing (Ping), Taylor Made Golf, Mizuno, Adams Golf, Orlimar Golf, Cleveland, Spalding Holdings, and others that fill niche markets.

Adams Golf and Orlimar Golf had successful launches capturing a significant market share in the fairway wood and specialty club market offering unique technological innovations and premium products. Other well-established club manufacturers have followed Callaway's "bigger is better" philosophy. Taylor Made Golf, Titlest, Ping, and others have designed oversized drivers that have caught on in popularity. In many respects, today's design and engineering for golf club manufacturing have led to a contest of who can make the biggest and longest driving club that technology and the rules of golf will allow. Premium clubs today not only offer technical innovation, forgiveness, power, distance, and accuracy but also are pushing the limits of the rules and the laws of physics.

CALLOWAY'S INTERNATIONAL MARKETING

For Callaway Golf, one of the largest American golf club equipment manufacturers, the world market is a very big part of its total market for clubs. Global sales were $837.6 million in 2000 with 40 percent of all sales coming from golfers in countries outside the United States, up from 35 percent in 1997. The severe downturn in the Japanese market, the second-largest economy globally and a huge golf market, hit Callaway and other equipment manufacturers hard. Japan's economy is not the only one experiencing a downturn. The U.S. and European economies have also slowed considerably. With many avid golfers tempted by new technology, improved products, and the next big thing, many golfers will forgo new club purchases during periods of tough economic times because golf equipment expenditures are discretionary.

International professionals, from England's Colin Montgomerie to Sweden's Annika Sorenstam, represent Callaway Golf. At the same time, Callaway claims hundreds of pros and over 7 million amateurs, worldwide, as players and representatives of their clubs. For Callaway Golf, golf is a global sport and the market is truly a global market.

THE ISSUES

In sports, it is often said that getting to the top is easier than staying there. Callaway Golf is faced with this challenge. Callaway Golf has the burdensome task of sustaining its phenomenal growth and leading market share against competitors that are in hot pursuit. Fast followers Orilmar and Adams have developed products that cut into Callaway's mainstay, the fairway wood and specialty wood market. Other big players in the equipment business are also after Callaway's market share and may pose a greater threat to Callaway's business. These companies are large enough and strong enough to survive any market slump and also have the resources to buy up smaller successful companies and the technology to provide popular products.

Technology drives this industry. In 1999, Karsten Manufacturing (Ping) released a driver that pushed the design and technical capabilities of product materials to the limit. Golf's ruling bodies—the United States Golf Association (USGA) in North America and the Royal and Ancient Golf Club of St. Andrews for the rest of the world—began an investigation as to whether new club designs exceeded or infringed on an obscure rule in golf. This rule, stating that no club shall exert or possess a "spring-like effect" on the ball when hit, had never received very much attention before. With competitors closing in on the limits of this spring-like effect or coefficient of resolution (COR), Callaway produced and marketed one of the first illegal or nonconforming drivers, the ERC. The ERC, named after Ely R. Callaway, was ruled nonconforming by the USGA (United States Golf Association) for exceeding its established COR limit. The ERC was approved for play in Europe and the rest of the world by the Royal and Ancient Golf Club of St. Andrews, because it had not yet established a reliable test for the "spring-like effect" in golf clubs. Thus the ERC and ERCII became one of the first clubs played by pros and amateurs competitively throughout the world, save the United States, Mexico, and Canada.

Golf continues to grow in popularity, particularly among youth, but the golf industry has taken a beating since 1998. For Callaway Golf, one of the largest current issues is the global economic condition. As countries experience struggling economies, golf, an expensive leisure luxury, becomes an activity people play less often or learn to enjoy with the equipment at hand. Well-made and maintained golf equipment can last for many years. So if times are tough, people can still play, but they'll probably play with the equipment they already own. Components and equipment improvements have made the game easier and more enjoyable to play. Also, the construction of more golf courses in the United States and worldwide has increased the opportunity for many people to play golf.[7]

Questions

1 What are the pros and cons of a global versus a multidomestic approach to marketing golf clubs for Callaway? Which approach do you believe would have more merit and why?
2 What are some of the significant environmental factors that could have a *major* impact on the marketing of golf clubs internationally? Describe each factor and what the nature of the impact would be.
3 What marketing mix recommendations would you have for Callaway as they attempt to increase international market share?

CASE D–8 HOM Furniture: Where Keen Observation Pays

"Some ideas are too good *NOT* to steal!" The speaker isn't a CIA agent but Wayne Johansen, CEO of HOM Furniture, a group of 10 furniture stores in the upper Midwest. Johansen isn't talking about anything illegal but is describing his approach to doing very practical, commonsense marketing research—visiting dozens of first-class retailers and then weaving the best of the ideas into HOM Furniture's operations. But that gets us ahead of the story.

HOW IT ALL BEGAN . . .

Wayne Johansen's life reads like an entrepreneurial case study. Right out of high school, Johansen started JC Imports, a wholesale import business built around jewelry and leather goods. The decision to add waterbeds to the merchandise mix proved to be a smart one and the import business was soon closed to focus on booming waterbed sales. But all good things must come to an end;

waterbeds don't wear out and the target audience of baby boomers was aging. When the market became saturated, Johansen, along with his brother, Rod, and Carl Nyberg converted their Water Bedroom stores to Total Bedroom stores. Ultimately, they wanted to expand into a full-line furniture company, but they needed larger store sizes, more warehouse capacity, and more working capital. So they took the first step in 1991 and HOM Oak and Leather stores were born. In 1997, their ultimate dream became reality as HOM Oak and Leather expanded into HOM Furniture, with sales of $30 million in 1996 growing to $120 million in 2001.

THE CONSUMER BUYING PROCESS

Success at HOM Furniture has been built upon keen understanding of how consumers buy furniture. Furniture is a product category characterized by "complexity and significant risk," explains Johansen. A furniture purchase must fit into the consumer's overall decorating scheme, coordinating with paint, wallpaper, draperies, and floor coverings. Women are the key decision makers and they believe that their home furnishings make a statement about whether they have good taste and social status. They fear a bad decision, relying more on the expertise of the salesperson and the selection available in the store, rather than on brand names.

HOM Furniture has responded with large and inviting stores in highly visible locations, featuring great selection and knowledgeable salespeople who specialize in a given department. The smell of fresh-baked cookies greets customers as they enter the store, drawing them into a race track–shaped layout of the different store departments. This provides maximum exposure to merchandise and creates an airy, open feeling.

MARKETING INFORMATION AT HOM

Very quickly, Johansen and his partners recognized the value of marketing information. Prior to the launch of HOM Furniture in 1997, they toured 70 of the top 100 U.S. full-line furniture stores to observe the practices that contribute most to success. Some of the successful ideas gleaned from these visits include fresh-baked cookies in the stores, the use of a "house" structure in the center of the stores, and the design of two-level stores.

This benchmarking activity continues today as HOM Furniture participates in a consortium of 14 furniture stores from the United States, Canada, and Mexico. Because the member stores do not directly compete with one another in their geographic area, they are free to share financial statements, sales data, and their best ideas. Meeting three times annually, the participants

spend the first day touring the host store and reviewing store advertising. The second day is reserved for the "best idea" contest. Each participant contributes $20 and the best idea takes the "pot."

Site location is widely recognized as critical to the success of any retail store. In order to reach a regional audience, HOM Furniture builds stores that are highly visible from the freeways leading into the city from all directions. With analytical assistance from a local newspaper, management can plot the location of all current customers on a map as well as determine the market potential within a given radius for any possible future store location. Assuming that a customer will shop at the HOM store nearest his or her home, HOM management can calculate the extent to which a future store will cannibalize business from existing stores.

This geographic analysis can be merged with MicroVision data from Claritas. MicroVision is a segmentation and consumer targeting system that classifies every U.S. household into 1 of 48 unique market segments, using demographic, lifestyle, socioeconomic, buying, media, and behavioral characteristics. For any given zip code, MicroVision provides a count of the number of households for each of the 48 market segments identified. This allows HOM's management to build stores in areas that are heavily populated with the types of consumers who like to shop at HOM Furniture stores.

Once the store is in operation, sales and productivity information is closely monitored. Management has easy access to a database that tracks sales by store, by department, by day of the week, and by hour of the day. In addition, the sales generated by each salesperson are recorded on a monthly basis. Productivity analysis is made possible through an electronic sensor mounted on the doorframe of the main entrance to each store to measure "door swings"—a very precise measure of customer visits. With door swing data by store, by day, and by hour, management can use sales per door swing as a measure of productivity and also relate door swings to ads, such as a Sunday insert in the local paper.

After the sale is complete, HOM Furniture wants to make sure that the customer is thoroughly satisfied. On average, a person buys $40,000 of furniture during a lifetime. A satisfied customer is more likely to be a repeat customer, worth thousands of dollars in future business. For that reason, HOM monitors the number of customer calls received and also the percentage of product sold that requires service. Expanding the system for measurement of customer satisfaction is one of Johansen's future priorities.[8]

Questions

1 (*a*) Identify the data sources HOM Furniture uses in its marketing information system. (*b*) Which would you classify as secondary data sources? (*c*) Which would be considered primary data sources?

2 When HOM Furniture advertises, it looks for a resulting spike in sales using their extensive database. (*a*) What are the advantages of this approach? (*b*) What are the possible shortcomings of this approach and how would you address them?

3 Assume that you have been hired as a marketing consultant by HOM Furniture's management. (*a*) What specific types of information should HOM collect to measure customer satisfaction with its stores and services? (*b*) For each type of information you identified in (*a*), how would HOM Furniture make use of that information to improve customer satisfaction?

CASE D–9   The Hummer: A Segmentation Challenge

What in the world is a Hummer? If you have seen one of the ungainly vehicles, you will not easily forget it. The Hummer, or Humvee as it was originally named, was designed for the U.S. Army as a jeep. This rugged vehicle is constructed of corrosion-proof aircraft aluminum. The chassis is made of massive, hollow girders, and hundreds of rivets cover the exterior and interior surface. At 6 feet 3 inches high, 15 feet 4 inches long, with giant front tires, and twice the diameter of a passenger car, the Hummer can splash through water 30 feet deep. It can climb 45-degree inclines, hills, and mountains. It is virtually unstoppable. Not surprisingly, it gets a whopping 11.5 miles to the gallon.

THE COMPANY

The Hummer is produced by AM General of South Bend, Indiana. AM General and its predecessor companies have been a leader in the design and manufacture of light- and medium-duty trucks for the military for over 50 years.

AM General has been bought, sold, and renamed numerous times. AM General's history is traced to Standard Wheel Company, a bicycle manufacturer, in Terre Haute, Indiana, that diversified into automobile manufacturing in 1903. AM General emerged from a spin-off of the American Motors Jeep Corporation, later acquired by LTV Corporation. Most recently AM General was purchased by its current owner, the Renco Group in 1992.

THE PRODUCT

The Hummer's history is much shorter than that of AM General. In 1979, AM General entered competition for the development of a high-mobility multipurpose wheeled vehicle (HMMWV) to meet the demanding standards of the U.S. Army.

The Army created a list of objectives for the vehicle. For instance, the Army wanted a vehicle that could climb a 60-degree grade without bogging down as well as traverse a 40-degree side slope with stability while carrying a 2-ton payload. The Army's requirements were for a new kind of vehicle, one that would be versatile, reliable, and easy to maintain. AM General engineers were not told *how* to reach these objectives but rather what was desired in the vehicle. AM General engineers then found unique design solutions to solve the problems created by the performance objectives.

The prototype Hummer was tested in the Nevada desert in July 1980, less than one year after its initial designs were drawn. After extensive testing, the Army awarded three contracts for test vehicles to General Dynamics, Teledyne, and AM General. Within 10 months, AM General delivered its Hummer prototypes to the Army. After five months of testing, the AM General Hummer was judged the superior product and AM General had an initial production contract of 55,000 vehicles over a five-year period.

Since production began in 1983, AM General has sold more than 110,000 Humvees or Hummers, as it was affectionately nicknamed, to the military. The Hummer replaced several vehicles in the U.S. Army's fleet including the jeep. Over 20,000 Hummers were used in the 1991 Gulf War alone where they were transformed into everything from ambulances to missile launchers.

The Hummer has many unique design features. Independent suspension for all four wheels avoids ground clearance limits of most conventional four-wheel-drive vehicles. The truck's wide track and well-distributed weight keep the center of gravity low preventing the truck from tipping over. Tire pressure can be adjusted on the go, from 15 psi in soft sand to 30 psi on asphalt, to obtain the best traction and handling on changing terrain.

THE CONSUMER MARKET

The development of the Hummer illustrates collaboration between one type of customer, the military, and AM General. The development of a new market for the Hummer—the consumer market—was the result of close interaction with selected consumers or perhaps one key consumer.

Believe it or not, Arnold Schwarzenegger is reportedly responsible for AM General's entry into the consumer market. Shortly after the Gulf War began, AM General's president, Jim Armour, received a call from Arnold Schwarzenegger. He thought his secretary was joking when she said "Arnold is on the phone." Armour recounts the conversation this way "This is Arnold. I want to see you." Armour told Schwarzenegger that he wouldn't sell Arnold the Hummer unless they were able to sell them to everyone. Arnold's response "What do I have to do to get you to sell them to the public?" From this, the development of the consumer version of the Hummer developed.

Arnold became the first civilian customer of the Hummer. But there have been many more. First sold in 1992, a number of different civilian models were available at Hummer dealerships around the country at hefty prices—currently around $80,000. Even with additional features, the civilian Hummer was still fairly spartan and appealed to a limited audience. AM General sold fewer than 1,000 Hummers in 2000.

The typical Hummer customers make $200,000 to $300,000 per year and are almost all men. Most buyers have two or three other cars. Reportedly, doctors buy Hummers but attorneys do not. Hummers sell well on the East Coast and West Coast but not in mid-America. Entrepreneurs, not corporate conformists, tend to buy the Hummer. Let's face it, this is not a vehicle to own if you want to be inconspicuous.

In December of 1999, AM General and General Motors reached an agreement giving GM exclusive ownership of the Hummer brand name worldwide. As part of this agreement, the two companies would jointly redesign the next generation of civilian Hummers. The original Hummer has been relabeled the Hummer H1 and AM General retains design responsibility for the H1 which will continue to be produced in Indiana. AM General will also manufacture the jointly designed H2. GM will assume all marketing and distribution responsibilities for the civilian Hummer. AM General will retain exclusive rights to the military market.

Automotive and business pundits have had mixed reviews of the GM H2 Hummer concept vehicle. It doesn't look much like a Hummer. It's a downsized Hummer SUV in an already crowded category. Rivals such as Porsche AG are already moving into the high-end SUV market, and there is plenty of competition in the mid- to lower end of the SUV market. In fact, the new H2 has more in common with GM's mass market Chevrolet Tahoe and Silverado than the original Hummer H1. Engine parts, underpinnings, steering wheel, door handles, and other parts for the H2 are shared with GM's SUVs and pickups.

GM's record on protecting brands while submitting to pressure to share parts hasn't been good. Cadillac's image was damaged when it became known that the parts were the same as those used in Chevrolet and Buick.

GM says that the target markets for the H2 are a combination of "rugged individualists" or wealthy baby boomers who will use the off-road capabilities of the vehicle and "successful achievers"—people who will probably never take to the hills because they wouldn't want to scratch the car.

Will consumers pay $50,000 for an H2? Will they think of it as a Hummer? What about the impact of the H2 on the traditional Hummer market segment? With the economy sputtering and concerns about SUV safety and gas mileage, GM may find it difficult to meet their ambitious sales goals of more than 100,000 Hummers by 2005, up from less than 1,000 in 2000.[9]

Questions

1   What type of market segmentation bases should be considered for the Hummer (*a*) in the consumer market and (*b*) in the business-to-business market?

2   What are the pros and cons of extending the Hummer's target markets with the H2?

3   How would AM General's marketing mix and positioning differ for its consumer market segments and a business-to-business segment such as targeting the Hummer to logging companies?

CASE D–10   Medtronic in China: Where "Simpler" Serves Patients Better

"I felt tremendous pressure to find markets and technologies to grow the business in other parts of the world," says Bobby Griffin, president of Medtronic Pacing Business. "Ninety-seven percent of Medtronic's products were being sold to twenty-seven percent of the world. I'd read books on China and *Business Week* articles about the success of General Electric and other companies that had gone into China with scaled-down products."

THE MARKET AND THE NEED

Medtronic is the world's leading medical technology company and sells products to alleviate heart arrhythmia and neurological disorders, such as heart pacemakers, defibrillators, and angioplasty balloon catheters. But in the early 1990s Medtronic sold only a few pacemakers in China, a country of 1.3 billion people. So Griffin interviewed a number of Chinese physicians. Their desires were very clear: They wanted a highly reliable, basic pacing device that would allow them to serve more people in need. "These doctors were motivated not by greed but by their desire to help and heal their patients," Griffin concluded. "Their relationships with their patients in the hospitals were touching. Instead of talking down to them from a standing position, they would get down on one knee and whisper in the patient's ear."

Griffin also found that only 4,000 cardiac patients a year were implanted with pacemakers in China—a small minority of the patients who needed them. "It was clear that a certain class of people in China could afford almost anything, while most could afford no treatment at all," Griffin said. "Yet more people in China could afford pacing than the populations of Germany and France combined. Of the millions of people living in the coastal cities and provinces of China, those in the middle class had $2,000 in disposable income. Ten thousand television sets were being sold every week, but health care is also vitally important."

THE NEW PACEMAKER FOR CHINA

As Griffin's plane lifted off from the Hong Kong airport, he recalled, "If we could build a pacemaker we could sell in China for $1,000 and still make our margins, we could serve many more people all over the world with a reliable product and still make a profit. I made up my mind to set an audacious goal. I'd shoot for a *radical* cost reduction in the product design."

Back at corporate headquarters, after a "You're crazy, Griffin!" reaction, Medtronic's head of development agreed to support the project. The project also received support from Medtronic's marketing organization: They liked the idea because the company could lead with an inexpensive product that could leverage sales of higher-end products later.

To meet Bobby Griffin's audacious goal, Medtronic chose its "Champion" pacemaker, a simplified version of the company's existing pacing systems that could meet specifications of cardiologists in China. Mechanical engineering design manager Bill Hooper had been support-

ing the Champion pacing system through Quest, a special program within the company that funded the work of engineers who wanted to develop projects that wouldn't otherwise receive funding. Hooper observed, "My dream was to see patients in less developed countries restored to full life in ways that had been available for years in more developed countries." His efforts exemplified Medtronic's mission: *To contribute to human welfare by application of biomedical engineering in the research, design, manufacture, and sale of instruments or appliances that alleviate pain, restore health, and extend life.* (See Figure 2–2 in Chapter 2.)

Hooper and electrical engineer Larry Hudziak had taken the current sophisticated technology and simplified it. "We wanted to reduce the cost to make it affordable in the Chinese market. By using a proven pacing lead technology for the coil, insulator, electrode and tine, we were able to save substantially. One of the most critical parts of the Champion, the lead wire, needed to flex whenever patients breathed, their hearts beat, or they moved. We chose a lead that had the best reliability of anything we make," Hooper explained.

The Champion design did not include more complex, state-of-the-art features like dual-chamber stimulation, activity sensors, or steroid-eluding leads. The Chinese physicians Bobby Griffin had met with considered these features unnecessary, preferring high quality, low cost, longevity, and ease of use. The design team had to work hard to reduce the cost of the Champion pacemaker, which could translate into a lower selling price. Medtronic engineers also designed the Champion so that it could be programmed externally with a simple magnetic device. By February 1995, the design was complete and the product had been tested (see photo on page 47).

ON-SITE IN CHINA: A NEW PLANT AND SALESFORCE

Medtronic realized that to ensure quality control, it needed to be directly involved in the production and selling process, and available when physicians implanted the pacemaker. Bill Hooper knew how to design facilities to cut costs, but it required an almost constant presence in Shanghai, where the plant was being built. Over a three-year period, Hooper made 19 trips, and Ron Meyer, vice president of a pacing group, made 26. They reported to each other via e-mail and phone calls. "The routine was grueling," Hooper recalls. "Check into the hotel, unpack, head out to buy water and walk for exercise, then back to your room. It was such a drill."

Building a new plant was not the only challenge facing Hooper and Meyer. Medtronic also needed a salesforce, including experienced heart surgeons, to contact and train Chinese physicians. Furthermore, with the plant located in Shanghai, on the eastern coast of China, they needed a distribution system capable of serving a country roughly the size of the United States (9.6 million square kilometers).

Hooper recalled that these were tough times for both of them: "We both had families. When I was doing algebra with my daughter on the phone in the middle of the night from China, I could remind myself, 'I'm here because of Medtronic's mission and my part in fulfilling that mission.' If I hadn't had that, I would have given up."[10]

Questions

1   Assess Medtronic's decision to develop and market the new Champion heart pacemaker in terms of the following reasons for new-product success: (*a*) "point of difference," (*b*) market attractiveness, (*c*) bad timing, and (*d*) economic access to doctors and patients.

2   Discuss the steps of the new-product process as they relate to the Champion Pacemaker.

3   New-product development is important to a company like Medtronic, but it is hard work, and often leads to failure. How can a company encourage its employees to take initiative, make a profit, *and* be ethically and socially responsible?

4   Relate Medtronic's decision to sell pacemakers in China to its corporate mission statement. (A portion is quoted in the case and the full text is in Figure 2–2.) How does the decision relate to these Medtronic stakeholders: (*a*) shareholders of Medtronic stock, (*b*) Medtronic employees, and (*c*) Chinese patients?

5   Medtronic chose to design and build a new low-priced, highly reliable, reduced-feature heart pacemaker in its Shanghai plant. What are the strengths and weaknesses of this decision from (*a*) a marketing viewpoint and (*b*) an ethical viewpoint?

CASE D–11   Yoplait USA: Managing a Successful Brand

"A little bit of constructive restlessness is good," says Chap Colucci, "because you can become too satisfied with your own success, with the status quo. You take your foot off the gas and things begin to stall." Colucci is vice president of marketing and sales at Yoplait USA, a subsidiary of General Mills, Inc. At General Mills, managing brands ranging from Pillsbury refrigerated baked goods, to Totino's pizza, to Betty Crocker desserts, to Big G cereals, is an important responsibility of its managers.

THE ORIGINAL IDEA

The idea for Yoplait began when top management at General Mills asked Steven M. Rothschild to head a team to investigate yogurt as a new business opportunity for the company. Rothschild's team found that in the United States yogurt had annual sales of $350 million with an annual growth rate of about 18 percent. The team also discovered that about 95 percent of the yogurt consumed in the United States was mixed with fruit or flavoring, and about 5 percent was plain. About 95 percent was consumed in 8-ounce cups. Finally, the team's

analysis indicated that the U.S. annual per capita consumption of yogurt was low (5 cups per person) compared with consumption in European countries (27 cups per person a year in France).

The industry was made up of four basic types of yogurt:

- Sundae style—fruit on the bottom of the cup.
- Swiss style—fruit blended throughout the cup to keep the fruit from settling on the bottom.
- Western style—fruit on the bottom and flavored syrup on the top.
- Frozen style—ice-cream or soft-custard form.

The various types of yogurt were available in 20 different flavors, and when refrigerated, had a shelf life of 21 to 60 days, depending on whether preservatives were added.

Rothschild and the team believed that a yogurt product would be a good match for the company because (1) it was a high-turnover branded item that would allow a significant profit margin; (2) it was a product for which the firm's skills in positioning, advertising, packaging, and promotion would provide an advantage over competition, and (3) it represented a business that would capitalize on trends resulting from long-term changes in consumer behavior. Based on the research, analysis, and conclusions of the team, General Mills decided to enter the yogurt market!

GETTING YOPLAIT STARTED AT GENERAL MILLS

General Mills estimated that it would take about three years to develop a new brand of yogurt. To save time it decided to buy the rights to market Yoplait yogurt in the

United States from Sodima, a large French company. This decision gave General Mills access to Yoplait's expertise and technology related to producing and distributing a refrigerated product. In return, Yoplait received profits from sales of its products in the United States.

At that time Yoplait was the best-selling yogurt in France. Marketing research revealed what consumers perceived as Yoplait's key benefits: (1) 100 percent natural yogurt without artificial sweeteners or preservatives, (2) Swiss style, with real fruit mixed throughout, and (3) outstanding taste with a creamy texture. In terms of U.S. competition, there was no national brand of yogurt at the time, but there was a two-tiered group of yogurt producers: (1) premium regional brands such as Dannon and Kraft, and (2) private-label brands produced by local dairies.

Yoplait USA moved quickly to gain acceptance for Yoplait as a national brand among American consumers. Yoplait USA positioned its yogurt as the "Yogurt of France" with creative TV commercials featuring personalities like Loretta Swit (from *MASH*) and Tommy Lasorda eating Yoplait and speaking French.

MANAGING THE BRAND

Yoplait experienced extraordinary success. As the brand grew, however, its managers became complacent and underestimated the competition from other brands such as Dannon. Although Yoplait was number two nationally, its market share and profitability began to decline. In an attempt to manage the product life cycle, Yoplait tried a Western-style version of its product, which failed. Eventually, a new vice president of marketing and sales, Chap Colucci, joined the Yoplait USA team and concluded that while the product had been successful during its introduction, the team was not pursuing strategies that would ensure continued growth.

Colucci conducted a situation analysis in preparation for developing a new marketing strategy for Yoplait USA. His analysis turned up some serious concerns, including:

1. *High retail prices.* Yoplait's price for a six-ounce cup was actually higher than competitors' eight-ounce cups. For example, the prices on Yoplait's 4 Pack were about 20 percent higher per cup than Dannon's and Kraft's 6 Pack.

2. *Low gross margins.* Margins had declined, at least partly because of high production and overhead costs.

3. *Unbalanced promotion spending mix.* Most promotional expenditures were directed at retailers and wholesalers rather than consumers.

4. *Lack of continued effective advertising.* Yoplait had been living off the great "Yogurt of France" series that launched the product without a similar creative follow-up campaign.

5. *Few coupons offered.* Yoplait had cut back on consumer coupons, while its competitors had heavy couponing.

6. *Few new products.* While Yoplait had developed a Lite product-line extension, there were very few new products in development.

7. *Geographic marketing organization.* Yoplait was organized geographically with three regions—Eastern, Central, and Western. This organization had caused marketing managers to focus on geography, not basic marketing.

These observations became the basis for developing new marketing strategies.

Colucci's brand management activities involved all elements of the marketing mix: improved pricing, more consumer promotion, new advertising, and new product line extensions. For example, Yoplait introduced a "grab-and-go" product called Go-Gurt for children, new flavors such as Orange Cream and Tropical Fruit, and a portable yogurt product for adults called Yoplait Exprèsse. Today, Yoplait is the number-one yogurt in the United States with 33.8 percent market share of a $1.86 billion market. Almost 43 percent of all people in the United States now consume yogurt!

Questions

1 What stages of the product life cycle has yogurt gone through in the United States since General Mills first evaluated it as a business opportunity? How have marketing activities changed at different stages of the product life cycle?

2 What activities did Yoplait undertake to manage the product's life cycle?

3 Chap Colucci's analysis suggested that Yoplait brand managers may have relied too long on the early success of the brand. What marketing actions would address each of the problems?

CASE D-12 Girl Scouts of America: Marketing a Nonprofit Organization

"I've got something for the girls of Savannah, and all America, and all the world, and we're going to start it tonight," said Juliette Gordon Low to a group of friends in 1912. She asked them to bring their daughters, little sisters, friends, and neighbors to her meeting. Her dream was to create an organization that would bring girls out of their home environments to serve in their communities. The result was the first meeting of the American Girl Guides, which a short time later became Girl Scouts of America (GSA)!

THE DREAM REALIZED

When Low founded GSA, she wanted young girls to be self-reliant and independent and to uphold the highest standards of citizenship and moral character. The many activities of GSA focused on young girls developing into wives and mothers, and merit badges were awarded for accomplishments such as dressmaking, homemaking, and being a hostess. By 1929, membership was over 200,000, and shortly after the Great Depression the Girl Scouts began selling cookies to help fund their nationwide organization. The organization continued to grow by focusing on traditional family life and received a congressional charter in 1950. In the 1960s, GSA followed the population migration away from the cities to the suburbs, and reached a membership of 3.9 million by 1969!

THE CHANGING ENVIRONMENT

The family, school, and work environments of girls and women were quickly changing, however. Divorce was changing the traditional family, opportunities for women to work outside the home were expanding, more married women were working, fewer children were being born, and the technology affecting everyday living was becoming more complex. The racial and ethnic composition in the United States was also changing as the number of African-Americans, Hispanics, and Asian-Americans grew.

In addition, fewer girls were becoming scouts, and GSA observed that girls who had become Girl Scouts as youngsters did not continue as they grew older. Many girls who had progressed from Brownies (the youngest group of 6- to 8-year-olds) to Juniors (ages 9 to 11) had dropped out before attaining the rank of Cadette at age 12, and thus never achieved the highest rank of Senior (ages 14 to 17). Membership began to decline and eventually reached approximately 2.5 million members.

MARKETING A NONPROFIT ORGANIZATION

While GSA was still the world's largest organization for girls, some people began to wonder if GSA's underlying principles had become obsolete. Could the changes in the environment explain the declining membership? GSA began asking typical marketing questions such as "What is our business?," "Who is our customer?," and "What does the customer value?" Market studies showed that girls had changed—they were now more interested in areas such as science, the environment, and business—but the Girl Scouts had not changed. It seemed that the scout troop organizational structure had contributed to the loss of scouts as they grew older. The troop format required frequent meetings that were difficult for teenagers as they became involved in a wider range of activities. An-

other disadvantage of the troop format was that it demanded considerable time from the adult troop leaders.

To adapt to the new environment, GSA adopted new approaches for attracting and retaining young girls. For example, GSA began recruiting girls in cities as well as the suburbs, and increased its emphasis on recruiting lower-income girls as well. GSA started reaching out to pregnant teenagers with a program dealing with career opportunities. GSA activities also have changed, as evidenced by the new merit badges. Today they are awarded in categories such as "Aerospace," "Businesswise," "Global Politics," "Oil Production," and "Computer Fun." The troop concept and requirement has been relaxed. Girls can now become scouts without joining a troop, provided they attend one official event per year. Once members, they are invited to participate in special interest projects that include field trips, guest speakers, and conferences.

These efforts have been described in a print, radio, and television public service campaign titled "Brainstorm," aimed at encouraging girls to become scouts and stay in the program even after they enter high school. The campaign included a 30-second TV message that covered sights and sounds related to ocean liners and travel, tap dancing, piano playing, airplanes, filmmaking, a space capsule taking off, and meeting young men.

GSA also implemented several other marketing strategies. For example, a Gift of Caring program was recently introduced to allow Girl Scout cookie customers to buy a "gift" box of cookies that the scouts then deliver to nursing home residents and hospitalized children. A new age group, called Daisy, for girls 5 years old or in kindergarten, was introduced to allow earlier participation. Finally, to reflect growing emphasis on physical fitness, GSA introduced a health and fitness national service project called GirlSports!

By encouraging equal access to all types of girls, focusing on contemporary issues, and becoming customer-oriented, the Girl Scouts of America reversed its membership trend and now serves more than 2.7 million girls. In addition, through its membership in the World Association of Girl Guides and Girl Scouts, GSA is part of a worldwide group of 10 million girls in 140 countries! To continue to grow, GSA (www.girlscouts.org), like most nonprofit organizations today, will need to continue improving its marketing expertise.

Questions

1 What unique elements of services (e.g., intangibility, inconsistency, inseparability, and inventory) are most evident in a nonprofit organization such as the Girl Scouts of America?
2 How did changes in the environment have an impact on membership at GSA?
3 What marketing actions did GSA take to reverse its decline in membership? What future actions should GSA consider to continue its growth?

CASE D-13   Health Cruises, Inc.: Estimating Cost, Volume, and Profit Relationships

Health Cruises, Inc. packages cruises to Caribbean islands such as Martinique and the Bahamas. Like conventional cruises, the packages are designed to be fun. But the cruise is structured to help participants become healthier by breaking old habits, such as smoking or overeating. The Miami-based firm was conceived by Susan Isom, 30, a self-styled innovator and entrepreneur. Prior to this venture, she had spent several years in North Carolina promoting a behavior-modification clinic.

Isom determined that many people were very concerned about developing good health habits, yet they seemed unable to break away from their old habits because of the pressures of day-to-day living. She reasoned that they might have a chance for much greater success in a pleasant and socially supportive environment, where good health habits were fostered. Accordingly, she established Health Cruises, Inc., hired 10 consulting psychologists and health specialists to develop a program, and chartered a ship. DeForrest Young, a Miami management consultant, became the chairperson of Health Cruises. Seven of Isom's business associates contributed an initial capital outlay totaling more than $250,000. Of this amount, $65,000 went for the initial advertising budget, $10,000 for other administrative expenses, and $220,000 for the ship rental and crew.

Mary Porter, an overweight Denver schoolteacher, has signed up to sail on a two-week cruise to Nassau, departing December 19. She and her shipmates will be paying an average of $1,500 for the voyage. The most desirable staterooms cost $2,200.

Mary learned of the cruise by reading the travel section of her Sunday newspaper on October 16. On that date, the Pittsford and LaRue Advertising Agency placed promotional notices for the cruise in several major metropolitan newspapers. Mary was fascinated by the idea of combining therapy sessions with swimming, movies, and an elegant atmosphere.

Pittsford and LaRue account executive Carolyn Sukhan originally estimated that 300 people would sign up for the cruise after reading the October 16 ads. But as of November 14, only 200 had done so. Isom and Health Cruises, Inc. faced an important decision.

"Here's the situation as I see it," explained a disturbed Ms. Isom at the Health Cruises board meeting. "We've already paid out more than a quarter of a million to get this cruise rolling. It's going to cost us roughly $200 per passenger for the two weeks, mostly for food. Pittsford and LaRue predicted that 300 people would respond to the advertising campaign, but we've only got 200.

"I see three basic options: (1) we cancel the cruise and take our losses; (2) we run the cruise with the 200 and a

few more that will trickle in over the next month; or (3) we shell out some more money on advertising and hope that we can pull in more people.

"My recommendation to this board is that we try to recruit more passengers. There are simply too many empty rooms on that ship. Each one costs us a bundle."

At this point, Carolyn Sukhan addressed the board: "I've worked out two possible advertising campaigns for the November 20 papers. The first, the limited campaign, will cost $6,000. I estimate that it will bring in some 20 passengers. The more ambitious campaign, which I personally recommend, would cost $15,000. I believe this campaign will bring in a minimum of 40 passengers.

"I realize that our first attempt was somewhat disappointing. But we're dealing here with a new concept, and a follow-up ad might work with many newspaper readers who were curious and interested when they read our first notice.

"One thing is absolutely certain," Sukhan emphasized. "We must act immediately if there's any hope of getting more people on board. The deadline for the Sunday papers is in less than 48 hours. And if our ads don't appear by this weekend, you can forget it. No one signs up in early December for a December 18 sailing date."

Isom interrupted, shaking her head. "I just don't know what to say. I've looked over Carolyn's proposals, and they're excellent. Absolutely first-rate. But our problem, to be blunt, is money. Our funds are tight, and our investors are already nervous. I get more calls each day, asking me where the 300 passengers are. It won't be easy to squeeze another $6,000 out of these people. And to ask them for $15,000—well, I just don't know how we're going to be able to justify it."[13]

Questions

1   What is the minimum number of passengers that Health Cruises must sign up by November 20 to break even with the cruise? (Show your calculations.)

2   Should Health Cruises go ahead with the cruise, since 200 passengers had signed up as of November 14?

3   Would it be worthwhile for Health Cruises to spend either $6,000 or $15,000 for advertising on November 20? If so, which figure would you recommend?

4   How realistic are Carolyn Sukhan's estimates of 20 more passengers for the $6,000 advertising campaign and 40 more passengers for the $15,000 campaign?

5   Should Health Cruises consider cutting its prices for this maiden voyage health cruise?

CASE D–14   Memorial Medical Emergency Clinic: Balancing Costs and Revenues

"We've been open for 11 months and have yet to break even in any one month," mulled Heather Waite as she scanned last month's revenue and expense summary for the Medical Emergency Clinic (MEC) operated by Memorial Hospital. As the administrator for MEC, Waite knows that something has to change. Even though Memorial is a nonprofit hospital, the charter for MEC stipulates that it has to be self-supporting in its second year of operation.

MEC was established to serve the health care needs of people who work in the central business district. The specific services offered by MEC included (1) preventive health care (such as physical examinations), (2) minor emergencies, (3) specialized employer services (such as preemployment examinations and workers' compensation injuries), and (4) primary health care services (for personal illnesses). A breakdown of average monthly service usage and the average charge for each service is as follows:

SERVICE	PERCENTAGE OF VISITS	AVERAGE CHARGE
Personal illness	39%	$25
Physical examinations	14	25
Workers' compensation	25	39
Employment or insurance examinations	19	47
Emergency	3	67

The weighted average charge per visit is $33.94, and the weighted average variable cost per visit is $5.67. Fixed costs per month average $17,500. The average number of visits per month is 590.

Since its opening, MEC has surveyed patients to find out how it might better serve their needs. Patient concerns fell into two categories: service hours and waiting time. To date, MEC has been open from 8 A.M. to 5 P.M., Monday through Friday. However, patients have requested extended hours, with an opening time of 7 A.M. and a closing time at 7 P.M. A second concern is waiting time, particularly during lunch hours (11 A.M. to 2 P.M.). A check of MEC records indicates that 70 percent of patient visits occur during this period, and most of these visits are for personal illnesses and examinations for various reasons. Further checking revealed that people actually left MEC because of congestion and did not return at a later date. Waite believes these concerns could be dealt with if MEC increased its personnel. Her plan is to add another

physician and support personnel to create two staffs. One staff could work from 7 A.M. to 3 P.M., and a second staff could work from 11 A.M. to 7 P.M. By using paramedical personnel and part-time medical assistants, she estimates that average monthly fixed costs will increase by only 25 percent, even with a raise in personnel salaries next year. The staff overlap at lunchtime will alleviate some of the congestion.

Still, Waite feels that something has to be done about the uneven demand for MEC's services during operating hours. She knows that personal physical examinations and employment and insurance examinations can be handled by appointment. Moreover, these services might be provided before or after normal working hours (before 8 A.M. or after 5 P.M.). Her interviews with employers and insurance companies revealed that they will schedule employment and insurance examinations during this period. Based on her interviews, she estimates that MEC could significantly modify its visit mix and number of patients in an average month. Specifically, she believes MEC will have an average of 749 patient visits per month if the hours were expanded. Almost all the additional visits will be for employment and insurance examinations. In addition, Waite received approval to increase the prices of MEC's major services. The new prices, which will become effective at the beginning of the second year of operation, and the forecast mix of patient visits are as follows:

SERVICE	PERCENTAGE OF VISITS	AVERAGE CHARGE
Personal illness	31%	$27
Physical examinations	11	37
Workers' compensation	20	41
Employment or insurance examinations	36	50
Emergency	2	70

Waite believes that the average variable cost per patient visit will be $6 next year, regardless of the mix of patient visits.

As she prepared her recommendation to the Memorial Hospital administrator, she identified at least two options to enable MEC to break even. She could simply institute the price increase, or she could increase prices, expand hours, and incur higher fixed costs. Whatever she recommends, she knows has to support her argument from both a profit and service perspective.[14]

Questions

1 How many visits below the break-even point is MEC at the present time?

2 Can MEC break even when the price increases are put into effect, assuming fixed costs remain unchanged, the visit mix is the same, but variable costs become $6 per visit?

3 Can MEC expand its hours, thereby increasing fixed cost, and break even given a price increase, the increased variable cost per visit, and the new patient visit mix expected by Waite?

CASE D–15   Starbucks Coffee: A Multichannel Strategy

What'll you have? Skinny latte, espresso, almond truffle mocha? How about a Raspberry Mocha Chip Frappuccino or Tazoberry and Cream? Consumers globally are increasingly turning to Starbucks to quench a growing thirst for specialty coffee and beverages.

THE COMPANY

Starbucks has been hugely successful. Net sales have grown from $800,000 in 1990 to an estimated $2.6 billion in 2001. Starbucks got its start in 1971 as a gourmet coffee bean store in Seattle. In 1987, Starbucks' current chief executive, Howard Schultz, opened the first stylish Starbucks coffee bar. The focus then and now has been on high-end gourmet coffees. Customers can buy fresh-roasted beans from around the world, gift packs, Starbucks coffee cups, sweets, as well as freshly brewed coffees. All coffee beans are roasted in-house to maintain quality. The company prides itself on buying top-quality beans. It vacuum packs the beans two hours after roasting and donates to charity any beans that go unsold seven days after opening the bag.

Starbucks employees are given over 24 hours of coffee-making training and lore. Starbucks maintains designers and architects in-house to develop, maintain, and update the hip, upscale image of the stores. All of this has led to the high-quality service that has built Starbucks' brand loyalty.

Citing concern about maintaining quality, Starbucks initially turned down lucrative franchising agreements for its coffee bars. As Starbucks moved into international markets, however, it utilized licensing agreements with local partners in addition to having company-owned stores—a departure from its original channel strategy. Starbucks even has licensed stores in North America. There were over 4,303 Starbucks stores in place globally as of May 2001. Roughly one-third of the international stores are company-operated, compared to almost 70 percent operated by licensees. The percentages are reversed for the North American market with only about 20 percent of store licensees. The company purposely opens stores near one another, even if it involves some cannibalization, in order to ensure intensive distribution coverage in attractive markets.

We're about to give airplane coffee a good name.

United is now serving Starbucks coffee in every class, on every flight worldwide. An improvement that makes perfect sense, coming from the more than 50,000 employees who own United. After all, we don't just work here. We drink the coffee, too. Come fly our friendly skies.

UNITED AIRLINES

Airports, hotels, and malls are all locations for Starbucks coffee bars. Another unique approach to distributing the product is developing special coffee blends for others. For example, Barnes and Noble bookstores have their own coffee bars in many locations and these coffee bars exclusively sell the Starbucks "Barnes and Noble coffee blend." United Airlines touts the fact that they now serve Starbucks coffee in every class on every flight worldwide.

Research also is a key part of Starbucks' success. A sophisticated point-of-sale system allows the company to track store and regional buying trends. The Starbucks real estate division sifts through data on potential markets and market characteristics for at least nine months prior to a store opening.

THE COFFEE MARKET

The coffee market wasn't always perking along. Some would argue that it still isn't. U.S. coffee consumption has declined 50 percent over the past 30 years—with discouraging trends for the youth market. Whereas 59 percent of people 55 to 64 are regular at-home coffee drinkers, only 31 percent of those 25 to 34 are regular coffee drinkers. Nationally, 47 percent of Americans consider themselves coffee drinkers.

The National Coffee Association claims that there were 105 million daily coffee drinkers and 34 million occasional coffee drinkers in the United States in 1991 with 113 million daily drinkers and 64 million occasional drinkers by 1999. Coffee consumption is expected to increase 7 percent by 2005, however, because of increasing average cup size (now up to 9 ounces) and the increase in the baby boomer population. Although specialty brews have boosted coffee consumption and have helped reposition a product category that had little differentiation, Americans now drink an average of 1.87 cups a day, a decline from the early 1960s when the average per capita daily consumption was over three cups.

THE COMPETITION

Today, Starbucks faces competition from a number of international, national, regional, and even local coffee bars and houses. Starbucks is credited with helping educate the public about specialty coffee creating the opening for large and small competitors. Major competitors include Diedrich Coffee, Inc., which produces the Gloria Jean's and Diedrich Coffee brands, as well as Tully's Coffee Corporation of Seattle. Even fast-food outlets such as Dunkin Donuts are improving their coffee offerings.

Starbucks had turned down opportunities to distribute its coffee through supermarkets until recently—this in spite of the fact that Starbucks' CEO considered supermarkets Starbucks' main competition. In 1998, Starbucks began test sales of ground and whole bean coffee in Chicago-area supermarkets. Kraft Foods entered a licensing agreement with Starbucks to place coffee in grocery stores across the country. Supermarkets sell about 70 percent of all coffee and are increasingly going upscale, selling whole beans to be ground in the store.

THE ISSUES

A major issue for Starbucks is the cost of coffee which can fluctuate wildly. Frost in Brazil, the world's largest coffee producer, can damage coffee plants for years. New bushes can take five years to mature. Commodity coffee prices doubled while specialty premium coffees briefly tripled in price as recently as the mid-1990s.

With increasing domestic competition, Starbucks has expanded to Europe and Asia. Starbucks has retail locations in Japan, Singapore, the Philippines, Taiwan, Thailand, the United Kingdom, New Zealand, and Malaysia. Starbucks opened its first store in Beijing, China, in 1999 partnering with Beijing Mei Da Coffee Co. Ltd., its distributor for wholesale operations in Beijing since 1994. Starbucks also opened its first outlet in the Middle East in Kuwait.

Frappucino, a blended coffee and milk drink served chilled or over ice, is a product developed by Starbucks in conjunction with PepsiCo. In spite of the fact that few Americans drank cold coffee prior to Frappucino's introduction as well as General Foods' market failure with a cold cappucino product called Cappio, Frappucino is gaining acceptance. Pepsi's venture with Lipton Tea Company produced the number one product in the ready-made iced-tea category. Starbucks has also developed Starbucks' coffee flavored ice cream in partnership with Dreyer's Grand Ice Cream, Inc. These products have made Starbucks a more significant brand within the grocery store channel. Starbucks also sells coffee and products such as espresso machines, coffee presses, music, and books through its coffee bars and its website www.starbucks.com. Starbucks also has a program to offer food service—coffee, specialty beverages, and other merchandise for a number of different markets including the college/university market, the hotel/casino market, hospital and health care market, as well as business cafeterias. Starbucks has designated "preferred providers" that perform as intermediaries for these market segments. Starbucks screens these select operators to ensure that they deliver the quality and service necessary to maintain the Starbucks experience.

Increasingly, North American consumers are following European consumers' concerns about genetically modified products. As the leader and most visible player in the domestic and increasingly global markets, Starbucks has been the focus of a number of protests. Various organizations have protested Starbucks' use of milk produced from cows treated with bovine growth hormone (rBGH) in its products and have promoted an end to the use of genetically engineered ingredients in all products. Consumers are also pressing for products that are produced by an environmentally and socially responsible method.

Starbucks is committed to providing rBGH-free milk alternatives in all company stores. The company has also worked with Conservation International to offer a coffee that thrives in shade (shade-grown Mexican coffee) that encourages farmers to preserve the forest environment of the endangered Chiapas cloud forest. Farmers earn 65 percent more than local prices for their crop and help protect the environment. Starbucks also offers organic and Fair Trade coffees in its commitment to providing consumers with products that also benefit local growers and the environment.[15]

1 What type of channel strategy is Starbucks currently employing? How does this channel strategy fit with Starbucks' products and positioning?

2 What is Starbucks' competitive advantage? Discuss whether you think this is a sustainable competitive advantage.

3 Starbucks has departed from its reliance on a corporate VMS (vertical marketing system) for its coffee bars, currently using channel partnerships for some of its ventures (such as its relationships with Barnes and Noble and with Dreyer's Grand Ice Cream) as well as franchising agreements in some markets that create a contractual VMS. What are the pros and cons of a corporate system versus a contractual (franchising) VMS? How have Starbucks' marketing and channel objectives and strategies changed over time as they have moved away from a channel based solely on a corporate VMS?

CASE D–16   Dell Computer Corporation: Leader in Supply Chain Management

From humble beginnings in a dorm room in Austin, Texas, Michael Dell has built the company that bears his name into a global phenomenon. Dell holds the number one market share position globally for computer systems and solutions.

Dell is the largest direct seller of computers in the world and one of the top global PC manufacturers. Dell had over $31.8 billion in sales in 2001, a 26.2 percent annual increase in sales. Dell offers PCs, notebooks, network servers, peripherals, and software. Over 90 percent of Dell's sales are to businesses and governmental customers. Dell's success is attributed in large part to its effective use of supply chain management.

What do customers want? They're looking for the latest innovations, competitive pricing, the configuration that will meet their application need, timely delivery, and support before and after sale. Dell carefully manages its supply chain to provide these deliverables to its customers.

Dell has closely aligned its suppliers with its direct channel strategy, resulting in dramatic improvements in inventory management and control. Dell has implemented supply chain management software from I2 that enables it to procure inventory from suppliers over the Web in real time and pull materials into the factories every two hours based on customer orders. Dell averages six days of inventory to supply operations and production. The newest Dell manufacturing plant is running with seven hours worth of inventory! This is important in an industry where component costs can decline 30 to 35 percent per year. This helps Dell take advantage of lower anticipated inventory costs in the future as well as minimizing the risk of holding obsolete parts in inventory. Dell "went negative" in its cash conversion cycle for the last several quarters. In other words, Dell gets paid faster than they pay.

No less significant have been Dell's efforts to work with vendors to reduce vendor cycle times—the time that elapses from Dell placing an order to receiving that order in a Dell manufacturing facility. Dell has launched valuechain.dell.com, a secure Extranet, that acts as a portal for Dell suppliers to collaborate in managing the supply chain. The Extranet provides information to each vendor on Dell's forecasted demand for the vendor's products, shares production schedules, and uses e-mail communication to make adjustments and changes.

The Dell website (www.dell.com) allows customers to shop online. Different online "stores" are available for different types of customers such as education, government, home/home office, and businesses. Shoppers can select the items they want and place them in their shopping basket. Once the order has been submitted, the website has the capability to check delivery dates and to even monitor the status of the order with its online tracking system.

Dell works closely with its customers. Dell achieves customer intimacy with daily contact and because of these relationships and customer input, is able to develop products on schedules that anticipate customer demand. Currently, Dell's more than 65,000 business and institutional customers worldwide use Dell's PremierDell.com Web pages for communication and information exchange.

Dell integrates all its electronic commerce and communication systems. Dell's system uses browser and Internet/Intranet technology as the interface for all applications. This makes it possible for every PC in the world to interact with Dell.

Dell utilizes decision support applications for modeling and simulating materials and factory scheduling to improve supply chain efficiency. For example, Dell can look out hours or days in advance, match this up with materials flow, and on the basis of this information, optimize a manufacturing plan to execute in the factory.

What does this all mean for the customer? Better service and lower costs—value which gives Dell an edge in the marketplace. Dell outperforms its competitors in inventory turnover. Its primary rivals—Gateway Incorporated, Compaq Computer Corporation, and Hewlett-Packard—have average inventories ranging from 16 to 62 days. No one can touch Dell in terms of sales per employee—Dell had sales per employee of $797,200 for the most recent fiscal year, much more than its nearest competitors which had sales per employee ranging from

$390,268 to $551,209. Dell's supply chain management provides a significant competitive advantage.[16]

Questions

1 Explain how Dell's approach to supply chain management satisfies the logistical objectives of minimizing logistics costs while maximizing customer service.

2 What are the supply chain management implications for Dell's competitors that primarily utilize an indirect channel strategy? What supply chain and marketing recommendations do you suggest for Dell given the competitive environment?

3 How does supply chain management relate to the marketing concept at Dell?

CASE D–17   Nordstrom, Inc.: Retailing in a Competitive Environment

Company lore says that John Nordstrom founded the department store that bears his name today using his stake from the Alaska gold rush. Whether the story is fact or fiction, the philosophy behind the company has made its success one of the real gold nuggets in U.S. retailing.

THE COMPANY

Started in Seattle in 1901 as a shoe store by Swedish immigrant, John Nordstrom, and a partner, Carl F. Wallin, the business prospered. In 1928, John Nordstrom sold his stake in the company to his three sons: Everett, Elmer, and Lloyd. Wallin sold his stake the following year. By 1959, Nordstrom was the largest independently owned shoe store in the United States. Nordstrom operated 27 stores in 1963. That same year Nordstrom acquired Best's Apparel, a decision that moved Nordstrom beyond shoes and launched it into women's fashions.

The third family generation took over Nordstrom management in 1970. At that point Nordstrom not only offered shoes but apparel and accessories for the entire family. Although Nordstrom went public as Nordstrom, Inc., in 1971, the Nordstrom family still retains controlling interest in the company. The fourth generation of the family now manages the company.

Nordstrom has grown from a single shoe store to more than 122 U.S. stores as well as more than 20 international boutiques and stores. Nordstrom also has an online shopping presence (nordstrom.com) to offer additional convenience to current and new customers. Nordstrom's 2001 annual sales of over $5.52 billion were up 7.9 percent. Expansion has moved it from the West Coast and Seattle area where Nordstrom has had a major presence to strategic locations throughout the country. Among the many new stores planned to open between 2002 and 2004 are those in Austin, Texas (Barton Creek Square Mall); Minneapolis, Minnesota (Maple Grove Center); Orem, Utah (University Mall); Durham, North Carolina (Streets at Southpoint); St. Louis, Missouri (West County Center); and Coral Gables, Florida (Village of Merrick Park). Nordstrom stores are generally located in major or regional malls and feature a wide selection of apparel and shoes for men, women, and children. Nordstrom stores may include a gift department and often a small restaurant. Nordstrom does not carry furniture, linens, housewares, electronics—items often found in department stores.

THE IDEA

The hallmark of Nordstrom is service. The initial philosophy of the two founders, still guiding Nordstrom today, was to offer the *very best* service, selection, quality, and value to the customer. This commitment to exceptional customer service has been combined with a managerial orientation that encourages and supports an entrepreneurial spirit among employees to react to customer needs.

Extraordinary tales are told of sales associates who went the extra mile to satisfy the customer. Reportedly a customer fell in love with a pair of Donna Karan slacks that had just gone on sale at the Nordstrom store in downtown Seattle. The salesperson, unable to track down the slacks at any of the other five Seattle-area stores, secured some petty cash from her department manager, ran across the street to the Frederick and Nelson Department Store where she bought the slacks at full price, and returned triumphantly to Nordstrom to sell them to the customer at the Nordstrom sale price.

Another fabled story is of a loyal Nordstrom customer who died with her Nordstrom account $1,000 in arrears. Nordstrom not only settled her account but also sent flowers to the funeral.

Nordstrom salespeople make the customer feel special. You won't find Nordstrom customers running to another part of the store to find a gift box (gift boxes are provided, complete with gift card and complimentary bow, in the department in which you make your purchase). One surprised father found that the Nordstrom's men's room had a changing table with complimentary diapers when he went inside to change his young son.

It is not unusual for a customer to receive a thank-you note from your Nordstrom salesperson, or phone calls or notes concerning new merchandise of particular interest to them. Salespeople keep customer books listing customer information such as likes and dislikes, sizes, and past purchases. This allows the salesperson to notify customers when merchandise arrives that could be of interest. One salesperson had the challenge of selling different "looks" to 40 different partners within the same 120-attorney office. It simply wouldn't do for the attorneys to show up in the office with the same suit!

Nordstrom is known not only for its salespeople but also for its generous guarantee return policy and welcoming, comfortable, and hassle-free store designs. One pleased spouse of a devoted Nordstrom customer wrote: "Of all the stores, Nordstrom was best. They gave a husband a place to rest."

THE ISSUES

In an increasingly competitive environment, Nordstrom's emphasis on building customer loyalty and retaining customers provides an advantage. While Nordstrom provides customers with what they consider an unsurpassed commitment to quality and value, increasing price competition and price-conscious consumers may be a threat.

Primary competition for Nordstrom could come from popular specialty stores such as Talbots or Ann Taylor for women's clothing; Brooks Brothers for men's clothing; Joseph Banks, Abercrombie and Fitch, and J. Crew for both men and women; and Kids Talbot and Gymboree for children. In addition, Nordstrom rec-

ognizes The Gap and Banana Republic as competitors. Because apparel specialty stores focus on more narrow product lines such as professional apparel, sportswear, or casual wear or by type of customer, the competition can be very diverse. In addition, traditional department stores such as Marshall Fields, Bloomingdale's, Nieman Marcus, and Saks are primary competitors. Department store competitors and specialty store competitors vary depending on the particular market and geographic location, because many are regional rather than national in scope. It is worth nothing that Nordstrom will experience competition not only from specialty stores for particular product lines (e.g., shoes), but also from stores offering broader lines such as traditional department stores. Continued geographic expansion can provide Nordstrom with additional opportunities for growth but also expose it to new competitors that may attempt to imitate Nordstrom's famous service and quality.[17]

Questions

1 How would Nordstrom be classified as a retail outlet in terms of form of ownership, level of service, and merchandise line?

2 What type of retail position does Nordstrom occupy? Who do you see as its primary competitors, given this position?

3 How do you reconcile Nordstrom's growth and success with the fact that department stores as a category are in the maturity stage of the retail life cycle? What implications are there for Nordstrom given the maturity of the category as well as the wheel of retailing concept?

CASE D–18   McDonald's Restaurants: An IMC Program to Reach Different Segments

"McDonald's outstanding success in Russia is a tribute to our Russian employees, suppliers, and, of course, our customers," comments George A. Cohon, senior chairman, McDonald's in Russia. It all started in 1976 at the Olympic Games in Montreal with a chance meeting between Cohon, who was then senior chairman of McDonald's Canada, and members of the Soviet Olympic delegation.

Fourteen years and countless meetings later, the 700-seat Pushkin Square restaurant in Moscow opened on January 31, 1990. The Pushkin restaurant still is the busiest McDonald's in the world, having served over 77 million customers during the first 11 years since its opening. But competition from Russian quick-service restaurant operators, such as Rostiks and Russian Bistro, is increasing. Therefore, the McDonald's team must continue to develop effective means of communicating with present and prospective customers.

ABOUT McDONALD'S IN RUSSIA

All McDonald's in Russia data in the case are as of March 2001. The amount of food McDonald's has served in Russia is staggering. Consider that in its first 11 years of operations in Russia, McDonald's has served:

- 300 million customers, over twice the 146 million population of Russia.
- 66 million Big Mac™ sandwiches, that if put side by side would be longer than the 3,476-kilometer diameter of the moon!

McDonald's currently has more than 70 restaurants in Russia, from Moscow and St. Petersburg to Nizhny Novgorod and Samara. McDonald's employs more than 6,000 Russians, or about 100 for each new restaurant that opens. Over 70 managers have successfully graduated

from its "Hamburger University" training course held at McDonald's head office in Chicago, part of the 2,000 hours of training they each receive. McDonald's in Russia also operates McComplex, a one-of-a-kind food-processing and distribution facility located in Moscow, which supplies products to restaurants not only in Russia, but also in Germany, Ukraine, Belarus, Austria, and the Czech Republic. It features dairy, bakery, pie, liquid, and meat lines, and has its own quality assurance laboratories to ensure that McDonald's strict food quality standards are met. McDonald's in Russia sources more than 75 percent of the raw ingredients it needs from over 100 independent suppliers in Russia and the Commonwealth of Independent States (CIS).

MCDONALD'S COMMUNITY EFFORTS

McDonald's has a philosophy of "giving back to the communities in which we serve" in the 120 countries in which it operates. In Russia, Ronald McDonald Children's Charities (Russia) operates the Ronald McDonald Centre, a sports and play facility for physically and mentally challenged children. Located in Moscow, the Ronald McDonald Centre hosts more than 1,500 children a week, conducting music, computer, and gym classes. In addition, McDonald's in Russia contributes to various charitable children's organizations to purchase items such as medical supplies and transportation equipment. Since opening 11 years ago, McDonald's in Russia has contributed more than $5 million U.S. to benefit Russian children in need.

WHAT MCDONALD'S MARKETS AND WHAT CUSTOMERS LOOK FOR

McDonald's restaurants were founded and continue to operate worldwide on the basis of the formula, Q, S, C, and V: quality, service, cleanliness, and value. The simple menu ensures convenience and quick service. McDonald's is the favorite restaurant of many Russian families, because McDonald's serves a high-quality meal, in a clean environment, with a smile, at a price families can afford.

Customers all over the world count on McDonald's for consistent taste and high-quality products, no matter where the restaurant is located. The McDonald's quality assurance program ensures that only the best quality products are served to its customers. This program begins with ensuring that only top-quality ingredients are used, that each food item is prepared in a consistent manner, and that the final product meets McDonald's exacting quality standards. For example, the components of a McDonald's Big Mac sandwich in Russia will undergo more than 98 quality checks before the final sandwich is presented to the customer. This ensures that every Big Mac sandwich tastes the same whether it is ordered by a customer in London, Tokyo, or Moscow.

McDonald's offers a curious marketing dilemma. Although the same meals are served to all customers, these same customers may be looking for strikingly different eating experiences on their restaurant visits! For example, a busy manager who only has enough time to "grab a quick lunch" is seeking a different eating experience than a young couple with a six-year-old child who is celebrating a special occasion. McDonald's also practices an "act local" strategy which allows its restaurants to cater to local tastes and laws. For example, its restaurants in Germany and France can serve beer—something prohibited in the United States.

DESIGNING AN INTEGRATED MARKETING COMMUNICATIONS (IMC) PROGRAM

These diverse customer segments, with their very different reasons for visiting a McDonald's restaurant, pose a special challenge for a McDonald's marketing manager responsible for designing and implementing an effective integrated marketing communications (IMC) program. Some of the key initial questions include:

- What are the key market segments that McDonald's might be trying to reach?
- What might each segment look for when it chooses to visit McDonald's?
- What appeals and messages might be used to attract each of these segments?
- What combination of promotional mix elements (advertising, personal selling, public relations, sales promotion, and direct marketing) could be used to reach each segment?

The decisions a McDonald's marketing manager must make become more complicated because the IMC program may vary from city to city. If McDonald's is entering a new city with its first restaurant, an IMC may be very costly. If McDonald's is adding several more restaurants in Moscow, the IMC costs can be spread across the more than 20 outlets it promotes.[18]

Questions

1 Consider these four distinct market segments for McDonald's meals in Russian cities in which it has outlets: a family with young children, busy businesspeople, an older couple,

and foreign tourists who are already familiar with McDonald's. For each segment (*a*) identify the special benefit or appeal McDonald's has to offer and (*b*) compose a 10- to 12-word promotional message that might be used to reach it.

2 For the first McDonald's restaurant to open in a city, what element of an integrated marketing communications (IMC) program might be used to reach (*a*) a family with young children and (*b*) busy businesspeople?

3 For the McDonald's restaurants in Moscow, what element of an integrated marketing communications (IMC) program might be used to reach (*a*) an older couple and (*b*) foreign tourists?

CASE D-19 Volkswagen: The "Drivers Wanted" Campaigns

Volkswagen's comeback in the United States is an amazing marketing story. VW demonstrated that it was possible to recover from a poor reputation with exciting new automobile designs combined with a lively and engaging promotional program. The promotional program's success was due to creation of a unified image for the Volkswagen brand while developing the personalities of each of its separate car models.

VW HISTORY

Volkswagen originally designed the Beetle in pre–World War II Germany as a people's car—"volks" people "wagen" car. It provided dependable, reliable, and economical transportation. The car was first sold in the United States in 1949 with a list price of $800. The car was a commercial success around the world with more than 21 million built, more than any other car in history. It was the best-selling and most-loved car in U.S. auto history. However, by 1979 VW had discontinued sales of the Beetle in the United States. Why?

Volkswagen automobiles had personality—the cuddly Beetle, the counterculture Microbus—but increasingly began to seem dowdy and unpretentious, inconsistent with VW's attempts to reposition itself and its brands as more upscale. Also, many original designs were unlikely to meet growing U.S. safety standards as well as increasing performance standards. Some pundits accused Volkswagen of trying to act like General Motors—appealing to a mass market—and finally credited them with recognizing that Volkswagen has to be Volkswagen.

Volkswagen's U.S. sales, at their peak in 1970 at 570,000 cars, fell to only 49,500 in 1993. Many wrote off Volkswagen and expected them to go the way of Renault and Fiat in the U.S. automotive market. However, by 1999 Volkswagen sales had increased to 316,000 cars.

THE COMEBACK

VW unveiled its new Beetle concept car at the 1994 Detroit Automobile Show. Although the car wasn't scheduled for shipment for two more years, the excitement and anticipation of the Beetle got buyers into showrooms to check out the redesigned Golfs, Passats, and Jettas.

Redesigning cars wasn't enough. Volkswagen unveiled a dynamite advertising campaign using Boston-based Arnold Communications. Arnold Communications has won countless advertising awards for its Volkswagen advertisements including honors from the Association of Independent Commerical Producers, Clios, Addys, ANDYs, Effies, and Cannes Lions.

Using the launch of the new Beetle, Arnold Communications not only generated tremendous interest and enthusiasm for that model but also sent buyers back to Volkswagen showrooms to check out other models. Advertising ran in print and television media geared to the Volkswagen target audience.

The "Drivers Wanted" umbrella tag line runs across all campaigns. However, a key to the Arnold Communications strategy was development of a personality for each of the Volkswagen automobile models. Marketing research played an important role in defining the target audience for each VW model.

For example, the Jetta wagon's target demographics are active, tend to be hikers and outdoor types, with an average age of 31. A recent television advertisement shows the VW Jetta wagon parked next to a tent in a quiet wilderness as the sun rises. We hear voices and finally see a couple emerge from the vehicle—not the tent! Other Jetta wagon commercials build on the "70-cubic-feet" theme and benefits and emphasize the lifestyle characteristics of the target audience. VW spent nearly $100 million in 2000 on Jetta advertising in the United States, where it is the top-selling European brand.

Overall, Volkswagen spent about $350 million on U.S. advertising in 2000.

"Round for a Reason" is the current theme for the Beetle. One ad shows ancient Roman aqueducts as a voice explains how they have stood for centuries because of the engineering marvel—the arch. The Beetle pulls in under the arch as the announcer says "To this day, modern man has yet to improve on the design."

The Beetle's target audience is described as confident, unique, and not afraid of being the center of attention. Since 60 percent of current Beetle buyers are women, Volkswagen is launching a concerted effort to go after men. The convertible Beetle—expected in late 2002—and the new limited-edition Sport model Beetle are expected to attract more male customers.

The VW Euro Van is getting its first U.S. TV campaign with a $10 million effort. "Our awareness for this vehicle is almost nothing" says Karen Marderosian, manager of advertising and marketing at VW. The Euro Van is VW's only truck. It entered the U.S. market in 1992 when the VW brand was in serious decline. Underpowered and overpriced at the time, the newly designed Euro Van has better performance (from 140 to 200 hp) and better value (2001 prices start at $26,500 down from $33,000 for the earlier model).

The new Euro Van campaign is all about freedom. It shows parents driving through desolate locations while talking to their children with geographic names like Denver and Dakota. They pick up a hitchhiker who pitches his "Phoenix" sign in the back with the other signs including Denver and Dakota. This campaign is supplemented with a direct-mail piece to 300,000 Microbus and VW car owners and print ads in national outdoor, lifestyle, and financial magazines and newspapers in 13 key markets. The primary customers for the Euro Van are outdoorsy VW loyalists, concentrated in the Northwest and Southwest, primarily married adults ages 35 to 49 with children.

Overall, Volkswagen customers tend to have high incomes, and are well educated, self-confident, full of life, and fun loving and unpretentious. The segmentation is based more heavily on lifestyle and behavior than demographics. Volkswagen customers are "young at heart," "interested in trying new things," and "very popular on the West and East Coasts and in the sort of centers of the country where there are a lot of educational institutions." The message is "what we're about is what you're about."

Volkswagen also invests in sales training. They recognize that this is a high-involvement purchase and that the salespeople need to project an image of a company that customers want to do business with. Volkswagen holds annual sales meetings but has also tried sending specially outfitted trailers around the country for four-hour interactive presentations to local salespeople.

The Internet is an important element in the Volkswagen promotional program. Given the demographics and psychographics of the VW customer, it is not surprising that a high percentage of this audience uses the Internet. Volkswagen has found that customers want rapid response, new content, and access to information as they conduct research. Many come to the Volkswagen site through third-party sites such as a ratings magazine site where unbiased evaluations of automobile performance can be obtained. Volkswagen has even made special limited-color edition Beetles available for sale online. Consumers can go to the Volkswagen website (www.vw.com) and configure the car and create a personalized "MyVW" page. VW has no plans for direct sales, so once buyers complete the transaction via the Internet they are directed to dealerships to complete the transaction.

What's next for Volkswagen? Their success with the retro Beetle has led to an ambitious plan to launch a twenty-first century remake of its old VW bus. Watch for it![19]

Questions

1 What are the primary promotional objectives for Volkswagen? What are the promotional objectives for the Euro Van? How do you expect Volkswagen and Euro Van objectives to change over time?

2 How did Volkswagen use integrated marketing communications to market the Volkswagen brand? What are the strengths and weaknesses of each element of the promotional mix and how do they correspond to Volkswagen's promotional objectives? What role did the New Beetle play in marketing the brand overall?

3 Volkswagen's promotional program has heavily emphasized a pull promotional strategy versus a push promotional strategy. Why? Is this emphasis likely to change over time?

CASE D–20 Field Furniture Enterprises: Making Promotion Trade-Offs

Edward Meadows, president of Field Furniture Enterprises, met with representatives of Kelly, Astor & Peters Advertising (KAP) and Andrew Reed, Field's vice president of marketing and sales, to discuss the company's advertising program for 2000. The KAP representatives recommended that Field Furniture increase its advertising in shelter magazines (such as *Good Housekeeping* and *Better Homes and Gardens*, which feature home improvement ideas and new ideas in home decorating) by $300,000 and maintain the expenditures for other promotional efforts at a constant level during 2000. The rationale given for the increase in advertising was that Field Furniture had low name recognition among prospective buyers of furniture, and it intended to introduce new styles of living and dining room furniture. Reed, however, had a different opinion as to how Field Furniture should spend the $300,000. He thought it was necessary to (1) hire additional salespeople to call on the 30 new retail stores to be added by the company in 2000, (2) increase the funds devoted to cooperative advertising, and (3) improve the selling aids given to retail stores and salespeople.

THE COMPANY

Field Furniture is a medium-sized manufacturer of medium- to high-priced living and dining room furniture. Sales in 1999 were $50 million. The company sells its furniture through 1,000 furniture specialty stores nationwide, but not all stores carry the company's entire line. This fact bothered Meadows because, in his words, "If they ain't got it, they can't sell it!" The company employs 10 full-time salespeople, who receive a $50,000 base salary annually and a small commission on sales. A company salesforce is atypical in the furniture industry because most furniture manufacturers use selling agents or manufacturer's representatives who carry a wide assortment of noncompeting furniture lines and receive a commission on sales. "Having our own sales group is a policy my father established 30 years ago," noted Meadows, "and we've been quite successful having people who are committed to our company. Our people don't just take furniture orders. They are expected to motivate retail salespeople to sell our line, assist in setting up displays in stores, coordinate cooperative advertising plans, and give advice on a variety of matters to our retailers and their salespeople."

In 1999, Field spent $2.45 million for total promotional expenditures, excluding the salary of the vice president of marketing and sales. Promotional expenditures were categorized into four groups: (1) sales expense and administration, (2) cooperative advertising programs with retailers, (3) trade promotions, and (4) consumer advertising. Cooperative advertising allowances are usually spent on newspaper advertising in a retailer's city and are matched by the retailer's funds on a dollar-for-dollar basis. Trade promotion is directed toward retailers and takes the form of catalogs, trade magazine advertisements, booklets for consumers, and point-of-purchase materials such as displays for use in retail stores. Also included in this category is the expense of trade shows. Field Furniture is represented at two trade shows a year. Consumer advertising is directed to potential consumers through shelter magazines. The typical format used in consumer advertising is to highlight new furniture and different living and dining room arrangements. Dollar allocation for each program in 1999 was as follows:

PROMOTIONAL PROGRAM	EXPENDITURE
Sales expense and administration	$ 612,500
Cooperative advertising	1,102,500
Trade advertising	306,250
Consumer advertising	428,750
Total	$2,450,000

THE INDUSTRY

The household wooden furniture industry is composed of more than 5,000 firms. Industry sales at manufacturers' prices were $10 billion. California, North Carolina, Virginia, New York, Tennessee, Pennsylvania, Illinois, and Indiana are the major U.S. furniture-producing areas. Although Ethan Allen, Bassett, Henredon, and Kroehler are the major furniture manufacturers, no one firm captured more than 3 percent of the total household wooden furniture market.

The buying and selling of furniture to retail outlets centers around manufacturers' expositions at selected times and places around the country. At these marts, as they are called in the furniture industry, retail buyers view manufacturers' lines and often make buying commitments for their stores. However, Field's experience has shown that sales efforts in the retail store by company representatives account for as much as half the company's sales in a given year. The major manufacturer expositions are held in High Point, North Carolina, in October and April. Regional expositions are also scheduled in June through August in locations such as Dallas, Los Angeles, New York, and Boston.

Company research on consumer furniture-buying behavior indicated that people visit several stores when shopping for furniture, and the final decision is made jointly by a husband and wife in about 90 percent of furniture purchases. Other noteworthy findings are as follows:

- Eighty-four percent of buyers believe "the higher the price, the higher the quality" when buying home furnishings.
- Seventy-two percent of buyers browse or window shop in furniture stores even if they don't need furniture.
- Eighty-five percent read furniture ads before they actually need furniture.
- Ninety-nine percent agreed with the statement, "When shopping for furniture and home furnishings, I like the salesperson to show me what alter-

natives are available, answer my questions, and let me alone so I can think about it and maybe browse around."

- Ninety-five percent get redecorating ideas from shelter magazines.
- Forty-one percent have written to order a manufacturer's booklet.
- Sixty-three percent feel they need decorating advice for "putting it all together."

BUDGETARY ISSUES

After the KAP Advertising representatives made their presentation, Reed again emphasized that the incremental $300,000 should not be spent for consumer advertising. He noted that Field Furniture had set as an objective that each salesperson would make six calls per year at each store and spend at least four hours at each store on

every call. "Given that our salespeople work a 40-hour week, 48 weeks per year, and devote only 80 percent of their time to selling due to travel time between stores, we already aren't doing the sales job," Reed added. Meadows agreed but reminded Reed that the $300,000 increment in the promotional budget was a maximum the company could spend, given other cost increases.[20]

Questions

1   How might you describe furniture buying using the purchase decision process described in Chapter 5?
2   How might each of the elements of the promotional program influence each stage in the purchase decision process?
3   What should Field's promotional objectives be?
4   How many salespeople does Field need to adequately service its accounts?
5   Should Field Furniture emphasize a push or pull promotional strategy? Why?

CASE D–21   Mattel, Inc.: Barbie.com and Multichannel Marketing

"We've been at the forefront of marketing for 40 years, so we have to be at the forefront of this new medium," says Christina DeRosa, vice president of website and media content for Mattel's Barbie/Girls' Division. "The Internet has become a very compelling part of a girl's life. When that happens to your customer base, you have to think about it," she added.

Ms. DeRosa is explaining why Mattel ventured into interactive and multichannel marketing with its Barbie.com website and first-ever Barbie catalog in the fall of 2000. "It's still too early to tell what will work and what won't," says Adrienne Fontanella, president of the Barbie/Girls' division. "But if we didn't do this, we'd be like a house without a refrigerator in the future."

THE TOY AND GAME INDUSTRY

The toy and game industry (excluding video games) is big business. Worldwide sales exceed $55 billion. The largest toy and game market is North America, which accounts for 43 percent of worldwide industry sales. A child in the United States receives about $400 worth of toys and games per year on average. The average annual expenditure per child outside the United States is $34.

U.S. chain stores are the principal distributors of toys and games. General merchandise stores like Wal-Mart stores, Kmart, and Target register 35 percent of retail sales. Toy chains, such as Toys "Я" Us, account for 25 percent of retail sales. Other retailers (toy, hobby, and game stores, department stores, and food and drug outlets) record 35 percent of sales. Four percent of toys and

games are sold through catalogs and one percent is sold on the Internet. Wal-Mart stores is the number 1 toy retailer, followed by Toys "Я" Us, Kmart, and Target, which sell toys and games through their retail stores and on their own websites.

The worldwide toy and game industry is dominated by two U.S. toy makers: Mattel and Hasbro. Japan's Bandai Company and Sanrio, as well as Denmark's LEGO Company, are also major toy makers with annual sales exceeding $1 billion.

THE COMPANY

Mattel is the house that the Barbie doll built. Headquartered in El Segundo, California, Mattel is the world's largest toy maker with sales just under $5 billion in 2000. In addition to marketing the world's best-selling toy—the Barbie doll (which accounts for 28 percent of company sales)—Mattel produces Fisher-Price toys, Hot Wheels cars, and action figures and toys based on Disney movies and the Harry Potter children's books.

Mattel's toys are sold around the world. However, 71 percent of company sales emanate from the United States. Almost all of Mattel's sales are made through toy stores and retailers—Toys "Я" Us and Wal-Mart stores alone account for 40 percent of Mattel's retail sales. In 1998, Mattel bought the mail-order firm Pleasant Company that markets American Girl–brand books, dolls, and clothing. Mattel's senior management planned to use American Girl as a platform to expand all Mattel brands into direct marketing saying that the acquisition would allow Mattel to generate as much as $1 billion in direct-to-customer sales. A secondary benefit of directing marketing was to reduce Mattel's reliance on retailers for sales.

THE ISSUES

Mattel's fall 2000 launch of a Barbie website and catalog was the company's most recent attempt at interactive and multichannel marketing. In the fall of 1998, Mattel introduced a Barbie website that featured My Design Barbie at www.barbie.com. Visitors could specify the features for their very own personalized Barbie doll, including hairstyle, eye and hair color, skin tone, clothes, and accessories. The custom-made doll was manufactured by Mattel and shipped to the buyer within six to eight weeks of the order date. However, this first effort by Mattel was modified and the My Design feature was dropped. Also, Mattel's large retailers complained about the website because of the potential for competition with their stores.

The new Barbie.com and catalog initiative was developed with the intention of accommodating retailer concerns. For example, Mattel voluntarily limited the number of products it made available in its catalog and on its website. Prices were deliberately set 15 percent higher than the suggested retail price in stores. On each catalog, Mattel listed, according to zip code, the nearest retailers where Mattel products were sold and prominently displayed the Barbie.com website address. The website featured Wal-Mart stores and Toys "Я" Us as retailers. Finally, Mattel didn't advertise the commerce features of the Barbie website. Still, Mattel's efforts did not accommodate everyone. "We're supposed to be partners and this is obviously competitive," said one top toy retail executive.[21]

Questions

1 What would a diagram of Mattel's multichannel strategy for Barbie look like? (*Hint*: Refer to Chapter 21, Figure 21–6.)

2 Visit the Barbie.com website at www.barbie.com. Is Barbie.com primarily a transaction or promotional website?

3 What type of channel conflict is Mattel trying to minimize with its approach to interactive and multichannel marketing? (*Hint*: Look again at Chapter 15, Conflict in Marketing Channels.) Why do you think Mattel, as the world's largest toy maker, believes it has to accommodate its large retailers?

CASE D–22   BP Connect™: Gasoline, Convenience, and . . . Just-Baked Bread!

"Before developing BP Connect™, we did extensive research to find exactly what consumers wanted in a convenience and fuel store," says Jack Burdett, senior vice president of retail marketing for BP plc.

Burdett is referring to a full-scale prototype of BP Connect's 4,200-square-foot convenience food-gasoline station constructed in an Atlanta warehouse in July 2000. Reactions of U.S. consumers touring the Atlanta prototype were overwhelmingly positive. BP spent $7 million developing the BP Connect concept and will spend $4.4 billion during the next four years to update old or build new BP Connect stations worldwide. In December 2000, BP Connect outlets opened in London, England, and Lisbon, Portugal, to enthusiastic reviews. The first BP Connect stations in the United States opened in 2001 in Indianapolis, Cleveland, and Atlanta.

THE COMPANY

BP plc—often shortened to simply BP—is the world's largest producer and marketer of petroleum products. BP is also the largest gasoline retailer in the United States with 17,500 stations, or about 15 percent of the market. Since 1998, BP has spent $120 billion to acquire Amoco, ARCO, and Burmah Castrol, making it the largest retailer of petroleum products in the world. At the end of 2000, BP served 10 million customers per day globally with 28,000 branded retail sites, including 4,300 AM/PM™ convenience stores.

Initially, Amoco was going to be the brand identity used in the United States. However, according to Doug Ford, BP's CEO for retailing and marketing worldwide, that decision was changed after BP conducted focus

groups. Consumers preferred the new BP logo and color scheme but still wanted the quality products that Amoco sells. Therefore, while BP will rebrand its BP and Amoco sites, it will continue to offer branded Amoco gasoline. However, because ARCO's customers are different than BP's or Amoco's, BP will also retain the very successful AM/PM™ convenience stores and ARCO-branded gasoline staions.

TRENDS IN CONVENIENCE STORE AND GASOLINE RETAILING

Several major trends currently affect both traditional convenience store and petroleum retailing worldwide:

- *Mergers and acquisitions.* During the past several years, BP and other major oil firms, such as Exxon (Mobil) and Total (PetroFina & Elf), have merged with or acquired one or more of their competitors.
- *Convergence.* Since 1977, the percentage of gasoline stations in the United States that are also convenience stores has gone from 5 percent to 45 percent. To improve profitability, convenience stores and gasoline retailers have encroached on each other's domain by offering products and services typically sold by the other.
- *Competition.* In the United States, large supermarket chains (such as Albertson's, in partnership with ARCO, which is owned by BP), mass merchandisers (such as Wal-Mart), and membership organizations (such as Costco or Sam's Club), have added retail petroleum operations to their product-service mix that are located on their parking lots.
- *Convenience.* Changes in lifestyle and shopping behavior has resulted in a greater demand for time and place convenience by consumers. Gasoline retailers have replaced the old "gas and cigarettes" strategy with a "scrambled merchandising" strategy that offers consumers several unrelated product lines in a single retail outlet, such as food, car washes, ATM banking, and new payment technologies (Exxon Mobil's Speedpass) to speed up the payment transactions.
- *Branding.* A growing number of petroleum retailers are using brand management to create a consistent, global, and proprietary image that enables firms to differentiate their offerings from those of competitors to gain a competitive advantage.
- *Co-branding.* Co-branding involves the pairing of brand names into a coherent image from two or more marketers to capitalize on the strengths of each that appeals to a firm's target consumers. Convenience store and petroleum marketers have developed relationships with fast-food restaurants (such as Taco Bell, Blimpie's, etc.) and other food, beverage, and nonfood firms in order to satisfy more consumer needs immediately, instead of having them buy the same brand elsewhere.

THE BP CONNECT CONCEPT

Based on the results of marketing research—much at the prototype outlet in Atlanta—BP Connect stores will feature:

- *A new logo.* The BP shield and Amoco torch will be replaced by a new logo that BP hopes will enhance its corporate image as a "green," environmentally friendly company.
- *Solar panels.* BP is the world's largest producer of solar power, so BP Connect will use renewable electricity generated from solar panels in its curved canopy to provide 10 to 20 percent of the power needed to operate the station.
- *High-tech pumps, and twenty-first century information technology.* Instead of traditional rectangular pumps, BP Connect stations will have curved ones that include an 8-inch touch screen to display news, weather, sports scores, and promotions; enable consumers to order food inside while pumping gas and to pay with a debit/credit card; and print travel maps from in-store Internet kiosks.
- *Sectional design.* Using a wide, open-aisle design, BP Connect will be divided into five sections: food service, beverage, impulse-buying with snacks, convenience-store, and Internet kiosk. Lighting will change with each section. In-store offerings will include fresh fruit and produce, a bakery, and a Wild Bean Coffee quick-serve restaurant. Some stores will have attached car washes.

BP plans on spending $200 million to let its BP Connect stores link to the Internet, which will let drivers check traffic congestion at the gas pumps or go inside and—for a fee—use the Web at a kiosk. The goal: Help BP generate half its retail sales from nonfuel items within five years.

THE MARKETING ISSUES

The BP Connect rollout strategy for the new stations represents a massive investment. Not only is there huge competition from other petroleum companies, but convenience store, supermarket, and mass-merchandiser chains are moving into the gasoline business. In addition, following the September 11, 2001, attacks, the demand for energy plummeted, oil prices fell by a third, and oil company profits fell.[22]

In answering the following questions, assume you are a marketing consultant to BP, assisting it with its BP Connect global rollout strategy for the next three years.

Questions

1 Conduct a SWOT (strengths, weaknesses, opportunities, threats) analysis for the BP Connect concept—looking forward globally to the next three years.

2 Consider these two elements of the BP Connect concept described above: high-tech pumps and twenty-first century information technology; and the sectional design. Assess these from the point of view of consumers in: (*a*) the United States, (*b*) Western Europe, and (*c*) Eastern Europe.

3 In the United States, how might BP conduct marketing research on the two elements of BP Connect identified in question 2 above?

GLOSSARY

above-, at-, or below-market pricing Pricing based on market price.

accelerated development The second stage of the retail life cycle, characterized by rapid increases in market share and profitability.

accessory equipment Support goods, such as tools and office equipment, usually purchased in small-order sizes by buyers.

account management policies Policies that specify whom salespeople should contact, what kinds of selling and customer service activities should be engaged in, and how these activities should be carried out.

action item list An aid to implementing a market plan, consisting of three columns: (1) the task, (2) the name of the person responsible for completing that task, and (3) the date by which the task is to be finished.

adaptive selling A need-satisfaction sales presentation that involves adjusting the presentation to fit the selling situation.

administered vertical marketing systems Achieve coordination at successive stages of production and distribution by the size and influence of one channel member rather than through ownership.

adoption Through a favorable experience on the first trial, a consumer's repeated purchase and use of the product or brand.

advertising Any paid form of nonpersonal communication about an organization, good, service, or idea by an identified sponsor.

advocacy advertisements Institutional advertisements that state the position of a company on an issue.

air freight forwarders Firms that market air express services to the general public. Also called express companies.

all-you-can-afford budgeting Allocating funds to promotion only after all other budget items are covered.

allowances Reductions from list or quoted prices to buyers for performing some activity.

anchor stores Well-known national or regional stores located in regional shopping centers.

ancillary services The degree of service or support required after the sale of a product.

approach stage In the personal selling process, the initial meeting between the salesperson and prospect, where the objectives are to gain the prospect's attention, stimulate interest, and build the foundation for the sales presentation itself and the basis for a working relationship.

aseptic packaging Germfree packaging that allows products to be sealed in paper containers and stored for extended periods of time without refrigeration.

assurance Dimension of service quality—the knowledge and courtesy of employees and their ability to convey trust and confidence.

atmosphere A store's ambiance or setting.

attitude A learned predisposition to respond to an object or class of objects in a consistently favorable or unfavorable way.

average revenue The average amount of money received for selling one unit of a product.

awareness The consumer's ability to recognize and remember the product or brand name.

baby boomers The generation of children born between 1946 and 1964.

back translation Retranslating a word or phrase into the original language by a different interpreter to catch errors.

backward integration Practice in the corporate vertical marketing system in which a retailer also owns a manufacturing operation.

bait-and-switch advertising An advertising practice in which a company shows a product that it has no intention of selling to lure the customer into the store and sell him a higher-priced item.

balance of trade The difference between the monetary value of a nation's exports and imports.

banner ads Strip ads in online advertising that usually contain a company or product name or some kind of promotional offer.

barriers to entry Business practices or conditions that make it difficult for new firms to enter the market.

barter The practice of exchanging goods and services for other goods and services rather than for money.

basing-point pricing Selecting one or more geographic locations (basing point) from which the list price for products plus freight expenses are charged to buyers.

behavioral learning The process of developing automatic responses to a situation built up through repeated exposure to it.

beliefs A consumer's subjective perception of how well a product or brand performs on different attributes; these are based on personal experience, advertising, and discussions with other people.

benchmarking Discovering how others do something better than your own firm so you can imitate or leapfrog competition.

bidder's list A list of firms believed to be qualified to supply a given item.

billboards The most common form of outdoor advertising.

blanket branding (see multiproduct branding)

blended family Formed by the merging into a single household of two previously separated units.

bots Electronic shopping agents or robots that comb websites to compare prices and product or service features.

brand equity The added value a given brand name gives to a product beyond the functional benefits provided.

brand extension The practice of using a current brand name to enter a completely different product class.

brand loyalists Online consumer lifestyle segment who regularly visit their favorite book-marked websites and spend the most money online.

brand loyalty A favorable attitude toward and consistent purchase of a single brand over time.

brand manager (see product manager)

brand name Any word, "device" (design, shape, sound, or color), or combination of these used to distinguish a seller's goods or services.

brand personality A set of human characteristics associated with a brand name.

branding Activity in which an organization uses a name, phrase, design, or symbols, or combination of these, to identify its products and distinguish them from those of competitors.

breadth of product line   The variety of different items a store carries.

break-even analysis   A technique that analyzes the relationship between total revenue and total cost to determine profitability at various levels of output.

break-even chart   A graphic presentation of the break-even analysis.

break-even point (BEP)   Quantity at which total revenue and total cost are equal and beyond which profit occurs.

brokers   Independent firms or individuals whose principal function is to bring buyers and sellers together to make sales.

build-to-order (BTO)   Manufacturing a product only when there is an order from a customer.

buildup forecast   Summing the sales forecasts of each of the components to arrive at the total forecast.

bundle pricing   The marketing of two or more products in a single "package" price.

business analysis   Involves specifying the features of the product and the marketing strategy needed to commercialize it and making necessary financial projections.

business analysis stage   Step 4 of the new-product process, which involves specifying the product features and marketing strategy and making necessary financial projections to commercialize a product.

business culture   Comprises the effective rules of the game, the boundaries between competitive and unethical behavior, and the codes of conduct in business dealings.

business firm   A privately owned organization that serves its customers in order to earn a profit.

business goods   Products that assist directly or indirectly in providing products for resale (also known as B2B goods, industrial goods, or organizational goods).

business marketing   The marketing of goods and services to commercial enterprises, governments, and other profit and not-for-profit organizations for use in the creation of goods and services that they then produce and market to other business customers as well as individuals and ultimate consumers.

business plan   A road map for the entire organization for a specific future period of time, such as one year or five years.

business portfolio analysis   Analysis of a firm's strategic business units (SBUs) as though they were a collection of separate investments.

business unit   An organization that markets a set of related products to a clearly defined group of customers.

business unit goal   A performance target the business unit seeks to reach to achieve its mission.

business unit level   Level at which business unit managers set the direction for their products and markets.

business unit mission   A statement specifying the markets and product lines in which a business unit will compete.

buy classes   Three types of organizational buying situations: new buy, straight rebuy, and modified rebuy.

buyer turnover   How often new buyers enter the market to buy a product.

buyers   Role in the buying center with formal authority and responsibility to select the supplier and negotiate the terms of the contract.

buying center   The group of people in an organization who participate in the buying process and share common goals, risks, and knowledge important to a purchase decision.

buying criteria   The factors buying organizations use when evaluating a potential supplier and what it wants to sell.

buzz   Word-of-mouth behavior in marketspace.

canned sales presentation   A memorized, standardized message conveyed to every prospect.

capacity management   Integrating the service component of the marketing mix with efforts to influence consumer demand.

case allowance   A trade-oriented sales promotion giving a discount on each case ordered during a specific time period.

cash and carry wholesaler   A limited-service merchant wholesaler that takes title to merchandise but sells only to buyers who call on it, pay cash for merchandise, and furnish its own transportation for merchandise.

cash discount   Price reduction to encourage retailers to pay their bills quickly.

category killers   Specialty discount outlets that focus on one type of product, such as electronics or business supplies, at very competitive prices. They often dominate the market.

cause-related marketing   Occurs when the charitable contributions of a firm are tied directly to the customer revenues produced through the promotion of one of its products.

caveat emptor   The legal concept of "let the buyer beware" that was pervasive in American business culture before the 1960s.

cease and desist order   An order issued to a company by the Federal Trade Commission (FTC) to stop practices it considers unfair.

cells   Boxes in a table or cross tabulation.

central business district   The oldest retail setting, the community's downtown area.

channel captain   A marketing channel member that coordinates, directs, and supports other channel members; may be a producer, wholesaler, or retailer.

channel conflict   Arises when one channel member believes another channel member is engaged in behavior that prevents it from achieving its goals.

channel of communication   The means (e.g., a salesperson, advertising media, or public relations tools) of conveying a message to a receiver.

channel partnership   Agreements and procedures among channel members for ordering and physically distributing a producer's product through the channel to the ultimate consumer.

Child Protection Act (1966)   A federal consumer protection law.

Children's Online Privacy Protection Act (1998)   A law requiring parental permission before collecting personal information from minors.

Children's Television Act (1990)   An act that limits the maximum amount of advertising during children's television programs.

choice board   An interactive, Internet/Web-enabled system that allows individual customers to design their own products and services.

Clayton Act (1914)   A law that forbids certain actions that are likely to lessen competition, although no actual harm has yet occurred.

Clean Air Act (1990)   A law to curb acid rain and air pollution.

click-and-mortar   Online consumer lifestyle segment consisting of female homemakers who tend to browse retailer websites, but actually buy products in traditional retail outlets.

closed-end question   Requires respondents to select one or more response options from a set of predetermined choices.

closing stage   The stage in the personal selling process that involves obtaining a purchase commitment from a prospect.

co-branding   The pairing of two brand names of two manufacturers on a single product.

code of ethics   A formal statement of ethical principles and rules of conduct.

cognitive dissonance   The feeling of postpurchase psychological tension or anxiety a consumer often experiences.

cognitive learning   Making connections between two or more ideas or simply observing the outcomes of others' behaviors and adjusting your own accordingly.

cold canvassing   Generating leads in person or by telephone from a directory.

collaborative filtering   A process that automatically groups people with similar buying intentions, preferences, and behaviors and predicts future purchases.

combination compensation plan   A compensation plan whereby a salesperson is paid a specified salary plus a commission based on sales or profit generated.

commerce   A website's ability to conduct sales transactions for products and services.

commercial online services   Companies that provide electronic information and marketing services to subscribers who are charged a monthly fee.

commercialization   Positioning and launching a new product in full-scale production and sales.

communication   (1) The process of conveying a message to others, which requires six elements: a source, a message, a channel of communication, a receiver, and the processes of encoding and decoding.(2) Online, the dialogue that unfolds between a website and its users.

community   Website design element encouraging user-to-user communications hosted by the company to create virtual communities.

community shopping center   A retail location that typically has one primary store (usually a department store branch) and 20 to 40 smaller outlets, serving a population of consumers who are within a 10- to 20-minute drive.

company forecast   (see sales forecast)

comparative advertisements   Show one brand's strengths relative to those of competitors.

competencies   An organization's special capabilities, including skills, technologies, and resources that distinguish it from other organizations.

competition   The alternative firms that could provide a product to satisfy a specific market's needs.

competitive advantage   A unique strength relative to competitors, often based on quality, time, cost, or innovation.

competitive advertisements   The objective of these messages is to persuade the target market to select the firm's brand rather than that of a competitors.

competitive institutional advertisements   Promote the advantages of one product class over another and are used in markets where different product classes compete for the same buyers.

competitive parity budgeting   Matching the competitors' absolute level of spending or the proportion per point of market share.

complexity   The technical sophistication of the product and hence the amount of understanding required to use it.

computer-assisted retailing   A retailing method whereby customers order products over computer linkups from their home after viewing items on the TV or on their computer monitor.

computer-mediated buying   The use of Internet technology to seek information, evaluate alternatives, and make purchase decisions.

concept tests   External evaluations of a product idea that consist of preliminary testing of the new product idea (rather than the actual product) with consumers.

conference selling   A form of team selling where a salesperson and other company resource people meet with buyers to discuss problems and opportunities.

connection   Website design element that is the network of formal linkages between a company's site and other sites.

consolidated metropolitan statistical area (CMSA)   The largest designation in terms of geographical area and market size, made up of several primary metropolitan statistical areas (PMSAs) that total at least 1 million people.

constraints   The restrictions, such as time and money, placed on potential solutions by the nature and importance of the problem.

consultative selling   Focuses on problem definition, where the salesperson serves as an expert on problem recognition and resolution.

consumer behavior   The actions a person takes in purchasing and using products and services, including the mental and social processes that precede and follow these actions.

Consumer Bill of Rights (1962)   Codified the ethics of exchange between buyers and sellers, including the right to safety, to be informed, to choose, and to be heard.

consumer ethnocentrism   The tendency to believe that it is inappropriate, indeed immoral, to purchase foreign-made products.

consumer goods   Products purchased by the ultimate consumer.

consumer-oriented sales promotion   Sales tools used to support a company's advertising and personal selling efforts directed to ultimate consumers; examples include coupons, sweepstakes, and samples.

Consumer Product Safety Act (1972)   A law that established the Consumer Product Safety Commission to monitor product safety and establish uniform product safety standards.

consumer socialization   The process by which people acquire the skills, knowledge, and attitudes necessary to function as consumers.

consumerism   A grassroots movement started in the 1960s to increase the influence, power, and rights of consumers in dealing with institutions.

content   All digital information included on a website, including the presentation form—text, video, audio, and graphics.

contest   A sales promotion in which consumers apply their skill or analytical or creative thinking to win a prize.

context   A website's aesthetic appeal and functional look and feel reflected in site layout and design.

continuity programs   Sales promotions used to encourage and reward repeat purchases by acknowledging each purchase made by a consumer and offering a premium as purchases accumulate.

continuous innovations   No new behaviors must be learned to use these new products.

continuous schedule   When seasonal factors are unimportant, advertising is run at a continuous schedule throughout the year; also called steady scheduling.

contract assembly A firm contracts with a foreign firm to assemble (not manufacture) parts and components that have been shipped to that country.

contract manufacturing A firm contracts with a foreign firm to manufacture products according to stated specifications.

contracting A strategy used during the decline stage of the product life cycle in which a company contracts the manufacturing or marketing of a product to another firm.

contractual system Independently owned stores that band together to act like a chain.

contractual vertical marketing system Independent production and distribution firms integrate their efforts on a contractual basis to obtain greater functional economies and marketing impact than they could achieve alone.

control group A group not exposed to the experimental variable in an experiment.

controlled distribution minimarkets Test markets run in smaller test areas that electronically monitor product purchases at checkout counters for more careful testing at reduced costs.

convenience goods Items that the consumer purchases frequently and with a minimum of shopping effort.

cookies Computer files that a marketer can download onto the computer of an online shopper who visits the marketer's website.

cooperative advertising Advertising programs by which a manufacturer pays a percentage of the retailer's local advertising expense for advertising the manufacturer's products.

corporate chain A form of retail ownership with multiple outlets under common ownership.

corporate culture A system of shared attitudes and behaviors held by the employees that distinguish an organization from others.

corporate goals Strategic performance targets that the entire organization must reach to pursue its vision.

corporate level Level at which top management directs overall strategy for the entire organization.

corporate philosophy The values and "rules of conduct" for running an organization.

corporate takeover The purchase of a firm by outsiders.

corporate vertical marketing system The combination of successive stages of production and distribution under a single ownership.

corporate vision A clear word picture of the organization's future, often with an inspirational theme.

corrective advertising FTC action requiring a company to spend money on advertising to correct previous misleading ads.

cost focus strategy Involves controlling expenses and, in turn, lowering prices, in a narrow range of market segments.

cost leadership strategy Using a serious commitment to reducing expenses that, in turn, lowers the price of the items sold in a relatively broad array of market segments.

cost of goods sold Total value of the products sold during a specified time period.

cost per thousand (CPM) The cost of reaching 1,000 individuals or households with an advertising message in a given medium. (M is the Roman numeral for 1,000.)

cost-plus fixed-fee pricing A pricing method where a supplier is reimbursed for all costs, regardless of what they turn out to be, but is allowed only a fixed fee as profit that is independent of the final cost of the project.

cost-plus percentage-of-cost pricing A fixed percentage is added to the total unit cost.

cost-plus pricing The practice of summing the total unit cost of providing a product or service and adding a specific amount to the cost to arrive at a price.

countertrade The practice of using barter rather than money for making international sales.

coupons Sales promotions that usually offer a discounted price to consumers, which encourages trial.

credence properties Characteristics that the consumer may find impossible to evaluate even after purchase and consumption.

cross-cultural analysis The study of similarities and differences among consumers in two or more nations or societies.

cross-docking Practice of unloading products from suppliers, sorting products for individual stores, and quickly reloading products onto trucks for a particular store.

cross-functional teams A small number of people from different departments in an organization who are mutually accountable to a common set of performance goals.

cross-tabulation Method of presenting and relating data having two or more variables to analyze and discover relationships in the data.

cue A stimulus or symbol perceived by consumers.

cultural ethnocentricity The belief that aspects of one's culture are superior to another's.

cultural symbols Things that represent ideas and concepts.

culture The set of values, ideas, and attitudes of a homogeneous group of people that are transmitted from one generation to the next.

cumulative quantity discounts Apply to the accumulation of purchases of a product over a given time period, typically a year.

currency exchange rate The price of one country's currency expressed in terms of another country's currency.

customary pricing A method of pricing based on tradition, a standardized channel of distribution, or other competitive factors.

customer contact audit A flowchart of the points of interaction between consumer and service provider.

customer experience The sum total of interactions that a customer has with a company's website.

customer relationship management (CRM) The process of identifying prospective buyers, understanding them intimately, and developing favorable long-term perceptions of the organization and its offerings so that buyers will choose them in the marketplace.

customer service The ability of logistics management to satisfy users in terms of time, dependability, communication, and convenience.

customer value The unique combination of benefits received by targeted buyers that includes quality, price, convenience, on-time delivery, and both before-sale and after-sale service.

customerization The growing practice of customizing not only a product or service but also personalizing the marketing and overall shopping and buying interaction for each customer.

customization The ability of a website to modify itself to— or be modified by—each user.

customized interaction Promotional element used in personal selling between a seller and a prospective buyer.

customs Norms and expectations about the way people do things in a specific country.

data The facts and figures pertinent to the problem, comprised of primary and secondary data.

data mining The extraction of hidden predictive information from large databases.

deal A sales promotion that offers a short-term price reduction.

deceptive pricing A practice by which prices are artificially inflated and then marked down under the guise of a sale.

decider Role in buying center with the formal or informal power to select or approve the supplier that receives the contract.

decision A conscious choice from among two or more alternatives.

decision making The act of consciously choosing from alternatives.

decision-making unit (DMU) The people in a household or an organization's buying center who are involved in the decision to buy a product.

decline stage The fourth and last stage of the product life cycle when sales and profits begin to drop.

decoding The process of having the receiver take a set of symbols, the message, and transform them back to an abstract idea.

deletion Dropping a product from the company's product line.

delivered pricing A pricing method where the price the seller quotes includes all transportation costs.

demand curve The summation of points representing the maximum number of products consumers will buy at a given price.

demand factors Factors that determine consumers' willingness and ability to pay for goods and services.

demographics Describing the population according to selected characteristics such as their age, gender, ethnicity, income, and occupation.

department Group at the functional level where specialists create value for the organization.

depth of product line The store carries a large assortment of each item.

derived demand Demand for industrial products and services driven by, or derived from, demand for consumer products and services.

desk jobber (see drop shipper)

development Turning the idea on paper into a prototype.

dichotomous question A fixed alternative question that allows only a "yes" or "no" response.

differentiation focus strategy Using significant points of difference in the firm's offerings to reach one or only a few market segments.

differentiation positioning Positioning a product in a smaller market niche that is less competitive.

differentiation strategy Requires innovation and significant points of difference in product offerings, brand image, higher quality, advanced technology, or superior service in a relatively broad array of market segments.

diffusion of innovation The process by which a product diffuses, or spreads, through the population.

direct channel A marketing channel where a producer and ultimate consumer deal directly with each other.

direct exporting A firm selling its domestically produced goods in a foreign country without intermediaries.

direct forecast Estimating the value to be forecast without any intervening steps.

direct investment A domestic firm actually investing in and owning a foreign subsidiary or division.

direct marketing Promotional element that uses direct communication with consumers to generate a response in the form of an order, a request for further information, or a visit to a retail outlet.

direct marketing channels Allow consumers to buy products by interacting with various advertising media without a face-to-face meeting with a salesperson.

direct orders The result of direct marketing offers that contain all the information necessary for a prospective buyer to make a decision to purchase and complete the transaction.

discontinuous innovations Make the consumer learn entirely new consumption patterns in order to use the product.

discounts Reductions from list price that a seller gives a buyer as a reward for some buyer activity favorable to the seller.

discretionary income The money that remains after paying for taxes and necessities.

disintermediation Channel conflict that arises when a channel member bypasses another member and sells or buys products direct.

disposable income The money a consumer has left after paying taxes to use for food, shelter, and clothing.

distribution center Designed to facilitate the timely movement of goods and represent a very important part of a supply chain.

diversification A strategy of developing new products and selling them in new markets.

downsizing Reducing the content of packages without changing package size and maintaining or increasing the package price.

drive A need that moves an individual to action.

drop shipper A merchant wholesaler that owns the merchandise it sells but does not physically handle, stock, or deliver; also called a desk jobber.

dual distribution An arrangement by which a firm reaches buyers by employing two or more different types of channels for the same basic product.

dumping When a firm sells a product in a foreign country below its domestic price or below its actual cost.

durable good An item that usually lasts over an extended number of uses.

dynamic pricing The practice of changing prices for products and services in real time in response to supply and demand conditions.

dynamically continuous innovations Only minor changes in behavior are required to use these new products.

early adopters The 13.5 percent of the population who are leaders in their social setting and act as an information source on new products for other people.

early growth The first stage of the retail life cycle, when a new outlet emerges as a sharp departure from competitive forms.

early majority The 34 percent of the population who are deliberate and rely on personal sources for information on new products.

ebivalent newbies Online consumer lifestyle segment consisting of newcomers to the Internet who rarely spend money online but seek product information.

economic espionage The clandestine collection of trade secrets or proprietary information about a company's competitors.

Economic Espionage Act A law that makes the theft of trade secrets by foreign entities a federal crime in the United States.

economic infrastructure A country's communications, transportation, financial, and distribution systems.

economy The income, expenditures, and resources that affect the cost of running a business and household.

efficient consumer response (see quick response)

eight-second rule   Customers will abandon their efforts to enter and navigate a website if download time exceeds 8 seconds.

80/20 rule   A concept that suggests 80 percent of a firm's sales are obtained from 20 percent of its customers.

elastic demand   A situation where a 1 percent decrease in price produces more than a 1 percent increase in quantity demanded, thereby actually increasing sales revenue.

electronic commerce   Any activity that uses some form of electronic communication in the inventory, exchange, advertisement, distribution, and payment of goods and services.

electronic data interchange (EDI)   Combine proprietary computer and telecommunication technologies to exchange electronic invoices, payments, and information among suppliers, manufacturers, and retailers.

electronic marketing channels   Employ the Internet to make goods and services available for consumption or use by consumers or industrial buyers.

e-marketplaces   Online trading communities that bring together buyers and supplier organizations.

emotional intelligence   The ability to understand one's own emotions and the emotions of people with whom one interacts on a daily basis.

empathy   Dimension of service quality—caring individualized attention provided customers.

encoding   The process of having the sender transform an abstract idea into a set of symbols.

environmental factors   The uncontrollable factors involving social, economic, technological, competitive, and regulatory forces.

environmental scanning   The process of continually acquiring information on events occurring outside the organization to identify and interpret potential trends.

ethics   The moral principles and values that govern the actions and decisions of an individual or group.

ethnographic research   Observational approach to discover subtle emotional reactions as consumers encounter products in their "natural use environment."

euro-branding   The strategy of using the same brand name for the same product across all countries in the European Union.

eurostyle   A no frills, monochrome, geometric look to product design.

evaluation   The consumer's appraisal of the product or brand on important attributes.

evaluative criteria   Factors that represent both the objective attributes of a brand and the subjective ones a consumer uses to compare different products and brands.

everyday fair pricing   Retail strategy to try to create value for customers through service and the total buying experience.

everyday low pricing   (1) The practice of replacing promotional allowances with lower manufacturer list prices. (2) Retailing strategy that emphasizes consistently low prices and eliminates most markdowns.

evoked set   The group of brands that a consumer would consider acceptable from among all the brands in the product class of which he or she is aware.

exchange   The trade of things of value between buyer and seller so that each is better off after the trade.

exclusive dealing   An arrangement a manufacturer makes with a reseller to handle only its products and not those of competitors.

exclusive distribution   Only one retail outlet in a specific geographical area carries the firm's products.

exclusive territorial distributorship   A manufacturer grants a distributor the sole rights to sell a product in a specific geographic area.

experience curve pricing   A method of pricing based on the learning effect, which holds that the unit cost of many products and services declines by 10 percent to 30 percent each time a firm's experience at producing and selling them doubles.

experience economy   Economy in which companies compete for customers by offering enjoyable, memorable experiences rather than traditional service transactions.

experience properties   Can only be discerned after purchase or during consumption.

experiment   Obtaining data by manipulating factors under tightly controlled conditions to test cause and effect.

experimental group   A group exposed to the experimental variable in an experiment.

exporting   Producing goods in one country and selling them in another country.

express warranties   Written statements of a manufacturer's liabilities for product deficiencies.

external secondary data   Published data from outside the firm or organization.

exurbs   The remote suburbs to which the population began to shift in the 1990s.

facilitators   Intermediaries that assist in the physical distribution channel by moving, storing, financing, or insuring products.

fad   A product that experiences rapid sales on introduction and then an equally rapid decline.

failure fee   A penalty payment made by a manufacturer to compensate the retailer for sales its valuable shelf space never made.

Fair Packaging and Labeling Act (1966)   A law that requires manufacturers to state on the package the ingredients, volume, and identity of the manufacturer.

family branding   (see multiproduct branding)

family life cycle   The distinct phases that a family progresses through from formation to retirement, each phase bringing with it identifiable purchasing behaviors.

Farm Bill (1990)   Legislation that sets the standards for organic foods and products that use the term "organic."

fashion product   A product that is introduced, declines, and then seems to return. Life cycles may last years or decades.

fast prototyping   A "do it, try it, fix it" approach to new products used in software development, encouraging continuing improvements even after the initial design.

fear appeals   Advertising messages suggesting to the consumer that he or she can avoid some negative experience through the purchase and use of a product.

Federal Cigarette Labeling and Advertising Act (1967)   An act that requires health warnings on cigarette ads and packages.

feedback   The communication flow from receiver back to the sender that helps the sender know whether the message was decoded and understood as intended.

feedback loop   Consists of a response and feedback.

field experiment   A test of marketing variables in actual store or buying settings.

field of experience   Similar understanding and knowledge; to communicate effectively, a sender and a receiver must have a mutually shared field of experience.

field warehouse A specialized public warehouse that takes possession of a firm's goods and issues a receipt that can be used as collateral for a loan.

finance allowance A trade-oriented sales promotion paying retailers for financing costs or financial losses associated with consumer sales promotions.

fixed alternative question Requires respondents to select one or more response options from a set of predetermined choices.

fixed cost The sum of expenses of the firm that are stable and do not change with the quantity of product that is produced and sold.

flexible-price policy Setting different prices for products and services depending on individual buyers and purchase situations. Also called dynamic pricing.

flighting schedule Periods of advertising are scheduled between periods of no advertising to reflect seasonal demand. Also called intermittent schedule.

FOB (free on board) Refers to the point at which the seller stops paying transportation costs.

FOB origin pricing A method of pricing where the title of goods passes to the buyer at the point of loading.

FOB with freight-allowed pricing A method of pricing that allows the buyer to deduct freight expenses from the list price of the goods, so the seller agrees to pay, or "absorb," the transportation costs. Also called freight absorption pricing.

focus group An informal session of 6 to 10 past, present, or prospective customers in which a discussion leader, or moderator, asks their opinions about the firm's and its competitors' products.

follow-up stage Making certain the customer's purchase has been properly delivered and installed and difficulties experienced with using the product are addressed.

Food, Drug, and Cosmetic Act (1938) A law that prevents the adulteration or misbranding of these three categories of products.

forced distribution markets (see selected controlled markets)

Foreign Corrupt Practices Act A law that makes it a crime for U.S. corporations to bribe an official of a foreign government or political party to obtain or retain business in a foreign country.

forgetting rate The speed with which buyers forget a brand if advertising is not seen.

form of ownership Distinguishes retail outlets based on whether individuals, corporate chains, or contractual systems own the outlet.

form utility The value to consumers that comes from production or alteration of a good or service.

formula selling presentation Providing information in an accurate, thorough, and step-by-step manner to inform the prospect.

forward buying A response to discounts offered by manufacturers in which retailers purchase more merchandise than they plan to sell during the promotion. The remaining stock is sold at a regular price later, or diverted to another store.

forward integration Practice in corporate vertical marketing system in which a producer also owns retail shops.

four I's of service Four unique elements to services: intangibility, inconsistency, inseparability, and inventory.

four P's (see marketing mix)

franchising Contractual arrangement between a parent company (a franchisor) and an individual or firm (a franchisee) that allows the franchise to operate a certain type of business under an established name and according to specific rules.

freight consolidators (see freight forwarders)

freight forwarders Firms that accumulate small shipments into larger lots and then hire a carrier to move them, usually at reduced rates.

frequency The average number of times a person in the target audience is exposed to a message or advertisement.

FTC Act (1914) A law that established the Federal Trade Commission (FTC) to monitor deceptive or misleading advertising and unfair business practices.

full-service agency An advertising agency providing the most complete range of services, including market research, media selection, copy development, artwork, and production.

full-service retailer Provides many services to its customers.

full warranty A statement of liability by a manufacturer that has no limits of noncoverage.

functional groupings Organizational groupings such as manufacturing, marketing, and finance, which are the different business activities within a firm.

functional level Level at which groups of specialists *actually* create value for the organization.

gap analysis An evaluation tool that compares expectations about a service offering to the actual experience a consumer has with the service.

gatekeeper Role that controls the flow of information in the buying center.

General Agreement on Tariffs and Trade (GATT) An international treaty intended to limit trade barriers and promote world trade through the reduction of tariffs.

general merchandise stores Stores that carry a broad product line with limited depth.

general merchandise wholesaler A full-service merchant wholesaler that carries a broad assortment of merchandise and performs all channel functions.

Generation X The 15 percent of the U.S. population born between 1965 and 1976— a period also known as the baby bust.

Generation Y Americans born after 1976, the year that many baby boomers began having children. Also described as the echoboom and the baby boomlet.

generational marketing The use of marketing programs designed for the distinct attitudes and consumer behavior of the cohorts, or generations, that make up the marketplace.

generic brand A no-name product with no identification other than a description of contents.

generic business strategy Strategy that can be adopted by any firm, regardless of the product or industry involved, to achieve a competitive advantage.

geographic information systems (GIS) Technology that records different layers of data on the same map.

geographical groupings Organization groupings in which a unit is subdivided according to geographical location.

global competition Exists when firms originate, produce, and market their products and services worldwide.

global consumers Customer groups living in many countries or regions of the world who have similar needs or seek similar features and benefits from products or services.

global marketing strategy The practice of standardizing marketing activities when there are cultural similarities and adapting them when cultures differ.

goal A targeted level of performance to be achieved, often by a specific time.

government units   The federal, state, and local agencies that buy goods and services for the constituents they serve.

gray market   A situation where products are sold through unauthorized channels of distribution; also called parallel importing.

green marketing   Marketing efforts to produce, promote, and reclaim environmentally sensitive products.

gross domestic product   The monetary value of all goods and services produced in a country during one year.

gross income   The total amount of money made in one year by a person, household, or family unit.

gross margin   Net sales minus cost of goods sold.

gross rating points (GRPs)   A reference number for advertisers, created by multiplying reach (expressed as a percentage of the total market) by frequency.

growth stage   The second stage of the product life cycle characterized by rapid increases in sales and by the appearance of competitors.

harvesting   When a company retains the product but reduces marketing support costs.

head-to-head positioning   Competing directly with competitors on similar product attributes in the same target market.

hierarchy of effects   The sequence of stages a prospective buyer goes through from initial awareness of a product to eventual action (either trial or adoption of the product). The stages include awareness, interest, evaluation, trial, and adoption.

high learning product   A product for which significant education of the customer is required and there is an extended introductory period.

hooked, online, and single   Online consumer lifestyle segment consisting of young, affluent, and single consumers who bank, play games, and spend more time online than any other segment.

horizontal conflict   Disagreements between intermediaries at the same level in a marketing channel.

horizontal price fixing   When two or more competitors explicitly or implicitly set prices.

humorous appeals   Advertising messages implying either directly or more subtly that a product is more fun or exciting than competitors' offering.

hunter-gatherers   Online consumer lifestyle segment consisting of married baby boomers with children at home who use the Internet like a consumer magazine to compare products and prices.

hypermarket   A large store (over 200,000 square feet) offering a mix of 40 percent food products and 60 percent general merchandise.

hypothesis   A conjecture or idea about the relationship of two or more factors or what might happen in the future.

hypothesis evaluation   Research to test ideas discovered in the hypothesis generation stage to help recommend marketing actions.

hypothesis generation   A search for ideas that can be evaluated in later research.

idea generation   Developing a pool of concepts as candidates for new products.

idle production capacity   When the service provider is available but there is no demand.

implied warranties   Assign responsibility for product deficiencies to the manufacturer.

inbound telemarketing   The use of toll-free telephone numbers that customers can call to obtain information about products or services and make purchases.

inconsistency   A unique element of services—because services depend on the people who provide them, their quality varies with each person's capabilities and day-to-day job performance.

independent retailer   A retail outlet owned by an individual.

indirect channel   A marketing channel where intermediaries are inserted between the producer and consumers and perform numerous channel functions.

indirect exporting   A firm selling its domestically produced goods in a foreign country through an intermediary.

individual interviews   A single researcher asks questions of one respondent.

industrial distributor   Performs a variety of marketing channel functions, including selling, stocking, delivering a full product assortment, and financing.

industrial espionage   The clandestine collection of trade secrets or proprietary information about a company's competitors.

industrial firm   An organizational buyer that in some way reprocesses a good or service it buys before selling it again to the next buyer.

industrial goods   Products that assist directly or indirectly in providing products for resale (also called B2B goods, business goods, or organizational goods).

industry   A group of firms offering products that are close substitutes for each other.

industry potential   (see market potential)

inelastic demand   A situation where a 1 percent decrease in price produces less than a 1 percent increase in quantity demanded.

Infant Formula Act (1980)   A federal consumer protection law.

influencer   Role in the buying center that affects the buying decision, usually by helping define the specifications for what is bought.

information technology   Designing and managing computer and communication networks to provide a system to satisfy an organization's needs for data storage, processing, and access.

infomercials   Program-length (30-minute) advertisements that take an educational approach to communication with potential customers.

in-house agency   A company's own advertising staff, which may provide full services or a limited range of services.

innovators   The 2.5 percent of the population who are venturesome and highly educated, use multiple information sources, and are the first to adopt a new product.

inseparability   A unique element of services—the consumer cannot (and does not) separate the deliverer of the service from the service itself.

inside order takers   Typically answer simple questions, take orders, and complete transactions with customers. Also called salesclerks.

installations   Support goods, consisting of buildings and fixed equipment.

institutional advertisements   Advertisements designed to build goodwill or an image for an organization, rather than promote a specific good or service.

intangibility   A unique element of services—services cannot be held, touched, or seen before the purchase decision.

integrated marketing communications The concept of designing marketing communications programs that coordinate all promotional activities—advertising, personal selling, sales promotion, public relations, and direct marketing—to provide a consistent message across all audiences.

intensive distribution A firm tries to place its products or services in as many outlets as possible.

interactive marketing Two-way buyer-seller electronic communications in a computer-mediated environment in which the buyer controls the kind and amount of information received from the seller.

interest An increase in the consumer's desire to learn about some of the features of the product or brand.

intermodel transportation Combining different transportation modes to get the best features of each.

internal marketing The notion that a service organization must focus on its employees, or internal market, before successful programs can be directed at customers.

internal secondary data Data that have already been collected and exist inside a business firm or organization.

Internet An integrated global network of computers that gives users access to information and documents.

Internet marketing channels Channels that employ the Internet to make goods and services available for consumption or use by consumers or industrial buyers.

intertype competition Competition between very dissimilar types of retail outlets.

introductory stage The first stage of the product life cycle in which sales grow slowly and profit is minimal.

inventory (1) Physical material purchased from suppliers, which may or may not be reworked for sale to customers. (2) A unique element of services—the need for and cost of having a service provider available.

involvement The personal, social, and economic significance of the purchase to the consumer.

ISO 14000 Worldwide standards for environmental quality and green marketing practices.

ISO 9000 Registration and certification of a manufacturer's quality management and quality assurance system.

job analysis A study of a particular sales position, including how the job is to be performed and the tasks that make up the job.

job description Written document that describes job relationships and requirements that characterize each sales position.

joint venture An arrangement in which a foreign company and a local firm invest together to create a local business, sharing ownership, control, and profits of the new company.

jury of executive opinion forecast Asking knowledgeable executives inside the firm about likely sales during a coming period.

jury test A pretest in which a panel of customers is shown an advertisement and asked to rate its attractiveness, how much they like it, and how much it draws their attention.

just-in-time (JIT) concept An inventory supply system that operates with very low inventories and requires fast, on-time delivery.

keiretsu Japanese channel relationship that bonds producers and intermediaries together.

label An integral part of the package that typically identifies the product or brand, who made it, where and when it was made, how it is to be used, and package contents and ingredients.

laboratory experiment A simulation of marketing-related activity in a highly controlled setting.

laggards The 16 percent of the market who have fear of debt, use friends for information sources, and accept ideas and products only after they have been long established in the market.

Lanham Act (1946) A law that provides for registration of a company's trademarks.

late majority The 34 percent of the population who are skeptical, below average in social status, and rely less on advertising and personal selling for information than do innovators or early adopters.

laws Society's values and standards that are enforceable in the courts.

lead The name of a person who may be a possible customer.

lead generation The result of a direct marketing offer designed to generate interest in a product or a service, and a request for additional information.

lead time Lag from ordering an item until it is received and ready for use or sale. Also called order cycle time or replenishment time.

learning Those behaviors that result from (1) repeated experience and (2) thinking.

level of service The degree of service provided to the customer by self-, limited-, and full-service retailers.

licensing A contractual agreement whereby a company allows another firm to use its brand name, patent, trade secret, or other property for a royalty or fee.

lifestyle A mode of living that is identified by how people spend their time and resources (activities), what they consider important in their environment (interests), and what they think of themselves and the world around them (opinions).

Likert scale A fixed alternative question in which the respondent indicates the extent to which he or she agrees or disagrees with a statement.

limited-coverage warranty A manufacturer's statement indicating the bounds of coverage and noncoverage for any product deficiencies.

limited-line store A retail outlet, such as a sporting goods store, that offers considerable assortment, or depth, of a related line of items.

limited-service agency Specializes in one aspect of the advertising process such as providing creative services to develop the advertising copy or buying previously unpurchased media space.

limited-service retailer Provides some services such as credit and merchandise return.

line extension The practice of using a current brand name to enter a new market segment in its product class.

line positions People in line positions, such as senior marketing managers, have the authority and responsibility to issue orders to the people who report to them, such as product managers.

logistics Those activities that focus on getting the right amount of the right products to the right place at the right time at the lowest possible cost.

logistics management The practice of organizing the cost-effective flow of raw materials, in-process inventory, finished goods, and related information from point of origin to point of consumption to satisfy customer requirements.

logo "Device" (design, sound, shape, or color) or other brand name that cannot be spoken.

loss-leader pricing Deliberately selling a product below its customary price to attract attention to it.

lost-horse forecast Starting with the last known value of the item being forecast, listing the factors that could affect the forecast, assessing whether they have a positive or negative impact, and making the final forecast.

low learning product A product for which sales begin immediately because little learning is required by the consumer and the benefits of purchase are readily understood.

macromarketing The study of the aggregate flow of a nation's goods and services to benefit society.

Magnuson-Moss Warranty/FTC Improvement Act (1975) An act that regulates the content of consumer warranties and also has strengthened consumer rights with regard to warranties through class action suits.

mail-order retailer A retailing operation in which merchandise is offered to customers by mail.

maintained markup The difference between the final selling price and retailer cost; also called gross margin.

major account management The practice of using team selling to focus on important customers so as to build mutually beneficial, long-term, cooperative relationships. Also called key account management.

make-buy decision An evaluation of whether components and assemblies will be purchased from outside suppliers or built by the company itself.

mall intercept interviews personal interviews of consumers while on visits to shopping centers.

management by exception A tool used by a marketing manager that involves identifying results that deviate from plans, diagnosing their cause, making appropriate new plans, and taking new actions.

manufacturer branding The producer dictates the brand name using either a multiproduct or multibranding approach.

manufacturer's agents Work for several producers and carry noncompetitive, complementary merchandise in an exclusive territory; also called manufacturer's representatives.

manufacturer's branch office Carries a producer's inventory and performs the functions of a full-service merchant wholesaler.

manufacturer's sales office Does not carry inventory, typically performs only a sales function, and serves as an alternative to agents and brokers.

marginal analysis A continuing, concise trade-off of incremental costs against incremental revenues.

marginal cost The change in total cost that results from producing and marketing one additional unit.

marginal revenue The change in total revenue obtained by selling one additional unit.

markdown Discounting a product when it does not sell at the original price and an adjustment is necessary.

market People with the desire and with the ability to buy a specific product.

market-based groupings Organizational groupings that utilize specific customer segments.

market development Selling existing products to new markets.

market growth rate The annual rate of growth of the specific market or industry in which a firm or SBU is competing; often used as the vertical axis in business portfolio analysis.

market modification Strategy in which a company tries to find new customers, increase a product's use among existing customers, or create new use situations.

market orientation Focusing organizational efforts on (1) continuously collecting information about customers' needs and competitors' capabilities, (2) sharing this information across departments, and (3) using the information to create customer value.

market penetration A strategy of increasing sales of present products in their existing markets.

market potential Maximum total sales of a product by all firms to a segment during a specified time period under specified environmental conditions and marketing efforts of the firms (also called industry potential).

market-product grid Framework to relate the segment of a market to products offered or potential marketing actions by the firm.

market segmentation Aggregating prospective buyers into groups, or segments, that (1) have common needs and (2) will respond similarly to a marketing action.

market segments The groups that result from the process of market segmentation; these groups ideally (1) have common needs and (2) will respond similarly to a marketing action.

market share The ratio of sales revenue of the firm to the total sales revenue of all firms in the industry, including the firm itself.

market testing Exposing actual products to prospective consumers under realistic purchase conditions to see if they will buy.

marketing The process of planning and executing the conception, pricing, promotion, and distribution of ideas, goods, and services to create exchanges that satisfy individual and organizational objectives.

marketing audit A comprehensive, unbiased, periodic review of the strategic marketing process of a firm or a strategic business unit (SBU).

marketing channel Individuals and firms involved in the process of making a product or service available for use or consumption by consumers or industrial users.

marketing concept The idea that an organization should (1) strive to satisfy the needs of consumers (2) while also trying to achieve the organization's goals.

marketing decision support system (MDSS) A computerized method of providing timely, accurate information to improve marketing decisions.

marketing mix The marketing manager's controllable factors, the marketing actions of product, price, promotion, and place that he or she can take to solve a marketing problem.

marketing orientation When an organization focuses its efforts on (1) continuously collecting information about customers' needs and competitors' capabilities, (2) sharing this information across departments, and (3) using the information to create customer value.

marketing plan A road map for the marketing activities of an organization for a specified future period of time, such as one year or five years.

marketing program A plan that integrates the marketing mix to provide a good, service, or idea to prospective buyers.

marketing research The process of defining a marketing problem and opportunity, systematically collecting and analyzing information, and recommending actions to improve an organization's marketing activities.

marketing strategy   The means by which a marketing goal is to be achieved, usually characterized by a specified target market and a marketing program to reach it.

marketing tactics   The detailed day-to-day operational decisions essential to the overall success of marketing strategies.

marketspace   An Internet/Web-enabled digital environment characterized by "face-to-screen" exchange relationships and electronic images and offerings.

markup   The amount added to the cost of goods to reach the final selling price.

mass customization   Tailoring goods or services to the tastes of individual customers on a high-volume scale.

mass selling   Promotional elements used with groups of prospective buyers: advertising, sales promotion, and public relations.

materials handling   Moving goods over short distances into, within, and out of warehouses and manufacturing plants.

matrix organization   A method of organizing that combines market-based groupings with product groupings.

mature households   Households headed by people over 50 years old.

maturity stage   The third stage of the product or retail life cycle in which sales increase at a declining rate and profit declines.

measures of success   Criteria or standards used in evaluating proposed solutions to the problem.

Meat Inspection Act (1906)   A law that provides for meat products be wholesome, unadulterated, and properly labeled.

mechanical observational data   Data collected by electronic or other impersonal means, such as meters connected to television sets in viewers' homes.

merchandise allowance   A trade-oriented sales promotion reimbursing a retailer for extra in-store support or special featuring of the brand.

merchandise line   How many different types of products a store carries and in what assortment.

merchant wholesalers   Independently owned firms that take title to the merchandise they handle.

message   The information sent by a source to a receiver in the communication process.

methods   The approaches that can be used to solve all or part of a problem.

metropolitan statistical area (MSA)   (1) A city having a population of at least 50,000 or (2) an urbanized area with a population in excess of 50,000 with a total metropolitan population of at least 100,000.

micromarketing   How an individual organization directs its marketing activities and allocates its resources to benefit its customers.

mission   A statement of the organization's scope.

missionary salespeople   Sales support personnel who do not directly solicit orders but rather concentrate on performing promotional activities and introducing new products.

mixed branding   A firm markets products under its own name and that of a reseller because the segment attracted by the reseller is different from its own market.

modified rebuy   A buying situation in which the users, influencers, or deciders in the buying center want to change the product specifications, price, delivery schedule, or supplier.

monopolistic competition   A competitive setting in which many sellers compete with their products on a substitutable basis.

monopoly   A competitive setting in which only one firm sells the product.

moral idealism   A personal moral philosophy that considers certain individual rights or duties as universal, regardless of the outcome.

motivation   The energizing force that causes behavior that satisfies a need.

multibranding   A manufacturer's branding strategy giving each product a distinct name.

multichannel marketing   The blending of different communication and delivery channels that are mutually reinforcing in attracting, retaining, and building relationships with consumers.

multichannel retailers   Utilize and integrate a combination of traditional store formats and nonstore formats such as catalogs, television, and online retailing.

multidomestic marketing strategy   A multinational firm's offering as many different product variations, brand names, and advertising programs as countries in which it does business.

multiple-zone pricing   The price to all buyers within any one zone is the same, but prices across zones vary depending on the transportation cost to the zone and the level of competition and demand within the zone.

multiproduct branding   A company uses one name for all products; also called blanket or family branding.

national character   A distinct set of personality characteristics common among people of a country or society.

need   That which occurs when a person feels deprived of food, clothing, or shelter.

need-satisfaction presentation   A selling format that emphasizes probing and listening by the salesperson to identify needs and interests of perspective buyers.

new buy   The first-time purchase of a product or service, involving greater potential risk.

new-product concept   A tentative description of a product or service a firm might offer for sale.

new-product process   The sequence of activities a firm uses to identify business opportunities and convert them to a salable good or service.

new-product strategy development   Defining the role for a new product in terms of the firm's overall corporate objectives.

news conference   A publicity tool consisting of an informational meeting with representatives of the media who are sent advance materials on the content.

news release   A publicity tool consisting of an announcement regarding changes in the company or the product line.

noise   Extraneous factors that can work against effective communication by distorting a message or the feedback received.

noncumulative quantity discounts   Price reductions based on the size of an individual purchase order.

nondurable good   An item consumed in one or a few uses.

nonprobability sampling   Using arbitrary judgments to select the sample so that the chance of selecting a particular element may be unknown or zero.

nonprofit organization   A nongovernmental organization that serves its customers but does not have profit as an organizational goal.

nonrepetitive decisions   Those decisions unique to a particular time and situation.

North American Industry Classification System (NAICS)   Provides common industry definitions for Canada, Mexico, and the United States, which facilitate the measurement of economic activity in the three member countries of NAFTA.

Nutritional Labeling and Education Act (1990) A federal consumer protection law.

objections Excuses for not making a purchase commitment or decision.

objective and task budgeting A budgeting approach whereby the company (1) determines its promotion objectives, (2) outlines the tasks to accomplish these objectives, and (3) determines the promotion cost of performing these tasks.

objectives Targeted levels of performance to be achieved, often by a specific time.

observational data Facts and figures obtained by watching, either mechanically or in person, how people actually behave.

odd-even pricing Setting prices a few dollars or cents under an even number, such as $19.95.

off-peak pricing Charging different prices during different times of the day or days of the week to reflect variations in demand for the service.

off-price retailing Selling brand-name merchandise at lower than regular prices.

oligopoly A competitive setting in which a few companies control the majority of industry sales.

one-price policy Setting one price for all buyers of a product or service. Also called fixed pricing.

one-price stores A form of off-price retailing in which all items in a store are sold at one low price.

online consumers The subsegment of all Internet/web users who employ this technology to research products and services and make purchases.

open-ended question A question that allows respondents to express opinions, ideas, or behaviors in their own words.

opinion leaders Individuals who exert direct or indirect social influence over others.

order getter A salesperson who sells in a conventional sense and identifies prospective customers, provides customers with information, persuades customers to buy, closes sales, and follows up on customers' use of a product or service.

order taker Processes routine orders or reorders for products that were already sold by the company.

organizational buyers Those manufacturers, wholesalers, retailers, and government agencies that buy goods and services for their own use or for resale.

organizational buying behavior The decision-making process that organizations use to establish the need for products and services and identify, evaluate, and choose among alternative brands and suppliers.

organizational buying criteria The objective attributes of the supplier's products and services and the capabilities of the supplier itself.

organizational goals Specific objectives a business or nonprofit unit seeks to achieve and by which it can measure its performance.

original markup The difference between retailer cost and initial selling price.

outbound telemarketing Using the telephone rather than personal visits to contact customers.

out-of-home TV Reaches 20 million viewers in bars, hotels, offices, and campuses each week.

outside order takers Visit customers and replenish inventory stock of resellers, such as retailers or wholesalers.

Pacific Rim The area of the world consisting of countries in Asia and Australia.

packaging Any container in which a product is offered for sale and on which label information is communicated.

panel A sample of consumers or stores from which researchers take a series of measurements.

parallel development An approach to new product development that involves cross-functional team members who conduct the simultaneous development of both the product and the production process, staying with the product from conception to production.

partnership selling The practice whereby buyers and sellers combine their expertise and resources to create customized solutions; commit to joint planning; and share customer, competitive, and company information for their mutual benefit, and ultimately the customer. Sometimes called enterprise selling.

patent Exclusive rights to the manufacture of a product or related technology granted to a company for 17 years.

penetration pricing Setting a low initial price on a new product to appeal immediately to the mass market.

penturbia The smaller towns to which the population began to shift in the 1990s.

per se illegality An action that by itself is illegal.

perceived risk The anxieties felt because the consumer cannot anticipate the outcomes of a purchase but believes that there may be negative consequences.

percentage of sales budgeting Allocating funds to advertising as a percentage of past or anticipated sales, in terms of either dollars or units sold.

perception The process by which an individual selects, organizes, and interprets information to create a meaningful picture of the world.

perceptual map A means of displaying or graphing in two dimensions the location of products or brands in the minds of consumers.

permission marketing The solicitation of a consumer's consent (called "opt-in") to receive e-mail and advertising based on personal data supplied by the consumer.

personal selling The two-way flow of communication between a buyer and seller, often in a face-to-face encounter, designed to influence a person's or group's purchase decision.

personal selling process Sales activities occurring before and after the sale itself, consisting of six stages: (1) prospecting, (2) preapproach, (3) approach, (4) presentation, (5) close, and (6) follow-up.

personality A person's consistent behaviors or responses to recurring situations.

personalization The consumer-initiated practice of generating content on a marketer's website that is custom tailored to an individual's specific needs and preferences.

piggyback See truck-rail.

piggyback franchising A variation of franchising in which stores operated by one chain sell the products or services of another franchised firm.

pioneering advertisements Tell people what a product is, what it can do, and where it can be found.

pioneering institutional advertisements Used for announcements about what a company is, what it can do, or where it is located.

place-based media Advertising messages in locations that attract a specific target audience such as airports, doctor's offices, and health clubs.

place utility   The value to consumers of having a good or service available where needed.

planning gap   The difference between the projection of the path to reach a new goal and the projection of the path of the results of a plan already in place.

point-of-purchase displays   Product displays taking the form of advertising signs, which sometimes actually hold or display the product, and are often located in high-traffic areas near the cash register on the end of an aisle.

points of difference   Those characteristics of a product that make it superior to competitive substitutes.

Poison Prevention Packaging Act (1970)   A federal consumer protection law.

population   The universe of all people, stores, or salespeople about which researchers wish to generalize.

portals   Electronic gateways to the World Wide Web that supply a broad array of news and entertainment, information resources, and shopping services.

portfolio test   A pretest in which a test ad is placed in a portfolio with other ads and consumers are questioned on their impressions of the ads.

possession utility   The value of making an item easy to purchase through the provision of credit cards or financial arrangements.

posttests   Tests conducted after an advertisement has been shown to the target audience to determine whether it has accomplished its intended purpose.

power center   A huge shopping strip with multiple anchor (or national stores), a convenient location, and a supermarket.

preapproach stage   The stage of the personal selling process that involves obtaining further information about the prospect and deciding on the best method of approach.

precycling   Efforts by manufacturers to reduce waste by decreasing the amount of packaging they use.

predatory pricing   Charging a very low price for a product with the intent of driving competitors out of business.

premium   A sales promotion that consists of merchandise offered free or at significant savings over its retail price.

presentation stage   The core of the personal selling process; its objective is to convert the prospect into a customer by creating a desire for the product or service.

prestige pricing   Setting a high price so that status-conscious consumers will be attracted to the product and buy it.

pretests   Tests conducted before an advertisement is placed to determine whether it communicates the intended message or to select among alternative versions of an advertisement.

price   The money or other considerations (including other goods and services) exchanged for the ownership or use of a good or service.

price discrimination   The practice of charging different prices to different buyers for goods of like trade and quality. The Clayton Act as amended by the Robinson-Patman Act prohibits this action.

price elasticity of demand   The percentage change in quantity demanded relative to a percentage change in price.

price fixing   A conspiracy among firms to set prices for a product.

price lining   Setting the price of a line of products at a number of different specific pricing points.

price war   Successive price cutting by competitors to increase or maintain their unit sales or market share.

pricing constraints   Factors that limit the latitude of price a firm may set.

pricing objectives   Expectations that specify the role of price in an organization's marketing and strategic plans.

primary data   Facts and figures that are newly collected for the project.

primary demand   Desire for the product class rather than for a specific brand.

primary metropolitan statistical area (PMSA)   An area that is part of a larger consolidated metropolitan statistical area that has a total population of 1 million or more.

prime rate   The rate of interest banks charge their largest customers.

private branding   When a company manufactures products but sells them under the brand name of a wholesaler or retailer (often called private labeling or reseller branding).

proactive strategies   New product strategies that involve an aggressive allocation of resources to identify opportunities for product development.

probability sampling   Using precise rules to select the sample such that each element of the population has a specific known chance of being selected.

product   A good, service, or idea consisting of a bundle of tangible and intangible attributes that satisfies consumers and is received in exchange for money or some other unit of value.

product advertisements   Advertisements that focus on selling a good or service and take three forms: (1) pioneering (or informational), (2) competitive (or persuasive), and (3) reminder.

product (or program) champion   A person who is able and willing to cut red tape and move the program forward.

product class   The entire product category or industry.

product counterfeiting   Low-cost copies of popular brands not manufactured by the original producer.

product development   A strategy of selling a new product to existing markets.

product differentiation   A strategy with two different but related meanings. Its broadest meaning involves a firm's using different marketing mix activities, such as product features and advertising, to help consumers perceive the product as being different and better than competing products. Its narrower meaning involves a firm's selling two or more products with different features targeted to different market segments.

product form   Variations of a product within the product class.

product item   A specific product as noted by a unique brand, size, or price.

product life cycle   The stages a new product goes through in the market place: introduction, growth, maturity, and decline.

product line   A group of products that are closely related because they satisfy a class of needs, are used together, are sold to the same customer group, are distributed through the same outlets, or fall within a given price range.

product line groupings   Organizational groupings in which a unit is responsible for specific product offerings.

product line pricing   The setting of prices for all items in a product line.

product manager   A person who plans, implements, and controls the annual and long-range plans for the products for which he or she is responsible.

product mix   The number of product lines offered by a company.

product modification   Altering a product's characteristic, such as its quality, performance, or appearance, to try to increase and extend the product's sales.

product placement   Using a brand-name product in a movie, television show, video, or a commercial for another product.

product positioning   The place an offering occupies in consumers' minds on important attributes relative to competitive offerings.

product repositioning   Changing the place a product occupies in a consumer's mind relative to competitive products.

production goods   Items used in the manufacturing process that become part of the final product.

profit   The reward to a business firm for the risk it undertakes in offering a product for sale; the money left over after a firm's total expenses are subtracted from its total revenues.

profit equation   Profit = Total revenue − Total cost, or Profit = (Unit price × Quantity sold) − Total cost.

profit responsibility   The view that companies have a simple duty—to maximize profits for their owners or stockholders.

profitability analysis   A means of measuring the profitability of the firm's products, customer groups, sales territories, channels of distribution, and order sizes.

program schedule   Shows the relationships through time of the various program tasks.

promotional allowance   Cash payment or extra amount of "free goods" awarded sellers in the channel of distribution for undertaking certain advertising or selling activities to promote a product.

promotional mix   The combination of one or more of the promotional elements a firm uses to communicate with consumers. The promotional elements include: advertising, personal selling, sales promotion, public relations, and direct marketing.

promotional websites   Advertise and promote a company's products and services and provide information on how items can be used and where they can be purchased.

prospect   A customer who wants or needs the product.

prospecting stage   In the personal selling process, the search for and qualification of potential customers.

protectionism   The practice of shielding one or more sectors of a country's economy from foreign competition through the use of tariffs or quotas.

protocol   A statement that, before product development begins, identifies (1) a well-defined target market; (2) specific customers' needs, wants, and preferences; and (3) what the product will be and do.

psychographics   The analysis of consumer lifestyles (activities, interests, and opinions).

Public Health Cigarette Smoking Act (1971)   An act that prohibits advertising tobacco products on radio and television.

public relations   A form of communication management that seeks to influence the feelings, opinions, or beliefs held by customers, prospective customers, stockholders, suppliers, employees, and other publics about a company and its products or services.

public service announcement (PSA)   A publicity tool that uses free space or time donated by the media.

publicity   A nonpersonal, indirectly paid presentation of an organization, good, or service.

publicity tools   Methods of obtaining nonpersonal presentation of an organization, good, or service without direct cost. Examples include news releases, news conferences, and public service announcements.

pull strategy   Directing the promotional mix at ultimate consumers to encourage them to ask the retailer for the product.

pulse schedule   A flighting schedule is combined with a continuous schedule because of increases in demand, heavy periods of promotion, or introduction of a new product. Also called burst schedule.

purchase decision process   The stages a buyer passes through in making choices about which products and services to buy.

purchase frequency   The frequency of purchase of a specific product.

pure competition   A competitive setting in which every company has a similar product.

pure monopoly   One seller who sets the price for a unique product.

push strategy   Directing the promotional mix to channel members to gain their cooperation in ordering and stocking a product.

qualified prospect   An individual who wants a product, can afford to buy it, and is the decision maker.

quality   Those features and characteristics of a product that influence its ability to satisfy customer needs.

quantity discounts   Reductions in unit costs for a larger order.

questionnaire data   Facts and figures obtained by asking people about their attitudes, awareness, intentions, and behaviors.

quick response   An inventory management system designed to reduce the retailer's lead time, thereby lowering its inventory investment, improving customer service levels, and reducing logistics expense.

quota   A restriction placed on the amount of a product allowed to enter or leave a country.

rack jobber   A merchant wholesaler that furnishes racks or shelves to display merchandise in retail stores, performs all channel functions, and sells on consignment to retailers.

rating (TV or radio)   The percentage of households in a market that are tuned to a particular TV show or radio station.

reach   The number of different people or households exposed to an advertisement.

reactive strategies   New product strategies that are defensive approaches in response to competitors' new items by developing new products.

rebate   A sales promotion in which money is returned to the consumer based on proof of purchase.

receivers   Consumers who read, hear, or see the message sent by a source in the communication process.

reciprocity   An industrial buying practice in which two organizations agree to purchase each other's products and services.

recycling   The use of technological developments to allow products to go through the manufacturing cycle several times.

reference groups   People to whom an individual looks as a basis for self-appraisal or as a source of personal standards.

regional marketing   Developing marketing plans to reflect specific area differences in taste preferences, perceived needs, or interests.

regional rollouts   Introducing a new product sequentially into geographical areas to allow production levels and marketing activities to build up gradually.

regional shopping centers   Consists of 50 to 150 stores that typically attract customers who live within a 5- to 10-mile range, often containing two or three anchor stores.

regulation   Restrictions state and federal laws place on business with regard to the conduct of its activities.

reinforcement A reward that strengthens a response.

reinforcement advertisement Used to assure current users they made the right choice.

relationship marketing Linking the organization to its individual customers, employees, suppliers, and other partners for their mutual long-term benefits.

relationship selling The practice of building ties to customers based on a salesperson's attention and commitment to customer needs over time.

relative market share The sales of a firm or SBU divided by the sales of the largest firm in the industry; often used as the horizontal axis in business portfolio analysis.

reliability Dimension of service quality—ability to perform the promised service dependably and accurately.

reminder advertisements Used to reinforce previous knowledge of a product.

reminder institutional advertisements Simply bring a company's name to the attention of the target market again.

repeat purchasers People who tried the product, were satisfied, and bought again.

repetitive decisions Decisions repeated at standard intervals during the work year.

repositioning Changing the place an offering occupies in a consumer's mind relative to competitive offerings.

requirement contract A contract that requires a buyer to purchase all or part of its needs for a product from one seller for a period of time.

resale restrictions A supplier's attempt to stipulate to whom distributors may resell the supplier's products and in what specific geographical areas or territories they may be sold.

reseller A wholesaler or retailer that buys physical products and resells them again without any processing.

response (1) In behavioral learning, the action taken by a consumer to satisfy a drive. (2) In the feedback loop, the impact the message had on the receiver's knowledge, attitudes, or behaviors.

responsiveness Dimension of service quality—willingness to help customers and provide prompt service.

restructuring (reengineering or streamlining) Striving for more efficient corporations that can compete globally by reducing duplicate efforts in multiple company locations, closing or changing unprofitable plants and offices, and laying off employees.

retail life cycle The process of growth and decline that retail outlets, like products, experience.

retail positioning matrix Positions retail outlets on two dimensions: breadth of product line and value added.

retailer-sponsored cooperative Small, independent retailers form an organization that operates a wholesaler facility cooperatively.

retailing All activities involved in selling, renting, and providing goods and services to ultimate consumers for personal, family, or household use.

retailing mix In retailing strategy, the (1) goods and services, (2) physical distribution, and (3) communications tactics chosen by a store.

return on investment (ROI) The ratio of after-tax net profit to the investment used to earn that profit.

returns Refunds or credit granted a customer for an item returned to the seller.

reverse auction A buyer communicates a need for a product or service and would-be suppliers are invited to bid in competition with each other.

reverse logistics A process of reclaiming recyclable and reusable materials, returns, and reworks from the point of consumption or use for repair, remanufacturing, redistribution, or disposal.

reverse marketing The deliberate effort by organizational buyers to build relationships that shape suppliers' products, services, and capabilities to fit a buyer's needs and those of its customers.

rich media Online promotion, such as banner advertising, that utilizes the audio, video, and interactive capabilities of the Internet to attract more attention from viewers and to provide an element of entertainment to the message.

Robinson-Patman Act (1936) An act that makes it unlawful to discriminate in prices charged to different purchasers of the same product, where the effect may substantially lessen competition or help to create a monopoly.

sales analysis A tool for controlling marketing programs using sales records to compare actual results with sales goals and to identify strengths and weaknesses.

sales component analysis A tool for controlling marketing programs that traces sales revenues to their sources, such as specific products, sales territories, or customers. Also called microsales analysis.

sales engineer A salesperson who specializes in identifying, analyzing, and solving customer problems and who brings know-how and technical expertise to the selling situations, but does not actually sell goods and services.

salesforce automation The use of technology to make the sales function more effective and efficient.

salesforce survey forecast Asking the firm's salespeople to estimate sales during a coming period.

sales forecast The maximum total sales of a product that a firm expects to sell during a specified time period under specified environmental conditions and its own marketing efforts (also called company forecast).

sales management Planning the selling program and implementing and controlling the personal selling effort of the firm.

sales plan A statement describing what is to be achieved and where and how the selling effort of salespeople is to be deployed.

sales promotion A short-term inducement of value offered to arouse interest in buying a good or service.

sales response function Relates the expense of marketing effort to the marketing results obtained. Measures of marketing results include sales revenue, profit, units sold, and level of awareness.

samples (1) Some elements taken from the population or universe, or (2) a sales promotion offering the product free or at a greatly reduced price.

sampling (1) the process of selecting elements from a population, or (2) the process manufacturers use of giving away free samples to introduce a new product.

scrambled merchandising Offering several unrelated product lines in a single retail store.

screening and evaluation The third stage of the new product process which involves internal and external evaluations of the new-product ideas to eliminate those that warrant no further effort.

search properties Tangible properties, such as color, size, and style, which can be determined before purchase.

seasonal discounts   Price reductions to encourage buyers to stock inventory earlier than their normal demand would require.

secondary data   Facts and figures that have already been recorded before the project at hand.

selected controlled markets   These sites, also referred to as forced distribution markets, are where a market test for a new product is conducted by an outside agency and retailers are paid to display the new product.

selective comprehension   Interpreting information so that it is consistent with your attitude and beliefs.

selective demand   Demand for a specific brand within the product class.

selective distribution   A firm selects a few retail outlets in a specific geographical area to carry its products.

selective exposure   Occurs when people pay attention to messages that are consistent with their attitudes and beliefs and ignore messages that are inconsistent.

selective perception   A filtering of exposure, comprehension, and retention.

selective retention   The tendency to remember only part of all the information one sees, reads, or hears, even minutes after exposure to it.

self-concept   The way people see themselves and the way they believe others see them.

self-liquidating premium   Merchandise offered at a significant cost savings over its retail price, self-liquidating because the cost charged to the consumer covers the cost of the items.

self-regulation   An alternative to government control where an industry attempts to police itself.

self-service   The extreme end of the service continuum because the customer performs many functions and little is provided by the outlet.

selling agent   Represents a single producer and is responsible for the entire marketing function of that producer.

semantic differential scale   A rating scale in which the opposite ends have one- or two-word adjectives that have opposite meanings.

seminar selling   A form of team selling where a company team conducts an educational program for a customer's technical staff, describing state-of-the-art developments.

semiotics   The field of study that examines the correspondence between symbols and their role in the assignment of meaning for people.

sensitivity analysis   Asking "What-if . . ." questions to determine how changes in a factor like pricing or advertising affect marketing results like sales revenue or profits.

service continuum   A range from the tangible to the intangible or good-dominant to service-dominant offerings available in the marketplace.

services   Intangible activities, benefits, or satisfactions that an organization provides to consumers in exchange for money or something else of value.

sex appeals   Advertising messages suggesting to the audience that the product will increase the attractiveness of the user.

share points   Percentage points of market share; often used as the common basis of comparison to allocate marketing resources effectively.

shelf life   The time a product can be stored before it spoils.

Sherman Anti-Trust Act (1890)   A law that forbids (1) contracts, combinations, or conspiracies in restraint of trade and (2) actual monopolies or attempts to monopolize any part of trade or commerce.

shopping goods   Items for which the consumer compares several alternatives on criteria such as price, quality, or style.

shrinkage   Breakage and theft of merchandise by customers and employees.

simulated test markets (STM)   A technique that simulates a full-scale test market but in limited fashion.

single-line store   A store that offers tremendous depth in one primary line of merchandise; for example, a running shoe store.

single-source data   Information provided by a single firm on household demographics and lifestyle, purchases, TV viewing behavior, and responses to promotions like coupons and free samples.

single-zone pricing   All buyers pay the same delivered price for the products, regardless of their distance from the seller; also known as uniform delivered pricing or postage stamp pricing.

situation analysis   Taking stock of where the firm or product has been recently, where it is now, and where it is headed in terms of the organization's plans and the external factors and trends affecting it.

situational influences   The purchase situation affects the purchase decision process through five situational influences: (1) the purchase task, (2) social surroundings, (3) physical surroundings, (4) temporal effects, and (5) antecedent states.

Six Sigma   A means to "delight the customer" by achieving quality through a highly disciplined process to focus on developing and delivering near-perfect products and services.

skimming pricing   The highest initial price that customers really desiring the product are willing to pay.

slotting fee   Payment manufacturer makes to place a new item on a retailer's shelf.

social audit   A systematic assessment of a firm's objectives, strategies, and performance in the domain of social responsibility.

social class   The relatively permanent, homogeneous divisions in a society into which people sharing similar values, lifestyles, interests, and behavior can be grouped.

social forces   The demographic characteristics of the population and its values in the environment.

social responsibility   The idea that organizations are part of a larger society and are accountable to that society for their actions.

societal marketing concept   The view that an organization should discover and satisfy the needs of its consumers in a way that also provides for society's well-being.

societal responsibility   Obligations that organizations have to the (1) preservation of the ecological environment and (2) general public.

solution   The best alternative that has been identified to solve the problem.

source   A company or person who has information to convey.

spam   Electronic junk mail or unsolicited e-mail.

specialty goods   Items that a consumer makes a special effort to search out and buy.

specialty merchandise wholesaler   A full-service merchant wholesaler that offers a relatively narrow range of products but has an extensive assortment within the product lines carried.

specialty outlet   Limited- and single-line stores that carry depth of product line, either in related items or in one primary line of merchandise.

splitting 30s   Reducing the length of a standard commercial from 30 seconds to 15 seconds.

staff positions People in staff positions have the authority and responsibility to advise people in the line positions but cannot issue direct orders to them.

stakeholder responsibility The concept of social responsibility that focuses on the obligations an organization has to those who can affect achievement of its objectives.

stakeholders Individuals or groups, either within or outside an organization, that relate to it in what it does and how well it performs.

standard markets Sites where companies test market a product through normal distribution channels and monitor the results.

standard markup pricing Adding a fixed percentage to the cost of all items in a specific product class.

Starch test A posttest that assesses the extent of consumers' recognition of an advertisement appearing in a magazine they have read.

statistical inference Drawing conclusions about a population from a sample taken from that population.

stimulus discrimination A person's ability to perceive differences in stimuli.

stimulus generalization When a response elicited by one stimulus (cue) is generalized to another stimulus.

stimulus-response presentation A selling format that assumes the prospect will buy if given the appropriate stimulus by a salesperson.

stock keeping unit (SKU) A unique identification number that defines an item for ordering or inventory purposes.

storage warehouses Goods are intended to rest for some time, as in the aging of products or in storing of household goods.

store audits Measurements of the sales of the product in stores and the number of cases ordered by a store from the wholesaler.

straight commission compensation plan A compensation plan where the salesperson's earnings are directly tied to the sales or profit generated.

straight rebuy Reordering an existing product or service from the list of acceptable suppliers, probably without checking with users or influencers.

straight salary compensation plan A compensation plan where the salesperson is paid a fixed fee per week, month, or year.

strategic alliances Agreements among two or more independent firms to cooperate for the purpose of achieving common goals.

strategic business unit (SBU) A decentralized profit center of a large firm that is treated as though it were a separate, independent business. *See also* **business unit**

strategic channel alliances A practice whereby one firm's marketing channel is used to sell another firm's products.

strategic marketing process The approach whereby an organization allocates its marketing mix resources to reach its target markets.

strip location A cluster of stores serving people who live within a 5- to 10-minute drive.

subbranding Combines a family brand with a new brand.

subcultures Subgroups within the larger, or national, culture with unique values, ideas, and attitudes.

subliminal perception Means that you see or hear messages without being aware of them.

supercenters Combine a typical merchandise store (typically 70,000 square feet) with a full-size grocery.

supplies Support goods similar to consumer convenience goods, consisting of products such as stationery, paperclips, and brooms.

supply chain A sequence of firms that perform activities required to create and deliver a good or service to consumers or industrial users.

supply chain management The integration and organization of information and logistic activities across firms in a supply chain for the purpose of creating and delivering goods and services that provide value to customers.

supply partnership A relationship that exists when a buyer and its supplier adopt mutually beneficial objectives, policies, and procedures for the purpose of lowering the cost and/or increasing the value of products and services delivered to the ultimate consumer.

support goods Items used to assist in producing other goods and services.

survey of buyers' intentions forecast Asking prospective customers whether they are likely to buy the product during some future time period.

survey of experts forecast Asking experts on a topic to make a judgment about some future event.

sustainable competitive advantage A strength, relative to competitors, in the markets served and the products offered.

sustainable development Conducting business in a way that protects the natural environment while making economic progress.

sweepstakes Sales promotions consisting of a game of chance requiring no analytical or creative effort by the consumer.

SWOT analysis An acronym describing an organization's appraisal of its internal strengths and weaknesses and its external opportunities and threats.

synergy The increased customer value achieved through performing organizational functions more efficiently.

tangibles Dimension of service quality—appearance of physical facilities, equipment, personnal, and communication materials.

target market One or more specific groups of potential consumers toward which an organization directs its marketing program.

target pricing Manufacturer deliberately adjusting the composition and features of a product to achieve the target price to consumers.

target profit pricing Setting an annual target of a specific dollar volume of profit.

target return-on-investment pricing Setting a price to achieve a return-on-investment (ROI) target.

target return-on-sales pricing Setting a price to achieve a profit that is a specified percentage of the sales volume.

tariff A government tax on goods or services entering a country primarily serving to raise prices on imports.

team selling Using an entire team of professionals in selling to and servicing major customers.

technology Inventions or innovations from applied science or engineering research.

telemarketing Using the telephone to interact with and sell directly to consumers.

Telephone Consumer Protection Act (1991) A law focusing on telemarketing abuses.

television home shopping   Possible when consumers watch a shopping channel on which products are displayed, then place orders over the telephone or the Internet.

test marketing   The process of offering a product for sale on a limited basis in a defined area to gain consumer reaction to the actual product and to examine its commercial viability and the marketing program.

theater test   A pretest in which consumers view test ads in new television shows or movies and report their feelings on electronic recording devices or questionnaires.

third-party logistics providers   Firms that perform most or all of the logistics functions that manufacturers, suppliers, and distributors would normally perform themselves.

time-sensitive materialists   Online consumer lifestyle segment who regard the Internet as a convenience tool for buying music, books, and computer software and electronics.

time utility   The value to consumers of having a good or service available when needed.

timing   The issue of deciding when to discount the price of merchandise.

top-down forecast   Subdividing an aggregate forecast into its principal components.

total cost   The total expense incurred by a firm in producing and marketing a product. Total cost is the sum of fixed cost and variable cost. In physical distribution decisions, the sum of all applicable costs for logistical activities.

total logistics cost   Expenses associated with transportation, materials handling and warehousing, inventory, stockouts, order processing, and return goods handling.

total revenue   The total money received from the sale of a product.

trade (functional) discounts   Price reductions to reward wholesalers or retailers for marketing functions they will perform in the future.

trade feedback effect   A country's imports affect its exports and exports affect its imports.

trade name   A commercial, legal name under which a company does business.

trade-oriented sales promotions   Sales tools used to support a company's advertising and personal selling efforts directed to wholesalers, distributors, or retailers. Three common approaches are allowances and discounts, cooperative advertising, and salesforce training.

trademark   Identifies that a firm has legally registered its brand name or trade name so the firm has its exclusive use.

Trademark Law Revision Act (1988)   A legislative change to the Lanham Act allowing a company to secure rights to a name before actual use by declaring an intent to use the name.

trading down   Reducing the number of features, quality, or price.

trading up   Adding value to a product (or line) through additional features or higher-quality materials.

traditional auction   A seller puts an item up for sale and would-be buyers are invited to bid in competition with each other.

traffic generation   The outcome of a direct marketing offer designed to motivate people to visit a business.

transactional websites   Electronic storefronts.

trend extrapolation   Extending a pattern observed in past data into the future.

trial   The consumer's actual first purchase and use of the product or brand.

truck jobber   Small merchant wholesalers who have a small warehouse from which they stock their trucks for distribution to retailers. They handle products such as bakery items, dairy products, and meat.

truck-rail   Popular intermodal transportation, also called piggyback or trailer on flat car (TOFC).

tying arrangement   A seller requires the purchaser of one product also to buy another item in the line.

ultimate consumers   The people—whether 80 years or 8 months old—who use the goods and services purchased for a household.

uncontrollable factors   (see environmental factors)

uniform delivered pricing   The price the seller quotes includes all transportation costs.

unit train   A train that is dedicated to one commodity (often coal), using permanently coupled cars that run a continuous loop from a single origin to a single destination and back.

unit variable cost   Variable cost expressed on a per unit basis.

unitary demand   Exists when the percentage change in price is identical to the percentage change in quantity demanded.

universal product code (UPC)   A number assigned to identify each product, represented by a series of bars of varying widths for scanning by optical readers.

unsought goods   Items that the consumer either does not know about or knows about but does not initially want.

usage rate   Quantity consumed or patronage—store visits—during a specific period; varies significantly among different customer groups.

users   People in the organization who actually use the product or service purchased by the buying center.

utilitarianism   A personal moral philosophy that focuses on the "greatest good for the greatest number" by assessing the costs and benefits of the consequences of ethical behavior.

utility   The benefits or customer value received by users of the product.

value   Specifically, value can be defined as the ratio of perceived benefits to price (Value = Perceived benefits/Price).

value added   Dimension of the retail positioning matrix that refers to elements such as location, product reliability, or prestige.

value analysis   A systematic appraisal of the design, quality, and performance of a product to reduce purchasing costs.

value consciousness   The concern for obtaining the best quality, features, and performance of a product or service for a given price.

value-pricing   The practice of simultaneously increasing service and product benefits and maintaining or decreasing price.

values   Personally or socially preferable modes of conduct or states of existence that are enduring. The beliefs of a person or culture; when applied to pricing, the ratio of perceived quality to price (Value = Perceived benefits/Price).

variable cost   The sum of the expenses of the firm that vary directly with the quantity of product that is produced and sold.

vending machines   Make it possible to serve customers when and where stores cannot.

vendor-managed inventory   An inventory management system whereby the supplier determines the product amount and assortment a customer (such as a retailer) needs and automatically delivers the appropriate items.

venture teams Multidisciplinary groups of marketing, manufacturing, and R&D personnel who stay with a new product from conception to production.

vertical conflict Disagreement between different levels in a marketing channel.

vertical marketing systems Professionally managed and centrally coordinated marketing channels designed to achieve channel economies and maximum marketing impact.

vertical price fixing The practice whereby sellers are required not to sell products below a minimum retail price. Also called resale price maintenance.

viral marketing An Internet/Web-enabled promotional strategy that encourages users to forward marketer-initiated messages to others via e-mail.

want A need that is shaped by a person's knowledge, culture, and individual characteristics.

warehouse A location, often decentralized, that a firm uses to store, consolidate, age, or mix stock; house product-recall programs; or ease tax burdens.

warehouse clubs Large retail stores (over 100,000 square feet) that require a yearly fee to shop at the store.

warranty A statement indicating the liability of the manufacturer for product deficiencies.

wasted coverage People outside a company's target audience who see, hear, or read the company's advertising.

web communities Websites that allow people to congregate online and exchange views on topics of common interest.

weighted-point system A method of establishing screening criteria, assigning them weights, and using them to evaluate new product ideas.

wheel of retailing A concept that describes how new retail outlets enter the market as low-status, low-margin stores and gradually add embellishments that raise their prices, and status. They now face a new low-status, low-margin operator, and the cycle starts to repeat itself.

whistle-blowers Employees who report unethical or illegal actions of their employers.

wholesaler-sponsored voluntary chain A wholesaler that develops a contractual relationship with small, independent retailers to standardize and coordinate buying practices, merchandising programs, and inventory management efforts.

word of mouth People influencing each other during their face-to-face conversations.

workload method A formula-based method for determining the size of a salesforce that integrates the number of customers served, call frequency, call length, and available selling time to arrive at a salesforce size.

World Trade Organization A permanent institution that sets rules governing trade between its members through a panel of trade experts who (1) decide on trade disputes between members and (2) issue binding decisions.

World Wide Web A part of the Internet that supports a retrieval system that formats information and documents into Web pages.

yield management pricing The charging of different prices to maximize revenue for a set amount of capacity at any given time.

CHAPTER NOTES

CHAPTER 1

1. Data in Figure 1-1 are based on statistics published by the National Sporting Goods Association and the Sporting Goods Manufacturers Association.
2. Website for the U.S. Patent and Trademark Office
3. Steven A. Meyerowitz, "Surviving Assaults on Trademarks," *Marketing Management,* no. 1 (1994), pp. 44–46; and Carrie Goerne, "Rollerblade Reminds Everyone That Its Success Is Not Generic," *Marketing News* (March 2, 1992), pp. 1–2.
4. "The Case for Brands," *The Economist* (September 8, 2001), p. 11; "Who's Wearing the Trousers?" *The Economist* (September 8, 2001), pp. 26–28; Gerry Khermouch, "The Best Global Brands," *Business Week* (August 6, 2001), pp. 50–64.
5. Peter D. Bennett, *Dictionary of Marketing Terms,* 2nd ed. (Lincolnwood, IL: NTC Publishing Group, 1995), p. 166.
6. Richard P. Bagozzi, "Marketing as Exchange," *Journal of Marketing* (October 1975), pp. 32–39; and Gregory T. Gundlach and Patrick E. Murphy, "Ethical and Legal Foundations of Relational Marketing Exchanges," *Journal of Marketing* (October 1993), pp. 35–46.
7. Robert M. McMath and Thom Forbes, *What Were They Thinking?* (New York: Times Business, 1998), pp. 3–22.
8. McMath and Forbes, pp. 181–82.
9. "And You Thought Atomic Fireballs Were Hot," *Time* (June 18, 2001), p. 20; "'Sweet Just Got Smart' as Pfizer Launches Body Smarts," *Pfizer Review* (Summer 2001), p. 5.
10. Peter Lewis, "Toro! Toro! Toro!" *Fortune* (July 9, 2001), p. 171.
11. Stephen H. Wildstrom, "Finally, Flat Is Better," *Business Week* (September 24, 2001), p. 20.
12. *Consumer Finance: College Students and Credit Cards* (Washington, DC: U.S. General Accounting Office, June 2001); "The Power of Plastic," *CBS News* (July 10, 2001); "Students Hooked on Credit," *CBS News* (January 19, 2001); Kristin Tillotson, "Credit-Card Debt Is Pushing Youth into Bankruptcy," *Star Tribune* (June 3, 2001), pp. A1, A20; James Surowiecki, "The Credit Card Kings," *The New Yorker* (November 27, 2000), p. 74; Theresa Luong, "A Tidy Savings," www.onmagazine.com (July 2001), pp. 58–59.
13. E. Jerome McCarthy, *Basic Marketing: A Managerial Approach* (Homewood, IL: Richard D. Irwin, 1960); and Walter van Waterschoot and Christophe Van den Bulte. "The 4P Classification of the Marketing Mix Revisited," *Journal of Marketing* (October 1992), pp. 83–93.
14. James Surowiecki, "The Return of Michael Porter," *Fortune* (February, 1999), pp. 135–38; and Kathleen M. Eisenhardt and Shona L. Brown, "Time Pacing: Competing in Markets That Won't Stand Still," *Harvard Business Review* (March–April 1998), pp. 59–69.
15. Werner J. Reinartz and V. Kumar, "On the Profitability of Long-Life Customers in a Noncontractual Setting: An Empirical Investigation and Implications for Marketing," *Journal of Marketing* (October 2000), pp. 17–35; "What's a Loyal Customer Worth?" *Fortune* (December 11, 1995), p. 182.
16. Michael Treacy and Fred D. Wiersema, *The Discipline of Market Leaders* (Reading, MA: Addison-Wesley, 1995); Michael Treacy and Fred Wiersema, "How Market Leaders Keep Their Edge," *Fortune* (February 6, 1995), pp. 88–89; and Michael Treacy, "You Need a Value Discipline—But Which One?" *Fortune* (April 17, 1995), p. 195.
17. Susan Fournier, Susan Dobseha, and David Glen Mick, "Preventing the Premature Death of Relationship Marketing," *Harvard Business Review* (January–February 1998), pp. 42–51.
18. The material on Rollerblade's current marketing strategy is based on a personal interview with David Samuels and with information from the Rollerblade website, and Rollerblade sales materials.
19. Leigh Muzlay, "Shoes that Morph from Sneakers to Skates Are Flying out of Stores," *The Wall Street Journal* (July 26, 2001), p. B1; The SGMA Report 2000, "The U.S. Athletic Footwear Market Today," which is published by the Sporting Goods Manufacturers Association.
20. Robert F. Keith, "The Marketing Revolution," *Journal of Marketing* (January 1960), pp. 35–38.
21. *Annual Report* (New York: General Electric Company, 1952), p. 21.
22. John C. Narver, Stanley F. Slater, and Brian Tietje, "Creating a Market Orientation," *Journal of Market Focused Management,* no. 2 (1998), pp. 241–55; Stanley F. Slater and John C. Narver, "Market Orientation and the Learning Organization," *Journal of Marketing* (July 1995), pp. 63–74; and George S. Day, "The Capabilities of Market-Driven Organizations," *Journal of Marketing* (October 1994), pp. 37–52.
23. The definition of customer relationship management is adapted from Rajendra K. Srivastava, Tasadduq A. Shervani, and Liam Fahey, "Marketing, Business Processes, and Shareholder Value: An Embedded View of Marketing Activities and the Discipline of Marketing," *Journal of Marketing* (special issue, 1999), pp. 168–79.
24. Michael E. Porter and Claas van er Linde, "Green and Competitive Ending the Stalemate," *Harvard Business Review* (September–October 1995), pp. 120–34; Jacquelyn Ottman, "Edison Winners Show Smart Environmental Marketing," *Marketing News* (July 17, 1995), pp. 16, 19; and Jacquelyn Ottman, "Mandate for the '90s: Green Corporate Image," *Marketing News* (September 11, 1995), p. 8.
25. Shelby D. Hunt and John J. Burnett, "The Macromarketing/Micromarketing Dichotomy: A Taxonomical Model," *Journal of Marketing* (Summer 1982), pp. 9–26.
26. Philip Kotler and Sidney J. Levy, "Broadening the Concept of Marketing," *Journal of Marketing* (January 1969), pp. 10–15.
27. "Marketing Museums: When Merchants Enter the Temple," *The Economist* (April 21, 2001), pp. 64–66; Lisa Snedeker, "Putting Their Money on Monets," *Star Tribune* (August 16, 2001), p. F16.
28. Based on "The State Hermitage Museum," a case written by Olga Saguinova, Michael J. Vessey, and William Rudelius appearing in Rudelius et al., *Marketing,* 1st Russian ed. (Moscow: DeNovo Publishing Company, 2001), pp. 594–96; Peter Baker, "Historically Rich Russia Struggles to Attract Tourists," *Star Tribune* (September 9, 2001), p. G5.
29. John A. Byrne, "Caught in the Net," *Business Week* (August 27, 2001), pp. 114–16; Gary Gentile, "eToast," *Star Tribune* (March 3, 2001), pp. D1, D2.

Rollerblade: This case was written by William Rudelius and Giana Eckhardt.

CHAPTER 2

1. www.benjerry.com.
2. Blair S. Walker, "Good-Humored Activist Back to the Fray," *USA Today* (December 8, 1992), pp. 1B–2B.
3. Jim Castelli, "Finding the Right Fit: Are You Weird Enough?" *HR Magazine* (September 1990), pp. 38–39.
4. "Ben & Jerry's Homemade, Inc.," news release (Burlington, VT, April 12, 2001).

5. Roger A. Kerin, Vijay Mahajan, and P. Rajan Varadarajan, *Contemporary Perspectives on Strategic Marketing Planning* (Boston: Allyn & Bacon, 1990), chapter 1; and Orville C. Walker, Jr., Harper W. Boyd, Jr., and Jean-Claude Larreche, *Marketing Strategy* (Burr Ridge, IL: Richard D. Irwin, 1992), chapters 1 and 2.

6. Theodore Levitt, "Marketing Myopia," *Harvard Business Review* (July–August 1960), pp. 45–56.

7. Norman Spaulding and Jay Lorsch, *Medtronic, Inc.* (Boston, MA: Harvard Business School, 1944), pp. 2–3.

8. Kenneth E. Goodpaster and Thomas E. Holloran, "Anatomy of Spiritual and Social Awareness: The Case of Medtronic, Inc." Third International Symposium on Catholic Social Thought and Management Education, (Goa, India, 1999), p. 9.

9. Charles W. L. Hill and Gareth R. Jones, *Strategic Management: An Integrated Approach,* 4th ed. (Boston: Houghton Mifflin, 1998), pp. 37–38.

10. Goodpaster and Holloran, pp. 9–11.

11. "Ben & Jerry's Homemade, Inc.," news release (Burlington, VT, November 20, 2000).

12. George Stalk, Phillip Evans, and Lawrence E. Shulman, "Competing on Capabilities. The New Rules of Corporate Strategy," *Harvard Business Review* (March–April 1992), pp. 57–69.

13. Roger A. Kerin and Robert A. Peterson, *Strategic Marketing Problems: Cases and Comments,* 8th ed. (Englewood Cliffs, NJ: Prentice Hall), pp. 2–3; and Derek F. Abell, *Defining the Business* (Englewood Cliffs, NJ: Prentice Hall, 1980), p. 18.

14. Christopher Meyer, *Fast Cycle Time* (New York: Free Press, 1993); and Michael E. Porter, *Competitive Advantage* (New York: Free Press, 1985).

15. W. Edwards Deming, *Out of the Crisis* (Cambridge, MA: MIT Center for Advanced Engineering Study, 1986).

16. Michael Totty, "Making the Sale," *The Wall Street Journal* (September 24, 2001), p. R6.

17. Adapted from "The Experience Curve Reviewed, IV. The Growth Share Matrix of the Product Portfolio" (Boston: The Boston Consulting Group, 1973).

18. Kerin, Mahajan, and Vardarajan, p. 52.

19. Strengths and weaknesses of the BCG technique are based largely on Derek F. Abell and John S. Hammond, *Strategic Market Planning: Problem and Analytic Approaches* (Englewood Cliffs, NJ: Prentice Hall, 1979); and Yoram Wind, Vijay Mahajan, and Donald Swire, "An Empirical Comparison of Standardized Portfolio Models," *Journal of Marketing* (Spring 1983), pp. 89–99.

20. J. Scott Armstrong and Roderick J. Brodie, "Effects of Portfolio Planning Methods on Decision Making: Experimental Results," *International Journal of Research in Marketing* (Winter 1994), pp. 73–84.

21. H. Igor Ansoff, "Strategies for Diversification," *Harvard Business Review* (September–October 1957), pp. 113–24.

22. Hill and Jones, chapters 1–3.

23. Totty, p. R6.

24. Linda Swenson and Kenneth E. Goodpaster, *Medtronic in China (A)* (Minneapolis, MN: University of St. Thomas, 1999), pp. 4–5.

25. Peter Nulty, "Kodak Grabs for Growth Again," *Fortune* (May 16, 1994), pp. 76–78.

26. Mark Maremont, "Kodak's New Focus," *Business Week* (January 30, 1995), pp. 63–68.

27. Daniel Eisenberg, "Kodak's Photo Op," *Time* (April 30, 2001), pp. 46–47.

28. Michael Ryan, "Kodak's Big Moment," *Smartbusinessmay.com* (July 2001), pp. 79–84.

29. Mike Musgrove, "'Y' Factor: A Camera that Tapes and Plays," *Washington Post* (March 24, 2001), p. E1.

30. John R. Wilke and James Bandler, "New Digital Camera Deals Kodak a Lesson in Microsoft's Ways," *The Wall Street Journal* (July 2, 2001), pp. A1, A6.

Specialized Bicycle Components, Inc.: This case was written by Giana Eckhardt.

APPENDIX A

1. Personal interview with Authur R. Kydd, St. Croix Venture Partners.

2. Examples of guides to writing marketing plans include: William A. Cohen, *The Marketing Plan* (New York: Wiley, 1995); Mark Nolan, *The Instant Marketing Plan* (Santa Maria, CA: Puma Publishing Company, 1995); and Roman G. Hiebing, Jr., and Scott W. Cooper, *The Successful Marketing Plan*, 2nd ed. (Lincolnwood, IL: NTC Business Books, 1997).

3. Examples of guides to writing business plans include the following: Rhonda M. Abrahms, *The Successful Business Plan: Secrets & Strategies.* 3rd ed. (Grants Pass, OR: The Oasis Press/PSI Research, 2000); Joseph A. Covello and Brian J. Hazelgren, *The Complete Book of Business Plans* (Naperville, IL: Sourcebooks, 1995); Joseph A. Covello and Brian J. Hazelgren, *Your First Business Plan*, 3rd ed. (Naperville, IL: Sourcebooks, 1998); and Angela Shupe, ed., *Business Plans Handbook*, vols. 1–4 (Detroit: Gale Research, 1997).

4. Abrahms, *The Successful Business Plan*, p. 30.

5. Some of these points are adapted from Abrahms, pp. 30–38; others are adapted from William Rudelius, *Guidelines for Technical Report Writing* (Minneapolis, MN: University of Minnesota, undated).

6. The authors are indebted to Randall F. Peters and Leah Peters for being allowed to adapt elements of a business plan for Paradise Kitchens, Inc., for the sample marketing plan and for their help and suggestions.

CHAPTER 3

1. David Kirkpatrick, "In Napster's Void: You've Got Misery!" *Fortune* (April 2, 2001), pp. 144–146; and Devin Leonard, "Don't Call Them Napster," *Fortune* (June 25, 2001), p. 44.

2. Chris Taylor, "More Pain for Napster," *Time* (April 16, 2001), p. 43; and Monica Roman, "Napster Gets Some Big Buddies," *Business Week* (June 18, 2001), p. 46.

3. Mathew Grimm, "Java Straight Up," *American Demographics* (February 2001), pp. 66–67; Rebecca Gardyn, "Grounds for a New Strategy," *American Demographics* (June 2001), pp. 15–17; Susannah Meadows, "The Water of the Moment," *Newsweek* (July 30, 2001), p. 40; and Michael Arndt, "McLatte and Croissant?" *Business Week* (April 2, 2001), p. 14.

4. Eric Nee et al, "10 Tech Trends to Bet On," *Fortune* (March 19, 2001), pp. 58–84; Christine Gorman, "Repairing the Damage," *Time* (February 25, 2001), pp. 53–58; Catherine Arnst, "The Rebirth of a Cancer Drug," *Business Week* (July 9, 2001), pp. 95–102; Steve Jarvis, "Internet Privacy at the Plate, Net Names, Taxes on Deck Too," *Marketing News* (January 1, 2001), pp. 12–14; Dana James, "Outlook 2000: A Look at the Trends That Will Shape the New Year," *Marketing News* (January 17, 2000), p. 9; Brent Schlender, "Peter Drucker Takes the Long View," *Fortune* (September 28, 1998), pp. 162–73; Annetta Miller, "The Millennial Mind-set," *American Demographics* (January 1999), pp. 60–65; and Harry S. Dent, Jr., *The Roaring 2000s* (New York: Simon and Schuster, 1998).

5. Nicholas Kulish, "Census 2000: The New Demographics," *The Wall Street Journal* (May 15, 2001), p. B1.

6. U.S. Bureau of the Census, "Current Population Report, Residential Population Projections" (March 1996).

7. Jennifer Cheeseman Day, "Population Projections of the United States by Age, Sex, Race, and Hispanic Origin: 1995–2050," in U.S. Bureau of the Census, "Current Population Reports" (March 1996), p. 25.

8. Lisa Vickery, Kelly Greene, Shelly Branch, and Emily Nelson, "Marketers Tweak Strategies as Age Groups Realign," *The Wall Street Journal* (May 15, 2001), pp. B1, B4.

9. Toddi Gutner, "Generation X: To Be Young, Thrifty, and in the Black," *Business Week* (July 21, 1997), p. 76; Howard Gleckman, "Generation $ Is More Like It," *Business Week* (November 3, 1997), p. 44; Karen Ritchie, "Marketing to Generation X," *American Demographics* (April 1995), pp. 34–39; and Diane Crispell," Generations to 2025," *American Demographics* (January 1995), p. 4.

10. Beck, "Generation Y: Next Population Bulge Shows Its Might"; and Susan Mitchell, "The Next Baby Boom," *American Demographics* (October 1995), pp. 22–31.

11. Charles D. Schewe, Geoffrey E. Meredith, and Stephanie M. Noble, "Defining Moments: Segmenting by Cohorts," *Marketing Management* (Fall 2000), pp. 48–53; Alison Stein Wellner, "Generational Divide," *American Demographics* (October 2000), pp. 53–58; J. Walker Smith and Ann Clurman, *Rocking the Ages*, (New York: HarperCollins Publishers, 1997); Kevin T. Higgins, "Generational Marketing," *Marketing Management* (Fall 1998) pp. 6–9; and Geoffrey Meredith and Charles Schewe, "The Power of Cohorts," *American Demographics* (December 1994), pp. 22–31.

12. Vanessa O'Connell, "Advertisers Are Cautious as Household Makeup Shifts," *The Wall Street Journal* (May 15, 2001), pp. B1, B4; Jason Fields and Lynne M. Casper, "America's Families and Living Arrangements," Current Population Reports: U.S. Bureau of the Census (June 2001); Ken Bryson and Lynne M. Casper, "Household and Family Characteristics: March 1997," U.S. Department of Commerce (April 1998); and U.S. Bureau of the Census, "Current Population Survey" (March 1998).

13. Joan Raymond, 'The Ex-Files," *American Demographics* (February 2001), pp. 60–64; Diane Crispell, "Dual-Earner Diversity," *American Demographics* (July 1995), pp. 32–37.

14. Marc J. Perry and Paul J. Mackun, "Population Change and Distribution," Census 2000 Brief: U.S. Bureau of the Census (April 2001); Paul Campbell, "Population Projection: States, 1995–2025," Current Population Report, U.S. Department of Commerce (May 1997).

15. Harry S. Dent, Jr., *The Roaring 2000s*, (New York: Simon and Schuster, 1998), p. 211.

16. Eduardo Porter, "Even 126 Sizes Don't Fit All," *The Wall Street Journal* (March 2, 2001), pp. B1, B4: William H. Frey, "Micro Melting Pots," *American Demographics* (June 2001), pp. 20–23; and Peter Francese, "American at Mid-Decade," *American Demographics* (February 1995), pp. 23–29.

17. "Resident Population of the United States: Estimates by Sex, Race, and Hispanic Origin, with Median Age," U.S. Bureau of the Census (December 28, 1998).

18. Zachary Schiller, "Stalking the New Consumer," *Business Week* (August 28, 1989), pp. 54–62.

19. William Frey, "The Diversity Myth," *American Demographics* (June 1998), pp. 39–43; and Jeffery D. Zbar, "In a Diverse Hispanic World, Image Counts," *Advertising Age* (April 3, 1995), pp. 518–19.

20. This discussion is based on Rebecca Gardyn, "Granddaughters of Feminism," *American Demographics* (April 2001), pp. 43–47; Judith Langer, "Behind the Looking Glass," *American Demographics* (February 2001), pp. 53–59; and Ginia Bellafante, "Feminism: It's All about Me!" *Time* (June 29, 1998), p. 62.

21. Edward B. Keller and Thomas A. W. Miller, "Re-mapping the World of Consumers," *American Demographics* (October 2000), pp. S1–S20; and Sandra Yin, "Making a Healthy Choice," *American Demographics* (July 2001), pp. 40–41.

22. Jill Smolowe, "Do You Still Know Me?" *Time* (September 12, 1994), p. 60; and Judann Dagnoli, "Value Strategy to Battle Recession," *Advertising Age* (January 7, 1991), pp. 1, 44.

23. Peter Brimelow, "The Education Paradox," *Forbes* (July 6, 1998), pp. 178–79.

24. James Cooper, Kathleen Madigan, and James Mehring, "Welcome to the Growth Recession," *Business Week* (July 2, 2001), pp. 87–90.

25. "The Index of Consumer Sentiment," Survey Research Center, University of Michigan (1998); and Blayne Cutler, "The Feel-Good Index," *American Demographics* (September 1992), pp. 56–60.

26. Bureau of Labor Statistics and the Bureau of the Census, "Annual Demographics Survey," (March 2001), Table HINC–01; "Money and Income in the United States," Current Population Reports: U.S. Census Bureau (September 2000).

27. Don Carlson, "The Old Economy in the New Economy," *Business Week* (November 13, 2000), p. 42H; Owen Ullmann, "Forget Saving, America. Your Job Is to Spend," *Business Week* (December 28, 1998), p. 54; Gene Koretz, "Savings' Death Is Exaggerated," *Business Week* (September 14, 1998), p. 26; and Marcia Mogelonsky, "No More Food, Thanks," *American Demographics* (August 1998), p. 59.

28. Berna Miller, "Fun Money," *American Demographics* (March 1997), p. 33.

29. Elizabeth Corcoran, "The Next Small Think," *Forbes* (July 23, 2001), pp. 96–106; Michael J. Mandel and Robert D. Hof, "Rethinking the Internet," *Business Week* (March 26, 2001), pp. 117–122; Catherine Arnst, "The Birth of a Cancer Drug," *Business Week* (July 9, 2001), pp. 95–102; Clint Willis, "25 Cool Things You Wish You Had and Will," *Forbes ASAP* (June 1, 1998), pp. 49–60.

30. Neil Gross, Peter Coy, and Otis Post, "The Technology Paradox," *Business Week* (March 6, 1995), pp. 76–84.

31. Leon Jaroff, "Smart's the Word in Detroit," *Time* (February 6, 1995), pp. 50–52.

32. Clint Willis, "25 Cool Things You Wish You Had and Will," *Forbes ASAP* (June 1, 1998), pp. 49–60.

33. Jim Carlton, "Recycling Redefined," *The Wall Street Journal* (March 6, 2001), pp. B1, B4; Stephanie Anderson, "There's Gold in Those Hills of Soda Bottles," *Business Week* (September 11, 1995), p. 48; Maxine Wilkie, "Asking Americans to Use Less Stuff," *American Demographics* (December 1994), pp. 11–12; and Jacquelyn Ottman, "New and Improved Won't Do," *Marketing News* (January 30, 1995), p. 9.

34. International Trade Administration definition reported in A. J. Campbell, "Ten Reasons Why Your Company Should Use Electronic Commerce," *Business America* (May 1998), p. 12; Andrew Urbaczewski, Leonard M. Jessup, and Bradley C. Wheeler, "A Manager's Primer on Electronic Commerce," *Business Horizons* (September-October 1998), pp. 5–16; and Ravi Kalakota and Andrew B. Whinston, *Electronic Commerce: A Manager's Guide* (Reading, MA: Addison-Wesley 1997).

35. Michael J. Mandel and Robert D. Hof, "Rethinking the Internet," *Business Week* (March 26, 2001), pp. 117–122; Steve Hamm, David Welch, Wendy Zellner, Faith Keenan, and Peter Engardio, "E-biz: Down but Hardly Out," *Business Week* (March 26, 2001), pp. 126–130; and Spencer E. Ante, Amy Borrus, and Robert D. Hof, "In Search of the Net's Next Big Thing," *Business Week* (March 26, 2001), pp. 140–141.

36. Henry Goldblatt, "The End of the Long Distance Club," *Fortune* (May 26, 1997), p. 30; and "Wheel of Fortune," *The Economist* (November 21, 1998), p. 53.

37. DeAnn Weimer, "Don't Be Shocked by Surges in the Price of Power," *Business Week* (July 27, 1998), p. 33

38. John Wilke, Ted Bridis, and Nick Wingfield, "Microsoft Scores a Big Legal Victory," *The Wall Street Journal* (June 29, 2001), pp. B1, B3: Steve Hamm, Amy Cortese, and Susan B. Garland, "Microsoft's Future," *Business Week* (January 19, 1998), pp. 59–68.

39. Michael Porter, *Competitive Advantage* (New York: Free Press, 1985); and Michael Porter, *Competitive Strategy* (New York: Free Press, 1980).

40. Catherine Arnst, "For Lucent, a Shining Moment," *Business Week* (April 21, 1997), p. 126.

41. David L. Birch, *The Job Generation Process* (Cambridge, Mass.: MIT Program on Neighborhood and Regional Change, 1979).

42. "A New Copyright Law?" *Business Week* (August 3, 1998), p. 45.

43. Karl Taro Greenfield, "Meet the Napster," *Time* (October 2, 2000), pp. 60–68; and Michael Schrage, "What If Napster Were Based in China?" *Fortune* (May 28, 2001), p. 194.

44. James Heckman, "Laws That Take Effect—and Some Likely to Return—in 1999 Mean Marketers Must Change Some Policies," *Marketing News* (December 7, 1998), pp. 1, 16.

45. Dorothy Cohen, "Trademark Strategy Revisited," *Journal of Marketing* (July 1991), pp. 46–59.

46. Paul Barrett, "High Court Sees Color as Basis for Trademarks," *The Wall Street Journal* (March 29, 1995), p. A6; Paul Barrett, "Color in the Court," *The Wall Street Journal* (January 5, 1995), p. A1; and David Kelly, "Rainbow of Ideas to Trademark Color," *Advertising Age* (April 24, 1995), pp. 20, 22.

47. Dick Mercer, "Tempest in a Soup Can," *Advertising Age* (October 17, 1994), pp. 25–29.

48. Mark McFadden, "The BBB on the WWW," *HP Professional* (September 1997), p. 36.

Flyte Time Productions, Inc.: This case was written by William Rudelius based on personal interviews with Jimmy Jam and Terry Lewis, and the following sources: Jon Bream, "Flyte Tyme Is Still Ticking After 20 Years of Hits," *Star Tribune* (April 29, 2001), pp. F1, F7; "Jimmy Jam and Terry Lewis Make Flyte Tyme Studios No. 1," *Business Wire* (August 21, 2001).

CHAPTER 4

1. "Our Commitment to Preventing Alcohol Abuse and Underage Drinking," www.beeresponsible.com; "Packaging," www.anheuser-busch.com, downloaded May 28, 2001.

2. For a discussion of the definition of ethics, see Eugene R. Lazniak and Patrick E. Murphy, *Ethical Marketing Decision: The Higher Road* (Boston: Allyn & Bacon, 1993), chapter 1.

3. Verne E. Henderson, "The Ethical Side of Enterprise," *Sloan Management Review* (Spring 1982), pp. 37–47. See also, Joseph L. Badaracco, Jr., *Defining Moments: When Managers Must Choose Between Right and Right* (Boston: Harvard Business School Press, 1997).

4. "Just How Honest Are You?" *Inc.* (February 1995), p. 104.

5. "Exporting Death," *Time* (April 13, 1998), p. 63; Ray O. Werner, "Marketing and the Supreme Court in Transition, 1982–1984," *Journal of Marketing* (Summer 1985), pp. 97–105; and Jane Bryant Quinn, "Computer Program Deceives Consumers," *Dallas Morning News* (March 2, 1998), p. B3.

6. "The Trust Factor," *American Demographics* (February 2001), p. 27; "Not Quite at the Bottom of the Barrel," *Advertising Age* (December 17, 2001), p. 21; *U.S. Employee Perceptions of Ethics in Organizations* (Indianapolis, IN: Walker Information, 1998).

7. See, for example, Lawrence B. Chonko, *Ethical Decision Making in Marketing* (Thousand Oaks, CA: Sage, 1995).

8. Thomas Donaldson, "Values in Tension: Ethics Away from Home," *Harvard Business Review* (September–October 1996), pp. 48–62.

9. "Levi Only Comfortable Dealing with Countries That Fit Its Image," *Dallas Morning News* (January 9, 1995), p. D2. See also William Beaver, "Levi's Is Leaving China," *Business Horizons* (March–April 1995), pp. 35–40.

10. P. Steidmeir, "The Moral Legitimacy of Intellectual Property Claims: American Business and Developing Country Perspectives," *Journal of Business Ethics,* vol. 12 (1993), pp. 157–64; Dan T. Swartwood and Richard J. Hefferman, *Trends in Intellectual Property Loss, Survey Report* (Alexandria, VA: American Society for Industrial Security, 1998).

11. "Agents Wage War on Piracy," *Dallas Morning News* (December 12, 2001), p. 10D; Bryan W. Husted, "The Impact of National Culture on Software Piracy," *Journal of Business Ethics,* vol. 26 (2000), pp. 197–211.

12. Vern Terpstra and Kenneth David, *The Cultural Environment of International Business,* 3rd ed. (Cincinnati: South-Western Publishing, 1991), p. 12.

13. "Carnivore in the Cabbage Patch," *U.S. News & World Report* (January 20, 1997), p. 69.

14. "Three Ad Agencies Settle FTC Charges of Deceptive Car-Leasing Commercials," *The Wall Street Journal* (January 21, 1998), p. B2.

15. "The Battle over Web Privacy," *The Wall Street Journal* (March 21, 2001), pp. B1, B4.

16. For an extensive examination on slotting fees, see Paul N. Bloom, Gregory T. Gundlach, and Joseph P. Cannon, "Slotting Allowances and Fees: Schools of Thought and Views of Practicing Managers," *Journal of Marketing* (April 2000), pp. 92–109. Also see, "FTC Pinpoints Slotting Fees," *Advertising Age* (February 26, 2001), p. 52.

17. This discussion contains statistics reported in Carolyn F. Siegel, "Introducing Marketing Students to Business Intelligence Using Project-Based Learning on the World Wide Web," *Journal of Marketing Education* (August 2000), pp. 90–98.

18. "P&G Expected to Get About $120 Million in Settlement of Chewy-Cookie Lawsuit," *The Wall Street Journal* (September 11, 1989), p. B10.

19. These examples are highlighted in Thomas W. Dunfee, N. Craig Smith, and William T. Ross, Jr., "Social Contracts and Marketing Ethics," *Journal of Marketing* (July 1999), pp. 14–32; and Andy Pasztor, *When the Pentagon Was for Sale: Inside America's Biggest Defense Scandal* (New York: Scribner, 1995).

20. www.transparency.de, downloaded May 25, 2001.

21. Thomas Donaldson, "The Corporate Ethics Boom: Significant, or Just for Show?" *Knowledge@Wharton,* downloaded February 25, 2001; "Doing Well by Doing Good," *The Economist* (April 22, 2000), pp. 65–67.

22. "Good Grief," *The Economist* (April 8, 1995), p. 57.

23. "Ethics Programs Aren't Stemming Employee Misconduct, Study Indicates," *The Wall Street Journal* (May 11, 2000), p. A1.

24. *The 2000 National Business Ethics Survey* (Washington, DC: Ethics Resource Center, 2000); "Simon Says, 'Behave!'" *Success* (January 2000), p. 21.

25. J. Badaracco, Jr., and A. Webb, "Business Ethics: A View from the Trenches," *California Management Review* (Winter 1995), pp. 8–28; "Workers Who Blow the Whistle on Bosses Often Pay a High Price," *The Wall Street Journal* (July 18, 1995), p. B1; and Randi L. Sims and John P. Keenan, "Predictors of External Whistleblowing: Organizational and Intrapersonal Variables," *Journal of Business Ethics* (March 1998), pp. 411–30.

26. Savior L. S. Nwachukwu and Scott J. Vitell, Jr., "The Influence of Corporate Culture on Managerial Ethical Judgments," *Journal of Business Ethics,* vol. 17 (1997), pp. 757–76; and Ismael R. Akaah and Daulatram Lund, "The Influence of Personal Values and Organizational Values on Marketing Professionals' Ethical Behavior," *Journal of Business Ethics,* vol. 13 (1994), pp. 417–30.

27. For an extensive discussion on these moral philosophies, see R. Eric Reidenbach and Donald P. Robin, *Ethics and Profits* (Englewood Cliffs, NJ: Prentice Hall, 1989); Chonko, *Ethical Decision Making;* and Lazniak and Murphy, *Ethical Marketing Decisions.*

28. "3M's Big Cleanup," *Business Week* (June 5, 2000), pp. 96–98.

29. James O. Wilson, "Adam Smith on Business Ethics," *California Management Review* (Fall 1989), pp. 59–72; and George M. Zinkhan, Michael Bisesi, and Mary Jane Saxton, "MBAs: Changing Attitudes toward Marketing Dilemmas," *Journal of Business Ethics,* vol. 8 (1989), pp. 963–74.

30. Alix M. Freedman, "Bad Reaction: Nestlé's Bid to Crash Baby-Formula Market in U.S. Stirs a Row," *The Wall Street Journal* (February 16, 1989), pp. A1, A6; and Alix Freedman, "Nestlé to Drop Claim on Label of Its Formula," *The Wall Street Journal* (March 13, 1989), p. B5.

31. Robert B. Reich, "The New Meaning of Corporate Social Responsibility," *California Management Review* (Winter 1998), pp. 8–17.

32. Harvey S. James and Farhad Rassekh, "Smith, Friedman, and Self-Interest in Ethical Society," *Business Ethics Quarterly* (July 2000), pp. 659–74.

33. "Beating the Odds in Biotech," *Newsweek* (October 12, 1992), p. 63.

34. For an extended description of the Perrier decision, see "Perrier—Overresponding to a Crisis," in Robert F. Hartley, *Marketing Mistakes and Successes,* 8th ed. (New York: Wiley, 2001), pp. 127–37.

35. "Anatomy of a Recall," *Time* (September 11, 2000), pp. 29–32; "Firestone Begins Ad Campaign," *Dallas Morning News* (April 8, 2001), p. D1.

36. Harvey Meyer, "The Greening of Corporate America," *Journal of Business Strategy* (January–February 2000), pp. 38–43; Irina Maslennikova and David Foley, "Xerox's Approach to Sustainability," *Interfaces* (May–June 2000), pp. 226–33. Also see, Philemon Oyewale, "Social Costs of Environmental Justice Associated with the Practice of Green Marketing," *Journal of Business Ethics,* vol. 29 (2001), pp. 239–51; and Ajay Menon and Anil Menon, "Environpreneurial Marketing Strategy: The Emergence of Corporate Environmentalism as Market Strategy," *Journal of Marketing* (January 1997), pp. 51–67.

37. *The ISO Survey of ISO 9000 and ISO 14000 Certificates* (Geneva, Switzerland: International Organization for Standardization, 2000).

38. For an extended discussion on this topic, see P. Rajan Varadarajan and Anil Menon, "Causes-Related Marketing: A Coalignment of Marketing Strategy and Corporate Philanthropy," *Journal of Marketing* (July 1988), pp. 58–74. The examples given are found in "The Socially Correct Corporation," *Fortune* (July 24, 2000), special section; and "The Wider Benefits of Backing a Good Cause," *Marketing* (September 2, 1999), pp. 18–22.

39. "Saving the Earth, One Click at a Time," *American Demographics* (January 2001), pp. 30–34; "The Socially Correct Corporation"; and "The Wider Benefits of Backing a Good Cause."

40. These steps are adapted from J. J. Carson and G. A. Steiner, *Measuring Business Social Performance: The Corporate Social Audit* (New York: Committee for Economic Development, 1974). See also Sandra Waddock and Neil Smith, "Corporate Responsibility Audits: Doing Well by Doing Good," *Sloan Management Review* (Winter 2000), pp. 75–84.

41. "A World of Sweatshops," *Business Week* (November 6, 2000), pp. 84–86.

42. "Who's Responsible?" *American Demographics* (December 1999), p. 17; Meyer, "The Greening of Corporate America"; Waddock and Smith, "Corporate Responsibility Audits."

43. "Factoids," *Research Alert* (December 1, 2000), p. 4; Paul Bernstein, "Cheating: The New National Pastime?" *Business* (October–December 1995), pp. 24–33; and "Penny for Your Thoughts," *American Demographics* (September 2000), pp. 8–9.

44. "A Lighter Shade of Green," *American Demographics* (February 2000), p. 24

45. "Schism on the Green," *Brandweek* (February 26, 2001), p. 18.

46. "FTC Stands by Regs for 'Green' Ad Claims," *Advertising Age* (October 7, 1996), p. 61.

CHAPTER 5

1. "Women in the Automotive Industry" and "He Said, She Said," www.womanmotorist.com, downloaded August 28, 2001; "Selling Cars to Women: Make & Model, Experience at Dealership Matter More," www.diversity.com, downloaded May 7, 2001; "A Sweet Deal," *American Demographics* (January 2000), pp. 10–11.

2. James F. Engel, Roger D. Blackwell, and Paul Miniard, *Consumer Behavior,* 9th ed. (Fort Worth, TX: Dryden Press, 1998).

3. For thorough descriptions of consumer expertise, see Joseph W. Alba and J. Wesley Hutchinson, "Knowledge Calibration: What Consumers Know and What They Think They Know," *Journal of Consumer Research* (September 2000), pp. 123–56; and Joseph W. Alba and J. Wesley Hutchinson, "Dimensions of Consumer Expertise," *Journal of Consumer Research* (March 1987), pp. 411–54.

4. For in-depth studies on external information search patterns, see Sridhar Moorthy, Brian T. Ratchford, and Debabrata Tulukdar, "Consumer Information Search Revisited: Theory and Empirical Analysis," *Journal of Consumer Research* (March 1997), pp. 263–77; Joel E. Urbany, Peter R. Dickson, and William L. Wilkie, "Buyer Uncertainty and Information Search," *Journal of Consumer Research* (March 1992), pp. 452–63; and Sharon E. Beatty and Scott M. Smith, "External Search Effort: An Investigation across Several Product Categories," *Journal of Consumer Research* (June 1987), pp. 83–95.

5. "Portable CD Players Ratings," *Consumer Reports* (July 2001), p. 43.

6. For an extended discussion on evaluative criteria, see Del J. Hawkins, Roger J. Best, and Kenneth A. Coney, *Consumer Behavior,* 8th ed. (Burr Ridge, IL: Irwin/McGraw-Hill, 2001), pp. 566–83.

7. John A. Howard, *Buyer Behavior in Marketing Strategy,* 2nd ed. (Englewood Cliffs, NJ: Prentice Hall, 1994), pp. 101, 128–89. For an extended discussion on consumer choice sets, see Allan D. Shocker, Moshe Ben-Akiva, Bruno Boccara, and Prakesh Nedungadi, "Consideration Set Influences on Consumer Decision Making and Choice: Issues, Models, and Suggestions." *Marketing Letters* (August 1991), pp. 181–98.

8. William J. McDonald, "Time Use in Shopping: The Role of Personal Characteristics," *Journal of Retailing* (Winter 1994), pp. 345–66; Robert J. Donovan, John R. Rossiter, Gillian Marcoolyn, and Andrew Nesdale, "Store Atmosphere and Purchasing Behavior," *Journal of Retailing* (Fall 1994), pp. 283–94; and Eric A. Greenleaf and Donald R. Lehman, "Reasons for Substantial Delay in Consumer Decision Making," *Journal of Consumer Research* (September 1995), pp. 186–99.

9. Ruth N. Bolton, "A Dynamic Model of the Duration of the Customer's Relationship with a Continuous Service Provider: The Role of Satisfaction," *Marketing Science,* vol. 17 (1998), pp. 45–65; and Ruth N. Bolton and James H. Drew, "A Multistage Model of Customers' Assessment of Service Quality and Value," *Journal of Consumer Research* (March 1991), pp. 376–84.

10. Jagdish N. Sheth, Banwari Mitral, and Bruce Newman, *Consumer Behavior* (Fort Worth, TX: Dryden Press, 1999), p. 22.

11. Frederick F. Reichheld and Thomas Teal, *The Loyalty Effect* (Boston: Harvard Business School Press, 1996); "What's a Loyal Customer Worth?" *Fortune* (December 11, 1995), p. 182; Patricia Sellers, "Keeping the Buyers You Already Have," *Fortune* (Autumn–Winter 1993), p. 57. For an in-depth examination of this topic, see Werner J. Reinartz and V. Kumar, "On the Profitability of Long-Life Customers in a Noncontractual Setting: An Empirical Investigation and Implications for Marketing," *Journal of Marketing* (October 2000), pp. 17–35.

12. Rahul Jacob, "The Struggle to Create an Organization for the 21st Century," *Fortune* (April 3, 1995), pp. 90–99.

13. "Customers, 800-Lines May Not Connect," *The Wall Street Journal* (November 20, 1990), p. B1.

14. For an overview of research on involvement, see John C. Mowen and Michael Minor, *Consumer Behavior,* 5th ed. (Upper Saddle River, NJ: Prentice Hall, 1998), pp. 64–68; and Frank R. Kardes, *Consumer Behavior* (Reading, MA: Addison-Wesley, 1999), pp. 256–58.

15. For an overview on the three problem-solving variations, see Hawkins, Best, and Coney, *Consumer Behavior,* pp. 506–07; Howard, *Buyer Behavior,* pp. 69–162.

16. Russell Belk, "Situational Variables and Consumer Behavior," *Journal of Consumer Research* (December 1975), pp. 157–63. Representative recent studies on situational influences are discussed in Mowen and Minor *Consumer Behavior,* pp. 451–75.

17. A. H. Maslow, *Motivation and Personality* (New York: Harper & Row, 1970). Also see Richard Yalch and Frederic Brunel, "Need Hierarchies in Consumer Judgments of Product Design: Is It Time to Reconsider Maslow's Hierarchy?" in Kim Corfman and John Lynch, eds. *Advances in Consumer Research* (Provo, UT: Association for Consumer Research, 1996), pp. 405–10.

18. Arthur Koponen, "The Personality Characteristics of Purchasers," *Journal of Advertising Research* (September 1960), pp. 89–92; Joel B. Cohen, "An Interpersonal Orientation to the Study of Consumer Behavior," *Journal of Marketing Research* (August 1967), pp. 270–78; and Rena Bartos, *Marketing to Women around the World* (Cambridge, MA: Harvard Business School, 1989).

19. Terry Clark, "International Marketing and National Character: A Review and Proposal for an Integrative Theory," *Journal of Marketing* (October 1990), pp. 66–79; and John-Benedict E. M. Steenkamp, "The Role of National Culture in International Marketing Research," *International Marketing Review*, vol. 18, no. 1 (2001), pp. 30–44.

20. For an interesting analysis of self-concept, see Russell W. Belk, "Possessions and the Extended Self," *Journal of Consumer Research* (September 1988), pp. 139–68.

21. Myron Magnet, "Let's Go for Growth," *Fortune* (March 7, 1994), p. 70.

22. This example provided in Michael R. Solomon, *Consumer Behavior*, 4th ed. (Upper Saddle River, NJ: Prentice Hall, 1999), p. 59.

23. For further reading on subliminal perception, see Anthony G. Greenwald, Sean C. Draine, and Richard L. Abrams, "Three Cognitive Markers of Unconscious Semantic Activation," *Science* (September 1996), pp. 1699–1701; Dennis L. Rosen and Surendra N. Singh, "An Investigation of Subliminal Embedded Effect on Multiple Measures of Advertising Effectiveness," *Psychology & Marketing* (March/April 1992), pp. 157–73; and Kathryn T. Theus, "Subliminal Advertising and the Psychology of Processing Unconscious Stimuli: A Review of the Research," *Psychology & Marketing* (May–June 1994), pp. 271–90.

24. "GOP Commercial Resurrects Debate on Subliminal Ads," *The Wall Street Journal* (September 13, 2000), p. B10; " I Will Love This Story," *U.S. News & World Report* (May 12, 1997), p. 12; "Dr. Feelgood Goes Subliminal," *Business Week* (November 6, 1995), p. 6; and "Firm Gets Message Out Subliminally," *Dallas Morning News* (February 2, 1997), pp. 1H, 6H.

25. "Customer Loyalty: Going, Going . . . ," *American Demographics* (September 1997), pp. 20–23; *Brand-Driven Marketers Are Beating Themselves in the War against Price-Based and Private Label Competition* (New York: Bates USA, 1994).

26. Martin Fishbein and I. Aizen, *Belief, Attitude, Intention and Behavior: An Introduction to Theory and Research* (Reading, MA: Addison-Wesley 1975), p. 6.

27. Richard J. Lutz, "Changing Brand Attitudes through Modification of Cognitive Structure," *Journal of Consumer Research* (March 1975), pp. 49–59. See also Mowen and Minor, *Consumer Behavior*, pp. 287–88.

28. "Pepsi's Gamble Hits Freshness Dating Jackpot," *Advertising Age* (September 19, 1994), p. 50.

29. "The Marketing 100: Colgate Total," *Advertising Age* (June 29, 1998), p. 544.

30. www.future.sri.com, downloaded January 3, 2002; Eric Arnould, Linda Price, and George Zinkham, *Consumers* (Burr Ridge, IL: McGraw-Hill/Irwin, 2002), pp. 285–90; and "The Frontiers of Psychographics," *American Demographics* (July 1996), pp. 38–43.

31. See, for example, Lawrence F. Feick and Linda Price, "The Market Maven: A Diffuser of Marketplace Information," *Journal of Marketing* (January 1987), pp. 83–97; and Peter H. Block, "The Product Enthusiast: Implications for Marketing Strategy," *Journal of Consumer Marketing* (Summer 1986), pp. 51–61.

32. "Survey: If You Must Know, Just Ask One of These Men," *Marketing News* (October 25, 1992), p. 13.

33. "Maximizing the Market with Influentials," *American Demographics* (July 1995), p. 42; also see, "I'll Have What He's Having," *American Demographics* (July 2000), p. 22.

34. "Put People Behind the Wheel," *Advertising Age* (March 22, 1993), p. S-28.

35. "Importance of Image," *The Wall Street Journal* (August 12, 1985), p. 19; and "What Soviets Think: A Gallup Poll," *Advertising Age* (February 28, 1990), p. 46.

36. Representative recent work on positive and negative word of mouth can be found in Robert E. Smith and Christine A. Vogt, "The Effects of Integrating Advertising and Negative Word-of-Mouth Communications on Message Processing and Response," *Journal of Consumer Psychology,* vol. 4 (1995), pp. 133–51; Paula Bone, "Word-of-Mouth Effects on Short-Term and Long-Term Product Judgments," *Journal of Business Research,* vol. 32 (1995), pp. 213–23; Chip Walker, "Word of Mouth," *American Demographics* (July 1995), pp. 38–45; and Dale F. Duhan, Scott D. Johnson, James B. Wilcox, and Gilbert D. Harrell, "Influences on Consumer Use of Word-of-Mouth Recommendation Sources," *Journal of the Academy of Marketing Science* (Fall 1997), pp. 283–95.

37. "We Will Bury You . . . with a Snickers Bar," *U.S. News & World Report* (January 26, 1998), p. 50ff.; "A Beer Tampering Scare in China Shows Peril of Global Marketing," *The Wall Street Journal* (November 3, 1995), p. B1; and "Pork Rumors Vex Indonesia," *Advertising Age* (February 16, 1989), p. 36.

38. For an extended discussion on reference groups, see Wayne D. Hoyer and Deborah J. MacInnis, *Consumer Behavior,* 2nd ed. (Boston: Houghton Mifflin, 2001), chapter 15.

39. For an extensive review on consumer socialization of children, see Deborah Roedder John, "Consumer Socialization of Children: A Retrospective Look at Twenty-Five Years of Research," *Journal of Consumer Research* (December 1999), pp. 183–213.

40. "Get 'em While They're Young," *Marketing News* (November 10, 1997), p. 2.

41. This discussion is based on "The American Family in the 21st Century," *American Demographics* (August 2001), p. 20; Suraj Commuri and James W. Gentry, "Opportunities for Family Research in Marketing," *Academy of Marketing Science Review* (Online), downloaded September 15, 2000; and J. Paul Peter and Jerry C. Olson, *Consumer Behavior and Marketing Strategy,* 5th ed. (Burr Ridge, IL: Irwin/McGraw-Hill, 1999), pp. 341–43.

42. Diane Crispell, "Dual-Earner Diversity," *American Demographics* (July 1995), pp. 32–37.

43. "There She Is . . . ," *American Demographics* (August 2001), p. 6; "Wearing the Pants," *Brandweek* (October 20, 1997), pp. 20, 22; and "Look Who's Shopping," *Progressive Grocer* (January 1998), p. 18.

44. "Call it 'Kid-fluence,'" *U.S. News & World Report* (July 30, 2001), pp. 32–33; "Special Report: Superstars of Spending," *Advertising Age* (February 20, 2001), pp. S1, S10; Teen Research Unlimited, www.teenresearch.com, downloaded September 4, 2001.

45. Harold R. Kerbo, *Social Stratification and Inequality* (Burr Ridge, IL: McGraw-Hill, 2000). For an extensive discussion on social class, see Arnould, Price, and Zinkhan, *Consumers,* chapter 6.

46. "An Almost Invisible $1 Trillion Market," *Business Week* (June 11, 2001), pp. 151.

47. For a summary of representative research on African-American consumers, see Solomon, *Consumer Behavior,* pp. 444–45; Mowen and Minor, *Consumer Behavior,* pp. 597–98; "The Forgotten Baby Boom," *American Demographics* (February 2001), pp. 46–51; and "Divide and Culture," *Brandweek* (January 29, 2001), pp. 16–18.

48. "Primary Colours," *The Economist* (March 17, 2001), pp. 27–28.

49. "Habla English?" *American Demographics* (April 2001), pp. 54–57; "The New Age of Ethnic Marketing," *Brandweek* (March 19, 2001), pp. 24–28; "Marketing to Hispanics," *Advertising Age* (August 24, 1998), pp. S1–S27; "Marketing to Hispanics," *Advertising Age* (September 18, 2000), pp. S1–S28.

50. "Asian Demographic Gets Attention," www.diversityinc.com, downloaded June 5, 2001; "A Yen for Brands," *Brandweek* (January 5, 1998), p. 17; "Spending: Ethnic Consumers are 30% of Met Life's Business," *Advertising Age* (November 20, 2000), p. S11.

CHAPTER 6

1. Interview with Kim Nagele, JCPMedia, June 8, 2001.

2. Peter LaPlaca, "From the Editor," *Journal of Business and Industrial Marketing* (Summer 1992), p. 3.

3. This figure is based on *Statistical Abstract of the United States: 2000* 120th ed. (Washington, DC: U.S. Census Bureau, 2000).

4. "FAA Announces Contract for New Workstations," *Dallas Morning News* (April 30, 1999), p. 16H.

5. *2002 NAICS United States Manual* (Washington, DC: Office of Management and Budget, January 2002).

6. An argument that consumer buying and organizational buying do not have important differences is found in Edward F. Fern and James R. Brown, "The Industrial/Consumer Marketing Dichotomy: A Case of Insufficient Justification," *Journal of Marketing* (Spring 1984), pp. 68–77. However, most writers on the subject do draw distinctions between the two types of buying. See, for example, Michael D. Hutt and Thomas W. Speh, *Business Marketing Management*, 7th ed. (Fort Worth, TX: Dryden Press, 2001); and H. Michael Hayes, Per V. Jenster, and Nils-Erik Aaby, *Business Marketing: A Global Perspective* (Chicago: Richard D. Irwin, 1996).

7. This listing and portions of the following discussion are based on F. Robert Dwyer and John F. Tanner, Jr., *Business Marketing*, 2nd ed. (Burr Ridge, IL: McGraw-Hill/Irwin, 2002): Edward G. Brierty, Robert W. Eckles, and Robert R. Reeder, *Business Marketing*, 3rd ed. (Upper Saddle River, NJ: Prentice Hall, 1998); and Frank G. Bingham, Jr., *Business Marketing Management* (Lincolnwood, IL: NTC, 1998).

8. "Latin Trade Connection," *Latin Trade* (June 1997), p. 72.

9. "Rumble Over Tokyo," *Business Week* (April 2, 2001), pp. 80–82; "Fedex Chooses Airbus 380," airwise.com (January 16, 2001); "Qatar Opts for Super Jumbo," airwise.com (March 1, 2001); and "Understanding the Next 20 Years," airbus.com/products/A380_Market (downloaded April 22, 2001).

10. "The Business Case for Diversity," diversityinc.com, accessed May 15, 2001.

11. "Sears, Roebuck and Co.: Minority Suppliers Energize Growth and the Bottom Line," *Forbes* (April 20, 1998), special section, p. 14; and interview with Bruce Ackerman, President, Anthony Mark Hankins Designer, May 8, 2001.

12. For a study of buying criteria used by industrial firms, see Daniel H. McQuiston and Rockney G. Walters, "The Evaluation Criteria of Industrial Buyers: Implications for Sales Training," *Journal of Business & Industrial Marketing* (Summer/Fall 1989), pp. 65–75. See also, "What Buyers Look For," *Sales & Marketing Management* (August 1995), p. 31.

13. "Small Firms Flock to Quality System," *Nation's Business* (March 1998), pp. 66–67.

14. Michael R. Leenders and David L. Blenkhorn, *Reverse Marketing: The New Buyer-Supplier Relationship* (New York: Free Press, 1996).

15. "Chrysler's Neon," *Business Week* (May 3, 1993), p. 119.

16. "$35 Million Machine: Wires Not Included," *Newsweek* (April 15, 1995), p. 25.

17. This discussion is based on ibm.com/procurement/html/ principles_practices, downloaded April 18, 2001; and Hayes, Jenster, and Aaby, *Business Marketing: A Global Perspective.*

18. "EDS Jars Rivals, Wins Big Defense Deal," *The Wall Street Journal* (October 9, 2000), p. A4.

19. This discussion is based on James C. Anderson and James A. Narus, *Business Market Management* (Upper Saddle River, NJ: Prentice Hall, 1999); Neil Rackham, Lawrence Friedman, and Richard Ruff, *Getting Partnering Right* (New York: McGraw-Hill, 1996); and Joseph P. Cannon and Christian Homburg, "Buyer-Supplier Relationships and Customer Firm Costs," *Journal of Marketing* (January 2001), pp. 29–43.

20. Thomas V. Bonoma, "Major Sales: Who Really Does the Buying?" *Harvard Business Review* (May–June 1982), pp. 11–19. For recent research on buying centers, see Morry Ghingold and David T. Wilson, "Buying Center Research and Business Marketing Practices: Meeting the Challenge of Dynamic Marketing," *Journal of Business*

& Industrial Marketing, vol. 13, no. 2 (1998), pp. 96–108; and Philip L. Dawes, Don Y. Lee, and Grahame R. Dowling, "Information Control and Influence in Emerging Buying Centers," *Journal of Marketing* (July 1998), pp. 55–68.

21. Paul A. Herbig, *Handbook of Cross-Cultural Marketing* (New York: The Halworth Press, 1998).

22. Jule M. Bristor, "Influence Strategies in Organizational Buying: The Importance of Connections to the Right People in the Right Places," *Journal of Business-to-Business Marketing*, vol. 1 (1993), pp. 63–98.

23. These definitions are adapted from Frederick E. Webster, Jr., and Yoram Wind, *Organizational Buying Behavior* (Englewood Cliffs, NJ: Prentice Hall, 1972), p. 6.

24. "Can Corning Find Its Optic Nerve?" *Fortune* (March 19, 2001), pp. 148–50.

25. Representative studies on the buy-class framework that document its usefulness include Erin Anderson, Wujin Chu, and Barton Weitz, "Industrial Purchasing: An Empirical Exploration of the Buy-Class Framework," *Journal of Marketing* (July 1987), pp. 71–86; Morry Ghingold, "Testing the 'Buy-Grid' Buying Process Model," *Journal of Purchasing and Materials Management* (Winter 1986), pp. 30–36; P. Matthyssens and W. Faes, "OEM Buying Process for New Components: Purchasing and Marketing Implications," *Industrial Marketing Management* (August 1985), pp. 145–57; and Thomas W. Leigh and Arno J. Ethans, "A Script-Theoretic Analysis of Industrial Purchasing Behavior," *Journal of Marketing* (Fall 1984), pp. 22–32. Studies not supporting the buy-class framework include Joseph A. Bellizi and Philip McVey, "How Valid Is the Buy-Grid Model?" *Industrial Marketing Management* (February 1983), pp. 57–62; and Donald W. Jackson, Janet E. Keith, and Richard K. Burdick, "Purchasing Agents' Perceptions of Industrial Buying Center Influences: A Situational Approach," *Journal of Marketing* (Fall 1984), pp. 75–83.

26. See, for example, R. Vekatesh, Ajay Kohli, and Gerald Zaltman, "Influence Strategies in Buying Centers," *Journal of Marketing* (October 1995), pp. 61–72; Gary L. Lilien and Anthony Wong, "An Exploratory Investigation of the Structure of the Buying Center in the Metal Working Industry," *Journal of Marketing Research* (February 1984), pp. 1–11; and Wesley J. Johnston and Thomas V. Bonoma, "The Buying Center: Structure and Interaction Patterns," *Journal of Marketing* (Summer 1981), pp. 143–56. See also, Christopher P. Puto, Wesley E. Patton III, and Ronald H. King, "Risk Handling Strategies in Industrial Vendor Selection Decisions," *Journal of Marketing* (Winter 1985), pp. 89–98.

27. "Evolution, Not Revolution," *Forbes* (May 21, 2001), pp. 38–39; "Business Connections: The Wired Way We Work," *Newsweek* (April 30, 2001), p. 59; and "Behind the Crystal Ball," *The Industry Standard* (March 26, 2001), pp. 81–83.

28. This discussion is based on Mark Roberti, "General Electric's Spin Machine," *The Industry Standard* (January 22–29, 2001), pp. 74–83; "Smart Business 50," *Smart Business* (November 2000), pp. 121–50; and "Grainger Lightens Its Digital Load," *Industrial Distribution* (March 2001), pp. 77–79.

29. "Internet Trading Exchanges: E-Marketplaces Come of Age," *Fortune* (April 15, 2001), special section; and "Private Exchanges May Allow B-to-B Commerce to Thrive After All," *The Wall Street Journal* (March 16, 2001), pp. B1, B4.

30. This discussion is based on "B2B . . . to Be?" *Forbes* (August 21, 2000), pp. 125–30; "e-Marketmakers: How Digital Marketplaces are Shaping the Future of B2B Commerce," Forrester Research, downloaded May 25, 2001; and Steven Kaplan and Mohanbir Sawhney, "E-Hubs: The New B2B Marketplaces," *Harvard Business Review* (May–June, 2000), pp. 97–103.

31. "A Little Guy's Marketplace," *Time* (November 27, 2000), pp. B15–B20; Eric Young, "Web Marketplaces that Really Work," *Fortune/CNET Tech Review* (Winter 2002), pp. 78–86.

32. This discussion is based on "Let's Build an Online Supply Network!" *The Wall Street Journal* (April 17, 2000), pp. B1, B4.

33. Robyn Meredith, "Harder Than the Hype," *Forbes* (April 16, 2001), pp. 188–94; "Some Assembly Required," *Business 2.0* (February 12, 2001), pp. 25–29.

34. A major portion of this discussion is based on Robert J. Dolan and Youngme Moon, "Pricing and Market Making on the Internet," *Journal of Interactive Marketing* (Spring 2000), pp. 56–73; and "Auctions Have Taken the Internet by Storm," *Dallas Morning News* (January 25, 2001), pp. 1F, 9F.

35. Bob Tedeschi, "GE Has a Bright Idea," *Smart Business* (June 2001), pp. 86–91.

36. Sandy Jap, "Going, Going, Going," *Harvard Business Review* (November–December, 2000), p. 30.

Lands' End: This case is based on information available on the company website (www.landsend.com) and the following sources: Robert Berner, "A Hard Bargain at Lands' End?" *Business Week* (May 28, 2001), p. 14; Rebecca Quick, "Getting the Right Fit—Hips and All—Can a Machine Measure You Better Than Your Tailor?" *The Wall Street Journal* (October 18, 2000), p. B1; Stephanie Miles, "Apparel E-tailers Spruce Up for Holidays," *The Wall Street Journal* (November 6, 2001), p. B6; Dana James, "Custom Goods Nice Means for Lands' End," *Marketing News* (August 14, 2000), p. 5.

CHAPTER 7

1. Personal interview with Dr. Daniel E. Cohen, chief executive officer and Kirk P. Hodgdon, vice president, Business Development of CNS, Inc., June 8, 2001.

2. These estimates are based on data from *International Trade Statistics 2001* (Geneva: World Trade Organization) and trend projections by the authors. Trade statistics reported in this chapter also came from this source, unless otherwise indicated.

3. Masaaki Kotabe and Kristiaan Helsen, *Global Marketing Management,* 2nd ed. (New York: Wiley, 2001), p. 440.

4. "Bartering Gains Currency in Hard-Hit Southeast Asia," *The Wall Street Journal* (April 6, 1998), p. A10; and Beatrice B. Lund, "Corporate Barter as a Marketing Strategy," *Marketing News* (March 3, 1997), p. 8.

5. Michael E. Porter, *The Competitive Advantage of Nations* (New York: The Free Press, 1990), pp. 577–615. For another view that emphasizes cultural differences, see David S. Landes, *The Wealth and Poverty of Nations* (New York: Norton, 1998).

6. Barry Shapiro, "Economic Espionage," *Marketing Management* (Spring 1998), pp. 56–58; "More Spies Targeting U.S. Firms," *Dallas Morning News* (January 12, 1998), pp. 1D, 4D.

7. Dennis R. Appleyard and Alfred J. Field, Jr., *International Economics,* 4th ed. (Burr Ridge, IL: McGraw-Hill/Irwin, 2001), chapter 15; "Rougher Sailing Across the Atlantic," *Business Week* (July 27, 1998), p. 29.

8. "A Fruit Peace," *The Economist* (April 21, 2001), pp. 75–76; Gary C. Hufbauer and Kimberly A. Elliott, *Measuring the Cost of Protection in the United States* (Washington, DC: Institute for International Economics, 1994).

9. "It Ain't Just Peanuts" *Business Week,* (December 18, 1995), p. 30.

10. This discussion is based on information provided by the World Trade Organization, at www.wto.org, downloaded April 20, 2001.

11. "Industrial Evolution," *Business Week* (April 27, 1998), pp. 100–01.

12. "Betting on Free Trade," *Business Week* (April 23, 2001), pp. 60–62; and Gary S. Becker, "It's Time for NAFTA to Look Farther South," *Business Week* (January 8, 2001), p. 28.

13. www.juniper.net/company, May 1, 2001; and General Mills, Inc., *Annual Report,* 2000.

14. For an excellent overview of different types of global companies and marketing strategies, see Warren J. Keegan, *Global Marketing Management,* 6th ed. (Upper Saddle River, NJ: Prentice Hall, 1999), pp. 43–54.

15. "Global Companies Don't Work; Multinationals Do," *Advertising Age* (April 18, 1994), p. 23; and David Benady, "Unilever in Global Ad Shake-Up," *Marketing Week* (February 11, 1999), p. 7.

16. Elissa Moses, *The $100 Billion Allowance: Accessing the Global Teen Market* (New York: Wiley, 2000); "Tracking Asia's Teens," *AdAge Global* (December 2001), pp. 26–27; "MTV Returns to Japan," *AdAge Global* (September 2000), p. 10; and "Bennetton Bounces Back," *Brandweek* (February 12, 2001), pp. 1, 8.

17. For an extensive discussion on identifying global consumers, see Jean-Pierre Jeannet and H. David Hennessey, *Global Marketing Strategies,* 4th ed. (Boston: Houghton Mifflin, 1998).

18. This discussion is based on "Behind the Crystal Ball," *The Industry Standard* (March 26, 2001), pp. 81–83; "The World's Online Populations, www.cyberatlas.com, downloaded April 15, 2001; "Fast Stats," *The Industry Standard* (November 27–December 4, 2000), p. 164; Majority of Users will be Non-English Speakers," www.nua.ie, downloaded April 10, 2001; and "Global E-Commerce Approaches Hypergrowth," Forrester Research Press Release, April 25, 2000.

19. For comprehensive references on cross-cultural aspects of marketing, see Paul A. Herbig, *Handbook of Cross-Cultural Marketing* (New York: The Halworth Press, 1998); and Jean-Claude Usunier, *Marketing Across Cultures,* 2nd ed. (London: Prentice Hall Europe, 1996). Unless otherwise indicated, examples found in this section appear in these excellent sources.

20. "McDonald's Adapts Mac Attack to Foreign Tastes with Expansion," *Dallas Morning News* (December 7, 1997), p. 3H; and "Taking Credit," *The Economist* (November 2, 1996), p. 75.

21. This discussion is based on Tipton F. McCubbins, "Somebody Kicked the Sleeping Dog—New Bite in the Foreign Corrupt Practices Act," *Business Horizons* (January–February, 2001), pp. 27–32; Russell R. Miller, *Doing Business in Newly Privatized Markets* (Westport, CT: Quorum Books, 2000), chapter 12.

22. "Clash of Cultures," *Brandweek* (May 4, 1998), p. 28. See also R. L. Tung, *Business Negotiations with the Japanese* (Lexington, MA: Lexington Books, 1993).

23. These examples appear in Del I. Hawkins, Roger J. Best, and Kenneth A. Coney, *Consumer Behavior,* 8th ed. (Burr Ridge, IL.: McGraw-Hill/Irwin, 2001), chapter 2.

24. "Greeks Protest Coke's Use of Parthenon," *Dallas Morning News* (August 17, 1992), p. D4.

25. "Japanese Products are Popular in the U.S.," *Research Alert* (November 17, 2000), p. 8; and "Buying American," *American Demographics* (March 1998), pp. 32–38.

26. "Geo Gaffes," *Brandweek* (February 23, 1998), p. 20.

27. "Global Thinking Paces Computer Biz," *Advertising Age* (March 6, 1995), p. 10.

28. "Nike Recalls Shoes Bearing Logo That Muslims Found Offensive," *Associated Press Newswire,* (June 25, 1997).

29. "Marketing by Language: Oracle Trims Teams, Sees Big Savings," *Advertising Age International* (July 2000), pp. 4, 38.

30. Terrence A. Shimp and Subhash Sharma, "Consumer Ethnocentrism, Construction and Validation of the CETSCALE," *Journal of Marketing Research* (August 1987), pp. 280–89.

31. Subhash Sharma, Terrence Shimp, and Jeongshin Shin, "Consumer Ethnocentrism: A Test of Antecedents and Moderators," *Journal of the Academy of Marketing Science* (Winter 1995), pp. 26–37; Joel Herche, "A Note on the Predictive Validity of the CETSCALE," *Journal of the Academy of Marketing Science* (Summer 1992), pp. 261–64; Richard G. Netemeyer, Srinivas Durvasula, and Donald R. Lichtenstein, "A Cross-National Assessment of the Reliability and Validity of the CETSCALE," *Journal of Marketing Research* (August 1991), pp. 320–27; and Jill Gabrielle Klein, Richard Ettenson, and Marlene D. Morris, "The Animosity Model of Foreign Product Purchase: An Empirical Test in the People's Republic of China," *Journal of Marketing* (January 1998), pp. 89–100.

32. This discussion is based on "So You Really Want To Do Business in China?" *Forbes* (July 24, 2000), pp. 92–96; "Coke Pours into Asia," *Business Week* (October 21, 1996), pp. 22–25.

33. "Selling in Russia: The March on Moscow," *The Economist* (March 18, 1995), pp. 65–66.

34. "Rubles? Who Needs Rubles?" *Business Week* (April 13, 1998), pp. 45–46.

35. "Betting on a New Label: Made in Russia," *Business Week* (April 12, 1999), p.122; "Russia and Central–Eastern Europe: Worlds Apart," *Brandweek* (May 4, 1998), pp. 30–31; "We Will Bury You . . . with a Snickers Bar," *U. S. News & World Report* (January 26, 1998), pp. 50–51.

36. Chip Walker, "The Global Middle Class," *American Demographics* (September 1995), pp. 40–47.

37. "Consumer Abroad: Developing Shopaholics," *U. S. News & World Report* (February 10, 1997), p. 55.

38. "Mattel Plans to Double Sales Abroad," *The Wall Street Journal* (February 11, 1998), pp. A3, A11.

39. Philip R. Cateora and John L. Graham, *International Marketing*, 11th ed. (Burr Ridge, IL: McGraw-Hill/Irwin, 2002), p. 560; and "Honda Takes Currency Hit in Europe," *The Wall Street Journal* (March 28, 2001), p. A16.

40. "Currency Troubles Halt P&G Shipments to Turkey," *Advertising Age* (March 5, 2001), p. 32.

41. "EU Turning Into Battleground over More Curbs on Marketing," *Advertising Age* (September 18, 2000), p. 60; "Europe Forges Ahead with Web Innovations," *Marketing News* (August 14, 2000), p. 8; "Will East Asia Slam the Door?" *The Economist* (September 12, 1998), p. 88.

42. *The ISO Survey of ISO 9000 and ISO 14000 Certificates* (Geneva, Switzerland: International Organization for Standardization, 2000).

43. For an extensive and recent examination of these market entry options, see, for example, Johny K. Johansson, *Global Marketing: Foreign Entry, Local Marketing, and Global Management*, 2nd ed. (Burr Ridge, IL: McGraw Hill/Irwin, 2000); Keegan, *Global Marketing Management*; Kotabe and Helson, *Global Marketing Management*; and Cateora and Graham, *International Marketing*.

44. Based on an interview with Pamela Viglielmo, director of international marketing, Fran Wilson Creative Cosmetics; and "Foreign Firms Think Their Way into Japan," www.successstories.com/nikkei, downloaded March 24, 2001.

45. www.boeing.com, downloaded May 1, 2001.

46. "A Little Guy's Marketplace," *Time* (November 27, 2000), pp. B15ff.; *Small & Medium Sized Exporting Companies: A Statistical Profile* (Washington, DC: International Trade Administration, December 1999).

47. "Made in Taiwan," *Forbes* (April 2, 2001), pp. 64–66.

48. "McDonald's Reports Global Results," *Corporate Press Release* (January 24, 2001).

49. Avraham Shama, "Entry Strategies of U.S. Firms to the Newly Independent States, Baltic States, and Eastern European Countries," *California Management Review* (Spring 1995), pp. 90–109.

50. Miller, *Doing Business in Newly Privatized Markets*, p. 53.

51. "China's Coming Telecom Battle," *Fortune* (November 27, 2000), pp. 209–14; "Mercedes: Made in Alabama," *Fortune* (July 7, 1997), pp. 150ff.; and "Car Power," *Business Week* (October 23, 2000), pp. 72ff.

52. "Harley-Davidson Establishes Wholly-Owned Italian Subsidiary," *Company News Release* (October 13, 2000); and Shama, "Entry Strategies of U.S. Firms."

53. The examples in this section are found in "The Color of Beauty," *Forbes* (November 22, 2000), pp. 170–76; "It's Goo, Goo, Goo, Goo Vibrations at the Gerber Lab," *The Wall Street Journal* (December 4, 1996), pp. A1, A6; Donald R. Graber, "How to Manage a Global Product Development Process," *Industrial Marketing Management* (November 1996), pp. 483–98; and Herbig, *Handbook of Cross-Cultural Marketing*.

54. Jagdish N. Sheth and Atul Parvatiyar, "The Antecedents and Consequences of Integrated Global Marketing," *International Marketing Review*, vol. 18, no. 1 (2001), pp. 16–29. Also see, D. Szymanski, S. Bharadwaj, and R. Varadarajan, "Standardization versus Adaptation of International Marketing Strategy: An Empirical Investigation," *Journal of Marketing* (October 1993), pp. 1–17.

55. This discussion is based on John Fahy and Fuyuki Taguchi, "Reassessing the Japanese Distribution System," *Sloan Management Review* (Winter 1995), pp. 49–61; and Edward Tse, "The Right Way to Achieve Profitable Growth in the Chinese Consumer Market," *Strategy & Business* (Second Quarter, 1998), pp. 10–21.

56. "Stores Told to Lift Prices in Germany," *The Wall Street Journal* (September 11, 2000), pp. A27, A30.

57. "Rotten Apples," *Dallas Morning News* (April 7, 1998), p. 14A.

58. "Parallel Imports: A Grey Area," *The Economist* (June 13, 1998), pp. 61–62; and "When Grey Is Good," *The Economist* (August 22, 1998), p. 17.

CNS Breathe Right® Strips: This case was prepared by Giana Eckhardt. Sources: *CNS, Inc. 1997 Annual Report* (Minneapolis, MN: CNS, Inc., 1998); and personal interviews with Dr. Daniel E. Cohen and Kirk P. Hodgdon of CNS.

CHAPTER 8

1. John Horn, "Studios Play Name Games," *Star Tribune* (August 10, 1997), p. F11.

2. *2000 US Economic Review*, Worldwide Market Research Department, Motion Picture Association of America, pp. 14, 16.

3. Willow Bay, "Test Audiences Have Profound Effect on Movies," *CNN Newsstand & Entertainment Weekly* (September 28, 1998). See www.cnn.com/SHOWBIZ/Movies/9809/28/screen.test/.

4. Thomas R. King, "How Big Will Disney's 'Pocahontas' Be?" *The Wall Street Journal* (May 15, 1995), pp. B1, B8.

5. Richard Turner and John R. Emshwiller, "Movie-Research Czar Is Said by Some to Sell Manipulated Findings," *The Wall Street Journal* (December 26, 1993), p. A1.

6. Helene Diamond, "Lights, Camera . . . Research!" *Marketing News* (September 11, 1989), pp. 10–11; and "Killer!" *Time* (November 16, 1987), pp. 72–79.

7. Jeff Stickler, "Titanic Director Was Floating on Air after Local Test," *Star Tribune* (December 26, 1997), pp. D1, D2.

8. "The Top Grossing Movies of All Time at the Worldwide Box Office," The Internet Movie Database, Ltd. See www.us.imdb.com/Charts/worldtopmovies.

9. Carl Diorio, "Tracking Projectings: B. O. Calculations an Inexact Science," *Variety* (May 24, 2001). See www.variety.com/index.asp?layout=story&articleid=VR1117799996.

10. For an expanded definition, consult the American Marketing Association's website at www.ama.org/about/ama/markdef.asp; for a researcher's comments on this and other definitions of marketing research, see Lawrence D. Gibson, "Quo Vadis, Marketing Research?" *Marketing Research* (Spring 2000), pp. 36–41.

11. John Cloud, "How the Furby Flies," *Time* (November 30, 1998), pp. 84–85; Joseph Pereira, "To These Youngsters, Trying Out Toys Is Hardly Kids' Play," *The Wall Street Journal* (December 17, 1997), pp. A1, A11; and Toy of the Year Awards, 2000," *Family Fun* (November 2000). See www.family.go.com/entertain/toys/feature/famf1000toymethod_led/famf1000toymethod_led.html.

12. Lawrence D. Gibson, "Defining Marketing Problems," *Marketing Research* (Spring 1998), pp. 4–12.

13. Laurence N. Gold, "High Technology Data Collection for Measurement and Testing," *Marketing Research* (March 1992), pp. 29–38; and information obtained from the websites of Information Resources, Inc. (www.infores.com) and AC Nielsen (www.acnielsen.com).

14. Joe Schwartz, "Back to the Source," *American Demographics* (January 1989), pp. 22–26; and Felix Kessler, "High-Tech Shocks in Ad Research," *Fortune* (July 7, 1986), pp. 58–62.

15. "What TV Ratings Really Mean," Nielsen Media Research website, pp. 1–8. See www.nielsenmedia.com/whatratingsmean/.

16. "Nielsen Media Research Estimates 105.5 Million TV Households in the U.S.," Nielsen Media Research news release (August 21, 2001), p. 1.

17. "Arbitron TV, Cable and Radio Audience Meter Passes Important U.S. Test Milestone," Arbitron news release (July 19, 2001), pp. 1–3. See www.arbitron.com/portable_people_meters/ and "Media Advisory: Arbitron's Portable People Meter System," Nielsen Media Research news release (July 19, 2001), p. 1. See www.nielsenmedia.com/newsreleases/releases/2001/arbitron+PPM.htm.

18. Mark Maremont, "New Toothbrush Is Big-Ticket Item," *The Wall Street Journal* (October 27, 1998), pp. B1, B6; Emily Nelson, "P&G Checks Out Real Life," *The Wall Street Journal* (May 17, 2001), pp. B1, B4.

19. Gerry Khermouch, "Consumers in the Mist," *Business Week* (February 26, 2001), pp. 92, 94.

20. Jonathan Eig, "Food Industry Battles for Moms Who Want to Cook—Just a Little," *The Wall Street Journal.* (March 7, 2001), pp. A1, A10; Susan Feyder, "It Took Tinkering by Twin Cities Firms to Saver Some Sure Bets," *Minneapolis Star Tribune* (June 9, 1982), p. 11A.

21. Constance Gustke, "Built to Last," *Sales and Marketing Management* (August 1997), pp. 78–83.

22. Michael J. McCarthy, "Food Companies Hunt for a 'Next Big Thing' but Few Can Find One," *The Wall Street Journal* (May 6, 1997), pp. A1, A6.

23. "Focus on Consumers," General Mills Midyear Report, Minneapolis, MN (January 8, 1998), pp. 2–3.

24. Bruce Stanley, "Redesigning Heinz Ketchup label Is a Kid's Job," *Marketing News* (June 9, 1997), p. 5.

25. Michael J. McCarthy, "Stalking the Elusive Teenage Trendsetter," *The Wall Street Journal* (November 19, 1998), pp. B1, B10; Elizabeth Canning Blackwell, "What Do Teens Really Want?" *North Shore Magazine* as cited in *TRU in the News* (see www.teenageresearch.com/NewsView.cfm?edit_id=60); and Teenage Research Unlimited press releases: "Teens Spend $155 Billion in 2000," (January 25, 2001).

26. Roy Furchgott, "For Cool Hunters, Tomorrow's Trend Is the Trophy," *The New York Times* (June 28, 1998), p. 10; Emily Nelson, "The Hunt for Hip: A Trend Scout's Trail," *The Wall Street Journal* (December 9, 1998), pp. B1, B6; Public Broadcasting System's *Frontline* website "The Merchants of Cool" (from a telecast dated February 27, 2001): "What's It Like Hunting for 'Cool?'" (see www.pbs.org/wgbh/pages/frontline/shows/cool/etc/hunting.html); and Patrick Goldstein, "Untangling the Web of Teen Trends," *Los Angeles Times* (November 21, 2000), p. F1.

27. Joshua Grossnickle and Oliver Raskin, "What's Ahead on the Internet," *Marketing Research* (Summer 2001), pp. 9–13; Gordon A. Wyner, "Life (on the Internet) Imitates Research," *Marketing Research* (Summer 2000), pp. 38–39.

28. The Wendy's questionnaire is adapted from one originally developed by Robert Joffe, now at the University of Redlands.

29. Wendy Zellner, "Look Out, Supermarkets—Wal-Mart Is Hungry," *Business Week* (September 14, 1998), pp. 98–100; Richard McCattery, "Wal-Mart Rumbles in the Supermarket Jungle," The Motley Fool (March 7, 1998); See www.fool.com/news/foth/2000/foth000307.htm; and Wal-Mart news releases: "Our 1,000 Supercenter," (August 22, 2001).

30. Steve Alexander, "Data Mining," *Star Tribune* (August 17, 1997), pp. D1, D5.

31. The step 4 and step 5 discussion was written by David Ford and Don Rylander of Ford Consulting Group, Inc.

32. Mark A. Moon, John T. Mentzer, Carlo D. Smith, and Michael S. Garver, "Seven Keys to Better Forecasting," *Business Horizons* (September–October 1998), pp. 44–52.

33. "2000 Survey of Buying Power and Media Markets," *Sales and Marketing Management* (New York: Bill Communications, Inc.), pp. 62, 118, 122, 133, 194–195.

34. Interview with Bill McKee, Manager–Corporate Communications/Public Relations, Xerox Corporation and annual reports available at www2.xerox.com/go/xix/about_xerox/T_archive.jsp?view=annual_reports.

Ford Consulting Group: This case was written by David Ford.

CHAPTER 9

1. Material on sneakers is based on the SGMA Report 2000, "The U.S. Athletic Footwear Market Today," which is published annually by the Sporting Goods Manufacturers Association (www.sgma.com) based on a study by the NPD Group (www.npd.com). NPD polls 35,000 consumers and over 3,500 retailers to provide this information.

2. Ibid.

3. Ibid.

4. Ibid.

5. Matt Forney, "Harry Potter, Meet 'Ha-li Bo-te,'" *The Wall Street Journal* (September 21, 2000), p. B1; and Gerry Khermouch, "Buzzzz Marketing," *Business Week* (July 30, 2001), pp. 50–56.

6. David Leohnardt, "Two-Tier Marketing," *Business Week* (March 17, 1997), pp. 82–90.

7. "Special Report on Mass Customization: A Long March," *The Economist* (July 14, 2001), pp. 63–65.

8. Dana James, "Custom Goods Nice Means for Lands' End," *Marketing News* (August 14, 2001), pp. 5–6; Greg Morago, "Customizing for the Masses," *Star Tribune* (July 10, 2000), pp. E1, E3; Alex Witchel, "Custom Blend of Fragrance Is Most Personal," *Star Tribune* (July 10, 2000), pp. E1, E3; and Louise Lee, "Can Levi's Be Cool Again?" *Business Week* (March 13, 2000), pp. 144–48.

9. "Keeping the Customer Satisfied," *The Economist* (July 14, 2001), pp. 9–10.

10. "Will the U.S. Chicken Out on Russia," *Fortune* (November 23, 1998), pp. 52–53.

11. See www.fallschurch.claritas.com.

12. Amber Holst, "Online Grocer Peapod Feels Chill of Its Rivals' Failures," *The Wall Street Journal* (July 23, 2001), p. B6; Chris Taylor, "E-Grocers Check Out," *Time* (July 23, 2001), p. 65; Peapod.com news release dated July 16, 2001.

13. The discussion of fast-food trends and market share is based on: *National Consumer Survey© Choices 3 Crosstabulation Report: Fast-Food Restaurants* (New York: Simmons Market Research Bureau, Inc., Spring 2001).

14. Ibid.

15. Jennifer Ordonez, "Taco Bell Chef Has New Tactic: Be Like Wendy's," *The Wall Street Journal* (February 23, 2001), pp. B1, B4; and Jennifer Ordonez, "An Efficiency Drive: Fast-Food Lanes Are Getting Even Faster," *The Wall Street Journal* (May 18, 2000), pp. A1, A10.

16. The discussion of Apple's segmentation strategies through the years is based on information from its website: www.apple-history.com/history.html.

17. Jim Carlton, "Apple to Post Profit Again on Sales Gains," *The Wall Street Journal* (January 6, 1999); pp. A3, A8.

18. Dennis Sellers, "Business Journal: Digital Hub Plan Just Might Work," *MacCentral* (January 16, 2001), Mac Publishing, LLC.

19. Wes George, "Opinion: Apple's Business Strategy," *MacCentral* (January 16, 2001), Mac Publishing LLC.

20. Kevin Lane Keller, "The Brand Report Card," *Harvard Business Review* (January–February 2000), pp. 147–57.

21. Rebecca Winters, "Chocolate Milk," *Time* (April 30, 2001), p. 20.

Nokia: This case was written by Michael Vessey and Steven Hartley based on information available on the company website (www.nokia.com); correspondence with Keith Nowak; a personal interview with Paul Dittner of Gartner Dataquest; Ari Bensinger, "Weaker Signals for Mobile Phone Firms," *Business Week Online,* April 6, 2001; "The Cellular Telecommunications

& Internet Association's Wireless Industry Survey," see www.wow-com. com; "Nokia's First Imaging Phone Marks Start of Multimedia Messaging Era," Nokia press release, November 19, 2001; "New Nokia 6340 Handset to Enable Roaming Across TDMA, GSM Networks," Nokia press release, January 7, 2002; "Nokia Unveils a New Active Category for Mobile Phones," Nokia press release, November 19, 2001; "Users Say 'No Thanks' to Mobile Advertising Unless Vendors Take Right Approach," In-Stat Group press release, October 31, 2001, see www.instat.com.

CHAPTER 10

1. Personal interview with Kenneth M. Hart, Ph.D., 3M, 2001.
2. Ibid.
3. Terry Fiedler, "3M Innovation to Be Tested," *Star Tribune* (December 10, 2000), pp. D1, D11.
4. Definitions within this section are adapted from Peter D. Bennett, *Dictionary of Marketing Terms*, 2nd ed. (Lincolnwood, IL: NTC Publishing Group, 1995) and Committee on Definitions, *Marketing Definitions: A Glossary of Marketing Terms* (Chicago: American Marketing Association, 1985).
5. Julia Angwin, "Latest Dot-Com Fad Is a Bit Old-Fashioned: It's Called Profitability," *The Wall Street Journal* (August 14, 2001), pp. A1, A6.
6. Ronald Grover, Tom Lowry, and Larry Armstrong, "TV Guy Henry Yuen of Gemstar-TV Guide Wants to Take Control of Your Television," *Business Week* (March 12, 2000), pp. 66–76; and Steve Jarvis, "Interactive TV Now Pioneering Marketing Option," *Marketing News* (August 27, 2001), pp. 1, 19, 20.
7. Clayton M. Christensen, *The Innovator's Dilemma: When Technologies Cause Great Firms to Fail* (Cambridge, MA: Harvard Business School Press, 1997); and Stephen A. Butscher and Michael Laker, "Market-Driven Product Development," *Marketing Management* (Summer 2000), pp. 48–53.
8. Greg A. Stevens and James Burley, "3,000 Raw Ideas = 1 Commercial Success!" *Research-Technology Management* (May–June 1997), pp. 16–27.
9. R. G. Cooper and E. J. Kleinschmidt, "New Products—What Separates Winners from Losers?" *Journal of Product Innovation Management* (September 1987), pp. 169–84; and Robert G. Cooper, *Winning at New Products*, 2nd ed. (Reading, MA: Addison-Wesley, 1993), pp. 49–66; and Thomas D. Kuczmarski, "Measuring Your Return on Innovation," *Marketing Management* (Spring 2000), pp. 25–32.
10. Greg Burns, "Has General Mills Had Its Wheaties?" *Business Week* (May 8, 1995), pp. 68–69.
11. John Gilbert, "To Sell Cars in Japan, U.S. Needs to Offer More Right-Drive Models," *Star Tribune* (May 27, 1995), p. M1.
12. Marcia Mogelonsky, "Product Overload?" *American Demographics* (August 1998), pp. 5–12.
13. Amy Merrick, "As 3M Chief, McNerney Wastes No Time Starting Systems Favored by Ex-Boss Welch," *The Wall Street Journal* (June 5, 2001), pp. B1, B4; see General Electric's website (www.ge.com) for an in-depth explanation of Six Sigma that 3M and other Fortune 500 companies use to improve quality: "The Road to Customer Impact: What Is Six Sigma?"
14. Eric von Hippel, Stefan Thomke, and Mary Sonnock, "Creating Breakthroughs at 3M," *Harvard Business Review* (September–October 1999), pp. 47–57.
15. Morgan L. Swink and Vincent A. Mabert, "Product Development Partnerships: Balancing Needs of OEMs and Suppliers," *Business Horizons* (May–June 2000), pp. 59–68.
16. Alec Klein, "The Techies Grumbled, but Polaroid's Pocket Turned into a Huge Hit," *The Wall Street Journal* (May 2, 2000), pp. A1, A10.
17. Otis Port, "Xerox Won't Duplicate Past Errors," *Business Week* (September 29, 1998), pp. 98–101.
18. Dennis Berman, "Now Tennis Balls Are Chasing Dogs," *Business Week* (July 23, 1998), p. 138.
19. Gary Hammel, "Innovation's New Math," *Fortune* (July 9, 2001), pp. 130–31.
20. Gardiner Harris, "With Big Drugs Dying, Merck Didn't Merge—It Found New Ones," *The Wall Street Journal* (January 10, 2001), pp. A1, A10.
21. Bill Vlasic, "When Air Bags Aren't Enough," *Business Week* (June 8, 1998) pp. 84–86; and Arthur J. Cummins, "Detroit Faces Crunch Time: Designing Gentler SUV's," *The Wall Street Journal* (February 25, 1998), pp. B1, B9.
22. Jack Neff, "White Bread, USA." *Advertising Age* (July 9, 2001), pp. 1, 12, 13.
23. Tom Molson and George Sproles, "Styling Strategy," *Business Horizons* (September–October 2000), pp. 45–52.
24. Jennifer Ordonez, "How Burger King Got Burned in Quest to Make the Perfect Fry," *The Wall Street Journal* (January 16, 2001), pp. A1, A8.

Palm Inc.: This case was written by Michael Vessey and Steven W. Hartley.

CHAPTER 11

1. quakeroats.com, downloaded August 20, 2001; "FTC Lets Pepsi–Quaker Oats Deal Proceed," *The Wall Street Journal* (August 2, 2001), p. A3; "Sue Wellington: She's Got Game," *Brandweek* (October 16, 2000), pp. M52–M62; and "The Gatorade Guys," *Sports Illustrated* (July 2, 2001), pp. 96–97.
2. For an extended discussion of the generalized product life-cycle curve, see David M. Gardner, "Product Life Cycle: A Critical Look at the Literature," in Michael Houston, ed., *Review of Marketing 1987* (Chicago: American Marketing Association, 1987), pp. 162–94; and Donald R. Lehmann and Russell S. Winer, *Product Management*, 3rd ed. (Burr Ridge, IL: McGraw-Hill/Irwin, 2002), pp. 261–65.
3. Glenn Rifkin, "Mach 3: Anatomy of Gillette's Latest Global Launch," *Strategy & Business* (Second Quarter 1999), pp. 34–41.
4. Orville C. Walker, Jr., Harper W. Boyd, Jr., and Jean-Claude Larréché, *Marketing Strategy*, 3rd ed. (New York: Irwin/McGraw Hill, 1999), p. 231.
5. Portions of the discussion on the fax machine industry are based on "The Technology That Won't Die," *Forbes* (April 5, 1999), p. 56; "Facsimile Is Still Preferred Method of Communication," *Purchasing Online* downloaded April 13, 2001; "Think Fax: The Technology, Not the Machine," *Purchasing Online* downloaded June 15, 2001; and "Atlas Electronic Corporation," in Roger A. Kerin and Robert A. Peterson, *Strategic Marketing Problems: Cases and Comments*, 8th ed. (Upper Saddle River, NJ: Prentice Hall, 1998), pp. 494–506.
6. "There's No Replacement—Not Even E-Mail," *Purchasing Online*, downloaded June 15, 2001; "Fax Is Still a Favorite, Despite the Alternatives," *Computing Canada* (June 25, 1999), pp. 62–65; and "We've All Got Mail," *Newsweek* (May 15, 2000), p. 73k.
7. "Why Coke Indulges (the Few) Fans of Tab," *The Wall Street Journal* (April 13, 2001), pp. B1, B4.
8. "Gillette's Edge," *Brandweek* (May 28, 2001), p. 5.
9. "How to Separate Trends from Fads," *Brandweek* (October 23, 2000), pp. 30, 32.
10. "Video-Game Sales Fell in 2000, Following Years of Record Growth," *The Wall Street Journal* (January 16, 2001), p. B6; "Video-Game Industry Is Seen Expanding at a Rapid Clip Next Five Years," *The Wall Street Journal* (May 25, 2001), p. B7; and "Video-Game Sales Surge More Than 30%," *The Wall Street Journal* (July 26, 2001), p. B10.
11. Everett M. Rogers, *Diffusion of Innovations*, 4th ed., (New York: Free Press, 1995).
12. Jagdish N. Sheth, Banwasi Mitral, and Bruce Newman, *Consumer Behavior* (Fort Worth, TX: Dryden Press, 1999).
13. "When Free Samples Become Saviors," *The Wall Street Journal* (August 14, 2001), pp. B1 B4.

14. For a historical perspective on the product/brand manager system, see George S. Low and Ronald A. Fullerton, "Brands, Brand Management, and the Brand Manager System: A Critical-Historical Evaluation," *Journal of Marketing Research* (May 1994), pp. 173–90.

15. "Haggar, Farah, Levi's Iron Out the Wrinkles," *Advertising Age* (March 6, 1995), p. 12; and "V-Rod Expands Harley-Davidson's Line as First Performance Custom Motorcycle," *Company Press Release* (July 12, 2001).

16. "Mass-Market Brands See More Upscale Heads," *Advertising Age* (September 25, 2000), p. S16.

17. "That's Dried Plums to You," *Dallas Morning News* (February 2, 2001), p. 2D; and Kenneth Li, "Power Player," *The Industry Standard* (September 2000), pp. 138–48.

18. "P&G's Soap Opera: New Ivory Bar Hits the Bottom of a Tub," *The Wall Street Journal* (October 23, 1992), p. B11.

19. Philip R. Cateora and John L. Graham, *International Marketing*, 11th ed.(Burr Ridge, IL: McGraw-Hill/Irwin, 2002), p. 359; and "Sneaker Company Tags Out-of-Breath Baby Boomers," *The Wall Street Journal* (January 16, 1998), pp. B1, B2.

20. "More People Are Eating for Health," *Research Alert* (October 20, 2000), pp. 5–6; "Calcium Craze Invading Two New Food Categories," *Advertising Age* (March 20, 2000), p. 28; and "Juice Marketers Boost Health Claims," *Advertising Age* (November 13, 2000), p. 46.

21. "It's Crunch Time," *Brandweek* (January 29, 2001), p. 3; Bag of Chips Not All That," *Dallas Morning News* (January 5, 2001), pp. 1D, 3D; "Don't Raise the Price, Lower the Water Award," *Brandweek* (January 8, 2001), p. 19.

22. This discussion is based on Kevin Lane Keller, *Strategic Brand Management* (Upper Saddle River, NJ: Prentice Hall, 1998); and Jennifer L. Aaker, "Dimensions of Brand Personality," *Journal of Marketing Research* (August 1997), pp. 347–56. See also Susan Fournier, "Consumers and Their Brands: Developing Relationship Theory in Consumer Research," *Journal of Consumer Research* (March 1998), pp. 343–73.

23. For an extended treatment of brand equity, see David A. Aaker, *Building Strong Brands* (New York: Free Press, 1996).

24. This discussion is based on Kevin Lane Keller, "Building Customer-Based Brand Equity," *Marketing Management* (July–August 2001), pp. 15–19.

25. This discussion is based on Roger A. Kerin and Raj Sethuraman, "Exploring the Brand Value–Shareholder Value Nexus for Consumer Goods Companies," *Journal of the Academy of Marketing Science* (Winter 1998); pp. 260–73; "P & G Sells to Cadbury Hawaiian Punch Label in $203 Million Accord," *The Wall Street Journal* (April 16, 1999), p. B2; and "Will Triarc Make Snapple Crackle?" *Business Week* (April 28, 1997), p. 64. Also see "The Best Global Brands," *Business Week* (August 6, 2001), pp. 50–64.

26. "Licensed to Thrive," *Advertising Age* (June 19, 2000), p. 16; and "Walt Disney Finalizes Licensing Deals with Rival Toy Makers Hasbro and Mattel," *The Wall Street Journal* (September 21, 2000), p. B16.

27. "Losing the Name Game," *Newsweek* (June 8, 1998), p. 44.

28. "A Good Name Should Live Forever," *Forbes* (November 16, 1998), p. 88.

29. Rob Osler, "The Name Game: Tips on How to Get It Right," *Marketing News* (September 14, 1998), p. 50; and Keller, *Strategic Brand Management*. See also Pamela W. Henderson and Joseph A. Cote, "Guidelines for Selecting or Modifying Logos," *Journal of Marketing* (April 1998), pp. 14–30; and Chiranjeev Kohli and Douglas W. LaBahn, "Creating Effective Brand Names: A Study of the Naming Process," *Journal of Advertising Research* (January–February 1997), pp. 67–75.

30. "Buying the Ranch on Brand Equity," *Brandweek* (October 25, 1992), p. 6; and "Kellogg Changes Name of Controversial Cereal," *Marketing News* (August 19, 1991), p. 22.

31. "A Survey of Multinationals," *The Economist* (June 24, 1995), p. 8.

32. John A. Quelch and David Kenny, "Extend Profits, Not Product Lines," *Harvard Business Review* (September–October 1994), pp 153–60.

33. For an overview of brand equity and brand extensions, see Vicki R. Lane, "Brand Leverage Power: The Critical Role of Brand Balance," *Business Horizons* (January–February 1998), pp. 25–84; and David C. Court, Mark G. Leitter, and Mark A. Loch, "Brand Leverage," *The McKinsey Quarterly*, no. 2 (1999); pp. 100–10.

34. "When Brand Extension Becomes Brand Abuse," *Brandweek* (October 26, 1998), pp. 20, 22.

35. Stephanie Thompson, "Brand Buddies," *Brandweek* (February 23, 1998), pp. 22–23ff. For an in-depth discussion on co-branding, see Akshay R. Rao and Robert W. Ruekert, "Brand Alliances as Signals of Product Quality," *Sloan Management Review* (Fall 1994), pp. 87–97.

36. "Unilever Pares Down to Leading Brands," *Mergers and Acquisitions* (April 2001), pp. 18–22.

37. "Brand X No Longer Plan B for Shoppers," *Dallas Morning News* (July 14, 2001), p. 2F. Also see David Dunne and Chakravarthi Narasimhan, "The New Appeal of Private Labels," *Harvard Business Review* (May–June 1999), pp. 41–52.

38. "Kodak Pursues a Greater Market Share in Japan with New Private-Label Film," *The Wall Street Journal* (March 7, 1995), p. B11.

39. www.pez.com. downloaded August 30, 2001; "The National Peztime," *The Dallas Morning News* (October 9, 1995), pp. 1C, 2C; David Welch, *Collecting Pez* (Murphysboro, IL: Bubba Scrubba Publications, 1995); and "Pez Dispense with Idea It's Just for Kids," *Brandweek* (September 26, 1996), p. 10.

40. "Just the Facts," *Research Alert* (July 2001), p. 5.

41. "L'eggs Hatches a New Hosiery Package," *Brandweek* (January 1, 2001), p. 6.

42. "Coca-Cola Finds Success Trading New for the Old," *The Wall Street Journal* (March 24, 1995), p. B5.

43. Lawrence L. Garber, Jr., Raymond R. Burke, and Morgan Jones, "The Role of Package Color in Consumer Purchase Consideration and Choice," *Marketing Science Institute*, Report No. 00-104, 2000.

44. Cateora and Graham, *International Marketing*, pp. 369–72.

45. "Asian Brands Are Sprouting English Logos in Pursuit of Status, International Image," *The Wall Street Journal* (August 7, 2001), p. B7C.

46. This discussion is based, in part, on Barry N. Rosen and George B. Sloane, III, "Environmental Product Standards, Trade and European Consumer Goods Marketing," *Columbia Journal of World Business* (Spring 1995), pp. 74–86; "Life Ever After," *The Economist* (October 9, 1993), p. 77; and "How to Make Lots of Money, and Save the Planet Too," *The Economist* (June 3, 1995); pp. 57–58. See also Stuart L. Hart, "Beyond Greening: Strategies for a Sustainable World," *Harvard Business Review* (January–February 1997), pp. 66–77; and Ajay Menon and Anil Menon, "Enviropreneurial Marketing Strategy: The Emergence of Corporate Environmentalism as Market Strategy," *Journal of Marketing* (January 1997), pp. 51–67.

47. Paula Mergenbagen, "Product Liability: Who Sues?" *American Demographics* (June 1995), pp. 48–54; and "Bottled Up," *The Economist* (December 17, 1994), p. 69.

48. For representative research on warranties, see Joydeep Srivastava and Ansuuree Mitra," Warranty as a Signal of Quality: The Moderating Effect of Consumer Knowledge on Quality Evaluations," *Marketing Letters* (November 1998), pp. 327–36; Melvyn A. Menezes and John A. Quelch, "Leverage Your Warranty Program, *Sloan Management Review* (Summer 1990), pp. 69–80; and "Broken? No Problem," *U.S. News & World Report* (January 11, 1999), pp. 68–69.

BMW: This case was written by Giana Eckhardt based on company interviews.

CHAPTER 12

1. "One-of-a-Kind Music and Dining Experience Ready to 'Rock' the Live Music Capital of the World," *PR Newswire* (June 25, 2001);

"Hard Rock Café Reveals Its Own Treasures in New Book," *PR Newswire* (June 18, 2001); Stefani Eads, "A New Beat at the Hard Rock," *Business Week* (October 9, 2000), p. 166; Jeffrey A. Trachtenberg, "Ballad of a Mad Café," *Forbes* (November 19, 1984), pp. 288, 290.

2. B. Joseph Pine and James H. Gilmore, *The Experience Economy,* (Boston: Harvard Business School Press); Rachel Brand, "Selling an Experience," *Denver Rocky Mountain News* (December 10, 2000), p. 1G; "The Personal Touch," *The Economist* (November 11, 2000); Jane E. Zarem, "Experience Marketing," *Folio* (October 2000); Scott MacStravic, "Make Impressions Last: Focus on Value," *Marketing News* (October 23, 2000), p. 44.

3. Survey of Current Business: Annual Revision of the National Income and Product Accounts (Washington, DC: U.S. Department of Commerce, August 2001); United States Department of Labor News, (Washington, DC: Bureau of Labor Statistics, August 2001); Michelle Conlin, Joseph Weber, A. T. Palmer, and Liz Garone, "Jobs: How Long Can Service Pick Up the Slack?" *Business Week* (February 19, 2001), pp. 34–35.

4. Joe Catalano, "At Your Service," *Newsday* (February 16, 2001), p. C6; John Ewoldt, "Dollars and Sense," *Star Tribune* (December 9, 1999), p. 1E; Susan Carey, "Web Site Promises Air-Traffic Control—for Passengers," *The Wall Street Journal* (June 1, 2001), p. B1; Daren Fonda, "Patently Absurd," *Time* (August 27, 2001), p. 17.

5. Janet R. McColl-Kennedy and Tina White, "Service Provider Training Programs at Odds with Customer Requirements in Five Star Hotels," *Journal of Services Marketing,* vol. 11, no. 4 (1997), pp. 249–64; Ellyn A. McColgan, "How Fidelity Invests in Service Professionals," *Harvard Business Review* (January–February 1997), pp. 137–43; and Frederick F. Reichheld and W. Earl Sasser, Jr., "Zero Defections: Quality Comes to Services," *Harvard Business Review* (September–October 1990), pp. 105–11.

6. Christopher H. Lovelock and George S. Yip, "Developing Global Strategies for Service Businesses," *California Management Review* (Winter 1996), pp. 64–86.

7. Stephen W. Brown, "The Move to Solutions Providers," *Marketing Management* (Spring 2000), pp. 10–11.

8. Christopher H. Lovelock and George S. Yip, "Developing Global Strategies for Service Businesses," *California Management Review* (Winter 1996), pp. 64–86.

9. Mark Hyman, "Hardball Software," *Business Week* (June 4, 2001), p. 16; Bill Saporito, "New Ball Games," *Time* (September 3, 2001), pp. 64–71; Tim Taylor, "Audience Info the Key to Sports Marketers," *Marketing News* (January 18, 1999), p. 10; Subir Bandyopadhyay and Mario Bottone, "Playing to Win," *Marketing Management* (Spring 1997), pp. 9–19; Aviv Shoham, Gregory M. Rose, and Lynn R. Kahle, "Marketing of Risky Sports: From Intention to Action," *Journal of the Academy of Marketing Science* (Fall 1998), pp. 307–21; and Allen St. John, "Who's on Deck?" *American Demographics* (October 1998), pp. 60–71.

10. Matthew L. Meuter, Amy L. Ostrom, Robert I. Roundtree, and Mary Jo Bitner, "Self-Service Technologies: Understanding Customer Satisfaction with Technology-Based Service Encounters," *Journal of Marketing* (July 2000), pp. 50–64.

11. "Nonprofit Activities," *The Nikkei Weekly* (October 30, 2000); and Paul Magnusson, "It's Open Season on Nonprofits," *Business Week* (July 3, 1995), p. 31.

12. Michael Gibb, "Inject New Life into Nonprofits' Marketing Program," *Marketing News* (October 23, 2000), p. 47.

13. Joan Oleck, "Cookies and High Tech," *Business Week* (March 12, 2001), p. 16; Ani Hadjian, "Follow the Leader," *Fortune* (November 27, 1995), p. 96.

14. Gene Del Polito, "Thinking of the P.O. Box," *Advertising Age* (June 11, 2001), p. 22; William Dowell, Chandrani Ghosh, and Bruce van Voorst, "Zapping the Post Office," *Time* (January 19, 1998), pp. 46–47; and Anne Faircloth, "The World Takes on the USPS," *Fortune* (July 24, 1995), p. 28.

15. Keith B. Murray, "A Test of Services Marketing Theory: Consumer Information Acquisition Activities," *Journal of Marketing* (January 1991), pp. 10–25.

16. Dawn Iacobucci, "An Empirical Examination of Some Basic Tenets in Services: Goods-Services Continua," Teresa Swartz, David E. Bowen, and Stephen W. Brown, eds., in *Advances in Services Marketing and Management,* vol. 1 (Greenwich, CT: JAI Press), pp. 23–52; and Valerie A. Zeithaml, "How Consumer Evaluation Processes Differ between Goods and Services," in James H. Donnelly and William R. George, eds., *Marketing of Services* (Chicago: American Marketing Association, 1981).

17. Michael J. Dorsch, Stephen J. Grove, and William Darden, "Consumer Intentions to Use a Service Category," *Journal of Services Marketing,* no. 2 (2000), pp. 92–117; and Murray, "A Test of Services Marketing Theory."

18. John Ozment and Edward Morash, "The Augmented Service Offering for Perceived and Actual Service Quality," *Journal of the Academy of Marketing Science* (Fall 1994), pp. 352–63.

19. A. Parasuraman, Valerie A. Zeithaml, and Leonard L. Berry, "Reassessment of Expectations as a Comparison Standard in Measuring Service Quality: Implications for Further Research," *Journal of Marketing* (January 1994), pp. 111–24; and Leonard L. Berry, *On Great Service* (New York: Free Press, 1995).

20. Valerie A. Zeithaml, A. Parasuraman, and Leonard L. Berry, *Delivering Quality Service* (New York: Free Press, 1990); and Stephen W. Brown and Teresa Swartz, "A Gap Analysis of Professional Service Quality," *Journal of Marketing* (April 1989), pp. 92–98.

21. Amy Ostrom and Dawn Iacobucci, "Consumer Trade-Offs and the Evaluation of Services," *Journal of Marketing* (January 1995), pp. 17–28; and J. Joseph Cronin, Jr., and Steven A. Taylor, "Measuring Service Quality: A Reexamination and Extension," *Journal of Marketing* (July 1992), pp. 55–68.

22. Stephen W. Brown, "Practicing Best-in-Class Service Recovery," *Marketing Management* (Summer 2000), pp. 8–9; Stephen S. Tax and Stephen W. Brown, "Recovering and Learning from Service Failure," *Sloan Management Review* (Fall 1998), pp. 75–88; Stephen S. Tax, Stephen W. Brown, and Murali Chandrashekaran, "Customer Evaluations of Service Complaint Experiences: Implications for Relationship Marketing," *Journal of Marketing* (April 1998), pp. 60–76; Stephen W. Brown, "Service Recovery Through IT," *Marketing Management* (Fall 1997), pp. 25–27; and Leonard L. Berry and A. Parasuraman, "Listening to the Customer—The Concept of a Service-Quality Information System," *Sloan Management Review* (Spring 1997), pp. 65–76.

23. Vicki Clift, "Everyone Needs Service Flow Charting," *Marketing News* (October 23, 1995), pp. 41, 43; Mary Jo Bitner, Bernard H. Booms, and Mary Stanfield Tetreault, "The Service Encounter: Diagnosing Favorable and Unfavorable Incidents," *Journal of Marketing* (January 1990), pp. 71–84; Eberhard Scheuing, "Conducting Customer Service Audits," *Journal of Consumer Marketing* (Summer 1989), pp. 35–41; and W. Earl Susser, R. Paul Olsen, and D. Daryl Wyckoff, *Management of Service Operations* (Boston: Allyn & Bacon, 1978).

24. Leonard L. Berry, "Relationship Marketing of Services—Growing Interest, Emerging Perspectives," *Journal of the Academy of Marketing Science* (Fall 1995), pp. 236–45; Mary Jo Bitner, "Building Service Relationships: It's All about Promises," *Journal of the Academy of Marketing Science* (Fall 1995), pp. 246–51; Kevin P. Gwinner, Dwayne D. Gremler, and Mary Jo Bitner, "Relational Benefits in Services Industries: The Customer's Perspective," *Journal of the Academy of Marketing Science* (Spring 1998), pp. 101–14; Susan Fournier, Susan Dobscha, and David Glen Mick, "Preventing the Premature Death of Relationship Marketing," *Harvard Business Review* (January–February 1998), pp. 42–51; and John V. Petrof, "Relationship Marketing: The Wheel Reinvented?" *Business Horizons* (November–December 1997), pp. 26–31.

25. Thomas S. Gruca, "Defending Service Markets," *Marketing Management,* no. 1 (1994), pp. 31–38; and Leonard L. Berry, Jeffrey S. Conant, and A. Parasuraman. "A Framework for Conducting a Services Marketing Audit," *Journal of the Academy of Marketing Science* (Summer 1991), pp. 255–68.

26. Patriya Tansuhaj, Donna Randall, and Jim McCullough, "A Services Marketing Management Model: Integrating Internal and External Marketing Functions," *Journal of Sciences Marketing* (Winter 1998), pp. 31–38.

27. Christian Gronroos, "Internal Marketing Theory and Practice," in Time Bloch, G. D. Upah, and V. A. Zeithaml, eds., *Services Marketing in a Changing Environment* (Chicago: American Marketing Association, 1984).

28. Ibid.

29. March C. Gilly and Mary Wolfinbarger, "Advertising's Internal Audience," *Journal of Marketing* (January 1998), pp. 69–88.

30. Sandy Allen and Ashok Chandrashekar, "Outsourcing Services: The Contract Is Just Beginning," *Business Horizons* (March–April 2000), pp. 25–34.

31. Dan R. E. Thomas, "Strategy Is Different in Service Businesses," *Harvard Business Review* (July–August 1978), pp. 158–65.

32. Haim Oren, "Branding Financial Services Helps Consumers Find Order in Chaos," *Marketing News* (March 29, 1993), p. 6; and Leonard L. Berry, Edwin F. Lefkowith, and Terry Clark, "In Services, What's in a Name?" *Harvard Business Review* (September–October 1998), pp. 28–30.

33. Frederick H. deB. Harris and Peter Peacock, "Hold My Place, Please," *Marketing Management* (Fall 1995), pp. 34–46.

34. Christopher Lovelock, *Services Marketing* (Englewood Cliffs, NJ: Prentice Hall, 1991), pp. 122–27.

35. Kent B. Monroe, "Buyer's Subjective Perceptions of Price," *Journal of Marketing Research* (February 1973), pp. 70–80; and Jerry Olson, "Price as an Informational Cue: Effects on Product Evaluation," in A. G. Woodside, J. N. Sheth, and P. D. Bennett, eds., *Consumer and Industrial Buying Behavior* (New York: Elsevier North-Holland, 1977), pp. 267–86.

36. Kirk Johnson, "A Flip Side to E-Z Pass: East River Tolls and Rush-Hour Prices," *The New York Times* (August 2, 1997), p. 21.

37. Robert E. Hite, Cynthia Fraser, and Joseph A. Bellizzi, "Professional Service Advertising: The Effects of Price Inclusion, Justification, and Level of Risk," *Journal of Advertising Research,* vol. 30 (August–September 1990), pp. 23–31; William R. George and Leonard L. Berry, "Guidelines for the Advertising of Services," *Business Horizons* (July–August 1981), pp. 52–56; and Eugene M. Johnson, Eberhard E. Scheuing, and Kathleen A. Gaida, *Profitable Service Marketing* (Homewood, IL: Dow Jones-Irwin, 1986).

38. Kathleen Mortimer, "Services Advertising: The Agency Viewpoint," *Journal of Services Marketing,* no. 2 (2001), pp. 131–46; and Sak Onkvisit and John J. Shaw, "Service Marketing: Image, Branding, and Competition," *Business Horizons* (January–February 1989), pp. 13–18.

39. *Bates and O'Sheen v. State of Arizona,* 433 U.S. 350, pp. 351–95 (1977): and "Supreme Court Opens Way for Lawyers to Advertise Prices for Routine Services," *The Wall Street Journal* (June 28, 1977), p. 4.

40. "Blond Ambition," *ABA Journal* (January 1996), p. 12.

41. Joe Adams, "Why Public Service Advertising Doesn't Work," *Ad Week* (November 17, 1980), p. 72.

42. Steve Rosenbush and Peter Elstrom, "8 Lessons from the Telecom Mess," *Business Week* (August 13, 2001), p. 60; Pallavi Gogoi, "What's Next–The Bank of Burger King?" *Business Week* (June 18, 2001), p. 150; Christopher Palmeri, "California: It Didn't Have to Be This Way," *Business Week* (January 22, 2001), p. 40; and Peter Coy, Stephanie Anderson Forest, Michael Arndt, and Ushma Patel, "Dark Days Ahead?" *Business Week* (May 14, 2001), p. 42.

43. Timothy J. Mullaney, "Online Pics: A Sure Shot," *Business Week* (September 3, 2001), p. EB12; Adam Leitzes and Joshua Solan, "Use Napster Alternative LimeWire," *Forbes* (June 25, 2001), p. 56; Ginny Parker, "Looking for Prince Charming? In Japan, Check Your Cell Phone," *Time* (June 4, 2001), p. 88; Tim Larimer, "Internet I-mode," *Time* (March 5, 2001), pp. 54–56; Leyland Pitt, Pierre Berthon, and Richard T. Watson, "Cyberservice: Taming Service Marketing Problems with the World Wide Web," *Business Horizons* (January–February 1999), pp. 11–18; J. M. Stifle, "Best of the Web: Dating," *Forbes* (June 25, 2001), p. 109.

DigitalThink: This case was adapted by Monica Noordam and Steven Hartley from a case titled "LearningByte International" written by Giana Eckhardt. Sources: Personal interviews with Umberto Milletti and Shelly Berkowitz; DigitalThink's website, (www.digitalthink.com); Lisa Vaas, "The E-Training of America," *PC Magazine* (December 26, 2001).

CHAPTER 13

1. Wendy Zellner, "Where the Net Delivers: Travel," *Business Week* (June 11, 2001), pp. 142–43.

2. Ibid.

3. Timothy Matanovich, Gary L. Lillien, and Arvind Rangaswamy, "Engineering the Price-Value Relationship," *Marketing Management* (Spring 1999), pp. 48–53.

4. Leyland F. Pitt, Pierre Berthon, Richard T. Watson, and Michael Ewing, "Pricing Strategy and the Net," *Business Horizons* (March–April, 2001), pp. 45–54.

5. Lisa Gubernick, "The Little Extras that Count (Up)," *The Wall Street Journal* (July 12, 2001), pp. B1, B4; Donald V. Potter, "Discovering Hidden Pricing Power," *Business Horizons* (November–December, 2000), pp. 41–48.

6. www.lamborghini.itg.net and www.kbb.com.

7. Adapted from Kent B. Monroe, *Pricing: Making Profitable Decisions* 2nd ed. (New York: McGraw-Hill, 1990), chapter 4. See also David J. Curry, "Measuring Price and Quality Competition," *Journal of Marketing* (Spring 1985), pp. 106–17.

8. Numerous studies have examined the price-quality-value relationship. See, for example, Jacob Jacoby and Jerry C. Olsen, eds., *Perceived Quality* (Lexington, MA: Lexington Books, 1985); William D. Dodds, Kent B. Monroe, and Dhruv Grewal, "Effects of Price, Brand, and Store Information on Buyers' Product Evaluations," *Journal of Marketing Research* (August 1991), pp. 307–19; and Roger A. Kerin, Ambuj Jain, and Daniel Howard, "Store Shopping Experience and Consumer Price-Quality-Value Perceptions," *Journal of Retailing* (Winter 1992), pp. 235–45. For a thorough review of the price-quality-value relationship, see Valerie A. Ziethaml, "Consumer Perceptions of Price, Quality, and Value," *Journal of Marketing* (July 1998), pp. 2–22.

9. Roger A. Kerin and Robert A. Peterson, "Throckmorten Furniture (A)" *Strategic Marketing Problems: Cases and Comments,* 9th ed. (Englewood Cliffs, NJ: Prentice Hall, 1998), pp. 235–45.

10. Mike Dodd, "Cards Hold 50 Years of Memories," *USA Today* (March 27, 2001), pp. 1A, 2A; J. C. Conklin, "Don't Throw Out Those Old Sneakers, They're a Gold Mine," *The Wall Street Journal* (September 21, 1998) pp. A1, A20.

11. Daniel Levy, Mark Bergen, Shautanu Dutta, and Robert Venable, "The Magnitude of Menu Costs: Direct Evidence from Large U.S. Supermarket Chains," *The Quarterly Journal of Economics* (August 1997), pp. 791–825.

12. David Wessel, "The Price Is Wrong, and Economics Are in an Uproar," *The Wall Street Journal* (January 2, 1991) pp. B1, B6.

13. Gordan A. Wyner, "New Pricing Realities," *Marketing Research* (Spring 2001), pp. 34–35.

14. Ron Winslow, "How a Breakthrough Quickly Broke Down for Johnson & Johnson," *The Wall Street Journal* (September 18, 1998), pp. A1, A5.

15. Adam Cohen, "No Split but Microsoft's a Monopolist," *Time* (July 9, 2001), pp. 36–38.

16. Akshay R. Rao, Mark E. Bergen, and Scott Davis, "How to Fight a Price War," *Harvard Business Review* (March–April 2000), pp. 107–16.

17. Bruce Orwall, "Hollywood's Costs Rose 8% in 2000 to a Record High," *The Wall Street Journal* (March 7, 2001), p. B6; and Bruce Orwall, "Theater Consolidation Jolts Hollywood Power Structure," *The Wall Street Journal* (January 21, 1998), pp. B1, B2.

18. Frank Bruni, "Price of Newsweek? It Depends," *Dallas Times Herald* (August 14, 1986), pp. S1, S20.

19. Vanessa O'Connell, "How Campbell Saw a Breakthrough Menu Turn into Leftovers," *The Wall Street Journal* (October 6, 1998), pp. A1, A12.

20. Janice Revell, "The Price Is Not Always Right," *Fortune* (May 14, 2001), p. 240; Indrajit Sinha, "Cost Transparency: The Net's Real Threat to Prices and Brands," *Harvard Business Review* (March–April 2000), pp. 43–50; Walter Baker, Mike Marn, and Craig Zawada, "Price Smarter on the Net," *Harvard Business Review* (February 2001), pp. 122–27.

21. www.airbus.com.

22. For an overview of price elasticity studies, see Ruth N. Bolton, "The Robustness of Retail-Level Elasticity Estimates," *Journal of Retailing* (Summer 1989), pp. 193–219.

23. Dominick Salvatore, *Managerial Economics in a Global Economy* 4th ed. (Fort Worth: Harcourt College Publishers, 2001), p. 111.

24. Rick Andrews and George R. Franke, "Time-Varying Elasticities of U.S. Cigarette Demand, 1933–1987," *AMA Educator's Conference Proceedings* (Chicago: American Marketing Association, 1990), p. 393.

25. Linda Himelstein, "Webvan Left the Basics on the Shelf," *Business Week* (July 23, 2001), p. 43.

Washburn International: The case is based on information and materials provided by the company.

CHAPTER 14

1. "Product News," gillette.com, downloaded June 15, 2001; "New Duracell Ultra with M3 Technology Is Now Available in North America; Breakthrough Design Makes Duracell Ultra the Most Powerful Battery in the World, Even More Powerful," *The Gillette Company Press Release,* September 26, 2000; "Duracell Makes Best Alkaline Battery Better with Duracell Ultra 3 Design," *The Gillette Company Press Release,* January 25, 2000.

2. "Nintendo Gamecube Set at Mass Market Price of $199.95"; "Dedicated Gameplay System Launches November 5, 2001, with Six First-Party Titles Priced at $49.95," *Nintendo of America, Inc., Press Release,* May 21, 2001.

3. For the classic description of skimming and penetration pricing, see Joel Dean, "Pricing Policies for New Products," *Harvard Business Review* (November–December 1976), pp. 141–53. See also, Reed K. Holden and Thomas T. Nagle, "Kamikaze Pricing," *Marketing Management* (Summer 1998), pp. 31–39.

4. Jean-Noel Kapferer, "Managing Luxury Brands," *The Journal of Brand Management* (July 1997), pp. 251–60.

5. "Time Is Money," *Forbes* (September 18, 2000), pp. 178–85.

6. "Premium AA Alkaline Batteries," *Consumer Reports* (March 21, 2001), p. 54; Kemp Powers, "Assault and Batteries," *Forbes* (September 4, 2000), pp. 54, 56; "Razor Burn at Gillette," *Business Week* (June 18, 2001), p. 37.

7. See, for example, V. Kumar and Robert P. Leone, "Measuring the Effects of Retail Store Promotions on Brand and Store Substitution," *Journal of Marketing Research* (May 1998), pp. 178–85; and "AT&T Simplifies Price Tiers," *Dallas Morning News* (November 5, 1997), p. 1D.

8. "Why That Deal Is Only $9.99," *Business Week* (January 10, 2000), p. 36. For further reading on odd-even pricing, see Robert M. Schindler and Thomas M. Kilbarian, "Increased Consumer Sales

Response Through Use of 99-Ending Prices," *Journal of Retailing* (Summer 1996), pp. 187–99; Mark Stiving and Russell S. Winer, "An Empirical Analysis of Price Endings with Scanner Data," *Journal of Consumer Research* (June 1997), pp. 57–67; and Robert M. Schindler, "Patterns of Rightmost Digits Used in Advertised Prices: Implications for Nine-Ending Effects," *Journal of Consumer Research* (September 1997), pp. 192–201.

9. For an overview on target pricing, see Stephan A. Butscher and Michael Laker, "Market Driven Product Development," *Marketing Management* (Summer 2000), pp. 48–53.

10. Thomas T. Nagle and Reed K. Holden, *The Strategy and Tactics of Pricing,* 3rd ed. (Englewood Cliffs, NJ: Prentice Hall, 2002), pp. 243–49.

11. Kent B. Monroe, *Pricing: Making Profitable Decisions,* 2nd ed. (New York: McGraw-Hill, 1990), pp. 326–27. For a recent discussion of this topic, see Ramarao Desiraju and Steven M. Shugan, "Strategic Service Pricing and Yield Management," *Journal of Marketing* (January 1999), pp. 44–56.

12. Robert J. Dolan and Hermann Simon, *Power Pricing: How Managing Price Transforms the Bottom Line* (New York: Free Press, 1996), p. 249.

13. Peter M. Noble and Thomas S. Gruca, "Industrial Pricing: Theory and Managerial Practice," *Marketing Science,* vol. 18, no. 3 (1999), pp. 435–54.

14. George E. Belch and Michael A. Belch, *Introduction to Advertising and Promotion,* 5th ed. (New York: Irwin/McGraw-Hill, 2001), p. 93.

15. For a comprehensive discussion on the experience curve, see Roger A. Kerin, Vijay Mahajan, and P. Rajan Varadarajan, *Contemporary Perspectives on Strategic Market Planning* (Boston: Allyn and Bacon, 1990), chapter 4.

16. "Hewlett-Packard Cuts Office-PC Prices in Wake of Moves by Compaq and IBM," *The Wall Street Journal* (August 22, 1995), p. B11.

17. "Retailers Using Cut-Rate Videos as Lures," *Dallas Morning News* (October 4, 1995), p. 5H.

18. "Cheap Thrills for Shoppers," *Newsweek* (April 16, 2001), p. 45.

19. This discussion is based on "How Technology Tailors Price Tags," *The Wall Street Journal* (June 21, 2001), p. A1; Robert D. Holf, "The Buyer Always Wins," *Business Week* (March 22, 1999), pp. EB26–EB28.

20. "How Dell Fine-Tunes Its PC Pricing to Gain Edge in a Slow Market," *The Wall Street Journal* (June 8, 2001), pp. A1, A8.

21. "Are Black Shoppers Treated Unfairly? An Expensive New Reason to Care," DiversityInc.com, downloaded June 5, 2001; Ian Ayres and Peter Siegelman, "Race and Gender Discrimination in Bargaining for a New Car," *The American Economic Review* (June 1995), pp. 304–21; and "Goodbye to Haggling," *U. S. News & World Report* (October 20, 1997), p. 57.

22. Monroe, *Pricing,* p. 34.

23. Jagmohan S. Raju, Raj Sethuraman, and Sanjay K. Dhar, "National Brand-Store Brand Price Differential and Store Brand Market Share," *Pricing Strategy & Practice,* vol. 3, no. 2 (1995), pp. 17–24.

24. "The Price Is Not Always Right," *Fortune* (May 14, 2001), p. 240.

25. For an extended discussion about price wars, see Akshay R. Rao, Mark E. Bergen, and Scott Davis, "How to Fight a Price War," *Harvard Business Review* (March–April 2000), pp. 107–16.

26. For an extensive discussion on discounts, see Monroe, *Pricing,* chapters 14 and 15.

27. Kenneth C. Manning, William O. Bearden, and Randall L. Rose, "Development of a Theory of Retailer Response to Manufacturers' Everyday Low Cost Programs," *Journal of Retailing* (Spring 1998), pp. 107–37; "Everyday Low Profits," *Harvard Business Review* (March–April 1994), p. 13; Stephen J. Hoch, Xavier Dreze, and Mary E. Purk, "EDLP, Hi-Lo, and Margin Arithmetic," *Journal of Marketing* (October 1994), pp. 16–27; and Tibbett Speer, "Do Low Prices Bore Shoppers?" *American Demographics* (January 1994), pp. 11–13. See also Philip Zerillo and Dawn Iacobucci, "Trade

Promotions: A Call for a More Rational Approach," *Business Horizons* (July–August 1995), pp. 69–76; and Barbara E. Kahn and Leigh McAlister, *The Grocery Revolution: The New Focus on the Consumer* (Reading, MA: Addison-Wesley Educational Publishers, 1996).

28. Dorothy Cohen, *Legal Issues in Marketing Decision Making* (Cincinnati, OH: South-Western, 1995).

29. "Six Vitamin Firms Agree to Settle Price-Fixing Suit," *The Wall Street Journal* (October 11, 2000), p. B10.

30. "Price Fixing," *USA Today* (March 7, 2000), p. C1.

31. "Predatory Pricing: Cleared for Takeoff," *Business Week* (May 14, 2001), p. 50.

My Own Meals: Sources: Personal interview with Mary Anne Jackson; Mike Duff, "New Children's Meals: Not Just Kids Stuff," *Supermarket Business* (May 1990), p. 93; Heidi Parson, "MOM, Incorporated," *Poultry Processing* (August–September 1989); Lisa R. Van Wagner, "Kids' Meals: The Market Grows Up," *Food Business* (May 20, 1991); Mary Ellen Kuhn, "Women to Watch in the 90's," *Food Business* (September 10, 1990); and Arlene Vigoda, "Small Fry Microwave Meals Become Big Business," *USA Today* (June 4, 1990); My Own Meals, Inc. website (www.myownmeals.com); Tom Richman, "The New American Start-up," *Inc.* (September, 1998), p. 54; Jerry Stroud, "Kids Specially Targeted in New Prepared-Dinner Market Effort," *St. Louis Post-Dispatch* (May 29, 1989), p. 5.

CHAPTER 15

1. avoncompany.com, downloaded July 25, 2001; Rochelle Kass, "Experimental Beauty," *The Journal News* (July 21, 2001), pp. 1D, 2D; Nanette Byrnes, "Avon: The New Calling," *Fortune* (September 18, 2000), pp. 136–48; "Retail Makeover," *Dallas Morning News* (May 9, 2001), p. 2D; and "Cosmetic Firms Try Change of Face," *Dallas Morning News* (September 19, 2000), p. 4D.

2. See Peter D. Bennett, ed., *Dictionary of Marketing Terms,* 2nd ed. (Chicago: American Marketing Association, 1996).

3. PepsiCo, Inc., *Annual Report,* 1997.

4. Donald V. Fites, "Make Your Dealers Your Partners," *Harvard Business Review* (March–April 1996), pp. 84–95.

5. This discussion is based on Bert Rosenbloom, *Marketing Channels: A Management View,* 6th ed. (Fort Worth, TX: Dryden Press, 1999), pp. 452–58.

6. *2000 Economic Impact: U.S. Direct Marketing Today* (New York: The Direct Marketing Association, 2001).

7. For a discussion on strategic channel alliances, see P. Rajan Vandarajan and Margaret H. Cunningham, "Strategic Alliances: A Synthesis of Conceptual Foundations," *Journal of the Academy of Marketing Science* (Fall 1995), pp. 282–96; and Johny K. Johansson, "International Alliances: Why Now?" *Journal of the Academy of Marketing Science* (Fall 1995), pp. 301–4. The examples appear in "Pepsi, Ocean Spray Renew Deal; Fruitworks Expands," *Brandweek* (April 6, 1998), p. 14; and "GM Pondering Consolidations in Field Marketing," *Advertising Age* (May 11, 1998), p. 4.

8. General Mills, Inc., *Annual Report,* 2000.

9. For an extensive discussion of wholesaling, see Louis W. Stern, Adel I. El-Ansary, and Anne T. Coughlan, *Marketing Channels,* 5th ed. (Upper Saddle River, NJ: Prentice Hall, 1996), chapter 3.

10. For an overview of vertical marketing systems, see Lou Peltson, David Strutton, and James R. Lumpkin, *Marketing Channels* (Chicago: Irwin, 1997), chapter 14.

11. Statistics provided by the International Franchise Association, July 31, 2001.

12. For a review of channel partnering, see Robert D. Bussell and Gwen Ortmeyer, "Channel Partnerships Streamline Distribution," *Sloan Management Review* (Spring 1995), pp. 85–96. See also Jakki J. Mohr and Robert E. Spekman, "Perfecting Partnerships," *Marketing Management* (Winter/Spring 1996), pp. 35–43.

13. Edwin R. Rigsbee, *The Art of Partnering* (Dubuque, IA: Kendall/Hunt Publishing, 1994), pp. 82–83.

14. "Target to Join Party, Sell Tupperware in Stores," *Dallas Morning News* (July 18, 2001), p. 2D.

15. Kroger, Inc., *Annual Report,* 2000.

16. For an interesting discussion of distribution intensity, see Gary L. Frazier and Walfried M. Lassar, "Determinants of Distribution Intensity," *Journal of Marketing* (October 1996), pp. 39–51.

17. Joshua Levine and Matthew Swibel, "Dr. No," *Forbes* (May 28, 2001), pp. 72–76.

18. "Radio Shack Campaign Touts Its RCA Alliance," *Advertising Age* (June 5, 2000), p. 61; "Radio Shack, Compaq Pact Is Extended," *Dallas Morning News* (April 20, 2000), p. 2D.

19. "Apple to Open 25 Retail Stores This Year in a Bid to Reach Out to New Customers," *The Wall Street Journal* (May 16, 2001), p. B8; "Strip Malls Are Gateway Country," *The Industry Standard* (November 27–December 4, 2000), pp. 82–86.

20. Jonathan Mandell, "Speed It Up Webmaster, We're Losing Billions Every Second," *The New York Times* (September 22, 1999), p. 58D.

21. "5 down 95 to Go," apple.com, downloaded July 25, 2001; "Apple Retail Stores Welcome over 7700 People in First Two Days," Apple Computer, Inc., press release, (May 21, 2001); and Cliff Edwards, "Sorry, Steve: Here's Why It Won't Work," *Business Week* (May 21, 2001), pp. 44–45.

22. "Gillette Tries to Nick Schick in Japan," *The Wall Street Journal* (February 4, 1991), pp. B3, B4.

23. This discussion is based on "Foreign Firms Think Their Way into Japan," *Nikkei Weekly* (September 20, 1999), pp. 8–9; John Fahy and Fuyuki Taguchi, "Reassessing the Japanese Distribution System," *Sloan Management Review* (Winter 1995), pp. 49–61; Michael R. Czinkota and Jon Woronoff, *Unlocking Japanese Markets* (Chicago: Probus Publishing, 1991), pp. 92–97; and "Japan Keeping U.S. Products out of Asia; Intricate Network Known as 'Keiretsu' Excludes Outsiders," *The Baltimore Sun* (November 9, 1997), p. 6F.

24. For a managerial discussion on channel conflict, see Christine B. Bucklin, Pamela A. Thomas-Graham, and Elizabeth A. Webster, "Channel Conflict: When Is It Dangerous?" *The McKinsey Quarterly* (Number 3, 1997), pp. 36–43.

25. "Black Pearls Recast for Spring," *Advertising Age* (November 13, 1995), p. 49.

26. Studies that explore the dimensions and use of power and influence in marketing channels include the following: Gul Butaney and Lawrence H. Wortzel, "Distributor Power versus Manufacturer Power: The Customer Role," *Journal of Marketing* (January 1988), pp. 52–63; Kenneth A. Hunt, John T. Mentzer, and Jeffrey E. Danes, "The Effect of Power Sources on Compliance in a Channel of Distribution: A Causal Model," *Journal of Business Research* (October 1987), pp. 377–98; John F. Gaski, "Interrelations among a Channel Entity's Power Sources: Impact of the Exercise of Reward and Coercion on Expert, Referent, and Legitimate Power Sources," *Journal of Marketing Research* (February 1986), pp. 62–67; Gary Frazier and John O. Summers, "Interfirm Influence Strategies and Their Application within Distribution Channels," *Journal of Marketing* (Summer 1984), pp. 43–55; Sudhir Kale, "Dealer Perceptions of Manufacturer Power and Influence Strategies in a Developing Country," *Journal of Marketing Research* (November 1986), pp. 387–93; George H. Lucas and Larry G. Gresham, "Power, Conflict, Control, and the Application of Contingency Theory in Channels of Distribution," *Journal of the Academy of Marketing Science* (Summer 1985), pp. 27–37; and F. Robert Dwyer and Julie Gassenheimer, "Relational Roles and Triangle Dramas: Effects on Power Play and Sentiments in Industrial Channels," *Marketing Letters,* vol. 3 (1992), pp. 187–200.

27. "FTC Pinpoints Slotting Fees," *Advertising Age* (February 26, 2001), p. 52; "Ca-ching," *Forbes* (June 12, 2000), pp. 84–85. Also see Paul N. Bloom, Gregory T. Gundlach, and Joseph P. Cannon,

"Slotting Allowances and Fees: Schools of Thought and Views of Practicing Managers," *Journal of Marketing* (April 2000), pp. 92–109.

28. For a comprehensive treatment of legal issues pertaining to marketing channels, see Dorothy Cohen, *Legal Issues in Marketing* (Cincinnati, OH: South-Western, 1995), chapters 12 and 13.

CHAPTER 16

1. David Simchi-Levi, Philip Kaminsky, and Edith Simchi-Levi, *Designing and Managing the Supply Chain* (Burr Ridge, IL: Irwin/McGraw-Hill, 2000), pp. 82–95; and H. Lee, V. Padmanabhan, and S. Whang, "The Bullwhip Effect in Supply Chains," *Sloan Management Review* (Spring 1997), pp. 93–102.

2. These estimates are given in James R. Stock and Douglas M. Lambert, *Strategic Logistics Management,* 4th ed. (Burr Ridge, IL: McGraw-Hill/Irwin, 2001), p. 5; and "U.S. Logistics Closing on Trillion Dollar Mark," *Business Week* (December 28, 1998), p. 78.

3. *What's It All About?* (Oakbrook, IL: Council of Logistics Management, 1993).

4. This example described in Simchi-Levi et al., *Designing and Managing the Supply Chain,* p. 5.

5. This discussion is based on Robert B. Handfield and Earnest Z. Nichols, *Introduction to Supply Chain Management* (Upper Saddle River, NJ: Prentice Hall, 1998), chapter 1.

6. This discussion is based on Robyn Meredith, "Harder than the Hype," *Forbes* (April 16, 2001), pp. 188–94; Robert M. Monczka and Jim Morgan, "Supply Chain Management Strategies," *Purchasing* (January 15, 1998), pp. 78–85; and Handfield and Nichols, *Introduction to Supply Chain Management.*

7. Major portions of this discussion are based on Sunil Chopra and Peter Meindl, *Supply Chain Management: Strategy, Planning, and Operations* (Upper Saddle River, NJ: Prentice Hall, 2001), chapters 1–3; and Marshall L. Fisher, "What Is the Right Supply Chain for Your Product?" *Harvard Business Review* (March–April 1997), pp. 105–17.

8. Eric Young and Mark Roberti, "The Swoosh Stumbles," *The Industry Standard* (March 12, 2001), pp. 47–49.

9. Portions of this discussion are based on Chopra and Meindl, *Supply Chain Management: Strategy, Planning, and Operations;* Nick Wingfield, "In the Beginning . . . ," *The Wall Street Journal* (May 21, 2001), p. R18; "Putting the 'E' Back in E-Business," *Information Week* (January 31, 2000), pp. 19–22. See also Richard A. Lancioni, Michael F. Smith, and Terence A. Oliva, "The Role of the Internet in Supply Chain Management," *Industrial Marketing Management,* vol. 29 (2000), pp. 45–46; and Donald J. Bowersox, David J. Closs, and M. Bixby Cooper, *Supply Chain Logistics Management* (Burr Ridge, IL: McGraw-Hill/Irwin, 2002), Chapter 10.

10. For an extensive listing and description of total logistics costs, see Stock and Lambert, *Strategic Logistics Management,* pp. 28–31.

11. Simchi-Levi et al., *Designing and Managing the Supply Chain,* p. 6.

12. Toby B. Gooley, "How Logistics Drive Customer Service," *Traffic Management* (January 1996), p. 46.

13. Faith Keenan, "Logistics Gets a Little Respect," *Business Week e-biz* (November 20, 2000), pp. EB113–EB126.

14. Michael Levy and Barton A. Weitz, *Retailing Management,* 4th ed. (Burr Ridge, IL: McGraw-Hill/Irwin, 2001), pp. 335–36; "A&P Bets the Store," *The Industry Standard* (May 14, 2001), pp. 46–49; and Ursula Y. Alvarado and Herbert Kotzab, "Supply Chain Management: The Integration of Logistics in Marketing," *Industrial Marketing Management,* vol. 30 (2001), pp. 183–98.

15. Jon Bigness, "In Today's Economy, There Is Big Money to Be Made in Logistics," *The Wall Street Journal* (September 6, 1995), pp. A1, A9.

16. Robert C. Lieb and Arnold Maltz, "What's the Future for Third-Party Logistics?" *Supply Chain Management Review* (Spring 1998), pp. 71–79.

17. Erik Schonfeld, "The Total Package," *eCompany* (June 2001), pp. 91–97; and "Compaq, UPS Unit Sign Network Pact," *Dallas Morning News* (April 21, 2000), p. 2D.

18. For an extensive description of transportation modes, see Douglas M. Lambert, James R. Stock, and Lisa Ellram, *Fundamentals of Logistics Management* (New York: Irwin/McGraw-Hill, 1998).

19. "Supply News: The Virtual Organization in our Future," www-1. ibm.com/procurement/supplynews/febsupplynews, downloaded February 1, 2001; Sheree DeCovny, "Electronic Commerce Comes of Age," *Journal of Business Strategy* (November/December 1998), pp. 38–44.

20. Jeffrey Davis and Martha Baer, "Some Assembly Required," *Business 2.0* (February 12, 2001), pp. 78–87.

21. Ronald Henkoff, "Delivering the Goods," *Fortune* (November 28, 1994), pp. 64–78.

22. Ken Cottrill, "Reforging the Supply Chain," *Journal of Business Strategy* (November/December 1997), pp. 35–39.

23. Fisher, "What Is the Right Supply Chain for Your Product?"

24. For an excellent overview on reverse logistics, see Edward J. Marien, "Reverse Logistics as Competitive Strategy," *Supply Chain Management Review* (Spring 1998), pp. 43–53.

25. Bruce Caldwell, "Reverse Logistics," www.informationweek.com, downloaded May 25, 2001; and "Return to Sender," *Modern Material Handling* (May 15, 2000), pp. 10–11.

26. Scott McMurry, "Life after Death," *eCompany* (December 2000), pp. 167–78; and Harvey Meyer, "The Greening of Corporate America," *Journal of Business Strategy* (January/February 2000), pp. 38–43.

27. Doug Bartholomew, "IT Delivers for UPS," *Industry Week*

Amazon.com: This case is based on material available on the company website, www.amazon.com, and the following sources: Robert D. Hof and Heather Green, "How Amazon Cleared That Hurdle," *Business Week* (February 4, 2002), p. 60; Heather Green, "How Hard Should Amazon Swing?" *Business Week* (January 14, 2002), p. 38: Robert D. Hof, "We've Never Said We Had To Do It All," *Business Week* (October 15, 2001), p. 53; "Amazon.com Selects Mercator E-Business Integration Brokers as Key Technology for Supply Chain Integration," *Business Wire* (November 28, 2000); Bob Walter, "Amazon Leases Distribution Center from Sacramento, Calif., Development Firm," *Sacramento Bee* (July 19, 2001).

CHAPTER 17

1. Laura Heller, "Target Gets Mod in Manhattan," *DSN Retailing Today* (August 20, 2001), p. 2; Alice Z. Cuneo, "On Target," *Advertising Age* (December 11, 2000), p. 1; "Target Lets Ads onto the Bag," *HFN* (August 20, 2001), p. 58; "Target and MJC: Sweet Game Plan," *DSN Retailing Today* (August 20, 2001), p. A4; Lesley O'Toole, "Target's Launch Party for Mossimo Hits the Mark," *In Style* (June 2001), p. 198; Amy Merrick, "Get Smart: Target Will Be First among Big Stores to Issue Cards," *The Wall Street Journal* (June 20, 2001), p. B6.

2. Kenneth Cline, "The Devil in the Details," *Banking Strategies* (November–December 1997), p. 24; and Roger Trap, "Design Your Own Jeans," *The Independent* (October 18, 1998), p. 22.

3. "Fortune 1000 Ranked within Industries," *Fortune* (April 16, 2001), p. F-54.

4. *Statistical Abstract of the United States,* 120th ed. (Washington, DC: U.S. Department of Commerce, Bureau of the Census, October 2000).

5. "Fortune Global 500 Ranked within Industries," *Fortune* (July 23, 2001), p. F15.

6. "Top Retailers Reinvent Themselves to Keep Pace," *PR Newswire* (July 5, 2001); William Echikson, Carol Matlack, and David Vannier, "American E-Tailers Take Europe by Storm," *Business Week* (August 7, 2000), pp. 54–55; "7-Eleven Wishes to Open 70 Stores in Denmark," *Borsen* (June 12, 2001), p. 12; "IKEA to Expand in the

U.S.," *Dagens Nyheter* (June 13, 2001), p. 2; "The Sun Never Sets on Wal-Mart's Retail Empire," *MMR* (December 18, 2000), p. 110; Lorrie Grant, "Global Reach Rings Up Earnings Boost for U.S. Retailers," *USA Today* (March 23, 1998), p. 7B; "Retailers Rush to Capture New Markets," *Financial Times* (March 13, 1998), p. 2.

7. "Retail Trade—Establishments, Employees, and Payroll," *Statistical Abstract of the United States,* 120th ed. (Washington, DC: U.S. Department of Commerce, Bureau of the Census, October 2000); Gene Koretz, "Those Plucky Corner Stores," *Business Week* (December 5, 1994), p. 26.

8. Christopher Palmeri, "Who's Afraid of Wal-Mart?" *Forbes* (July 31, 1995), p. 81.

9. Richard C. Hoffman and John F. Preble, "Franchising into the Twenty-First Century," *Business Horizons* (November–December 1993), pp. 35–43.

10. "How Widespread Is Franchising?" International Franchise Association (www.franchise.org), September 2001; John Ryans, Jr., Sherry Lotz, and Robert Krampf, "Do Master Franchisors Drive Global Franchising?" *Marketing Management* (Summer 1999), pp. 33–37.

11. "Franchise 500," *Entrepreneur* (January 2001); Scott Shane and Chester Spell, "Factors for New Franchise Success," *Sloan Management Review* (Spring 1998), pp. 43–50.

12. David Breitkopf, "From NCR, an Automated Checkout Line System," *The American Banker* (August 7, 2001), p. 10; "Food 4 Less Introduces U-Scan Self-Service Checkout at Hollywood Store," *PR Newswire* (February 13, 2001); Marc Rice, "Competition Fierce in Complex Business of Delivering Packages," *Marketing News* (May 22, 1995), p. 5.

13. "Can the Nordstroms Find the Right Style?" *Business Week* (July 30, 2001), p. 59; Cyndee Miller, "Nordstrom Is Tops in Survey," *Marketing News* (February 15, 1993), p. 12.

14. Aixa M. Pascual, "Can Office Depot Get Back On Track?" *Business Week* (September 18, 2000), p. 74.

15. Laurie M. Grossman, "Hypermarkets: A Sure-Fire Hit Bombs," *The Wall Street Journal* (June 25, 1992), p. B1.

16. Scott Carlson, "Wal-Mart Superstores Not Coming Soon to Minnesota's Twin Cities Area," *St. Paul Pioneer Press* (August 2, 2001); Barbara Thau, "Super Centered," *HFN* (April 23, 2001), p. 10; Wendy Zellner, "A Grand Reopening for Wal-Mart," *Business Week* (February 9, 1998), pp. 86–88; and Elliot Zwiebach, "With Renewed Financial Resources Kmart Is Starting on a Journey of Growth," *Supermarket News* (November 16, 1998), p. 1.

17. Ginny Parker, "Vending the Rules," *Time* (May 7, 2001), p. 24.

18. Julie Mitchell, "Electronic Payment Services Move beyond Tollbooths," *Investor's Business Daily* (August 30, 2001), p. 10; and Steve Scrupski, "Tiny 'Brains' Seen for Vending Machines," *Electronic Design* (December 1, 1998), p. 64F.

19. *U.S. Direct and Interactive Marketing Today,* 6th ed. (New York: Direct Marketing Association, October 2000); *Statistical Fact Book 2000* (New York: Direct Marketing Association, 2000); Ellen Neuborne, "Coaxing with Catalogs," *Business Week* (August 6, 2001), p. EB6.

20. Edward Nash, "The Roots of Direct Marketing," *Direct Marketing* (February 1995), pp. 38–40; and Edith Hipp Updike and Mary Kurtz, "Japan Is Dialing 1 800 BUYAMERICA," *Business Week* (June 12, 1995), pp. 61–64.

21. Monica Roman, "You Gotta Have a Catalog," *Business Week* (May 14, 2001), p. 56; Beth Viveiros, "Catalog and Internet Sales Grow More Quickly than Retail," *Direct* (July 2001); David Stires, "Office Depot Finds an E-Business That Works," *Fortune* (February 19, 2001), p. 232; and Diane Brady and Julia Cosgrove, "A Big Break for Your Postman," *Business Week* (September 10, 2001), p. 16.

22. "Intimate Brands Reports August Sales," *PR Newswire* (September 6, 2001); Christopher Palmeri, "Victoria's Little Secret," *Forbes* (August 24, 1998), p. 58; and Dyan Machan, "Sharing Victoria's Secrets," *Forbes* (June 5, 1995), pp. 132–33.

23. "Joe Namath, Franco Harris, Boomer Esiason, and Tim Brown Appear On Home Shopping Network during Super Bowl Week," *PR Newswire* (January 23, 2001); "Cover Girls Queen Latifah and Molly Sims Brush Up on Youth Volunteerism," *PR Newswire* (August 22, 2001); Carole Nicksin, "QVC Opens Up in Mall Space," *HFN* (August 20, 2001), p. 6; Chris Wynn and Tim Adler, "Battle for UK Home-Shopping Viewers Hots Up as QVC Gets Heavyweight Rival," *New Media Markets* (May 11, 2001).

24. Heather Green, "Where Did All the Surfers Go?" *Business Week* (August 6, 2001), p. 35; Steve Hamm, David Welch, Wendy Zellner, Faith Keenan, and Peter Engardio, "E-Biz: Down but Hardly Out," *Business Week* (March 26, 2001), pp. 126–30; Lewis Braham, "E-Tailers Are Clicking," *Business Week* (July 23, 2001), p. 73; "Will Wal-Mart Get It Right This Time?" *Business Week* (November 6, 2000), p. 104; and Raymond R. Burke, "Do You See What I See? The Future of Virtual Shopping," *Journal of the Academy of Marketing Science* (Fall 1997), pp. 352–60.

25. "Former Cendant Marketing Chief Will Help Company Leverage Core Media Products While Broadening Member Benefit Offerings," *PR Newswire* (February 21, 2001); Tim Mullaney, "And All the Price Trimmings," *Business Week* (December 18, 2000), p. 68; Mary J. Cronin, "Business Secrets of the Billion-Dollar Website," *Fortune* (February 2, 1998), p. 142; Robert D. Hof, Ellen Neuborne, and Heather Green, "Amazon.com: The Wild World of E-Commerce," *Business Week* (December 14, 1998), pp. 106–19; "Future Shop," *Forbes ASAP* (April 6, 1998), pp. 37–52; Chris Taylor, "Cybershop," *Time* (November 23, 1998), p. 142; Stephen H. Wildstrom, "Bots' Don't Make Great Shoppers," *Business Week* (December 7, 1998), p. 14; and Jeffrey Ressner, "Online Flea Markets," *Time* (October 5, 1998), p. 48.

26. Roger O. Crocket, "Let the Buyer Compare," *Business Week* (September 3, 2001), p. EB10.

27. "My Virtual Model Inc. Acquires EZsize," *PR Newswire* (June 21, 2001); Steve Casimiro, "Shop Till You Crash," *Fortune* (December 21, 1998), pp. 267–70; and De' Ann Weimer, "Can I Try (Click) That Blouse (Drag) in Blue?" *Business Week* (November 9, 1998), p. 86.

28. "Usability Study of PC and TV-Based Web Platforms Reveals Online Shopping Tasks Confuse, Frustrate Users," *PR Newswire* (September 5, 2001); Chris O'Malley, "No Waiting on the Web," *Time* (November 16, 1998), p. 76; B. G. Yovovich, "Webbed Feat," *Marketing News* (January 19, 1998), p. 1, 18; and Joseph Alba, John Lynch, Barton Weitz, Chris Janiszewski, Richard Lutz, Alan Sawyer, and Stacy Wood, "Interactive Home Shopping: Consumer, Retailer, and Manufacturer Incentives to Participate in Electronic Marketplace," *Journal of Marketing* (July 1997), pp. 38–53.

29. See cybercafes.com; Michelle Megna, "Wireless at Starbucks," *Daily News* (August 16, 2001), p. 12; "Pinet and Softstar Cooperate in Online Game Market," *China Post* (November 2, 2000).

30. Donna Bursey, "Targeting Small Businesses for Telemarketing and Mail Order Sales," *Direct Marketing* (September 1995), pp. 18–20; "Inbound, Outbound Telemarketing Keeps Ryder Sales in Fast Lane," *Direct Marketing* (July 1995), pp. 34–36; "Despite Hangups, Telemarketing a Success," *Marketing News* (March 27, 1995), p. 19; Kelly Shermach, "Outsourcing Seen as a Way to Cut Costs, Retain Service," *Marketing News* (June 19, 1995), pp. 5, 8; and Greg Gattuso, "Marketing Vision," *Direct Marketing* (February 1994), pp. 24–26.

31. Brian P. Murphy, "Giving Cold Calls the Cold Shoulder," *Business Week* (July 2, 2001), p. 12; and "TeleWatch to Help Control Unethical Telemarketing," *Telemarketing & Call Center Solutions* (April 1998), p. 28.

32. Nanette Byrnes, "The New Calling," *Business Week* (September 18, 2000), pp. 137–48.

33. Bill Vlasic and Mary Beth Regan, "Amway II: The Kids Take Over," *Business Week* (February 1, 1998), pp. 60–70.

34. Mathew Schifrin, "Okay, Big Mouth," *Forbes* (October 9, 1995), pp. 47–48; Veronica Byrd and Wendy Zellner, "The Avon Lady of the Amazon," *Business Week* (October 24, 1994), pp. 93–96; and Ann

Marsh "Avon Is Calling on Eastern Europe," *Advertising Age* (June 20, 1994), p. 116.

35. The following discussion is adapted from William T. Gregor and Eileen M. Friars, *Money Merchandizing: Retail Revolution in Consumer Financial Services* (Cambridge, MA: Management Analysis Center, Inc., 1982).

36. Nicole Harris, "Just For Feet Is Making Tracks," *Business Week* (July 20, 1998), pp. 70–72.

37. Gail Tom, Michelle Dragics, and Christi Holdregger, "Using Visual Presentation to Assess Store Positioning: A Case Study of JCPenney," *Marketing Research* (September 1991), pp. 48–52.

38. William Lazer and Eugene J. Keley, "The Retailing Mix: Planning and Management," *Journal of Retailing* (Spring 1961), pp. 34–41.

39. Francis J. Mulhern and Robert P. Leon, "Implicit Price Bundling of Retail Products: A Multiproduct Approach to Maximizing Store Profitability," *Journal of Marketing* (October 1991), pp. 63–76.

40. Gwen Ortmeyer, John A. Quelch, and Walter Salmon, "Restoring Credibility to Retail Pricing," *Sloan Management Review* (Fall 1991), pp. 55–66.

41. William B. Dodds, "In Search of Value: How Price and Store Name Information Influence Buyers' Product Perceptions," *Journal of Consumer Marketing* (Spring 1991), pp. 15–24.

42. Leonard L. Berry, "Old Pillars of New Retailing," *Harvard Business Review* (April 2001), pp. 131–37.

43. Neil Gross, "On beyond Shoplifting Prevention," *Business Week* (October 2, 2000), p. 170; and "A Time to Steal," *Brandweek* (February 16, 1999), p. 24.

44. Rita Koselka, "The Schottenstein Factor," *Forbes* (September 28, 1992), p. 104, 106.

45. Wendy Zellner, "Warehouse Clubs: When the Going Gets Tough . . ." *Business Week* (July 16, 2001), p. 60; "Warehouse Clubs Fine-tune Units," *Chain Drug Review* (June 29, 1998), p. 38; James M. Degen, "Warehouse Clubs Move from Revolution to Evolution," *Marketing News* (August 3, 1992), p. 8; Dori Jones Yang, "Bargains by the Forklift," *Business Week* (July 15, 1991), p. 152; and "Fewer Rings on the Cash Register," *Business Week* (January 14, 1991), p. 85.

46. Ira P. Schneiderman, "Value Keeps Factory Outlets Viable," *Daily News Record* (July 20, 1998), p. 10; Stephanie Anderson Forest, "I Can Get It for You Retail," *Business Week* (September 18, 1995), pp. 84–88; and Adrienne Ward, "New Breed of Mall Knows: Everybody Loves a Bargain," *Advertising Age* (January 27, 1992), p. 55.

47. Anne Faircloth, "Value Retailers Go Dollar For Dollar," *Fortune* (July 6, 1998), pp. 164–66.

48. Barry Brown, "Edmonton Makes Size Pay Off in Down Market," *Advertising Age* (January 27, 1992), p. 4–5.

49. James R. Lowry, "The Life Cycle of Shopping Centers," *Business Horizons* (January–February 1997), pp. 77–86; Eric Peterson, "Power Centers! Now!" *Stores* (March 1989), pp. 61–66; and "Power Centers Flex Their Muscle," *Chain Store Age Executive* (February 1989), pp. 3A, 4A.

50. Pierre Martineau, "The Personality of the Retail Store," *Harvard Business Review* (January–February 1958), p. 47.

51. Julie Baker, Dhruv Grewal, and A. Parasuraman, "The Influence of Store Environment on Quality Inferences and Store Image," *Journal of the Academy of Marketing Science* (Fall 1994), pp. 328–39; Howard Barich and Philip Kotler, "A Framework for Marketing Image Management," *Sloan Management Review* (Winter 1991), pp. 94–104; Susan M. Keaveney and Kenneth A. Hunt, "Conceptualization and Operationalization of Retail Store Image: A Case of Rival Middle-Level Theories," *Journal of the Academy of Marketing Science* (Spring 1992), pp. 165–75; James C. Ward, Mary Jo Bitner, and John Barnes, "Measuring the Prototypicality and Meaning of Retail Environments," *Journal of Retailing* (Summer 1992), p. 194; and Dhruv Grewal, R. Krishnan, Julie Baker, and Norm Burin, "The Effect of Store Name, Brand Name and Price Discounts on Consumers' Evaluations and Purchase Intentions," *Journal of Retailing* (Fall 1998), pp. 331–52.

For a review of the store image literature, see Mary R. Zimmer and Linda L. Golden, "Impressions of Retail Stores: A Content Analysis of Consumer Images," *Journal of Retailing* (Fall 1988), pp. 265–93.

52. Mary Jo Bitner, "Servicescapes: The Impact of Physical Surroundings on Customers and Employees," *Journal of Marketing* (April 1992), pp. 57–71.

53. Jans-Benedict Steenkamp and Michel Wedel, "Segmenting Retail Markets on Store Image Using a Consumer-Based Methodology," *Journal of Retailing* (Fall 1991), p. 300; and Philip Kotler, "Atmospherics as a Marketing Tool," *Journal of Retailing*, vol. 49 (Winter 1973–1974), p. 61.

54. Carole Nicksin, "Sears' New Ad Campaign to Stress Brand Image, Shopping Convenience," *HFN* (August 27, 2001), p. 4.

55. The wheel of retailing theory was originally proposed by Malcolm P. McNair, "Significant Trends and Development in the Postwar Period," in A. B. Smith, ed., *Competitive Distribution in a Free, High-Level Economy and Its Implications for the University* (Pittsburgh: University of Pittsburgh Press, 1958), pp. 1–25; see also Stephen Brown, "The Wheel of Retailing—Past and Future," *Journal of Retailing* (Summer 1990), pp. 143–49; and Malcolm P. McNair and Eleanor May, "The Next Revolution of the Retailing Wheel," *Harvard Business Review* (September–October 1978), pp. 81–91.

56. Peter Kiekmeyer, "McDonald's Bet Heavily on McCafe," *The Montreal Gazette* (August 28, 2001), p. D2; "McDonald's Adds Sourdough Line and Cheesecake to Revolving Menu Offerings," *PR Newswire* (August 9, 2001); David Farkas, "Drive-Thru in the Fast Lane," *Chain Leader* (July 2001), p. 40.

57. Bill Saporito, "What's for Dinner?" *Fortune* (May 15, 1995), pp. 51–64.

58. William R. Davidson, Albert D. Bates, and Stephen J. Bass, "Retail Life Cycle," *Harvard Business Review* (November–December 1976), pp. 89–96.

59. Gretchen Morgenson, "Here Come the Cross-Shoppers," *Forbes* (December 7, 1992), pp. 90–101.

60. Ranjay Gulati and Janson Garino, "Getting the Right Mix of Bricks and Clicks," *Harvard Business Review* (May–June 2000), pp. 107–114; Marshall L Fisher, Ananth Raman, and Anna Sheen McClelland, "Rocket Science Retailing Is Almost Here: Are You Ready?" *Harvard Business Review* (July–August 2000), pp. 115–24; Charla Mathwick, Naresh Malhotra, and Edward Rigdon, "Experiential Value: Conceptualization, Measurement and Application in the Catalog and Internet Shopping Environment," *Journal of Retailing* (Spring 2001), pp. 39–56; Lawrence M. Bellman, "Bricks and Mortar: 21st Century Survival," *Business Horizons* (May–June 2001), pp. 21–28; Zhan G. Li and Nurit Gery, "E-Tailing—for All Products?" *Business Horizons* (November–December 2000), pp. 49–54; Bill Hanifin, "Go Forth and Multichannel: Loyalty Programs Need Knowledge Base," *Marketing News* (August 27, 2001), p. 23.

61. Mary Kuntz, Lori Bongiorno; Keith Naughton, Gail DeGeorge, and Stephanie Anderson Forest, "Reinventing the Store," *Business Week* (November 27, 1995), pp. 84–96; and David Fischer, "The New Meal Deals," *U.S. News & World Report* (October 30, 1995), p. 66.

Mall of America: This case was written by David P. Brennan and is based on an interview with Maureen Cahill and materials provided by Mall of America.

CHAPTER 18

1. "Best Promoted Brands of 2001," *PROMO* (September 2001), pp. 55–62; "Daring Disney," *Advertising Age* (March 26, 2001), p. 20; Wayne Friedman, "Disney's Twist on Film Promo," *Advertising Age* (March 19, 2001), p. 3; Wayne Friedman, "Disney Sets $250 Mil Birthday Bash," *Advertising Age* (July 2, 2001), p. 1; Bob Garfield, "Disney's Quest for Boomers Shows a Bit of Imagineering," *Advertising Age* (August 13, 2001), p. 29; Stephanie Thompson, "The Mouse in the Food Aisle," *Advertising Age* (September 10, 2001),

p. 73; Lorraine Calvacca, "Mouse Trapping," *PROMO* (May 2001), p. 47; Stephanie Thompson, "A Disney Assist," *Advertising Age* (July 30, 2001), p. 39; Wayne Friedman, "Disney, Toys 'Я' Us Sign Cross-Media Deal," *Advertising Age* (June 18, 2001), p. 3; Chester Dawson, "Will Tokyo Embrace Another Mouse?" *Business Week* (September 10, 2001), p. 65; and David Jackson, "How to Build a Better Mouse-trap," *Time* (February 19, 2001), pp. 40–42.

2. Wilbur Schramm, "How Communication Works," in Wilbur Schramm, ed., *The Process and Effects of Mass Communication* (Urbana, IL: University of Illinois Press, 1955), pp. 3–26.

3. E. Cooper and M. Jahoda, "The Evasion of Propaganda," *Journal of Psychology*, vol. 22 (1947), pp. 15–25; H. Hyman and P. Sheatsley, "Some Reasons Why Information Campaigns Fail," *Public Opinion Quarterly*, vol. 11 (1947), pp. 412–23; and J. T. Klapper, *The Effects of Mass Communication* (New York: Free Press, 1960), chapter VII.

4. Cynthia L. Kemper, "Biting Wax Tadpole, Other Faux Pas," *The Denver Post* (August 3, 1997), p. G-04.

5. Adapted from *Dictionary of Marketing Terms*, 2nd ed., Peter D. Bennett, ed. (Chicago: American Marketing Association, 1995), p. 231.

6. Kusum L Ailawadi, Scott A. Neslin, and Karen Gedenk, "Pursuing the Value-Conscious Consumer: Store Brands versus National Brand Promotions," *Journal of Marketing* (January 2001), pp. 71–89;

7. B. C. Cotton and Emerson M. Babb, "Consumer Response to Promotional Deals," *Journal of Marketing*, vol. 42 (July 1978), pp. 109–13.

8. Robert George Brown, "Sales Response to Promotions and Advertising," *Journal of Advertising Research*, vol. 14 (August 1974), pp. 33–40.

9. Adapted from *Economic Impact: U.S. Direct Marketing Today* (New York: Direct Marketing Association, 1998), p. 25.

10. Siva K. Balasubramanian and V. Kumar, "Analyzing Variations in Advertising and Promotional Expenditures: Key Correlates in Consumer, Industrial, and Service Markets," *Journal of Marketing* (April 1990), pp. 57–68.

11. Don E. Schultz, "Consumer Marketing Changed by Advent of 29.8/7 Media Week," *Marketing News* (September 24, 2001), pp. 13, 15; Pamela Paul, "Getting Inside Gen Y," *American Demographics* (September 2001), pp. 43–49; Charles Pappas, "Ad Nauseam," *Advertising Age* (July 10, 2000), pp. 16–18; Dan Lippe, "It's All in Creative Delivery," *Advertising Age* (June 25, 2001), pp. s8, s9; and Kate Fitzgerald, "Viral Marketing Breaks Through," *Advertising Age* (June 25, 2001), p. s10.

12. Dunn Sunnoo and Lynn Y. S. Lin, "Sales Effects of Promotion and Advertising," *Journal of Advertising Research*, vol. 18 (October 1978), pp. 37–42.

13. John Palmer, "Animal Instincts," *PROMO* (May 2001), pp. 25–33.

14. J. Ronald Carey, Stephen A. Clique, Barbara A. Leighton, and Frank Milton, "A Test of Positive Reinforcement of Customers," *Journal of Marketing*, vol. 40 (October 1976), pp. 98–100.

15. James M. Olver and Paul W. Farris, "Push and Pull: A One-Two Punch for Packages Products," *Sloan Management Review* (Fall 1989), pp. 53–61.

16. Julia Flynn and Michael Oneal, "A Tall Order for the Prince of Beers," *Business Week* (March 23, 1992), pp. 66–68; and Patricia Sellers, "How Busch Wins in a Doggy Market," *Fortune* (June 22, 1987), pp. 99–111.

17. Fusun F. Gonul, Franklin Carter, Elina Petrova, and Kannan Srinivasan, "Promotion of Prescription Drugs and Its Impact on Physicians' Choice Behavior," *Journal of Marketing* (July 2001), pp. 79–90.

18. Joseph Weber, "Drug Ads: A Prescription for Controversy," *Business Week* (January 18, 1993), pp. 58–60.

19. Tom Duncan, "Is Your Marketing Communications Integrated?" *Advertising Age* (January 24, 1994), p. 26.

20. Kim Cleland, "Few Wed Marketing, Communications," *Advertising Age* (February 27, 1995), p. 10.

21. Don Schultz, "Objectives Drive Tactics in IMC Approach," *Marketing News* (May 9, 1994), pp. 14, 18; and Neil Brown, "Redefine Inte-grated Marketing Communications," *Marketing News* (March 29, 1993), pp. 4–5.

22. Richard Verrier, "Disney Seeks to Add China to Its World," *Los Angeles Times* (September 16, 2001), p. 3-1.

23. Robert J. Lavidge and Gary A. Steiner, "A Model for Predictive Measurement of Advertising Effectiveness," *Journal of Marketing* (October 1961), p. 61.

24. Brian Wansink and Michael Ray, "Advertising Strategies to Increase Usage Frequency," *Journal of Marketing* (January 1996), pp. 31–46.

25. "45th Annual Report: 100 Leading National Advertisers," *Advertising Age* (September 24, 2001), p. s1-s26.

26. Don E. Schultz and Anders Gronstedt, "Making Marcom an Investment," *Marketing Management* (Fall 1997), pp. 41–49; and J. Enrique Bigne, "Advertising Budget Practices: A Review," *Journal of Current Issues and Research in Advertising* (Fall 1995), pp. 17–31.

27. John Philip Jones, "Ad Spending: Maintaining Market Share," *Harvard Business Review* (January–February 1990), pp. 38–42; and Charles H. Patti and Vincent Blanko, "Budgeting Practices of Big Advertisers," *Journal of Advertising Research*, vol. 21 (December 1981), pp. 23–30.

28. James A. Schroer, "Ad Spending: Growing Market Share," *Harvard Business Review* (January–February 1990), pp. 44–48.

29. Jeffrey A. Lowenhar and John L. Stanton, "Forecasting Competitive Advertising Expenditures," *Journal of Advertising Research*, vol. 16, no. 2 (April 1976), pp. 37–44.

30. Daniel Seligman, "How Much for Advertising?" *Fortune* (December 1956), p. 123.

31. James E. Lynch and Graham J. Hooley, "Increasing Sophistication in Advertising Budget Setting," *Journal of Advertising Research*, vol. 30 (February–March 1990), pp. 67–75.

32. Jimmy D. Barnes, Brenda J. Muscove, and Javad Rassouli, "An Objective and Task Media Selection Decision Model and Advertising Cost Formula to Determine International Advertising Budgets," *Journal of Advertising*, vol. 11, no. 4 (1982), pp. 68–75.

33. Don E. Schultz, "Olympics Get the Gold Medal in Integrating Marketing Event," *Marketing News* (April 27, 1998), pp. 5, 10.

34. "The Fellowship of the New Line," *PROMO* (September 2001), p. 84; and "Sneak Preview of Trailer for New Line Cinema's 'The Lord of the Rings: The Fellowship of the Ring'" *PR Newswire* (September 21, 2001).

35. Kate Fitzgerald, "Beyond Advertising," *Advertising Age* (August 3, 1998), pp. 1, 14; Curtis P. Johnson, "Follow the Money: Sell CFO on Integrated Marketing's Merits," *Marketing News* (May 11, 1998), p. 10; and Laura Schneider, "Agencies Show That IMC Can Be Good for Bottom Line," *Marketing News* (May 11, 1998), p. 11.

36. *Economic Impact: U.S. Direct Marketing Today* (New York: Direct Marketing Association, 2000), pp. 24–30.

37. "The Columbia House Company Selects Akamai EdgeSuite to Support Growing Online Business," *Business Wire* (September 5, 2001); "Back to College Market Fuels Growth in Internet Commerce and Traffic," *Business Wire* (September 10, 2001); and Carol Krol, "Columbia House Looks Down the Road for Gains from Play," *Advertising Age* (March 1, 1999), p. 20.

38. *Statistical Fact Book '98* (New York: The Direct Marketing Association, 1998).

39. Robert Berner, "Going that Extra Inch," *Business Week* (September 18, 2000), p. 84.

40. Adapted from *Economic Impact: U.S. Direct Marketing Today* (New York: Direct Marketing Association, 1998), pp. 25–26.

41. Carol Krol, "Club Med Uses E-Mail to Pitch Unsold, Discounted Packages," *Advertising Age* (December 14, 1998), p. 40.

42. "Rising to the Top," *PROMO* (September 2001), pp. 46–62.

43. Jean Halliday, "Taking Direct Route," *Advertising Age* (September 7, 1998), p. 17.

44. Julie Tilsner, "Lillian Vernon: Creating a Host of Spin-offs from Its Core Catalog," *Business Week* (December 19, 1994), p. 85; and Lisa Coleman, "I Went Out and Did It," *Forbes* (August 17, 1992), pp. 102–4.

45. Alan K. Gorenstein, "Direct Marketing's Growth Will Be Global," *Marketing News* (December 7, 1998), p. 15; Don E. Schultz, "Integrated Global Marketing Will Be the Name of the Game," *Marketing News* (October 26, 1998), p. 5; and Mary Sutter and Andrea Mandel-Campbell, "Customers Are Eager, Infrastructure Lags," *Advertising Age International* (October 5, 1998), p. 12.

46. Juliana Koranten, "European Privacy Rules Go into Effect in 15 EU States," *Advertising Age* (October 26, 1998), p. S31; and Rashi Glazer, "The Illusion of Privacy and Competition for Attention," *Journal of Interactive Marketing* (Summer 1998), pp. 2–4.

47. Douglas Wood and David Brosse, "Mulling E-Mail Options," *PROMO* (September 2001), p. 18; Kathleen Cholewka, "Making E-Mail Matter," *Sales and Marketing Management* (September 2001), pp. 21, 22; "$2.1 Billion Will Be Spent on E-Mail Marketing by Year-End 2001," *Direct Marketing* (August 2001), p. 7; Arlene Weintraub, "When E-Mail Ads Aren't Spam," *Business Week* (October 16, 2000), p. 112; "Opting Out of E-Mail Ads Isn't So Easy to Do," *Business Week* (November 6, 2000), p. 20; "With E-Mail Marketing, Permission Is Key," eStatNews (on emarketer.com), September 2001.

CHAPTER 19

1. Daniel Eisenberg, "Making Brands Magically Appear," *Time* (July 23, 2001), p. 46; Christine Y. Chen, "TiVo Is Smart TV," *Fortune* (March 19, 2001), p. 124; Lee Gomes, "I Want My PC-TV—Two Products Take Baby Steps toward Ideal," *The Wall Street Journal* (August 16, 2001), p. B1; Khanh T. L. Tran, "TiVo, Sonicblue Still See the Bright Side," *The Wall Street Journal* (August 31, 2001), p. B3; Jennifer L. Schenker, "Death of a Salesman," *Time* (June 4, 2001), p. 54.

2. David A. Aaker and Donald Norris, "Characteristics of TV Commercials Perceived as Informative," *Journal of Advertising Research,* vol. 22, no. 2 (April–May 1982), pp. 61–70.

3. Larry D. Compeau and Dhruv Grewal, "Comparative Price Advertising: An Integrative Review," *Journal of Public Policy & Marketing* (Fall 1998), pp. 257–73; and William Wilkie and Paul W. Farris, "Comparison Advertising: Problems and Potentials," *Journal of Marketing* (October 1975), pp. 7–15.

4. Jennifer Lawrence, "P&G Ads Get Competitive," *Advertising Age* (February 1, 1993), p. 14; Jerry Gotlieb and Dan Sorel, "The Influence of Type of Advertisement, Price, and Source Credibility on Perceived Quality," *Journal of the Academy of Marketing Science* (Summer 1992), pp. 253–60; and Cornelia Pechman and David Stewart, "The Effects of Comparative Advertising on Attention, Memory, and Purchase Intentions," *Journal of Consumer Research* (September 1990), pp. 180–92.

5. Bruce Buchanan and Doron Goldman, "Us vs. Them: The Minefield of Comparative Ads," *Harvard Business Review* (May–June 1989), pp. 38–50; Dorothy Cohen, "The FTC's Advertising Substantiation Program," *Journal of Marketing* (Winter 1980), pp. 26–35; and Michael Etger and Stephen A. Goodwin, "Planning for Comparative Advertising Requires Special Attention," *Journal of Advertising,* vol. 8, no. 1 (Winter 1979), pp. 26–32.

6. Lewis C. Winters, "Does It Pay to Advertise to Hostile Audiences with Corporate Advertising?" *Journal of Advertising Research* (June/July 1988), pp. 11–18; and Robert Selwitz, "The Selling of an Image," *Madison Avenue* (February 1985), pp. 61–69.

7. Mary Lou Quinlan, "Women: We've Come a Long Way, Maybe," *Advertising Age* (February 22, 1999), p. 46.

8. Jean Halliday, "Of Hummers and Zen," *Advertising Age* (August 6, 2001), p. 29.

9. "Claritin Springs into Allergy Season with New Consumer Programs," *PR Newswire* (February 20, 2001).

10. Ira Teinowitz, "Self-regulation Urged to Prevent Bias in Ad Buying," *Advertising Age* (January 18, 1999), p. 4.

11. Bob Donath, "Match Your Media Choice and Ad Copy Objective," *Marketing News* (June 8, 1998), p. 6.

12. "Arnold Worldwide Drives Away with $100,000 MPA Kelly Award for Its Volkswagen Beetle Campaign," *Business Wire* (May 22, 2001); Christine Tierney, Andrea Zammert, Joann Muller, and Katie Kerwin, "Volkswagen," *Business Week* (July 23, 2001), pp. 60–68.

13. Kate Maddox, "ARF Forum Examines Internet Research Effectiveness," *Advertising Age* (January 11, 1999), p. 28.

14. Demetrios Vakratsas and Tim Ambler, "How Advertising Works: What Do We Really Know?" *Journal of Marketing* (January 1999), pp. 26–43.

15. Wayne Friedman, "Second Down," *Advertising Age* (September 3, 2001), p. 3; Bonnie Tsui, "Bowl Poll," *Advertising Age* (February 5, 2001), p. 33; Rich Thomaselli, "Open Season," *Advertising Age* (August 27, 2001), p. 3; Kate Fitzgerald, "Bud's Super 'Bowl'," *Advertising Age* (January 15, 2001), p. 20; Bob Garfield, "Super Bowl Ads Score," *Advertising Age* (January 29, 2001), p. 3.

16. Hillary Chura and Kate MacArthur, "Flat Colas Anxiously Watch Gen Yers Switch," *Advertising Age* (September 25, 2000), p. S10; Kate MacArthur, "Campbell Wins Sepracor Acc't," *Advertising Age* (June 25, 2001), p. 3.

17. Michael S. LaTour and Herbert J. Rotfeld, "There Are Threats and (Maybe) Fear-Caused Arousal: Theory and Confusions of Appeals to Fear and Fear Arousal Itself," *Journal of Advertising* (Fall 1997), pp. 45–59.

18. Bob Garfield, "Allstate Ads Bring Home Point about Mortgage Insurance," *Advertising Age* (September 11, 1989), p. 120; and Judann Dagnoli, "'Buy or Die' Mentality Toned Down in Ads," *Advertising Age* (May 7, 1990), p. S-12.

19. Hank Kim and Scott Hume, "Positioning: Blue Cross, Kaiser Permanente Ads Play Big on HMO Trust Factor," *Brandweek* (September 14, 1998); Jeffrey D. Zbar, "Fear!" *Advertising Age* (November 14, 1994), pp. 18–19; John F. Tanner, Jr., James B. Hunt, and David R. Eppright, "The Protection Motivation Model: A Normative Model of Fear Appeals," *Journal of Marketing* (July 1991), pp. 36–45; Michael S. LaTour and Shaker A. Zahra, "Fear Appeals as Advertising Strategy: Should They Be Used?" *The Journal of Consumer Marketing* (Spring 1989), pp. 61–70; and Joshua Levine, "Don't Fry Your Brain," *Forbes* (February 4, 1991), pp. 116–17.

20. "Operating Strategy," BeBe website (www.bebe.com); Betsy McKay, "New Diet Coke Campaign Plays Up Sex," *The Wall Street Journal* (March 23, 2001), p. B7; Emily Nelson, "Forget Supermodels," *The Wall Street Journal* (March 30, 2001), p. B1.

21. Anthony Vagnoni, "Best Awards," *Advertising Age* (May 28, 2001), pp. S1–18; Dana L. Alden, Wayne D. Hoyer, and Chol Lee, "Identifying Global and Culture-Specific Dimensions of Humor in Advertising: A Multinational Analysis," *Journal of Marketing* (April 1993), pp. 64–75; and Johny K. Johansson, "The Sense of 'Nonsense': Japanese TV Advertising," *Journal of Advertising* (March 1994), pp. 17–26.

22. Alice Z. Cuneo, "Creative That Endures," *Advertising Age* (January 29, 2001), pp. 1, S1-6.

23. "Ronald McDonald Models Milk Mustache," *PR Newswire* (September 11, 2001); "Image of the Week," *Advertising Age* (February 26, 2001), p. 56; Rich Thomaselli, "Air Ball?" *Advertising Age* (October 1, 2001), p. 3; Mercedes Cardona, "Venus and Serena Become Avon's New Leading Ladies," *Advertising Age* (January 22, 2001), p. 8; Jeffri Chadiha and Joel Stratte-McClure, "M'm-M'm-Bad," *Sports Illustrated* (June 4, 2001), p. 31; Paul Lukas, "Got Milk? Got Books? Got a Clue?" *Fortune* (September 7, 1998), p. 40; Brian D. Till and Terence A. Shimp, "Endorsers in Advertising: The Case of Negative Celebrity Information," *Journal of Advertising* (March 22, 1998), p. 67; and Alan R. Miciak and William L. Shanklin, "Choosing Celebrity Endorsers," *Marketing Management* vol. 3, no. 3, pp. 51–59.

24. Jean Halliday, "Exotic Ads Get Noticed," *Advertising Age* (April 9, 2001), p. S4.

25. "Domestic Advertising Spending by Medium," *Advertising Age* (September 24, 2001), p. S12.

26. Giles D'Souza and Ram C. Rao, "Can Repeating an Advertisement More Frequently than the Competition Affect Brand Preference in a Mature Market?" *Journal of Marketing* (April 1995), pp. 32–42.

27. Vicki R. Lane, "The Impact of Ad Repetition and Ad Content on Consumer Perceptions of Incongruent Extensions," *Journal of Marketing* (April 2000), pp. 80–91.

28. Katherine Barrett, "Taking a Closer Look," *Madison Avenue* (August 1984), pp. 106–9.

29. Joe Mandese, "Out-of-Home TV: Does It Count?" *Advertising Age* (January 18, 1993), p. 53.

30. Joe Mandese, "'ER' Tops Price Charts, Regis Wears the Crown," *Advertising Age* (October 2, 2000), pp. 1, 24.

31. Surendra N. Singh, Denise Linville, and Ajay Sukhdial, "Enhancing the Efficacy of Split Thirty-Second Television Commercials: An Encoding Variability Application," *Journal of Advertising* (Fall 1995), pp. 13–23; Scott Ward, Terence A. Oliva, and David J. Reibstein, "Effectiveness of Brand-Related 15-Second Commercials," *Journal of Consumer Marketing*, no. 2 (1994), pp. 38–44; and Surendra N. Singh and Catherine Cole, "The Effects of Length, Content, and Repetition on Television Commercial Effectiveness," *Journal of Marketing Research* (February 1993), pp. 91–104.

32. Cliff Edwards, "Is TiVo's Signal Fading?" *Business Week* (September 10, 2001), p. 72; Jacqueline M. Graves, "The Fortune 500 Opt for Infomercials," *Fortune* (March 6, 1995), p. 20; and William McCall, "Infomercial Pioneer Becomes Industry Leader," *Marketing News* (June 19, 1995), p. 14.

33. Cara Beardi, "Radio's Big Bounce," *Advertising Age* (August 27, 2001), p. S2.

34. "Change in Number of Magazine Titles," *Marketing News* (July 2, 2001), p. 11; R. Craig Endicott, "Past Performance Is Not a Guarantee of Future Returns," *Advertising Age* (June 18, 2001), pp. S1, S6; and George R. Milne, "A Magazine Taxonomy Based on Customer Overlap," *Journal of the Academy of Marketing Science* (Spring 1994), pp. 170–79.

35. Julia Collins, "Image and Advertising," *Harvard Business Review* (January–February 1989), pp. 93–97.

36. Samir Husni, "Good Ideas Gone Awry," *Advertising Age* (October 23, 2000), p. S26.

37. Jeffery D. Zbar, "Papers Tackling Sprawl," *Advertising Age* (April 30, 2001), pp. S6, S7; Heather Holliday, "Papers, TV Stations Extend War to Web," *Advertising Age* (April 30, 2001), p. S8; Mary Ellen Podmolik, "Urban Tabloids Snare Hipper Young Readers," *Advertising Age* (April 30, 2001), p. S2; and Kim Cleland, "Online Soon to Snare 100-plus Newspapers," *Advertising Age* (April 24, 1995), p. S6.

38. Sandeep Krishnamurthy, "Deciphering the Internet Advertising Puzzle," *Marketing Management* (Fall 2000), pp. 35–39; Judy Strauss and Raymond Frost, *Marketing on the Internet: Principles of Online Marketing* (Englewood Cliffs, NJ: Prentice Hall, 1999), pp. 196–249; and Maricris G. Briones, "Rich Media May Be Too Rich for Your Blood," *Marketing News* (March 29, 1999), p. 4.

39. Heather Green and Ben Elgin, "Do e-Ads Have a Future?" *Business Week* (January 22, 2001), p. EB46; Ellen Neuborne, "For Kids on the Web, It's an Ad, Ad, Ad, Ad World," *Business Week* (August 13, 2001), p. 108; Ellen Neuborne, "Beyond the Banner Ad," *Business Week* (December 11, 2000), p. 16; Laurel Wentz, "Moo-It-Yourself," *Advertising Age* (July 9, 2001), p. 28.

40. Dana Blankenhorn, "Bigger, Richer Ads Go Online," *Advertising Age* (June 18, 2001), p. T10; Patricia Riedman, "Poor Rich Media," *Advertising Age* (February 5, 2001), p. 26; Heather Green, "Net Advertising: Still the 98-Pound Weakling," *Business Week* (September 11, 2000), p. 36; Thom Weidlich, "Online Spots—A New Generation," *Advertising Age* (July 30, 2001), p. S10.

41. Arch G. Woodside, "Outdoor Advertising as Experiments," *Journal of the Academy of Marketing Science,* vol. 18 (Summer 1990), pp. 229–37.

42. Ronald Grover, "Billboards Aren't Boring Anymore," *Business Week* (September 21, 1998), pp. 86–90; and Marc Gunther, "The Great Outdoors," *Fortune* (March 1, 1999), p. 150–57.

43. James Betzold, "Jaded Riders Are Ever-Tougher Sell," *Advertising Age* (July 9, 2001), p. S2.

44. Charles R. Taylor and Weih Chang, "The History of Outdoor Advertising Regulation in the United States," *Journal of Macromarketing* (Spring 1995), pp. 47–59; Cyndee Miller, "Outdoor Advertising Weathers Repeated Attempts to Kill It," *Marketing News* (March 16, 1992), pp. 1, 9; Ricardo Davis, "Outdoor Ad Giants Trim Pay to Agencies," *Advertising Age* (January 18, 1993), p. 54; and Patricia Winters, "Outdoor Builds New Areas to Replace Tobacco and Liquor," *Advertising Age* (October 12, 1992), pp. 5–24.

45. Ed Brown, "Advertisers Skip to the Loo," *Fortune* (October 26, 1998), p. 64; John Cortex, "Growing Pains Can't Stop the New Kid on the Ad Block," *Advertising Age* (October 12, 1992), pp. 5–28; Allen Banks, "How to Assess New Place-Based Media," *Advertising Age* (November 30, 1992), p. 36; and John Cortex, "Media Pioneers Try to Corral On-the-Go Consumers," *Advertising Age* (August 17, 1992), p. 25.

46. "It's An Ad, Ad, Ad, Ad World," *Time* (July 9, 2001), p. 17; "Triton, Secora in Alliance for Advertising on ATMs," *Marketing News* (June 5, 2000), p. 12; Joan Oleck, "High-Octane Advertising," *Business Week* (November 29, 1999), p. 8.

47. Sehoon Park and Minhi Hahn, "Pulsing in a Discrete Model of Advertising Competition," *Journal of Marketing Research* (November 1991), pp. 397–405.

48. Peggy Masterson, "The Wearout Phenomenon," *Marketing Research* (Fall 1999), pp. 27–31; Lawrence D. Gibson, "What Can One TV Exposure Do?" *Journal of Advertising Research* (March–April 1996), pp. 9–18.

49. Rob Norton, "How Uninformative Advertising Tells Consumers Quite a Bit," *Fortune* (December 26, 1994), p. 37; and "Professor Claims Corporations Waste Billions on Advertising," *Marketing News* (July 6, 1992), p. 5.

50. Jack Neff, "Feeling the Squeeze," *Advertising Age* (June 4, 2001), pp. 1, 14–15; Laura Q. Hughes, "Measuring Up," *Advertising Age* (February 5, 2001), pp. 1, 34.

51. The discussion of posttesting is based on William F. Arens, *Contemporary Advertising,* 6th ed. (Burr Ridge, IL: Richard D. Irwin, 1996), pp. 181–82.

52. David A. Aaker and Douglas M. Stayman, "Measuring Audience Perceptions of Commercials and Relating Them to Ad Impact," *Journal of Advertising Research*, vol. 30 (August/September 1990), pp. 7–17; and Ernest Dichter, "A Psychological View of Advertising Effectiveness," *Marketing Management*, vol. 1, no. 3 (1992), pp. 60–62.

53. David Kruegel, "Television Advertising Effectiveness and Research Innovation," *Journal of Consumer Marketing* (Summer 1988), pp. 43–51; and Laurence N. Gold, "The Evolution of Television Advertising Sales Measurement: Past, Present, and Future," *Journal of Advertising Research* (June/July 1988), pp. 19–24.

54. "A Cautionary Tale," *PROMO'S 9th Annual Sourcebook* (2002), pp. 12–14.

55. Magid M. Abraham and Leonard M. Lodish, "Getting the Most out of Advertising and Promotion," *Harvard Business Review* (May–June 1990), pp. 50–60; Steven W. Hartley and James Cross, "How Sales Promotion Can Work for and against You," *Journal of Consumer Marketing* (Summer 1988), pp. 35–42; Robert D. Buzzell, John A. Quelch, and Walter J. Salmon, "The Costly Bargain of Trade Promotion," *Harvard Business Review* (March–April 1990), pp. 141–49; and Mary L. Nicastro, "Break-Even Analysis Determines Success of Sales Promotions," *Marketing News* (March 5, 1990), p. 11.

56. Betsy Spethmann, "Going for Broke," *PROMO* (August 2001), pp. 27–31; Mathew Kinsman, "Bad Is Good," *PROMO* (April 2001), pp. 71–74; "Nowhere to Go but Up," *PROMO'S 9th Annual Sourcebook* (2002), pp. 22–23.

57. Kapil Bawa and Robert W. Shoemaker, "Analyzing Incremental Sales from a Direct-Mail Coupon Promotion," *Journal of Marketing* (July 1998), pp. 66–78.

58. Roger A. Strang, "Sales Promotion—Fast Growth, Faulty Management," *Harvard Business Review*, vol. 54 (July–August 1976), pp. 115–24; and Ronald W. Ward and James E. Davis, "Coupon Redemption," *Journal of Advertising Research*, vol. 18 (August 1978), pp. 51–58. Similar results on favorable mail-distributed coupons were reported by Alvin Schwartz, "The Influence of Media Characteristics on Coupon Redemption," *Journal of Marketing*, vol. 30 (January 1966), pp. 41–46.

59. "Competing with Coupons," *Marketing News* (March 15, 1999), p. 2; and Larry Armstrong. "Coupon Clippers, Save Your Scissors," *Business Week* (June 20, 1994), pp. 164–66.

60. Michael Scroggie, "Online Coupon Debate," *PROMO* (April 2000); "Coupon Fraud Indicted," *PROMO* (June 2000); "Experts Warn about E-Coupon Fraud," *Brandmarketing* (June 2000), p. 38; "Nine Steps to a Fraud-Proof Rebate Form," *PROMO* (December 1994), p. 16; Kerry Smith, "The Promotion Gravy Train," *PROMO* (August 1995), pp. 50–52; Christopher Power, "Coupon Scams Are Clipping Companies," *Business Week* (June 15, 1992), pp. 110–11; and Kerry J. Smith, "Coupon Scam Uncovered in Detroit," *PROMO* (December 1992), pp. 1, 45.

61. Carrie MacMillan, "Creature Features," *PROMO* (October 2001); Dan Hanover, "Not Just for Breakfast Anymore," *PROMO* (September 2001).

62. "Rising to the Top," *PROMO* (September 2001), pp. 46–62.

63. Lorraine Woellert, "The Sweepstakes Biz Isn't Feeling Lucky," *Business Week* (March 22, 1999), p. 80.

64. Carrie MacMillan, "Star Makers," *PROMO* (August 2001), pp. 75–78.

65. Edward Kabak, "Staking Out the States," *PROMO* (October 2001); Richard Sale, "Sweeping the Courts," *PROMO* (May 1998), pp. 42–45; and Fred C. Allvine, Richard D. Teach, and John Connelly, Jr., "The Demise of Promotional Games," *Journal of Advertising Research*, vol. 16 (October 1976), pp. 79–84.

66. "Best Activity Generating Brand Awareness/Trial," *PROMO* (September 2001), p. 51; "Brand Handing," *PROMO's 9th Annual Sourcebook* (2002), p. 32.

67. Dan Hanover, "Pay Dirt," *PROMO* (July 2001), pp. 25–26.

68. Cyndee Miller, "P-O-P Gains Followers as 'Era of Retailing' Dawns," *Marketing News* (May 14, 1990), p. 2.

69. Jeff Neff, "Floors in Stores Start Moving," *Advertising Age* (August 20, 2001), p. 15.

70. Sholnn Freeman, "Big Three Auto Makers Call on Rebates, Financing Bargains to Sell More Vehicles," *The Wall Street Journal* (May 10, 2001), p. A4; "Walking the Tight Rope, Rebates Remain a Love Em or Hate Em Proposition," *PROMO* (March 2001).

71. Marvin A. Jolson, Joshua L. Wiener, and Richard B. Rosecky, "Correlates of Rebate Proneness," *Journal of Advertising Research* (February–March 1987), pp. 33–43.

72. Paula Lyon Andruss, "Survivor Packages Make Real-Life Money," *Marketing News* (March 26, 2001), p. 5; Wayne Friedman, "Eagle-Eye Marketers Find Right Spot, Right Time," *Advertising Age* (January 22, 2001), p. S2; David Goetzl, "TBS Tries Virtual Advertising," *Advertising Age* (May 21, 2001), p. 8; James Poniewozik, "This Plug's for You," *Time* (June 18, 2001) p. 76–77; "Never Say Never Again," *PROMO* (October 2001), p. 16.

73. Danon Darlin, "Junior Mints, I'm Going to Make You a Star," *Forbes* (November 6, 1995), pp. 90–94.

74. This discussion is drawn particularly from John A. Quelch, *Trade Promotions by Grocery Manufacturers: A Management Perspective* (Cambridge, MA: Marketing Science Institute, August 1982).

75. Michael Chevalier and Ronald C. Curhan, "Retail Promotions as a Function of Trade Promotions: A Descriptive Analysis," *Sloan Management Review*, vol. 18 (Fall 1976), pp. 19–32.

76. G. A. Marken, "Firms Can Maintain Control over Creative Co-op Programs," *Marketing News* (September 28, 1992), pp. 7, 9.

77. "Safetyforum.com and Public Citizen Report: NHTSA Forces Firestone to Recall Defective Tires, Expand Wilderness ATs Recall," *PR Newswire* (October 5, 2001); Cindy Skrzycki and Frank Swoboda, "Firestone Refuses Voluntary Recall," Safetyforum.com (July 20, 2001); Jim Suhr, "Tire Recall Response Time Defended," Safetyforum.com (August 10, 2000).

78. Scott Hue, "Free 'Plugs' Supply Ad Power," *Advertising Age* (January 29, 1990), p. 6.

79. Mike Harris, "Earnhardt's Lap Belt Was Broken," Safetyforum.com (February 23, 2001); and Marc Weinberger, Jean Romeo, and Azhar Piracha, "Negative Product Safety News: Coverage, Responses, and Effects," *Business Horizons* (May–June 1991), pp. 23–31.

80. Irving Rein, Philip Kotler, and Martin Stoller, *High Visibility* (New York: Dodd, Mead, 1987); and Steven Colford, "Ross Perot: A Winner after All," *Advertising Age* (December 21, 1992), pp. 4, 18.

81. Michael Treacy and Fred Wiersema, "Customer Intimacy and Other Value Disciplines," *Harvard Business Review* (January–February 1993), pp. 84–93.

82. Gerry Khermouch and Tom Lowry, "The Future of Advertising," *Business Week* (March 26, 2001), p. 139; D. J., "Outlook 2001: Advertising," *Marketing News* (January 1, 2001), p. 10.

83. Betsy Spethmann, "McFallout," *PROMO* (October, 2001), pp. 31–38.

84. "Kid Stuff," *PROMO*, vol. 4 (January 1991), pp. 25, 42; Steven W. Colford, "Fine-Tuning Kids' TV," *Advertising Age* (February 11, 1991), p. 35; and Kate Fitzgerald, "Toys Star-Struck for Movie Tie-Ins," *Advertising Age* (February 18, 1991), p. 3, 45.

85. Herbert J. Rotfeld, Avery M. Abernathy, and Patrick R. Parsons, "Self-Regulation and Television Advertising," *Journal of Advertising*, vol. 19, no. 4 (1990), pp. 18–26.

The Fallon Worldwide case© was written by Mark T. Spriggs and William Rudelius based on interviews with Fallon personnel and materials on the Lee Dungarees and BMW promotional campaigns provided by Lee, BMW, and Fallon. The BMW case history is used with permission of BMW of North America, LLC.The BMW name and logo are registered trademarks.

CHAPTER 20

1. Kathleen Cholewka, "Xerox's Savior?" *Sales & Marketing Management* (April 2001), pp. 36–42; "Anne Mulcahy Named Xerox Chief Executive Officer," www.xerox.com, downloaded July 26, 2001; and "She's Here to Fix the Xerox," *Business Week* (August 6, 2001), pp. 47–48.

2. "Who's the Boss," *Sales & Marketing Report* (May 2001), p. 7.

3. "America's 25 Best Sales Forces," *Sales & Marketing Management* (July 2000), pp. 57–85.

4. For recent representative research on and commentary on relationship selling, see James Boles, Thomas Brashear, Danny Bellenger, and Hiram Barksdale, Jr., "Relationship Selling Behaviors: Antecedents and Relationship with Performance," *Journal of Business & Industrial Marketing*, vol. 15, no. 2/3 (2000), pp. 141–53; Neil Rackham, *Rethinking the Sales Force* (New York: McGraw-Hill, 1999); and Barton A. Weitz and Kevin D. Bradford, "Personal Selling and Sales Management: A Relationship Marketing Perspective," *Journal of the Academy of Marketing Science* (Spring 1999), pp. 241–54.

5. David W. Cravens, "The Changing Role of the Sales Force," *Marketing Management* (Fall 1995), pp. 49–57.

6. Douglas J. Dalrymple, William L. Cron, and Thomas E. DeCarlo, *Sales Management*, 7th ed. (New York: Wiley, 2001), pp. 55–57.

7. For a perspective on types of selling, see Thomas R. Wotruba, "The Evolution of Personal Selling," *Journal of Personal Selling & Sales Management* (Summer 1991), pp. 1–12. See also René Y. Darmon, "A Conceptual Scheme and Procedure for Classifying Sales Positions," *Journal of Personal Selling & Sales Management* (Summer 1998), pp. 31–46.

8. Christen Heide, *Dartnell's 31st Salesforce Compensation Survey 2000* (Chicago: Dartnell Corporation, 2000), p. 176.

9. "What a Sales Call Costs," *Sales & Marketing Management* (September 2000), p. 80.

10. "Keep Calling!" *Sales & Marketing Report* (May 2001), p. 3.

11. For representative research and commentary on team selling, see Keith A. Chrzanowski and Thomas W. Leigh, "Customer Relationship Strategy and Customer-Focused Teams," in Gerald J. Bauer et al., *Emerging Trends in Sales Thought and Practice* (Westport, CT: Quorum Books, 1998); and Mark A. Moon and Susan Forquer Gupta, "Examining the Formation of Selling Centers: A Conceptual Framework," *Journal of Personal Selling & Sales Management* (Spring 1997), pp. 31–41.

12. Neil Rackham, Lawrence Friedman, and Richard Ruff, *Getting Partnering Right* (New York: McGraw-Hill, 1996), pp. 47–48; and "The Selling Game," *The Wall Street Journal* (March 29, 1994), p. A1.

13. For a brief overview on prospecting, see "The Best Way to Prospect," *Sales & Marketing Management* (January 1998), p. 80.

14. Carol J. Loomis, "Have You Been Cold-Called?" *Fortune* (December 16, 1991), pp. 109–15.

15. "Corporate Cultures: Clearing Customs," *SKY Magazine* (July 1995), pp. 35–40.

16. "Don't Call Laws Raise False Hope for Peace, Quiet," *The Wall Street Journal* (December 22, 2000), pp. B1, B4.

17. "Out of the Cold: Banned from Cold Calling, Amex Financial Reps Have to Warm Up to Referrals," *Selling* (May 1996), pp. 22–24.

18. Paul. A. Herbing, *Handbook of Cross-Cultural Marketing* (New York: Holworth Press, 1998).

19. "What Do Customers Hate about Salespeople?" *Sales & Marketing Management* (June 2001), pp. 43–51.

20. "Japanese Business Etiquette," *Smart Business* (August 2000), p. 55.

21. For an extensive discussion on adaptive selling, see Barton Weitz, Stephen B. Castleberry, and John F. Tanner, Jr., *Selling: Building Partnerships*, 4th ed. (Burr Ridge, IL: McGraw-Hill/Irwin, 2001), chapter 6.

22. F. Robert Dwyer and John F. Tanner, *Business Marketing*, 2nd ed. (Burr Ridge, IL: McGraw-Hill/Irwin, 2002), p. 400.

23. "America's 25 Best Sales Forces," *Sales & Marketing Management.*

24. For an extensive discussion of objections, see Charles M. Futrell, *Fundamentals of Selling* (New York: Irwin/McGraw-Hill, 2002), chapter 10.

25. Philip R. Cateora and John L. Graham, *International Marketing*, 10th ed. (New York: Irwin/McGraw-Hill, 1999), pp. 128, 131; and Herbing, *Handbook of Cross-Cultural Marketing*, p. 60.

26. Theodore Levitt, *The Marketing Imagination* (New York: Free Press, 1983), p. 111.

27. "Leading Edge," *Sales & Marketing Management* (July 1995), p. 13. See also "Focus on the Customer," *Fortune* (September 7, 1998), special advertising section.

28. *Management Briefing: Sales and Marketing* (New York: Conference Board, October 1996), pp. 3–4.

29. "Why It Pays to Be Curious," *Sales & Marketing Management* (August 1998), p. 76.

30. Alan J. Dubinsky, Marvin A. Jolson, Ronald E. Michaels, Masaaki Katobe, and Chae Un Lim, "Ethical Perceptions of Field Sales Personnel: An Empirical Assessment," *Journal of Personal Selling & Sales Management* (Fall 1992), pp. 9–21; and Alan J. Dubinsky, Marvin A. Jolson, Masaaki Katobe, and Chae Un Lim, "A Cross-National Investigation of Industrial Salespeople's Ethical Perceptions," *Journal of International Business Studies* (Fourth Quarter 1991), pp. 651–70.

31. See Gilbert A. Churchill, Jr., Neil M. Ford, Orville C. Walker, Jr., Mark W. Johnson, and John F. Tanner, Jr., *Sales Force Management*, 6th ed. (Burr Ridge, IL: Irwin/McGraw-Hill, 2000), pp. 101–4.

32. Churchill et al., *Sales Force Management*, pp. 110–13. Also see Arun Sharma, "Who Prefers Key Account Management Programs? An Investigation of Business Buying Behavior and Buying Firm Characteristics," *Journal of Personal Selling & Sales Management* (Fall 1997), pp. 37–30; Dan C. Weilbaker and William A. Weeks, "The Evolution of National Account Management: A Literature Perspective," *Journal of Personal Selling & Management* (Fall 1997), pp. 49–50; and Paul Dishman and Philip S. Nitse, "National Accounts Revisited," *Industrial Marketing Management* (January 1998), pp. 1–9.

33. Several variations of the account management policy grid exist. See, for example, Dalrymple, Cron, and DeCarlo, *Sales Management*, pp. 173–74; Churchill et al., *Sales Force Management*, pp. 190–92.

34. Patricia Sellers, "How to Remake Your Sales Force," *Fortune* (May 4, 1992), p. 103. See also "Look Who's Calling," *Sales & Marketing Management* (May 1998), pp. 43–46.

35. This discussion is based on Dalrymple, Cron, and DeCarlo, *Sales Management*, pp. 325–31.

36. See, for example, "What Do Customers Hate about Salespeople?" *Sales & Marketing Management;* "What Buyers Look For," *Sales & Marketing Management* (August 1995), p. 31; and "The Best Sales Reps Will Take On Their Bosses for You," *Purchasing* (November 7, 1996), p. 81.

37. Weitz, Castleberry, and Tanner, *Selling*, p. 21. For further reading see Daniel Goleman, "What Makes a Leader?" *Harvard Business Review* (November–December 1998), pp. 93–102; A. Fisher, "Success Secret: A High Emotional IQ," *Fortune* (October 26, 1998), pp. 293–98; and Daniel Goleman, *Working with Emotional Intelligence* (New York: Bantam, 1999).

38. *Statistical Abstract of the United States*, 120th ed. (Washington, DC: U.S. Department of Commerce, 2000). See also, Lucette B. Comer, J. A. F. Nicholls, and Leslie J. Vermillion, "Diversity in the Sales Force: Problems and Challenges," *Journal of Personal Selling & Marketing* (Fall 1998), pp. 1–20; and *Occupational Outlook Quarterly* (Washington, DC: U.S. Department of Labor, Fall 2001).

39. "America's 25 Best Sales Forces," *Sales & Marketing Management.*

40. "Training #9010: Overview and Statistics," *Sales Marketing Network,* www.infonow.com, downloaded January 5, 2001.

41. See, for example, Nora Wood, "What Motivates Best?" *Sales & Marketing Management* (September 1998), pp. 71–78; Melanie Berger, "When Their Ship Comes In," *Sales & Marketing Management* (April 1997), pp. 60–65; William L. Cron, Alan J. Dubinsky, and Ronald E. Michaels, "The Influence of Career Stages on Components of Salesperson Motivation," *Journal of Marketing* (January 1988), pp. 78–82; Pradeep K. Tyagi, "Relative Importance of Key Job Dimensions and Leadership Behaviors in Motivating Salesperson Work Performance," *Journal of Marketing* (Summer 1985), pp. 76–86; and Richard C. Beckerer, Fred Morgan, and Lawrence Richard, "The Job Characteristics of Industrial Salespersons: Relationship of Motivation and Satisfaction," *Journal of Marketing* (Fall 1982), pp. 125–35.

42. This breakdown is given in Dalrymple, Cron, and DeCarlo, *Sales Management*, p. 476.

43. "Mary Kay's Off-Road Bonus," *Business Week* (April 6, 1998), p. 8.

44. "Number Crunching," *Sales & Marketing Management* (September 2000), pp. 79–88.

45. For further reading, see Goutam N. Challagolla and Tasadduq A. Shervani, "A Measurement Model of the Dimensions and Types of Output and Behavior Control: An Empirical Test in the Salesforce Context," *Journal of Business Research* (July 1997), pp. 159–72; and Gregory A. Rich, William H. Bommer, Scott B. McKenzie, Philip M. Podsakoff, and Jonathan L. Johnson, "Apples and Apples or Apples and Oranges? A Meta-Analysis of Objective and Subjective Measures of Salesperson Performance," *Journal of Personal Selling & Sales Management* (Fall 1999), pp. 41–52.

46. "Measuring Sales Effectiveness," *Sales & Marketing Management* (October 2000), p. 136; "Quota Busters," *Sales & Marketing Management* (January 2001), pp. 59–63.

47. Melissa Campanelli, "Eastman Chemical: A Formula for Quality," *Sales & Marketing Management* (October 1994), p. 88; William Keenan, Jr., "What's Sales Got to Do with It?" *Sales & Marketing*

Management (March 1994), pp. 66–70; and Cravens, "The Changing Role of the Sales Force," *Marketing Management.*

48. "Costly Lessons Abound with SFA Programs," *Marketing News* (April 9, 2001), pp. 5–6.

49. Cravens, "The Changing Role of the Sales Force," *Marketing Management.*

50. Robert L. Lindstrom, "Training Hits the Road," *Sales & Marketing Management,* part 2 (June 1995), pp. 10–14.

51. "Going Mobile, Part 2," *Sales & Marketing Management* (June 1994), p. 5.

52. "Supercharged Sell," *Inc. Tech* (November 1998), pp. 42–50.

53. "Intranets Grow Up," *Sales & Marketing Management* (December 2000), p. 105.

Reebok: This case was written by Giana Eckhardt.

CHAPTER 21

1. Rafi A. Mohammed, Robert J. Fisher, Bernard J. Jaworski, and Aileen M. Cahill, *Internet Marketing: Building Advantage in a Networked Economy* (Burr Ridge, IL: McGraw-Hill/Irwin, 2002); and Yoram Wind, Vijay Mahajan with Robert E. Gunther, *Convergence Marketing* (Upper Saddle River, NJ: Prentice Hall, 2002).

2. "NPD e-Visory Report Shows Offline Sales Benefit from Online Browsing," *The NPD Group Press Release* (July 21, 2001).

3. Jupiter Media Matrix, "Industry Projections," www.jmm.com, downloaded September 22, 2001.

4. "Strip Malls Are Gateway Country," *The Industry Standard* (November 27–December 4, 2000), pp. 82–86.

5. "The Five-Year Forecast," *The Industry Standard* (March 26, 2001), pp. 82–83.

6. Michael Weiss, "Online America," *American Demographics* (March 21, 2001), pp. 53–60.

7. Mohammed et al., *Internet Marketing.*

8. Adrian J. Slywotzky, "The Age of the Choiceboard," *Harvard Business Review* (January–February 2000), pp. 40–41.

9. Christine Bittar, "Reflect: A Palatable Model," *Brandweek* (April 2, 2001), pp. 18–24; and "Reflect.com Shines Despite Downturn," *Silicon Valley Business iNK* (May 4, 2001), pp. 31–32.

10. For a description of collaborative filtering and similar types of systems, see Ward Hanson, *Principles of Internet Marketing* (Cincinnati, OH: South-Western College Publishing, 2000), pp. 207–19.

11. Michael Grebb, "Behavioral Science," *Business 2.0* (March 2000), p. 112.

12. Alan Rosenspan, "Participation Marketing," *Direct Marketing* (April 2001), pp. 54–66.

13. "More Web Users Wage a Guerrilla War on Nosy Sites," *U.S. News & World Report* (August 28, 2000), p. 59.

14. This discussion is drawn from Jeffrey F. Rayport and Bernard J. Jaworski, *e-Commerce* (Burr Ridge, IL: McGraw-Hill/Irwin MarketspaceU, 2001); and Mohammed et al., *Internet Marketing.*

15. *Home Computers and Internet Use in the United States* (Washington, DC: U.S. Census Bureau, September 2001), p. 3.

16. "Statistics: U.S. Online Shoppers," Shop.org. downloaded September 14, 2001.

17. "The Clicks-and-Bricks Way to Buy That Car," *Business Week* (May 7, 2001), pp. 128–30; and *The Next Chapter in Business-to-Consumer E-Commerce* (Boston: The Boston Consulting Group, March 2001).

18. "Statistics: U.S. Online Shoppers," Shop.org.

19. "The 90/20 Rule of e-Commerce: Nearly 90% of Online Sales Accounted for by 20% of Consumers," *Cyber Dialogue Press Release,* September 25, 2000.

20. Weiss, "Online America," *American Demographics.*

21. This discussion is based on "A Hard Sell Online? Think Again," *Business Week* (July 12, 1999), pp. 142–43; Paul Foley and David Sulton, "Boom Time for Electronic Commerce—Rhetoric or Reality?" *Business Horizons* (September–October 1998), pp. 21–30;

and Forrester Research estimates reported in "Briefing: Business to Consumer," *Red Herring* (June 1, 2001), p. 54.

22. "Branding on the Net," *Business Week* (November 2, 1998), pp. 78–86.

23. "How to Lose a Customer in a Matter of Seconds," *Fortune* (June 12, 2000), p. 326.

24. Jerry Wind and Arvind Rangaswamy, "Customerization: The Next Revolution in Mass Customization," *Journal of Interactive Marketing* (Winter 2001), pp. 13–32.

25. Mohammed et al., *Internet Marketing.*

26. "Global Babble," *Forbes* (October 15, 2001), p. 51.

27. "What's So New about the 'New Economy'? Glad You Asked . . ." *Business 2.0* (August/September 2001), p. 84.

28. For references on buzz and viral marketing, see "Buzz Marketing," *Business Week* (July 30, 2001), pp. 50–56; Renée Dye, "The Buzz on Buzz," *Harvard Business Review* (November–December 2000), pp. 139–46; "The Cool Kids Are Doing It. Should You?" *Business 2.0* (November 2001), pp. 140–41; "This Is One Virus You Want to Spread," *Fortune* (November 27, 2000), pp. 297–300; and "Why Are These CEOs Smiling?" *Time* (November 5, 2001), pp. Y1–Y4.

29. "Now Is the Price Right?" *Smart Business* (February 2001), pp. 36–38; and "Price Isn't Everything," *The Wall Street Journal* (July 12, 1999), p. R20.

30. Weiss, "Online America," *American Demographics.*

31. "Branding on the Net," *Business Week.*

32. "Exposure in Cyberspace," *The Wall Street Journal* (March 21, 2001), p. B1; "Today's Privacy Policies Don't Protect e-Shoppers, Advocate Charges," *Computer World* (April 24, 2001), pp. 42–43; Pamela Paul, "Mixed Signals," *American Demographics* (July 2001), pp. 45–49; and "It's My Life," *The Wall Street Journal* (October 29, 2001), p. R9.

33. Clay Hathorn, "Online Business: Trying to Turn Cookies into Dough," *Microsoft Internet Magazine Archive,* www.microsoft.com, downloaded February 15, 1999.

34. This discussion is based on "By the Numbers: Buying Breakdown," *The Wall Street Journal* (September 24, 2001), p. R4; "Factoids," *Research Alert* (November 17, 2000), p. 4; and Weiss, "Online America," *American Demographics.*

35. Weiss, "Online America," *American Demographics.*

36. "NPD e-Visory Report Shows Offline Sales Benefit from Online Browsing," *The NPD Group Press Release.*

37. "Eddie Bauer's Banner Time of Year," *Advertising Age* (October 1, 2001), p. 55.

38. For an extended discussion on leveraging multiple channels with multichannel marketing, see Ranjay Gulati and Jason Garino, "Get the Right Mix of Bricks and Clicks," *Harvard Business Review* (May–June 2000), pp.107–14.

39. "Office Depot Finds an E-Business That Works," *Fortune* (March 25, 2001), p. 98.

40. *Multi-Channel Integration: The New Retail Battleground* (Columbus, OH: PricewaterhouseCoopers, March 2001); and Richard Last, "JC Penney Internet Commerce," presentation at Southern Methodist University (February 12, 2001).

41. Michael Krantz, "Click Till You Drop," *Time* (July 20, 1998), pp. 34–39.

42. *Multi-Channel Integration: The New Retail Battleground.*

43. "Don't Cut Back Now," *Business Week e-biz* (October 1, 2001), p. EB 34.

44. *Fighting Fire with Water—from Channel Conflict to Confluence* (Cambridge, MA: Bain & Company, July 1, 2000).

45. "Can the Internet Hot-Wire P&G?" *Smart Business* (January 2001), pp. 69–79.

46. Tom Duncan, *IMC: Using Advertising and Promotion to Build Brands* (New York: McGraw-Hill, 2002); and Larry Chiagouris and Brandt Wansley, "Branding on the Internet," *Marketing Management* (Summer 2000), pp. 35–38.

47. *The Next Chapter in Business-to-Consumer E-Commerce: Advantage Incumbent* (reference cited).

America Online, Inc.: This case was written by Michael Vessey and Steven Hartley based on information from the AOL Time Warner corporate website (www.aoltimewarner.com) and the America Online company website (www.corp.aol.com) and the following sources: "AOL's Sputtering Online Growth Engine," *Business Week* (January 21, 2002), p. 37; Catherine Yang and Tom Lowry, "AOL Time Warner Aiming Too High?" *Business Week* (September 10, 2001), p. 98; Catherine Yang and Hay Greene, "AOL vs. Microsoft," *Business Week* (August 13, 2001), p. 28; Amy Borrus, "AOL's Point Man in the Web War," *Business Week* (July 2, 2001), p. 56; Jay Greene, "Why AOL Nixed a Microsoft Deal," *Business Week* (July 2, 2001), p. 58; Robert Barker, "A Yardstick for AOL Time Warner," *Business Week* (February 26, 2001), p. 124; Monica Roman, "AOL, Sony, and the Connected Home," *Business Week* (November 26, 2001), p. 51; Monica Roman, "AOL's Sprint into Long Distance," *Business Week* (December 10, 2001), p. 42.

CHAPTER 22

1. Richard Gibson, "A Cereal Maker's Quest for the Next Grape-Nuts," *The Wall Street Journal* (January 23, 1997), pp. B1, B7.

2. David Leonhardt, "Cereal-Box Killers Are on the Loose," *Business Week* (October 12, 1998), pp. 74–77.

3. *1997 General Mills Annual Report* (Minneapolis: General Mills, Inc., 1997), p. 5.

4. *2000 General Mills Annual Report* (Minneapolis: General Mills, Inc., 2000), p. 2; *2000 Kellogg's Annual Report* (Battle Creek: Kellogg Company, 2000), p. 7; Alejandro Bodipo-Memba, "Kellogg's Concedes Top Spot to Rival," *Detroit Free Press* (February 22, 2001) (see www.freep.com/newslibrary to access the article online).

5. H. D. Cantu, "Kellogg's Teaching Tony the Tiger Spanish," *Corvallis Gazette-Times* (February 25, 2000), p. C5; and *2000 General Mills Annual Report* (Minneapolis: General Mills, Inc., 2000), pp. 2–3, 12–13.

6. Ellen Neuborne, "MMM! Cereal for Dinner," *Business Week* (November 24, 1997), pp. 105–6.

7. Ann Merrill, "Pillsbury Acquisition a Done Deal," *Star Tribune* (October 24, 2001), pp. A1, A10.

8. Roger A. Kerin, P. Rajan Varadarajan, and Robert A. Peterson, "First-Mover Advantage: A Synthesis, Conceptual Framework, and Research Proposition," *Journal of Marketing* (October 1992), pp. 33–52; and Pankaj Ghemawat, "Sustainable Advantage," *Harvard Business Review* (September–October 1986), pp. 53–58.

9. Murali K. Mantrala, Prabhakant Sirha, and Andris A. Zoltners, "Impact of Resource Allocation Rules on Marketing Investment-Level Decisions and Profitability," *Journal of Marketing Research* (May 1992), pp. 162–75.

10. Vanitha Swaminathan, Richard J. Fox, and Srinivas K. Reddy, "The Impact of Brand Extension Introduction on Choice," *Journal of Marketing* (October 2001), pp. 1–15; Deborah Roedder-John, Barbara Loken, and Christopher Joiner, "The Negative Impact of Extensions: Can Flagship Products Be Diluted?" *Journal of Marketing* (January 1998), pp. 19–32; and Akshay R. Rao, Lu Qu, and Robert W. Ruekert, "Signalling Unobservable Product Quality through a Brand Ally," *Journal of Marketing Research* (May 1999), pp. 258–68.

11.. This discussion and Figure 22–3 are adapted from Stanley F. Stasch and Patricis Longtree, "Can Your Marketing Planning Procedures Be Improved?" *Journal of Marketing* (Summer 1980), p. 82; by permission of the American Marketing Association.

12. Terry Fledler, "Soul of a New Cheerios," *Star Tribune* (January 28, 1996), pp. D1, D4; and Tony Kennedy, "New Cheerios about to Sweeten Cereal Market," *Star Tribune* (July 25, 1995), pp. 1D, 2D.

13. Adapted with permission of The Free Press, a Division of Macmillan, Inc., from *Competitive Advantage: Creating and Sustaining Superior Performance* by Michael E. Porter. Copyright 1985 by Michael E. Porter.

14. William B. Wertner, Ic, and Jeffrey L. Kerr, "The Shifting Sands of Competitive Advantage," *Business Horizons* (May–June, 1995), pp. 11–17.

15. Michael Treacy and Fred Wiersoma, "How Market Leaders Keep Their Edge," *Fortune* (February 5, 1995), pp. 88–89.

16. Keith Naughton and Bill Viasie, "The Nostalgia Boom," *Business Week* (March 23, 1998), pp. 58–64; and David Woodruff and Keith Naughton, "Hard Driving Boss," *Business Week* (October 5, 1998), pp. 82–90.

17. J. Martin Fraering and Michael S. Minor, "The Industry-Specific Basis of the Market Share-Profitability Relationship," *Journal of Consumer Marketing*, vol. 11, no. 1 (1994), pp. 27–37.

18. Zachary Schiller, Greg Burns, and Karen Lowry Miller, "Make It Simple," *Business Week* (September 9, 1996), pp. 96–104.

19. Richard Siklos and Catherine Yang, "Welcome to the 21st Century," *Business Week* (January 24, 2000), pp. 36–47; and Carol J. Loomis, "AOL + TWX = ???" *Fortune* (February 7, 2000), pp. 81–84.

20. John Greenwald, "Slice, Dice, and Devour," *Time* (October 26, 1998), pp. 64–66.

21. Stratford Sherman, "How Intel Makes Spending Pay Off," *Fortune* (February 22, 1993), pp. 57–61.

22. Ann Merrill, "A Lot to Digest," *Star Tribune* (October 26, 2001), pp. D1, D2.

23. Jonathan Eig, "General Mills Intends to Reshape Doughboy in Its Own Image," *The Wall Street Journal* (July 18, 2000), pp. A1, A8; Julie Forster, "The Lucky Charm of Steve Sanger," *Business Week* (March 26, 2001), pp. 75–76; *2000 General Mills Annual Report*, pp. 1–13; Joseph L. Bower, "Not All MAs Are Alike—and That Matters," *Harvard Business Review* (March 2001), pp. 92–101.

24. *2000 General Mills Annual Report*, pp. 8–13.

25. Lee Ginsburg and Neil Miller, "Value-Driven Management," *Business Horizons* (May–June 1992), pp. 23–27; Richard L. Osborn, "Core Value Statement: The Corporate Compass," *Business Horizons* (September–October 1991), pp. 28–34; and Charles E. Watson, "Managing with Integrity: Social Responsibilities of Business as Seen by America's CEOs," *Business Horizons* (July–August 1991), pp. 99–109.

26. Carl W. Stern and George Stalk, Jr., eds., *Perspectives on Strategy from the Boston Consulting Group* (New York: Wiley, 1998), pp. 13–42.

27. Reprinted by permission of the *Harvard Business Review*. An exhibit from "Making Your Marketing Strategy Work" by Thomas V. Bonoma (March/April 1984), Copyright ©1984 by the President and Fellows of Harvard College; all rights reserved; and Charles H. Noble and Michael P. Mokwa, "Implementing Marketing Strategies: Developing and Testing a Managerial Theory," *Journal of Marketing* (October 1999), pp. 57–74.

28. Julia Angwin, "Latest Dot-Com Fad Is a Bit Old-Fashioned: It's Called Profitability," *The Wall Street Journal* (August 14, 2001), pp. A1, A6; Jerry Useem, "Dot-Coms: What Have We Learned," *Fortune* (October 30, 2000), pp. 82–96.

29. Jeffrey A. Krames, *The Jack Welch Lexicon of Leadership* (New York: McGraw-Hill, 2002), pp. 54–56, 105–8, 187–88; Robert Slater, *Jack Welch and the GE Way* (New York: McGraw-Hill, 1999), pp. 59–68, 77–88, 279–86; Nicholas Stein, "The World's Most Admired Companies," *Fortune* (October 2, 2000), pp. 183–91; and Jim Rohwer, "GE Digs into Asia," *Fortune* (October 2, 2000), pp. 165–78.

30. Daniel Roth, "This Ain't No Pizza Party," *Fortune* (November 9, 1998), pp. 158–64.

31. Thomas J. Peters and Robert H. Waterman, Jr., *In Search of Excellence: Lessons from America's Best-Run Companies* (New York: Harper & Row, 1982).

32. Tom Peters, "Winners Do Hundreds of Percent over Norm," *Minneapolis Star Tribune* (January 8, 1985), p. 5B; and Ben Rich and Leo Janos, *Skunk Works* (Boston: Little Brown, 1994), pp. 51–53.

33. The scheduling example is adapted from William Rudelius and W. Bruce Erickson, *An Introduction to Contemporary Business*, 4th ed. (New York: Harcourt Brace Jovanovich, 1985), pp. 94–95.

34. Peter Galuska, Ellen Neuborne, and Wendy Zeliner, "P&G's Hottest New Product: P&G," *Business Week* (October 5, 1998), pp. 92–96.

35. Robert W. Ruekert and Orville W. Walker, Jr., "Marketing's Interaction with Other Functional Units: A Conceptual Framework and Empirical Evidence," *Journal of Consumer Marketing* (Spring 1987), pp. 1–19. Shikhar Sarin and Vijay Mahajan, "The Effect of Reward Structures on the Performance of Cross-Functional Product Development Teams," *Journal of Marketing* (April 2001), pp. 35–53; and Amy Edmondson, Richard Bohmer, and Gary Pisano, "Speeding Up Team Learning," *Harvard Business Review* (October 2001), pp. 125–32.
36. Nelson D. Schwartz, "Colgate Cleans Up," *Fortune* (April 16, 2001), pp. 179–80.

The Golden Valley Microwave Foods case was written by Thomas J. Belich and Mark T. Spriggs based on personal interviews with Jack McKeon and Frank Lynch, and company data they provided.

APPENDIX C

1. Denny E. McCorkle, Joe F. Alexander, and Memo F. Diriker, "Developing Self-Marketing Skills for Student Career Success," *Journal of Marketing Education* (Spring 1992), pp. 57–67.
2. Joanne Cleaver, "Find A Job through Self-Promotion," *Marketing News* (January 31, 2000), pp. 12, 16; and James McBride, "Job-Search Strategies to Begin the Next Millenium," *Planning Job Choices: 1999,* 42nd ed. (Bethlehem, PA: National Association of Colleges and Employers, 1998), pp. 14–18.
3. Julie Rawe, "What Will Be the 10 Hottest Jobs?" *Time* (May 22, 2000), pp. 70–71; "Five 'New Economy' Careers for Liberal Arts Majors," *Job Choices in Business: 2002,* 45th ed. (Bethlehem, PA: National Association of Colleges and Employers, 2001), pp. 11–13.
4. *Job Choices in Business: 2002,* 45th ed. (Bethlehem, PA: National Association for Colleges and Employers, 2001), p. 10.
5. Nicholas Basta, "The Wide World of Marketing," *Business Week's Guide to Careers* (February–March 1984), pp. 70–72.
6. Paula Lyon Andruss, "So You Want to Be a CEO?" *Marketing News* (January 29, 2001), pp. 1, 10.
7. "Average Yearly Salary Offers," *Salary Survey* (Bethlehem, PA: National Association of Colleges and Employers, Summer 2001), pp. 6–7.
8. "Tomorrow's Jobs," *Occupational Outlook Handbook* (Indianapolis, IN: JIST Works, 2001), p. 4; and "Charting the Projections 1998–2008," *Occupational Outlook Quarterly* (Washington, DC: U.S. Department of Labor, Winter 1999–2000), p. 11.
9. Linda M. Gorchels, "Traditional Product Management Evolves," *Marketing News* (January 30, 1995), p. 4; "Focus on Five Stages of Category Management," *Marketing News* (September 28, 1992), pp. 17, 19; and Sandy Gillis, "On the Job: Product Manager," *Business Week's Guide to Careers* (April–May 1988), pp. 63–66.
10. Phil Moss, "What It's Like to Work for Procter & Gamble," *Business Week's Guide to Careers* (March–April 1987), pp. 18–20.
11. David Kirkpatrick, "Is Your Career on Track?" *Fortune* (July 2, 1990), pp. 38–48.
12. Robin T. Peterson, "Wholesaling: A Neglected Job Opportunity for Marketing Majors," *Marketing News* (January 15, 1996), p. 4.
13. "Advertising," *Career Guide to America's Top Industries* (Indianapolis, IN: JIST Works, 1994), pp. 142–45.
14. "The Climb to the Top," *Careers in Retailing* (January 1995), p. 18.
15. "Playing the Retail Career Game," *Careers in Retailing 2001* (New York: DSN Retailing Today, January 2001), pp. 4, 6.
16. "2001 Salary Survey," *Sales and Marketing Management* (May 2001), pp. 47–50.
17. Milan Moravec, Marshall Collins, and Clinton Tripoli, "Don't Want to Manage? Here's Another Path," *Sales and Marketing Management* (June 1990), pp. 62–75.
18. Robin T. Peterson, "Startup Careers through Rep Firms," *Marketing News* (August 4, 1997), p. 8.
19. William Keenan, Jr., "America's Best Sales Forces: Six at the Summit," *Sales and Marketing Management* (June 1990), pp. 62–72.

20. Kathleen Cholewka, "Do No Disturb: A New Way to E-Mail?" *Sales and Marketing Management* (November 2001), pp. 21–22; and "Best E-Business Strategy," *Sales and Marketing Management* (September 2001), p. 28.
21. Michael R. Wukitsch, "Should Research Know More about Marketing?" *Marketing Research* (Winter 1993), p. 50.
22. "Market Research Analyst," in Les Krantz, ed., *Jobs Rated Almanac,* 3rd ed. (New York: Wiley, 1995).
23. Joshua Grossnickle and Oliver Raskin, "What's Ahead on the Internet," *Marketing Research* (Summer 2001), pp. 9–13.
24. Carolyn D. Marconi, "Desperately Looking for New Talent Is a Recurring Theme," *Marketing Research* (Spring 2000), pp. 4–6.
25. Susan B. Larsen, "International Careers: Reality, Not Fantasy," *CPC Annual: A Guide to Employment Opportunities for College Graduates,* 36th ed. (Bethlehem, PA: College Placement Council, 1992), pp. 78–85; and Hal Lancaster, "Global Managers Need Boundless Sensitivity, Rugged Constitutions," *The Wall Street Journal* (October 13, 1998), p. B1.
26. John W. Buckner, "Working Abroad at Home," *Managing your Career* (Spring 1992), pp. 16–17.
27. Lisa Bertagnoli, "Marketing Overseas Excellent for Career," *Marketing News* (June 4, 2001), p. 4.
28. "Your Job Search Starts with You," *Job Choices: 1996,* 39th ed. (Bethlehem. PA: National Association of Colleges and Employers, 1995), pp. 6–9; Hugh E. Kramer, "Applying Marketing Strategy and Personal Value Analysis to Career Planning: An Experiential Approach," *Journal of Marketing Education* (Fall 1988), pp. 69–73; Alan Deutschman, "What 25-Year-Olds Want," *Fortune* (August 27, 1990), pp. 42–50; and Dawn Richerson, "Personality and your Career," *Career Woman* (Winter 1993), pp. 46–47.
29. Arthur F. Miller, "Discover Your Design," in *CPC Annual,* vol. 1 (Bethlehem, PA: College Placement Council, 1984), p. 2.
30. Robin T. Peterson and J. Stuart Devlin, "Perspectives on Entry-Level Positions by Graduating Marketing Seniors," *Marketing Education Review* (Summer 1994), pp. 2–5.
31. Callum J. Floyd and Mary Ellen Gordon, "What Skills Are Most Important? A Comparison of Employer, Student, and Staff Perceptions," *Journal of Marketing Education* (August 1998), pp. 103–9; "What Employers Want," *Job Outlook '98* (Bethlehem, PA: National Association of Colleges and Employers); and Andrew Marlatt, "Demand for Diverse Skills Is On Upswing," *Internet World* (January 4, 1999).
32. Diane Goldner, "Fill In the Blank," *The Wall Street Journal* (February 27, 1995), pp. R5, R11.
33. Karen Epper Hoffman, "Recruitment Sites Changing Their Focus," *Internet World* (March 15, 1999); Pamela Mendels, "Now That's Casting a Wide Net," *Business Week* (May 25, 1998): and James C. Gonyea, *The Online Job Search Companion* (New York: McGraw-Hill, 1995).
34. Peter Cappelli, "Making the Most of On-Line Recruiting," *Harvard Business Review* (March 2001), pp. 139–46.
35. Ronald B. Marks, *Personal Selling* (Boston: Allyn & Bacon, 1985), pp. 451–62.
36. Constance J. Pritchard, "Small Employers—How, When and Who They Hire," *Job Choices: 1996,* 39th ed. (Bethlehem, PA: National Association of Colleges and Employers, 1995), pp. 66–69.
37. Leonard Felson, "Undergrad Marketers Must Get Jump on Networking Skills," *Marketing News* (April 8, 2001), p. 14; and Wayne E. Baker, *Networking Smart* (New York: McGraw-Hill, 1994).
38. John L. Munschauer, "How to Find a Customer for Your Capabilities," in 1984–1985 *CPC Annual,* vol. 1 (Bethlehem, PA: College Placement Council, 1984), p. 24.
39. C. Randall Powell, "Secrets of Selling a Résumé," in Peggy Schmidt, ed., *The Honda How to Get a Job Guide* (New York: McGraw-Hill, 1984), pp. 4–9.
40. Ibid., p. 4.
41. Adapted from Ibid., pp. 4–9.

42. Joyce Lain Kennedy, "Computer-Friendly Résumé Tips," *Planning Job Choices: 1999,* 42nd ed. (Bethlehem, PA: National Association of Colleges and Employers, 1998), p. 49; and Joyce Lain Kennedy and Thomas J. Morrow, *Electronic Résumé Revolution* (New York: Wiley, 1994).

43. Arthur G. Sharp, "The Art of the Cover Letter," *Career Futures,* vol. 4, no. 1 (1992), pp. 50–51.

44. Perri Capell, "Unconventional Job Search Tactics," *Managing Your Career* (Spring 1991), pp. 31, 35.

45. Julie Griffin Levitt, *Your Career: How to Make It Happen* (Cincinnati: South-Western Publishing, 1985).

46. Deborah Vendy, "Drug Screening and Your Career," *CPC Annual* (Bethlehem, PA: College Placement Council, 1992), pp. 61–62.

47. Dana James, "A Day in the Life of a Corporate Recruiter," *Marketing News* (April 10, 2000), pp. 1, 11.

48. Marks, *Personal Selling,* p. 469.

49. Terence P. Pare, "The Uncommitted Class of 1989," *Fortune* (June 5, 1989), pp. 199–210.

50. Bob Weinstein, "What Employers Look For," in Peggy Schmidt, ed., *The Honda How to Get a Job Guide* (New York: McGraw-Hill, 1985), p. 10.

APPENDIX D

1. The Burton Snowboards case was prepared by Linda Rochford from the following sources: Burton Snowboards corporate website: product information and news www.burton.com; Hoovers Online Burton Snowboards capsule www.hoovers.com; National Sporting Goods Association website: www.nsga.org/public/articles/index.cfm?cat=136 (May 28, 2001); Sitour USA, Ski Industry Demographics: www.sitourusa.com; Dr. George Ahlb-Sumer, "An Ounce of Prevention: Should Injury Statistics in Snowboarding Affect the Industry?" Snowboarding-Online.com, *SnowBiz* (February 29, 2000).

2. The Clearly Canadian case was adapted and updated by Steven Hartley from a case originally written by Frederick G. Crane for *Marketing,* 4th Canadian ed. (McGraw-Hill Ryerson, 2000), and from the following sources: Jonathan Cronin, "Redefining a Category," *Beverage Aisle* (June 15, 2001), p. 62; "Clearly Canadian Launches Summer Campaign for Reebok Fitness Water," *Business Wire* (July 5, 2001); "Clearly Canadian Announces International Listings for New Package," *Canadian Corporate Newswire* (December 13, 2000); "BevNET.com's Top Ten Hottest Beverages," *PR Newswire* (July 11, 2000); Judith Crown, "Quaker's Big Gulp Snapple Buy Ultimate Test for Smithburg," *Crain's Chicago Business* (November 7, 1994), p. 1; Clearly Canadian Beverage Corporation, *Annual Report 2000;* Clearly Canadian Beverage Corporation, *Annual Report 1999;* Clearly Canadian website: www.clearly.ca.

3. The Jamba Juice case was prepared by Linda Rochford from the following sources: Nancy Rivera Brooks, "How to Get A Business Loan," *Los Angeles Times* (May 16, 1993); David Eddy, "Juice Club: Smoothin' Its Way to Success," *San Luis Obispo County Telegram–Tribune* (April 23, 1993); Jamba Juice Corporate website and press releases: www.jambajuice.com; Kinney Littlefield, "Slurp to Heart's Content at Juice Club," *The Orange County Register* (April 23, 1993); Beth Lorenzini, "Turn Up the Juice," *Restaurants and Institutions* (February 1, 1995), p. 113; Janet Moore, "Juicy Prospects," *Minneapolis Star Tribune* (August 27, 2001), pp. D1–D2; Louis Trager, "Get Ready for Juice Bars, at a Corner Nearby Soon," *San Francisco Examiner* (1995).

4. The Ford and Firestone case was prepared by Linda Rochford from the following sources: David Barboza, "Bridgestone/Firestone to Close Tire Plant at Center of Huge Recall," *The New York Times* (June 28, 2001), p. C.1; Keith Bradsher, "Ford Intends to Replace 13 Million Firestone Wilderness Tires," *The New York Times* (May 23, 2001), p. C.1; Keith Bradsher, "Ford Wants to Send Drivers of Sport Utility Vehicles Back to School," *The New York Times* (July 4, 2001), p. A.9; John Greenwald, "Tired of Each Other," *Time* (June 4, 2001), pp. 51–56; Phil Meyerowitz," SUV Chic: The Rugged and the

Reckless," *The New York Times* (July 7, 2001) p. 12; www.fordexplorerrollovers.com/time_line.htm.

5. "The Johnsons Buy a Food Processor" case was prepared by Roy D. Adler, professor of marketing at Pepperdine University, Malibu. Copyright by Roy D. Adler. Reproduced with permission.

6. The Honeywell, Inc., case was prepared by Roger A. Kerin based on company sources. Used with permission.

7. The Callaway Golf case was prepared by Paul H. Sandholm and Linda Rochford from the following sources: Callaway Golf company capsule, Hoovers Online; "Callaway: Average Golfer Has a Right to Make a Choice," *Golfweek* (August 28, 2001), pp. 20–21; Doug Ferguson, Associated Press golf writer, "Drapeau Sets Out to Replace an Icon at Callaway" (July 31, 2001); Hoovers Online: hoovnews.hoovers.com/; James Achenbach, "From Hickory Stick to Callaway, Ely Sought to Please Golfers," *Golfweek* (July 14, 2001), p. 26–27; Gene Yasuda, "Silver Lining in Carlsbad," *Golfweek* (May 5, 2001), p. 21; Gene Yasuda, "Callaway Golf Earnings Take 39 Percent Hit," *Golfweek* (August 4, 2001), p. 25.

8. The HOM Furniture case was prepared by Kathy Chadwick based on interviews with Wayne Johansen and internal HOM Furniture materials.

9. The Hummer case was prepared by Linda Rochford from the following sources: Stuart F. Brown, "Quest for the Boojum," *Popular Science* (July 1995), p. 77–81; "What's a Hummer? Aah! Thought You'd Never Ask," *Fortune* (October 2, 1995), p. 146; "His Summer in a Hummer," *Fortune* (October 2, 1995), pp. 154–155; AM General website and press releases: www.amgmil.com; Hoover's Online AM General capsule: www.hoovers.com/; Gregory L. White, "GM's New Baby Hummer Shares Its Toys with Chevy," *The Wall Street Journal* (April 10, 2001), pp. B1, B4.

10. The Medtronic in China case was prepared by Mark T. Spriggs and Kenneth E. Goodpaster based on Medtronic annual reports and three Medtronic cases: Medtronic in China (A), (B), and (C) prepared by research assistant Linda Swenson under the supervision of Kenneth E. Goodpaster (Minneapolis–St. Paul, MN: University of St. Thomas, 1999).

11. The Yoplait USA case was prepared by William Rudelius and Steven Hartley based on personal interviews with Chap Colucci and Steven M. Rothschild, materials available on the company website (www.generalmills.com), and the following sources: "General Mills Celebrates Acquisition of Pillsbury," *Business Wire* (November 1, 2001); Melissa Levy, "General Mills Meets Earning Estimates, Unveils Products," *Star Tribune* (June 28, 2000), p. 1D; "Active Market For Active Cultures," *Dairy Field* (April, 2000), p. 18.

12. The Girl Scouts of America case was prepared by Roger A. Kerin and Steven Hartley based on information available on the organization's website (www.girlscouts.org) and the following sources: Carol Wolfram, "Girl Scouts Have Got the Cookies," *The Times-Picayune* (January 17, 2002), p. 26; Joan Oleck, "Cookies and High Tech," *Business Week* (March 12, 2001), p. 16; and Kathryn Linderman, "Girl Scouts Founder Juliette Gordon Low: Her Determination Gave Girls Their First Taste of Leadership," *Investor's Business Daily* (September 28, 2001), p. 5.

13. The Health Cruises, Inc. case was prepared by Maurice Mandell and Larry J. Rosenberg. Reprinted by permission of Prentice Hall, Inc.

14. The Memorial Medical Emergency Clinic case was prepared by Roger A. Kerin based on company sources. Used with permission.

15. The Starbucks case was prepared by Linda Rochford from the following sources: "What's the Buzz?" *Seattle Post–Intelligencer* (December 14, 1999): seattlepi.nwsource.com/lifestyel/coff14.shtml; Jane McCabe, "Is There Any Hope Out There?" from the editor's desk, Tea and Coffee Trade online (April/May 2001): www.teaandcoffe.net/0401/editor.htm; Jennifer Minnich, "Activists Protest Starbucks' Products," *Daily Herald,* p. A9 and HarkTheHerald.com; Hoovers Online: hoovers.com/capsules/15745.html, capsules on Tully's Coffee Corporation, Peet's Coffee & Tea, Inc., Starbucks' Corporation, New World Coffee–Manhattan Bagel, Inc., Diedrich Coffee, Inc.; Starbucks' Corporate Home Page: starbucks.com, product information and press releases.

16. The Dell Computer case was prepared by Linda Rochford from the following sources: Dell website: www.dell.com, "Dell at a Glance," "Dell's Supply Chain," "Service Porfolio Summary"; Gale Group Business and Company Resource Center, Dell Computer Corporation: galenet.galegroup.com.

17. The Nordstrom case was prepared by Linda Rochford from the following sources: Brian Silverman, "Shopping for Loyal Customers," *Sales and Marketing Management* (March 1995), p. 96–97; Robert Spector and Patrick D. Mc Carthy, *The Nordstrom Way: The Inside Story* of *America's #1 Customer Service Company* (New York: Wiley, 1996); Nordstrom website www.nordstrom.com; hoovers.com Nordstrom company capsule.

18. The McDonald's in Russia case was prepared by Sarah Casanova of McDonald's Canada and Michael J. Vessey based on internal McDonald's reports and the McDonald's website information: www.mcdonalds.com/.

19. The "Volkswagen: Drivers Wanted" case was prepared by Linda Rochford from the following sources: Christine Tierney and Joann Muller, "Another Trip Down Memory Lane," *Business Week* (July 23, 2001), p. 62–63; Karl Greenberg, "Arnold Unveils Push for Jetta," *Adweek New England Advertising Week* (May 7, 2001), p. 7; "Volkswagen Beetle," *Adweek Eastern Edition* (May 14, 2001), p. 33; Jean Halliday, "VW Relaunches Euro Van in the US: First TV Push in Nearly a Decade Set to Counter Lack of Awareness," *Advertising Age* (July 9, 2001), p. 3; Roberta Bernstein, "Car Guys," *Shoot*

(December 10, 1999), p. 48; Andy Cohen, "VW Is Riding High," *Sales and Marketing Management* (March 1999), p. 19; Jean Halliday, "VW Targets Web-Savy with Online Beetle Offer," *Advertising Age* (May 8, 2000), p. 18; Ralph Kisiel, "VW Seeks Male Buyers to Raise New Beetle Sales," *Advertising Age* (January 22, 2001), p. 6; Mickey Alam Khan, "Volkswagen Wants 'Oops'-Free Sales Push," *Marketing News* (May 8, 2000), p. 4.

20. The Field Furniture case was prepared by Roger A. Kerin based on company sources. Used with permission.

21. The Mattel, Inc. case was prepared by Roger A. Kerin from the following sources: "Mattel, Inc.," Hoover's company profile: www.hoovers.com; *World Toy Facts and Figures—2000* (New York: International Council of Toy Industries, 2001); "Mattel Inc. Delivers the Ultimate in Toy Design," *Business Wire* (November 4, 1998); "Selling Barbie Online May Pit Mattel vs. Stores," *The Wall Street Journal* (November 17, 2000), pp. B1, B4.

22. The BP Connect™ case was prepared by Michael J. Vessey and William Rudelius from the following sources: William Echikson, "When Oil Gets Connected," *Business Week e.biz* (December 3, 2001), pp. EB28–EB30; Martha Hamilton, "Giving Drivers Their Fill: Service Stations Modernized as BP Consolidates Merged Oil Firms," (July 25, 2000), downloaded from *The Washington Post;* Alexei Barrionuevo and Ann Zimmerman, "Latest Supermarket Special—Gasoline," *The Wall Street Journal* (April 30, 2001), pp. B1, B4.

CREDITS

CHAPTER 1

p. 2, Courtesy of Rollerblade, Inc.; p. 6, Courtesy of Rollerblade, Inc.; p.10 (left), Courtesy of New-ProductWorks; p. 10 (center) Courtesy of New-ProductWorks; p. 10 (right) ©Brian Hagiwara; p. 13 (left), Courtesy Wal-Mart Stores, Inc.; p. 13 (right) ©Lands' End, Inc. Used with permission; p. 16, 18, *All* Courtesy of Rollerblade, Inc.; p. 21 (right), Courtesy American Library Association; p. 21 (center), Wisconsin travel ad. Courtesy Wisconsin Department of Tourism; p. 21 (right), Courtesy Polo Ralph Lauren Corporation; p. 25, Courtesy of Rollerblade, Inc.

CHAPTER 2

p. 30, ©Dawn Villella/Wide World Photo; p. 32, Courtesy Medtronic; p. 40 (top), Courtesy Microsoft Corporation; p. 40 (bottom) Courtesy Aurora Foods, Inc.; p. 43, Courtesy Rick Armstrong; p. 44, ©M. Hruby; p. 47, Courtesy Medtronic; p. 53, Courtesy Specialized Bicycles.

APPENDIX A

pp. 59, 63, 65, 67, 68, ©1996 Paradise Kitchens Inc. All photos and ads reprinted with permission.

CHAPTER 3

p. 72, Courtesy Apple Computer; p. 77 (left) ©The Procter & Gamble Company. Used by permission; p. 77 (center), Courtesy T. Rowe Price; Photo/Getty Images; p. 77 (right) Photograph by Michael Martin. Reproduced courtesy of Ask Jeeves, Inc. and Grey Worldwide San Francisco; p. 81, Courtesy Saturn Corporation; Agency: Publicis & Hal Riney; p. 83, Figure 3–5: *Surveys of Consumers*, Survey Research Center, The University of Michigan. Reprinted with permission; p. 84 (top), ©2001 CACI Marketing Systems; p. 84 (bottom) Courtesy Westin Hotels & Resorts; Agency: Cole & Weber/Seattle; Photographers: Kathleen Norris Cook and Tim Bieber/Image Bank Northwest and Tony Stone Images; p. 85 (left), Courtesy of Sony Electronics, Inc.; p. 85 (center) Courtesy Zenith Electronics Corporation; p. 85 (right) Courtesy EchoStar Communications Corporation; p. 87 (left), Courtesy Tomra North America; p. 87 (right), Courtesy of Lever Brothers Company; p. 89, Courtesy Lotus Development Corporation, an IBM company; p. 91, ©Wide World Photos; p. 92, ©M. Hruby; p. 93, Courtesy of Better Business Bureau, Inc.; p. 96, 97, Courtesy Flyte Time.

CHAPTER 4

p. 98, Courtesy Anheuser-Busch Companies; p. 103, Rex USA; p. 104, (2001) Michelle Delsol; p. 105, Courtesy Transparency International;

p. 106–7, Figure 4–3 reprinted with permission from the *AMA Code of Ethics* published by the American Marketing Association; p. 111, Tony Stone; p. 112, Courtesy McDonald's Corporation; p. 113, ©Anastasia T. Vrachnos.

CHAPTER 5

p. 120, Courtesy Jaguar Cars, Inc.; Agency: Young and Rubicam/Irvine; p. 124, ©PhotoEdit; p. 125, Courtesy Kimberly-Clark Worldwide, Inc.; p. 127, ©Tropicana Products, Inc.; p. 130, Courtesy Inscape for Time Warner Interactive; p. 131 (left), "FRESH STEP® is a registered trademark of The Clorox Pet Products Company. Used with permission; p. 131 (right) ©2001 Mary Kay, Inc. Photos by Grace Huang\for Sarah Laird; p. 133 (left) Courtesy Colgate-Palmolive Company; p. 133 (right) The Bayer Company; p. 134, Courtesy SRI Consulting Business Intelligence/VALS™ Program; p. 135, Figure 5–6, VALS™, SRI Consulting Business Intelligence (SRIC-BI), Menlo Park, CA. VALS™ is a trademark of SRI Consulting Business Intelligence. Reprinted with permission; p. 137, Courtesy Omega SA; p. 139, Figure 5–7, Patrick G. Murphy and William A. Staples, "A Modernized Family Life Cycle," *Journal of Consumer Research*, January 1979, p. 17. Reprinted with permission of The University of Chicago Press; p. 140, Courtesy of Haggar Clothing Co.; ©1997 Haggar Clothing Co.; p. 142, Courtesy Bonne Bell, Inc.; p. 143, ©M. Hruby; p. 145, 146, Courtesy of Ken Davis Products, Inc.

CHAPTER 6

p. 148, Courtesy JCPenney; p. 151, Courtesy Corning, Inc.; p. 152, Courtesy of the United States Department of Commerce Bureau of the Census; p. 155, Courtesy Airbus; p. 156, Courtesy Anthony Mark Hankins; p. 157, Courtesy Harley-Davidson; Agency: Carmichael Lynch; Photographer: Paul Wakefield/Bernstein Andriulli; p. 159, Dan Bosler/Tony Stone; p. 162, Courtesy Allen-Bradley Company, Inc.; p. 165, Courtesy of Covisint, L.L.C.

CHAPTER 7

p. 170, Courtesy CNS, Inc.; p. 175 (left), Courtesy Sony Electronics, Inc.; p. 175 (right) Courtesy of Bruno Magli; p. 177, The Image Bank; p. 180, Courtesy ALMAP/BBDO Sao Paulo; p. 181, Photo: O. Toscani; Courtesy United Colors of Benetton; p. 182, Courtesy Nestlé S.A.; p. 184 (left)., Travelpix/FPG International; p. 184 (right) Antonio Rosario/The Image Bank; p. 186, ©Dennis Cook/AP Wide World Photos; p. 187, ©1993 Mary Beth Camp/Matrix International, Inc.; p. 188, Courtesy of The Coca-Cola Com-

pany; p. 189, Figure 7–5, *American Demographics* Magazine, © 1995. Reprinted with permission; p. 190, Courtesy The PRS Group; p. 193, Courtesy of Sanyu Boh, Ltd.; p. 194, Courtesy McDonald's Corporation; p. 196, Courtesy The Gillette Company; p. 199, Courtesy CNS, Inc.; p. 200, United Press Syndicate.

CHAPTER 8

p. 202, "Lord of the Rings" Copyright 2001, New Line Productions, Inc. All rights reserved. Poster appears courtesy of New Line Productions, Inc.; p. 206, "Lord of the Rings" Copyright 2001, New Line Productions, Inc. All rights reserved; p. 208, Courtesy Fisher-Price; p. 209, Courtesy Fisher-Price; p. 210, ©M. Hruby; p. 215, Courtesy Nielsen Media Research; p. 216 (left), Courtesy The Gillette Company; p. 216 (center), Courtesy 3M; p. 216 (right), Courtesy Skechers USA; p. 216, Figure 8–4: Reprinted with permission of Nielsen Media Research; p. 217, Figure 8–5: Reprinted with permission of Nielsen//NetRatings; p. 218, Courtesy Teenage Research Unlimited; p. 222, Courtesy Wendy's International, Inc.; p. 224, Courtesy Fingerhut Corporation; p. 225, Courtesy Tony's Pizza Brand Group of Schwan's Consumer Brands North America.

CHAPTER 9

p. 236, ©Brent Jones; p. 237, Courtesy Heelys™, Heeling Sports Limited; p. 238 (left, center), ©M. Hruby; p. 238 (right), Courtesy Heelys™, Heeling Sports Limited; p. 242, ©M. Hruby; p. 243, All Courtesy Street & Smith's Magazine; p. 244, Courtesy Customatix; p. 246 (top), DILBERT reprinted by permission of United Features Syndicate, Inc.; p. 246 (bottom), Courtesy Mac-Gray; p. 248, Figure 9–5: National Consumer Survey© Choices 3 Crosstabulation Report: Fast-Food Restaurants (New York: Simmons Market Research Bureau, Inc., Spring 2001). Reprinted with permission; p. 249, Figure 9–6: National Consumer Survey© Choices 3 Crosstabulation Report: Fast-Food Restaurants (New York: Simmons Market Research Bureau, Inc., Spring 2001). Reprinted with permission; p. 249, Photo by John Abbott; p. 250, Courtesy Xerox Corporation; p. 253, Courtesy Wendy's International, Inc.; p. 254, 256, Courtesy Apple Computer; p. 259 (left), Courtesy of Buick Motor Division; p. 259 (center), Courtesy of Oldsmobile; Agency: Leo Burnett; p. 259 (right), ©M. Hruby; p. 262, Courtesy Nokia.

CHAPTER 20

p. 528, Courtesy Xerox Corporation; p. 531, ©John Madere; p. 533, Mitch Kezar/Stone; p. 535, Courtesy Xerox Corporation; p. 537, Einzig Photography; p. 538, CB Productions/ Corbis Stock Market; p. 540, Ken Ross/FPG International; p. 542, Color Day Production/The Image Bank; p. 548, Courtesy of Mary Kay; p. 551, Both photos Courtesy of Toshiba America Medical Systems and Interactive Media; p. 550, Jose Peleaz/The Stock Market; p. 554, Courtesy of Reebok International Ltd.

CHAPTER 21

p. 558, ©tom white.images; p. 561 (left), Courtesy Orbitz; p. 561 (right), ©2001 Hertz System, Inc. Hertz is a registered service mark and trademark of Hertz System, Inc.; p. 564, Figure 21–2: From *Internet Marketing: Building Advantage in a Networked Economy*, Mohammad, Fisher et al. Copyright © 2002 by The McGraw-Hill Companies, p. 573, ©Matt Mahurin Inc.; p. 579, 580, Courtesy America Online.

CHAPTER 22

p. 582, ©M. Hruby; p. 585, ©M. Hruby; p. 588, Figure 22–3: Reprinted with permission from *Journal of Marketing,* published by the American Marketing Association, Summer 1980, p. 82; p. 590 (left), Courtesy Wal-Mart, Inc.; p. 590 (right), Courtesy of Volkswagen of America, Inc.; p. 593, Figure 22–6: Reprinted with permission from The Free Press, a division of Simon & Schuster, from *Competitive Advantage: Creating and Sustaining Superior Performance* by Michael E. Porter. Copyright © 1985 by Michael E. Porter; p. 594, ©M. Hruby; p. 595, Courtesy of Papa John's International; p. 596, ©M. Hruby; p. 598, GE Lighting Group; p. 600 (bottom), Courtesy Lockheed; p. 600 (top), 2002 General Motors Corporation. Used with permission GM Media Archives; p. 602, Figure 22–9: Reprinted by permission of Harvard Business Review. An exhibit from "Making Your Marketing Strategy Work," by Thomas V. Bonoma, March-April 1984. Copyright © 1984 by the President and Fellows of Harvard College, all rights reserved; p. 602, Figure 22–10: From an *Introduction to Contemporary Business*, 4th edition, by W. Rudelius, W.B. Erickson © 1985. Reprinted with permission of South-Western College Publishing, a division of Thomson Learning. Fax 800-730-2215; p. 603, Figure 22–11: From an *Introduction to Contemporary Business*, 4th edition, by W. Rudelius, W.B. Erickson © 1985. Reprinted with permission of South-Western College Publishing, a division of Thomson Learning. Fax 800-730-2215; p. 606, ©M. Hruby; p. 610, Courtesy Golden Valley; p. 625. Reprinted with permission.

APPENDIX C

p. 613, Figure C–1: *Careers in Marketing* by David W. Rosenthal and Michael A. Powell ©1984, pp. 352-54, by permission of Pearson Education, Inc., Upper Saddle River, NJ; p. 614, Paul Elledge; p. 615, Employment Branding Advertisement for Xerox Corporation developed by JWT Specialized Communications/Chicago; p. 616, Toyota Motor North America, Inc.; p. 619 (top), Reprinted from Job Choices 2002, with permission of the National Association of Colleges and Employers, copyright holder; p. 624, Thatch cartoon by Jeff Shesol; Reprinted with permission of Vintage Books; p. 626, ©Imagebank.

APPENDIX D

p. 630, Courtesy Kingpin Snowboarding; p. 632, Courtesy Clearly Canadian; p. 641, Courtesy HOM Furniture; p. 645, ©M. Hruby; p. 650, Courtesy United Airlines; p. 660, Courtesy British Petroleum.

NAME INDEX

COMPANY/PRODUCT INDEX

SUBJECT INDEX

MCGRAW-HILL/IRWIN SERIES IN MARKETING

Arens
*CONTEMPORARY ADVERTISING,
8/E*

Arnould, Price & Zinkhan
CONSUMERS, 1/E

Bearden, Ingram & LaForge
*MARKETING: PRINCIPLES &
PERSPECTIVES, 3/E*

Belch & Belch
*ADVERTISING & PROMOTION: AN
INTEGRATED MARKETING
COMMUNICATIONS APPROACH,
5/E*

Bingham & Gomes
*BUSINESS MARKETING
MANAGEMENT, 2/E*

Boyd, Walker, Mullins & Larreche
*MARKETING MANAGEMENT: A
STRATEGIC DECISION-MAKING
APPROACH, 4/E*

Cateora & Graham
INTERNATIONAL MARKETING, 11/E

Cole & Mishler
*CONSUMER AND BUSINESS
CREDIT MANAGEMENT, 11/E*

Cravens & Piercy
STRATEGIC MARKETING, 7/E

Cravens, Lamb & Crittenden
*STRATEGIC MARKETING
MANAGEMENT CASES, 7/E*

Crawford & Di Benedetto
*NEW PRODUCTS MANAGEMENT,
7/E*

Dolan
*MARKETING MANAGEMENT: TEXT
AND CASES, 1/E*

Duncan
*IMC: USING ADVERTISING AND
PROMOTION TO BUILD BRANDS,
1/E*

Dwyer & Tanner
BUSINESS MARKETING, 2/E

Eisenmann
*INTERNET BUSINESS MODELS:
TEXT AND CASES, 1/E*

Etzel, Walker & Stanton
MARKETING, 12/E

Futrell
*ABC'S OF RELATIONSHIP
SELLING, 7/E*

Futrell
FUNDAMENTALS OF SELLING, 7/E

Hair, Bush & Ortinau
MARKETING RESEARCH, 2/E

Hawkins, Best & Coney
CONSUMER BEHAVIOR, 8/E

Johansson
GLOBAL MARKETING, 3/E

Johnston & Marshall
*CHURCHILL/FORD/WALKER'S
SALES FORCE MANAGEMENT, 7/E*

Kerin, Berkowitz, Hartley & Rudelius
MARKETING, 7/E

Lehmann & Winer
*ANALYSIS FOR MARKETING
PLANNING, 5/E*

Lehmann & Winer
PRODUCT MANAGEMENT, 3/E

Levy & Weitz
RETAILING MANAGEMENT, 4/E

Mason & Perreault
THE MARKETING GAME!, 3/E

McDonald
*DIRECT MARKETING: AN
INTEGRATED APPROACH, 1/E*

Mohammed, Fisher, Jaworski & Cahill
*INTERNET MARKETING: BUILDING
ADVANTAGE IN A NETWORKED
ECONOMY, 1/E*

Monroe
PRICING, 3/E

Pelton, Strutton & Lumpkin
*MARKETING CHANNELS: A
RELATIONSHIP MANAGEMENT
APPROACH, 2/E*

Perreault & McCarthy
*BASIC MARKETING: A GLOBAL
MANAGERIAL APPROACH, 14/E*

Perreault & McCarthy
*ESSENTIALS OF MARKETING: A
GLOBAL MANAGERIAL
APPROACH, 8/E*

Peter & Donnelly
*A PREFACE TO MARKETING
MANAGEMENT, 9/E*

Peter & Donnelly
*MARKETING MANAGEMENT:
KNOWLEDGE AND SKILLS, 6/E*

Peter & Olson
CONSUMER BEHAVIOR , 6/E

Rayport & Jaworski
*INTRODUCTION TO E-COMMERCE,
1/E*

Rayport & Jaworski
E-COMMERCE, 1/E

Rayport & Jaworski
CASES IN E-COMMERCE, 1/E

Richardson
INTERNET MARKETING, 1/E

Roberts
*INTERNET MARKETING:
INTEGRATING ONLINE AND
OFFLINE STRATEGIES, 1/E*

Spiro, Stanton & Rich
*MANAGEMENT OF A SALES
FORCE, 11/E*

Stock & Lambert
*STRATEGIC LOGISTICS
MANAGEMENT, 4/E*

Ulrich & Eppinger
*PRODUCT DESIGN AND
DEVELOPMENT, 2/E*

Walker, Boyd, Mullins & Larreche
*MARKETING STRATEGY: A
DECISION-FOCUSED APPROACH,
4/E*

Weitz, Castleberry & Tanner
*SELLING: BUILDING
PARTNERSHIPS, 4/E*

Zeithaml & Bitner
SERVICES MARKETING, 3/E

A Wealth of Student Resources

Whether preparing for an exam, researching marketing topics, or extending your knowledge through application, the Kerin/Berkowitz/Hartley/Rudelius author team provides you with a tremendous toolkit of print, online, and CD-ROM based study tools.

Packaged Free with Your Textbook: Student CD-ROM to Accompany Kerin et al., MARKETING 7/e

This CD-ROM contains a Narrated Concept Review for each chapter of the book. This study outline features narrations of all key concepts in the text. It also contains Self Quizzes with Feedback for each chapter and Marketing Planning Software that helps guide you in the preparation of a marketing plan.

Print Study Guide (ISBN: 0072469013)

A printed study guide is available that helps you prepare for tests and goes beyond mere memorization. It contains chapter outlines for note taking, sample tests, application questions and exercises, critical thinking questions, and concept review flash cards. This study aid can be ordered through your bookstore or by calling customer service at 1-800-262-4729.